W9-ARI-835

ALSO BY HAL ERICKSON

*Syndicated Television: The First Forty
Years, 1947–1987* (1989)

*Baseball in the Movies: A Comprehensive
Reference, 1915–1991* (1992)

*Religious Radio and Television in the
United States, 1921–1991: The Programs
and Personalities* (1992)

AND PUBLISHED BY McFARLAND

Television Cartoon Shows

Television
Cartoon Shows

An Illustrated Encyclopedia,
1949 through 1993

BY HAL ERICKSON

McFarland & Company, Inc., Publishers
Jefferson, North Carolina, and London

British Library Cataloguing-in-Publication data are available

Library of Congress Cataloguing-in-Publication Data

Erickson, Hal, 1950–
    Television cartoon shows : an illustrated encyclopedia, 1949
through 1993 / by Hal Erickson.
        p.   cm.
    Includes bibliographical references and index. ∞
    ISBN 0-7864-0029-3 (lib. bdg. : 50# alk. paper)
    1. Animated television programs — United States — Encyclopedias.
I. Title.
PN1992.8.A59E74   1995
791.45′3 — dc20   94-23878
                                                          CIP

Manufactured in the United States of America

McFarland & Company, Inc., Publishers
  Box 611, Jefferson, North Carolina 28640

Dedicated to the
"Krystal Set" gang: Some kids
never grow up

Acknowledgments

First off, oceans of love and showers of kisses to my wife Joanne, who's lived with this project from the outset. Not only that, but she proofread the manuscript (1500-plus pages) with the expert assistance of her longtime friend (and mine, too), Cari Bobke. Both of you ladies are due a fancy dinner. Don't wake me up when you get home.

Also thanks to my research assistants: John Bierman, who's forgotten more about cartoons and comic books than most people will ever learn (though he's forgotten nothing about what's *in* this book); and my son Peter, whose expert commentary on the current television animation scene belies the "ten year old mentality" onus that producers have imposed on the viewers. Peter is 10 years old, and he's already smarter than most producers. (My other son, Brian, prefers Garth Brooks to cartoons. That's material for another book.)

Most of the illustrations in this book are from the author's own collection—a very eclectic one, as you will plainly see. Many of the gaps in my photo files were admirably and eagerly filled by my good friend Jim Feeley. Additional photographs were provided by Mark Zimmerman, just in the nick of time. Extra thanks to Wayne and Rita Hawk for the donations from their own enormous cartoon memorabilia collection; and to William A. Ruiz of DIC Entertainment.

As I mentioned earlier, much of my research took the form of sitting through hundreds of cartoons. This is not a job for loners, and I take pleasure in thanking those who aided me in this labor, and who diligently kept their VCRs running whenever mine were overloaded: Richard and Ruth Denamur; Gary and Denise Elfe; my parents, Pete and Pudge Erickson; and Laura Kuiper. For generously sharing several years' worth of past cartoon taping sessions, I offer profuse thanks to Carl Bobke and Jeff Messderman.

Information was solicited from several people in the entertainment industry. A handful of the kindest and most helpful are listed below and offered a mass thank-you: Michael Bell; Marie Ceccino of New World; Nancy Fox of AFTRA; Celia Hamilton of the Alliance of Canadian Cinema, Television and Radio Artists; Jack Krieger and Mike Weiden of All-American Television; Fred Patten; William A. Ruiz (again!) of DIC Entertainment; Susan Silo; Kath Soucie; Ken Spears of Ruby-Spears; and the staff of NBC Audience Services.

And, as they used to say on *Rocky and His Friends*, I thank a host of others (for a variety of reasons), among them Ron Killian, Larry Koellner, Mark Longley, Lee Matthias, Roger Sorenson, and the staff of Shokus Video.

Now check your dignity and maturity at the door. You're 12 years old again, your whole life is ahead of you, and you've got to get home right away or you'll miss *George of the Jungle*. And have fun. That's what cartoons are supposed to be all about.

HAL ERICKSON
Milwaukee, June 1994

Table of Contents

Introduction

Please don't ask me how much I love cartoons. After four years of being buried beneath an avalanche of animation, I honestly don't know *how* I feel about them any more.

This book came about as the result of an indirect challenge. In his revised 1987 edition of the landmark cartoon history book *Of Mice and Magic*, Leonard Maltin noted that there was not, up to that time, a book devoted to cartoons made for television. I took up the cudgel. I was going to change all that. I was gone in the head.

Nobody likes a whiner, especially one who whines in print, so I will not detail all the bumps, potholes amd detours on the road to completing this book. I began my research in late 1989 (actually a little earlier than that, if you count the notes that I recorded for my book *Syndicated Television*). I finished my text in 1994 — just in time for the publisher's deadline.

This effort entailed reading, researching, collating, collecting, sending off letters, picking the brains of my friends and colleagues, begging, imploring, cajoling, renting videos, recording videos, and watching — watching — WATCHING one television cartoon after another. Sometimes it was fun. Other times, I would rush to the window and scream "Let me out! I'm as sane as you are!"

As the book took shape, I realized I was not completely alone in my field of so-called expertise. Historian George Woolery had already written his 1983 two-volume work on children's television, while Jeff Lenburg came out with his revised *Encyclopedia of Animated Cartoons* in 1991. A renewal of interest in television cartoons (brought about by an overall improved product) resulted in numerous fan magazines' sprouting up, some specialized, some general. All the above-mentioned works were valuable research tools, but Leonard Maltin's basic statement of 1987 was still true: there was no all-encompassing book devoted *exclusively* to made-for-television animation. Until now.

There is much more to be written on the subject than has previously been published, especially since, from the time of the January 1990 cut-off date in Jeff Lenburg's book to the end of 1993, over 100 new cartoon programs have premiered on television. Also, the television cartoon industry now has more network and cable conduits than ever before, including an entire cable service devoted to animation, Ted Turner's Cartoon Network. That is proof enough to me that an insatiable audience for television cartoons exists out there, somewhere. I hope my book will go some distance in satisfying its appetite.

As far as I can determine, this book has the most extensive production credits of any previous television animation reference. Some of the credit listings were gleaned from existing sources (Lenburg, Woolery, and television encyclopedist extraordinaire Vincent Terrace). Some were discovered by combing through trade magazines, pressbooks and promotional material. But most of this information was gathered by personally viewing virtually all of the cartoon series included between these covers—and by keeping a steady finger on the VCR "pause" button as the closing credits whizzed by.

I regret that the production information is not thorough for some of the series. Some programs had skimpy on-screen credits, some no credits at all, many were inadequately documented in print, and others were simply unavailable to me. Still, at least 90 percent of the entries in this book are as complete as they are going to be until some other foolhardy soul decides to update and expand upon my information in a future television cartoon history.

As much as I had intended an impersonal, scholarly work, I confess that my opinions run rampant throughout the book. Frankly, no one seems capable of meeting the subject of television animation halfway—especially not the "All TV Cartoons Are Garbage" contingents, so secure in their opinions that they refuse to compromise by watching television cartoons at any point in their lives.

While I brought some preconceptions to this book (though none as spiteful as the "garbage" one cited above), I have discovered that changing one's mind never killed anybody. The first rule I learned was not to condemn television animation outright simply because it is not up to the standards of theatrical cartoons. Plagued as they are by attenuated budgets, precious little production time, and the added creative handicaps imposed by sponsors and network censors, it is miraculous that the makers of television cartoons can get anything done at all, either good or bad. Theatrical animation producers enjoy the (comparative) luxuries of time, budget and relaxed regulation; television producers can only shrug in resignation and do the best possible job under the circumstances. So instead of moaning that television cartoons should all aspire to Disney level, it is better to appreciate how much is accomplished on television with the tools at hand.

Rule number two: "Never typecast." It is so unfairly facile to vent one's spleen at the largest and most successful cartoon firms: "Hanna-Barbera shows are worthless" or "DIC wouldn't know a good cartoon if it fell over one." Those who make such smug empirical statements forget that *any* major assembly-line entertainment unit, from a prolific cartoon company to a big movie studio to a national television network, is bound to spew out a dog from time to time. Hanna-Barbera and DIC have been besmirched because they are among the largest targets. Critics disdainful towards television cartoons in the first place will downgrade the genuine accomplishments of such studios, playing up the failures to "prove" their criticism. To begrudge the major cartoon firms a few clinkers is to disregard the fact that, without such giants in the field, there would be no television cartoon industry. The success of the Hanna-Barberas and DICs has made possible a marketplace for the "geniuses" and "mavericks" of the animation world: the Jay Wards, the Bob Clampetts, the John Kricfalusis.

Conversely, never assume that the mantle of "brilliance" automatically guarantees an unending stream of superlative product. Remember that while Jay Ward had his *Rocky and His Friends*, he also had his disappointing *Hoppity Hooper*; and who can tell how the quality of his work might have suffered had he been working along the same mass-production lines as Hanna-Barbera? Remember also that though animation veteran Arthur Leonardi was largely responsible for the wonderful *Shelley Duvall's Bedtime Stories*, he was also one of the principal instigators of the miserable *Problem Child*. Best not to typecast *anyone* in the television animation field, either studio or individual.

In this, I have tried to be fair. If a program is excellent, I will say so. If it reeks to high heaven, I will say that. This is done on a show by show basis, without suggesting that any studio or individual producer is totally consistent either in hits or misses. Hanna-Barbera deserves as much commendation for *The Flintstones* as it does condemnation for *Shazzan!* DIC has every reason to be proud of *Inspector Gadget*, and every reason to hang its head for *Lady Lovelylocks and the Pixietails*. And though Film Roman can take many of the bows for *Garfield*, it also must take some of the blame for *Cro*.

The last-named series brings up a final rule I've learned while working on this book: "Be wary of anything that's supposed to be good for you." *Cro* and *Captain Planet and the Planeteers* are the most recent examples of programs designed more for the benefit of pressure groups and savants than for viewers. It is, of course, possible to produce a cartoon series with wholesome educational value and still manage to entertain, as witness *Schoolhouse Rock*, *Valley of the Dinosaurs*, and *Widget, the World Watcher*. That this is not done more often is due to the humorless intrusiveness of certain "media watchdogs," one more flock of predators bearing down upon television cartoon producers, denying them leeway to do their best work.

And the best of that work can be wonderful indeed.

Television Cartoon Shows: A History

This introductory survey of television cartoon shows covers some 65 years; to include everything that happened in that period would turn this book into a two-volume set, and reduce me to gibbering. The following overview touches exclusively on the historical milestones, the major trends and the extreme high and low points of the television-cartoon industry. It is provided as a frame of reference, not as a textbook in itself.

Details on specific cartoon programs and their significance (if any) in the overall scheme of television animation will be found in the individual essays in the alphabetical section of this book, which immediately follows this historical overview.

ARCHEOLOGICAL EXCAVATIONS

Here is an easy one for any cartoon fan. The clues: The year was 1928. The central figure was a small, black and white anthropomorphic cartoon animal character. The event was a major technological advance in the world of entertainment.

If you responded "Mickey Mouse in Walt Disney's *Steamboat Willie*, the first sound cartoon," you chose *one* of the correct answers.

In 1928 the Radio Corporation of America (RCA) began testing its 60-line scanning speed television screen for potential long-range broadcasting. The RCA engineers needed a figure to stand before the television camera under extremely bright, hot illumination for hours at a time, so that experiments could be made to transmit the image from New York to Kansas. The first "TV stars" were human beings, but no one could withstand the heat or the boredom of the responsibility beyond a few hours. The RCA people then hit upon a solution: utilizing a small statue of an immediately recognizable figure so that the Kansas receiving station would know instantly if transmission was successful.

The figurine would have to be defined in sharp, extreme black and whites for proper picture fidelity. And it would have to move, so that the technicians could check the efficiency of their focusing equipment on a moving figure. Thus, the foot-tall statue was placed on a turntable and rotated before the camera for hours, then days, on end. And when the primitive 60-line cameras and receivers gave way to more sophisticated systems, the RCA people retained their little figurine as a test pattern. The model was used throughout the 1930s as the television picture continually improved before settling on the industry standard of 525 scan lines in 1941. The model's image became an ongoing reassurance to technicians, who measured their progress by the smiling visage of that little rotating figurine.

You have seen that image reproduced in hundreds of books on television history, and in motion picture form whenever PBS or some other culturally minded broadcast service has chosen to map the saga of television. At the time the image was chosen, it was the single most popular face in the realm of animated cartoons. It was Felix the Cat.

How convenient it would be to get lofty or whimsical here, using Felix as a segue into the theory that cartoons and television were "made for each other" from the outset—that from the crudest beginnings in the late 1920s, it was a "given" that television would turn out to be a greater conduit for animation than theatrical exhibition. Felix did indeed act as a sort of harbinger, but the ultimate significance of his presence has little to do with loftiness or whimsy. That plaster of Paris pussycat was propped up before the cameras only out of necessity, after the human volunteers gave up the job. *This* was the precedent set in 1928. Animated cartoons would eventually gravitate to television not out of any artistic or aesthetic motivation, but because it was *necessary* for them to do so. Without television, the cartoon would have probably ceased to exist. With television, the cartoon would not only survive but also post a profit—the most potent motivating force of all.

Throughout television's Caveman Era of the 1930s and 1940s, cartoons were hardly a priority. When they did appear on the small screen, they functioned as they did theatrically—as "extra added attractions" to round out the bill for the main feature. Pioneer television technicians were more concerned with seeing how far the image could be broadcast (the first coaxial television cable was constructed in 1936, linking New York with Philadelphia), how portable the equipment could be (the mobile television unit, created by RCA's own National Broadcasting Company—NBC—in 1937, got its first real workout with coverage of a fire in 1938), and how best to demonstrate the practicality of television as home entertainment (the most spectacular display of this occurred at the New York World's Fair of 1939). The emphasis was on "live" events as they happened: breaking news stories, theatrical presentations, sports. And just as radio of the era was resistant to recordings, early television tended to shy away from film. Radio tried to avoid records because the networks and sponsors wanted to maintain complete financial and creative control over the talent (why play a record over and over for the enrichment of the artist, without the network or sponsor getting a dime?); television veered away from film because the big movie studios weren't about to give away what they could sell.

Still, early television needed something to test the quality of film-to-tube transfers and to fill up the time between "Big Events." In the late 1930s and early 1940s, this meant a reliance upon second-rate "B" pictures from independent producers, cheap short subjects and industrial films, and of course whatever cartoons the broadcasters could get their hands on. Copyright laws regarding 16-millimeter home movie prints of theatrical cartoons prohibited public exhibition for profit—but there were no laws blocking telecasts of these privately owned prints. And since the most popular attractions on the 16-millimeter cartoon market were the silent and early-talkie prints of Walt Disney cartoons, it was Disney who got the most exposure in television's embryonic years.

Disney in fact figured into two early-television milestones. In May of 1939, NBC's New York flagship station W2XBS (once the home of the ever-spinning Felix the Cat doll) offered its first regular schedule of evening programs. Amidst the cooking shows, news broadcasts, musical recitals and college baseball games was a sneak preview of the Disney cartoon *Donald's Cousin*, which was released to theatres a few days after its television bow— the first true "TV premiere" of any motion picture. And in September of that year, so the story goes, the British Broadcasting Corporation, then pursuing the policy of scheduled broadcasts even more aggressively than the United States, was running the 1933 Disney featurette *Mickey's Gala Premiere*— when suddenly, halfway through a gag sequence, the plug was pulled and the BBC went dark. War had been declared, and all British television service was halted until VE Day in May of 1945. At that point, the BBC reportedly signed back on the air with *Mickey's Gala Premiere*—picking up exactly where the cartoon had halted six years earlier! (Another version of this legend involves a BBC newsman being knocked off the "telly" in 1939, and then reappearing in 1945 by declaring "Now, as I was saying before I was so rudely interrupted. . . ." I'll use this alternate version if I ever write a book about BBC newscasters.)

Virtually all cartoon activity on television in the 1930s appeared by way of the movies. There was no real reason to create brand-new animation for television, any more than there was any reason for first-run film presentations. The attractiveness of the whole television concept was its ability to turn the audience into eyewitnesses as events unfolded "live," not to dole out second-hand experience via film. The solitary example of creating animation exclusively for television took place in April 1938, over (again!) W2XBS. "Willie the Worm," adapted from a famous children's poem by Disney employee Chad Grothkopf, was a rudimentary exercise in cutout and cel animation—but it did move, and like most cartoons of the era, it moved to a musical beat. One hopes that Willie fully entertained the 50 or so New York and Pennsylvania households that owned television sets.

No cartoon worms inched their way across the ethos when W2XBS changed its call letters to WNBT and began regular commercial broadcasts on July 1, 1941 — the same day that WCBW, the Manhattan flagship of the Columbia Broadcasting System (or CBS) came into being. The only thing resembling a children's program that day was WNBT's *Uncle Jim's Question Bee*. Nor were cartoons a top-drawer attraction on any of WNBT's subsequent telecasts, which came to an end in BBC fashion when the United States entered World War II on December 8, 1941. The 10 television channels then on the air went dark, allowing television technicians to concentrate their skills on the war effort.

One of the few entrepreneurs who pursued commercial television during the war years was Allen B. DuMont, who had been conducting his own experimental broadcasts since 1931 and who in 1939 had put the first all-electronic television receivers on the market. DuMont inaugurated New York's Channel 5, WABD (now WNYW) in 1944. Among WABD's earliest on-air personalities was ventriloquist Paul Winchell, establishing DuMont's early leadership in the field of children's programming. Winchell, however, preferred sharing airtime with his dummies Jerry Mahoney and Knucklehead Smif rather than with the old, duped-down animated cartoons then available on the nontheatrical scene. Though Paul Winchell would eventually host several cartoon series in the 1950s and 1960s, and would from 1969 onward establish himself as one of the most prolific cartoon voice-actors, animated art was absent on those 1940s Winchell telecasts.

When network television resumed full force in 1946, NBC and DuMont were in the forefront, while CBS, then deeply involved in the development of color television, held back until 1947. The American Broadcasting Company (ABC), an offshoot of the NBC radio chain, had no New York affiliate until 1948 and had to share space on DuMont's WABD until that time. Since NBC's television service was regarded as an adjunct of its radio network, it is not surprising that the first postwar NBC programs would reflect some of the more popular radio genres: variety shows (*Musical Merry-Go-Round*), sportscasts (*Gillette's Cavalcade of Sports*), soap operas (*Faraway Hill*), and late-afternoon children's programming — which in NBC's case consisted of *Puppet Playhouse* (later *Howdy Doody*) and *Junior Jamboree* (featuring future television headliners Kukla, Fran and Ollie). DuMont also had a brace of kids' shows: *Oky Doky Ranch*, which like *Puppet Playhouse* starred a cowboy puppet, and *Small Fry Club*.

Small Fry Club took shape as a local WABD program under the guidance of DuMont producer "Big Brother" Bob Emery during Christmas week of 1946. Emery, at heart a radio announcer, was more comfortable sequestered in a broadcast booth than before the cameras. When Emery's DuMont contribution went weekly as *Movies for Small Fry* in March of 1947, Big Brother Bob remained unseen, functioning only as narrator of old silent movies. Among those antiques was a package of *Aesop's Fables* cartoons, produced in the late 1920s by Paul Terry. Once Emery became an on-camera star when the retitled *Small Fry Club* graduated to a daily DuMont networker a month after its debut, the filmed attractions no longer needed the services of a narrator: Most of the cartoons by then were talkies, like the *Aesop's Fables* and

Tom and Jerry series (the latter a pair of human characters, not MGM's cat-and-mouse team), produced by Paul Terry's onetime boss Amadee J. Van Beuren. The Van Beuren cartoon package, containing most of that studio's sound output from 1929 to its demise in 1936, was the first Hollywood animated property to be televised on a regular basis.

After *Small Fry Club* had run the cartoons past the saturation point in 1951, the Van Beurens, along with a bundle of early Walter Lantz Studio productions, were syndicated (sold directly to local stations, rather than net-workcast) as the *Unity Pictures Theatrical Cartoon Package*, an appendage of Unity's enormous manifest of old, independently produced movies and short subjects. Additional Van Beuren releases were syndicated by Official Films (the leading home-movie distributor of the period), following network exposure from 1950 through 1952 on ABC's *TV Tots Time*. Film historian Leonard Maltin noted in 1980 that he "was among the many children whose earliest television experiences included multiple viewings of [Van Beuren's] *Sunshine Makers, Toonerville Trolley* and *Parrotville Post Office.*"

Add this writer's name to that list of children, and include in the sensory experience such oft-run Van Beurens as Tom and Jerry's *Wot a Night* (1931) and the haunting, hallucinatory *Pastrytown Wedding* (1934), and you can see why so many of us warped Baby Boomers grew up with an insatiable appetite for dancing mice and talking bears.

TRAILBLAZERS

Cartoons were therefore a vital part of children's television from 1947 onward—but as with the Disney offerings in the 1930s, these were retreads, not made-for-television animated shorts. *Small Fry Club* did telecast original films on occasion, but these showcased puppets and marionettes, regarded at the time as having more resale value than cartoons thanks to the popularity of such video puppets as Howdy Doody and Judy Splinters. The major animation houses and their distributors—Disney/RKO, Terrytoons/20th Century–Fox, Paramount/Famous Studios, Walter Lantz/Universal, MGM, Warner Bros., and Columbia (distributor for Screen Gems Studios, then UPA)—were flourishing in the theatrical market. If the major studios evinced no interest in venturing into television, why should the cartoonists? Independent animators like Shamus Culhane and the Jam Handy Organization did not have the financial wherewithal to produce 26 to 52 television cartoons a year. And besides, advertising work (commercials, public service announcements) was a more readily lucrative endeavor.

One distributor who presaged a burgeoning market for fresh filmed television fare was Jerry Fairbanks, who together with fellow independents Frederick Ziv and Hal Roach was a principal supplier of film filler to local television stations in the late 1940s and early 1950s. Fairbanks had begun his career in theatrical short subjects, marketing a combination cartoon/live action series of one-reelers titled *Speaking of Animals* (in which footage of animals was overlaid with animated lip movements, to give the appearance that the beasts were spouting wisecracks) through the facilities of Paramount Pictures. Fairbanks calculated that the increasing popularity of double features would soon squeeze short subjects off the big screen. Rather than allow his product to wither on the vine theatrically, Fairbanks moved his activities to television, licensing several 10–30 minute properties directly to the small screen between 1947 and 1949: *Public Prosecutor*, starring John Howard as the first filmed television detective; *Goin' Places with Uncle George*, a serialized cutdown of an old Paramount travelogue hosted by veteran character actor Dick Elliot; *Jackson and Jill*, the first filmed sitcom; and *Variety Musicale*, a 15-minute musical program filmed in Mexico to avoid American union restrictions. Jerry Fairbanks was able to assemble his product swiftly and cheaply by means of his patented Multicam system, wherein the action was filmed from several different angles by three (and sometimes five) cameras rather than taking up valuable studio time for new set-ups and retakes.

Among Jerry Fairbanks' wares was a children's program, targeted for potential Saturday morning exposure (the A.M. hours were all but ignored until 1950, on the theory that the more affluent adults purchasing sets were too busy to watch before 5 P.M.). "I don't recall anything special about Saturday morning at that point except that the networks had some vague idea that they wanted programs for kids," recalled Fairbanks to children's television historian Gary Grossman in 1981. "That's why we developed *Crusader Rabbit* and sold our *Speaking of Animals* films to television." *Crusader Rabbit* was a pilot project from aspiring animators Jay Ward, a real estate man, and Alex Anderson, nephew of Terrytoons head man Paul Terry. This serialized story of an adventuresome rabbit and his comic sidekick Rags the Tiger was but one of several cartoon concepts pitched to Fairbanks in hopes that the producer would help Ward and Anderson gain a foothold in the otherwise closed-door animation industry. Considering the fact that "animation" on *Crusader Rabbit* was pared to the bone—the stories unfolded in static, still poses, with movement occurring on the average of once every four seconds—Fairbanks probably latched onto this concept as much for its economy as its cleverness. In fact, the whole operation, from Ward's and Anderson's storyboards concocted in the San Francisco garage of Ward's mother to Fairbanks' Los Angeles–based sound recording sessions, came to the munificent sum of $2500 for each 19.5 minutes' worth of cartoonery (each individual *Crusader* episode was four minutes long, which came to an allotment of approximately $500 an episode). Lucille Bliss, the voice of Crusader Rabbit, would observe over 40 years later that Fairbanks' recording sessions were conducted between 9 P.M. and 4 A.M. because studio space was cheapest during those hours; for her efforts, Bliss was awarded $5.00 per cartoon.

Jerry Fairbanks' pennypinching grew from the realization that he was not going to see a lot of sponsor revenue for *Crusader*. Since the radio days, sponsors had always paid less for children's programming because the kids' peak tune-in hours were Saturday morning from 10 A.M. to noon (EST) and between 4 and 6 P.M. on weekdays—hours during which most adult consumers were out of the room. At the time of *Crusader Rabbit* (1949), only 9 percent of the population owned televisions, which whittled available sponsor money down even further. "At the rock-bottom prices the networks and stations were able to pay for programming then, we had to develop shortcuts" noted Jerry Fairbanks some thirty years later. Indeed, these earliest of television cartoons were labelled "short cut animation" by an industry for whom the term "limited animation" had not yet been coined.

    Crusader Rabbit was ready for broadcast by late 1949. The series was test-marketed in selected cities the following year; the first documented telecast was over Los Angeles' NBC affiliate on Tuesday (not Saturday), August 1, 1950. The remaining four NBC owned-and-operated stations picked up the series, including New York's WNBT—which had been W2XBS back in the "rotating Felix" days. Though the series was the first popular made-for-TV cartoon, it was not, technically, the first such production to be seen. That honor was reserved for *Tele-Comics*, a package of adventure cartoons first syndicated by Vallee Video in late 1949.

    Like *Crusader Rabbit*, *Tele-Comics'* appeal was its cheapness. The series was created as a continuum for a profitable form of children's radio entertainment: the daily cliffhanging serial. Certain live programs like DuMont's *Captain Video* were able to unfold in chapter-play form, but the limited range of the networks at the time (there was still no "live" linkup past Chicago) narrowed the potential audience—and also the profits. To film a daily serial for nationwide distribution at that time would have been far beyond the financial limits of most production firms. *Tele-Comics* was designed as an economical alternative to "real" action, a method of exploiting the action-adventure format without tying up a lot of money consuming on- and off-camera talent. By utilizing nonmoving comic strip panels and a handful of radio actors, *Tele-Comics* was able to embrace several action genres at a fraction of its cost as a "live" property; also, it could be played repeatedly, without expensive restaging. Since the series never pretended to be anything more than illustrated radio, viewers were willing to accept the limitations of *Tele-Comics* and enjoy the series on its own terms—and to fill in production gaps with their radio-fostered imagination skills.

    Though *Crusader Rabbit* would have been the more likely candidate with its links to the NBC o-and-o's, it was *Tele-Comics* which NBC chose as its very first network cartoon series—but not before changing its name to the more proprietary *NBC Comics*. Telecast from September 18, 1950, through March 30, 1951, *NBC Comics* made back its cost almost instantly, and survived in syndication (as *Tele-Comics* again) until the end of the 1950s. So why did *NBC Comics*, together with *Crusader Rabbit*, not immediately open the gates for a steady stream of original television cartoons?

    Again, the answer was largely a matter of money. Despite a growing dependency on film fare, it was still less expensive by about 66 percent to stage a live children's program in the early 1950s. Most such programs sidestepped scripts, sets and actors, preferring the "Uncle" or "Captain" host who presided over a studio audience. The live hosts had one main advantage over participants of filmed dramatic series: They could pitch the sponsor's product directly into the camera without dropping character, and do it over and over without interrupting a nonexistent plotline. Cartoon characters could conceivably do this too, but not without expensively re-animating the footage whenever the sponsor changed its sales pitch — or whenever the sponsor changed, period.

Another reason for the dearth of new cartoon material was public demand. Children enjoyed cartoons, to be sure, but they enjoyed puppet shows, live outer-space adventures and old western movies even more. Those were the merchandising fields mined by the television producers of the early 1950s.

Thus, from 1951 through 1954, only two other television cartoon properties joined *Crusader Rabbit* and *Tele-Comics* on the tube. Both were tied in with television's never-ending search for novelty, to allay fears that children (and adults) would tire of television once its newness had worn off. Television Screen Production's *Jim and Judy in Teleland*, produced between 1949 and 1950 in the wake of *Crusader* and syndicated in 1953, was a mélange of cutout animation (jogging cardboard figures past the screen to create the illusion of movement) and limited cel art, depicting the serialized adventures of two all–American kids. It also attempted to fulfill the fantasies of the first "TV generation" by showing Jim and Judy gain access to "Teleland" by climbing right into their television receiver.

A more successful 1953 venture was Ariel Productions' *Winky Dink and You*. Unlike *Jim and Judy*, this series had its roots in past "audience participation" radio programs, where the kids at home were encouraged to join in the games, contests and quizzes conducted from the radio studio. These were usually conceived with the ulterior motive of pushing the sponsors' products. Children's show producers Jack Barry, Dan Enright and Ed Friendly were approached by an advertising agency which wanted to encourage children to draw pictures in conjunction with a television series — a clever means of promoting a line of drawing kits, in the fashion of the popular Jon Gnagy home-artist series (*You Are an Artist, Learn to Draw*, etc.). To avoid the static quality of aiming a camera at an artist drawing on an easel, Jack Barry and his associates suggested that the on-screen pictures be animated. Gradually this evolved into a pointy-headed cartoon sprite named Winky Dink.

"Using simplified stop-motion animation-limited animation in its crudest form, we presented Winky Dink's cartoon story," Jack Barry recalled to Gary Grossman in the early 1980s. "At some point in the adventure, the kids would see something like Winky Dink and his pet dog Woofer come up to a river with no way of getting across. So we'd say, 'Okay, boys and girls, quickly get your crayons and draw a little boat. . .' I'd show them right where to draw it, it would appear that Winky Dink would then get into it and go across the river."

The Winky Dink Magic TV Kit, 50 cents at toy stores everywhere, would facilitate the kids' home artistic skills. The viewer was encouraged to stretch a sheet of clear acetate across the television screen and draw directly upon it with washable crayons. Jack Barry would later insist it was his hope to foster "interactive television" in this manner — though as newspaper humorist Dave Barry (no relation) would observe in 1994, the most "interactive" aspect of this project occurred whenever parents reacted to their kids' forsaking the acetate sheet and drawing straight onto the television screen.

Winky Dink and You is fondly remembered by graybeard television addicts like myself, even though most of us caught on early that its *raison d'être* was commercialism rather than art. Somehow it did not matter back in the 1950s that 90 percent of television was a glorified advertising supplement (dancing cigarette cartons, singing detergent containers, etc.) so long as we were fully entertained in the process. *Winky Dink* does however illustrate our premise that most made-for-television cartoons were created out of necessity rather than artistic considerations. Chances are Jack Barry and his confreres would never have animated Winky Dink at all had there been a better method to sell those kits.

By the middle of the 1950s, necessity would also prompt animation's "big guns" to enter the television fray — and in so doing open up a market that really hadn't existed before.

ENTER THE "MAJORS"

Walt Disney had been courted by the television networks as early as 1950, but Hollywood's foremost cartoon producer disliked the medium's "bad showmanship" inherent in its constant commercial interruptions. Disney insisted that his annual Christmas specials, inaugurated in 1951, be telecast with the sponsor's name mentioned only at the beginning and end of each program, with no interior advertisement. Come 1954, however, Disney was less resistant to commercial television, and for the most fundamental of reasons: his bank account. The producer's dream of a Disneyland amusement park could not be realized without the input of outside financial backing. The upstart ABC television network (which had gone coast-to-coast in 1953), anxious to amplify its schedule with quality programming in order to achieve parity with the long-entrenched CBS and NBC, approached Disney with a mutual backscratching deal. If ABC would agree to pump money into Disneyland, Walt Disney in turn would produce a weekly, full-hour anthology series for ABC.

Though the subsequent *Disneyland* was, at base, a 60-minute advertisement for Disney and his wares (reviewers dubbed the series' "documentary" on the studio's *20,000 Leagues Under the Sea* as "The Long, Long Trailer"), Walt Disney himself was committed to wrapping up the package in the most professional, entertaining manner possible. In making the best, slickest commercial on television, Disney also turned out the medium's finest filmed anthology series — not as an afterthought, but with the deliberation and pre-planning of the true showman. As a result, *Disneyland* offered the most accomplished animated work ever seen on television. True, much of it was re-edited from Disney's theatrical shorts, but the studio bridged the old footage with rich, fully animated new cartoonwork. The motives were both aesthestic and practical: With the decreasing market for movie-theatre short subjects and with his feature length cartoons consuming as much as three to six years' production time, Disney was able to keep his animation staff busy on a day-to-day basis with television work. Some of the best animation of *Disneyland*'s inaugural season showed up in an otherwise live-action episode, "Man in Space," which when released theatrically was nominated for an Academy Award.

Crucial to *Disneyland*'s success was its timeslot. Had the series shown up on one of the older networks (CBS, NBC or DuMont), Disney's reputation as a children's entertainer might have consigned the program to Saturday morning or, at best, the "culture ghetto" of late Sunday afternoon. But ABC recognized Disney's value, so *Disneyland* was slotted in Wednesday prime time, 7:30 to 8:30 P.M. EST. It was on early enough to grab the youngsters before bedtime, and late enough to qualify as adult programming. Despite the fact that ABC had only 13 prime affiliates in 1954 (in most markets, the network shared a channel with NBC or CBS), *Disneyland* staged an almost instant ratings coup, outperforming such longtime favorites as Arthur Godfrey and Perry Como in some key cities. It was the first network series that truly fulfilled the entertainment needs of all viewer demographic groups, from six years old to 76. By the time of its second season (1955-56), *Disneyland* was the fourth highest rated program on television—just below Ed Sullivan, just above Jack Benny—and the *only* ABC offering to break into the Top 25.

Disneyland proved that major studio animation could flourish on a well-publicized network basis, but Disney was too much the showman to confine his series to cartoons. Mickey Mouse and Donald Duck were obliged to share time with Davy Crockett, *True Life Adventures* animal documentaries, and serialized cutdowns of Disney's best live-action films. Conversely, Paul Terry of Terrytoons had *only* cartoons to offer. But he had well over 1,000 of these, just ripe for plucking and tossing into the television barrel. A businessman first, last, and always, Terry was fond of noting that while Disney was the Tiffany's of cartoondom, Terrytoons was the Woolworth's. True enough, but a five-and-dime zircon can have as much resale value as a jeweled setting if it is promoted properly.

The first major sale of Terrytoons predated the Disney deal, when General Foods bought television rights to a package of late silent and early talkie cartoons in 1953—most of these starring a hayseed character named Farmer Al Falfa. Like many early television releases of theatrical films, the production origins of the Terrytoons were heavily camouflaged with refilmed opening credits, new titles, and even a renamed hero: Farmer Al Falfa was transformed into Farmer Gray. Terrytoons' distributor, 20th Century–Fox, insisted upon this so that the older cartoons would not represent competition to the newer Terrytoons releases; it would not be smart business to suggest that kids could satisfy themselves with television releases at the expense of the still-saleable Terrytoons theatrical shorts. This first Terrytoons batch showed up on a twice-weekly, 15-minute CBS afternoon program, *Barker Bill's Cartoon Show*, which ran from 1953 through 1956. *Barker Bill* was a success, prompting an even bigger 1953 sale for Paul Terry: CBS bought the entire Terrytoons backlog for 3.5 million dollars—more than Terry had ever seen in all his forty years in the business—and a few years later purchased the studio itself.

But CBS bided its time, waiting to see how *Disneyland* would fare before giving its Terrytoons package a full-fledged 30-minute weekly display. On December 10, 1955, the network unveiled the fully sponsored *Mighty Mouse Playhouse* on Saturday mornings, where it remained a top ratings-grabber for 12 years. Here CBS had a popular, immediately recognizable central character to assure its leadership in the children's show field—and most attractively, the property was already bought and paid for, without the exigencies of residual payments or new talent fees. It was the beginning of the end of "live" kids' programming on Saturday mornings.

Another established cartoon studio followed suit with a major television sale. In 1955, Guild Films purchased the television rights to Warner Bros.' black-and-white Looney Tunes, produced between 1930 and 1943 and headlining such favorites as Porky Pig and Daffy Duck. Officially, this package premiered in April of 1955, but didn't make its biggest sales push until after Disney and Terrytoons mapped out the marketable territory. As with the earliest Terry releases, Guild was obliged to disguise the fact that Warner Bros. had anything to do with *Looney Tunes* with reshot credits and interior edits of all references to Warners (notably the W-B Shield logo which pops up out of nowhere in *Porky in Wackyland*); the studio had not yet issued its feature film backlog to television, and wasn't about to "legitimize" the competition by advertising itself on the tube.

By late 1955, Warners and, indeed, most of the major studios were openly wooing television. Disney's success was only part of the reason. The 1949 Supreme Court ruling against block booking—the studios' practice of promising their "A" product to theatres on the proviso that those theatres also run their "B" and "C" films—had led to the governmental decree that the studios divest themselves of their movie-theatre chains and thus break up the monopoly that the "majors" had enjoyed for years. Without a guaranteed outlet for their product, the studios were forced to turn to television. At first, this was accomplished in the Disney manner of doling out selected filmclips of earlier triumphs: thus in 1955 was born ABC's *MGM Parade*, a hodgepodge of vignettes from such hits as *Captains Courageous* and *The Philadelphia Story*, which the network ran just following *Disneyland* on Wednesday evenings. That same year, CBS telecast (*again* on Wednesdays!) *The 20th Century–Fox Hour*, wherein the studio offered brand new hour-long adaptations of the best of its past theatrical films. And finally in 1955, ABC's *Warner Bros. Presents* (squeezed off Wednesdays and telecast Tuesdays) rotated three weekly adaptations of old Warners feature triumphs: *King's Row*, *Casablanca* and *Cheyenne*. All of the above-mentioned programs emulated Disney in brazenly promoting their studios' current product. None of the programs exhibited Disney's graceful expertise at combining self-aggrandizement with entertainment value.

In 1956, most of the studios commenced releasing their pre–1948 films to television (the cutoff date was dictated by the Screen Actors Guild's insistence upon payment of residuals for anything produced during the "TV era"—that is, anything after 1948). Most old movies were issued through the studios' television subsidiaries. Columbia's product was handled by the studio's own Screen Gems; the pre–1948 Warner Bros. movies, controlled via a complicated legal arrangement by United Artists, were distributed to television by UA's subsidiary Associated Artists Productions (A.A.P.); and 20th Century–Fox films were released to television by National Telefilm Associates (N.T.A.), a firm partly owned by Fox. The three above-mentioned television syndicators also handled the bulk of major-studio cartoons. Screen Gems was responsible for television play of Columbia's *Scrappy*, *Krazy Kat* and *Phantasies* cartoon series of the 1930s and 1940s. Warners' *Merrie Melodies* cartoons were handled by A.A.P., with the *Bugs Bunny* vehicles receiving the most promotion. National Telefilm Associates could not issue the 20th Century–Fox Terrytoon releases, since these were controlled by CBS, so the distributor made a deal with Paramount Pictures (which did not issue its backlog to television until late 1958) in conjunction with U.M.&M. Television Corp. to release Paramount's *Little Lulu*, *Betty Boop*, *Screen Songs*, *Color Classics*, *Puppetoons*, and others—the majority of Paramount's Max Fleischer, George Pal and Famous Studios product.

Two potent Paramount properties slipped through N.T.A.'s fingers. Max Fleischer's expensive *Superman* cartoons of the early 1940s were legally controlled by the comic-book firm National Periodicals, and separately licensed to Motion Pictures for Television, which also had syndicated the live-action *Superman* television series. And the Paramount *Popeye the Sailor* cartoons, the studio's most valuable animated commodity, were sold by King Features, the newspaper chain which owned the Popeye character, to A.A.P.

As a result, A.A.P. found itself with the hottest combination ticket in the cartoon field: *Bugs Bunny* and *Popeye*. When both properties were made available to television in late 1956, local stations in the largest markets, taking their cue from Disney's marketing strategy, saw to it that the A.A.P. package attained the best and most prestigious timeslots possible. Big cities like New York and Los Angeles were able to support independent television channels (stations not affiliated with any network), and these independents, eager to bite away at the networks, ran their *Popeye*s and *Bugs Bunny*s in the early evening hours, rather than confining them to the less sponsor-attracting afternoon slots. According to the weekly "local top ten" tallies compiled by *Broadcasting Magazine* and *Variety* in the late 1950s, the A.A.P. cartoons were guaranteed to rack up big ratings—often *the* top ratings in their timeslot. In fact, Chicago's independent channel WGN-TV did so well with their prime-time, full color *Bugs Bunny Show* that the station continued running the daily cartoon series until the early 1960s, at which time its producer was a youngish cartoon buff by the name of Fred Silverman.

BILL AND JOE

The 1956-1957 television season represented an Elysian Field for the cartoon fan. The Disney manifest could be seen sporadically on *Disneyland* and via a daily cartoon serving on ABC's *Mickey Mouse Club*; Terrytoons' *Mighty Mouse* was joined by the studio's *Heckle and Jeckle* on CBS' Saturday morning schedule; and Popeye, Bugs Bunny, Porky Pig, Betty Boop and such were crowding the airwaves on a local basis. But these were all theatrical hand-me-downs; where were the fresh, new, made for television cartoons?

They weren't there because no one felt the need. Both Disney and Terrytoons were producing occasional television animation, but not on a large basis. Disney, as mentioned, liked to use *Disneyland* as a combination training and exercise program for his staff. Terrytoons was owned by CBS which, like Disney, felt it should get value for money by keeping the staff busy on occasion. When CBS decided to go head-to-head on Wednesdays with *Disneyland* in the summer of 1956, it was with a package of readymade Terrytoons under the umbrella title *CBS Cartoon Theatre*. Since *Disneyland* had a host (Walt Disney himself), *Cartoon Theatre* would also have a host: 31-year-old Dick Van Dyke. To sustain the cartoon connection in the live-action sequences, the network ordered its Terrytoons staffers to produce a few "bumpers" in which Heckle and Jeckle or Dinky Duck would appear to be conversing with Van Dyke. And when Bob Keeshan, CBS' *Captain Kangaroo* on weekday mornings, made it clear that he was dissatisfied with the frequently vulgar and violent early-talkie theatrical cartoons that plagued children's programs, CBS obliged Keeshan with a wholesome, nonviolent Terrytoons first-run featurette, *Tom Terrific*. These cartoons established a base on *Captain Kangaroo* for a handful of other television cartoons from both Terrytoons (*Adventures of Lariat Sam*) and independents (Sam Singer's *The Adventures of Pow Wow*).

On the whole, television executives were happy with the financial kickbacks on theatrical cartoon retreads, and did not feel a need to request new material. The single instance in the 1956-57 season that an entire half-hour of fresh cartoons was required occurred when CBS, again hoping to tap the *Disneyland* audience, commissioned the award-winning cartoon firm United Productions of America (UPA) to assemble a Sunday late-afternoon series built around UPA's popular character Gerald McBoing Boing. The request was logical from a financial standpoint. United Productions of America had popularized the "limited animation" form, using the least amount of movement to tell its stories in a stylized, minimalist fashion. This style not only cost less than most cartoonmaking, but it represented a deliberate break from the Disney "full animation" technique which, so far as UPA was concerned, made cartoons move so realistically that the animator was denied any form of personal artistic expression. The stature of UPA in the animation community impressed CBS, but CBS was most impressed by the cost factor; figuring that the limited-animation technique was also quicker and cheaper than the

Disney method, the network went to UPA in hopes of attaining Disney prestige at a fraction of the cost and time.

To its credit, CBS heavily advertised *Gerald McBoing Boing* and gave it a leg-up by telecasting the series in color, a luxury denied ABC's *Disneyland*. The problem was that UPA's theatrical product appealed more to the intelligentsia than the average cartoon fans: the studio was strong on mood, technique and design, but weak on charismatic star characters and slapstick gags—the principal sales angles of such favorites as Popeye, Mighty Mouse and Bugs Bunny. Mr. Magoo, UPA's one major, bankable "star," was absent on *Gerald McBoing Boing*; the studio's distributor Columbia refused to cut into Magoo's theatrical profits by issuing him to television. *Gerald McBoing Boing* had an on-and-off career for the next two years over CBS, but while it received the plaudits of critics and parents' groups, it failed to establish a profit base that might have encouraged further made-for-TV cartoons.

Still, 1957 saw a small spurt of television-cartoon activity. Impressed by the success of Popeye and company, Shul Bonsall bought the rights to the old *Crusader Rabbit* property and ground out a thrifty new full-color *Crusader* package, animated by the television-commercial factory TV Spots. Richard H. Ullman decided to break into the "franchise" business (selling a program concept to local stations, which would then be responsible for production costs) as popularized by Claster Productions' *Romper Room*, and to do so commissioned a parsimonious outer-space cartoon, *Colonel Bleep*, to be shown as a component on a franchised children's program, *Uncle Bill's TV Club*. And Art Clokey's *Gumby*, an added-attraction feature of *The Howdy Doody Show* which utilized stop-motion animation (puppet models manipulated by hand, then filmed one frame at a time to simulate movement), was bundled into its own half-hour weekly in March 1957 as NBC's Saturday morning answer to *Mighty Mouse*.

Matters began to congeal in the fall of 1957. Kellogg's cereals, impressed at the manner in which ABC's late-afternoon daily *Mickey Mouse Club* had turned the comparatively tiny toy firm of Mattel into a major commercial competitor, decided to invest in the afternoon children's television field. Kellogg's could not buy time on *Mickey Mouse* because of competing cereal sponsorship on the Disney series, but attained the next best thing when ABC dropped the expensive first half hour of the 60 minute *Club* to make room for its own less costly package of five half-hour filmed series, each to be run once a week in the 5:00 P.M. (EST) timeslot. Four of the five ABC afternoon attractions were reruns of earlier syndicated and prime time series, and two of these had built-in Kellogg's sponsorship: *Superman* and *Wild Bill Hickok*. Kellogg's wanted a third 5 P.M. series, and it wanted a cartoon program, in hopes of achieving the excellent results which greeted General Foods' patronage of *Mighty Mouse Playhouse* and *Heckle and Jeckle*.

At the same time, theatrical cartoon producer Walter Lantz was seeking a prestige entree into network television for his hefty backlog of cartoon shorts. Lantz, Kellogg's and ABC pooled their energies, and the result was *The Woody Woodpecker Show*, a 17-episode series comprised of old Lantz cartoons, bridged with newly animated commercial lead-ins and "behind the scenes" pieces on animation techniques hosted (in Disney fashion) by Lantz himself. Only a season or so earlier ABC had practically no afternoon service: now it had a nearly unbeatable Thursday afternoon lineup: *American Bandstand* at 4 P.M., *Woody Woodpecker* at 5, *Mickey Mouse Club* at 5:30.

Woody Woodpecker was welcome, but still represented only a sliver of newly shot animation for television. Then there was NBC's Saturday-morning *Ruff and Reddy*, which the network had plunked opposite CBS' *Mighty Mouse Playhouse* in hopes of syphoning off the cartoon-fan contingent. Originally, *Ruff and Reddy* was to have been constructed on the same lines as *Mighty Mouse* and *Woody Woodpecker*—a half hour made up of old theatrical releases. Unfortunately, NBC did not have anything to run. John Mitchell, head of sales for Columbia Pictures' television division Screen Gems, pitched his parent studio's manifest of 1930s and 1940s cartoons to NBC. Aware that these Columbia cartoons were among the least appealing short subjects ever released by a major Hollywood studio, Mitchell also offered NBC the added attraction of brand new cartoons—produced, it was carefully emphasized, by the same people who had been doing the Oscar-studded *Tom and Jerry* series for MGM.

From the various Hollywood cartoons readied for television sales in 1956, the MGM product, *Tom and Jerry* included, was conspicuously absent. This is because MGM cartoons were still posting considerable profits in the theatres, and the studio had no desire to undercut this with any television sales. Historically MGM had been more resistant to television than any other studio, viewing the Great Glowing Cathode as the unfairest of competition—the free kind. But the march of postwar progress was against MGM. Increasing production costs and tax levies resulted in budget slashes and layoffs at this formerly most extravagant of studios. In 1956, MGM posted its first financial loss in its 32-year history. Also in 1956, the MGM pre–1948 film package was licensed to television.

Elsewhere on the MGM lot, William Hanna and Joseph Barbera, who had started with the MGM animation division as part of the artist/writer pool in the 1930s, had been appointed to head that division in 1955 upon the retirement of longtime cartoon producer Fred Quimby. With the *Tom and Jerry* and *Droopy* cartoons representing some of the very few surefire money-makers for MGM in this troubled period, and with their budgets increased while other studio expenditures were being diminished, Hanna and Barbera had every reason to feel secure. But "security" and "Hollywood" are oxymor-onic terms: In early 1957, MGM decided it could make just as much money reissuing its old cartoons, eliminating the need for any new product. And so it came to pass that Bill Hanna and Joe Barbera showed up one bright spring morning for work, only to be told by a functionary of the bookkeeping department to clean out their desks and vacate the premises post-haste.

Bill and Joe desperately tried to convince the MGM brass that they could continue to produce cartoons at a drastically reduced price, by stream-

The Hanna-Barbera Stock Company. *Clockwise from top left:* Pixie and Dixie, Huckleberry Hound, George Jetson, Quick Draw McGraw, Doggie Daddy, Astro, Fred Flintstone, Yogi Bear and Boo Boo (with pic-a-nic basket), Augie Doggie (with clapper), Ranger Smith (behind tree), Wilma Flintstone, Scooby-Doo, and Barney Rubble.

lining the operation to the most limited of movements and by cutting down production time. After all, had not UPA shown that this technique could be saleable? Though MGM executive Eddie Mannix was impressed by Hanna and Barbera's moneysaving blueprints, he shook his head, saying, "There is no future in cartoons." After several weeks of slammed doors at other studios, Bill and Joe decided to set up their own independent animation firm.

Hanna and Barbera had one strong ally from the old MGM days, director George Sidney, with whom the team had worked on the 1945 musical *Anchors Aweigh* (the one wherein Gene Kelly dances with a cartoon mouse) and who functioned as president of Bill and Joe's studio in its earliest days. George was the son of L. K. Sidney, a close and trusted friend of Columbia Pictures president Harry Cohn. Thanks to this link, Hanna-Barbera was able to set up a meeting at Columbia, thereby arranging for the production of a pilot television cartoon, to be bankrolled by Screen Gems. Harry Cohn got only as far as viewing the pilot's pencil test (the rough animated drawings prepared for the inkers and painters responsible for the finished cartoon) when he abruptly shouted with his usual charm and tact, "Get rid of them! Just drop the whole idea!" But Screen Gems' John Mitchell had faith in the television-cartoon concept: He had already shipped the same footage to NBC, who were eager to use the Hanna-Barbera project as a wraparound for their otherwise unappetizing Columbia cartoon package. Roger Muir, one of *Howdy Doody's* producers, entered the picture, offering to produce the live part of the program, hosted by Jimmy Blaine and a couple of puppets.

Hanna-Barbera's contribution to this confection were the short, serialized adventures of a small cat named Ruff and a tall dog named Reddy. Premiering December 14, 1957, *The Ruff and Reddy Show* established many of Hanna-Barbera's trademarks: cut-to-the-bone animation (even more simplified than the plan the producers had submitted to Eddie Mannix, thanks to Columbia's insistence that each five-minute *Ruff and Reddy* cost less than $3000); compartmentalized character design, wherein neckties and cuffs separated heads and hands from the bodies, allowing Hanna-Barbera to animate only that part of the body that moved rather than the entire figure; and heavy reliance upon dialogue and versatile voiceover work, here provided by future Hanna-Barbera stalwarts Daws Butler and Don Messick.

The impact of *Ruff and Reddy* was immediate on its appreciative young audience, less so on the television industry. A January 1958 *TV Guide* article titled "Are Children's Shows Through?" listed the difficulties that such worthwhile programs as *Captain Kangaroo, Susan's Show, Watch Mr. Wizard* and *Let's Take a Trip* had in lining up sponsors. Each network affiliate, we were told, carried such programs at a loss because of their cost and the lack of commercial support. The notion that television cartoons might attract sponsors and cut down on ongoing costs (once the cartoons were produced, they could be run forever at little additional expense) was not mentioned. In fact, cartoons themselves were not mentioned at all.

A *Variety* article later in 1958 did address the potential of television animation, noting the audience response to *Tom Terrific* and *Ruff and Reddy*, but more or less decreed that there was no necessity to churn out new animation when such "old" material as *Popeye* and *Bugs Bunny* was doing so well on a local basis. The article also discussed the merits of full versus limited animation, coming to the same conclusion as most television executives of the time: Kids can't tell the difference. Reading between the lines, one could note a secondary conclusion: Why rack our brains over what kids will buy, when the big money was in adult prime time? The *TV Guide* article had also pointed out the lack of percentage in gearing new product solely for children. CBS executive James Aubrey was quoted as preferring "broad, general" programs aimed at the widest possible age range, and did not believe in telling either affiliates or sponsors, "Here's a show you won't like if you're over 10 years old."

Hanna-Barbera must have taken stock of this attitude as it prepared its second television release, *Huckleberry Hound*. The program would be sponsored by Kellogg's, which this time around opted for syndication rather than the ABC network, because it was possible to corral more local markets on a station-by-station basis rather than relying on ABC's comparatively puny affiliate lineup. Kellogg's was established as a children's sponsor. Thus, cartoons were strictly for kids—at least they *were* until the Hanna-Barbera promotional staff went to work. Even before *Huckleberry Hound* was released, the "adult" aspects of the series—notably its flippant dialogue and occasional lampoons of popular television and movie genres—were trumpeted and amplified. Several local markets responded by picking up the series for prime time berths (or very near prime time), purchasing splashy newspaper ads to herald Huck. And once the series did score a hit, Hanna-Barbera issued authenticated statistics indicating that a goodly percentage of the *Huckleberry Hound* audience was of voting, or at least draft age.

Hanna-Barbera had thus not only created a market for television cartoons, but had also created a wide-range market with the potential for attracting adult advertisers. The influence of Hanna-Barbera can best be measured by the number of made-for-television cartoons produced between 1958 and 1960. In 1958, there were *Huckleberry Hound* and a minor-league *Crusader Rabbit* imitation, *Spunky and Tadpole*. From January through December of 1959, television trade magazines were peppered with ads for new cartoon properties: Hanna-Barbera's *Quick Draw McGraw*, Larry Harmon's *Bozo the Clown*, Joe Oriolo's *Felix the Cat* (there's that feline again!), Jay Ward's *Rocky and His Friends*, New World's *Mel-o-Toons* and Cambria's *Clutch Cargo*. These were not tiny promos tucked into corners (the fate of *Spunky and Tadpole*) but full-page-spread invitations to pick up and profit from these properties; *Felix the Cat* boasted an ad campaign comparable to a Cinerama spectacular. And in 1960, the floodgates opened further: *Q. T. Hush, Courageous Cat, Deputy Dawg, The Nutty Squirrels, King Leonardo, Dick Tracy*, and brand-new *Popeye* and *Mr. Magoo* packages.

A 1977 piece on Saturday morning cartoons written by Mark Nardone for Workman Press' *TV Book* acknowledged Hanna-Barbera's responsibility for initiating the television-cartoon movement—and in so doing, consigned the studio to the ash heap. "Hanna-Barbera proved to the networks that by cutting corners (actually chunks), it was possible to make cartoons cheaply enough for television's needs. They deserve thanks for nothing." Nardone chronicles all of Hanna-Barbera's artistic "crimes," reserving his words of praise for Bob Clampett's *Beany and Cecil* and Jay Ward's *Rocky* (both admittedly praiseworthy). Had his thesis that all Saturday morning cartoonery was trash allowed him objectivity, Mark Nardone could have observed that had Hanna-Barbera not constructed a market for television animation from scratch in the first place, there would have been no *Beany and Cecil* or *Rocky*. They deserve thanks for plenty.

1960–1965: THE GOLD RUSH

The much-maligned ABC network, like Hanna-Barbera, is also due some praise for securing the future of television cartoons. Although the network's treatment of the brilliant *Rocky and His Friends* was cavalier at best, careless at worst (juggling its timeslot, running serialized episodes out of sequence), for the most part ABC was more committed to cartoonery than either NBC or CBS. *Disneyland*, now titled *Walt Disney Presents*, was still dominating the ratings as the 1960s commenced, though Disney was concentrating more on live-action westerns and adventure programs and less on cartoons. *Matty's Funday Funnies*, a package of Paramount/Famous Studios theatrical cartoons fully sponsored by Mattel Toys (which benefited tremendously from the merchandising of Paramount's *Casper the Friendly Ghost*), managed to make an otherwise comatose late Sunday afternoon timeslot lucrative enough to encourage ABC to expand its entire weekend morning and afternoon schedule. And in the fall of 1960, ABC unveiled Hanna-Barbera's *The Flintstones*, not as an afternoon children's program, but as a prime time adult series (Though not the *first* cartoon prime-timer as sometimes suggested, *Flintstones* was the first to be telecast as late as 8:30 P.M., traditionally the kid-adult cutoff point).

Sensing a trend that would pick up where the once popular but now-flagging "western" craze left off, ABC also had two other cartoon shows in its 1960-61 evening schedule: Warner Bros.' *The Bugs Bunny Show* (featuring post–1948 Warners cartoons never before seen on television, bridged with newly shot animation) and *Matty's Funday Funnies*, now occupying the 7:30 P.M. Friday slot where *Walt Disney Presents* (moved to Sundays to combat NBC's new *Shirley Temple Theatre*) had reigned supreme since 1958. Though only *Flintstones* was a grade-A hit, the ABC anschluss, together with the ongoing syndicated popularity of Hanna-Barbera's *Huckleberry Hound, Yogi Bear* and *Quick Draw McGraw*, prompted a renaissance in the cartoon industry, which the major studios (like MGM) had been in the process of writing off with a curt "No future."

Twenty-five Hollywood production companies were busy tossing off animation in mid–1961, amassing a budget in excess of $33,000,000. While much of this activity was concentrated in advertising, a lot of cartoon work was also being geared for entertainment. New properties included *The Alvin Show, Top Cat, Calvin and the Colonel, Space Angel*; from Canada's Rankin-Bass, *Tales of the Wizard of Oz* and *The New Adventures of Pinocchio*; and from Britain's Halas and Batchelor, *Snip Snap* and *Foo Foo*. In production or on the horizon were *Touche Turtle, Lippy the Lion, Wally Gator, Beetle Bailey, Krazy Kat, Snuffy Smith* and *The Mighty Hercules*.

In the fall of 1961, network prime time schedules cleared space for the established *Flintstones* and *Bugs Bunny Show*, with *Rocky and His Friends* emigrating from ABC to NBC, thence given a 7 P.M. Sunday colorcast as *The Bullwinkle Show*. *Calvin and the Colonel* was run by ABC on Tuesdays at 8:30, and *Top Cat* in the same slot on Wednesdays. Earlier on Wednesday evening, CBS joined the club with *The Alvin Show*. And on Saturday or Sunday early evening (depending on the market), Mattel had folded *Matty's Funday Funnies* and latched on to a new merchandising Eldorado, *Beany and Cecil*. But the anticipated prime time cartoon trend never really materialized. Audiences who enjoyed *The Flintstones* regarded the newer cartoon arrivals as mere pretenders to the throne, and tuned in instead to sitcoms, variety shows and the *true* new trend of the early 1960s, the "psychological" or "problem" drama (*Ben Casey, Dr. Kildare, The Defenders*, etc.). But cartoons were still more than welcome during the Saturday morning and late afternoon children's hours—especially since the networks needed something to counteract the increasing costs of live-action kids' programs.

Saturday morning in fact became the Port of Wayfaring Cartoons. In 1961, only Total Television's *King Leonardo* (NBC) and the evergreen *Mighty Mouse* (CBS) were run in that period, the rest of the morning given over to human beings. But in mid–1962, *The Alvin Show* commenced Saturday morning reruns, allowing its producers (Format Films/Bagdasarian Productions) to recoup its costs and permitting CBS a viable commercial property at a now-reasonable price (the program had already been paid for; no new moneys need change hands outside of residuals). By September of 1962, only *The Flintstones* and Hanna-Barbera's new *The Jetsons* were seen in prime time. *The Bullwinkle Show*, as much a victim of NBC interference as its CBS *Lassie* competition, had been shunted to Sunday afternoon; Walt Disney, now on NBC, pursued diversification, with only a smattering of cartoon episodes. Saturday morning was now the refuge of *Alvin*, *Top Cat* and *Bugs Bunny* reruns from the evening hours (joined in January 1963 by *Beany and Cecil* rebroadcasts); of *King Leonardo*, first-run on Saturdays but now itself in rerun; and of 1957's *Ruff and Reddy*, exhumed on the coattails of Hanna-Barbera's latter-day prominence.

From here on, producers and distributors would set their sights on Saturday morning and the sponsors who dwelt therein. The 1963 lineup in that pocket of time included *Top Cat*, *Alvin*, *Bugs Bunny*, *Mighty Mouse*, *Beany and Cecil*, *Ruff and Reddy*, incoming repeats of *The Jetsons*, *Quick Draw McGraw* and *Bullwinkle*, and three new programs, Terrytoons' *Hector Heathcote*, Total Television's *Tennessee Tuxedo*, and Harveytoons' *New Casper Cartoon Show*. None of these would have been big performers in nighttime, but all were automatic money machines for the kiddie trade—and except for *Heathcote*, *Tennesse Tuxedo* and *Casper* not one extra cent for new animation was required.

The year 1964 represented a last stand for prime time cartoons (except for the very brief surfacing in 1970 of the summer replacement series *Where's Huddles?*). Hanna-Barbera sought to alter its comedy image somewhat with *Jonny Quest*, an elaborate weekly animated adventure series for ABC. United Productions of America, acting upon the marvelous ratings performance of its 1962 one-hour animated special *Mr. Magoo's Christmas Carol*, mounted an ambitious weekly anthology of dramatized literary classics, *The Famous Adventures of Mr. Magoo*, for NBC. However, 1964 turned out to be the Year of the Spy, and both *Jonny Quest* and *Famous Adventures* were deemed as Ghosts of Seasons Past rather than up-to-date fodder for the *Man from U.N.C.L.E.* generation. The only new cartoons to score significant successes in 1964 were on Saturday morning (Total TV's *Underdog*, Jay Ward's *Hoppity Hooper*, Ed Graham's *Linus the Lionhearted*) and in syndication (Hanna-Barbera's *Magilla Gorilla* and *Peter Potamus*).

Somewhat unobtrusively, one wave of the future was signalled with another 1964 cartoon release (actually available in 1963, but not sold on a nationwide basis until a year later): *Astro Boy*, a daily half-hour science fiction cartoon. One of the reasons that so many cartoons were so readily available in the early 1960s was that a large contingent of animation staffers had been cut loose from the major Hollywood studios, who were closing down their cartoon divisions as the market for short subjects evaporated. These cartoon veterans were eagerly picked up by Hanna-Barbera, Bob Clampett, Format Films and other firms, and though they were frustrated on a creative level, the oldtimers were willing to learn shortcut techniques to survive. Still, the Cartoonists Union demanded lofty wages for their services. Total Television and Jay Ward Productions stemmed this by shipping their animation to Mexico, but even here costs were increasing. *Astro Boy* was produced in Japan at rock-bottom prices, with the Japanese Mushi Studios handling virtually all production responsibilities, from storyboard and character design onward. Best of all, it was saleable to an American audience. Though the Japanese imports were few in the middle years of the 1960s — *Astro Boy, Gigantor, The Eighth Man, Cyborg Big "X," Kimba the White Lion, Marine Boy, Prince Planet,* and everyone's favorite, *Speed Racer* — a marketplace was slowly being established, leading up to the inevitable decision that American production costs could be defrayed or dropped altogether by relying upon what the industry would tag "Japanimation."

September 1965: No new prime time cartoons appeared; only *The Flintstones* survived from the olden days, and it was destined for cancellation. New to Saturday morning network television were *Secret Squirrel, Atom Ant* and *Milton the Monster.* The first two programs, produced by Hanna-Barbera, exhibited the loss of spirit that was beginning to fester in the television animation world. Neither program contributed anything new comically that had not already been seen on H-B's *Huckleberry Hound, Yogi Bear* or *The Flintstones.* They appeared to be going through their motions by rote: The same background art, the same tired "rhyming" jokes, the same homogenized character design. Hal Seeger's *Milton the Monster,* together with the syndicated 1965 releases *Roger Ramjet* and *The New Three Stooges,* exhibited another shortcoming of animation in this period: solid comic ideas and clever production design compromised by budget restrictions and lack of preparation time. On one hand, we had animators with the facilities but without the desire; on the other, we had the desire but limited facilities. The overall attitude of the networks was "Who cares, as long as there's lots of animation for us to advertise?" Hence the new programs on Saturday were outnumbered by reruns of the old. Even the one "new" success on CBS was old: MGM's *Tom and Jerry* backlog.

Conversely, ABC had King Features' *The Beatles.* This package of new cartoons based on the likenesses and songs of the Fab Four made up in style and energy what it lacked in full animation. *The Beatles* established a still-thriving trend towards animating "live" properties with guaranteed appeal, leading to future projects like *The Jackson 5ive, The Osmonds, New Kids on the Block, Kid 'n Play* and *Hammerman* on the musical side, *Laurel and Hardy, Laverne and Shirley, Fonz and the Happy Days Gang, Mork and Mindy, The Gary Coleman Show* and *Wishkid Starring Macaulay Culkin* from the comedy world, and *Harlem Globetrotters, Hulk Hogan's Rock 'n' Wrestling,* and *Pro-Stars* from the sports arena.

Additionally, *The Beatles* reclaimed much of the adult audience that had been abandoning cartoons in the last few seasons. One of those adults viewed *The Beatles* less as an entertainment than as a challenge — a challenge to this man to enervate the Saturday morning "garbage pile" (his own words) and turn it into a network ratings battleground on the same scale as prime time.

1965-1969: THE GOLDEN GUT

The shape of Fred Silverman's television career was predetermined before he had even set foot in a studio. His college thesis dwelt (with admiration) on the manner in which ABC television had risen in stature through "counterprogramming" — running westerns while the other networks were running variety shows, scheduling detective series opposite sitcoms, and so forth. Silverman remained faithful to this concept while working at Chicago's independent WGN in the early 1960s, adding his own brilliant showmanship savvy: By generously publicizing what WGN had to offer (network reruns, old movies) and counterprogramming against the city's three competing network affiliates, he managed to make the WGN manifest seem an attractive and alluring alternative from "the usual" on the networks. Silverman performed the same ratings magic when he moved to New York City "indie" WPIX-TV, augmenting his technique with audience-rousing contests and giveaways.

In both Chicago and New York, Fred Silverman took an active hand in building up not only the adult lineup, but the children's programming. Silverman was a businessman, a realist, a seerlike forecaster of popular television trends (his talent in this respect has led to the nickname "The Man with the Golden Gut"), and a certified adult; still, he brought to his job the wide-eyed enthusiasm of the child within. Put succinctly, the man loved cartoons. Jack Schneider, one of Fred's colleagues in his later network days, would regard the annual development meeting of the Saturday morning schedule as a "high point": "It would consist of storyboards, and he would play all the parts in his version of the dialects and voices of the characters. He threw himself into it with such gusto. . . . His enthusiasm was infectious. He cared about those characters." And it is said that one of the principal reasons Fred Silverman married his first wife is that both he and she were voracious fans of Bugs Bunny.

Silverman was hired as director of CBS' daytime programming in 1964, at a time when the network regarded cartoons as a simplistic sop for the kiddie trade. Just as in his future prime time career, Silverman was determined to take whatever he had been put in charge of and force it to function to the utmost of its potential — even if it consisted of nothing more than CBS' throwaway Saturday morning schedule.

But how to combat NBC and ABC in a manner that would truly turn the 8 to 12 A.M. Saturday shift into a big-time contender? Silverman took one look at ABC's *The Beatles* and had the answer. If counterprogramming could work in the evening hours, why not apply it to daytime? Ironically, ABC itself helped provide Fred Silverman with the solution via that network's phenomenally popular live-action *Batman* series. *Batman* made the television industry "superhero conscious" in the same manner that it had earlier been western- and spy-conscious. And what better genre to exploit in Saturday mornings, the land of wall-to-wall cartoonery, than the Superhero genre, which had its very roots in cartoons and comic books?

And with this thought in mind, Fred Silverman sought out the High Lama of all comic superheroes, Superman. Shortly before all this—1965, to be exact—the new cartoon studio Filmation was created by radio announcer Norm Prescott, a veteran of the Larry (*Bozo the Clown*) Harmon animation team named Lou Scheimer, and onetime Disney animator Hal Sutherland. Through displays of chutzpah rivalling Fred Silverman's, the tinker-toy Filmation firm managed to grab the television rights for Superman from National Periodicals. Silverman had CBS pick up *Superman*, launching not only his blitzkrieg against the other networks but the prosperous 20-year career of Filmation, which in due time rivalled and often surpassed Hanna-Barbera in terms of television cartoon output.

As for Hanna-Barbera itself, Fred Silverman sought out that studio for an original superhero character, *Space Ghost*, taking paternal interest over the character's developnent. Starting with *Superman* and *Space Ghost*, Silverman set about busting *The Beatles* with his "Superhero Saturday," linking up reruns of *Mighty Mouse* and *Underdog* with another new Hanna-Barbera series, *Frankenstein Jr. and the Impossibles*, and the cartoon debut of *The Lone Ranger* (Format Films). Fred Silverman's efforts were rewarded with the all-time best Saturday morning ratings that CBS had ever posted.

The overall industry results would not be felt until the 1967-68 season— but when the returns were in, there was no doubt that CBS led the pack with adventure cartoons: returnees *Space Ghost, Superman* (now teamed with *Aquaman*), *Lone Ranger, Frankenstein Jr.*, newcomers *Moby Dick and the Mighty Mightor, Shazzan!, The Herculoids*, and ABC carryover *Jonny Quest*. The ABC lineup included *The Fantastic Four, Spiderman* and *King Kong* (though ABC's commitment to comedy cartoons was maintained with *Beatles, Casper*, and the last network shot from Jay Ward, *George of the Jungle*). Armed to the teeth was NBC, with *Samson and Goliath, Birdman and the Galaxy Trio*, and—saints preserve us—*Super President*.

There was slightly more variety on Saturday mornings than the above tally would suggest, but the fact was that men and women of extraordinary strength, bedecked in capes, masks and cowls, were the dominant factors of the 1967 cartoon world. At this juncture, the top-rated network animated shows were bringing in a total of $50,000,000 per year. Advertising rates on these programs were as high as $9750 per minute. The average weekly audience was 14 million children. It was fun while it lasted. Unfortunately for fans of this sort of entertainment, it was too much fun to last.

"IT'S FOR YOUR OWN GOOD"

The correlation between violence in the Popular Arts and real-life violence is a subject for an argument that no one ever completely wins or loses. We will make three observations before moving on as dispassionately as possible. (A) The subject is hardly a new one. Long before there were television cartoons, sociologists were attacking the theatre, the dime novels, silent movies, talking pictures, radio, comic strips and comic books, as generating a lust for violence or perversity amongst youngsters. (B) The operative word in Popular Arts is "popular." If entertainment containing violence was ignored by the public, it would be ignored by the pundits, especially those who enjoyed seeing their names in the papers. (C) Whenever an "expert poll" is conducted to compile statistics linking the amount of violence on television with the increase of violence on the streets, it is amazing that the conclusions reached are *exactly* the conclusions the pollsters had set out to prove. When Frederick Wertham interviewed youngsters to prove that comic books fostered juvenile delinquency in the early 1950s, he was careful to confine his interviews to juvenile delinquents. Nowhere in Wertham's written theses was found a straight-A student who happened to enjoy comic books. See? That *proves* it!

The year 1968 was described as "the worst yet" in terms of television cartoon mayhem by the National Association for Better Radio and Television (later known as the National Association for Better Broadcasting, or NABB). This was also the year that George Gerbner, hailed at the time as the "foremost expert on TV violence," began charting the "violence quotient" in network kidvid, dutifully lumping pie-throwing and Wile E. Coyote's descents into the Grand Canyon together with fistfights and gunshots (Gerbner was still at it in 1994, monitoring the amount of violence on cable television, which unlike "free TV" was subsidized by people who assumed that they would be left alone to watch what they wanted so long as they paid for it. Beautiful dreamers). Senator John Pastore, never one to shy away from a photo opportunity, likewise entered the fray with his subcommittee activities vis-à-vis television violence.

Cartoon creators understandably countered all criticism by pointing out that kids had always craved action and adventure, and the purpose of cartoons was to fill that craving as entertaingly as possible. Additionally, violence was often as not *implied* rather than displayed outright, or it was of so unrealistic a nature that any discerning child would recognize the difference between a cartoon and real life. That argument *might* hold water, agreed Peggy Charren, organizer of the newly formed Action for Children's Television (ACT). But why was there virtually nothing *but* superheroes on Saturday morning? And whatever happened to the entreaties of former FCC chairman Newton Minow, who had made headlines with his 1961 assessment of television as a "vast wasteland," asking in the same speech, "Is there no room in television to teach, to inform, to stretch, to enlarge the capacities of our children?"

Network executives pointed to the advances of public television and to such earlier cartoon attempts at "edu-tainment" as Mattel's syndicated *The Funny Company* and Total Television/CBS' *Tennessee Tuxedo*. Then they pointed to the ratings. "We'd love to give the kids *Reading Room* or *A Day at the Planetarium*," declared NBC's daytime programming head Larry White. "We'd be applauded by many — and watched by no one." When the sterling example of CBS' *Captain Kangaroo* was invoked, the executives quickly noted that *Kangaroo* had always been a "loss leader," and that it could not have existed without the so-called animated garbage on Saturday morning paying the bills and enabling CBS to absorb the loss.

All room for argument was closed off after the 1968 assassinations of Martin Luther King and Robert F. Kennedy, and the civil unrest and street rioting that further stained that tumultuous year. Television violence would *have* to be curbed to set an example, and that meant bringing the cartoon superhero cycle to an end. The reseponse of NBC was to remove virtually all of its adventure cartoons from the 1968-69 lineup, retreating to light humor: The network's *Banana Splits Adventure Hour*, produced by Hanna-Barbera, was touted heavily as the single most significant swingback to comedy and harmless adventure. Over at CBS, Fred Silverman also chopped away at the adventure lineup, creating a whole new trend towards teen-oriented musical comedy with Filmation's *The Archies* — which was so popular that it spawned innumerable imitations on all three networks.

In 1968 and then 1969, Silverman, in league with Hanna-Barbera, unveiled two more enduring cartoon formats on CBS, also ripe for imitation. In 1968 *Wacky Races* gave the illusion of perpetual, pulse-pounding adventure on wheels, softened by nonthreatening slapstick; this "never-ending race" formula was being emulated as late as 1990 with the *Fender Bender 500* segments on Hanna-Barbera's *Wake Rattle and Roll*. And 1969's *Scooby-Doo, Where Are You?* likewise coupled comedy with adventure, taking the sting out of violent events, evildoers and the Supernatural by showing such terrors to be fraudulent, exposed as shams by a big, loveable, stupid, funny dog. *Scooby-Doo* was Silverman's way of saying, "It's all an illusion, folks, so have fun and stop worrying" — and was successful enough to lead to a wealth of *Scooby-Doo* ripoffs and wanna-bes. *Scooby* also worked wonders for its developers, a pair of Hanna-Barbera writers named Joe Ruby and Ken Spears, who thanks to their new industry prestige were able to break away and form their own cartoon studio in 1978.

Simply upgrading the comedy content with *Scooby-Doo* and his friends, however, was not enough for the clean-up-TV people. The Public Broadcasting System's *Sesame Street*, introduced in 1969, had shown that education could be entertaining *and* popular; could the networks, shown the lighted path by PBS, at least try to come up to *Sesame Street* standards? Well, they certainly tried between 1970 and 1973 with a whole raft of lighthearted live-action instructional programs: *Hog Dog, Curiosity Shop, Take a Giant Step, Jambo*. But the cartoons emanating from the four major animation houses (Hanna-Barbera, Filmation, Rankin-Bass, DePatie-Freleng) still pulled down the big ratings and advertising dollars — and, with such conspicuous edu-tainment exceptions as *Tomfoolery*, *Schoolhouse Rock* and *Fat Albert and the Cosby Kids* (forerunners of one of the best "good for you" network cartoons of all, 1984's *Muppet Babies*), cartoon series were disinclined to broaden the experience of the Saturday morning audience beyond the usual singing teenagers and crimefighting comedy animals.

The do-gooders summoned their forces again in the early 1970s, led by FCC chairman Nicholas Johnson, who was so aghast at the Saturday morning lineup that he labelled the programmers "evil men" and "child molesters." *Variety*, which generally excused mediocrity so long as it showed a profit, joined in the chorus with an extensive 1973 article by Bill Greeley which assessed what was then being offered as children's entertainment: "Weird creatures abound, but they are mutants of the old grotesque monsters and freaks that saturated the schedule before the public caught on. There are giggling apes and fire-snorting dragons afraid of mice, crying lions and bats with a comedic flair. . . . Much of the new cartoon products could be classed as situation comedy. It's not children's programming. It's sort of shrunken adult programming."

Greeley continued in this vein, condemning the "cheap hip talk," "cliche sayings" and the overall Saturday morning atmosphere as "almost unanimously witless, heartless, charmless, tasteless and artless." Similar articles in other publications came to the same conclusion.

Once more, the networks circled the wagons and defended themselves. Many cited the new representation of ethnic groups on the cartoons in the 1972-73 season: the Native American male lead on NBC's *Sealab 2020*, the racial mix on ABC's *Kid Power*, the African American cast on CBS's *Fat Albert*. As for the so-called overdose of mindless slapstick, CBS' Alan Ducovny played "J'Accuse!," pointing out that the networks would not have beefed up comedy had they not been forced to tone down action and adventure (There were even threatened FCC reprisals to stations telecasting reruns of "excessively violent" cartoons like *Batman* and *Aquaman*). Every time CBS had wanted to show a dilemma in terms of natural conflict or threat, the pressure groups had thwarted them. "I feel it's wrong to protect children from experiencing this. It's also futile. Children do see this on other programs. Why shouldn't they see them on Saturday mornings?"

An argument might be made that *Fat Albert* was able to depict successfully realistic conflicts and urban dangers, tempered with goodnatured humor. But that program required a strong and costly writing and psychological-advisory lineup to accomplish this, and the resultant expense would have been prohibitive if all Saturday morning cartoons were equally costly.

Could not the more powerful kids' show sponsors pick up that cost? Not in 1973—not when the pressure people were after sponsors with the same diligence as their attack on program content.

The love affair between sponsors and cartoons was long-standing: 1953's *Winky Dink and You*, for all of Jack Barry's declarations of "educational value," was put together for the purpose of selling a home crayon–art kit. Some of the most fondly remembered 1960s cartoon shows were created at the command of the sponsor: ABC's *Beany and Cecil* (1961) would not have debuted without a prior merchandising agreement between producer Bob Clampett and Mattel Toys; CBS' *Linus the Lionhearted* (1964) was designed to promote the sugar cereals of Post; and, back on ABC, both *Hot Wheels* and *Sky Hawks* were created to ballyhoo the toy car and aircraft lines of (again) Mattel.

A 1969 National Association of Broadcasters ruling, sparked at the insistence of such groups as Action for Children's Television, decreed that the sweetheart tie-in between sponsor and program would have to end — that the so-called "half hour cartoon commercial" would no longer be tolerated. This led to a drop-off of Saturday morning ads for sugared cereals and vitamin pills, and a government dictated cutback on the amount of advertising time permitted on kidvid. Local children's show hosts were dealt a death blow in 1972, when the NAB dictated that these hosts could no longer promote commercial products while in character on their programs.

Thus, while cartoons remained moneymakers, a principal flow of income, the sponsor, was being narrowed to a trickle. The cost of an animated half hour, once fixed in the early 1960s at about $30,000, would climb to $100,000 by 1978. Without commensurate sponsorial feedback, the producers were forced to cut animation corners and reduce the number of yearly episodes from 26 to as few as 10. Small wonder that critics had plenty of ammunition against television cartoons in this period: "They're cheap looking! And they're almost all reruns!"

1975–1983: MEDICINE-COATING THE SUGAR

Cartoon producers had every right to be as truculent as the critics. Rushing to outrate one another, the networks of the 1970s were imposing strict deadlines on the studios — still insisting that cartoon makers hack out what one harried producer described as "animation by the yard." Cutbacks in the number of commercials permissible in any given timeslot resulted in the once lucrative half-hour format reaping less profits in the mid-to-late 1970s than program "blocks" of 60, 90 and even 120 minutes. "Funshine Saturday" of 1974 was the catchall label given to ABC's full morning of animation, pitched to sponsors as a cluster rather than as individual programs; seven years later this group mentality persisted on ABC with the network's "It's a Comedy Blockbuster" and "90 Minutes of Action and Comedy" cartoon blocks, run back-to-back for three hours on the Saturday morning schedule. With too much work and too little time, there was no luxury to develop new animation methods to improve the quality.

Hanna-Barbera was frequently cited during this period as the sole perpetrator of poor animation, but in fact the studio was merely working along the same budgetary considerations as everyone else. At first, the studio was proud of how it could produce so much with so little, even insisting that inexpensive limited animation was ideal for its own creative vision. "There was too much technique in the movie days, too much time spent in trying to make animal characters move as naturally as real animals," Joe Barbera noted in 1961. "Well, that's not our idea of what a cartoon is supposed to be. A cartoon should have its own personality, its own feeling, its own way of moving." By 1969, the studio had given up the "creativity" argument, observing that shortcut animation was simply the most adaptable form for the television medium. "When we first started limited animation, it disturbed me. Then when I saw some of the old cartoons on TV, I saw that, actually, limited animation came off better on the dimly lit television screen than the old fully animated drawings."

At the peak of critical condemnation of television cartoons in the late 1970s, Hanna-Barbera was forced to concede (somewhat) that its assembly line methods were more cost-effective than visually satisfying. "It is unfortunate that more money can't be spent," Bill Hanna was quoted as saying in 1977. "As it is, I think we do a fair job in character design, we do a decent job in background, and I think where we fall short is in the actual animation."

Could poor television animation be compensated for with original story material and dynamic new characters? Again, the time-and-budget strictures prohibited extensive development of original ideas, and there was never any certainty if the New and Different would catch on with the increasingly fickle audience (a fickleness admittedly stemming from disappointment over the worst Saturday morning offerings of the 1970s). From 1972 onward, producers and networks played safe by dipping into past successful concepts (called "insurance policies" because of their already established audience following), which led not only to rank imitations of other cartoons but of live-action nighttime programs as well. Sometimes, as with Filmation's *Star Trek* series for NBC, this could be done with class and distinction. Most of the time you ended up with *The Brady Kids, The Partridge Family 2200 AD, The New Adventures of Gilligan, My Favorite Martians* and *The Oddball Couple* — most exhibiting quality ranging from passable to dismal, and none coming close to the appeal of the originals. Herb Klynn, producer of *The Alvin Show* and the animated *Lone Ranger*, cited reluctance on the part of the networks to test out new concepts. "We can create so much through animation, but try to show the networks. Most people I bring ideas to have no creative insight at all."

In fairness, networks were not so much unimaginative as fearful. The pressure-group edicts prohibiting the sort of comic and action content that had been permitted in earlier years (wild slapstick, cliffhanging tension) also decreased the impetus to work at full creative capacity. Story content and program premises were now overseen by network Standards and Practices divisions, eager to second-guess the FCC, the ACT, the NABB, and the rest of that alphabet soup — avoiding outside legislation with rigid self-censorship. "Script and story boards must meet the network's guidelines," said Alan Wurtzel, vice president of ABC's Standards and Practices in the early 1980s. "We're seeing the work at every step of the process." It was not merely the overtly violent moments that were snipped. Anything that a child at home might, in the farthest reaches of the imagination, imitate—from dropping an anvil out a window to dunking a cat into spaghetti—was vetoed from the outset.

Not content with scooping the guts out of new cartoons, the networks began bowdlerizing the old ones. From the mid–1970s onward, it was virtually impossible to find an old theatrical Warner Bros. cartoon being telecast on any of the networks without several of the more "brutal" gags removed— usually such horrific moments as Elmer Fudd getting a comic-opera gunblast in the face, emerging with no more damage than a charcoaled countenance.

And how was this network butchery rewarded? The very people that supposedly would be appeased by this activity were the ones who condemned it! In assessing the dry-cleaned *Daffy Duck Show* in 1980, a panel of children's television experts bemoaned the "old cartoon favorites cut up into unintelligible segments. Surely the kids will notice." Small wonder that cartoon creativity from 1975 to 1983 was virtually nonexistent. How could you create anything with impunity when the tongue-cluckers kept changing the rules?

One potentially positive byproduct of the networks' heightened sensitivity was the decision to provide "pro-social" vignettes in each cartoon program, encompassing such topics as safety, health, history and science. Programs like CBS' revived *Popeye* (Hanna-Barbera) and *Mighty Mouse* (Filmation) ended each episode with a 30-second animated "bite" in which the characters would offset useful advice to the home audience: Avoid overloading electrical outlets, stay away from strange automobiles, eat a balanced breakfast, protect the environment, and so on. Science fiction cartoons (of which there were plenty after the *Star Wars* films jump-started *that* genre) contributed to this vein by offering brief astronomical and technological lessons, sometimes utilizing the "alien" characters common to such programs to illustrate lessons of tolerance and coexistence. And Filmation's *Tarzan/ Lone Ranger/Zorro* series of the early 1980s provided quick informational factoids on jungle life, the history of the American West, and the Spanish language. Unfortunately, while some of these prosocial bites came off with sincerity, most appeared to be hastily inserted with an eye-dropper and wedged in with a shoehorn—a fleeting conscious-stricken afterthought, or a forced apology, for *not* educating the viewers within the body of the program.

THE EARLY 1980S: FROM *SMURFS* TO SYNDICATION

By 1981, network cartoons were a kaleidoscope of *Scooby Doo* and *Star Wars* progeny, animated sitcom spinoffs and unadventurous adventure. No one was truly proud of the landscape, and one network, NBC, was seriously considering stemming diminishing Saturday-morning returns by dropping all its cartoons and expanding its news programming to weekends. Re-enter Fred Silverman, who since last we saw him at CBS had switched to ABC, turning that once moribund network into America's number one entertainment machine of the 1970s. (During that time Silverman did ABC daytime an enormous favor by encouraging continuance of his beloved animated superhero format with new episodes of the "hero rally" *Superfriends*.) Now Silverman was in charge of NBC, hoping to make magic for the third time. Fred's first move was to rescue NBC's Saturday morning animation; to do this, he brought in a property that though internationally successful since 1957, had only recently broken into the American market by way of stuffed dolls and toys. *The Smurfs*, produced by old Silverman cronies Hanna and Barbera, was the saving turnaround for the NBC children's programming division—and in fact was its biggest-ever Saturday morning hit. Once *The Smurfs* impacted, the old copycat strategy geared up. Playthings and greeting-card icons like the Care Bears, My Little Pony and Rainbow Brite added animation to their marketplace saturation. More mature "toys"—namely video games, the latest preteen craze—provided subject matter for such network cartoons as *Pac-Man, Saturday Supercade, Dungeons and Dragons, Dragon's Lair* and *Pole Position*.

But were these not tail-wagging-the-dog properties, commercial products turned into cartoon shows as a means of selling those products—the very things abandoned by law back in the *Linus the Lionhearted* and *Hot Wheels* days? Well, not really—so long as the programs were not sponsored by the products animated. *The Smurfs* was therefore permitted provided that no "Smurfs" products were advertised on the series.

Meanwhile, changes were being made in the world of governmental legislation. In 1981, Mark Fowler was appointed chairman of the FCC. Reflecting the overall Reagan-era laissez-faire attitude towards big business, Fowler regarded television not as art or as a teaching tool but as an entertainment appliance: "A toaster with pictures." If toy manufacturers, videogame firms, movie producers and cereal companies wanted to transform their licensed characters into cartoons, so be it, as long as the public wanted it. "Let the marketplace decide" was Fowler's credo.

Into this arena entered two 1983 cartoon properties: *He-Man and the Masters of the Universe* and *Inspector Gadget*. Mattel had plans to imitate the "Smurfs" strategy of encouraging sales of its "He-Man" action figure (an ad man's term for "a doll boys can play with because it's never *called* a doll") with a cartoon series. The ABC network was approached, but backed off; despite Mark Fowler's relaxed attitude, ABC had not forgotten the trouble it had incurred from the FCC over Mattel's earlier *Hot Wheels*. So Mattel bypassed the networks entirely, submitting its new *He-Man* series to non-network local syndication, "stripping" the program by running it Monday through Friday. There was a secondary consideration here: By avoiding the network Standards and Practices hobgoblins, Mattel and its production company Filmation would have more freedom so far as the new series' action-adventure content was concerned.

At the same time, former Hanna-Barbera story supervisor Andy Heyward was establishing himself as an animation titan. A small French production firm called DIC (an anagram for Diffusion, Information and Communication), which had been turning out European animation since 1976, was seeking to crack the U.S. market. Heyward was originally hired to translate DIC founder Jean Chalopin's French for potential American buyers, but it soon became obvious that the young cartoon executive's true destiny lay in marketing and merchandising. By 1983, Andy Heyward had sold his own concept, a bungling bionic detective named Inspector Gadget, as a cartoon character and potential action figure. Having recently escaped the network battlefields, Heyward determined that more money, and more creative leeway, were to be had in the world of syndication. *Inspector Gadget* not only proved that a demand existed for original Monday-through-Friday syndicated animation, but that costs could be kept to a minimum by utilizing extensive computer animation, hiring Hollywood's unionized animators on a program-by-program basis rather than retaining an expensive year-round staff, and farming most animation work to studios in the Orient (DIC's detractors frequently jibed that the corporate initials stood for "Do It Cheap").

He-Man and the Masters of the Universe and *Inspector Gadget* opened up a lucrative late-afternoon, first-run syndicated market that had only been spottily successful in the past (1966's *Marvel Superheroes* and 1978's *Battle of the Planets* had been the last significant daily syndicated strips). Moreover, syndication offered greater saturation potential for toy merchandisers. There was still the FCC edict that action figures could not be advertised on programs based on those figures; however, it *was* perfectly acceptable for a toy firm to schedule its programs in one syndicated timeslot, then sell advertisements for the toys dramatized on those programs in *other* timeslots within the buying station's broadcast day—*every* day, rather than merely weekly. Regular viewers of that station would make the link between program and product subliminally, without the series' producers overtly breaking any FCC rules.

Also in 1983, the Claster Company, with animation provided by Marvel Productions (formerly DePatie-Freleng), introduced cartoon adaptations of the Claster-owned Hasbro Toy products *G.I. Joe* and *Transformers*. These programs, coupled with Mattel's *He-Man* and its sequel *She-Ra*, ensured that toys-cum-cartoons would dominate the syndicated scene for the next three seasons, as witness *ThunderCats, Silverhawks, Galaxy Rangers, Challenge of the GoBots* and so many others.

In addition to fostering a trend, Claster deployed a moneysaving method to test whether or not its series would go over with the audience: The cartoon mini-series, consisting of a "pilot" adventure which could be telecast in a single two-hour slot or as a five-part daily "special event." This pilot would then be rebroadcast all over the country to stimulate viewer interest; should the viewers indeed be stimulated, production would commence on the daily, 65-episode cartoon series proper. By test marketing the pilot as an "event," Claster avoided the crippling cost of a full season's worth of episodes for a program that might not ever take off. One future cartoon series to benefit from the cautiousness of a five-part miniseries introduction was Murikami-Wolf-Swenson's phenomenally successful *Teenage Mutant Ninja Turtles*.

It was not just a series of cagey promotional moves that made syndication a viable market in the early 1980s. Since the beginning of the decade, there had been a surge of new independent UHF television stations (covering channels 14 through 69, as opposed to Channels 2 through 13 on the VHF band). Three hundred such stations had signed on the air in the three years prior to the *He-Man–Inspector Gadget–G.I. Joe–Transformers* group debut. Mattel-Filmation, Claster/Hasbro, and DIC were the first cartoon and merchandise factories to exploit this new marketing territory. By 1985, Hanna-Barbera had grabbed a piece of the action with *The Funtastic World of Hanna-Barbera*, the first weekly 90 minute syndicated "block" of animation (a stake-claiming technique carried over from the Saturday morning network program blocks).

And in 1987, Disney took the syndicated plunge with *DuckTales*. The studio proved that in a market glutted with hasty cartoonwork and sketchy scriptwriting on the theory that "kids don't notice," top-quality animation and strong story values would enhance audience appeal — if only animators were willing to risk higher budgets. *DuckTales* further proved that the cartoon characters need not be animated toys and action figures to flourish. Disney's ad copy for its syndicated entree underlined this: "He Men were yesterday . . . robots were today . . . ghosts may be tomorrow, but . . . Disney is Forever." The studio's success with *DuckTales* encouraged creation of its own long-running daily "block," *The Disney Afternoon*, which would feature at one time or another *Chip 'n' Dale's Rescue Rangers, Tale Spin, Gummi Bears, Darkwing Duck* and *Goof Troop*.

The increased demand for daily syndicated product breathed life into another aspect of animation, alluded to in earlier notes on *Astroboy*. "Japanimation," or "Anime" (Annie-May) as it is known in Japan, briefly thrived on the syndie scene of the mid–1980s with such imported dailies as *Robotech, Macron 1, Captain Harlock* and *Tranzor Z*. Many animation fans despaired at the thought of cartoonery moving farther than ever from Hollywood. (Most of the studios were by this time farming out virtually all animation to Japan, Korea, Taiwan and the Philippines; the sole all–American holdout, Filmation, finally gave up and began relying upon foreign artisans shortly before the company was bought out and dissolved in 1989.) Other viewers, caught up in the quirky rhythms, unorthodox storylines and multilayered characterizations in the Japanese product, formed a strong cult following around "Anime" — one worthy of an encyclopedic book in itself.

While the made-in-Japan craze levelled off before the end of the 1980s, the import responsibilities enriched several small distributors to the point of equality with the bigger animation companies. One such distributor, the Canadian-based Saban company, became a cartoon producer in its own right, ultimately setting up a European studio in 1991 which yielded such recent moneymakers as *Amazin' Adventures* and *X-Men*.

DIAL 900–CABLE ME

In the mid–1980s, networks and syndication were joined by a hitherto untapped and underestimated market for fresh animation: the cable television industry. A decade earlier, such a market would have been not only untapped but illegal; when cable began offering its own channels and networks rather than merely retransmitting commercial broadcasts to "fringe" areas otherwise not served by local stations, the FCC insisted that the new cable channels could not run commercial or entertainment programs. Cable was supposed to confine itself to "the public interest." Broadcast mogul Ted Turner changed this attitude in the mid–1970s by using satellite technology to transform a dying Atlanta UHF independent channel into "Super Station" WTBS—a commercial entertainment service deliberately aimed at nationwide (and ultimately worldwide) cable. As the FCC loosened cable restrictions in the early 1980s, more and more satellite-cast services followed Turner's lead.

For media watchdogs, this increase in cable activity cried out for the diversification and improved quality they had been demanding from the networks—specifically in terms of children's television. In 1979, two cable services were set up for the express purpose of providing fresh family-oriented programming: Nickelodeon, from the Warner-Amex home entertainment empire, and Calliope, a joint venture of United Artists and Columbia. Nickelodeon's intention was to broadcast 13 to 14 hours a day, minus commercials. To quote the service's trade advertisements, "It's hearty, wholesome programming that will delight PTAs, community groups and just plain anxious parents . . . as well as the kids." Nickelodeon's centerpiece was the daily five-hour *Pinwheel*, a potpourri of puppets, live action, interractive entertainment, audience participation, soft-sell instruction—and cartoons, produced in studios all over the world. Calliope promised a similar ongoing children's service.

Several older cable firms, notably the Christian Broadcasting Network, or CBN (a "basic-cable" service—that is, one offered along with several other services for a basic monthly charge), and Home Box Office (HBO) and Showtime (both "pay cable" services acquired by viewers by paying an extra amount over and above the basic fee) joined Nickelodeon and Calliope in the early 1980s by providing commercial-free animation. The Christian Broadcasting Network, a religious operation, came forth in 1982 with two made-in-Japan Biblical cartoon series: *Superbook* and *Flying House*. And between them, HBO and Showtime offered foreign productions of broader appeal, notably *Thunderbirds 2086* and *Danger Mouse*.

As the decade progressed, marketplace realities set in. Both Nickelodeon and CBN were forced to accept commercial advertising and to widen their program selection to survive. Calliope never really got off the ground as a separate service; the concept was absorbed by the USA Cable Network, which was still running a *Calliope* children's series into the 1990s, albeit as one of many regular programs aimed at kids *and* adults. Only the Disney

Channel, created in 1983, was able to supply 24 commercial-free hours, but viewers were required to pay extra for the privilege.

Still, Nickelodeon remained loyal to the notion of giving exposure to cartoon series that allegedly did not have the saleability or significant appeal to an audience over the age of eight that would otherwise earn them a major network or syndicated slot. Most of these programs were originally telecast outside the United States, and many were distributed by the up-and-coming Canadian firms Saban and Cinar: *Belle and Sebastian, Mysterious Cities of Gold, Spartakus, Adventures of the Little Koala, Maya the Bee, The World of David the Gnome*, and many others. The Christian Broadcasting Network — which by 1990 was seeking to expand its audience by downpedalling religiosity and changing its name to the Family Channel — was content to stock up with reruns of cancelled network and syndicated cartoon programs. Eventually it, too, distinguished itself with first-run animation: *Wowser, Heroes on Hot Wheels, Swiss Family Robinson* and *The Legend of Prince Valiant*.

Pay-cable's HBO and Showtime were both willing to showcase new animation that, like the Nickelodeon lineup, was limited in commercial or popular appeal but was still worth a glance or two. As the 1980s became the 1990s, the pay-cable animation scene included such drolleries as Britain's *Henry's Cat*, such careful literary adaptations as Japan's *Tales of Little Women* and the Russian-English *Shakespeare: The Animated Tales*, and a brace of children's book adaptations animated by the Canadian-French concern Nelvana/ Ellipse: *Babar* and *The New Adventures of Tintin*.

Nelvana, a Toronto-based studio whose creation was financed by credit cards in 1971, had made an auspicious U.S. debut with its syndicated *Nelvanamation* specials in 1978. The company exercised significant skill in producing comparatively low-cost but high-quality cartoons, and in adapting the distinctive artistic and comic styles of the various suppliers from whom the company had secured exclusive animation rights (*Babar* creator Jean De Brunhoff, *Tintin* mentor Herge). These studio trademarks created an overwhelming demand for Nelvana's services in cable, network and syndication, as witness such recent (and diverse) hits as *Beetlejuice, Care Bears, Rupert* and *Eek! the Cat*. The output in the late 1980s to early 1990s of Nelvana and other upstart firms like Klasky-Csupo, Film Roman, Murikami-Wolf-Swenson (later Fred Wolf Productions) and Gunther-Wahl began to have a trickle down effect on the (relatively) older companies like Hanna-Barbera, Ruby-Spears, and Marvel, who found they would have to upgrade their animation styles and freshen their comedy content to keep apace with the younger companies in the business.

Meanwhile, in the late 1980s young people were being regaled by an animation smorgasbord that had been inaccessible to their elders. Thanks to cable television, together with the blossoming home videocassette industry, animation lovers young and old were able to sample the best of the old theatrical days (the Disney Channel, the Turner services' repeats of *Bugs Bunny, Popeye* and *Tom and Jerry*, and videotape packages of forgotten delights from such antediluvian cartoonmakers as Ub Iwerks and

Van Beuren); to pick and choose favorites from three decades of past television-cartoon productions (Hanna-Barbera's extensive backlog was still turning a profit, as were Jay Ward's *Rocky* and *Bullwinkle*, UPA's *Mr. Magoo* and the Filmation–Marvel–Ruby-Spears "superhero" canon); and to select new first-run favorites (*Inspector Gadget, Beetlejuice, Muppet Babies*, and much much more). This animation onslaught created a "cartoon literate" audience, one which through collective popular-culture consciousness could fondly invoke every animation cliche, every slapstick setpiece, every popular character catchphrase.

Whether this heightened cartoon savvy was good or bad is best left to pedants and sociologists, but it did result in an eager paying audience for the 1988 theatrical film which (according to many historians) single-handedly revitalized popular demand for top-quality animation: *Who Framed Roger Rabbit?* The film relied on one's thorough understanding of cartoon terminology and technique to succeed, and might not have been produced a few years earlier on the basis that "It's too inside. No one will get it." But nothing was too "inside" for an audience weaned on the 24-hour cultural and sensory assault of cable television, where virtually every aspect of the overall Human Experience (including how humans entertained themselves) was available — if only the viewer was willing to burrow past all those home shopping channels.

THE 1990S: CARTOONS, CARTOONS EVERYWHERE. . .

Another new player entered the television cartoon game in 1990. The Fox Television Network, after a rocky start with *The Joan Rivers Show* in 1986, made enormous headway in subsequent years with a diet of hip, young adult–oriented programming, establishing the network as a prime contender even though it had only half the nationwide coverage of NBC, CBS or ABC. One of the hottest properties developed in Fox's formative years was an offshoot of a "between the acts" cartoon attraction on the network's *The Tracy Ullman Show*. This matured into *The Simpsons*, one of the first half hour animated shows to be targetted for prime time since the "nighttime cartoon" heyday of the early 1960s. *The Simpsons*, based on a series of cutting-edge panel cartoons by artist Matt Groening, was typical Fox Network fare: irreverent, topical, satirical, scatological, censor-baiting, and aimed squarely at the 18- to 34-year-old audience demographic group. The fact that it was a cartoon also guaranteed a preteen following, though adult "clean TV" advocates condemned *The Simpsons* as unsuitable for any age.

Once firmly entrenched in prime time, Fox sought to expand its coverage to weekday mornings and afternoons. In the old Fred Silverman counterprogramming spirit, Fox knew that it would trail the Big Three networks if its daytime shows merely imitated the soap operas and game shows already established in that period. The success of *The Simpsons*, together with the determination of Fox children's programming head Margaret

The Fox Network Cartoon Family. *Clockwise from top left:* Tom & Jerry Kids, Beetlejuice, Bobby *(Bobby's World)*, Chester Cheetah (from a yet-to-be-seen series), The *Taz-Mania* cast, Batman, and Babs Bunny *(Tiny Toon Adventures)*.

Loesch to develop a strong animation manifest for the network, led to the creation of the Fox Children's Network (FCN)—the first new daily network service for kids since ABC's *Discovery* in 1963. As with the *Joan Rivers Show*, the inauguration of FCN's lineup was shaky, kicking off with the lukewarm, barely completed daily half-hour *Peter Pan and the Pirates* in the fall of 1990. Faring better were the Saturday morning FCN programs: *Bobby's World*, *Tom and Jerry Kids*, and *Attack of the Killer Tomatoes*, each assembled in the fashion of *The Simpsons* with enough knowledgeable contemporary humor to please adults as well as children (though even on Saturdays there were conspicuous first-season failures like *Zazoo U* and *Piggsburg Pigs*).

Fox's share of the Saturday morning viewership would expand as the 1990s progressed with such winners as *Taz-Mania, Eek! the Cat* and *X-Men*.

Indeed, the impact of Fox's weekend invasion literally drove the bottom-rated NBC network out of the cartoon business. Once NBC's last animated series, *Wishkid Starring Macaulay Culkin*, folded in the fall of 1992, the network that had pioneered Saturday morning cartoons buckled under the triple threat of Fox, CBS (with its *Teenage Mutant Ninja Turtles* and *Garfield*) and ABC (with its Disney first-runs and Warner Bros. reruns). All of NBC's animation was swept away, in favor of a two-hour news program — just as it had intended to do before *Smurfs* reprieved its cartoon schedule in 1981.

But let us get back to 1990: Though not yet one of the grownups, Fox refused to act its age in pursuit of establishing a showcase for the new FCN daily package. The first move the network made was to take on the mighty Disney, accusing that powerful studio of unfairly strongarming local stations into purchasing the entire four-program *Disney Afternoon* as a block (all four shows, or no shows), thereby freezing out the competition. In so doing, Fox won the respect — and eventually, the output — of the new Warner Bros. Animation division. Like the FCN shows, Warners' daily, syndicated *Tiny Toon Adventures* (executive producer, Steven Spielberg) was founded on the assumption that a sophisticated audience, capable of grasping any and all inside jokes and pop-culture gags that the producers could think up, existed for cartoons. Though Warners producer Jean MacCurdy admitted that the studio would never have been emboldened to offer a daily syndie cartoon series in 1990 without Disney's *DuckTales* paving the way, Warners echoed Fox's recriminations against Disney's monopoly tactics. The fact that the early-morning, late-afternoon local market could stir up so heated a battle was proof enough that television cartoons of the 1990s would be treated with more industry respect than in past seasons.

Disney's controversial return to the block-booking practices of the 1950s had a positive effect by default on another young cartoon concern, Calico/Zodiac. Several local stations publicly announced that they had bought C/Z's *Widget, the World Watcher* and *Mr. Bogus* precisely because of the new company's genteel business tactics; these stations would rather purchase a soft-sell Calico/Zodiac product than be manhandled into allowing Disney to map out their entire afternoon schedule.

Both *Widget* and *Bogus* represented a return to the soil so far as television-cartoon program content was concerned: Both characters were created chiefly because the producers themselves were entertained by them. Many of the earliest made-for-TV animation properties, including Jay Ward's *Crusader Rabbit* and Hanna-Barbera's *Huckleberry Hound*, grew from the personal tastes and preferences of the creators. Like the best theatrical cartoons, these earlier programs were *creator-driven*. They were not, like such 1980s projects as *He-Man* and *Transformers*, commissioned to sell pre-existing toy products, nor were they designed to perpetuate the careers of comic book characters like *Batman* and *Superman*. The cartoon producer thought up the idea, then brought that idea to fruition because he himself believed in the idea; storyboards were not predetermined by network committees, publishers or advertising partnerships.

As cartoonmaking became largely a matter of merchandising, the creator-driven cartoon became an endangered species. Some of the "pre-fab" cartoons of the 1960s, 1970s and 1980s were well worth having; one of the best and most successful properties of the late 1980s, *Teenage Mutant Ninja Turtles*, originated not in the think-tanks of its animation company Murikami-Wolf-Swenson, but in the basement of two hungry comic book artists—as a comic book. While Fred Wolf could take justifiable pride in ordering the cosmetic improvements that made the animated *Turtles* far more popular than they had ever been in the comics, the fact remained that he could not in all good conscience call himself the creator. Few cartoonists in the television field could share Warner Bros. director Chuck Jones' philosophy: "These cartoons were never made for children. Nor were they made for adults. They were made for *me*."

But the creator-driven cartoon would make a pronounced comeback in the 1990s—principally through the good graces of two interrelated cable services, Nickelodeon and Music Television (MTV). Eager to stockpile its own warehouse of original cartoons, Nickelodeon unveiled three brand-new animated half hours on August 11, 1991: *Doug, Rugrats* and *Ren and Stimpy*. Though most of the animation work on the three programs was shipped overseas, the concept of each new program was born with its creator or creators: *Doug's* Jim Jinkins, *Rugrat's* Arlene Klasky, Gabor Csupo and Paul Germain, and *Ren and Stimpy's* John Kricfalusi. From storyboard to cel, the characters and their antics were determined by the artists and writers, rather than by such outside forces as comic books and toy companies. Though Nickelodeon would ultimately exercise proprietary influence on these series, it was obvious to the viewer that *Doug, Rugrats* and *Ren* were products of individuals who loved, enjoyed and cared about cartoons, rather than a team of jaded ad executives who saw animation as merely a means to a selling end.

Exhibiting the same daring and aplomb with which it had built the music-video industry from the ground up, the MTV cable network (which owned Nickelodeon) took the creator-driven concept beyond all existing television perimeters. *Liquid Television*, premiering over MTV in July of 1991, could well be labelled the Art-House Animation Festival of the Air. Supervised by the San Francisco cartoon firm (Colossal) Pictures (the parentheses are part of the name), *Liquid Television* served up a weekly diet of the most outrageously radical animation ever seen on any commercial television service. The series' contents (analyzed in detail within the reference section of this book) were creator-driven to beat the band. Some were *literally* individual visions, because the producer was also the principal (and sometimes the only) animator. Conventional storytelling, character development, censorial taboos and social amenities were disdained on *Liquid Television*, which per its title flowed from one free-form animation bite to the next, providing a forum for virtually all forms of movie cartoonery: cel art, cutouts, stop-motion puppetry, computer animation, and eye-popping, seamless combinations of cartoons and live action. But while *Liquid Television* proved that television was ready for such experimentation, it also revealed that a good portion of the audience was not. Viewer preference leaned towards those animated segments with recognizable characters, cogent scenarios, and easily graspable comedy or adventure elements. The most popular segment of *Liquid Television* was also its simplest (in every sense of the word): the estimable *Beavis and Butt-Head*, which in early 1993 was spun off into its own half hour.

While for the most part television cartoons were still in the hands of studio and network executives, the attractiveness and profitability of cable television's creator-driven product encouraged a similar if less spectacular trend on mainstream television. The Fox Network's *Eek! The Cat* was lovingly supervised by its creator Savage Steve Holland, while Donovan Cook's *Two Stupid Dogs* and the Tremblay brothers' *SwatKats* were both produced through the facilities of Hanna-Barbera with the promise (thus far honored) that the programs' destinies would remain in the hands of the creators rather than the studio. These early–1990s projects would seem to bode well for future animation *auteurs* who hope to get their personal cartoon statements on the television screen with a minimum of corporate "improvements"—though the example of *Ren and Stimpy* creator John Kricfalusi, whose series was yanked from his hands by Nickelodeon after several well-publicized clashes over story content and missed deadlines, might well squelch any dreams of creative autonomy.

Certain nuances aside, the overall television animation field of the early 1990s was littered with hangovers from past seasons. There were copycat programs, most aspiring to be *Teenage Mutant Ninja Turtles*; animated comic-book characters, with *X-Men* one of the best of this type and *Batman: The Animated Series* unequivocally *the* best; videogame spinoffs like *Video Power*, *Sonic the Hedgehog* and *Double Dragon*; revivals of previous entertainment-industry successes both animated and "live," such as *Pink Panther*, *The Addams Family*, *Back to the Future* and *Conan the Adventurer*; cartoonized celebrities (*Hammerman*, *New Kids on the Block*); and "retro" series depicting popular cartoon characters as children (*Yo Yogi*, *Tom and Jerry Kids*). There were also futile bids to snatch up some of the *Simpsons* magic in prime time (*Capitol Critters*, *Fish Police*), just as *Flintstones* had previously encouraged an equally unsuccessful animated drive into the evening hours of the 1960s.

Cable television maintained its willingness to exhibit the offbeat and nontraditional, only now it was hard to determine whether such programs were originally geared for cable or had been conceived as direct-to-videotape projects. *Shelley Duvall's Bedtime Stories*, *American Heroes and Legends*, *We All Have Tales*, *The World of Peter Rabbit and Friends* and other such series blurred the distinction between the cable market and the video stores: Some cable "premieres" had previously done service on the rental shelves, while others were released simultaneously to both cable and home video markets. None of this really mattered, of course, so long as the quality of these programs maintained a decent level. But the dual-market approach tended to cheapen the term "Children's Classic," applying it to old video releases of negligible quality which happened to offer animated versions of well-known fairy tales and legends, or to failed television series which were re-edited into "movies" and misleadingly retitled to suggest tenuous relationships to better, more popular projects in the "classic" field.

To cartoon fans, it mattered not the source of the animation, but simply that it was there. "Give us plenty of cartoons, and we'll decide what we like and what we don't" was the viewer philosophy of the early 1990s. The notion that deciding what was good for the public should be left in the hands of the public was anathema to those self-appointed barometers of taste, the pressure groups. Having remained loud but relatively ineffective throughout the Mark Fowler years, the professional do-gooders found the FCC more receptive in 1990 when that organization created the Children's Television Act. Part of this act's purpose was (again) to limit the number of commercials on children's programming; part of it was (yet again!) to stem what was perceived as an increase in violence and objectionable material—a perception usually on the part of people who did not watch the cartoons that they were so roundly condemning. When the Los Angeles *Times* editorialized against "exploding heads" on Saturday morning cartoons, one wondered whose planet's programs the *Times* was monitoring.

Some clean-TV zealots expected the FCC ruling to impose punishments on cartoon programs that contained "smut"—specifically programs like *The Simpsons*, *Ren and Stimpy* and *Beavis and Butt-Head*, all of which revelled in raunchy subject matter that made some parents uncomfortable (and none of which was specifically aimed at children: *Beavis and Butt-Head* in fact carried a "mature entertainment" disclaimer). Did that mean that the FCC should also purify daily soap operas, which trafficked in goings-on that made the "bad" cartoons look like *Bambi*, and which were run in timeslots easily accessible to youngsters? Good gracious, no. Shelter the kids from animated vulgarity, but don't take away my *General Hospital*!

But the Children's Television Act went beyond mere antiviolence and antismut. To be thoroughly "FCC Friendly," cartoon programs would be encouraged to be educational. This would have been acceptable if the pressure groups were calling for a broad education (of the sort that would have been the responsibility of parents and schools back in the days when people took responsibility for their own children). But such was not quite the case. The "education" expected to be promoted had to fall within the boundaries of political correctness. If a villain appeared on an FCC-friendly cartoon show, he or she could not be a mere petty crook or just plain grouch. The heavy would have to be a narcotics merchant, a bigot, a crooked land developer, a wicked forest despoiler, an evil polluter. The heroes were no longer simply seeking to save the life and limb of themselves and their friends: Now they were expected to save the environment, save the whales, save the world. Ted Turner's *Captain Planet and the Planeteers* (syndicated in 1990) was the most extreme example of the politically correct cartoon series—and as expected, it played more like a propaganda leaflet than a television show.

"We've been through all this before," noted Joe Ruby of Ruby-Spears regarding the ramifications of the Children's Television Act. "In the seventies it amost killed children's programming. You had to remove everything from a show that made it entertaining. As a result, ratings went so low you couldn't make any money. The FCC can say whatever it wants about what kids should watch, but if kids don't like a show, they won't go near it."

Margaret Loesch, president of the Fox Children's Network, chose to continue regarding cartoons as entertainment rather than an ax-grinding conduit for special interest groups. "Recently, I was saying something to my husband, and he said, 'Oh you'd better watch it! That's not politically correct.' I said, 'That's great, because I don't want to be politically correct.'" It was not that Loesch was against including educational gracenotes in her cartoons; she simply didn't want to be forced to do this in a pedantic manner. When given the opportunity of rushing the FCC-friendly cartoon series *Where in the World Is Carmen Sandiego?* on the air, she chose to wait until the program's production company had turned out a first-rate product rather than a slapdash quickie. "I'm not going to slop a show on the air and appease the FCC just because it's educational. It's got to be entertaining."

Just where the Children's Television Act will lead cartoons is open to conjecture. One very prominent animation firm has — ominously — published a set of "new standards" wherein it promised, among other things, to avoid slapstick that might be imitated by the viewers and to show the consequences of "anti-social" behavior. It was but a step away from the sort of timorous self-censorship that all but destroyed the television cartoon industry in the 1970s.

But whatever content problems might be faced by television cartoons in the 1990s, one cannot deny that most of the finished product will look and sound better than anything in past seasons. Enhanced and improved production techniques, and an influx of talented creative people who have adored cartoons since childhood, have in recent years resulted in smoother animation, richer background art, more sharply etched characterizations, and an abundance of belly-laugh comedy. Also, state-of-the-art television receiving and transmitting equipment — embracing full stereo sound and high-definition television screens — has ensured that the murkiness and fuzziness which greeted cartoon broadcasts of the 1950s and early 1960s can truly be regarded as ancient history. Additionally, those new receivers are going to have to be kept primed for the sheer volume of animation already being telecast and still to come. The CBS network, along with ABC, Fox, HBO, Showtime, Nickelodeon, the Disney Channel, Turner, the Family Channel, the USA Network, the Sci-Fi Channel and innumerable syndication firms are all providing first-run animated fare for both the discriminating animation buff and pure cartoon fan.

And in October 1992, the marketplace dominance of animation was brought home with the creation of Ted Turner's Cartoon Network, the world's first 24-hour animation service. Though the Cartoon Network devoted its formative months to reruns from the Hanna-Barbera, Warner Bros. and MGM vaults owned by Turner, we are being promised brand new, "hang the cost" cartoon productions in the future — and say what you like about the man (as this writer has done concerning the pretentious *Captain Planet*) Ted Turner keeps his promises.

Wrapping up an overview of a subject covering 65 years, like television cartoons, is tricky. Happily, the industry has done it for the author. In the fall of 1993, the Film Roman studio announced that it had secured the rights for a series of newly animated *Felix the Cat* cartoons.

The Shows
(An Introductory Note)

This section covers all made-for-television cartoon series telecast between January 1, 1949, and December 31, 1993. Each entry is listed in the following manner: By title; network or cable affiliation; premiere date; date of final telecast (if any); production and or voice credits; and a synopsis and critique.

The "official" titles are used when applicable. If the words "Adventures of" or variations therein are part of the title, or the producer or production company is included, it will be alphabetized accordingly. Thus, you will find *Galaxy Rangers* under its full title *Adventures of the Galaxy Rangers*; *Superted* as *The Further Adventures of Superted*; *Around the World in Eighty Dreams* as *Saban's Around the World in Eighty Dreams*; *Gummi Bears* as *Disney's Adventures of the Gummi Bears*; and *Gravedale High* as *Rick Moranis in Gravedale High*. This does not apply to titles in which the producer or production company's name has been contractually tacked on to the main credit, even though the series' official name does not reflect this obligation. *Animaniacs* and *Tiny Toon Adventures* are listed under their own names, minus the *Steven Spielberg Presents* qualification (which is barely noticeable on screen—except perhaps to Spielberg). Similarly, *Peter Pan and the Pirates* is listed under "P" and not as *Fox's Peter Pan and the Pirates*, since the series carried the name of its network essentially for publicity purposes. Alternate titles, both official and unofficial, are cross-referenced for reader convenience.

Series with multiple spinoffs or sequels are treated within single entries. It would tax this book to the bursting point to list such satellite programs as *Everything's Archie* and *U.S. of Archie* individually; therefore, they have been listed (along with their individual credits and telecast dates) in the body of the entry on *Archie*. You will find similar multiple listings within the entries of such programs as *The Flintstones*, *Scooby Doo* and *Yogi Bear*.

Separate programs offered in omnibus "blocks" with catchall titles like *Amazin' Adventures* and *Funtastic World of Hanna-Barbera* are listed on a case by case basis. *Funtastic World* has run nearly ten seasons with a large, ever-changing manifest, and thus its individual programs (*Galtar and the Golden Lance, Young Robin Hood,* etc.) are given their own alphabetized entries. Conversely, the *Marvel Action Universe* block ran only a single season, so for the sake of convenience its separate half hour series (*Dino Riders, Robotix*) are listed as part of the block title. Again, such multiple listings are alphabetically cross-referenced.

The network or cable affiliation is listed whenever a program was first-run on a nationwide network or cable hookup, or whenever a series changed networks. *Scooby-Doo,* for example, premiered on CBS but eventually moved to ABC; this move is reflected in the listing. *Scooby-Doo'*s syndicated reruns, and its subsequent afterlife in cable television repeats, are not listed, but are referred to in passing in the series entry itself.

When a series has continued to telecast first-run episodes in cable, these are acknowledged. *My Little Pony* began life in syndication, but was subsequently telecast with new episodes on the Disney Channel under the title *My Little Pony Tales.*

The following networks and cable services will be found in these pages:

NETWORK: ABC (American Broadcasting Company)
CBS (Columbia Broadcasting System)
Fox (Fox Television Network)
NBC (National Broadcasting Company)
PBS (Public Broadcasting System).
CABLE: CBN (Christian Broadcasting Network—later known as The Family Channel)
Disney (The Disney Channel)
Family Channel (see above listing for CBN)
HBO (Home Box Office)
MTV (Music Television)
Nickelodeon
Sci-Fi Channel
Showtime
TBS (Atlanta Superstation WTBS)
USA (The USA Network)
(The Cartoon Network, ironically, is not included. It had offered no first-run TV cartoons as of December 31, 1993).

Many cartoon programs were not networkcast, but were sold directly to local stations or regional sponsors. These programs are designated as "Syndicated."

Premiere dates include month, day and year if the program debuted on network, cable or syndication on the same day throughout the United States. The premieres of most syndicated programs (which debuted at the convenience of individual local stations), and of several cable series (whose precise debut dates were not indicated in my sources), are listed by the month and year, or simply by year.

Production information includes the name of the studio(s) or production company (or companies), technical credits (producer, director, writer, etc.) and voice credits. Role designations are listed when known, with the actor's name followed by the character name in parentheses. Example: Mel Blanc (Heathcliff). If there are no technical or voice credits listed, it is because I was unable to determine this information in my research.

This listing includes those cartoon programs specifically made for television. For the most part, programs consisting entirely of theatrical cartoons are not listed. For example, do not look for *Heckle and Jeckle* to be listed as such, since the CBS telecasts of *Heckle and Jeckle* were comprised of theatrical releases. *Heckle and Jeckle* did appear in made-for-television cartoons, but only as a component of *The New Adventures of Mighty Mouse* — and thus are listed under *Mighty Mouse*. In the same vein, the only *Mighty Mouse* cartoons listed herein are those made for television. This also applies to such onetime theatrical properties as *Felix the Cat, Out of the Inkwell, Popeye*, and *Tom and Jerry*.

No rule exists without exceptions. Programs primarily comprised of theatrical releases like *The Bugs Bunny Show, CBS Cartoon Theatre, Jokebook* and *The Woody Woodpecker Show* are included in these listings, for special reasons duly noted in their entries.

Network series that were locally syndicated under different titles are not acknowledged. *Captain Inventory*, to choose one example from many, was Hanna-Barbera's syndicated blanket title for a group of "superhero" cartoon networkers like *The Fantastic Four* and *Shazzan!*, none of which had enough episodes to "strip" — that is, to run Monday through Friday — but which could be rerun on a rotating daily basis. Since there was never really any series titled *Captain Inventory*, the programs included in this package are listed separately.

However, a handful of "component" features culled from network programs were rebroadcast under different titles *on the networks*. These are recognized by title and broadcast dates (*Aquaman, Rubik the Amazing Cube*), though the reader is encouraged to look up full production information under the original titles (e.g., *Aquaman* under *Superman*).

Which brings us to the word "component." This word refers in these pages to secondary cartoon packages appearing regularly within the body of a "main" series. *Snooper and Blabber* and *Augie Doggie and Doggie Daddy* were regular weekly component features of the Hanna-Barbera half hour series *Quick Draw McGraw*, and as such are analyzed within the entry on *Quick Draw*. Most component cartoons are cross-referenced in the text, with such notable exceptions as the components of such programs as *Liquid Television* and *Lunch Box*, which are telecast on a sporadic rather than a regular basis. I have also confined component cross-referencing to cartoons which have been rebroadcast under their own titles (until recently, the Family Channel actually had an *Augie Doggie and Friends*). Since the individual components of Jay Ward's *Rocky and His Friends* and *George of the Jungle* are seldom run individually, they are listed only within the context of their parent programs.

"Special" cartoon programs are listed conditionally. Certain groups of specials like *HBO Storybook Musicals*, *Nelvanamation* and *World of Peter Rabbit and Friends*, though not telecast on a set weekly basis, were nonetheless packaged and sold as a group rather than as individual programs; these can be found in the text under their umbrella titles. Yearly or seasonal specials such as the *Garfield*, *Madeline*, and *Peanuts* telecasts are referred to only when they bear a relation to a regular series; the *Peanuts* specials, for example, are mentioned in the entry on *The Charlie Brown and Snoopy Show*. One-shot cartoon specials like *The Bear Who Slept Through Christmas*, *Mouse on the Mayflower* and *Rikki Tikki Tavi* are not listed.

Live-action network and cable children's programs which telecast only theatrical cartoons and or utilized animation on a secondary or peripheral basis, are not given separate listings. This applies to programs like *The Small Fry Club* from the 1940s, *Barker Bill* from the 1950s, *Cartoonies* from the 1960s, *ABC Afternoon Specials* from the 1970s, *Pinwheel* and *Calliope* from the 1980s, and *Chip 'n' Pepper's Surf's Up Saturday* from the 1990s. Network series like *My World and Welcome to It* (1969) and *The Duck Factory* (1984), which featured newly produced animation as an added attraction but which were essentially "live," are also omitted.

The Shows

ABBOTT AND COSTELLO. Syndicated: 1967. Hanna-Barbera/RKO-Jomar. Voices: Bud Abbott (Himself), Stan Irwin (Lou Costello), Mel Blanc, Hal Smith, John Stephenson, Don Messick, Janet Waldo.

Abbott and Costello was one of a brief spate of 1960s cartoons which cashed in on that decade's nostalgia craze by animating popular movie comedy teams of bygone days (see also *Laurel and Hardy* and *The New Three Stooges*). 156 five minute cartoons featuring the likenesses of Bud Abbott and Lou Costello were churned out by Hanna/Barbera in a style charitably described as journeyman. Abbott and Costello purists are of the opinion that these cartoons should never have been made; opinions from nonpartisans of the team range from "dreary" to "brainless."

It is all but impossible to tell these cartoons apart. Virtually every one of them features the tubby Costello being pursued by some bugeyed monster or giant sized garden pest, screaming what seems to be his only line of dialogue, "HEY AB-BOTTTT," at the top of his lungs. None of the classic verbal exchanges which brought the real Abbott and Costello to fame in the first place are evident. Harold Schechter summed this misbegotten project up best: "There are worse children's [programs] on the market than this one. But not many."

Abbott and Costello's solitary redeeming factor was that it gave much needed work to an ill and impoverished Bud Abbott, who rallied his strength long enough to provide the voice for his cartoon alter ego. While the gravelly, sardonic Abbott intonations were welcome, the comedian's health had deteriorated to the point that he sounded far older than his 71 years. The voice of Lou Costello (who'd died in 1959) was supplied by Las Vegas nightclub manager and future *Tonight Show* producer Stan Irwin, a close friend of both Abbott and Costello's who displayed a wicked gift for mimickry in conjuring up his old pal Lou's childish whine.

THE ABC SATURDAY SUPERSTAR MOVIE/THE NEW SATURDAY SUPERSTAR MOVIE. ABC: 9/9/1972–8/31/1974. Produced by Hanna-Barbera, Rankin-Bass, Warner Bros., Universal, Filmation, King Features and Fred Calvert Productions.

The *ABC Saturday Superstar Movie*, a cartoon anthology series, came into being so that Hanna-Barbera (who produced the bulk of *Superstar Movie*'s first season) and a host of other leading cartoon producers could test a number of venerable properties for potential new series sales.

Amidst such tried and true cartoon characters as Yogi Bear (represented by Hanna-Barbera's *Yogi's Ark Lark*), Popeye (King Features' *Popeye Meets the Man Who Hated Laughter*) and Porky Pig and Daffy Duck (Warner Bros./Filmation's *Daffy Duck and Porky Pig Meet the Groovie Goolies*), a handful of favorite live action sitcom characters were given a go at "pilots" for possible animated weeklies. Occasionally the people who'd originally appeared in these sitcoms provided voices for their animated counterparts: Marlo Thomas on *That Girl in Wonderland* (Rankin-Bass) and Juliet Mills and Richard Long on *Nanny and the Professor* (Fred Calvert Productions), for example. The

51

entire pre-adult "gang" from *The Brady Bunch* (*you* know their names!) did their own voices on *The Brady Kids on Mysterious Island* (Filmation), the pilot for a cartoon series which actually did make it to the regular Saturday morning lineup. Other warmed over live action creations were represented on such *Superstar Movies* as Fred Calvert Productions' *Lassie and the Spirit of Thunder Mountain*, Hanna-Barbera's *Lost in Space* and *Gidget Makes the Wrong Connection*, and Universal Television's *The Mini-Munsters*.

Some of the more enjoyable *Superstar Movies* were one-shots not designed for extended weekly lives, featuring recognizable personalities both factual and fictional. These included *Robin Hoodnik* and the two-part *Oliver and the Artful Dodger* (both Hanna-Barbera), and perhaps the best of the batch, Rankin-Bass' *Willie Mays and the Say-Hey Kid*, a fantasy reminiscent of the 1951 feature film *Angels in the Outfield*, with Mays engagingly supplying the voice for his animated "self."

In all, 19 *Saturday Superstar Movies* were made, 16 for the 1972-73 season, and three more for 1973-74, just barely enabling ABC to palm off the series' rerun-studded second season as *The New Saturday Superstar Movie*.

ABC WEEKEND SPECIALS. ABC: 9/10/77–. Animated producers: Hanna-Barbera, Ruby-Spears, DIC, Rick Reinert Productions, Marvel Productions, many others.

This Saturday anthology series, which was first telecast sporadically before solidifying into a weekly offering in 1979, consisted primarily of newly filmed live action dramas, as well as repeats from ABC's highly regarded *ABC Afterschool Specials* (q.v.). Occasionally, 60-minute animated specials produced by various studios were also telecast.

Among the cartoon contributions to *ABC Weekend Specials* were a number of multipart productions, spread out over two or more weeks and later released as videocassette "features": *The Trouble with Miss Switch* (1980) and *Miss Switch to the Rescue* (1982), a brace of two-part stories from Ruby-Spears Productions about a benevolent witch; *Scruffy* (Ruby-Spears 1980), a three parter about the adventures of an orphaned puppy; and *Liberty and the Littles* (DIC 1986), three weeks' worth of

the elfish characters seen on the weekly ABC cartoon half hour *The Littles* (q.v.). Several of the animated hours attempted to apprise children of the dangers facing wildlife and nature at the hands of insensitive humans: the aforementioned *Scruffy* warned dog owners not to abandon their pets, while Rick Reinert Productions' *The Bollo Caper* (1985) attacked thoughtless trappers who selfishly sought the pelts of endangered species. Even a comic episode like Marvel Productions' *Monster Bed* had a moral lurking about somewhere (don't be afraid of what you don't understand). In sum total, the cartoons seen on the *ABC Weekend Special* endeavored to enrich the minds of youngsters by encouraging them to think, reason, and—above all—read, as witness the several *Cap'n O.G. Readmore* installments (Reinert Productions, 1985–1988), in which an erudite cat and his "Friday Night Book Club" demonstrated the pleasures inherent in the Printed Word.

Still plugging away as of this writing, *ABC Weekend Specials'* first-run animated offerings dwindled as the cartoon studios worked full blast for syndication and cable, but a few new cartoon gems occasionally surfaced. One pleasant entry from April 24, 1993, *Legend of Lochnagar*, was based on a story by Britain's Prince Charles, who took time off from his hectic private life to host the episode in person.

THE ADDAMS FAMILY. NBC: 9/7/1973–8/30/1975. Hanna-Barbera. Executive producers, William Hanna and Joseph Barbera. Produced by Iwao Takamoto. Directed by Charles Nichols. Story by Bill Raynor, Bob Atkinson, Jack Mendelsohn, Myles Wilder, Dick Comby, Gene Thompson. Story direction by Jim Carmichael, Carl Fellberg, Dave Hanan, Fred Crippen, Jan Green, Don Sheppard. Animation director, Carl Urbano. Animation supervision by James A. Pabian. Character design by Takashi Masunaga. Series created by David Levy; based on the cartoons by Charles Addams. Music by Hoyt Curtin; musical direction by Paul DeKorte. Voices: Lennie Weinrib (Gomez Addams); Janet Waldo (Morticia Addams/Granny); Jackie Coogan (Uncle Fester); Ted Cassidy (Lurch); Jodie Foster (Pugsley); Cindy Henderson (Wednesday). And Josh Albee, John Carver, Pat Harrington Jr., Bob Holt, John Ste-

phenson, Don Messick, Herb Vigran, Howard Caine.
—THE ADDAMS FAMILY. ABC: 9/12/1992–. Fils-Cartoons/Hanna-Barbera. Executive producers: David Kirschner, Mark Young. Produced by Ron Myrick. Creative consultant: The Lady Colyton. Supervising director, Ray Patterson. Directed by Robert Alvarez, Don Lusk, Carl Urbano. Original theme music by Vic Mizzy. Musical score by Guy Moon. Voices: John Astin (Gomez); Nancy Linari (Morticia); Debi Derryberry (Wednesday); Jeannie Elias (Puggsley); Rip Taylor (Uncle Fester); Carol Channing (Granny); Jim Cummings (Lurch); Pat Fraley (Cousin Itt); Edie McClurg (Mrs. Normanmeyer); Rob Paulsen (Mr. Normanmeyer); Dick Beals (N. J. Normanmeyer); and Ruth Buzzi, Ernest Harada, Anna Marie Horsford, Erv Immerman, Brian Mitchell, Marion Ramsey, Hal Rayle, Susan Silo, Marcelo Tubert, Renee Victor, Marcia Wallace, Anderson Wong, Michael Bell, Earl Boen, Julie Brown, Hector Elizondo, Dick Gautier, Peter Cullen, Candy Houston, Gordon Hunt, Nick Jameson, Vicki Juditz, Page Leong, Ian Monfrette, Charles Nelson Reilly, Bob Ridgely, Pamela Segall, Marsha Warfield, Frank Welker.

When *New Yorker* cartoonist Charles Addams began drawing his rather ghoulish "family" in the 1940s, the characters had no names. Addams' creations were a gnomish, wide-eyed father; his statuesque, spiderlike wife; his children, an overweight little boy and a voodoo doll-shaped little girl; and a vaguely defined pair of in-laws, one a witch type straight out of *Macbeth* and the other an egg-bald uncle or grandfather. There was also the family butler, who looked more like a factory second from Frankenstein Castle. They all seemed to have spawned from the 1932 tongue in cheek horror film *The Old Dark House*, which depicted an equally eccentric but malevolent Victorian family. Addams' family was not so much malevolent as morbidly mischievous, though one wonders if the Christmas carollers whom the Addams clan were preparing to douse with boiling oil in one of their earliest *New Yorker* appearances accepted this lighthearted Yuletide prank in the spirit in which it was intended.

The first TV incarnation of Addams' creations was the 1964 live action ABC comedy series *The Addams Family*. Now compelled to name his creatures, Addams chose "Gomez" for the father, "Morticia" for the mother, "Pugsley" and "Wednesday" for the kiddies, "Uncle Fester" and the deceptively benign "Grandmamma" for the elder relations, and "Lurch" for the lurching butler. There was also a new character, a disembodied hand named "Thing" who popped out of a box on a table to deliver mail, telephones, and cigars, and to perform other useful single handed services. A whimsical combination of traditional sitcomery with bizarre and offbeat trappings (notably their horror-museum of a mansion) and convoluted family values (in the very first episode, Gomez and Morticia took their local school system to task for teaching their children the "sick" story of a nice dragon killed in cold blood by a knight in shining armor), *The Addams Family* lasted only two seasons, but developed a cult following which allowed for a robust rerun syndication existence. Charles Addams' financial harvest was bountiful, although *New Yorker* editor William Shawn, snobbishly determining that the artist had sold out to the masses, never allowed Addams to feature his "family" characters in the magazine's pages again.

The *Addams Family* remained moribund until 1973, when two new projects surfaced. One, a tepid musical version of the original series, died aborning when the 42 underwriting TV stations involved in the project turned a unanimous thumbs down. The second was a Saturday morning half hour cartoon series, produced by Hanna-Barbera (with animation reportedly farmed out to Britain's Halas and Batchelor and Canada's Rankin-Bass) which had had a test run the previous season as a 60-minute entry on *The New Scooby-Doo Movies* (see *Scooby-Doo*). While the original stars of *The Addams Family*—John Astin, Carolyn Jones, Jackie Coogan and Ted Cassidy—had provided voices for the *Scooby Doo* one shot, the only original cast members who signed on for the *Addams Family* cartoon series were Coogan (as Uncle Fester) and Cassidy (as Lurch). Lennie Weinrib replaced John Astin as Gomez Addams, providing a mellifluous "Reginald Van Gleason" voice for the character. Another of the new voice artists was 11-year-old Jodie Foster, here cast in the male role of Pugsley by virtue of her low, raspy vocal range. Janet Waldo, who played Morticia (complete with an ear-shattering scream) and Granny on the 1973 series, would recall in later years that Jodie Foster behaved with the same straightforward professionalism that would be the hallmark of the Oscar-winning actress' adult career; this attitude was especially handy in keeping recording time down whenever chain-smoking Jackie Coogan spoiled a take with a coughing spasm.

Hanna-Barbera forsook the mansion-bound ambience of the live action series and opted to put the Addams Family on the road, in the style of *Scooby-Doo*. To that end, the family was provided with a "haunted" camper (optional moat and bats included), which allowed them to skulk from state to state, and even underwater. Along for the ride was a menagerie of funny animals: Kitty-Cat the Lion, Mr. V the Vulture, Alley the Alligator, and Ocho the Octopus, who doubled as windshield wiper for the Addams' camper.

The National Association for Better Broadcasting was pleased with the result, noting that *The Addams Family* and Filmation's *Star Trek* (q.v.) were practically the only live-to-cartoon series to retain "the flavor of the original." I don't know what the NABB was smoking, but the *Addams Family* cartoons I've seen from the 1970s were dismally animated and cliche-ridden, their ineptitude underscored by a repellant laughtrack. The plots were depressingly cut from the usual Hanna-Barbera "formula" cloth: the family joins a circus, the family thwarts a shipboard robbery, Puggsley enters a broken-down nag in the Kentucky Derby. Worse still, the wryly demonic nature of the live-action Addams clan was botched by making their cartoon counterparts ingenuous buffoons, who (like *The Munsters*) can't understand why everyone else is frightened of them, and who stupidly misinterpret every move made by the series' various villains as a gesture of kindness and generosity. Rescuing the 17 half-hour *Addams Family* cartoons from complete worthlessness was the faithful character design adherence to Charles Addams' original *New Yorker* panels.

This *Addams Family* ran on NBC until 1975. Then, thanks to the phenomenally successful *Addams Family* theatrical movie released in 1991, the old property was given a second animated round in 1992, again courtesy of Hanna-Barbera. Some new twists, notably transforming Wednesday into Pugsley's older sister to allow for "kid brother" jokes, were blended with the time-tested, audience-approved elements of both the 1960s TV series and the 1991 feature film. John Astin, the original Gomez, returned to the fold in this new *Addams Family*, which also nostalgically reinstated Vic Mizzy's snapping-finger musical theme and that fiendishly furnished family mansion — now a dwelling with an anthropomorphic "life" of its own.

Alas, this ambitious new project fell prey to banality and formularization early on — this time in the shape of a newly created set of hostile yuppie neighbors, the Normanmeyers, who each week did their best to purge the community of Happydale Heights of the unorthodox Addamses. To the studio's credit, Hanna-Barbera tried to adopt the gag-a-minute, nonsequitur style of Warners' *Tiny Toons* (q.v.) for the new *Addams Family* series, but this chicken salad technique was at odds with H-B's traditional "beginning middle and end" approach to storylines; it was hard to get involved with the plot when one was trying to follow the throwaway jokes. "Overkill" was the key word here. Example: the Normanmeyers were incensed that the Addams mansion was cluttered with gothic kitsch, yet the Normanmeyer house was decorated in equally atrocious taste, with everything from telephones to wall paintings designed in the style of boxer shorts, reflecting the fact that Mr. Normanmeyer was the "underwear king" of his business community. Both the original live action *Addams Family* and the 1973 cartoon series thrived on the basic joke of the Addamses' alternate life style. But what was the point on the new *Addams* series if everyone else in Happydale Heights was just as wacked out as the "wacky" neighbors?

Equally problematic were other stylistic choices. In direct opposition to the dank Doomsday color schemes of the *Addams* movie, the new *Addams Family* was incongruously prettied up with bright, happy hues. The verbal humor was likewise at odds with the original concept; in place of the graveyard wit of Charles Addams, we had such 1990s-style scatology as having Uncle Fester blow his nose, contemplate his handkerchief, and announce "I'll save that for my collection." Although the computer-enchanced animation and background layout far outclassed anything on the 1973 series, the new Hanna-Barbera *Addams Family* was still something of a letdown to devout Charles Addams disciples. The rest of America was less finicky. As of 1993, 3.5 million viewers were tuning in weekly to *The Addams Family*, making it ABC's number one Saturday morning program — and in fact the highest-rated program of its kind on all four major networks.

THE ADVENTURES OF BATMAN see BATMAN

THE ADVENTURES OF GULLIVER. ABC: 9/14/1968–9/5/1970. Hanna-Barbera. Produced and directed by William Hanna and Joseph Barbera. Music: Hoyt Curtin. Voices: Jerry Dexter (Gary Gulliver); Herb Vigran (Tagg); John Stephenson (Thomas Gulliver/Captain Leech/King Pomp); Ginny Tyler (Flirtacia); Allan Melvin (Bunko); Don Messick (Egger/Glum).

So far as the cartoon industry is concerned, the eponymous hero of 17th century author Jonathan Swift's *Gulliver's Travels* never got any farther than Lilliput. You'll find no Yahoos or Houyhnhnms and no land of Brobdingnag in Max Fleischer's 1939 animated feature version of the story (which spends nearly two reels showing the industrious Lilliputians tying poor Gulliver to the ground). Nor did Hanna/Barbera's 1968 Saturday morning TV series explore Swift's dark satirical message concerning the follies of humanity as exemplified by giants and humanized horses. To the cartoon makers, Lilliput — the land in which the normal sized Gulliver towered like a colossus over the tiny Lilliputians — was the end-all and be-all of Swift's story.

In fact, Hanna-Barbera's 17-episode *The Adventures of Gulliver* threw out almost everything *but* the Lilliputians. In this version, the hero is Lemuel Gulliver's teenaged son Gary — his surname a tipoff that the stories were updated to the 20th century — who set out to find his lost explorer father. Just like Pop, Gary was shipwrecked (in the company of his regulation Hanna-Barbera dog companion, Bib) on the isle of Lilliput, where he spent half his time rescuing the citizens from a deadening parade of giant sized monsters, and the other half protecting his treasure map from King Leech, a villainous character whom Jonathan Swift had impulsively omitted from the original novel. Other characters included King Pomp, his daughter Flirtacia, and a con man named Bunko. Enough said. (see also *Saban's Gulliver's Travels*.)

THE ADVENTURES OF HOPPITY HOOPER see HOPPITY HOOPER

THE ADVENTURES OF JONNY QUEST see JONNY QUEST

Lariat Sam and Tippytoes.

THE ADVENTURES OF LARIAT SAM. CBS: 9/10/1962–8/27/1965. Terrytoons/Robert Keeshan Associates. Produced by Bill Weiss. Directed by Arthur Bartsch, Robert Kuwahara, Connie Rasinski and Dave Tendlar. Voices: Dayton Allen.

Lariat Sam was first shown as a component of CBS' long-running live-action children's daily *Captain Kangaroo* (see also *The Adventures of Pow Wow* and *Tom Terrific*). Produced by Terrytoons, each three part adventure (13 stories in all) starred Lariat Sam, a naive cowboy who couldn't see anything but good in anybody. Sam's cohort, a derby-hatted horse named Tippy-Toes, was a bit more clearheaded than Sam, but still inclined toward the idealistic, preferring poetry to wild west mayhem. Sam's principal antagonist was Badlands Meeney, whose name said it all. Played strictly for laughs, *Lariat Sam* rode clear of excess violence (per its title, the hero's weapon of choice was his lariat), and as such appealed most to the four- to seven-year-old contingent.

THE ADVENTURES OF POW WOW. CBS: 1957. Syndicated: 1958. Sam Singer/Tempitoons/Screen Gems.

A feature of the daily CBS kiddie series *Captain Kangaroo* (see also *The Adventures of Lariat Sam* and *Tom Terijfc*), *The Adventures of Pow Pow* consisted of 26 five-minute cartoons tracing the exploits of a pint-sized Indian boy. Each episode, enacted without dialogue, endeavored to teach the hero (and, hopefully, the home audience) a valuable Life Lesson. During its network run, *Pow Wow* was also syndicated by Screen Gems to 11 TV markets not serviced by CBS. Though scarcely politically correct by today's standards, *Pow Wow* was widely popular among the baby boomers of the late 50s, as evidenced by the singing of the cartoon's theme song by John Candy on a 1983 episode of *Second City TV*.

THE ADVENTURES OF RAG-GEDY ANN AND ANDY. CBS: 9/17/1988–9/1/1990. A CBS Animation Production. Voices: Christina Lange (Raggedy Ann); Josh Rodine (Raggedy Andy); Kath Soucie (Raggedy Cat); Dana Hill (Raggedy Dog); Ken Mars (Camel with the Wrinkled Knees); Tracy Rowe (Marcella); Charlie Adler (Grouchy Bear); Katie Leigh (Sunny Bunny).

Animated cartoon adaptations of Johnny Gruelle's famed 1917 children's story "Raggedy Ann and Andy," and its ancillary line of ragdoll playthings, have ranged from three enjoyable theatrical shorts from the Max Fleischer/Famous Studios factory in the 1940s to a dismally dull 1977 feature film (initially slated for TV's *Hallmark Hall of Fame*). Producer Chuck Jones fared best with a brace of leisurely half hour animated specials, produced for CBS in 1978 and 1979 and featuring flawless vocal contributions by June Foray and Daws Butler in the leading roles.

Hoping to capitalize on the "cute doll" craze inflicting the TV cartoon market in the 1980s, CBS commissioned a new, 13-episode *Raggedy Ann and Andy* series for the 1988-89 season. All the old favorites were in attendance, including the Camel with the Wrinkled Knees, Kracklin the Wizard, and the little girl Marcella, the principal "human" character from the original stories. The CBS series detailed the doll characters' adventures in Raggedyland, a Tolkien-like world replete with fairies and dragons. Adults were satisfied with this newest incarnation of an old favorite, though *TV Guide*'s James Morrow chastised the "mild sexism" inherent in the fact that it was Raggedy Andy rather than Raggedy Ann who took most of the physical risks in the adventures. But children of 1988, not overly familiar with the 70-year-old Raggedy Ann saga perceived—correctly so—that the new *Raggedy Ann and Andy* series owed far too much to *The Smurfs* (q.v.) and its various imitators to be totally enjoyed on its own merits.

THE ADVENTURES OF SONIC THE HEDGEHOG see SONIC THE HEDGEHOG

THE ADVENTURES OF TEDDY RUXPIN. Syndicated: 1987 (five-episode "pilot" syndicated 1986). Alchemy II, Inc./Worlds of Wonder Productions/DIC. Produced by Andy Heyward, Jean Chalopin, Alison Clayton, W. H. Stevens Jr., M. H. Cloutier and Christopher Brough. Directed by Chris Schouten. Created by Ken Forsse. Creative supervisors, Jean Chalopin and W. H. Stevens Jr. Script coordinators, Lori Crawford, Gail Chapple, Bill Ruiz, Patricia Hicks. Story editors, Jack Mendelsohn, Brian Jeffrey Street, Doug Stratton. Written by Mary Crawford, Derek Diorlo, Dan Lalando, Mary MacKay-Smith, Patrick A. McCarthy, Stephen McLoughlin, Carol Bruce Mendelsohn, Ron Ross, Doug Stratton, Brian Jeffrey Street, Alan Templeton. Story consultants, Phil Baron and Lenny Levit. Associate producers, Jack Spillum and Dave Mepham. Music score arranged by Andrew Huggart; songs composed by George Wilkins. Alchemy II Production Staff: Larry Larsen, Sandi Vidan, Jodie Resnick. Voices: Phil Barron (Teddy Ruxpin); John Stocker (Newton Gimmick);

Will Ryan (Grubby); John Koensgen (Tweeg); Robert Bockstael (L.B. Prince Aran); Holly LaRoque (Leota); Abby Hagyard (Aruzia); Pierre Paquette (Wooly Whatsit); Pier Kohl.

Teddy Ruxpin seemed like a good idea in 1985. In an age of "interactive" toys, what better gift for a child than a teddy bear who not only spoke but also told long, complicated stories? This was accomplished by planting an audiocassette player deep within Teddy Ruxpin's inner workings. The child had merely to pop in a prerecorded cassette and an afternoon's entertainment was had by all (it was almost like really having friends!). Test-marketing on Teddy Ruxpin was so high that a new company, Worlds of Wonder, was created specifically to market the doll. The $93 million sales in its first year of production was exceeded—far beyond the dreams of its creators—by Teddy Ruxpin's $300 million profitability in 1986.

But by 1987, it was clear that children were growing rapidly impatient sitting still with a doll for hours on end, nor could they be enthralled forever by a tape player which stared back at them. Also, the very explicitness of the prerecorded adventures threw the whole idea of "use your imagination" right out the window. Additionally, microchip technology made Mr. Ruxpin's bulky innards obsolete virtually the moment the toy glutted the market. Its sales falling off disastrously, the Teddy Ruxpin doll ended up one of the more daunting disappointments of the 1980s, bringing despair to the bankrupt Worlds of Wonder and its thousands of investors, and resulting in half-price overstock sales for many Christmases to come.

At any rate, DIC's daily, 65-episode The Adventures of Teddy Ruxpin was a diverting cartoon derivation of the toy which inspired it, though its cannibalization of elements previously utilized in such projects (discussed elsewhere in this book) as Raggedy Ann and Andy, Pandamonium, Winnie the Pooh, Paddington Bear, Babar, Peter Potamus and virtually every "elf on a quest" story written since Tolkien's Ring trilogy, robbed the series of any real originality. The plot of Teddy Ruxpin featured Teddy, his absent-minded "creator" Newton Gimmick and his octopede pal Grubby embarking in an elaborate airship to find the secret behind a recently unearthed cache of magic crystals, each la-

belled with virtues like "Loyalty" and "Friendship." The good characters included King Nogburt, the toylike Princess Azuria and Prince Aran, the musclebound Wooly Whatsit, and the peaceful citizens of the Land of Grundo. The villains included the lizardlike Gutangs and a cartel known as M.A.V.O. (Monsters and Villains Organization). Top badguy Tweeg was very funny, especially whenever he burst into song after winning a round against Teddy Ruxpin.

The series' animation was acceptable, and the characters were likable and remarkably soft-spoken (except for the villains)—and far more compelling than the somewhat stolid Teddy Ruxpin plaything which prompted their creation. But once the toy took a marketplace nosedive, so did the expensive Adventures of Teddy Ruxpin.

In 1993, the Teddy Ruxpin doll made a comeback of sorts, packaged with a companion line of cartoon videocassettes starring the likes of Teenage Mutant Ninja Turtles (q.v.) and other popular properties. This time, Teddy responded to the on-screen dialogue. Also this time, there was no Teddy Ruxpin cartoon series. Once bitten, DIC was twice shy.

THE ADVENTURES OF THE GALAXY RANGERS. Syndicated: 1986. Transcom Media/Gaylord Productions/ITF Enterprises. Animation by TMS (Tokyo Movie Shinsha) Entertainment. Executive producer: Abe Mandell. Produced by Robert Mandell. Associate producer: Eleanor Kearney. Story editors: Owen Lock, Christopher Rowley. Writers: Henry Beck, Veronica Chapman, Brian Daley, Laurel Davis, Tom De Haven, Mick Farren, Daniel Fiorella, James Luceno, Robert Mandell, John Rawlins, Laura Robson, Christopher Rowley, Shelley Shapiro, Josepha Sherman, Cy Voris. Music by Phil Galdston, John Van Tongeren, Peter Wetzler. Voices: Jerry Orbach (Zachary Foxx); Hubert Kelly (Doc Hartford); Laura Dean (Nikko/Aliza and Jessica Foxx); Doug Preis (Goose/Mogel the Space Sorceror/The General/Nimrod/Jackie Subtract/Bubblehead the Memory Bird); Robert Bottone (Zozo/Squeegie/GV/Little Zach Foxx/Brappo); Maia Danziger (Maya/Annie Oh/Mistwalker); Earl Hammond (Cmdr. Joseph Walsh/Lazarus Slade/Capt.

Kidd/Wildfire Cody/ King Spartos); Auben Kelly (Roy); Henry Mandell (Waldo/Geezi the Pedulont/Q Ball/Larry/Scarecrow/Kilbane/Crown Agent); Alexander Marshall (Buzzwang); Corinne Orr (Queen of the Crown/The Kiwi Kids); Ray Owens (Macross).

One of three "outer space westerns" delivered to the cartoon syndie market in 1986 and 1987 (see also *Bravestarr* and *Saber Riders and the Star Sheriff*), the daily *Adventures of the Galaxy Rangers* was arguably the most enjoyable, simply because it refused to take itself too seriously.

Galaxy Rangers was set in 2086. Two peaceful aliens, Waldo Zeptic of the planet Ando and Zozo from the planet Kyrin, have received help from the World Federation of Earth in thwarting an intergalactic outlaw syndicate. In return, Zeptic and Zozo gratefully provided the Earth with the plans for the first hyperdrive space vehicle. With this formidably armed conveyence, the World Federation was able to form BETA—the Bureau of Extra-Terrestrial Affairs—in conjunction with the League of Planets. Keeping the peace for BETA was the skipper of the hyperdrive, Captain Zachary Foxx, whose authority was assured by the awesome power of his bionic arm. Fox's crew included Nikko, a girl with extrasensory powers; Doc Hartford, a computer whiz; and Goose, the pilot. *Star Trek* redux? Only if one remembers that NBC often described *Star Trek* as "*Wagon Train* in outerspace." The Galaxy Rangers dressed and behaved in the manner of Wild West lawmen of the 1880s, albeit equipped with the technology of the 2080s (while incidentally representing many of the "generic spaceship crew" stereotypes of the 1980s). Just as in frontier days gone by, these planet hopping peacemakers were not to be trifled with: their motto was "No Guts, No Glory."

Additional allies included BETA commander Joseph Walsh; a diminutive pair of alien "Kiris"; the Galaxy Rangers' robot horses, Voyager and Mel, both of whom could out-talk any Mister Ed in the universe; and grizzled old prospector Roy McIntyre and his mechanical Burro. Leading the villains were the infamous Queen of the Crown, and her Darth Vader-like lieutenant, Seven-Zero; sidelines antagonists included mercenary robot parrot Captain Kidd. The bone of contention between heroes and heavies (other than domination of the Galaxy) was the Star Stone, an ore more precious than gold. The heroes had an advantage over the baddies with their Ranger badges, which were possessed of powers and abilities far beyond those of your average tin star.

The 65-episode *Adventures of the Galaxy Rangers* could well have been ponderous (certainly the animation leaned in that direction at times), but the juxtaposition of deliberately selected Western cliches with high tech space jargon and paraphernalia was played out with the sort of larger than life exuberance that made the *Star Wars* films so much fun.

The Little Koala (of *Adventures of the Little Koala*), when he was still called "Kolbea."

THE ADVENTURES OF THE LITTLE KOALA. Nickelodeon, 6/1/1987–. Cinar/Viacom. Originally produced by Tohokushinsha Film Co., Ltd. Executive producer: Michelle Charest. Produced by R. A. Weinberg. Musical producer: Andrea Perreault. Theme song by Pierre Daniel Rheault. Lyrics by Liz Joyce. Theme performed by Sonja Ball, Sharl Chaskin, Maxie Vaughann. Voices: Steven Bednarski (Roobear); Phillip Pretten (Kiwi); Tim Webber (Floppy); Barbara Poggemiller (Mimi); Bronwen Mantel (Pamie/Miss Lewis); Ian Finley (Nick); Morgan Hallet (Laura); Cleo Paskal (Betty); A. J. Henderson (Walter); Jane Woods (Mommy); Walter Massey (Papa); Rob Roy (Colt); Dean Hagopian (Horsie); Arthur Grosser (Duckbill).

The Little Koala was Roobear (originally "Kolbea"), who lived in a vaguely Australian environment with his parents and little sister Laura. Roobear's best pals were Mimi and Nick, penguins; Floppy and Pamie, rabbits; Betty, another koala; Duckbill, a platypus; and Kiwi, a . . . kiwi. Adventures were of a nonthreatening "moral lesson" nature, but still there had to be a Menace. The bane of Roobear's existence was a trio of Dead End Kid foxes — Walter, Colt, and Horsie — ever anxious to embroil our marsupial hero in their misdeeds.

The 26 *Little Koala* half hours, attractively drafted in a soft, muted color scheme reminiscent of old-fashioned children's book illustrations, were telecast on a daily basis, one of several foreign made cartoon releases shown exclusively in the United States over the Nickelodeon cable service.

ADVENTURES OF THE LITTLE MERMAID FANTASY *see* **THE LITTLE MERMAID**

THE ADVENTURES OF THE LITTLE PRINCE. Syndicated: 1982. Jambre/Gallerie International Films Productions/Jason Syndication. English adaptation produced by Jameson Brewer. Director and editorial supervisor, Franklin Coford. Associate producers, Irving Klein and Sherman Price. Written by Jameson Brewer, Peter Germano, Helen Swain, Richard Shaw, Jerry Thoms, Muriel Germano. Special effects by Fritz Miller Animation Graphics. Music composed and conducted by Dale Schacker. Voices: Julie McWhirter Dees, Katie Leigh (The Little Prince); Hal Smith (Swiftee the Space Bird); Bob Ridgely, Janet Waldo, Walker Edmiston, Pamela Ziolowski.

Judging by a survey of the most popular Christmas gift selections, Antoine de St.-Exupéry's 1942 book *The Little Prince* is an imperishable favorite of female liberal arts students the world over. To be sure, this slim little allegory of a young extraterrestrial monarch who leaves his home asteroid "B-612" to encounter various personifications of human frailties and strengths, does have its own peculiar charm. Among its fans have been such diverse celebrity types as actor James Dean and authors Anne Morrow Lindbergh and Anais Nin. Certainly its subtext of innocence lost was a potent message to its first readers, citizens of a Nazi-occupied France. Yet *The Little Prince* has proven devilishly difficult to adapt to film. An early attempt, which was to have been a collaboration between Orson Welles and Walt Disney Studios, fell apart after Disney proclaimed "there is not room on

this lot for two geniuses!" The excruciating 1974 live action film version, with songs by Lerner and Loewe and direction by Stanley Donen, proved that there was even less room for three geniuses.

However, Jambre/Gallerie's animated, 25-episode *Adventures of the Little Prince*, produced in 1978 for French television, was a pleasant surprise, despite its many departures from the original. The series carried an onscreen disclaimer that it was "not directly based on the book itself," a statement instantly borne out by the artwork, which looked nothing like St. Exupery's illustrations but instead emulated the wide eyes, gapless toothy grins and sharpened background angles typical of Japanese animation (none of the Japanese production team was given screen credit, but the series' heritage was obvious). The important character of the airplane pilot who flew the Little Prince from moral lesson to moral lesson — a character which St. Exupery, an air ace who died in World War II, based upon himself — was replaced with the more "kiddie-accessible" character of Swiftee the Space Bird; the Prince did his planet-hopping on the tails of conveniently passing comets. And the symbolism and allegory of the original gave way to more straightforward adventures involving good guys, bad guys, and the occasional last minute rescue — though the series steered clear of intensity and violence. With all its alterations and emendations, TV's *Little Prince* managed to retain some of the fragile whimsy of the source material by gently emphasizing such universal values as friendship, honesty, generosity, forgiveness, and real courage vs. phony bravado. The only real mis-step (occurring only in the English-language version of the series) was the French-accented narrator, who came off like a roadhouse imitation of Maurice Chevalier.

Expertly reedited by Frank Coford (who spliced in new 3D-like establishing shots of a clay model representing the Prince's planet) and adapted for English speaking audiences by veteran Disney and Hanna-Barbera scripter Jameson Brewer, *The Adventures of the Little Prince* was first shown in the U.S. in 1982 over ABC's owned and operated TV stations in New York and Los Angeles, where the half hour series swept the ratings. The prosocial, nonviolent nature of the project enabled *Little Prince* to earn a recommendation from the National Education Association. In 1985, the series gained even wider audience acceptance when it was picked up by the Nickelodeon cable service, while several French-speaking Canadian cable networks helped make the show a hit above the U.S. border.

If *The Little Prince* seems a bit precious and pokey to audiences geared to the slick cynicism of *The Simpsons*, please remember that it is this same leisurely ambience which has kept Antoine de St.-Exupéry's original book in circulation for nearly fifty years.

THE ADVENTURES OF TIN TIN *see* **TIN TIN**

Bubba of the T-Rex family band.

THE ADVENTURES OF T-REX.

Syndicated: September 1992. Gunther-Wahl/Kitty Film/Créativité et Développement/All American Communications. Created by Michael Wahl and Lee Gunther. Developed for television by Michael Wahl, Lee Gunther and Jean Chalopin. Executive producers: Michael Wahl, Lee Gunther and Hidenori Tagu. Co-executive producer: Mark Taylor. Produced by Rudy J. Zamora, Xavier Picard

and Shigekazu Ochiai. Associate producers: Karen Marach and Robert Winthrop. Directed by Stephen Martiniere. Story editor, Peter Lawrence. Original character design by Saturo Tsuda. Creative consultant: Takashi. Music by Robert J. Walsh. Animation produced at KK&D Asia, Madhouse Studios, Philippine Animation Studio, Mook Co., Samke Animation and Hung Long Productions. Voices: Kathleen Barr, Michael Beattie, Gary Chalk, Jennifer Chopping, Ian Corlett, Michael Dobson, Kevin Hayes, Phil Hayes, Janyce Jaud, Allesandro Juliani, Annabel Kershaw, Scott McNeil, Robert O. Smith, Venus Terzo, Dale Wilson.

The *Adventures of T-Rex* was set in Rep City, the Big Apple of one of those "alternate evolution" worlds popularized by the TV series *Dinosaurs*, in which civilized reptiles comprised the ruling class. Five Tyrannosaurus brothers — Buck, Bubba, Bugsy, Bruno and Bernie — hatched into this world prematurely with invisible "enhanced" powers, had formed a singing group which, unbeknownst to everyone but eccentric inventor Professor Edison, frequently transformed itself into a super crimefighting team known as T-Rex. The quintet's most elusive enemy was Rep City's "Big Boss" Graves, who headed a crime cartel known as The Corporation. T-Rex set forth in its souped-up Rexmobile on a weekly basis to battle the forces of evil — still managing to make it to their sold-out concerts on time, and to conceal their secret identities even to the person closest to them, their vocalist sister Ginger.

Sounds a lot like *Teenage Mutant Ninja Turtles* (q.v.), doesn't it? Perhaps with a dash of *Alvin and the Chipmunks* (q.v.) thrown in. But to hear the publicity mills of Gunther-Wahl Productions, not to mention the promotional crews of the 95 TV stations over which the 52-episode *The Adventures of T-Rex* premiered in the fall of 1992, the concept was the most original, outlandish, and hilarious to come down the pike in years. As an added selling point, much was made of the fact that each member of T-Rex was blessed with an imitation celebrity voice. The timid, parsimonious Bernie, for example, sounded a little like Jack Benny. while the other four dino siblings sort of sounded like Peter Falk, Jimmy Durante, Art Carney (or maybe Yogi Bear?) and Jimmy Carter.

When *T-Rex* started production, several of the voice imitations were of different celebrities, as reflected by the characters' original names: Bing, Benny, Jimmy and Jackie.

But beyond the vocal distinctions and the diverse skin colors among the reptilian crimebusters, the series failed to develop the sort of distinctive characterizations that added so much charm to *T-Rex*'s Chipmunk and Ninja Turtle role models.

In fact, despite the herculean efforts of the Gunther-Wahl publicity team, *The Adventures of T-Rex* had very little at all to recommend it in terms of humor, excitement, or even passable animation. About the only real movement on *T-Rex* occurred in the optical "wipes" which moved the worn-out storylines from scene to scene.

ALF. NBC, 9/26/1987 (starting date postponed from 9/12)–9/2/1989.

–ALF TALES. NBC, 9/16/1989–8/25/1990. Alien Productions/DIC/Saban Productions. Created by Tom Patchett and Paul Fusco. Executive producers: Tom Patchett, Bernie Brillstein, Paul Fusco. ALF TALES developed by David Cohen, Roger S. H. Schulman. Directors: Dan Riba (ALF), Kevin Altieri (ALF TALES). Story editors: Duane Capizzi (ALF), Alicia Marie Schudt (Both series). Music by Haim Saban and Shuki Levy. Voices: Paul Fusco (Alf, a.k.a. Gordon Shumway); Peggy Mahon (Flo); Paulina Gillis (Augie/Rhoda); Thick Wilson (Larson Petty/Bob); Dan Hennessey (Sloop); Rob Cowan (Skip); Ellen-Ray Hennessey (Stella); Noam Zylberman (Curtis); and Michael Lampos, Marla Lukofsky, Stephen Ouimette, Harvey Atkin, Jayne Eastwood, John Stocker, Don Francks, Debra Theaker, Greg Morton, Nick Nichols, Gren Swanson, Len Carlson, Ray Kahnert, Eva Almos, Linda Sorenson.

Alf was based on NBC's surprise-hit live action sitcom of 1986, which for four seasons followed the adventures of diminutive dogfaced alien Gordon Shumway, forced to flee from his self-destructing planet of Melmac to the safety of planet Earth. Taken in by the nonplussed Tanner family, Gordon was renamed Alf, an acronym for Alien Life Form. Though 229 years old, Gordon/Alf was a party animal teenager by his home planet's standards, and as such comported himself in an in-

destructibly immature manner until the series' final cliffhanging episode of 1990, when he was captured by the American military. The series' cancellation that same year left Alf's fate unresolved.

The NBC network cartoon version of *Alf* avoided these plot complications by setting itself up as a "prequel" to the nighttime series. The animated *Alf*, with voice provided (as ever) by series cocreator Paul Fusco, still resided on Melmac, still going by the name of Gordon Shumway (his age was adjusted to 193 — after all, he was fresh out of high school); the rest of the Shumway family included dad Bob, mom Flo, brother Curtis and sister Augie. While the live action *Alf* was offbeat and amusing enough, the 26-episode cartoon counterpart was zany in the extreme, taking uproarious scattershots at any satirical target that tickled the writers' fancies. A prime example of the *Alf* technique was the first-season episode "20,000 Years in Driving School," in which Alf/Gordon's punishment for a speeding ticket was a soujourn at a hard-time instructional driving camp. Before long, the whole affair had evolved into a lampoon of *Cool Hand Luke*, with such choice moments as Our Hero being "de-loused" in a carwash. Delivering a subliminal traffic safety message entertainingly, *Alf* managed a trick often attempted but seldom realized by other cartoon series of its era — it was prosocial without ever losing its sense of humor.

In the fall of 1988, the half-hour *Alf* expanded to sixty minutes with an additional component titled *Alf Tales*, in which the protagonists from the earlier series appeared in "fractured" versions of fairy tales, fables, classic movies and assorted legends. *Alf Tales* became a half hour series unto itself in 1989, its 21 rerun installments replacing its animated "parent" program. After running their network course in 1990, reruns of both *Alf* and *Alf Tales* were added to the weekday cartoon lineup of cable TV's Family Channel.

ALL-NEW DENNIS THE MENACE *see* **DENNIS THE MENACE**

ALL-NEW EWOKS *see* **THE EWOKS AND STAR WARS DROIDS ADVENTURE HOUR**

ALL-NEW GUMBY *see* **GUMBY**

Alvin, standing (uncharacteristically) behind Simon, with Theodore at far right.

ALL-NEW PINK PANTHER SHOW *see* **PINK PANTHER**

ALL-NEW POPEYE HOUR *see* **POPEYE**

ALL-NEW POUND PUPPIES *see* **POUND PUPPIES**

THE ALL-NEW SCOOBY AND SCRAPPY-DOO SHOW *see* **SCOOBY-DOO**

THE ALL-NEW SUPER FRIENDS HOUR *see* **SUPERFRIENDS**

THE ALVIN SHOW. CBS: 10/14/1961–9/5/1962; 6/23/62–9/18/65 (weekend repeats). NBC: 3/10/1979–9/1/1979 (repeats of the CBS series, shown under the title ALVIN AND THE CHIMPUNKS). Format Films/Bagdasarian Productions. Ex-

ecutive producer: Herbert Klynn. Associate producer, Leo Salkin. Production executive, Bud Getzler. Directed by Osmond Evans, Rudy Larriva, Gil Turner and Alan Zaslove. Story by Leo Salkin, Cal Howard, Bob Kurtz, Ed Nofzinger, Dale Hale, Jan Strejohn, Al Bertino, Jack Cosgriff, Bill Danch, Chris Jenkyns, Dick Kinney, Tedd Pierce. Art director, Jules Engel. Production design: Sam Weiss, Vern Jorgensen, Ernie Nordli, Dale Barnhart, Cullen Houghtaling. Musical direction by Johnny Mann. Original music by Ross Bagdasarian. Voices: Ross Bagdasarian (Alvin/Simon/Theodore/Dave Seville/Sam Valiant); Shepard Menken (Clyde Crashcup); June Foray (Daisy Belle, other voices); Lee Patrick (Mrs. Frumpington); Joe Besser (Dragon); and Paul Frees, Bill Lee, Johnny Mann, William Sanford, Reg Dennis.

—**ALVIN AND THE CHIMPUNKS.** NBC: 9/17/1983–9/1/1990. (Title changed

to THE CHIPMUNKS in 1988.) Syndicated by Lorimar in 1988. Fox: 9/14/1992–. (Previously shown afternoons on several Fox stations.)
—CHIPMUNKS GO TO THE MOVIES. NBC: 9/8/1990–9/7/1991. Bagdasarian/Ruby-Spears. Producers and composers: Ross Bagdasarian Jr. and Janice Karman. Directed by Charles A. Nichols. Story editors: Cliff Ruby, Elana Lesser. Music by Dean Elliot; music supervised by Paul DeKorte. Vocal and music arrangements: Howard Pfeiffer. Voices: Ross Bagdasarian Jr. (Alvin/Simon/Theodore/Dave Seville); Janice Karman (Jeanette/Brittany/Eleanor); Dody Goodman, Katie Leigh, Doreen Murphy, Johnny Haymer, Jack Engart, Frank Welker, Pat Fraley, Derek Barton, Peter Cullen, Kerrigan Mahan, Julie McWhirter Dees, Thom Watkins, Alan Young, Tress MacNeille, Ken Sansom, Phillip Clarke.

Even though many cartoon historians credit *The Beatles* (q.v.) as the first animated TV series based on a bestselling recording group, *The Beatles* was preceded by four years by *The Alvin Show*—and what matter if the "group" represented on this series was actually comprised of a single person?

That single person was Ross Bagdasarian, a performer of many talents who until the mid-1950s hadn't quite found his showbiz niche. Bagdasarian had started as a stage actor (in the original 1939 production of *Time of Your Life*, written by his cousin William Saroyan), then moved on to singing, composing, and motion pictures (he played the struggling songwriter in Alfred Hitchcock's 1954 classic *Rear Window*), before nearly chucking it all due to lack of lasting success. Bagdasarian decided to give the business one more go, changing his professional name to David Seville. A rousing little dialect ditty titled "Come On-a My House" that Bagdasarian/Seville had penned for Rosemary Clooney in 1953 had become a top ten hit, convincing the songwriter that his future lay in novelty songs—which led to his sinking every penny of his savings into a home tape recording unit. In 1957, the composer's "Witch Doctor" defied all doomsaying declarations from such trendwatchers as Los Angeles disc jockey Peter Potter—who predicted that the song had "no future"—and turned into another smash, compelling otherwise sane music fans to repeat *ad infinitum* the song's tender refrain of "Ooh, eeh, ooh ahh ahh, ting, tang, walla walla bing bang."

Part of the charm of "Witch Doctor" was Bagdasarian's experimentation with speeded-up voices (accomplished by recording at 16 rpm, then replaying at 33⅓). Liberty Records suggested that the songwriter take this device a few steps farther in his next recording. Bagdasarian did so by preparing a three track "harmony" Christmas song, with his own voice singing all three parts. It was the songwriter's children who suggested that the high-pitched results sounded like a bunch of singing chipmunks (Bagdasarian's original name for the threesome was to have been The Butterflies!), though the composer's agents circulated another story claiming that Bagdasarian was inspired by a recalcitrant chipmunk confronted on a busy California highway.

As a tribute to his recording label, Bagdasarian named the singers of "The Chipmunk Song" after Liberty executives Alvin Bennett and Simon Warnoker and the studio's chief engineer Theodore Keep. With the astonishing success of "The Chipmunk Song" in the winter of 1958 (four million copies were sold), Alvin and the Chipmunks were launched on a career which would reap 38 million sales, 11 gold records and five Grammy awards.

Several attempts were made to create visual counterparts of the Chipmunks between 1959 and 1960, ranging from three roughhewn puppets designed by Bob (*Beany and Cecil*) Clampett which appeared on *The Ed Sullivan Show*, to a terrifying trio of snake-eyed, ratfaced monstrosities dreamed up by Dell comic books. The softer, more lovable groundhogish chipmunks (wearing body length sweaters which gave them a more childlike appearance) that ultimately gained worldwide fame were designed by the staff of Format Films, a TV animation house formed in 1959 by Herb Klynn, Jules Engel, and several fellow expatriates from UPA Studios (see *Dick Tracy* and *Mister Magoo*). The *Alvin Show* was nearly two years in development before its 1961 CBS premiere—it was Format's biggest project to date, compelling Herb Klynn to farm out some of the work to Jack Kinney Productions—allowing enough time for an imitation-chipmunk group, *The Nutty Squirrels* (q.v.), to beat Format to the punch with its own syndicated cartoon package (another prominent Chipmunk ripoff recording group, "The Grasshoppers," remained mercifully unseen).

Because it was felt that Bagdasarian's creations had proven "adult" appeal, CBS used *The Alvin Show* as its entree into the prime time cartoon market opened up in 1960 by *The Flintstones* (q.v.). As it turned out, the weekly half hour series was best enjoyed and digested by undiscriminating children. To anyone over the age of 10, Alvin's adventures were neither very amusing nor well paced, due in part to the problem of timing Bagdasarian's speeded-up voices to the cartoon action; one could follow a rhythmic beat when singing, but it was virtually impossible to determine the comic pacing of one's dialogue when speaking twice as slowly as normal. More entertaining were the brief weekly segments wherein the Chipmunks' recent recordings were visualized by the animators—a very early example of the "music video" technique. And far funnier than anything else on *The Alvin Show* were the weekly seven-minute escapades of pompous scientist Clyde Crashcup, who, through the use of a magic pencil and with the help of his pint-sized, virtually mute assistant Leonardo, "invented" such things as baseballs, bathtubs, birthdays and housewives. Crashcup's voice, supplied by Shepard Menken, was so accurate an imitation of comic actor Richard Haydn's radio-based "Edwin Carp" characterization that it's a wonder the curmudgeonly Haydn never brought about legal action.

While falling short of its potential (especially considering that one of the writers, Chris Jenkyns, was a principal contributor to *Rocky and His Friends* [q.v.]), *The Alvin Show* did succeed in cementing the basic characterizations of its stars for a generation of cartoon fans. Alvin was the egocentric rebel, Simon the bespectacled, cool-headed intellectual, and Theodore the giggling baby brother of the family; David Seville was the easily flustered father figure, trying his best to maintain decorum and instill a sense of responsibility and professionalism into his rodent foster children. The *Alvin Show* might not have been the best cartoon series on the 1961 market, but the characters were distinctive, memorable and, above all, immensely appealing. The upshot of this appeal was a booming traffic in

Alvin spinoff toys, dolls, and games— assuring that, though the series died in prime time opposite *Wagon Train* on NBC and *The Steve Allen Show* on ABC, *The Alvin Show* would be provided a secure berth on CBS' Saturday-morning lineup in the fall of 1962. There the series' 26 episodes were repeatedly rebroadcast for four ratings-grabbing seasons.

The Chipmunks' last album was released in 1967; five years later, Ross Bagdasarian was dead. The composer's son Ross Jr., after briefly pursuing a career in law, took it upon himself in 1977 to revitalize the Chipmunks. Though the original *Alvin Show* rerun package had remained in lucrative syndication, few were particularly interested in a Chipmunk comeback, with two significant exceptions: NBC TV head Fred Silverman, who tested the waters for an *Alvin* renaissance by repeating the old CBS series on his home network in 1979; and an actress-singer named Janice Karman, who formed a production company with the younger Bagdasarian and ultimately became his wife.

What sparked real industry interest in the "new" Chipmunks was a stunt pulled off by an East Coast radio deejay, who out of boredom began running a disco tune at top speed, characterizing the squeaky-squealy results as "Chipmunk punk." The stunt became a regular feature on the deejay's program, eventually gaining enough popularity to spawn a brand-new Chipmunk album from the Ross Bagdasarian Jr. production team in 1980, titled—*Chipmunk Punk*. Brisk sales enabled this album to go platinum, which led to an animated special, *A Chipmunk Christmas*, produced by Chuck Jones and telecast over NBC on December 14, 1981. And *this* led to a weekly Saturday morning series on the same network, *Alvin and the Chipmunks*, produced by Bagdasarian Productions through the facilities of Ruby-Spears, in the fall of 1983.

There had been changes over the years. Chuck Jones redrafted the original Format Films Chipmunk designs, resulting in a more cuddly appearance. The shifting sands of musical tastes determined that Alvin, Simon and Theodore would no longer sing ballads or folk songs but would instead re-emerge as rock concert artists. And as a nod to the equal rights sentiments

The Chipmunks, still complicating the life of David Seville (1980s edition).

of the 1980s, coproducer Janice Karman created three female counterparts to the Chipmunks: an Australian singing group called "The Chippettes," comprised of ego-driven Brittany, sensible Jeanette, and flighty Eleanor.

The scriptwriters for the new *Alvin and the Chipmunks* experimented with fresh satiric material, covering everything from a takeoff of the ABC detective series *Moonlighting* to an ersatz "rock documentary" a la Rob Reiner's feature film *This Is Spinal Tap*. As a result, the new series was slicker, faster, and more consistently amusing than the old *Alvin Show*, lasting seven first-run seasons and playing to an average weekly audience of ten million. In 1988, the first four NBC seasons, together with a handful of new half hour installments, entered daily strip syndication; the network version continued unabated under a new title, *The Chipmunks*. Ever seeking to broaden the series' appeal, Bagdasarian included blockbuster-movie parodies—with titles like "Funny We Shrunk the Adults" and "Batmunk"—in the fall of 1990 with a still newer title, *Chipmunks Go to the Movies*. After a season of these (interspersed with *Alvin* reruns from previous seasons), NBC cancelled, leaving the Chipmunks networkless for the first time in eight years.

Taking up the slack, the Fox Children's Network plucked the *Alvin and the Chipmunks* reruns from syndication and resettled the property into its Fall 1992 weekday afternoon lineup. This, in addition to such projects as the 1987 theatrical feature film *The Chipmunk Adventure* (which wound up on the American Movie Classics cable service!) and the 1992 CD album *Chipmunks in Low Places*, in which the stars rendered a string of recent country and western hits ("Achy Breaky Heart" is a stitch), has kept alive and kicking a property that started as a simple novelty tune over thirty years ago—and has. outlived its creator by a full two decades.

AMAZIN' ADVENTURES. Syndicated: 9/7/1992–. DIC/Saban/Bohbot.

Bohbot's *Amazin' Adventures*, a two hour syndicated cartoon block comprised of four half hour weeklies, was telecast weekend mornings over 143 stations which carried the series starting in September of 1992. For further details, see separate listings for *Double Dragon, King Arthur and the Knights of Justice, The Hurricanes, Mighty Max, Saban's Around the World in Eighty Dreams, Saban's Gulliver's Travels* and *The Wizard of Oz*.

THE AMAZING CHAN AND THE CHAN CLAN. CBS: 9/9/1972–9/22/1974. Hanna-Barbera/Leisure Productions. Executive producers, William Hanna and Joseph Barbera. Creative director, Iwao Takamoto. Animation director, Charles Nichols. Music by Hoyt Curtin. Voices: Keye Luke (Charlie Chan); Bob Ito (Henry Chan); Brian Tochi (Alan Chan); Stephen Wong, Lennie Weinrib (Stanley Chan); Virginia Ann Lee, Cherilyn Lee, Leslie Juwai (Suzie Chan); Cherilyn Lee, Leslie Juwai (Mimi); Leslie Kunamota, Jodie Foster (Anne); Michael Takamoto, John Gunn (Tom); Jay Jay Jue, Gene Andrusco (Flip); Debbie Jue, Beverly Kushida (Nancy); Robin Toma, Michael Morgan (Scooter); Don Messick (Chu Chu the dog); and Lisa Gerretsen, Hazel Shermet, Janet Waldo, Len Wood.

Charlie Chan, novelist Earl Derr Biggers' shrewd and unfailingly polite Honolulu-based Chinese detective, has attained folklore stature thanks to the 47 theatrical films featuring the character made between 1926 and 1949. More recent attempts to revitalize Chan haven't been quite as successful as these earlier films. A 1957 TV series starring J. Carroll Naish suffered from too many attempts to "modernize" the aphorism-spouting private eye; a 1971 TV movie starring Ross Martin was so bad that it sat unreleased on the shelf for eight years; and it can be said with some assurance that the 1981 atrocity *Charlie Chan and the Curse of the Dragon Queen* is not listed in the current resumes of its stars Peter Ustinov, Angie Dickinson and Michelle Pfeiffer.

Keeping in mind these recent live action failures, it's a bit unfair to take Hanna-Barbera's *The Amazing Chan and the Chan Clan* to task for being less than brilliant (the National Association for Better Broadcasting's precise words in describing the series were "inept, shallow, and tiresome"). Not that this 16-episode cartoon series was really worthwhile, but it was really no worse than any of the other youth-oriented Hanna-Barbera network projects of the early 1970s — though it might have been interesting to see what Terrytoons, the studio where the concept of an updated Charlie Chan first came into being, would have done with the character. In keeping with H-B tradition, the old property was "freshened" with lots of 70s slang words and the inclusion of a comic relief family dog named Chu Chu. The stories followed the lead of the cartoon studio's popular *Scooby-Doo* (q.v.) by populating the 30-minute plotlines with any number of mystery villains, none of whom were any match for those "meddling kids." In this instance, the kids were ten in number, a carryover from the original Charlie Chan (that is, the original *movie* Chan), who at one point boasted of 12 offspring — most of whom tried to emulate their dad by exhibiting their own haphazard crime solving skills. In the tradition of practically every other cartoon series of 1972, the Chan Clan often broke into rock songs at the drop of dad Charlie's panama hat.

The one distinguishing feature of *The Amazing Chan and the Chan Clan* was that, for the first time in media history, the leading character was portrayed by a genuine Chinese; Canton-born Keye Luke provided the voice of Charlie. Luke had, of course, played Charlie's Number One Son in several 20th Century–Fox Chan films in the 1930s, and at the time of *Amazing Chan*'s production the 67-year-old actor made a statement as to how proud his "Pop" would have been that he was carrying on the family tradition — though, truth to tell, Keye Luke himself was prouder of his more artistically fulfilling supporting roles in the concurrently produced live-action TV series *Kung Fu* and *Anna and the King*.

THE AMAZING THREE. Syndicated: 1967. Mushi Productions/Erika Productions. Created by Osamu Tezuka. Voices: Jack Grimes, Corinne Orr, Jack Curtis.

Created by prolific Japanese comic artist Osamu Tezuka (see notes on *Astro*

Boy), W3 was a sci-fi/adventure comic strip which made its newspaper bow early in 1965. In June of that year, a weekly, half hour animated version of W3 premiered over Japanese television, where it remained in distribution for the next 12 years. The "W" in the title stood for "Wonder"; the Wonder Three was a trio of extraterrestrials sent by the Galactic Congress to chart the future of the warmongering planet Earth. Should they determine Earth to be too dangerous for the rest of the galaxy to survive, the game plan was to destroy the planet. Once earthbound, the three aliens assumed the forms of a rabbit, a horse and a duck, and in these guises formed a strong friendship with a young male Earthling. Setting aside their original intentions, the Wonder Three united with the Earth boy to combat evil.

In the wake of the successful American runs of the earlier Osamu Tezuka/Mushi Productions cartoon series Astro Boy and Kimba the White Lion (q.v.), it was decided to bring W3 to the states. Joe Oriolo Productions re-edited and rescripted 52 episodes of the Japanese production to conform with American time limits and broadcast standards (though the violence quotient was still impressive). The major characters were given Americanized names—the rabbit was now "Bonnie," the horse "Ronnie," the duck "Zero" and the Earthling "Kenny Carter"—the voices of the characters were dubbed into English, and the series was retitled The Amazing Three. Sales were respectable in the larger TV markets, but Amazing Three didn't match the popularity of earlier Tezuka/Mushi imports.

AMERICAN HEROES AND LEGENDS. Showtime: 10/8/1992–. Rabbit Ears Video. Executive producers: Mike Pogue, Mark Sottnick. Produced by Ken Hoin. Directed by C. W. Rogers. Animation camera/editor: Mark Forker.

American Heroes and Legends was the first weekly program from Rabbit Ears Video, though hardly the company's premiere TV attraction. Rabbit Ears was formed in 1985 by former high school teacher Mark Sottnick, who conceived the notion of adapting famous children's stories for the burgeoning videocassette market. Lacking the budget for full animation, Sottnick and his wife (and partner) Doris settled upon a technique previously utilized to some degree by such projects as Clutch Cargo (q.v.) and Curious George (q.v.). The stories were illustrated by still-picture drawings, which dissolved from one picture to another as the plotline progressed. There was some panning (moving the camera from one side to another) and zooming (adjusting the camera lens to make the picture seem closer), and occasionally a cardboard cutout would be "jogged" across the screen to create the illusion of movement; otherwise, the stories were not animated in the literal sense. But it wasn't vital to Mark Sottnick whether or not the images moved. To Sottnick, the story was the selling point, and it was his mission to introduce children to the joys of rich verbal storytelling, and to attain the ability to "follow" a tale even when the words weren't easy to understand—a marked contrast to the minimalist "oof-argh-uggh" dialogue generally heard on the superhero cartoons of 1985.

To sustain audience interest in Sottnick's first project, a visualization of The Velveteen Rabbit for PBS, the producer needed a first-rate storyteller. Oscar winning actress Meryl Streep was coaxed to narrate Velveteen Rabbit at a nominal fee, and the result was a 60-minute "instant classic," which won Parent's Choice and Action for Children's Television awards and which still is making the video-rental and telecast rounds. Partly out of gratitude for the titular character who launched his company, and partly to invoke the imagery of a busy television receiver adorned with a pre-cable antenna, Mark Sottnick named his company Rabbit Ears.

In its first years of existence, the company concentrated on cassettes, narrated by stellar Hollywood and Broadway talent and scored by top recording artists from the entire musical stylistic spectrum. In 1989, the first of 18 half-hour Rabbit Ears children's story adaptations appeared on Showtime pay-cable's sporadically scheduled Storybook Classics. This project was followed in 1991 by another off-and-on Showtime/Rabbit Ears attraction, We All Have Tales, consisting of 13 "international" children's legends. Both of these projects were released on video simultaneously with their TV telecasts (Another Rabbit Ears endeavor, a group of Bible tales called Greatest Stories Ever Told, was pretty much confined to the rental stores catering to church groups). Finally in 1992, Rabbit Ears was given regular weekly exposure with *American Heroes and Legends*, originally telecast early Wednesday evenings, back-to-back with another Showtime animated series, *A Bunch of Munsch*.

The 13 *Heroes and Legends* half hours covered tales drawn from a variety of ethnic and regional true stories and folk tales. Some were in the "Paul Bunyan" spirit of round-the-campfire hyperbole, such as Eric Metaxa's *Stormalong*, wherein comic actor John Candy articulated the tall tale of New England sea captain Alfred Bulltop Stormalong who, among his many accomplishments, "cried the Great Salt Lake into existence." Similarly, and backed by the boisterous music of B. B. King, Denzel Washington described "the Guaranteed, Gold Plated 99.9 percent truth" about railroad man John Henry.

Other stories were based in truth, though in the tradition of director John Ford, it was decided that concentrating on legend rather than fact would make for a more rousing story. In this spirit, Nicholas Cage narrated *Davy Crockett*, complemented with music by David Bromberg; Keith Carradine related John Howard Kunstler's version of the life of Annie Oakley, with music supplied by Los Lobos; radio personality Garrison Keillor had his way with the fact-based legend of Johnny Appleseed; and Graham Greene (the Native American actor, not the British author!) delineated the tale of *Squanto and the First Thanksgiving*.

But while stories like "Rip Van Winkle" were narrated fancifully by *American Heroes and Legends'* all-star voice lineup (which included Anjelica Huston in its otherwise boys-only fraternity), the series could tell a story "straight" if the subject matter required it. Case in point: Morgan Freeman's reading of *Follow the Drinking Gourd* (music by Taj Mahal), a slightly gilded but otherwise factual yarn of the Underground Railroad which rescued thousands of slaves in the antebellum years.

Though none of these stories was fully animated, the producers did wonders with conveying "life" to still pictures. Some of the choicest moments occurred during Danny Glover's reading of *Brer Rabbit and the Lion* (music: Dr. John), which managed to suggest a "3-D" effect by simply placing a cutout of Brer Rabbit in just the right perspective.

Like all Rabbit Ears projects, *American Heroes and Legends* used its visuals as a stimulant rather than distraction in pursuing Mark Sottnick's avowed purpose: to revitalize the ancient and honorable art of pure storytelling.

AMIGO AND FRIENDS *see* **CANTINFLAS**

ANIMANIACS (a.k.a. **STEVEN SPIELBERG PRESENTS ANIMANIACS**). Fox: 9/20/1993–. Warner Bros./ Amblin. Executive producer, Steven Spielberg. Executive in charge of production, Jean MacCurdy. Senior producer, Tom Ruegger. Produced by Rich Arons and Sherri Stoner. Directed by Rusty Mills, Dave Marshall, Gary Hartle, Rich Arons, Barry Caldwell, Michael Gerard, Alfred Gimeno, Bob Kline, Jerry Lerew, Audu Paden, Greg Reyna, Lenord Robinson, Chris Brandt, Jeffrey De Grandis, Jon McClenahan. Supervising story editors, Tom Ruegger, Paul Rugg, Sherri Stoner. Story editors, Peter Hastings and Tom Hinton. Written by Paul Rugg, Tom Ruegger, Nicholas Hollander, Peter Hastings, John P. McCann, Deanna Oliver, Randy Rogel, Sherri Stoner. Music by Richard Stone, Carl Johnson. Theme song by Richard Stone and Tom Ruegger. Animation facilities: Wang Film Production Co., Ltd., Tokyo Movie Shinsha Ltd., Akom Films, Freelance Animation, Startoons. Voices: Rob Paulsen (Yakko/Pinky); Jess Harnell (Wakko); Tress MacNeille (Dot); Frank Welker (Ralph Org); Maurice LaMarche (The Brain); Chick Vennera (Pesto); Sherri Stoner (Slappy); Bernadette Peters (Rita); and Jim Cummings, Michael McKean, many others.

Animaniacs was designed as the successor to Warner Bros. Animation's *Tiny Toon Adventures* (q.v.) — and as such, it set itself the goal of being even funnier and zanier than its predecessor. Senior producer Tom Ruegger suggested publicly that he considered *Tiny Toon* merely a grade school warm-up to *Animaniacs*, and that the new show would be deliberately aimed at the adults who'd taken *Tiny Toon* to their hearts.

The premise of the daily half-hour program was established in its opening scene, shot as a mock black and white newsreel of

The Animaniacs: zany to the "max."

the 1930s. We were told that three bizarre animal-like characters were created at that time by Warner Bros.' star animator (drawn as a porcine caricature of the immortal Tex Avery), but that their subsequent starring cartoons were so crazy and incoherent that no theatre wanted to book them. Embarrassed, the studio locked the trio in the water tower that dominated (and still dominates) the Warner back lot. But in the 1990s, the long-dormant cartoon threesome escaped.

These were the Animaniacs, also known as the "Warner Brothers"—not Warner *Bros.* (the official spelling of the studio name), and in fact not all brothers. This W.B. contingent included Yakko, the verbal one; Wakko, the slapsticky one; and a girl, Dot, whose routine consisted of feigned cuteness. That's *who* they were — but *what* were Animaniacs? Certainly not human, and decidedly not of any recognizable species. Tom Ruegger would only describe their nebulous pedigree as "an homage to the Warner Bros. cartoons of the 30s when they made these generic characters, and you didn't know what the heck they were."

Whatever their lineage, the Animaniacs were inveterate anarchists, running roughshod over the Warner studios and dropping sight gags and verbal volleys on anyone who dared cross their path. The humans that crossed most often were Viennese studio psychiatrist Dr. Scratchensniff and his voluptuous nurse (whose presence always warranted a quasi-phallic reaction from Yakko and Wacko); Big Babboon, a studio guard; and a pint-sized CEO who described the Animaniac invasion as the worst thing to happen to the

studio since it produced *Don't Tell Mom The Babysitter's Dead.* The Animani-antics were often set to music, with original songs on a par with the series' theme song: "We're Animaniacs/ And we're zany to the Max/ So just sit back and relax/'Til you collapse/We're Animaniacs." Let's just ignore the lyric that rhymes "Animaniacs" with "Bill Clinton and His Sax."

Each episode presented either one half-hour adventure, or two to three short cartoons, featuring a rotating group of component stars. These secondary characters included cat and dog Rita and Runt, girl and dog Mindy and Buttons and their robot nemesis Mr. Skullhead, the Hip Hippos, Chicken Boo, and a female counterpart to Tex Avery's Screwball Squirrel (see *Droopy, Master Detective*) named Slappy — also a purported refugee of the 1930s whose cartoons went unreleased and unappreciated.

In keeping with the series' ongoing parade of pop culture references — jokes about Shirley MacLaine and Jack Nicholson abounded, while Soviet ex-premier Gorbachev was seen walking the streets disconsolately with a sign reading "Will Sell Secrets for Food" — one component was titled "The Goodfeathers." The stars were three mildly larcenous pigeons, takeoffs on the profanity-spouting Mafiosa in the 1990 film *Goodfellas.* The principal Goodfeather, "Pesto," was based on the mercurial psycho hit man played in *Goodfellas* by Joe Pesci.

And there were also "Pinky and the Brain," a pair of laboratory rats (for Acme Labs, of course) who'd been experimented upon once too often. Pinky had been rendered a babbling goofball, while the dome-browed Brain, who sounded like Orson Welles, had been converted to a criminal genius bent on taking over the world — provided he could ever get out of his cage. Most of the above-mentioned *Animaniacs* costars were introduced in a first-episode Disney lampoon, narrated by Jim Cummings in his fruitiest Sterling Holloway tones.

Steven Spielberg was executive producer of *Animaniacs*, personally supervising each script. It was hard to miss the Spielberg touch. The series was fully and sumptuously animated, its character and background design painstakingly recreating the "look" of the Warners cartoon heyday of the 1940s and 1950s. But as with some of Spielberg's past projects, it was lavishness at the expense of inspiration. Here, as on *Tiny Toon Adventures*, Spielberg didn't seem to believe that full animation was not always in the best interest of comedy. The vintage Warner Bros. cartoon product only animated the most necessary and pointed movements: a double take, a slow burn, a raised eyebrow, a hurried escape. By animating *everything* in a fluid, realistic fashion, *Animaniacs* blunted its comic sting and looked more like one of the overproduced Disney cartoons of the 1950s, which likewise sacrificed humor for technique (see *Tiny Toon Adventures* for the animators' reactions to Spielberg's insistence on too-busy cartoon-work).

Also, the misbehavior of the three Animaniacs would have worked better had it looked as impulsive and off the cuff as the antics of Bugs Bunny and Daffy Duck. Instead, the characters worked so hard at being zany that their cartoons took on a studied, contrived air. By trying to force its laughs, *Animaniacs* resembled those 1970s comedy films which tried to hide their lack of truly amusing material or appealing characters with noise, destruction and aimless scurrying about—just like Steven Spielberg's most notorious movie misfire, *1941*.

The best *Animaniacs* component was "Pinky and the Brain," simply because it returned to Warner Bros. cartoon basics. We knew that the Brain's world-domination plans were doomed to failure, and so we watched in anticipatory delight as the rodents' best laid schemes went painfully awry, resulting in humiliation for the Brain and additional headlumps for the already punchdrunk Pinky. It was basic "Wile E. Coyote" frustration comedy, and it worked beautifully because of its straight-line simplicity.

Make no mistake, *Animaniacs* was a funny and frequently brilliant outing. Still, the series might have gotten even louder and longer audience reaction had it relaxed long enough to trust the comedy material and not jam it down our throats. But a Steven Spielberg project must traditionally be bigger than anything surrounding it—and never mind that "Bigger" is not always interchangeable with "Better."

ANIMATOONS. Syndicated: 1967. Radio and Television Packagers/Anima-toons/Language Arts Films. Narrator: Nancy Berg.

Not offering much in the way of innovative animation, *Animatoons* was a nonetheless laudable package of 22 cartoon shorts in which model/actress Nancy Berg narrated such fondly remembered stories as "Peter and the Wolf" and "Ali Baba and the Forty Thieves," along with some newer samplings of children's literature. The series' distributors issued teaching guides to interested schools in an effort to hone the younger viewers' reading and cognitive skills.

AQUAMAN. CBS: 9/14/1968–9/7/1969. National Periodicals/Filmation. (See *Superman* for production and voice credits.)

After a year's run as a component of CBS Saturday-morning series *The Superman/Aquaman Hour* (see *Superman* for further details), *Aquaman* was spun off into a separate half-hour Sunday morning weekly, comprised of 36 seven-minute cartoon repeats from *Superman/Aquaman* and an additional 18 animated shorts—also culled from the earlier series—featuring such National Periodical comic book "guest stars" as The Teen Titans, The Green Lantern, Atom and Hawkman.

THE ARABIAN NIGHTS *see* **THE BANANA SPLITS ADVENTURE HOUR**

ARCHIE. (The following entry lists all cartoon series starring the ARCHIE characters.)
—**THE ARCHIE SHOW.** CBS: 9/14/1968–9/6/1969.
—**THE ARCHIE COMEDY HOUR.** CBS: 9/13/1969–9/5/1970. Both series produced by Filmation Studios. Executive producers: Lou Scheimer, Norman Prescott. Directed by Hal Sutherland. Art director, Don Christensen. Musical supervision by Don Kirschner. Music by Yvette Blais and Jeff Michael. Written by Bob Ogle (both series); additional writers, ARCHIE COMEDY HOUR: Jim Mulligan, Jim Ryan, Bill Danch, Jack Mendelsohn, Chuck Menville, Len Janson. Voices: Dal McKennon (Archie/Mr. Weatherbee/Salem/Mr. Andrews/Mr. Lodge/Coach Cleats/Chuck Clayton); John Erwin (Reggie/Hexter/Irwin/Dad); Jane Webb (Betty/Veronica/Sabrina/Big Ethel/Miss Grundy/Aunt Hilda/Aunt Zelda/Hagatha); Howard

Morris (Jughead/Big Moose/Pops/Dilton Doily/Hot Dog Jr.).

—ARCHIE'S FUN HOUSE FEATURING THE GIANT JUKE BOX. CBS: 9/12/1970–9/4/1971. Production and voice credits virtually the same as THE ARCHIE SHOW and THE ARCHIE COMEDY HOUR. Writers: Jim Ryan, Bill Danch.

—ARCHIE'S TV FUNNIES. CBS: 9/11/1971–9/1/1973. Production credits same as earlier shows. Additional writing credit: Ken Sobol. Voices, "TV FUNNIES" sequences: Dal McKennon (Captain/Hans/Kayo/Chief/Sam Ketchum/Pat Patton/B. O. Plenty); Howard Morris (Inspector/Fritz/Sluggo/Sandy/Moon Mullins); Jame Webb (Mama/Miss Della/Fritzi Ritz/Gravel Gertie); John Erwin (Dick Tracy/Alvin/Smokey Stover).

—EVERYTHING'S ARCHIE. CBS: 9/8/1973–1/26/1974. Production credits same as earlier series, minus Don Kirschner. Voice credits the same as THE ARCHIES.

—U.S. OF ARCHIE. CBS: 9/7/1974–9/5/1976. Production and voice credits same as EVERYTHING'S ARCHIE, with following additions: Directors: Don Townsley, Lou Zukor, Rudy Larriva, Bill Reed. Writers: Chuck Menville, Len Janson, Bill Danch, Jim Ryan, Marc Richards. Don Christensen now listed as Creative Producer. Music producer on this and future ARCHIES programs: Jackie Mills.

—THE NEW ARCHIE / SABRINA HOUR. NBC: 9/10/1977–11/5/1977. Fils-Cartoons/Filmation. Most production credits same as earlier programs. Don Christensen now producer. Directors: Marsh Lamore, Don Townsley, Rudy Larriva. Associate producers/story editors: Jim Ryan, Bill Danch. See separate entry on SABRINA for voice credits for that component.

—ARCHIE'S BANG-SHANG LALAPALOOZA SHOW. NBC: 11/26/1977–1/28/1978. Fils-Cartoons/Filmation. Production credits same as NEW ARCHIE/SABRINA HOUR. Additional credit: Director, Bill Reed. Voice credits the same as on the earlier productions, with following additions: Jose Flores (Carlos); Don Messick (Harvey); Treva Frazce (Ophelia).

—THE NEW ARCHIES. NBC: 9/12/1987–9/3/1988; 11/12/1988–2/4/1989. Saban/DIC. Executive producers: Andy Heyward, Haim Saban. Produced and directed by Jim Simon. Supervising producers: Robby London, Ellen Levy. Story editor: Kimmer Ringwald. Script coordinator: Lori Crawford. Production supervisor: Winnie Chaffee. Animation supervisor: Than Vu. Music by Haim Saban and Shuki Levy. Voices: J. Michael Roncetti (Archie); Karen Burthwright (Amani); Lisa Coristine (Betty); Alyson Court (Veronica); Michael Fantini (Jughead); Marvin Goldhar (Mr. Weatherbee); Jazzmin Lausanne (Big Ethel); Linda Sorenson (Miss Grundy); Greg Swanson (Coach); Sunny Bensen Thrasher (Reggie); Colin Waterman (Eugene) and Victor F. Erdos.

When CBS mogul Fred Silverman commissioned *The Archie Show* in 1968 to counter pressure group accusations that Saturday morning cartoons were excessively violent, his actions were hardly unprecedented. The original Archie Comics line, which began in 1941 with the twenty-second issue of MLJ Publications' *Pep Comics*, was conceived by publisher John Goldwater and artist Bob Montana as a lighthearted "antidote" to such blood and thunder affairs as *Superman* and *Batman*. And in 1954, the *Archie* magazines were held up by comic book publishers as shining examples of how the funny-book business was cleansing itself of the damaging influence on youth allegedly perpetrated by horror and crime comics. In fact, *Archie* artist Bob Montana, a man with a well documented puritanical streak, had helped draft the stringent Comics Code which effectively eliminated all "scare" comics.

Fred Silverman's 1968 "cleansing" decision did a world of good for the Saturday morning cartoon merchants. The "down with kiddie TV" concerns were satisfied that CBS had veered away from violence and concentrated its efforts on harmless slapstick humor. And as luck would have it, *The Archie Show* was a hit, grabbing 75 percent of the audience and paving the way for such equally lucrative teen-comedy projects as *Scooby-Doo* and *The Jackson Five* (see individual entries on these titles).

As mentioned, the saga of 17-year-old Archie Andrews and his assorted friends and family members began in 1941. John Goldwater may have come up with the basic "All American Teenager" format (based after a fashion on the popular *Henry Aldrich* radio series), but it was 21-year-old

Archie strums his way into our hearts.

artist Bob Montana who fleshed out the characters by drawing upon the personalities of his own Massachusetts high school acquaintances. Carrot-topped Archie, for example, was based upon Montana himself, while Mr. Weatherbee, principal of Archie's Riverdale High, was patterned after the artist's own high school principal, who'd warned the boy that he'd never amount to anything if he didn't stop drawing pictures. Wise guy Reggie Mantle was taken from a rich kid acquaintance of Montana's; blonde Betty Cooper was a composite of two girls the artist had dated; and wealthy brunette Veronica Lodge drew her name from Veronica Lake, one of Montana's favorite movie stars, and the celebrated Lodge family of Boston, who'd once hired the teenaged Montana to paint murals in the basement of the Lodge mansion.

The most compelling character in the *Archie* menagerie was the hero's best friend, Jughead Jones, who looked like a droop-eyed dolt but who possessed a wicked wit and a keen observation of the human condition. Jughead was also the only character in the comic books who was not at all interested in the opposite sex, preferring hamburgers to heavy petting. Bob Montana claimed that Jughead was purely the product of imagination, and that he'd never really known anyone like him; but Bob's widow Peg Bertholet would remember a high school chum of Montana's by the name of Skinny Lenahan, who purportedly possessed many of Jughead's peculiar traits.

In both magazine and newspaper strip form (the strip commenced in 1947), not to mention its late 1940s incarnation as a radio series, *Archie* was never anything deeper than a "gag" comic, with no purpose beyond making its audience chuckle. It doggedly avoided innovation either in content or characterization; its teenaged and adult cast members were drawn from every "Campus Comedy" cliche known to mankind. Yet it had charm and consistency, and filled an ongoing reader demand for laughter *sans* substance which sustained *Archie* through a multitude of spinoff comic magazines, and which enabled Archie Comics to grow into a major publishing house (at last count in 1992, there were 31 titles in its manifest, including the phenomenal *Teenage Mutant Ninja Turtles* [q.v.]). All the same, the property never quite made it as a live action TV project. Several proposed *Archie* sitcoms were announced over the years, one or two of them even getting to the pilot-film stage (the format was unquestionably a primary influence on the popular CBS series *Dobie Gillis*, which ran from 1959 through 1963). But as it turned out, *Archie's* TV success would manifest itself in pen and ink rather than flesh and blood.

Not only did the 1968 animated version of *Archie* put Filmation Studios firmly on the map, but it created a new Top Ten singing group. It was decided that as a lure for potential teenage viewers above and beyond CBS' two- to 11-year old "target" audience, *The Archie Show* would emulate the live-action NBC series *The Monkees* by incorporating rock tunes into each episode's "dance party" closing segment. To that end, CBS engaged *Monkees* mentor Don Kirschner to produce the musical portion of the program. Kirschner commissioned a bubble-gum ballad titled "Sugar Sugar" for the series, and tried to inveigle his own Monkees to perform it. But though this four-man band had been organized from whole cloth under the guidance of Kirschner, the Monkees were beginning to have artistic aspirations of their own — and refused to have anything to do with "Sugar, Sugar." Kirschner then hired studio musician Ron Dante (later the editor of the erudite periodical *Paris Review*) and utility singer Toni Wine to record the song. Thus were born "The Archies," whose first single, the selfsame "Sugar Sugar," managed to beat out the Rolling Stones for the number one top selling plateau in early 1969—though it might be worth noting that the first "Archies" record album, advertised in *TV Guide* at the time of *The Archie Show*'s premiere, did *not* include "Sugar Sugar."

The *Archie Show* was not what one could call inspired. Its sledgehammer humor, executed in a fragmented fashion imitative of NBC's *Rowan and Martin's Laugh-In*, was made doubly obvious by the overuse of a canned laughtrack, and the potentially endearing traits and catchphrases of the characters (notably Principal Weatherbee's oft repeated "I don't see that. I *don't* see that!") were likewise pummelled into weariness. But as has been proven so many times before by such programs as *Mighty Mouse* (q.v.) and *Mister Magoo* (q.v.), young children seem to thrive on repetition and predictability, so Filmation sagely chose not to tinker with this basic element of the series' success. The studio did, however, play fast and loose with the series' format; as Filmation executive Norm Prescott explained it at the time, "We always have to look for other ways to utilize the characters in new forms to regenerate interest. Sometimes we succeed, sometimes we fail."

After a season's worth of half hour programs, *The Archie Show* expanded to 60 minutes in 1969 (its name changed accordingly to *The Archie Comedy Hour*), the better to attract wider sponsorship. In one of these elongated second season installments, Sabrina the Teenage Witch, created for the Archie comics line in 1962, was introduced to television (after a failed attempt by Filmation to secure cartoon rights for a better-known TV sorceress, Samantha of the live-action *Bewitched*), resulting in a weekly spinoff spotlighting this spellbinding young lady (see *Sabrina and the Groovie Ghoulies*). For its third season, *The Archie Comedy Hour* was cut back to 30 minutes and given yet another title, *Archie's Fun House Featuring the Giant Jukebox*; Sabrina was gone, and the titular Jukebox became the center of attention, spewing forth sketches, blackout gags (some written by two blackout specialists from *Rowan and Martin's Laugh-In*, Jack Mendelsohn and Jim Mulligan) and songs to an appreciative live-action studio audience.

In 1971, the property metamorphosed into *Archie's TV Funnies*. This precursor (sort of) to the MTV format had Archie and his pals in charge of a TV studio, switching on various monitor screens to follow the short subject adventures of several other popular comic strip characters: Chester Gould's Dick Tracy (see individual entry on this character), Russell Myers' Broom Hilda, Marty Links' Emmy Lou, Frank Willard's Moon Mullins, Sidney Smith's The Gumps, Howie Post's The Dropouts, Bill Holman's Smokey Stover, Ernie Bushmiller's Nancy and Sluggo, and Rudolph Dirks' the Captain and the Kids (see also *The Fabulous Funnies*). Two seasons later, there was yet another format shakeup: now the "outside" comic strip characters were eliminated, now the title was *Everything's Archie*, and now the series consisted exclusively of repeats from earlier *Archie* seasons.

Finally, Filmation decided to pump new blood into the flagging property by joining in the national Bicentennial mania of 1974–76. As *U.S. of Archie*, the series featured the "ancestors" of its familiar characters in 16 recreations of great historical events. The installment featuring Harriet Tubman of Underground Railroad fame was one of the few times in the *Archie* output that an African American was ever given a prominent role to play (though several black supporting characters, notably Chuck Clayton, had recently been included in Archie's circle of friends). Its lofty ambitions laid low by unimaginative execution and wearisome distortions of historical facts, *U.S. of Archie* drove the final nail in the coffin of a once thriving concept. This newest variation of a rapidly aging theme was so unsuccessful that CBS moved it to Sunday mornings within a few months of its debut; there it languished in rerun form until its cancellation in 1976.

After two years of rerun syndication (during which time several episodes were redubbed with more up-to-date music), *The Archies* was revived for network play when CBS whiz-kid Fred Silverman moved to NBC. The *New Archie/Sabrina Hour* was the mixture as before (with a few reruns from the CBS days tossed in), albeit with a new Hispanic character named Carlos plunked into the Riverdale student body. As in 1970, teen witch Sabrina was whiskbroomed off to her own series (this time titled *Super Witch*), leaving the "new" Archie with a thirty minute slot and an almost desperately flashy moniker, *Archie's Bang-Shang Lalapalooza Show*, a variation on the title of a 1968 "Archies" song. But times had changed. The hot sensation of the soft-rock 1960s was the fossilized dinosaur of the disco-dominated 1970s. Besides, everyone was watching the Bugs Bunny and Road Runner cartoons over on ABC. By January of 1978, it was all over for Archie and company.

Still, the *Archie* comic books maintained their audience, adhering to the tried and true while making casual nods to more enlightened social values. For example, the character of Big Moose, an athlete previously written off as monumentally stupid, was finally diagnosed as being dyslexic, providing a more positive role model to "slow" readers who might identify with Moose. And Jughead's cynical misanthropy was tempered by his compassionate involvement with a group of handicapped children.

But *Archie*'s television career remained under wraps until 1987, when NBC, emulating such recent "stars as children" projects as *The Muppet Babies* (q.v.) and *The Flintstone Kids* (see *The Flintstones*), teamed with DIC and Saban to come up with *The New Archies*. This 26-episode effort recast the teenaged *Archie* characters as nine-year-old kids—hardly an innovation, since Archie Comics had been churning out the adventures of *Little Archie* since 1956 (inasmuch as the "Little" aspect of the *Archie* saga was conceived *in toto* by publisher John Goldwater rather than by artist Bob Montana, the closing credits of *The New Archies* were wholly justified in stating that the series was based on characters created by Goldwater alone). Several commendable efforts were made to breathe some nuance into the 46-year-old property, notably the suggestion of a romance between Principal Weatherbee and Riverdale School's star instructor Miss Grundy. There was also a more pronounced ethnic mix than in earlier seasons, exemplified by the inclusion of African-American classmates Eugene and Amani. But the humor quotient was still locked into the pig bladder level of the *Archie* of the 1960s, and the plotlines were leisurely to the point of inducing slumber.

Archie prospered into the 1990s in comic-book form (its largest readership was, as ever, concentrated in the six- to 13-year-old female demographic), and there was even a 1990 live action TV movie, *To Riverdale and Back Again*, in honor of the property's upcoming Golden Anniversary. As for the animated *Archie* . . . well, you might get a few bucks at the half-price store for your old 45-rpm copy of "Sugar Sugar."

AROUND THE WORLD IN EIGHTY DAYS. NBC: 9/9/1972–9/1/ 1973. Air Programs International/D. L. Taffner. Produced by Walter Hucker. Directed by Richard Slayenski. Written by Chet Stover. Music by John Sangster. Voices: Alastair Duncan (Phileas Fogg); Ross Higgins (Passepartout); Max Obenstein (Mr. Fix); and Owen Weingott.

One of the first Australian imports to American television, *Around the World in 80 Days* was a disappointingly sluggish 16-episode, half-hour series that was faithful neither to the letter nor the spirit of Jules Verne's 1872 novel. A new twist was added in having globetrotting hero Phileas Fogg set out on his wager to girdle the world in eighty days at the behest of Lord Maze, father of Fogg's sweetheart Belinda. Maze's plan was to cause Fogg to lose the bet, thereby losing the hand of his daughter; to that end, the nobleman hired Mister Fix—no longer the police inspector of the original, but a stereotypical crooked sharpster—to see that Phileas and his manservant Passepartout did not achieve their goal.

The animated Phileas Fogg retained none of the delightfully cultured sang froid of David Niven's characterization in the Oscar-winning 1956 film version of *Around the World* (which coincidentally made its TV debut the same week in 1972 that its animated counterpart premiered on NBC's Saturday morning lineup). The cartoon Fogg rapidly rendered himself tiresome by speaking in rhymed epigrams a la *Underdog* (q.v.)—hardly surprising, since the chief writer for *Around the World in 80 Days* was former *Underdog* scrivener Chet Stover. Fogg's most often repeated maxim, for example, was "The motto of the wise is: Be prepared for surprises." To which we respond: "*What* suprises?" (see also *The Cattanooga Cats* for another variation of the Verne original, *Around the World in 79 Days*.)

AROUND THE WORLD IN EIGHTY DREAMS *see* **SABAN'S AROUND THE WORLD IN EIGHTY DREAMS**

ARTHUR AND THE SQUARE KNIGHTS OF THE ROUND TABLE. Syndicated: 1968. Air Programs International.

A precursor to the *Danger Mouse* (q.v.) and *Count Duckula* (q.v.) brand of British nonsense humor, *Arthur and the Square Knights of the Round Table* was a rousing send-up of the Camelot legend, replete with clumsiness and wisecrackery in both the heroes' and the villains' camps. Sir Lancelot, for example, was portrayed as a literal-minded dunderhead (he did just what you expect when invited to "break bread"); thus it was only fair that his wicked counterpart, The Black Knight, be equally dimwitted. Little throwaway touches such as the title of the wicked sorceress Morgana's magic spell book, *Merlin's Book of Spells, Incantations and Barbecue Cooking*, were indicative of the comic grace notes that made this series a hit in its native country.

Jeff Lenburg has reported that a package of seven-minute *Arthur and the Square Knights of the Round Table* cartoon shorts made it into American syndication in 1968. If so, it's positively criminal in this writer's opinion that no TV station picked it up in Milwaukee.

ASTRO AND THE SPACE MUTTS *see* SPACE STARS

ASTRO BOY. Syndicated: 1963. Mushi Productions/Video Promotions, Inc./NBC Films and Screen Gems. Created and produced by Osamu Tezuka. English adaptation written and directed by Fred Ladd. Music by Tatsuo Takai; lyrics by Don Rockwell. Voices: Billie Lou Watt (Astro Boy/Astro Girl); Ray Owens (Dr. Elefun); Peter Fernandez; Gilbert Mack.

Mention *Astro Boy* to any middle-aged Japanese male and you're likely to get a quizzical or even a hostile look. Mention *Tetsuan-Atoma* and you'll witness the same warm glow that comes over the face of most middle-aged American males when they're reminded of *Li'l Abner, Steve Canyon* or *Buz Sawyer*. For long before it was rechristened *Astro Boy* for the American market, artist Osamu Tezuka's *Tetsuan-Atoma* was the most popular comic book in Japan, as well as one of the longest running newspaper strips (1951–1968) in the country's history.

The project began as *Atom-Taishi* ("Am-

bassador Atom"), but soon adopted its more familiar title, which translates as "Mighty Atom." The plotline, set in the twenty-first century, concerned the Institute of Science's Dr. Tenma, who out of grief over the traffic accident death of his own young son built a jet powered robot in the dead boy's image. The robot, Tetsuan-Atoma, had in addition to the usual super-strength and ability to fly the capacity for human emotions. But Dr. Tenma soon became irritated that his mechanical "son" would never grow into manhood, and eventually sold the creature to a circus (shades of *Pinocchio*). Here he was adopted by kindly Dr. Ochanomizu, whose goodness and altruism inspired Tetsuan-Atoma into adopting a life of crimefighting—a not inconsiderable task, since his foes included mad doctors, space aliens, mind control freaks and an evil giant robot known as "Colosso."

Though his work went in a diametrically opposite direction, Osamu Tezuka was a big fan of American animators Walt Disney and Max Fleischer. As an homage to these cartoon giants, Tezuka drew nearly all his characters with huge, saucer-like eyes—a style soon adopted by virtually every Japanese animator. It is for this reason, and not because of a distorted Asian perspective of how Occidental eyes are shaped (as has sometimes been suggested), that the characters in *Astro Boy* and other Japanimation efforts all seem to have optical elephantiasis.

The animated cartoon version of *Tetsuan-Atoma*, which served as the premier attraction of Osamu Tezuka's recently established Mushi Productions, debuted on Fuji TV on January 1, 1963, as Japan's first TV cartoon series, and later moved to the NKK Network. In all, 193 half hour episodes were produced. When NBC Films purchased the series for American TV (it was originally slated for the NBC network, but there was no room that year), rights were secured to 153 installments; ultimately, only 104 programs made it to the States—still more than enough for a Monday through Friday syndicated strip. Like the other non–Japanese distributors among the twenty nations carrying the series, NBC Films adapted the project for domestic consumption. Dr. Ochanomizu was renamed "Dr. Elefun," a tribute to his impressive nasal appendage; Tetsuan-Atoma was named "Astro Boy," a variation of "Astor Boynton," who in the NBC Films version was the son of Dr. Boynton, formerly Dr. Tenma. In most other countries, the series was rechristened *Mighty Atom* (with Dr. Tenma renamed Dr. Atom), but a conflict with an obscure American comic book character of that name prompted NBC Films to break with international tradition. (As the series progressed, Dr. Ochanomizu/Elefun constructed a sister-companion for the titular hero, named "Astro Girl" in the American version.)

While *Astro Boy* was re-edited and redubbed to conform to American broadcast policies, much of the casual sadism of the original remained intact. Surprisingly, considering the youth market for which it was aimed, the morbid opening episode sequence involving the death of Astor Boynton was left untouched, as was the curiously cruel "black" humor surrounding Dr. Boynton's eventual descent into gibbering madness. These and other no-nonsense touches elevated *Astro Boy* from the usual kiddie adventure cartoon rut, encouraging adults to join in on the excitement.

Although the animation was primitive to the point of nonexistence — the series popularized the Japanese cartoon technique of simulating movement by flat-cutting and lap-dissolving from pose to pose, rather than using inbetween or "smear" animation — *Astro Boy* moved with swiftness, vigor, intelligent plot development, and a welcome dash of knockabout humor. It became a major syndication hit, knocking the competition out of the box in major markets like New York and Los Angeles. Even in smaller markets where the lack of independent television channels confined the series to weekly rather than daily exposure, *Astro Boy* performed exceedingly well. The series prompted an onslaught of Japanese-made cartoons on the U.S. market, enriching Mushi and establishing the careers of many other aspirant animation houses.

The grandaddy of all lovable android cartoon series, *Astro Boy* isn't seen too much today, due to its black and white status in a color-hungry TV world and the fact that Mushi's bankruptcy in 1972 somewhat bollixed up U.S. distribution rights (Osamu Tezuka tried to make a 1980s comeback with a new, full-color *Astro Boy*, but the spirit was gone and the updated series failed miserably; Tezuka

died in 1986). It can safely be said, however, that no matter what one's personal feelings are regarding such Japanese products as *Speed Racer*, *The Eighth Man*, *Kimba the White Lion*, *Battle of the Planets*, *Robotech* and *Voltron* (see individual entries on these series), chances are none of these projects would have made a dent outside their home base had it not been for the pioneering popularity of *Astro Boy*.

THE ASTRONUT SHOW. Syndicated: 1965. Terrytoons/CBS Films/Viacom. Produced by Bill Weiss. Directed by Connie Rasinski, Dave Tendlar, Arthur Barisch, Robert Kuwahara and Cosmo Anzilotti. Voices: Dayton Allen (Astronut and others); Bob McFadden (Oscar Mild and others); Lionel Wilson; John Myhers.

Astronut, a friendly pint-sized extraterrestrial who lived with (and frequently confounded) meek Earthling Oscar Mild, was introduced in an episode of Terrytoons' earlier cartoon series *Deputy Dawg* (q.v.). The affable alien's syndicated spinoff series consisted of theatrical cartoon shorts mixed in with made-for-TV episodes — which, in the tradition of *Deputy Dawg*, were subsequently distributed to movie theatres. Terrytoons' distributor CBS Films (and its successor, Viacom) filled out the 26-week, half hour *Astronut Show* with a batch of six-minute cartoons — again geared to the dual market of TV and moviehouses — featuring such characters as Luno the Flying Horse, Sad Cat, James Hound, Possible Possum, and two "stars" previously telecast over Terrytoons' *Hector Heathcote Show* (q.v.): Hashimoto the Mouse and Sidney the Elephant.

THE ATOM ANT / SECRET SQUIRREL SHOW. NBC: 10/2/1965–12/31/1966; 9/9/1967–9/7/1968.
   —THE ATOM ANT SHOW. NBC: 1/7/1967–9/2/1967.
   —THE SECRET SQUIRREL SHOW. NBC: 1/7/1967–9/2/1967. Hanna-Barbera/Screen Gems. Produced and directed by William Hanna and Joseph Barbera. Animation director, Charles Nichols. Music by Hoyt Curtin. Components: **1. ATOM ANT.** Voices: Howard Morris and Don Messick (Atom Ant). **2. SECRET SQUIRREL.** Voices: Mel Blanc (Secret Squirrel); Paul Frees (Morocco Mole). **3. SQUIDDLY DIDDLY.** Voices: Paul

Oscar Mild is amused by Astronut's bad habits.

Frees (Squiddly Diddly); John Stephenson (Chief Winchley). **4. THE HILLBILLY BEARS.** Voices: Henry Corden (Paw Rugg); Jean VanderPyl (Ma Rugg/Floral Rugg); Don Messick (Shag Rugg). **5. WINSOME WITCH.** Voices: Jean VanderPyl (Winsome Witch). **6. PRECIOUS PUPP.** Voices: Don Messick (Precious Pupp); Janet Waldo (Granny Sweet). (*See also* TWO STUPID DOGS.)

Hanna-Barbera's first project for NBC in the 1960s was the 60-minute Saturday morning *Atom Ant/Secret Squirrel Show*, consisting of two separate half-hour cartoon series.

Atom Ant continued the H-B tradition of three six-minute cartoon components bundled together under the title of one of these components. The eponymous hero was a helmeted, scientific, superpowered ant, capable of lifting a piano with his little pinky; the character's catchphrase was "Up and at 'em, Atom Ant." His power was derived from a pair of atomized eyeglasses — a plot device also deployed by

Hal Seeger's like-vintage *Fearless Fly* (see *Milton the Monster*). The other headliners on *Atom Ant* included Precious Pupp, another of Hanna/Barbera's seemingly endless supply of demonic, raspy-laugh dogs, who lived at 711 Pismo Place with his motorcycle riding mistress Granny Sweet; and "The Hillbilly Bears," comprised of industriously lazy Paw Rugg (who never spoke when mumbling would do), pipe smoking Maw Rugg, and kids Floral and Shagg, all of whom could be counted upon to render a country tune or two in between their efforts to avoid steady work. *Atom Ant* may have been cookie-cutter in concept and execution, but it remained vibrant in the memory of at least one impressionable youngster, who grew up to become rock star Adam Ant.

The principal star of *Atom Ant* was a takeoff on the then-burgeoning superhero craze. In a similar vein, the title character of *Secret Squirrel* was a lampoon of the James Bond–*Man from U.N.C.L.E.* mania sweeping the nation in 1965. Secret Squirrel of the Double-Q Agency was a trenchcoated, gadget laden superspy, seldom seen without his aide-de-camp Morocco Mole, a myopic Peter Lorre type; master villains included such miscreants as Yellow Pinky, based on you know who. Considering the lampoon potential of *Secret Squirrel*, the cartoons were disappointingly tame and barren of inventiveness. Too often, the gadgetry utilized by heroes and villains narrowed down to such graybeard standbys as the Outsized Stick of Dynamite.

Fleshing out each of the 13 weekly *Secret Squirrel* half hours were the adventures of Squiddly Diddly, yet another *Yogi Bear*–inspired character. This time it was a sailor-capped squid who wished to escape his "cage" (a Marineland-type aquarium) in order to see the real world (Squiddly wanted a showbiz career). The high point of this component was Hanna-Barbera's effort to animate all six of Squiddly's tentacles independent of one another; now *that* was funny. Rounding out *Secret Squirrel* were the exploits of Winsome Witch, the most endearing and enjoyable character of this particular Hanna-Barbera batch. "Winnie" was a Fairy Godmother School dropout who undauntedly buzzed around the city on her broomstick in search of people on whom she could bestow good deeds.

The *Atom Ant/Secret Squirrel Show* retained its 60-minute status until the first week of 1967, when NBC's wedging of Hanna-Barbera's *The Flintstones* (q.v.) into its Saturday morning lineup, coupled with the network's rescheduling of H-B's *Space Kiddettes* (q.v.), split *Atom Ant/Secret Squirrel* into two half hours, retitled after the Messrs. Ant and Squirrel respectively. In the fall of 1967, the two entities were reunited into one, and *The Atom Ant/ Secret Squirrel Show* was rerun unmolested over NBC until September of 1968. The series' six component cartoons (26 episodes per character) were later included in H-B's syndicated *Banana Splits* (q.v.) daily strip, where it became even more difficult for non-devotees of Hanna-Barbera to distinguish one cartoon character from another. Later on, most of the *Atom Ant/Secret Squirrel* characters made guest appearances on such all-star H-B extravaganzas as *Yogi's Treasure Hunt* (see *Yogi Bear*). And in 1993, a modernized Secret Squirrel starred in all-new adventures on Hanna-Barbera's *Two Stupid Dogs* (q.v.).

THE ATTACK OF THE KILLER TOMATOES. Fox: 9/8/1990–8/1993. Four Square Productions/Marvel Productions/Fox Children's Network. Executive producers: Joe Taritero, Steve Peace, John DeBello. Produced in association with American Film Technologies. Produced by Richard Trueblood. Story editor: Flint Dicce. Music by Shuki Levy. Theme song by John DeBello. Voices: John Astin, Thom Bray, S. Scott Bullock, Cam Clarke, Chris Guzer, Maurice LaMarche, Chuck McCann, Rob Paulsen, Neil Ross, Susan Silo, Kath Soucie.

The 1979 feature film *The Attack of the Killer Tomatoes* was a rarity: a bad movie that was *intended* to be a bad movie. Producer/director/writer John DeBello deliberately set out to make a "cult" film, a parody of those cheapjack 1950s horror movies (*Robot Monster, Plan 9 from Outer Space*, et al.) that have developed cults because of their innate awfulness. The resultant *Killer Tomatoes* did in fact make it to many subsequent All-Time Worst Movie festivals, though like its predecessors, the film's highlights were not the idiotic contrivances of its "Cannibal Tomato" plotline but such unintentional moments as the out-of-control helicopter which figured prominently in the opening scenes.

Fox's weekly, half-hour cartoon version of *Attack of the Killer Tomatoes* retained John DeBello's relentlessly silly theme song and the film's basic premise of garden vegetables running amok and attacking mankind. But unlike the movie, the TV version was definitely not a cheap, quickie undertaking. Starting with its third season in 1992, *Killer Tomatoes* was Fox's first fully computer-generated cartoon program—a far more expensive process than the usual foreign-made TV animation, but worth the extra expenditure, at least on surface level. The computer work allowed for sharper background detail, more fluidity of camera and character movement, and a "three dimensional" quality usually lacking in the two dimensional Saturday morning TV world. American Film Technologies, a San Diego–based firm specializing in the colorization of old black and white films, was the outfit engaged by Marvel Productions to render movement on *Killer Tomatoes*. In justifying the extra cost incurred by American Technologies,

Marvel executive Margaret Loesch noted that the result was at least one cartoon series on American television that didn't have to farm out its animation to foreign companies, thereby providing more work for U.S. artists and technicians.

Not everyone in the cartoon industry was enthusiastic over *Attack of the Killer Tomatoes'* heavy reliance on computer art. Savage Steve Holland, creator of Fox's *Eek! The Cat* (q.v.), deemed the results "horrific," bemoaning the loss of the "beauty of ink and paint."

BABAR™

Babar and the Royal Family.

Its artistic shortcomings aside, *Attack of the Killer Tomatoes* was a mild but amusing monster movie spoof, told in weekly cliffhanger fashion. A certain Dr. Putrid T. Gangrene (voiced by John Astin, who portrayed this character in two theatrical *Killer Tomatoes* sequels) diabolically developed humanized tomatoes in his lab in order to conquer the world. Alas, his creations, led by head tomato Zoltan, got the better of the Doc and his lamebrained assistant Igor, overtaking the populace all by their little leafy selves and establishing their own juicy junta. It was up to the Killer Tomato Task Force—teenagers Wilbur, Jud, Tara, Sam and Phil-Al, newscaster Whitley White, a "Friendly Tomato" nicknamed F. T., and a Woody Allen-esque shnook known as "The Tomato Guy" because of his traumatic childhood experiences with Dr. Gangrene—to make the world safe for the 56 other Heinz varieties. *Attack of the Killer Tomatoes* was good for three seasons before audience interest waned and the program was chopped off at the roots by Fox.

AUGIE DOGGIE AND DOGGIE DADDY *see* **QUICK DRAW McGRAW**

BABAR. HBO: 4/9/1989–9/1993. Family Channel (reruns): 9/1993–. Nelvana/Ellipse/Clifford Ross Company/CBC. Produced by Patrick Loubert, Michael Hirsh, and Clive A. Smith. Executive in charge of production, Deborah Bernstein. Supervising producer, Lenora Hume. Line producer and director, Peter Hudecki. Assistant director, Kate Shepard. Story editors: Peter Sauder, J. D. Smith. Theme music and score by Milan Kymlicka. Creative consultant, Clifford Ross. Produced in conjunction with The Family Channel

(Canada), Telefilm Canada, Télévision Quatre Saisons, Canal + FR3. Voices: Gordon Pinsent (Adult Babar); Gavin Magrath (Young Babar); Dawn Greenhaigh (Queen Celeste); Tara Charendoff (Young Celeste); Stephen Ouimette (Pompadour); Chris Wiggins (Cornelius); John Stocker (Basil); Elizabeth Hanna (The Old Lady); Alan Stewart-Coates (Rataxes); Corinne Koslo (Lady Rataxes); Lisa Yamanaka (Flora); Bobby Becker (Pom); Amos Crawley (Alexander); and Gareth Bennett, Michael Fantini, Gordon Halsey, Ian Heath, Keith Knight, Maxine Miller, Wayne Robson, Robert Hoist, Barbara Hamilton, Dan Hennessey, Michael Longstaff, Marsha Moreau, Joe Roncetti, Noel Slater.

Babar, the benevolent elephant king who with his cousin-consort Queen Celeste ruled over the animals of the Great Forest, was created by French author/artist Jean DeBrunhoff in 1931. The royal pachyderm's illustrated adventures have been translated into a multitude of languages, with most versions retaining the schoolboy script style in which DeBrunhoff charmingly penned his prose. Children have always delighted in the well ordered world of Babar's domain, while more politically aware adults have tended to rain on the parade by pointing out DeBrunhoff's implicit glorification of the old French colonial system in Africa.

The cartoon *Babar* made his bow in a 1968 NBC special produced jointly by Bill Melendez Associates and Jean DeBrunhoff's American publisher, Random House (negotiations were handled by DeBrunhoff's son Laurent, who'd been writing Babar books since his father's death in 1937); both this and a followup 1971 special were narrated by Peter Ustinov. The first regular TV adaptation of *Babar* was in the form of a late 1970s series of French language live action shorts, with actors dressed in marionette-like costumes. In 1986, it was back to animation when Canada's Nelvana Studios, in concert with the CBC, produced still another one-shot special, *Babar and Father Christmas.* The special was telecast in the States over Home Box Office.

Nelvana was responsible for a subsequent 1989 animated feature, *Babar: the Movie*, which flashed back to the elephant's childhood. The same flashback premise (described favorably by one critic as "*Wonder Years* for elephants") was utilized when Nelvana and the CBC reteamed, with the participation of the Clifford Ross Company, to produce an expensive 52-week series for Canadian consumption in 1988. In most of the stories, the adult Babar related a landmark childhood experience—the death of one of Babar's elephant chums at the hands of hunters was a particularly powerful episode—to provide a strong moral lesson for his sons and daughter. Babar's supporting (and supportive) cast, who also appeared in the flashbacks to give the elephant's stories more credibility to his children, included faithful family retainer Pompadour and irascible prime minister Cornelius.

Once more, it was HBO that brought the property to the United States, for which the cable company was honored with a 1989 Ace award. Unlike many TV spinoffs of theatrical features, *Babar* lost none of its quality when diminished to the 21-inch screen, and in fact the television version often surpassed the movie. Even the occasional dependence on the banal "hero vs. heavy" formula indigenous to weekly television was adroitly handled: Babar's eternal foe, the covetous Lord Rataxis of Rhinoland, usually found his delusions of grandeur shattered by his kind and fair-minded wife. Best of all, *Babar* managed to pull off the delicate trick of retaining the simplicity of Jean DeBrunhoff's childlike book illustrations, all the while adopting a more colorful and sophisticated graphic design.

In 1993, reruns of *Babar* were run on a daily basis over the basic-cable Family Channel service, in tandem with another Nelvana adaptation of a beloved European comic strip, *Rupert* (q.v.).

BACK TO THE FUTURE. CBS: 9/14/1991–8/14/1993. Amblin/Wang Film Production Co., Ltd./Z.M. Productions/ Universal Pictures. Created by Bob Zemeckis and Bob Gale. Executive producers: Frank Marshall, Kathleen Kennedy. Directed by Bob Gale. Live-action sequences produced by Zaloom-Mayfield. Technical advisor for live-action sequences: Bill Nye. Music by Michael Tavera. Voices: Dan Castellaneta (Doc); David Kaufman (Marty); Thomas F. Wilson (Biff); Josh Weiner (Jules); Troy Davidson (Verne); Danny Mann (Einstein); Mary Steenburgen (Clara); and Joe Alaskey, Adrienne Alexander, Jack Angel, Arthur Burghardt, Carlos Carrasco, William Galloway, Linda Gary, Paige Gosney, Benji Gregory, Deb Lacasta, Jack Lynch, Lily Mariye, Andee McAfee, Conan McCarty, Brian Mitchell, Dustin Morgan, Billy O'Sullivan, Hal Rayle, Susan Silo, John Stewart. Cast (live-action): Christopher Lloyd (Doc); Bill Nye (The Science Guy).

Back to the Future was the umbrella title of three brisk, extremely profitable science fiction comedy films produced between 1984 and 1989 by Steven Spielberg's Amblin Productions. The brainchild of Robert Zemeckis (who directed the trilogy) and Bob Gale, the *Future* films related the adventures of 1980s teenager Marty McFly and flamboyantly eccentric scientist "Doc" Emmett Brown, who through the facility of Doc's time travelling DeLorean automobile travelled back to the 1950s (in the original *Back to the Future*), forward to the 21st century (*Back to the Future II*), and backward again to the Old West of the 1880s (*Back to the Future III*). Each film took a lighthearted glance at the "history is inviolate" concept, which theorized that each minor alteration in the events of the Past or Future would have cataclysmic or beneficial consequences in the Present. Despite the moans and wails of "fantastic fiction" specialists like Harlan Ellison, who weren't happy with the logic liberties taken by the plots, the three *Future* flicks were enormous moneymakers, each film blessed with eye-popping, state of the art special effects—not to mention *con brio* acting performances by Michael J. Fox as Marty and Christopher Lloyd as Doc.

Given the theoretically limitless advantages the animated cartoon has over the live action film in making the impossible probable, CBS' weekly *Back to the Future* cartoon TV series was a major letdown, and not only because the animation was flat and uninvolving. The time displacement concept of the *Future* films was shunted off in favor of a cavalcade of Saturday-morning banality: Adolescent wishes fulfilled to the detriment of the wisher, computer game heroes and villains brought to life, and tired lessons in "being yourself" and "covet not thy neighbor's goods." The freewheeling back-and-forth chronology in the films was sacrificed by locking the characters—drawn mostly from the third *Future* film, which introduced the characters of Doc's 19th-century wife Clara and their sons Jules and Verne—into a standard suburbanite Present.

Critics applauded the accuracy with which past historical events were depicted on *Back to the Future*, but this was small compensation to unsatisfied animation buffs. The results were especially disheartening when one realizes that *Back to the Future* executive producers Frank Marshall and Kathleen Kennedy were concurrently in charge of the consistently brilliant *Tiny Toon Adventures* (q.v.), which made a practice of studiously avoiding the TV cartoon cliches which clutched *Future* in a death grip.

The most entertaining moments of TV's *Back to the Future* were the live action educational wraparounds featuring Christopher Lloyd reprising his role as Doc, narrating the scientific facts and oddities demonstrated by Bill Nye The Science Guy (spun off into his own syndicated series in 1993). According to the CBS publicity, Lloyd was also supposed to have supplied the voice of the cartoon Doc, just as Michael J. Fox had been slated to give voice to his animated counterpart. As it happened, the only carryovers from the films who dubbed in their cartoon likenesses were Thomas F. Wilson as fleabrained school bully Biff (given an equally repulsive young son in the TV series), and Oscar-winning actress Mary Steenburgen, who seemed to be having a high old time supplying the vocal intonations of Doc's feisty frontierswoman wife Clara.

BAGGY PANTS AND THE NITWITS. NBC: 9/10/1977–10/28/1978. DePatie-Freleng. Produced by David DePatie and Friz Freleng. Directed by

Robert McKimson, Sid Marcus, Spencer Peel, Brad Case, Gerry Chiniquy. Head writer: Robert Ogle. Music by Doug Goodwin, Steven DePatie. Voices: Arte Johnson (Tyrone); Ruth Buzzi (Gladys); and Joan Gerber, Joe Besser, Frank Nelson.

This DePatie-Freleng Saturday morning package consisted of 13 half-hour installments, each featuring two cartoon components. "Baggy Pants" was a laudable effort to emulate the success of DePatie-Freleng's earlier *Pink Panther* (q.v.) by creating a nonspeaking, pantomimic character as a contrast to the usual dialogue-laden kiddie TV syndrome. Unfortunately the role model for the studio's silent-cat character was Charlie Chaplin, a resolutely flesh-and-blood personality who'd been proving impossible to successfully capture in ink and paint ever since the first Chaplin animated cartoons back in 1916. Another roadblock to the survival of "Baggy Pants" was that the average kid of the late 1970s had no idea who Charlie Chaplin was, and thus couldn't relate to this derivative TV creation.

More familiar to contemporary audiences were the characters starring in the second component. "The Nitwits" were Tyrone and Gladys, the "dirty old man" and "frumpy spinster" characters created respectively by Arte Johnson and Ruth Buzzi for NBC's hit comedy-variety series *Rowan and Martin's Laugh-In* (1968–1973). The "masher in the park" subtext was understandably downplayed for the cartoon series (Tyrone lost his last name of "Horneigh" for reasons that should be obvious), and Tyrone and Gladys were recast as retired superheroes who were called back to active duty. Arte Johnson and Ruth Buzzi were signed up to provide the voices; Johnson was also credited as one of the writers. The "Nitwits" cartoons themselves were average to mediocre, though it was good for a weekly laugh to see the superannuated superheroes flying through the air while still wearing their traditional *Laugh-In* costumes (you'd never see Superman wearing a tacky overcoat nor Wonder Woman sporting a hairnet).

BAILEY'S COMETS. CBS: 9/8/1973–8/31/1975. DePatie-Freleng. Produced by David H. DePatie and Friz Freleng. Created by Joe Ruby and Ken Spears. Directed by Robert McKimson, Sid Marcus, Spencer Peel and Brad Case. Music by Doug Goodwin and Eric Rogers. Voices: Carl Esser (Barnaby Bailey); Robert Holt (Dude); Sarah Kennedy (Bunny); Karen Smith (Candy); Jim Begg (Wheelie); Kathi Gori (Sarge); Frank Welker (Pudge); Daws Butler (Dooter Roo, a helicopter pilot); Don Messick (Gabby, a reporter).

A nod to the ongoing popularity of roller derbies, as well as a variation on the "never ending contest" theme developed by Hanna-Barbera's *Wacky Races* (q.v.), DePatie-Freleng's *Bailey's Comets* was the story of a five member roller team captained by Barnaby Bailey. The Comets were participants in a round-the-world skating competition centered around a $1,000,000 buried treasure; clues to the whereabouts of the booty were given in rhyme each week. Predictably, the Comets were often the only honest contestants; in the simplified world of 1970s TV cartoons, the losers invariably lost because they were crooked and nasty (this *could* very well be real life, though not in this writer's real life). Stopovers during the race included the Philippines, Transylvania, Loch Ness and the Amazon. The Comets' opponents included such colorfully named rapscallions as The Roller Bears, the Broomer Girls, the Dr. Jeckell/ Hydes, the Cosmic Rays, the Yo Ho Hos, the Texas Flycats—and so it went, two ten-minute adventures per week for 17 weeks.

Bailey's Comets moved from Saturday mornings to Sundays in January 1974. The series survived two seasons, although the second year consisted exclusively of reruns from year one. If anyone was entertained by all this, it certainly wasn't the National Association for Better Broadcasting, which wrote off *Bailey's Comets* as "a waste of time."

THE BANANA SPLITS ADVENTURE HOUR. NBC: 9/7/1968–9/5/ 1970. Hanna-Barbera. Executive producers, William Hanna and Joseph Barbera. Produced by Edward J. Rosen. Associate animation producers, Alex Lovy, Lew Marshall and Art Scott. Animation director, Charles A. Nichols. Production design, Iwao Takamoto. Animation stories by Neal Barbera, Walter Black, Tom Dagenais, Bill Luiz, Joe Ruby, Ken Spears, Dalton Sandifer. Music by Ted Nichols,

David Mook and Hoyt Curtin. Arranged by Jack Eskrew. "Tra La La Song" by Ritchie Adams and Mark Barkan. Associate live-action producer, Don Sandberg. Wraparound sequences directed by Tom Boutross. "Danger Island" directed by Richard Donner. Locations: Fouad Said. Live-action sequences written by Jack Hanrahan, Jimmie Young, Ellis Kadison and Anthony Spinner. Costumes and sets created by Krofft Enterprises. COMPONENTS: Cartoon: 1. THE THREE MUSKETEERS. Voices: Bruce Watson (D'Artagnan); Barney Phillips (Porthos); Don Messick (Aramis); Jonathan Harris (Athos); Teddy Eccles (Tooly); Julie Bennett (The Queen/Constance). 2. THE ARABIAN KNIGHTS. Voices: Henry Corden (Bez); Paul Frees (Evil Vangore); Frank Gerstle (Raseem); Shari Lewis (Princess Nidor); Jay North (Prince Turhan); John Stephenson (Fariik/ Bakaar). 3. THE MICRO VENTURE. Voices: Don Messick (Prof. Carter); Patsy Garrett (Jill Carter); Tommy Cook (Mike Carter). 4. THE HILLBILLY BEARS. (See *The Atom Ant/Secret Squirrel Hour.*) Additional voices: Rick Lancelot, Daws Butler, Jay Larrimore, Allan Melvin, Thomas Poole, Robert Smith, Paul Winchell. Live-action segments: 1. BANANA SPLITS. Wraparound voices: Paul Winchell (Fleegle); Daws Butler (Bingo); Allan Melvin (Drooper); Don Messick (Snorky). 2. DANGER ISLAND. Cast: Frank Aletter (Prof. Irwin Hayden); Ronne Troup (Leslie Hayden); [Jan] Michael Vincent (Link Simmons); Rockne Tarkington (Morgan); Kahana (Chongo); Victor Eberg (Mu-Tan); Rodrigo Arrendondo (Chu).

Sponsored by Kellogg's Cereals, which managed to get a "presenting" credit in the opening titles, *The Banana Splits Adventure Hour* was Hanna/Barbera's first televised effort to combine live action with animation (an earlier sitcom pilot, *I'll Take Manhattan*, had gone nowhere). Perhaps "combined" is too grandiose a term since, except for the *Micro Venture* segment in which cartoon characters were intercut with blown-up microscope photography, the animated and "live" components of *Banana Splits* operated independently of one another. At any rate, it was an ambitious project, and initially a moneymaker.

The Banana Splits, an anthropomorphic animal singing group, hosted the weekly

Saturday morning series. These characters—Fleegle the dog, Drooper the lion, Bingo the gorilla and Snorky the baby elephant—were portrayed by actors in costume (designed by Krofft Enterprises of *H. R. Pufnstuf* fame), with voices supplied by Hanna/Barbera regulars Paul Winchell, Daws Butler, Don Messick and Allan Melvin. Their segments consisted of disposable soft rock songs, purposely abysmal puns and punchlines, slapstick sketches, and lots of scampering about with toy motorcycles and automobiles—sort of a masquerade party version of *The Monkees* or *Rowan and Martin's Laugh-In*, complete with "boink" and "bop" sound effects and an appreciative prerecorded laughtrack. The resemblance to *Laugh-In* was further solidified when one of that series' dancers, Byron Gillian, was hired to choreograph the Banana Splits' production numbers.

Coproducer Joseph Barbera would later explain to TV historian Gary Grossman why the Banana Splits sequences were performed live, and not animated as had been planned: "The show simply evolved when we decided to make some of the characters we were drawing larger and thereby give them more charm." This decision was made about nine months before the program's premiere—at which time the singing group hadn't even been given a name yet.

The charming shenanigans of the "Splits" served as buffers for several short cartoon and live-action components: the animated *The Three Musketeers* and *The Arabian Knights*, the "live" *Danger Island*, and the aforementioned hybrid *Micro Venture*. *Musketeers* resurrected the time-honored Dumas characters with such freshly minted villains as Duke LaVal and the "Evil Jester." The charcoal-pencil background art of Walt Peregoy and the rotoscoped animation in the horse-riding sequences were the best aspects of this pedestrian entry. Otherwise, the thrill quotient in *Three Musketeers* was bogged down with predictable plots, uninspiring duel scenes, rubber-stamp character design (the Musketeers more or less looked and moved alike), and an overreliance on stock Hanna-Barbera music themes culled from *Jonny Quest* (q.v.), *The Flintstones* (q.v.) and—most anachronistically—*The Jetsons* (q.v.).

Far better was the tongue-in-cheek *Arabian Knights*, wherein young and handsome Prince Turhan and young and beautiful Princess Nidor teamed with three middle-aged and homely magicians for the purpose of wresting Turhan's throne away from the evil Bakaar. Once again, Walt Peregoy's background art, impressionistic and colorful, was superb, but unlike *Three Musketeers*, these backgrounds were matched by the excellence of the animation and the rich variety of character design. With a "magical" premise and a complete set of original characters, the Hanna-Barbera staff was allowed more flexibility and imagination than was possible in the comparatively hidebound *Musketeers*. Adding to the fun was a spirited new musical score, reminiscent of Rimsky-Korsakov's "Scheherezade" themes.

Micro Venture, the one *Banana Splits* component deliberately intended as "educational," was a four-part take on the popular miniaturized scientist film *Fantastic Voyage* (1966), with Professor Carter and his offspring cruising in their micro-dune buggy through a world of live-action cells, protozoa, and supermagnified animal life. One *Micro Ventures* installment, "Backyard Jungle," came across like a rough draft for the elaborate 1989 comedy-fantasy film *Honey, I Shrunk the Kids*. An additional *Banana Splits* component, *The Hillbilly Bears*, consisted of rebroadcasts from the 1966 Hanna-Barbera weekender *The Atom Ant/Secret Squirrel Show* (q.v.).

On the whole, the animated material on *Banana Splits* took second place to the chaotic vigor of the live action *Danger Island*, a surrealistic farrago of shipwrecked scientists, underclad damsels in distress, gold-toothed pirates and combative natives. The raggedy hand-held camerawork and VegoMatic editing of *Danger Island* held the attention even when the audience had no clue about what was going on. This project was directed by Richard Donner of *Superman* and *Lethal Weapon* fame, who in 1981 would fondly describe the "feel" of *Danger Island* as seeming to be "totally improvised on Acapulco Gold."

While certainly chock-full of action, suspense and danger, the various components of *Banana Splits Adventure Hour* steered clear of the brutality and violence that some observers perceived as being de rigueur on Saturday morning television;

indeed, the series had been deliberately designed as an answer to the glut of pugnacious cartoon superheroes then dominating the networks. *Banana Splits* was trumpeted by NBC as the show that would revitalize Saturdays with a "new concept in entertainment . . . for children of all ages." This concept was of course hardly new (vide *Howdy Doody, Captain Kangaroo,* and a myriad of live action programs of the 1950s) but the Hanna-Barbera series was nonviolent and laugh-provoking enough for several mothers of *Banana Splits'* youthful fans to write grateful letters to the producers, thanking them for entertaining rather than frightening their children. Still, the series faltered after a prosperous first year, a fact that Joe Barbera attributed to the lack of variety in the background sets used for the Banana Splits bumpers, which led viewers to believe that they were watching reruns of these segments rather than new installments. Hanna-Barbera would rectify this error in its later "costume" series *The Skatebirds* (q.v.), for which several segments were filmed in such theme parks as Six Flags Over Texas and Coney Island—later known as Kings Island—in Cincinnati (the studio had also shot fresh new location footage of the Banana Splits for off-network syndication).

While only two seasons' worth of programs were produced for NBC, *Banana Splits* became a staple of local weekday lineups in the early 1970s under the title *Banana Splits and Friends.* The series' manifest of cartoons and live shorts was augmented for syndication with reruns of other Hanna/Barbera properties, among them *Atom Ant, Secret Squirrel, Precious Pupp, Squiddly Diddly, Winsome Witch* and *The New Adventures of Huck Finn* (see separate entries under these titles).

BANANAMAN. Nickelodeon, 1989–. 101 Productions. Writers and voice artists: Graeme Garden, Bill Oddie, Tim Brooke-Taylor.

Seen in the United States over the Nickelodeon cable network, *Bananaman* was a zoned-out sendup of cartoon superheroes from Britain's 101 Productions. The hero was an unprepossessing fellow named Eric Wimp who gained his superstrength through daily ingestion of bananas, causing him to blossom forth in full yellow tinted costume—replete with banana peel

gloves. The villains were similarly endowed with unusual powers and similarly garbed in pointlessly flashy uniforms. None of the characters, however, had spent any time learning to speak proper grammar or to avoid bungling the simplest physical effort.

Based on a character created for Britain's *Nutty Comics* magazine in 1980, the *Bananaman* episodes were priceless five-minute chunks of the nonsense humor which the British seem to do so effortlessly. The voice actors–head writers were Graeme Garden, Bill Oddie and Tim Brooke-Taylor, three leading lights of English sketch comedy who'd previously scripted such British TV classics as *Doctor in the House* and *The Goodies,* as well as BBC radio's *I'm Sorry, I'll Read That Again.* (Bill Oddie had also worked on a 1978 children's TV program, presciently titled *Saturday Banana.*)

BARBAPAPA. Syndicated: 1981. Polyscope (Netherlands)/LBS Communications. Executive producers: Annette Tilson, Talus Taylor. Supervising producer, Ralph Berliner. Written by Jerome Alden. Animation by Jorn Jenson and Per Lygum. Music by Ed Kalehoff. Voices: Allen Swift (Storyteller); Ann Costello; Alexander Marshall.

Similar to the world-renowned Belgian comic strip characters "The Stroumpfs" (see *The Smurfs*), the Netherlands' Barbapapas were a family of tiny troll-like creatures who grew straight from the ground like blades of grass and who were endowed with the ability to change shape and form. Most of the main characters had variations of "Barba" in their names, with the exception of Irving the Dog (adopted, no doubt). Though available for American syndication as early as 1977, the weekly half hour *Barbapapa* wasn't given a go in the U.S. until its distributor, LBS Communications, had made an impression with another Dutch cartoon import, *Dr. Snuggles* (q.v.).

THE BARKLEYS. NBC: 9/9/1972–9/1/1973. DePatie-Freleng. Produced by David H. DePatie and Friz Freleng. Directed by Steven DePatie, Bob McKimson, Sid Marcus and Spencer Peel. Music by Doug Goodwin and Eric Rogers. Voices: Henry Corden (Arnie Barkley); Joan Gerber (Agnes Barkley); Julie

McWhirter (Terry Barkley); Steve Lewis (Chester Barkley); Gene Andrusco (Roger Barkley); and Frank Welker, Bob Holt, Don Messick, Bob Frank and Michael Bell.

The *Barkleys*, an NBC Saturday morning series, brought the word "derivative" to hitherto unscaled heights. The Barkley family, a pack of humanized bulldogs, was headed by outspoken blowhard Arnie Barkley, an ultraconservative type who was constantly matching wits with his more liberally inclined wife and offspring, or with the neighboring Beagle family. This much DePatie/Freleng borrowed (a nicer word than "swiped") from the groundbreaking CBS sitcom *All in the Family*. Arnie Barkley was a bus driver, just like Ralph Kramden on *The Honeymooners*, which many TV chroniclers have pinpointed as a primary influence for *All in the Family*'s blue collar format. Arnie's voice was provided by Henry Corden, who'd later replace Alan Reed as the voice of Fred Flintstone, star of the animated *The Flintstones* (q.v.), which like *All in the Family* drew much of its inspiration from *The Honeymooners*. The one vital difference between *The Barkleys* and its live action ancestors was that *The Barkleys* was cancelled and forgotten after 13 lackadaisical half hour episodes, while reruns of *The Honeymooners* and *All in the Family* still flourish mightily.

At the time of *The Barkley*'s release, Saturday morning kidvid was under fire for its carbon-copying of prime time series themes; *Variety* condemned the entire spectrum of animated series as "shrunken adult programming." Defending his product, George Heinemann, vice president of NBC children's programming in 1972, would own up to only one direct "shrinking": Heinemann admitted that *The Barkley*'s Henry Corden had been instructed to imitate Carroll O'Connor for his voicework as Arnie Barkley. This was to Heinemann "the closest I come to that charge." Note the word "charge"; the poor vice president had been so browbeaten by criticism that he probably was persuaded that imitation was a capital crime. Were that the case, all three networks' prime time executives would have been left twisting slowly in the wind long before 1972.

BARNYARD COMMANDOS. Syndicated: 9/4/1990–9/7/1990. Those Charac-

ters from Cleveland/Murikami-Wolf-Swenson/Sachs-Finley. Supervising producer, Fred Wolf. Produced and directed by Bill Wolf. Animation directors, Bill Hutten, Tony Love, Kent Butterworth. Story editors, Rowby Goren, Jack Mendelsohn. Theme by Chuck Lorre and Dennis C. Brown. Music by Dennis C. Brown and Larry Brown. Overseas supervisor, James Mason. Voice director, Susan Blu. Voices: Scott Bullock, Thom Bray, Pat Fraley, Paul Kreppel, John Mariano, Bob Ridgely, Lenny Weinrib, Danny Wells.

Barnyard Commandos was an abbreviated cartoon miniseries, consisting of four episodes instead of the usual five; it was syndicated on Labor Day week of 1990, thus Monday was pre-empted. To say that *Commandos* was a ripoff of *Teenage Mutant Ninja Turtles* (q.v.) would be charitable. The property wanted with every fibre of its being to be *Turtles* in mammal skins, right down to the soundalike theme music.

The premise of *Barnyard Commandos* concerned two uniformed animal armies, doing battle in an otherwise placid barnyard: on one side, were the pigs, on the other the sheep. These antagonists were known respectively as Platoon of Rebel Killers, or P.O.R.K.S., and the Rebel Army of Military Sheep, or R.A.M.S. Despite their guerilla nicknames, neither side was truly imbued with the killer instinct; the enemies bombarded one another with nothing more deadly than "swill bombs" and eggs.

The P.O.R.K.S. had platoon members like Capt. Lard, Sgt. Hammond Eggar, the obligatory "Phil Silvers" type), Private Porker and Captain McChopper. The R.A.M.S. included Woolly Bully, Gen. Carrotcrusher and Pvt. Bellwether. To fake each other out, the two armies deployed secret codes: The P.O.R.K.S. spoke in "Pork Latin," while the R.A.M.S. communicated in "Baa Code," which sounded like the blubbery babblings of Mushmouth on *Fat Albert and The Cosby Kids* (q.v.). The P.O.R.K.S.' rallying cry was "Porker Power," the R.A.M.S.' was "Ramalamadoo." The warring livestock conducted their maneuvers on battlefields so surrealistic that it was hard to tell whether the "war" was supposed to be real or just a product of the characters' choleric imaginations.

It was equally hard to believe that the

same production team that produced the delightful *Teenage Mutant Ninja Turtles* was responsible for *Barnyard Commandos*, which did so much so badly. The characters, already ugly as sin to begin with, were so poorly drawn that some viewers couldn't distinguish the pigs from the sheep.

Unlike *Turtles*, which was careful to build up audience empathy with its otherwise unattractive protagonists, there was no one to "root" for on *Barnyard Commandos*. Neither P.O.R.K.S. nor R.A.M.S. were clearly defined as heroes or villains (perhaps so the merchandisers who built the toy tie-ins could promote the action figures from *both* armies as the "good guys"), and the two armies were unified not by friendship and fidelity but by mutual crassness and stupidity. Additionally, the miniseries aimed and misfired at the "pop culture parody" milieu of *Turtles* by having each episode incorporate specific movie takeoffs; one episode was titled "Applecalypse Now."

Barnyard Commandos failed as a *Teenage Mutant Ninja Turtles* clone simply because it trashed the very elements that made *Turtles* succeed: well-defined characters whom the audience cared about, solid and (within context) credible story values, and carefully integrated moments of genuine humor. Mercifully, the toys and action figures that *Barnyard Commandos* was designed to promote also failed, so we were spared any further visits from the P.O.R.K.S. and R.A.M.S. once the miniseries ran its course. In short—but not short enough—*Barnyard Commandos* was one big, noxious swill bomb.

BATFINK. Syndicated: 1967. Hal Seeger/Screen Gems. Written by Dennis Marks, Heywood King, Martin Taras. Musical director, Win Sharples. Voices: Frank Buxton (Batfink); Len Maxwell (Karate); and Bob McFadden.

When *Mad* magazine set about lampooning the immensely popular TV series *Batman* in 1966, it did so with great trepidation: How does one spoof a program that is *already* a spoof? (*Mad*'s solution was to concentrate on the absurder aspects of Robin the Boy Wonder constantly having his teenage social life interrupted by being compelled to don costume and fight crime.) No such apprehension bothered Hal Seeger, producer of the syndicated cartoon series *Batfink*. Seeger just jumped in and started swimming. And drowned.

Batfink, a package of 100 five-minute cartoon shorts (generally bundled together five at a time for a weekly half hour), avoided legal confrontation from *Batman*'s publisher National Periodicals by making its hero not a man dressed as a bat but a *genuine* bat, one equipped with steel wings and "Super Sonic Sonar" hearing. Instead of a "Boy Wonder" sidekick, Batfink's compadre was a Japanese martial arts expert named Karate (a snatch of *The Green Hornet* here). The primary villain was a guy given the pure-1960s moniker Hugo a Go Go. Other villains were drawn from the realm of fairy tales and legends: Robber Hood, Old King Cruel, Beanstalk Jack, Brother Goose, and Daniel Boom. The series' animation was lamentable, which wouldn't have mattered had *Batfink* been funny. But except for the campy voice work of Frank Buxton (an aficionado of old radio adventure programs who knew just how to get the proper imperious superhero timbre in his throat), *Batfink* was only sporadically amusing—and never as chucklesome as the original *Batman* live action series.

But what *Batfink* lacked in style and humor it made up for in pacing. The swiftness of the action was due mostly to the driving musical direction of Paramount veteran Win Sharples, who took a page from the repertoire of Warner Bros. orchestrator Carl Stalling by incorporating several compositions written by bandleader Raymond Scott. According to Scott historian Irwin Chusid, 46 *Batfink* episodes included new arrangements of such big-band classics as "The Toy Trumpet," "Dinner Music for a Pack of Hungry Cannibals," and that masterpiece of assembly-line pulsation, "Powerhouse," which had been used so often in Warner Bros. cartoons of the 1940s that it practically became that studio's signature. The Raymond Scott pieces were not chosen for any artistic reason; Win Sharples controlled the rights to the songs at the time of *Batfink*, and merely employed them to earn royalties when the series was syndicated. Still, it was fun to hear the tunes again, even in Sharples' erratic, surrealistic arrangements for his five-piece "orchestra."

Batman swings into the 1990s.

BATMAN. (The following entry lists all the animated series featuring the character of Batman.)
—THE BATMAN/SUPERMAN HOUR. CBS: 9/14/1968–9/6/1969.
—THE ADVENTURES OF BATMAN AND ROBIN. CBS: 9/13/1969–9/6/1970. Filmation/National Periodicals. Executive producer, Alan Ducovny. Produced by Lou Scheimer and Norman Prescott. Directed by Hal Sutherland. Voices: Olan Soule (Bruce Wayne-Batman/Alfred); Casey Kasem (Dick Grayson-Robin); Jane Webb (Barbara Gordon-Batgirl/Catwoman); Ted Knight (Alfred, Narrator and several villains). (For voice credits of SUPERMAN cartoons, see *Superman.*)
—SUPER FRIENDS. ABC: 9/8/1973–8/30/1975; 2/21/1976–9/3/1977 (see separate listing on this title).
—THE NEW ADVENTURES OF BATMAN. CBS: 2/10/1977–9/10/1977. Filmation. Executive producers, Lou Scheimer, Norman Prescott. Produced by Don Christensen. Directed by Don Townsley, Ed Friedman, Gwen Wetzler, Kay Wright, Marsh Lamore and Lou Zukor. Music by Yvette Blais, Jeff Michael.

Voices: Adam West (Bruce Wayne-Batman); Burt Ward (Dick Grayson-Robin); Melendy Britt (Barbara Gordon-Batgirl); Lennie Weinrib (Bat-Mite and Several villians); Lou Scheimer (Bat-Mite).
—THE ALL-NEW SUPERFRIENDS HOUR. ABC: 9/10/1977–9/2/1978 (see separate listing on SUPER FRIENDS).
—THE BATMAN/TARZAN ADVENTURE HOUR. CBS: 9/10/1977–9/2/1978. Credits same as THE NEW ADVENTURES OF BATMAN, with additional voice credit of Robert Ridgely as Tarzan.
—CHALLENGE OF THE SUPER FRIENDS. ABC: 9/8/1978–9/15/1979 (see separate listing for SUPER FRIENDS).
—TARZAN AND THE SUPER SEVEN. CBS: 9/9/1978–8/30/1980 (see separate listing on this program).
—THE WORLD'S GREATEST SUPER FRIENDS. ABC: 9/22/1979–9/27/1980 (see separate listing for SUPER FRIENDS).
—BATMAN AND THE SUPER SEVEN. NBC: 9/27/1980–9/5/1981 (see separate listing on TARZAN production and voice credits).
—SUPER FRIENDS: THE LEGEND-

ARY SUPER POWERS SHOW. ABC: 9/8/1984–8/31/1985 (see separate listing on this program).
– THE SUPER POWERS TEAM: GALACTIC GUARDIANS. ABC: 9/7/1985–8/30/1986 (see separate listing on SUPER FRIENDS for information on the two programs listed above).
– BATMAN: THE ANIMATED SERIES. Fox: September 6, 1992–. Warner Bros. Television. Executive producers: Jean MacCurdy, Tom Ruegger. Produced and developed by Bruce W. Timm, Eric Radomski and Alan Burnett. Directed by Kevin Altieri, Boyd Kirkland, Frank Paur, Eric Radomski, Dick Sebast, Dan Riba, Bruce W. Timm and Kent Butterworth. Based on characters created by Bob Kane. Story editors: Laren Bright, Sean Derek, Marty Pasko, Michael Reaves and Paul Dini. Theme music by Danny Elfman. Background music by Todd Haven. Voice director, Andrea Romano. Animation facilities: Don Yang Animation, Akom Productions Co., Spectrum Animation, Studio Junio, Sunrise, Tokyo Movie Shinsha, Blue Pencil S. I. Voices: Kevin Conway (Batman-Bruce Wayne); Melissa Gilbert-Brinkman (Batgirl-Barbara Gordon); Clive Revill, Efrem Zimbalist Jr. (Alfred); Loren Lester (Robin-Dick Grayson); Lloyd Bochner (Mayor Hamilton); Bob Hastings (Comissioner Gordon); Bobby Costanzo (Harry Fox/Harvey Bullock); Diana Muldaur (Leslie Thompkins); Brock Peters (Lucius Fox); Mark Hamill (The Joker/other villains); Adrienne Barbeau (Catwoman-Selena Kyle); Paul Williams (The Penguin); Roddy McDowall (The Mad Hatter); Michael Ansara (Mr. Freeze); John Glover (The Riddler); Richard Moll (District Attorney Dent-Two Face); Diane Pershing (Poison Ivy); Helen Slater (Talia); Alan Rachins (Clock King); Ron Perlman (Clay Face); Ed Asner (Roland Dugget); Michael York (Count Vertigo); Treat Williams (Prof. Milo); Marc Singer (Man-Bat); Meredith MacRae (She-Bat); David Warner (Ra's Al Ghul); Arlene Sorkin (Harley Quinn); Ray Buktenika (Dr. Hugo Strange); Mari Devon (Summer Gleason); Michael Pataki (Sewer King); Ingrid Olin (Renee Montoya); George Murdock (Boss Biggis); John Vernon (Rupert Thorne); Mickey Dolenz (Min and Max); Eugene Roche (Arnold Stromwell); Michael Gross (Lloyd Ventris); Michael Des Barres (Nostromos); Aron Kincaid (Killer Croc); Kimmy Robertson (Alice); Paddy Edwards (Maggie Paige); Bud Cort (Josiah Wormwood); Thomas Wilson (Tony Zucco); Robert Ito (Kyodai Ken); Harry Hamlin (Cameron Kaiser/Romulus); Robby Benson (Wilkes); Ed Begley Jr. (Charlie Collins); Jeff Bennett (HARDAC); William Sanderson (Karl Rossum); Leslie Easterbrook (Randa Duane); Joseph Maher (Dr. Emile Dorian); Jim Cummings (Tygrus); George Dzundza (Ventriloquist); Richard Dysart (Batman's Psychiatrist); Matt Frewer (Sidney Debris); Dorian Harewood (Riley); Marilu Henner (Veronica Vreeland); Julie Brown (Zatana); Joseph Campanella (Dr. Thorne); Steve Siskind (Maxie Zeus); Kate Mulgrew (Red Claw); Adam West (The Grey Ghost); Paul Winfield (Earl Cooper); and Tim Curry, Rene Auberjonois, Levar Burton, Paul Dooley, Herb Edelman, Ken Howard, Heather Locklear, Kevin McCarthy, Sam McMurray, Melissa Manchester, Tim Matheson, Joe Piscopo, John Rhys-Davies, Vincent Schiavelli, Peter Scolari, Loretta Swit, Jean Smart, Jay Thomas, Marcia Wallace, William Windom, Angel Harper, Joe Leahy, John Delancie, Walter Olekiwicz, Bruce W. Timm, Neil Ross, Frank Ross, Frank Welker, Steve McGowan, Danny Mann, Goh Misawa, Ron Taylor, Takayo Fisher, Laurie Johnson, Nicholas Savalas, Carmen Zapata, Seth Green, Josh Weiner, Alan Roberts, Ernie Hudson, Roger Rose, Pat Fraley, Zale Kessler, Steve Franken, Steve Bulin, Barry Gordon, Maurice LaMarche, Chao-Li Chi, Brian Cummings, Ed Gilbert, Pat Musick, Peter Renaday, Jim Cummings, Beverleigh Banfield, Bob Clothworthy, Linda Dangcil, Lynette Mettey.

Although artist/writer Bob Kane's *Batman* had been knocking around in DC comic books since 1939's *Detective Comics* #27, an animated version of Batman wasn't forthcoming until after the astounding ratings coup of ABC television's 1966 live action sendup of the comic book crimefighter. Batman and his "boy wonder" sidekick Robin—who as we all know are really millionaire Bruce Wayne and his youthful ward Dick Grayson—made their TV cartoon entree in much the same way as they'd appeared on radio back in the late 1940s: as guests in another superhero's house. Radio's Batman had appeared exclusively on the *Superman* radio serial; similarly, the animated *Batman* was a component to Filmation's animated *Superman* series in 1968 (q.v.), which somewhat grudgingly changed its title to *The Batman/Superman Hour*.

Filmation's version of Batman was perhaps not "rubbish," as designated by the National Association for Better Broadcasting, but neither was it memorable. In their favor, the *Batman* cartoons managed to copy the energetic pacing of the comic-book storylines, and in terms of design remained faithful to the comic artists' renditions of the heroes and villains. But the animated Batman and Robin existed as soulless cardboard cutouts, springing to "life" only when battling such traditional costumed foes as the Joker, the Penguin, the Riddler, Mr. Freeze, Catwoman and Simon the Pieman. The 17 12-minute Filmation cartoons were stylistically closer to the original comics than ABC's live action *Batman*, but hardly as much fun. The animated property made the rerun rounds on the CBS network under the title *The Adventures of Batman and Robin* in 1969, which included 17 new adventures, many costarring the Caped Crusader's distaff counterpart Batgirl — also known as Barbara Gordon, daughter of the police commissioner of Batman's home base, Gotham City.

Once more, the new cartoons added little to the Batman legend except to prolong its TV exposure. After 1970, all the Filmation *Batman* series were put into local syndication, where they remained until various pressure groups virtually banished the package on the grounds of "excessive violence" — a curious criticism, since these tired efforts weren't excessively anything, except excessively loud.

Except for guest appearances on *The Brady Kids* (q.v.) and *Scooby-Doo* (q.v.), the cartoon *Batman* was put in mothballs until 1973, when he and Robin became part of a crimefighting team of DC Comics headliners (among them Superman, Wonder Woman, Aquaman, Plastic Man and The Green Lantern) on Hanna-Barbera's *Super Friends*. Sixteen half hours were produced, of better quality and wider story variety than the earlier Filmations and highlighted with some enjoyably sarcastic banter between the various headlining heroes, but unfortunately locked in the Hanna-Barbera "formula" trap. The project withered after 13 weeks, only to receive a shot in the arm in 1976 vis-à-vis the popularity of ABC's live action primetimers *Six Million Dollar Man* and *Wonder Woman*, which made superheroes "hot" once more. Back came Hanna-Barbera with 1977's *All-New Superfriends Hour*, which begat 1978's *Challenge of the Superfriends*, wherein the increasingly topheavy roster of heroes was pitted against the League of Doom; this property was retitled *World's Greatest Superfriends* in 1979. Batman was in harness throughout, but now was just one of the "boys" instead of a stellar attraction in his own right, and as such lost a lot of his individuality. (See notes on *Superfriends* for more on the above-mentioned series.)

While all this Hanna-Barbera activity was in full gear, Filmation developed a CBS Saturday morning project called *The New Adventures of Batman*, which at least had the saving graces of restoring Batman to solo star status, and of voiceover work from ABC's onscreen Batman and Robin of the 1960s, Adam West and Burt Ward. (Ever since the cancellation of the "live" Batman back in 1968, West and Ward had made frequent press statements asserting their desire to play challenging roles beyond Batman and Robin. But actors do have to eat.) Batgirl was back for the *New Adventures*, although her voice was not provided by West and Ward's primetime costar Yvonne Craig, who'd left acting for the more financially satisfying world of real estate. A new addition to *New Adventures* was Bat-Mite, a gremlinish mascot first introduced in the Batman comic books of the 1950s as a "fourth dimension" denizen a la Superman's Mr. Mxylzlpltk. Otherwise *New Adventures of Batman* was the "same old same old," better animated and with more elaborate background art, but not a whole lot more distinguished than the earlier Filmation efforts.

Before long, Batman was sharing his star dressing room again, this time with an even older property, Edgar Rice Burroughs' Tarzan. First there was Filmation's *Batman/Tarzan Adventure Hour* in 1977, which resurfaced in rerun form as a component of *Tarzan and the Super Seven* a year later; Batman and Tarzan functioned in their own half-hour installments (Batman's were rebroadcast from his *New Adventures of Batman*), which then popped up in *Tarzan and the Super Seven* amongst the newly animated travails of "Isis and the Freedom Force," "Micro Woman and Super Stretch," "Webwoman" and "Manta and Moray." In 1980, the entire collection of *Super Seven* reruns moved over to NBC. (See separate *Tarzan* entry for details on the above-mentioned series.)

And then came another round of *Super Friends* adventures for ABC, newly produced by Hanna-Barbera in 1984 as *Super Friends: The Legendary Super Powers Show,* which was rechristened one year later as *Super Powers Team: The Galactic Guardians* (see separate entry on *Super Friends* for information on these series). Batman was by now utterly robbed of all his uniqueness, not only by being thrown in the pot with all the other caped and costumed heroes but by constantly being labelled a "super" hero. Bob Kane's distinction way back in 1939 was to create Batman as a normal fellow whose heroics stemmed from self-motivated physical fitness and keenly cultivated intelligence, not because he was endowed from birth, or through mutation, with superhuman advantages.

It seemed by the time *Super Powers Team* was cancelled in 1986 that Batman had worn out his TV welcome and would never be satisfactorily transferred to animation. But that was a premature assumption. The year 1986 also saw the debut of artist Frank Miller's graphic novel *Batman: The Dark Knight Returns*—a grim, adult oriented comic book which in turn inspired the dark grittiness and mordant humor of the spectacularly successful 1989 theatrical feature *Batman: The Movie,* directed by Tim Burton (see *Beetlejuice* [q.v.] for more on Burton).

In the summer of 1992, *Batman Returns,* the sequel to that 1989 blockbuster, accrued the biggest opening day gross in Hollywood history. Meanwhile, reruns of the live action *Batman* sendup of the 60s were still turning a profit in syndication and on cable TV, their appeal enhanced by new color prints which restored their pictorial quality to mint condition. These facts, combined with the recently energized late afternoon "fringe time" TV cartoon audience, encouraged the Fox Network in 1992 to green-light Warner Bros. Animation for an expensive new *Batman* cartoon daily.

Warners didn't have to look far within its organization for the right men for the *Batman* job. Alan Burnett, a story editor on Warners' *Tiny Toon Adventures* (q.v.), had drawn up a précis on a *Batman* pilot series while working on H-B's 1984 edition of *Super Friends.* Burnett fine-tuned this project with Bruce Timm and Eric Radomski, *Tiny Toon* colleagues who'd likewise loved *Batman* with a passion since childhood and had independently dreamed up their own pilot. Responding to industry rumors that Fox was going to commission a new non-comedy cartoon series, Warners executive producer Jean MacCurdy gave Timm and Radomski the go-ahead to prepare a two-minute sample reel; the animators had been offered several potential projects, and one of them happened to be their beloved *Batman.* It was on the basis of that pilot reel alone that *Batman: The Animated Series* was sold—and once Timm, Radomski and Burnett had wrapped up production on *Tiny Toon* in late 1991, the project was off and going full throttle.

Batman: The Animated Series was not an emulation of the earlier, juvenile cartoons from Hanna-Barbera and Filmation, nor did it take the "camp" approach of the live action *Batman* series. Nor, in fact, was it specifically based on the Tim Burton movies, though Burton had previewed the project and given it his blessing. The 1992 edition of *Batman* drew much of its inspiration from the aforementioned Frank Miller graphic comics; producers Jean MacCurdy and Tom Ruegger eliminated most of the inner turmoil and fascistic tendencies demonstrated by Miller's "dark knight" (and also cut out any on-camera killings), but kept the film noir quality of the artwork. MacCurdy referred to the style of the 1992 series as "Dark Deco," an apt description for the bold, sharp lines of the character artwork, the streamlined forced perspective backgrounds designed by Ted Blackman, and the nocturnal, spider-shadow ambience of the whole project. To further sustain the look of the series, Timm and Radomski hit upon the inspired notion of painting the backgrounds on black paper, providing just the right gloomy tonality to the color texture.

"What we really have here is an animated drama," producer MacCurdy explained. "I think it may be the only animated series that takes a dramatic, rather than strictly action-adventure approach." Emmy winner Paul Dini, one of the *Batman* directors, amplified Mac-Curdy's statement. To Dini, the series' style played "with the basic idea of what Batman is: a shadowy, unknown creature of the night who strikes out in the darkness."

Batman: The Animated Series was such a break from the normal run of superhero cartoons (which took themselves seriously, but on more of a "fun for all ages" level) that many TV critics celebrated the program as a strictly adult fantasy, along the lines of the recent live action CBS weekly *Beauty and the Beast*. So bowled over were critics by the results that they even suggested *Batman* was the first animated effort to utilize so dramatic an approach — quite forgetting that Max and Dave Fleischer had been doing much the same thing, and with remarkably similar character and background design, 50 years earlier in their theatrical *Superman* cartoon shorts. The debt to the Fleischers was, however, publicly acknowledged by the creators of the new *Batman*, who also cited the influence of the 1926 Fritz Lang sci-fi silent film *Metropolis* and the chromelike artwork seen on Russian propaganda posters.

Storylines retained the Gotham City setting, the dual identity concept and the splendidly caparisoned villains. There were at least two pronounced carryovers from the recent *Batman* movies: the Prokofiev-style theme music composed by Danny Elfman — whose style was admirably captured by the series' conductor Shirley Walker — and the strengthening of the character of Alfred, Bruce Wayne/Batman's loyal retainer. Some of the best and most pointed dialogue was spoken by the pragmatic, precise Alfred, whose voice was supplied by British actor Clive Revill in the pilot episode, and thereafter by Efrem Zimbalist Jr.

As voiced by TV actor Kevin Conway (a costar of Fox's live action *Rachel Gunn RN*), Batman was not the enigma portrayed in the films by Michael Keaton but someone whose emotions were never far from the surface. Other familiar regulars included Robin (added at the behest of Jean MacCurdy, much to the dismay of Timm, Radomski and their colleagues, who weren't that enamored of the Boy Wonder), Commissioner Gordon, and such perennial baddies as the Riddler,

the Joker, the Penguin and Catwoman. To win converts among hardcore Batman fans, the new series had the good sense to revitalize several of Batman's original comic-book foes, some of them making their first screen appearances: Dr. Strange, Poison Ivy, Count Vertigo and many others. Timm and Radomski had been given carte blanche by DC Comics the use of any of the publisher's comic book villains — so long as they'd made their debuts in Batman's "home" publication, *Detective Comics*.

As was the case with the 1960s *Batman* live action series, movie and TV celebrities lined up to take on these nefarious roles (many of these famous performers had already flexed their vocal muscles with the California-based Radio Workshop). Thus we were treated to Adrienne Barbeau as Catwoman, Mark Hamill as the Joker, Paul Williams as the Penguin, Richard Moll as Two-Face, Michael Ansara as Mr. Freeze and Michael York as Count Vertigo, along with contributions by Ed Asner, Treat Williams, John Glover, Tim Curry, Rene Auberjonois, and a veritable honor roll of others. Two piquant links between the 1966 and 1992 editions of *Batman* were provided by Roddy McDowell, who played "The Bookworm" in 1966 and "The Mad Hatter" in 1992; and by the original TV Batman, Adam West, who in the animated episode "Beware the Gray Ghost" supplied the voice of a washed-up TV hero who happened to be Bruce Wayne's boyhood idol!

These last-mentioned harkbacks were hardly the only "inside" references to be found on the new *Batman*. By the fall of 1993, connoisseurs of the series were staging their own "trivial pursuit" contests, tallying up the in-jokes and publishing annotated lists in such animation fan magazines as *Animato* and *Wild Cartoon Kingdom*. My personal favorite *Batman* gags include the name of the cyborg manufacturer in the two-part episode "Heart of Steel" — Rossum, the same name given the ill-fated inventor in the grandaddy of all cyborg dramas, Karel Capek's 1923 play *R.U.R.* I also got a kick out of the license plate on an automobile in "The Mechnanic," embossed with the proud motto "Gotham: The Dark Deco State."

Batman: The Animated Series premiered as a special half hour on Sunday, September 6, 1992, and one day later settled into a weekday slot at 4:30 or 5 P.M. in most cities. The program performed so brilliantly (deflecting viewer complaints that not enough half hours had been made prior to its debut) that Fox used selected episodes to beef up its Saturday morning lineup, and then in December announced that *Batman* would be made a 7:00 P.M. attraction on Sundays. Although the series' ratings buckled under the weight of CBS' *60 Minutes*, the nighttime *Batman* still held enough of a viewership for Fox to stay with that timeslot for five months—while still maintaining its lucrative weekday schedule. A second season, which reintroduced Batgirl to the fold, was not only inevitable but, to its fans, mandatory. Such was the popularity of *Batman: The Animated Series* that Fox commenced production of a fully animated *Batman* theatrical feature, released during Christmas week of 1993.

If you've been faithfully tape recording the daily *Batmans*, none of the above entry is of any surprise to you. But you *might* be surprised to learn that your video collection may, even as we speak, be out of date. So devoted to their work are the creators of *Batman: The Animated Series* that they'll go back during the various rerun cycles and *re*-animate sequences that hadn't satisfied them during the series' first run.

BATTLE OF THE PLANETS. Syndicated: 1978. Gallerie International/ Tatsunoko Productions/Sandy Frank. American version credits: Executive producer, Jameson Brewer. Produced and directed by David Hanson. Script adaptation: Jameson Brewer, Alan Dinehart III. Written by Jameson Brewer, Harry Winkler, Sid Morse, Howard Post, William Bloom, Richard Shaw, Kevin Coates, Alan Susin, Muriel Germano. Music by Hoyt Curtin. Voices: Alan Young (7-Zark-7/Keyop); Keye Luke (Zoltar); Casey Kasem (Mark Venture); Janet Waldo (Princess); Ronnie Schell (Jason); Alan Dinehart III (Tiny).
—G-FORCE. TBS: Mid–1980s. Gallerie/ Tatsunoko/Turner Entertainment. Voices: Sam Fontana (Ace Goodheart); Cameron Clarke (Dirk Daring); Jan Rabson (Hootie); Barbara Goodson (Agatha June/Pee Wee); Bill Capizi (Galactor).

Gatchaman ("Gander Man") was a well received Japanese cartoon series which ran in its own country from October 1972 to September 1974. Its space travel format was a surefire ratings grabber in Japan, but chances for an American sale were slim in the mid–1970s due to a drive during that period to purge U.S. television of overly violent sci-fi kids' programs. The fantastic popularity of the first *Star Wars* film in 1977 made the genre almost impossible to ignore, however, and soon several American cartoon companies were drawing up plans to get their characters suited up, helmeted, and rocketed into the stratosphere. The first producer on the syndicated scene was gameshow distributor Sandy Frank, who acquired the readymade *Gatchaman*, hired Hanna/Barbera veterans Jameson Brewer and Alan Dinehart III to adapt the scripts into English, edited out the more graphically violent passages, commissioned new animation of an R2D2-like robot character named "7-Zark-7" to narrate and bridge the continuity gaps left by the trimming, and retitled the whole package *Battle of the Planets*. Total cost to Sandy Frank: $4.5 million. It was, as *TV Guide* reported in 1985, more than was necessary, but Frank was a man willing to overspend if he foresaw a gigantic return.

Set in the year 2020, the Sandy Frank version of *Gatchaman* centered around the exploits of G-Force, a protective squad commandeered by Mark Venture (a character name wrought in the mold of *Star Wars* leading actor Mark Hammill) and consisting of four war orphans: Jason, Tiny, The Princess (another bow to *Star Wars*) and Keyop. Headquartered beneath the seas of Earth at Center Neptune, the G-Force spent the better part of its time rallying together with the cry "Transmute!" (translation: get on your uniforms!), the better to stem the megalomaniacal inclinations of Zoltar, insidious leader of the withering planet Spectra, whose wicked denizens were forced to conquer new worlds and galaxies in order to survive.

Eighty-five half-hour episodes of *Battle of the Planets* (whittled down from the 100 original *Gatchamans*) were ready for Monday through Friday telecasts by the spring of 1978. However, the kiddie TV market's swing back to violence and suspense by the end of the 70s rather mitigated the bowdlerized *Battle*'s impact, the end result being that Sandy Frank nearly lost his original heavy investment. Commenting on his mistimed nonviolent approach, Mr. Frank, the distributor of *The Dating Game* and *The $1.98 Beauty Show*, ascribed the error to "my damn high ideals." Still, thanks to a razzle-dazzle promotional push ("I sold it like the Second Coming"), the producer was able to clear $15 million in sales.

Although ratings weren't bad, *Battle of the Planets* had only a so-so first run, regularly beaten out by older cartoons and network reruns (the property has since done better in reissue and cable sales). The mild reaction to *Battle* effectively halted American distribution of the sequel to *Gatchaman*, which premiered over Japanese television in 1978 under the title *Gatchaman F*.

This last named property didn't make it to the States until the mid–1980s, when Ted Turner's TBS cable superstation acquired six episodes of the sequel, grafted on new soundtracks and renamed the leading characters once again: Mark Venture was now "Ace Goodheart," Jason was "Dirk Daring," and the Princess "Agatha June," indicating the generally derisive tone of the new adaptations. As *G-Force*, *Gatchaman F* failed to make any impact whatsoever in America, while reruns of the original *Gatchaman/Battle of the Planets* were still playing profitably in a number of local markets.

THE BEAGLES. CBS: 9/10/1966–9/2/1967. Total TV/Lancelot Productions. Executive producer: Treadwell Covington. Voice credits unavailable, but probably included George Irving and Allan Swift.

This much we can agree on: *The Beagles*, the final release from Total TV Productions (see *King Leonardo and His Short Subjects*), concerned the serialized trials and tribulations of two canine rock musicians, Stringer and Tubby. Beyond this, all past histories of TV cartoon series are dead wrong. The *Beagles*, despite its title, was not a parody of the Beatles. Stringer and Tubby were in fact takeoffs on Dean Martin and Jerry Lewis, both in physique and general deportment. And this is all that's worth discussing about this half hour CBS time-waster.

BEANY AND CECIL (a.k.a. MATTY'S FUNNIES WITH

BEANY AND CECIL). ABC: 1/6/1962–12/19/1968. Bob Clampett Productions/Snowball Studios. Executive producer, ACR Stone. Produced and created by Bob Clampett. Directed by Art Scott. Written by Bob Clampett, Eddie Maxwell, Al Bertino, Jack Bonestell, Jack Hannah, Dick Kinney and Dale Hale. Music by Jack Roberts, Hoyt Curtin, Bob and Sody Clampett, Eddie Brandt, Melvin Lenard and Marrigold Music Co. Voices: Jim MacGeorge (Captain Horatio Huffenpuff/Beany Boy); Irv Shoemaker (Cecil/Dishonest John); and Joan Gerber, Daws Butler, Don Messick, Paul Frees, Bob Clampett, Bobby Clampett, Sody Clampett, Eddie Brandt and Freddy Morgan. Guest-star voices included Robert Clary, Arlene "Chatterbox" Harris, Sammee Tong, Mickey Katz, and Gonzales-Gonzales.

—**BEANY AND CECIL.** ABC: 9/10/1988–10/8/1988. Bob Clampett Productions/DIC Enterprises. Produced and directed by John Kricfalusi. Story editors, Chuck Lorre and Paul Dini. Voices: Mark Laurence Hildreth (Beany Boy); William Werstine [Billy West] (Cecil); James A. MacGeorge (Captain Huffenpuff); Maurice LaMarche (Dishonest John).

Bob Clampett, one of Warner Bros.' most accomplished cartoon directors of the 1930s and 1940s (*Porky in Wackyland* and *Coal Black and De Sebben Dwarfs* were but two of the many Clampett-directed classics), was never a man to come up with an idea and then not run with it. He was unable during his Warners days to build a series of cartoons around his pet concept of a friendly sea serpent—though the character made a cameo appearance in the 1939 Porky Pig cartoon *Christopher Columbus Jr.*—but the idea served him well in the early, experimental days of Los Angeles television, when anyone with even a germ of a novelty was allowed to prove his worth before the black and white camera eye.

Together with a daunting array of creative talents including actor/satirist Stan Freberg, voice artist Daws Butler, and writer and future *Rocky and His Friends* (q.v.) coproducer Bill Scott, Bob Clampett blossomed forth in February of 1949 with an elaborate daily puppet show, *Time for Beany*, over Paramount Studios' KTLA-TV. This series of serialized 15-minute adventures starred talespinning Captain Horatio Huffenpuff of the good ship

Leakin' Lena; his nephew Beany Boy, so named for his propellor headgear; and Beany's erstwhile companion, Cecil the Seasick Sea Serpent. The fly in the ointment to these adventures was Dishonest John, a mustachioed villain (reportedly based on one of Clampett's bosses at Warners) who declared his presence with a sneering "Nya Ha Ha." *Time for Beany* had something for everyone: thrilling adventures for the kids coupled with knowledgable showbiz and political inside jokes for the grownups. Indeed, the most vocal fan following for *Beany* included such overaged adolescents as Lionel Barrymore (who, legend has it, had to watch the show at his local tavern because his employer, MGM Studios, prohibited its contractees from owning TV sets), Groucho Marx, and Albert Einstein! In 1950, Paramount Television began distributing *Time for Beany* kinescopes—films taken directly off the TV screen—to the rest of the country, a package that remained in active syndication until at least 1958. As icing on the cake, the series was honored with Emmy awards in 1950 and 1952.

But by the end of the 1950s, puppet shows weren't the hot properties that they'd once been, nor were American theatrical animated cartoons the stellar attractions they'd been in years past. Determined to keep his hand in animation and to perpetuate his favorite creation, Bob Clampett, with the backing of Associated Artists Productions head Elliot Hyman, set about producing five *Beany and Cecil* cartoons, distributed in Australia, Canada and Europe by Associated Artists' parent company, United Artists, in 1959.

Stylistic differences between such theatrical films as *Beany and Cecil Meet Billy the Squid* and the later made-for-television *Beany and Cecil* cartoons will be immediately obvious to fans of the TV version. The character design in the earliest shorts is based more closely upon the original puppets—sometimes to the point of grotesqueness, with ugly fixed grins on the faces of Captain Huffenpuff and Dishonest John. Animation in these theatrical cartoons is fuller, background art richer and color schemes brighter than in the television efforts. And the voices not only sound slightly more subdued than on TV, but they resonate as though recorded in an echo chamber. Moreover, there were departures from the later characteriza-

tions and format of the TV series (As in the puppet version, Uncle Captain didn't believe in sea serpents) that had to be edited out when the theatrical *Beany and Cecil*s were absorbed into the 78-cartoon package put together by Clampett for the ABC network in 1960 and 1961.

Sponsored by Mattel Toys and first shown in January 1962 under the title *Matty's Funnies with Beany and Cecil*, the series was the successor to *Matty's Funday Funnies* (1959–1961), a weekly ABC offering of post–1948 Paramount/Famous Studios theatrical cartoons (see notes on *Casper the Friendly Ghost*). As such, Clampett was obliged to include Mattel's corporate mascots Matty Mattel and Sister Belle in the "bumper" animation between cartoons. Matty and Belle would be edited out when *Beany and Cecil* went into multisponsored weekend morning reruns in January of 1963, just as the Mattel-commissioned theme music, another carryover from *Funday Funnies*, would be rewritten.

The alliance with Mattel had an enormous lasting effect on the continuing success of Clampett's characters. Beany's headwear of choice, together with such related toys as the "Beanycopter," were for many years some of Mattel's biggest Christmastime sellers; as a result, the Beany character remained vivid in the public consciousness long after the series shut down production. Clampett later claimed he had no idea, nor was it intended, that the beany would "take off" as a saleable commodity—a statement that seems to be at odds with the producer's overemphasis on the propellored prop in the original *Beany and Cecil* opening credits.

As for the *Beany and Cecil* cartoons themselves, opinions are divided. Many older Clampett fans feel that the cartoons were but pale shadows of the original *Time for Beany*, citing their lack of story development (an allowable luxury for a daily 15-minute serial but hard to pull off within a single 6-minute cartoon), the short-changing of such three-dimensional *Time for Beany* puppet creations as Tearalong the Dotted Lion and Thunderbolt the Wondercolt by reducing their characterizations to caricatures, and the loss of the adlibbed dialogue so generously supplied on the live series by Stan Freberg and Daws Butler. Other fans, having grown up with the cartoons while witnessing only a smattering of surviving *Time for Beany* kinescopes out of continuity and context, feel that the extra preparation that went into the cartoons resulted in far sharper dialogue and slicker comedy turns than were possible back in the puppet days. Both opinions have value. It can't be denied that the cartoons seemed loud, pushy and selfconscious compared to the wry, whimsical *Time for Beany*; at the same time, *Beany and Cecil* was one of the best-looking TV programs on the market in 1962, and virtually the only cartoon series of its era outside of *Rocky and His Friends* (q.v.) that behaved as though there was a viewership with intelligence and sophistication beyond the *Flintstones* level.

Bob Clampett would complain in later years that he was forever under the thumb of network and sponsorial censorship, which recoiled in horror whenever a contemporary reference or satirical jab was made for fear that one person (or sponsor) out of a thousand would be offended. And yet, *Beany and Cecil* got away with stuff that other TV producers would not even touch. First and foremost, Clampett treated us to friendly swipes at Saint Disney: Disneyland was lampooned as "Beanyland," Davy Crockett became "Davy Cricket" with patented coonskin cap intact, and Snow White and the Seven Dwarfs were transformed into the sizzling Vegas lounge act "So What and the Seven Whatnots"—each Whatnot a caricatured 1962 celebrity. As early as the pre–TV *Beany and Cecil Meet Billy the Squid*, Clampett was genially tweaking Uncle Walt's nose by showing Captain Huffenpuff joining the rats in leaving his sinking ship, "disguising" himself with a round-eared Mickey Mouse Club cap!

Less genial were Clampett's frequent gibes at advertisers, authority figures, and especially selfstyled TV watchdogs: Whenever Cecil was being severely pummelled by Dishonest John, he'd pause, look at the audience, and ask dryly, "Do you think there's too much violence on television?" *Beany and Cecil*'s celebrity takeoffs, ranging from a bald eagle in the image of hairless comic Jack E. Leonard to a Three Stooges clone called "The Three Headed Threep," were so broadly drawn that they seemed to cry out "If you don't like it, sue us." And the series included more 1960s pop-cultural references than can possibly be repeated (or appreciated) here—an aspect of cartoon humor avoided by some TV animators of that era, who worried that too much contemporary comedy would "date" their product and hurt future rerun sales.

Even more bold was Clampett's fascination with dialect humor, a definite taboo on many TV series at the time, who were reeling under attacks from a variety of ethnic pressure groups. If Clampett thought a Jewish Indian was funny, he'd have a Jewish Indian, and hang the consequences. While skirting the boundaries of good taste, Clampett's *Beany and Cecil* was in its own way as jauntily irreverent as the Warner Bros. cartoon output of the 1930s and 1940s, which poked fun at every celebrity, minority group, and public foible with such impartiality that few were offended and many came back for more.

Beany and Cecil was taken off ABC after its seventh rerun cycle in 1968; then there was a long dry period during which the series was seldom seen at all, though it ostensibly was available for syndication. Thanks to its circle of loyal fans, its merchandising, and Bob Clampett's ceaseless self-promotion (he began taking credit for creating so many classic cartoon characters that fellow Warner Bros. alumnus Chuck Jones was moved to publish a formal "cease and desist" protest), *Beany and Cecil* assumed legendary status. The series was put back in circulation by popular demand in 1983, a year before Clampett's death, when RCA-Columbia packaged the 78 cartoons into several volumes of home videocassettes.

Then there was DIC Enterprises' 1988 revival of *Beany and Cecil* for the ABC network, which was astonishingly successful in capturing the spirit of the Clampett original. Producing and directing this version was Ralph Bakshi protégé John Kricfalusi, who'd later create *The Ren and Stimpy Show*. Of his experience with the new *Beany and Cecil*, Kricfalusi—who idolized Bob Clampett, and wanted more than anything to emulate his hero's old panache—made the characteristic comment that "I learned first-hand how cartoons got to be so suck-y over the years." Some cartoon buffs (notably those who've resisted the current *Ren and Stimpy* cult worship) have suggested that Kricfalusi's notoriously slow working methods, and his seeming inability to meet deadlines, were the principal reasons that DIC's *Beany and Cecil* lasted only five half-hour episodes.

(For the record, two of John Kricfalusi's *B and C* collaborators, artist Bruce Timm and story editor Paul Dini, would go on to bigger things with Fox's 1992 *Batman* [q.v.]; and actor Billy West, who'd later do the voice of Kricfalusi's Stimpy, was heard on the 1988 series as Cecil the Seasick Sea Serpent.)

The failure of DIC's remake did not, however, bode ill for the original. Bob Clampett's *Beany and Cecil* of the 1960s was returned to local syndication in 1989, where it outrated all competition in its first five major TV markets.

THE BEATLES. ABC: 9/25/1965–4/20/ 1969. Al Brodax/King Features. Executive producer, Al Brodax. Character design by Peter Sander and Jack Stokes. Animation facilities, TVC Studios. Voices: Paul Frees (John Lennon/George Harrison); Lance Percival (Paul McCartney/Ringo Starr).

If you don't know the history of the Beatles, then you've been hibernating since 1963 (or maybe you weren't born until 1974, in which case, take notes). Anyway, the initial wave of Beatlemania was peaking in 1965, so it was determined to get as much merchandising value out of the Liverpool Lads as quickly as possible, before the bubble would theoretically burst. Al Brodax, the head of King Features Syndicate's television division who'd already brought such King Features newspaper properties as *Popeye* (q.v.) and *Beetle Bailey* (see *King Features Trilogy*) to the screen, was elected by ABC to develop an animated series based on the Beatles. Brodax set to work, enlisting the corps of artisans from the British-based TVC studios—which would later produce the influential Beatles animated feature *Yellow Submarine* (1968), directed by TVC head George Dunning—and the staff of Australia's Astransa company. Swept up in this project was toy manufacturer A. C. Gilmer, who had visions of untold wealth resulting from Beatle tie-ins. Capitol Records also had a major piece of the action in exchange for the rights to "visualize" the actual Beatles recordings for TV.

Caricatures of the four moptops were swiftly drafted by cartoon artists Peter Sander and Jack Stokes. Unlike a lot of celebrity tie-in animation art, the results were not slapdash likenesses, but artists' renderings that gave careful consideration and weight to each Beatle's personality. John Lennon was drawn as the most aggressive of the bunch, the leader both vocally and physically; George Harrison was designed in a casual, lopsided, leaning fashion; Paul McCartney was the poised fashion plate; and Ringo Starr was the droopy, dishevelled, childlike Beatle. These artistic impressions were gleaned from multiple viewings of director Richard Lester's brace of Beatles flicks, *A Hard Day's Night* (1964) and *Help!* (1965). The hectic, fast-cut directorial style Lester imposed on these films also carried over into the animated *Beatles*, giving the series its breezy pace and comic impudence.

Each half hour episode of *The Beatles* contained two short cartoons. Each cartoon would be titled after the Beatles song hit highlighted and illustrated during its running time. The plotline's relation to the song content was often tenuous but somehow always logical: In the very first program, for example, "I Want to Hold Your Hand" served as the leitmotif for a lovestruck octopus. As intermissions between these weekly features, the Beatles were heard in two singalong sequences, their song lyrics appearing line by line in "Bouncing Ball" fashion on the screen—a valuable service to fans in those days before lyrics were printed on the album covers. These in-between sequences sustained the humor quotient on the program by relying heavily on slapstick and punning dialogue. One of the most fondly remembered bits involved Ringo's being reprimanded for the grammatical gaffe of dropping his "G's" at the end of words, a running gag which culminated in a large "G" landing on the hapless drummer's head.

On the subject of dialogue, a note on the voicework: While the actual Beatles were heard during the songs, actors Paul Frees and Lance Percival—the latter a popular British comedian and one of the original cast members of the BBC's satirical revue *That Was the Week That Was*—supplied the boys' speaking voices. Paul Frees sounded exactly like Paul Frees, as he usually did when attempting a celebrity impression, but Lance Percival's work was amusingly accurate, especially his droll rendition of Ringo Starr.

Despite the anticipated dropoff in audience interest, *The Beatles* did better than anyone expected, grabbing 52 percent of its Saturday morning audience and forcing rival CBS executive Fred Silverman to counterprogram with superhero cartoons. *The Beatles'* ratings dropped off during the 1966-67 season thanks to strong competition from CBS's *Space Ghost* (q.v.), but the program remained in active production for three full years, weathering even the tempest of 1966, when John Lennon's public declaration that the Beatles were more popular than Jesus was taken out of context and resulted in wholesale pressure-group banning of the boys' albums (while some bloodhounds were able to yank the Beatles from local radio stations, they were less successful in convincing ABC to black out one of its biggest weekend moneymakers). For its last two network seasons, *The Beatles* appeared exclusively in reruns, though it was still in production during the time that the group began to move out of its "teen idol" period and branched into more mature works like "Eleanor Rigby" and "Nowhere Man"—both of which were dutifully dished up by King Features in incongruously lighthearted animated form.

A nostalgic favorite, *The Beatles* was extensively replayed in the late 1980s over the MTV cable network. One lasting legacy of the series is indirect. In keeping with the style of the rest of the program, the "King Features" logo appeared at the beginning of each episode with a snatch of Beatles music heard in the background. This explains why subsequent King Features TV releases—including all 28 *Blondie* movies of the 1930s and 1940s—were heralded with a musical fanfare lifted from Lennon and McCartney's "Love Me Do."

BEAVIS AND BUTT-HEAD. MTV: May 17, 1993–. An MTV Networks Production. Creative supervisor/creator/designer/writer: Mike Judge. Executive producer, Abby Terkuhle. Produced by John Andrews. Supervising producer, Christina Norman. Associate producers, Nick Litwinko and John Lynn. Video segments produced by Trez Bayer and Susie Lynn. Script supervisor, Tiny Hong. Written by Mike Judge, Joe Stillman, Chris Kreski, Glenn Eichler, Geoff Whelan, David Felton. Animation facilities: J. J. Sedelmaier Productions, U.S. Animation TM Hollywood. All voices: Mike Judge.

This one wouldn't have even gotten past the title on mainstream TV. *Beavis and Butt-Head*, a pair of lamebrained adolescent rock music fans, were originally named Bobby and Billy when created by Mike Judge—a former physics major and musician described in the credits as "some guy from Texas"—as stars of the short subject "Frog Baseball," a one-shot component of the MTV cable channel's *Liquid Television* (q.v.), in September of 1992. Somehow this demented duo, which made the stars of the movie *Wayne's World* seem like MENSA members by comparison, was deemed worthy of a starring half hour, daily MTV series. *Beavis and Butt-Head* debuted in May of 1993 after production delays had scuttled its anticipated March premiere (the few completed episodes were sporadically run in March, but the full manifest of 29 "officially" entered the MTV schedule in May).

Each episode featured the scatology-spouting protagonists—both dressed in repulsive "death rock" tee shirts—in two short cartoons; some of the more cerebral of these showed the boys throwing up on a dog, dropping a bowling ball from a third-story window, pulling the legs off grasshoppers, and dropping a stick of TNT down a toilet. The rest of the program was made up of old and new music videos, upon which Beavis and Butt-Head would comment insinuatingly and libelously in a manner similar to what might have transpired had Siskel and Ebert grown up watching MTV and nothing else. Phrases like "This sucks!" and "Look at his butt!" flew like shrapnel through the boys' basement headquarters. The only stimulant to their alleged brains would be in the form of one of the many underdressed females appearing in MTV's catalogue. After watching one particularly sensuous video, Beavis (or was it Butt-Head?) was heard to say, "I'm gettin' a stiffie!"—pure Noël Coward in comparison to their usual patois.

In fact, Beavis and Butt-Head seemed to spend 95 percent of every half hour (a lot better drawn, designed and scripted than the acne-ridden "stars" would seem to deserve) glued to their flickering old TV tube, snickering moronically over the slightest sexual connotation. If *Beavis and Butt-Head* can be said to have a catchphrase, it was the stars' unison dirty giggle: "Huhuh-huh-huh-huh-huh-huhuh-huhuh."

To many grownups—those who missed the satirical point of a cartoon about two warped MTV addicts being produced *for* MTV addicts—watching this series was like being condemned to sit in the back of a school bus for all eternity. This assessment should give a good indication of the age range of *Beavis and Butt-Head's* biggest fans, who rapidly made the series MTV's top-rated attraction, garnering ten times as many viewers as its standard rock-video manifest. Magazine articles, and then magazine covers, lavished attention on the two "B"s—a publicity blitz followed up by T-shirts, toys, an all-star CD album (the boys' rendition of "I Got You Babe" with Cher must be seen to be believed), plans to make the characters "regulars" on David Letterman's late-night show, and a paperback book, titled *Beavis and Butt-Head: This Book Sucks* (Truth in advertising at last). *B & B* creator Mike Judge took all this adulation in stride, greatly amused by the lunatic aspect of sudden fame: "All of a sudden I was reading contracts that said 'Butt-Head' on the top. It's pretty weird."

Campaigners for "clean TV" couldn't have had a better target than *Beavis and Butt-Head* had they invented the boys themselves. Terry Rakolta's Americans for Responsible Television labelled the program "irresponsible and reckless," while such old reliable complainants as Senator Ernest Hollings and Rev. Donald Wildmon spread the word to their flocks to start letter-writing campaigns calling for the series' immediate demise. The only good to result from this activity is that in the excitement, people completely forgot similar campaigns against such "scandalous" cartoon series as *Ren and Stimpy* (q.v.) and *The Simpsons* (q.v.). Pressure group cannonades peaked in the fall of 1993, thanks to one of those unforeseeable tragedies which will always fuel the do-gooder brigades of the world. A five-year-old boy, playing with matches, set fire to his family's mobile home, killing his younger sister. The boy's mother took to the airwaves blaming the tragedy solely on *Beavis and Butt-Head*, citing an episode in which the tittering teens lit up a match and chortled "Fire is cool! Huhuhuhuhuh...."

Scattered reports that the five-year-old had had a history of setting fires, and that the child's home hadn't even been wired for cable TV, were disregarded in the rush to condemn *all* TV as dangerously violent, with *Beavis and Butt-Head* in danger of dying for television's sins. (Let's not pursue the question as to why any parent would leave a preschool child home alone watching MTV. The media has already squeezed that lemon dry.)

With millions in merchandising and a potential film deal at stake, MTV couldn't drop the series entirely without taking a bath. At the same time, some dramatic, decisive action was called for. Boldly casting its mercenary instincts to the winds, MTV dropped *Beavis and Butt-Head*—dropped it from its 7 P.M. (EST) nightly timeslot, while still running the program several times later in the evening. But, hey, they *also* went and spliced out all references to fire on the show. A shame they couldn't excise the boys' neanderthal giggle while they were at it.

Beavis and Butt-Head would wind up an eventful 1993 being nominated for cable TV's ACE awards—not as a cartoon series, but in the "comedy series" category. Looks like MTV had the last "Huh-huhhuh-huh-huhhuh-huh."

BEETLEJUICE. ABC: 9/9/1989-9/5/1992. Fox: November 1991-September 1993. Geffen Film Co./Tim Burton Inc./Nelvana/Warner Bros. Executive producers, David Geffen and Tim Burton. Produced by Michael Hirsh, Patrick Loubert and Clive A. Smith. Directed by Robin Budd. Coordinating producer, Stephen Hodgins. Executive in charge of Nelvana production, Stanford Blum. Supervising producer, Lenora Hume. Developed by Tim Burton; consultants, Michael Bender and Larry Wilson. Story editors: Patsy Cameron, Todd Anasti. Art director, John Halfpenny. Theme music by Danny Elfman. Score composed and produced by Acrobat Music. Mixed media segments by Calibre Digital Designs Inc. Voices: Stephen Ouimette (Beetlejuice); Alyson Court (Lydia Deetz); Roger Dunn (Charles Deetz); Elizabeth Hanna (Delia Deetz); and Len Carlson, Tara Charendoff, Robert Coit, Ray Landry, Faith Hampshire, Ron Rubin, Paulina Gillis, John Stocker, Joseph Sherman, Colin Fox, Dan Hennessey.

Beetlejuice was a darkly uproarious 1988

Beetlejuice in action.

film farce directed by Tim Burton. Seven years earlier, Burton had been a Disney animator, back when the floundering studio was still mired in the past and hadn't revitalized itself with *The Little Mermaid* and *Beauty and the Beast*. "The place was weird at the time," he noted later, "a lot of bitterness and fear and not a lot of direction." Even if he hadn't been dismissed early on, Burton probably would have bolted out of frustration after having all his progressively imaginative concepts rejected by the hidebound Disney higher-ups of the era (one such notion ultimately took shape as 1993's *The Nightmare Before Christmas*). Ultimately, Tim Burton broke into the bigtime with a "cartoon" feature that happened to be totally live-action: *Pee-wee's Big Adventure* (1985), a dreamlike lampoon of the classic Italian neorealistic drama *The Bicycle Thief* starring man/child comedian Pee-wee Herman.

Big Adventure, which amalgamated the reality of flesh and blood with the flights of fancy indigenous to animation, solidified Burton's style, which can best be described as what one might expect if a nine-year-old comic book fan of heightened intelligence were let loose in a major film

studio with *carte blanche* to direct any film he chose. Tim Burton was older than nine, but only physically. With coolheaded craftsmanship, he turned out successful, elaborate motion pictures which redefined the limits of real life within the realm of unbridled preteen imagination.

This was the style Burton brought to *Beetlejuice*, which told of a newly deceased married couple whose chance of happiness in the afterlife was in the grimy hands of an otherworldly confidence trickster—a yellow haired, flatulent creature of mismatched parts, rotten teeth and horrendous taste in clothes, named "Beetlejuice" in honor of his favorite junk food, live beetles. The film's amoral Beetlejuice lied, cheated and connived with shameless exuberance, ultimately outsmarting himself because of his misguided obsession with a suicidal teenage girl named Lydia Deetz. Tim Burton provided Michael Keaton (later the star of Burton's *Batman* films) with the role of a lifetime as Beetlejuice, and made a star out of Wynona Ryder, who played the melancholy Lydia.

Although hardly suitable for very young children, *Beetlejuice* nonetheless attracted an enthusiastic kiddie fan following. The preordained result was a weekly half hour animated cartoon series, produced by Tim Burton Inc. in association with the comparatively conservative animation firm Nelvana Ltd. (as a bonus, the series featured "mixed media" advertising parodies produced by Calibre Digital Designs, adroitly blending cartoon, computer and puppet animation). TV's *Beetlejuice* was nicer and far less gross than his cinema counterpart, though he still leaned towards the outrageous in both comportment and personal hygiene. The emphasis in the series was on Beetlejuice's now benign relationship with Lydia Deetz—no longer the potential suicide of the film, but still a young lady whose fascination with the occult and supernatural isn't quite sympatico with her upwardly mobile parents or the other residents of suburban Peaceful Pines.

Lydia's earthly scrapes and predicaments would frequently compel Beetlejuice to seek solutions in the Neitherworld, a beautifully animated Daliesque landscape populated with such creepy crawlers as skeletal physical fitness maven Jacques LaLean, Doomie the Dogbrained Car, TV commercial huckster Barry

Menot (pronounced mee-not), and a band of unholy boy scouts, the Sappy Face Ghouls. And these were the *good* guys. The villains, whose activities threatened to thrust both Beetlejuice and Lydia into a purgatory existence even more undesirable than the Neitherworld, included such delightful deviants as cowboy Jesse Germs and Scuzzo the Clown. Sorry, parents, there wasn't a lot of socially redeeming activity in this neighborhood, but there were plenty of laughs and pop-cultural gibes at celebrities like Woody Allen and Jack Nicholson.

Beetlejuice performed well in its Saturday morning ABC slot, and even better when new episodes were telecast daily by the Fox network starting in 1991. The Fox episodes broadened the series' scope to include parodies of fairy tales and favorite motion pictures, each given the special touch of Beetlejuice's "magic juicing finger" (don't ask). By 1992, the series was the fifth most popular daytime cartoon show with children ages five to 11 — and the *third* most popular with teenagers. Its ratings and its 1990 Emmy award for "Outstanding Animated Program" were certainly deserved: Unlike many other TV cartoons based on live action films *(Back to the Future, The Original Ghostbusters)*, *Beetlejuice* was one of the few animated series to equal and even occasionally improve upon its source material — an indication that Tim Burton's onscreen production credit was more than just honorary.

BELLE AND SEBASTIAN. Nickelodeon: June 1984–1990. MK Company/ Visual 80 Productions/Toho Co. Ltd.

Belle and Sebastian, a Japanese-produced series of 52 half hour cartoons, was based on a popular live action British Broadcasting Corporation TV serial of 1966, written and directed by French film actress Cecile Aubrey. Best described as a European *Lassie, Belle and Sebastian* told of the warm relationship between a dog — in this case a large white "wild" sheepdog named Belle — and Sebastian, a young boy abandoned by gypsies in the French alpine village of Saint-Martin and adopted by elderly mountain man Cesar. Plotlines were complicated with a soap-opera subplot involving Cesar's daughter Angelina (Sebastian's surrogate mother), her brother Jean, and the emotional wedge driven between brother and sister by a handsome young stranger named Norbert.

Unlike the stories in *Lassie*, Sebastian did not have to be extracted by a smarter pet from an endless parade of dangerous situations thanks to the lad's foolhardiness and lack of respect for his elders. The perils in *Belle and Sebastian* were due to the alpine terrain (some superb background art here), the bitter winter weather, and the insensitivity of people who tended to shun Sebastian because of his parentless status. Adopting a deceptively relaxed pace, the series demonstrated how two sensitive, caring souls could survive in a difficult, sometimes hostile environment.

Consigned to the Sunday afternoon ghetto by the Nickelodeon cable service, *Belle and Sebastian* nonetheless attained enough fan support to remain on American television for six seasons. Its potent story values, strong character development and excellent draftsmanship cry out for a release to videocassette.

THE BERENSTAIN BEARS. CBS: 9/14/1985–9/5/1987. Joe Cates Co. Ltd./ Southern Star Productions/Hanna-Barbera Australia. Produced by Buzz Potamkin. Developed for TV by Joe Cates. Creative director, Chris Cuddington. Associate producer, Gordon Kent. Animation directors, Jon McClenahan and Darrell Van Citters. Story editor, Rowby Goren. Music by Elliot Lawrence. Executive in charge of production, Keith Amor. Voices: Ruth Buzzi (Mama); Brian Cummings (Papa Q. Bear); Christina Lange (Sister); David Mendenhall (Brother); Frank Welker (Raffish Ralph); and John Rodine, and Marissa Mendenhall.

The *Berenstain Bears* — Papa, Mama, Brother and Sister — started in the mid-1970s as the hollow tree–dwelling protagonists of a series of children's books by writer/illustrators Stan and Jan Berenstain, who previously had forged a long career of panel cartoons revolving around the adventures of suburban children. In the *Bears* books, simple storylines would demonstrate in entertaining fashion the values of responsibility and consideration for others. The Berenstains avoided condescension and sugarcoating, tackling subject matter ranging from division of family chores to the more serious dilemma of keeping children clear of unchaperoned weekend parties. The books were complemented by a series of animated specials produced by the Cates Brothers Company for NBC, which ran sporadically from 1979 through 1984. All five of these specials were early entries in the children's videocassette market, where they were well received for their inherent prosocial content—though video critic Harold Schechter took the tapes to task for the Bear children's tendency to welcome "friendly strangers" without regard for personal safety.

When the property was transformed into a weekly series for CBS in 1985, it retained its positive values (and even answered Schechter's concern over the "stranger" issue in one episode), though some of its special qualities were diluted by the necessity of churning out a new half hour program a week, two separate plotlines per program, for two seasons. The weekly *Berenstain Bears* kept the "Beartown" and "Bear Country" setting and the strong indivisible ties between the various members of the Bear family, and their strong friendship with such neighbors as Mayor Horace T. Honeypot, Big Paw Bear, and eccentric scientist Actual Factual. But too often, *Berenstain Bears* settled for warmed-over situation comedy devices, usually initiated by Raffish Ralph, a strawhatted con man and petty crook who cheerfully described himself as "rotten to the core" (maybe he should have read one of the Berenstain books and gotten wise to himself). Ralph's "get rich quick" schemes and his currying favor with the evil Weasel McGreed gang threatened to plunge the denizens of Beartown into poverty and despair (their economy was based on honey rather than money), and in one installment nearly caused the metropolis to collapse during an earthquake! The Raffish Ralph–motivated episodes were okay, but *The Berenstain Bears* worked best when concentrating on family values—one of the few cartoon shows of the 1980s where the "prosocial" aspects worked better than the straight-out comedy.

BEST OF SCOOBY-DOO see **SCOOBY-DOO**

BEVERLY HILLS TEENS. Syndicated: 1987. K K & D/DIC Enterprises/ Access Syndication. Executive producer, Andy Heyward. Supervising producer, Robby London. Supervising director,

Michael Maliani. Animation director, Bruno Bianchi. Producer for KK&D, Tetsuo Katayama. Story editors, Jack Mendelsohn, Jack Olesker, Mike O'Mahoney, Brynne Stephens. Developed by Jack Olesker, Michael Maliani and Barry O'Brien. Music by Haim Saban and Shuki Levy. Production supervisor, Eric S. Rollman. Voices: Michael Beattie (Buck/ Wilshire); Karen Bernstein (Tara/Jett); Hadley Kay (Radley/Guitar); Corrine Koslo (Nikki Darling); Mary Long (Larke/ Dog); Stephen McMulkin (Pierce Thorndyke); Tracy Moore (Jillian/Bianca/Blaise); Jonathan Potts (Troy); Mark Saunders (Gig/Dad); Joanne Schellenberg (Switchboard); Linda Sorenson (Fifi); Michelle St. John (Shanelle Spencer); and Terry Hawkes, and Sean Roberge.

Somehow it was logical that a half hour cartoon series about a bunch of filthy rich teenagers would begin and end in the waning days of the "Gelt Without Guilt" 1980s. The protagonists of *Beverly Hills Teens* were more than comfortably well off; they lived in mansions the size of European dukedoms, attended a palatial high school with marbled halls and Louis XIV furnishings, cruised the mall with battalions of servants, and tooled around their Beverly Hills neighborhoods in chauffeur-driven limousines equipped with backseat swimming pools. And there you have the story—and the single joke—of *Beverly Hills Teens*.

With a premise dragged kicking and screaming from *Richie Rich* [q.v.], humorless scripts, unappealing characters and listless animation, the daily *Beverly Hills Teens* was doomed to last but a single syndicated season (reruns popped up as part of Access Syndication's *Maxie's World* [q.v.] package in 1989). This left the "wealthy teen" field wide open for Fox Television's live action nighttime series *Beverly Hills 90210* a few seasons later. Time will tell if this constitutes progress.

THE BIG WORLD OF LITTLE ADAM. Syndicated: 1964. Little Adam Productions, Inc./Banner Films. Produced by Fred Ladd. Voices: John Megna (Little Adam), Craig Seckler (Wilbur).

Bespectacled Little Adam and his littler brother Wilbur appeared in the animated wraparounds of this series, which was chiefly comprised of officially sanctioned color documentary film from the files of the National Aeronautics and Space Administration. The *Big World of Little Adam* was NASA's valentine to the first generation of the Space Age—back in the days before the Shuttle was commonplace, when parents let their kids get up at 4 A.M. to await the countdown for the latest manned rocket launch.

Frequently mistitled "Big World of Little Atom" in earlier reference books, *The Big World of Little Adam* is one of those utterly obscure properties that is liable to be written off by the casual researcher as never having gotten past a pilot episode. Yet the 110 five-minute *Little Adam* episodes sold quite well on a regional basis in 1964, a syndicated career halted only when the series was rendered anachronistic by NASA's rapid technological advances. The voice of Little Adam was supplied by John Megna, brother of actress Connie Stevens and a very busy performer in his own right; he is perhaps best remembered for his role as the heroine's intellectual young neighbor in *To Kill a Mockingbird* (1962).

BIGFOOT AND THE MUSCLE MACHINE *see* **SUPER SUNDAY**

BIKER MICE FROM MARS. Syndicated: 1993. New World Family Filmworks/Brentwood Television Funnies/Marvel/Worldwide Sports & Entertainment/Genesis. Executive producers, Rick Ungar and Norman Singer. Produced and directed by Tom Tataranowicz. Executive in charge of production, Michealine Cristini. Produced in association with Worldwide Sports and Entertainment Inc. Created by Rick Ungar. Developed for TV by Frank Ward, Dennis McCoy, Pamela Hickey and Mike Young. Story editor, Bob Forward. Motorcycles designed by Rick Cascelli. Music by Will Anderson. Overseas animation facilities, Philippine Animation Studio Inc. Overseas supervisor, Larry Cariou. Voices: Dorian Harewood (Modo); Rob Paulsen (Throttle); Ian Ziering (Vinnie); Leeza Miller-McGee (Charlie); Morgan Sheppard (Lawrence Limburger); Susan Silo (Dr. Karbunkle); Jess Harnell (Sweet Georgie Brown); Brad Garrett (Grease Pit); and Neil Ross.

The *Biker Mice from Mars* were three muscular humanized rodents, space-cycling leaders of a Martian revolt against the conquering Plutarkians. The latter race had (A Warning For Us All!) destroyed their own planet through greed-motivated ecological rape, and afterwards zipped through the universe using their ill-gotten wealth to buy up other planets, then gutting them and wiping out the citizenry to make room for themselves. The three Biker Mice—evidently the last of their breed—were visually-impaired Throttle, one-armed Modo and half-faced Vinnie, all three victims of the mutilating lab experiments of evil Plutarkian Dr. Karbunkle.

Pursued through the cosmos by the enemy, the Biker Mice varoomed in space bikes towards earth, where they landed in Chicago, crashing through the scoreboard at "Quigley Field," home of the Chicago "Nubbs." Here is where they made their earthly headquarters, with friendly "Last Chance Garage" owner Charley—very much a girl, despite the name—acting as their go-between with the human race. Charley had problems of her own in the person of eco-villain Lawrence Limburger, a millionaire land developer who wanted to use the garage as cornerstone for his latest environment-ravaging project. The Mice recognized the "human" Limburger as one of their Plutarkian enemies, sent by his superiors to strip the Earth of its natural riches and decimate the populace. In league with Limburger was another old enemy, Dr. Karbunkle, who wanted to pick up his sadistic lab experiments where he'd left off. Other henchmen included the moronic Greasepit and a cybernaut Schwarzenegger soundalike called—and we're not one bit surprised—The Exterminator.

Those familiar with *Teenage Mutant Ninja Turtles* (q.v.) will easily recognize its numerous similarities with *Biker Mice from Mars*: mixed-species heroes, Megalomaniac villains, dumdum secondary baddies, beautiful young woman acting as the Mice's liaison with the world (the counterpart to *Turtles* heroine April O'Neil) and so on. Add to these such other *Biker Mice* liftings from *Turtles* as the Mice's fondness for junk food (hot dogs and root beer in place of the Turtles' pizza), rock music (from bogus groups like "Metallican" and "Guns and Noses") and rallying cries along the lines of "Let's Rock—And Ride!" and "It's tail-whippin' time!" The most pronounced resemblance between the two properties was the light-

Vinnie from *Biker Mice from Mars*.

hearted, self-mocking tone. When offered cheese as a snack, the Biker Mice recoil in disgust; and upon being introduced to Charlie, who expresses surprise at the sight of pumped-up vermin, the Mice reply, "Well, what did you expect—turtles?"

Most producers of the "animal superhero" programs created in the wake of *Teenage Mutant Ninja Turtles*, notably *The Adventures of T-Rex* (q.v.) and *Swat Kats* (q.v.), bent over backward in print insisting that these were not imitations. In this respect, the creators of *Biker Mice from Mars* were refreshingly candid. Not only did they readily admit that their series was designed to emulate *Turtles*, but they also proclaimed that the weekly half-hour *Biker Mice* was deliberately commissioned to be the *Turtle*'s successor.

In 1992, *Teenage Mutant Ninja Turtles* was showing signs of faltering, producing a mere $200 million in merchandising profits compared to a 1991 highpoint of $1 billion. Though the series continued producing a handful of new episodes for its CBS network timeslot, the syndicated ver-

sion was terminated. Merchandisers wanted to keep the ball rolling, so a call went out for a new *Turtles*. Rick Ungar, president of Marvel Productions (riding high in 1993 with *X-Men*) responded with *Biker Mice from Mars*, which not only emphasized the aforementioned *Turtles* earmarks but even emulated the pattern of the earlier program's publicity buildup by premiering the Mice in the summer of 1993 in comic book form. To make certain that the public would be saturated by these latest superfolk, 130 American companies were granted licenses to market *Biker Mice* paraphernalia (including several struggling smaller companies who'd been left out of the *Turtles* windfall) while both Sega and Nintendo began assembling video games—all before the first episode had premiered. The logic behind this was to accelerate the five years' work that it took to popularize *Teenage Mutant Ninja Turtles*—to whip up a *Biker Mice from Mars* craze in less than five months.

Biker Mice secured playdates in 94 percent of the U.S., with Marvel sending out tyro promotional teams to the biggest markets. In Chicago, where the action of *Biker Mice* was set, three actors dressed as the flap-eared heroes made an appearance in Quigley—er, Wrigley Field at a game between the New York Mets and the Chicago Nubbs—er, Cubs. One of the Biker Mice wannabes actually threw out the first ball. That the Cubs subsequently lost to the Mets was all but ignored in the stunt's newspaper coverage (nobody likes an omen). The independent UHF outlet carrying *Biker Mice* in Chicago, WPWR-TV (after a tough and expensive bidding war with three other channels), was so confident of a hit that it ran the cartoon series in prime time—with a downplayed contingency plan to shuffle the Mice to daytime if the series couldn't cut it.

If you liked *Teenage Mutant Ninja Turtles*, you might have been partial to this energetic but second-string derivation. Newspaper critics were none too friendly to *Biker Mice from Mars*—not because of its underdeveloped animation, but because it was perceived as wallowing in mindless violence, this at a time when cartoon makers had promised on bended knee to soften this aspect of TV animation. Marvel's Rick Ungar was quick to defend his baby by noting that no one was ever killed on *Biker Mice*. Like all other producers of his ilk, he called the series an "action show." Moreover, Ungar insisted that everything he'd put into the program was at the command of youngsters from whom he'd elicited suggestions. "You'd be amazed at how many things are in this series because kids told me they should be," said the producer, amazed.

This bowing to the will of the 7–11 crowd sorely offended *Biker Mice*'s critics. While the kids might have cherished dialogue blasts like "Shut up, scumball!" adults were less enchanted. Nor were they convinced that *Biker Mice* would entertain anyone over the age of nine. Most critics echoed the Chicago *Tribune*'s Jennifer Mangan, who "failed to find" the two to seven jokes per episode that Rick Ungar claimed he'd aimed over the heads of the youngsters for the amusement of the grownups. We can't say as of this writing if *Biker Mice from Mars* will fulfill its destiny as successor to the *Teenage Mutant Ninja Turtles* throne—but *we* can't always find those two to seven jokes either.

BILL AND TED'S EXCELLENT ADVENTURES. CBS: 9/15/1990–8/31/1991. Fox: 9/14/1991–9/5/1992. Big Star International Co./Spectrum Animation Studios/DIC/Orion TV/Nelson Entertainment. Creative supervisor and executive producer, Andy Heyward. Executive producer, Robby London. Produced and directed by Stan Philips. Story editor, Judy Rothman. Music by Murray McFadden, Timothy Mulholland. Supervising music editor, John Mortarotti. Voices: Keanu Reeves (1990-91 season only); Alex Winter (1990-91 season only); George Carlin (1990-91 season only); and Evan Richards, Christopher Kennedy, Don Lake, Alison Court, Dan Hennessey, Ray Kahnert, Susan Boyd, Tara Charendoff, Paulina Gillis, Marilyn Lightstone, Judy Marshak, Greg Morton, Susan Roman, Andrew Sabiston, Stuart Stone, Greg Swanson and Marlow Vella.

Bill and Ted's Excellent Adventure was an endearingly stupid 1989 comedy film with a premise far more mature than most of its fans. The eponymous heroes, residents of the California community of San Dimas, were a pair of airheaded teens in danger of flunking their high school history finals, which would end their dreams of forming a rock group called "The Wild Stallions." Enter Rufus, a visitor from the future, who offered to help the boys pass their exams. Rufus had a vested interest: His futuristic society worshipped (in the true religious sense) the music that Bill and Ted would write and produce once they did form their band; without that music, Rufus' civilization would not exist. Thus the boys were transported by their new mentor to various past historical events through the facilities of a time-travelling telephone booth. In the end, Bill and Ted pass their exam with flying colors by producing such "eyewitnesses" as Napoleon, Lincoln, Socrates and Joan of Arc!

Before embarking on an even better movie sequel, 1991's *Bill and Ted's Bogus Journey*, the *Excellent Adventure* production team combined forces with DIC Productions to create a weekly, half hour Saturday morning cartoon series based on the film. For its first season on CBS, *Bill and Ted's Excellent Adventures* (note the plural—they had 13 weeks to fill) had the advantage of voice work from the film's three stars: Alex Winter as Bill, Keanu Reeves as Ted and George Carlin as Rufus. That these performers were replaced by "regular" TV cartoon voice artists for the series' second season on the Fox Network didn't really matter much, because the animated *Bill and Ted* never truly captured the ingratiating goofiness of the original film. The time travel premise was still in force, with the added "history is inviolate" twist of the boys having to make sure past events came to fruition lest the altered chronology wreak havoc on their own existences. Unfortunately, while the animation was smoothly handled, the scriptwriting was very standard and the characterizations pat and predictable. Add *Bill and Ted's Excellent Adventures* to such equally tepid TV projects as *Back to the Future* (q.v.) and *Toxic Crusaders* (q.v.) and you have a disturbingly evergrowing list of cartoon series based on hit fantasy movies which failed to equal the impact of their live-action sources.

THE BIONIC SIX. Syndicated: 1987. LJN Toys/TMS Entertainment/MCA TV. Producers: Yutaka Fujioka, Sachiko Tsuneda, Gerald Baldwin. Voices: Norman Bernard (J.D. Bennett); Carol Bilger (Helen Bennett); Bobbi Block (Meg Bennett); Jennifer Darling (Madame O); Jim MacGeorge (Dr. Scarab); Hal Rayle (Eric

Bennett); Neil Ross (F.L.U.F.F.I.); John Stephenson (Jack Bennett/Klunk); Brian Tochi (Bunji Bennett); Frank Welker (Glove/Mechanic/Chopper); and Shuko Akune, Bever-Leigh Banfield, Susan Blu, Arthur Burghardt, Michael Mish, Howard Morris, Alan Oppenheimer, and Michael Sheehan.

The *Bionic Six* began as a weekly syndicated series in April of 1987, then matriculated into a biweekly and finally a daily by September of that year. The series centered around the peacekeeping activities of two bionic (part-human, part-machine) crimefighters named Bionic One and Bionic Two (the mind boggles at such inspiration), who were thrust into parenthood by adopting four multiracial orphans — all of whom, like "Mom" and "Dad," enjoyed extraordinary powers thanks to an electronic device worn around the wrist. The six superheroes — bearing nicknames like I.Q. and Sport One — adopted the suburban guise of the "Bennett" family, occasionally bursting into rock music in the manner of the late and unlamented Partridges. The villain, who evidently attended the same postgraduate course in Megalomania as all the other animated science fiction baddies, was Dr. Scarab.

Conceived by Japan's LJN Toys (see also *Hello Kitty's Furry Tales Theatre* and *ThunderCats*) in hopes of marketing action figures and video games based on the leading characters, *The Bionic Six* was gone by 1989. Its last episode was titled "That's All, Folks"; there were those who would have chosen the more befitting "That's Enough, Folks."

BIRDMAN AND THE GALAXY TRIO. NBC: 9/9/1967–12/28/1968. Hanna-Barbera. Produced and directed by William Hanna and Joseph Barbera. Story directors: Art Davis, Paul Sommer. Animation director, Charles Nichols. Character design by Alex Toth. Music by Hoyt Curtin and Ted Nichols. Animators included Ed Love and Bill Hutten. Production supervisor, Howard Hanson. Voices: Keith Andes (Ray Randall, a.k.a. Birdman); Don Messick (Falcon 7/Vapor Man); Dick Beals (Birdboy); Virginia Eiler (Galaxy Girl); Ted Cassidy (Meteor Man). *Birdman and the Galaxy Trio* was created for Hanna-Barbera by gifted comic book artist Alex Toth (see *Space*

Angel). This 18-episode, half hour Saturday morning adventure series featured ordinary mortal police investigator Ray Randall, who was endowed by the Egyptian sun god Ra with super powers, foremost among these the gift of flight and the ability to summon up solar energy beams through his knuckles. In the company of his young sidekick Birdboy and his eagle Avenger, Birdman (aka Ray Randall) fought the obligatory neverending battle against evil and "spread the light of justice into the darkest recesses of the human soul," at the behest of his superior officer, Falcon 7.

The Galaxy Trio, whose seven-minute exploits were sandwiched between the two weekly *Birdman* cartoon shorts, were also blessed with astonishing powers: Vapor Man could take on any gaslike form, literally becoming a human cloud; Galaxy Girl was able to journey throughout space without giving the laws of gravity a second thought; and Meteor Man was a Hulklike creature of enormous strength, principally manifested in his outsized right fist. Why these characters needed a spaceship (the Condor Seven) is problematic, since the Galaxy Trio seemed perfectly capable of traversing the heavens without any mechanical support.

Though the dialogue was overbaked and the leading character was burdened with having to sing his own name in a sappy tenor warble ("BIIIirRrdMaAannnn!"), the accomplished preproduction model and layout sheets of Alex Toth helped to lift the quality of *Birdman and the Galaxy Trio* ever so slightly above average. The series might have had a second season had not its dependence upon violent action made it a prime target for the media-monitor spoilsports, who strongarmed NBC into cancelling all its adventure cartoon series in 1968.

THE BISKITTS. CBS: 9/17/1983–9/1/1984; 5/30/1985–9/7/1985. Hanna-Barbera. Produced by Art Scott. Directed by Ray Patterson, Oscar Dufau, George Gordon, Carl Urbano, John Walker and Rudy Zamora. Music supervision by Paul DeKorte. Voices: Darryl Hickman (Waggs); B.J. Ward (Lady); Dick Beals (Scat); Kathleen Helppie (Sweets); Bob Holt (Spinner/Bump/Flip); Kip King (Shecky); Jerry Houser (Shiner); Peter Cullen (Scratch/Fang/Dog Foot); Kenneth

Mars (Max/Fetch/Snarl); Jennifer Darling (Wiggle); Marshall Efron (Mooch); Henry Gibson (Downer); and Mark L. Taylor.

Hanna-Barbera's *The Biskitts* was a period piece about a bunch of tiny puppies (as tall as a dog biscuit, hence the title) who guarded the crown jewels of Biskitt Castle's recently deceased monarch. Protecting the treasure under the leadership of top Biskitt Waggs were such steadfast canines as Lady, Blabber, Scat, Bump, Bones, Shiner, Flip, Downer, Mooch, and Wiggle (this last-named character was an anachronistic "valley girl" type). King Max, the cruel ruler of neighboring Lower Suburbia and the brother of the Biskitts' late king, did his worst to snatch the treasure, aided by his own team of bowwows — Fang and Snarl — and his clumsy jester Shecky (the significance of the jester's name was lost on anyone who hadn't grown up watching comic Shecky Greene haunt the talk shows of the 1960s). An additional nemesis, whose interest in the Biskitts was culinary rather than monetary, was the ravenous Scratch the wildcat.

This enormous cast of characters was out of work when *The Biskitts* ceased production after 14 half hour episodes: cute animals were, after all, only cute animals. Hanna-Barbera had already covered the "mini-creature" concept one year earlier with *Shirt Tales* (q.v.) and would do the same to better effect years later with *Pound Puppies* (q.v.).

BLACKSTAR. CBS: 9/12/1981–9/11/ 1982. Filmation. Executive vice president in charge of creative affairs, Joe Mazzuca. Director in charge of animation, Gwen Wetzler. Directed by John Armstrong, Ed Friedman, Lou Zukor, Marsh Lamore, Marja Dahl, Shelby Kelly, Ernest Schmidt, Louis Chavras. Story editor, Tom Ruegger. Music by Yvette Blais and Jeff Michael. Voices: George DiCenzo (Blackstar); Pat Pinney (Balkar/Terra/Klone); Frank Welker (Gossamear/Burble/Rif); Alan Oppenheimer (Carpo/Overlord); Linda Gary (Mara).

Astronaut John Blackstar, sucked through a black hole in space, found himself on the planet Sagar, where with the help of laser-powered sorceress Mara he aided in the rebellion against the despotic Overlord of the Underworld (who looked like a talking totem pole), battling monsters all the while. Most of the rest of

Blackstar was a sponge of past inspiration. From *Star Wars* came the "battle against the Empire" angle and the fact that the Overlord was the spiritual evil twin to Blackstar, just as *Star Wars*' Darth Vader and Obie Wan Kanobe were two opposites from the same power source (*Blackstar's* theme music was also as close to *Star Wars*' opening fanfare as one could get without being sued). From the "sword and sorcery" genre came Blackstar's noble dragon-steed Warlock and Blackstar's source of super strength, the Power Star. From *The Hobbit* came the tree-dwelling Trobbits, the dwarves of Sagar (packaged in a Disneyesque grouping of seven), while the dwarves' speeded-up voices invoked memories of *Alvin and the Chipmunks*. And from the live action TV series *Space: 1999* came the "elf warrior" Klone, who like Catherine Schell on *Space: 1999* was able to metamorphose into various life forms (he also looked a lot like *Star Trek's* Mr. Spock). Steal from many, it's research. Or it's *Blackstar.*

The single truly original aspect of the series was never seen by the viewers. According to Filmation historians Michael Swanigan and Darrell McNeil, Blackstar was supposed to have been African American . . . a *genuine* "black star." But CBS, which honored racial balance more in the breach than in the observance, felt that this might frighten potential sponsors, so Blackstar totally negated the meaning of his name by turning white (albeit with a deep suntan).

The otherwise derivative *Blackstar* would itself be consciously imitated a few years later as Filmation's *He-Man and the Masters of the Universe* (q.v.). Recognizing the similarity, Filmation put the 13 *Blackstar* episodes in syndication after striking gold with *He-Man* late in 1983. This time around, the "original" managed to look even less original than it had in 1981, and its abysmal animation — even by Filmation's none too exacting standards — was all the more glaring. One beneficial by-product of *Blackstar* is that it represented the first TV cartoon work for artist/writer Bruce Timm, later one of the principal motivators behind the brilliant *Batman: The Animated Series* (q.v.) — which had as executive producer another *Blackstar* veteran, Tom Ruegger. Timm's artistic finesse and Ruegger's expansive storytelling skills would be far better served by *Batman* than they were on *Blackstar*, where any glimmer of ambition and talent was stifled by nonexistent production values.

BLAST-OFF BUZZARD *see* **THE C. B. BEARS**

BOBBY'S WORLD. Fox: 9/8/1990–. Film Roman Productions/Fox Children's Television Network. Executive producers: Howie Mandel and Phil Roman. Created by Howie Mandel. Developed for TV by Jim Stahl and Jim Fisher. Produced by Mitch Schauer. Directed by Berny Wolf and Ron Myrick. Story editor: Dianne Dixon. Music by John Tesh. Main title music by John Tesh and Michael Hanna. Animation produced at Wang Film Productions and Cuckoo's Nest Studios. Live action sequences: Produced by John Calas. Directed by John Peter. Written by Howie Mandel. Voices: Howie Mandel, Gail Matthias, Charity James, Frank Welker, Tino Insara, Benny Grant, Gary Owens, Debi Derryberry, Dan Castellaneta, Miriam Flynn, John Moschitta.

Bobby's World was the invention of funnyman Howie Mandel, who'd been utilizing the character of his four-year-old alter ego "Bobby" for years in his comedy act. For the purposes of the cartoon series, Bobby was given the last name Generic — pronounced with emphasis on the first syllable — and Mandel's fondness for R-rated material was obliterated. Bobby lived with his bullheaded father, his cliché-spouting mother (the first visibly pregnant woman on a Saturday morning cartoon), his taunting older brother Derek and his whiny sister Kelly. The boy's best friends were his neighbor Jackie, his sheepdog Roger, and occasionally his loudmouthed Uncle Ted. Each weekly half hour illustrated a devastating dilemma facing Bobby, who used his rather expansive imagination to determine the best methods of solution; Bobby's unfettered Walter Mittyesque daydreams were the real "World" of the title. The voice of Bobby was supplied by Howie Mandel, whose facility in the falsetto range had previously served him well in providing the intonations for "Gizmo" in the 1984 movie *Gremlins*. Mandel also appeared in the live action wraparounds of each animated *Bobby's World*, setting up the premise at the beginning of the show and trad-

ing quips with the cartoon Bobby at the end.

This Film Roman production was the series selected by Fox Children's Network president Margaret Loesch as her network's entree into the world of Saturday morning "block" programming in the fall of 1990. Considering its lack of familiar characters and its comparatively soft nature (soft even when dealing with something as provocative as a child's reaction to the death of a loved one), *Bobby's World* was according to Loesch "a risk because it doesn't have some of the elements that kids find popular right now, like you would find in [*Teenage Mutant*] *Ninja Turtles* [q.v.] and *Ghostbusters* [q.v.], but it's got something special." That "special" quality of juxtaposing the banalities and iniquities of real life with the limitless imagination of a child wasn't new to *Bobby's World*, having previously been explored by such theatrical cartoons as UPA's *Christopher Crumpet* and Warner Bros.' *From A to Z-Z-Z-Z*, and by the evergreen TV series *Muppet Babies* [q.v.]. But the impressionistic "1950s" background design, broadly delineated character art, and rollercoaster pacing made *Bobby's World* impossible to ignore. Its only drawback was uneven scriptwork, which frequently failed to sustain the strength of the premise and the visuals.

To date, Howie Mandel's brainchild has survived four seasons, and though its "kid's viewpoint" concept has been matched and surpassed by Nickelodeon's *Doug* (q.v.) and *Rugrats* (q.v.), *Bobby's World* has more than held its own — even when playing way over its target audience's head by serving up takeoffs on adult-oriented films like *Misery* and *Psycho*.

THE BOING BOING SHOW *see* **THE GERALD McBOING BOING SHOW**

BONKERS. Disney Channel: 2/1993–9/1993. Syndicated: September 1993. Walt Disney Television/Buena Vista. Supervising producers, Robert Taylor and Bob Hathcock. Produced by Hank Tucker, David Schwartz. Coproducer/supervising story editor, Duane Cappizi. Directed by Roy Wilson. Story editors, Carter Crocker and Ralph Sanchez. Written by John Behnke, Rob Humphrey, Jim Peterson. Animation directors: Carole Beers, Vincent Bassols, Charles A. Nichols, Bob

The cast of *Bobby's World*, with creator Howie Mandel.

Shellhorn, James T. Walker, Terence Harrison. Music by Mark Watters. Theme music produced, arranged and written by Randy Petersen and Kevin Quinn. Voice director, Ginny McSwain. Animation facilities: Sunwoo Animation, Kennedy Cartoons Inc. (Manila). Sunwoo director, Park Dong Kwun. Kennedy director, Jim Kennedy. Voices: Jim Cummings (Bonkers/ Sgt. Lucky Piquel); and Jeff Bennett, Earl Boen, Corey Burton, Carla DeVito, Brad Garrett, Dana Hill, Maurice LaMarche, Alan Oppenheimer, Ron Perlman, Bob Ridgely, Neil Ross, and April Winchell.

Bonkers D. Bobcat, the hyperactive "former 'toon star" first seen on Disney's CBS series *Raw Toonage* (q.v.), was given his own weekly, half hour starring series on the Disney Channel pay-cable service in April of 1993. The uninhibited but well-meaning polka-dotted Bonkers was here working on behalf (?) of the Tinseltown (Disney-ese for "Hollywood") Police Force. This was purely a political move: Bonkers had inadvertently saved A-list Tinseltown resident Donald Duck from harm, and politically ambitious Police Chief Kennifkey thought he might elicit the "Toon vote" in the future mayoral race by putting the Bobcat on the force.

This didn't sit well with long-suffering human detective Sgt. Lucky Piquel, who found himself teamed with Bonkers (Disney veteran Jim Cummings did the voices of both Bonkers and Piquel — perhaps this prolific voice artist's finest hour). Foremost among several oil-and-water problems with the Bonker/Piquel coupling was the fact that a toon and a human were capable of doing entirely different physical feats — and consequently suffered entirely different degrees of pain. In short, Bonkers could survive an anvil on the noggin, but the results were disastrous for Piquel. Here was the series' "prosocial" point — that cartoons weren't real life and vice versa — although the message didn't overwhelm the laughter as on other moralizing TV toons.

All this was an extension of the central situation of the 1988 live-and-cartoon feature film *Who Framed Roger Rabbit*, which served as the unofficial model for *Bonkers* (the film was set in "Toontown"). And just as in *Roger Rabbit*, the principal characters rubbed shoulders with a number of Toon celebrities — mostly several well-established Disney creations like Scrooge McDuck, the Mad Hatter from *Alice in Wonderland* (1951), and the derby-hatted spook who first appeared in the 1937 Mickey Mouse vehicle *Lonesome Ghosts*. Mickey himself figured in one episode in which an unscrupulous movie producer tried to woo the legendary Mouse away from Disney with a fat, fringe-benefit contract.

This last pop-cultural conceit was typical of *Bonkers*, which had more cutting-edge verbal wit than the usual Disney product. In fact, at times the series looked like a Warner Bros. project, what with its scattershot satirical snipes at anything that moved. In typical Disney fashion, the "hip" gags on *Bonkers* were never arbitrary or nonsequitur, but instead tightly bound to the storyline. In one excellent example, Bonkers and Lt. Piquel were put in charge of a Toon Rehabilitation Program, designed to reform "rogue" toon characters and get them back in the mainstream. Their subject was a Tasmanian Devil take-off named "The Louse," who ate everything in sight while the two cops diligently studied their namby-pamby "toon psychology" book. Within a carefully paced yet gag-packed half hour, the episode managed to skewer political hacks, Warner Bros.' tendency to forgo plotlines in favor of mindless mayhem, misguided political correctness, Leon Buscaglia and Dr. Spock. This kitchen-sink approach didn't always work (the Disney people weren't psychologically suited to it), but when *Bonkers* was on target—as in the afore-mentioned episode—it was pure gold.

Bonkers was harder to pull off than most other Disney TV properties. The series had to be 100 percent animated in order to illustrate the radical contrast between the "real" and the "toon" characters: Lucky Piquel and the other human characters had to move in a smoother, more lifelike fashion than the helter-skelter Bonkers, who in turn moved at a different pace than the *other* Toons. As a result, the production team (which included facilities in Asia and the Philippines) frequently had to put in Golden Time to get the episodes finished on schedule. Even so, the expected Disney gloss and finesse was in full flower; it helped to compensate for the fact that the *Bonkers* characters, though undeniably funny, weren't nearly as appealing as those on such other Disney TVers as *DuckTales* and *Chip 'n' Dale's Rescue Rangers* (see individual entries on these series).

BOTS MASTER. Syndicated: 1993. Nuoptix/Avi Arad/Créativité et Développement/All-American Television. A co-production of Créativité et Développement/Avi Arad/ABC SA/AB Productions/Telecast Intl./Nuoptix Corp. 3-D. Executive producers, Jean Chalopin and Avi Arad. Produced by Mark Taylor and Xavier Picard. Associate producer, Victor Villegas and Christine Blache. Directed by Xavier Picard. Written by Jean Chalopin. English story adaptation by Jack Olesker. Design by Finn Torquin. Music by Alain Garcia, produced by Saban International Paris. Animation produced by KK C&D Asia; US Production director, Toshiyuki Hiruma. Animation director, Shigeo Koshi. Animation producer, Takahiko Tsuchiya. 3-D Scenes: system by Nuoptix; produced by Metropolitan Entertainment, Metrocel Animation, Pixi Box. Voices: Ian Corlett, Richard Cox, Mike Donovan, Steve Guilinetti, Mark Hildreth, Janyce Jaud, Surya Keller, Terry Klassen, Sam Kouth, Rob Lehane, Gusse Mankuma, Pamela Martin, Crystaleen Obray, Kim Restell, Chelan Simmons, Dale Wilson.

Bots Master (originally titled *Z Z Bots*) was at first glance a routine humanized-robots daily half hour. Set in the future, the series predicted that androids and cybernauts would have all the manual-labor and transportation jobs, allowing humans more free time. The Robot Megafact Corporation, better known as The Corp, built most of these "Bots." But the Corp's Dr. Hisss, Lord Paradim and Lady Frenzy had a hidden "take over the world" agenda, with robots being clandestinely prepared for the event. Computer geek Zig Zulander—"ZZ"—was wise to the Corp, but was powerless by himself, since the conglomerate had several important political and media people in its pocket. Aided by little sister Blitzy, the outcast ZZ fought the Corp and its team of "Humabots" (malevolent mutants led by a pile of nuts and bolts named Freen) by utilizing his own team of benign bots: Tools, Ninju, Twig, and several others, their names extensions of their personalities and skills ("Bats" was a baseball bot, "Bogie" a golf bot, and so on).

Heard this song before? Well, yes, except—*Bots Master* owned the distinction of being the first cartoon series regularly telecast in 3-D (earlier experiments with the stereoptic process on *Yo Yogi* [see *Yogi Bear*] had been intermittent). Within each episode there was a two-minute 3-D sequence, wherein the home viewers were cued to put on their special glasses with the words "Laser Time," then instructed to remove their specs with the phrase "Game Over." Though not brilliantly animated, these 3-D vignettes, produced by the Nuoptix Company, were the best and sharpest ever available to American television (Nuoptix had established itself with a spectacular 3-D demonstration during the halftime festivities of Super Bowl XXIII in 1989—and since that time had improved its already remarkable process). As a bonus, the scenes were processed to avoid the double-vision effect that might cause eyestrain to those not lucky enough to have the necessary glasses.

Bots Master had so much going for it on the technical end that it seems almost ungrateful to complain that its scripts and animation were mired in cliché and predictability. Perhaps the producers should have been warned that story and production deficiencies were what killed off the 3-D movie craze of the early 1950s. *Bots Master*, despite its visual dynamics, had little to offer for the vast majority of 2-D TV viewers.

BOZO THE CLOWN. Syndicated: 1959. Larry Harmon Productions/Ted Ticktin Productions/Jayark Films. Animation directed by Paul Fennell. Voices: Larry Harmon (Bozo/Butchy Boy); Paul Frees (Almost everybody else).

Bozo the Clown became an animated series as an afterthought. The Bozo character first drew breath in a series of Capitol children's records of the 1940s, their dustjackets decorated with pop-up pictures of "The World's Most Famous Clown." An early attempt to produce a live action Bozo TV series, directed by comedy film veteran Leslie Goodwins in 1951, did little more than gather dust. It was up to merchandising tyro Larry Harmon to develop Bozo into superstar status upon purchasing the property in 1956. With the energy that inspired co-workers to nickname him "The White Tornado," Harmon vowed to "Bozo-ize the world," and to that end created a line of toys, comic books and related merchandise. He then franchised the "Bozo" character to TV stations throughout the world, allowing these stations, for a fee, to develop local "audience participation" kiddie shows with built-in

universal appeal and an instantly recognizable "star" (a similarly spectacular franchise success story had occured earlier with the Claster Company's *Romper Room*). For many years, Harmon personally trained the many local personalities who'd don the frizzy red fright wig, white "Grock" makeup and blue clown costume that were Bozo trademarks. At its peak in the mid–1960s, "Bozo mania" embraced 240 TV markets worldwide. Even as these words are being written in 1993, one of the last surviving *Bozo* shows, a long-running extravaganza seen over Chicago "Superstation" WGN and starring Joey D'Auria, has a three-year waiting list for studio audience tickets.

To keep the viewers "Bozo conscious," Larry Harmon determined that even the cartoons carried on his series would spotlight the corny clown. Accordingly, the entrepreneur set up Larry Harmon Productions, an animation house overseen by director Paul Fennell and numbering among its staff two guiding lights of the future Filmation studio: producer Lou Scheimer and director Hal Sutherland. The 156 five-minute color *Bozo* cartoons cranked out by Harmon between 1958 and 1961 were described in the trade papers as boasting "magnificent animation." The animated *Bozo* was an irredeemably obnoxious creature, given to doubling over with laughter at fadeout time over the slightest of jokes and speaking most of his dialogue in irritating rhymed couplets. Bozo's pal Butchy Boy was an adenoidal cipher, and the clown's adventures were the sort of tired old clichéd situations—Bozo battles spies, Bozo gets stuck on a runaway motorbike, Bozo helps Little Bo Peep locate her sheep—that even the most banal Hanna-Barbera scripts of the era would have avoided. The one lasting legacy of these cartoons was Bozo's cry of "Whoaaaa, Nellie," a phrase allegedly coined by "Roller Derby" host Richard Lane in the late 1940s and since adopted by many a middle aged sports announcer.

Nevertheless, the *Bozo* cartoons filled a need in the product-hungry late 1950s, and became even more valuable when TV went "full color" in the mid–1960s. Less successful were several attempts within the Bozo package to spin off the Coyote-like character of "Wacko Wolf" into his own starring series. Gradually, the cartoons were weeded out of the many local *Bozo* dailies, with such audience participation events as the "Grand Prize Game" (accurately tossing five ping-pong balls into five cups to win such fabulous prizes as a cake decorated with Bozo's countenance) leaving little if any room for cartoons. If you really must satisfy your curiosity, the original *Bozo* shorts are available on cassette from Celebrity Video. You've been warned.

THE BRADY KIDS. ABC: 9/16/1972–8/31/1974. Filmation. Executive consultant and creator: Sherwood Schwartz. Produced by Lou Scheimer and Norm Prescott. Directed by Hal Sutherland. Written by Marc Richards. Music by Yvette Blais and Jeff Michael. CAST: Maureen McCormick, Erika Scheimer (Marcia); Barry Williams, Lane Scheimer (Greg); Eve Plumb (Jan); Christopher Knight, Keith Allen (Peter); Susan Olsen (Cindy); Mike Lookinland (Robbie); Larry Storch (Marlon the Magic Bird/ Ping/ Pong); Jane Webb (Babs); "Lassie" (Moptop).

The *Brady Bunch*, the *Leave It to Beaver* of the 1970s generation, has in recent years attained cult status. Reruns of the series (produced from 1969 and 1974) still top the ratings in several local markets, and we've recently witnessed the publication of at least five books devoted to the subject, including one "tell all" opus by former *Brady* star Barry Williams. There's even an ongoing live "readers theatre" production in Chicago wherein actors recite *Brady Bunch* scripts on a nightly basis. A sure method of determining a person's age is to see how much of the *Brady Bunch* theme song can be recited from memory; a surer method is to see how many storylines of the series' 120 episodes can be recounted, line for line and plot twist for plot twist. Whether all this latter-day adulation is due to the *Brady Bunch*'s inherent quality or due to the latent kinkiness of the series' premise—a widow with three daughters marries a man with three sons, all of whom live under the same roof as brothers and sisters even though the proximities in the kids' ages could very well lead to relationships of a more delicate sort—is a matter best left to sociologists of the 1970s.

In any event, *The Brady Bunch* proved that success cannot be gained by osmosis. Otherwise, the now-obscure half hour cartoon series *The Brady Kids* would be right up in there in the same valhalla of "TV Classics."

The *Brady Kids* shared the same theme music, the same six kid characters (their voices provided during the first season by the same six kid actors), the same executive producer (Sherwood Schwartz) and even the same "checkerboard" opening-title design as its live action prototype. Gone were Mr. and Mrs. Brady and Alice the housekeeper, replaced by a bunch of cartoony family pets: Moptop the dog, Marlon the magic bird, and Ping and Pong the panda astronauts. We generally saw the Brady kids when they were congregating in their treehouse to rehearse their gigs as a family rock band. And there were weekly "dance sessions," featuring songs you'd never heard before and would never hear again. The *Brady Kids* owed less to *The Brady Bunch* than it did to the live action *Partridge Family* and the animated *Archie Show* (q.v.)—in fact, some of the original *Archie* animation was redressed (in typical Filmation fashion) for the musical numbers on the *Brady Kids*.

When challenged in 1973 to demonstrate that TV cartoon series had redeeming values, ABC's then-vice-president of children's programs Michael Eisner pointed with pride to a *Brady Kids* episode in which the white-bread Bradys cleaned up a littered inner city neighborhood. This uplifting plotline was evidently missed by the National Association for Better Broadcasting, which assessed the 22-episode *Brady Kids* thusly: ". . . [T]his animated version has even less substance than its live-action progenitor." And that, to many less charitable situation comedy fans, is less than zero.

BRAVESTARR. Syndicated: 1987. Filmation. Produced by Lou Scheimer and Arthur H. Nadel. Directed by John Grusd, Marsh Lamore, Lou Kachivas, Ed Friedman, Lou Zukor. Creative advisor: Arthur H. Nadel. Series writer/ developer: Bob Forward. Music by Frank Becker. Voices: Charlie Adler (Scuzz/Deputy Fuss); Susan Blu (Judge B.J.); Pat Fraley (Marshal Bravestarr); Ed Gilbert (30-30/Shaman); and Erik Gundin, Alan Oppenheimer, and Erika Scheimer.

Bravestarr was Filmation's contribution to the cartoon outer space western trend of 1986–1987 (see also *Adventures of the*

Galaxy Rangers and *Saber Riders and the Star Sheriff*)—and, incidentally, Filmation's very last TV production. The strong silent hero of the title, Marshal Bravestarr, drew his super powers from the combined strength of the Puma, the Hawk, the Wolf and the Bear; he also had a few robotic traits, such as his ability to see with computerized information being fed into his range of vision, in the manner of Arnold Schwarzenegger's "Terminator." Bravestarr kept the peace on the planet of New Texas in the 24th century, his authority backed up by his pal Thirty-Thirty, an Equestroid (that's cartoonese for a muscular talking horse who wielded a mean sixgun). Also on hand were Deputy Fuss, a pintsized alien of indeterminate origin, and a female magistrate named B.J.

Occasional visits were paid by Bravestarr's elderly Indian mentor Shaman (a word meaning "medicine man"), who has taught the Marshal the value of physical mightiness tempered by a sense of morality and justice. The holy grail sought by good guys and bad guys alike on *Bravestarr* was Kerium, an otherworldly precious ore in the tradition of *Adventures of the Galaxy Rangers'* "Star Stone." Bravestarr's opposition in the villain's camp was Tex-Hex, leader of the Carrion Bunch. Tex-Hex, whose bony visage was reminiscent of Skeletor on *He-Man and the Masters of the Universe* (q.v.), was actually only the hired gun of an evil cartel known as Stampede (Most of these characters' action figure counterparts from Mattel toys were on the shelves in December of 1986, nearly a year before the TV series' premiere).

The premise was viable, the graphics watchable, the animation serviceable. What held *Bravestarr* back from being totally enjoyable was its sermonizing. Gordon H. Berry, prosocial technical advisor on many animated series of the mid-1980s, more than earned his keep on *Bravestarr*. To its credit, the series didn't offer 22 minutes of mindless mayhem with a "valuable lesson" sanctimoniously squeezed into its last 30 seconds, as was standard practice. The lessons learned on *Bravestarr*—the value of friendship, the efficacy of tolerance, the wisdom of avoiding artificial stimulants like drugs and alcohol, the sagacity of knowing when not to resort to brute strength, etc.—were solidly integrated

into the plotlines of the daily series' 65 half hours. The trouble was, most of the *Bravestarr* episodes were nothing *but* lessons, hammering their points home in the blunt style of a homeroom detention teacher. Young viewers, having endured eight hours' worth of classroom activity, didn't cotton to being preached at for an additional half hour when *Bravestarr* signed on in the late afternoon.

Considering the series' overall lack of subtlety, it's amazing that the single most positive aspect of *Bravestarr* was all but ignored in the series' publicity by both Dr. Gordon Berry and the Filmation people (and curiously, by an otherwise thorough recent book on the history of Filmation). It was unmistakable from Bravestarr's demeanor, his reverence of spiritual advisor Shaman, his facial structure and his skin pigmentation that the Marshal was a Native American. As such, Bravestarr was one of the very few representatives of his ethnic group ever to star as the hero in an American TV series of *any* kind. This respectful and noncondescending treatment of one of the most maligned of minorities was not only passed over in Filmation's press handouts for *Bravestarr*, but to my knowledge it wasn't even picked up on by the media critics of 1987 who were eternally griping that certain racial types were either ignored or misrepresented on television. *Bravestarr* was "politically correct" even before that term was in common usage—and everybody missed it!

BREEZLY AND SNEEZLY *see* PETER POTAMUS

BUCKY AND PEPITO. Syndicated: 1959. Samsing Creations/Trans-Artists Productions. Produced by Sam Singer. Voice talent: Dallas McKennon.

I defer to cartoon historian Jeff Lenburg on the subject of *Bucky and Pepito*—and to a popular late night radio personality on Chicago's WGN, who confirmed that she'd seen the series in childhood. It was Lenburg who established that the series was about an imaginative young lad named Bucky and his inventor pal Pepito; it was the WGN radio host who further recalled that the eight-minute *Bucky and Pepito* cartoon adventures centered around Bucky and his burro.

Available for syndication in early 1959

(as confirmed by its copyright entry), *Bucky and Pepito* made the rounds at least until the mid–1960s, a time during which most old black and white TV cartoons were squeezed out by newer color-filmed properties. I *know*, therefore, that *Bucky and Pepito* existed — I just don't remember it.

BUCKY O'HARE AND THE TOAD WARS. Syndicated: 1991.

Abrams Gentile/Sunbow/Claster/Marvel Productions. Produced in association with Continuity Comics and IDDH. Based on the graphic novel illustrated by Michael Golden. Animation by Akom Production Co. and Studio Idom Angouleme. Music by Doug Katsaros. Voices: Long John Baldry, Jay Brazeau, Gary Chalk, Doc Harris, Simon Kendall, Sam Kouth, Terry Klassen, Scott McNeil, Shane Meier, Jason Michas, Richard Newman, Doug Parker, Margot Pindvic, David Steele, Dale Wilson.

Originated in 1978 by artist/writers Larry Hama and Michael Golden, Bucky O'Hare, a heroic galaxy-hopping green rabbit, became a "graphic novel" star for Pacific Comics' *Echo of Futurepast* (later published by Continuity Comics) in 1984. This was the same year as the debut of the *Teenage Mutant Ninja Turtles* comic book, a concept which in fact Bucky O'Hare predated. Nonetheless, one can visualize the bull session in 1990 that convinced Marvel Productions to go ahead with its animated TV series *Bucky O'Hare and the Toad Wars*: "How's this? *Ninja Turtles* meet *Star Wars!*"

The intrepid O'Hare was skipper of the space cruiser "Righteous Indignation," vanguard vessel for the peacekeeping organization S.P.A.C.E. (Sentient Protoplasm Against Colonial Encroachment). Bucky's crew included first mate Jenny (a "witchcat"), gunner Deadeye Duck, Bruiser the gorilla, and adolescent android Blinky. The Righteous Indignation cruised the Aniverse, a limitless extraterrestrial frontier populated solely by non-humans. The antagonists were amphibians from the planet Genus, who devoted their spare time to enslaving other planets; these (literally) coldblooded creeps were led by an enormous android toad named Complex. The human factor was represented by 10-year-old Willy DuWitt, who lived in

a parallel universe (that is to say *our* universe) and who occasionally passed through a dimensional warp in his bedroom wall to assist Bucky O'Hare and Company.

The 1991 cartoon series was overseen by the Claster Company's Hasbro Toys division, which predictably had an extensive line of Bucky O'Hare action figures on the shelves practically before the series was off the storyboards. *Bucky O'Hare* certainly had potential, notably in the satiric slant given the Toad civilization: The evil amphibians used the Toad Network, a 24-hour cable TV service offering such entertainment as *Toadally Hidden Video* and *21 Hop Street*, as a conduit for their secret messages. Ultimately, however, the derivative nature of the whole project, coupled with the uncomfortably xenophobic atmosphere stirred up by the series' anti-toad sentiments, worked against its acceptance by an increasingly restless young audience. After 13 episodes, Claster replaced *Bucky O'Hare* in syndication with *Conan the Adventurer* (q.v.).

BUFORD AND THE GALLOPING GHOST. NBC: 2/3/1979–9/1/1979.

Hanna-Barbera. Executive producers, William Hanna and Joseph Barbera. Produced by Art Scott. Directed by Ray Patterson, Oscar Dufau, George Gordon, Carl Urbano, John Walker and Rudy Zamora. Music by Hoyt Curtin. Voices: Frank Welker (Buford Bloodhound/Nugget Nose); Pat Parris (Cindy Mae/Rita); Dave Landsburg (Woody); Marilyn Schreffler (Wendy); Frank Nelson (Mr. Fuddy); Henry Corden (Sheriff Dupres); Roger Deltz (Deputy Goofer).

Two cartoon components made up the 13-week Saturday morning offering *Buford and the Galloping Ghost*. "The Buford Files" starred a Gomer Pyle type private eye bloodhound who solved mysteries with his teenaged chums Cindy Mae and Woody. Buford's nose not only sniffed out wrongdoers, but flashed red when locating its quarry. The character was something of a backwoods *Scooby-Doo* (q.v.) — and if you were in the mood for further *Scooby* derivations, there was also this series' second component, "The Galloping Ghost." Instead of a large dog protagonist who was afraid of ghosts, there was a large horse protagonist who *was* a ghost: Nugget Nose,

You know who.

also known as Mergatroyd, who "lived" on a dude ranch owned by Fenwick Fuddy, and who assisted teenaged ranch workers Rita and Wendy in—yes—solving mysteries.

Both "Buford Files" and "Galloping Ghost" had been introduced in September of 1978 on Hanna-Barbera's *Yogi's Space Race* (see *Yogi Bear*).

THE BUGS BUNNY SHOW. ABC: 10/1/1960–9/25/1962; Rerun 9/1962–9/1968; CBS: 9/11/1971–9/1/1973; ABC: 9/8/1973–8/30/1975. Warner Bros. Written and produced by Chuck Jones and Friz Freleng. New segments directed by Jones, Freleng, Robert McKimson, Maurice Noble, Gerry Chiniquy, Hawley Pratt, Robert Tronson, Ken Harris, Abe Levitow and Tom Ray. Theme music by Jay Livingston and Mack David. Additional music (new sequences): Milt Franklyn. Voices: Mel Blanc, Arthur Q. Bryan, Daws Butler, June Foray, Julie Bennett, Stan Freberg, Billy Bletcher, Bea Benaderet.

The *Bugs Bunny Show* was two years'

worth of prime time network exposure for a select package of vintage Warner Bros. cartoons, many starring the titular Oscar-winning rabbit who'd been a studio mainstay since 1940. United Artists Television controlled virtually all the WB product made before 1949; thus *The Bugs Bunny Show* was "confined" to such classic post–1949 efforts as *One Froggy Evening, The Rabbit of Seville, Duck Amuck, Scarlet Pumpernickle, Three Little Bops,* and practically the entire "Road Runner" output up to 1961. The reason this essentially retrospective series is included in a book on made-for-TV cartoons is that the Warner Bros. artisans went to the trouble of filming at least 4½ minutes of "bumper" animation for each of the 52 nighttime *Bugs Bunny Shows*—and also turned out commercials for the series' principal sponsor, General Foods (many of these directed by the peerless Tex Avery).

Never mere filler to take up space between cartoons, the new material was as well produced as the original shorts, and sometimes just as funny. Generally, the bumpers were designed to illustrate the unifying theme of the evening's three theatrical short-subject offerings: music, pets, culture, automobile travel, and so forth. Occasionally the new footage helped knit the old animation into some sort of continuity. Two particularly good examples were the premiere episode of October 1, 1960, which expanded 1957's *Show Biz Bugs* to fill nearly an entire half hour, and the second-season installment "Stage Couch" (12/26/1961), wherein three "Sylvester and Tweety" cartoons were unified by having Sylvester the cat relate his misadventures with Tweety Bird to a Viennese psychiatrist. One such pastiche episode, "Satan's Waitin'" (10/17/1961), used its combination of new and old footage to tell of Yosemite Sam's efforts to stay out of Hades; this episode was then pared down to seven minutes and released as a 1963 theatrical cartoon, *Devil's Feud Cake*. As on the series, it was virtually impossible for the untrained eye to detect the seams between the 1950s material and the 1960s embellishments, though *Devil's Feud Cake* shared the same weak, unsatisfying fadeout gag as "Satan's Waitin'." This was a failing in common with many otherwise excellent *Bugs Bunny Show* episodes, which couldn't seem to come up with really good wrap-ups for their cartoon compilations—indicating that longtime Warners scriptwriters Warren Foster and Michael Maltese, then employed at Hanna-Barbera, were perhaps as indispensable as they seemed to be.

Mel Blanc was back on hand to provide voicework for *The Bugs Bunny Show*, though it was fortunate indeed that he'd polished off most of his recording sessions before his near-fatal auto accident of January 1961, or else there probably wouldn't have been any new material at all. The weekly program was overseen by Chuck Jones and Friz Freleng, with individual sequences directed by an honor guard of Warners veterans. The *Bugs Bunny Show* went the weekend morning rerun route in the fall of 1962, where, hopscotching between ABC and CBS and frequently cobilled with another Warners property as *The Bugs Bunny/Road Runner Show*, it remained until 1975. Its success ✻ spawned a whole slew of Warner Bros. network cartoon packages, which mopped up the ratings while providing new generations with some of the best Hollywood

animation of all time—marching to immortality to the tune of Jay Livingston and Mack David's unforgettable *Bugs Bunny Show* opening theme music, "This Is It."

THE BULLWINKLE SHOW *see* **ROCKY AND HIS FRIENDS**

A BUNCH OF MUNSCH. Showtime, 10/14/1992–. Cinar/CTV/Showtime/MacLean Hunter Television Ltd. Based on the works of Robert Munsch, illustrated by Michael Martchenko, published by Annick Press. Executive producer, Micheline Charest. Produced by Ronald A. Weinberg. Supervising producer, Cassandra Schafhausen. Supervising director, Peter Sander. Directed by Greg Bailey. Story editor, Peter Landecker. Line producer, Lesley Harris. Music by Jeff Fisher and Jeff Zahn. Theme music by Jeff Zahn and Judy Rothman. Animation produced by Crayon Animation. Animation facilities: Stanfield Animation, HanHo Huengup Co. Ltd., Akom Production Co. Ltd. Produced with participation of Telefilm Canada. Voices: Amy Fulco, Sonja Ball, Kathleen Fee, Rick Jones, Tamar Kozlov, Liz MacRae, Michael Rudder, Harry Strandjofski, Eramelinda Bouquer.

A *Bunch of Munsch*, based on the wry award-winning children's stories of Canadian humorist Robert Munsch, premiered in the fall of 1992 as half of a 60-minute cartoon block on the Showtime cable service (the other half was Rabbit Ear Video's *American Heroes and Legends*). Munsch himself appeared in the opening and closing title sequences; he did not, however, host this hostless half hour.

Aimed at the four- to eight-year-old crowd, *Bunch of Munsch* used gentle satire and light fantasy to shed light on otherwise problematic social issues: peer pressure, sexual and ethnic stereotypes, personal safety and hygiene, cooperation and understanding. *Munsch* was animated in a "soft" style, successfully transferring the distinctive artistic technique of Munsch's illustrator Michael Martchenko to the requirements of animation. The storylines (usually two per half hour) were faithful renditions of such Munsch classics as "The Paper Bag Princess," wherein the title character pulled a deliberate cliché-reversal by rescuing a handsome prince from a dragon, then gave the prince the boot when he complained she looked "messy"; "Thomas' Snowsuit," the tale of a boy ashamed of his grungy winter wardrobe; and "Angela's Airplane," a cautionary fable of what might happen if one presses the wrong buttons on the wrong machinery.

Predictably, this calculatedly prosocial and genteel project—which carefully siphoned out the harmless scatology, mostly in the form of "fart jokes," that Robert Munsch had included in his original stories to amuse his young audience—earned the plaudits of TV critics (notably those of *The New York Times*) and watchdog groups alike, even winning a few specialized awards. To be sure, *A Bunch of Munsch* was commendable. It's just that it could have been a bunch better. One diminishing aspect of the series was its insistence upon including original songs in each adventure; the tunes were jaunty but unmemorable (not to mention over-arranged), and all tended to sound alike— just as Cinar's character and background design remained too much the same from week to week. A second problem was *Munsch's* unvaried caricaturing of adults as loud, pigheaded jerks, which sent out a curious mixed message: Why should kids aspire to improve themselves (as the series preached), if the best they could hope for would be to turn into ignoramuses like their elders? (This goofus-grownup element was one of the charms of the Munsch originals, but didn't play as well when literalized on film.)

But *Bunch of Munsch* at its best was well worth having. My favorite sequences were "Pigs," all about a group of learned swine who commandeer a school bus, and "David's Father," which had as its titular hero an amiable giant. Perhaps my sensitivity towards the series' faults was prompted by the critical reaction to *Bunch of Munsch*, which sometimes suggested that it was virtually the *only* worthwhile cartoon effort of the 1992-93 season—outclassing the likes of *Batman: The Animated Series*, *Dog City* and *Goof Troop*! (See individual entries on these series.)

THE BUNGLE BROTHERS *see* **KWICKY KOALA**

BUTCH CASSIDY AND THE SUN DANCE KIDS. NBC: 9/8/1973–8/31/1974. Hanna-Barbera. Produced by Alex Lovy. Directed by William Hanna and Joseph Barbera. Music supervision: Paul DeKorte. Voices: Chip Hand (Butch); Judy Strangis (Merilee); Mickey Dolenz (Harvey); Tina Holland (Steffy); Frank Welker (Elvis); John Stephenson (Mr. Socrates); and Cam Clarke, Hans Conried, Alan Oppenheimer, Virginia Gregg, Ross Martin, Pamela Peters, Frank Maxwell and Henry Corden.

Avoiding a lawsuit by the simple expedient of breaking up one word and pluralizing its title, the weekly half hour *Butch Cassidy and the Sun Dance Kids* (produced late in 1971 but not telecast until 1973) had nothing whatever to do with the 1969 feature film of almost the same name—nor anything to do with Western bandits, for that matter. Under the aegis of the "World Wide Talent Agency," young Butch Cassidy headed a rock group known as the Sun Dance Kids, comprised of Merilee, Harvey, Steffy, and a dog named Elvis. A rock group, just like Filmation's *The Archies* (q.v.). And this rock group just like *The Archies* was actually a band of government agents who hopped from place to place solving crimes. A bunch of teenagers and a dog solving crimes, just like Hanna-Barbera's *Scooby-Doo* (q.v.). And like a lot of Saturday morning cartoon series of the early 1970s that were either just like *The Archies* or just like *Scooby-Doo* or just like both, the cliché-ridden *Butch Cassidy and the Sun Dance Kids* was cancelled after a single 13-week season. Just like that.

CADILLACS AND DINOSAURS. CBS: 9/18/1993–. Nelvana/Galaxy Films/DeSouza Productions. Based on character concepts created by Mark Schultz. Originally published by Kitchen Sink Press. Executive producers: Steven E. DeSouza, Michael Hirsh, Sasha Hatari, Patrick Loubert. Co-executive producer, Toper Taylor. Supervising producer, Stephen Hodgins. Line producer, Patricia R. Burns. Consultants, Denis Kitchen and John Byers. Music by John Tucker. Additional production facilities: Another Push Pin Planning Co. Ltd. Voices: David Keeley (Jack); Susan Roman (Hannah), Bruce Tubbe (Mustapha); Dawn Greenhaigh (Scharnhorst); Tedd Dillon (Hammer); Colin O'Meara (Wrench); Frank Pellegrino (Vice); David Fox (Kirgo); Don Francks (Grith/Hobbs); Kristina Nicoll (Dahlgren); Philip Williams (Toulouse);

Lenora Zann (Mikla); Don Dickinson (Noe).

The starting point of *Cadillacs and Dinosaurs* was artist Mark Schultz' late–1980s alternative comic book, *Xenozoic Tales*. A former advertising draftsman, Schultz had always wanted to break loose artistically in the richly detailed, melodramatic manner of oldtime EC Comics artists Wallace Wood and Will Elder. He also held great affection for Edgar Rice Burrough's environment-friendly "Tarzan" stories and for Mel Gibson's *Mad Max* films, a series of violent adventures about a post-apocalyptic society dependent on motor transportation for status and survival.

Mark Schultz combined all these elements in *Xenozoic Tales*. The comic book's continuity was set in the 26th century, 500 years after the global warming hastened by ecological rape had resulted in cataclysmic natural upheavals—icecap meltings, volcanoes, earthquakes—which wiped out most of mankind. The survivors were driven underground while the Earth's surface burned. One of the leading groups was the Mechanics, a quasireligious society made up of machinists and engineers; the group's code of living was the Machinatio Vitae—"The Machinery of Life." When people were able to resurface on a cooled-down globe in 2500 or so (Earth by then had two moons, thanks to tidal conditions), they discovered that excessive flooding had turned the once-concrete City in the Sea (formerly New York City) into a land of bountiful foliage and sustenance. With no need for machinery in this new Eden, the Mechanics lost power to the Council of Governors, a semi-benevolent bureaucracy. Crime was in the hands of the Poachers, who lived in the lush forests surrounding the City in the Sea—which were also populated by dinosaurs (now called "Chevattes," a variant of the French word for horse) who'd managed to regenerate while domesticated mammals were still underground.

Hero Jack Tenrec was the last of the "old-blood" Mechanics, his family having been killed by renegade poacher Hammer Terhune. Jack's mentor was "Obi Wahn Kenobe" type Grith, a reptilian spirit who urged Tenrec to "trust the Machinery of Life"—to reintroduce beneficial technology to the brave new world and not resort to Poacher-style violence. Tenrec

believed in the Mechanics' ability to use benign technology—principally computers and flying machines—to maintain the 26th century's balance of nature, but he opposed revival of "bad" technologies—warmaking weaponry and ecologically unfriendly machinery—that would destroy nature. Cruising the "Xenozoic era" landscape in his reconditioned 1953 Cadillac, Tenrec, his computer-geek pal Mustapha Cairo and research scientist Hannah Dundee (from the land of Wassoon, a.k.a. Washington DC, home of the world's remaining scholars) joined forces to uphold the good qualities of the new world and to link up the various pockets of civilization throughout what was left of America.

In addition to Hammer Terhune and his equally dangerous brothers Wrench and Vice, Tenrec was opposed by Wilhelmina Scharnhorst, the spokesperson for the Council of Governors. Scharnhorst's hidden agenda was to overthrow her fellow governors and set up her own dictatorship. To do this, she felt she had to "modernize" the world by proving that society was no longer reliant on nature alone to survive—this "proof" consisting of pillaging the land of its riches with the same environmental mismanagement that had brought about cataclysm in the first place. Thus Scharnhorst needed to discredit Tenrec and his Mechanics, or to clandestinely have him killed by her secret ally Hammer Terhune.

Whew! What a backstory, skillfully set forth by Mark Schultz. *Xenozoic Tales* was too labyrinthine for most publishers, and only alternative-comic pioneer Dennis Kitchen had enough faith to publish the property. Schultz' comic subsequently won several industry awards, but more importantly it made money, and this is what attracted a number of movie producers to *Xenozoic Tales*. Galaxy Films came up with the proposal that Kitchen and Schultz found had most long-run potential: Rather than drop the property on the moviegoing public with one, big movie—a movie that might die at the boxoffice, killing *Xenozoic* at the get-go—Galaxy opted for the *Teenage Mutant Ninja Turtles*' (q.v.) slow and steady buildup. First, the cult comic book; next, a weekly half hour TV cartoon series; next, the attendant toy/action figure merchandising of the TV version; next, a stream of video games; and *finally*, after the public had been thoroughly inundated by the property, the inevitable big-budget movie spectacular.

But that title had to go. "Xenozoic" was incomprehensible to the average viewer, and besides, any cartoon series with an "X" in the title would automatically be labelled a cheap imitation of the popular X-Men (q.v.). Latching on to Jack Tenrec's mode of transportation and the presence of dinosaurs in the narrative, Galaxy came up with Cadillacs and Dinosaurs. This would involve special permission from General Motors, but it was worth it to achieve the punchier title—and, incidentally, to suggest a tenuous resemblance to 1993's summer-movie megahit Jurassic Park.

Nelvana Studios was chosen for Cadillacs and Dinosaurs because of its past success in adapting comic books and strips to television without losing the style and flavor of the originals (see Babar, Rupert and Tin Tin). Happily, the studio captured succinctly the grim, rough-edged alternative comic "look" of Xenozoic Tales: slightly misshapen characters, funereal shadows, razor-edged silhouettes against the ravaged landscapes. What Nelvana was unable to duplicate was Schultz's talent for conveying physical pulchritude, both male and female. In the books, Jack Tenrec and especially Hannah Dundee were lovingly drawn with the most beautiful, supple bodies this side of a romance-novel cover. Nelvana didn't quite grasp this, rendering hero and heroine in flat, less alluring fashion. Still, the studio earned points for the overall striking visual style of Cadillacs and Dinosaurs, which was more successful in celebrating its vigorous comic-book original than the slicker X-Men. Even when the animation wasn't quite up to the concept, at least the series looked great.

Likewise admirable was the input of executive producer Steven E. DeSouza, the scripter of such no-nonsense film actioners as The Running Man, Commando, and the two Die Hard pictures. Instead of overloading the narrative with the comic book's topheavy backstory, DeSouza and his writers revealed important plot elements piecemeal, little by little per episode, allowing exposition to grow naturally from the dialogue and situations. To do this, of course, he had to trust that viewers would tune in each week to the serialized Cadillacs and Dinosaurs to see what plot secrets each episode would uncover.

Though the series was described by Nelvana president Michael Hirsh as "the grittiest, hardest-hitting action-adventure show on TV," Stephen DeSouza could not indulge in the violent excesses of his film work without being pilloried by both CBS' standards and practices and the nation's many clean-up-TV concerns. To that end, DeSouza—and the animators—conveyed an illusion of nonstop violent action while deemphasizing weapons and seeing to it that no one onscreen was killed. Any mayhem in Cadillacs and Dinosaurs had to be justified by the plot—and it had to be made clear that Jack Tenrec never really strayed from his nonviolence policy, moving into action only to defend himself or his friends. The program also had to be more all-pleasing than the comic book, straddling fans of Xenozoic Tales on one end and the usual preteen cartoon devotees on the other. Usually, the show succeeded in playing as an "adult" property while still appealing to, and not alienating, the younger viewers.

None of these accomplishments was pulled off without a hitch, and occasionally Cadillacs and Dinosaurs seemed weighted down with too many obligations to too many viewers and critics. Additionally, in its attempts to be both verbally and visually sophisticated, the show frankly slowed down to a plod at times, logjammed with unnecessary bantering dialogue and a too-busy background design. But it deserved "A" for Effort, and Cadillacs and Dinosaurs had a better chance of survival than its stylistic sister program, Hanna-Barbera's 1991 Pirates of Dark Water (q.v.), thanks to the progress made by X-Men and Batman: The Animated Series in breaking down audience resistance to intricate plotlines, nontraditional artwork, and character complexities.

THE CALIFORNIA RAISINS. CBS: 9/16/1989–9/8/1990. Murikami-Wolf-Swenson. Produced by Fred Wolf. Voices: Cam Clarke, Dorian Harewood, Jim Cummings, Brian Mitchell, Cree Summer, Rebecca Summers, Gailee Heideman, Michelle Mariana, Todd Tolces, Brian Cummings.

The California Raisins were introduced in 1987 on a series of commercials for the California raisin growers (you were expecting maybe the California kumquat growers?), superbly staged via stop-motion model animation by "Claymation" king Will Vinton. The Raisins' "Motown" sound, ultracool dance movements, finger-snapping rhythm and priceless facial gestures sold raisins by the bushel basket and opened up a cottage industry of merchandising for Vinton's anthropomorphic fruit. "Raisinmania" culminated in two extremely entertaining network specials, 1987's *Claymation Christmas Celebration* and 1989's *History of the Raisins*, the latter incorporating a sly lampoon of avaricious talent agents who suck their hapless clients dry while surrounding themselves with creature comforts.

Murikami-Wolf-Swenson's 1989 animated cartoon version of *The California Raisins* was an extension of this "talent vs. management" principle, showing the puckered protagonists on tour and at home in their lavish penthouse, ever on the outs with their manager, an overt disciple of conspicuous consumption. Added to the concept was the notion of giving the four raisins names: Stretch, Bebop, A.C. and Red. But there was something missing—notably the captivating personalities with which Will Vinton had imbued his original "Claymation" raisins. As a weekly half hour cel-animation series, the 13-episode *California Raisins* was flat and uninvolving; and, coming as it did from a cartoon studio that had previously made millions with a quartet of ninja turtles, *Raisins* seemed to suffer from a bad case of wanting to be *The Teenage Mutant Prunes*.

CALVIN AND THE COLONEL.
ABC: 10/3/1961–10/31/1961; 1/27/1962–9/22/1962. Kayro/Revue. Produced and written by Joe Connelly and Bob Mosher. Production executive, Al Almatezio. Music by George Bruns. Animation by Creston Studios/TV Spots. Animation producers, Bob Ganon, Sam Nicholson, Gerald Ray. Animation directors, Chuck McKimson, John Walker. Supervising animators, Tom McDonald, John Sparey, Bob Bemiller, Ben Washam, Volus Jones, Jim Davis, Harvey Toombs. Art director, Norm Gottfredson. Voices: Freeman Gosden (Col. Montgomery J. Klaxton); Charles Correll (Calvin J. Burnside); Virginia Gregg (Maggie Belle); Beatrice Kay (Sister Sue); Gloria Blondell (Gladys); June Foray (Myrtle); Paul Frees (Oliver Wendell Clutch); Joe Flynn (Nephew Newton); and Barney

Phillips, Frank Gerstle, Elvia Allman and Frank Nelson.

Freeman Gosden and Charles Correll, creators of the longrunning (1927–1960) radio series *Amos 'n' Andy*, found themselves—after years of being celebrated as brilliant performers—at the center of an unwelcome controversy in the early 1960s. On *Amos 'n' Andy*, Gosden and Correll, both Caucasian, had portrayed two African Americans, Amos Jones and Andy Brown. The series flourished at a time when "blackface" humor using comically exaggerated dialects was acceptable. But when *Amos 'n' Andy* made it to television in 1951, everything started to unravel. Gosden and Correll were compelled to hire black actors to portray their radio creations, and the producers' insistence upon coaching these actors in the "proper" way to play their roles sparked accusations of racism and stereotyping. Television's *Amos 'n' Andy* (1951–1953) was successful both on the CBS network and in reruns, but not without ceaseless recriminations of groups such as the NAACP. By 1961, it looked as though the highly profitable *Amos 'n' Andy* reruns were going to be yanked from distribution (as indeed they were five years later). Freeman Gosden and Charles Correll determined to keep their property alive—even if it meant donning animal skins.

The result was a weekly, half hour animated ABC network series, produced by Kayro/Revue and by Gosden and Correll's longtime scriptwriters Joe Connelly and Bob Mosher (then employed as producerwriters of *Leave It to Beaver*). It was still essentially *Amos 'n' Andy*, and in fact bore that very title when announced in the trade papers in early 1961, but the black characters had become anthropomorphic animals and the series debuted under the title *Calvin and the Colonel*. Calvin J. Burnside, a cigar smoking bear, was a lumbering Lothario patterned after *Amos 'n' Andy*'s Andrew Brown. Montgomery J. Klaxton, a glib con-artist fox who owned a ramshackle real estate agency, was not far removed from *A and A*'s favorite character, George "Kingfish" Stevens. The dialects used by Gosden and Correll to dub the characters' voices could now pass as merely "Southern," thereby sidestepping accusations of racism (at times, Calvin Burnside had no accent whatsoever). As *Variety* put it in its review of *Calvin and*

120   Camp Candy

the Colonel, "Amos 'n' Andy are back but instead of worrying the NAACP, they'll probably bother the ASPCA." The supporting cast of *Calvin and the Colonel*, also animalized, were likewise cut from the *Amos 'n' Andy* cloth. The Colonel's wife Maggie Belle was the cartoon counterpart to the old series' Sapphire, Kingfish's spouse; Sister Sue, Maggie Belle's sibling, was the pen and ink image of the original "Momma," Kingfish's barge-like mother-in-law; and Oliver Wendell Clutch, a crafty attorney weasel, was a diluted version of *Amos 'n' Andy*'s resident shyster, Algonquin J. Calhoun. Paul Frees' voiceover for Clutch avoided the ethnic dialect, offering a characterization reminiscent of Digger O'Dell, the "friendly undertaker" played by John Brown on the old radio sitcom *The Life of Riley*.

This writer recalls being impressed by the level of wit in the *Calvin and the Colonel* scripts when the series debuted in the fall of 1961. Impressive it was, and small wonder; the series' storylines were drawn verbatim from the half hour *Amos 'n' Andy* radio shows written by Connelly and Mosher in the late 1940s and early 1950s. Even the opening episode, "The Television Job," was virtually word for word the same script as an *Amos 'n' Andy* radiocast of 1952. Critics at the time resented this wanton recycling of old material, though praise was heaped upon the animation work by Creston Studios, a firm previously responsible for the 1957 revival of *Crusader Rabbit* (q.v.). The Creston artists preferred a brazenly exaggerated UPA style to the more conservative renditions of the Hanna-Barbera school, utilizing impressionistic background art with deliberately sloppy splashes of color (lost on viewers during the series' black and white ABC run) and forced-perspective settings. So modernistic were Creston's visuals that they often played havoc with the "aged in the wood" quality of the scriptwork.

Calvin and the Colonel died in a Tuesday prime time slot opposite *Dobie Gillis* on CBS and *Alfred Hitchcock* on NBC—and to add to the dilemma, the producers couldn't deliver scheduled episodes on time, causing no end of confusion to readers of *TV Guide*. The ABC network panicked, and after six weeks, *Calvin and the Colonel* was pulled off the schedule. The series was officially put on "hiatus," a Latin word which usually translates as

"You'll never see this turkey again." But a firm commitment for 26 episodes had already been made between ABC and Revue, so in January of 1962, *Calvin and Colonel* returned to fill a Saturday evening gap left by the cancellation of the adventure series *The Roaring Twenties*. There the cartoon weekly clung to life opposite the one-two punch of *Bonanza* on NBC and *Perry Mason* on CBS, until taps finally blew in September of 1962.

In a way, it was too bad; with 33 years' worth of *Amos 'n' Andy* material at hand, *Calvin and the Colonel* might have gone on forever, treating viewers to years of superlative limited animation work courtesy of Creston Studios. But *Amos 'n' Andy* had frankly run its course no matter what new pelt it was wrapped in; additionally, the cartoon series' visuals leaned towards the "talking head" approach, with all action stopping dead in its tracks for long banter sequences. So it came to pass that *Calvin and the Colonel* was in 1962 consigned to MCA's "B" list of syndicated rerun packages.

CAMP CANDY. NBC: 9/9/1989–9/7/1991. Syndicated: 1992. Frostback Productions/DIC (1st season); Frostback/Saban/Worldvision (later seasons). Executive producers: Andy Heyward and John Candy (1st season); Haim Saban and John Candy (later seasons). Produced and directed by Winston Richard. Created by Joel Andryc and Ellen Levy. Theme song written by Harry Nilsson; sung by Nilsson and John Candy. Incidental music by Shuki Levy. Story editor: Betty Birney. Executive in charge of production: Eric Rollman. Animation produced by Sei Young Studios Ltd. Voices (both versions): John Candy (Himself); Lewis Arquette (Rex); Valri Bromfield (Nurse Molly); Danny Mann (Chester). Additional voices, DIC version: Tom Davidson (Iggy); Danielle Ferrandes (Robin); Willow Johnson (Vanessa); Andrew Seebarin (Rick); Chiara Zanni (Alex). Additional voices, Saban version: Christopher Candy, Jennifer Candy, Victoria Carroll, George Coe, E.G. Daily, Michael Green, Jess Harnell, Michael Horse, Tito Insana, David L. Lander, Katie Leigh, Eugene Levy, Andrea Martin, Gail Matthius, Roddy McDowall, Candi Milo, Hal John Smith, Kath Soucie, Dave Thomas, William Windom, Marcia Wallace.

John Candy, arguably the most likable of the *Second City TV* comedy troupe graduates, usually seemed to have trouble translating his audience rapport to the big screen. With the notable exception of *Uncle Buck* (1989), Candy's feature film vehicles were woefully routine, enlivened only by the presence of the corpulent star. Nor was the 1989 Saturday morning half hour cartoon series *Camp Candy* a truly suitable showcase for the actor's talents.

Co-produced by Candy, who'd once been a camp counselor, the animated weekly trod familiar farcical ground. It was set in a ramshackle summer camp on the shores of Lake Cacciatore (an old Indian name?), where a caricatured version of the star acted as owner, counselor, chief cook and bottle washer, aided and abetted by Nurse Molly. The ethnically mixed Camp Candy kids, who ran the usual gamut from practical joker to bespectacled nerd, were Rick, Robin, Alex, Binky, Vanessa and Iggy. The land occupied by Camp Candy was dearly coveted by sleazy condo developer Rex de Forrest, who with the help of his brainless assistant Chester was diligent in his underhanded efforts to chase Candy and company off the property. The series had a strong pro-ecology slant, making the proceedings superficially worthwhile. But those expecting an extension of John Candy's inspired brand of humor were disappointed by *Camp Candy*'s undercooked scripts and lukewarm punchlines. Thankfully, the series had enough flashes of social and political satire, and occasional very effective comic and dramatic vignettes, to compensate for its overall blandness.

The network version of *Camp Candy* was handled by DIC Productions, while Saban Entertainment was responsible for the later syndicated episodes. The high point of the 1989–1991 network run was the series' winning the Humanitas Award for the 1991 half hour "Wish Upon a Fish," a determinedly nonmaudlin story about a leukemia-stricken young camper. This honor was not, however, the chief reason that *Camp Candy* was revived for strip syndication in 1992. According to its own publicity, the project was warmed up in order to attract more young male viewers to daytime television. John Candy's fan following was biggest with preteen boys, so it was *Camp Candy* which Worldvision

chose to distribute as its entry in the *Teenage Mutant Ninja Turtles* (q.v.) ratings sweepstakes.

The syndicated *Camp Candy* contained the added filip of John Candy's live action educational wraparounds, in which the star would discuss with warm nonchalance a fact or two about the great outdoors and the animal life dwelling therein (These wraparounds were Candy's own idea, and not merely a balm to the FCC). Adding to the enjoyment—just as in the network days—was the voiceover work by several of Candy's *Second City TV* cohorts, including Eugene Levy, Andrea Martin and Dave Thomas, who on occasion recreated their favorite *SCTV* characters. But considering the talent involved, *Camp Candy* wasn't half as good as it should have been.

Cantinflas—cartoon style.

CANTINFLAS. Syndicated: 1980–1982. Televisa SA/Hanna-Barbera/Diamex S.A. Distributed in the United States by Viacom. Voices (English language ver-

Nature communes with John Candy in *Camp Candy*.

sion): Don Messick (Cantinflas, a.k.a. Amigo), John Stephenson (Narrator).

Produced in Mexico by Hanna-Barbera and Diamex S.A., *Cantinflas* was a series of 104 six-minute comic/educational cartoons, in which a monkeylike character based on the enormously popular Mexican film comedian Cantinflas explored the natural wonders of the Earth and its galactic neighbors. The spindly, mustachioed star also conducted guided tours of such man-made wonders as the Aztec Pyramids, and on occasion visited famous personalities of the past: Galileo, Shakespeare, Napoleon, Helen of Troy, and even Dante Alighieri, author of *The Divine Comedy* (Cantinflas doused the flames of Dante's Inferno with a fire extinguisher!). Unlike the studio's *Laurel and Hardy* (q.v.) and *Abbott and Costello* (q.v.) cartoons, Hanna-Barbera's animated Cantinflas came surprisingly close to the cheeky, charismatic screen persona of his real-life counterpart.

Sporadic sales of *Cantinflas* were made in the United States, first under the title *Amigo and Friends* with 52 episodes dubbed in English, and later under the original title in a bilingual format (52 cartoons in English, 52 in Spanish). According to cartoon chronicler Jeff Lenburg, the series' greatest fan following was international; dubbed into at least six different languages, *Cantinflas* enjoyed vast, worldwide success.

CAPITOL CRITTERS. ABC: 1/28/1992–3/14/1992. Steven Bochco Productions/Hanna-Barbera. Created by Steven Bochco, Nat Mauldin and Michael Wagner. Executive consultant, Steven Bochco. Executive producer-writer, Nat Mauldin. Co-executive producer, David Kirschner. Supervising producer, Davis Doi. Produced by Dayna Flanagan. Directed by Robert Alvarez. Animation producer, James Wang. Animation directors, Robert Alvarez, Joan Drake, Joanne Romersa, Allen Wilzbach. Overseas animation directors, Julian Harris and John Conning. Music by Bruce Broughton. Voices: Neil Patrick Harris (Max); Bobcat Goldthwait (Muggle); and Patric Zimmerman, Patti Deutsch, Dorian Harewood, Charlie Adler, Chick Vennera, Joan Gerber, Brian Cummings, Brian Mitchell, Michael Bell,

Jennifer Darling, Tim Curry, Paul Eiding, B. J. Ward, Rob Paulsen.

Having learned nothing from the tepid results of the first nighttime cartoon boom following *The Flintstones* (q.v.) in 1961, the major TV networks insisted upon capitalizing on the success of Fox's *The Simpsons* (q.v.) in 1990 by announcing plans for a whole manifest of new prime time animated series. One of the few projects that got past the drawing board was *Capitol Critters* (originally titled *Aristocritters*). The spiritual leader behind this project was producer Stephen Bochco, whose two most successful live action TV series, *Hill Street Blues* and *St. Elsewhere*, tended to make people forget about his lengthier list of failures. Even when such misbegotten Bochco projects as *Bay City Blues* were cited by critics, their comments were qualified by the fact that the producer was undeniably a man of courage, willing to risk chancy and noncommercial series concepts rather than "go with the flow" of standard TV fare. In fact, at the time *Capitol Critters* made its January 1992 debut, Bochco was just recovering from the drubbing received by his 1990 series, *Cop Rock*, in which police and criminals alike regularly interrupted their activities to burst into songs and production numbers! In its own way, *Capitol Critters* was equally as "courageous" as *Cop Rock*—and equally as disastrous.

Produced in collaboration with Hanna-Barbera, the weekly half hour *Capitol Critters* was the story of Max, a young Nebraska mouse who was sole survivor of a guerilla attack on his family by a band of heartless human exterminators (featured in a grim opening episode which one review described as looking "more like a CNN war report than a kid's cartoon"). The orphaned Max went to live with his relatives in Washington DC, who dwelt with a variety of vermin in the basement of the White House. Max's new "family" included Berkeley, a leftover hippie mouse; Trixie, a brash feminist Brooklyn rodent; Moze, a street smart cockroach; Jammet, a "crazed combat veteran" squirrel; and Mugger, a laboratory rat whose psyche had been addled by constant scientific experimentation.

The storylines dealt in a brand of kneejerk political satire reminiscent of the "kids vs. establishment" films of the 1960s and 1970s. Each week, Stephen Bochco took it upon himself to educate his viewers in matters of race prejudice, drug abuse, post–Vietnam depression and the corruption factor of absolute power. Typical of the *Capitol Critters* party line was a gag in which members of the Senate (shown from the waist down, like all the other human characters on the series) were seen weathering a filibuster by reading comic books and dirty magazines. Bochco's publicity machine claimed that the soundtracks of the cartoon series weren't put together until the very last minute to allow for hot, current political commentary ("You will even hear actual recordings of press conferences with [President] Bush," insisted executive producer Nat Mauldin in a 1991 *TV Guide* interview). Still, *Capitol Critters* was obsessed with jokes about the long-gone Richard Nixon and Ronald Reagan—including at least one doddering reference to Bonzo.

Hanna-Barbera's Taiwan-produced animation was quite good, even if obviously patterned after the artwork in Don Bluth's feature film *An American Tail*. Also commendable was the voice work, particularly *Doogie Howser, M.D.* star Neil Patrick Harris as Max and especially gonzo comedian Bobcat Goldthwait as the ballistic Mugger. But *Capitol Critters* was out of the box after only seven of its proposed 13 episodes—two of which were shown as "previews" during the series' first week on the air.

Part of *Capitol Critters*' problem was its smug Hollywood liberal "Think as we think or be damned" stance (even the cats chasing the mice were identified as Republicans!). If *The Simpsons* could attack sacred cows, the reasoning went, so could *Capitol Critters*. Ignored was the fact that *The Simpsons* picked its satirical targets from *all* parts of the social spectrum, not merely the politically "incorrect"—and it sustained its exuberant outrageousness by offering a bottomless supply of rapid sight gags and throwaway one-liners which kept its breathless viewers laughing rather than becoming truly offended. *Capitol Critters* took the partisan attitude of a "single issue" office seeker, then doled out its "controversial" jokes with an emphatic slowness that suggested the producers felt the audience was not so much unsophisticated as lamebrained.

Or perhaps the producers were never sure what audience they really wanted.

For all its "adult" humor, the artwork and character design of *Capitol Critters* seemed geared for a preteen audience—a suspicion confirmed by the line of *Capitol Critters* toys and action figures that prematurely, and unprofitably, popped up on store shelves before the series had even taken hold. At a time when politicians were decrying a lack of "family values," one newsmagazine's TV critic suggested that *Capitol Critters* failed because it was *too* family oriented.

CAPTAIN AMERICA see THE MARVEL SUPER HEROES

CAPTAIN CAVEMAN AND THE TEEN ANGELS. ABC: 3/8/1980–6/12/ 1980. Hanna-Barbera. Executive producers, William Hanna and Joseph Barbera. Produced by Alex Lovy. Directed by Charles Nichols. Music by Hoyt Curtin. Musical supervision by Paul DeKorte. Voices: Mel Blanc (Captain Caveman); Vernee Watson (Dee Dee); Marilyn Schreffler (Brenda); Laurel Page (Taffy). (*See also* listings on *The Flintstones* and *Scooby-Doo.*)

Drawing inspiration from *Charlie's Angels*, from the superhero sagas of other cartoon and comic book creators, and from its own *The Flintstones* (q.v.), Hanna-Barbera unleashed *Captain Caveman and the Teen Angels* in 1977 as an eight-minute component of the Saturday morning series *Scooby's All-Star Laff a Lympics* (see *Scooby-Doo*). Captain Caveman was a hirsute stone-ager, frozen for millions of years in a block of ice and thawed out in the late 20th century by an "Angels" aggregation of three teenaged girls: Brenda, the smart one (also the black one on this series); Dee Dee, the funloving one; and Taffy, the silly, frightened one. An unprepossessing, hairy runt of a man, the Captain was armed with a "club of tricks" and an arsenal of super powers which were at the ready whenever the girls would exclaim "Captain Caveman!" in unison. Our hero, who spoke in a Tonto-like guttural ("Me love junk food") supplied by voice artist Mel Blanc, was a character encouraged and nurtured by ABC president Fred Silverman, eternally on the outlook for a new *Scooby-Doo* from Hanna-Barbera.

Was there a funny animal sidekick? Need you ask? It was Cave Bird, who acted as the Captain's property master, handing "Cavey" the various clubs and rocks necessary to cartoon crime control.

Captain Caveman and the Teen Angels attracted enough of a following to warrant its own 16-episode series in 1980. Although his starring career was rather short, Captain Caveman resurfaced as a supporting character on the NBC Hanna-Barbera offering *The Flintstones Comedy Show* (see *The Flintstones*) in the fall of 1980. Here we learned that "Cavey" was actually Chester, a mildmannered copy boy for the powerful prehistoric newspaper *The Daily Granite*, where Wilma Flintstone and Betty Rubble had recently taken jobs. And in 1986, Captain Caveman was entertainingly included—along with his elementary-school-age son Cavey Jr.—as a component of *The Flintstone Kids* (see, again, *The Flintstones*).

CAPTAIN FATHOM. Syndicated: 1967. TV III/Cambria. Produced by Dick Brown. Directed by Clark Haas. Voices: Warren Tufts (Captain Fathom); and Margaret Kerry, Hal Smith, Tom Brown, and Nel LeFebvre.

Cambria Productions eschewed its "Syncro-Vox" process (combining cartoons with live action footage of the characters' mouths) previously used on the company's *Clutch Cargo* (q.v.) and *Space Angel* (q.v.), for a new streamlined method of giving still pictures the illusion of movement called "Superanivision." This was the process utilized on Cambria's *Captain Fathom*, an underwater adventure opus featuring a submarine captain and a cotillion of seabound characters known as the Argonauts. There were 195 five-minute serialized color cartoons produced in the Superanivision process for local syndication in 1966 (An abortive pilot for *Captain Fathom*, still employing Syncro-Vox, had been shot in 1962).

In some markets, the *Captain Fathom* package was shown as one of the various components of *Captain Sailor Bird*, a grabbag of short animated subjects hosted in cartoon wraparounds by a talking parrot, which was distributed by Sterling Films beginning in 1960 to TV stations that didn't have the budgetary wherewithall to develop their own local kiddie shows. Other "canned host" wraparound syndies of the era included United Artists Television's *Big Mac and His Magic Train* and the Detroit-based *B'wana Don* (See also *Col-*

onel Bleep for a further example of "package" programming).

CAPTAIN HARLOCK AND THE QUEEN OF 1000 YEARS. Syndicated: 1985. Harmony Gold/Ziv International. Created by Reiji Matsumoto. Animation by Toei Studios.

Captain Harlock was a shaggy-haired, scarred, eyepatched buccaneer who, after all the oceans on earth had been destroyed in the 30th century, conducted his piracy in outer space. A "man without a country" surrounded by several loyal friends, Harlock sometimes fought on behalf of the resistance against the aliens who'd overtaken the earth — usually when there was something in it for him. The Captain was the star of two half-hour adventure cartoons created in Japan by Reiji Matsumoto, the artist responsible for *Space Cruiser Yamato* (see *Star Blazers*). The fact that Captain Harlock was a maverick who owed no allegiance to any one flag and answered to no ruling class made him an instantly appealing character to fans of "rebel" comic heroes, and it was this appeal that overcame the property's overall lack of animation finesse.

The two original Harlock series were *Space Pirate Captain Harlock*, featuring serialized adventures with enticing titles like "The Woman Who Burns Like Paper," and *Harlock and the Queen*, the saga of the Captain's battles against the empress of a dying planet who was set upon colonizing the Earth. When *Harlock* was released by Harmony Gold and Ziv International to non–Japanese markets, the two packages were meshed into one in order to fill up a daily syndicated strip. The American title was *Captain Harlock and the Queen of 1000 Years*, the "pirate" angle — and Harlock's essentially vengeful nature — played down in the sound dubbing and removed from the title so as not to subject the series to potential adult pressure-group criticism.

Fans of the original *Harlock* bemoaned the editing process as damaging the integrity of the project. General audiences, confused by the murky continuity of the abridged version, tuned out in droves, and *Captain Harlock and the Queen of 1000 Years* was a failure in the U.S., killing a multitude of tie-in merchandising deals that had been in the planning stages. But as in the case of other cult cartoon favorites like *Robotech* (q.v.), *Captain*

Harlock's true disciples kept the torch lit in the form of comic books and extensive background articles in the "Anime" fanzines catering to Japanimation devotees.

CAPTAIN N: THE GAME MASTER. NBC: 9/9/1989–9/1/1990.

– CAPTAIN N: THE ADVENTURES OF THE SUPER MARIO BROS. 3. NBC: 9/8/1990–9/7/1991.

– CAPTAIN N AND THE NEW SUPER MARIO WORLD. NBC: 9/14/1991–7/25/1992.

– CAPTAIN N AND THE VIDEO GAME MASTERS. Syndicated: 1992. Nintendo/DIC. Executive producer, Andy Heyward. Supervising producer, Michael Maliani. Directed by Chuck Patton. Story editor, Dorothy Middleton. Music by Michael Tavera. Music editor, Stuart Goetz. Live action sequences produced for Squire Productions by Jamie Edlin. Directed by Kit Hudson. Voices: Matt Hill (Captain N/ Narrator); Gary Chalk (King Hippo, others); Alessandro Juliani (Kid Icarus); Andrew Kavadas (Simon Belmont); Doug Parker (Megaman and Megamite); Venus Terzo (Lana); Levi Stubbs Jr. (Mother Brain); Tomm Wright (Duke); and Doc Harris, Andrew Marados, Jonathan Potts, Cindy Preston, Frank Welker, Long John Baldry, Don Brown, Len Carlson, Barb Chula, Violet Crumble, Marcie Goldberg, Anthony Holland, Lee Jeffrey, Al Jorden, Annabelle Kershaw, Colin Meachum, Shane Meier, Alvin Sanders, Mark Weatherly, Kurt Weldon. Live action cast: Dorian Barag (Kevin Keene); Louie the dog (Duke). (See *Super Mario Bros.* for credits of that component.)

Captain N: The Game Master was like its predecessor *Super Mario Bros.* (q.v.) based on a popular Nintendo home video game, with "audience/sponsor identification" built right in by making the hero, Kevin Keene (seen at the beginning of each program in a live-action sequence), a teenaged Nintendo champ. Kevin and his dog Duke were sucked into their home video unit and ended up in Videoland, a high-tech sword and sorcery parallel world where the boy assumed the superhero identity of Captain N. The remainder of each weekly half hour was an enactment of a previously marketed Nintendo game, with Captain N and his cohorts battling the lineup of computerized villains who tried to appropriate the "Sun Stone," the chief source of power in Videoland. The Captain's allies included beauteous Princess Lana (aren't any of the girls in these programs merely ladies in waiting?); vainglorious Simon Belmont, who both resented and relied upon Captain N's skill with a control pad; Megaman and Kid Icarus, a robot and a cupid type respectively (both pretty homely galoots, compared to the perfectly proportioned Captain, Lana and Simon); and Megaman's pintsized robonic chum Megamite.

Heading the villains was "The Mother Brain," a rap-talking, disembodied slab of gray matter who sounded a lot like the cannibalistic talking plant from the musical film version of *Little Shop of Horrors* — no surprise, since both brain and plant were given voice by actor Levi Stubbs Jr. (The character name, by the way, was an inside joke: The Mother Brain was the name given the Japanese offices of Nintendo's CEO.) Other baddies included the Dragon Lord, Mother Hippo and the Eggplant Wizard. The character names may have sounded like so much applesauce to a parent, but all were familiar monickers to young Nintendo fans.

What *Captain N* lacked in real humor it made up for in execution of concept. The series was designed and performed like a neverending video arcade contest, with Captain N unsheathing his Nintendo joystick to "rearrange" the plotline, or pressing the buttons of his control pad to freeze the action, speed it up, and slow it down — a true video game master, even though the Captain was the video game himself. One could not disagree that *Captain N* delivered exactly what it promised.

In 1990, *Captain N* teamed up with Nintendo's other star attraction for a 60-minute NBC weekender titled *Captain N: The Adventures of Super Mario Bros. 3* (see *Super Mario Bros.*), with the Captain and the Marios appearing in their own back-to-back half hours. Included in this mélange were the adventures of three other Nintendo properties: Zelda, Gameboy and Link. The series was retitled *Captain N and the New Super Mario World* in 1991, then disappeared in July of 1992 when NBC dropped virtually all its cartoon shows in favor of a two-hour Saturday morning news block. In September 1992, the syndicated weekday strip *Captain N and the Video Game Masters* debuted (minus the *Mario Bros.*), which com-

bined old *Captain N* episodes with new ones.

CAPTAIN PLANET AND THE PLANETEERS. TBS and Syndication: 9/10/1990–. TBS/TPS/DIC. TBS production staff: Original idea by R. E. (Ted) Turner. Executive producer, Barbara Y. E. Pyle. Executive in charge of operations, Roger Mayer. Executive in charge of production, Vivian Schiller. Series concept written by Phil Harnage. DIC production staff: Executive producers, Andy Heyward, Robby London and Nicholas Boxer. Supervised by Stacy Gallishaw. Produced by Cassandra Schafhausen. Produced and directed by Jim Duffy. Script coordinator, Lori Crawford. Story editors, Pat Allee and Ben Hurst. Music supervision by Joanne Miller. Main title music and score by Tom Worral. End music by Murray McFadden and Timothy Mulholland. End lyrics by Nicholas Boxer. Music editor, Stuart Goetz and Daniel J. Johnson. Voice director, Marsha Goodman. Executive in charge of operations, Brian A. Miller. Executive in charge of whole production, Thierry P. Laurin; assistant, Kimberly R. Frances. Hanna-Barbera version (THE NEW ADVENTURES OF CAPTAIN PLANET): Executive producers, Nick Boxer and Barbara Pyle. Produced by Cos Anzilotti. Story editors, Sean Catherine Derek, Laren Bright. Executive in charge of production: Roger Mayer. Main title animation by DIC/TBS. Supervising animation directors, Joanne Romersa and Ray Patterson. Animation directors: Don Lusk, Carl Urbano, Robert Alvarez, Frank Andrina, Allen Wilzbach, Joan Drake, Ken Southworth, Richard Bowman, Ernesto Lopez, Art Scott, Rebecca Bristow, Daniel De LaVega, Zeon Davush, Constantine Mustatea. Main title and score by Thomas Chase and Steve Rucker. End title music and lyrics the same as DIC version. Production facilities: Fils-Cartoons; overseas supervisor, Chris Cuddington. Logo animated by Crawford Designefx. Voice direction: Gordon Hunt, Ginny McSwain, Kris Zimmerman. Voices: David Coburn (Captain Planet); Levar Burton (Kwame); Joey Dedio (Wheeler); Janice Kawaye (Gi); Scott Menville (Ma-Ti); Kath Soucie (Linka); Frank Welker (Sushi the Monkey); Whoopi Goldberg, Margot Kidder (Gaia). "Polluting Perpertrators" ("Eco-Villains" in the press book): Ed

Captain Planet.

Asner (Hoggish Greedly); Mary Kay Bergman, Meg Ryan (Dr. Blight); S. Scott Bullock (Argos Bleak); James Coburn (Looten Plunder); Tim Curry, David Rappoport (MAL); Jeff Goldblum, Maurice LaMarche (Verminous Skumm); John Ratzenberger (Rigger); Martin Sheen (Sly Sludge); Sting, David Warner (Zarm); Dean Stockwell, Maurice La Marche (Duke Nukem); Cam Clarke (Ooze); Frank Welker (Leadsuit); and Malcolm McDowell, Edmund Gilbert and Jim Cummings. Additional guest voices: Ed Begley Jr., Danice McKellar, Lou Rawls, Floyd Red Crow Westerman, Vanna White, Phyllis Diller, Danny Glover, Charlie Schlatter, Dennis Weaver, Fred Savage, Franklin Ajaye, Hector Elizondo, Neal Patrick Harris, Robert Ito, Louis Gossett Jr., Ricki Lake, Robby Romero, Elizabeth Taylor, Robby Benson, Kadeem Hardison, Helen Hunt, Marilyn McCoo, Brock Peters, Dionne Warwick. And Real Andrews, Ephrain Figueroa, Clayton Halsey, A. L. Jamal, Sal Lopez, Danny Mann, Anna Mathias, Candy Milo, Brian Mitchell, Barbara Sammeth, Allan Shearman, Mong-Ling Tzu, Marcelo Tubert,

April Winchell, Anderson Wong, Christina Avila, Michael Bell, Peter Cullen, Linda Dangcil, Robert Foxworth, David Hayter, George Hearn, Candy Houston, Page Leong, Rene Levant, Marilyn Lightstone, Jean Marsden, Andee McAfee, Tonio Melendez, Nick Omana, Rob Paulsen, Corey Rand, Don Reed, Robert Ridgely, Neilson Ross, Rodney Saulsberry, Pepe Serna, Brian Tochi, Marcia Wallace, B.J. Ward, Eugene Williams.

Captain Planet and the Planeteers was one of media mogul Ted Turner's most conspicuous contributions to the pro-ecology movement, which, thanks to such organizations as the Environmental Media Association and the Rainforest Foundation, had become the show business "Cause *Du Jour*" of the late 1980s — culminating in the high profile "Earth Day" celebration in May of 1990.

The weekly half hour *Captain Planet*, produced in collaboration with DIC Enterprises, was at base traditional superhero fare. Five young people, each possessing a special power, pooled their energies once a week to summon an all-powerful single entity. This "united we stand" concept had been used before on such animated programs as *G.I. Joe*, *Voltron*, and *Saber Riders and the Star Sheriff* (see individual entries on these series). The twist here was that each of the five protagonists was endowed with a power of Nature that would benefit the Earth's damaged environment and thwart those "polluting perpetrators" (the series' description of its villains) who would destroy every bit of plant and animal life if given half a chance.

The heroic quintet was made up of a variety of ethnic types: Wheeler, an American, represented "Fire"; Ma-Ti, a Native American, could conjure up the power of "Heart," or compassion; Gi, an Asian, worked on behalf of "Water"; Linka, an East European, was an agent of "Wind"; and Kwame, an African, was the personification of "Earth," or soil. The powers held by these young people were transmitted through their finger rings; when all five called upon their powers simultaneously, the result was Captain Planet, who looked like the Jolly Green Giant but was in fact the invulnerable embodiment of all the heroes' skills. The Captain's motto, aimed primarily at home viewers, was "The Power Is Yours." Spiritual guidance for the

Captain Planet team was handled by Gaia, a Mother Nature type. Comic relief was the province of Sushi, a monkey. Though the characters depicted on *Captain Planet* were grounded in fantasy, the scripts were gone over with a biodegradable fine-toothed comb by a team of ecological consultants in pursuit of scientific accuracy.

Ted Turner was able to rally extensive prerelease enthusiasm for *Captain Planet* by announcing that a truckload of celebrities had signed on to contribute their voices—at Screen Actors' Guild scale salaries—for the noble cause of saving the Planet. Whoopi Goldberg and Levar Burton were among the heroes; Ed Asner, James Coburn, Martin Sheen, Sting, Dean Stockwell, and a host of other notables from Tinseltown's liberal wing dusted off their most underhanded scene-stealing tricks to play the villains, who were given such names as Hoggish Greedley, Verminous Skumm, Duke Nukem and Sly Sludge. At one point Tom Cruise intended to participate in the series as Captain Planet himself, but previous commitments forced him to bow out. (Autograph fans needn't have bothered hanging around the dubbing studios of *Captain Planet* hoping to see an unending parade of glitterati. Most of the stars didn't show up for the principal dubbing, due to workloads and union rules which set a four-hour limit on recording sessions; a "stand-in" filled in the lines for the convenience of the other actors until the star was free to loop his or her dialogue in a separate recording date.)

Utilizing every facet at the disposal of his intimidatingly efficient promotional team and sales staff, Ted Turner not only locked *Captain Planet* into the schedule of his own world-girdling TBS superstation, but also managed to syndicate the series to 223 markets. The series gained even more valuable press coverage in early 1992 when it presented an AIDs awareness episode, starring the voices of Elizabeth Taylor and *Doogie Howser, M.D.* star Neal Patrick Harris.

Now let's digress. Suppose there was a cartoon adventure series with undue emphasis on graphic violence. Suppose the heroes were all good looking, and the villains all hideously ugly. Suppose that the dialogue on this program was never spoken below the level of a shout; that the sound effects were exclusively of the bang-crunch-kaboom-aiyeee! variety; and that

the protagonists were invariably placed in life threatening perils guaranteed to induce nightmares in the youngest viewers. It stands to reason that, were such a cartoon series put on the market, the "clean up TV" brigades would be ceaseless in their efforts to have the show removed. "No violence! No hyperbole! No demeaning juxtapositions of 'beauty' with 'goodness', and 'ugly' with 'evil'! And above all, no scare tactics deliberately designed to terrify the kiddies!" And yet, when *Captain Planet and the Planeteers* made its bow in the fall of 1990, not a peep was heard from the kiddie-TV monitor groups. *Captain Planet*, you see, was politically correct. The environmental movement was sacrosanct, and anything done in its behalf equally so. So except for a somewhat xenophobic article in *Reader's Digest* (which complained that the "foreigners" on the series were more attractive than the Americans), mainstream TV reviewers and media monitors considered *Captain Planet* above criticism.

Well, not here it isn't—nor was the series allowed to escape scot-free by the more specialized animation magazines aimed at hardcore cartoon addicts. *Captain Planet* was a major letdown for one big reason. Never mind that there's a big difference between entertaining and proselytizing. Forget that the villains were rendered utterly unbelievable by having them caricatured in the manner of the worst agitprop "protest" films of the 1960s. (Hoggish Greedly was such an Establishment pig that he literally oinked!) Ignore the fact that the series implied that you're nobody if you're not a superhero (another traditional "taboo" for the Action for Children's Television crowd). *Captain Planet and the Planeteers* fell short of greatness because, despite the vaunted importance of the project, the budgetary input from the Turner machine, the generous time allotted to preplanning, and the amount of talent involved, the series' animation was on the same level as a flashing neon sign at a pizza parlor.

Conditions improved somewhat in 1993 when production for *Captain Planet*'s fourth season moved from DIC to Hanna-Barbera, at which time the Ted Turner people decided to modify their preaching tactics. The animation itself wasn't much better, but the stories were more exciting and involving, and the leading characters were less dogmatic and more fallible. The Duke Nukems and Hoggish Greedlys still motivated many of the sporadically violent plotlines on *The New Adventures of Captain Planet*, but now most of the antagonists—construction engineers, local businessmen and the like—were more misguided than evil, people who ravaged the air and despoiled the land because the Planeteers hadn't yet shown up to set them right. Best of all, "good" and "evil" was not split into two camps by physical appearance. Outside of the regular "polluting perpetrators," characters were drawn as human beings rather than stereotypes.

The closing "Planeteers Alert" 30-second segments were likewise less strident than in earlier seasons. Where once the Planeteers virtually commanded viewers to boycott fur factories and order their parents to drop red meat completely from the dinner menu, the kids at home were now advised to quietly set a good example by their own behavior, and to respectfully write to their governmental representatives in the fight against plundering the planet. The new, improved 1993 *Captain Planet*, while still far from perfect, definitely deserved its awards from the Environmental Protection Agency, and *almost* made one forget the excesses of the series' first three seasons.

Even before its attitude turnaround, *Captain Planet* paid its way. Ratings were strong, though Turner Broadcasting's insistence that it was the highest rated cartoon show on the market was protested by other animation firms who pointed out that *Captain Planet* was run twice a week in most markets, and this coupled with TBS' own weekly exposure meant that the series had three times as many chances to accrue an audience than the average once-a-week animated series. Whatever the case, the kids tuned in.

The question remaining: Did kids tune in to the earliest *Captain Planet and the Planeteers* seasons because they believed in the message, or because they were finally permitted to watch an excessively violent program that had been thoroughly cleared and approved by their elders? We may never know; we *do* know that a viable proecological message *can* be presented with full entertainment value and quality animation consistently intact. Take a look at the 1992 Don Bluth animated feature *Ferngully* sometime. Or look at another

TV cartoon series, *Widget* (q.v.), which did just what *Captain Planet* did, did it better, and didn't wrench its muscles patting itself on the back.

THE CARE BEARS. Syndicated: 1985. Those Characters from Cleveland/DIC Enterprises/SFM. Executive producers, Jean Chalopin, Andy Heyward, Tetsuo Katayama. Directed by James A. Simon. Director of animation, Hideo Nishimaki. Creative supervisor, Jean Chalopin. Script supervisor, Lori Crawford. Story editors, Sandy Fries, Jack Olesker, Francis Moss. Written by Eleanor Burian-Mohr, Randal Case, Howard R. Cohen, Matt Geller, Jack Hanrahan, Don Hart, Shelly Karol, Francis Moss, Jack Olesker, Bruce Reisman. Characters developed by Ralph Shaffee, Linda Edwards, Tom Schneider. Character design, Doug McCarthy, Rachel Brenner, Judie Martin, Richard Moore. Voice directors, Marsha Goodman, Dan Hennessey, Jennifer Goldie. Main title music, Bob Chimbel, Merry Loomis. Sound effects by Sizz Sound Creation Co., Ltd.

—**THE CARE BEAR FAMILY.** ABC: 9/13/1986–1/23/1988. Syndicated: 1988. The Saul Group/Nelvana/SFM. A Neil B. Saul Presentation. Produced by Michael Hirsch, Patrick Loubert, Clive A. Smith. Supervising producer, Leonard Hume. Line producers, Peter Hudecki and Stephen Hodgins. Creative consultants, Jack Chojnacki, Hervey Levin. Directed by Joseph Sherman, Laura Shepherd, David Marshall. Story editors, Peter Hudecki, John De Klein. "Care Bears Countdown" composed and performed by John Sebastian. Score by Tom Szczesniak, Ray Parker, Jim Morgan, Patricia Cullen, Acrobat Music. Produced in association with Global Television Network and Telefilm Canada. Animation facilities: Wang Production Co., HanHo Heung Up, Shanghai Animation Film Studio. Voices (all series): Bob Dermie (Grumpy Bear); Dan Hennessey (Brave Heart Lion/Loyal Heart Dog/Good Luck Bear); John Stocker (Mr. Beastley); Melleny Brown (Birthday Bear); Luba Goy (Lotsa Heart Elephant/Gentle Heart Lamb), Billie Mae Richards (Tenderheart Bear). Additional voices, 1985 series: Laurie Waller Benson (Bedtime Bear); Linda Sorenson (Love a Lot Bear); Janet Lane Green (Wish Bear); Patrice Black (Share Bear); Terry Sears (Champ Bear);

Eva Almos (Swift Heart Rabbit); Jim Henshaw (Bright Heart Raccoon); Marla Lukovsky (Playful Heart Monkey); Louise Vallance (Proud Heart Cat); Pauline Renny (Cozy Heart Penguin/Treat Heart Pig); and Jayne Eastwood, Len Carlson, and Joyce Gordon. Additional voices, 1986 and 1988 series: Tracey Moore, Susan Roman, Chris Wiggins, Tara Charendoff, Terri Hawkes, Adam Simpson, Sunny Thrasher, Noam Zylberman.

The *Care Bears* cartoons were what former Paramount animation director Myron Waldman referred to as "Ooooh ... ahhhh" pictures. They weren't meant to elicit laughs or shudders, but instead sighs of "oooh" and "aaah" from their audience. In this respect, they certainly succeeded.

The Care Bears were created in 1981 by a division of American Greeting Cards, "Those Characters from Cleveland," who'd struck pay dirt with their child-oriented *Strawberry Shortcake* (q.v.) line and were looking for a project that would attract children of both sexes, not just girls. The result was the Care Bear family, a collection of irresistibly cute little fat bruins with *Everyman*-like descriptive names such as "Tenderheart," "Funshine," "Grumpy Bear" and "Cheerbear." Ooooh. Each lookalike bear—and each of their "cousins," who were drawn from other animal species like Elephants, Lions and Monkeys—had an identifying symbol like a sun or a flower emblazoned on his or her tummy. Ahhhh. The Care Bears and their families lived in the Heavenly land of Care-a-lot, whence they'd travel to earth by way of a rainbow or their "cloudmobile" to ward off gloom, depression and ill will by projecting multicolored hearts from their midsections. Oooooh. Ahhhhh.

This was a very "soft" project, very attuned to the sensitivity-dominated early 1980s. The Care Bears' popularity as a greeting card attraction led to a highly rated animated TV special, *The Care Bears in the Land Without Feelings* (1983); this in turn prompted an amazingly profitable theatrical feature, *The Care Bears Movie* (1985), which spawned two sequels.

A syndicated weekly half-hour series followed in 1985: DIC's *The Care Bears*, a pink confection which was squarely aimed at preschoolers. Even the villains (mostly insensitive adults) sounded as though they were holding back, as though telling a bed-time story to a two-year-old. This series was succeeded by an ABC Saturday morning half hour, Nelvana's *The Care Bear Family*, which per its title added innumerable new characters to the property—so many that, at times, the Care Bears threatened to outnumber the audience. After one first-run and one rerun season, Nelvana syndicated *The Care Bears Family* under its original, simpler *Care Bears* title, with new episodes interspersed with the old. The Nelvana installments, which were more densely plotted and designed for a slightly older demographic group than the DIC episodes, introduced the "Caring Meter," which pinpointed just where in the world the Bears were needed most. Another new element was a regular villain, who in contrast to the "Tenderhearts" and "Bravehearts" of Care-a-Lot was named (groan!) No-Heart. This miscreant was assisted by a beast named Beastley—a sorely needed comedy relief.

What can one say? All the various *Care Bears* incarnations delighted their target audience—and though children had a tendency to quickly outgrow the Bears, there were new potential fans being born every day, equally willing to plunk down in front of the TV and to coax Mommy and Daddy to buy the myriad of *Care Bears* toys and dolls. For adults, there wasn't much to recommend the property. Most grownups emerged from a *Care Bears* viewing feeling as though they'd just been smothered in maple syrup.

Intriguingly, both the DIC and the Nelvana *Care Bears* inspired a great deal of creative animosity among rival cartoon companies. Film Roman, producers of *Garfield and Friends* (q.v.), came up with a delectably devastating parody: "The Buddy Bears," a trio of grinning-idiot animals who'd viciously pummel and humiliate anyone who didn't share their tender, loving philosophy. After *Garfield* set this irreverent tone, those animation buffs turned off by the whole *Care Bears* concept were treated to such lampoons as the "Dummi Bears" on Klasky-Csupo's *Rugrats* (q.v.) and—the cruelest and funniest takeoff of all—the masochistic "Squishy Bearz" on Savage Steve Holland's *Eek! the Cat* (q.v.).

CARTOON CLASSICS SERIALS. Syndicated: 1958. Radio and Television Packagers/ Banner Films.

Following the late–1950s success of Hanna-Barbera's *Huckleberry Hound* (q.v.), several TV distribution companies scrambled to find fresh, saleable cartoon product. One bountiful source was the output of the European animation industry, which with a little bit of trimming and a whole lot of dubbing could be redressed for American consumption. Many of the "instant" full-color cartoon packages of this period consisted wholly of foreign short subjects, notably Jayark's *Storybook Cartoons*. Some distributors took overlength animated shorts (Europeans were fond of the 20- to 30-minute timespan, as opposed to the standard Hollywood six-minute cartoon) and re-edited them into serialized adventures. As late as the mid–1970s, a number of local stations were still running a package of this nature from Flamingo Films, wherein foreign cartoons were "Americanized" to the point of absurdity. A classic example was Flamingo's serialization of the 1956 Czech cartoon featurette *The Creation of the World*, in which, so as not to offend anyone, a character obviously meant to be God was identified by the American narrator as "The Old Man with the Beard."

Banner Films' *Cartoon Classics Serials* is listed herein principally because it was one of the few syndicated animation anthologies to include at least two American-made properties. *Space Explorers* and *The New Adventures of The Space Explorers*, each running 26 cliffhanging episodes (five minutes per installment), were originally produced as educational films for the classroom circuit under the guidance of Dr. Franklyn Branley, associate astronomer of Hayden Planetarium. The "stars" were erstwhile astronauts Jim Perry and Professor Nordheim, but the real attractions to the sputnik-happy kids of the period were the lovingly detailed background renditions of various planets, constellations and nebulae. The remainder of *Cartoon Classics Serials* was the expected roundup of fairy tale adaptations, of which more were added when Banner Films expanded the package in the mid–1960s.

CARTOON FUN *see* **HOPPITY HOOPER**

CASPER AND THE ANGELS *see* following entry

CASPER THE FRIENDLY GHOST. (This entry lists only the two first-run TV cartoon series featuring the character of Casper the Friendly Ghost.)

—**THE NEW CASPER CARTOON SHOW.** ABC: 10/5/1963–1/30/1970. Harvey Films/Paramount Cartoon Studios. Directed by Joe Oriolo, I. Sparber, Seymour Kneitel, Sam Buchwald. Music by Win Sharples. Voices: Ginny Tyler (Casper); and Allen Swift, Jack Mercer, and Sid Raymond.

—**CASPER AND THE ANGELS.** NBC: 9/22/1979–5/3/1980. Hanna-Barbera. Executive producers, William Hanna and Joseph Barbera. Produced by Art Scott and Alex Lovy. Creative producer, Iwao Takamoto. Directed by Ray Patterson, George Gordon, Carl Urbano, Oscar Dufau. Story supervisor, Jim Ryan. Story editor, Bob Ogle. Story by Jack Bonestell, Patsy Cameron, Gary Greenfield, Bob Ogle, Dick Robbins. Story direction by Don Christiansen, George Singer, Sukbdev Dail. Music by Hoyt Curtin, Paul DeKorte. Voices: Julie McWhirter (Casper); Laurel Page (Minnie); Diane McCannon (Maxie); John Stephenson (Harry Scary/Commander); and Rick Dees, Bob Hastings, Jim MacGeorge, Ronnie Schell, Hal Smith, Frank Welker, Paul Winchell.

Casper the Friendly Ghost began as a one-shot theatrical cartoon produced in 1945 by Paramount/Famous Studios, titled simply *The Friendly Ghost*. This innocuous little tale of a youthful spectre who chose not to frighten people but instead to make friends was conceived by Famous Studios animator Joe Oriolo, who would be associated on and off with Casper for the next 20 years, despite the galling fact that Paramount paid him a mere $175 for the concept and pocketed millions in merchandising for themselves. The *Friendly Ghost* set a pattern that would be followed ever afterward: the little wraith's attempts at making friends with various humans and animals were invariably greeted by fear (a bug-eyed double take and the exclamation "A G-G-Ghost!"), until the boy spirit's kindness and courageousness would win over the mortals, who were most often represented by a small child or an imperiled small animal. No followup to *The Friendly Ghost* was produced until *There's Good Boos Tonight* in 1948; this was followed by *A-Haunting We Will Go* in 1949,

Unmindful of skin disease (mainly because of a lack of skin), Casper the Friendly Ghost catches some rays.

wherein the ghost was finally given the name of Casper.

At the time, there was criticism for making a hero out of a baby ghost, but such was the infant mortality rate of the late 1940s that the notion of a young life terminated before maturity was less unsettling than it is today. To modern audiences, the earliest *Casper* cartoons seem surprisingly grim: In *The Friendly Ghost*, the protagonist spends half the running time trying to kill himself (!), while in *There's Good Boos Tonight* Casper's only friend, a baby fox, is shot to death—only to be happily reunited with the boy by becoming a ghost itself.

Casper the Friendly Ghost became a series proper in 1950, the "death" angle was downplayed, and Casper was designed to look less like a small child and more like a rounded "toon" character. Sixty-two *Casper* cartoons were produced by Paramount/Famous (and its successor, Paramount Cartoon Studios) from 1950 to 1959, virtually all telling the same story repeatedly. Nonetheless, the cartoons were consistently popular, and Casper ended up the most durable of Paramount/Famous' animated characters— beaten out only by *Popeye the Sailor*

(q.v.), who unlike Casper was a character originally created outside the studio.

For several years, fans were treated to *two* Caspers. First, there was the misunderstood spirit of the cartoons; and second, there was the well-adjusted, socially accepted Casper who'd started appearing in Harvey comic books in 1952. Harvey's Casper resided in the Enchanted Forest, where no one was frightened of him and everyone loved him. He was given a new set of chums—all of them eventually spun off into their own comic book series— including Wendy the Good Little Witch, talking horse Nightmare, and "tuff" little derby-hatted ghost Spooky (who would make occasional animated cartoon appearances during the late 1950s). The "scary" ghosts of the cartoons who provided contrast to the non-scary Casper were personified in the comics as The Ghostly Trio, who weren't so much fearsome as mischievous. The Harvey version of *Casper* was even more child-oriented than the animated version, and thanks to his monthly appearances, he was better known to many children of the late 1950s than the theatrical cartoon Casper. The stylistic schism between Paramount/Famous and Harvey was made obvious only when the *Casper* cartoons were released to television in 1959 as part of a package of Paramount/Famous releases (now owned by Harvey, who had purchased the rights in perpetuity) which showed up on ABC as the weekly *Matty's Funday Funnies*, sponsored by Mattel toys.

When Harvey commissioned Paramount Cartoon Studios to produce a new series of *Casper* shorts for TV, the decision was made to follow the style of the comic books rather than the theatrical releases. The Enchanted Forest, Wendy, Spooky, Nightmare and The Ghostly Trio were brought to the small screen *in toto*—sometimes in filmed versions of the original comic book stories. The *New Casper Cartoon Show* premiered in the fall of 1963, interspersing fresh seven-minute *Casper* cartoons with several Paramount/Famous theatrical releases made between 1959 and 1962. In terms of animation style and comic content, there was very little difference between the TV cartoons and the movie-house product at this time; in fact, a number of Paramount releases were deliberately prepared for both markets. *The New Casper Cartoon Show* was perhaps less repetitious than the older *Casper* shorts, but the animation and background work was several levels below that of the Paramount releases of the early 1950s (though still well drafted in comparison to other TV-cartoon work of the period). The series remained in reruns on ABC for six seasons, capturing ratings and attracting a lot of advertising—despite the fact that the program itself was bland and unambitious, its most memorable aspect being a peppy hoedown-style theme song.

Casper's next network stint was 1979's *Casper and the Angels*, produced by Hanna-Barbera with all of that studio's late–1970s clichés, tired jokes and prerecorded laughtracks in attendance. Casper now dwelt in 2179 A.D., where with the help of comic-assistant spook Harry Scary, he aided a pair of toothsome young female members of the Space Police, Mini (flighty white girl) and Maxi (sensible black girl), in collaring extraterrestrial lawbreakers.

Mini and Maxi received their orders via two-way TV from "The Commander," a plot device that has led several media historians to label *Casper and the Angels* a ripoff of the live-action *Charlie's Angels*. But Hanna-Barbera had not yet begun to pilfer. The cartoon series not only stole from *Charlie's Angels*, but also leeched off *Laverne and Shirley*—most obviously in the character of the malaprop-spouting, redheaded Mini, who was drawn to look exactly like *Laverne and Shirley's* Penny Marshall. And just in case we missed that allusion, the girls were saddled with two "Lenny and Squiggy" style dopey male cops, Nerdly and Fungo. In addition, *Casper and the Angels* yanked inspiration from Hanna-Barbera's earlier futuristic *The Jetsons* (q.v.)—*and* from the Standard Cartoon Lexicon Department (voice-imitation division) by having red-nosed spectre Harry Scary sound like poor, overused comedian Ed Wynn.

Casper was evidently shoehorned into the proceedings as a "selling angle" to NBC; there was absolutely no reason for his being on *Casper and the Angels* at all. Even worse, where once the character was mildly cloying, Hanna-Barbera's Casper was downright irritating, slurring his dialogue in a manner suggesting a mouthful of wet tissue paper. The single neat stylistic touch in this styleless farrago was to have Casper continually float like a "real" ghost, his feet never touching the floor. Otherwise, *Casper and the Angels* was an empty hole on the TV screen, deservedly "ghostbusted" after one season's worth of 13 half hours (two 11-minute "adventures" per show). A panel of children's TV experts assembled by *TV Guide* in 1980 were right on target when writing off *Casper and the Angels* as "boring . . . An excuse to show women in tights."

After *Casper and the Angels*, the Friendly Ghost was only sporadically seen, thanks to some knotty legal tangles involving Harvey's TV rights to its comic book characters. When last we called on Casper in 1991, he was headlining a syndicated rerun package of old Paramount/Famous and Harvey TV cartoons. Evidently to sidestep residual payments, the voice tracks and musical scores of these cartoons have all been redubbed, with "offensive" material (often the funniest gags) carefully sliced out for the more sensitive 1990s.

THE CATTANOOGA CATS. ABC: 9/6/1969–9/5/1970; 9/13/1970–9/5/1971. Hanna-Barbera. Produced by William Hanna and Joseph Barbera. Directed by Charles Nichols. Music by Hoyt Curtin;

musical direction by Paul DeKorte. Components: 1. **THE CATTANOOGA CATS** (Live action). Voices: Bill Callaway (Country); Casey Kasem (Groovey); Jim Begg (Scotts); Julie Bennett (Kitty Jo/Cheesie). 2. **MOTORMOUSE AND AUTOCAT.** Voices: Dick Curtis (Motormouse); Marty Ingels (Autocat). 3. **IT'S THE WOLF.** Voices: Paul Lynde (Mildew Wolf); Daws Butler (Lambsy); Allan Melvin (Bristol Hound). 4. **AROUND THE WORLD IN 79 DAYS.** Voices: Bruce Watson (Phileas Fogg Jr.); Janet Waldo (Jenny Trent); Don Messick (Hoppy/Smirky); Daws Butler (Crumden); Allan Melvin (Bumbler).

Cattanooga Cats, a Hanna-Barbera Saturday morning hour invoking memories of 1968's *The Banana Splits Adventure Hour* (q.v.), featured live action sequences as buffers for three component cartoons. The titular cats—Cheesie, Kitty Jo, Scoots, Country and Groovey—hosted each program; like the Banana Splits, the Cattanooga congregation consisted of people in animal costumes who doubled as a rock group.

The cartoon components included *Motormouse and Autocat*, a "neverending race" saga in the manner of H-B's earlier *Wacky Races* (q.v.), with a dash of *Tom and Jerry* thrown in; Motormouse, Southern-accented proprietor of the Spin Your Wheels garage, was in eternal competition with professional rodent-eradicator Autocat and the feline's vehicle "The Mouse Stomper." *Around the World in 79 Days* was a throwback to the studio's *Adventures of Gulliver* (q.v.) conceit of recasting a classic novel with modern-day teenagers, in this case Phileas Fogg Jr. and his friends Jenny and Hoppy (no Inspector Fixx or Passepartout on this slightly abbreviated world trip). And *It's the Wolf* was an amusing retread of a venerable formula: a crafty wolf named Mildew outsmarted by a "helpless" lamb named Lambsy, whose great ally was a Dean Martin-like sheepdog, Bristol Hound.

Hanna-Barbera obviously had high hopes for the last-named component. *It's the Wolf* was honored with a prime time "sneak preview" just before its fall 1969 debut, and its dialogue was peppered with a catchphrase that Hanna-Barbera undoubtedly believed would catch on with kids in the tradition of Fred Flintstone's "Yabba Dabba Doo" and Yogi Bear's "Smarter than the average bear."

Whenever Lambsy would spot the ravenous Mildew, he'd shout "It's the wul-luff! That's who it is! It's the wul-luff!" But neither the catchphrase nor the characters ever really caught on. Only 17 installments of *Cattanooga Cats* were filmed. The program was cleft in twain for its second, all-rerun season; *Cattanooga Cats*, retaining *Around the World in 79 Days*, was moved to a Sunday half hour, while *Motormouse* branched off into his own Saturday series, with *It's the Wolf* in tow.

Overlooking its script banalities, *The Cattanooga Cats* was distinguished with bright visuals. *It's the Wolf* was drawn in a mockingly "sweet" fashion, its soft, cloud-like artwork providing sharp counterpoint to the slapstick antics of the protagonists, and to the withering sarcasm of Paul Lynde as the voice of Mildew Wolf. And *Motormouse* was rendered in a style described by H-B background designer Walt Peregoy as "lyrical." Motormouse and Autocat were inked with thinner outlines than usual for Hanna-Barbera, giving the characters the charmingly ragged appearance of a soft-pencil sketch, while their rapid-fire adventures were played out before vividly colored "fantasy" backdrops that added a tincture of whimsy to the proceedings. Also worth cherishing were Walt Peregoy's own private jokes, such as the Picasso painting hanging in Autocat's grungy garage!

THE C.B. BEARS. NBC: 9/10/1977–9/2/1978. Hanna-Barbera. Executive producers, William Hanna and Joseph Barbera. Creative producer, Iwao Takamoto. Directed by Charles Nichols. Music supervision by Paul DeKorte. Components: 1. **C.B. BEARS.** Voices: Daws Butler (Hustle); Henry Corden (Bump); Chuck McCann (Boogie); Susan Davis (Charlie). 2. **BLAST-OFF BUZZARD AND CRAZY LEGS.** No voices. 3. **HEYYY, IT'S THE KING.** Voices: Lennie Weinrib (The King/Yukayuka); Sheldon Allman (Big H); Marvin Kaplan (Skids); Don Messick (Clyde); Susan Silo (Zelda); Ginny McSwain (Shenna). 4. **POSSE IMPOSSIBLE.** Voices: Daws Butler (Big Duke/Stick); Chuck McCann (Blubber); Bill Woodson (Sheriff). 5. **SHAKE RATTLE AND ROLL.** Voices: Paul Winchell (Shake); Lennie Weinrib (Rattle); Joe E. Ross (Roll); Alan Oppenheimer (Sidney Merciless). 6. **UNDERCOVER ELEPHANT.**

Voices: Daws Butler (Undercover Elephant); Bob Hastings (Loud Mouse); Mike Bell (Chief).

This Saturday-morning 1970s time capsule from Hanna-Barbera managed to compress most of the cultural aberrations of its period. The headlining component of the weekly, hour-long *The C.B. Bears* starred three crimesolving bruins—Hustle, Bump and Boogie—who were dispatched in their personalized garbage truck to their various assignments by an unseen lady named Charlie (*Charlie's Angels* in drag) via Citizen's Band radio—an electronic fad of the era that had already been plugged to death by country/western singers.

Four more short components filled out the *C.B. Bears* hour. *Heyyy, It's the King* was an anthropomorphic animal twist on the Fonzie character popularized on the sitcom *Happy Days*, here reconceived as a "cool" lion. The King motored his hot rod through a series of 1950s adventures with his pal Skids the alligator. *Shake Rattle and Roll* was yet another H-B effort to duplicate the success of its own *Scooby-Doo* (q.v.); instead of mortals being annoyed by ghosts, this one had three ghosts—spectral innkeepers—trying to avoid being annoyed by mortals. As in past Hanna-Barbera projects, the voicework carried the bulk of the humor. Shake sounded like Hugh ("Woo Woo") Herbert, Rattle like Lou Costello, and Roll like Joe E. Ross' "Gunther Toody" character on *Car 54 Where Are You?*—not much of a stretch, since Roll's voice was supplied by Ross himself.

The other three components bypassed "up to date" references by drawing upon genres proven popular on the syndicated rerun market of the mid-1970s. *Posse Impossible* was a bumbling-cowboy opus in the tradition of the 1960s series *F Troop*. *Undercover Elephant* (a gold star for that title alone!) was an espionage spoof starring a trenchcoated pachyderm with a passion for rather ineffective disguises. And *Blast-Off Buzzard* was a throwback to the old Warner Bros. Road Runner–Coyote cartoons, this time featuring a buzzard chasing a snake named Crazylegs.

C.B. Bears was so locked into its 1977 time frame that the 13-episode series was rendered as disposable as tissue for future generations (though *Undercover Elephant* reruns popped up as filler on the Disney

Channel run of H-B's *Wake, Rattle and Roll* [q.v.]). The one component really worth noting was *Blast-Off Buzzard*, a courageous attempt to develop an all-pantomime series by Hanna-Barbera, who had previously relied heavily upon dialogue humor to compensate for animation shortcomings.

CBS CARTOON THEATRE. CBS: 6/13/1956–9/5/1956. Terrytoons/CBS Films. Host (live action): Dick Van Dyke.

CBS Cartoon Theatre deserves mention in this book for historical reasons: It was the first prime time network animated cartoon series (*The Flintstones*, sometimes cited as the first, made its debut in 1960). And that's as far as any innovation went. Hastily slapped together as a replacement for the failed western series *Brave Eagle*, *CBS Cartoon Theatre* had both eyes on the "family" market created by ABC's *Disneyland*—and in fact was scheduled directly opposite Disney's Wednesday evening weekly.

Unlike the expensive *Disneyland*, however, CBS' series was economically assembled from elements the network already had under its nose. A package of animated Terrytoons theatrical shorts, recently purchased lock, stock and barrel by CBS from Paul Terry, was featured, with interlocutory comments by host Dick Van Dyke, whom the network had under contract as a utility performer eminently suitable for daytime shows, quiz programs, and summer replacements. In emulation of *Disneyland*, Van Dyke traded dialogue with such animated characters as Heckle and Jeckle and Gandy Goose in between the shorts—but CBS' claim that the combination of live action and cartoon was accomplished through a "special process" was somewhat mitigated when viewers noted that the host was standing in a standard "den" set, speaking to cartoon characters who appeared on a wall sized screen, with no interraction between real and unreal whatsoever.

CBS STORYBREAK. CBS: 3/30/ 1985–1/4/1986; 1/3/1987–10/26/1991; 9/18/ 1993–. Host: Bob Keeshan.

CBS Storybreak was an outgrowth of a regular feature on CBS' *Captain Kangaroo* series dating back to the early 1960s, wherein the Captain would introduce limited-animation adaptations of popular children's stories produced by various studios. Material on *Storybreak* ranged from venerable ("Raggedy Ann and Andy and the Camel with the Wrinkled Knees") to brand-new ("Harry, the Fat Bear Spy"); the story that seemed to be everybody's favorite was 1985's "How to Eat Fried Worms"—*exactly* what its title described! Bob Keeshan, minus his "Captain Kangaroo" makeup, hosted the *CBS Storybreak* Saturday morning weekly, consisting of 26 anthologized animated half hours. New cartoon material was incorporated in the 1993 *Storybreak* revival (the series had been bumped in 1991 in favor of *Inspector Gadget* [q.v.]), which was seen whenever CBS didn't have a pre-empting Saturday sports event.

The "illustrated book" format of *CBS Storybreak* would later resurface on such pay-cable series as *We All Have Tales* (q.v.) and *Shelley Duvall's Bedtime Stories* (q.v.).

THE CENTURIONS. Syndicated: 1985. Ruby-Spears/Worldvision. Produced by Larry Huber. Animation supervisor, Russell Mooney. Story editors: Ted Pedersen, Dick Sebast and Rick Hoberg. Creative consultants: Gil Kane, Jack Kirby and Doug Wildey. Production design supervision by John Dorman. Music composed and produced by Udi Harpaz. Voices: Vince Edwards (Jake Rockwell); Diane Pershing (Crystal Kane); Pat Fraley (Max Ray/Dr. Wu); Bob Ridgely (Rex Charger); Neil Ross (Ace McCloud); Ron Feinberg (Doc Terror); Edmund Gilbert (Hacker); Jennifer Darling (Amber); and Bill Martin, Mona Marshall, John Stephenson, Alan Oppenheimer, Frank Welker, Mea Martineau, Tress MacNeille, Keone Young, David Mendenhall, Pat Pinney, Stacy McLaughlin.

The *Centurions*, a daily syndicated half hour, was one of the few cartoon outer space series to star a strong female character. Crystal Kane, following her father's footsteps as a crimefighting computer scientist, rallied her "Centurions"—computer generated battlers—to oppose renegade mutant software whiz Dr. Terror, his scurrilous sidekick Hacker, and the Doc's evil Doom Drones. The hero team included Jake Rockwell (voiced by TV's onetime "Dr. Ben Casey" Vince Edwards), Ace McCloud (given the same last name as the hero of the 1960s cartoon series *Space Angel*, perhaps in a fit of

nostalgia), Max Ray, Rex Charger and Amber. A two-hour special version of *Centurions* was sliced into five serialized parts and run as part of the daily package under the title "Man or Machine."

Like most animated space operas of its era, *The Centurions* was heavily indebted to *Star Wars*, with its metallic-voiced "Darth Vader" villain, its multidimensional graphics in the battle scenes (plenty of spaceship pursuits between rocky crags, a la the climactic *Star Wars* confrontation), and the inclusion of "mascot" characters—only instead of robots, the series featured a dog named Shadow and an orangutan named Lucy. Shortcomings in animation, story values and originality were compensated for by an exhaustingly fast pace and some excellent character artwork and background design. No doubt contributing to the polished veneer of *Centurions* was its team of artist/writer "creative consultants": *Jonny Quest* creator Doug Wildey, Marvel Comics co-founder and *X-Men* mentor Jack Kirby, and famed freelancer Gil Kane, of *Scarlet Avenger*, *Green Lantern* and *Conan* fame (this team would also work on such other "serious" Ruby-Spears efforts as *Chuck Norris' Karate Kommandos* [q.v.] and *Rambo* [q.v.]).

Honoring its prosocial obligations, Ruby-Spears ended each *Centurions* episode with a 30-second lesson in astronomy and space travel. These were extremely well drawn and a lot less patronizing than similar advisories on other like-vintage adventure cartoon series.

CHALLENGE OF THE GOBOTS. Syndicated: 1984. Hanna-Barbera/Tonka Toys/TeleRep. Executive producers, William Hanna and Joseph Barbera. Co-executive producer, Joe Taritero. Executives in charge of production, Jayne Barbera and Jean MacCurdy. Produced by Kay Wright. Creative supervisor and story editor, Jeff Segal. Associate story editor, Kelly Ward. Supervising director, Ray Patterson. Directed by Art Davis, Oscar Dufau, Volus Jones, Don Lusk, Rudy Zamora, Alan Zaslove. Assistant directors, Robert Goe, Bill Hutten, Rick Leon, Tony Love, Dick Patterson, Tim Walker. Story direction by Robert Taylor, Kent Butterworth, Roy Wilson, Rhoydon Sishido, Michael Swanigan, Peter Von Sholly, Rich

Chidlaw, Larry Latham, Marlja Dial, Dale Barnhart, Tom Sito, George Scribner, Bill Kroyer. Animation supervision, Richard Bowman, Gary Hurst, Willard Kitchen, Mark Simon. Production supervisor, Lynn Hoag. Design supervision, Davis Doi. Character design by Michael McHugh and Tony Sgroi. Music by Hoyt Curtin; musical supervision by Paul DeKorte. Animation facilities: Cuckoo's Nest Studio, Wang Film Production Co., Ltd. Tonka production staff: Patrick S. Feeley, Lois Hanrahan, Ray McDonald. Voices: Lou Richards (Leader-1); Art Burghardt (Turbo); Frank Welker (Scooter); Bernard Erhard (Cy-Kill); Bob Holt (Cop-Tur); Marilyn Lightstone (Crasher); Morgan Paull (Matt Hunter); Leslie Speights (A.J. Foster); Sparky Marcus (Nick Burns); Rene Auberjonois (Dr. Braxis); Brock Peters (General Newcastle); and Adrienne Alexander, Lewis Arquette, Bever-Leigh Banfield, Jered Barclay, Eddie Barth, Robin Braxton, Candy Brown, Steve Bulin, Howard Caine, Bill Callaway, Ken Campbell, Philip Lewis Clarke, Selette Cole, Henry Corden, Regis Cordic, Peter Cullen, Jennifer Darling, Jerry Dexter, George DiCenzo, Richard Dysart, Paul Eiding, Phil Hartman, Darryl Hickman, Erv Immerman, David Jolliffe, Zale Kessler, Peter Leeds, Norma McMillan, Tress MacNeille, Ken Mars, Bill Martin, Walter Mathews, Gail Matthius, Amanda McBroom, Jow Medaus, Alan Melvin, Scott Menville, Sidney Miller, Noelle North, Soon-Teck Oh, Alan Oppenheimer, Laurel Page, Rob Paulsen, Peter Renaday, Robert Ridgely, Josh Rodine, Shavar Ross, Marilyn Schreffler, Michael Sheehan, Steve Susskind, Mark Taylor, Brian Tochi, Les Tremayne, Manu Tupou, B. J. Ward, Kelly Ward, Kirby Ward, Jimmy Weldon, Eric Williams, Keone Young, Ted Ziegler. The world of toy manufacturing is a small one, where trends are pounced upon, precipitated and imitated in the time it takes to wink. At virtually the same instant in the early 1980s that Mattel's robot-cum-vehicle *Transformers* (q.v.) hit the market, Tonka Toys was on the spot with its own line of robotic characters who could transform themselves into automobiles, tanks, trains, helicopters and the like (one character named "Scales" crossed over into Paganism and metamorphosed into a serpent!). Tonka's action figures

were called "The GoBots," which like the Transformers were duly enlisted as daily cartoon stars on the half-hour *Challenge of the GoBots* (after a five-part "special" syndicated a year before the series' debut—also just like *Transformers*).

The GoBots, headed by Leader-1, came from the planet GoBotron, where for centuries they had been locked in deadly combat with the Renegades, a band of rogue robots commandeered by Cy-Kill ("Cy-Kill" as in "cycle." And another character was named "Cop-Tur." You get the idea). The Renegades referred to themselves as The Guardians, for it was as benevolent "guardians" of GoBotron that they had originally been designed—until Cy-Kill's insurrection altered the status quo. This "helpful robot turned harmful" theme would later be played out to fuller effect on 1993's *Exo-Squad* (q.v.), created by Jeff Segal—who, as it happened, had been "creative supervisor" on *Challenge of the Gobots*.

The GoBots and the Renegades thoughtfully brought their battle to planet Earth, the same path trod by Mattel's Transformers and Decepticons. Since it was the intention of the Renegades to enslave the world, the GoBots were on the humans' side, and vice versa: Leader-1's second in command was handsome human Matt Tracker.

Let's save time by breaking down the team lineups:

HEROES (GoBots): Leader-1, Scooter, Smallfoot (a female), Turbo.

HEROES (Human): Matt Tracker, General Newcastle, little kids A. J. (girl) and Nick (boy).

VILLAINS (Renegades All): Cy-Kill, Crasher, Pressure, Loco, and a few special guest goons.

With fewer marketable characters and thinner plotlines than *Transformers, Challenge of the GoBots* found itself locked in second place for most of its 65-episode run. (A theatrical animated feature with an "all-star" voice cast, *Gobots: Battle of the Rock Lord*, was released in 1986, at which time the TV series was winding down.) Compensating for its script and character shortcomings were *GoBots'* occasional bursts of comedy, evidence that Hanna-Barbera (who coproduced the series with Tonka) would always be more comfortable with humor than with "straight" adventure. My own favorite *Challenge of the*

Gobots vignettes include the outsized monocle worn by "mad scientist" robot Dr. Braxis, and Cy-Kill's self-satisfied sentiment after a particularly destructive bit of skullduggery: "Isn't mayhem wonderful?"

CHALLENGE OF THE SUPER FRIENDS *see* SUPER FRIENDS

THE CHARLIE BROWN AND SNOOPY SHOW. CBS: 9/17/1983–8/3/1986.

Mendelson-Melendez/Charles Schultz/United Features. Produced by Lee Mendelson and Bill Melendez. Written by Charles M. Schultz. Directed by Dick Horn and Steven C. Melendez. Music by Ed Bogas and Desiree Goyette. Voices: Brian Kersten, Bret Johnson (Charlie Brown); Angela Lee, Heather Stoneman (Lucy); Bill Melendez (Snoopy); Victoria Hodges, Gini Holtzman (Peppermint Patty); Jeremy Schoenberg (Linus); Kevin Brando, Danny Colby (Schroeder); Michael Dockery, Keri Holzman (Marcie); Jason Muller [Mendelson] (Rerun); Mary Tunnell (Frieda); Carl Steven (Franklin); Dana Ferguson (Little Girl); Desiree Goyette (Singer of theme song); Joseph Chemay and Joey Harrison Scarbury (Singers).

Charles Schultz' "Peanuts" comic strip characters had been welcome visitors to TV ever since a series of Ford Motor Co. ads produced by Disney veteran Bill Melendez in the early 1960s. That welcome was extended further after 1965's *A Charlie Brown Christmas*, coproduced by Melendez and former TV documentary maker Lee Mendelson, inaugurated a series of consistently fine half-hour animated specials. So cherished have these seasonal specials become over the years that it's sobering to discover that the first *Peanuts* special very nearly didn't get made. It had been turned down by virtually everyone in the TV hierarchy, most of them echoing CBS executive James Aubrey's complaint that Charlie Brown was "a loser."

While the specials never failed to score superlative ratings, Charles Schultz, Lee Mendelson and Bill Melendez had for years avoided a regular weekly *Peanuts* series for fear that the property's unique brand of whimsy would be diluted by overexposure and by being adapted into a traditional half hour cartoon cliché festival. There was also the concern that the carefully preplanned limited animation style adopted by Mendelson and Melendez, which seemed so "right" for Schultz' children characters on the specials, would be forsaken for the usual soulless Saturday morning assembly line look.

In 1983, Schultz, Mendelson and Melendez finally took the plunge with the weekly *Charlie Brown and Snoopy Show*. Contrary to expectation—and despite an overreliance on slapstick and formula plotlines—the series for the most part maintained Mendelson and Melendez' high standards. The potentially talent-draining problem of creating a 30-minute script once a week for the *Peanuts* crowd was avoided by presenting the characters in short seven-minute segments and blackout gags, capturing the chuckle per day ambience of Schultz' newspaper strip. The *Peanuts* characters seen on *Charlie Brown and Snoopy* included the "boy and his dog" title characters, along with fussbudget Lucy, blanket toting Linus, piano prodigy Schroeder, tomboy Peppermint Patty, and "naturally curly hair" girl Frieda. A pair of relatively new characters—"new" in the sense that most of the *Peanuts* cast had been solidified in the mid–1950s—also appeared: Franklin, a black child, and Rerun, Linus and Lucy's younger brother. Conspicuously absent was the eternally dirty "Pig Pen," whose careless hygienic habits were not in keeping with the network-approved, squeaky clean approach taken by *Charlie Brown and Snoopy.*

In the tradition of the *Peanuts* specials, grownup characters never appeared on *Charlie Brown and Snoopy,* nor was the voiceover work done by adult child imitators. The characters' voices were provided by genuine children, who to retain their freshness were permitted to record their dialogue one line at a time rather than being required to memorize, an on-site adult voice coach gently suggesting variations in the line readings (a practice still used on programs like *Dennis the Menace* [q.v.] which rely upon child actors). Because of the kids' naturally maturing vocal chords, there was quite a cast turnover when the series entered its second season. One voice artist who survived both first-run seasons was also the only actor who'd been in the *Peanuts* specials of the 1960s, and indeed the only adult actor ever heard on the series: *Charlie Brown and Snoopy* coproducer Bill Melendez, who supplied the giggles, simpers and howls of Snoopy the dog.

Repeats of *Charlie Brown and Snoopy* were included in the package of *Peanuts* specials purchased by the Disney Channel in 1993. (See also *This Is America, Charlie Brown*.)

CHIP 'N' DALE'S RESCUE RANGERS.

Disney Channel: August 27, 1988–September 1989. Syndicated: Fall 1989. Walt Disney/Buena Vista Television. Produced at Walt Disney Television Animation and Sun Woo Animation. Produced by Tad Stones and Alan Zaslove. Supervising director, Alan Zaslove. Directed by John Kimball and Bob Zamboni. Supervising story editor, Tad Stones. Story editor: Bryce Malek. Written by Dev Ross and Tad Stones. Theme music and lyrics by Mark Mueller. Music composed and conducted by Glen Daum. Voices: Corey Burton, Peter Cullen, Jim Cummings, Tress MacNeille, Rob Paulsen.

Having watched its $20,000,000 investment in 1987's *DuckTales* (q.v.) pay off in spades, Walt Disney Television invested $28,000,000 in its 1989 half hour TV series *Chip 'n' Dale's Rescue Rangers*, which joined *DuckTales* as the second half hour of the daily syndicated "Disney Afternoon." *Chip 'n' Dale's Rescue Rangers* represented the first time that Disney created a first-run syndie series featuring the studio's "primary" characters. Whereas the cast of *DuckTales* was comprised principally of characters created for the Disney comic books, *Rescue Rangers* starred two of Disney's star theatrical cartoon attractions: Chip and Dale, the fast-talking little chipmunks introduced in 1943 and first given "above the title" billing in 1951's *Chicken in the Rough*.

Beyond their basic character design and high-pitched voices, TV's Chip and Dale bore little resemblance to their childishly mischievous theatrical counterparts. In the tradition of Steven Spielberg's "Indiana Jones" films, the stars of *Rescue Rangers* were globetrotting soldiers of fortune, subjected to one perilous predicament after another. Unnoticed by the "big" world, the chipmunks would fly from assignment to assignment in their Ranger Plane (a jerrybuilt balloon gondola), solving small crimes before the cases got too

large for the human constabulary to control. Chip and Dale's Rescue Rangers team, headquartered in a hollow tree, was an affectionate amalgam of several adventure movie stereotypes: feisty female inventor/weapons specialist Gadget (a mouse); talespinning Aussie oldtimer Monterey Jack (a bigger mouse); a comic relief fly named Zipper; and a less frequently seen companion, Cajun crocodile bodyguard Sewer Al. The villains were likewise drawn from the nonhuman world—notably the covetous Fat Cat.

Like *DuckTales, Chip 'n' Dale's Rescue Rangers* was consummately produced and written; its Korean animation work, strictly supervised by Disney's Hollywood staff, succeeded in putting most other overseas output to shame. Also like *DuckTales, Rescue Rangers* was introduced to syndication (after an earlier pay-cable run on the Disney Channel) with a two-hour special, accompanied by what Disney described as "the largest national marketing and promotional campaign ever to launch an animated television strip." And, again also like *DuckTales, Chip 'n' Dale's Rescue Rangers* was a cash cow for everyone concerned, paving the way for such future syndicated Disney triumphs as *Tale Spin, Darkwing Duck*, and *Goof Troop* (see individual entries).

CHUCK NORRIS' KARATE KOMMANDOS.

Syndicated: 1986. Ruby-Spears/Worldvision. Executive producers, Joe Ruby and Ken Spears. Produced by Larry Huber. Directed by Charles A. Nichols and John Kimball. Story editors, Bob Distefano and Ted Field. Story direction by Dick Sebast, Xam! Productions Inc. and Jaime Diaz. Creative consultants, Doug Wildey, Gil Kane, Jack Kirby and Alfredo Alcala. Voice director, Michael Hack. Music by Udi Harpaz. Voices: Chuck Norris (Himself); Robert Ito (Tabe); Sam Fontana (Reed); Mona Marshall (Too-Much); Kathy Garver (Pepper); Alan Oppenheimer (The President); Bill Martin (The Claw); Keone Young (Super Ninja); and Linda Gary, Rodney Kagayama, Bob Ridgely, Michael Chain and James Avery.

Part of a cycle of 1980s adventure cartoons based on "real life" characters (see also *Mister T, Rambo* and *Hulk Hogan's Rock 'n' Wrestling*), Ruby-Spears' *Chuck Norris' Karate Kommandos* was a five-part, half hour syndicated series in which the popular karate expert/film star supplied the voice for his own animated likeness. Chuck Norris portrayed a special agent for the president, assigned to thwart the unspeakable machinations of an "invisible criminal empire" called Vulture, operated by The Claw and his chief lieutenant, the masked Super Ninja.

Answering to his immediate superior "Mister Director," Norris embarked on his missions with five highly trained Karate Kommandos: beautiful young woman Pepper, Samurai warrior Kimo, teenaged ninja Reed, sumo wrestler Tabe, and diminutive Too-Much, a kid character reminiscent of "Short Round" in the 1985 film *Indiana Jones and the Temple of Doom* (Too-Much was not *Karate Kommandos'* only lifting from the "Indiana Jones" saga). Following the usual 22 minutes of chopsocky action, the real Chuck Norris would offer a 30-second bit of prosocial advice to his young and impressionable audience, dictated and approved by a resident psychiatrist/technical advisor. "Violence is my last option," observed Norris at one point. "But that's the one we tuned in for!" the kids at home unanimously replied.

Except for some well-rotoscoped fight scenes in which the animators traced over live-action footage of Chuck Norris in action, *Chuck Norris' Karate Kommandos* was virtually indistinguishable from Ruby-Spears' other movie-icon-turned-cartoon star of 1986, *Rambo* (q.v.). Both projects began as miniseries, both had the same team of major comic-book artists as "creative consultants," both favored fist-and-gun marathons over plotlines, and both were blatant imitations of the "specialist team" concept popularized on the hit animated series *G.I. Joe* (q.v.). Perhaps *Rambo* graduated to a full-fledged series while *Karate Kommandos* began and ended with its first five episodes because it was less expensive for Ruby-Spears to license the rights for a fictional character than for a factual movie star. Or perhaps it was because the more literate viewers steered clear of a series that spelled "Commando" with a "K."

THE CLUE CLUB. CBS: 8/14/1976–9/3/1977; 9/10/1978–9/2/1979. Hanna-Barbera. Produced by William Hanna and Joseph Barbera. Creative producer, Iwao Takamoto. Directed by Charles Nichols.

Music by Hoyt Curtin. Musical direction by Paul DeKorte. Voices: David Jolliffe (Larry); Bob Hastings (D.D.); Patricia Stitch (Pepper); Tara Talboy (Dotty); Paul Winchell (Woofer); Jim MacGeorge (Wimper); John Stephenson (Sheriff Bagley).

Hanna-Barbera's overstocked "teenage detective" barrel found itself with another occupant in 1976. The *Clue Club* was a 16-episode, half hour Saturday morning series about a foursome of young crime-solvers (goodlooking Larry and Pepper, and funnylooking D.D. and Dotty) who sought to emulate Sherlock Holmes—but not so much as to bring about legal action from the Conan Doyle estate. This series' requisite harkback to Hanna-Barbera's *Scooby-Doo* (q.v.) was a pair of cowardly Southern bloodhounds, Woofer (a braggart who wore a Holmeslike deerstalker hat) and Wimper (who slept a lot, just like the audience). The fact that Hanna-Barbera was hoping for a repeat of the *Scooby-Doo* success was verified when the *Clue Club* reruns were briefly retitled *Woofer and Wimper, Dog Detectives* in September of 1978, before reverting to the original title.

Anything new here at all? Well, one of the "Clue Club" members, a girl named Dotty, was an egghead computer wizard—one of the earliest examples of a cartoon stereotype that would glut the kid's show market in the high tech 1980s.

CLUTCH CARGO. Syndicated: 1959. Cambria Productions. Produced by Dick Brown. Created by Clark Haas. Special technical effects by Ed Gillette. Voices: Richard Cotting, Ned LeFebvre (Clutch Cargo); Margaret Kerry (Spinner/Paddlefoot); Hal Smith (Swampy).

Released during the first syndicated cartoon boom of 1958–1961, *Clutch Cargo's* eponymous hero was a cliff-jawed, musclebound aviator/author who found adventure in all corners of the world in the company of his young ward Spinner and his dachshund Paddlefoot. These adventures were distributed by Cambria Films in five-minute cliffhanger installments, suitable for Monday through Friday serialization; the 130 episodes could also be organized into self-contained weekly half hour doses. So far, so good. Another cartoon adventure series. Well, not quite—not quite a cartoon, that is.

Created by comic strip artist Clark Haas

in the image of Roy Crane's popular newspaper serial *Buz Sawyer* (on which Haas had worked as assistant), *Clutch Cargo* was in effect a comic strip itself. "We are *not* making animated cartoons," declared Haas in 1961, and truer words were never spoken. All "movements" were governed by special effects maestro Ed Gillette, utilizing cardboard cutouts and moveable character figures. If someone walked on the series, his or her cutout likeness was shot from the waist up and jogged across the background, like a hand puppet. If there had to be a moving prop like a windmill or propellor, a cardboard windmill or propellor was poked through the background and moved by hand. And if a character smoked a cigarette, real smoke was seen. Haas described the project as "motorized movement," pointing out proudly that the *Clutch Cargo* production staff was able to turn out cartoons at one-fifth the cost of Hanna-Barbera's product.

Many of the effects seen on *Clutch Cargo* were attractive and well above average for 1959 television. The background art by Charlie Christiansen was on a par with a good Sunday comic supplement (and the best of these in 1959 were very good indeed). Some of the landscape shots had a virtual 3-D quality; this was accomplished with a four layer multi-plane system developed by Ed Gillette, which allowed the background paintings to be photographed slightly out of focus in comparison to the cut-out shrubbery and foliage in the foreground, giving such scenes the illusion of realistic depth. But that's not what you and I remember *Clutch Cargo* for, is it? The project's centerpiece was Syncro-Vox (sometimes spelled Synchro-Vox), a process invented by Ed Gillette to be used on "talking animal" advertisements in the early 1950s. Syncro-Vox was a method of combining actual lip movements of the voice actors with the faces of the cartoon characters; a closeup of the live actor, with all but the lips masked, would be shot, then superimposed over the drawings. The bizarre results are better seen than described. Suffice it to say that it was necessary for the actors to wear heavy makeup in order to blend with their cartoon counterparts, which wasn't so bad when the lips belonged to Margaret Kerry (actress wife of *Clutch Cargo* producer Dick Brown), but

seemed a little androgynous when the heavily rouged jaws of one of the male actors appeared.

In an interview with Karl Cohen in *Animato* magazine, *Cargo* actor Hal Smith recalled that the recording sessions not only required him to apply red lipstick, but also to be strapped in a chair which held his head rigidly in place in order to allow his mouth to be filmed without undue jiggle. Producer Dick Brown told Cohen that the "live" film was then projected with an interlocking camera device onto the artwork cels in progress; the film was flashed one frame at a time to permit the artists to match slight changes of facial expression with the lip movements.

Clutch Cargo was popular enough in the early 1960s for several newspaper syndicates to approach Cambria Productions in hopes of applying Syncro-Vox and "motorized movement" to their most popular comic strip characters (imagine Dick Tracy with lipstick). As it happened, the only followup to reach the production stage was *Space Angel* (q.v.), just as nonmobile as *Clutch* but a vastly superior series. Both programs made money for Cambria and satisfied the children's audience they were geared for.

But not all children. Many baby boomers—this author included—remember being attracted by the offbeat gimmickry of *Clutch Cargo* at first, then being bored to tears by the uninspiring dialogue and molasses-like progress of the storylines. The most positive note concerning *Clutch Cargo* was that a school for the deaf employed 16-mm prints of the series as a teaching tool for lipreading techniques.

Clutch Cargo disappeared from syndication in the mid–1970s, and many of those who'd watched the series began to believe *Clutch* never existed at all, but that the residual memory of the series was the residual effect of a collective bad drug trip during college. And then in 1990, cable's Comedy Channel revived *Clutch Cargo*, along with such other cultural flotsam and jetsam as the TV marionette-adventure program *Supercar* and the theatrical short subject series "Joe McDoakes," as part of an ongoing effort to introduce modern viewers to the kitsch of past decades. Described by *TV Guide* as an "animated aberration," *Clutch Cargo* once more won the hearts of the youth of America—this time as an object of laughter.

COLONEL BLEEP. Syndicated: 1957. Richard H. Ullman Inc./Soundac Color Productions. Created and written by Robert D. Buchanan. Animation director, Jack Schleh. Technical director, Bob Biddlecom. Narrator: Noel Taylor.

Rendered in a style best described as Early Cereal Commercial, *Colonel Bleep* followed the semicomic interplanetary exploits of its title character, a peacekeeper of the Planet Futura (misspelled "Pheutora" in earlier sources, probably due to the narrator's pronounced Southern accent) who was headquartered on Zero Zero Island. Colonel Bleep, who looked like a helmeted embryo, travelled in space and also journeyed back and forth in time. To that end, Bleep deputized two "experts" from Earth to help him better understand the manners and mores of different historical periods: Squeek, a small-boy puppet, was from The Present (the 1950s, that is, which explained his "TV cowboy" costume), while Scratch, a superstrong caveman, was uniquely suited to handle the distant past, since he'd taken a long nap during Evolution. The main heavy of the piece was the shadowy Dr. Destructo, who toiled endlessly to conquer the universe. Not far behind Destructo in the villainy department was Captain Patch, a displaced pirate.

While the series' sole voice artist Noel Taylor was principally used as narrator, it is not true that the characters of *Colonel Bleep* never spoke dialogue, as has been previously reported. And though its frenetic pace and severely limited animation might lead the modern viewer to conclude that the series was filmed in Japan in the early 1960s, the 104 six-minute *Colonel Bleep* episodes were actually produced at the Soundac Studios of Miami, Florida, in the late 1950s—one of the first TV cartoon series to be filmed in color.

In 1993, *Colonel Bleep* animation director Jack Schleh told interviewer Karl Cohen that the character derived his name from the "bleep bleep" sound made by Russia's Sputnik satellite, and that this inspiration occurred while the first group of *Bleep* cartoons were being completed. If so, the character christening must have been a *very* last-minute decision, since while Sputnik was launched in October of 1957, many of the cartoons carry a copyright date of 1956!

Originally designed as part of a franchised children's show package titled *Uncle Bill's TV Club*, *Colonel Bleep* most often played as "filler" for the Uncle Bill or Captain Bob or Aunt Susie who happened to be your local kiddie host. Due to the saleability of anything filmed in color in the 1960s, the series remained alive in syndication long after the space-travel format had become antiquated; as late as 1970, New York City's WNBC-TV was running *Colonel Bleep* on Saturday mornings. And thanks to the recent rediscovery of the series' original negatives, we may be due a *Colonel Bleep* renaissance in the 1990s—launched by the "guest appearance" of a *Bleep* episode in the 1993 theatrical cartoon-compilation film *The Speed Racer Movie* (see *Speed Racer*).

COMIC STRIP. Syndicated: 1987. Rankin-Bass/Lorimar-Telepictures. Executive producers, Arthur Rankin Jr. and Jules Bass. Supervising producer, Lee Dannacher. Script supervisor, Peter Lawrence. Project planning: Leisure Concepts Inc. Music by Bernard Hoffer. Character design by Michael Germakian, Bob Camp and Pepe Moreno. Animation by Pacific Animation Corp.; in charge of production, Hasaki Iizuka. Psychiatric consultants, Dr. Robert Kuisis Ph.D., Dr. Patricia M. Carey, Ph.D. Components: 1. **KARATE KAT.** Voices: Robert McFadden, Earl Hammond, Maggie Jakobson, Gerriane Raphael, Larry Kenney. 2. **MINI-MONSTERS.** Voices: Robert McFadden, Jim Meskimen, Maggie Jakobson, Seth Green, Jim Brownold, Josh Blake, Danielle DuClos, Peter Newman. 3. **STREET FROGS.** Voices: Gordy Owens, Gary V. Brown, Tanya Willoughby, Carmen De Lavallade, Ron Taylor, Daniel Wooten, Donald Acree, Robert McFadden. 4. **TIGERSHARKS.** Voices: Robert McFadden, Earl Hammond, Larry Kenney, Peter Newman, Jim Meskimen, Jim Brownold, Camille Banora.

No sooner had Hanna-Barbera struck paydirt with its 90-minute weekend cartoon omnibus *Funtastic World of Hanna-Barbera* (q.v.) than did other producers announce that they, too, would come up with syndicated Sunday morning animation marathons. Rankin-Bass' contribution was

The Comic Strip (see also Marvel's *Super Sunday*). In the tradition of its Hanna-Barbera role model, *Comic Strip* offered four self-contained half hour series, suitable for *en masse* weekend telecasts or as individual daily "strips" (hence the blanket title).

Relatively speaking, the best of the components was "Karate Kat." Though its title misled youngsters that they were about to see a parody of the hit theatrical feature *The Karate Kid*, "Karate Kat" was actually a spoof of TV private detective shows, starring an inept feline martial arts expert ("I'm lean, I'm mean, a Karate Machine") who worked for the McClaw Detective Agency. Fellow gumshoes included "Big Mama" Katie McClaw, the proprietor; Japanese weapons whiz Katmandu; dim-witted Cat Gut; and a brace of leggy females—the denser of the two, Meow-Baby, being the only McClaws employee who took the vain Karate Kat to be the supercop he imagined himself.

The remaining components were serviceable but forgettable. "The Street Frogs" (originally "The Street Kids"), starring a quartet of worldly young crime-solving amphibians, was a rap-talking precursor to *Teenage Mutant Ninja Turtles* (q.v.). "The Mini-Monsters" headlined the mischievous offspring of Dracula, The Wolfman, The Mummy, The Invisible Man and the Frankenstein Monster: Dracky, Wolfie, Mumm-O, Blank-O, and Franklin respectively. These monstrosities befriended a pair of young mortals named Sherman and Melissa at a ghoulish summer resort, Camp Mini-Mon. This was a variation on the old Hanna-Barbera series *Drak Pack* (q.v.), which in turn would be revitalized on H-B's "Monster Tails" (see *Wake, Rattle and Roll*).

Finally there was "Tigersharks" (originally "Sea Angels"), the most serious of the *Comic Strip* components, which featured a band of musclebound super-heroes able to transform themselves into fishlike beings. When trade-paper announcements were made about the coming *Comic Strip* in October of 1985, a fourth component titled "Spellsinger" was in the planning stage; this was subsequently dropped.

Twenty-five two-hour installments of *Comic Strip* were produced, enough for five weeks' worth of daily viewing should a local TV station be inclined to divide up the package into four separate series. Each component's star (or stars) was featured in two 11-minute episodes, overseen for suitable content by a team of "psychiatric consultants"—though one wonders just what prosocial purpose prompted these worthies to okay the plot device of having *Karate Kat's* Katie McClaws turn out to be the ex-wife of the town's top criminal!

Despite entertaining scripts—particularly those written for *Karate Kat* by newspaper comic strip veteran Leonard Starr—and clever character design (among the artists was future *Ren and Stimpy* [q.v.] contributor Bob Camp), none of the individual components of *Comic Strip* had any real staying power, and the project was off the market by the fall of 1988.

COMMANDER McBRAGG *see* **TENNESSEE TUXEDO**

THE COMPLETELY MENTAL MISADVENTURES OF ED GRIMLEY. NBC: 9/10/1988–9/2/1989. Hanna-Barbera. Produced by William Hanna, Joseph Barbera, and Martin Short. Voices: Martin Short (Ed Grimley); Joe Flaherty (Count Floyd); Catherine O'Hara (Miss Malone); Jonathan Winters (Mr. Freebus/Roger Gustav); Andrea Martin (Mrs. Freebus); Frank Welker (Sheldon); Danny Cooksey (Wendell Gustav); and Dave Thomas.

Ed Grimley, the "ultimate nerd" created by Martin Short for *Second City TV* and *Saturday Night Live*, was given a shot at his own Saturday morning animated vehicle in 1988. Short himself provided the voice of the feckless Mr. Grimley (reportedly as a means of entertaining his own cartoon-fan children), while several of the comic actor's "Second City" compadres also took part in the voicework and appeared with Short in live-action buffers between segments. Joe Flaherty was heard and seen in the live-action scenes as tacky TV horror movie host Count Floyd, star of "Count Floyd's Scary Stories"; Catherine O'Hara enacted the cartoon role of Ed's lovely actress neighbor Miss Malone; and Andrea Martin did the voice of Ed's hostile landlady Mrs. Freebus. Dave Thomas likewise showed up in scattered supporting roles. The legendary Jonathan Winters, mentor of many an improvisational comic (Martin Short included), contributed a voice-over as one of the Gustav Brothers, a brace of unidentical twins who acted as "Mr. Wizard"-style interpreters of Grimley's 13 adventures.

The *Completely Mental Misadventures of Ed Grimley* scored points with critics for its very funny scriptwork and its affectionate treatment of "out of mainstream" character types. Had this series taken off, Hanna-Barbera would have followed up with the cartoon capers of another "real world" comedian, Whoopi Goldberg. But much of the satire on *Ed Grimley*—notably Count Floyd's being stuck with hosting a package of determinedly nonfrightening films, a frequent plight of TV "Shock" emcees of the 1950s and 1960s—was aimed at the over-30 crowd with deliberate cartoon parodies of schlock scare pictures of the 1950s, and as such was lost on the usual Saturday morning kiddie contingent (later, of course, such "over their heads" Saturday A.M. cartoons as *Eek! the Cat* (q.v.) and *Bobby's World* (q.v.) would flourish). NBC cancelled the series in September 1989; ironically, its replacement was *Camp Candy* (q.v), a project featuring still another of Martin Short's Second City colleagues, John Candy.

CONAN THE ADVENTURER. Syndicated: September 1992. Conan Properties/Graz Productions/Sunbow/Claster. Executive producers: Joe Bacal, Tom Griffin, C. J. Kettler. Produced by Will Meugniot. Executive in charge of Graz Productions: Jim Graziano. Supervising animation directors, Karen Peterson, Graham Morris. Art director, Russ Heath. Assistant art director, Nick Cuti. Creative consultant/story editor: Christy Marx. Creative director, Joe Bacal. Title song by Chase/Rucker Productions. Executive in charge of production, Carole Weizman. Produced through the facilities of Akom Productions. Akom directors staff: Kyung-Chook Sah, Young-Wook Yeo, Heung-Sun Oh, Sung-Chil Kim, Seung-Jin Oh. Voices: Kathleen Barr, Michael Beattie, Jim Burnes, Gary Chalk, Mike Donovan, John Pyper Ferguson, Janyce Jaud, Scott Mc-Neil, Richard Newman, Doug Parker, Alec Willows.

Conan, barbarian warrior from the land of Cimmeria, was created for *Weird Tales* magazine by Robert E. Howard in 1932. The project's heavy reliance on sword and sorcery, coupled with the musclebound protagonist's utterly antisocial demeanor, forced comic book publishers to shy away from Howard's creation for many years. With the relaxing of restrictions on comic book subject matter in the late 1960s, Marvel Comics began to see possibilities in Conan. The company bought the rights to Howard's character in 1970, and the resultant periodical was a hit, principally with teens and young adults. Marvel writer Roy Thomas and illustrators Barry Smith, Gil Kane and John Buscema retained Conan's rough edges and mercenary nature, while tempering the character's tendency to kill first and ask questions later. Still, Conan was too much the barbarian for mass media consumption. While Arnold Schwarzenegger cemented his reputation on a brace of *Conan* theatrical films in the early 1980s, TV would still have to mature a bit before the character could make a satisfying home screen debut.

As it turned out, it was Conan who did the maturing. Sunbow/Claster's 13-week animated series of 1992 reflected that spiritual growth process in its title: no longer the Barbarian, our hero was now *Conan the Adventurer.* Elements that had been developed by Marvel to "motivate" Conan's brutal misanthropy were now fully utilized by Sunbow/Claster to cleanse the character and make him a misunderstood victim of circumstance and a selfless crusader for justice, rather than a ruthless campaigner for his own comfort and convenience. The cartoon Conan was a young nobleman whose family had been turned to stone by the despicable Rathamon, head of the Serpentmen. Conan was then captured and enslaved, whereupon he made friends with those similarly oppressed. The rest of the serialized adventures delineated Conan's struggle to escape his bondage, to thwart the villains, to establish freedom in Cimmeria and to restore his family to "human" status.

Conan the Adventurer premiered over 103 stations as Claster/Sunbow's hasty replacement for its failed syndicated series of 1991, *Bucky O'Hare and the Toad Wars* (q.v.). Emulating its kid-oriented predecessor, *Conan* was geared less for the hardcore Robert E. Howard devotees than it was for the 11- to 15-year-old demographic group. The program became a daily in 1993, with 52 new episodes put together by France's JetLag Productions (see also

He didn't smile like that in the pulp novels: *Conan the Adventurer.*

Heroes on Hot Wheels); plans were also drawn up that year for a network spinoff series spotlighting Conan's preteen friends, "The Barbarian Kids" (isn't that a bit redundant?). *Conan the Adventurer* certainly satisfied its target audience, and though the animation was merely adequate, its variety of color and attention to detail in the background art were particularly pleasing. But it was a far cry from the bulging-bicep *Conan* pulps of the good, gory old days.

COOL McCOOL. NBC: 9/10/1966–8/31/1969. Cavalier Productions/King Features. Executive producer: Al Brodax. Created by Bob Kane. Animation by TVC; animation produced by George Dunning. Voices: Bob McFadden (Cool McCool); Chuck McCann (Number One/Riggs); Carol Corbett (Friday).

Cool McCool, the second TV cartoon project from *Batman* creator Bob Kane, was more entertaining than the first (see *Courageous Cat*) but still too derivative to fully stand on its own merits. Inspired by the secret agent spoof *Get Smart, Cool*

McCool starred a bungling crimesolver who somehow always managed to collar his man. McCool, like Maxwell Smart, answered to a long-suffering superior, here named Number One; the equivalent to Smart's "Sorry about that, chief!" was McCool's oft-repeated assurance "That will *never* happen again, Number One." And if Maxwell Smart could have a "shoe telephone," Cool McCool was perfectly justified in possessing a transistorized mustache.

To avoid an all-out ripoff, Cool McCool sounded nothing like *Get Smart* star Don Adams. Instead, he spoke in a manner reminiscent of comedian Jack Benny (in 1983, the *Cool McCool* concept would be revived more successfully by DIC's *Inspector Gadget* [q.v.], which *did* feature the voice of Don Adams). Each of the 20 *Cool McCool* half hours featured two short adventures spotlighting the star. A third component recalled the exploits of Cool's equally inept father, Keystone Kop clone Harry McCool.

Produced by King Features executive Al Brodax (see also *The Beatles, The King*

Features Trilogy and *Popeye the Sailor*), *Cool McCool* was mildly funny but generally uninspired. The series was occasionally effective in invoking the "film noir" milieu and forced-perspective art of its mentor Bob Kane. At other times, the backgrounds were too busy for the audience to appreciate what was going on in the foreground—a surprisingly clumsy graphic choice from the series' British animation staff at TVC Studios, who'd done such excellent work on Brodax' *The Beatles*.

Cool McCool was in production for only a year. After its initial run in the 1966-67 season, network reruns bounced back and forth between Saturday and Sunday mornings until 1969.

C.O.P.S. Syndicated: 1988. CBS (as CYBER C.O.P.S.) 3/27/1993–9/4/1993. DIC Enterprises/Claster. Executive producer: Andy Heyward. Supervising producer, Robby London. Produced by Richard Raynis. Executives in charge of production: Richard Raynis and Winnie Chaffee. Directed by Kevin Altieri. Supervising story editor, Bruce Shelley. Art director, Alex Stevens. Animation supervisor, Gun Chic Chung. Public service announcements ("COPS for Kids") produced and directed by Terri B. Akman; written by Phil Harnage. Voices: Ken Ryan (Baldwin P. "Bulletproof" Vess); Jane Schoettle (Rafaella Diamond, alias Nightshade); Brent Titcomb (Rock Crusher); Mary Long (Tina "Mainframe" Cassidy); Paul de la Rosa (Berserko); Nick Nichols (Buttons McBoomBoom/ Rex "Bowzer" Pointer); Dan Hennessey (Turbo Tu-Tone); Jeri Craden (Whitney Morgan); Darren Baker (Hardtop); Paulina Gillis (Ms. Demeanor); John Stocker (P. J. "Longarm" O'Malley); Ron Rubin (Dr. Badvibes); Len Carlson (Brandon Babel, alias The Big Boss/Mace); Marvin Goldhar (Squeeky); Peter Keleghan (Bullseye); Elizabeth Hanna (Mirage); Ray James (David E. "Highway" Harlson/Barricade); and Noah Zylberman, Ray Kahnert, Ruth Springford, Jon Roncetti, Michael Fantini, Barbara Hamilton.

C.O.P.S. was one of two daily police-force cartoon series released to the syndicated market in 1988 (see also *Police Academy*), and as such was dismissed by viewers who didn't care much for the "peacekeeper" genre. Actually, *C.O.P.S.*

had potential—though it was a potential left unrealized by the dishearteningly flat animation style.

Set in 2020 in corruption-ridden Empire City, *C.O.P.S.* was heavily inspired by the 1986 feature film *RoboCop* (which spawned an animated series of its own—see *Marvel Action Universe*). Virtually all the characters, including the bit players, were either bionic creations (part human, part cyborg) or endowed with computer-based skills. The title's initials stood for Central Organization of Police Specialists, overseen by hero/narrator Baldwin P. "Bulletproof" Vess, a former F.B.I. operative. Each member of the C.O.P.S. team—whose battle cry was "It's crime fighting time!"—had a special techno-generated peacekeeping talent, implicit in the nicknames. "Highway" was a warp-speed highway patrolman; "Longarm" was endowed with crookcatching long arms (amazing, isn't it?); "Sundown" was a bionic Wild West type; and "Mainframe" (originally "Powderkeg") was a female computer expert. Let's get the other C.O.P.S. out of the way as quickly as possible: Hardtop, Mirage, Bullseye, Mace, Barricade, Updraft and Buttons McBoom-Boom. And there was Bowzer, a K-9 officer who owned a robot pooch named Blitz. These characters were far more amusing than their names—honest they were.

In keeping with the "high tech" concept (and the series' heavy reliance on *Dick Tracy*-style literalism), the heavies were likewise semiautomated, likewise blessed with descriptive character names: Berserko, Rockcrusher, Ms. Demeanor, Turbo Tu-Tone, Dr. Badvibes, and Nightshade. With all this galloping gimmickry, it's almost a relief to report that the top villain, "The Big Boss," was an old fashioned Edward G. Robinson type.

Despite its "beat the concept to death" approach, *C.O.P.S.* scored with a sturdy inner lining of social satire. Empire City's ineffectual Mayor Davis would invariably stymie the C.O.P.S. team and unwittingly aid the cause of the villains through his foolhardy cost-cutting attempts. One of his most ruinous notions was to commission a team of robot meter maids, who ended up imposing life imprisonment for the slightest traffic infractions while letting the real criminals off scot-free (the manufacturer of these robots was, of course, in the pocket of the Big Boss). Other half hour episodes likewise illustrated the problem of maintaining law and order in a community more concerned with frugality, appeasement and red tape than in real solutions. The satiric thrust of *C.O.P.S.* was aimed more at adult victims of civic government stupidities than at children, though the series fulfilled its prosocial obligations with its daily "C.O.P.S. for Kids" tips on how to best serve the community and to avoid becoming a crime victim. These 30-second bites were produced in cooperation with the National Crime Prevention Council, U.S. Department of Justice, National Center for Missing and Exploited Children, Project DARE (an anti-drug program), International Juvenile Officer's Association and the California Highway Patrol. Local stations were encouraged by DIC/Claster to create their own "C.O.P.S. for Kids" tips and telecast them during the closing minutes of each *C.O.P.S.* installment.

Unfortunately, the 65 *C.O.P.S.* episodes were animated in such a static fashion that viewers seldom stuck around long enough to revel in the slyly lampoonish plotlines. The series was on and off before Hasbro could fully capitalize on the individual skills of the C.O.P.S. members by converting them into a series of toy action figures — which was, dare we suggest, the ultimate motivation for putting *C.O.P.S.* on the air in the first place. In March of 1993, the program (and its merchandising) was given a second chance in rerun form as a Saturday morning CBS network entry, retitled *Cyber C.O.P.S.*

COUNT DUCKULA. Nickelodeon: 2/8/1988–. Cosgrove-Hall Productions/Thames Television. Executive producer, John Hambley. Produced by Mark Hall and Brian Cosgrove. Director and associate producer, Chris Randall. Animation director, Dan Whitworth. Written by Jimmy Hibbert. Music by Mike Harding. Voices: David Jason (Count Duckula); Jack May (Igor); Brian Trueman (Nanny); Jimmy Hibbert (Von Goosewing); Barry Clayton (Narrator); Doreen Edwards, Mike Harding (Theme song vocals); and Ruby Wax.

Right! *Count Duckula* was a billed, feathered and webfooted takeoff on a famous horror legend. Wrong! It wasn't a takeoff on "Frankenstein."

It was a dark and stormy night. Igor, the hulking majordomo of Castle Duckula, was hard at work trying to revive the last of a line of vampire ducks, who'd been suspended in eternal sleep by a ray of sunshine centuries earlier. Blood was the principal ingredient needed for returning the corpse to life. But, no! Instead of blood, the dormant Count Duckula was accidentally given a transfusion of fresh red tomato catsup. The result was a vegetarian vampire — a likeable chap who sounded more like Daffy Duck than Bela Lugosi, who would rather pursue a showbiz career than preside over his rotting castle, and who was not the least interested in sinking his fangs in anyone's jugular. Poor Igor was stuck with taking Count Duckula all over the world in hopes of stirring memories of his master's bloodsucking heritage — just one waddle ahead of tireless vampire hunter Dr. Von Goosewing, who always seemed to have a hammer and stake tucked away in his overnight bag (and whose niece Vanna was enamored of the hapless Count). About the only "normal" regular on *Count Duckula* was the Count's devoted Nanny, who managed to retain her good nature and calm demeanor in the face of the most appalling circumstances.

Originally produced in England in the mid-1980s by the same cartoon craftspeople who also gave us *Danger Mouse* (q.v.), *Count Duckula* was a droll 52-week foray into *Monty Python* territory (with but scant resemblance to an earlier "Duckula," created in the 1970s by American comic book artist Scott Shaw!). The series' own special brand of "nut" humor was maintained even during the closing credits of each half hour episode, wherein the viewer could find the name of one Hal E. Gator, billed as the series' animal trainer.

THE COUNT OF MONTE CRISTO. Syndicated: 1974. Halas and Batchelor/RAI Television. Voices: George Roubicek, Jeremy Wilkin, Bernard Spear, Peter Hawkins, Miriam Margoyles, Jean England, David de Keyser.

Alexandre Dumas' classic tale of sweet revenge was given the "superhero" treatment on this animated 17-week, half hour series, produced for European television in England and Italy and syndicated on a limited basis in the United States. The Count of Monte Cristo was no longer a middle-aged prison escapee seeking retribution against those who had wronged him, but a robust young man fighting for truth and justice. Accompanying the Count in his do-gooding were his friends, comic relief Rico and hulking former slave Jacopo.

COURAGEOUS CAT AND MINUTE MOUSE. Syndicated: 1960. Sam Singer Productions/Prime TV/Trans Artists/TeleFeatures. Produced by Marvin Woodard and Ruben Timmins. Directed by Sid Marcus and Ruben Timmins. Music by Johnny Holiday. Voices: Bob McFadden.

Batman creator Bob Kane anticipated the spoofery inherent in the 1966 live action TV series based on the Caped Crusader by dreaming up his *own* spoof in 1960, which resulted in a package of 100 five-minute cartoons. In place of Batman and Robin were the caped and cowled Courageous Cat and Minute Mouse. Their base of operations was Empire City, not Gotham City. And instead of such colorfully costumed foes as the Riddler and the Penguin, Courageous Cat and Minute Mouse did battle with the likes of Foxy Fox, Professor Shaggy Dog, and Rodney Rodent—but most often with Flat-Face Frog, an Edward G. Robinson-style gangster who seemed to be in every other episode.

Courageous Cat had a gimmick. You couldn't miss it. It was pulled out and played beyond its worth at every opportunity. The gimmick was Courageous Cat's Catgun, which with a flick of the trigger could be converted into a parachute, an umbrella, a bulletproof shield, a ladder, a can opener—and on rare occasions, a gun. The ceaseless repetition of this single joke was rendered even unfunnier by the plodding animation style, with the series' occasional good gags sacrificed to hesitant, jerky character movement. In all fairness, *Courageous Cat* did have at least one sure-fire laugh provoking aspect. Unlike the police commissioner of *Batman*, who would make an effort to solve a crime before calling in the Cowled One, the bulldog police chief on *Courageous Cat* would throw in the towel almost before the crime was even committed, going so far as to plead for Courageous and Minute's help via radio bulletins and newspaper headlines. It was perversely refreshing to see a police official on a superhero series surrender so

willingly to the fate of being rescued by someone wearing tights.

Other than that, *Courageous Cat* was a drag. Still, it *was* in color and certainly capable of enthralling the small children for whom it was designed, so the property sold well during its first syndicated run. Later on in the 1960s, the popularity of the *Batman* TV series gave *Courageous Cat* a renewed spurt of profitability, at least until its target audience grew up.

CRAZY CLAWS see KWICKY KOALA

CRO. ABC: 9/18/1993–. Film Roman/ CTW. Partial funding by National Science Foundation. Executive producers, Franklin Getchell, Marjorie Kalins, Phil Roman. Executive in charge of production, Bill Schultz. Produced by Bob Richardson. Story editor and voice director, Mark Zaslove. Supervising director, Dave Brian. Directed by James West, Milt Gray, Kyle James, Swinton Scott, Bob Nesler. Executive editor, Edward G. Atkins, Ph.D. Research director, Susan L. Mendelsohn, Ph.D. [10 Ph.D.s on advisory staff!]. Animation facilities: Sunwoo Animation Co. Ltd. and Anivision America, Inc. Overseas production supervisor, James Miko. Music and main title theme by Stacy Widelitz. Based on the book *The Way Things Work* by David Macaulay. Developed for television by Mark Zaslove. Voices: Max Casella (Cro); and Charlie Adler, Ruth Buzzi, Jim Cummings, Tress MacNeille, Candy Milo, Laurie O'Brien, April Ortiz, Jane Singer, Jussie Smollet, and Frank Welker.

Since its formation in 1969, the Children's Television Workshop had been linked with PBS, overseeing and helping finance such quality programs as *Sesame Street* and *The Electric Company*. It was therefore with understandable pride that ABC gave full-force publicity to the fact that the Workshop had chosen the network for its very first non-PBS Saturday morning effort. To the tongue-cluckers disdaining the move into the world of commercial television, Franklin Getchell, executive producer for Children's TV Workshop, explained that the move was "to reach as many kids as we could . . . we had to go where the kids go—to Saturday morning programs." To allay the fears of those who felt the workshop had sold out, assurances were made that the maiden

ABC effort would have abundant educational merit.

The property decided upon was *The Way Things Work*, a lavishly illustrated coffee-table book written in 1988 by David Macaulay. In nonpatronizing but enjoyable terms, Macaulay chronicled the history of technology, partly through lovingly detailed illustrations, and partly through the "diary" of an enterprising Cro-Magnon man, who was discovering for literally the first time the Way Things Work: pulleys, levers, wheels, screws, springs and such natural phenomena as Light and Sound. The book took the readers—and its caveperson protagonist—straight into the world of nuclear energy and mass communications, explaining everything with clear-eyed accuracy. Throughout the book, Mankind's emergence into the 1980s was counterpointed with the narrator/diarist's capture and domestication of the "Great Woolly Mammoth," who served purposes as varied as beast of burden, household pet, and "model" for such inventions as TV and movie cameras.

"We made a conscious decision to create programming that we felt would have wide entertainment appeal, with content," said Marjorie Kalins, Children's Television Workshop vice president. "We're demystifying science, and bringing it right to kids so they can have fun with it." To allow the CTW leeway to produce the best program possible under the pressure-cooker circumstances of weekly half-hour cartoonery, ABC gave the organization an 18-month lead time to develop and produce *The Way Things Work*.

After all that time, and with the added incentive of a $7 million grant from the National Science Foundation, one might have hoped that the CTW and its coproducers Film Roman would have come up with something more worthwhile than the resultant series, retitled *Cro*. This cartoonization of the Macaulay original turned the book's supporting character into its star and subjugated the book's star to a stooge. *Cro* was not so much about cave boy "Cro" as about his intellectual mentor: A woolly mammoth named Phil. According to *Cro*, the Cromagnon hero and his Neanderthal foster family—grunt-speaking Nandy, Uhg, Ogg, and Bob the pet monkey—would never have mastered machinery and tools (not to mention understanding the phases of the moon, the buoyancy of water, and the intricacies of musical instruments) had it not been for a pack of benevolent talking mammoths! And we of the Modern Age would never have known about Cro and his era had not Phil been quick-frozen in a block of ice and revived in the 20th century.

Beyond the eco-correct admonition that we shouldn't destroy endangered animal species because we have so much to learn from them, the "history" presented on *Cro* made the scriptwriting on *The Flintstones* (q.v.) look like H. G. Wells. Everyone spoke in pop-culture patois, the Neanderthals swapping 1990s slang in an Early Tonto dialect. The "modern" jokes were on the level of the Neanderthals' flossing their teeth and the mammoths' admission that their favorite music was the banal ballad "Feelings"—this on a program ostensibly aimed at impressionable six- to 11-year-olds. And as a "hook" to grab a wider demographic audience range, the characters in the modern sequences—wherein Phil explained to his 20th century scientist rescuers what life was like millions of years ago—were ethnic stereotypes. Dr. C was an excitable Hispanic woman, and her young assistant Mike was a rap-spouting African American. The dialogue and byplay in the modern sequences were metered to a Hip-Hop beat—a WASP's notion of how to "reach" young urban kids.

Cro was trivial, patronizing and misleading in a manner that Children's Television Workshop had sagaciously avoided in its PBS work. The weekly half-hour series even insulted one's common sense by suggesting that the only threat to Cro-Magnon man's wellbeing was a scraggly pack of "Dire Wolves," headed by saber-toothed Selene and his two Runyonesque henchwolves. These characters were drawn as comic-opera buffoons, inept enough to assure that *Cro* could never be accused of frightening its audience. And the producers were *proud* of this subliminal invitation to children everywhere to cuddle up to those snarling predatory animals in their own environment.

The producers also "Cro'ed" about how brilliantly they'd blended comedy, music and education, when in fact the story stopped dead in its tracks every time an educational bite about science or technology was played out. Maybe the Children's Television Workshop should have reviewed some *Electric Company* reruns, just to remind themselves how once upon a time they'd done this sort of thing correctly.

Incredibly, media critics and educators were blind to *Cro's* many flaws, overpraising the series to the skies. Perhaps this was out of gratitude that CTW came off its pedestal to honor ABC with its presence, or perhaps the critics and pundits never read David Macaulay's original book. To be sure, *Cro* did show kids "the way things worked." It also showed how some adults evidently viewed children—as Cro-Magnons and Neanderthals who needed a "mammoth" educational organization to lead them out of darkness.

CRUSADER RABBIT. Syndicated: 1949 and 1957. 1949 release credits: Television Arts Productions/Jerry Fairbanks. Produced, directed and written by Jay Ward and Alex Anderson. Voices: Lucille Bliss (Crusader Rabbit); Vern Loudon (Rags). 1957 release credits: Creston Studios/TV Spots. Produced by Shul Bonsall. Voices: GeGe Pearson (Crusader Rabbit); Vern Loudon (Rags); Russ Coughlan (Dudley); Roy Whaley (Narrator).

In recent years, *Crusader Rabbit* has assumed legendary status. It was the first animated series made exclusively for the small screen; it was the first project of *Rocky and His Friends* (q.v.) mentor Jay Ward; it was, discounting the theatrical features of "Hopalong Cassidy," the first notable syndicated children's television success; and it was the first TV cartoon program to indulge in adult satire. Yet when seen today, the series invariably disappoints. That's because until very recently, most people who saw the few samples of *Crusader Rabbit* available on the videocassette market weren't really seeing the original *Crusader* at all, but an empty shell of the character filmed nearly ten years after his inception.

The first incarnation of the character occurred in 1948 in the makeshift garage studios of two lifelong chums, both aspiring animators: Alex Anderson, nephew of Terrytoons' Paul Terry, and business major Jay Ward. Anderson and Ward were possessed with the notion that the fledgling TV industry was just the place to blaze new animation trails: To that end, they came up with several character concepts

(see notes on *Rocky and His Friends*). Jerry Fairbanks, a contract releaser of theatrical "novelty" short subjects (*Speaking of Animals, Unusual Occupations* et al.) was approached by Anderson and Ward, who'd incorporated as "Television Arts Productions." Fairbanks showed minimal interest in most of the pair's ideas, but was intrigued by the potential of one new cartoon character, a do-gooding rabbit who wished to emulate the noble Crusaders of old. The distributor commissioned Television Arts Productions to make a 15-part "pilot" serial headlining this character, and thus *Crusader Rabbit* came to be.

Fairbanks began test-marketing the black and white series to local stations in late 1949, but the first 195 episodes of *Crusader Rabbit* weren't "officially" put in syndication until a Los Angeles channel bought the package in 1950. Previously, the NBC network had evinced interest in the project but ultimately turned it down as a coast-to-coast attraction, though first dibs for *Crusader Rabbit* went to the five owned and operated NBC channels. The series sold well, but a number of legal tangles involving NBC, Jerry Fairbanks and Television Arts turned the early career of *Crusader* into a spotty one, and the cartoons were off the air as much as on in the first half of the 1950s.

When Jay Ward decided to abandon animation for the world of real estate, Television Arts Productions was dissolved. The *Crusader Rabbit* property was sold in 1956 to Shul Bonsall, the owner of TV Spots, which up until that time had specialized in animated commercials. Through the facilities of TV Spots' Creston Studios, Bonsall cranked out 260 five-minute, color, cliffhanging installments of *Crusader Rabbit*.

The Shul Bonsall version is the package that received the widest distribution in the 1950s, and thus is the *Crusader Rabbit* most clearly remembered by the majority of baby boomers. It is from this package that one of the few videotape examples of the series resurfaced in the 1980s, a public domain 20-part adventure titled "Sahara Today, Gone Tomorrow." Viewers watching this sample tend to be mildly amused, but unimpressed. Could this be the fabled, pioneering *Crusader Rabbit*—this chintzy, halfhearted effort that can't even match the Hanna-Barbera cartoons from the same time period?

No. The real *Crusader* is best represented by the series' very first storyline, "Crusader Rabbit vs. The State of Texas," happily committed to cassette by Rhino Home Video in 1991. Here all the elements that made the series so appealing in 1950 are in evidence. We meet Crusader Rabbit, a delightfully pugnacious resident of Galahad Glen who, unhappy with his lot as a cute woodland creature, aspires to greatness as a "good deed" doer. Unfortunately, his efforts come acropper due to his lack of physical strength. All this changes when Crusader, the "brains," meets Ragland T. Tiger, the "brawn." At first wary of this natural predator, Crusader befriends the softhearted Rags (a softness that has spread to his head), and as a team the pair are able to continue their strongarm quest for truth and justice. The first quest takes them to Texas, where all jackrabbits are being deported due to an acute shortage of carrots. As the story weaves through 15 picaresque installments, Alex Anderson and Jay Ward provide a sometimes gentle, ofttimes pointed satire of several hallmarks of the late 1940s: class prejudice, "hard sell" TV and radio advertising, Hollywood's distortion of the Old West, and the cult of Celebrity (the state of Texas brings in a high-profile hunter, Frank Sawbuck, to head the Rabbit and Hare Removal Department).

Animation is not the strong suit in the first *Crusader Rabbit*s. No more than four poses are seen within any five seconds of screen time (sometimes not even that many); most often, movement is conveyed by rapid cutting from scene to scene, or "simulated" by the energetic narration, the evocative musical score and the two-reel comedy sound effects. It isn't really important, however, how often the characters move. What gives this project exuberance is its impeccable sense of timing. The setups, punchlines and throwaway gags occur at such "right" moments that the series stands as a model of brilliant comic editing. Adding to the fun is the character of Crusader Rabbit himself. After years of relatively mild mannered TV cartoon characters like Huckleberry Hound and Scooby-Doo, it's a real eye opener to see this furry little bunny from four decades ago, who charges unprovoked into a room and threatens to punch out all comers. This guy doesn't just have adventures — he's *making* the adventures.

And of course there was the dialogue and narration — never quite as barbed as the material used on Jay Ward's later *Rocky and His Friends*, but still chock full of such future Ward trademarks as deliberately horrible puns, a high level of literacy (Crusader and Rags are not mere heroes but "idealists") and the characters' tendency to address directly, and sometimes vehemently argue with, the narrator. How much of this style is due to Jay Ward and how much is due to his partner Alex Anderson or even distributor Jerry Fairbanks is currently a matter of debate (Anderson partisans claim that it was he, not Ward, who was the main idea man, while Jerry Fairbanks indicated in interviews given to writer Gary Grossman in the early 1980s that it was Fairbanks himself who set the comic tone of the series); the point is that the original *Crusader Rabbit* assumed its audience was intelligent enough to go along for any ride the writers had in mind. It never, ever talked down to its fans — an exhilarating quality *Crusader Rabbit* held in common with the best of the so-called "kid's" programming in TV's formative years, notably the puppet series *Time for Beany* (see *Beany and Cecil*), *Kukla, Fran and Ollie* and *Johnny Jupiter.*

When Shul Bonsall took over *Crusader Rabbit* in 1957, the still very limited animation was better produced, but many of the qualities that made the 1949 version so irresistible were forsaken. To be sure, there was still the random joke at the expense of such contemporary phenomena as Ed Sullivan and flying saucers, and puns were still very much in evidence (chapter titles included "Miles to the Galleon," "Apes of Rath" and "Inflamed Heel"). But the old flair was missing. The voiceover narration, previously blasted out full force, was now spoken in a kindly whisper. Worse, Crusader Rabbit was no longer the fearless instigator of his adventures, but a benign creature who tended to be sucked into the adventures after they'd commenced. But possibly the weakest element of the Bonsall *Crusaders* was the villainy. The perennial heavy was Dudley Nightshade, a woebegone holdover from the silkhatted "me proud beauty" type of Victorian melodramas. Poor Dudley seemed so certain that his schemes were foredoomed from the start, and possessed so whiny and cracking a voice, that there was never any real menace for Crusader and Rags to play off. One of the major advantages of Jay Ward's successors to the Rabbit and the Tiger, Rocky and Bullwinkle, is that they were challenged by one of the great comic-villain creations of all time, the supremely confident, deliciously nasty Boris Badenov. The lack of a good "Boris" on the 1957 version of *Crusader Rabbit* rendered the project virtually interchangeable with most of the other "soft" children's entertainment of the late 1950s.

The original black and white *Crusader Rabbit* was shelved in favor of the lesser color episodes—which turned out to be a smart business move during the 1960s color TV boom, when the Bonsall package became a hot commodity for color-hungry station managers. The Bonsalls remained in active syndication at least until 1970, reaping a large profit for the distributor but scuttling the reputation earned with the brilliant Ward-Anderson *Crusaders*. It would be two decades before the 1949 edition of *Crusader Rabbit* would once again be made available to regale lovers of intelligent cartoonmaking and to win new fans, 90 percent of whom weren't even alive when the series was taken out of circulation back in the 70s.

CURIOUS GEORGE. Produced: 1979–1982. First shown in the U.S. in 1984 on Nickelodeon. Lafferty, Harwood and Partners/Milktrain Productions. Narrator: Jack Duffy.

Curious George was scarcely animation at all. Based on the eternally popular children's books inaugurated in 1941 by H. A. and Margaret Ray, these Canadian-produced adventures of a precocious monkey and his resourceful master, known only as The Man in the Yellow Hat, were most often merely filmed still pictures (with occasional flailing arms, shifting eyes and nodding heads) patterned directly after the book illustrations. Nonetheless, the main character has always been appealing and the stories moved along energetically, so *Curious George* provided a welcome five minutes of entertainment when the Nickelodeon cable network began running the cartoons on a nationwide basis as part of its *Pinwheel* morning program in 1985; later, Nickelodeon repackaged these cartoons as a half hour daily offering. *Curious George* also flourished over the Disney Pay Cable lineup as a compo-

nent of the daily *Lunch Box* starting in 1989.

CYBORG BIG "X." Syndicated: 1965. Tokyo/Global/Transglobal.

Created in 1963 by Osamu Tezuka (see *Astro Boy*), "Big X" was a daily Japanese science-fiction comic strip about a young boy named Akira, who was transformed into a cyborg by Axis scientists; the villains then proceeded to plant Akira's brain in the carcass of a huge robot. Naturally, the Axis plans for using the robot for world conquest backfired when the robot, Big X, absorbed Akira's good qualities and became an agent for Right, proving that "the pen was mightier than the sword"— especially if one had a special magnetized crime-fighting pen like the one wielded by Big X. Fifty-nine animated episodes of *Big X* were commissioned for Japanese television and broadcast in prime time from August 3, 1964, through October 4, 1965. *Big X* was dubbed into English and made available for American distribution during its Japanese run, though most U.S. markets didn't pick it up until 1967, at which time the series was retitled *Cyborg Big "X."* The half hour series suffered from being filmed in black and white, the kiss of death for many children's series distributed in the color-conscious late 60s. Like most other "humanized robot" cartoon imports of its period, however (see also *Eighth Man, Gigantor* and *Mighty Mister Titan*), *Cyborg Big "X"* performed well in Los Angeles, San Francisco, and other cities where large Japanese communities flourished.

DANGER MOUSE. Nickelodeon 6/4/1984–. Syndicated: 1984. Cosgrove-Hall Productions/Thames Television/Taffner. Produced by Mark Hall and Brian Cosgrove. Directed by Brian Cosgrove. Created and written by Brian Trueman. Storyboards by Keith Scobie. Music by Mike Harding. Voices: David Jason (Danger Mouse/Colonel K/Nero); Terry Scott (Penfold); Edward Kelsey (Baron Silas Greenback); Brian Trueman (Stiletto).

The relentlessly ribtickling *Danger Mouse*, from the same British production company responsible for the equally hilarious *Count Duckula* (q.v.), proved beyond doubt that the American producers of *Tiny Toons* (q.v.) and *The Simpsons* (q.v.) didn't have a monopoly on Collective

Cultural Consciousness. *Danger Mouse* was an illustrated encyclopedia of spoofery, skewering past entertainment properties and present public institutions. The title of the weekly half hour cartoon was purposely evocative of *Danger Man*, the excellent British spy series starring Patrick McGoohan which ran in the U.S. as *Secret Agent*. *Danger Mouse* was at base a takeoff on the James Bond school of gimmicky espionage, a fact made immediately obvious by Danger Mouse's boss Colonel K, whose name conjured up memories of Bond's superior "M." The titular character, a musclebound white mouse, sported an eyepatch, a bit of exotica lifted from another English TV series of blessed memory, the Boris Karloff vehicle *Colonel March of Scotland Yard*. The fearless Danger Mouse was coupled with a timorous assistant, a mole named Penfold, who seemed to be cut from the same cloth as British character comedian Roy Kinnear, an actor frequently cast in similar "scared sidekick" roles. Danger Mouse and Penfold lived in a Baker Street mailbox, a cockeyed variation of the police call box used as a base of operations on the internationally popular TV science fiction serial *Dr. Who*. The number one heavy of *Danger Mouse* was Baron Silas Greenback, a frog character who some observers say was patterned after English entertainment mogul Sir Lew Grade. The Baron's efforts at world domination were almost always thwarted by incredibly stupid and irritatingly apologetic henchmen, whose thick provincial dialects and thicker wits echoed the best low-comedy turns in the good old days of the British Music Halls.

There's more. *Danger Mouse* boasted a bombastic narrator, who in true *Rocky and His Friends* (q.v.) fashion frequently argued with the on-camera talent. The narrator also followed the course charted by *Monty Python's Flying Circus*—and *The Goon Show* before that—by frequently regressing from the plotlines to recite bits of poetry, sing a syrupy cheer-up song, describe the beauties beheld during his last vacation abroad, or gripe about his minuscule paycheck. Another *Monty Python* carryover was the "Terry Gilliam" style of nonsequitur background design; artists Malcolm Turner, Danny Roper and Diane Wren must have stayed up nights thinking of such throwaway gags as having an outer space scene dotted with floating

debris ranging from "road closed" signs to the Statue of Liberty. This was typical of the overall irreverence of *Danger Mouse*, which like the live action series *Get Smart* used its spy format as a starting point for wide-ranging social satire, lampooning everything from civil service red tape to the common market. While never forgetting its younger audience, *Danger Mouse* was at heart a show for grownups—at least for those who'd grown up casting a jaundiced eye at the subject matter satirized on the series.

While each episode overflowed with comic invention, *Danger Mouse* marched to its own beat in terms of pacing and plot development. Where an American cartoon program would "cut to the chase" almost immediately for fear of losing its audience, Danger Mouse could—and did—spend nearly half an episode trying to extricate his automobile from a user-unfriendly parking structure. So unorthodox was the series' rhythmic sense that *Danger Mouse* didn't make it to the U.S.A. until three years after its 1981 British debut—and even then, local stations still avoided buying the 65-episode series, complaining it was too "different" for afterschool audiences. Dauntless Thames Television distributor D.L. Taffner then took his wares directly to the young and hungry Nickelodeon cable service, where *Danger Mouse* scored an almost instant hit and built up a large fan following. As of this writing, the series still rakes in ratings as a daily and weekend Nickelodeon attraction—and perhaps it was the deliberately oddball quality of *Danger Mouse* and its cousin *Count Duckula* which inspired Nickelodeon to develop its own lineup of out-of-the-norm cartoon series (see *Doug, Ren and Stimpy* and *Rugrats*).

DARK WATER *see* **PIRATES OF DARK WATER**

DARKWING DUCK. Disney Channel: Spring 1991. Syndicated: September 1991. ABC: 9/7/1991–9/4/1993. Disney/ Buena Vista Television. Supervising producers: Tad Stones, Alan Zaslove. Produced by Alan Zaslove. Animation directors: Chris Bradley, Ian Harrowell, Henry Neville. Story editor, Kevin Crosby Hoops. Theme music by Steven Nelson and Thom Sharp. Music by Phillip Giffen. Animation facilities: Walt Disney Television Animation (Australia) and PTY Limited. Voices: Jim Cummings (Darkwing Duck, aka Drake Mallard/Negaduck/ Moliarty/Cousin Globby); Hamilton Camp (Gizmo Duck); Christine Cavanaugh (Gosalyn Mallard); Danny Mann (J. Gander Hooter); Terry McGovern (Launchpad McQuack); Rob Paulsen (Steelbeak); Katie Leigh (Honker Muddlefoot); Jim Cummings (Herb Muddlefoot); Susan Tolsky (Blinky Muddlefoot); Dan Hill (Tank Muddlefoot); Ron Feinberg (Agent Gryslikoff); Dan Castellanta (Megavolt); Kath Soucie (Morgana Macawber/ Aunt Nasty); Kenneth Mars (Tuscernini); Frank Welker (Meraculo Macawber); and Maggie Roswell, Roddy McDowall, Tim Curry, Victoria Carroll, Andrea Martin, Marty Ingels, Jerry Houser, Teresa Ganzel.

Darkwing Duck (original title: *Double-O Duck*), a daily, half hour spinoff of the Disney series *DuckTales* (q.v.), was added to the syndicated "Disney Afternoon" block in the fall of 1991. The lead character was Drake Mallard, mild mannered and middle-aged resident of the town of St. Canard. Unbeknownst to everyone but close pal Launchpad McQuack (a crossover character from *DuckTales*), Mallard was also the cloaked-and-masked Darkwing Duck, a crimefighter whose nocturnal appearances and sudden disappearances prompted the local constabulary to believe that Darkwing was himself a criminal (shades of *The Green Hornet*).

This shadowy figure was described by the Disney press agent machine as "the terror that flaps in the night; the scouring pad that scrubs the stains of crime." In other words: Get Down, Get Silly, and, to quotation Darkwing Duck (who stole the quotation from Arsenio Hall), "Let's get dangerous!" Other prominent waterfowl in the cast of *Darkwing Duck* included Drake Mallard's nine year old adopted daughter Gosalyn; her intellectual young friend Honker Muddlefoot; Darkwing's great rival Gizmo Duck—a.k.a. Fenton Crackshell, who like Launchpad McQuack hailed from nearby Duckburg; and that stain of crime himself, the evil Steel Beak of F.O.W.L. (the Fiendish Organization of World Larceny).

Jim Cummings, the voice of Darkwing Duck, regarded the character as one of his favorites. "He is just a wonderful, humorous departure from Disney," noted Cum-

mings to the Chicago *Tribune*. "Darkwing Duck couldn't be more sarcastic. He's a wiseguy, self-centered and has an ego the size of Montana." How true; at times it sounded as though Darkwing was really Daffy Duck, working under an alias to avoid contract conflict with Warner Bros.

Maintaining the same high animation and scripting standards as the rest of the "Disney Afternoon" components, *Darkwing Duck* did tend to play safe with its surefire superhero spoofery, and at other times strained a bit too hard to maintain the "laugh a minute, thrill a minute" quality of its companion series *DuckTales, Chip 'n' Dale's Rescue Rangers* (q.v.) and *Tale Spin* (q.v.)—the sign of a good formula wearing thin. Still, there was plenty to delight the ear and eye, notably the happily harmonious relationship between dialogue and visuals. In an episode titled "A Brush with Oblivion," Darkwing Duck and friends found themselves supernaturally trapped in the paintings hanging in an art gallery. As they made their way from frame to frame, the characters' bodies assumed the highly varied styles of Picasso, Seurat and Dali—and all the while, Darkwing and his companions made rueful comments about suddenly growing a third eye or being reduced to colored dots.

Darkwing Duck's adult fans included Dolores Morris, vice president of creative development and TV animation for Disney. Quoted in the Chicago *Tribune*, Morris observed that Darkwing's adopted child Gosalyn was "a breakthrough character. She has a point of view, a mind of her own. She's very feisty, a very positive girl character. I don't know who actually developed her, but whether it was a man or a woman, it wouldn't have happened without a sensibility that cartoons have to change. They can't be so male-oriented, so boy-oriented." Morris' comments were true enough, yet it's surprising that she would single out Gosalyn as a "breakthrough" when in fact the Disney organization had been creating strong, positive female characters for quite some time before *Darkwing Duck*, including Gadget in *Chip 'n' Dale's Rescue Rangers*, Becky and Molly in *Tale Spin*, and Belle in the theatrical feature film *Beauty and the Beast* (admittedly released after the premiere of *Darkwing Duck*, yet obviously in development for several years before that).

Muttley in the cockpit, Yankee Doodle Pigeon in the air, Dick Dastardly in high dudgeon.

Shortly after its syndicated debut in September 1991, *Darkwing Duck* also joined the lineup of Saturday morning ABC network cartoons, where it remained for two seasons. The ABC package consisted of 13 new episodes originally telecast over the Disney Channel in the spring of 1991 but not included in the 65- episode syndication manifest.

DASTARDLY AND MUTTLEY IN THEIR FLYING MACHINES.
CBS: 9/13/1969–9/4/1971. Hanna-Barbera. Produced and directed by William Hanna and Joseph Barbera. Associate producer, Alex Lovy. Animation director, Charles Nichols. Story by Larz Bourne, Dalton Sandifer, Michael Maltese. Story directors: Alex Lovy, Bill Perez. Production design by Iwao Takamoto. Character design by Jerry Eisenberg. Background styling by Walt Peregoy. Music by Ted Nichols and Hoyt Curtin. Song "Stop That Pigeon" by Bill Hanna and Hoyt Curtin. Voices: Paul Winchell (Dick Dastardly/The General); Don Messick (Muttley/Yankee Doodle Pigeon/Klunk/Zilly).

In a sense, one can thank Charles Schultz and his *Peanuts* comic strip for Hanna-Barbera's *Dastardly and Muttley.* Schultz' mid–1960s running gag involving Snoopy's imaginary airplane battles against World War I fighting ace Baron Von Richtoffen prompted a renewal of public interest in the "War to End All Wars" and its airborne combatants. Hanna-Barbera, with the enthusiastic encouragement of CBS executive Fred Silverman, latched onto the "Red Baron" gimmick, threw in elements of the studio's own *Wacky Races* (q.v.) and *Precious Pupp* (see *The Atom Ant/Secret Squirrel Show*), and the resultant soufflé was titled *Dastardly and Muttley in Their Flying Machines*—a title reminiscent of the 1965 "spectacular" comedy film *Those Magnificent Men in Their Flying Machines*.

Dick Dastardly, introduced as a nogoodnik motorist on *Wacky Races*, was in his own starring series a World War I–style flyer (evidently operating in the present) for an unnamed enemy country. Ordered by a never-seen general to intercept and hopefully neutralize the steadfast American courier Yankee Doodle Pigeon—who had a RED satchel, WHITE body and BLUE helmet—Dastardly enlisted the negligible aid of his "Goof-Up Squadron," consisting of cowardly mechanic Zilly and his bizarre companion Klunk, who like UPA's *Gerald McBoing Boing* (q.v.) spoke only in sound effects. Also carried over from *Wacky Races* was Dastardly's duplicitous doggie companion Muttley, he of the raspy snicker (just like Precious Pupp) and grumbled griping. It probably goes without saying that Dick Dastardly and his motley airborne crew were never able to keep Yankee Doodle Pigeon from his swiftly appointed rounds. Each *Dastardly and Muttley* contained two breathlessly paced seven-minute cartoons featuring the entire cast, plus an additional "Magnificent Muttley" adventure wherein the cackling canine would imagine himself a dauntless hero. In between these segments were brief comic blackouts, titled "Wing Dings."

This enjoyable but repetitive formula was recycled for 17 weeks in first run, and for two years in reruns. But even that wasn't enough: The characters of Dastardly and Muttley continued to resurface on several future H-B series, including *Wake Rattle and Roll* (q.v.), and *Yo, Yogi!* (see *Yogi Bear*) — appearing in the latter as teenagers! Say what one will about Hanna-Barbera's rigid adherence to formula, one cannot deny that they were able to successfully squeeze every drop of value out of any property.

Dastardly and Muttley was originally titled *Stop That Pigeon*, the title of a song that was warbled by an offscreen Dick Dastardly whenever Yankee Doodle Pigeon streaked across the sky with Dastardly's jerrybuilt fleet of flying machines in hot pursuit. The lyrics of this tender ballad's refrain consisted entirely of the repeated phrase "Stop the Pigeon!" Even the words to the theme song of *The Jetsons* (q.v.) were more sophisticated and intricate.

DAVEY AND GOLIATH. Syndicated: 1961. Clokey Productions/United Lutheran Church in America. Produced by Art Clokey. Directed by Art Clokey and Ray Peck. Voices: Norma McMillan, Nancy Wible (Davey Hanson); Hal Smith (Goliath); and Richard Beals.

Davey and Goliath was a series of 64 15-minute films produced by Art Clokey of *Gumby* (q.v.) fame. As with his earlier creation, Clokey animated the puppet characters on *Davey and Goliath* with a stop-motion process known as Pixilation, adjusting the figures ever so slightly from one frame exposure to the next to give the illusion of movement. Unlike the footloose and fancy free *Gumby*, *Davey and Goliath* was more sedate and down to earth; in fact, at times it was downright sluggish. There were also episodes in which the limited animation was dispensed with altogether in favor of toy models and stock "live" footage ("Jeep in the Deep" is a prime example of this). But the true worth of *Davey and Goliath* was measured not by its pace or production values but by its purpose. Financed and released by the United Lutheran Church in America, the series was essentially a religious cartoon — though it never evangelized nor pummelled the audience over the head with its religiosity.

The uncluttered, nonaggressive storylines of *Davey and Goliath* spotlighted 11-year-old Davey Hanson, who lived with his parents John and Mary and his lookalike sister Sally. Davey's best friend was his dog Goliath, who was able to speak in a languid, low drawl — but who only spoke to Davey. Davey and Goliath confronted adventures and crises seemingly predestined to test their faith in family values, friendship, and above all, God. Each week the pair would emerge from their latest escapade a little wiser in the ways of the world, with their trust in and love of the Almighty strengthened.

Some of the *Davey and Goliath* episodes (notably "Lost in a Cave," "The Waterfall" and "All Alone") would place one of the characters in a dangerous situation, the explicit message being that some dangers could be avoided with a little more common sense — and the *implicit* message being that the character's ultimate rescue had as much to do with prayer as with pluck. Other episodes like "The Runaway" would have Davey briefly decide that he was unloved by those closest to him, only to be set aright by circumstances and by the suggestion of Divine providence. And *Davey and Goliath* was one of the few animated series to deal with death, specifically the demise of a beloved relative which severely strained Davey's belief in God's good grace — something that all child viewers would have to endure eventually themselves, so better to confront the issue head-on rather than couch it in euphemisms.

The best and most substantial *Davey and Goliath* installments were those involving prejudice. In "Polka Dot Tie," a boy is cruelly shunned because of his manner of dress, while in "The Shoemaker" the Hanson children are senselessly resentful of a family of foreigners. In these and similar episodes, the folly of blind hatred is made abundantly clear without ever resorting to the self-righteous unsubtleties frequently seen on adult prime time "message" programs.

Though basically religious in nature, *Davey and Goliath* never overtly stumped for membership in the Lutheran Church; indeed, the series' only specifically Lutheran trademark was its theme music, "A Mighty Fortress Is Our God," a hymn written by Martin Luther himself. The plotlines on *Davey and Goliath* contained lessons applicable to any religious persuasion, and it was this universality that enabled TV station managers to book the series without feeling like agents for a denomination which they themselves may not have embraced. Originally produced between 1959 and 1960, *Davey and Goliath* was first distributed nationally in January of 1961, and while it didn't reach the valuable New York City market for nearly two years, the series was an instant syndicated success. Many TV stations, favoring technology to theology, used the color-filmed series to test their newly acquired color equipment in those earliest years of tinted television.

Davey and Goliath ceased regular production due to lack of funding early on, but later resurfaced for a series of six half-hour specials, produced between 1965 and 1977: "Christmas Lost and Found," "New Year Promise," "Happy Easter," "School . . . Who Needs It?," "To the Rescue," and "Halloween Who Dun It." The original program is still in circulation as of this writing. It has been dubbed into several languages and is seen worldwide, though in recent years exposure to *Davey and Goliath* in the United States has been pretty much limited to those local stations and cable services offering full-time religious programming.

DAVID THE GNOME *see* **THE WORLD OF DAVID THE GNOME**

DEFENDERS OF THE EARTH.
Syndicated: 1986. King Features/Marvel. Produced by Margaret Loesch, Lee Gunther and Bruce Paisner. Supervising producer, Karl Geurs. Produced by John Ahern, Rick Hoberg, Bill Hutten, Glen Johnson, Tony Love, Lee Orgel, Don Sheppard. Director of production, David J. Corbett. Production manager, Barbara L. Stoddard. Supervising directors, Ray Lee and John Gibbs. Directed by Warren Batchelder, Brad Case, Joan Case, Gerry Chiniquy, Charlie Downs, Bill Extes, Milton Gray, Bob Kirk, Al Kouzel, M. Flores Nichols, Karen Peterson, Tom Ray, Barbara Shellhorn, Bob Treat. Art director, Ray Hoffman. Supervising story editor, Tony Pastor. Story editors, Bryce Malek, Dick Robbins, Larry Parr, Alan Swayze. Music composed and conducted by Rob Walsh. Main title music by Rob Walsh and Tony Pastor. Main title lyrics by Stan Lee. King Features production executives, Austin Hearst and James R.

McGee. Child psychological consultants: Joyce C. Mills, Ph.D., Richard J. Crowley, Ph.D. Voices: William Callaway, Adam Carl, Ron Feinberg, Buster Jones, Loren Lester, Sarah Partridge, Diane Pershing, Lou Richards, Peter Mark Richman, Dion Williams.

Produced in 1985 but not syndicated until a year later (the local-station manifests were full), *Defenders of the Earth* spotlighted the offspring of famous comic strip adventure heroes. The proud parents were four characters from the files of the King Features newspaper syndicate, only one of whom had previously trod the TV animation trail: space traveller Flash Gordon, created in 1934 by Alex Raymond and previously the star of *The New Adventures of Flash Gordon* (q.v.). Mandrake the Magician and his assistant Lothar were created by Lee Falk and Phil Davis, also in 1934; Mandrake's peculiar powers of prestidigitation, usually pulled off by "gesturing hypnotically," were frequently used to fight crime. Likewise righting wrongs was a 1936 creation from Lee Falk, this time in collaboration with Ray Moore: The Phantom, the masked, seemingly immortal "Ghost Who Walks" of the African jungles.

The children involved in *Defenders of the Earth* were Flash Gordon's son Rick; The Phantom's daughter Jedda, the only second-generation character on the series who'd actually sprung from the original strip; Lothar's son Lothar Jr., known to his friends as L.J.; and Kshin, a 10-year-old boy who'd been adopted by Mandrake. (Earlier published reports that the characters included Phantom's son Kit Walker Jr. and Flash's daughter Jedda were based on prerelease information offered by trade papers in 1985.) Kshin was oriental and L.J. was black, allowing *Defenders of the Earth* to offer a multicultural and multiracial good-guy team — with the obligatory comic relief, a furball alien named Zuffy.

An additional note for all you completists: Technically speaking, the Phantom was *also* the son of a famed comic strip superhero — none other than The Phantom! Since the backstory of the comic strip stretched back 200 years to the founding of the Phantom dynasty, the character seen on *Defenders of the Earth* was (we were somberly informed in the closing credits) the *twenty-seventh* Phantom.

Animation fans are as of this writing awaiting "Number 28" in the much-anticipated cartoon series *Phantom 2040*, originally slated for a fall 1993 berth on the Fox Network but rescheduled at the last minute for 1994.

Defenders was set in 2015, wherein Flash Gordon's perennial nemesis, Ming the Merciless of planet Mongo, threatened to enslave the human race. Each of the second-generation heroes possessed a special talent to confound the ruthless Ming: L.J. had extraordinary strength, Kshin was a martial arts expert, Rick Gordon was a science whiz, and Jedda dabbled in telekinesis and the occult. To hone their skills to fullest effect, the younger Defenders trained in a "virtual reality" holographic room in which they were conditioned to wriggle out of simulated life-threatening situations. While this room and other elements of the series — the talking female computer Dynax, the Defenders' "Monitor" space vehicle — were futuristic, many of the basic problems confronting the Defenders were not, and the series often managed within its daily, half hour limitations to address dilemmas facing the home viewers of The Present. One episode which drew particular praise from various special interest groups, "The Deadliest Battle" (first telecast February 13, 1987), involved the rehabilitation of Flash Gordon's son Rick, who was dangerously close to becoming a drug addict.

Well-intentioned though it was, *Defenders of the Earth* had a great deal wrong with it. For starters, two of the familiar parental figures were hampered with demeaning personality quirks. The normally down-to-earth Mandrake was redefined as an effete, egotistical snob, with a most unbecoming yellow streak when it came to physical danger (sometimes he required rescuing by a newly conceived female character, the beautiful whip-wielding adventuress Atascadero). The Phantom, also more accessible and friendly in his comic strip, was on *Defenders* a taciturn, narrowminded Clint Eastwood type whose grim determination to honor ancient superstitions and cultural taboos often placed his companions in undue peril. While these changes didn't benefit the original characters one iota, *Defenders of the Earth* did include at least one welcome harkback to the Mandrake of old:

Unlike the antiseptic hypnotist the character had become in his last years in the funny papers, the animated Mandrake regained the truly supernatural powers he'd enjoyed when created back in 1934.

Other so-called improvements reflected the influence of "fantastic" entertainments outside the King Features realm. Ming the Merciless now looked like a *Star Trek* Klingon; he camped out in "Ice Station Earth," a flipside version of Superman's Fortress of Solitude; and Ming's minions included Garax, a heavy-breathing robot not unlike *Star Wars*' Darth Vader, and "bad" computer Octoron, an exaggeration of HAL 9000 in *2001: A Space Odyssey*.

In other words, the producers of *Defenders of the Earth* didn't trust their King Features source material enough not to borrow from other sources. The whole project was in fact struggling desperately to imitate DC/Hanna-Barbera's *Superfriends* (q.v.) and Marvel's *Fantastic Four* (q.v.) TV series — not to mention the long-running Marvel comic book *X-Men* (q.v.). Unfortunately, *Defenders'* four leading characters didn't have the same natural rapport with each other as did the DC and Marvel stars. Add to the aforementioned shortcomings *Defenders of the Earth's* leaden pace and dull animation, and the result was a regrettable waste of a lot of potent comic-character talent.

Most everybody and everything involved with *Defenders of the Earth* would be better served elsewhere: Producer Margaret Loesch as an executive of the Fox Network, supervising producer Karl Geurs at the Disney studio, writers Bill Hutten and Tony Love with *Teenage Mutant Ninja Turtles* (q.v.), title-song lyricist Stan Lee at his own Marvel Publications, and the whole "young crimefighting team" concept in 1993's TV version of *X-Men*.

DENNIS THE MENACE. Syndicated: 1985. CBS: 1/2/1988–9/10/1988. DIC/DFS/General Mills. Produced by Jean Chalopin, Andy Heyward and Tetsuo Katayama. Directed by Michael Maliani. Animation director, Masanori Miura. Story editors: Jack Mendelsohn, David B. Garren, Steve Granat, Bob Logan. Music by Shuki Levy and Haim Saban. Voices: Brennan Thicke (Dennis the Menace); Brian George and Maurice LaMarche (Henry Mitchell); Louise Vallance and Marilyn Lightstone (Alice Mitchell); Phil

Hartman and Maurice LaMarche (Mr. Wilson); Phil Hartman (Ruff); Jeannie Elias (Margaret/ Joey/ Tommy); Marilyn Lightstone (Martha Wilson); Hank Sound (Dick/Jim); Sharon Noble, Riva Spier.
—ALL-NEW DENNIS THE MENACE. CBS: September 11, 1993–. General Mills/DIC. Executive producer, Andy Heyward. Story editor and series developer, Sean Roche. Executive in charge of production, Brian A. Miller. Production supervisors, Stacy Gallishaw and RaNae Bonella. Associate producers, Kent Meredith and Kurt Weldon. Script coordinator, Lori Crawford. Music by Tom Worral; supervised by Joanne Miller and Monica Wakefield; edited by Stuart Goetz. Production facilities: Sae Rom Production Co., Ltd. Overseas director, Gary Scott. Based on the comic strip by Hank Ketcham. Voice director, Susan Blu. Voices: Adam Wylie (Dennis); Greg Burson (Mr. Wilson), Jeannie Elias (Alice); June Foray (Mrs. Wilson); Dan Gilvezan (Henry); and Katie Leigh, Anna Mathias, Jack Angel, Alyce Beasley, Bob Bergen, Greg Berger, Eileen Brennan, Roger Bumpass, Frank Buxton, Hamilton Camp, Brian Cummings, Jennifer Darling, Linda Gary, Michael Gough, Danny Mann, Mona Marshall, Chuck McCann, Michael Mish, Pat Musick, Wayne Powers, Jan Rabson, Hal Rayle, Jack Roth, Eugene Roche, Roger Rose, Maggie Roswell, John Rubinow, Kevin Schon, Roger Scott, Susan Silo, David Sterry, and Doug Stone.

Dennis the Menace began as a daily Hall Syndicate newspaper panel by artist Hank Ketcham on March 12, 1951. Ketcham's four-year-old, cowlick-haired tyro (based on his own son) quickly gained popularity with the postwar "instant parent" crowd, and by 1952 had earned a Sunday color page. *Dennis* became something of a cottage industry for Ketcham, spawning several paperback reprints of his daily escapades, a series of well-received comic books for Fawcett, and one well remembered "Baby Sitter's Guide," ostensibly written by little Dennis Mitchell, which became a fixture of *Scholastic* magazine book clubs for years. The character matriculated into a live action sitcom star in 1959. Screen Gems did an admirable job of locating actors who were living images of the comic strip Dennis' parents, Henry and Alice Mitchell (the players were Herbert Anderson and

Gloria Henry), and for the purposes of the plotlines the studio converted Dennis' eternally grouchy one-dimensional neighbor Mr. Wilson into a fussy social climber, well acted by Joseph Kearns. Dennis, alas, was not the angel-faced little demon of the newspapers; as portrayed by Jay North, the character was softened into an impulsive but basically benign kid, whose attempts to be friendly and helpful always seemed to backfire. By the time TV's *Dennis the Menace* had rolled into its fourth and final season, Dennis Mitchell was giving lectures on civic responsibility, and it was Mr. Wilson (now played by Gale Gordon) who was childish and mischievous.

Reruns of the original series remained in lucrative circulation for years, and this, coupled with the ongoing popularity of the newspaper strip, encouraged DIC Enterprises, General Mills, and DFS Distribution to collaborate on a daily, syndicated *Dennis the Menace* cartoon series in 1984 (a year earlier, Ruby-Spears had produced a one-shot animated special, *Dennis the Menace: Mayday for Mother*, for NBC). The DIC artists succeeded in matching Hank Ketcham's rough-edged, deceptively slapdash style in bringing Dennis to life. Happily, the cartoon Dennis was as much a hellraiser as his newspaper counterpart, declaring his presence in each episode by careening destructively down the street on a skateboard—an entrance later adopted by an even more diabolical animated kid, Bart Simpson (see *The Simpsons*). Similarly, Mr. Wilson returned to his curmudgeonly comic-strip roots; his longsuffering voice, which sounded like Paul Ford from the old "Sgt. Bilko" series, was supplied by versatile *Saturday Night Live* regular Phil Hartman. Dennis himself was given an equally satisfying voice in the person of child actor Brennan Thicke, son of TV talk show host Allan Thicke and singer Gloria Loring. The animated Dennis, together with his friends Margaret, Tommy and Joey, and his good ol' dog Ruff, were swept up in a scope of adventures undreamed of by the Hank Ketcham daily, ranging from international espionage to excursions into the past and confrontations with famous storybook characters. Saving the relentlessly roistering Dennis Mitchell from being roundly condemned by "clean up TV" campaigners was the fact that each plotline ended with Dennis saving the day and making things come out right, then reappearing in the last 30 seconds of each episode to deliver the standard prosocial advice to his kiddie audience. *Dennis the Menace* more than paid the rent for DIC, increasing its syndication profits 100 percent in 1986, the year after its premiere, and twice that by 1987. Nonetheless, when a deal was struck to make additional *Dennis* episodes for CBS in 1987, the eternally frugal network would only offer a $150,000 licensing fee per episode—some $100,000 less than was needed. Andy Heyward, a DIC executive, agreed to CBS' financial terms, then arranged with his syndicated sponsor General Mills to make up the rest of the necessary funding. In return, General Mills received domestic syndication rights to the series. Heyward came out best in the bargain, securing foreign sales revenues—no mean slice of cash considering that *Dennis* was then being seen all over the world, dubbed into seven languages. And while the program's network career was brief, *Dennis the Menace* was as of 1993 still a premier syndicated attraction, frequently telecast as a lead-in for local independent stations' blocks of Disney, Warners and Fox cartoon programming. The series' stock in the industry was strengthened when a feature length, live action *Dennis the Menace* movie, written and directed by John (*Home Alone*) Hughes and starring no less than Walter Matthau and Joan Plowright (Lady Olivier!) as Mr. and Mrs. Wilson, readied itself for release in the summer of 1993.

That particular *Dennis* sank like a stone at the boxoffice, but this didn't stop CBS from premiering *The All-New Dennis the Menace* (again from DIC and General Mills) in the fall of the same year. Publicity promised that the new episodes would have a rougher, slapstickier look than the 78 *Dennis* half hours of the 1980s, in emulation of the movie. Dream on! Except for a few trendily scatological "vomit" jokes, Dennis was back to his sitcom personality of the 1960s: a well-meaning buttinsky who was fundamentally smarter than the adults. And he joined the ranks of the politically correct. Dennis learned that macho wasn't courage, that girls are always right and boys are always wrong, and I can't go on, do you hear?

When the Dennis of the nineties *did* behave in the manner of old, it was less in the tradition of Hank Ketcham and more in the miniature-adult mode of child actor Macaulay Culkin, complete with uncharacteristically mature wisecracks (the voice of Dennis this time around was Adam Wylie, a regular on the CBS prime time series *Picket Fences*). The best aspect of the *All-New Dennis the Menace* was its musical score, which utilized Mozart's "Marriage of Figaro" overture as its main theme and the strains of Mendelsohn, Grieg and Beethoven as incidental music.

DENVER, THE LAST DINOSAUR. Syndicated: 1988. Calico/World Events. Executive producer and creator, Peter Keefe. Produced and directed by Tom Burton. Music by Dale Schacker. Animation by Dinosaur Animation Productions and Sei Young Productions. Voices: Pat Fraley (Denver); Adam Carl (Wally/Jeremy); Cam Clarke (Mario/Shades); Brian Cummings (Morton Fizzback/Professor Funt); Rob Paulsen (Chet/Motley); Kath Soucie (Heather/Casey); and Jack Angel, Tress MacNeille, Diane Pershing, Fred Scott, James Swodec, Townsend Coleman, Jan Rabson, B. J. Ward, Frank Welker.

Denver, the Last Dinosaur, a briefly popular weekly half hour, revolved around the antics of the title character, a "party animal" relic of the Paleozoic era who was revived in the 20th century when a group of skateboarding teenagers inadvertently cracked a petrified dinosaur egg. Denver was then adopted and sheltered by his new group of friends, who included Jeremy, Wally, Heather, Shades and Mario. *Denver, the Last Dinosaur* was recommended by the National Educational Association, but surely this was not a reaction to *Denver's* loose grouping of human beings with dinosaurs (there are theories around and about that atmospheric conditions and bacteria would prohibit such a coexistence) nor its cut and dried animation style. One would suspect that the NEA approved most heartily of *Denver's* pro-ecological, anti-capitalistic stance, as represented by the ongoing efforts of the series' villain, a slimy showbiz promoter named Morton Fizzback, to capture and then exploit the elusive Last Dinosaur.

The principal significance of *Denver, the Last Dinosaur*, beyond its being one of the few entries in the short "dinosaur 'toon"

Deputy Dawg gets a dressing down from the Sheriff, much to the delight of Vincent Van Gopher and Ty Coon.

trend of the late 1980s (see also *Dink, the Little Dinosaur* and *Dinosaucers*), was that it represented the half-hour syndicated series breakthrough for its home studio, Calico Entertainment—though in fact it was the company's second such venture, since the five-episode *Vytor, the Starfire Champion* (q.v.), while not released until January of 1989, was Calico's first 30-minute effort. For information on subsequent Calico projects, see the entries in *Mr. Bogus, Twinkle the Dream Being*, and *Widget the World-Watcher.*

DEPUTY DAWG. Syndicated: 1960. NBC: 9/11/1971–9/2/1972. Terrytoons/CBS Films. Produced by Bill Weiss. Created and written by Larz Bourne. Directed by Dave Tendlar, Bob Kuwahara, Connie Rasinski, Bill Tytla, George Gordon, and Ralph Bakshi. Additional screenplays by Jack Mercer, Cal Howard, Chris Jenkyns, T. Hee, Dick Kinney and Al Bertino. Voices: Dayton Allen, Lionel Wilson.

The word "bucolic" seems to have been invented for Deputy Dawg, a fat, slow witted southern sheriff who kept the peace in a tiny Mississippi swampland community. The canine starpacker spent half of his time tracking down such friendly miscreants as Muskie the Muskrat, Vincent Van Gopher and Ty Coon the Raccoon, and the other half trying to curry favor

with his human boss, the Sheriff. In later episodes, Deputy Dawg found himself the bashful subject of hero worship from his lookalike little nephew Elmer. Created by longtime Terrytoons writer/animator Larz Bourne, Deputy Dawg was deemed worthy of his own series of six-minute cartoons, specially produced for television. Packaged into a half hour weekly with an accompanying manifest of theatrical Terrytoon shorts, Bourne's creation premiered in 47 markets—mostly in the South and Midwest, mostly in the 6 P.M. to 7 P.M. timeslot—in the fall of 1960, thanks to the strong sponsorship of Lay's Potato Chips. Much of the rest of the country settled for the 104 *Deputy Dawg* cartoons as solo "fillers," minus the rest of the Terrytoons package.

The rigors of maintaining a heavy TV production schedule—heavier than the studio had ever previously experienced—obliged Terrytoons, for the first time in its 45 year history, to go outside its own employee pool for directing and writing talent. This may explain why the *Deputy Dawg* series was so erratic: Each fast-paced, well scripted cartoon entry was almost invariably followed by a loser. Blame for the lesser episodes cannot be levelled at the limited animation style itself, which though inexpensive-looking was neatly and nicely stylized. Nor could any criticism be aimed at the sublime voice work of comedian Dayton Allen, who indulged his fondness in the bizarre by utilizing offbeat celebrity imitations for his characters: Deputy Dawg sounded like Frank Fontaine's "Crazy Guggenheim" character (whom Fontaine was calling "John L. C. Sivoney" back in 1960); Vincent Van Gopher was the vocal twin of prolific character actor Percy Helton; and supporting characters tended to sound like such unique performers as Groucho Marx and Hugh Herbert.

As a TV property, *Deputy Dawg* survived three seasons; by 1963, some of the better installments were being directed by young Terrytoons staffer Ralph Bakshi, on the threshold of bigger things. The series was so popular that a number of movie theater managers, principally in Texas, demanded that Terrytoons issue *Deputy Dawg* cartoons for theatrical release. Already swamped with work, the studio took the simple expedient of releasing a handful of made-for-TV cartoons to movie houses and drive-ins, where they made money even though the simplistic animation style tended to look crude and cheap on the Big Screen.

After a healthy syndicated run, its cash flow enhanced by lucrative toy merchandising contracts, *Deputy Dawg* reemerged as *The Deputy Dawg Show* on NBC in 1971, again bundled into a 30-minute package with older Terrytoons releases.

DEVLIN. ABC: 9/11/1974–2/15/1976. Hanna-Barbera. Executive producers, William Hanna and Joseph Barbera. Creative producer, Iwao Takamoto. Directed by Charles Nichols. Music by Hoyt Curtin. Voices: Mike Bell (Ernie Devlin); Mickey Dolenz (Tod Devlin); Michele Robinson (Sandy Devlin); Norman Alden (Hank); and Philip Clarke, Don Diamond, Sarina Grant, Bob Hastings, David Jolliffe, Robby Lester, Stanley Livingston, Derrell Maury, Barney Phillips, Fran Ryan, John Stephenson, John Tuell, Ginny Tyler, Don Weiss and Jesse White.

If you've ever wondered what *Speed Racer* (q.v.) would have looked like had Hanna-Barbera produced it, we submit for your approval *Devlin*, a Saturday morning network half hour. Daredevil stunt motorcyclist Ernie Devlin, together with his orphaned, speed-happy sister Sandy and brother Tod, were the principal attrac-

tions in a travelling circus, where in addition to their cycling duties they were saddled with the financial and emotional tribulations attending the lives of "gypsy" entertainers.

Perhaps to deflect pressure-group complaints about the Devlins' death defying stuntwork, Hanna-Barbera inserted a number of safety tips within the body of each episode. This sort of caution also prompted two pre-release cosmetic changes on *Devlin*. The series was originally titled *Wild Wheels*, but the network didn't like the name — too "dangerous." And the leading character's name was changed from Dare Devlin to Ernie Devlin: According to Hanna-Barbera, ABC "made us drop the 'Dare' because of what [it] called 'image problems.'"

The 17 *Devlin* episodes were strictly assembly-line animation work, though the series boasted some expertly delineated and relatively realistic character design. As was typical of such Hanna-Barbera network projects, the second season of *Devlin*, telecast Sundays, consisted exclusively of repeats.

DICK TRACY. Syndicated: 1961. UPA. Executive producers, Henry G. Saperstein and Peter DeMet. Produced by Glan Heisch. Supervising director, Abe Levitow. Directed by Ray Patterson, John Walker, Steve Clark, Clyde Geronomi, Jerry Hathcock and Paul Fennell (among others). Animation by Ed Solomon and Xenia. Music by Carl Brandt. Based on the comic strip by Chester Gould. Voices: Everett Sloane (Dick Tracy); and Mel Blanc, Benny Rubin, Paul Frees, Jerry Hausner, Johnny Coons, June Foray, and Joan Gardner.

An audience favorite since his Chicago *Tribune* newspaper-strip inception in 1931, Chester Gould's jutjawed plainclothes detective Dick Tracy has been a welcome visitor to all branches of the entertainment world. The first of three live action *Dick Tracy* serials was produced by Republic in 1937; from 1945 to 1947 a quartet of low-budget but highly stylized B pictures headlining Tracy were filmed by RKO Radio; and in 1951, Dick Tracy made his TV debut on a live (as opposed to film) weekly half hour network series, starring the best of the movie Tracys, Ralph Byrd. This last project was converted to a filmed, syndicated TV package in 1951 by Snader-Goldstone Productions (the team later responsible for, of all things, Liberace's longrunning TV program), which flourished until Byrd's death in 1952. And of course there was the *Dick Tracy* radio series, which fluctuated between a weekly half-hour format and a daily serial from 1935 to 1948.

The near-impressionistic Chester Gould artwork and the strip's colorful lineup of impossibly grotesque villains—Flattop, Pruneface, Mumbles, B-B Eyes, The Blank, et al.—make one wonder why nobody ever put together an animated *Dick Tracy* until 1960, though this might have been due to Gould's understandable obsession with getting the biggest financial kickback possible. United Productions of America was lucky enough to make the one offer that Gould couldn't refuse, and it was UPA who produced the 130 five-minute *Dick Tracy* cartoon package, designed and planned as a followup to the studio's successful *Mr. Magoo* (q.v.) TV series. Chester Gould himself supervised the pilot cartoon—something he would later regret, for in wishing to make the property accessible to the widest audience, he gave in to UPA's notion of gearing Dick Tracy to younger audiences instead of playing the character "straight" (Gould had also bowed to the lowest common denominator when each successive radio adaptation of *Dick Tracy* in the 1930s and 1940s turned out to be more juvenile than the last).

Missing on the TV *Dick Tracy* was the original strip's sobriety and meticulous attention to accuracy in police procedure and crime-lab paraphernalia—except occasionally in the 30-second "Crimestoppers" features used as bumpers between cartoons. On the whole, the UPA version was as farcical as Al Capp's celebrated Tracy parody "Fearless Fosdick." Dick Tracy himself barely appeared at all. At the beginning of each cartoon, Tracy would be seen talking over an intercom, saying—in the voice of onetime Orson Welles associate Everett Sloane—"Okay, chief, I'll get on it right away" (This opener was designed as a tie-in to the local *Dick Tracy Show* hosts, who usually dressed up as policemen and were expected to introduce each cartoon by barking "Calling Dick Tracy!" into their own prop intercoms). The detective would then activate his two-way wrist radio to

summon one of his deputies, who as it developed would be the *real* star of the cartoon. Tracy's four assistants were pure buffoons, as far removed from Gould's original concept as another galaxy: Corpulent beat cop Heap O'Calorie, martial arts expert Joe Jitsu, marathon runner Go Go Gomez—who as "Manuel Tijuana Guadalajara Tampico Gomez, Junior" had first been seen as a penny-ante conman in the *Mister Magoo* cartoons—and the one "funny animal" of the lot, police dog Hemlock Holmes.

Once Tracy decided who'd headline the adventure at hand, the anointed deputy would follow a pattern that varied but little from cartoon to cartoon. Heap O'Calorie (given an "Andy Devine" voice by kiddie show host Johnny Coons) would be discovered stealing apples at a local market when called by Tracy over his wrist radio; he would then seek out "street" information from beatnik informant Nick, who tapped out Morse code on his bongos. Go Go Gomez (whom Mel Blanc provided with his legendary "Si ... Sy ... Si" Hispanic dialect) would be taking a siesta in his hammock or romancing a senorita when Tracy called, then would dart through the city streets at super speed. Hemlock Holmes (his voice a carbon copy of Cary Grant's, courtesy of Jerry Hausner) would assemble his "Retouchables," a motley Keystone Kop crew, who'd then run en masse into their patrol wagon and speed off—forever leaving poor Hemlock behind. Japanese Joe Jitsu (voice by master dialectician Benny Rubin) didn't have a traditional "opening," but somewhere in every one of his adventures he'd be seen effortlessly tossing his opponents about judo-style, all the while politely murmuring "So sorry ... Excuse please."

Thus it was that each *Dick Tracy* cartoon was comprised of anywhere from 20 to 25 percent of stock animation footage, used over and over. Similarly repetitious were the plotlines, especially one device which occurred at the halfway point of every story: The deputy would cry "Hold everything!," all action would stop cold, and the deputy, no matter what peril he was facing, would report his progress via wrist-radio to Tracy—thus allowing the local TV stations to use this break in the action to run an additional commercial, if so inclined. The footage leading up to the "Hold everything" gag would be used as a

Dick Tracy.

reminisced how they'd fed a ship's captain and crew to their pet shark, while in another cartoon, The Brow and Oodles were seen escaping from prison, still strapped in their electric chairs! But for the most part, UPA reduced Gould's rogues gallery to the same kiddie level as the rest of *Dick Tracy*, mainly by giving the villains clichéd comedy-cartoon voices: B-B Eyes sounded like Edward G. Robinson, Flattop like Peter Lorre, The Brow like James Cagney, Pruneface like Boris Karloff, and Sketch Paree like every "Powerful Pierre" Frenchman since the birth of animation.

Dick Tracy wouldn't have been worth all the space allotted to it here except that it was enormously popular. Several TV stations, basking in the profits accrued by UPA's *Mister Magoo*, were willing to purchase *Tracy* in 1961 without even screening its pilot, and were well rewarded for this foresight. The series, which benefited from its color photography and strong tie-ins with such merchandisers as Mattel Toys and American Character Products, did exceptionally well in big-city markets, notably in Dick Tracy's birthplace of Chicago, where independent station WGN-TV ran the program Monday through Friday in prime time. The rate of attrition vis-à-vis *Dick Tracy*'s predictability was rather swift, but a new young audience unfamiliar with its formula was always available every few years, so the series remained a strong sales item into the 1970s. It might have even survived into the 1980s had not the characters of "Joe Jitsu" and "Go Go Gomez" been deemed stereotypical and offensive by several ethnic activist groups.

pre-credits "preview" for the cartoon, eating up even more time and permitting UPA to shoot no more than three and one-half minutes of new animation per five-minute short subject. Having had the distinction of separating itself from assembly-line formula in its theatrical cartoons, UPA retrogressed full scale to that formula in *Dick Tracy*.

Virtually all that remained of "vintage" Chester Gould were the villains, who for the purposes of the streamlined plotlines were paired off, like wrestling tag teams: Flattop and B-B Eyes, Stooge Viller and Mumbles, Sketch Paree and the Mole, Pruneface and Itchy, and the Brow and Oodles (one "solo" villain was specially invented for the animated series: Cheater Gunsmoke, whose face was obscured by a cloud of cigar fumes). United Productions did an admirable job of accurately recreating Gould's original drawings, occasionally allowing the characters to be just as homicidal as their comic-strip counterparts: In one episode, Pruneface and Itchy gleefully

End of story? Not quite. Dick Tracy resurfaced in 1971 as one of several comic-strip characters appearing in vignettes on Filmation's *Archie's TV Funnies* (see *Archie*); these were at least closer in spirit to the original than UPA's, and were bolstered by the presence of several of Tracy's newsprint supporting characters, including Pat Patton, Tess Trueheart, Junior Tracy and the Moon Maid. And in 1990, the release of Warren Beatty's monster-budget *Dick Tracy* feature film prompted UPA's new distributor to repackage the old cartoons for a brief syndicated run. This time around, local stations were given the option whether or not to telecast the "racist" Joe Jitsu and Go Go Gomez installments; not surprisingly, these were rejected outright by virtually every independent channel in California.

DINGBAT AND THE CREEPS *see* **HEATHCLIFF**

DINK, THE LITTLE DINOSAUR. CBS: 9/16/1989–8/24/1991. Ruby-Spears. Executive producers, Joe Ruby and Ken Spears. Produced by Larry Huber. Directed by Bill Hutten and Tony Love. Story editor, Ralph Sanchez. Animation supervisor, John Conning. Associate producer, Scott McLaughlin. Director of production design, Ric Gonzalez. Storyboard supervisor, Cosmo Anzilotti. Background layout supervision, Larry Nikolai. Background styling, Eric Semones. Voice director, Ginny McSwain. Music by John DeBray. Developed by Chris Weber and Karen Wilson. Voices: R. J. Williams (Dink); Andee McAfee (Amber); Ben Granger (Shyler); S. Scott Bullock (Flapper); Frank Welker (Scar/Crusty); and Dana Hill, and Nancy Cartwright.

Conceived in the shadow of Don Bluth's animated feature *The Land Before Time* (1988), *Dink, the Little Dinosaur* entered the Saturday morning network sweepstakes for a two-season run in 1989. Like the hero of the Bluth film, TV's Dink was a young, wide-eyed, mischievous apatosaurus (or brontosaurus) of the Cretaceous period, trying to cope with and make sense of the still-forming Earth around him. Dink's friends included a wise old turtle named Crusty (who sported white sideburns!), as well as several Disneyesque renditions of such species as the pteranodon, corythosaurus and edaphorsaurus. The scriptwriters made the sweeping assumption that these very different dinos would have lived together peacefully — except of course for the traditionally villainous Tyranno the Tyrannosaurus.

Two short episodes were seen per 30-minute program, both prechecked for accuracy by a team of dinosaur experts (who were of course willing to look the other way regarding Dink's cartoonish appearance, human emotions, power of speech, and physical dexterity). Parallels drawn by *Dink, the Little Dinosaur* between the prehistoric protagonist's respect for nature and modern mankind's misuse of it were hidden only to viewers who couldn't read. Further satisfying the Political Correctness Patrol, Dink and his friends learned lessons about prejudice, tolerance, cooperation, and other matters of utmost concern to dinosaurs.

The preaching persisted with an educational segment introduced in *Dink, the Little Dinosaur*'s second season: The weekly "Factasaurus," offering viewers statistics and trivia about the individual dinosaur type spotlighted on each episode.

DINO BOY *see* **SPACE GHOST AND DINO BOY**

DINO RIDERS *see* **MARVEL ACTION UNIVERSE**

DINOSAUCERS. Syndicated: 1987. Lightyear Entertainment/KK&D/DIC/Coca-Cola/LBS. Executive producers: Andy Heyward, Benjamin Meiniker, Michael E. Uslan. Produced by Michael Maliani. Directed by Stephen Martiniere. Story editors: Diane Duane, Byrnne Stephens. Original character drawings: Craig Benjamin. Music by Haim Saban and Shuki Levy. Voices: Len Carlson (Quackpot/Allo), Rob Cowan (Tricero), Marvin Goldhar (Bonehead/Bronto-Thunder), Dan Hennessey (Genghis Rex/Plesio), Ray Kahnert (Steggio), Gordon Masten (Styraco), Don McManus (Brachio), Barbara Redpath (Sara), Simon Reynolds (Ryan), John Stocker (Terrible Dactyl/Ankylo), Leslie Toth (David), Chris Wiggins (Dimetro), Thick Wilson (Ichthyo), Richard Yearwood (Paul).

Dinosaucers, a daily syndicated strip, was the *Transformers* (q.v.) formula in lizard skin. Instead of a group of outer-space robots bringing their eons-old battle to planet Earth, the heroes and villains of *Dinosaucers* were extraterrestrial dinosaurs, who extended their neverending war on doomed planet Reptillion to our own Big Blue Marble — all in the ultimate offscreen hope of promoting a line of action figures and toys. The good Dinosaucers included Allo, Terry and Icky, and others whose nicknames invoked various species. The villains, or "Tyrannos" (why does everyone assume that meateating dinosaurs were automatically evil?) were led by Genghis Rex.

The Dinosaucers' human allies on Earth were the Secret Scouts, a teen contingent made up of David, Sara, Paul and Ryan. Not your normal prehistoric creatures, the dino characters were fully equipped with state-of-the-art technology, included a "Fossilizer" gun that froze one's enemy in his tracks. The saving grace of the series was that it was sometimes funny on purpose — but more often, as in one deathless episode titled "Lochs and Bay Gulls" which tried to satirize the Loch Ness Monster and the movie *Casablanca* all at once, it was funny by accident. Whatever the case, the world wasn't ready for militant reptiles in 1987 — *Teenage Mutant Ninja Turtles* would impact the following year — so *Dinosaucers* was extinct (I *had* to say it) after a single first-run season, excavated in cable-rerun form in 1989 on the Family Channel.

DIPSY DOODLE. Syndicated: 1974. WJW-TV/SFM/General Foods. Executive Producer: Bob Huber. Live-action cast: Karen League Barrett, Sandy Faison, Jon Freeman, Michael McGee, Harry Gold, Emil Herrera, Helen Leonard.

Dipsy Doodle was an animated-cartoon country bumpkin who laid claim to being a direct descendant of the "original" Yankee Doodle. Most of the rest of the hour-long *Dipsy Doodle Show* featured a cast of live performers, doing the sort of quasi-educational entertaining expected of children's shows of the era. Produced in Cleveland, *Dipsy Doodle* was given a single shot at national coverage in December of 1974, one of many entries in American television's two-year bicentennial celebration.

DIRTY DAWG *see* **KWICKY KOALA**

THE DISNEY AFTERNOON *see* **BONKERS, CHIP 'N' DALE'S RESCUE RANGERS, DARKWING DUCK, DISNEY'S ADVENTURES OF THE GUMMI BEARS, DUCKTALES, GOOF TROOP and TALE SPIN**

DISNEY'S ADVENTURES OF THE GUMMI BEARS. NBC: 9/14/1985–9/2/1989. Syndicated: 1990. The Disney Channel: 1991–.
— **DISNEY'S GUMMI BEARS/WINNIE THE POOH HOUR.** ABC: 9/9/1989–9/1/1990. Walt Disney Animation/Buena Vista. Produced by Arthur Vitello, Tad Stones and Alan Zaslove. Associate producer, Tom Ruzicka. Directed by Arthur Vitello and Alan Zaslove. Story editors, Jymn Magnon, Tad Stones. Animation

supervisors: David Block, Bob Zamboni, John Ahern. Assistant directors, Kent Holaday and Randy Chaffee. Supervising editor, Robert S. Birchard. Music coordinator: Chris Montan. Music theme by Silvesher and Silvesher. Music composed and conducted by Thomas Chase and Steve Rucker. Animation facilities: TMS Entertainment, Walt Disney Animation Japan. Voices: Corey Burton (Gruffi Gummi/Toadie/Gigglin), Roger C. Carmel (Sir Tuxford), Brian Cummings (Chillbeard Jr., Knight of Gummadon), Jim Cummings (Chummi), Walker Edmiston (Sir Thornberry), David Faustino (Knight of Gummadon), June Foray (Granni Gummi/The Most Peaceful Dragon in the World/Mobile Tree/Councilor Woodale), Bob Holt (Giant with the Wishing Stone/Dom Gordo of Ghent), Christian Jacobs, Brett Johnson (Cavin), Katie Leigh (Sunni Gummi/Mobile Tree), Chuck McCann (Tadpole/Sir Tuxford), Tress MacNeille (Marsipan/Great Oak/Mother/Lady Bane), Howard Morris (Sir Ponch), Lorenzo Music (Tummi Gummi/Bubble Dragon), Noelle North (Cubbi Gummi/Princess Calla/Mobile Tree), Alan Oppenheimer (Knight of Gummadon), Pat Parris (Trina/Aquarianne), Rob Paulsen (Gusto), Will Ryan (Unwin/Gad/Zook/Ogres/King Carpie), Michael Rye (King Gregor/Duke Igthorn/Gowan/Malsinger), Bill Scott (Gruffi Gummi/Toadie/Sir Tuxford/Angelo Davini/Ogre), Lennie Weinrib (Zorlock), Frank Welker (Ditto/Chillbeard Jr./Mervyns/Mother Griffin), Paul Winchell (Zummi Gummi/Slumber Sprite/Clutch/Tuck/Giggalin); and Hamilton Camp, and Kath Soucie.

When Disney decided to enter the world of mass produced TV animation full-force in 1985, things did not seem to bode well for cartoon lovers. Instead of bringing one or all of the old Disney favorites to the small screen for weekly half hour doses, the studio opted to follow a trend established by — shudder — Hanna-Barbera. *Disney's Adventures of the Gummi Bears* was not only designed to promote a line of confections and toys designed by the Heide candy company, but it also seemed to be a blatant ripoff of Hanna-Barbera's *The Smurfs*. How dare Disney offer its longtime disciples something as shamelessly commercial, as simperingly imitative as a cartoon world populated by cute little medieval bears, their names all based on the word "Gummi"? Storm the gates and force-feed the Disney staffers on their own tripe!

But *Gummi Bears* surprised all and turned out to be well worth having — perhaps below the usual Disney standards (an expected by-product of farming its animation to outside studios), but a property that transcended its derivative roots and was able to stand on its own two paws. It was the same situation that faced the 1954 Disney cartoon short *Toot, Whistle, Plunk and Boom*, which seemed at first to be an uninspired imitation of the upstart UPA Studio but which by fadeout time proved to be as worthy a Disney product as any cartoon from the "Golden Age."

The weekly series was set in the medieval kingdom of Dunwym, a land beset with such traditional fairytale urban blight as evil knights, despotic nobility in the person of Duke Igthorn, a wicked and omnipotent sorceress, cloddish giants, and various enemies on land (trolls) and in the air (the flying Carpies). Someone had to save the kingdom, and since Tolkien wasn't around any more to summon up his Middle Earth heroes, Dunwyn ended up relying on the Gummi Bears. These magical, supposedly mythical bruins had a long history told in song and legend, passed from generation to generation by such benign elders as Granni Gummi. With a few healthy swigs of Gummiberry juice, the Gummi Bears were able to set forth to save their land with the help of a human boy named Cavin, who allowed the Bears access to locales where they might otherwise be imprisoned or done away with. The 65 episodes were overabundant with the sort of occult mysticism and magical spells that irritated many born-again Christian critics of Saturday morning cartoons, but which delighted Disney fans of all ages.

Rescuing *Gummi Bears* from being a mere *Smurfs* clone were the series' well-delineated characters (both heroes and villain), an abundance of marvellous background art by Disney stylist Gary Eggleston, and some very sharp, savvy scripting, setting a pattern for ceaseless "inside" jokes that would over the next decade become something of a trademark in Disney animation, culminating in the cultural-reference-per-second fest in the 1992 animated feature *Aladdin*. The seemingly gratuitous but carefully integrated

in-jokes on *Gummi Bears* ranged from the appearance of Mickey Mouse and Donald Duck as bath toys in an episode irresistibly titled "Someday My Prints Will Come," to voice actress June Foray, playing Granni Gummi, being permitted to exclaim "Hokey smoke!" — an affectionate throwback to Foray's previous life as Rocket J. Squirrel (see *Rocky and His Friends*).

Gummi Bears lasted four first-run seasons on NBC, where it habitually ranked #1 in its timeslot — and incidentally sold a lot of Gummi Bear candy. For its fifth season, the program moved to ABC and was combined in a 60-minute slot with another Disney property, *The New Adventures of Winnie the Pooh* (q.v.). In 1990, the whole *Gummi Bears* rerun package was transferred to syndication as part of the studio's "Disney Afternoon," aligned with *DuckTales, Chip 'n' Dale's Rescue Rangers* and *Tale Spin* (see individual entries on these titles). While not losing any of its lustre, *Gummi Bears* seemed out of kilter with the rest of the Disney Afternoon. It looked overproduced compared to the more streamlined "Afternoon" components, plus it was the only one of the four programs not to offer serialized plotlines. A far better showcase for *Gummi Bears* opened up when the series was appropriated for the Disney Channel pay cable service, where it remains as of this writing.

DOCTOR SNUGGLES. Syndicated: 1981. KidPix/LBS. Executive producer, Jeffrey O'Kelley. Produced by Joop Visch. Directed by Mel Price. Written by Richard Carpenter and Paul Halas. Music by Kon Leray. Voices: Peter Ustinov, Owen Griffiths, John Challis.

Produced in the Netherlands, *Dr. Snuggles* was a whimsical little weekly half hour starring a kindly "Dr. Doolittle" type veterinarian who hopped from adventure to adventure on his pogo stick. Not only did Snuggles talk to the animals — he talked to *everything*, sharing conversations with trees, doormats, furniture, stepladders and even his own doctor's bag. Sidelines characters included Granny Toots, Miss Nettles the housekeeper, Mathilda Junkbottom the robot maid, Knobby the Mouse, Dennis the badger, and Benjy and Freddy the rabbits. Most of the voices were supplied with a seemingly limitless

Dog City: **Eliot Shag and entourage.**

variety of characterizations by Peter Ustinov.

The sort of genteel fare that would in later years be best suited for a morning berth on the Nickelodeon cable service, *Dr. Snuggles* was distributed far and wide in 1981, usually broadcast on weekends as an independent-station alternative to the networks' alleged obsession with animated slapstick and violence.

DODO—THE KID FROM OUTER SPACE. Syndicated: 1965. Halas and Batchelor/Fremantle.

The highly regarded British animation house of Halas and Batchelor, best known to Americans as the guiding force of the 1955 cartoon-feature version of George Orwell's *Animal Farm* (that's the one with the happy ending), briefly broke into American distribution in the 1960s with a handful of projects (see also *Foo Foo* and *Snip Snap*). *DoDo—The Kid from Outer Space*, consisting of 78 color half hours, looked and sounded a lot like such Japanese science-fiction cartoon imports as *Astro Boy* (q.v.) and *The Amazing Three* (q.v.)—perhaps deliberately so. The weekly series featured DoDo, his pet Compy, and researcher Professor Fingers, all of whom hailed from the "atomic" planet Hena Hydro. Seldom seen outside the major markets, *DoDo—The Kid from Outer Space* managed a lengthy run on several NBC owned and operated stations from 1966 through 1970.

DOG CITY. Fox: 9/19/1992–. Nelvana/ Henson Productions/Channel 4/Global Television Network/Autonomous Stations of Spain/Canal-Spain. Executive producers: Michael K. Frith, Brian Henson, Patrick Loubert, Michael Hirsh, Clive A. Smith. Produced by Stephen Hodgins. Directed by John Van Bruggen. Story editors: Peter Sauder, J. D. Smith. Written by Laraine Arkow, Terrie Collins, Robert Schechter and Gary Sperling. Theme music by Phil Balsam. Additional production facilities: Hanho Heung Up Co. Ltd. Voices: Ron White (Ace Heart), Elizabeth Hanna (Chief Rosie O'Gravy), John Stocker (Bugsy), James Rankin (Frisky), Howard Jerome (Bruiser), Paulina Gillis (Kitty), Stephen Ouimette (Mad Dog). Muppet performers: Kevin Clash (Eliot Shag), Fran Brill (Colleen), Joey Mazzarino (Artie), Brian Meehl (Bruno); and Martin P. Robinson, David Rudman and Don Reardon.

Amidst all the hype attending the Fox Network's invasion of the Saturday morning cartoon field, Henson Productions' *Dog City*, based on a live-action sketch first seen in 1989 on NBC's *The Jim Henson Hour*, slipped in virtually unnoticed and unheralded—a real surprise, since this weekly half hour amalgam of live "muppet" action and animation was certainly among the best of Fox's offerings. The premise of *Dog City* is easier described than accomplished: Juxtaposing the traditional *film noir* private-eye genre with a cartoon world populated almost exclusively by talking canines. That Henson Productions—commandeered in this instance by the late Jim Henson's son Brian—and Nelvana Studios managed to remain doggedly (ouch!) faithful to the premise, and keep things unfailingly funny at the same time, was enough to compensate for any number of second-rate cartoon series from less inspired filmmakers.

Ace Heart, the star of *Dog City*, was a trenchcoated Philip Marlowe type, given to lines like "I knew the dame was trouble the moment she sat down and uncrossed her hind legs." Ace tried to solve mysteries as discreetly as possible for his nervous clients, aided by his chums Eddie the newsie, Bugsy, Frisky, Bruiser and Kitty; his police force nemesis was the beauteous Chief Rosie O'Gravy. The hardboiled hound's adventures usually leaned toward the supernatural, in the tradition of Nelvana's earlier *Beetlejuice* (q.v.).

Dog City employed the engaging framing device of showing Ace Heart's exploits being drawn on a cartoon storyboard before our eyes. The artist was Eliot Shag, a live-action Muppet dog whose own life was as rocky as his creation's; Eliot was constantly interrupted in his work by his girl friend Colleen and by various pals, loan sharks and angry landlords (all of whom were unwitting role models for Shag's cartoon characters). Eliot interacted with Ace Heart, trading quips and insults with his "dog star," who was always complaining about the scrapes Eliot dreamed up for him. Once in a while, the artist got even by putting Ace in an inescapable situation or having one of his trusted cartoon cohorts turn into a mad killer or vampire—only to rescue the chastened detective at the very last moment. (Was *Dog City* really "The Brian Henson Story," perhaps?)

The best aspect of *Dog City* was that, unlike the black-nosed residents of Disney's Duckburg, Henson's stars were not merely doglike humans but real dogs with real dog instincts—manifested in one episode by having all the characters drop their Raymond Chandler demeanor and jargon in order to snarl menacingly at a human mailman. Most wonderful was the series' ability to convey a canine point of view without losing sight of the detective parody, and vice versa: When Ace Heart did the standard detective bit of ordering his young pal Eddie to stay in the car while Ace investigated, Eddie replied, "Okay. But don't keep the windows rolled up again."

The scriptwork on the series was so sharp that one could have forgiven any sloppy animation or artwork. But even here the Henson/Nelvana people didn't disappoint: *Dog City* was as stylish as any live-action episode of *Magnum P.I.* or *Miami Vice*, its beautifully rendered backgrounds melding perfectly with its caricatured leading characters. *Dog City* was proof positive that in the long run, the new breed of TV cartoonmakers in the 1990s was the best thing that happened to television since the remote control button.

DON COYOTE AND SANCHO PANDA. Syndicated: 1990 (as part of FUNTASTIC WORLD OF HANNA-BARBERA). Hanna-Barbera. Co-produced by RAI (Radiotelevisione Italiana Raiuno). Executive in charge of production, Jayne Barbera. Executive producers,

William Hanna and Joseph Barbera. Co-executive producer, Paul Sabella. Story editors, Don Nelson and Arthur W. Alsberg. Voices: Michael Bell, Gregg Berger, Lauree Berger, Sorrell Booke, Thom Bray, Ruth Buzzi, Hamilton Camp, Townsend Coleman, Didi Conn, Peter Cullen, Brian Cummings, Tim Curry, Keene Curtis, Jennifer Darling, Barry Dennen, Hector Elizondo, Bernard Erhard, Steve Franken, George Furth, Teresa Ganzel, Brad Garrett, Joan Gerber, Henry Gibson, Ed Gilbert, Jim Gilstrap, Jonathan Harris, Phil Hartman, Jerry Houser, Helen Hunt, Renae Jacobs, Tony Jay, Arte Johnson, Jean Kasem, Stacy Keach Sr., Zale Kessler, Alan Lurie, Sherry Lynn, Ken Mars, Allan Melvin, Sidney Miller, Pat Musick, Stacey Melkin, Allan Oppenheimer, Ron Palillo, Julie Payne, Henry Polic II, Peter Renaday, Bob Ridgely, Joan Roberts, Joe Ruskin, Michael Rye, Avery Schreiber, Susan Silo, Kath Soucie, Kristofer Tabori, Jeffrey Tambor, Marcelo Tubert, Len Weinrib, Frank Welker.

Coproduced by Hanna-Barbera and Italy's RAI TV network, *Don Coyote and Sancho Panda* ran in Europe a year before its 1990 American premiere as a half-hour component of *The Funtastic World of Hanna-Barbera* (q.v.). It probably isn't necessary to delineate the series' particular anthropomorphic-animal twist on Miguel Cervantes' original *Don Quixote*, which is implicit in the title (a time-travel subtheme not covered by Cervantes was also explored). The most refreshing aspect of *Don Coyote* was the lead character's "Good Soldier Schweik" demeanor. Thanks to plain dumb luck, Don Coyote always managed to rout the villains, who as a result considered the harmless old fellow such a threat that they united their efforts to put him out of the way—and in so doing, succeeded only in tripping themselves up. Don Coyote may have been one of the few cartoon "heroes" who never really *did* anything, but who nevertheless always came out on top. As in the Peter Sellers movie *Being There*, the protagonist became what those around him assumed him to be. Kinda esoteric stuff for Sunday morning cartoon time, don't you think?

DONKEY KONG and DONKEY KONG JR. *see* **SATURDAY SUPERCADE**

DOUBLE DRAGON. Syndicated: 1993 (as part of AMAZIN' ADVENTURES). DIC/Bohbot. Executive producers, Andy Heyward, Robby London, Avi Arad, Byron Cook. Produced and directed by Chuck Patton. Executive in charge of production, Brian Miller. Production supervisors, Stacy Gallishaw and RaNae Bonela. Associate producer, Kurt Weldon. Adapted for animation by Phil Harnage and Chuck Patton. Script coordinator, Lori Crawford. Music by Clark Patton. Music editor, John Mortarotti. Executive in charge of production for Bohbot, Allen J. Bohbot. Animation produced by Sae Rom Plus One, Ltd. Double Dragon is a trademark of Technos Japan Corporation, exclusively licensed to Tradewest, Inc. Voices: Jim Byrnes, Gary Chalk, Mike Donovan, Scott McNeil, Wezley Morris, French Tichner, Cathy Weseluck.

Based on the Komani video game, *Double Dragon*, a 1993 addition to Bohbot's weekend *Amazin' Adventures* (q.v.) package, bore out its title with twin-brother leading men: Jimmy and Billy Lee, separated at birth and united in their eighteenth year. Dark-haired Billy was the protégé of the Oldest Master of the Dragonmasters, an order of laser-wielding ninjas headquartered in the Chinatown section of Metro City. Decked out with superpowered vehicles and bulging pectorals, the Dragonmasters defended the weak, used wits over brute strength in thwarting the wicked, and devoted their spare time to meditation. Their prime enemy was the Shadowboss, functionary of the Shadow of Evil crime syndicate, which had at its disposal a bottomless supply of high-tech weaponry and thick-skulled henchmen (notably blocklike Bubbo and wacko Wild Willie).

After being appointed a special Metro City deputy by Patrolperson Marian Martin, Billy Lee used his martial arts school as a haven for the helpless—and it was there that his blond twin brother Jimmy stumbled in one evening, claiming that he was being pursued by the Shadowboss. It didn't even take a casual knowledge of Rafael Sabatini's novel *The Corsican Brothers* to figure out before the end of the first episode that Jimmy Lee *was* the Shadowboss—Billy's Doppelganger, as devoted to evil as Billy was to good. And since Billy and Jimmy shared each other's pain, neither brother could destroy the

Doug (right) and Porkchop contemplate their individual destinies.

other without fatal consequences to himself. This was but one aspect of the "mirror image" theme pervading *Double Dragon*: for every good laser weapon there was a "bad" one, for every souped-up hero's vehicle there was an equally powerful villain's vehicle, and on it went.

After a handful of episodes, however, Billy and Jimmy Lee found themselves working together against the Shadow of Evil. So there went the premise, right? Wellll . . . it depended on which version of the "Double Dragon" videogame one happened to have at home. In some versions, the Lee boys were allies rescuing fair damsels, while in others, Billy and Jimmy were mortal enemies.

One could get a general idea of the tenor of things on the weekly, half-hour *Double Dragon* by listening as Billy Lee declared that "Violence is the last refuge of the ignorant"—minutes before being sucked into an orgy of violence (but no killing, thank you!). It was the old Cecil B. De-Mille syndrome: Show people it's bad to sin by illustrating sin as entertainingly as possible.

Double Dragon occasionally rose from its clonelike resemblance to TV's other cartoonizations of popular videogames (the "mirror image" concept again, perhaps?) thanks to the care and skill of direc-

tor Chuck Patton, a veteran of the comic-book *Justice League of America* artists pool and recent contributor to the DIC miniseries *Swamp Thing* (q.v.).

DOUG. Nickelodeon: 8/11/1991–. Jumbo Pictures ("Grade A Quality")/Ellipse/ Nickelodeon. Supervising producer and director: Tony Eastman. Produced by Melanie Grisanti. Directed by John Paratore. Original character created by "Doug" executive producer Jim Jinkins and Joe Aaron. Executive producers: David Campbell, Christine Martin, David Martin. Supervising producer, Brad Gunther. Written by Alan Silberberg, Lisa Melamed and Alicia Marie Schudt. Music by Dan Sawyer and Fred Newman. Animation facilities: Han Ho Studios. Voices: Billy West, Constance Shulman, Doug Preis, Alice Playten, Fred Newman, Becca Lish, Greg Lee, Steve Higgins, Jim Brownold, Doris Belack, John Lee, Bruce Bailey Johnson, Patience Jarvis, Julie Halston, Fran Brill.

The inaugural series of Nickelodeon's 1991 foray into first-run animation, *Doug* was simpler and gentler than its two companion cartoon series (see *Ren and Stimpy* and *Rugrats*), but no less praiseworthy. *Doug* was the weekly story of 11-year-old Doug Funnie, the new kid in the small town of Bluffington. Doug lived with his parents, his "Sixties Activist" older sister Judy, and his faithful dog Porkchop. New friends of Doug's included sweet Patty Mayonnaise, whom our hero worshipped from not so afar, and Doug's confidant Mosquito "Skeeter" Valentine. Foremost among his new foes were school bully and all-around jerk Roger Klotz (whose "Eddie Haskell" persona was not the only thing *Doug* borrowed from the old live-action *Leave It to Beaver* series), and Vice Principal Bone, a Don Knotts clone whose strict adherence to rules and regulations was guaranteed to cause agony for Doug and his friends, and ultimately to backfire on the pompous Mr. Bone.

Most of Doug's adventures consumed the entire half hour, while a few were doled out in two 15-minute chunks per program. Whatever the case, the throughline of *Doug* was the eternal dilemma of fitting in with the status quo: trying to be "one of the guys," avoiding public humiliation, constructing a decent science project, standing up to school bureaucracy, camouflaging a facial pimple, gathering up nerve to ask a girl out to the school dance, and so on. It was a central premise with which any member of the audience from kindergartner to middleager could identify, and it was clear that the one person who most identified with Doug was *Doug's* creator, former Children's Television Workshop employee Jim Jinkins. The series' protagonist was a diarist and fledgling cartoonist who often cast himself in his scribbled adventures, usually as caped superhero "Quailman" or as a tuxedoed, *sang froid* James Bond type named "Smash Adams." At the end of each episode, Doug's essential decency and sense of right won out, usually at the expense of the braying Roger Klotz. Doug was the smart, nice kid we all wanted to be—the one who got himself out of jeopardy through wits rather than fisticuffs or some other form of negative physical exertion. "*Doug* is nice, warm and funny," praised Peggy Charren of Action for Children's Television, "and it doesn't talk down."

At times, *Doug* was a little *too* nice. To keep audience interest piqued, Jumbo Pictures and Ellipse (the series' production companies) adopted a visual style that can best be labelled "quirky." Each character on the series was a different color — not just white, black or yellow, but also

blue, orange, purple and green. The color choices had nothing to do with the characters' personalities, but instead helped to make the steady flow of onscreen bodies appear to be individuals instead of the usual TV-animation paper dolls. Another eccentric production touch (toned down after the first few episodes) was to give some characters only one eyebrow, which reflected those characters' thought processes.

Perhaps *Doug's* most bizarre trademark was the series' obsession with meat products. In addition to the aforementioned pet dog Porkchop, there was an entire half hour devoted to Doug's intense dislike of liver and onions. Another storyline dealt with a student-vs.-vice principal clash over an inedible luncheon delicacy called "Magic Meat." And in a Halloween episode, costume-party guests arrived dressed as everything from a mutton leg to a pot roast. Neither this nor any of *Doug's* other peculiarities ever detracted from the series' storylines, characters or overall appeal. As with the personal directorial touches of *auteurs* like John Ford, Howard Hawks and George Lucas, the odd little quirks of the Jumbo/Ellipse staff merely added depth and texture to the series.

After a season in the weekend morning and afternoon lineups, *Doug* was rewarded with a Saturday evening prime time slot in the fall of 1992, holding his own despite the competition of his louder and more demonstrative neighbors *Ren and Stimpy* and *Rugrats*—not to mention the frenetic live-action Nickelodeon attractions *Roundhouse* and *Are You Afraid of the Dark?*

DRAGON WARRIOR. Syndicated: 1990. Saban/LBS. Executive producer, Haim Saban. Supervising producer, Winston Richard. Associate producer, Eric S. Rollman. Story editor, Robert V. Barron. Music by Haim Saban and Shuki Levy. Animation facilities: Nippon Animation Studios. Voices: Long John Baldry, Jay Brazeau, Jim Byrnes, Gary Chalk, Marcy Goldberg, Sam Kouth, Shelley Lefler, Duff McDonald, Richard Newman.

Unveiled by Nintendo in 1986, "Dragon Quest," a combination of two personal-computer games, was the company's most complicated and costly videogame to date. Its debut was heralded by a sword-and-sorcery backstory in a Japanese boys' magazine to tantalize video addicts, and its resultant big sales prompted Nintendo to create three "Dragon Quest" sequels. A weekly half-hour cartoon series followed, produced by Japan's Nippon Animation Studios in 1989 and released in the U.S. by LBS Communications the following year, under the title *Dragon Warrior*.

The thirteen serialized *Dragon Warrior* episodes emulated the videogame format by being titled as "Levels": The first install-ment was "Level One: Ariahan Village," the second was "Level Two: Departure," the third "Level Three: Leebe Village," and so on until "Level Thirteen: Najimi Tower." Introduced in Level One was 16-year-old Abel, who was compelled by cir-cumstance to seek and destroy Baramos, a huge, horrible winged creature who bore the "Voice of Doom." Baramos had threat-ened to expose mankind to the apocalyptic fury of the Great Dragon by means of a magical amulet called the Red Stone. It's likely that Abel would have steered clear of all this had not his closest childhood friend, 15-year-old girl Tiala, been the latest descendant of the family charged with guarding the Red Stone—making her subsequent kidnapping by Baramos all but inevitable. If you're wondering why some-one in Tiala's family hadn't simply tossed the Red Stone in the dumpster to avoid potential disaster, the answer is simple: Then there wouldn't have been any *Dragon Warrior*.

Various good and bad characters peo-pled the series, but outside of Baramos and his coward-bully servant Moor (who looked like an ulcerated toad), most of the regulars were "good." There was Abel's close pal MocoMoco, larger than Abel but not quite as athletic. There was Daisy, described by *Dragon Warrior*'s press release as a "macho miss" (I'd like to have seen *that!*), introduced in "Level 4: Girl Warrior Daisy." And for the sake of griz-zled humor, there was Janac the wizard, a mustachioed, pipe-puffing old soak with not a few eccentric character flaws.

Written and produced with traditional Japanimation ebullience, and blessed with a solid premise aimed squarely at the 11- to 14-year-old market, *Dragon Warrior* should have been at least a modest suc-cess. Sadly, the series was vanquished after six months—not by Baramos or the Great Dragon but because of generally weak timeslots (most independent sta-tions, overloaded with product in 1990,

shunted the series to the least accessible of the Sunday-morning hours) and an overall drop of public interest in the original Nintendo videogame.

DRAGON'S LAIR. ABC: 9/8/1984–4/27/1985. Ruby-Spears. Executive pro-ducers, Joe Ruby and Ken Spears. Di-rected by Charles A. Nichols. Music by John DeBray. Music supervision by Paul DeKorte. Voices: Arthur Burghardt (Cinge); Michael Mish (Timothy); Fred Travalena (King Ethelred); Bob Sarlatte (Dirk the Daring); Ellen Gerstel (Princess Daphne); Marilyn Schreffler (Assorted Voices); Clive Revill (Storyteller); Peter Cullen (Bertram).

Dragon's Lair arrived close to the end of the first "animated video game" phase in the Saturday morning network cartoon business. The characters in this 13-week extravaganza were King Ethelred, a me-dieval monarch; the King's noblest knight, Dirk the Daring, and his stalwart white horse Bertram; Princess Daphne, an occa-sionally distressed damsel; and Cinge, a ferocious (but not terribly ferocious look-ing) dragon. Villains included an assort-ment of "ice monsters," "bat demons" and similar nemeses.

Though the scripts were wryly written with tongue firmly in cheek, none of the *Dragon's Lair* installments could match the intricate graphics and euphoric excite-ment of the original Cinematronics video game—which, incidentally, was designed in 1983 by the gifted animation producer Don Bluth (*An American Tail, Secret of NIMH, The Land Before Time*, et al.).

THE DRAK PACK. CBS: 9/6/1980–9/5/1981. Hanna-Barbera. Executive pro-ducers, William Hanna and Joseph Barbera. Produced by Art Scott. Directed by Chris Cuddington. Music by Paul De-Korte. Voices: Jerry Dexter (Drak Jr.); Bill Callaway (Frankie/ Howler); Alan Op-penheimer (Big D); Hans Conried (Dr. Dred); Julie McWhirter (Vampira); Chuck McCann (Mummy Man); Don Messick (Toad/Fly).

Here's a switch that's brand new to any-one who hasn't seen *The Addams Family* or *The Munsters*: The monsters on *Drak Pack* were the good guys. Anticipating the later cartoon offerings "Mini Monsters" (see *Comic Strip*) and "Monster Tails" (see *Wake, Rattle and Roll*), the heroes on this

Hanna-Barbera half hour were teenaged descendants of the Famous Monsters of Movieland. Drak Jr., the leader, was the great-grandson of Dracula; Frankie was a relative of Frankenstein; and Howler was a member of the Wolfman family. To make up for the misdeeds of their forefathers, the Drak Pack became crimefighters, battling Dr. Dred of O.G.R.E. (Organization of Generally Rotten Enterprises). Dr. Dred girdled the globe in his Dredgible — we're really in Hanna-Barbera territory now—accompanied by his stooges Vampira, Mummy Man, Toad and Fly.

The Drak Packers thwarted their enemies by changing into superpowered clones of their ancestors (shades of the live-action *The Incredible Hulk*), through the simple expedient of clasping their hands together and shouting "Wacko!" Audiences responded by shouting "No! No!" and by switching their TV dials to the more popular Hanna-Barbera efforts on ABC (*Scooby's Laff-a-Lympics*) and NBC (*Jonny Quest*).

DRAWING POWER. NBC: 10/11/1980–5/16/1981. Newall and Yohe Productions. Animated segments by Kim and Gifford Animation. Actors (live action): Bob Kaliban (Pop); Lenny Schultz (Lenny); Kari Page (Kari).

From the same production company that brought us *Schoolhouse Rock* (q.v.) came NBC's *Drawing Power*, a series of animated/live action educational half hours sandwiched between the more traditional Saturday morning offerings. Three human animation artists, headed by an elderly cartoonist named Pop, delivered little instructional bits of animation—"Cartoons with a conscience," was the animators' description, just as if animators really talked that way. Featured were such characters as Dewey Decimal in cartoons bearing such titles as "Bus Stop," "Pet Peeves," "Professor Rutabaga," "The Book Report," "What Do You Do Dad/Mom?" and "Superperson U." All in all, *Drawing Power* was a worthy effort from the days when the FCC forced the networks to care as much about their viewers' minds as their bank accounts.

DROIDS: THE ADVENTURES OF R2D2 AND C3PO *see* **THE EWOKS**

DROOPY, MASTER DETECTIVE. Fox: 10/2/1993–. Hanna-Barbera/Turner Entertainment. Executive producers: William Hanna, Joseph Barbera. Produced by Joseph Barbera, Don Jurwich, Larry Huber, Kay Wright. Story editors, Don Jurwich, Neal Barbera. Storyboard supervision: Jerry Eisenberg, Bob Singer. Supervising animation directors, Joanna Romersa, Ray Patterson. Animation Directors: John Kafka, Robert Alvarez, Don Lusk, Carl Urbano, Ed Love, Allen Wilzbach, Frank Andrina, Joan Drake, Dan Hunn, David Michener, Margaret Nichols, Sam Nicholson, Jay Sarbry, Art Scott, Ken Southworth, Paul Sommer. Design supervision, Bob Onorato, Scott Jeralds. Main title theme: Music by Gary Lionelli, lyrics by Joseph Barbera. Production facilities: Fils-Cartoons (Philippines), Mr. Big Cartoons (Australia). Overseas animation directors, John Rice and Steve Lumley. Based on characters created by Tex Avery. Voices: Charlie Adler, William Callaway, Teresa Ganzel, Don Messick, Frank Welker, Brandon Adams, Joe Alaskey, Patricia Alice Albrecht, Lewis Arquette, Rene Auberjonois, Michael Bell, Gregg Berger, Sheryl Bernstein, Susan Blu, Sorrell Booke, Charlie Brill, Nicole Brown, Scott Bullock, Arthur Burghardt, Greg Burson, Hamilton Camp, Nancy Cartwright, Marsha Clark, Selette Cole, Townsend Coleman, Danny Cooksey, Bud Cort, Jesse Corti, Peter Cullen, Brian Cummings, Jim Cummings, Tim Curry, Jennifer Darling, Mari Devon, Nancy Dussault, Maggie Egan, June Foray, Patrick Fraley, Brad Garrett, Kathy Garver, Joan Gerber, Barry Gordon, Archie Hahn, Phil Hartman, Pamela Hayden, George Hearn, Dana Hill, Jerry Houser, Charity James, Nick Jameson, Tony Jay, Arte Johnson, Vicki Juditz, Zale Kessler, Kip King, Paul Kreppel, Maurice LaMarche, David Lander, Nancy Linari, Allan Lurie, Sherry Lynn, Tress MacNeille, Kenneth Mars, Chuck McCann, Edie McClurg, Diane Michelle, Brian Mitchell, Alan Oppenheimer, Bibi Osterwald, Gary Owens, Patricia Parris, Rob Paulsen, Pat Pinney, Henry Polic II, Tony Pope, Hal Rayle, Clive Revill, Bob Ridgely, Kimmy Robertson, Stuart Robinson, Roger Rose, Neil Ross, Ronnie Schell, Susan Silo, Sarah Silverman, Hal Smith, Michael Stanton, Kath Soucie, Sally

Struthers, Barbara Stuart, Marcelo Tubert, Janet Waldo, B. J. Ward, Jimmy Weldon, Jane Wiedlin, Lee Wilkoff, April Winchell, Paul Winchell, Jo Anne Worley, Kris Zimmerman, Patric Zimmerman.

Droopy, Master Detective was a spinoff component of Fox's *Tom and Jerry Kids* (q.v.), with 13 new seven-minute episodes added to the already existing 13 from the earlier series. The star was (you win!) Droopy, the diminutive deadpan basset hound created for the MGM cartoon studio by Tex Avery in 1943's *Dumb Hounded*, and later spotlighted in his own MGM series between 1949 and 1952. Seldom moving a muscle and never speaking above a murmur (originally supplied by Bill Thompson in his mump-cheeked "Wallace Wimple" voice, as heard on radio's *Fibber McGee and Molly*), Droopy spent most of his screen time confounding the insidious schemes of a crooked Wolf or a covetous Bulldog named Spike. Spike or the Wolf would pull off some slick piece of chicanery, only to discover—with accompanying "horror" reaction, generally a drop-to-the-floor jaw or strung-out eyeballs—that the ubiquitous Droopy was always a step or two ahead of the game. Unlike other cartoon stars like Bugs Bunny and Daffy Duck who instigated the action in their vehicles, Droopy would pop up unannounced after the action had commenced. The character was a living punchline.

In fact, Droopy was a better punchline than a star; his weaker films were made so by the fact that he simply wasn't as effective as a plot motivator as he was at messing up the plotting of the villains. This problem persisted into Droopy's TV career, both on Filmation's 1979 *The Tom and Jerry Comedy Show* (q.v.) and Hanna-Barbera's *Tom and Jerry Kids*. Though the latter series' *Droopy*s were consummately animated by the newly expanded Hanna-Barbera staff, they lacked a strong central character, a fact made clearer by the addition of Droopy's lookalike, soundalike young son Dripple. After the first few gags involving Droopy's and Dripple's lack of facial reaction to the most appalling of events, and after dutifully trotting out Droopy's laconic catchphrases "Hello, you happy people" and "You know what? That makes me mad," there was really nowhere for the cartoons to go. Harking back to the MGM days, the best

and funniest bits went to the supporting cast—notably the hyperactive Wolf (named McWolf on the Hanna-Barbera version), who still pounded himself with mallets and tore his hair out with the best of them, and a curvaceous human female, a direct descendant of the impossibly sexy "Red" in the old MGM cartoons, named Ms. VaVoom.

While Droopy and Dribble held down a variety of jobs and interests on *Tom and Jerry Kids*, they were rechannelled as trenchcoated hard-boiled gumshoes on *Droopy, Master Detective*. The atmosphere was suitably *film noir*, replete with looming shadows, venetian-blinded windows, garish neon signs and wet city streets. Droopy and Dripple struck just the right incongruous note in these surroundings, drolly satirizing the central situations usually found on *Dragnet* and Clint Eastwood's *Dirty Harry* movies. Once again, however, the premise was worth only one or two shots before repetition—and attrition—set in. And despite vast improvements in Hanna-Barbera's animation technique, the studio still suffered from its tendency to ooververbalize the humor. In the studio's earlier days, verbal comedy *had* to compensate for animation shortcomings; but now, with better designed and more elaborate sight gags, Hanna-Barbera couldn't seem to shake the habit of having the characters comment upon and underline each joke until the humor was effectively smothered to death.

Wedged between the two Droopy vehicles on each half hour *Droopy, Master Detective* were the new adventures of another "back from the dead" Tex Avery creation, Screwball (a.k.a. Screwy) Squirrel. Dropped from the MGM roster after a scant half-dozen cartoons in 1946 because he was considered too maniacal even for the Avery unit, Screwball would seem to have been ideally attuned to the no-brakes cartoon atmosphere of the 1990s generated by *Ren and Stimpy* (q.v.) and *Beavis and Butt-Head* (q.v.). Certainly the new cartoons' basic premise was surefire: The sociopathic squirrel vs. truculent public park attendant Dweeble (with a Storm-Trooper Teutonic accent) and Dweeble's "Which way did he go, George?" dumb dog Grappley. And the dialogue at times approached brilliance: "I'm just a leisure suit in the thrift shop of life," sighed Screwball Squirrel at one point.

But the amiable anarchy which had once flowed so smoothly from the psyche of Tex Avery seemed forced and strained in Hanna-Barbera's hands. Like Warner Bros.' *Animaniacs* (q.v.), the new *Screwball Squirrel* cartoons struggled to recapture the old magic by substituting noise and clutter for inspiration. And again, as in the *Droopy* sequences, there was way too much dialogue. A mere handful of voice-over artists like Bill Thompson and John Brown was all that was necessary to bring the classic MGM cartoons of the 1940s to life. *Droopy, Master Detective*, with only seven main characters, was somehow obliged to maintain an on-call roster of *one hundred and one* voice actors.

I know what you're thinking: Better to have Hanna-Barbera trying too hard than not trying at all. Still, *Droopy, Master Detective*, hilarious though it could be, left most of its viewers pining for the less pretentious lunacies of the original Tex Avery *Droopy* cartoons — and for just a few more variations on the one-note character of Droopy himself.

DUCKTALES. Syndicated: 1987. Walt Disney Animation/Buena Vista Television. Supervising producer (first season): Fred Wolf. Produced by supervising director Bob Hathcock Jr. Co-producers/story editors: Alan Burnett, Ken Koonce, David Wiemers. Written by Mark Seidenburg and Allan Burnett. Directed by James T. Walker and James Mitchell. Art director, Mark Mueller. Music composed and conducted by Ron Jones. Animation facilities: Tokyo Movie Shinsha (TMS). Voices: Alan Young (Scrooge McDuck); Russi Taylor (Huey/Dewey/Louie/Webby); Chuck McCann (Duckworth/Burger and Bouncer Beagle); Brian Cummings (Doofus); Hamilton Camp (Gizmo Duck, a.k.a. Fenton Crackshell); Hal Smith (Gyro Gearloose/ Flintheart Glomgold); Frank Welker (Bubba/Big Time/Baggy Beagle); Terry McGovern (Launchpad McQuack/Baby Face Beagle); June Foray (Ma Beagle/ Magica De Spell); and Howard Morris, Kath Soucie.

DuckTales, Walt Disney Television Animation's first daily syndicated effort, proved to the world that, to quote Disney Television Animation president Gary Krisel, "a high quality series with incentive characters and storylines could almost single-handedly revitalize a floundering segment of the television business." From *DuckTales*' inception onward, one saw fewer and fewer half-hour "action figure" cartoon commercials of the *GI Joe* (q.v.) and *He-Man* (q.v.) variety in daily syndication, and more and more comedy — comedy that, for a change, was genuinely funny to virtually all age groups.

Disney decided to rely upon several of its "secondary" characters for *DuckTales* — characters who'd achieved their greatest fame in Disney's comic books and newspaper strips, as opposed to such "primary" theatrical stars as Mickey Mouse and Goofy (Donald Duck, one of the "primaries," did, however, make a number of guest appearances in *DuckTales*' first season). Most of the series' characters were the residents of the town of Duckburg immortalized for the Disney comic books by brilliant artist/writer Carl Barks — known merely as "The Good Artist" to his fans for many years, since it was Disney's company policy to cloak its print cartoonists in anonymity.

Back in 1937, Carl Barks had contributed gags to a script for a proposed Disney cartoon feature written by Homer Brightman and Harry Reeves, titled *Donald Duck Finds Pirate Gold*. Though never filmed, the screenplay was adapted in 1942 by Bob Karp, an idea man for the daily Donald Duck newspaper strip, into a 64-page Dell comic book, illustrated by Barks and fellow Disney studio employee Jack Hannah. When Dell hired Barks away from Disney a year later, the artist's first assignment was the "Donald Duck" segment in the monthly *Walt Disney's Comics and Stories*. The stories in this periodical were continuations of the "adventurous quest" vein in *Pirate Gold*. Eventually the plotlines were centralized into the Duckburg setting, which Barks populated with such unforgettable citizens as inventor Gyro Gearloose, handyman Gus Goose and his erstwhile employer Grandma Duck, Donald Duck's infuriatingly lucky cousin Gladstone Gander, and the larcenous Beagle Boys, criminals so brazen that they'd walk the streets while wearing their burglar masks and prison serial numbers (176-167, 176-617, 176-671 and 176-761). In December of 1947 came Barks' masterpiece of characterization, Donald's incredibly wealthy Uncle Scrooge — properly spelled $crooge — McDuck.

DuckTales: In various states of excitement are Uncle Scrooge (with top hat), Bubba (with hair), and Huey, Dewey and Louie.

DuckTales: "Unca" Scrooge conspires with his nephews (I can't tell Huey, Dewey and Louie apart without their different colored sweaters).

Carl Barks retired in 1966, but his Duckburg stories remained in circulation through reprints and private collections ever afterward, establishing Scrooge McDuck as a cult figure. The World's Richest Duck made his animated-cartoon debut in the 1967 Disney featurette *Scrooge McDuck and Money,* in which his Scots dialect was rather hollowly rendered by Paul Frees. It was up to comic actor Alan Young to bring depth, bite, and a touch of warmth to Scrooge in the 1983 Disney short subject *Mickey's Christmas Carol*; and it was Alan Young who was tapped for the permanent job of McDuck's voice when the cantankerous webfooted "centrifugillionaire" was chosen as the central character of *DuckTales.*

Scrooge's role on the daily half-hour series was a globetrotting adventurer, usually searching for ways and means of increasing his already astounding fortune. McDuck travelled in the company of Donald Duck's nephews Huey, Dewey and Louie — who despite their many screen appearances were still considered "secondary" Disney characters because they'd first appeared in the Donald Duck comic strip in 1937, a full year before their film debut. In the interest of coherence, the three nephews no longer spoke in the nearly unintelligible squawk provided by the late Clarence Nash in the theatrical cartoons, but were made more articulate by voice actress Russi Taylor. Gyro Gearloose was frequently seen on *DuckTales,* as were the Beagle Boys, now given names instead of merely numbers (Baggy, Burger, Big Time, Bouncer, and a new sibling, Baby Face) and joined by their equally underhanded mother. Other carryovers from the comic books were Gladstone Gander, as damned lucky as ever, and "saucy sorceress" Magica De Spell. New to *DuckTales* were Mrs. Beakley, governess to Huey, Dewey and Louie after "Unca Donald" joined the navy; Mrs. Beakley's spunky, eternally imperiled granddaughter Webbigail "Webby" Vanderduck; Launchpad McQuack, Scrooge's daredevil airplane pilot/adventurer-for-hire, and Launchpad's aptly named sidekick Doofus; Flintheart Glomgold, Scrooge's duplicitous business rival; Bubba, a primitive "cave duck" adopted during one of the adventures; and mildmannered Fenton Crackshell, who sometimes transformed himself into gadget-happy super-

hero Gizmo Duck. Carl Barks may have retired long before *DuckTales,* but his muse certainly hadn't left the building.

Though generally discussed in glowing terms, *DuckTales* was criticized by a few sourpusses for its deliberate echoes of popular live-action adventure films *Romancing the Stone* and (especially) *Raiders of the Lost Ark*; each five part *DuckTales* adventure was a dangerous quest of some sort or other to some distant land or other, just like the above-mentioned boxoffice hits. Even the lettering of *DuckTales'* opening title card was similar to the familiar advertising graphics of the two films. Remember, though, that the directors of *Romancing* and *Raiders* — Robert Zemeckis and Steven Spielberg, respectively — have publicly acknowledged their childhood devotion to comic books. Surely some of the comics devoured by young Bobby Z. and Stevey S. included those early *Pirate Gold*-style adventures (modestly labelled "novelettes" by Carl Barks) spotlighting Donald Duck, his nephews, and his Uncle Scrooge. Thus, *Romancing the Stone* and *Raiders of the Lost Ark* were as much homages to Disney — and by extension *DuckTales* — as the other way around.

But if all *DuckTales* had to offer were thrills and spills, it would have been interchangeable with the rest of the afternoon animation product. What really sold the series was laughter — not the pretested, timid, derivative old jokes recycled on much of the Hanna-Barbera and Filmation output, but laugh-out-loud laughter. As with the classic theatrical cartoons of the 1940s and 1950s, one sensed that the producers of *DuckTales* were entertaining themselves as much as the audience, rather than cynically doling out the usual tired routines on the theory that kids will laugh at anything if you're noisy enough.

The fulsome comic content of *DuckTales* is no surprise when one considers that the production staff was overstocked with seasoned comedy specialists. The program's first-season supervising producer was Fred Wolf, whose skill at blending thrills, laughter and strong story values would culminate in the later *Teenage Mutant Ninja Turtles* (q.v.) for his own company, Murikami-Wolf-Swenson. *DuckTales'* supervising directors included Bob Hathcock, who like Wolf ran his own firm, Incredible Films, Inc. The son of Jerry

Hathcock, a 50-year veteran of the animation game, Bob Hathcock had started as an assistant animator at Disney before manning a director's chair at Hanna-Barbera, where he worked on most of that company's comedy series, ultimately earning an Emmy for his work on *The Smurfs* (q.v.). Additional supervisory direction for *DuckTales* was in the hands of story editors Ken Koonce and David Wiemers, a remarkably productive team who had previously won a Humanitas award for their efforts on TMS Entertainment's *Galaxy High School* (q.v.) and an Emmy for their tenure on Marvel's *Muppet Babies* (q.v.), and who would later function as story editors/producers on another top-notch Disney daily, *Chip 'n' Dale's Rescue Rangers* (q.v.).

Still, comedy was not unique to *Duck-Tales* in afternoon syndication. Already established in the fall of 1987 were such humorous efforts as *Heathcliff, Inspector Gadget*, and the two *Ghostbusters* series (see individual entries on these programs). What put *DuckTales* in the lead was summed up a few paragraphs ago by Disney executive Gary Krisel in a single word: Quality. Though the sheer body of work — 65 episodes the first season, 30 new episodes each season thereafter — required Disney to farm out its animation to overseas studios, *DuckTales* was scrupulously supervised by the Hollywood Disney staff to keep it from falling too far below the established studio standard. To be sure, the series wasn't quite up to the lofty heights of Disney's theatrical cartoon work (this was obvious when comparing the 1989 animated feature *DuckTales: The Movie, Treasure of the Lost Lamp* to Disney's like-vintage *The Little Mermaid*); still, *DuckTales*, budgeted at approximately $100,000 per episode more than the usual daily animated strip, looked a whole lot better than almost anything else on the market in 1987.

To paraphrase the "voice" in the movie *Field of Dreams*: If you build a better product, the people will come. *DuckTales* debuted at the top of the ratings heap, maintaining a 60 percent lead over its nearest animated competitor. And at the beginning of the 1990s, *DuckTales* became the lynchpin of a syndicated "Disney Afternoon" two-hour programming block — the success of which sparked a Golden Age of TV-cartoon creativity from Warner Bros.

(see *Tiny Toon Adventures*), Nelvana (see *Beetlejuice*) and a whole crop of new animation houses (see *Ren and Stimpy* and *The Simpsons*. Any chance you get).

THE DUDLEY DO-RIGHT SHOW. ABC: 4/27/1969–9/6/1970. Producers Associates for Television. (See *King Leonardo* and *Rocky and His Friends* for production credits.)

The *Dudley Do-Right Show* was a rerun package of cartoons from Jay Ward Productions' *The Bullwinkle Show* (see *Rocky and His Friends*) headlining headstrong Constable Do-Right of the Mounties. Also seen herein were rebroadcasts of three other *Bullwinkle* components, "Aesop and Son," "Fractured Fairy Tales" and "Peabody's Improbable History." When *The Dudley Do-Right Show* left the network for syndication, it was retitled *Dudley Do-Right and His Friends* — those "friends" being King Leonardo, Odie Cologne and The Hunter, component characters from Total Television's *King Leonardo and His Short Subjects* (q.v.). This cartoon mulligan's stew has unfortunately led many historians to believe that Jay Ward was somehow responsible for *King Leonardo*, but we won't let him take the rap for that in *this* book.

THE DUKES. CBS: 2/5/1983–11/5/1983. Hanna-Barbera. Executive producers, William Hanna and Joseph Barbera. Produced by Kay Wright. Directed by Oscar Dufau and Bob Hathcock Jr. Written by John Bradford, Benny Ferman, Clive Ferman, O. Grady, John Graham, Orville Hampton, Tom Ruegger and David Tudman. Voices: Sorrell Booke (Boss Hogg); John Schneider (Bo Duke); Tom Wopat (Luke Duke); Catherine Bach (Daisy Duke); Denver Pyle (Uncle Jesse); James Best (Sheriff Rosco Coltrane); Christopher Mayer (Vance Duke); Frank Welker (Flash/Smoky/General Lee).

One wonders why Hanna-Barbera would make a cartoon out of the popular live action CBS comedy-melodrama *The Dukes of Hazzard*. It should be clear to anyone who's ever seen that program that it was *already* a cartoon.

If you've never seen *Dukes of Hazzard*, here's the lowdown. The weekly hour-long series revolved around the Duke family, a "Tobacco Road" aggregation who lived in Hazzard County in some mercifully unnamed southern state. Uncle Jesse Duke was the father-figure, watching out for his adult charges Bo Duke, Luke Duke, and Daisy Duke, who were cousins even though they looked more like unrelated winners of the Malibu Beautiful Abdomen Contest. Bo and Luke were aficionados of auto racing, their pride and joy being a souped-up 1969 Dodge Charger nicknamed the General Lee. Each week for 143 weeks, the Dukes used their automotive expertise to outwit Hazzard County's comically corrupt political boss Hogg and inept Sheriff Rosco Coltrane. *Dukes of Hazzard* was a top-ten attraction from 1979 to 1982, offering daredevil car chases to the kiddies and a plentitude of pulchritude to the daddies in the person of the curvaceous Daisy Duke. As for story content and wittiness of dialogue—well, it's best to say that *Dukes of Hazzard* was the sort of series for which the phrase "No-Brainer" was coined.

It was the kiddies to whom Hanna-Barbera's *The Dukes* was pitched when it showed up as a midseason entry on the CBS Saturday morning manifest in February of 1983 (it replaced the last half hour of the formerly 90-minute *Bugs Bunny/ Road Runner Show*). The actors who'd played the roles of Boss Hogg, the Dukes, and Sheriff Coltrane were engaged to give voice to their cartoon counterparts. One hopes that Catherine Bach (Daisy Duke) was flattered when Hanna-Barbera followed its usual pattern of making the cartoon version of her character even sexier than in real life—in fact, she was a knockout! (See also *Jeannie* and the animated version of Elizabeth Montgomery's *Bewitched* character on the *The Flintstones* for other examples of Hanna-Barbera's cosmetic miracles.) In keeping with the studio's beloved "never ending race" concept (see *Wacky Races, Yogi's Space Race,* and any number of Hanna-Barbera efforts), the animated Dukes were sent on an auto race around the world, the better to win enough money to pay the mortgage on the Duke homestead. Mortgage-holder Boss Hogg, of course, exercised the usual prerogative of all flies in the ointment, and tried to sabotage the Duke boys' chances for success.

Whatever uniqueness there was in the original *Dukes of Hazzard* was quickly dispensed with on *The Dukes*; Hanna-Barbera succeeded in reducing the property

to its usual assembly line standards, right down to giving the Dukes the inevitable funny dog (Flash), whose voice was supplied by the inevitable Frank Welker. For a disturbing example of Hanna-Barbera homogenization, take a look at author Ted Sennett's coffee-table book *The Art of Hanna-Barbera*. On page 222, there's a picture of the cast of *The Dukes*, and on page 216, there's a picture of the cartoon cast of *Mork and Mindy* (q.v.), together with a still of the dramatis personae of Hanna-Barbera's *Fonz and the Happy Days Gang* (q.v.). Each picture is taken from an animated derivation of a popular live action, prime time networker; each picture shows a lineup of characters in various "look at me!" poses; and each picture features a pet dog. "Interchangeable" is the term that comes to mind.

Somehow *The Dukes* squeaked into the CBS fall 1983 cartoon lineup, but only for about a month. It was replaced by *Plasticman* (q.v.), ironically produced by former Hanna-Barbera employees Joe Ruby and Ken Spears. Only 20 episodes of *The Dukes* made it past the drawing board. About 20 too many.

DUNGEONS AND DRAGONS.
CBS: 9/17/1983–8/30/1986; 6/20/1987–9/5/ 1987. Dungeons & Dragons Entertainment Group/TSR Inc./Marvel Productions. Executive producers, David DePatie and Lee Gunther. Produced by Gary Gygax and Don Richardson. Directed by John Gibbs, Gerry Chiniquy, Milt Gray, Tom Ray, Nelson Shin. Music by Johnny Douglas and Rob Walsh. Voices: Willie Aames (Hank); Donny Most (Eric); Katie Leigh (Sheila); Toni Gayle Smith (Diana); Adam Rich (Presto); Ted Field III (Bobby); Sidney Miller (Dungeon Master); Peter Cullen (Venger).

Created by Tactical Studies Rules (TSR) in 1974, "Dungeons and Dragons" was an enormously popular fantasy board game, in which the players assumed various "personae" and embarked on imaginary medieval sword-and-sorcery quests. The game became a center of controversy when it was revealed that some teen and preteen "D and D" aficionados seemingly had trouble separating fantasy from reality, playing out the game beyond the board and into the streets, seeking out potentially dangerous hiding places from their "enemies," and refusing to behave in any

Eek! the Cat   181

manner other than their fictional roles. As always, psychologists and sociologists blamed Dungeons and Dragons itself rather than the home environment or pre-existing emotional disturbances that might have caused these youngsters to feel the need to withdraw from the real world.

In comparison, Marvel's animated, weekly half hour version of *Dungeons and Dragons* caused very little animosity in the psychiatric world, although it must be noted that it premiered the same year (1983) that *Newsweek* magazine was prompted to offer an article titled "Kidvid: A National Disgrace." In retrospect, the only real "disgrace" of the cartoon *Dungeons and Dragons* is that it was produced on the same quickie level as most other Saturday morning offerings of its period.

The plotline of the series took elements of the original board game to illustrate a typical "teen adventure" yarn. Six young people — Sheila, Hank, Eric, Diana, Bobby and Presto — embarked on an amusement park ride which turned out to be a one-way trip into the fantasy land of Dungeons and Dragons. In order to find the way out, each youngster was compelled to assume a "role" (with appropriate costume) and play the game — making certain to keep at least one step ahead of the Venger, "the Ultimate Source of Evil." As a balm to in-teractively inclined audience members, each *Dungeons and Dragons* episode pro-vided sundry clues and riddles — the hand-iwork of the benign Dungeonmaster, "The Protector of All That Is Good" — which permitted home viewers to play the game right along with the characters. The Marvel production staff may not have ex-celled in terms of animation, but the stories, which pitted the protagonists against such fearsome foes as the two-headed Demodragon, were involving enough for the series to survive three first-run seasons — 26 episodes in all. *Dungeons and Dragons* was rerun in late 1987, but by that time the audience's fascination with the original board game had cooled and the series disappeared without protest.

The most interesting aspect of this otherwise standard project was its cast of voice actors. A trio of onetime TV child and teen stars could be found on the call-sheets: Adam Rich and Willie Aames of *Eight Is Enough* and Donny Most of *Happy Days*. Going back in entertainment history a bit further, the actor who supplied the

voice of the Dungeonmaster was Sidney Miller, himself a former child actor of the 1930s, who from 1955 to 1959 was the prin-cipal director of Disney's *Mickey Mouse Club*.

DYNOMUTT, DOG WONDER *see* **SCOOBY-DOO**

EEK! THE CAT. Fox: 9/19/1992–11/13/1993.
— **EEK! AND THE TERRIBLE THUN-DERLIZARDS.** Fox: 11/20/1993–. Fox Childrens Network/Savage Studios, Ltd./ Nelvana. Executive producer: Savage Steve Holland. Supervising producers, Bill Kopp and Stephen Hodgins. Produced by Patrick Loubert, Michael Hirsch and Clive A. Smith. Directed by John Half-penny. Animation supervisor, Rick Mar-shall. Musical theme and score by Nathan Wang. Animation facilities: Wang Film Production Co., Studio D. Voices: Bill Kopp (Eek the Cat); and Charlie Adler, Curtis Armstrong, E. G. Daily, Cam Clarke, Dan Castellaneta, Jaid Barrymore, Savage Steve Holland, Elinor Donahue, Tawny Kitaen, Brad Garrett, Gary Owens, Jason Priestly, Buck Henry, Phil Hartman, Kertwood Smith, many others.

Fox's *Eek! the Cat* was a bizarre, dreamlike animated series best described as the misadventures of a neurotic cat — a compulsive dogooder whose efforts always resulted in catastrophe. *Eek!* was the deadly alien spawn of animator Bill Kopp and Kopp's longtime friend, director Savage Steve Holland, who'd already dem-onstrated his guerilla-warfare sense of humor in such theatrical films as *Better Off Dead* and *One Crazy Summer*, and in the late lamented 1987 Fox network series *The New Adventures of Beans Baxter* (a per-sonal favorite of mine, though evidently not of anyone else).

Eek!, who never spoke when screaming hysterically would do, lived with a family consisting of an oddball Mom devoted to audiotape Berlitz lessons (in an increas-ingly incomprehensible foreign language) and a particularly hideous little brother and sister team — J. B. and Wendy Eliza-beth — who spent most of their waking hours figuring out ways to agonize and tor-ture their pet without tipping Mom off. Eek! seemed to spend half his life falling from high places in the honored tradition of Wile E. Coyote; the other half was spent

Eek! the Cat.

mooning over his next door neighbor, a corpulent kitty named Annabelle who was guarded by a vicious pit bull appropriately named Sharkey. Though nearly never being rewarded for his good deeds, Eek! nonetheless did his utmost to protect his abusive family, notably in the episode "Cape Fur," wherein he tried vainly to warn his masters about the intentions of a supposedly cute little bunny rabbit—who was actually a tattooed burglar, pyromaniac, and aspiring serial killer!

Anyone familiar with the work of Savage Steve Holland shouldn't be surprised at the content of Eek! the Cat; for Holland, this was subtle. The director carried several traits of his live-action projects into Eek!, notably by stocking the voiceover personnel with a number of his favorite performers. Tawny Kitean, toothsome leading lady of many an R-rated, torn-blouse adventure film, was atypically cast as the overweight Annabelle. On the opposite end of the spectrum, there was Elinor Donahue, onetime teenage "Princess" of Father Knows Best, whose skill at playing addlepated suburbanite moms had already been tapped by Holland on Beans Baxter and who just before her Eek! tenure had portrayed Chris Elliot's ditzy mother on the live-action Fox series Get a Life.

And, believe it or not, Eek! was semiautobiographical. Eek!'s extraordinary bad luck was drawn from Steve Holland's hor-

rendous experiences with his own pet cats, all of whom met with exotic deaths; one was accidentally poisoned by radiator fluid, another fell out a 15-story window in pursuit of a bird, and a third was reportedly carried off by a large hawk. Only slightly less benighted was Eek! supporting character Elmo the Elk, who forever elicited Eek!'s advice and assistance—with consequences that in real life would have resulted in instant Elkburgers.

Holland's Eek! the Cat partner in crime Bill Kopp had once attended the California Institute of the Arts. At fellow student Savage Steve's instigation, Kopp joined Holland in quitting the Institute's traditional character animation program, signing up instead for an experimental animation class, where the pair honed their twisted, stream-of-consciousness storytelling technique. The Holland/Kopp style can be summed up in the Eek! the Cat scene transition wherein Eek! jumps into a gigantic meatball, which in a pullback shot is revealed to be atop an even more gigantic football. It was a step beyond Monty Python lunacy into the realm of Holland/Kopp gibbering insanity.

The producers' impatience with formula and cliché was manifested in a sidebar attraction on Eek! the Cat. Eek's! young owners were often seen glued to the TV, watching the exploits of a faux cartoon congregation known as The Squishy Bearz. Not content with merely lampooning the cardboard sweetness of The Care Bears (q.v.) (as was the purpose of the "Buddy Bears" on Garfield and Friends [q.v.] and the "Dummi Bears" on Rugrats [q.v.]), Holland and Kopp took sadistic delight in thrusting the Squishy Bearz in as many horrendous, life-threatening perils as possible, usually involving some sort of apocalyptic explosive device.

Part of the fun in cartoonmaking for Holland and Kopp was challenging Fox's Broadcast Standards and Practices Department, which, though far more liberal than its counterparts at ABC, NBC and CBS, nonetheless had its patience sorely tested by Eek! the Cat. Of the hapless BS&P lady assigned to the production, Bill Kopp cheerfully observed, "She has to know every swear word, every offensive gesture and every sexual deviance, plus every slang word for all of it."

Some of the lady's blue-pencil remarks made their way into an Entertainment

Weekly article ("Censor Overload," June 11, 1993), indicating what she was up against. In the original script for an episode titled "Catsanova," she wrote the following request: "Please don't show Cupid using a switchblade knife, an illegal weapon. How about an ax or chainsaw?" The script for "Road Trip" was returned to the producers with this footnote: "Please substitute a teacher's name that isn't a form of cancer." And in "Eek vs. the Flying Saucers," the network lady dictated, "It will not be acceptable for the alien King, Queen and Princess to resemble a toilet, urinal, and roll of toilet paper, and to discuss the way Earthlings treated them 'like filth' on their visit to our planet." One suspects that Holland and Kopp deliberately stuck these overtly puerile bits in their scripts as a bargaining chip, so that in exchange for cutting the offending lines, they'd be permitted to include an equally repulsive but less censorable vignette somewhere else in the script. It's a "beat the censor" game as old as Hollywood itself.

Though never *so* offensive that it repulsed its audience (as Nickelodeon's *Ren and Stimpy* [q.v.] was wont to do), the breezily wacked-out *Eek! the Cat* was perfectly attuned to the audiences inundated by *Home Alone* the 1990s. Perhaps this would have resulted in a merchandising blitz—had Savage Steve Holland taken this aspect of the cartoon business more seriously and designed something beyond the stuffed Eek! doll. Or maybe merchandising just wasn't worth the effort: Quoted in *Animato* magazine, Holland mused "[Eek!] is sort of a hard guy to grasp into . . . Eek!'s thing is really just being nice, and how do you translate it into a t-shirt? It's not easy."

In 1993, Fox improved *Eek! the Cat's* erratic ratings by moving the series to an earlier, more advantageous time slot. Savage Steve Holland's plans around this time included introducing a 15-minute component to the series utilizing a team of *Eek!* supporting characters: three New Age dinosaurs (from 135 million years ago) named Day Z. Cutter, Doc, and Bo "Diddly" Squat—the last-named the meanest of the bunch, described in the Savage Studios synopsis as "kind of a dinosaur version of Bill Kopp, only he's got more reptile skin." The result—delayed from its proposed September 1993 unveiling to November due to interference from Fox, the loss of Bill Kopp to Disney's *Marsupilami* (q.v.), and a brief communications breakdown between Holland and Nelvana Studios—was *Eek! and the Terrible Thunderlizards*. The serialized storylines of this revamped *Eek!* involved the titular dinosaur trio as ex-convict "SWAT dinos," sent out by their high-tech superiors to rid the prehistoric landscape of those pesky cavemen critters Bill and Scooter.

And there's more! Even as we write, Savage Steve Holland is hoping to spin off the hapless Squishy Bearz into *their* own separate component, set in a rundown theme park featuring such attractions as "The Lake of Dirt" and "The Lawsuit Waiting to Happen Roller Coaster." As Eek! the Cat would put it: "Kum Ba Ya!"

THE EIGHTH MAN. Syndicated: 1965. TCJ Animation Center/ABC Films. Producer: Mitsuteru Tokoyama. U.S. adaptation by Joe Oriolo Studios.

8-Man was the title of a Japanese comic strip which first appeared on a weekly basis in April of 1963. Written by science-fiction specialist Kazumasa Hirai and drawn by Jiro Kuwata, the strip was the story of Detective Rachiro Azuma, who after being killed by the notorious gangster Mukade was recreated by the brilliant Dr. Tani in the form of a humanized robot. The new creation, 8-Man, retained Azuma's memory, sense of justice, and range of emotions, as well as his personal appearance; the difference was that the "new" Azuma was an atomic-powered marvel with approximately one thousand times the strength of any ordinary mortal. To maintain his power, 8-Man recharged his atomic energy supply with tiny strength pills, which in keeping with the relatively adult approach of the original strip were in the form of cigarettes. The android was also able to confound criminals by changing his facial features; according to Japanese comic strip historian Hisao Kato, 8-Man's favorite disguise was as the villain's gun moll!

In addition to greatly influencing the "friendly robot" Japanese comic-strip creations to come, *8-Man* was converted into a 52-episode, half hour animated TV series by producer Mitsuteru Tokoyama. These were shown in black and white in their home country, but color prints were struck when *8-Man* was picked up for American distribution by ABC Films. At that time, the title was changed to *The Eighth Man* (the original title must have sounded too much like "8-Ball" for ABC Films' taste), the dialogue redubbed and the episodes reedited, and the character names changed. Detective Rachiro Azuma became "Peter Brady" and his robot alter ego was imaginatively called "Tobor"; the evil Mukade was rechristened "Saucer Lip" (*there's* a name to strike fear in the hearts of law enforcement officers everywhere!); Dr. Tani was given the new name "Professor Genius"; and whatever the police chief of "Metro City" was called in the original *8-Man*, to American audiences he was known as Chief Fumblethumbs. These subtle and witty character names bore the hallmark of Joe Oriolo Studios, which did the redubbing on *Eighth Man* and which previously had turned out the equally overbaked *Felix the Cat* (q.v.) TV cartoons. Oriolo even went so far as to impose a banal *Felix*-like theme song over the series' opening titles; "Call Tobor-r-r-r-r, the EIGHTH MAN!" is all I can remember of this little ditty.

Battling local crooks, international spies and superhuman beings with stiff-armed impunity in such episodes as "The Horrible Honeybees," "The Gold Beetle of the Orient" and "Evil Jaw and the Devil Germs," *The Eighth Man* remained in syndication until the early 1970s; in this respect, it outlasted the original *8-Man* comic strip, which ended in 1968. If *Eighth Man's* concept sounds familiar, it's because the whole "android detective" idea was resurrected to spectacular effect by the 1985 theatrical feature film *Robocop*—which in turn was itself converted into a weekly cartoon series (which see).

EMERGENCY + FOUR. NBC: 9/8/ 1973–9/4/1976. Mark VII/Fred Calvert Productions/Universal Television. Produced by Fred Calvert, Michael Caffey and Janis Diamond. Directed by Michael Caffey. Music by Soundtrack Music Company. Voices: Kevin Tighe (Roy DeSoto); Randolph Mantooth (John Gage); Sarah Kennedy (Sally/Carol Harper); David Jolliffe (Mathew Harper); Donald Fullilove (Jason Philips); Peter Haas (Randy Alrich); and Richard Paul, and Jack DeLeon.
Emergency ran from 1972 through 1977 as a prime time live action adventure series on NBC. Produced by Jack Webb's Mark VII Productions, the 60-minute weekly was an eleventh hour replacement for two failed sitcoms, but managed to regain its timeslot's ratings and enjoy an even longer afterlife in syndicated reruns. The episodes were centered at Squad 51 of the Los Angeles County Fire Department, where a team of paramedics were on call in case of (what else?) emergency. When NBC commissioned a cartoon spinoff of *Emergency*—the network had found that its biggest fans were aged 11 and under—two of the original cast members, Kevin Tighe and Randolph Mantooth, were hired to do voicework for their animated likenesses. Absent were the remaining *Emergency* stars Robert Horton, Bobby Troup, and Julie London (who'd developed a distaste for soundproof recording booths during her years as a singer). In their place was a quartet of youngsters: Sally (later replaced by Carol), Randy, Jason and Matt, who offered assistance to the adult team. *Emergency + Four* also featured a dog named Flash, a myna bird named Charlemagne, and a monkey named Bananas—all of whom must have completed their paramedic training, else why would their presence have been tolerated at Squad 51?

Opinions varied as to the quality of the 22 *Emergency + Four* episodes. Janis Diamond, one of the series' producers, was quoted by Jeff Lenburg as claiming that local fire prevention organizations across America clamored for videotapes of the episodes, so worthwhile and educational was their content. Conversely, the National Association for Better Broadcasting declared that the "educational aspects of illustrating rescue techniques do not come across," and wrote off the whole project as "unrealistic." Whatever the case, *Emergency + Four* was cancelled by NBC at the same time it looked as though the original *Emergency* would also leave the airwaves in the fall of 1976. The "live" *Emergency* was renewed for another season at the last minute; no such rescue awaited *Emergency + Four*.

EVERYTHING'S ARCHIE see AR-CHIE

THE EWOKS. ABC: 9/7/1985–2/22/ 1986.

—DROIDS: THE ADVENTURES OF R2D2 AND C3PO. ABC: 9/7/1985–2/22/1986.
—THE EWOKS AND STAR WARS DROIDS ADVENTURE HOUR. ABC: 3/1/1986–11/1/1986.
—THE ALL-NEW EWOKS. ABC: 11/8/1986–9/5/1987. Lucasfilm/Nelvana Ltd. Executive producer, Mikki Herman. Produced by Michael Hirsh, Patrick Loubert and Clive A. Smith. Supervising producer, Lenora Hume. Directed by Ken Stephenson. Animation directors, Mike Fallows, Gord Stanfield, John Laurence Collin. Voice director, Rob Kirkpatrick. Music by Stewart Copeland, Derek Holt, Patricia Cullen, David Greene, David Shaw. Production facilities: Hanho Heung-Up and Mi-Hahn Productions. Voices (EWOKS segments, 1985): Jim Henshaw (Wicket); John Stocker (Widdle/Hoom/Dulok Scout); Greg Swanson (Weechee/Jinda Boy); Eric Peterson; (Teebo/Murgoob), Paul Chato (Paploo); Richard Donat (Deej); Nonnie Griffin (Shodu); Leanne Coppen (Winda/Baby Nippet); Cree Summer Francks (Princess Kneesaa); Taborah Johnson (Latara); Doug Chamberlain (Logray); George Buza (Chief Chirpa/Lumat/Nah-Kee); Pam Hyatt (Aunt Bozzie); Michael Fantini (Baby Wiley); Paulina Gillis (Ashma); Don McManus (Chukah-Trok/Bondo); Antony Parr (Erphram); Pauline Rennie (Kaink); Ron James (Mring); Hadley Kay (Ubel/Shaman's Nephew); Rob Cowan (Punt); Jackie Burroughs (Morag); Glori Gage (Singing Maiden); Alan Fawcett (Trebla); Desmond Ellis (Rock Wizard); Joe Matheson (Zut); Diane Polley (Dobah); Myra Fried (Hoona); Dan Hennessey (King Corneesh/Trome 1); Meleny Brown (Urgana); Don Francks (Dulok Shaman); Marvin Goldhar (Trome 2); Peter Blais (Trome 3). Voices (DROIDS segments): Anthony Daniels (R2D2 and C3PO electronic sounds); Graham Haley (C3PO Guide Track); Andrew Sabiston, Dan Hennessey, Lesleh Donaldson, Terri Hawkes, Maurice Godin, Michael Kirby, Marvin Goldhar, Toby Tarnow, George Buza, Ken Pogue, Long John Baldry, Donny Burns, Milah Cheylov, Taborah Johnson, Donny Burns, Michael Lefebvre, Don Francks, Don McManus, John Stocker, Graeme Campbell, Cree Summer Francks, Jamie Dick, Christopher Young, Chris Wiggins, J. Gordon Masten, Winston Reckert, Barry

Green, Rob Cowan, Jan Austin, Peter MacNeill, Eric Peterson, Michael Kirby, Pam Hyatt. Voices (ALL-NEW EWOKS segments, 1986): Denny Delk (Wicket); Jim Cranna (Teebo); Sue Murphy (Latara); Esther Scott (Shodu); Rick Cimino (Logray); and Michael Pritchard, Bob Sarlatte, Morgan Upton, Lucille Bliss, Richard Nelson, Dan St. Paul, and Richard Devon.

About the only merchandising aspect untapped by the *Star Wars* industry up to 1985 was the animated cartoon. *The Ewoks* took care of that. This animated series was regarded by most observers as a spinoff of the third *Star Wars* film, *Return of the Jedi* (1983), which introduced the furry, gnomish Ewoks as fierce defenders of their home moon Endor, and subsequently as allies of the *Star Wars* heroes against the insidious Empire (space constrictions do not allow me to relate the entire *Star Wars* saga; if you haven't seen director George Lucas' film trilogy by this time, go to the video store and do yourself a favor). Actually, *The Ewoks* was more a direct derivation of the 1984 TV movie *The Ewok Adventure*, produced by George Lucas and directed by Jon Korty. The film was heavier on special effects than on the story values which so enriched the original *Star Wars*, but it was a hit, resulting in two 1985 projects: a live action sequel, *Ewoks: The Battle for Endor*; and the animated *Ewoks*, collaboratively produced by Lucasfilm and Canada's Nelvana Ltd.

Each half-hour *Ewoks* episode headlined the eponymous hirsute residents of the "forest moon" Endor, now metamorphosed into teenagers to make them compatible with the rest of the Saturday morning cartoon stars. Led by bold scout Wicket, the Ewoks and their friends Princess Kneesaa and Latra travelled from adventure to adventure, learning a little about themselves, each other, and the basic values of loyalty and friendship. Nelvana's animation was fair if not faultless, and the characters were interesting if not fascinating. Kids and adults who hadn't already travelled the similar "alternate world" path found in the novels of J.R.R. Tolkien were suitably entertained.

The ABC weekly *Ewoks* telecast was followed by another half-hour *Star Wars* derivation, also produced by Lucasfilm/Nelvana, *Droids: The Adventures of R2D2 and C3PO*. The leading characters were of course the Mutt-and-Jeff robots who appeared in all three *Star Wars* films, now divested of their human companions Luke Skywalker, Han Solo, Princess Leia et al. and off on their own. Unlike *Ewoks*, the *Droids* adventures consumed as many as four consecutive weekly installments—self-contained connecting narratives, minus the expected cliffhanger climaxes. Again, production values were slightly better than the usual Saturday morning run, but still a second-rate substitute for the depth and imagination of the original films.

On March 1, 1986, the two above-mentioned series were combined into one single 60-minute weekly, *The Ewoks and Star Wars Droids Adventure Hour*. Contrary to expectations raised by this title, the Ewoks and Droids still appeared within their own respective stories, with no crossovers. In this form, the series lasted until the fall of 1986; it was okay, but too unremarkable and too expensive to survive intact. The *Droids* portion was dropped, and a new group of 21 episodes, featuring fresh voiceover talent, was run by ABC as *The All-New Ewoks*. This package veered more toward the simplified *Smurfs* brand of humor than in the first season, and as such was even less memorable than its hour-long *Ewoks/Droids* predecessor.

EXO-SQUAD. Syndicated: 1993. Universal Cartoon Studios, Inc./MCA TV. Executive producer, Will Meugniot. Created by Jeff Segal. Developed by Will Meugniot, Eric Lewald, Eric Semones, Michael Torres, Mark Hoffmeier. Executive story editor, Eric Leward. Supervising director, Graham Morris. Animation directors, Richard Bowman, Milton Gray, Emory Myrick, Eric Peterson, Kevin Petrilak. Music by Mark Tavera. Animation by Akom Production Co. Ltd. Overseas animation supervisor, Dennis Woodyard. Voices: Robby Benson (Lt. J. T. Marsh); and Lisa Ann Beley, Michael Benyaer, Richard Newman, John Payne, Michael Donovan, Teryl Rothery, Rob Morton, Janyce Jaud, Wally Marsh, Garrison Chrisjohn, Karin Konovan, Ken Camroux, Sudsey Clark, Sylvia Biller, Jason Geffney.

Exo-Squad was designed in 1993 to launch the Universal Family Entertainment Network, a potential competitor to the established Disney and Warner Bros. TV cartoon dynasties. Universal's cartoon

CEO Jeff Segal was well grounded in the animation world, having written and produced for Hanna-Barbera and other major firms. Though he'd gained much of his industry prestige with his work (in collaboration with future *Batman* [q.v.] producer Alan Burnett) on H-B's award winning *The Smurfs* (q.v.), Segal's interest lay not in cute little Earthbound sylvanians but in big ugly robots and outer-space themes. In the early 1980s, Segal had handled the English adaptation of the Japanese extraterrestrial series *Ultraman*, and in 1984 he was the creative force behind Hanna-Barbera's *Challenge of the GoBots* (q.v.). The producer's fondness for and familiarity with *Ultraman*-style Japanimation, coupled with his experience with the "good robot gone bad" throughline of *GoBots*, served him well when he left his senior vice president post at Hanna-Barbera to found and commandeer Universal Cartoon Studios. Jeff Segal's first big project was the weekly, syndicated *Exo-Squad*—a labor of love, intended as the apotheosis of all renegade-robot half hours.

The series was set in the 22nd century. Earth had already colonized several "Homeworld" planets like Venus, Mars, and Jupiter, initially using convict labor to work the land. But too many criminals had escaped, establishing their own pirate communities. As a result, scientists were compelled to master robot technology to perform manual labor on the Homeworlds. The artificial humans, called Neosapiens, were perfect pieces of genetic engineering: They were strong, did as they were told, never required sex and never needed to go to the bathroom. But things didn't progress as smoothly as hoped. Once the Neosapiens developed human-like intelligence, they began demanding rights and liberties (analogies between the robots and America's own African slaves were hard to miss). An insurrection occurred, resulting in the Neosapien takeover of the Homeworlds, but this was quickly put down—with the concession that the "better" robots would be permitted some degree of freedom.

Exo-Squad took place 50 years after the rebellion, at which time the squad of the title patrolled the skies to protect the Earth from the aforementioned human space pirates, notably John Simbaka's Pirate Clans of Saturn. Operating from their home satellite Ameron, the Exo-Squad was headed by Lt. J. T. Marsh, whose loyal bodysuit-clad crew included Alec, Maggie Weston (tech specialist), Kaz, Nara (stock young idealist) and benign Neosapien Marsala. Marsh also tried to maintain a tenuous friendship with Chicago cop Sean Napier, who'd lost his Exo-Squad post due to his terrible temper. The Exo-Squad traversed the skies with personalized robot weapon/vehicles called E-Frames, which the Squad members "wore" in the manner of the powerlifters in the *Alien* films.

Some of Exo-Squad's toughest battles were not with pirates but with the government bureaucracy and political corruption that festered throughout the Earth. Into this dirty-fingered atmosphere stepped Phaeton, charismatic leader of the Neosapiens, who preached a doctrine of peaceful coexistence to the human higher-ups. But once gaining political respectability, Phaeton turned out to be the proverbial smiler with a knife. He successfully staged a Neosapien takeover of the Earth, enslaving the populace (now called "Terrans") and renaming Chicago Phaeton City. Suddenly the Exo-Squad were themselves considered "outsiders" with the clarion-call motto "Who Dare, Win!", they set about battling the Neosapiens in order to reclaim Earth for humankind. Played against this were the shifting loyalties of the human space pirates and the mixed emotions of those Neosapiens like Marsala who'd remained loyal to Exo-Squad—and of course J. T. Marsh's own mixed feelings about the tempestuous ex–Squader Sean Napier, who now became indispensable in thwarting the robots.

Jeff Segal's devotion to Japanese-produced cartoon series was obvious in *Exo-Squad*. The episodes were sequential, like the serialized *Robotech* (q.v.)—several weeks went by before the actual Neosapien takeover—while the "piracy" angle had previously been part and parcel of Japan's *Captain Harlock* (q.v.). But *Exo-Squad* was no mere ripoff of Japanamation; nor was it simply an inverse variation of Fox's popular *X-Men* (q.v.)—with the "freaks" as the ruling class and the humans on the outs, rather than the other way around—as a casual glance might suggest. Segal and his staff (including executive producer Will Meugniot, who held that same office on *X-Men*) worked overtime to

give *Exo-Squad* its own distinct identity, not with broad, sweeping strokes but through little throwaway grace notes. A small example: the series' modernistic trappings weren't the usual "gee it's great to be here in the future" obvious gimmickry, but little background touches like holographic street-gang graffiti.

The Neosapien characterizations were likewise adroitly handled. In the manner of old Hollywood "epics," the Neosapiens' names were derived from the classic Greek and Roman days—Phaeton, Praetorius, Livanus, Draconia, Typhon, Shiva and Livia—and in true Laurence Olivier/*Spartacus* fashion, the robots spoke in "Stage British" dialect. Beyond this surface emulation of earlier cinematic clichés, *Exo-Squad* took a multilayered turn by choosing not to make the Neosapiens purely villainous. The robots simply could not be judged on human terms because they weren't humans, and they operated on an entirely different moral level. At times, Phaeton's own peculiar logic came close to seducing the audience into thinking that the Neosapien way was indeed the best way—a deliberate parallel to the situation when Hitler took over Germany.

While insisting that *Exo-Squad* was not in any way derivative of *X-Men* or *Batman: The Animated Series* (q.v.), Jeff Segal allowed that his series wouldn't have been possible without the preordained *Batman/X-Men* audience."This is a smart group. If you look at the kids who are fans of *X-Men*, *Batman* and *Star Trek*, we're talking about a relatively enlightened, smart audience. Mindless action is *not* sufficient. They'll respond to a complex story that's fundamentally the battle between good and evil." (Perhaps this can explain why 1991's *Pirates of Dark Water* [q.v.], which in many ways resembled the texture and format of *Exo-Squad*, failed despite its quality animation and story values. The audience for this sort of entertainment hadn't been cultivated yet.)

Exo-Squad, though consummately produced, wasn't above criticism. The beautifully designed characters, weaponry and space vehicles were basically unsubtle bids to the toy and action figure market, though they were at least built logically into the plotlines. The animation level soared in the battle sequences, but the movement of the Earthbound characters dropped into the usual jerk-and-spurt

Saturday morning cartoon syndrome. And the scriptwork, despite the writers' every effort to depict the Neosapiens three-dimensionally, sometimes betrayed an unattractive "don't trust anyone different" streak—which, given the allegorical subtext of the series, could be translated by more impressionable viewers into an apologia for racism.

Still, *Exo-Squad* was a distinguished kickoff for the Universal Family Entertainment Network. Jeff Segal announced at the time of the series' 1993 premiere that if it clicked, *Exo-Squad* would be the foundation of a TV-cartoon empire devoted to developing topnotch adaptations of such established Universal properties as *Jurassic Park, Phantom of the Opera, Creature from the Black Lagoon* and *Jaws.* And perhaps, somewhere down the line, Segal would even answer every child's prayer and resurrect *Woody Woodpecker* (q.v.).

THE FABULOUS FUNNIES. NBC: 9/9/1978–9/8/1979. Filmation. Executive producers: Lou Scheimer, Norm Prescott. Produced by Don Christansen. Directed by Kay Wright, Ed Friedman, Gwen Weltzer, Marsh Lamore, Lou Zukor. Written by Jim Ryan, Bill Danch, Sam Simon, Buzz Dixon. Music by Yvette Blais. Voices: June Foray (Broom Hilda/Sluggo/Ooola/Hans/Fritz); Robert Holt (Alley Oop/Gaylord/Foozy/Der Captain); Jayne Hamil (Nancy/Emmy Lou); Alan Oppenheimer (King Guzzle/Irwin/Der Inspector/Grelber).

Fabulous Funnies was an extension of a concept Filmation had previously used on *Archie's TV Funnies* (see *Archie*): a weekly "omnibus" series featuring several popular comic-strip characters in their own seven-minute TV cartoons. (Earlier reports that the newly filmed cartoons on *Fabulous Funnies* were in fact occasionally interspersed with repeats from the earlier *Archie* series are erroneous.)

The well established characters used herein were Broom Hilda, the love-starved, cigar smoking witch created by Russell Myers in 1970; Alley Oop, the roughhouse caveman introduced by V. T. Hamlin in 1932, along with Alley Oop's girl friend Ooola, his boss King Guzzle, and his pal Foozy, who also acted as *Fabulous Funnies'* host; Nancy and Sluggo, those round-domed preteen dispensers of middle class mediocrity first seen in Ernie Bushmiller's "Fritzi Ritz" in the 1930s before spinning

off into Nancy's own strip in 1940; and the oldest property on *Fabulous Funnies,* the Captain and the Kids (the kids being the sociopathic Hans and Fritz), who under the alternate sobriquet "The Katzenjammer Kids" had been around since 1898!

Tom K. Ryan's "Tumbleweeds," also scheduled to appear weekly, showed up on the first program only to be yanked when it was discovered that no one at Filmation had secured the cartoon rights for the character from Ryan! This one-and-only "Tumbleweeds" episode has, however, recently been released to videotape.

Fabulous Funnies found itself especially prone to criticism. Oddly, the complaints came not from comic-strip purists, who actually were rather pleased with the improvements made on the otherwise wearisome Nancy and Sluggo (possibly the handiwork of *Funnies* staff writer Sam Simon, who years later did better for himself as a producer on *The Simpsons*). Nor were there any gripes about the animation, which was surprisingly good for Filmation, or the comedy content, since the cartoons—especially the Broom Hilda episodes—were actually pretty funny. *Fabulous Funnies* came under fire for casting its characters in the role of prosocial purveyors. Each cartoon would set up a social or ecological dilemma, which the characters would solve in a method approvable to any "clean up TV" pressure group. One would think there would be rejoicing in the adult camp for offering this obviously well intentioned effort to upgrade the quality of Saturday morning TV. Instead, the ungrateful wretches complained that *Fabulous Funnies'* little prosocial missives were unsubtle and, to quote the Los Angeles *Times,* "heavy-handed."

What, pray tell, did the media critics *expect* when such marvelously uninhibited, havoc-wreaking characters like Alley Oop and the Katzenjammer Kids were required to warn the kids at home to behave like responsible ladies and gentlemen? Especially in the case of the Katzenjammers, the whole point of newspaper strips in the first place was to give rule-bound children (and adults!) a cathartic outlet for their latent antisocial tendencies. With the noblest motivations in mind, *Fabulous Funnies* managed to rob its characters of their very reason for being.

Children were no happier than the

critics, as it turned out; *Fabulous Funnies* lasted only 13 episodes. But it was not the end of trying to force proper behavior down the throats of cartoon fans, as we would find out in the even *more* pro-socially minded 1980s.

FAMILY CLASSICS THEATRE. CBS: Premiered 11/14/1971. —**FAMILY CLASSIC TALES.** CBS: Premiered 11/15/1975. Air Programs International/Hanna-Barbera Productions.

The above-mentioned *Family Classic* projects were not weekly series, but two separate packages of seasonal specials, some produced by Australia's Air Programs International, others by Hanna-Barbera. In all, there were 24 hour-long animated specials: 13 on *Family Classics Theatre* and 11 on *Family Classic Tales.* Several of these were first-run, while some of the offerings bearing the *Family Classics* banner were rebroadcasts of prime time network holiday specials. The titles included "Tales of Washington Irving," "The Prince and the Pauper," "Robinson Crusoe," "Gulliver's Travels," "Robin Hood," "A Christmas Carol," several samplings of Jules Verne ("20,000 Leagues Under the Sea," "Mysterious Island," "Journey to the Centre of the Earth"), and a few illustrated biographies of such notables as Daniel Boone and Davy Crockett.

Animation was for the most part on the level of the average "superhero" cartoon and the dialogue was frequently simplified into infantilism—though as a group, the Jules Verne adaptations were more intelligently presented and a degree or so better produced than the other *Family Classics.* The 60-minute specials went into local syndication immediately following network exposure, and in recent years have popped up with great frequency on Nickelodeon's *Weekend Special* anthology.

FAMILY DOG. CBS: 6/23/1993–7/21/1993. Original special: 2/16/1987 (as part of "Amazing Stories"). Production companies, 1987 special: Hyperion-Kushner-Locke/Amblin/Universal. Production companies, 1993 series: Amblin/Universal/Warner Bros. Credits, 1993 series: Executive producers, Steven Spielberg and Tim Burton. Writer/executive producer: Dennis Klein. Created by Brad Bird. Produced by Chuck Richardson. Supervising pro-

ducer, Steve Hodgins. Directed by Chris Buck, Clive A. Smith. Theme composed and conducted by Danny Elfman. Additional music, Steve Bartek. Supervising animators: Klay R. Hall, Ron Hughart, Becky Bristow. Additional animation facilities: Wang Film, Nelvana. Additional material by Paul Dini, Sherri Stoner. Animation directors: Robin Budd, Steve Whitehouse. Voices on 1987 special: Stan Freberg (Father); Mercedes McCambridge (Mother); Scott Menville (Billy); Annie Potts (Baby Sister); and Jack Angel, Brooke Ashley, Brad Bird, Marshall Efron, and Stanley Ralph Ross. Voices on 1993 TV series: Martin Mull (Father, aka Skip Binford); Molly Cheek (Bev); Zak Huxtable Epstein (Billy); Cassie Cole (Buffy); Danny Mann (Dog). And Bruce Gill, Deanna Oliver, Charlie Adler, Mary Kay Bergman, Jim Dugan, Dan Gilvezan, Aaron Luftig, Norman Parker, Kevin Schon, Kimberly Scott, Lynn Marie Stewart, and Eric Welch.

Family Dog, the story of a much maligned but ever-optimistic pet canine and his monumentally insensitive human owners, had been dreamed up by future *Simpsons* (q.v.) contributor Brad Bird back in his California Institute of the Arts days. In 1986, Bird was able to interest megadirector/cartoon fanatic Steven Spielberg in the premise, with the result being a fully animated, half hour *Family Dog,* broadcast February 16, 1987, over Spielberg's much-touted TV anthology *Amazing Stories.* The episode generated more industry chitchat than any of the series' other low-rated installments, and a *Family Dog* series might have developed then and there had the marketplace been responsive to prime time cartoons in 1987. But it would take the 1990 success of *The Simpsons* to regenerate *Family Dog,* by which time Steven Spielberg and fellow fantasy director Tim Burton (see *Beetlejuice*) had taken over the project as executive producers.

An official announcement was made at the Grammy Awards ceremonies in February 1991 that *Family Dog* would shortly evolve into a weekly; by this point, the project had undergone a very difficult three-year gestation. Brad Bird's basic "dog's eye view" concept had been retained, as had the boorish nature of the dog's owners, the Binford family, but Bird was too busy with other cartoon work to involve himself in the series. Now the reins were held firmly by Spielberg, who characteristically wanted the series to put all previous TV cartoon outings to shame. Also characteristically, Spielberg began spending money by the bushel basket to "improve" the property, bloating the originally overpriced $650,000 per episode budget to well over $1 million. A source close to Spielberg was quoted as saying, "He wanted to show somebody that this is the show he wanted to produce. So he wanted to at least get one or two episodes that would say, 'This is Family Dog.' If it's successful, and we get a chance to make more episodes, this is what it's going to be like."

We were warned. Family Dog began exhibiting the troublesome creative shortcomings that had plagued some of the earlier projects Spielberg had produced and/or directed. The cynical attitude between owners and pet was softened to allow the still-unnamed title character to rescue the unrescuable kids from perilous situations. The humor regressed from the inherent comedy of characterization to instant-reaction scatological gags involving anatomy and "doggie doo" piles (one episode highlighted a steaming cluster of elephant poop). And in the tradition of the ill-fated Hook, Spielberg went the "star" route by replacing the superb but unknown Doug Coffin in the role of the Family Dog's adult owner Mr. Binford with the more bankable comic actor Martin Mull.

A major tactical misstep was hiring comedy writer Dennis Klein, who, though eminently suitable for his chores on HBO's adult-minded The Larry Sanders Show, floundered in the cartoon format. Not only was Klein totally unfamiliar with the technique of blocking out his action to fit the animator's storyboards, but he didn't even own a dog—and had to ask his friends and associates all about "typical" doggie behavior. But Klein's unsuitability came in second to Family Dog's most terminal flaw: After all the money that flowed through the project, the first three episodes looked appallingly cheap—far below the standard set by Spielberg's Tiny Toon Adventures, which cost one-fifth as much.

In January of 1992, it was painfully clear from a private preview showing that Family Dog was in sorry shape, and the lead character was coming off as flat, dull and unfunny (save for the excellence of voice artist Danny Mann's barks, grunts and yelps for the Dog). Spielberg and Bur-

ton's answer to the problem was one that a congressman might envy: Instead of cutting their losses, they lavished even more money to repair the damage. Two million dollars was devoted to having Nelvana Studios reanimate key scenes and redub voices and sound effects. Family Dog was now superficially better, but the animators still couldn't lick the problem that the Binford family was so repulsively selfish that audience interest in their adventures was nil (this had worked for the 1987 pilot, but was hard to maintain for a series; even the supposedly dysfunctional Simpsons had an underlying warmth and devotion to one another). Likewise injurious was the lack of strong story values: one Family Dog installment spent a soporific 15 minutes showing the Dog trying to cross a busy highway.

Family Dog might have been shelved forever had not the creators hoped that the monster success of Spielberg's 1993 film Jurassic Park might rub off on a cartoon series with the same producer's name attached. In June of that year, five of the ten completed Dogs were played off on CBS in prime time, with the promise that the remaining five would see the light of day should audiences take to the project. What happened can be summed up in four words: "It ain't The Simpsons." Audiences in 1993 had been conditioned for something better, and something better Family Dog was not. Television critics tried their best to mine some gold from the dross, praising the UPA-like production design, the admittedly impressive full animation, and the fluid intricacy of the point-of-view shots at the dog's level. But technique alone can't carry a show if the stories and characters are turnoffs, so Family Dog was euthanized in mid–July.

THE FAMOUS ADVENTURES OF MR. MAGOO see **MR. MAGOO**

FANGFACE. ABC: 9/9/1978–9/8/1979. Ruby-Spears/Filmways. Executive producers, Joe Ruby and Ken Spears. Produced by Jerry Eisenberg. Directed by Rudy Larriva. Music by Dean Elliot. Voices: Jerry Dexter (Sherman "Fang" Fangworth); Susan Blu (Kim); Frank Welker (Biff); Bart Braverman (Puggsy).

Fangface was the first cartoon series produced by Joe Ruby and Ken Spears, shortly after the team used the prestige they'd earned developing *Scooby-Doo* (q.v.) for Hanna-Barbera to allow them to set up their own studio. It's too bad that *Fangface* wasn't a worthier debut for Ruby-Spears, but you've got to cut your teeth—or fangs—somewhere.

Fangface was in reality a normal, slightly idiotic teenager named Sherman Fangworth, who because of the Fangworth family "curse" had the unsettling habit of transforming into a werewolf at the first glance of a full moon—or even a picture of a full moon. No Lon Chaney Junior he, Fangface was a benign lycanthrope who solved crimes—and in the tradition of *Scooby-Doo*, this ersatz canine did his crimesolving in the company of several high schoolers, including Kim (a girl), Biff and Puggsy. These last two characters were patterned after Leo Gorcey and Huntz Hall of the "Bowery Boys" films; the other principal celebrity imitator on the series was Fangface himself, who sounded a lot like Joe E. Ross ("Ooh! Ooh!") of *Car 54, Where Are You?* fame. The villains of the piece were, like the hero, monsters—albeit the malevolent variety, bearing such names as "The Heap." Despite its obsession with the Unearthly, *Fangface* was supposed to be a comedy. The laughtrack told us so.

Surprisingly, the numbingly nonintellectual *Fangface* briefly became an object of intellectual scrutiny. In their book *Children and Television: A Semiotic Approach* (Stanford University Press, 1986), Robert Hodge and David Tripp, a team of structural theorists, dissected *Fangface*'s opening credit sequence to study the "semiotics" in its 50 seconds of screen time—that is, to analyze everything in the sequence that was a form of communication. The authors noted that the picture of Fangface wearing a hat was a "syntagm"—a linear order of signs designed to "represent" something. An animal with a hat represented Fangface's oddness as a semihuman, which led to the "paradigmatic" of the sequence—a group of visual signs within the signs. Fangface's dual existence as an animal and a human made him both normal and abnormal; one of the paradigms within this theory was the fact that Fangface wore his hat backwards, representing the "reverses" in his makeup.

After 17 syntagm-filled half hour epi-

sodes, *Fangface* bit the big one, only to resurface in 1979 as the "Fangface and Fangpuss" segment of Ruby-Spears' *The Plasticman Comedy/Adventure Show* (q.v.). For a more successful utilization of the "I Was a Funny Teenage Werewolf" theme, see the notes on the animated TV version of the Michael J. Fox film *Teen Wolf.*

THE FANTASTIC FOUR. ABC: 9/9/ 1967–8/30/1969;   9/7/1969–8/30/1970. Hanna-Barbera. Executive producers: William Hanna and Joseph Barbera. Produced by Alex Lovy. Associate producer, Lewis A. Marshall. Directed by Charles A. Nichols. Written by Phil Hahn and Jack Hanrahan, based on an idea by Stan Lee and Jack Kirby. Character design: Alex Toth, Bob Singer. Music by Ted Nichols and Hoyt Curtin. Voices: Gerald Mohr (Reed Richards—Mr. Fantastic); Jo Ann Pflug (Sue Richards—Invisible Girl); Paul Frees (Ben Grimm—The Thing/Dr. Doom); Jac Flounders (Johnny Storm—The Human Torch).

—**THE NEW FANTASTIC FOUR.** NBC: 9/9/1978–9/1/1979. DePatie-Freleng/Marvel. Supervised by David DePatie and Friz Freleng. Created for television by Stan Lee. Animation director, Brad Case. Storyboards by Jack Kirby and Lew Marshall. Written by Stan Lee, Roy Thomas, Christie Marx, Bob Stitzel and Bob Johnson. Music by Dean Elliot; conducted by Eric Rogers. Voices: Mike Road (Mr. Fantastic); Ginny Tyler (Invisible Girl); Ted Cassidy (The Thing); Frank Welker (Herbie); John Stephenson (Dr. Doom); and Hal Smith, Dick Tufield, Don Messick, Gene Moss, Nancy Wible, Joan Gerber, and Vic Perrin. (*See also* THE FLINTSTONES.)

With a "superhero cycle" imposed on Saturday morning cartoons by CBS executive Fred Silverman in the late 1960s, the other networks wasted no time following suit. It was for ABC that Hanna-Barbera joined forces with Stan Lee of Marvel Comics to come up with a half hour animated version of Marvel's *Fantastic Four.*

The "Four" was originally the result of a brainstorming session between Stan Lee and artist Jack Kirby in 1961—which, legend has it, was inspired by a golf game. It seems that a higher-up at DC Comics was on the links with another comic book executive, and between tee-offs the two men were expressing amazement at the success of DC's *Justice League of America* (see *Superfriends*), a 1940s property which had recently staged a revival. The DC man was remarking upon what a grand business idea it had been to spotlight a superhero "team" like the Justice League. The other comic-book man reportedly rubbed his chin and murmured, "Hmmmm . . . a team. . . ."

The other man was, so the story goes, Stan Lee, who'd recently left his hired-writer job at Atlas Publications to set up his own company, Marvel Comics. Lee's proposed variation on the *Justice League* "team," cooked up in conjunction with Marvel cohort Jack Kirby, became *The Fantastic Four*, which represented not only the first official Marvel property, but also the first of many Marvel-based super-powered individuals whose personal problems tended to get in the way of their crimefighting.

Scientist Reed Richards was *Fantastic Four*'s Mister Fantastic, whose flexible skin enabled him to stretch and squash in and out of any scrape (a "straighter" variation on Jack Cole's satirical *Plasticman* [q.v.]). Richards' wife Sue was Invisible Girl, whose invisibility on the cartoon series was depicted by having her drawn transparently, with thick white inklines. Sue's younger brother was Johnny Storm, whose propensity for bursting into controllable flames earned him the alias "The Human Torch" (a character of the same name had already been seen as early as 1939 in the pages of Marvel's predecessor Timely Comics; at that time he wasn't human at all, but an android). And finally there was the Richards' close friend Ben Grimm, nicknamed "The Thing" because of his ability to transform into an orange-colored rocklike being resembling Marvel's "Hulk" (this character later re-emerged as an *Archie*-inspired comedy teenager on Hanna-Barbera's *Fred and Barney Meet the Thing*; see notes on *The Flintstones*). On the first episode of Hanna-Barbera's *Fantastic Four*, it was explained that the quartet's talents were the after-effects of a bombardment of cosmic rays endured by the Richards' rocketship.

Comic book artist Alex Toth was given the task of transferring the original Marvel character designs to the small-screen version of *Fantastic Four*; he succeeded primarily in streamlining the project into a virtual carbon copy of Hanna-Barbera's

earlier *Jonny Quest* (q.v.). Most of the human frailties that gave the "Four" their three-dimensionality in the comic books — Reed Richards' insensitivity, Sue Richards' childishness, Johnny Storm's impetuous-ness — were dispensed with so as not to bog down the action packed plotlines. Only Ben Grimm, a.k.a. The Thing, carried over his often debilitating oversensi-tivity concerning his physical appearance from the Marvel pages to the TV screen. At that, his constant grumbling was played for laughs rather than pathos or character depth.

Fantastic Four scored on its graphics and snappy dialogue, but even at its best the series wasn't sufficiently different from the usual Hanna-Barbera syndrome to warrant further discussion. The 20 epi-sodes were repeated on ABC until 1970, and thereafter in syndication, before fading from the scene (it was briefly rebroadcast on the TNT Cable Network in 1993, the same year that a live action *Fantastic Four* motion picture was in pro-duction, with Alex Hyde-White as Mr. Fantastic).

A new *Fantastic Four* — cleverly titled *The New Fantastic Four* — made its appear-ance on NBC in 1978, this time copro-duced by Marvel and DePatie-Freleng. (To win back the animation rights, Marvel was forced to give up *Godzilla* [q.v.] to Hanna-Barbera.) Three of the "Four" re-mained in this fresh version. Johnny Storm/The Human Torch was gone; the TV rights had been signed away by Marvel to Universal Television in anticipation of a separate "Human Torch" weekly series which, as it developed, was never pro-duced. In Storm's place was a flippant jet-propelled robot, which was called HER-B (Humanoid Electronic Robot — B Model), and spelled "Herbie" in the closing credits. (Incidentally, he'd had a few other names before the series was released: Jack Kirby's original character design sheets named the robot "Z-Z-1-2-3," while net-work publicity heralded the character as "CHX RL-3," or "Charlie the Computer.") This latest version of the crimebusting quartet was whisked from caper to caper in a flying auto called the Fantastacar — which like the talking robot was the sort of gimmickry that seemed destined for toy-store incarnations.

Though the spectre of merchandising loomed large over *The New Fantastic Four*, this version was closer to the "feel" of a Marvel comic book—both verbally and visually—than the Hanna-Barbera *Four*. This was because Stan Lee himself wrote many of the scripts (adapted from the comic book continuities, as the Hanna-Barbera episodes had been), while *Fantastic Four* co-creator Jack Kirby supervised the storyboards which mapped out the cartoon action shot by shot. To meet the requirements of network "standards and practices," violence was downplayed in favor of strong characterization—even perennial villain Dr. Doom was quite fair-minded and reasonable in comparison to other Saturday morning baddies—with emphasis on Stan Lee's trademarked wiseguy dialogue. Lee's quippish sense of humor was especially evident in the character of The Thing, who came off like a mutant Rodney Dangerfield. The Thing also represented some of the best work of actor Ted Cassidy (see *The Addams Family, Godzilla* and *New Adventures of Huckleberry Finn*), who provided a subtle, naturalistic reading to what otherwise could have been a standardized "tough lug" character.

Unfortunately, superheroes were (temporarily) on the outs in Saturday morning TV in 1978, plus new NBC head Fred Silverman wasn't fond of the Marvel series. The *New Fantastic Four* lasted only 13 installments; it wasn't even afforded the courtesy of an extra rerun season on NBC.

FANTASTIC MAX. Syndicated: 1988. Hanna-Barbera. Co-produced by Kalisto, Inc., and Booker Pictures. Created by Mike Young. Designed and coproduced by Dave Edwards. Coproduced by John Parkinson. Story editors: Mark Young and Kelly Wood. Music by Clark Gassman and Michael Tavera. Voices: Ben Ryan Ganger (Fantastic Max); Nancy Cartwright (FX); Gregg Berger (A. B. Sitter); Gail Matthius (Mom); Paul Eiding (Dad); Elisabeth Harnois (Zoe); and Rene Auberjonois, Sorrell Booke, Philip Boute, Hamilton Camp, Townsend Coleman, Jennifer Darling, Jerry Dexter, Joanie Gerber, Dorian Harewood, Dana Hill, Jerry Houser, Arte Johnson, Michael Lembeck, Aaron Lohr, Laurence Luckinbill, Danny Mann, Ken Mars, Nan Martin, Chuck McCann, Howard Morris, Lorenzo Music, Rob Paulsen, Henry Polic II, Larry Riley, Ronnie Schell,

Avery Schreiber, Howard Stevens, Andre Stojka, B. J. Ward, Edward Winter.

Added to the weekend syndie package *Funtastic World of Hanna-Barbera* (q.v.) in 1988, *Fantastic Max* was a fast paced science-fiction comedy. The star was a normal Earthling preschooler who, after taking an accidental ride on a spaceship, returned to the bosom of his family with unusual talents and some *very* unusual playmates. Max was now able to traverse from Earth to Beyond and back again with impunity, armed against enemies with his special four-ply diaper and safety pin, which doubled as weapons and dispensers of superpowers. The boy's alien cohorts, who appeared to be mere bedtime toys to Max's parents and sister Zoe, were A. B. Sitter, a prissy robot, and FX, a walking special-effects generator.

Patterned somewhat after another *Funtastic World* component, *The New Adventures of Superted* (q.v.), *Fantastic Max* was a charmingly frantic half hour, with the freshly enervated Hanna-Barbera gag-writing staff working full blast for satisfying results.

FANTASTIC VOYAGE. ABC: 9/14/ 1968–9/5/1970. Sci-Fi Channel (reruns): 9/1992–. Filmation. Executive producers: Lou Scheimer, Norm Prescott. Directed by Hal Sutherland. Story editor, Ken Sobol. Music by Gordon Zahler. Voices: Marvin Miller (Scientist Corby Birdwell); Jane Webb (Erica Stone); Ted Knight (Cmdr. Jonathan Kidd/Prof. Carter).

Fantastic Voyage was inspired by the 1966 20th Century–Fox feature film of the same name. Expanding upon its parent project, the weekly half hour cartoon *Voyage* was all about a team of government scientists, led in this instance by scientist Corby Birdwell and Commander Jonathan Kidd, members of the Combined Miniature Defense Force who were miniaturized in order to expedite their submarine journey not only through the human blood system (as in the film) but in otherwise inaccessible areas around the world and throughout the universe. The principal attractions of the feature film were the superlative special effects and the sight of Raquel Welch in a skintight diving suit. The animated *Voyage* couldn't do much to recreate Ms. Welch—the character of biologist Erica Lane was drawn more along the lines of Saturday morning TV stan-

Fantastic Max and his retinue take up space surfing.

dards and practices—but the Filmation crew did reasonably well imitating the giant-sized blood cells and mammoth arterial passages seen in the original film. The draftsmanship can be regarded as the precursor to Filmation's "straight" approach to the *Star Trek* (q.v.) cartoon series, anticipating that later project's advantages (realistic design) as well as its shortcomings (underdeveloped animation).

For the purposes of playing down to its audience, the cartoon *Fantastic Voyage* was hoked up with the mystical, turbaned Guru, who was described as a "master of mysterious power." It was the clichéd elements like the Guru and the continual intervention of miniature enemy spies and space monsters that allowed the National Association of Better Broadcasting to dismiss the 17-week *Fantastic Voyage* as "formula junk."

FAT ALBERT AND THE COSBY KIDS.

CBS: 9/9/1972–8/25/1984 (retitled THE NEW FAT ALBERT SHOW on 9/8/1979). NBC: 2/11/1989–9/2/1989 (reruns). Syndicated: 1984. Filmation. Executive producer: William H. Cosby Jr. Produced by Norm Prescott, Lou Scheimer and Arthur H. Nadel. Directed by Hal Sutherland, Lou Zukor, Don Christensen, Bob Arkwright, Don Townsley, John Armstrong, Kent Butterworth, Ed Friedman, Lou Kachivas, Marsh Lamore, Ernie Schmidt, Kay Wright. Music by the Horna-Mahana Corporation. Voices: Bill Cosby (Fat Albert/Mush Mouth/Dumb Donald/Weird Harold/Brown Hornet/Leroy/Mudfoot); Gerald Edwards (Weird Harold); Jan Crawford (Russell/Bucky); Eric Suter (Rudy/Devery); and Keith Allen, Pepe Brown, Erika Carroll, Lane Vaux, and Lou Scheimer.

Comedian Bill Cosby built most of his professional reputation in the 1960s upon humorous reminiscences of his childhood, particularly his memories of such schoolyard chums as Cryin' Charlie, Junior Barnes, Old Weird Harold, and especially an earthquake-inducing young man named Fat Albert. Somehow Cosby's recollection of Albert's "Hey, hey, HEYYYY!" instantly conjured up vivid mental pictures of the brash, goodnatured fat kids that all of us grew up with (and possibly flattered those grownups who *were* the brash, goodnatured fat kids). Fat Albert inevitably graduated to the animated cartoon via a 1969 NBC special, *Hey, Hey, Hey, It's Fat Albert*, coproduced by Bill Cosby and Filmation. In this half hour visualization of Cosby's famed "street football" routine, Albert was drawn as something of a human dirigible, literally bursting out of his clothes. But by the time Filmation had convinced Cosby that the character had weekly series potential, the Fat One was drawn along more realistic "overgrown kid" lines—though he was still the biggest boy on the block.

This wasn't the only change made when *Fat Albert and the Cosby Kids* premiered as a CBS Saturday morning series in 1972. The biggest change was in the whole concept of animating a "live" property. Usually when such a metamorphosis took place in the 1960s and 1970s, it was done for the crass purpose of merchandising a hot commodity, of squeezing out the last drop of profitability before that property cooled down. While the animation and writing were occasionally above average (see *The Beatles*), for the most part the cartoon versions of the originals added little to their popularity or charm, and frequently brought the originals down to the same banal level as most of the rest of weekend TV (see—if you can stand it—*Laurel and Hardy*, *Abbott and Costello*, or more recently, *Wishkid Starring Macaulay Culkin*).

But Bill Cosby wasn't interested in merely perpetuating a line of Fat Albert merchandise, nor in simply keeping his name in the public's consciousness. Intensely concerned with the disillusionment and disenfranchisement facing children of 1972—particularly minority children trapped in urban ghettos—Cosby wanted *Fat Albert* to teach a set of educational and moral values to its audience. But he was still a showman, and as such relied on the Filmation writing crew to keep the series entertaining: as he would say in his weekly live-action introduction to the show, "Stick around and have fun . . . and if you aren't careful, you might learn something."

To meet both requirements, Filmation not only hired some of the best gag writers and cartoon directors in the business, but also enlisted the advice of ten prominent psychologists and philosophers from UCLA. As Filmation executive Lou Scheimer explained to kiddie-show historian Gary Grossman, the UCLA team "worked with our writers in the selection of story material, character development and character relationships." Such a liaison always runs the risk of bleeding-heartism or pretentiousness—one need only glance at recent daily cartoon shows with technical advisors who either indulge in overkill or wedge their "vital message" in the last 30 seconds of each episode—but the concept of combining traditional cartoon people with educators was so fresh and innovative in 1972 that everyone did their best to simply do their job rather than grandstand or proselytize. And while Filmation ultimately returned to business as usual in its later biff-bang-pow cartoon series, for a long while the company maintained an equitable balance between entertainment and education in its product, notably in its live action comic book derivations *Shazam!* and *Isis*.

Fat Albert and the Cosby Kids revolved around the antics of a group of nice, albeit trouble-prone, Philadelphia black kids: Fat Albert, the Cosby boys (Bill and wisecracker Russell), showoff Rudy, Weird Harold, Dumb Donald (hat eternally pulled over his eyes), Mushmouth (the one with the peculiar speech impediment which implanted a "B" sound in every syllable), and atmosphere kids Bucky and Devery. Many of the storylines were pure "Little Rascals," with the kids running the gamut from building their own playthings to vying over the attentions of a pretty girl or raising money for a worthy cause. But this was 1972, not 1932; often as not the kids were confronted with such contemporary perils as truancy, the dropout rate, drugs and street crime (our heroes were always blameless; generally the troublemakers were "outsiders" or duplicitous adults). An unstressed additional element to *Fat Albert* was the background art; the gang's homes were lower-middle-class shabby, the streets were strewn with litter and garbage, and the kids' favorite hangout was a junkyard. The fact that Fat Albert and company were able to retain their humor, gentle nature and overall likability in this rundown inner city atmosphere could only emit positive messages to real-life children likewise entrapped in dingy poverty.

But *Fat Albert's* message was aimed at all children rather than just those in reduced circumstances. Many of the issues confronted on the series were those with which most of the home viewers could identify, among them peer pressure, handicaps, learning disabilities and respect for others' cultural heritage. Two of the best *Fat Albert* episodes, "TV or Not TV" (1976) and "Sweet Sorrow" (1979), dealt respectively with a child addicted to television to the detriment of his mental and physical well being (imagine *any* nighttime TV series doing that!), and with the sudden death of a beloved relative. Refreshingly, many of the problems posed on *Fat Albert* were not resolved within 22 minutes' screen time; Bill Cosby would appear in live action footage to explain that there were some emotional wounds that would take a lot of time to heal. Any children's

program that posed dilemmas and then refused to offer up easy answers was a rare bird indeed, and this was recognized by the various awards organizations in the entertainment world: *Fat Albert and the Cosby Kids* was honored with the Ohio State Award, a commendation from Action for Children's Television, and an Emmy—this last awarded in 1985, at which time the series was out of production and in reruns!

While we're on that last subject, we must note that Bill Cosby, notoriously difficult to please, was not altogether happy with *Fat Albert*—not because of any defects in production, but of CBS's reluctance to order more new episodes after the first season. From 1973 onward, the most Filmation was ever allowed to produce was between six to eight new installments per year, the rest of the season filled out with reruns. In 1974, 1977 and 1978, *no* new *Fat Alberts* were produced, which meant that not only would Filmation lose out on extra rental fees, but that the studio's series ran the risk of losing its freshness due to constant repetition of older episodes. When Cosby and Lou Scheimer complained to CBS, they were told flatly that the series was doing just fine in rebroadcasts, so why go to the expense of producing 17 fresh installments per year? As a result, only 54 *Fat Albert* episodes were completed throughout its 12 seasons on CBS, with an additional 50 half hours produced when the series went into strip syndication in 1984.

This last-mentioned move into the offnetwork market was welcomed by Bill Cosby because it allowed him to tackle subject matter that was denied him by the censors during the CBS years. One of the most forceful syndicated *Fat Alberts* was a harrowing episode in which the gang, peripherally involved in a minor crime, were convinced to remain on the side of the law by being taken to a prison for a "Scared Straight" session. For the rest of the episode, a battery of hardened convicts verbally assaulted the terrified boys with threats, profanity, and sexual invitations. To drive the point home, Cosby saw to it that the cartoon criminals used *exactly* the sort of language they'd use in real life—after carefully prefacing the episode with a live-action disclaimer, warning the audience that what they'd be seeing wouldn't be pretty. (Another new element to the syndicated version, a silly "good ole boy" lawyer called the Legal Eagle, was, conversely, a singularly uninspired "improvement.")

While always worthwhile, *Fat Albert* was not perfect. The animation was frequently unimaginative and elementary, with certain scenes—particularly a shot of the Gang cheering—used over and over again to lower the budget. Most episodes were afflicted with a tiresome holdover from Filmation's *Archie* (q.v.), in which the Gang would sing an original rock song, accompanying themselves on makeshift instruments. (The "singing" Fat Albert sounded nothing at all like the "talking" one.) And in the final network episodes, the longwinded preaching of the Gang's favorite TV superhero, "The Brown Hornet" (a much funnier concept on Cosby's record albums), served only to beat to death each week's Important Lesson—an element of the series that previously had been handled with skill and subtlety.

But the good intentions and ultimate salutary results of *Fat Albert* more than made up for its faults. And most importantly, the series never turned into a mere conduit for merchandising. During the first season, Filmation's Lou Scheimer and Norm Prescott had licensed the Fat Albert characters for lunch boxes and T-shirts, but, as Prescott told Gary Grossman, "when we saw *Fat Albert* suddenly emerge as a meaningful character who . . . became a symbol for good things, we never renewed any of those contracts. We said the hell with it, we're just not interested in just making money and jeopardizing what this character has become." To that end, Filmation released licensing rights to only three very carefully selected outlets: McGraw-Hill, a publishing firm that used Albert and his buddies in an audio-visual teaching program for grammar schools; Dell Publishing, which novelized the *Fat Albert* scripts for the purpose of encouraging kids to learn to read without resorting to comic book balloons and captioned pictures; and a line of low-sugar cookies, which were made within strict nutritional and healthful guidelines. "If he can't be associated with something good," concluded Prescott, "then we're not interested in licensing him."

Fat Albert and the Cosby Kids ended its first run in 1985; the series was brought back in rerun form in February 1989 on NBC—where Bill Cosby's prime time sitcom was then the number one attraction. The following September, *Fat Albert* was consigned to the USA Cable Network, still remaining a justifiable source of pride for Bill Cosby, Filmation, and TV monitor groups such as Action for Children's Television. Although it didn't exactly change the world, *Fat Albert and the Cosby Kids* certainly enriched that corner of the world it chose to occupy for nearly two decades.

FEARLESS FLY *see* **MILTON THE MONSTER**

FELIX THE CAT. Syndicated: 1960. Joe Oriolo Productions/Trans-Lux. Produced and directed by Joe Oriolo. Voices: Jack Mercer.

Few cartoon characters have maintained as distinguished a reputation for so long a period of time as Felix the Cat. Created by Pat Sullivan, Otto Messmer and John King as an adjunct to the *Paramount Screen Magazine* newsreel in 1919, the resourceful little black cat was signed for a solo series first by Pathé in 1920, and then by pioneering animation distributor M. J. Winkler in 1921. *Felix Saves the Day* (1922) was the first in a popular series of one-reel cartoons released internationally by Winkler, which under the aegis of master showman Pat Sullivan were assembled by such celebrated cartoon craftsmen as Raoul Barre, Bill Nolan, Al Eugster and Rudy Zamora. The felicitous feline's famous stunt repertoire, most notably his mobile, removable tail which functioned at various times as everything from a vaulting pole to a question mark, cemented his image in the collective consciousness of silent movie fans the world over—until 1929, when Sullivan's hesitancy to convert to sound brought an abrupt end to the series. Even though he missed that technological advance, Felix remained at the forefront of another media event when, in 1928, a toy statue of the cat was chosen to test RCA's experimental 60-line television transmitter—making Felix the Cat the first bonafide television star.

After a handful of attractively animated but undistinguished sound cartoons produced in Technicolor by Van Beuren Studios in 1936, Felix was retired, save for a series of clever comic books. It was television that brought the character back to full public view again. In 1958, Joe Oriolo, the Paramount animation artist who'd developed *Casper the Friendly Ghost* (q.v.), was illustrating the Felix comics when he was tapped by Trans-Lux to produce a series of four-minute Felix cartoons for TV. During the next two years, the Oriolo studios ground out 260 color cartoons—a number which we'd label astonishing had the results been of astonishing quality. No such luck. The new *Felix the Cat* succeeded only in trashing the character's reputation for brilliance. Cartoon critic Harold Schechter perhaps overstated the case when he observed, "It's hard to imagine a worse set of cartoons," but not by much.

The TV *Felix* was offered in cliffhanger form, most stories running two episodes. Why anyone bothered to come up with separate titles for these things is a mystery, for every *Felix* story was virtually the same: The precocious pussy was assaulted by the two main villains, the Professor (human) and Rock Bottom (a bulldog), or occasional guest heavies like the Master Cylinder. These reprobates usually wished to liquidate Felix in order to steal the cat's legendary Bag of Tricks, an unprepossessing carpetbag wherein was packed an assortment of tools, magic tricks, escape devices, thinking caps, "instant holes" and the like. Felix's erstwhile allies included the Professor's bespectacled, egghead nephew Poindexter (named after Joe Oriolo's attorney!) and Vavoom, an odd little Eskimo who was able to blast holes in mountains with the force of his voice.

The stories moved at a pace that made a snail look like Speed Racer. The lethargy was emphasized by the incongruously peppy background music, lifted bodily from the Paramount *Popeye* and *Casper* cartoons scored by Win Sharples; and by Joe Oriolo's insistence that voice actor Jack Mercer (who in happier times had been the voice of Popeye) speak v-e-r-y s-l-o-w-l-y, one syllable at a time, in order to consume film footage which would otherwise have to be more elaborately animated and thus push the project over its already skintight budget. (Mercer wasn't happy with this assignment, nor did he enjoy having to continually switch voicegears from high to low pitch rather than

"loop" each character separately.) As a result of this slavishly measured pace, Felix and company moved and spoke like robots from a bad 1950s science fiction movie. Complaints that the cartoons were overly violent—many storylines wound up with Felix and the villains trying to do each other in—were perhaps mitigated by the fact that the series' sluggishness couldn't remotely build up any tension or suspense, but that's small compensation for the overall mediocrity.

Pat Sullivan, the man contractually billed as Felix's sole "creator," was reported to have insisted in 1959 that modern audiences wouldn't be able to tell the difference between the old *Felix* of the 1920s and the new *Felix* of 1960. The fact that Sullivan had been dead for several years didn't stop the publicity flacks from confusing him with whoever really made that statement; but whoever *did* say it, the sad thing is that he might have been right. Incredible as it seems, the listless TV version of *Felix the Cat* left a big impression on children growing up during the 1960s. One lasting legacy was the character name "Poindexter," which along with "Mr. Peabody" (see *Rocky and His Friends*) became a schoolyard nickname for any overly bright kid. Indeed, a preteen actor by the name of Randall Yothers, who starred in the 1970s children's series *Cliffwood Avenue Kids* and *Tony the Pony*, chose to adopt Poindexter as his professional monicker. (And how about punk-rock singer Buster Poindexter—real name David Johansen—while we're on this subject?)

The other hangover from the TV *Felix* was its jaunty theme song, which promised expansively that "You'll laugh so much your sides will ache/Your heart will go pitter-pat." It's difficult to find any American TV fanatic born after 1955 who can't recite this ditty from memory. Few, however, can recall experiencing aching sides or pitter-pat heartbeats.

Just why the "new" *Felix the Cat* was so successful is worthy of intense study; one hopes it doesn't prove the cynical TV-producer theory that kids will swallow anything served up to them. At any rate, the character's durability enabled Trans-Lux to market its 260 cartoons far and wide, especially during the color TV boom of the mid–1960s. Some local stations were so pleased with the results that they

Felix the Cat laughs so much his sides will ache (saving the audience the pain).

renewed their *Felix* contracts until past 1970. The profitability of the series kept the character alive for a whole generation of viewers who wouldn't have been caught dead watching an old, silent, black and white *Felix*. This success stretched into at least 1987, when Joe Oriolo's son Don produced a computer enhanced, feature-length *Felix* TV special, intended as a pilot for a potential new series. It's a shame that the series didn't develop; the younger Oriolo managed to salvage whatever marginal charm the 1960 TV *Felix* had had by dressing it up with first class animation and character design. If nothing else, Don Oriolo proved that there might be a dance left in the old cat after all. (Certainly Film Roman thought so in 1994 when the studio prepared its own pilot for a daily *Felix* syndicated series.)

A final shot: Some six months before Oriolo/Trans-Lux's *Felix the Cat*'s official January 1960 debut, the cartoons were telecast round the clock at the American National Exhibit in Moscow, as an example for Russian observers of "typical" U.S. television fare. Small wonder that Premier Khrushchev believed he could bury us.

FENDER BENDER 500 *see* **WAKE, RATTLE AND ROLL**

FESTIVAL OF FAMILY CLASSICS. Syndicated: 1972. Rankin/Bass. Production facilities: Mushi Studios. Music by Maury Laws. Voices: Carl Banas,

Len Birman, Bernard Cowan, Peg Dixon, Keith Hampshire, Peggi Loder, Donna Miller, Frank Perry, Henry Raymer, Billie Mae Richards, Alfie Scopp, Paul Soles. *Festival of Family Classics* was an occasionally stodgy but basically satisfying series of 18 hour long animated specials, syndicated to local stations. Subject matter was firmly entrenched in the classics, including the oft-filmed "Around the World in Eighty Days" and "Snow White and the Seven Dwarfs." Most of these were done straight, but there were such occasional diversions as the comic slant given to "Cinderella"—in which Prince Charming was a hopeless bungler—and "Robin Hood," the latter a wholly new chapter to the venerable legend involving a "boy and his dog" subplot. Also explored were such tall-tale regulars as Johnny Appleseed and Paul Bunyan.

In all, *Festival of Family Classics* was one of the better "cultural" cartoon offerings of the 1970s (for similar projects, see *ABC Weekend Specials* and *Family Classics Theatre*). The series also represented the last stand of Japan's Mushi Studios (see notes on *Astro Boy*), which before its early 1970s financial collapse provided animation facilities for *Festival*'s parent producing company, Rankin-Bass of Canada.

FIEVEL'S AMERICAN TAILS. CBS: 9/12/1992–9/11/1993. Universal/Amblin TV/Nelvana. Executive producers: Frank Marshall, Kathleen Kennedy. Executive production consultant and creator, David Kirschner. Produced by Patricia Loubert, Michael Hirsh, Clive A. Smith, Lawrence Zelig Jacobs. Supervising producer, Stephen Hodgins. Story editors, Chris Hubbell and Sam Graham. Animation facilities: Wang Film Production Co., Ltd., Bartel Animation, Hollywood Cartoon Company. Theme music by Robert Irving and Hank Saroyan. Music by Milan Kymlicka. Voices: Dom DeLuise (Tiger); Lloyd Battista (Papa); Dan Castellaneta (Chula the Spider); Cathy Cavadani (Tanya); Philip Glasser (Fievel); Gerrit Graham (Cat R. Waul); Kenneth Mars (Sweet William); Arthur Burghardt (Hambone); Carlos Carrasco (Jorge); Alex Dent (Fernando); Cynthia Ferrer (Miss Kitty); Paige Gosney (Stanley); Danny Mann (Dog); Patty Parris (Aunt Sophie); Lisa Picotte (Lorna Holcombe); Hal Rayle

(Clint Mousewood); Rolland Thompson (Jack).

Fievel Mousekewitz, a young, 19th century Jewish immigrant mouse, was introduced in Don Bluth's 1986 cartoon feature *An American Tail*. Though the film suffered from Bluth's usual shortcomings vis-a-vis story development and murky color design, the animation itself was well up to Disney standard, the characters were ingratiating if somewhat unmemorable, and the songs were appealing (one of the tunes, "Somewhere Out There," received an Oscar nomination). As a result, *American Tail* was a major financial success both for Bluth and executive producer Steven Spielberg—whose grandfather, incidentally, was named Fievel. A sequel followed five years later: *An American Tail: Fievel Goes West*, which per its title took the Mousekewitz family out of the Lower East Side and transplanted them in the great American frontier. This feature didn't do nearly as well as its predecessor, but did provide the groundwork for a 1992 weekly Saturday morning half hour, *Fievel's American Tails*, coproduced by Canada's Nelvana Ltd., Spielberg's Amblin Entertainment, and Universal Television. Don Bluth was not involved in this project, though it bore the name of Fievel's original creator David Kirschner (late of Hanna-Barbera) as "executive production consultant."

In the series, Fievel (voiced as in the films by Philip Glasser) continued his adventures in the frontier community of Green River, in the company of onetime foe but latterly good friend Tiger the Cat (Dom DeLuise, also repeating his motion picture voiceover chore; DeLuise was also credited for "special oohs and ahhs," whatever that means). The Mousekewitz family members—Fievel, his parents, and his nonspeaking baby sister Tanya—were proud owners of a violin shop, purveying to a trade largely comprised of fellow immigrant animals: Hispanic Jorge, Australian Jack, and so forth. The traditional black-hat villainy was in the hands of Cat R. Waul, an erudite confidence trickster whose two life goals were fleecing the multicultural community and making a dinner out of Fievel and his family. Cat R. Waul was aided in his skulking by Chula, a rusty-voiced spider, and Sweet William, an oafish bandit. While nominal protection against these predators was offered by

a character named Clint Mousewood (ouch!), Fievel managed to wriggle out of most of his perils by utilizing his wits. Frequently, solutions to impossible problems were solved by Fievel's ability to read—a gentle tie-in with the "Reading Is Fundamental" public service project, for which Fievel Mousekewitz was the 1992 spokesmouse and for which he hosted a weekly "Reading Buddy" segment on the series.

Fievel's American Tails was well and lovingly animated, with some strikingly gorgeous Western landscape background art (also a plus factor in ABC's like-vintage cartoon weekly, *The Wild West C.O.W.-Boys of Moo Mesa* [q.v.].) Yet it fell short of perfection thanks to pokey pacing and repetitive jokes—precisely the antithesis of the *American Tail* theatrical features, which were paced too frenetically and were far too overstocked with irrelevant gags to be completely satisfying. But better that we had an imperfect Fievel than no Fievel at all. *Fievel's American Tails* was consistently cheerful and enjoyable, as well as one of the few non–Fox Network, non–Disney projects to flourish in the fiercely competitive kidvid scene of 1992—but not, worse luck, for long. Ratings dwindled by the middle of 1993, and the series was quietly cancelled in the fall of that year (though plans were drawn to package a new group of *American Tails* for a possible 1994 airdate).

FISH POLICE. CBS: 2/28/1992–3/13/1992. Hanna-Barbera. Executive producers, David Kirschner, Benjamin Melnicker, Michael E. Uslan. Co-executive producers, Melissa Goldsmith and Paul Sabella. Produced by Larry Huber and Jeanne Romano. Based on the comic book by Steve Moncuse. Character art and design, Rick Schneider. Supervising animation director, Ray Patterson. Animation director, Joanna Romersa. Music by James Horner. Voices: John Ritter (Inspector Gil); Edward Asner (Chief Abalone); JoBeth Williams (Angel); Megan Mullaly (Pearl); Hector Elizondo (Clams Calimari); and Georgia Brown, Jonathan Winters, Buddy Hackett, Robert Guillaume, Tim Curry, Charlie Schlatter, Frank Welker, and Rob Paulsen.

In 1960, Hanna-Barbera's *The Flintstones* (q.v.) sparked a brief trend in prime time, half hour cartoon series. In 1992, the success of *The Simpsons* (q.v.) precipitated a similar trend—only this time, Hanna-Barbera did not lead but followed, first with *Capitol Critters* (q.v.) and then with *Fish Police*. The latter project premiered on the same evening that two other notable TV disasters, *Scorch* (a talking dragon) and *Nightmare Cafe* (an anthology about restless ghosts), made their debuts: February 28, 1992. A date which will live in indifference.

The genesis of *Fish Police* was respectable enough. The project was based on a series of "alternative" comic books created in 1985 by Steve Moncuse, in which traditional detective stories were juiced up by having all the characters drawn as carp rather than human beings. Beyond the inherent humor of the concept, Moncuse's storylines were complex, Raymond Chandlerish *film noir* mysteries that could have held up on their own without the piscatorial gimmickry. Characteristically, Hanna-Barbera downpedalled the detective angle while playing up the comedy; it was in this spirit that the studio described the series' visual style as "fish noir." On paper, *Fish Police* seemed fairly hip, and soon media critics were quoting the best gags—one-liners like "I said 'Inspector Gil', not inspect her gills," a place of worship known as "Our Church of the Holy Mackerel," etc.—until incessant repetition robbed these gags of their risibility.

Generous preshow print space was also devoted to *Fish Police*'s voice actors. Instead of drawing upon TV's pool of reliable vocal talent, Hanna-Barbera went the celebrity route of engaging John Ritter as Inspector Gil, JoBeth Williams as "fin fatale" songstress Angel, Ed Asner as Chief Abalone, Hector Elizondo as mad doctor Calamari, and Buddy Hackett as a crab cabbie. Other such luminaries were Robert Guillaume and Jonathan Winters enacted the various good and bad little fishies—including the likes of Clams Casino, Mussels Marinara, and Sharkster—who happened to float by. However, many of the best lines went not to the megastar "name" actors but to *Fish Police* supporting voice artist Georgia Brown as a prickly, much-married police secretary.

After a publicity blitz which blanketed CBS' 1992 Winter Olympics coverage, *Fish Police* opened. To its credit, the animation was much more fluid than Hanna-Barbera followers were accustomed to.

Studio CEO David Kirschner informed *TV Guide* that Hanna-Barbera's Taiwan production facilities turned out at least 22,000 animation cels per half hour, as opposed to the standard 15,000: "We wanted more animation, so that you can see someone blow the hair out of their eyes, see their fingers curl." Overall, the artwork was terrific, with such excellent isolated setpieces as an Edward Hopper takeoff showing Inspector Gil sitting alone in an art-deco café. (The bluesy background music of James Horner in such scenes was another plus.)

And, yes, it was funny. For a while. Long enough for people to get *really* tired of all those fish jokes. And long enough for Steve Moncuse fans to realize that the density and wit of the original comic books would be jettisoned in favor of such all too typical Hanna-Barbera bits as having Inspector Gil's police badge turn out to be a hyperactive starfish. Even those unfamiliar with Moncuse were unsatisfied. The series didn't connect with cartoon fans who wondered why such lush animation and overblown comedy content was inappropriately applied to such gritty subject matter; nor did it appeal to detective-show fans, who couldn't understand why the plotlines weren't simply acted out with people rather than sea life. Never managing to cultivate a following, *Fish Police* was dead in the water after only three episodes.

This isn't to say, however, that the concept of a detective series played out by nonhuman characters wasn't a viable one. One need only see Henson Productions' infinitely superior *Dog City* (q.v.) for proof of that.

(Footnote: A similar Canadian series, aimed at children, was produced in 1988 by Cine Group under the title *Sharky and George*.)

FLASH GORDON *see* **THE NEW ADVENTURES OF FLASH GORDON**

THE FLINTSTONES. (This entry consists of all TV series pertaining to the "Flintstones" characters.)
—THE FLINTSTONES. ABC: 9/30/ 1960–9/2/1966. NBC: 1/7/1967–9/5/1970 (reruns). Hanna-Barbera/Screen Gems. Produced by William Hanna and Joseph Barbera. Directed by William Hanna, Joseph Barbera, Alex Lovy, Charles A.

Nichols, others. Written by Joseph Barbera, William Hanna, Michael Maltese, Warren Foster, R. Allen Safian, Barry Blitzer, Tony Benedict, Herb Finn, Jack Raymond, Sid Zelinka, Arthur Phillips, Joanna Lee, Bill Idelson, Rance Howard, Phil Hahn, Jack Hanrahan, R.S. Allen and Harvey Bullock (among others). Music by Hoyt Curtin. Voices: Alan Reed (Fred Flintstone); Mel Blanc, Daws Butler (Barney Rubble/Dino); Jean VanderPyl (Wilma Flintstone/Pebbles Flintstone); Bea Benaderet, Gerry Johnson (Betty Rubble); John Stephenson (Mr. Slate, others); Don Messick (Bamm Bamm/Arnold the Newsboy/others); Verna Felton (Wilma's Mother); Harvey Korman (The Great Gazoo); and Hal Smith, Walker Edmiston, Herbert Vigran, Herschel Bernardi, Howard McNear, Frank Nelson, June Foray, Howard Morris, Naomi Lewis. "Guest star" voices: Hoagy Carmichael, Ann-Margret, Tony Curtis, James Darren, Elizabeth Montgomery, Dick York, Jimmy O'Neill, The Beau Brummels.

—PEBBLES AND BAMM BAMM. CBS: 9/11/1971–9/2/1972; 5/1973–9/1973 (reruns); 2/1974–9/1974 (reruns); 3/1975–9/1976 (reruns). Hanna-Barbera. Produced by William Hanna and Joseph Barbera. Creative producer, Iwao Takamoto. Directed by Charles Nichols. Written by Joel Kane, Woody Kling, Howard Morganstern, Joe Ruby, Ken Spears. Music by Hoyt Curtin. Voices: Sally Struthers (Pebbles Flintstone); Jay North (Bamm Bamm Rubble); Lennie Weinrib (Moonrock); Mitzi McCall (Penny); Gay Hartwig (Wiggy/Cindy); Carl Esser (Fabian).

—THE FLINTSTONES COMEDY HOUR. CBS: 9/9/1972–9/1/1973; 9/8/1973–1/26/1974 (reruns, in 30 minute format and retitled THE FLINTSTONES SHOW). (Program consisted of reruns of PEBBLES AND BAMM BAMM, with four new episodes included.) Hanna-Barbera. Produced by Joseph Hanna, William Barbera and Iwao Takamoto. Music by Hoyt Curtin. Voices: Mickey Stevens, Sally Struthers (Pebbles Flintstone); Jay North (Bamm Bamm Rubble); Alan Reed (Fred Flintstone); Mel Blanc (Barney Rubble/Zonk/Stub); Jean VanderPyl (Wilma Flintstone); Gay Hartwig (Betty Rubble/Wiggy); John Stephenson (Mr. Slate/Noodles); Mitzi McCall (Penny); Lennie Weinrib (Moonrock/Bronto); Carl Esser (Fabian).

—THE NEW FRED AND BARNEY SHOW. NBC: 2/3/1979–9/15/1979. Hanna-Barbera. Executive producers, William Hanna, Joseph Barbera. Produced by Alex Lovy. Creative producer, Iwao Takamoto. Directed by Ray Patterson, Carl Urbano, Oscar Dufau and George Gordon. Music by Hoyt Curtin. Voices: Henry Corden (Fred Flintstone); Mel Blanc (Barney Rubble); Jean VanderPyl (Wilma Flintstone); Gay Autterson (Betty Rubble).

—FRED AND BARNEY MEET THE THING. NBC: 9/22/1979–12/1/1979. Same cast and production credits as THE NEW FRED AND BARNEY SHOW. Additional credits: "The Thing" created for television by Stan Lee; written by (among others) Jim Ryan, Ray Parker, Tex Avery and Doug Booth. Additional voices: Joe Baker (The Thing); Wayne Norton (Benjy Grimm); Noelle North (Kelly); Marilyn Schreffler (Betty/ Miss Twilly); John Erwin (Ronald Radford); John Stephenson (Stretch/Dr. Harkness); Art Metrano (Spike); Michael Sheehan (Turkey).

—FRED AND BARNEY MEET THE SHMOO. NBC: 9/8/1979–11/15/1980. Same cast and production credits as FRED AND BARNEY MEET THE THING. Additional credits: "The Shmoo" created by Al Capp. Additional voices: Frank Welker (The Shmoo); Dolores Cantu-Primo (Nita); Chuck McCann (Billy Jo); Bill Edelson (Mickey).

—THE FLINTSTONES COMEDY SHOW. NBC: 11/22/1980–9/5/1981. Hanna-Barbera. Executive producers, William Hanna and Joseph Barbera. Executives in charge of production, Jayne Barbera and Margaret Loesch. Produced by Alex Lovy and Carl Urbano. Directed by Ray Patterson, George Gordon and Rudy Zamora. Story supervisor, Ray Parker. Story editors, Tex Avery, Doug Booth, Chuck Couch, Chuck Menville, Ray Parker, Duane Poole, Dick Robbins, Cliff Roberts, Tom Shale. Writers (among many others): Don Christensen, Don Glut, Jack Kinney, Jack Mendelsohn, Bob Ogle, Virgil Partch. Story directors included Chris Jenkyns, Bill Perez. Recording directors, Gordon Hunt, Alex Lovy; assistant, Ginny McSwain. Animation supervision, Jay Sarbry, Bob Hathcock. Music by Hoyt Curtin; musical direction by Paul DeKorte. Voices: Henry Corden (Fred Flintstone); Mel Blanc (Barney Rubble/Dino); Jean VanderPyl (Wilma Flint-

stone); Gay Autterson (Betty Rubble/ Wiggy); Russi Taylor (Pebbles Flintstone/ Cave Mouse); Michael Sheehan (Bamm Bamm); Ken Mars (Lou Granite); Lennie Weinrib (Sgt. Boulder/Moonrock); John Stephenson (Slate); Mitzi McCall (Penny); Don Messick (Schleprock); Charles Nelson Reilly (Frank Frankenstone); Ruta Lee (Hidea Frankenstone); Zelda Rubinstein (Atrocia Frankenstone); Paul Reubens [Pee-wee Herman] (Freaky Frankenstone); Frank Welker (Rockjaw); Joe Baker (Captain Caveman); and Rene Auberjonois, Mitzi McCall, Frank Nelson, Marilyn Scheffler, Lurene Tuttle, and Paul Winchell.
— THE FLINTSTONES FAMILY ADVENTURES. NBC: 10/4/1981–10/18/1981. Hanna-Barbera. (Repeats of three FLINTSTONES COMEDY SHOW episodes.)
— FLINTSTONE FUNNIES. NBC: 9/18/1982–9/8/1984. Hanna-Barbera. (Repeats of various components of THE FLINTSTONES COMEDY SHOW.)
— THE FLINTSTONE KIDS. ABC: 9/13/1986–10/22/1988; 1/6/1990–5/26/1990. Syndicated: 1990 (on FUNTASTIC WORLD OF HANNA-BARBERA). Hanna-Barbera. Produced by Kay Wright. Supervising director, Ray Patterson. Directed by Art Davis, Don Lusk, Carl Urbano and Rudy Zamora. Creative design by Iwao Takamoto. Story editors: Arthur Alsberg, John Klodin, Don Nelson, Lane Raichett. Title design by Bill Perez. Musical direction by Hoyt Curtin. Production facilities: Wang Film Productions, Cuckoo's Nest Studios. Voices: Scott Menville (Freddy, 1st season); Lennie Weinrib (Freddy, 2nd season/ Commissioner); Hamilton Camp (Barney/Flab Slab); Elizabeth Lyn Fraser (Wilma, 1st season); Julie Dees (Wilma, 2nd season/Micky/ Mica/Tarpit Tommy); B.J. Ward (Betty/ Miss Rockbottom); Mel Blanc (Robert Rubble/Captain Caveman/Dino); Henry Corden (Ed and Edna Flintstone); Jean VanderPyl (Doris Slaghoople); Marilyn Scheffler (Flo Rubble/Rocky Ratrock); Frank Welker (Nate Slate/Stalagbite); Susan Blu (Dreamchip Gemstone/Granite Janet); Ken Mars (Narrator); Bumper Robinson (Philo Quartz); Rene Levant (Officer Quartz); Charles Adler (Cavey Jr.); and Bever-Leigh Banfield, Jon Bauman, Michael Bell, Jim Cummings, Rick Dees, Dick Erdman, Takayo Fisher, Pat Fraley, June Foray, Arte Johnson, Buster Jones, Aron Kincaid, Allan Lurie, Tress MacNeille, Janet May, Howard Morris, George O'Hanlon, Rob Paulsen, Michael Rye, John Stephenson, Beau Weaver, and Patric Zimmerman.

The *Flintstones*, its characters, its catchphrases, its theme music and even its flaws and shortcomings have in the last three decades surpassed the household-word category and entered the realm of folklore. A whole generation of TV viewers has reached maturity under the assumption that the Flintstones have always existed. Not quite. There had to be a starting point somewhere.

In 1959, Hanna-Barbera productions had three series in active production: *Ruff and Reddy* for NBC, *Huckleberry Hound* and *Quick Draw McGraw* for Kellogg's cereals and syndication (see individual entries on these series). John Mitchell, vice president of Hanna-Barbera's distributor Screen Gems, had a suggestion: Since a fair portion of the H-B audience was adult, why not fashion a cartoon program with adults in mind? And, after having gone the usual "humanized animals" route with such previous characters as Huck Hound and Yogi Bear, why not create a cartoon with animated people? Hanna-Barbera agreed.

This new project would be the first made-for-TV half hour prime time animated series (the two previous evening-hour cartoon shows, *CBS Cartoon Theatre* [q.v.] and *Gerald McBoing Boing* [q.v.], were mainly comprised of theatrical shorts). A lot of time and money would be invested in this effort, so Hanna-Barbera covered its bets by relying on tried-and-true formulae for the series' content, so as not to be *so* radical that audiences would tune out. It was decided that the new animated project would be a situation comedy, a very fertile genre in the late 50s and early 60s. Hanna and Barbera had always been big fans of Jackie Gleason's *The Honeymooners*, so it was determined that their new cartoon series would emulate the Gleason formula of a blowhard blue collar man, his beleaguered wife, and his wacky best pal who was also married. (This was a departure from the initial concept for the proposed Hanna-Barbera series: a takeoff on Chic Young's *Blondie* comic strip.)

Hanna-Barbera now had the premise and the characters; the next step was to create an offbeat, "probable impossible" setting which would justify the animated-cartoon format. Legend has it that the producers tried out their four principal characters as Pilgrims, Ancient Romans, Cowboys, Native Americans and Eskimos before Hanna-Barbera artists Dan Gordon and Ed Benedict came up with their preliminary "cave man" sketches. Another story goes that Hanna and Barbera were stumped for an approach to their new series until one of their artists, on a whim, began to doodle a "prehistoric" automobile.

While it's probably true that there was a lot of trial and error before the Stone Age milieu was decided upon, it's also true that the juxtaposition of modern life with the Prehistoric era had been a surefire laugh-getter since at least 1914, when Charlie Chaplin donned a bearskin and starred in *His Prehistoric Past*. As late as 1958, the newspaper comic strip *B.C.* was earning laughs by putting modern jargon in the mouths of cave dwellers. The Stone Age angle was a natural, since the Dawn of Man was historically ambiguous enough to allow a fuller array of anachronistic gags than would have been possible had Hanna-Barbera locked their characters into a more definite, better chronicled time period. And by avoiding making their characters a distinct ethnic group like Indians or Eskimos, Hanna and Barbera also avoided the burgeoning pressures from special-interest groups; after all, how can a Neanderthal Man sue? Like the *Honeymooners* format, the caveman concept was a time-tested and reasonably safe method to ensure a wide audience appeal. (Incidentally, the caveman approach must have been decided upon by the end of 1959, since the earliest pre-production press coverage of *The Flintstones* occurred in February 1960.)

The leading characters of the new series were originally called the Flagstones, a name which stuck through a two-minute "sample" cartoon (in which Fred Flagstone looked more like a talking mortar shell than the Fred we've come to know and love) until the spring of 1960. At that point, it was decided that the name was too close to the Flagstons, the family depicted in the newspaper comic strip *Hi and Lois*. There was a brief period in which the moniker "Gladstone" was considered, before this was dropped in def-

erence to the Walt Disney character Gladstone Gander and the name "Flintstone" was finalized. The principal players were Fred Flintstone, a bombastic but basically goodnatured construction worker who lived in the town of Bedrock; Wilma Flintstone, Fred's down to earth spouse; happy-go-lucky Barney Rubble, Fred's best friend and next-door neighbor; and Betty Rubble, who like *The Honeymooners'* Trixie Norton was a nondescript foil for her friend Wilma's schemes and an object for husband Barney's affection. In the project's early stages, a fifth character existed, Fred Flintstone Jr. (a fact long suppressed by Hanna-Barbera and only recently uncovered in *The Encyclopedia of Cartoon Superheroes*), but this precocious offspring only got as far as the preliminary pencil sketches and the first *Flintstones* children's book before it was determined that Fred and Wilma would remain, for the time being, childless.

Despite the enthusiastic support of Screen Gems' John Mitchell, *The Flintstones* was vetoed by both CBS and NBC: too different, too oddball. But ABC, the perennial also-ran network, was more receptive. By bucking the trends of the "big two" networks with creative counter-programming, ABC had been doing all right of late. A half hour animated cartoon was indeed "counter" enough to thrive on the basis of novelty value alone—the same novelty value that had allowed ABC to get a leg up in the business with its Western series and Disney programs. Best of all, *The Flintstones* was the perfect antidote to the anti-violence lobbyists who were then plaguing network television; as one executive encapsulated the Hanna-Barbera series, "At least it doesn't have blood and guts running in the alley."

The next challenge was to obtain prime time sponsorship—no small task, in that no pilot episode had yet been filmed, compelling the producers to use pencil sketches to promote the series; and the traditional advertisers for cartoon shows were such kiddie-oriented concerns as cereal companies and soft drink manufacturers. But after many arduous sales sessions, *The Flintstones* was picked up by Miles Laboratories, makers of One-a-Day Vitamins (who would eventually introduce a line of children's chewable vitamins designed in the shapes of the Flintstones characters), and by the Reynolds Tobacco

Company—the latter definitely *not* in the kidvid trade. And yes, the Flintstones characters were expected to hawk the wares of their sponsors in animated commercials. Some of the biggest-selling items in the current home video market are the original *Flintstones* commercials wherein Fred and Barney are seen puffing away on Winston cigarettes, musing over the pleasures of filter blend smoking.

Even with a network hookup and full sponsorship, *The Flintstones* was still a crap shoot. No one could have told at the time whether the show would be a hit or whether its lofty $65,000-per-episode budget—pretty steep by 1960 standards— would send Hanna-Barbera into receivership. But after the premier showing on September 30, 1960, of "The Flintstone Flyer" (one of the two half-hour pilots), all those involved with *The Flintstones* could rest easy. Despite very mixed reviews, the new program was a success, ranking 18th in the ratings—one notch higher than NBC's moneyspinning western *Bonanza*.

The principal appeal of *The Flintstones* was not in its animation style nor its rather timeworn plotlines but in the old reliable "time displacement" concept. Even critics who were cool to the series marvelled at the finesse and variety of the gags Hanna and Barbera were able to glean out of linking the Stone Age with the Space Age, from Fred Flintstone's suburban cave and foot-propelled "automobile" to the various and sundry modern conveniences fashioned out of stone and wood.

Throughout the phenomenal six-season run of *The Flintstones*, the program remained fresh by observing the fads, foibles and personalities of its era through a comically exaggerated Stone Age perspective. The race for space was satirized in 1960's "The Astra-Nuts." The commercialization of Rock 'n' Roll was a frequent satiric subject, from the lampoon of Elvis' Col. Parker in the first season's "The Girl's Night Out" to the *à clef* version of the Beatles' Brian Epstein ("Eppy Brianstone") in the last season's "No Biz Like Show Biz." Fast-buck film promoters were given a going over in such episodes as "The Monster from the Tar Pits" (1961) and "Fred Meets Hercurock" (1965). The status-seeking mania was attacked in "Social Climbers" (1962) and "The Big Move" (1963). A subject as serious as Alcoholics Anonymous was fair game for a witty takeoff, "Food

Anonymous," in 1961's "Fred Flintstone— Before and After." And television itself was mercilessly ribbed via spoofs of such popular series as *Peter Gunn* (redubbed "Perry Gunnite"), *Perry Mason* ("Perry Masonry"), *Burke's Law* ("Boulder's Law"), *Candid Camera* ("Peekaboo Camera"), *Sing Along with Mitch* ("Hum Along with Herman") and *Flipper* ("Dripper").

In the midst of all these takeoffs, genuine celebrities would from time to time make "guest" appearances on *The Flintstones* by supplying their voices to their cartoon-caricatured forms. The first such guest was Hoagy Carmichael, who appeared under his own name in the second-season opener "The Hit Songwriters," and even composed a special tune for that episode, "Yabba Dabba Doo," based on Fred Flintstone's frequent bellow of delight. Later guest stars had their names altered to conform with the Stone Age setting: Thus Ann-Margret became Ann-Margrock, while Tony Curtis was transformed into Stoney Curtis. In one episode, 1965's "Samantha," Elizabeth Montgomery and Dick York lent their voices to cartoon versions of their *Bewitched* characters Samantha and Darrin Stevens—the first time that a live action series ever crossed over to a non-live program. All these guest appearances added to the ongoing appeal of *The Flintstones*—and additionally set a precedent for later celebrity turns on Hanna-Barbera's *Scooby-Doo* (q.v.) in the 1970s and the Fox Network's *The Simpsons* (q.v.) in the 90s.

As a bonus, there were any number of gags predicated on the practice of using domesticated animals (including dinosaurs, perpetuating Hollywood's fractured historical conceit that Brontosauri and Pterodactyls coexisted with Mankind a million years ago) as kitchen utensils, cleaning equipment, hedge trimmers and the like. Ted Sennett's book on Hanna-Barbera includes a compilation of the clever lines spoken by these overworked creatures after performing one task or another (a bird employed as an alarm clock mutters "I'll be glad when real roosters develop. I'll be able to sleep in the morning.")—though to nonpartisans of *The Flintstones*, it seemed that far too often the writers relied on the hackneyed "Eh! It's a living."

This last warmed-over witticism points out the basic flaw of *The Flintstones*: Once it set up its engaging premise, the value of the program was occasionally worn down through repetition and laziness (it's hard to use the word "lazy" when describing a program that sprang literally from the drawing board each week, but this unfortunately was the impression left by the weaker *Flintstones* outings). Longtime viewers were inevitably disappointed by the producers' habit of making every fast-talking con man or promoter sound like Phil Silvers. Mother-in-law and rolling pin jokes abounded, none of them any more amusing or original than they'd been in the days of two-reel comedies. Punch lines would be delivered and then redelivered and re-redelivered just to make sure we didn't miss the point — a common Hanna-Barbera shortcoming. Corner cutting in the animation department (admittedly necessary) resulted in innumerable scenes in which Fred, running through his living room, scurried past the same furniture three or four times.

And one nagging question was never answered by any *Flintstones* script, causing many a sleepless night for more than one impressionable youngster: How in the world were the B.C.-vintage Flintstones able to celebrate Christmas? "Every weekly series has a few Christmas shows" seemed to be the attitude of the producers. "Who cares about our meticulously developed premise?"

Overall, however, *The Flintstones* was a remarkable achievement. It survived in a TV market resistant to anything new or different (one of its many industry awards was a citation as "Most Unique [sic] Series"), and later weathered an onslaught of copycat prime time cartoon series in the years just after its debut. Though its animation was cut to the bone and the draftsmanship only fair, audiences accepted the *Flintstones* characters as real, living beings worth caring about. And at its best, the series was one of the most consistently entertaining and succinctly written programs on TV; there was seldom any "waste footage" on a *Flintstones* episode, and rarely a dull moment. To those who watch the show today and wonder how the program could have been promoted — and accepted — as an adult cartoon series, we can only point out examples of some of the allegedly "adult" live-action series of the 1960–66 period (try sitting through *The Dennis O'Keefe Show* or *Wendy and Me*

sometime) and observe that *The Flintstones* was, by comparison, a monument to maturity.

Adding immeasurably to the likability of *The Flintstones* was its cast of voice artists. Alan Reed, whose radio credits included the Shakespearian "Fallstaff Oppenshaw" on *The Fred Allen Show*, Luigi's overbearing pal Pasquale on *Life with Luigi* and the heroine's ulcerated boss on *My Friend Irma*, brought just the right blend of bombast, bluff and big-heartedness to Fred Flintstone (after Daws Butler took a growlier whack at the character in the *Flagstones* pilot). Mel Blanc was encouraged by the producers to imitate Art Carney's Ed Norton when providing the voice for Barney Rubble (who was after all modelled on Norton) but opted instead for a nasal, chipper intonation that was perfect contrast to Fred Flintstone's gravelly gruffness — though Blanc later lowered his "Barney" voice to match the inflections of Daws Butler, who'd briefly subbed for Blanc in 1961 while Mel was recovering from his near-fatal auto accident. Jean VanderPyl, whose principal claim to fame was her portrayal of Margaret Anderson on radio's *Father Knows Best* (the role later essayed by Jane Wyatt on TV), expertly alternated cynicism with compassion as Wilma Flintstone. And Bea Benaderet brought a lot more sparkle to Betty Rubble than the thankless role deserved — at least until she left *The Flintstones* in 1963 to devote all her energies to her own starring series, *Petticoat Junction*, and was replaced in the role of Betty by onetime Dallas TV puppet-show host Gerry Johnson (who in turn would later be replaced by Gay Hartwig and Gay Autterson).

The loss of Bea Benaderet was not the only change *The Flintstones* underwent during its six seasons. Some alterations were cosmetic. As the seasons progressed, Fred Flintstone and company looked less like the rough-hewn cavepersons they appeared to be in the earlier episodes (In the first show, Fred's haircut and posture look like something out of a Paleozoic museum exhibit, while Betty Rubble dolls up for a night on the town by putting a bone in her hair) and more like streamlined, "soft" cartoon characters, suitable for conversion into Ideal Toys' line of dolls, models and board games. Also, the first two *Flintstone* seasons had a different opening sequence and theme song than those that most modern viewers are familiar with. As the soundtrack boomed forth composer Hoyt Curtin's "Rise and Shine" (which closely resembled "This Is It," the theme music of Warner Bros.' *The Bugs Bunny Show* [q.v.]), the earliest episodes of *The Flintstones* opened with scenes of Fred driving home on the freeway, stopping in the middle of downtown traffic to allow a mastodon-powered fire engine to clang past, pausing at a dry cleaner's to pick up his other suit (his *other* suit?), slowing down at a newsstand to purchase a copy of "The Daily Slate" (which he evidently never paid for), and then pulling—or crashing—into his garage. (This introduction, which ended with a segue into a plug for the sponsor of the week, was for many years available only to private collectors until it was dug up only by the Cartoon Network in May of 1994 as part of a *Flintstones* marathon.) The opening we're most accustomed to, showing Fred, Barney and their families heading to the drive-in while an offscreen chorus sings "Meet the Flintstones," wasn't introduced until season three in the fall of 1962, when the program switched from black-and-white to color telecasts.

One particular change radically altered both approach and attitude toward *The Flintstones*. In late 1962, the producers acted upon the suggestion of Joe Barbera's wife Sheila that Fred and Wilma should have a baby. After lengthy discussions concerning the baby's sex (Fred Flintstone Jr. had long been forgotten), Pebbles Flintstone made her debut on the February 22, 1963, episode, "Dress Rehearsal." This was one of the highest-rated *Flintstones* of all, as well as a particular favorite of Jean VanderPyl's, the voice of Wilma. The actress had been pregnant while recording the installment, and reportedly gave birth in real life the same day that Pebbles was born onscreen (shades of *I Love Lucy!*).

The arrival of Pebbles dictated several changes for *The Flintstones*; the most immediate was the insertion of new animated introductions for the fall 1962 episodes repeated in the summer of 1963 which alluded to Fred and Wilma's lack of children (these vignettes were telecast but once on the network, and were never syndicated). By September of 1963, viewers noted that the series had attained a whole new sensibility. There were fewer episodes involving the wives' jealousies or the

husbands' plans to skip out on the girls for a night on the town. The "rough edges" of some of the earlier programs (including lovely Wilma's startling violent streak, resulting in blows to the head for Fred or anyone else who got in her way!) were smoothed into domestic respectability. And with the oncoming surge of toys and dolls tied in with the Pebbles character—who was created essentially for merchandising purposes—it was clear that *The Flintstones* was an "adult" cartoon no longer. Once the series dropped the sponsorship of Reynolds Tobacco in 1963, picked up the more youth-oriented Welch's Grape Juice and Skippy Peanut Butter as advertisers, and moved its time slot from 8:30 P.M. to 7:30 at the beginning of its fourth season, *The Flintstones* became a kiddie show.

There were still some strong satirical barbs in the next few seasons—notably a 1964 James Bond takeoff, "Dr. Sinister," written by future *Bob Newhart Show* and *M*A*S*H* contributor Bill Idelson—but the emphasis was shifted to baby Pebbles and the Flintstones' array of animal pets, from Dino the dog-like dinosaur to a "hopasaurus" named Hoppy. As an added merchandising tool, as well as a method to keep Barney and Betty Rubble from taking a back seat to Fred's extended family, the Rubbles adopted a child of their own, a boy named Bamm Bamm—"the world's strongest baby."

By season six, it seemed as though *The Flintstones* could do nothing better than repeat ideas from its previous five seasons. But Hanna-Barbera provided a shot in the arm to the flagging property by creating The Great Gazoo, a diminutive space creature from the future assigned by his planet to observe the manners and mores of Earthlings—particularly Fred and Barney, whom Gazoo imperiously designates as "Dum Dums" (the alien's cocky demeanor was perfectly realized by Harvey Korman's voiceover work). In most of the Gazoo episodes, the little creature allows Fred and Barney to let their most craven and avaricious dreams come true, the better to prove to them that they're best off in their own back yards. Principal writer for the Great Gazoo adventures was Joanna Lee, later a leading light of the "issue of the week" school of TV movies.

The *Flintstones* ended its 156-episode prime time run in the fall of 1966 with

Wilma and (probably) her "Hooverstone."

respectable but sagging ratings. That same year, a theatrical feature length cartoon, a spy spoof titled *A Man Called Flintstone*, kept the characters in first-run public view a little bit longer. By 1967, reruns of *The Flintstones* were in local syndication, where the property made more money for Hanna-Barbera than it ever had during its tenure at ABC.

In 1970, CBS executive Fred Silverman approached Hanna-Barbera with the notion of reviving *The Flintstones* in a form that would emulate the success of CBS' teen-oriented *The Archies* (q.v.). Thus it was that Pebbles Flintstone and Bamm-Bamm Rubble abruptly attained teenager status, acquired a whole bunch of Archielike chums who could be organized into a rock band at a moment's notice, and became headliners on their own Saturday morning half-hour, *Pebbles and Bamm-Bamm*. Pebbles' voice was supplied by Sally Struthers, an unknown in 1970 who would achieve stardom with *All in the Family*, which premiered long before the first *Pebbles and Bamm-Bamm* episode made its bow on September 11, 1971. Conversely, Bamm-Bamm's voice belonged to a star on the downswing—Jay North, who

hadn't retained the heights he'd enjoyed back in the early sixties as star of *Dennis the Menace*.

None of the 20 *Pebbles and Bamm-Bamm* episodes was as memorable as the original *Flintstones* outings, nor did any hit songs evolve from the new series' incessant musical score. Where *The Flintstones* had been an innovation, *Pebbles and Bamm-Bamm* was merely product. Still, it got by on the nostalgia wave prevalent in the early seventies and lasted in network reruns for several seasons, both under its own title and as a component of a 1973 CBS series, *The Flintstones Comedy Hour*.

When Fred Silverman moved to NBC in 1978, he automatically went to work revamping its Saturday morning schedule. It was inevitable that he'd turn to Hanna-Barbera once more to bring *The Flintstones* back to life. *The New Fred and Barney Show* premiered in February of 1979. It was the mixture as before except for a few changes: Pebbles and Bamm-Bamm were returned to infant status; Henry Corden had replaced Alan Reed (who died in 1977) as the voice of Fred Flintstone; and the program wasn't very funny. The mediocrity of the new *Fred and*

Fred Flintstone meets the Stone Age head on.

Barney episodes was thrown into sharper relief by the 13 original *Flintstones* episodes included in the package to fill out the season.

The property was, however, still a valuable one; like *Pebbles and Bamm-Bamm*, *The New Fred and Barney Show* survived a number of seasons in rerun form, mostly as part of two "umbrella" programs which included a brace of 20th century characters based on comic strip originals. *Fred and Barney Meet the Thing* included component adventures based *very* loosely on a Marvel Comics creation. The star of these cartoons was nerdy high school kid Benjy Grimm, who, whenever he pressed his ring fingers together and shouted "Thing Ring, do your thing!" turned into "The Thing," an orange-colored superhero who talked like a longshoreman and looked like a walking rockpile (see the entry on *The Fanatastic Four* for a more faithful-to-the-source version of this character). *Fred and Barney Meet the Shmoo* was a 90-minuter which included not only "The Thing" but also cartoons previously aired on the H-B series *The New Shmoo* (q.v.). Just to keep the record straight, Fred and Barney and The Thing only "met" the Shmoo and the

Thing in the bumper vignettes between cartoons, never sharing an adventure. (How could they, since the characters existed in different time-frames?) Both Thing and Shmoo trod the tired cartoon-show route of crimesolving, thereby adding nothing truly creative to the *Flintstone* saga.

In 1980, NBC elongated that saga with *The Flintstones Comedy Show*, a Saturday morning hour and a half comprised of six segments: "The Flintstone Family Adventures," "Captain Caveman," "Bedrock Cops," "Pebbles, Dino and Bamm-Bamm," "Dino and the Cavemouse," and "The Frankenstones." The "Family Adventures" (three of which were later repeated in prime time) covered many fads and foibles of the 80s, including celebrity diets, energy shortages and recreational vehicles. Also reflecting the 80s was the fact that Wilma and Betty entered the work force, as reporters for the *Daily Granite*—edited, naturally, by Lou Granite. The *Granite* also figured into the "Captain Caveman" sequences, in which a humble copy boy transforms into a superhero; this was a carryover character from an earlier H-B Saturday series, *Captain*

Caveman and the Teen Angels (q.v.). "Bedrock Cops," a parody of such live-action series as *Starsky and Hutch* and *CHiPS*, cast Fred and Barney as inept reserve police officers, working shoulder to shoulder with a battalion of prehistoric Shmoos, adapted from *Fred and Barney Meet the Shmoo*. "Pebbles, Dino and Bamm-Bamm" was preoccupied with solving mysteries, in the tradition of *Scooby-Doo* (q.v.); the two *Flintstones* offspring were herein restored to teenagers after their brief reversion to babyhood on *The New Fred and Barney Show*. "Dino and the Cavemouse," developed by animation giant Tex Avery shortly before his death, allowed the Flintstones' faithful family pet his own vehicle, a wacky "Tom and Jerry" derivation. And "The Frankenstones" was a spinoff of a pair of 1980 *Flintstones* prime time specials, featuring a bizarre family of bolt-necked monsters who frequently took time out to render a rock 'n' roll tune.

"The Frankenstones" was the best of the new components, and a refreshing break from the usual "friendly monster who thinks everyone else is abnormal" formula, worn thin on such previous Hanna-Barbera outings as *The Addams Family* (q.v.). Frank Frankenstone was a sarcastic, ill-tempered creature (portrayed vocally by a specialist in ill-tempered sarcasm, Charles Nelson Reilly) who carried on a hilariously snotty feud with neighbor Fred Flintstone. The lines given to Frankenstone and his goodnatured wife Hidea (supplied with a delectable "dirty laugh" by actress Ruta Lee) were some of the sharpest and funniest heard on any *Flintstones* incarnation in years. The verbal humor was evenly matched by the grotesquely imaginative visual design of the Frankenstone home, which carried its own raincloud and was overrun with utterly indescribable stone-age monstrosities of all shapes and colors. While most of *The Flintstone Comedy Show* was banal and repetitious enough to make one wonder why 40 people were hired for the writing staff (including the brilliant surrealist magazine cartoonist Virgil "Vip" Partch), the "Frankenstones" sequences more than made up for the rest of the show with a generous supply of gut-deep laughs.

One ingredient of *The Flintstone Comedy Show* could pass as educational, had the FCC pressed the issue. Between the main components, the leading "actors" were shown giving tips to the home audience on how to draw cartoons—Hanna-Barbera's somewhat self-serving equivalent to a home learning course (did *you* know that Fred Flintstone was merely a circle piled atop two squares?). In the same vein, Fred Flintstone could be seen conducting "scrambled face" contests, inviting the kids at home to identify mixed-up photos of famous historical personalities. This was about as "interactive" as *Flintstones* would ever get.

Watching these latter-day *Flintstones* revivals is reminiscent of watching the 1970s reunion specials of *The Honeymooners*. It's nice to see familiar old friends back at work, but the writing is erratic, the production values are lavish one moment and shabby the next, the efforts to be contemporary seem strained, and everyone is beginning to get flabby and paunchy. There were some bright moments, but all in all the newer versions of *The Flintstones* were lukewarm affairs coasting on their nostalgic appeal; the same was true of the 1987 two-hour TV movie *The Jetsons Meet the Flintstones* (see also *The Jetsons*).

The most recent weekly incarnation of the property was ABC's 1986 Saturday-morning outing, *The Flintstone Kids*. All of the previous "mythology"—notably the 1964 *Flintstones* installment "Bachelor Daze," which recalled in flashback that Fred and Barney met their future wives while all of them were in their early twenties—was cast to the four winds with the *Flintstones Kids'* premise that Fred, Barney, Wilma, Betty and even Dino had all been friends in childhood. New characters introduced on this program included neighborhood bully Ronald Ratrock, wealthy little Dreamchip Bluestone, and aspiring gumshoe Philo Quartz—the first continuing black character in Flintstone history. Returnees from the *Flintstones* of old were Captain Caveman (with son Cavey Jr.) and Nate Slate, who would ultimately mature into Fred Flintstone's construction-executive boss.

Two well written segments during the 22-episode run of *Flintstone Kids* were "Flintstone Funnies," in which the leading characters were allowed to indulge in wild imaginary adventures, and "Dino's Dilemma," wherein we were told stories from a dinosaur-eye view. The best moments were the "Captain Caveman and Son" sequences, which were presented as a show within a show, representing the Flintstone Kids' favorite TV program. These marvelously offbeat vignettes played comic havoc with superhero traditions—the Captain's secret headquarters were heralded by a sign announcing that they were *not* the Captain's secret headquarters—and with the glass wall between viewers and TV characters (the Captain frequently exchanged dialogue with the Bedrock kiddies, threatening at times to stop the show if they didn't calm down).

Thanks to newly developed computer processes, the animation on *Flintstone Kids* was a notch above the haphazard Hanna-Barbera work of the late 70s and early 80s. Because it abandoned the old half-hour plotlines in favor of ten-minute vignettes, the series was capable of entertaining its target audience of children with shorter attention spans; and, every once in a while, *Flintstone Kids* had something to offer for those viewers older than ten. The series made one significant cultural contribution: An anti-drug program telecast over ABC on September 15, 1988, *The Flintstone Kids "Just Say No" Special*, which in the grand old tradition included a takeoff on a current rock celebrity, in this instance "Michael Jackstone."

Flintstones Kids was replaced with *Animal Crack-ups* by ABC in the summer of 1990, slipping into rerun syndication in September of that year as part of the weekend two-hour block *The Funtastic World of Hanna-Barbera*. At that point, 30 years into the existence of the property, one would think that all possible revival potential of *The Flintstones* would have been squeezed dry. That supposition would not take into consideration Hollywood's they'll-love-it-twice mentality. Even as this paragraph is being written in mid–1994, a live action *Flintstones* feature film is being shipped to theatres after being tackled by no fewer than 35 screenwriters, starring John Goodman as Fred Flintstone and Rick Moranis as Barney Rubble (Fred's mother-in-law is played by Elizabeth Taylor. Some men call her mad).* And we've already seen the long-anticipated "Pebbles marries Bamm-Bamm" prime time special, *I Yabba Dabba*

Do (ABC: February 7, 1993) with Pebbles walking down the aisle in an "Oscar DeLaRocka" original gown (some jokes never change)—followed after a respectable length of time by the obligatory "Pebbles is a mommy" special, *Hollyrock-a-Bye Baby* (ABC: December 5, 1993).

Thus, it's a safe bet that the original *Flintstones* and all its progeny of the 70s and 80s will pervade the consciousness of TV watchers worldwide for years to come—thanks to specials, spinoffs, local reruns, videocassettes, cable TV, movie merchandising and the neverending series of animated commercials for Post Fruity Pebbles cereal, in which Barney Rubble will continue to devise methods of depriving Fred Flintstone of his breakfast until the Crack of Doom.

FLUKEY LUKE *see* **MILTON THE MONSTER**

FLYING HOUSE *see* **SUPERBOOK**

FONZ AND THE HAPPY DAYS GANG. ABC: 11/8/1980–9/18/1982. Hanna-Barbera. Executive producers, William Hanna and Joseph Barbera. Produced by Don Jurwich. Directed by Ray Patterson, George Gordon and Rudy Zamora. Story supervisor, Ray Parker. Story editors, Tom Swale and Hank Poole. Story directors, Gary Hoffman, Emilie Kong, Dick Sebast and Don Sheppard. Animation supervisor, Bob Hathcock. Background supervision, Al Gmuer. Voice direction, Gordon Hunt and Ginny McSwain. Music by Hoyt Curtin. Music supervision by Paul DeKorte. Executives in charge of production, Jayne Barbera and Margaret Loesch. Voices: Henry Winkler (Fonzie); Ron Howard (Richie Cunningham); Donny Most (Ralph Malph); Frank Welker (Mr. Cool); Didi Conn (Cupcake); and Marlene Aragon, Rene Auberjonois, Ken Mars, Amanda McBroom, Mitzi McCall, Don Messick, Henry Polic, Stanley Ralph Ross, Kathryn Leigh Scott and Susan Silo.

Happy Days was one of those "pantheon" sitcoms that, like *I Love Lucy*, *The Honeymooners*, *All in the Family* and *Cheers*, really needs no introduction. On the offchance that you're not familiar with the series, I'll just note that *Happy Days*

The live-action Flintstones turned out to be one of the major hits of the summer 1994 movie season. And Taylor was terrific!

was the story of a late–1950s family called the Cunninghams, and of Richie Cunningham's closest friend, a leatherjacketed garage mechanic born Arthur Fonzarelli, but better known as "Fonzie." From 1974 through 1983, *Happy Days* was the premier mortgage-lifter for the previously underdog ABC network; it also made an international celebrity out of an introspective young character actor named Henry Winkler, who played the gloriously extroverted "Fonz."

A half hour cartoon version was a "given" in this case. What was suprising was that it took so long to make it to the air. Hanna-Barbera's *Fonz and the Happy Days Gang* debuted over ABC in the fall of 1980 — by which time the parent *Happy Days*, though still a ratings reaper, had cooled a bit as a national sensation. This may be one of the reasons why *Fonz and the Happy Days Gang* survived only two seasons and 24 episodes, while *Happy Days* ultimately clocked in at 254 programs. The other reasons all had to do with that familiar intangible known as "Quality."

Fonz and the Happy Days Gang offered cartoon caricatures of Richie Cunningham, Fonzie, and their mutual friend Ralph Malph (but not very accurate renditions; Richie, for example, looked like Dick York from *Bewitched*). The actors who originated these roles — Ron Howard, Henry Winkler, and Donny Most — were engaged to do the voiceover work, with "guest appearance" billing; intriguingly, Howard and Most had already left the nighttime *Happy Days* in 1980 to pursue newer career vistas. Hanna-Barbera performed its usual Saturday morning makeover by taking Fonz and his pals out of their natural habitat of Milwaukee, Wisconsin, in 1957 and hurling them into a flying time machine, piloted by "girl from the future" Cupcake (her voice supplied by Didi Conn, who like Henry Winkler was a darling of the 1970s thanks to her work in the feature film *Grease*). Cupcake could shoot rainbow-colored rays from her fingers and was able to conjure up instant disguises for Fonz and his gang — usually such inefficient cover-ups as Groucho glasses and vegetable-shaped bodysuits. She was also prone to expostulating space-age expletives like "Travelling time-warps!", "Cosmic Comets," and (the one that was the limit of this viewer's patience) "Leaping Logarithms!"

And what would a Hanna-Barbera live-TV derivation be without a funny talking dog? The resident canine of *Fonz and the Happy Days Gang*, in emulation of master Fonzie, went by the name of "Mr. Cool," even copying Fonz's familiar "Heeeeyyy!" thumbs-up gesture (I didn't know that dogs *had* thumbs). Mr. Cool was the series' comedy relief. Comedy relief on a comedy show....

Inasmuch as this cartoon half-hour weekly transported the *Happy Days* kids to various moments of world history, ABC was able to pass the series off as educational. In a way, this was true: Watch *Fonz and the Happy Days Gang* and you'll learn your lesson in a real hurry. Actually, we can be a little fairer than that. The fine background work by Art Gmuer was careful to convey accurately the farflung locations and time periods in each episode, and the costuming of the non-*Happy Days Gang* supporting characters was designed with proper historical and cultural detail (except for the female characters, who generally bared more leg than was suitable for most of the episode's time-frames).

All the positive aspects of *Fonz and the Happy Days Gang* were, however, compromised by the flat animation work and the poorly drawn principal characters. As an added handicap, in order to save time preparing animation cels, the same poses and gestures were recycled for each episode. Maybe that's why Fonz and his buddies breezed through their many perils with the same pasty grins on their faces. (See also *The Mork and Mindy/Laverne and Shirley/Fonz Hour*.)

FOO FOO. Syndicated: 1961. Halas and Batchelor/Interstate Television. Produced and directed by John Halas and Joy Batchelor.

Hungarian-born John Halas and his wife Joy Batchelor maintained the best and busiest animation house in England in the 1950s and 60s, producing everything from short subjects to feature films like *Animal Farm* (1956) and *Ruddigore* (1967). But since most of their output was commissioned work for industrial firms and public service organizations, Halas and Batchelor tended to follow the dictates of their clients, and never quite developed a distinctive style of their own.

Foo Foo, a series of 32 five-minute cartoons produced in 1960 and distributed to the U.S. in 1961, was typical of the Halas and Batchelor styleless style. This package of shorts, about a cute little transparent man living in a pencil-sketch world with his chubby girlfriend Mimi and his chief rival Gogo, closely resembled the output of the UPA studios (see *Dick Tracy* and *Mister Magoo*), while the character design was reminiscent of Ernest Pintoff's *Flebus*, a theatrical series distributed by Terrytoons. *Foo Foo* was released by Interstate Television in tandem with another Halas-Batchelor project, a stop-motion series called *Snip Snap* (q.v.).

FOOFUR. NBC: 9/13/1986–9/3/1988. Hanna-Barbera/Sepp International Studios. Executive producers, Freddy Monnickendam, William Hanna and Joseph Barbera. Executive in charge of production, Jayne Barbera. Created by Phil Mendez. Produced by Paul Sabella. Supervising director, Ray Patterson. Directed by Paul Sommer, John Kimball, Bob Goe and Oscar Dufau. Animation directors, Jay Sarbry, Frank Andrina, Joan Drake, Oliver Callahan, Rick Leon, Don Patterson, Joanna Romersa, James T. Walker. Story editors, Mark Young, Arthur Alsberg, Don Nelson. Creative design, Iwao Takamoto. Story directors, Bob Taylor, Rhoydon Shushido, Mitch Schauer, Lew Marshall, Richard Bowman, Jesse Casio, Roy Wilson, Joel Seibel, Jim Willoughby, John Brown. Recording director, Roy Hunt. Music by Hoyt Curtin; musical direction by Paul DeKorte. Animation facilities, Toei Animation. Voices: Frank Welker (Foofur); Christina Lange (Rocky); Susan Tolsky (Annabell); Pat Carroll (Hazel); Don Messick (Pepe); Allan Melvin (Chucky); Susan Blu (Dolly); David Doyle (Mel); Jonathan Schmock (Fritz-Carlos); Dick Gautier (Louis); Chick Vennera (Sam); Peter Cullen (Baby); Bill Callaway (Burt); Eugene Williams (Fencer); Susan Silo (Mrs. Escrow); Michael Bell (Harvey); and David Ackroyd, Roscoe Lee Browne, Hamilton Camp, Cheryl Chase, Peter Cullen, Jim Cummings, Jennifer Darling, Leo DeLyon, Walker Edmiston, Miriam Flynn, George Furth, Henry Gibson, Scott Grimes, Edan Gross, Jonathan Harris, Phil Hartman, Jerry Houser, Vincent Howard, Allan Lurie, Jim MacGeorge, Robert Mandan, Terry McGovern, Brian Mitchell, Lynne Moody, Pat Musick, Louis Nye,

Rob Paulsen, Percy Rodrigues, Alexandra Stoddart, Larry Storch, Sal Viscuso, B. J. Ward, Lennie Weinrib.

Foofur was a blue, bony, Phil Harris-like bloodhound who inherited an old mansion in the town of Willowby from his late master, and then with the help of his niece Rocky turned the place into a haven for his down-and-out buddies. A true democrat, Foofur opened the doors of his home to a variety of species: Louis the bulldog, a former "street gang" member who sounded like *The Honeymooners'* Ralph Kramden; Annabell the vain and flighty sheepdog; foreign-accented Fritz-Carlos and Carol Channing soundalike Hazel, the two resident "aristocrats"; and even a jive-talking alley cat named Fencer.

Many of Foofur's half hour adventures (two seasons' worth) concerned his ongoing hide-and-seek with Mrs. Escrow, a ditsy real estate agent who wanted to sell the mansion. Mrs. Escrow was unaware of the dogs' presence, and couldn't understand what it was that scared potential customers away from the house. Escrow's scrawny chihuahua Pepe *did* understand, however, and used this leverage to exact blackmail from Foofur, though his skullduggery usually backfired. Other antagonists included the three Rat Brothers, who insisted that they owned the mansion via "squatter's rights" — though the Rats could be counted upon to align themselves with Foofur when the dogs were imperiled by animal-abusing humans.

The second of Hanna-Barbera's collaborations with Belgian comic book artist Freddy Monnickendam (see *The Snorks*), *Foofur* was the latest in a series of "warm and fuzzy" cartoons virtually begging to be taken to the children's hearts and homes in the form of dolls, toys and action figures. In other words, it was the *Smurfs* (q.v.) or *Pound Puppies* (q.v.), 1986 edition. That *Foofur* occasionally transcended its derivative nature was a tribute to the Hanna-Barbera staffers, who injected the series with sundry endearing little touches. A few personal favorites: pedigreed pooch Fritz-Carlos' absurd handlebar mustache and Continental habit of calling everyone "darling"; the theme song of the old TV series *Secret Agent* used as background music during one of Foofur's covert rescue missions; a basic-training takeoff in which the dogs were seen attacking dummies dressed as cops; and a circus monkey named Huxley.

FRAGGLE ROCK (a.k.a. JIM HENSON'S FRAGGLE ROCK).

NBC: 9/12/1987–9/3/1988. Jim Henson/ Marvel Productions. Executive producers, Jim Henson and Margaret Loesch. Coproducer and conceptual design, Michael K. Frith. Produced by Mike Jones. Story editors, John Semper and Cynthia Friedlob. Supervising director, Ray Lee. Key director, Kim Peterson. Directed by Vonnie Batson, Rudy Cataldi, Charlie Downs, Eileen Dunn, Bob Kirk, Al Kouzel, Margaret Nichols, Stan Phillips, Tom Ray, Bob Trent, Neal Warner, John Wilson, Warren Batchelder. Score composed and conducted by Rob Walsh. Produced in association with Akom Production Co. Production supervisor, Jean Mac-Curdy and Jim Graziano. Executive in charge of production, Lee Gunther. Voices: Bob Bergen (Wembley); Townsend Coleman (Gobo/Archibald/Wrench); Barbara Goodson (Wingnut); Mona Marshall (Mokey/Cotterpin); Patti Parris (Ma Gorg); Rob Paulsen (Boober/ Sprocket/Marjory); Pat Pinney (Travelling Matt/Pa Gorg/Flange); John Stephenson (Doc/Philo/Gunge); Stu Rosen (Storyteller).

Fraggle Rock, a live action half hour series from muppet meister Jim Henson, debuted on January 10, 1983 — the first children's series released exclusively to Home Box Office (HBO). The only "real" person in the proceedings was a scientist named Doc, beneath whose house dwelt a curious, miniature race of cloth characters, all of whom lived within a single rock. The 18-inch-tall, radish-loving Fraggles were carefree and impulsive; their six-inch friends the Doozers were the industrious "worker ants" of the community; and the Gorgs—Ma, Pa, Junior—were the gross, despotic and fairly stupid ruling class (or so they believed) of Fraggle Rock. As always, Henson was able to balance the elements of the series that would most appeal to children with the more mature asides designed to amuse the adults; prominent in this latter category was Henson's use of movie-technician jargon for the character names as Gobo, Travelling Matt—whose muppet counterpart introduced the cartoons—and Sprocket. Ever stressing the basic values of friendship,

trust, cooperation and honesty, *Fraggle Rock* was a marked contrast to HBO's standard R-rated fare, and as such was a hit for six seasons with viewers and children's-television activists alike. In 1986, the 96-episode *Fraggle Rock* earned an even larger audience share when reruns commenced over the TBS basic cable service.

Jim Henson and Marvel Productions assembled 1987's half hour cartoon version of *Fraggle Rock*, utilizing many of the same technicians, artists and educational advisors who'd made a hit out of Henson/ Marvel's *Muppet Babies* (q.v.)—and, by rights, should have had a lifespan comparable to that earlier series. The inclusion of all the favorite characters and of one well-written original song per adventure (some stories ran the full 30 minutes, others only half that time) was well within the Henson tradition of quality.

Alas, NBC's animated *Fraggle Rock* lost much of the charm of the original by the very virtue of its being animated. Without the presence of the "live" muppet characters, the special magic of unbridled movement and fullfledged characterization manifested in a group of cloth creations was gone, and the Fraggles were just another bunch of furry little cartoon drawings. The series also had the miserable luck to be scheduled opposite CBS's blockbusting *Pee-wee's Playhouse*—and since this was long before Pee-wee Herman's unfortunate night out at the movies, viewers were far more interested in "I know you are—but what am I?" than in the adventures of the Fraggles. Only 24 new *Fraggle Rocks* were produced before Henson and Marvel decided to concentrate the bulk of their energies on the still-thriving *Muppet Babies. Fraggle Rock* reruns would resume in the early 1990s as part of the Disney Channel weekend schedule.

FRAIDY CAT see UNCLE CROC'S BLOCK

FRANKENSTEIN JR. AND THE IMPOSSIBLES. CBS: 9/10/1966–9/7/ 1968.

—THE SPACE GHOST/FRANKENSTEIN JR. SHOW. NBC: 11/27/1976–9/3/ 1977. Hanna-Barbera. Produced by Joseph Hanna and William Barbera. Directed by Charles Nichols. Music by Hoyt Curtin; musical direction by Ted Nichols. Voices: Ted Cassidy (Frankenstein Jr.); Dick Beals

(Buzz Conroy); John Stephenson (Prof. Conroy); Don Messick (Multi-Man); Paul Frees (Fluid Man); Hal Smith (Coil Man). (See also *Space Ghost and Dino Boy.*)

Actually, the only true Frankenstein Jr. would be Basil Rathbone, who played the title role in the 1939 feature film *Son of Frankenstein.* But Hanna-Barbera, like everyone else, ignored the fact that Mary Shelley's original Frankenstein was the scientist and not the scientist's monster creation. So it was that H-B's *Frankenstein Jr.* was himself a monster of sorts: a 30-foot-tall mechanical man, outfitted with the regulation superhero cape and mask — undoubtedly to disguise the fact that he was a 30-foot-tall mechanical man. Junior could blast off like a rocket, shoot heat-rays from his eyes, and take on a battalion of villains all at once — but only when activated by a radar ring worn by the monster's inventor, Buzz Conroy (himself a "Junior," the son of Professor Conroy). Buzz and Junior would take flight from their mountaintop headquarters with a cry of "Allakazoom" (I don't remember *any* of this in the Mary Shelley novel), the better to do battle with such minions of evil as Dr. Spectro and Mr. Menace (Dennis' father?). Why a 30-foot robot would need an arsenal of "James Bond" style weaponry is best left to wiser heads than ours, but such was the case in *Frankenstein Jr.,* which after all *was* played primarily for laughs. (Buzz called his pet monster "Frankie," and the villains were given to growling "Curses!")

The Impossibles, who appeared in two seven-minute adventures during each *Frankenstein Jr. and the Impossibles* half hour, were moptopped members of a rock group. Well, not really a rock group. They were really three superheroes named Fluid Man, Multi-Man and Coil Man, who pretended to be a rock group called the Impossibles in order to thwart criminals in secret. Actually, the trio looked more like teenaged versions of the Three Stooges (Coil Man was the fat one, Multi-Man the "Larry" and Fluid Man the moptopped leader of the group), whose unique abilities of turning one's legs into springs (that was Coil Man), duplicating oneself into infinity (Multi-Man) and self-liquifying (Fluid Man) enabled them to poke and jab such miscreants as the Fiendish Fiddler and the Diabolical Daubler. Is it necessary at this point to observe that ABC's live-action *Batman* premiered some nine months before the appearance of *Frankenstein Jr. and the Impossibles?* Oh, before we forget; the Impossibles drove the "Impossicar" and communicated with their superior, a guy named Big D, through a two-way TV concealed in the band's guitar.

The principal source for the above entry was Ted Sennett's book *The Art of Hanna-Barbera.* What's frightening is that I remembered many of the details concerning the 18-episode *Frankenstein Jr. and the Impossibles* without Ted Sennett's help — and confirmed these memories through recent viewings of the series over cable TV. (See *Space Ghost and Dino Boy* for information on the all-rerun package *The Space Ghost/ Frankenstein Jr. Show*).

FRED AND BARNEY MEET THE SHMOO and **FRED AND BARNEY MEET THE THING** *see* **THE FLINT-STONES**

FREEDOM FORCE *see* **TARZAN**

FROGGER *see* **SATURDAY SUPER-CADE**

THE FUNKY PHANTOM. ABC: 9/11/1971–9/1/1972. Hanna-Barbera. Produced and directed by William Hanna and Joseph Barbera. Music by John Sangster. Voices: Daws Butler (Jonathan Muddlemore, aka "Musty"); Mickey Dolenz (Skip); Tommy Cook (Augie); Tina Holland (April); Jerry Dexter, and Julie Bennett.

More ghosts and crimefighting kids from Hanna-Barbera, who'd cornered this particular market with *Scooby-Doo* (q.v.), *Funky Phantom* might be considered a derivation of the 1946 Abbott and Costello comedy *The Time of Their Lives* — if it wasn't for the fact that *Time of Their Lives* was itself a derivation (of sorts) of Oscar Wilde's *The Canterville Ghost.*

The "Phantom" was Jonathan Muddlemore, a Revolutionary-era New Englander who in 1776 had escaped from the Redcoats by scooting into an old mansion and hiding in a grandfather clock. The clock door became securely locked, entrapping poor Muddlemore. Nearly two centuries later, the ghost of Muddlemore was still imprisoned in the clock — until three teenagers, seeking shelter from a storm, stumbled into the old mansion. In a twinkling, the teen trio — April, Skip and Augie — found the clock and freed the shivering spectre. To make amends for his long-ago cowardice, Muddlemore (nicknamed "Musty") aided the teens in fighting 20th century villains — all the while regaling them with his name-dropping anecdotes about the Colonial founding fathers.

Yes, there were funny animals. The kids had a dog named Elmo, while Muddlemore owned a cat named Boo, who like his master had been entombed in the clock and was himself a ghost. Yes, the kids had a jalopy with a cute name. It was a jeep called the Looney Duney. Yes, this was a Hanna-Barbera comedy cartoon of the 1970s, and as such had an omnipresent laughtrack. And yes, the grownups despised *Funky Phantom*. "Poor history — poorer show," clucked the National Association for Better Broadcasting. The kids weren't too impressed either; *Funky Phantom* spooked its way through only 17 episodes before being cancelled after one season. Reruns showed up on *The Godzilla/Dynomutt Hour with Funky Phantom* (see *The Godzilla Show*) in 1980. This time *Funky Phantom* dematerialized after a mere two months. Who says children have no taste?

THE FUNNY COMPANY. Syndicated: 1963. Funny Company Productions/Ken Snyder Productions/Mattel. Associate producer, Leo Salkin. Animation producer, Sam Nicholson. Voices: Dick Beals (Buzzer Bell/Shrinkin' Violet); Robbie Lester (Polly Plum); Nancy Wible (Merry Twirter/Jasper National Park); Ken Snyder (Terry Dactyl); Hal Smith (Dr. Todd Goodheart/Belly Laguna/Dr. Van Upp); Tom Thomas (Broken Feather); Bud Hiestad (Weisenheimer).

When the call went forth in early 1963 for children's programs with an educational slant, Mattel Toys' advertising representative Cy Schneider teamed with cartoon producer Ken Snyder to come up with a product that would allow the educational angle to be properly sugarcoated with solid entertainment value. Digging deep into past inspirations, Schneider and Snyder decided to revive the old "Little Rascals" kid's club format for their foray into what they labelled "edu-tainment" — and the result was *The Funny Company*.

Operating from an underground clubhouse, the Company, led by an enterprising lad named Jasper National Park, organized community service activities, public performances, fundraising work projects and instructional field trips for themselves — and of course, for those of us out in videoland. Jasper's childhood cohorts included Buzzer Bell, Polly Plum, Merry Twirter and Shrinkin' Violet (so named for her tendency to miniaturize whenever she was frightened). Adult chums and chaperones included kindly inventor Dr. Todd Goodheart and a brace of Native Americans named Super Chief (due to the fact that the Chief "spoke" only with the baleful sound of a railroad horn) and Broken Feather. The club's mascot was Terry Dactyl, a small flying lizard who cracked jokes and performed celebrity imitations (he did a mean Stan Laurel). Complicating all the Funny Company's do-goodery were villains along the lines of mad doctor Belly Laguna and mobster Cheese Lasagna.

The centerpiece of all 260 *Funny Company* escapades was the Weisenheimer, a talking computer which, in typical mid-1960s fashion, was almost as large as the clubhouse itself. The Weisenheimer would dispense live-action educational film clips (generally culled from existing industrial and promotional shorts) while narrating the cogent points of interest in each film. Contrary to earlier published reports, these filmclips were not offered as buffers between the five-minute *Funny Company* episodes, but were in fact incorporated in the middle of each cartoon itself. Thus the cartoon was the wraparound to the "live" film, rather than the other way around.

The jokes on *Funny Company* weren't bad, the character and background design were a positive echo of the best of UPA (even if the limited animation technique was less than positive), and the cartoons were welcomed with open arms by those adult special interest groups who'd demanded "edu-tainment" in the first place. Mattel barter-sponsored *Funny Company* in most major markets, seeing to it that the series would get choice timeslots (preferably on stations with colorcasting facilities), excellent press coverage and strong promotional tie-ins. Each station running the series was sent a packet of *Funny Company* paraphernalia, from

"Keep Smiling" buttons (invoking the Company's motto) to 45-rpm recordings of the cartoons' opening and closing theme music. *Funny Company* was successful enough to establish a whole subgenre of cartoons enhanced with live-action instructional vignettes, as witness *The Big World of Little Adam, Max the 2000 Year Old Mouse, The Wonderful Stories of Professor Kitzel* and *The Spirit of Freedom* (see individual entries on these series).

THE FUNTASTIC WORLD OF HANNA-BARBERA. Syndicated: 1985. Hanna-Barbera. Executive producers: William Hanna, Joseph Barbera, Jayne Barbera.

Telecast on Saturdays and Sundays, *The Funtastic World of Hanna-Barbera* was the first effort by any cartoon manufacturer to create a "block" of syndicated programming: a package of several separate half hour series designed to be telecast one after another in the course of a single morning or afternoon. Judging by the copycat efforts of other producers (see *Super Sunday, The Comic Strip* and *Marvel Action Universe*), and Disney's ultimate adaptation of the "block" concept to include daily rather than weekly series (see *Bonkers, Chip 'n' Dale's Rescue Rangers, Darkwing Duck, DuckTales, Goof Troop* and *Tale Spin*), *Funtastic World* was a hit, putting Hanna-Barbera back in the "innovator" category they'd occupied back in the days of *Huckleberry Hound* (q.v.) and *The Flintstones* (q.v.).

For details on the various *Funtastic World* components from 1985 through 1993, see separate entries on the following: *Don Coyote and Sancho Panda, Fantastic Max, The Flintstones* (for *The Flintstone Kids*), *The Further Adventures of Superted, Galtar and the Golden Lance, Jonny Quest, The Midnight Patrol, Paddington Bear, The Paw Paws, The Pirates of Dark Water, Richie Rich, Sky Commanders, The Snorks, Swat Kats, Two Stupid Dogs, Yogi Bear* (for *Yogi's Treasure Hunt* and *Yo, Yogi*), and *Young Robin Hood.*

THE FURTHER ADVENTURES OF DR. DOOLITTLE. NBC: 9/12/1970–9/4/1971. DePatie/Freleng/20th Century–Fox. Produced by David DePatie and Friz Freling. Directed by Arthur Leonardi. Music by Doug Goodwin and Eric Rogers. Voices: Robert Holt (Dr.

Doolittle); Hal Smith (Tommy Stubbins); Len Weinrib (Sam Scurvy); Don Messick, Barbara Towers (Various Animals); Ronnie Fellon, Colin Julian, Annabell (Grasshoppers).

It's astounding that 20th Century–Fox, after nearly collapsing under the weight of its blunderbuss musical film version of Hugh Lofting's *Dr. Doolittle* (1967), would want to perpetuate the property by releasing a "Further Adventures" cartoon series in 1970. Evidently the contracts had already been signed and the DePatie-Freleng animated talent had already been committed to the series. The *Further Adventures of Dr. Doolittle* was better than the cinematic disaster which inspired it, but only by default.

Dr. Doolittle, it will be remembered, was a kindly British medico who developed a method of talking to animals simply by learning their various languages. The original Lofting novels took Doolittle on worldwide journeys aboard his little sailing vessel, the *Flounder*, interacting with sundry animal and human affairs. The cartoon version complicated things with such Saturday-morning "improvements" as a megalomaniac villain named Sam Scurvy and a "lunar kitten" named Mooncat. Musical contributions were offered by an anthropomorphic soft-rock group called The Grasshoppers. Seventeen half hours came and went before *The Further Adventures of Dr. Doolittle* went no further.

Predictably, adult critics were displeased, echoing the National Association for Better Broadcasting's assessment of *Dr. Doolittle* as "formula junk." Some complainers went after the series for what could be regarded as the wrong reason; these were the people who moaned that the cartoon series was a "travesty" of the Hugh Lofting novels. Did those people really want to see a weekly reenactment of the implicit defense of British imperialism and class snobbery contained in the original *Dr. Doolittle*? One wonders what critical reaction would have been to an animated rendition of the infamous episode in the first *Doolittle* book, wherein the good doctor was roundly congratulated for coming up with a scientific formula which turned black men white! (See also *The Voyages of Dr. Doolittle*.)

THE FURTHER ADVENTURES OF SUPERTED. Syndicated: 1988.

Hanna-Barbera/Telin, Ltd. Executive producers, William Hanna and Joseph Barbera. Executive in charge of production, Jayne Barbera. Supervising producers, Jeff Segal and Bruce David Johnson. Produced by Charles Grosvenor and Licia Therese Rester. Story editors, Kelly Ward and Mark Young. Supervising director, Ray Patterson. Directed by Bob Alvarez, Bob Sommers. Animation directors, Oliver Callahan, Bob Alvarez, Joanna Romersa. Recording directors: Gordon Hunt (U.S.), Mike Young (U.K.). Main character design by Dave Edwards. Animation supervisors, John Rice and Roman Klys. Music by John Debney and Hoyt Curtin. Produced in association with S4C and Siriol Animation. Original character copyright 1982 Petalcraft. Voices: Danny Cooksey (Superted); Patrick Fraley (Spottyman); Charles Adler, George Ball, Earl Boen, Hamilton Camp, Phillip Clarke, Peter Cullen, Bernard Erhard, Jerry Houser, Georgi Irene, Marvin Kaplan, Brian Mitchell, Pat Musick, B. J. Ward, Frank Welker. (Earlier reports that Victor Spinetti worked on the American version of *Superted* are not borne out by the closing credits.)

Introduced in the 1988-89 *Funtastic World of Hanna Barbera* (q.v.) weekend lineup, *The Further Adventures of Superted* was the Americanized sequel to a 1979 TV series coproduced in Cardiff, Wales, by Siriol Animation Studio and the Disney Company. The original economically produced Welsh 10-minute episodes, distributed to the U.S. in 1983 exclusively on home videotape, involved a defective stuffed teddy bear who was taken under the wing of a "Spottyman" (who looked like a banana with a mohawk haircut) from the planet Spot, and then endowed with super powers courtesy of cosmic dust from a magic cloud. With his newfound powers came full "hero" costume, jet-powered boots and all, which Superted wore *under* his bear pelt. Battling such baddies as Texas Pete, the Skeleton and the Bulk and spewing such expletives as "Bubbling blackmange!" and "Pulsating prunes," Superted and his friends Spottyman, Spotty's sister Blotch, and Speckle the Hoparoo, carried on the noble deadpan tradition of British nonsense humor. *Superted* boasted such added attractions as a self-enamored *Danger Mouse* (q.v.) type narrator, and the top-rank voicework of

gifted British comic actors Roy Kinnear and Victor Spinetti.

If Hanna-Barbera's half hour *Further Adventures of Superted* didn't quite scale the hilarious heights of its Welsh predecessor, it wasn't from lack of trying. The animation — farmed out by Hanna-Barbera to a Central American studio — was fuller and more ornate than the original, with Superted's elaborate bear-shaped treehouse and two-way TV communications system effectively yanking the property out of the humble crags of Cardiff and plunking it into the garish, creature comfort-attuned Hollywood Hills (Superted matched his new California-ized surroundings with the All American Boy voiceover work of Danny Cooksey). The storylines likewise played to a more cosmopolitan audience, eschewing the droll adventure-story satire of the Welsh version in favor of Hanna-Barbera's own raucous brand of pop culture parody. One of the more engaging *Further Adventures* had Texas Pete committing several seemingly unrelated crimes — all logically linking up to his desire to become a rhinestone-studded country and western singing star.

But in gaining slickness, the 13-episode *Further Adventures of Superted* lost the intimate charm of the Siriol version, while its lampoonish emulation of the *Star Wars* films turned the series into merely the latest of a long line of similarly inspired cartoon weeklies. Thankfully, a few holdover moments from the Welsh *Superted* poked through the canvas from time to time, not the least of which was the pompously omnipotent narrator. Some of the better bits belonged to Texas Pete's minion Skeleton, a whining "nance" character who delivered lines like "I'm tired of working my fingers to the bone. What do I have to show for it? Bony fingers." *Further Adventures of Superted* never quite matched the consistent humor level of its Siriol days, but it definitely had its moments.

THE GALAXY GOOF-UPS see **HUCKLEBERRY HOUND and YOGI BEAR**

GALAXY HIGH SCHOOL. CBS: 9/13/1986-9/5/1987; 1/2/1988-8/27/1988. TMS Entertainment. Executive producer, Yutaka Fujioka. Produced by Barry Glasser and Gerald Baldwin. Developed by

Chris Columbus (creative consultant). Story editors: Ken Koonce and David Wiemers. Music composed and performed by Don Felder. Voices: Susan Blu (Aimee Brighttower); Hal Rayle (Doyle Cleverlobe); John Stephenson (Beef Bonk); Pat Carroll (Biddy McBrain/Katrina); Nancy Cartwright (Gilda Gossip/ Flat Freddy); Gary Christopher (Earl Eccchhh); Gino Conforti (Ollie Oilslick/ Reggie Unicycle); Jennifer Darling (Wendy Garbo/Booey Bubblehead); Pat Fraley (Coach Frogface/Sludge); Henry Gibson (Aimee's Locker/Doyle's Locker); Danny Mann (The Creep); Neilson Ross (Rotten Ronald); David L. Lander (Milo De Venus); Howard Morris (Prof. Mac-Greed/Prof. Icenstein/Luigi LaBounci).

Galaxy High School took the "multiculturalism" encouraged in late-1980s children's television to the nth degree. Teenaged earthlings Doyle Cleverlobe and Aimee Brighttower (the series characters' personality traits were implicit in their names, as the above cast list will indicate) found themselves exchange students in an extraterrestrial high school on the Flotor asteroid; here they came face to face not only with a myriad of races, colors and cultures, but with animals, vegetables and minerals as well. The sophomores were tomatoes (not "killer" tomatoes—that wouldn't come until 1990), the tentacled class gossip dished her dirt with five mouths, the school bully was a choice cut of beef, the kids' lockers talked back to them, the physical education coach was a frog, and the student body included a humanized unicycle, a "flat" boy, and a blob of oil. That these many diverse types could peacefully coexist was a point that had been made for years by the various incarnations of the live-action series *Star Trek*—though never quite in such broadly comic terms.

The best of the thirteen half hour *Galaxy High Schools* was a refreshingly nondogmatic antidrug endeavor, "Brain Blaster." The episode won a Humanitas award for the series' story editors, Ken Koonce and David Wiemers, who later moved to Disney's *DuckTales* (q.v.).

THE GALAXY RANGERS see ADVENTURES OF THE GALAXY RANGERS

GALTAR AND THE GOLDEN LANCE. Syndicated: 1985 (as part of

FUNTASTIC WORLD OF HANNA-BARBERA). Hanna-Barbera. Executive producers, William Hanna and Joseph Barbera. Produced by Bob Dranko and Berny Wolf. Creative supervisor, Joe Taritero. Story editor, Neal Barbera. Creative design, Iwao Takamoto. Supervising director, Ray Patterson. Directed by Don Lusk, Ray Patterson and Alan Zaslove. Animation directors, "Lefty" Callahan, Bob Goe and Jay Sarbry. Story directors, Floyd Norman, Alex Fierro, Bob Singer, Rick Estrada, Mike Vosberg, Rich Chidlaw. Recording director, Gordon Hunt. Musical director, Hoyt Curtin. Animation facilities, Wang Film Production Co., Ltd., Cuckoo's Nest Studios. Executives in charge of production, Jayne Barbera and Jean MacCurdy. Voices: Lou Richards (Galtar); Mary McDonald Lewis (Galeeta); Brock Peters (Tormack); Bob Arbogast (Ither); Barry Dennen (Krimm); George DiCenzo (Otar); Don Messick (Pandat); Bob Frank (Rak); David Mendenhall (Zork); Frank Welker (Tuk/Thork/ Koda); and Chris Afarian, Joe Alaskey, Jon Bauman, Michael Bell, Barry Dennen, Joan Gardner, Helen Hunt, Roth Manning.

For its inaugural 1985-86 season, *Funtastic World of Hanna-Barbera* offered as one of its components *Galtar and the Golden Lance*, an outer space "sword and sorcery" affair featuring a thonged-and-breastplated superhunk named Galtar. Searching for the vile Tormack (this series' resident "Darth Vader," distinguished by his amber-tinted artificial eye and cobalt blue beard), the despot responsible for the death of his parents, Galtar aligned himself with beautiful princess Goleeta and her feisty little brother Zork. Goleeta and Zork also had a score to settle with Tormack, who'd stolen their magical golden shield. Tormack in turn coveted Galtar's equally magical double-edged golden lance, for whosoever possessed both lance and shield would be all-powerful, omnipotent, and all that other J.R.R. Tolkien stuff.

Throughout *Galtar*'s 20 half-hour episodes, both Galtar and Tormack battled an unending parade of mutants and extraterrestrials in their quest to vanquish each other. And both hero and villain had to deal as best they could with a brace of comic relief dwarves: Rak and Tuk, bumbling father-and-son mercenaries who excused their chronic doublecrossing as "the

Dramatis personae: *Galtar and the Golden Lance.*

only work we know." As further indication that Hanna-Barbera hadn't completely abandoned comedy on *Galtar and the Golden Lance,* several of the "heavies" (the dwarves, Tormack's grovelling sorceror Krimm) lisped and sputtered their dialogue in the juicy tradition of such past cartoon giants as Sylvester the Cat and Daffy Duck.

Galtar and the Golden Lance was a conspicuously elaborate and richly detailed work from Hanna-Barbera, which by the mid–1980s had just begun to extricate itself from its 1970s reputation for rigormortis animation, sketchy artwork and uninspired character design. It was the beginning of a new era for Hanna-Barbera, whose animation quality (by way of its

Taiwanese production facilities) picked up tremendously and kept improving through-out the early 1990s. And though it would win no awards for originality—the story-line covered territory previously staked out by Conan the Barbarian in the pulp novels and comic books, Luke Skywalker in the *Star Wars* movies, and the hero of Marvel's cartoon syndie *He Man and the Masters of the Universe* (q.v.)—*Galtar and the Golden Lance* did manage to cop a 1988 Golden Reel Award for Animation and Sound Editing.

GARFIELD AND FRIENDS. CBS: 9/17/1988–. United Media/Mendelson Pro-ductions in association with Film Roman/ Paws, Inc. Produced by Bob Curtis and Bob Nesler. Directed by Jeff Hall and Tom Ray. Written by Mark Evanier and Shar-man DiVono, among others. Music by Ed Bogas and Desiree Goyette. Animation fa-cilities: Wang Film Production Co., Ltd./ Cuckoo's Nest Studios. Voices: Lorenzo Music (Garfield); Thom Huge (Jon/Binky/ Roy); Gregg Berger (Odie/Orson); Desiree Goyette (Nermal); Julie Payne (Liz/Lano-lin); Frank Welker (Sheldon/Booker/Bo); Pat Buttram (Cactus Jake); David L. Lan-der (Doc Boy); and June Foray, Jack Riley, Sharman DiVono, and William Woodson.

The throne once occupied by such car-toon kitties as Felix and Top Cat was in the 1980s the domain of two carryovers from the comic strips. To those who can't tell the difference: *Heathcliff* (q.v.) was the cocky, pugnacious cat. *Garfield* was the lazy, voracious one. Also the funnier one.

Created for the funny papers by Jim Davis in June of 1978, Garfield—named after Davis' grandfather—quickly became a worlwide moneymaker for the United Press Syndicate (seen in over 2000 newspapers), branching out into a series of paperback reprints which cracked the *New York Times* best seller list on 25 separate occasions! Either there were a lot of cat lovers out there, or *Garfield* fulfilled the non-feline fancier's long held suspicion that all cats are worthless parasites who spend all their time eating, sleeping, ar-rogantly playing off affection they don't deserve and secretly plotting domination against both the human and canine races.

Jim Davis' porcine pussy struck a responsive chord for whatever the reason, making inevitable the switchover to TV animation. Garfield crept into this field on

little cat feet by way of a series of yearly half hour CBS specials. The first of these, *Here Comes Garfield* (1982), was produced by old *Peanuts* (q.v.) hands Bill Melendez and Lee Mendelson (*Peanuts* was also a United Press property). The special won an Emmy, a feat repeated by *Garfield on the Town* (1983), *Garfield in the Rough* (1984), *Garfield's Halloween Special* (1985) and *Garfield: Babes and Bullets* (1988), this last a classy black-and-white *film noir* takeoff aimed at the adults who comprised the character's biggest fan following (Garfield's character was "Sam Spayed").

Though Lee Mendelson Productions re-tained its ties with the project, the *Garfield* specials of the mid–1980s became the re-sponsibility of a new firm, Film Roman, started by former *Peanuts* animator Phil Roman in 1984. Thanks to the clout of his four-paw attraction Garfield, Roman's struggling little company graduated to the big time, ultimately attaining such prize assignments as *Bobby's World* (q.v.) and *The Simpsons* (q.v.).

Contributing so much to the hairball charm of the *Garfield* specials was the voicework of actor and sitcom producer Lorenzo Music, who used his ever-in-ebriated Carlton the Doorman character from the 1970s series *Rhoda* to serve as the basis for the self-indulgent musings of Gar-field. (To convey visually the "thought balloons" used by Jim Davis for the cat's dialogue in the comic strip, the animators would keep Garfield's lips motionless, his words seemingly emanating from his sub-conscious.) Music claimed he'd started "researching" his role even before his 1982 debut, describing Garfield as "Carlton with fur. He's a selfish, lazy, arrogant, con-ceited, gluttonous slob—and I know how to do that."

A weekly *Garfield* series was heralded by CBS publicity in 1987, and premiered in half-hour form the following year, re-tooling as a full hour in 1989. Garfield's gang of regulars included sanctimonious, idealistic John Arbuckle, Garfield's bach-elor master, whose mission in life was to get his pet to do something daringly dif-ferent, like wake up before noon; Odie, a disgustingly affectionate dog with the wet-test tongue in the known Universe; Ner-mal, the world's most cloying cute cat, whose very existence was reason enough for Garfield to plot revenge against Na-ture; and occasional visitors like John's

Garfield exerts himself enough to smile — sort of.

brother Doc Boy, leathery westerner Cactus Jake, and Binky the Clown, the sort of yukka-yukka kiddie show host that Garfield never was, never would be.

Garfield appeared in two short episodes per 60-minute program (each installment buoyed by funky original background music by Ed Bogas and Desiree Goyette), and performed double duty in the quickie blackout gags that buffered the sequences. Many of the stories were traditional situation comedy fare, liberally laced with throwaway gags about such topics as the choiceless choices offered by cable television, or the hidden fact (based on sworn testimony!) that cats were alien invaders put on Earth with the power of mind control over humans. The best vignettes were wicked flights of fancy deliberately designed to ulcerate the CBS executives. Some of the episodes in the latter category involved the ongoing efforts of the network "suits" to get Garfield to make his program less pure entertainment and more "prosocial." One such bright corporate notion was to team Garfield with the Buddy Bears, three maniacally lovable bruins who would likely have been called the Care Bears flat out if the producers could have gotten away with it. So far as Garfield (and Film Roman) saw it, the

Buddy Bears were the Sunshine Boys from Hell, pummelling and brutalizing anybody who didn't see the light of their "love love love" approach. "Perverse" is the word that comes to mind here.

Sharing space with Garfield were characters who'd appeared in another, comparatively shortlived Jim Davis comic strip, *U.S. Acres* (which had been discontinued by the time of *Garfield*'s TV debut). These worthies were smartmouthed farm animals headlined by Orson the pig, Roy the Rooster, Sheldon the baby chick and Lanolin the Lamb. The *U.S. Acres* cast members were no less irreverent than Garfield; more than once the animals complained about being typecast as mere "livestock" by their scriptwriters. Two *U.S. Acres* seven-minute adventures appeared on each *Garfield and Friends* installment; the *Acres* menagerie also appeared in its own set of "between the acts" blackout gags.

Garfield and Friends rapidly became the hub around which the rest of CBS' morning lineup was built. Unlike its linear ancestor *Peanuts*, which found its appeal slightly diluted by the overfamiliarity of weekly visits, *Garfield* seemed to get better with each passing season. The series never earned the Emmies that its prototype yearly specials garnered, but *Garfield* managed to stay alive into the 1990s, CBS' strongest fortification against the Fox Network Saturday-morning *anschluss* of that decade.

THE GARY COLEMAN SHOW. NBC: 9/18/1982–9/10/1983. Gary Coleman Productions/Hanna-Barbera. Executive producers, William Hanna, Joseph Barbera. Produced by Art Scott. Directed by Ray Patterson, George Gordon, Bob Hathcock, Carl Urbano, Rudy Zamora. Voices: Gary Coleman (Andy LeBeau); Jennifer Darling (Angelica); Sidney Miller (Hornswoggle); Calvin Mason (Spence); LaShanda Dendy (Tina); Jerry Houser (Bartholomew); Lauren Anders (Chris); Julie McWhirter Dees (Lydia); Steve Schatzberg (Matt); Jeff Gordon (Haggle); Casey Kasem (Announcer).

Gary Coleman, the Macaulay Culkin of the 1970s, was the preteen star of the popular NBC sitcom *Diff'rent Strokes*. When time came to merchandise Coleman as a cartoon character, Hanna-Barbera and Gary Coleman Productions chose not to extenuate the *Diff'rent Strokes* milieu (as was later done with another adolescent-star sitcom, *Punky Brewster* [q.v.]) but instead to delve into the residue of Mr. Coleman's TV-movie career. From 1979 through 1983, the young actor appeared in a trilogy of films costarring adult performer Robert Guillaume: *The Kid from Left Field*, *The Kid with the Broken Halo* and *The Kid with the 200 I.Q.* It was 1982's *Broken Halo*, based on the old bromide about an apprentice angel who can't earn his wings until performing a series of truly good deeds, which was tapped as the springboard for *The Gary Coleman Show*.

Coleman provided the voice for his animated likeness, here named (as in the movie) Andy LeBeau. The original three good deeds of the movie were attenuated into 28 (two per half hour episode); instead of being answerable to Robert Guillaume as in the film, Andy/Gary had to account for himself to Heavenly superior Angelica (once again, the Hanna-Barbera Clever Character Names Division was on the job). The bad guy, sent by the Other Place to bedevil our hero, was named Hornswoggle (catch that first syllable); his voice was supplied by a former child actor, Sidney Miller, who must have stood by in amazement as he watched Gary Coleman make more money in a week than Miller had probably made the first 12 years of his life. That's assuming that Coleman's everpresent personal "representatives" let any of the other cast members get anywhere near the million dollar kid. (Coleman's early celebrity would catch up with him disastrously in his twenties, with numerous lawsuits between himself and his parents over residuals, but that's material for another book.)

Prefabricated programs like *The Gary Coleman Show* are virtually impossible to critique objectively. Gary Coleman was transformed into a cartoon because he was popular, not because he was essentially cartoonable; the stories were written in the same spirit of innovation and imagination that was evident in the rest of the series. The *Gary Coleman Show*, like its CBS Saturday morning competition *The Dukes* (q.v.)—also produced by Hanna-Barbera!—wasn't really a cartoon series at all, but merely an animated publicity pressbook.

GENTLE BEN. Syndicated: 1981. Gentle Ben Animation Co.

This entry originated with Jeff Lenburg. Reportedly, *Gentle Ben*, a live action series about a giant bear living with a Florida family which was produced by Ivan (*Flipper*) Tors and ran from 1967 through 1969, was the inspiration for a shortlived syndicated cartoon version. Perhaps it was this *Gentle Ben* which ran on Canadian cable television in the late 1980s.

GEORGE OF THE JUNGLE. ABC: 9/9/1967–9/6/1970. Fox: (reruns only) 9/19/1992–10/17/1992. Jay Ward Productions. Executive producers, Jay Ward, Bill Scott and Ponsomby Britt, O.B.E.(sic!). Directed by Gerald Baldwin, Frank Braxton, Pete Burness, Paul Harvey, Jim Hiltz, Bill Hurtz, Lew Keller, John Walker. Scripts by Chris Jenkyns, Jim MacGeorge, John Marshall, Jack Mendelsohn, Lloyd Turner. Music by Sheldon Allman and Stan Worth. Voices: Bill Scott (George/Tom Slick/Super Chicken/Gertie Growler); June Foray (Marigold/Ursula); Paul Frees (Ape/Fred/Narrator/Dick Two-Lane/Baron Otto Matic); and Daws Butler.

George of the Jungle was the last network stand of Jay Ward Productions before the studio resigned itself to the production of commercials. Like his earlier *Rocky and His Friends*, Ward's *George* had been in gestation long before its 1967 ABC debut; announcements had been made for several years of a planned Tarzan parody initially titled *Walter of the Jungle*, while one of the components of the series, *Super Chicken*, was being heralded in the trade papers as early as 1964. When *George* finally debuted—the hero's name was changed from Walter to what the producers determined to be "the flattest-sounding, non-Jungle name in the world"—it was only one of two first run cartoon networkers (*The Beatles* [q.v.] was the other) that played for laughs rather than straight-faced superhero thrills, and as such received more than usual attention from comedy fans and "clean up TV" advocates.

The weekly, half hour series offered three components. The "George of the Jungle" sequence was about a muscle-bound, muscleheaded lord of the apes who ruled benevolently over the Imgwee Gwee valley (live action attempts at Tarzan parodies usually missed the satirical point of an inept strong man by casting a slight, weak-looking actor as the hero). Like Tarzan before him, George had a very limited vocabulary, a voluptuous mate who'd been raised in the outside world, and several animal companions. In the latter category was an ape named Ape, who unlike George was meticulously educated and cultured, speaking in Ronald Colman pear-shaped tones; Shep, an elephant whom George took to be a "big, gray, peanut-eating dog"; and the Tooky-Tooky bird, which relayed messages throughout the jungle and was understood without difficulty by George and others, even though its vocabulary was limited to "Tooky-Tooky."

George's wife Ursula spent a goodly amount of time reminding her husband, who'd just blindly stepped out the front door, "George, we live in a tree"—always a shade too late (George also had problems with vine-swinging, as noted in the admonition "Watch out for that tree!" in the series' theme song). A certain amount of confusion has arisen since the *George of the Jungle*'s initial network run due to throwaway shots during the opening and closing title sequences, depicting Ursula doing a two-step with a girl who looked exactly like her. The accompanying song lyrics stated something that sounded like "Thella and Ursula stay in step," suggesting the unprecedented kinky notion that here was a Saturday morning kiddie show character with two wives! Even Jay Ward's most scholarly fans couldn't seem to unravel the mystery of George's "twin" mates, since Thella—or Bella, as some historians have written—never appeared in any of the 17 five-minute *George of the Jungle* installments.

The mystery would seem to have been cleared up by Walter Brasch's little-known but well researched 1983 book *Cartoon Monickers*. According to Brasch, the word that sounded like "Thella" was really "Fella," a carryover of a running gag concerning George's inability to discern his mate's sexual orientation. Whenever asked about Ursula, George would say something like "Ursula? He that funny-lookin' fella who never shave?" The shots of the two Ursulas were, perhaps, Jay Ward's way of underlining George's confusion and stupidity: To George, the voluptuous Ursula was just one of the "fellas," like his nonhuman pals Ape and Shep.

By the way ... according to *George*

director Bill Hurtz, Ursula was originally supposed to have been named Jane, but the Edgar Rice Burroughs estate didn't see the humor in this. "Ursula" was chosen for one of two reasons: Hurtz claimed that his daughter had a friend by that name, while *George of the Jungle* coproducer Bill Scott insisted that George's mate was inspired by actress Ursula Andress.

Well, Ursula is rapidly becoming a book in herself, so let's move ahead.

George of the Jungle's second component, "Super Chicken," headlined a mild mannered millionaire rooster, Pittsburgh's Henry Cabot Henhouse III, who assumed superhero status whenever downing a flagon of super-sauce. Joining in his worldwide adventures was Super Chicken's handyman and general factotum Fred, a timorous lion who sounded like Ed Wynn. Super Chicken's oft-spoken admonition to his right hand man, "You knew the job was dangerous when you took it, Fred!" became *George of the Jungle*'s most familiar catch phrase.

"Tom Slick," the third component, featured a Dudley DoRight-like, blue-eyed, stronglimbed and purehearted young hero, a race car driver who piloted his patented "Thunderbolt Grease Slapper." Tom's beloved was the virginal Marigold, whose syrupy demeanor was offset by Tom's grandmother (and chief mechanic), the salty Gertie Growler. Each week, Tom was pitted in a big race (one was described as "The Forthcoming Race," sponsored by Arnold Forthcoming), with running radio commentary from sportscaster Dick Two-Lane. The first episode—an unusually well animated and beautifully backgrounded cartoon—pitted Tom against a Phil Silvers-ish Arab sheik; later regular opponents included Bogart-like motorcycle bum Harley Angel and Teutonic trickster Baron Otto Matic. "Tom Slick's" best running gag was the reaction of the fans in the stands. Whether it be "Yay" or "Boo," the "vast crowd" never sounded like any more than three unenthusiastic people.

The "to be continued" serialized format of Ward's earlier programs had been vetoed by ABC, so each episode of the three *George of the Jungle* components was self-contained. This meant that Ward's tendency to drag a joke beyond its worth was muted, but it also meant that the producer was forced by running-time restrictions to go for quick reaction laughs rather than the subtle interwoven satire of *Rocky and His Friends*. Many of these laughs were solid, rich and gut-deep, ranging from such throwaways as "The Isle of Lucy" and "Receding Airlines," to an elaborate "Super Chicken" science fiction parody involving a gigantic mass of hair (the hero solved that one by worrying the monster into a state of baldness, whereupon the "big bald" got a job for life as the Houston Astrodome). As always, the brilliant dialogue tripped effortlessly from the tongues of Bill Scott and fellow voice actors Paul Frees, June Foray and Daws Butler—none of whom, curiously, received billing.

Lavishly designed in a manner new to the Jay Ward canon, *George of the Jungle* was often hysterically funny, and certainly a welcome step up from Ward's earlier *Hoppity Hooper* (q.v.). Still, there seemed to be a little something lacking. Perhaps it was the freshness and originality of *Rocky*—after all, *George* was merely one of several superhero parodies in the late 1960s. Whatever the reason, *George of the Jungle* was the only Jay Ward series ever to lose money for its network, and as such wound up in the syndication mills a little earlier than usual.

Seen today, *George of the Jungle* is as potent a laugh-grabber as ever. The trick is to *see* it today. Repeats of *George of the Jungle* on the Fox Network in the fall of 1992 warmed the hearts of many diehard Ward devotees and held out hope for a renewal of interest in the series, but this package wasn't given much of a chance; the reruns were telecast merely as a stopgap until Marvel's *X-Men* (q.v.) was ready for its long-delayed debut. So *George of the Jungle* was once more shelved by the networks—though, happily, several episodes are currently available to collectors and fans in a group of inexpensive videocassettes.

GERALD McBOING BOING SHOW (a.k.a. BOING BOING).

CBS: 12/16/1956–3/10/1957; 5/30/1958–10/3/1958. United Productions of America. Produced by Bobe Cannon. Associate producer, Bill Scott. Written and directed by Bobe Cannon, George Dunning, Ernest Pintoff, Fred Crippen, Jimmy Murikami, Jim Hiltz, Mordi Gerstein. Written by Bill Scott, Leo Salkin. Artwork by Aurie Battaglia, Dun Roman, Bob McIntosh. Music by Ernest Gold and Lyn Murray. Voices:

Bill Goodwin (Host); Marvin Miller; and Howard Morris.

Historians have noted that the *Gerald McBoing Boing Show* beat *The Flintstones* (q.v.) by two years as a made-for-TV prime time network cartoon series—even though its inaugural 1956 timeslot, 5:30 P.M. on Sunday evenings, wasn't nearly as "prime" as *The Flintstones* Friday 8:30 P.M. berth. *Gerald McBoing Boing* was also the first evening-hour network cartoon series to be telecast in color.

The genesis of *Gerald* was a theatrical cartoon directed by Bobe Cannon for United Productions of America in 1950. Gerald McBoing Boing was originally created by children's poet Dr. Seuss for a phonograph record; the record sold poorly, but Dr. Seuss still thought the character had potential, and took the notion to UPA. The deceptively simple story of *Gerald McBoing Boing* was that of a little boy whose efforts at speech resulted only in sound effects. "Boing boing" was his standard utterance, but Gerald could also emulate fire sirens and machine guns—all to the consternation of his silence-seeking parents. Shunned by friends and family because he was an "oddball" (do we begin to detect the message here?), Gerald finally realized a happy ending when he was signed as a human sound-effects machine by a radio network. *Gerald McBoing Boing* was a critical and financial hit, garnering praise from no less than *Time* magazine for its wryly humorous script by Phil Eastman and Bill (*Rocky and His Friends*) Scott, its bold utilization of "mood" colors and the forced perspective, borderless background design of Bill Hurtz. The character of Gerald McBoing Boing became, along with Mr. Magoo (q.v.), one of the mainstays of the UPA organization, though none of the three subsequent "Gerald" theatrical cartoons came close to the charm and nuance of the Oscar-winning original.

In 1956, the CBS television network commissioned UPA to come up with a *Gerald McBoing Boing* series, not so much to accrue big ratings (Sunday early evening, then as now, was ghetto time) as to bring an extra touch of prestige to an entertainment medium then under critical fire for its overall lack of prestige (wasn't this supposed to be the Golden Age of Television?). The weekly half hour series was conceived in the fashion of CBS' Saturday-morning Terrytoons collections: several short-subject components within each program. Longtime *Burns and Allen Show* announcer Bill Goodwin was engaged for "star insurance" as the host; Goodwin also functioned as the interpreter for Gerald's bizarre vocal emissions. While a handful of UPA theatrical shorts was incorporated into the series, much of the material on *Gerald McBoing Boing* was new, forcing producer Bobe Cannon to expand the skeletal UPA staff by hiring outside talent. "Talent" turned out to be an understatement, since the staff of *Gerald* included such animation noteworthies as Ernest Pintoff, who would later win a San Francisco Film Festival award for his Terrytoons short subject *Flebus* and who eventually became a "cult" live-action director; George Dunning, brilliant Canadian who in 1967 directed the matchless Beatles feature cartoon *Yellow Submarine*; and Fred Crippen, who took what he learned at UPA into the advertising game, and who ultimately turned out one of the 1960s' best TV-cartoon efforts, *Roger Ramjet* (q.v.).

Each *Gerald McBoing Boing* episode featured, in addition to the star, a whole slew of bright creations. There were the Twirlinger Twins, a brace of child entertainers who found it constitutionally impossible to remember their lines. There was Dusty of the Circus, who like Gerald had a singular vocal gift, the ability to talk to animals. And there were regular features like "Meet the Artist" (adventures rendered in the famous styles of past and present masters), "Meet the Inventor," and a seminal version of *Rocky and His Friends'* "Peabody's Improbable History," variously titled "Legends of America and the World" and "Mr. Longview Looks Back." This last effort may well have been the handiwork of future *Rocky* mentor Bill Scott, one of the original *Gerald McBoing Boing* scenarists who'd been assigned by UPA to act as associate producer and juice up the comedy content on an otherwise rather esoteric series.

As cartoon critic Leonard Maltin has observed, the strength of UPA was in its sheer variety of subjects, a strength diluted when their subject matter was formularized into regular series (*Mr. Magoo* certainly became less amusing the longer he was around). It's not surprising then

that some of the best vignettes on *Gerald McBoing Boing* were its one-shots. Two of the most enjoyable single efforts were Ernest Pintoff's superb literalization of Stan Freberg's satirical school anthem "Fight On for Old," and "The Matador and the Troubadour," the story of a flamenco-dancing bullfighter.

Gerald McBoing Boing was not a hit, thanks to the tendency of CBS affiliates to schedule more profitable syndicated reruns, wrestling matches and paid-time religious broadcasts in its Sunday timeslot. Nonetheless, the network held on bravely to the series at the behest of PTA groups and other such parental guidance specialists until March of 1957, then repeated the 13-episode package starting in May of 1958, after ABC's *Disneyland* (q.v.) had renewed interest in network cartoons. This time *Gerald McBoing Boing*, now simply *The Boing Boing Show*, had a more preferable 7:30 P.M. Friday timeslot, but it still ran a dead last to ABC's *Rin Tin Tin* and NBC's *Truth or Consequences*. By October of 1958, Gerald and his UPA cohorts had been consigned to the mothball fleet of Happy Memories; eventually, the "new" UPA approach of slapdash design and cheapjack production, exemplified by the TV versions of *Dick Tracy* and *Mister Magoo* (see individual entries on both series), pretty much buried the studio's "artistic" reputation.

Rebroadcasts of the various *Gerald McBoing Boing* components could be seen in the late 1980s on a USA cable network early-morning daily series, *The UPA Cartoon Show*, a highly mixed bag of some of the studio's best work (the theatrical shorts *Rooty Toot Toot*, *The Telltale Heart* and *Unicorn in the Garden*) and some of the worst (the TV *Magoos*).

THE GET-ALONG GANG. CBS: 9/15/1984–6/28/1986. Those Characters from Cleveland/Scholastic-Lorimar/DIC/LBS. Executive producers, Jean Chalopin and Andy Heyward. Creative supervision by Jean Chalopin and Lori Crawford. Supervising producer/director, Cullen Blaine. Story director, Allan Swayze. Written by Marc Scott Zicree, Larry Parr, Jack Olesker, Pamela Hickey, Dennis McCoy, George Hampton, Mike Moore, George Atkins, Bob Rosenfarb, John Ludin, Michael and Felicia Maliani. Characters created by Tony Byrd, Ralph Shaffee,

Muriel Fabion, Tom Jacobs, Linda Edwards, Mark Spangler. Music by Haim Saban and Shuki Levy. Voices: Bettina Bush, Timothy Gibbs, Georgi Irene, Nicky Katt, Robbie Lee, Sherry Lynn, Sparky Marcus, Chuck McCann, Scott Menville, Don Messick, Frank Welker, Donovan S. Freberg, Eva Marie Hesse.

The *Get-Along Gang* was an offshoot of a series of children's books and greeting cards featuring anthropomorphized, adolescent animals. As suggested by the title, the purpose of the books and cards, as well as the subsequent weekly cartoon series, was to show how various species (read: various human racial types) could coexist peacefully. The members of the Gang, who congregated at their Clubhouse Caboose in the small town of Greenmeadow, were leader Montgomery "Monty" Moose (I'm not the only one who thinks this antlered kid looks like the love child of Bullwinkle and Nell Fenwick. Note that one of the *Get-Along Gang* writers was ex–Jay Ward man George Atkins); Zipper the "hep" cat; Dotty the dog, a creature of exceptional strength; Woolma the vain lamb; and such various sundries as Bingo Beaver and Portia Porcupine.

Each character represented a recognizable human frailty: Bingo didn't like to play by the rules, Woolma was incredibly self-absorbed, Zipper was stubborn, Dotty was careless, and even cute little Portia could exhibit jealousy. As the gang's "voice of reason," Montgomery Moose was psychologically more secure than the others, but did have a tendency towards clumsiness.

Through example and experience, the Get-Along Gang learned lessons about greed, honesty, winning and losing, teamwork and toleration. The "Goofus" characters to the Get-Along Gang's bunch of "Gallants"—those scurvy types who never seemed to get the prosocial message—included Catchum Crocodile and Leland Lizard. The wisdom of presenting a "love one another" cartoon series which carefully divided animal species into "good" mammals and "bad" lizards might be questionable to some . . . but what the hell, lizards can't write protest letters.

No worldbeater in the animation department, *Get-Along Gang* did boast an appealingly "soft" overall design and occasionally good isolated sight gags. Most of the latter were tied in to the inescapable fact that, though the characters walked and talked like humans, they were after all animals: Montgomery Moose would get his antlers tangled in low-hung tree limbs, Bingo Beaver could hammer nails with his flat tail, and so forth.

Before settling into its weekly network slot, *Get-Along Gang* was heralded by a half-hour pilot episode produced by Nelvana Studios, with voicework by Charles Haid and Dave Thomas and theme music by John Sebastian. Some of the 26 *Get-Along Gang* half hours were repackaged after their CBS network run as components of a DIC/LBS weekend syndicated block, *Kideo TV* (q.v.).

G-FORCE *see* **BATTLE OF THE PLANETS**

GHOSTBUSTERS. Syndicated: 1986. Filmation/Tribune Broadcasting Company. Created by Mark Richards. Executive producer, Lou Scheimer. Executive vice president of creative affairs and vice president in charge of production: Arthur H. Nadel. Vice president in charge of production: Joseph A Mazzuca. Adapted for animation by Robby London and Barry O'Brien. Art director, John Grusd. Educational advisor, Dr. Gordon Berry. Voices: Patrick Fraley (Jake Kong Jr.), Peter Cullen (Eddie Spencer Jr.), Alan Oppenheimer (Prime Evil), Susan Blu (Futura), Linda Gary (Jessica), Erik Gunden (G.B./ Haunter); Erika Scheimer (Jessica's Nephew); Lou Scheimer (Tracy). (See also *The Real Ghostbusters*.)

The *Ghost Busters* (two words, not one) premiered as a live-action Saturday morning half hour in 1975. It was a harmless resuscitation of the "scare comedy" that had so well served such comedians as The Three Stooges, Abbott and Costello and The Bowery Boys. Though *The Ghost Busters* was aimed at children, executive producers Lou Scheimer and Norm Prescott saw to it that the casting would invoke nostalgic memories for older viewers. Starring were Forrest Tucker and Larry Storch, who'd been teamed before on the popular ABC sitcom *F Troop* (1965–67), and in the guest cast were such proven favorites as Anne Morgan Guilbert (Millie Helper of *The Dick Van Dyke Show*) and Huntz Hall, the latter a former Bowery Boy and thus part of the scare-comedy lineage mentioned a few sentences ago

How not to infringe a copyright: the "living logo" of Filmation's *Ghostbusters*. (Any resemblance to any other trademark, living or dead ... or at Columbia studios....)

(Hall wasn't the only tie-in with this venerable genre; *Ghost Busters'* director Norman Abbott was the nephew of Lou Costello's straight man Bud Abbott).

The premise of *Ghost Busters* concerned a team of detectives named Spenser, Tracy and Kong. Spenser was Larry Storch, Kong was Forrest Tucker, and Tracy was a gorilla (there's that scare-comedy tradition again!) played by Bob Burns in a monkey suit. These were the Ghost Busters, whose job it was to battle and contain the spirits of historical and fairy-tale characters, all to the accompaniment of a ubiquitous laughtrack. The series ended after a single season, and so far as its producing company Filmation was concerned, that was that—back to cartoons. And that would indeed have been that except for an extremely popular comedy film of 1984, *Ghostbusters*, starring Dan Aykroyd, Bill Murray and Harold Ramis as a ramshackle team of "paranormal investigators." With the videotape release of *Ghostbusters* delayed due to its theatrical run (video companies used to do that, once upon a time), Filmation decided to capitalize on the film's success with a property it had right under its nose. Wasting not one millisecond, Filmation

dug out its old *Ghost Busters* series and prepared a videocassette collection, adroitly titled *The Original Ghostbusters*. Columbia Pictures, distributors of the theatrical *Ghostbusters*, threatened legal action, a compliment returned by Filmation. Whatever the final settlement, the battle was fundamentally pointless in that the Filmation property barely resembled Columbia's, and vice versa.

The situation repeated itself in 1986 when Columbia and Filmation simultaneously decided to translate *Ghostbusters* into a half hour cartoon series. Once more, toothless legal volleys were fired, the result being that Columbia's project was sent out as *The Real Ghostbusters* (q.v.), while Filmation, after first flirting with *Filmation's Ghostbusters*, settled on the "original" *The Original Ghostbusters*. By the time the latter program was released, Filmation and Columbia had come to terms, and the "Original" project was billed both on-screen and in daily TV logs simply as *Ghostbusters*. The cartoon daily used the same main characters as Filmation's 1975 live-actioner, except that Eddie Spenser and Jake Kong were much younger and handsomer this time around (it was explained in the promotional material that the two stars were the *sons* of the live-action series' protagonists), and Tracy the Ape was occasionally able to grunt out what sounded like a word of dialogue, courtesy of an uncredited Lou Scheimer.

Again, the basic premise of the Ghostbusters' tracking down and thwarting legendary and historical spooks was followed, sometimes in the company of a TV reporter named Jessica (a smarter counterpart to *The Real Ghostbusters'* ditsy secretary Janine). Other new characters included sexy sorceress Futura, who acted as the Ghostbusters' dispatch person and liaison to the netherworld, and all-around spectral bad guy Prime Evil, who came off like an "Evening at the Improv" Darth Vader. The Original Ghostbusters were given a corporate logo (a circled closeup of a spirit which changed expressions from scene to scene) that was carefully designed not to resemble the Casper-like "no ghost zone" emblem of *The Real Ghostbusters,* and also a talking automobile called "G.B." that could fly through time and space. A harmlessly ghoulish grace note to the series was the "skeleton" motif used to decorate the Ghostbusters' office, including a skull-like telephone and a boney computer monitor.

Despite the morbidity of the subject matter, *Ghostbusters* was scrupulously nonviolent, leaning more towards the varsity-show silliness of Filmation's *Archie Show* (q.v.). It also bent over backward to fulfill the prosocial obligations set down by education advisor Dr. Gordon Berry, usually by unsubtly structuring messages into each episode. For example, the old "frog prince" yarn became a "Beauty is only skin deep" message, while the tale of a leprechaun jealously guarding his pot of gold turned into a tract on trusting one's friends.

Filmation's *Ghostbusters* did good business when first syndicated by Tribune Broadcasting on a daily basis in 1986, and achieved a boost in viewership by being run over Tribune's "superstation" WGN-TV and the broadcast group's five other TV outlets. But it lacked the instant-recognition merchandising connection with the Columbia *Ghostbusters* theatrical feature and the simultaneous network/syndication exposure that greeted *The Real Ghostbusters.* The series also fell prey to the deadening repetition of gags that often diminished the Filmation product (Prime Evil's inability to say the word "Ghostbusters" without wincing was funny—but not 10 or 11 times per episode). Within two years, the 65-episode *Ghostbusters* was off the market. As with Filmation's live *Ghost Busters* series in 1975, the Loss was not terribly deep—though on an asthetic level, one rather missed the catchy, well-designed montage sequences and scene transitions on the cartoon *Ghostbusters.*

G.I. JOE. (two separate series listed below)

—G.I. JOE: A REAL AMERICAN HERO. Syndicated: 1985 (original pilot special: 1983). Marvel/Sunbow/Claster. Produced by Joe Bacal. Five-part pilot (1983) produced by Joe Bacal, David De-Patie, Tom Griffin. Series creative director, Jay Bacal. Executive producers, Joe Bacal, Tom Griffin, Margaret Loesch. Executive in charge of production, Lee Gunther. Supervising director, Ray Lee. Directed by Robert Alvarez, Warren Batchelder, Brad Case, Joan Case, Rudy Cataldi, Gerry Chiniquy, Charlie Downs, Lilian Evans, John Freeman, Milton Gray, Bob Kirk, Bill Knoll, Norman McCabe, Bob Matz, Joe Morrison, Margaret Nichols, Karen Peterson, Thom Ray, Robert Shellhorn, Bob Trent, Neal Warner. Educational advisors: Robert L. and Anne Selman. Director of production, Jim Graziano. Supervising producers: Don Jurwich, Sam Weiss. Story editor, Buzz Dixon. Coproducer, Michael Charles Hill. Producers: Jim Duffy, Mark Glomack, Larry Houston, Alex Lovy, George Singer, John Walker, Dan Thompson. Music theme by Ford Kinder and Spencer Michlin. Theme by Robert J. Walsh and Johnny Douglas. Main title and end theme by Stephen Taylor. Voices: Jackson Beck (narrator), Charlie Adler, Jack Angel, Liz Aubrey, Michael Bell, Arthur Burghardt, Corey Burton, Bill Callaway, Peter Cullen, Brian Cummings, Pat Fraley, Hank Garrett, Dick Gautier, Ed Gilbert, Dan Gilvezan, Dave Hall, Zack Hoffman, Kene Holliday, Jerry Houser, Chris Latta, Loren Lester, Mary McDonald Lewis, Chuck McCann, Michael McConnohie, Rob Paulsen, Pat Pinney, Lisa Raggio, Bill Ratner, Hal Rayle, Bob Remus, Neil Ross, Will Ryan, Ted Schwartz, John Stephenson, B. J. Ward, Lee Weaver, Frank Welker, Stan Wojno, Keone Young.

—GI JOE. Syndicated: 1990 (Five-part pilot telecast 1989). DIC/Claster. Executive producers, Andy Heyward, Robby London. Produced by John Grusd. Directed by Jim Duffy and Chuck Paxton. Music by Stephen James Taylor. Musical editor, Stuart Goetz. Animation facilities: Sei Young Studios Ltd. Voices: Lee Jeffrey (Stalker); Suzanne Emmett-Balcom (Lady Jaye); Kevin Conway (Rock&Roll); Dale Wilson (Mutt); Jim Byrnes (Alley Viper); Ian Corlett (Gnaugahyde); Michael Benyaer (Scoop); Maurice LaMarche (Copperhead/Lowlight/Serpentor/Spirit/Destro); Chris Latta (Cobra Commander); Morgan Lofting (Baroness); Sgt. Slaughter (Himself); and Don Brown, Gary Chalk, Brent Chapman, Christopher Collins, Lisa Corps, Edmund Gilbert, Ted Harrison, Phil Hayes, Jerry Houser, Terry Klassen, Andrey Koening, Scott McNeil, Rick Polatruk, Alvin Sanders, William Taylor, David Wills, Bob Remus, Mark Acheson, Babs Chula, Gary Jones, Annabel Kershaw, Victoria Langston, Pauline Newstone, John Novak, Doug Parker, Tomm Wright, and Lee Jeffrey.

"G.I. Joe," once a generic term referring to a typical World War II soldier (the letters stood for "Government Issue"), was a name coined in 1942 for a comic panel drawn by Dave Breger, an artist for the American forces' *Yank* magazine. It slipped into the public domain thanks to the newspaper columns of war correspondent Ernie Pyle, and thus wasn't registered for copyright until Hasbro Toys, seeking to create a "Barbie doll for boys," came up with the G.I. Joe doll in 1964. Actually this was not so much a doll as one of the first "action figures"; kids could manipulate G.I. Joe by moving its arms and legs. Still, it was the Barbie-inspired expensive accessories—weaponry, helmets, uniforms—which really brought in the bucks for Hasbro, and G.I. Joe was a top seller until resistance to the Vietnam War prompted a dip in military playthings in the late 1960s. The property was revamped in 1969 to include more than one doll, a "fighting team" concept involving Joe's buddies that held fast until G.I. Joe was dropped entirely in 1978, a victim of an overall demilitarization of children's toys. When Joe was revived in 1982 during the hawkish Reagan administration, the toymakers returned to the "team" notion, this time as a bow to the *Star Wars* films

emphasizing the importance of a united front against a common foe. Hasbro now offered a five-man force, operating under the blanket name G.I. Joe—and the upshot, to no one's surprise, was five times as many sales.

It was this team, pumped up with several new enlistees, that made it to the drawing boards in a five-part series of half hour cartoon adventures, *G.I. Joe: A Real American Hero*, subsidized by Hasbro and produced by Marvel in 1983 (the miniseries was also easily adapted into a two-hour "TV movie"). This five-parter, together with a 1984 followup, made the syndication rounds for several years before the looser "toy-into-series" market, created by the laissez faire policies of new FCC head Mark Fowler and encouraged by the success of such other half hour quasi-advertisements as *The Smurfs* (q.v.) and *He Man and the Masters of the Universe* (q.v.), resulted in a full fledged daily *G.I. Joe* animated series.

The "Joes," as the combat team was known on this program, were assigned to take on the forces of the evil terrorist conclave COBRA, overseen by a Darth Vader-type masked villain named Destro and by a nasty feminine number called The Baroness. With world domination on its game plan, COBRA performed such mischief as attempting to control the weather, sabotage communications satellites and build doomsday weapons. But the Joes, led by Hawk (a.k.a. Clayton M. Abernathy), had the strength of thousands for they were pure in heart—and for all their deployment of heavy artillery, the Joes never killed or seriously injured anyone. In this way, Marvel/Hasbro could point with pride at the basic lack of real violence on *G.I. Joe*. Children didn't quite get the point, however, and it wasn't hard to find youngsters playing with their G.I. Joe toys and screeching "You die!" and "Eat lead!" Too bad the safe-TV watchdogs couldn't use mind control . . . but then, they'd be just as wicked and megalomanic as COBRA, wouldn't they?

This being 1985, *G.I. Joe* went through the usual motions of squeezing in a 30-second "valuable lesson," in the form of a tip from the National Child Safety Council, at the climax of each episode. A tip which, of course, was dutifully watched and followed by all the kids at home, when they weren't aiming their toy guns at the tube and shouting "Die, suckers!"

G.I. Joe lasted 90 episodes (some of these were the 1983 and 1984 trial balloons) before being aced off the market by an increasing upsurge in comedy-oriented cartoon dailies like *DuckTales* (q.v.). The series was revived in 1990, this time as an alliance between Hasbro and DIC Productions. (Once more, the project was hautboyed by a 1989 miniseries.) Though still locked in combat with COBRA, the new *G.I. Joe* was (in keeping with the times) kinder and gentler, its heroes deemphasizing violence in favor of quickwittedness, compromises, and convincing certain bad guys to see the light and give up. As a further nod to the new state of world affairs, G.I. Joe leader Stalker, clearly American, found himself accepting assignments and exchanging pleasantries with one Capt. Krimoff, clearly Russian (note the dropping of the subtitle "Real American Hero").

Some of the more aggressive moments on these new *Joe* installments were the live-action appearances of professional wrestler Sgt. Slaughter, a carryover from the 1985 show who functioned as the action figure's celebrity spokesman. Equally aggressive was the development staff on *G.I. Joe*, which saw to it that the fighting force was even larger than it had been in 1985. Kids found themselves assaulted from all sides by G.I. Joe personnel with such descriptive monickers as Snake-Eyes, Tripwire, Short Fuse, Torpedo, Lowlight, Scoop, Heavy Duty, Skydive, Iceberg, Lifeline, Rampart, Mainframe, Forester, Ripcord, Wetsuit, Cross-Country, Gung-Ho, Breaker, Iron Knife, Road Block, Grand Slam, Short Fuse, Grunt, Rock N Roll, Clutch, Steeler, Zap, Matt, Deep Six, and Joe Bullhorn. AND (gasp! pant! wheeze!) a few "G.I. Janes," female members of the squad like Scarlet and Cover Girl, who were afforded the full privileges of the once all-male fraternity—including the right to duck and dodge during the battle sequences.

To keep DIC's storyboards from becoming dangerously overpopulated, the various Joes appeared in repertory, some of them featured in all episodes, others only sporadically. The new *G.I. Joe* didn't last long in first-run daily syndication, but its influence was felt on its toy counterpart for several seasons thereafter. As duly noted

by increasingly elaborate, fully animated 30-second commercials run in key prime time slots, the Hasbro G.I. Joe playthings began fighting COBRA action figures in 1990, deploying such TV-to-toystore artillery as H.A.L. (Heavy Artillery Laser) and V.A.M.P. (Vehicle Attack/Multi Purpose). All one can say is W.O.W. (Worn Out Watching.)

GIGANTOR. Syndicated: 1966. TCJ Animation Center/Delphi Associates Inc./ Trans-Lux. American producers/adapters: Fred Ladd and Al Singer. Theme created by Lou Singer and Gene Raskin. Music coordinators, Dan Hart and George Craig. Supervising editor, P. A. Zavala. Titles designed by Robert E. Lee. Sound recording, Titra. Voices: Billie Lou Watt, Peter Fernandez, Gilbert Mack, Cliff Owens.

—**GIGANTOR.** Sci-Fi Channel: 1993. Tokyo Movie Shinsha Co. Ltd. Produced by Fred Ladd. Animation producers, Yasuji Takahashi, Shigeru Akagawa. Directed by Tetsuo Imazawa, Shigeo Hasegawa, Kazuyuki Hirokawa, Minoru Okazaki.

Gigantor was the American name for *Tetsujin 28GO*, a Japanese comic book character created in 1958 by Mitsuteru Yokoyama. The character's name translated literally as "Iron Man No. 28"; he (it?) was developed during World War II as a flying battle machine designed to combat Allied troops. The U.S. Air Force bombed the robot lab into rubble, and after the war the scientists responsible for Tetsujin 28GO, Doctors Kaneda and Shikisama, decided to rebuild their creation as an instrument of peace rather than war (which didn't stop the robot from mercilessly blasting villains out of the sky). The giant, helmeted flying robot became an agent of the Japanese police; the mechanism was operated by Dr. Kaneda's young son Shotaro. (Some of the elements prevalent in this concept resurfaced, uncredited, in the 1967 Hanna-Barbera cartoon series *Frankenstein Jr. and the Impossibles* [q.v.].)

Tetsujin 28G0 had a great deal of influence on the "lovable robot" school of Japanese comic art; the property was spun off into a radio series, a brief live action television program, and in 1963, a weekly half hour cartoon adventure from TCJ Animation Center, which ran on Japanese network TV for four seasons. American producers Fred Ladd and Al Singer, who spent most of their careers mining Japanese animation for domestic distribution, secured the rights for 52 episodes of *Tetsujin 28GO* in 1965. The producers went the *Astro Boy* (q.v.) route of editing out excessive violence—though the implied offscreen deaths of several bad guys were retained—and portions of the plotlines that wouldn't appeal to American fans. The character names were then "westernized": Dr. Kaneda became Dr. Sparks; his son Shotaro became Jimmy; and finally, since there already was an "Iron Man" on the market (see *Marvel Superheroes*), Tetsujin 28GO was not translated as Iron Man No. 28 but completely rechristened as Gigantor.

Like *Astro Boy*, *Gigantor* was chock full of futuristic thrills both in this world and in the Outer Limits; its character design ranged from the "straight" secret agent Dan Strong to the "silly" Inspector (who sounded like comic actor Frank Nelson in the American version); and it moved like sixty, satisfying viewers who were bored by the comparatively languid pace of many home-grown cartoons available in 1966. Most effective was *Gigantor's* breathtaking variety of offbeat camera angles, including at least one point-of-view shot from inside the villain's mouth!

Only its black and white photography prevented *Gigantor* from becoming as enduring an American hit as its companion Japanese imports *Speed Racer* (q.v.) and *Marine Boy* (q.v.). When cable TV's Sci-Fi Channel rebroadcast the original *Gigantor* in early 1993, distributor Fred Ladd was careful to computer-colorize the property to boost its saleability—and to whet the viewers' appetites for Sci-Fi's fall 1993 premiere of the new full-color *Gigantor* ("new" to the U.S., though it was actually produced in Japan in the early 1980s). While the character design and voicework of this latest *Gigantor* were on a par with the 1965 version, the animation was fuller and the violence level was amplified to suit the tastes of the 1980s and 1990s.

Thankfully *not* altered for *Gigantor's* revival was the original series' familiar calypso theme music. American producers had learned just how attached Japanimation addicts were to favorite theme songs when the new *Speed Racer* (q.v.) of 1993 came acropper by eliminating its beloved "Here He Comes/Here Comes Speed Racer" musical signature.

GILLIGAN'S PLANET *see* **NEW ADVENTURES OF GILLIGAN**

GLO FRIENDS *see* **MY LITTLE PONY**

THE GO GO GOPHERS. CBS: 9/14/ 1968–9/6/1969. Leonardo/Total Television. (See *Underdog* for production credits.)

Go Go Gophers, an all-rerun network package, consisted of two component features that had gone, gone, gone from Leonardo/Total TV's *Underdog* (q.v.): "Go Go Gophers" (but you *knew* that) and "Klondike Kat." As far as Klondike Kat was concerned, *Underdog's* loss was *Go Go Gopher's* loss.

THE GODZILLA POWER HOUR. NBC: 9/9/1978–10/28/1978. Toho/Benedict Pictures Corp./Hanna-Barbera. Executive producers, William Hanna and Joseph Barbera. "Jana of the Jungle" produced and created by Doug Wildey. Directed by George Gordon, Ray Patterson and Carl Urbano. Creative producer, Iwao Takamoto. Story editors, Dick Robbins and Duane Poole. Animation supervisors, Bill Neil, Jay Sarbry and Bob Goe. Music by Hoyt Curtin. Voices: Ted Cassidy (Godzilla/Montaro); Don Messick (Godzookey); Jeff David (Captain Carl Majors); Brenda Thompson (Dr. Quinn Darien); Al Eisenman (Pete); Hilly Hicks (Brock); B.J. Ward (Jana); Mike Bell (Dr. Ben Cooper). And Bill Boyett, Virginia Eiler, Ron Feinberg, Joan Gerber, Jane James, Casey Kasem, Ross Martin, Vic Perrin, Barney Phillips, Michael Rye, and Bill Woodson.

–GODZILLA AND THE SUPER 90. NBC: 11/4/1978–9/1/1979. Same credits as previous program. See individual listing on *Jonny Quest* for credits on *GODZILLA AND THE SUPER 90*.

–THE GODZILLA SHOW. NBC: 9/8/ 1979–11/3/1979. Rebroadcast 5/23/1981– 9/5/1981. Same credits as THE GODZILLA POWER HOUR, minus JANA OF THE JUNGLE credits.

–THE GODZILLA/GLOBETROTTERS ADVENTURE HOUR. NBC: 9/10/ 1979–9/20/1980. Same credits as THE GODZILLA SHOW. See HARLEM GLOBETROTTERS for additional credits.

–THE GODZILLA/DYNOMUTT HOUR WITH THE FUNKY PHANTOM. NBC: 9/27/1980–11/15/1980. Same credits as THE GODZILLA SHOW. See SCOOBY-

DOO and FUNKY PHANTOM for additional credits.

—THE GODZILLA/HONG KONG PHOOEY HOUR. NBC: 11/22/1980–5/15/1981. Same credits as THE GODZILLA SHOW. *See* HONG KONG PHOOEY for additional credits.

Depending on one's source, the name "Godzilla" was either a combination of "gorilla" and "kujira," the Japanese word for "whale," or it was Japanese slang for "big clumsy ox." At any rate, it was the nickname of an employee of Japan's Toho motion picture studio in 1954, around the time that the studio's special-effects wizard Eiji Tsuburaya came up with the notion of building a movie around a huge fire-breathing amphibian. With actor Haru Nakajima dressed in a lizard suit careening around a set resembling a miniature Tokyo, *Godzilla, King of the Monsters* was committed to film, achieving international success when Embassy pictures picked up the picture for non–Japanese distribution (the American version included new sequences starring Raymond Burr, filmed nearly two years after the picture's completion). So popular was the character that he/she/it went the "Rambo-Terminator" route of changing from mindless monster to beneficent friend of humanity in the many *Godzilla* sequels — and since the original monster was blown to smithereens in the first film, it was the newly designed Godzilla of *Gigantis the Fire Monster* (1959) who became the worldwide celebrity.

The "nice" Godzilla was also the star of Hanna-Barbera's 1978 *Godzilla Power Hour*—in fact, he was downright cuddly at times. The 400-foot-tall clumsy ox/gorilla-whale was now the tame companion of a group of researchers, headed by Captain Carl Majors and Dr. Quinn Darien (a female with a male name, in true 1950s sci-fi-flick fashion), whose mission was to investigate unexplained phenomena aboard an ocean vessel called the *Calico*. It seemed that the scientists had befriended Godzilla by rescuing the huge lizard's little nephew, a comic relief character named Godzookey.

Each *Godzilla Power Hour* contained a complete two-part adventure, the first part a "cliffhanger" leaving Godzilla and his cohorts imperiled until salvation arrived in Part Two. While certainly loud enough, these *Godzilla* shorts were crudely and carelessly animated, the smoothest cartoonwork showing up in the rotoscoped credit sequences. One would like to have seen what UPA Studios, whose head man, Henry G. Saperstein, had originally pitched a cartoon *Godzilla* to disinterested sponsors in the 1960s, might have done with the project. Then again, considering the lackadaisical UPA work on the TV versions of *Mr. Magoo* (q.v.) and *Dick Tracy* (q.v.), it's unlikely that the company would have improved upon Hanna-Barbera all that much.

Separating the two above-mentioned *Godzilla* segments was a weekly 30-minute cartoon starring a female Tarzan named Jana of the Jungle, created by comic strip artist Doug Wildey (who had worked for Atlas Comics in the 1950s, the same time that the publishing firm ran the similar *Jana of the Jungle*). Jana's pedigree had a lot in common with Tarzan's; she was lost in a South American jungle as a child after her father's boat sank in the Amazon, then was rescued and raised by an Indian warrior named Montaro. More attractive than Sheena, the previous queen of the jungle, Jana was another prime example of Hanna-Barbera's fondness for animating beautiful, long-stemmed blondes. Jana spent much of her adventure time searching for her lost father, with the assistance of her white jaguar Ghost, her comic-relief squirrel monkey Tico, and handsome American doctor Ben Cooper. Jana also enjoyed the tactical advantage of Montaro's magical "staff of power," her own super-powered necklace which doubled as a weapon against her foes, and the finely tuned ability to communicate with the most dangerous of jungle beasts.

So far as many animation fans were concerned, *Jana of the Jungle* could have stood on its own merits without the *Godzilla* name to bolster it. Doug Wildey's character designs were among his best—Jana managed to be wholesome and sexy all in one—and was enhanced by great vine-covered background art from Al Gmuer (who was still contributing first-rate work for Hanna-Barbera as late as 1993's *Captain Planet and the Planeteers* [q.v.]). But the network was far more interested in male fans than female, so *Jana* was brusquely downplayed in the series' publicity.

Two months after its 1978 Saturday morning debut, *The Godzilla Power Hour* was expanded to 90 minutes to accommodate repeats of another Doug Wildey/Hanna-Barbera creation, *Jonny Quest* (q.v.); the series' title was obligingly changed to *Godzilla and the Super 90*. The following season, *Jana of the Jungle* and *Jonny Quest* were gone, and 13 new episodes of *Godzilla* appeared solo under the title *The Godzilla Show*. Within two months, the "star" was sharing space with reruns of Hanna-Barbera's *The Super Globetrotters* (q.v.); now the series was called *The Godzilla/Globetrotters Adventure Hour*. This lasted until season three in 1980, at which time the Globetrotters dribbled off and the series was refashioned into *The Godzilla/Dynomutt Hour with the Funky Phantom*, an all-rerun package incorporating episodes of *Dynomutt, Dog Wonder* (see *Scooby-Doo*) and *Funky Phantom* (q.v.). A scant three months after this mélange was introduced, NBC fans were treated to a "new" series, *The Godzilla/Hong Kong Phooey Hour*, this time comprised of the 1979 *Godzilla* episodes as well as rebroadcasts of H-B's *Hong Kong Phooey* (q.v.). Finally, despite the studio's apparent belief that the giant amphibian couldn't carry a series by itself, the program cut out all its embellishments and returned as simply *The Godzilla Show* in May of 1981.

All that fuss for such a forgettable series. Well, there *was* at least one point of interest. Throughout all its retooling jobs, *Godzilla*'s voice was provided by Ted Cassidy, who during his tenure as "Lurch" on the live-action *The Addams Family* commented that he didn't want to be typecast in monster and supernatural roles, but who was condemned by Hollywood's typecasting system to portray little else than the roles he disliked during all his years in the Hanna-Barbera recording booth. At least Jana of the Jungle's articulate friend Montaro offered Ted Cassidy *some* chance to stretch.

GOLDIE GOLD AND ACTION JACK. ABC: 9/12/1981–9/18/1982. Ruby/Spears. Executive producers, Joe Ruby and Ken Spears. Produced by Jerry Eisenberg. Directed by Rudy Larriva and John Kimball. Supervising story director, John Dorman. Story directors, Kurt Conner, Mario Piluso, Dick Sebast, Lew Woodbury, Doug Wildey, Bill Way. Written by Buzz Dixon, Mark Evanier, Marty Pasko,

Christopher Vane, Ted Pedersen, Jeffrey Scott and Roy Thames. Story editor, Steve Gerber. Character design, Jack Kirby and Rick Gonzalez. Background layout supervisor, David High. Animation supervisors, Milt Gray and Bill Reed. Music by Dean Elliot. Voice director, Alan Dinehart. Animation facilities, Westwind Productions. Voices: Judy Strangis (Goldie Gold); Sonny Melendrez (Action Jack); Sam Bradshaw (Sam Gritt); and Henry Corden, Robert Ridgely, Peter Cullen, Alan Dinehart, Walker Edmiston, Lyle Talbot, Keye Luke, Terry McGovern, Shep Menken, Avery Schreiber.

Not a spinoff of *Richie Rich* (q.v.) as its title might suggest—even though it followed *The Richie Rich/Scooby-Doo Hour* on Saturday mornings—*Goldie Gold and Action Jack* was more a junior-grade derivation of such adult comic strips as Dale Messick's *Brenda Starr* and Peter O'Donnell and Jim Holdaway's *Modesty Blaise*. This all-but-forgotten weekly half hour was about a fabulously wealthy, fabulously beautiful blonde 18-year-old woman named Goldie Gold, publisher of *The Gold Street Journal*, an investigative magazine. Each week, Goldie, with the blessings of managing editor Sam Gritt, took time out for life-threatening exploits in the company of adventurer/intern reporter "Action" Jack Travis. Goldie Gold and Action Jack met all obstacles head-on through utilization of up to date James Bond-style gadgetry.

The 13 *Goldie Gold and Action Jack* adventures veered pretty strongly into "Indiana Jones" territory (one of many cartoon projects of the 1980s to plunder that bottomless bounty of inspiration). The series also endeavored to duplicate the tongue-in-cheek quality of the "Jones" films, with mixed results. Each time a potentially hilarious element was introduced—for example, Goldie Gold's mansion was so large that she had to ride a hang-glider from one room to another—the producers doublecrossed us by playing it dead straight. The resulting ambience of *Goldie Gold* either entertained the viewer or induced head-scratching noncomprehension—there seemed to be no middle ground. One thing everyone could agree on, however: The superior character design (by way of Marvel Comics mainstay Jack Kirby) far outclassed the series' lackadaisical animation and pot-holed plotlines.

Goldie Gold and Action Jack executive producers Joe Ruby and Ken Spears included one carryover from their Hanna-Barbera days: a pet dog (albeit not played for laughs), this one named Nugget—no relation to the "Nugget" who costarred in the *Big Boy* restaurant-giveaway comic books.

GOOBER AND THE GHOST CHASERS. ABC: 9/8/1973–8/31/1975. Executive producers, William Hanna and Joseph Barbera. Creative producer, Iwao Takamoto. Directed by Charles A. Nichols. Music by Hoyt Curtin. Musical director, Paul DeKorte. Voices: Paul Winchell (Goober); Ronnie Schell (Gilly); Jerry Dexter (Ted); Jo Ann Harris (Tina); Susan Dey (Laurie Partridge); Brian Forster (Chris Partridge); Suzanne Crough (Tracy Partridge); Danny Bonaduce (Danny Partridge); Alan Dinehart Jr.; Alan Oppenheimer.

"Give us another *Scooby-Doo!*" cried ABC to Hanna-Barbera in 1974. The producers obliged, and the result was the Saturday morning half-hour *Goober and the Ghost Chasers*. Goober was the sad-faced, sickly pet dog of junior reporters Gilly, Ted and Tina (their teenage voices supplied by comparatively venerated actors, including 40-something Ronnie Schell). Investigating phony paranormal phenomena for their own *Ghost Chasers* magazine—called the *Ghostly Review* in the first episode—Goober and the Ghost Chasers frequently enlisted the aid of caricatured "celebrities," most often the child actors from the live-action sitcom *The Partridge Family* (see also *Partridge Family: 2000 AD*). And yes, the perpetrators were nearly always non-ghosts, and they nearly always would have gotten away with whatever they were trying to get away with if it hadn't been for those meddling kids.

The one novelty of this highly imitative series was that Goober would become invisible whenever severely frightened. *Goober and the Ghost Chasers* itself became invisible after a single 17-episode season and a year's worth of Sunday morning reruns.

THE GOOF TROOP. Disney Channel: March 1992. Syndicated: September 1992. ABC: 9/12/1992–9/11/1993. Disney/Buena Vista Television. Produced by Walt

Disney Animation of Australia. Animation director, Ian Harrowell. Supervising producer and director, Robert Taylor. Story editor, Bruce Talkington. Music by Mark Watters. Theme song by Randy Patterson, Kevin Quinn, Robert Irving. Voices: Nancy Cartwright, Jim Cummings, Bill Farmer, Dana Hill, Rob Paulsen, Kath Soucie, Frank Welker, April Winchell.

Disney's 1992 offering to daily strip syndication, *The Goof Troop* went the usual Disney Channel cable debut and two-hour "special" route before settling into its Monday through Friday local berth and its simultaneous weekly Saturday morning slot on ABC. Like the earlier Disney series *Darkwing Duck* [q.v.], the ABC run consisted of *Goof Troop* episodes not seen in the daily series.

What was it all about? Check out the title, and there's half the story right there. Star of *Goof Troop* was Goofy, Disney's bucktoothed "everydog" who'd been working at the studio since his introduction as a supporting character (then named Dippy Dawg) in 1932. The Goofy of the new TV series was an extension of the character nurtured by such directors as Jack Kinney and Jack Hannah in the 1940s: the feckless suburbanite whose efforts to repair his home, tend his garden and engage in sporting activities were used as an instructional tool—to show the audience how *not* to do things.

According to *Goof Troop*, Goofy was a single parent, the father of 11-year-old Maximum "Max" Goof, whose outlook on life was apparently molded by overdoses of MTV. After years of tooling around the country, father and son moved into a picturesque small town neighborhood. This didn't sit well with Goofy's new neighbor, an Archie Bunker-style version of legendary Disney villain Peg Leg Pete (it was the more compassionate 1990s: the peg leg had been replaced with an undetectable prosthesis). Inordinately proud of his home-improvement skills, Pete was aghast that the eternally accident prone Goofy had moved in such close proximity, but ultimately accepted the new neighbor in a spirit of expansiveness that would never have been found in the Peg Leg Pete of the 1930s (though this "new-and-improved" Pete still tended to cheat at sports events). Included in the *Goof Troop* supporting-cast orbit were Pete's pragmatic wife Peg; Pete and Peg's son Pete Junior—or P.J.—

and daughter Pistol; and the town's hard-case, a Marlon Brando/"Wild One" motorcycle bum named Leech.

The *Goof Troop* didn't blaze any new cartoon trails, but still was another high watermark of Disney TV animation, its all-out slapstick balanced with a genteel parody of suburban status seeking and peer pressure, 1992 style. One hundred sixty-five local stations picked up *Goof Troop* on the basis of the Disney reputation alone; some ran it as a separate entity, others as part of the studio's already established "Disney Afternoon," which by now consisted of new *Darkwing Duck* episodes and rerun installments of *Chip 'n' Dale's Rescue Rangers* and *Tale Spin* (see individual entries on these series).

GRAVEDALE HIGH see RICK MORANIS IN GRAVEDALE HIGH

THE GREAT GRAPE APE see TOM AND JERRY

GRIMM'S FAIRY TALES. Nickelodeon: Sept. 1989–. Nippon Animation Company/Saban.

This collection of fast-moving hourlong versions of classic fairy tales (fast-moving so that the English language voice actors could match the rapid lip movements of the original Japanese animation) was broadcast on weekends as part of Nickelodeon's long-running *Special Delivery* anthology series. New wraparound animation, featuring a flying female elf, was shot to give the package a semblance of continuity.

GRIMMY see MOTHER GOOSE AND GRIMM

THE GROOVIE GOOLIES. CBS: 9/12/1971–9/3/1972; ABC: 10/25/1975–9/5/1976. Filmation. Executive producers: Lou Scheimer, Norman Prescott. Produced by Hal Sutherland. Voices: Howard Morris (Frankie/Wolfie/Mummy/Ghoulahand); Jane Webb (Hagatha/Aunt Hilda/Aunt Zelda/Bella La Ghostly/Broomhilda/Sabrina); Larry Storch (Count "Drac"/Ratzo); Larry Mann (Boneapart/Dr. Jekyll-Hyde/Batzo/Hauntleroy); Don Messick; Dal McKennon; John Erwin.

An indirect spinoff of *The Archies* (q.v.), that cornucopia of Saturday morning treats, *The Groovie Goolies* first appeared as supporting players on another *Archies* derivation, 1970's *Sabrina and the Groovie Goolies* (see *Sabrina the Teenaged Witch*). As usual, it was CBS Saturday morning executive Fred Silverman, Czar of All the Spinoffs, who suggested that the "Goolies" were strong enough for their own starring weekly.

The Groovie Goolies were all boarders of Horrible Hall, managed by Count Dracula, his wife Hagatha and his son Frankie (evidently named for an old family friend, whom bolt-necked Frankie resembled). The Dracula family and Horrible Hall's other residents were not at all interested in murder or mayhem, opting instead for practical jokery and *Archie*-like rock songs. If you really need to know the names of the rest of the Groovie Goolies, they were Wolfie the lovable lycanthrope; Boneapart the skittish skeleton; the two headed Dr. Jeckyll-Hyde; Mummy, the guess what, now gainfully employed as a TV announcer; and a host of assorted creeps named Ghoulahand, Hauntleroy, Ratzo and Batzo, the Mummies and the Puppies, and the Bare Bones Band (sounds like a Transylvanian prom night).

Horrible Hall's decor was dominated by an ambulatory Loveseat (who had a crush on "Count Drac") and a harmlessly carnivorous plant named Orville. Commandeering Horrible Hall's switchboard (on the "tel-a-bone") was Bella La Ghostly, who may have been one of the many reasons why the Bela Lugosi family went to court in the 1970s to win back exclusive rights to the name and likeness of the long-deceased horror film actor.

The *Groovie Goolies* were the recipients of the critical overkill that sometimes afflicts adult TV watchdogs who condemn all Saturday morning cartoons as "frightening" and "worthless." Well, *Groovie Goolies* at least wasn't frightening—how could you scare anyone by removing the teeth, the claws, and the guts of the famous monsters of filmland, then turning them into "revue actors" a la *Rowan and Martin's Laugh-In*?

THE GUMBY SHOW. NBC: 3/16/1957–11/16/1957. Syndicated: 1966. Art Clokey. Productions. Produced by Art Clokey. Written, directed and animated by Ray Peck and Pete Kleinow. Story editor, Ruth Goodell. Animation and puppet maker, Jim Danforth. Music by John

Seeley. Special effects by David Allen. Voices: Dallas McKennon, Art Clokey. —THE ALL-NEW GUMBY. Syndicated: 1988. Art Clokey Productions/Premavision/Lorimar. Produced, directed and written by Art Clokey. Lorimar's executive in charge, Jim Paratore. Gumby's Pal at Lorimar-Telepictures, Bob Bain. Assistant to executive producer, Gloria Clokey. Animation directors included Michael Belzer. Music composed by Jerry Gerber. Production coordinator, Ruth Goodell. Premavision administrative staff: Michael Hock, Stephanie Hock, Kevin Reher. Voices (1988): Dalmac Productions, Art Clokey, Gloria Clokey.

In *TV Guide*'s 1993 fortieth anniversary edition, *Gumby* was nominated as one of the best animated TV series of all time (the winner was *The Simpsons* [q.v.]). It's important to note the qualification "animated"— like *Davey and Goliath*, *Snip Snap* and *The New Adventures of Pinocchio* (see individual entries on these series), *Gumby* was not technically a cartoon show, but instead a miracle of stop-motion model animation. Was little green eraser-boy Gumby really the star of one of the best animated series of all time? Well, note that when animation aficionado Leonard Maltin makes an appearance as resident video critic on *Entertainment Tonight*, he frequently wears a Gumby button on his lapel. Try to find a film critic sporting a button for *Scooby-Doo* or *The Archies*. Yes, it's one of the best—to some, *the* best.

Gumby had its roots in the 1953 short subject *Gumbasia*, created by artist/animator Art Clokey. The clay shapes and models forming colorful geometric patterns in this film had no character names, nor any personalities for that matter. The character of Gumby would solidify (an inappropriate word for such a fluid character) in a group of clay-animation shorts first seen on NBC's live action *Howdy Doody* Saturday-morning series in 1957, and thereafter on his own NBC weekly, hosted by *Howdy* supporting actor and co-producer Bobby Nicholson (who was succeeded by kidvid icon Pinky Lee, on the rebound from his nearly fatal on-camera sinus attack).

Later in life, Art Clokey would recall the elements that went into the makeup of his rubbery creation. The name "Gumby" was derived from "Gumbo," a Southern term referring to the stickiness of soil following

a rain. The character's green color was drawn from grass, which Clokey insisted was in emulation of free-spirit poet Walt Whitman's "Leaves of Grass." And the curious upsweep of Gumby's pointed head was based on a haircut favored by Clokey's father. Whether or not all these images were really dancing in Art Clokey's head when time came to create Gumby, the important point is that the artist's heart and soul went into the creation—and the results reflected this dedication.

It's hard to describe the "plot" of any one *Gumby* episode for the same reason that it's hard to describe music to a deaf person. Each viewer contemplates *Gumby* and finds what he or she wants to find. To some, the storylines are pointless and stupid. To others, they are mildly amusing children's fantasies. To deep-dish *Gumby* devotees, however, such whimsical escapades as "Moon Trip," "The Fantastic Farmers" and "The Magic Wand" are surreal, dadaesque, existential, and . . . (fill in the blank with your own intellectual buzzword). Part of the fun was in watching Gumby stretch, shrink, disintegrate, roll into a ball, multiply, and in general glide weightlessly from gag situation to plot point to visual non sequitur with the brisk nonchalance of a two-year-old who fully accepts the absurdities of the world with the innocence of the untaught.

Contributing to the artistic excellence of Art Clokey's "pixillation" process (the name given to the animation technique utilized here and in Clokey's later, more sobersided *Davey and Goliath*) were a corps of brilliant technicians. Foremost of these were animated filmmaker Raymond Peck, who wrote and directed the bulk of the *Gumby* installments, and the superlative movie special-effects master Jim Danforth, who'd later contribute model and stop-motion on such projects as Ray Harryhausen's *Clash of the Titans* (1981) and his own *When Dinosaurs Ruled the Earth* (1967) and who was the guiding force for the unforgettable *Outer Limits* TV-episode shocker "The Zanti Misfits."

The initial *Gumby* package went into syndication in late 1959, mostly shipped to NBC affiliates with color facilities. A new syndicated package was prepared in 1966, with all the Gumby characters—Gumby's pony Pokey, his parents Gumba and Gumbo, Prickle the dinosaur, Nopey the dog, Goo the blue clay-girl, the nasty

Blockhead twins (G. and J.), King Ott of Roo and his nemesis the Black Knight, The Pesky Indians, Richard the Lion and Zveegee the mad scientist—back in harness. This time around the storylines made more sense, even though Gumby's behavior remained impulsively in defiance of all laws of gravity and physics.

The *Gumby* legend was kept alive in 1982 when the irreverent comedy series *Saturday Night Live* began running the old shorts as an absurdist memory jolt to the baby boomers comprising the series' biggest viewership. This was followed by repeats of 130 *Gumby* episodes on the Disney pay TV channel in 1983. Our most recent visit to Gumbyland occurred with a new daily 65-episode syndicated strip in 1988, consisting of new adventures with far more sophisticated animation than we'd seen in the *Gumby* of the 1950s and 1960s.* Art Clokey was back as producer, while Dal McKennon, the original voice of Gumby, trained several performers to play this part through his own Dalmac Productions.

That the high-speed 1988 *All-New Gumby* was a bit of a stylistic break from the measured pace of the older series was due less to Art Clokey than to his new staff. Stop-motion animator Michael Belzer was hired by Clokey as a *Gumby* director and told to speed up production to eight to ten seconds' worth of film per day. As Belzer told writer D.C. Denison, the staff would be compelled to stick to Clokey's dependable but flickery two-frames-per-movement technique in order to get the series finished on schedule. "[Clokey] wanted us to shoot in twos . . . I wanted to do it on ones; it looks much better. So what often happened was that I and the other animators would try to shoot on ones, but fast enough to keep up with a schedule that was based on twos." This streamlined production procedure worked beautifully, and the 18 months spent on *Gumby* proved valuable experience when Michael Belzer moved to the deadline-dominated rigors of the Pillsbury Doughboy commercials, and ultimately to MTV's groundbreaking animation anthology series *Liquid Television* (q.v.).

The new half hour *Gumby* was occasionally mired in good guy/bad guy for-

mula (the Blockheads were on practically every episode), but happily the old anything-goes spirit of the original survived intact. If anything, the visual puns and bizarre stretching, squashing and shrinking of the characters were carried even farther than in past *Gumbys* (Michael Belzer celebrated the venerable Gumster as "down and dirty"). As for the prosocial messages which were imposed upon other 1988 cartoon projects . . . Listen, experts! *Gumby* was a celebration of life and the spirit of living—of having no limits on creation or achievement because imagination has no such limits. You can't *get* more pro-social than that.

HAMMERMAN. ABC: 9/7/1991–9/5/ 1992. Bustin' Productions/DIC Enterprises. Produced by Kevin O'Donnell. Directed by Mike Maliani. Creative supervisor, Andy Heyward. Story editors: Reed and Bruce Shelley. Production facilities: Pacific Rim Animation. Voices: Hammer (Himself and Stanley); and Clark Johnson, Jeff Jones, Miguel Lee, Dean Wint, Susan Roman, Joe Markeson, Ron Rusta, Neil Crone, Louise Vallance, Carmen Twilte, Phil Aiken, Royal Morenz, Jason Burke, George Buza, Len Carlson, Rob Cowan, Michelin Emelle, Dan Hennessey, Mark Marut, Greg Morton, Jackie Richardson, Judith Scott, Enos Slue, Michael Stark, John Stocker, Marion Vella, and Richard Yearwood.

Hammerman was another weekly half hour cartoon series based on an actual celebrity, in this case 27-year-old "rap" singer Hammer (formerly M. C. Hammer), who in 1991 was the biggest-selling recording star in rap history. Hammer was one of the few rappers of the 1990s who worked "clean"—upbeat lyrics containing no profanity, sexism or race-bashing—and as such was held up as a role model to children by parents who otherwise shunned this particular brand of music. "I hope the image I do project is something that is a positive image," commented the singer at the time of *Hammerman's* debut in an interview with *Animation* magazine. "The cartoon itself is designed with a positive image in mind. In every episode there is always a moral. After the show, I expound on what has happened." Aware

The new Gumby *package also included several older episodes from the 1950s and 1960s, redubbed and rescored to make them compatible with the 1988 cartoons.*

that Saturday morning TV was regularly condemned as a poor substitute for parental guidance, Hammer told *Animation* that he'd be careful on his series *not* to set himself up as the viewers' surrogate father, and that the series would encourage strong parenting.

Hammer certainly poured a lot of himself into the project. He provided the voice for the principal character, a sensitive young children's recreation center employee named Stanley Kirk Burrell (Hammer's real name; his nickname came from a close resemblance to baseball great Hank Aaron, the "hammer man"). Stanley, a resident of urban-blighted Oaktown (Hammer grew up in a crime-ridden East Oakland [California] neighborhood), suddenly found his life turned around when a wise old scientist provided him with a pair of "Magic Dancin' Shoes"—each shoe with a voice and personality of its own. Once donning the footwear, Stanley became the superpowered Hammerman, aiding his young multiracial rec center pals against the forces of evil—personified by Oaktown's crooked Boss Grindenheimer, who ruled from behind prison bars using his equally shifty son as a surrogate.

While Grindenheimer motivated many of the plots—usually in a disappointingly banal and clichéd fashion—the major stumbling blocks facing Hammerman and his pals were such realistic plights as drug addiction, teenage gangs and pollution. Hammer himself was particularly proud of an episode in which a young graffiti "artist" is chastened when his artwork turns into an all-encroaching monster and nearly destroys the neighborhood. For those tuning for music rather than message, Hammer provided at least one song per week, and composed the series' theme music in collaboration with Felton Pilate. Those who still couldn't get enough of the star were encouraged (*not* during the *Hammerman* episodes, lest the FCC spank) to visit the local toy shop for the new Hammer dolls, part of Mattel's "Barbie's Celebrity Friend" line.

Although one could not fault the good intentions which went into the project, *Hammerman*'s animation was blah and its storylines meandering—the same shortcomings that were beginning to plague Hammer's songs and music videos by late 1991. The singer underwent a severe dip in popularity during the next year; by 1992,

both Hammer and *Hammerman* had joined The New Kids on the Block, 1990's hottest singing group (also repackaged in cartoon form), on the road to the Musical Hall of Obscurity.

THE HANNA-BARBERA NEW CAR-TOON SERIES *see* **LIPPY THE LION, TOUCHE TURTLE and WALLY GA-TOR**

THE HARDY BOYS. ABC: 9/6/1969–9/4/1971. Filmation/20th Century–Fox. Produced by Norm Prescott and Lou Scheimer. Directed by Hal Sutherland. Written by Ken Sobol, H. F. Mauberly, Eric Blair and David Melmoth. Music by Gordon Zahler. Voices: Dal McKennon (Frank Hardy/Chubby Morton); Byron Kane (Joe Hardy/Pete Jones/Fenton Hardy); Jane Webb (Wanda Kay Breckenridge/Gertrude Hardy).

In an era of teenaged cartoon detectives, Filmation came up with a pair of readymade youthful sleuths: Joe and Frank Hardy, heroes of several novels written in the 1930s, 1940s and 1950s by a staff of scriveners using the "house name" Franklin W. Dixon (actually a nom de plume for Edward D. Stratemeyer). The Hardy Boys, whose father Fenton was a police inspector, had already been dramatized on the small screen in an entertaining brace of live-action serials which appeared in the 1950s version of *The Mickey Mouse Club* (all together now for the theme song: "Gold doubloons and pieces of eight/all belong to Ap-ple-gate . . ."). At that time, the roles were taken by Tim Considine and Tommy Kirk. There would be a second live-action Hardy series in 1977 as an adjunct to the filmed adventures of Nancy Drew, a teenaged snoop created by Carolyn Keene (actually Stratemeyer again!). Parker Stevenson was Frank and Shaun Cassidy was Joe on this one.

In between these flesh and blood Hardys, Filmation offered a "new" twist on the old format in 1969, which wasn't really new at all but a continuum of a long-standing Saturday cartoon trend: the animated Hardy Boys were members of a rock group bearing their names (not so coincidentally, the concurrently published "Hardy Boys" novels of the late 1960s also gave the boys their own rock band). Other members of the "Hardy Boys Plus Three" were Pete and Chubby; rounding out the detecting "staff" was traditionally cute teen queen Wanda Kay Breckinridge. The guitar-strumming Hardys were booked on a world tour, allowing them entree to baffling (but nonviolent) crime cases on an international scale.

Two "firsts," courtesy of Filmation historians Michael Swanigan and Darrell McNeil: *The Hardy Boys* was the first network cartoon show to include public service announcements about health and safety in the body of each half hour episode—a precursor to the prosocial 1980s. It was also the first to include a young black character, Pete Jones, in the regular supporting cast (though the character was dubbed by Byron Kane—a white actor, and a middle-aged one at that!).

Maybe the songs performed by live actors in wraparound sequences were okay, but there wasn't a "Sugar Sugar" (see *The Archies*) in the bunch. And maybe the show was better than existing publicity stills (with the Hardys decked out in Nehru jackets and bell bottoms) indicate. But don't look for the trapped-in-the-70s *Hardy Boys* to make any classic cartoon revival festivals in the near future. As for the series' original network run, *The Hardy Boys* was scheduled opposite the Hanna-Barbera double threat of *Banana Splits* (q.v.) and *Scooby-Doo* (q.v.)—and thus virtually disappeared even before it appeared.

THE HARLEM GLOBETROTTERS. CBS: 9/12/1970–9/2/1972; 9/10/1972–5/20/1973. Hanna-Barbera. Executive producers and directors, William Hanna and Joseph Barbera. Creative producer, Iwao Takamoto. Animation director, Charles Nichols. Music by Hoyt Curtin. Voices: Stu Gilliam (Curly Neal); John Williams (Geese); Scatman Crothers (Meadowlark Lemon); Richard Elkins (Gip); Eddie "Rochester" Anderson (Bobby Joe Mason); Robert DoQui (Pablo); Nancy Wible (Granny).

—**GO GO GLOBETROTTERS.** NBC: 2/4/1978–9/2/1978. (Reruns of the 1970 HARLEM GLOBETROTTERS. See also credits for THE C.B. BEARS and THE HERCULOIDS.)

—**THE SUPER GLOBETROTTERS.** NBC: 9/22/1979–12/1/1979. Hanna-Barbera. Executive producers, William Hanna and Joseph Barbera. Produced by

Art Scott and Alex Lovy. Directed by Ray Patterson, George Gordon and Carl Urbano. Music by Hoyt Curtin. Voices: Stu Gilliam (Curly Neal/Sphere Man); John Williams (Geese Ausbie/Multi-Man); Adam Wade (Sweet Lou Dunbar/Gizmo Man); Scatman Crothers (Nate Branch/Fluid Man); Buster Jones (Twiggy Sanders/Spaghetti Man); Frank Welker (Crime Globe); Mike Rye (Announcer).

—**THE GODZILLA/GLOBETROTTERS ADVENTURE HOUR.** NBC: 11/10/1979–9/20/1980. (Same credits as THE SUPER GLOBETROTTERS. See GODZILLA for additional credits.)

The Harlem Globetrotters started as a standard pro basketball team in 1927, poking along with minimal success until team mentor Abe Saperstein dreamed up the idea of adding comedy and precision dribbling to the repertoire. By the mid–1950s the team was so famous that no fewer than two theatrical motion pictures had told its story. Many of the Globetrotters—notably Meadowlark Lemon—lasted so long on the team that they became as legendary as the team itself. The resultant merchandising ran the gamut from T-shirts to toys, but not even the visionary Abe Saperstein ever imagined that the amazing Trotters would make their weekly TV bow as a cartoon. And even had that notion crossed Saperstein's mind, he probably didn't have an inkling that the fabulous court jesters would have ultimately wound up as caped crusaders.

Fred Silverman, a CBS executive, assigned Hanna-Barbera the job of transferring the Globetrotters to pen and ink. In doing so, the studio created two milestones: the first cartoon series with an all-black cast, and the first to animate real-life athletes (a practice still practiced as late as *Prostars* [q.v.] in 1991). The *Harlem Globetrotters* used the names and likenesses of its main men Meadowlark Lemon, Curly Neal, Geese Ausbie, Bobby Joe Mason, etc.; since none of these superb athletes were as well equipped as actors, a corps of top black voice artists, including song-and-dance star Scatman Crothers and the inimitable, buzzsaw-throated Eddie "Rochester" Anderson, were employed to read the laugh lines. The animated Globetrotters no longer competed against the lineup of "stunt" teams used in their real life meets; now they were required to score points against teams made up of

The world (and the ball) at their fingertips: *The Harlem Globetrotters.*

his alter ego "Sphere Man"; also returning was Geese Ausbie, a.k.a. "Multi Man." Newer teammate/superheroes included Sweet Lou Dunbar ("Gizmo Man"), Nate Branch ("Fluid Man") and Twigger Sander ("Spaghetti Man"—and no, there was no "Meatball Man," though perhaps there should have been). Now the power-laden team was dispatched by the "Crime Globe" to battle evildoers throughout the universe. They spent 16 episodes doing so.

Had enough? Well, NBC hadn't; in December of 1979 the "new" Globetrotters were welded with Hanna-Barbera's "old" *Godzilla Power Hour* (q.v.), spawning *The Godzilla/Globetrotters Adventure Hour*. Whatever one's thoughts on all this, these ersatz appearances of the team were infinitely more pleasing than their later "live" appearance in the 1981 TV-movie atrocity *The Harlem Globetrotters on Gilligan's Island*. And probably all that kept Hanna-Barbera from creating a cartoon out of *that* was the fact that the *Gilligan* characters had been licensed to Filmation.

everything from robots to kangaroos. This being Hanna-Barbera Land, the team was also gifted with a chucklesome pet dog, unappetizingly named Dribbles. Twenty-two *Harlem Globetrotters* were assembled over a two-year period, and the series, hammocked between *Josie and the Pussycats* (q.v.) and *The Archies* (q.v.) on CBS's Saturday morning lineup, was a noteworthy success. Sometimes the kids at home laughed even without the help of the recorded laughtrack.

Viewers were bereft of the Globetrotters in 1973; the following year, a live action show featuring the real team, *The Harlem Globetrotters Popcorn Machine*, kicked off a two-year CBS run. The cartoon version was repeated as *Go Go Globetrotters* after Fred Silverman moved to NBC in 1978. When next we met the Hanna-Barbera Globetrotters on NBC in 1979, they'd evidently visited the NBA branch of Superman's Fortress of Solitude, for they had now metamorphosed into *The Super Globetrotters*. Meadowlark Lemon had retired, but Curly Neal was back, as was

HBO STORYBOOK MUSICALS.

HBO: 9/26?/1990–1992. Michael Sporn/ Italtoons/Radiotelevisione della Swizzera Italiana/HBO. Executive producer, Giuliana Nicodomi. Art director, Bridget Thorn.

Initially produced for European television in 1989-1990 by watercolor-animation specialist Michael Sporn, *The HBO Storybook Musicals* was a group of half-hour cartoon specials based on popular children's books. Like the various Rabbit Ears Video productions telecast on Showtime Cable (see *American Heroes and Legends, Storybook Classics, We All Have Tales*), the HBO project was released to video stores practically simultaneously with its broadcast schedule; and like Rabbit Ears, Michael Sporn was able to secure celebrity names to narrate his playlets.

First-season *HBO Storybook Musicals* included Tim Curry narrating "The Marzipan Pig," F. Murray Abraham reading "The Little Match Girl," Robert Klein bringing "Mike Mulligan and His Steam Shovel" to life, and Amanda Plummer relating the tale of "The Dancing Frog" (this last entry betrayed Michael Sporn's fondness for classic animation: the amphibian of the title looked just like Chuck Jones' *One Froggy Evening* star

Michigan J. Frog). Older children's literature was usually updated, though never with any damage to the source. One of the best first-season ventures was Hans Christian Andersen's "The Red Shoes," contemporized with black characters and a reggae soundtrack.

The limited but very stylish animation style which characterized *HBO Storybook Musicals* was carried over for its second season, which featured dramatizations of such stories as "The Ice Queen's Mittens" and "The Runaway Teapot." The series' respectful treatment of its source material and the various pedigrees of its star participants resulted in a great deal of critical adulation. Peggy Charren, the hypercritical head of Action for Children's Television, enthused over *HBO Storybook Musicals* ("Clever musical versions of books children love"), while Marilyn Droz of the Council for Children's TV and Media advised that the half hours were "worth taping because, like a well-loved book, children will enjoy these stories over and over again." Posterity has not recorded the reaction to Droz' recommendation of the various home video companies which had already prepared *HBO Storybook Musicals* cassettes, and were understandably averse to giving away what they could sell.

HEATHCLIFF:
—HEATHCLIFF AND DINGBAT. ABC: 10/4/1980–9/18/1981. Ruby/Spears. Executive producers, Joe Ruby and Ken Spears. Produced by Jerry Eisenberg. Directed by Rudy Larriva, Charles Nichols and John Kimball. Music by Dean Elliot. Supervising story editor, Gordon Kent. Story directors, Emily Kong, Alex Lovy and Tom Minton. Writers included Norman Maurer, Tony Benedict, Jack Hanrahan and Don Jurwich. Voices, HEATHCLIFF episodes: Mel Blanc (Heathcliff/Spike/Muggsy/Iggy/Mr. Schultz/Milkman); Julie McWhirter and Marilyn Schreffler (Sonja); Henry Corden (Clem/Digby/Dogsnatcher); June Foray (Crazy Shirley/Sonja/Grandma/Marcy); and Michael Bell, Melendy Britt, Rachel Blake, Joan van Ark, Joe Baker, Alan Oppenheimer, Shep Menken, Hal Smith, Alan Dinehart. Voices, DINGBAT AND THE CREEPS: Frank Welker (Dingbat); Don Messick (Nobody/Sparerib).

—HEATHCLIFF AND MARMADUKE. ABC: 9/12/1981–9/18/1982. Same production credits as HEATHCLIFF AND DINGBAT, with the additional credits of Scatman Crothers as performer of "Marmaduke" theme song and Gordon Kent as co-producer. Additional voice credits for MARMADUKE: Paul Winchell (Marmaduke/Phil Winslow); Russi Taylor (Dottie Winslow/Barbie Winslow/Billy Winslow/Missy); Marilyn Schreffler (Barbie's sister).

—HEATHCLIFF (a.k.a. HEATHCLIFF AND THE CATILLAC CATS). Syndicated: 1984. DIC/McNaught Syndicate/LBS. Executive producers: Jean Chalopin, Andy Heyward and Tom Katayani. Music by Haim Saban and Shuki Levy. Series created by Jean Chalopin, Bruno Bianchi. Developed by Jean Chalopin; assistants, Alan Swayze, Chuck Lorre. Head writer: Alan Swayze. Character design staffer: John Kricfalusi. Voices: Mel Blanc (Heathcliff); Donna Christie (Cleo/Iggy); Stanley Jones (Riffraff/Wordsworth/Milkman); Marilyn Lightstone (Sonja); Danny Mann (Hector/Fish Market Proprietor); Derek McGrath (Spike/Muggsy/Knuckles); Danny Wells (Bush/Raul); Ted Ziegler (Leroy/Mungo/Grandpa); Peter Cullen, and Jeannie Elias.

Heathcliff, the foot-high feline with an attitude, was created for the McNaught newspaper syndicate by comic artist George Gately in 1973, five years before the birth of Heathcliff's closest comic-strip cat rival, Garfield. Accordingly, Heathcliff's TV debut occurred several seasons before Garfield's, first as a network series, then as a separately produced syndicated daily.

To the nonfan, Heathcliff and Garfield are indistinguishable. Closer scrutiny reveals that, whereas Garfield is a fat, lazy house cat who is galvanized into action only when his space and solitude are threatened, Heathcliff is a pugnacious street cat—even though he has owners, the Nutmeg family—who battles all comers of all animal species just for the hell of it. Heathcliff also doesn't passively wait for his bowl to be filled by his master; he ducks and dodges through delicatessen, grocery store and fish market, seldom leaving empty pawed. This larcenous streak is an inheritance from his father, Pops Heathcliff, who wears convict stripes and who generally makes his comic-strip appearances in the form of "wanted" posters.

As the more physically aggressive of the two, Heathcliff should by rights have been easier to adapt to animation than the relatively cerebral Garfield. Yet Heathcliff's TV projects ran second to Garfield's in terms of knockabout comedy, though at least one of them was on equal footing so far as animation technique was concerned.

The first Heathcliff series was ABC's *Heathcliff and Dingbat* (1980), a Ruby-Spears half hour weekly. The combative cat was joined in his 27 short episodes by erstwhile girl friend Sonja, Spike the bulldog, and various frustrated human adversaries including milkmen and dogcatchers. The second component of the weekly *Heathcliff and Dingbat* featured a monster-parody contingent (without a comic strip pedigree) called "Dingbat and the Creeps." Headlining this collection of four- and six-minute installments were Dingbat, a vampire dog who sound like Curly Howard of the Three Stooges (his voice was provided by Frank Welker, whose previous "Curly" assignments included Hanna-Barbera's *Jabberjaw* [q.v.] and *Three Robonic Stooges* [see *Skatebirds*]); Sparerib, a.k.a. "Bonehead," a skeleton who sounded like Bela Lugosi; and Nobody, a bodyless pumpkin who was the voice double of Jimmy Durante. The Creepy trio worked out of a temporary employment agency, Odd Jobs Inc.—no doubt as Kelly Ghouls.

In 1981, the series was retitled *The Heathcliff and Marmaduke Show*. Joining the club was another McNaught syndicate comics star, Brad Anderson's giant Great Dane Marmaduke (which predated Heathcliff, having commenced in 1954). The principal *Marmaduke* gag, that of a king-sized dog with the temperament and emotions of an infant, was clearly meant by Ruby-Spears as an "answer" to Hanna-Barbera's *Scooby-Doo* (q.v.), which Joe Ruby and Ken Spears had developed over a decade earlier. In addition to his six-minute adventures, which alternated weekly with the "Dingbat" episodes, Marmaduke was also featured in two groups of 30-second bumpers: "Marmaduke Riddles" and "Marmaduke's Doggone Funnies," the latter sequences devoted to letters from Marmaduke's fans about their own funny pets.

Unfortunately, the cartoon Marmaduke wasn't *that* doggone funny—nor were the Dingbats or headliner Heathcliff. This was the era of network kidvid during which characters were prevented by wellmeaning media critics from cutting loose in full slapstick splendor—meaning that Heathcliff, so gloriously unrepentant a sinner in the funny papers, was warm, cute, and cuddly on TV. His ongoing tiffs with Spike the dog were depicted as harmless, nonvindictive fun; to make Heathcliff more lovable, the put-upon Spike was transformed by Ruby-Spears into a bully whom Heathcliff only wanted to befriend and play with. And whenever a stock slapstick routine had the guts to rear its head, it was always watered down, ostensibly to keep kids at home from imitating the routine. When, for example, Heathcliff indulged in the time-honored "hit the dog with a boulder using an innertube slingshot" bit, the gag was eviscerated by having well-meaning Heathcliff put the boulder atop the tightening tube in order to weigh the tube down and keep it from accidentally snapping in someone's face!

Things perked up for Heathcliff in 1984, when DIC Enterprises, fresh from their local-syndication triumph *Inspector Gadget* (q.v.), came up with a daily half hour syndie officially titled *Heathcliff and the Catillac Cats* (the cobilling was dropped for the series proper). Heathcliff was returned to his "rebel" status, reducing neighborhood merchants, dogs and postmen to quivering submission. When not at home with Grandpa, Grandma and young Iggy Nutmeg, Heathcliff hung out at the local junkyard with a passel of pussycat buddies, called the "Catillac Cats" in the publicity but seldom on the series: girl friend Sonja, vainglorious Cleo, intellectual Wordsworth, patsy Hector, dumdum Mungo, and con artist Riff Raff. The easily thwarted villain in the junkyard sequences was a hardcase mongrel named Leroy—a spoof of the old Jim Croce song "Bad Bad Leroy Brown," whose protagonist was "meaner than a junkyard dog." There were usually two 15-minute segments per episode, the second spotlighting Heathcliff's buddies, though sometimes Heathcliff's travails ate up the whole half hour. In 1985, several installments were strung together with new transitional footage of Heathcliff rabbeted in, and the result was that home-video "blockbuster," *Heathcliff: The Movie*.

On the whole, the 65-episode syn-dicated *Heathcliff* was a tremendous im-provement over the earlier ABC series, both in laugh content and draftsmanship. It wasn't quite as droll as the competing *Garfield and Friends*, nor did it ring true when the otherwise sociopathic Heathcliff appeared in those daily 30-second "pro-social" bites wherein he lectured the kids at home on proper pet care. Still, DIC's *Heathcliff* had at least one strong drawing card, the one successful holdover from the disappointing Ruby-Spears version: Mel Blanc, who celebrated his fiftieth year in showbiz by supplying the Bugs Bunnyish voice of Heathcliff. When Blanc let loose with such Heathcliffisms as "I come from a long line of ba-a-ad pussycats," it was the closest thing to Cartoon Heaven.

HECKLE AND JECKLE see CBS CARTOON THEATRE and THE NEW ADVENTURES OF MIGHTY MOUSE AND HECKLE AND JECKLE

THE HECTOR HEATHCOTE SHOW. NBC: 10/5/1963–9/25/1965. Ter-rytoons/CBS Films. Produced by Bill Weiss. Directed by Arthur Bartsch, Mar-tin B. Taras, Dave Tendlar, Connie Rasin-ski, Bill Tytla, Bob Kuwahara and Mannie Davis. Music by Phillip Scheib and Jim Timmens. Voices: John Myhers (Hector Heathcote/Hashimoto/Mrs. Hashimoto/Yuriko/Saburo); Dayton Allen (Sidney/Stanley/Cleo); Lionel Wilson (Sidney).

The *Hector Heathcote Show* combined new animated shorts with recently pro-duced Terrytoons theatrical cartoons. The title character, created by Eli Bauer and introduced in the 1959 Terrytoon *Minute and a 1/2 Man*, was a colonially garbed young fellow with a propensity for popping up during crucial moments in American history. Previously published reports that Hector Heathcote was a 20th century scientist who had invented a time machine are inaccurate. Hector was simply "there" at all the right times with no further ex-planation, and always wearing an 18th cen-tury tricorner hat—even when helping build the transcontinental railroad in the mid–1860s! Occasional appearances were made by Heathcote's bulldog Winston, who true to his name spoke in rounded Churchillian tones and who offered sage advice to his rather befuddled master. A fat lot of good that did; Hector Heathcote

never got the credit he deserved for changing the course of history, usually because he seldom accomplished what he'd originally set out to do (while trying to invent the airplane, for example, Hector inadvertently created the harvester, a vital but less glamorous contraption).

Other components on *The Hector Heathcote Show* were comprised of theat-rical cartoons with the occasional made-for-TV effort throw in, featuring a pair of Terrytoons stars of the 1958–1963 era: Hashimoto the Japanese mouse, created by Bob Kuwahara, and Sidney the 42-year-old "baby" elephant, the brainchild of onetime Terrytoons head man Gene Deitch. The theatrical shorts televised on *Hector Heathcote* had been showered with quite a few honors, more than Terrytoons was accustomed to. *Minute and a 1/2 Man* (1959) won first prize at the Venice Film Festival; *Hashimoto San* (1959) was se-lected for showing at Cannes; and *Sidney's Family Tree* (1959) was nominated for an Academy Award.

Such accolades were not bestowed upon the made-for-TV ventures, however. While the animation was wilder and more "modern" than the stodgily produced Ter-rytoons of the 1930s and 1940s, the studio still held fast to formula and repetition, just like in its *Mighty Mouse* (q.v.) days. Hashimoto was nearly always sucked into trouble by his mousey American newsman buddy G.I. Joe, and then extricating himself, his wife Hanako and his children Yuriko and Saburo thanks to his expertise in judo. Sidney the Elephant (who in some cartoons was supplied with a "Hugh Herbert" voice by comedian Dayton Al-len) was a mass of neuroses, invariably wreaking well-meaning havoc on his friends Stanley the Lion (who sounded like Ned Sparks—again thanks to Dayton Al-len) and Cleo the giraffe (who sounded like Carol Channing—Dayton Allen strikes again).

In all, 39 of the 71 cartoons broadcast during the two-year NBC run of *The Hector Heathcote Show* had previously been seen in theaters; the remaining 32 were ground out for television. While the difference in quality between the two packages was rather obvious to discerning cartoon fan-ciers, younger viewers didn't really mind. Or perhaps their minds were elsewhere; most kids were eagerly awaiting the next exciting episode of the "Supermariona-

Hector Heathcote—forever in the middle.

tion" series *Fireball XL-5*, which followed *Heathcote* on NBC's Saturday morning lineup. (See also *The Astronut Show*.)

HELLO KITTY'S FURRY TALE THEATER. CBS: 9/19/1987–9/3/1988. DIC Enterprises/MGM-UA Television. Executive producer, Andy Heyward. Produced and directed by Michael Maliani. Supervising producer, Robby London. Animation supervisor, Norman Drew. Production executive, Winnie Chaffee. Associate producers, John O'Sullivan Francis Jr., Krista Lynn Haimovitch, Lisa A. Salamone. Script supervisor, Lori Crawford. Adapted for animation and story edited by Phil Harnage. Written by Phil Harnage, Jack Hanrahan, Eleanor Burian-Mohr, Jim Lenahan, Martha Moran, Tony Marino, Pat Allee, Ben Hurst, Temple Mathews, Matt Uitz and Jack Olesker. Voice direction by Michael Hack. Title song written and performed by David Pomeranz. Music by Haim Saban

and Shuki Levy. Characters created by Sanrio Co. Ltd. Voices: Tara Charendoff (Hello Kitty); Sean Roberge (Tuxedo Sam); Noam Zylberman (Chip); Maron Bennett (My Melody); Carl Banas (Grandpa Kitty); Elizabeth Hanna (Mama Kitty/Grandma Kitty); Len Carlson (Papa Kitty); Cree Summer Francks (Catnip); Greg Morton (Grinder); Denise Pidgeon (Fangora).

"Hello Kitty," originally created in 1976, was an LJN Toys/Sanrio Co. furry animal doll. By the mid–1980s, "Kitty" was popular enough in its native Japan to encourage matriculation into an American cartoon series—and, it was hoped, into a mass media success commensurate with other doll-to-TV characters like *The Smurfs* (q.v.) and *The Care Bears* (q.v.). The series' premise was that soft 'n' cuddly Hello Kitty ran a repertory theatre with several of her animal friends, where she put on comic versions of famous legends, fables and fairy stories. Season subscribers to the

Furry Tale Theatre were treated to 26 15-minute productions (two per week), bearing such titles as "Wizard of Paws," "Cinderkitty," "Catula" and "How the Scrichnip Stole Christmas." Cast in these lightly amusing playlets were Hello Kitty's companions Tuxedo Sam, My Melody, Catnip, Grinder, Chip and Fangora; occasionally the manager/star nepotistically hired her Mama, Grandpa and Grandma Kitty.

As with *The Muppet Babies* (q.v.), which this series' concept resembled, the real-life personalities of Hello Kitty's acting troupe were reflected in the parts they played; the vain and covetous Catnip, for example, was nearly always cast as a villainess. This served, of course, to convince young viewers at home that all TV actors behaved exactly the same as their TV characters. Well, don't they?

H.E.L.P.! ABC: 1979-80. 8 Films/Dahlia Productions. A Phil Kimmelman production. Executive producers, Ken Greengrass and Phil Lawrence. Produced by Lynn Ahrens.

With *H.E.L.P.!*, a series of one-minute educational animated fillers sprinkled throughout ABC's 1979-80 Saturday morning schedule, the network assuaged its conscience concerning its more frivolous cartoon series (and also deflected criticism from ACT and similar groups). The title was an acronym for Dr. Henry's Emergency Lessons for People; the lessons herein centered on safety and first aid. All of the *H.E.L.P.!* vignettes were pre-screened by a team of respected medicos and educators—including Stanford University's Dr. Donald Roberts, a specialist in prosocial television—before being approved for telecast. *H.E.L.P.!* won a 1980 Emmy for "Outstanding Children's Informational/Instructional Programming—Short Format," an honor it shared with a similar animated package, *Schoolhouse Rock* (q.v.).

HELP! IT'S THE HAIR BEAR BUNCH. CBS: 9/11/1971-9/2/1972.

Hanna-Barbera. Executive producers, William Hanna and Joseph Barbera. Associate producer, Alex Lovy. Creative supervisor, Iwao Takamoto. Animation director, Charles A. Nichols. Story by Joel Kane, Woody Kling, Howard Morganstern, Joe Ruby, Ken Spears. Story direc-

tion by Brad Case, Cullen Houghtaling, Earl Klein, Lew Marshall, George Singer, Paul Sommer, Warren Tufts. Character design, Jerry Eisenberg. Musical director, Ted Nichols. Additional music by Hoyt Curtin. Voices: Daws Butler (Hair Bear); Paul Winchell (Bubi Bear); Bill Callaway (Square Bear); John Stephenson (Mr. Peevely); Joe E. Ross (Botch); and Don Messick, Hal Smith, Vic Perrin, Jeanine Brown, Joan Gerber, Janet Waldo, and Lennie Weinrib.

Grasping at a theme already time-honored through repetition on its previous series *Yogi Bear* (q.v.) and *Wally Gator* (q.v.)—that of domesticated animals wishing to escape their human-imposed environs and commiserate in the outside world—Hanna-Barbera came up with 1971's half hour *Help! It's the Hair Bear Bunch*. The Bunch, consisting of confidence trickster Hair Bear, double-talking Bubi Bear and Phil Harris soundalike Square Bear, were residents of Wonderland Zoo, Cave Block #9 (one of many lampoonish references to old prison-break movies). Refusing to live like mere animals, the Hair Bear Bunch converted their cave into a "luxury pad" complete with TV, refrigerator and reclining chairs. All this was kept from the scrutiny of Wonderland's by-the-book curator Peevely and dimwitted guard Botch by hiding the creature comforts behind rocks and revolving walls, in the manner of the live-action sitcom *Hogan's Heroes*. The Bunch managed to escape the zoo quite easily and often during the series' 16 episodes, usually to promote one of Hair Bear's scams at Peevely's expense. In this and most other respects (including Daws Butler's voice characterization for Hair Bear) *Help! It's the Hair Bear Bunch* was a takeoff on Phil Silvers' "Sgt. Bilko"—a chunk of comedy territory canvassed to better effect by Hanna-Barbera's earlier *Top Cat* (q.v.).

The weekly, half hour *Help! It's the Hair Bear Bunch* was just another timekiller during a rather fallow period of inspiration for Hanna-Barbera. The stories rambled, the characters were tiresome, and the laughtrack seemed to be having more fun than either the animators or the audience. Even so, *the Hair Bear Bunch* did produce one lasting Hanna-Barbera legacy: the vocal characterization of Peevely, who sounded just like *McHale's Navy* costar Joe

Flynn. In truth, it was Hanna-Barbera voice veteran John Stephenson who enacted Peevely. Stephenson was encouraged by the producers to do a Flynn-type voice, whereupon he asked why Hanna and Barbera didn't simply just hire Joe Flynn. "We did," they replied. "And he didn't sound right." John Stephenson retained "Joe Flynn" in his repertoire thereafter, most notably in Hanna-Barbera's *Yogi's Space Race* (see *Yogi Bear*).

Since the Hair Bears were drawn to look like hippies (or at least "square" TV's concept of hippies), it was decided to downplay the dated references to their hairiness when Hanna-Barbera syndicated the series in 1974. As a result, the reruns went out under the title *Yo Yo Bears*—ironic, in that "Yo Yo Bear" had been one of the proposed names for the Hair Bears' most obvious Hanna-Barbera ancestor, Yogi Bear.

HE-MAN AND THE MASTERS OF THE UNIVERSE. Syndicated: 1983. Filmation/Mattel/Group W. Executive producer, Lou Scheimer. Executive vice president, creative affairs, Arthur H. Nadel. Directed by Lou Zukor and Hal Sutherland. Vice president in charge of production, Joe Mazzuca. Written by Robby London, Tom Ruegger, Ron Schultz, Sam Schultz, Marc Scott Zicree, Larry Ditillo, Paul Dini, J. Michael Reaves, Byrnne Stephens, Anis Diamond, David Wise, Susan Stewart, Marc Richards, Mel Gilden, Jeffrey O'Hare, Douglas Booth, Arthur Browne, Jr. Music by Erika Lane, Shuki Levy, Haim Saban. Voices: John Erwin (He-Man/Ram-Man); Melendy Britt (She-Ra); Alan Oppenheimer (Skeletor/Marman/Beast Man); Linda Gary (Queen/Evil-Lyn/Sorceress/Teela); Lou Scheimer (Orko/King); Erik Gunden (Battlecat/Gringer/Man-at-Arms); George DiCenzo; Lana Beeson; Erika Scheimer; B. D. Bobb. —THE NEW ADVENTURES OF HE-MAN. Syndicated: 1990. JetLag Productions/DIC Enterprises. Executive producer, Andy Heyward. Produced by Mark Taylor and Akihero Ikeda. Directed by Kazuo Terade, Masanori Miura and Bernard Deyries. Developed by Jean Chalopin. Story advisors, Jean Chalopin and Jack Olesker. Story editor, Jack Mendelsohn. Music by Haim Saban and Shuki Levy; musical direction by Alex Dimitroff. Voice director, Susan Blu. Animation facilities: KK C&D/Parafrance Communications. Voices: Don Brown, Gary Chalk, Ted Cole, Tracy Eisner, Mark Hildreth, Anthony Holland, Campbell Lane, Doug Parker, Alvin Sanders, Venus Terzo.

He-Man and the Masters of the Universe was the first animated series to benefit directly from the relaxing of FCC rules under the Mark Fowler regime — and as a result became the cartoon property that changed the face of the syndicated cartoon market.

The daily series drank deeply from the well of *Star Wars*, with heavy gulps of "sword and sorcery" consumed in the process. Prince Adam was the handsome, part–Earthling regent of the planet Eternia, an idyllic orb threatened with subjugation from the irascibly power-hungry mutant of Snake Mountain, Skeletor—so named because of his skull-like countenance. Both hero and villain sought to gain entrance to Castle Greyskull, to obtain the wisdom of the Council of Elders. Prince Adam's advantage was the ability to transform into the superpowered He-Man, simply by holding his sword aloft and shouting "By the power of Greyskull!" With the help of magic weaponry and the counsel of Man-at-Arms (*He-Man*'s version of Obie Wahn Kenobee, *Star Wars*' "shaman" character), He-Man, bellowing his motto "I have the power!" was able to hold Skeletor at bay—but only for the length of each half hour episode, since the wicked sorceror-warrior was always back on the job within a few days.

There were others on the side of Good, including Prince Adam's twin sister Princess Adora, ruler of the Parallel world Etheria (introduced in the 1985 five-parter *Secret of the Sword* and later a series star in her own right—see *She-Ra, Princess of Power*); Man-at-Arms' daughter, warrior goddess Teela; the Sorceress, who despite her forbidding name was one of He-Man's most powerful allies; Duncan, a kindly scientist; Orko, He-Man's trollish comedy sidekick; the metamorphosing robot Man-E-Faces; Meckaneck the human periscope; and Adam's faithful but timorous green tiger Cringer, which with a little highpowered help became the mighty, armored "Battle Cat." Skeletor also had his allies, among them Evil-Lyn, Shotoki (the Mistress of the Night), the demon Negator, and the Gargon Warriors (who looked like Gargoyles). Quite an elaborate, and elaborately costumed, cast for a mere afternoon syndie of the early 1980s — but then, *He-Man* was more than a cartoon. "He-Man" had already been established as a line of action figures, rolling off the production lines of Mattel Toys. The character designs of He-Man and his confreres were drafted in 1981 by the artists at National Periodical's DC Comics line, and test-marketed in that publisher's *Superman* comic books, complete with a backstory about life on Eternia. Reader response was positive; the next step was to advertise He-Man on TV. Impressed by Filmation's similar *Blackstar* (q.v.) cartoon weekly, Mattel commissioned that studio to create a package of elaborate 30-second *He-Man* animated commercials, which resulted in strong toystore sales for the action figures. This in turn led to plans for a daily cartoon *He-Man* series as an additional marketing tool for the toys.

The ABC network, to whom *He-Man and the Masters of the Universe* was first pitched in 1982, turned the series down flat. Never mind that Mattel — keeping within FCC rules — had no intention of running advertisements for the He-Man toys during the series proper. The network had been burned badly by criticism and incipient litigation heaped upon it back in 1970 for *Hot Wheels* (q.v.), another series based on a Mattel product. The network had been pressured to remove this popular series from its lineup after being accused of using its airtime for "show-length commercials."

By 1983, however, FCC chairman Mark Fowler had modified several long-standing rules concerning children's TV commercialization, among them the rule against a series based on a particular toy product. So long as the "He-Man" figures were not advertised on the *He-Man* series itself, everything was on the square.

Richard Weiner Inc., Mattel's promotional firm, was sent out to convince local stations (ABC was still resistant) that *He-Man* could be a potent syndication item with built-in sponsor identification. This being 1983, a particularly dry year for fresh syndicated cartoon product (outside of DIC's *Inspector Gadget* [q.v.], local stations had to make do with network repeats), *He-Man* seemed particularly attractive — especially since distribution was being handled by the powerful and reliable Group W, which owned Filmation at that time. The sales were made — and

made, and made, until *He-Man and the Masters of the Universe* was the second-highest-rated kidvid syndie on the market, and its tie-in toy the second largest seller in the nation — beaten only by Mattel's evergreen Barbie doll.

Once established, the system of purchasing half-hour "cartoon commercials" was the method by which non-network children's programming prospered; ultimately, syndication bypassed the networks as the biggest marketplace for the four major animation houses. It can be said that without *He-Man* to show the way, there wouldn't have been any *DuckTales* (q.v.), nor any *Tiny Toons* (q.v.), nor any *Batman: The Animated Series* (q.v.).

Better animated and designed than most earlier Filmations (including its direct inspiration *Blackstar*), *He-Man* was careful to temper its action content with prosocial messages about tolerance and nonviolence. Most of these were implicit in the storylines, but Filmation and Group W wanted to make sure no one missed the messages lest the series be accused of motivationless mayhem (as it often was by those who never watched it). Thus, comic-relief Orko was on hand at the end of each episode with a spoken 30-second moral, supervised (as were many of these animated placebos) by Stanford University's Dr. Donald F. Roberts.

Dr. Roberts exercised even more control over the *New Adventures of He-Man* revival in 1990, by which time DIC Enterprises had succeeded the moribund Filmation as the production company. Under Roberts' guidance, what had once been a virile, vibrant property had been toned down to a "kinder and gentler" level. Skeletor, whose crankiness had been occasionally amusing on the older series, was reduced to a pure buffoon on the new *He-Man* — just one of the many team members of the Mutants, a creepy contingent engaged in athletic events and psychological games against He-Man and his fellow heroes on their new turf, the planet Primus. Deadly warfare was now merely good vs. bad sportsmanship, and a drop of red ink was spilled. The new *He-Man* also had an ecological bent; Prince Adam/He-Man tried to save Primus more through conservation than combat. All that hadn't been "improved" was the animation, a pale shadow of the (temporarily)

Henry's Cat celebrates the invention of sausage — or maybe cucumbers.

higher Filmation standards on the first *He-Man*.

The *New Adventures of He-Man* failed to catch on in the manner of its predecessor. Like the revived *G.I. Joe* (q.v.) that same year (1990), this was another past champion laid low by syndication's new emphasis on comedy and animal characters.

HENRY'S CAT. Showtime: 1990. Produced 1983. Videotape available 1986. Bob Godfrey Films Ltd. England. Created by Stan Hayward. Narration and Voices: Bob Godfrey (Dom DeLuise redubbed the videocassette version).

Henry never appeared on the British-produced *Henry's Cat*, but we certainly got a lot of that cat. The titular feline was a bedraggled orange creature of Cockney parentage, who, with such back-alley animal buddies as Chris Rabbit and Rambaba the sheep, would fantasize wild adventures: a Tarzan spoof, the *Star Wars*-inspired "Captain Goodcat," the Sherlock Holmes ripoff "The Case of the Pilfered Pearls," and the like. Most of these fanciful flights were the result of meticulous rehearsal conducted by Chris Rabbit, who wore a cardboard-cutout TV set on his head for the occasion. (Isn't that the way *real* directors do it?)

Henry's Cat was virtually a one-man operation produced by Bob Godfrey, an Australian-born animator best known internationally for his sidesplitting 1961 short *Do-It-Yourself Cartoon Kit*. Godfrey's trademarks included satiric, sarcastic narration and dialogue (one of the Cat's adventures was so vivid that the narrator suggested "He must have seen the movie! He must have read the book!") and a visual smorgasbord of cel paintings, cardboard cutouts, and magazine illustrations — stylistic choices which obviously influenced the output of *Monty Python's Flying Circus* cartoonist Terry Gilliam.

Always offbeat and sometimes hilarious, *Henry's Cat* premiered in the U.S. over the Showtime cable service in 1990, where it was erratically telecast in early-morning slots except for a prime-time brace of Christmas specials telecast in December 1991. Five years earlier, several of the Cat's ten-minute adventures had been packaged for the videocassette market — where, in a misguided Americanization effort, Bob Godfrey's droll narration was supplanted by the stridency of Dom DeLuise.

THE HERCULOIDS. CBS: 9/9/1967– 9/6/1969. Hanna-Barbera. Produced and directed by William Hanna and Joseph

Barbera. Music by Ted Nichols. Character design by Alex Toth. Voices: Mike Road (Zandor/Zok/Igoo/Tundra); Virginia Gregg (Tara); Teddy Eccles (Dorno); Don Messick (Gloop/Gleep).
—GO GO GLOBETROTTERS. NBC: 2/4/1978–9/2/1978. (Included reruns of the THE HERCULOIDS. See also credits for THE C.B. BEARS and THE HARLEM GLOBETROTTERS.)
—SPACE STARS. NBC: 9/12/1981–9/11/1982. (See separate entry.)

The *Herculoids* existed in an indefinite future on the primitive planet Quasar, where it was their mission to protect citizens both high-born (The King and Family) and low (the underground-dwelling Sand People) from extraterrestrial enemies. King Zandor, his wife Tara and his son Dormo were humans, while their Herculoid protectors were animals—though Zandor, an intellectual Tarzan type, was more than capable of fending for himself. The Herculoids themselves included Zok, a dragon with laser-equipped eyes and tail; Tundro the Tremendous, a dinosaur who had a cannon in his horn and ten legs for locomotion; Igoo, a hulking "rock ape"; and Gloop and Gleep, a pair of amoebalike blobs who were able to form themselves into any shape or size.

This package of 18 animated half hours—two episodes per show—was one of the most ambitious and least derivative of Hanna-Barbera's Saturday morning superhero efforts of the 1960s. The *Herculoids* benefited mightily from the input of comic book artist Alex Toth (see *Space Angel*), especially in the teasingly sexy character design of the humans, both female (Tara) *and* male (Zandor). As for the nonhumans, this was one cartoon series where the various alien entities really looked as though they'd come from other worlds instead of merely being drawn as exaggerated Earthlings: Gloop and Gleep, for example, resembled floating, translucent pancakes. As an intriguing precursor to the *Star Wars* school (still a decade in the future), *Herculoid*'s diverse life forms managed to coexist not only but to be eminently suited to each other's company, rather than providing uncomfortably comic contrasts. In the same vein, the "timeless" outer-space motif on *Herculoids* allowed futuristic space vehicles to land on Quasar's still-forming "Dawn of Man" landscape without a hint of anachronism.

Herculoids' storylines maintained the intelligence and texture of the visual style. It was not uncommon for Zandor to let a murderous villain off scot-free, on the proviso that the miscreant leave the planet and never return. Maintaining Quasar's wellbeing was Zandor's mission, not vengeance. Those chest-beating experts who wailed over "excessive violence" on Saturday morning TV in the 1960s probably passed over *Herculoids*—assuming it was nothing more than a new coat of paint on "Hercules"—and never gave this actionful but anti-violent series a break.

The series also boasted the exuberant but straight-faced voice work of *Jonny Quest* (q.v.) veteran Mike Road and radio actress extraordinaire Virginia Gregg (among her thousands of voiceover roles was the malevolent "Mother" in Hitchcock's *Psycho*). Hanna-Barbera regular Don Messick rose to the occasion with a self-described "vibrato" intonation that he'd first used in his teenaged radio days in Maryland for the voices of Gloop and Gleep.

In 1976, reruns of *The Herculoids* and two other Hanna-Barbera retreads, *The Harlem Globetrotters* (q.v.) and *The C.B. Bears*, and the result was NBC's *Go Go Globetrotters* (q.v.). New *Herculoids* episodes—none which came anywhere near the quality of the originals—were produced for a 1981 Hanna-Barbera portmanteau series, *Space Stars* (q.v.).

HERE COMES THE GRUMP. NBC: 9/6/1969–9/4/1971. DePatie-Freleng/Mirisch. Produced by David H. DePatie and Friz Freleng. Directed by Gerry Chiniquy, Art Davis, George Gordon, Sid Marcus, Hawley Pratt, Grant Simmons. Story supervision by John W. Dunn, Don Christensen, Nick George and Bill Lutz. Character design by Art Leonardi. Music by Doug Goodwin. Voices: Jay North (Terry); Stefanianna Christopher (Dawn); Rip Taylor (Grump); and Avery Schreiber, Marvin Miller, Larry D. Mann, Athena Lorde, and June Foray.

A rare instance of attempting a "fairy tale" milieu in the superhero-dominated late 1960s, *Here Comes the Grump* was the part–Tolkien, part–Seuss tale of a faraway land placed under the curse of Gloom. The instigator was the Grump, who was fed up with all the happiness and joy dispensed under the reign of the good Princess

Dawn. The basic plotline anticipated the many videogame-inspired cartoon series of the 1980s: American youth Terry Dexter was magically called upon to rescue Dawn, her dog Bib (actually not *really* a dog but a nondescript bubble of fur with a detachable nose and a propellor tail), and her land from the dour influence of the Grump. This entailed a search throughout the Land of 1000 Caves for the hidden Cave of the Whispering Orchids, wherein was secreted the Crystal Key, which would release the kingdom from the Gloom spell. For the next 17 episodes (two short adventures per half hour) Terry, Bib and Dawn trekked their way through such sort-of-legendary locales as Snow White City, Blunderland and the Lemonade Sea — all the while pursued by the Grump, astride his flying Jolly Green Dragon.

It all sounds precious and ponderous, but *Here Comes the Grump* was strictly slapstick, directed by such seasoned comedy men as Gerry Chiniquy, Art Davis and Sid Marcus. The Grump, who when described on paper comes off as the very personification of Menace, was actually a short, self-important jerk in the Daffy Duck mode, whose own greed and ambition invariably led to his downfall. There was a little "Wile E. Coyote" in his makeup as well, what with innumerable traps set for the heroes backfiring disastrously on the villain. Moreover, the Grump *looked* funny — an all-pink meanie decked out with an outsized handlebar mustache and a hand-me-down wizard's outfit. Rip Taylor, a "nut" comic who utilized wacky props and horrendous puns in his act (sort of an Aquarius-Age Gallagher), chose a gravelly, southern-fried mumble as the voice of the Grump, demonstrating the true comedian's knack for saying things funny rather than saying funny things.

Also played for laughs was the Grump's "sidekick," the Jolly Green Dragon, who despite his allegiance to the villain was a benign creature, grinning broadly even when abused by his disgruntled master — and belching fire only when one of his many allergies brought on a sneeze. This lighthearted approach extended to the various fantasy characters encountered by Terry and Dawn in their flight from the Grump. Several of these characters were humanized non-humans like trains, trees, bottles and balloons, and most of them were supplied with an abundance of gently satiric dialogue. One superb episode was set in a ghost town populated by talking houses and buildings, all displaying the more annoying characteristics of their former owners: a library spoke in harsh whispers, while "City Hall" refused to offer a direct answer to any question.

With all this comic competition, the "straight" leads — Terry and Princess Dawn — came off as nonentities, though it was amusing to watch the Princess haughtily try to pull rank on talking trees, doors, and wheels, who knew nothing and cared less about royal protocol. *Here Comes the Grump* moved too quickly and covered too much ground for anyone to worry about a dull hero and heroine — or the fact that each episode was all jokes and no plot. There was also a smorgasbord of visual treats to draw attention away from the negligible Terry and Dawn: the superb animation, the beautifully timed gags, and the colorful Wonderland-style background art. *Here Comes the Grump* was an ideal showcase for the crackerjack De-Patie-Freleng team, negating the widely held belief that all late–1960s TV cartoons were artistic disgraces.

Perhaps because it didn't "mean" anything and thus was considered to have no educational or socially redeeming values, *Here Comes the Grump* disappeared from the airwaves once Saturday morning network cartoons were forced to be "significant." This is one series that deserves to be better known; dig a little at the rental stores and you might find a few scattered episodes on videocassette. *Here Comes the Grump* was no *Rocky and His Friends* (q.v.) or *Beany and Cecil* (q.v.), but is definitely worth a second look.

HERO HIGH *see* **KID SUPER POWER HOUR WITH SHAZAM**

HEROES ON HOT WHEELS. Family Channel: 9/16/1991–8/28/1992. LaCinq/C & D/Jingle/Hit/CNC/Family Channel/LBS Communications. In association with Mattel. Executive producers: Christian Masson, Mark-Pierre Houlinjeane, Mark Taylor. Directed by Christian Ligman. Animation director, Eiji Okabe. Created by Jean Graton. Written by Dominique Prive, Patrick Vanetti. Story editors: Jack Olesker, Mark Taylor. English translation by Moneric Translators and

Kazumi Sawaguchi. U.S. production facilities: JetLag Productions. Additional overseas production facilities: KK C&D. Executive in charge of KKC&D Animation: Shigeru Akagawa, Hiroshi Toita. Music by Haim Saban and Shuki Levy. Musical direction: Alex Dimitroff. Voices: Ian James Corlett, Mike Donovan, Scott McNeil, Venus Terzo, Dale Wilson.

The second animated series to promote Mattel's "Hot Wheels" toy car line (see *Hot Wheels*), *Heroes on Hot Wheels* was a half hour adventure 'toon revolving around the exploits of the Shadow Jets. The Jets were a highly sophisticated and technically advanced team of space scientists and explorers, who doubled in their spare time as race car drivers. Handsome head driver Michael was the son of Dr. Valiant, leader of the scientists. Mike's assistants included his rolypoly Uncle Quincy, his close pal Steve Warson, and a monkey named Arthur. Dr. Valiant's second-in-command Prof. Kathy Durant veered away from the fast-track action, preferring the comparative safety of the scientific control booth (which, as devotees of the *Speed Racer*-style cartoon series can tell you, wasn't all that safe either). The villains were the usual bad drivers and poor sports; some were poachers, smugglers and evil scientists in the bargain.

Heroes on Hot Wheels was produced for French television, where it played for nearly two years before being picked up in 1991 for American Monday-through-Friday play by the Family Channel cable service. Though not mentioned in the English-language credits, the series did not spring solely from a desire to sell Mattel products, but was in fact the animated version of a Belgian adventure comic strip, "Michel Vaillant," which cartoonist Jean Graton introduced in *Tintin* (q.v.) magazine way back in 1957. Older than his "Mike Valiant" screen counterpart, Michel Vaillant was the son of the car manufacturer who'd created the "Vaillante" line which Michel raced in competition. Steve Warson was Michel's friendly American rival in the comic strip instead of his partner. Steve was always on excellent terms with Michel and his Vaillante racing team, who in turn were on *such* excellent terms with one another that Jean Graton was obliged to marry off Michel Vaillant in 1973 due to reader accusations that the strip advocated homosexuality! Though the "Hot Wheels" toys were not promoted in "Michel Vaillant," Graton had no qualms about accepting compensation for plugging other auto-related brand names in his panels.

American purchasers of the *Heroes on Hot Wheels* home videotapes were treated to an added bonus denied the Family Channel viewership. Each cassette packing box came equipped with a Mattel "Hot Wheels" Formula One, Dune Buggy or miniature Porsche.

HILLBILLY BEARS *see* **ATOM ANT**

HOKEY WOLF *see* **HUCKLEBERRY HOUND**

HONEY HONEY. CBN: 1984–1988. Toei Studios/MIC Modern Programs International. Executive producer, Juzo Tsubota. Directed by Takeshi Shirato.

Honey Honey, a Japanese half hour animated series, was all about a do-gooding little girl whose personality bore a marked resemblance to the bygone American comic strip moppet "Little Annie Rooney." Twenty-nine episodes were produced by Toei Studios and telecast in Japan as *The Wonderful Adventures of Honey Honey* from October 1981 through May 1982. The series' American run was limited to the early-morning and weekend children's lineup of the CBN cable service, where it flourished for at least four seasons. The sugary sweet *Honey Honey* should not under any circumstances be confused with another, far raunchier Japanese comic-strip effort: the sexy saga of an android high school student titled *Cutie Honey.*

HONG KONG PHOOEY. ABC: 9/7/1974–9/4/1976; NBC: 2/4/1978–9/2/1978.

—THE GODZILLA/HONG KONG PHOOEY HOUR. NBC: 11/22/1980–5/15/1981. Hanna-Barbera. Executive producers, William Hanna and Joseph Barbera. Creative producer, Iwao Takamoto. Directed by Charles A. Nichols. Executive story consultant, Myles Wilder. Story editor, Bill Raynor. Story by Fred Fox, Seaman Jacobs, Len Janson, Chuck Menville, Larz Bourne and Jack Mendelsohn. Recording director, Wally Burr. Backgrounds by Montealegre. Music by Hoyt Curtin and Paul DeKorte. Voices: Scatman Crothers (Penrod Pooch/Hong Kong Phooey); Joe E. Ross (Sgt. Flint); Kathi

Gori (Rosemary); Don Messick (Spot); and Richard Dawson, Ron Feinberg, Bob Holt, Casey Kasem, Jay Lawrence, Peter Leeds, Allan Melvin, Alan Oppenheimer, Bob Ridgely, Fran Ryan, Hal Smith, Jean Vanderpyl, Lee Vines, Janet Waldo, Frank Welker, Lennie Weinrib, and Paul Winchell. (For additional voice credits, see entry on GODZILLA.)

This pig-bladder spoof of live action detective shows (*not* a spoof of *Kung Fu*, as has sometimes been suggested) starred a meek dog janitor, Penrod Pooch, who worked in a metropolitan police station. No one on the force suspected that Penrod Pooch was secretly the robed and masked Hong Kong Phooey, "Number One Superguy" and "muscular master of the martial arts," who leaped into a filing cabinet to change into his baggy costume. As Hong Kong Phooey, he negotiated the city streets in his gadget-laden Phooeymobile with his long-suffering assistant, a cat named Spot, in search of criminal masterminds. Penrod/Phooey was armed with limitless self confidence gleaned from a correspondence course in self defense, exemplified by his always-handy manual "The Hong Kong Kung Fu Book of Tricks."

Alas, Hong Kong Phooey was not the brightest of hounds, and usually found himself up against it, at which point it became necessary to be rescued by the giggling, world-weary Spot, whose exasperated facial reactions in such circumstances rivalled those of Oliver Hardy. One of Spot's less glamorous tasks was to hike back to the police station and fetch Penrod's cumbersome filing cabinet—because it was the *only* place where Penrod felt comfortable transforming into Hong Kong Phooey.

The rest of the cast was comprised of humans: good guys Sgt. Flint and police switchboard operator Rosemary (who openly yearned for Hong Kong Phooey while virtually ignoring Penrod Pooch), and bad guys on the order of Mr. Pattycake (a combination jewel thief and cookie baker), The Malevolent Magician, and Mr. Tornado. Hong Kong Phooey was only called upon when such "tricky" criminals flourished—meaning, in the case of this series, once per week (or twice per week, since some half hours carried two short adventures).

Perhaps the most notable aspect of *Hong Kong Phooey* was that the voice of the central character, a devoted student of oriental martial arts, was supplied by a black actor, Scatman Crothers—who, may we add, was terrific. Sixteen half hour *Hong Kong Phooey* programs, all funny enough not to rely upon the series' moronic laughtrack, were run on ABC for two seasons. When that network's head honcho Fred Silverman defected to NBC, he rebroadcast his *Hong Kong Phooey* manifest together with reruns of Hanna-Barbera's *Godzilla* (q.v.). The result was a cartoon salad bearing the title *The Godzilla/Hong Kong Phooey Hour.*

HOPPITY HOOPER. ABC: 9/12/1964–9/2/1967. Jay Ward Productions/Producers Associates of Television. Produced by Jay Ward and Bill Scott. Producer for P.A.T., Peter Piech. Directed by Bill Hurtz, Pete Burness and Lew Keller. Written by Bill Scott, Chris Jenkyns. Animation by Gamma Productions; Sam Kai, animation supervisor. Executive producer: Ponsomby Britt, O.B.E. (sic!). (Commander McBragg episodes produced by Leonardo Television.) Voices: Chris Allen (Hoppity Hooper); Hans Conried (Prof. Waldo Wigglesworth); Bill Scott (Fillmore); Paul Frees (Narrator); and June Foray, Edward Everett Horton, Charlie Ruggles, Daws Butler and Kenny Delmar.

Several earlier television encyclopedias have listed Jay Ward's *Hoppity Hooper* as being released for syndication in 1962. Possibly it was *announced* for syndication in that year, but this writer recalls that the first official word on *Hoppity Hooper* occurred when voice actor Hans Conried referred to its upcoming ABC release on NBC's *Tonight Show* in the summer of 1964. Had there been any real plan to release it any earlier, Jay Ward, whose self-promotional skills were legendary, would certainly have gotten that tidbit to all major city newspapers before 1962 was half over.

Now that that's out of the way, *Hoppity Hooper* was Ward's third network series (see *Rocky and His Friends* for comment on that series and its followup *The Bullwinkle Show*), and the first released directly to Saturday mornings. Like *Rocky's* Frostbite Falls, Minnesota, *Hoppity's* plotline springboard was another fictional midwestern burg, Foggybog, Wisconsin. Hoppity Hooper (originally Hippity Hooper, a character name vetoed because it was too close to Warner Bros.' cartoon kangaroo Hippity Hopper) was a freshfaced young frog, who never walked when hopping would do and who lived alone in Foggybog until his home was invaded by snake-oil peddler Waldo Wigglesworth, a Shakespearian fox who passed himself off as Hoppity's uncle (what better way to attain free food and lodging?). Uncle Waldo's shill was the slowwitted Fillmore Bear, who inexplicably dressed in Confederate Army garb (his voice contained no trace of Southern heritage) and who occasionally broke up the action by blowing an offkey charge on his battered bugle.

The ABC Network wasn't keen on the lengthy continuing-story format established by Jay Ward on *Rocky and His Friends* — ABC had convinced itself that younger viewers in 1964 couldn't follow a plotline as long as *Rocky*'s 40-part "Jet Fuel Formula" — so the 26 stories on *Hoppity Hooper* were rigidly locked into a four-part format, the first two episodes serving as cliffhangers for the following week's concluding chapters. Lost, then, were the delightful plot convolutions and Dos Passos-like ramblings and non sequiturs that graced Jay Ward's "Rocky and Bullwinkle" adventures. Ward and coproducer Bill Scott were required to stick to the point, *sans* embellishments, in each *Hoppity* saga.

This didn't always adversely affect the comedy content, which at its best was as sharply satirical as the rest of the Ward-Scott output. My vote for the finest *Hoppity Hooper* would go to the four-part "Traffic Zone," a Rod Serling takeoff in which the characters stepped into a parallel universe where they all turned into huge vegetables. The storyline was a winner all the way, from the Serlingesque narration by Paul Frees to a screamingly funny Bob Newhart imitation — courtesy of Bill Scott — when the Mayor of Foggybog called the President for protection against "killer vegetables": "You . . . you say we should call the secretary of agriculture? . . . 'More in his line of work.' I — I see, sir . . ."

But for the most part *Hoppity Hooper*'s scripts weren't as zestful as earlier Jay Ward projects; there were too many misfire gags, too many long unfunny stretches between the best jokes. Perhaps this was because its writing staff consisted

of only two people (Bill Scott and Chris Jenkyns) instead of the large rotating team that had worked on *Rocky* and *Bullwinkle*. This sort of comedy is best created with a large number of top comic talents bouncing ideas off one another, resulting in innumerable jokes and sight gags both good and bad which could then be boiled down to the best of the batch.

Hoppity Hooper also lacked the strongest suit of the Rocky and Bullwinkle stories — dynamic heroes and villains to latch onto. Hoppity, a naive and generally passive character, was definitely no Rocket J. Squirrel, nor was Chris Allen's adolescent voice characterization of the friendly frog in the same league as June Foray's resourceful Rocky. Prof. Waldo Wigglesworth, whose get-rich-quick schemes and meticulously preplanned confidence scams motivated many of the plots, might in other circumstances have been a Boris Badenov-style recurring comic villain. Actor Hans Conried certainly gave his all to Waldo, pulling every stop out with the snorts, trilled "r's," and elongated vowels that he used whenever portraying a John Barrymore "ham." But Waldo was all bravado and no substance. Previous Ward heavies like Boris Badenov and Snidely Whiplash would occasionally pause and reveal hidden layers of characterization beyond their two-dimensional perfidy: Boris' toadying terror of his superior Fearless Leader, Snidely's morose soliloquies as to how little his villainy has gotten him in life, and the like. Waldo Wigglesworth was a flat, tiresomely bombastic plot catalyst, nothing more. Only Fillmore Bear, with his Bullwinkle-like speech patterns and his flashes of realization that he was indeed merely a TV cartoon character ("What would all them kids out there think of you if you ran out?" he remonstrated to Waldo at one juncture), was up to Jay Ward's usual standard.

Each *Hoppity Hooper* half hour incorporated "Fractured Fairy Tales" and "Peabody's Improbable History" reruns from the earlier *Rocky and His Friends* and *Bullwinkle Show*. Since the series was sponsored by General Mills, the cereal company decreed that the "Commander McBragg" sequences from another "Big G"–sponsored program, Leonardo Productions' *Tennessee Tuxedo and His Tales* (q.v.), be included on *Hoppity Hooper*. This package was syndicated locally in

1965 as *Uncle Waldo and His Friends*, even as the ABC version still played on Saturday mornings. The various *Hoppity* components reappeared in a 1967 ABC Sunday series, *Cartoon Fun*, with additional rerun segments of Jay Ward's "Aesop and Son" (again from *Rocky*).

HOT WHEELS. ABC: 9/6/1969–9/4/1971. Mattel/Pantomime Pictures. Executive producer, Ken Snyder. Produced by Jean Lindsay, Charles Phalen, Dick Reed and Paul Shively. Directed by Fred Crippen, Joe Bruno, George Singer and Irv Spector. Music by Jack Fascinato. Theme song performed by Mike Curb and the Curbstones. Voices: Bob Arbogast (Jack Wheeler/ Doc Warren); Melinda Casey (Janice Martin); Albert Brooks (Mickey Barnes/ Kip); Susan Davis (Ardeth Pratt); Casey Kasem (Tank Mallory/ Dexter Carter); Nora Marlowe (Mother O'Hara); Michael Rye (Mike Wheeler).

Hot Wheels was widely touted by ABC as a "pro-safety" cartoon series, something its indirect inspiration, the syndicated *Speed Racer* (q.v.), implicitly was not—at least not according to concerned-parent groups. The weekly half hour was created by Ken Snyder, utilizing a straight, realistic "Anamorphic" animation process far removed from the UPA-like modernistic approach he'd taken five years earlier with *Roger Ramjet* (q.v.). The all-human cast consisted principally of a teenaged auto racing club, populated by what the publicity boys were careful to point out were "responsible" teens. Middle aged Doc Warren supervised the Hot Wheels Club of Metro City, headed by young Jack Wheeler and numbering among its members pretty Janice Martin, studious Kip Chogi, rambunctious Mickey Barnes (voice provided by comedian Albert Brooks, whose brother Bob Einstein would ironically later portray foolhardy stuntman *Super Dave* [q.v.]), tomboy Ardeth Pratt, and mechanic Tank Mallory. The club's strict observance of safety and traffic rules was contrasted with the bad example set by reckless rival racers Dexter Carter and Stuff Haley. Peripheral educational material in the form of nature lessons and health tips was provided by the upright (but never boring) Hot Wheelers.

All of *Hot Wheels'* best prosocial intentions were ignored by the FCC, which perceived the series as an unabashed half hour advertisement for Mattel Toys' line of Hot Wheels miniature cars. The regulatory agency threatened to yank the series, insisting that there was an unbendable rule prohibiting program-length commercials (this was 1969, not 1989). This was contested by ABC, which pointed out that there'd been no prior commitment to Mattel when the series began production and that the Hot Wheels cars were never advertised on the *Hot Wheels* series; the network was eventually backed up on this by the National Association of Broadcasters. Nonetheless, FCC pressure compelled the networks to avoid future such commercial tie-ins for the next decade. *Hot Wheels* itself was cancelled after two lucrative seasons (17 half hours, two short adventures per program), not so much to appease the FCC as to clear the boards for Mattel's next merchandising campaign.

In 1991, FCC rules had relaxed sufficiently to allow cable's Family Channel to run a new Mattel-generated variation of the original *Hot Wheels* concept: *Heroes on Hot Wheels* (q.v.).

THE HOUNDCATS. ABC: 9/9/1972–9/1/1973. DePatie/Freleng. Executive producers, David DePatie and Friz Freleng. Directed by Sid Marcus, Robert McKimson, Spencer Peel and Brad Case. Voices: Daws Butler (Stutz); Aldo Ray (Muscle Mutt); Arte Johnson (Rhubarb); Joe Besser (Puddy Puss); Stu Gilliam (Dingdong); and Joan Gerber, and Michael Bell.

Unlike other DePatie-Freleng takeoffs on popular nighttime live action series (see *The Barkleys* and *The Oddball Couple*), *The Houndcats* was a spin on *two* such programs, one of them not at all popular. The principal inspiration was *Mission:Impossible*, which from 1966 to 1973 depicted the exploits of a highly trained team of troubleshooters and masters of disguise who'd execute deadly missions for the U.S. government. The *Houndcats* also drew upon CBS's *The Bearcats*, a very short-lived western version of *Mission: Impossible*, wherein a troubleshooting team (Rod Taylor and Dennis Cole) traversed the countryside in a Stutz Bearcat. By the time *The Houndcats* made its Saturday morning bow in September 1972, *The Bearcats* had already been dead and gone for nine months, killed off by competition from NBC's *Flip Wilson Show* and ABC's *Alias Smith and Jones*.

The *Houndcats'* premise: A crack team of specialized dogs and cats, whose individual talents never got in the way of their basic ineptitude (and vice versa), were assigned by the government to pull off impossible missions in the Old West. Stutz, the dog leader, was so named because he captained "Sparkplug," the team's Stutz Bearcat (and wore an early 20th century motorist's duster and goggles, just to show the kids at home that he was indeed in the driver's seat). Ding Dong was the southern-fried daredevil stunt dog; Muscle Mutt, a sheepdog, was the brawn supply; Rhubarb, a cat evidently named after the pugnacious pussy from the 1951 baseball comedy of the same name, was the inventor and electronics whiz; and Puddy Puss, the "cat of a thousand faces," was *The Houndcat*'s equivalent of *Mission: Impossible*'s Martin Landau—though the voice work by former Three Stooges member Joe Besser ("You cra-a-zy, you!") somewhat dissipated any resemblance to Landau (and as in *Mission* and the earlier "Undercover Elephant" sequences of Hanna-Barbera's *C.B. Bears* [q.v.]) the Houndcats got their marching orders from a tape recording which invariably self-destructed in a disastrous fashion each week.

While *The Houndcats* fell short of the success of *Mission: Impossible*, its 13 half hour episodes did manage to match the number produced for *The Bearcats*.

HUCKLEBERRY HOUND. The following entry lists all series featuring or starring Huckleberry Hound on a regular basis.

—**HUCKLEBERRY HOUND.** Syndicated: 1958. Hanna-Barbera/Screen Gems. Executive producers: William Hanna and Joseph Barbera. Produced by Art Scott. Production supervisor, Howard Hanson. Animation directed by Charles Nichols. Story director, Alex Lovy. Written by Warren Foster, Michael Maltese, Tony Benedict, Charles Shows, Dan Gordon (among others). Music by Hoyt Curtin. Components: 1. HUCKLEBERRY HOUND. Voices: Daws Butler (Huckleberry Hound). 2. PIXIE AND DIXIE. Voices: Daws Butler (Mr. Jinks/Dixie); Don Messick (Pixie). 3. YOGI BEAR (1958–61). Voices: Daws Butler (Yogi Bear); Don Messick (Boo Boo/Ranger

Smith). 4. HOKEY WOLF. Voices: Daws Butler (Hokey Wolf); Doug Young (Ding-a-Ling).

—**YOGI'S GANG.** ABC: 9/8/1973–8/30/1975. (*See* YOGI BEAR for further information.)

—**SCOOBY'S ALL-STAR LAFF-A-LYMPICS.** ABC: 9/10/1977–9/2/1978.

—**SCOOBY'S LAFF-A-LYMPICS.** ABC: 9/9/1978–9/3/1979; 6/12/1980–11/1/1980. (*See* SCOOBY-DOO for further information on above two series.)

—**YOGI'S SPACE RACE.** NBC: 9/9/1978–3/3/1979.

—**GALAXY GOOF-UPS.** NBC: 11/4/1978–1/27/1979.

—**YOGI'S TREASURE HUNT.** Syndicated: 1985 (as component of FUNTASTIC WORLD OF HANNA-BARBERA). (See *Yogi Bear* for cast and production credits of the above three series.)

—**WAKE, RATTLE AND ROLL.** Syndicated: 1990. (See individual entry on this series.)

—**YO YOGI.** ABC: 9/14/1991–7/25/1992. (See *Yogi Bear* for further information on this series.)

Having established itself in 1957 with NBC's *Ruff and Reddy* (q.v.), an animated project designed to serve as "filler" for a group of theatrical cartoons and a live host, the new firm of Hanna-Barbera yearned to create a series over which the studio would have total creative control—no network-imposed host, no "outside" cartoonwork. In early 1958, Kellogg's cereals, which had planted itself in afternoon TV "kidvid" time with an ABC network weekday lineup of adventure show reruns (*Superman*, *Sir Lancelot*, *The Buccaneers*, and *Wild Bill Hickok*), had realized that their biggest hit in this 5 P.M. timeslot was a new cartoon project, Walter Lantz's *Woody Woodpecker*. Suddenly Kellogg's was also interested in sponsoring fresh new animated fare (*Woody* was mostly made up of theatrical cartoons, but Walter Lantz's live sequences and the attendant "buffer" animation were new). Hanna-Barbera and Kellogg's were made for each other—despite a disastrous sales meeting in which several cartoons were screened for Kellogg's with mismatched soundtracks—and the resultant progeny of the two firms was the syndicated *Huckleberry Hound*.

Hanna-Barbera's brainstorm sessions included input from the 70 former MGM

After 29 years at Hanna-Barbera, Huckleberry Hound deserved to win the girl just once. This is from the 1987 special "The Good, the Bad and the Huckleberry Hound."

animation staffers working at the studio. It was decided to draw inspiration from the best of the MGM product, with several grace-notes to appeal to up-to-date 1958 TV fans and with both eyes on a tinier budget. Central character Huckleberry Hound was based in part on the resourceful Droopy, an MGM canine who remained unmoved and unperturbed by the most horrendous of catastrophes. There was also a bit of Disney's Goofy in that Huckleberry was an Everydog, taking on different professions and goals in each cartoon. According to publicity in early 1959, there had been plans to give the new Hound a different voice for each new "role": Bogart for adventure stories, Jack Webb for detective parodies, Gary Cooper for westerns, and so forth. This was forsaken in favor of a relaxed Southern drawl that actor Daws Butler had been using for years in his work with satirist Stan Freberg, and had been employed with excellent results in a 1953 MGM cartoon, *Three Little Pups*. (The voice also popped up in a number of Walter Lantz cartoons, emanating from the larynx of Gabby Gator, perennial foe of Woody Woodpecker.) When *Huckleberry Hound* would score a success in 1958, critics suggested that his voice

was "inspired" by comedian Andy Griffith—even though Butler's career predated Griffith's by at least ten years.

Once it was decided that the Hound would be a laid-back, bucolic character—as indicated by his unofficial (and off-key) theme song, "My Darling Clementine"—several rustic names were proposed and abandoned: Alfalfa Hound, Cactus Hound, and the like. "Huckleberry" was arrived at when the dog began to emerge from preliminary sketches with a blue skin color. Kellogg's liked the character design, but at first it vetoed the name on the grounds that Huckleberry was too long a name for children to remember. (How lucky we are that Mark Twain never worked for Kellogg's.)

Most of the humor in the *Huckleberry Hound* cartoons relied on Huck's deadpan reactions to events, such as the famous sequence when, after being flattened by a drawbridge outside a villain's castle, the Hound gathered his wits and murmured, without pain or rancor, "Man. That's a right heavy drawbridge." This was in line with Hanna-Barbera's economy-dictated policy of loading up on verbal humor in lieu of elaborate visual gags. Two of the best cartoon scriveners from the Warner

Bros. stall, Warren Foster and Michael Maltese, were hired to come up with punch lines that kept viewers laughing—and their minds off animation deficiencies and corner cutting.

A market for half hour cartoons had yet to be established, so the *Woody Woodpecker* format of three short cartoons per program was followed on *Huckleberry Hound*. Huck acted as host, introducing the various segments and exchanging small talk with the series' supporting characters in the openings and closings. (During the first season, Huck also interacted with Cornelius, the Kellogg's Corn Flakes rooster, who was later eliminated from the credits sequences on the theory that Kellogg's would not sponsor the program forever in reruns.) The Hound starred in his own cartoon, usually run as the closing act. The series' other two animated components were "Pixie and Dixie" and "Yogi Bear."

Pixie, the one with the bowtie, and Dixie, the one with the vest and southern accent, were mice on the run from Mr. Jinx, the house cat. While the clear inspiration here was the "Tom and Jerry" series produced by Hanna and Barbera in their MGM days, there were significant differences. For one thing, the characters talked. For another, the impulsive Tom was supplanted by hip-talking cat Mr. Jinx, a Marlon Brando type. Mr. Jinx was voice artist Daws Butler's favorite character because of his efforts to remain loose, flip, cool and rebellious despite his "establishment" function as the family mouse eradicator. Though Jinx took gleefully sadistic delight at thinking up methods to aggravate the "meeces" whom he hated "to pieces," he was such an appealing character that Hanna and Barbera allowed him to win a round or two against the mischievous meeces.

It was *Huckleberry Hound*'s third component, "Yogi Bear," that would ultimately gain the greatest success. Notes on this fascinating character will be found on his own separate entry in this book; it's enough here to note that, when *Huckleberry Hound* entered its third season in 1961 without Yogi Bear—who'd branched out to his own series—a separate rerun package was sent out by Kellogg's for prime time telecasting under the title *The Best of Huck and Yogi*.

Yogi's replacement on *Huckleberry Hound*, a Phil Silvers derivation named Hokey Wolf, first appeared in January 1961. Hokey and his little pal Dingaling spent most of their time trying to cadge free meals from the gullible; this threadbare premise was elevated by some fairly funny lines and by Daws Butler's virtuoso voicework as Hokey.

Kellogg's, in concert with Hanna-Barbera's distributor Screen Gems, chose to syndicate *Huckleberry Hound* in 1958 rather than return to the cereal firm's former ABC stomping grounds, reasoning that the network, which then had only about 85 affiliates, would not deliver up as many local markets as city-by-city distribution would. They were right, of course; within a year of its debut, *Huckleberry Hound* was playing in 192 out of the 263 existing TV markets—and entertaining an *international* audience of 16,000,000. The series was among the top 10 non-network programs in virtually every major city, quite a coup in an age when distributors considered children's programs the toughest to sell. But who ever said *Huckleberry* was merely a children's show? Yes, it had earned an Emmy—the first for a cartoon series—in the "outstanding achievement in the field of children's programming" category. Still, Hanna-Barbera's research revealed that the program had a significant chunk of adult viewership—65 percent of its audience, in fact—which in 1959 counted most with sponsors.

When this writer read these tidbits back in early 1960, he was nine years old, and had yet to meet anyone *over* the age of nine who'd admit to watching *Huckleberry Hound* regularly. Yet the record was there, as well as additional evidence. There was a throwaway query, "Is Huckleberry Hound really a dog?" in director Jack Webb's otherwise somber 1959 newspaper melodrama *-30-*. There was the vignette in 1961's *Breakfast at Tiffany's* wherein Audrey Hepburn nearly shoplifts a Huckleberry Hound mask. There was a scene in the 1960 feature comedy *Who Was That Lady?* in which Dean Martin and Tony Curtis, stepping out with a couple of good-time girls, enter a Chinese bar-restaurant where the television is playing a *Huckleberry Hound* episode (though this may have been less a reflection of its "adult" appeal than the fact that Columbia Pictures, Screen Gems' parent company, produced

Who Was That Lady?). And there was that real-life saloon in Seattle, where between 6 and 6:30 P.M. Thursday evenings a sign was posted: "No loud tinkling of glasses. No unnecessary conversation. No disturbing elements. No drinks served. BECAUSE WE'RE WATCHING HUCKLEBERRY HOUND."

Can this be the same *Huckleberry Hound* which, when seen today, seems draggy, only sporadically funny, and animated with as much fluidity as a NO VACANCY sign? But we're imposing 1994 values on a 1958 series, and to fully appreciate the impact of *Huckleberry Hound*, it is necessary to project oneself back to 1958. Most syndicated series of that period were variations on themes that had been established seasons earlier; even that year's most popular syndie, *Sea Hunt*, was basically a new coat of paint on an "adventurer for hire" format that had been utilized in such previous programs as *Crunch and Des*, *Waterfront*, *Whirlybirds* and *Soldiers of Fortune*. *Huckleberry Hound* was like nothing that had previously been seen in syndication: a full half hour of brand new cartoons, not merely as an appendage to some "Uncle" or "Captain" daytime kiddie host, but an entity standing on its own two feet. And most significantly, the series was not confined to the 4 to 5 P.M. TV children's show hours, but instead was telecast in most cities between 5:30 and 7 P.M.— hours in which the audience demographics began to enter the 19- to 34-year range. Some markets, notably Chicago, even ran *Huckleberry Hound* in prime time, when adult viewership was at its peak.

So here was a grownup audience, watching a program that wasn't a tired rehash of everyone else's western or private eye show or sitcom. Here was an audience basically unfamiliar with classic Hollywood cartoons (which, with exceptions like *Bugs Bunny* and *Popeye*, were not being telecast on a preferred-timeslot basis), and thus was wide open for a new group of appealing cartoon characters to grab its attention. And while it's true that *Huckleberry Hound* cannibalized many of its best gags from earlier MGM and Warners animated shorts, these gags were not in general circulation in 1958; thus they certainly *seemed* fresh.

And, by 1958's standards, *Huckleberry Hound* was very funny. Perhaps we're not patient enough nowadays to wait for a

character to comment humorously only after being prodded by a painful sight gag. And perhaps the sight of Yogi Bear reacting to an offense against his person by muttering "Sheesh!" is insufficient in a TV world where Bart Simpson is saying "Eat my shorts!" But this aging writer can tell you that such moments paid off in big, deep laughs back in a simpler day.

As to the matter of animation style: Most young viewers were raised to accept the fact that inexpensive TV animation could not begin to compare with the stuff we saw on *Disneyland* or down at the neighborhood movie house. Despite *Variety's* complaint about the "abbreviated animation" on *Huckleberry Hound*, kids were more forgiving in 1958. It was only when Hanna-Barbera and other studios began *over*producing cheap animation, with no end or improvement in sight, that viewers began to get queasy. But in 1958, *Huckleberry Hound* and *Ruff and Reddy* were virtually the only cartoons produced later than 1950 that we cartoon fanciers had available to us, so we didn't feel compelled to gripe. In fact, we were grateful that anyone cared enough to oblige us with new material.

Huckleberry Hound continued as a ratings-puller and merchandising gold mine for four seasons, toting up 57 first run episodes. But it was former *Huckleberry* supporting player Yogi Bear who became Hanna-Barbera's top gun, so much so that when Huckleberry Hound was revived in the late 1970s, the Hound was in Yogi's support. In later series like *Yogi's Gang*, *Yogi's Space Race*, and *Yogi's Treasure Hunt*, it was clear who was the star and who was the straight man. Still, Huck was always a welcome presence; like Disney's Mickey Mouse, he was kept around long after he'd ceased being the studio's biggest moneymaker simply because it was his series that had put Hanna-Barbera on the map. In 1988, the Hound was restored to pride of place in a syndicated two-hour western spoof, *The Good, The Bad and the Huckleberry Hound*, the inaugural entry in the studio's new series of specials, *Hanna-Barbera's Superstars 10*. Huck was on the payroll even into the 1990s, as one of many past H-B animal stars featured in the "Fender Bender 500" segments of the syndicated *Wake, Rattle and Roll* (q.v.).

HULK HOGAN'S ROCK 'N' WRESTLING! CBS: 9/14/1985–6/13/

1987. Titan Sports/WWF/DIC Animation City. Produced by Jean Chalopin, Andy Heyward and Tetsuo Katayama. Directed by Bruno Bianchi; assistant director, Michael Maliani. Developed by Jeffrey Scott; based on a concept created by Dave Wolff and Cyndi Lauper. Creative supervision by Andy Heyward and Jean Chalopin. Main title music and lyrics by Jim Steinman. Music by Score Productions. Music supervision by Mitch Wirth and Lynne McCleary. Animation supervisors: Hiroshi Toita and Shigeru Akagawa. Live action producer, Nelson Sweglar. Animation facilities: HanHo Heungup Studios, Wang Film Productions, Studio Shaft. Voices: Brad Garrett (Hulk Hogan); Charles Adler (Roddy); James Avery (Junkyard Dog); Lewis Arquette (Superfly Snuka); Jodi Carlisle (Moolah/Richter); George Di-Cenzo (Capt. Lou Albano); Ronald A. Feinberg (Andre the Giant); Pat Fraley (Hillbilly Jim); Ronald Gans (Volkoff); Ernest Harada (Mr. Fuji); Aron Kincaid (The Iron Sheik); Chuck Licini (Big John Studd); Joey Pento (Tino Santana); Neil Ross (Mean Gene). Live-action sequences: Hulk Hogan (Himself); Gene Okerlund (Himself).

Professional wrestling—the glittery, garish, gloriously unbelievable TV version, that is—achieved respectability in the early 1980s after years of "joke" status when entrepreneur Vince McMahon aligned several regional wrestling circuits into a single entity, the World Wrestling Federation. A heightened interest in the sport via new independent UHF stations and cable outlets resulted in a whole slew of high-rated weekly grappling matches from the WWF and such competitors as World Championship Wrestling (WCW), each with its own sets of Good Guys, Bad Guys, world champ titles and deadly rivalries. Those who scoffed at this renewed interest in wrestling and assumed it was a passing fancy were astounded when the annual "Wrestlemania" matches not only swept the ratings when telecast on pay-per-view cable starting in 1985, but also broke sales records when released in videocassette form.

Into this arena stepped *Hulk Hogan's Rock 'n' Wrestling*, a weekly cartoon half hour based on a notion by rock star Cyndi Lauper, who happened to be a diehard wrestling fan and manager of several WWF stars. The title character was Hulk

Hogan, he of the bulging biceps and platinum blonde tresses, who was then the reigning champ of the WWF (a title he'd successfully defend on and off into the 1990s). The Hulkster appeared in live-action comedy sketch wraparounds on *Rock 'n' Wrestling* in the company of "Mene" Gene Okerlund; even nonfans of the sport immediately recognized Okerlund as the slight, balding, pokerfaced announcer who remained unflappable when interviewing the most repulsive and roisterous of rasslers in between the weekly televised bouts. Hogan was also seen in live footage during the credits as a "pied piper," with an enthusiastic crowd of kids following him down the street.

Both Hogan and Mene Gene appeared in caricatured cartoon form in the series proper—their living images copied on the animation cels through a process called Hagiographication—in the company of such WWF luminaries as Andre the Giant, Captain Lou Albano (later a vocal contributor to another cartoon outing, *Super Mario Bros.* [q.v.]), Rowdy Roddy Piper, the Iron Sheik, Big John Studd and Junkyard Dog. None of these athletes provided their own voices; the producers, evidently having learned a lesson from the failure of the Muhammad Ali animated series *I Am the Greatest* (q.v.), saw to it that the WWFers were voiced by professional actors. We should also mention that *Hulk Hogan's Rock 'n' Wrestling* made a token gesture to female viewers (and, indirectly, the panting fans of women's wrestling) by arbitrarily writing in the characters of "nice" wrestlerette Richter and her "mean" counterpart Moola.

The "rock" part of the *Rock 'n' Wrestling* title was manifested in a weekly music video sequence, wherein the wrestlers were seen performing in a pantomimed action montage while a current rock tune was heard, with original singer intact, on the soundtrack. Additionally, the real wrestlers were seen on occasion in an elemental "dance hall" set, boogeying and lyp-synching to the newest hits (these sequences, along with Hulk Hogan's and Gene Okerlund's live intros, were removed from the syndicated package of *Rock 'n' Wrestling*, evidently to avoid excess residual payments and to pare the series' original 60-minute length down to 30). The music was easily the most entertaining aspect of the series, which for the most part was mired in the formula situational slapstick typical of Saturday morning cartoonery.

This isn't to minimize the input of the scriptwriters, who were stuck with a ticklish dilemma: How could they promote the series' prosocial message of teamwork and togetherness while still maintaining the down-and-dirty rivalries that flourished between the various wrestlers in "real" life? The usual answer was to have the "hero" and "heavy" wrestlers being *forced* to work together, accomplish the week's goal, then go right back to being "enemies." Sometimes this was funny; other times, notably whenever Hulk Hogan was reluctantly aligned with the caricatured Russian wrestler Volkoff—whose stupidity and chauvinism were among the more unfortunate vestiges of the old Cold War mentality—the results were downright insulting.

In short, *Hulk Hogan's Rock 'n' Wrestling* wasn't quite as entertaining as a real WWF wrestling weekly, where unreality and nonthink were elevated to art forms.

THE HUNTER *see* **KING LEONARDO**

THE HURRICANES. Syndicated: 1993 (as part of AMAZIN' ADVENTURES). Siriol Productions (Cardiff)/Scottish Television Enterprises/DIC/Bohbot. Executive producers, Andy Heyward, Robby London, Sandy Ross and Jeff Henry. Produced by Robin Lyons. Executive in charge of production, Brian A. Miller. Production supervisors, Stacy Gallishaw and RaNae Bonella. Associate producer, Lisa Salamone. Development writer, Phil Harnage. Script coordinator, Lori Crawford. Music by Michael Tavera, Reed Robbins, Mark Simon; music supervised by Joanne Miller. Animation facilities: Rainbow Animation Group. Overseas supervisors, S. J. Bleick and Sheldon Arnst. Executive in charge of production for Bohbot, Allen J. Bohbot. Voices: Chiara Zanni, Stuart Hepburn, Ian James Corlett, Michael Benyaer, Chris Humphreys, Jay Brazeau, Brent Chapman, Andrew Airlie, Carl Hibbert, Chris Gaze, Colin Heath, Peter Williams, Scott McNeil, Alvin Sanders, Candus Churchill, Carol Alexander, Christina Lippa, Gary Chalk, Kathleen Barr, Louise Vallance, Mark Hildreth, Wezley Morris, Roger Crossly, Jeannie Zahni.

The *Hurricanes* featured an "underdog" team of the World Soccer League, headquarted in the South American Hispanola Stadium. High schooler Amanda Carey had inherited the team, which had been a losing tax write-off for her father (who'd disappeared while flying over the Bermuda Triangle), and thus suffered severe morale and personality problems. Initially, the Hurricanes resisted taking orders from their teenaged owner, until Amanda turned the team into a winning commodity by luring the "notorious" soccer star Cal Howard out of retirement. After this, the Hurricanes were more than willing to follow the advice of Amanda—who in turn elicited advice from crusty-but-goldhearted Scottish team trainer Jock Stone.

Emphasizing the multicultural slant prevalent in many cartoon series of the early 1990s, the Hurricanes team was an ethnic melting pot: North Americans Cal Casey and Georgie Wright, Jamaican Rude Marley, Cockney Napper Thompson, Italian Dino Allegro, Japanese "Stats" (a math whiz), German Jorg, Brazilian Plato, Scotsman Andy and Spaniard Toro, among others. This polyglot quality of *Hurricanes* was carried to the announcer's booth, where an African American play-by-play sportscaster rap-talked to a worldwide radio audience. The only "specialized" group seemingly overlooked by *Hurricanes* were the animals—save for Amanda's pet dog Dribble (the name was just as nauseating 20 years earlier when applied to the canine mascot of Hanna-Barbera's *Harlem Globetrotters* [q.v.]).

No, we didn't forget the bad guys. Internationally despised multimillionaire Stavros Garkos was owner of the Gorgons, a "dirty" soccer team who tore down every sportsmanship ethic that the fair-play Hurricanes built up, and who deployed the most diabolical means imaginable to try to force Amanda to sell him her team. Garkos' prime henchmen were Gorgons' British star player Wynn Smythe and the vaguely oriental Genghis. Even the villains on *Hurricanes* were equal-opportunity employers.

The *Hurricanes*, co-produced with Cardiff-based Siriol Productions (see *The Further Adventures of Superted*) and Scottish Television Enterprises, was created because DIC head man Andy Heyward craved a weekly half hour series "that was purely international, and of course soccer is a natural." Soccer is also a sport that boasts a rabid fan following everywhere in the world *except* the United States — so accordingly, the series was first marketed internationally. By mid–1992, the series was the fastest-selling cartoon series in the world — before there'd been a single U.S. sale, and long before the first episode was even telecast!

Few were disappointed when *Hurricanes* finally premiered, however. Though animation was merely perfunctory in the dialogue sequences, the soccer games themselves exhibited a wealth of camera-angle ingenuity and raw energy — helped along by little chunks here and there of rotoscoped cartoonwork, traced over actual soccer filmclips.

The series satisfied American television's prosocial requirements (requirements not mandatory in the rest of the world, where cartoon series are served up minus apologies or social consciousness) by offering 30-second "Good Sportsmanship: The Ultimate Edge" episode closers — which in the spirit of good sportsmanship were underwritten by Spalding Sporting Goods, whose products were spotted throughout each *Hurricanes* episode. The ad campaign for *Hurricanes* stressed the series' positive messages (the ecological slant this time around was centralized in the negative example of land-despoiling Stavros Garkos), and also promised "lots of boy and girl appeal." This last assurance was curious, since principal female character Amanda appeared to harbor aspirations to be one of the "boys," even disguising herself in the first episode as a male Hurricane named Charlie Sands. And one final query: If *Hurricanes* did indeed want to broaden its appeal to female viewers, why then did the advertising art feature only the male characters?

I AM THE GREATEST: THE ADVENTURES OF MUHAMMAD ALI. NBC: 9/10/1977–1/28/1978; 2/11/1978–9/2/1978. Farmhouse Films/Fred Calvert Productions. Executive producer and director: Fred Calvert. Produced by Janis Diamond. Written by Fred Calvert and Janis Diamond. Music by Charles Blaker. Voices: Muhammad Ali (Himself); Patrice Carmichael (Nicky); Casey Carmichael (Damon); Frank Bannister (Himself); and Bob Arbogast, Michael Baldwin, Jim Brik, Booker Bradshaw, Dianna

Oyama Dixon, Joan Gerber, Peter Haas, Peter Haskell, Stanley Jones, James Levon Johnson, Gene Moss, Wali Muhammad, Richard Paul, David Roberts, and Paul Shively.

In his prime, boxer Muhammad Ali once noted — well, more than once — that his was the most recognizable face in all the world. But fame in one profession does not always guarantee expertise in another. Most of Ali's attempts at show business (his starring film *The Greatest*, his supporting role in the TV miniseries *Freedom Road*) revealed a man as clumsy with dialogue and acting technique as he was flawless in the ring. And yet the producers of the 1977 NBC cartoon series *I Am the Greatest: The Adventures of Muhammad Ali* had enough faith in Ali's huge fan following that they felt his providing the voice for his animated likeness wouldn't hurt the series *too* much.

The half-hour *I Am the Greatest* cast Ali in the role of a "modern Robin Hood" (the words used by most descriptions of this series, from contemporary publicity to latter-day TV encyclopedias), who interacted with his niece Nicky and nephew Damon and with his public relations man Frank Bannister, who like Ali supplied his own voice to the cartoon. It was the garrulous Ali's purpose in life to keep his young friends morally sound and to fight for the ill-used and the downtrodden; usually this took the shape of bucking The System, or, in keeping with the rest of Saturday morning TV, solving mysteries.

Thirteen episodes later, *I Am the Greatest: The Adventures of Muhammad Ali* was ignominiously yanked from its 9:30 A.M. NBC berth, replaced by the more durable *Pink Panther Show* (q.v.). The series had been regularly trounced by *Scooby's All-Star Laff-a-Lympics* (see *Scooby-Doo*) over at ABC and the live-action *Space Academy* from CBS. But stiff competition wasn't the only problem. *I Am the Greatest* was put together by the same team who'd brought us *Emergency + Four* (q.v.) in 1974, and suffered the same shortcomings: sagging plotlines, intrusive "kid" characters, lethargic animation. Character design, one of the better aspects of *Emergency + Four*, was poorly executed in *Greatest*: The animators' version of Muhammad Ali made the champ look more like a movie lobby display than a real human being. And as mentioned, Ali's listless line readings — even his famous poems lacked the old zip—helped an already desperate situation not at all. Perhaps the biggest problem was the show's title. It was hard to believe that the animated Muhammad Ali was in any way interested in the well-being of others on a series that revived the boxer's "I Am the Greatest" catchline from his cock-of-the-walk "Cassius Clay" days. (Evidently the NBC people who provided information to *TV Guide* felt the same way: that magazine listed the series as simply "Adventures of Muhammad Ali"—and later, just "Muhammad Ali.")

Still, there was some pressure back in 1978 by several activist groups to keep alive as many programs spotlighting minorities as possible. *I Am the Greatest* could not be revived on the network during its key timeslots with any hope of profit or extra ratings, but reruns did get played off at 7:30 A.M. (EST) Saturdays from February through September 1978—meaning that the greater part of the country, in the Central and Mountain time zones, were offered the series during the graveyard slot of 6:30 A.M.

INCH HIGH PRIVATE EYE. NBC: 9/8/1973–8/31/1974. Hanna-Barbera. Executive producers, William Hanna and Joseph Barbera. Associate producer, Alex Lovy. Creative producer, Iwao Takamoto. Directed by Charles Nichols. Story by Bill Raynor, Fred Fox, Seaman Jacobs, Myles Wilder, David Harmon, Gene Thompson. Story direction by Bill Carney, George Jorgensen, Earl Klein, Alex Lovy, Dan Milk, Dan Noonan, Vey Risto, Jay Sarbry, Don Sheppard, Paul Sommer. Character design by Jerry Eisenberg. Music by Hoyt Curtin. Musical direction by Paul De-Korte. Voices: Len Weinrib (Inch High); Kathy Gori (Lorie); Bob Luttrell (Gator); John Stephenson (Mr. Finkerton); Jean VanderPyl (Mrs. Finkerton); Don Messick (Braveheart); and Ted Knight, Jamie Farr, Vic Perrin, Janet Waldo, Alan Oppenheimer.

The concept of a miniaturized detective was not what one could call overused: From 1950 through 1960 the notion had been used but once in live action, on the forgotten syndicated series *World of Giants* (1960). Only cartoon makers seemed to be interested in the concept—such as Hanna-Barbera, who produced the weekly half hour networker *Inch High Private Eye* in 1973.

The shrunken shamus of the title, known only as "Inch High," was a bumbling gumshoe, complete with trenchcoat and snap brim hat. Inch High, who sounded like a cross between Jack Benny and Don Adams (with all of those comedians' abrasive qualities and none of their charm), worked for the Finkerton Detective Agency, whence he was dispatched, reluctantly, by the firm's husband and wife owners to solve the unsolvable and protect the unprotectable. In anticipation of the later DIC series *Inspector Gadget* (q.v.)—which like *Inch High Private Eye* had its comedy roots in the live action spy spoof *Get Smart*—Inch High's assistant and confidante was his pretty blonde niece Lorie, who was frequently in the company of her hayseed boy friend Gator. Braveheart, a resilient if thickwitted St. Bernard who carried Inch High's disguises and weaponry in the brandy keg around his collar, was the detective's "capable, cunning, canine companion in crime fighting." That was the series' Hanna-Barbera funny dog; could the Hanna-Barbera "funny vehicle" be far behind? Nope! Inch High and his assistants drove around in his silent Hushmobile, which looked like a jumbo frankfurter.

Unlike his predecessor on *World of Giants*, Inch High was not always thumb-sized. He became diminutive only after drinking a special potion (another example of the medicinal catalysts like the Proton Pills on *Roger Ramjet* [q.v.] and the Super Sauce on the "Super Chicken" episodes of *George of the Jungle* [q.v.] which network TV would later veto for fear of children at home assuming that pills of a more addictive variety would induce super strength). Complications arose when the potion would wear off at the most inopportune times—usually whenever Inch High was trying to make his escape from the villain's lair. In the episodes I've seen, however, this didn't happen. Inch High came acropper due to his own clumsiness and arrogance rather than chemical dependency.

Though lasting only 13 episodes (its NBC run was smack dab opposite a more popular Hanna-Barbera effort on CBS, *Yogi's Gang* [see *Yogi Bear*]), *Inch High Private Eye* had a healthy syndicated rerun life in various Hanna-Barbera "collection" packages. A recent glance at several episodes has revealed that the series' haphazardly applied recorded laughtrack (which reacted to sight gags only, ignoring the dialogue jokes) was a most annoying distraction, the main character was unlovable and obnoxious, and the "small" jokes were small in every sense of the word. As with many Hanna-Barberas of the early 1970s, *Inch High Private Eye*'s ragged animation was redeemed by the topnotch background art of Fernando Montealegre, who here employed a florid watercolor design.

THE INCREDIBLE HULK *see* **MARVEL SUPER HEROES** and **SPIDER-MAN**

THE INHUMANOIDS. Syndicated: 1986. Marvel/Claster/LBS. Executive producers, Joe Bacal, Margaret Loesch, Tom Griffin. Director of production, Jim Graziano. Executive in charge of production, Lee Gunther. Produced by Stephanie Burt. Co-producer, Flint Dille. Associate producer, Chris Pelzer. Story editor, Larry Parr. Creative director, Jay Bacal. Supervisor of directors, Ray Lee. Directed by Charlie Downs, Bob Kirk, Margaret Nichols, Bob Matz, Rudy Cataldi, Karen Peterson, Joe Harrison, Spencer Peel, Neal Warner, Lillian Evans, Stan Philips, Norman McCabe, Gerry Chiniquy, Warren Batchelder, Bob Trent, Brad Case, Joan Case, John Freeman, Tom Ray, Bill Knoll. Theme music by Kinder and Bryant. Music composed and conducted by Robert J. Walsh. Voices: Michael Bell, William Callaway, Fred Collins, Brad Crandall, Dick Gautier, Ed Gilbert, Chris Latta, Neil Ross, Stanley Ralph Ross, Richard Sanders, Susan Silo, John Stephenson.

The *Inhumanoids* was tested as a two-week component on Marvel's *Super Sunday* (q.v.) in January 1986 before debuting on a weekly basis in September of that year. It was one of the few half hour animated series of the 1980s to draw its title from the villains rather than the heroes. The Inhumanoids — also known as Mutors — were an ancient subterranean race who came to the Earth's surface to establish domination and destroy any obstacles in their path. The Earth Corps was the good-guy contingent called upon to rescue mankind.

Roll call for the Earth Corps: leader Herc D. Armstrong, leader of E. Corps who wore protective armor; Dr. Derek

Bright, designer of machinery; Auger, designer of vehicles; and Johnathan N. Slattery, a sportsman popularly known as "The Liquidator." Each character had "personalized" weaponry, extensions of his own personality which could be developed by Claster as accessories for the inevitable "action figures." The Earth Corps' high-tech, high-priced earthburrowing equipment was underwritten by the beautiful and wealthy Sandra Shore. Unbeknownst to Sandra, it was her own brother, Blackthorne Shore, who was responsible for the Inhumanoids' resurgence. An anti-environmental scoundrel, Blackthorne had made a deal with Metlar, ruler of Inhumanoids; he'd help the invaders take over the world, so he could subsequently overtake *them* and have all of "middle earth" to plunder for profit.

Not all the subterranean Mutors were bad. The good ones were mutated from trees, granite, and other "beneficial" natural splendors. The bad Mutors — those pesky Inhumanoids — worshipped at the altar of ecology-spoiling machinery; these were evolved from lizards, skeletons, and other such repulsive entities. Unfortunately, the bad guys had the power to take over the personalities of the "good" Mutors and the human beings; they could also bring statues to life and enlist them in their unholy army.

That's why it would take more than one half hour to squash *The Inhumanoids*. In fact, it took eight half hours. Though not the best that Marvel had to offer, the series exhibited some of the finer characteristics of that studio, utilizing such comic book techniques as split panels (two separate arenas of action on one screen, depicted within one frame) and long, looming, pitch-black shadows.

If this sounds overly somber and serious, be assured that *Inhumanoids* was often played for laughs. The Granite Mutors were snobs, referring to humans as "Earth slugs." The slugs — er, Earth Force members — were probably the most tremulous bunch of heroes in cartoondom, ever eager to avoid direct confrontation, and fighting only when an escape route didn't materialize. And in one of the best episodes, the Mutors captured every stone statue of a female figure in sight (they'd been infected with a love potion), with one of the baddies having the misfortune to abduct a rather bitchy Statue of Liberty!

Inhumanoids was, not unexpectedly, tied in with a line of Hasbro toy vehicles and action figures. It also managed to squeeze at least one *Inhumanoids* comic book out of Marvel Publications before its single season had run its course.

INSPECTOR GADGET. Syndicated: 1983. Nickelodeon: 10/3/1987–Fall 1992; CBS: 11/2/1991–8/31/1992. DIC/Fr3/Nelvana/Field Communications/LBS/TMS/ Cuckoo's Nest. Produced and written by Jean Chalopin and Andy Heyward. Created by Jean Chalopin, Andy Heyward and Bruno Bianchi. Directed by Harry Love, Bernard Deyries, Bruno Bianchi, Toshi Uuki, Philippe Landrot. Music by Haim Saban and Shuki Levy. Production facilities: DIC, Nelvana, and Cuckoo's Nest Studios. Voices: Don Adams (Inspector Gadget); Mona Marshall, Cree Summer Francks, Holly Berger (Penny); Frank Welker (Brain/Dr.Claw/Madcat); Maurice LaMarche (Chief Quimby); Townsend Coleman (Capeman); and Dan Hennessey, Greg Duffell, Jeannie Cradden, Meleny Brown.

Inspector Gadget was DIC Enterprises' Mickey Mouse—the lucky cartoon mascot upon which the DIC empire was built. The half hour series was the studio's first syndicated property, pitched in 1983 to local stations on a barter-sponsor basis. The head man at DIC, Andy Heyward, would later note that the direct-to-syndication route was prompted by anticipation of only a small percentage of rerun profits had the series been run on one of the networks; in local distribution, profits were shared equitably with the TV outlets carrying *Inspector Gadget*. Heyward's strategy paid off, establishing DIC among the foremost cartoon producers, right up there with Hanna-Barbera and Filmation.

We'll return to the business end of this property after we introduce you to Inspector Gadget. The Inspector was a bionic detective (half human, half machine), and had the series been a straight superhero adventure, that would have been the sole plot gimmick. The added twist was that Gadget was basically stupid, an habitual bumbler whose 13,000 built-in mechanical devices—elongated arms, propellored head, springlike legs, etc.—saved his synthetic hide whenever his thought processes failed him. Andy Heyward had conceived Gadget as an amalgam of all the

elements that had appealed to him as a child and as a staffer at Hanna-Barbera: children's toys, the Three Stooges, and the Scooby-Doo school of bumbling heroics. Additionally, he was armed with the confidence of the ignorant: "He's incredibly optimistic," Heyward observed in 1993. "No matter what's happening around him, the sun is always shining over Gadget's head."

Given this aspect of the character, it isn't hard to envision Inspector Gadget as a latter-day version of Maxwell Smart, the equally bumbling, equally superconfident secret agent of the 1960s TV spy spoof *Get Smart* (Peter Sellers' Inspector Clouseau also comes to mind, but that character had already been animated). With this pedigree, the only logical person to provide Gadget's voice was *Smart* star Don Adams. The presence of Adams paid off in a major publicity push, with fulsome coverage of *Inspector Gadget* on such showbiz-oriented series as *Entertainment Tonight*. Even though some snatches of the later *Gadget* dialogue sequences are voiced by someone who merely sounds (just barely) like Don Adams, it was the star's considerable input which really socked the series over with the viewing public.

Also like Maxwell Smart, Inspector Gadget was surrounded by a team of clearer-headed individuals who enabled the star to solve whatever crimes and mysteries were tossed his way. Gadget's preteen niece Penny, despite her habit of being kidnapped every other episode, was one of the most intelligent and resourceful female characters in cartoondom, piecing together puzzles and figuring out avenues of escape with the panache of *The Avengers'* Diana Rigg. Penny's dog was named Brain, and the name was more than appropriate; not only was the pooch swift on the graymatter and faster than a speeding auto, but he was also a master of disguise—including female impersonation, red lipstick and all!

Additional characters included Gadget's superior, Metro City's Chief Quimby, who invariably suffered from his employee's foolishness by being blown up in some inventive fashion after every secret meeting with the Inspector. Quimby's opposite number was The Claw, the thunder voiced leader of M. A. D. (Mean and Dirty), who in the manner of James Bond's Ernst Blofeld was never shown full-face and who was frequently in the company of an equally unsavory feline, Mad Cat. Every *Gadget* half hour episode ended with The Claw growling, "I'll get you next time, Gadget . . . next time!" while the closing credits rolled.

One would think that Gadget would be the last person in the world to be entrusted with the prosocial advisory vignettes which rounded out each episode . . . and one would be wrong. Inspector Gadget would explain to Penny the value of proper electrical wiring, pedestrian safety and the like with surprising conviction. That's because he taught by example — by accidentally demonstrating the disastrous results of not following his advice. Even in these parent group-imposed prosocial bites, the integrity of Inspector Gadget's resiliently boneheaded character was maintained.

Animation was expectedly limited on *Inspector Gadget*, but the character design was eyecatching and the comedy sequences meticulously timed and executed. The result was a series that showed a lot more production polish and vitality than some of the "straight" superhero series of the 1983-84 season. *Inspector Gadget* was an unqualified syndicated success, as indicated by the fact that 21 new daily episodes were commissioned after the traditional first 65. Even as the series continued its local run, rebroadcasts were licensed for six seasons by the Nickelodeon cable service, starting in 1987. Come 1991, these same episodes could be seen over the CBS network on Saturday mornings — and *still* they plugged away in syndication and on cable (most recently over the Family Channel, as the main attraction of Family's *Fun Town* weekend cartoon block. "The show has built up an amazing following," Heyward declared in 1993, "and today *Inspector Gadget* is stronger than he's ever been."

The property continues to turn a profit for DIC, and not only with the Gadget "action figure" toys for which the character was originally designed. In 1992, a CBS special, *Inspector Gadget Saves Christmas*, made what was intended to be the first of many annual Yuletide appearances (Don Adams was absent from this project). A comically subdued Inspector Gadget has been appointed official spokesperson for the National Center For Missing and Exploited Children, an organization in which

Andy Heyward has been actively involved since 1985. And as of this writing, a deal has been closed with Ivan (*Ghostbusters*) Reitman for a live action *Gadget* feature film. To quote the indestructible Inspector Gadget: "Wowsers!"

IRON MAN *see* **MARVEL SUPER-HEROES**

IT'S PUNKY BREWSTER. NBC: 9/14/1985–9/5/1987; 11/12/1988–9/2/1989. Ruby/Spears. Executive producers: Joe Ruby and Ken Spears. Voices: Soleil Moon Frye (Punky Brewster); Henry Warnimont (Henry Warnimont); Ami Foster (Margaux Kramer); Casey Ellinson (Allen Anderson); Cherie Johnson (Cherie); Frank Welker (Glomer). (*See also* MAXIE'S WORLD.)

It's Punky Brewster, NBC's 1985 bid to topple the competing *Thirteen Ghosts of Scooby-Doo* (see *Scooby-Doo*), was based on a live-action sitcom of the same title, minus the contraction "It's." On the original, Punky Brewster was a seven-year-old abandonee who lived in an empty apartment with her dog until discovered by apartment manager–professional photographer Henry Warnimont. Though a confirmed bachelor not terribly fond of kids, Henry took in the little girl and set about improving her environment and station in life. Punky's offbeat name was drawn from a childhood friend of NBC president Brandon Tartikoff's — who incidentally was well compensated for her "participation" in the project. (On the series, the writers had some sport with Tartikoff by naming Punky's pooch "Brandon.")

The live-action *Punky Brewster* ran on NBC from 1984 through 1986 (because it was telecast just after the Sunday sports events, some episodes ran a mere 15 minutes), then was entered into syndication with newly taped episodes. Such was the popularity of the project that, a year into the series' run, the animated *It's Punky Brewster* made its bow. The half hour weekly was for the most part unimaginative: The cartoon characters were slavishly designed after the originals, and the voices were provided by the live series' stars, including Soleil Moon Frye as Punky, George Gaynes as Henry, and Cherie Johnson, Ami Foster and Casey Ellison as Punky's schoolmates. A new character was added in the form of Glomer, a gremlinish entity who whisked Punky and company into worldwide adventures. Ruby-Spears was able to realize a respectable 42-episode manifest on *It's Punky Brewster*, rerunning the property through the 1988-89 season.

In September of 1989, Punky Brewster reared her tousled little head again when the Ruby-Spears reruns were packaged together with DIC's weekday syndicated *Maxie's World* (q.v.).

IT'S THE WOLF *see* **CATTANOOGA CATS**

THE ITSY BITSY SPIDER. USA: 9/1993–. Hyperion/Paramount. Created by Matt O'Callaghan. Developed for television by Willard Carroll and Matt O'Callaghan. Produced by David R. Cobb and Ron Rocha. Executive producers, Willard Carroll, Thomas L. Wilhite, Mike Mitchell. Associate producer, Ron Rocha. Directed by Mike Mitchell. Music by John O'Kennedy. Title song by William Finn. Art director, David McCamley. Animation facilities: Shanghai Morning Sun Animation Co., Ltd. and Wang Film Production Co., Ltd. Overseas director, Greg Sullivan. Voices: Frank Welker (Itsy/ Langston); Charlotte Rae (Adrienne Facts); Matt Frewer (The Exeterminator); Francesca Marie Smith (Leslie); Jonathan Taylor Thomas (George); and Margaret Cho, Joel Brooks, John Kassir, David Cobb, Mike Mitchell, Miriam Flynn, Gabrielle Boni, and Bradley Pierce.

As a cartoon character, the "Itsy Bitsy Spider" of children's-roundelay fame had a brace of incarnations before graduating to series status. A seminal "Itsy Bitsy" showed up in the animated credit titles of *The Elephant Show*, a live action Nickelodeon children's daily of the mid–1980s. Another version, developed by Whitman Publishing, appeared as protagonist of a 1990 Cinar Studios half hour special, *The Real Story of Itsy Bitsy Spider*. This one-shot featured *Cosby Show* costar Malcolm Jamal Warner as the voice of I. B. Spider, a mischievous misfit who attended an all-insect high school. Cinar's *Itsy Bitsy Spider* was one of a handful of Canadian specials broadcast in the U.S. over HBO cable in 1994 under the blanket title *The Real Story of—*. (Other entries gave the "lowdown" about such nursery rhyme perennials as Humpty Dumpty, the Little Teapot, the Three Little Kittens, and "O Christmas Tree.")

I.B. Spider's basic design—six legs rather than eight—was adopted for the 1992 theatrical cartoon short subject *Itsy Bitsy Spider*, written by *National Lampoon* mainstay Michael O'Donoghue and released by Hyperion/ Paramount as a companion piece to the animated feature film *Bebe's Kids*. It was this *Spider* that the USA cable network decided to use as its inaugural first-run cartoon character. Eighteen months of preparation went into Paramount/Hyperion's *Itsy Bitsy Spider*, which USA (with astonishingly little fanfare) released back-to-back with another new series, *Problem Child* (q.v.), as part as the service's Sunday morning *Cartoon Express*.

Itsy, a funloving, four-eyed wise-ass arachnid (high-pitched vocals courtesy of "weird animal" specialist Frank Welker) was the bane of the existence of pretentious grand dame Adrienne Facts. Originally identified merely as "The Piano Teacher," Adrienne (voice-acted with fire breathing fervor by Charlotte Rae, taking over from the theatrical cartoon's Andrea Martin) was also vaguely delineated as a dragon-lady cooking show host, and as a "Norma Desmond" washed-up Great Actress. Whatever her lot in life, Ms. Facts despised Itsy Bitsy (and not without reason—the little guy was a real pest), and thus aligned herself with a karate-champ "Exterminator," whose upper torso muscles were rivalled only by those in his head. One welcome novelty: the Exterminator, voice supplied by Matt Frewer, *didn't* sound like Arnold Schwarzenegger.

Only little girl Leslie and her young friend George truly enjoyed Itsy Bitsy's company, though even they expressed exasperation at the character's capriciousness and tendency to elaborate on the truth. Most of the 13 *Itsy Bitsy Spider* half hours pitted Leslie vs. Adrienne Facts and Adrienne's fat, pampered pussycat Langston, with Itsy resolving all plot difficulties in an orgy of destructive slapstick.

Itsy Bitsy Spider bore the heavy scatalogical influence of *Ren and Stimpy* (at commercial-break time, Itsy Bitsy entreated the home audience to "Go potty or something"), but this element, plus the intermittent Pop-culture jokes, seemed to strain desperately to be hip. At times, *Itsy Bitsy Spider* also suffered from wishing it were the nonsequitur-per-minute *Tiny Toons Adventures* (q.v.), without the strong reserve of established Warner Bros. cartoon characters to bolster these aspirations (The TV rights to Paramount's best remembered cartoon entities, notably *Betty Boop, Popeye* and *Casper,* had long ago been licensed to other companies). As for the FCC-dictated "Educational" portion, the scripts and background art of *Itsy Bitsy Spider* included throwaways about the importance of reading.

Never as funny as it wanted to be, *Itsy Bitsy Spider* was well animated and designed, and a lot more worthwhile than its USA network companion piece, the nausea-inducing *Problem Child* (q.v.).

JABBERJAW. ABC: 9/11/1976–9/3/1977; 9/11/1977–9/3/1978. Hanna-Barbera. Executive producers, William Hanna and Joseph Barbera. Creative producer, Iwao Takamoto. Associate producer, Alex Lovy. Directed by Charles Nichols. Storyboard directors, Don Jurwich, Michael O'Connor, Paul Sommer, Kay Wright. Story editor, Ray Parker. Story by George Atkins, Haskell Barkin, John Bates, Larz Bourne, Tom Dagenais, Robert Fisher. Music by Hoyt Curtin, Paul DeKorte. Created by Joe Ruby and Ken Spears. Voices: Frank Welker (Jabberjaw); Barry Gordon (Clamhead); Julie McWhirter (Bubbles); Pat Parris (Shelley); Tommy Cook (Biff); and Regis Cordic, Ron Feinberg, Gay Hartwig, Hettie Lynn Hurtes, Casey Kasem, Keye Luke, Don Messick, Vic Perrin, Barney Phillips, Hal Smith, John Stephenson, Janet Waldo, and Lennie Weinrib.

Blending the "teenage rock band" concept of *Josie and the Pussycats* (q.v.) with the "shark-mania" inspired by the 1975 feature film *Jaws, Jabberjaw* starred a great white shark who fronted a rock band. Jabberjaw was the 15-foot-tall drummer for the Neptunes, an otherwise all-human singing group playing dates in the 21st century multicultural undersea settlement Aquaworld. Hanna-Barbera took the "killer" whammy off Jabberjaw by depicting him as harmlessly excitable: he sounded like Curly Howard of Three Stooges fame ("nyuk nyuk nyuk," "woowoowoowoo," and "soitan'y" were second nature to him), while his catchphrase—"I don't get no respect!"—was lifted from Rodney Dangerfield. The remaining Neptunes were brawny Biff on lead guitar, kooky Clamhead on bass, birdbrained Gracie Allen soundalike Bubbles on the organ and stuck-up Shelley (who had an automated make-up kit) on the tambourine. There was no funny dog this time around to aid these typical Hanna-Barbera characters when they tangled with such piscatorial villains as The Octopus and Commander Shark, but The Neptunes *did* have a funny auto, the Aquacar.

The series was created by Joe Ruby and Ken Spears in the fashion of their earlier H-B contribution *Scooby-Doo* (q.v.)—including such *Scooby* trademarks as the Overgrown Funny Animal, the "Shaggy" type goofy teenager (Clamhead), and villains who played utterly straight in contrast to their comedy surroundings. *Jabberjaw* also borrowed a *Josie and the Pussycats* gimmick by playing the Neptunes' rock music over the chase scenes. Reaching even further into the Hanna-Barbera backlog, *Jabberjaw*'s bad guys, notably one megalomaniac named Dr. Lo, appeared to be leftovers from *Jonny Quest* (q.v.).

Jabberjaw was previewed the Friday evening before its official Saturday morning debut, as part of a cartoon preview sequence on NBC's Bill Cosby variety show *Cos.* Sixteen half hours were produced, then rebroadcast for the next two seasons. The Jabberjaw character was surprisingly durable—especially considering his series' paper-doll plotlines, omnipresent laughtrack and irritating human characters—and he bobbed to the surface again as one of the judges on H-B's *Laff-a-Lympics* (see *Scooby-Doo*). If nothing else, *Jabberjaw* affirmed the reputation of standup comic Frank Welker, whose hilarious Curly-like intonations resulted in increased demand for his vocal services on subsequent animated series.

THE JACKSON 5IVE. ABC: 9/11/1971–9/1/1973. Halas & Batchelor/Rankin-Bass/Motown. Produced by Arthur Rankin Jr. and Jules Bass. Directed by Robert Balser. Written by Romeo Muller, William J. Kennan, Hal Hackaday, Lou Silverstone and Sue Milbern. Music by Maury Laws. Voices: Sigmund "Jackie" Jackson, Toriano "Tito" Jackson, Jermaine Jackson, Marion "David" Jackson, Michael Jackson (Themselves); and Paul Frees, Edmund Silvers, Joe Cooper, Mike Martinez and Greg Grandy.

The Jacksons, that talented fivesome from Gary, Indiana, who became Motown's premier bubble-gum singing attraction in the 1970s, were featured in their own 23- episode half hour cartoon series beginning in 1971. Rankin-Bass produced the series, meaning that the publicity art which showed up in newspapers and magazines far surpassed the actual cartoon draftsmanship.

Storylines on *The Jackson 5ive* were little more than pegs upon which to hang the two songs per week, though a few of the plots, such as an episode in which the Jacksons try to keep their favorite park from being bulldozed, had merit so far as showing how working together for a good cause can result in happy endings (happier than, say, the Jackson family's real home life, which has since been thoroughly documented in depressing detail). Otherwise, it's safe to say that we never would have seen *The Jackson 5ive* after its 1973 cancellation had not the incredible popularity of Michael Jackson in the mid–1980s prompted Worldvision to syndicate the old series on a daily basis. While it doesn't hold up too well, *The Jackson 5ive* serves the historical purpose of reminding us what Michael looked like back in 1971 with his original nose.

JAMES BOND JR. Syndicated: 1991. Mac B., Inc./Murikami-Wolf-Swenson/Claster/MGM-UA. Executive producer, Fred Wolf. Supervising producer, Walt Kubiak. Produced and directed by Bill Hutten and Tony Love. Story editors: Jack Mendelsohn, Mark Jones, Brian Halek and Jeffrey Scott. Developed by Michael G. Wilson, Andy Heyward and Robby London. Theme music by Dennis C. Brown and Maxine Sellers. Background music by Dennis C. Brown and Larry Brown. Music supervision by John Mortarotti. Animation facilities: Danjaq SA and UA. Voices: Jeff Bennett, Corey Burton, Julian Holloway, Mona Marshall, Brian Mitchell, Jean Rabson, Susan Silo, Simon Templeman, Aride Talent, Eddie Barth, Cheryl Bernstein, Susan Blu, Susan Boyd, Hamilton Camp, Jennifer Darling, Mari Devon, Jane Downs, Paul Eiding, Jeannie Elias, Pat Fraley, Linda Gary, Ellen Gerstell, Ed Gilbert, Rebecca Gilchrest, Michael Gough, Gaille Heidemann, Vicki Juditz, Matt N. Miller, Pat Musick, Alan Oppenheimer, Samantha Paris, Tony Pope, Bob Ridgely, Maggie Roswell, Kath Soucie, B. J. Ward, Jill Wayne.

James Bond Senior was created by former British intelligence agent Ian Fleming in 1953 as the protagonist of the sexy spy novel *Casino Royale*. Only 3000 copies were sold, but the property had enough potential to warrant a yearly sequel, which Fleming churned out until his death in 1964. The gimmick here was Bond's "007" classification with British secret service, which gave him carte blanche to kill who he wanted when he wanted. Sales of the Bond books were brisk internationally and not bad in America, where a handful of people evinced interest in bringing the suave secret agent to the screen; but only a lukewarm hour-long TV adaptation of *Casino Royale*, wherein Barry Nelson was cast as *American* agent Jimmy Bond, resulted.

It wasn't until 1961 that producers Harry Saltzman and Albert Broccoli cast Sean Connery as James Bond in the modestly budgeted Jamaica-based thriller *Dr. No*. Luck of luck, around the same time the film premiered in America in early 1963, President Kennedy made a public statement — probably written and circulated by his public relations staff — that he enjoyed Fleming's "Bond" books. Not since President Eisenhower had endorsed Zane Grey had the words of a chief executive had such a salutary effect on pulp fiction. Ian Fleming died during the first wave of Bondmania, but the filmed sequels to *Dr. No*, produced like their literary counterparts on a yearly basis, turned into United Artists' biggest moneyspinners.

And, boy, did the youth of America eat these films up with a spoon! Ostensibly adult entertainments, the girl/gun/gadget-happy "Bond" films spawned a juvenile merchandising industry that even the overabundance of TV imitations (*Man from U.N.C.L.E.*, *Wild Wild West*, *I Spy*, et al.) could not slow down. There is hardly a middle aged American male alive today who didn't at one time or another plunk down hard-earned lawnmowing money for a Double-Oh-Seven toy gun or a scale model Aston Martin sportscar. Many of us would have given our eyes, our ears, and our baby brothers for a well-produced *James Bond* cartoon series back in 1965. Some of us still felt that way in the late 1980s, when announcements were made that Hanna-Barbera was going to produce a prime time animated *Bond* for network TV.

But it was not until 1990 that Murikami-Wolf-Swenson, fat and sassy from their *Teenage Mutant Ninja Turtles* (q.v.), collaborated with Mac B. Inc., MGM-UA television and the Claster Company to produce a daily syndicated half hour, tentatively titled *Young James Bond* and finally released in 1991 as *James Bond Jr.* No, the series didn't star the son of James; this was James Bond's 17-year-old nephew, who'd inherited the looks, the "cool," and not a little of the charisma of his celebrated uncle. The rationale for this "retro" teenaged variation of the Bond format was given by Mac B. Inc.'s John Parkinson. "You try to drag in a younger audience to increase your franchise," noted Parkinson. "Kids probably associate a little more closely with [junior versions] because they are that age themselves."

Empowered by what the pressbook described as "an unerring instinct for finding the action and doing what is right," James Jr. enrolled in Warfield Academy, a finishing school for aspiring secret agents, along with several other attractive teens of an equitable gender and racial mix. James Jr.'s fellow students included the progeny of many of James Bond Srs.' old companions. For example, nerdy computer whiz "I.Q." was the son of "Q," the scientist who'd created most of Bond Srs.' gimmicky weapons and accessories, while Gordo Leiter was the surfing-dude offspring of Bond Srs.' American CIA liaison Felix Leiter. The ladies included the American Phoebe Farragut and European teen jetsetter Erica Van Horton.

In keeping with tradition, young Bond was constantly imperiled by an enemy organization—not Bond Sr.'s SMERSH or SPECTRE, but a new bunch known as S.C.U.M.: Saboteurs and Criminals United in Mayhem. Quite a few of the S.C.U.M. operatives were old foes of Bond Sr., including Dr. No and Jaws (the metal-mouthed giant introduced in 1977's *The Spy Who Loved Me*), both of whom had been seriously dead at the end of their filmed adventures, or so we were led to believe. Other baddies were the usual assortment of cartoon characters whose names and personalities were interchangeable, notably the metaldomed Skullcap and fractured-French-speaking Dr. DeRange.

Worth noting were two holdovers from the old "Bond" films—one welcome, the other less so. Each *James Bond Jr.* opened with a pre-credits "teaser," giving viewers a tantalizing glimpse of the thrills to come, just as the movies did (and still do). Of more negligible value was the series' echo of the Bond films' tendency to rework Ian Fleming's highly individualized and resourceful heroines into mere arm ornaments and damsels in distress. It was disappointing that after creating the feisty April O'Neill for *Teenage Mutant Ninja Turtles*, Murikami-Wolf-Swenson would backtrack with the helpless "eek eek" girls on *James Bond Jr.* who seemingly couldn't walk into the hallway without requiring rescue. The series was itself rescued by some well-wrought background art, and especially by a sense of humor that matched the wryness of the first Bond. When, for example, a villain was destined for a bumpy airplane ride (non-fatal, since no one was licensed to kill on this program), James Bond Jr. emulated his elder relative by advising that the bad guy be "shaken, not stirred."

Equipped with the sort of gadgetry—including jet-propelled sneakers and skateboards, and James' combination Aston Martin/airplane—that suited itself to conversion into playthings from Claster's Hasbro toy division, *James Bond Jr.* opened on some 100 stations in September 1991. Confined by the contractual agreements of established syndicated programs which grabbed the best available timeslots, *Bond* was usually consigned to the very early morning hours where, according to Claster TV president John Claster, "it wasn't a monster success and it wasn't a failure. It was a decent performer." *James Bond Jr.*, spectacular success though it wasn't, was locked in on the basis of its producers' track record to a two-year, 65-episode deal, where it continued selling Hasbro's line of tie-in merchandise on a respectable level well into 1993.

JANA OF THE JUNGLE *see* **GODZILLA**

JANOSCH'S DREAM WORLD. Nickelodeon: 12/5/1993–. WDR Cologne/Cinar. European version: Produced by Enrico Platter. Director and art director, Uwe-Peter Damme, Jurgen Egenoff. Animation by Liz Mulleneisen. Designed by Klaus Pacholak, Adriana Van Rooyen.

Background by Dietmar Hoffman. Music by Wolfram Brunke. For Cinar (English version): Adaptation and voice direction by Arden Ryshpan. Voices (English-language version): Dean Hagopian, Terry Haig, Harry Hill, Terrence Labrosse Ross, Elizabeth MacRae, Howard Ryshpan, Sam Stone, Jane Woods.

"Janosch" was the pen name for the award winning German author/illustrator Horst Eckert. For the purposes of the half-hour cartoon anthology *Janosch's Dream World*, based on Eckert's works, Janosch was a storyspinning bear, telling very low-key, gentle stories about "dreams, magic and friendship" to his animal friends. The bear's alter ego Eckert was an art school dropout ("I had no talent") who didn't write his first Janosch book until 1963 when he was 32, and then didn't crack the best-seller list until his seventh book. Not surprisingly, then, most of the stories on *Janosch's Dream World* involved perseverance and self-trust. Each episode avoided the terminal "cutes" by inserting a jokey, punning Aesop's-fable moral, delivered as the curtain fell (literally) on Janosch and his chums.

A former industrial designer, Horst Eckert had once aspired to be a great painter. Eckert's evocative "Janosch" watercolor illustrations combined a designer's sense of composition (realistic backgrounds, correct perspective) with freeflowing imaginative fancies: anthropomorphised creatures, oddball animal-built mechanical contrivances and Grimm's Fairy Tale houses and buildings, all blending naturally with the "real" aspects of the artwork. These illustrations were flawlessly adapted into animation for *Janosch's Dream World* by Germany's WDR studios. Produced between 1988 and 1990, the series was first released to videocassette in the U.S. in the early 1990s, then began a 9:30 A.M. weekday run on the Nickelodeon cable service in late 1993. *Janosch's Dream World* fit right in with the Old World flavor of such other Nickelodeon cartoon offerings as *Maya the Bee*, *Littl' Bits* and *The World of David the Gnome* (see individual entries on these series).

JAYCE AND THE WHEELED WARRIORS. Syndicated: 1985. DIC Audiovisuel/WWP Productions/ICC Canada-France TV/SFM. Produced by Jean Chalopin, Denys Heroux, John Kemeny.

Executive producers: Jean Chalopin, Andy Heyward, Tetsuo Katayama. Executives in charge of production: Theiry Laurien, Kevin O'Donnell, Janan Roberts. Story editors: Jim Carlson, Haskel Barkin. Music by Haim Saban, Shuki Levy. Voices: Darin Baker (Jayce); Dan Hennessey (Audric/Monster Mind/Sawtrooper/Ko Kruiser); Valerie Politis (Flora); Len Carlson (Herc Stormsailer/Monster Mind/Terror Tank); Charles Joliffe (Gillian); Luba Goy (Oon); Giulio Kukurugya (Saw Boss); John Stocker (Monster Mind/Gun Grinner).

Jayce and the Wheeled Warriors was a daily, 65-episode syndicated space opera about a young man named Jason — or Jayce, to avoid confusion with the live-action series *Jason of Star Command* — who dwelt on an agrarian planet covered with vines and vegetables. Jason's father was Audric, a benevolent plant scientist whose attempts to create a food-supplying magic root ended disastrously when his creation grew out of control, thanks to an ecology-hating villain named Sawboss (so named because of his fondness for sawing down healthy foliage). The root transmogrified into several anthropomorphic evil entities, bent on carrying out Sawboss' plans of domination and destruction. These killer bushes were known as the Monster Minds.

Jayce was separated from Audric in the confusion, but knew that the combined power of his father's finger ring with his own would result in Good triumphant. To find his dad and thwart the Monster Minds, Jayce counted on the support of local wizard Gillian, and of Flora, a little girl created from plant life who was hypersensitive and thus able to "feel" danger, affection, etc. Oon, Jayce's robot, could think in flashbacks and flashforwards and could conjure up a holographic image of Jayce's advice-spouting father Audric (Stop me if you've heard this one before). Gillian remembered that a positive force, a team of warriors called the Lightning League, had protected their planet in the past and thus enlisted Jayce to re-invent the League with the good guys at hand. Jayce's own branch of the League was called the Wheeled Warriors because of their unusual vehicle, the Armed Force, which was multifaceted in its methods of wheel locomotion and weaponry. To haul the Armed Force and four other defensive wheeled vehicles throughout the Universe,

Jayce and his Warriors hired the Space Barge, captained by the nomadic, mercenary and fiercely independent Herc Stormsailer, and. . . .

NOW you recognize all this, don't you? It was that last character name that gave it away. It was *that* close to Luke Skywalker, wasn't it? That's right . . . *Jayce and the Wheeled Warriors* was yet another mutation off the *Star Wars* vine, complete with allknowing father figure, quest through space, and cute robot. And all that wheeled hardware? Merely confirmation that *Jayce and the Wheeled Warriors* was the latest half-hour toy commercial from the *Transformers* (q.v.) and *Challenge of the GoBots* (q.v.) school of kidvid merchandising.

JEANNIE. CBS: 9/8/1973–8/30/1975. Hanna-Barbera. Executive producers, William Hanna and Joseph Barbera. Creative producer, Iwao Takamoto. Animation directed by Charles Nichols. Written by Marion Hargrove, Austin Kalisch, Irma Kalisch, Sid Morse, Bill Cannings, Dave Ketchum, Bruce Shelley, Leonard Stadd, Arlene Stadd, Frank Waldman, Phyllis White, Robert White. Music by Hoyt Curtin. Musical direction by Paul DeKorte. Based on a character created by Sidney Sheldon. Voices: Julie McWhirter (Jeannie); Joe Besser (Babu); Mark Hamill (Corkey Anders); Bob Hastings (Henry Glopp); Arlene Golonka (Debbie); Mike Bell (Mark); Janet Waldo (Mrs. Anders); and John Stephenson, Sherry Jackson, Susan Silo, Tina Holland, Indira Dirks, Gay Hartwig, Vincent Van Patten, Ginny Tyler, Tommy Cook, Don Messick, Julie Bennett, and Sherry Alberoni.

First there was *I Dream of Jeannie*, a live action fantasy sitcom which ran on NBC from 1965 through 1970. Barbara Eden starred as the revealingly clad Jeannie, rescued from a bottle after 2000 years by a marooned astronaut, Tony Nelson (Larry Hagman). Jeannie followed Tony to Cocoa Beach, Florida, after his rescue, offering her services as a magical sprite for five full seasons. You've all seen the show, so we won't go on here, except to say that the series fulfilled an academic purpose: It demonstrated that bottled genies were born without navels.

I Dream of Jeannie was firmly established as an off-network rerun hit when Hanna-Barbera came up with a half hour animated spinoff in 1973, titled simply *Jeannie*. Catering to a younger audience, Hanna-Barbera obligingly shaved about 1,984 years off Jeannie's age, making her a sweet sixteen. Her rescuer/master wasn't an astronaut this time, but a teenaged surfer named Corkey (whose voice was supplied by Mark Hamill, about four years away from his own extraterrestrial career vis-a-vis *Star Wars*). An additional genie was present, acting as both guardian and comic relief: a fat bumbler named Babu, voiced by a past master at fat bumbling, comedian Joe Besser. The voice of Jeannie was provided by impressionist Julie McWhirter, who really did sound like what Barbara Eden must have sounded like in high school. The series utterly ignored the underlying innuendo of *I Dream of Jeannie* (though the leading lady was drawn with Hanna-Barbera's usual attention to pulchritudinous detail), relying instead on what some people considered typical teenaged trials and tribulations. Another alteration in the original was the manifestation of Jeannie's magic; instead of folding her arms and blinking as Barbara Eden did, the teen Jeannie pointed with her enchanted ponytailed hair.

A number of notable comedy veterans contributed to the scripts of the 16 *Jeannie* episodes, notably Marion Hargrove (whose son Dean later teamed with producer Fred Silverman—who'd commissioned *Jeannie* from Hanna-Barbera in the first place—for a series of *Perry Mason* TV movies in the 1980s) and the team of Leonard and Arlene Stadd (*Room 222*, *Love American Style* and many other series). But despite this talent input, *Jeannie* never really rose above its basic derivative level; even the "teen" concept was left over from an earlier project, *Pebbles and Bamm Bamm* (q.v.).

The National Association for Better Broadcasting was emphatic in its displeasure over *Jeannie*: "Whatever creative qualities there might have been in the original are missing from the Hanna-Barbera animated version. In making the characters younger the producers have gone too childish and silly even for the younger viewers for whom this is intended. A complete disregard or contempt for the intelligence of the viewing children and adolescents." The original *I Dream of Jeannie* was, of course, widely renowned for its high level of drawing-room wit.

Children and adolescents evidently didn't feel terribly insulted. *Jeannie* played its first season with the highest rating in its Saturday morning timeslot—beating out even the superior *Star Trek* (q.v.) cartoon series.

JEM. Syndicated: 1986 (previously syndicated 1985 as component of SUPER SUNDAY [q.v.]). Sunbow/Wildstar/Wildfire/Claster. Produced by Joe Bacal, Margaret Loesch and Tom Griffin. Creative direction by Joe Bacal. Executive in charge of production: Lee Gunther. Supervising producer, Gwen Wetzler. Produced by Marja Miletic Dahl, Don Thompson, Will Meugniot. Directed by Jim Graziano. Story editor/coproducer, Roger Slifer. Story editor, Christy Mark. Music by Robert J. Walsh. Theme song "Truly Outrageous" by Ford Kinder and Anne Bryant. Voices: Britta Phillips (Jem); Ellen Bernfield (Pizazz); and Charlie Adler, Patricia Albrecht, Tammy Amerson, Marlene Aragon, Allison Argo, Bobbie Block, Catharina Blore, Susan Blu, Anne Bryant, Angela Capelli, Kim Carlson, T. K. Carter, Cathy Cavadini, Linda Dangcil, Louise Dorsey, Walker Edmiston, Diva Grey, Deanise Goyette, Lauri Groves, Michael Horton, Ford Kinder, Jeff Kinder, Ullanda McCullough, Cindy McGee, Cathie Marcuccio, Samantha Newark, Noelle North, Neil Ross, Jack Roth, Michael Sheehan, Terri Textor, Florence Warner, and Valerie Wilson.

JEM was arguably the first cartoon series directly affected by the style and substance of the MTV cable network. At *JEM*'s core was a female rock group fronted by a beautiful young lady named Jerica Benton. Jerica, an executive for Starlight Music and also in charge of the Starlight Orphanage for Girls, discovered that her late scientist father had developed a holographic device which imbued people with supernatural powers. Bombarded by the device's computerized pulsations, Jerica Benton turned into JEM, rock artist supreme, and it was in this guise that she organized several of Starlight's teenaged charges into a group called the Holograms. Many of the episodes dealt with the Holograms' professional and personal battles with less savory rival bands, notably a girl group known appropriately as the Misfits, led by hardcase Pizazz. Other groups were likewise populated with the less attractive forms of show-business fringies, usually representing such deadly sins as vanity (in the person of a selfish teen named Rapture), greed and duplicity. Through methods both human and superhuman, JEM was usually able to keep her own band on the right path and to teach her antagonists a thing or two about proper behavior. (In one episode, JEM deflected a potential enemy by teaching her how to read!)

The series' principal attraction was with preteen girls who entertained notions of showbiz careers, and *JEM* certainly catered to this demographic group with its flashy costumes, garish lighting effects and mock-MTV rock videos (complete with a little slug at the left hand corner of the screen bearing the name of the group, the song, and the recording label). But the series was very careful to warn the more impressionable fans of the pitfalls and dangers of professional entertaining. The best *JEM* episodes took a cold-eyed and trenchant look at dishonest business managers, manipulative record executives, "bought" lawyers, false friends and empty promises. This harsh approach to the realities of the business gave *JEM* a mature edge that previous fluffy rock-band series like *Josie and the Pussycats* (q.v.) lacked entirely.

JEM began as a component of Marvel's *Super Sunday* (q.v.) in September 1985; within a few months, a song from the series, "Truly Outrageous," had scored a major hit with the junior-high crowd. By May of 1986, *JEM* was permitted to branch out into its own weekly half hour independent of *Super Sunday*, and in the fall of that year, it was syndicated on a daily basis. The series lasted two first-run seasons, retaining its freshness and showbiz savvy despite the dip in animation quality and reliance upon fantasy-toon clichés forced upon the producers by the intensified production schedule. Some of the *JEM* episodes were recycled as part of Marvel's syndicated *Maxie's World* (q.v.) in 1989, while the original series endured in cable syndication, where it was still flourishing in 1993 as part of the USA Network weekend lineup.

THE JETSONS. ABC: 9/23/1962–9/8/1963; 9/21/1963–4/18/1964 (reruns); 9/18/1982–4/2/1983 (reruns). CBS: 9/26/1964–

George, Elroy, Jane and Judy Jetson, relaxing from the rigors of life in the future; with Rosey the Robot (standing), Astro the dog, and pet alien Orbity (a character added for *The Jetsons'* 1985 revival).

9/18/1965 (reruns); 9/13/1969–9/4/1971 (reruns). NBC: 10/2/1965–9/2/1967 (reruns); 9/11/1971–9/4/1976 (reruns). Syndicated: 1985. Hanna-Barbera. NETWORK VERSION: Produced and directed by William Hanna and Joseph Barbera. Animation director, Charles Nichols. Music by Hoyt Curtin. Written by Michael Maltese, Warren Foster, Harvey Bullock, Larry Markes and Tony Benedict. Voices: George O'Hanlon (George Jetson); Penny Singleton (Jane Jetson); Mel Blanc (Spacely); Daws Butler (Elroy Jetson); Janet Waldo (Judy Jetson); John Stephenson (Cogswell); Don Messick (Astro); Jean VanderPyl (Rosie the Robot); and Howard Morris, Hal Smith, Herschel Bernardi, Dick Beals, Joan Gardner, among others. SYNDICATED VERSION: Executive producers, William Hanna and Joseph

Barbera. Produced by Bob Hathcock. Associate producers, Jeff Hall, Alex Lovy. Executives in charge of production, Jayne Barbera, Jean MacCurdy. Creative supervisor, Joe Taritero. Story editors, Arthur Alsberg, Tony Benedict, Don Nelson, Art Scott. Supervising director, Ray Patterson. Directed by Art Davis, Oscar Dufau, Carl Urbano, Rudy Zamora, Alan Zaslove. Animation directors, Don Patterson, Don Lusk, Bob Goe, Rick Leon, Irv Spence. Animation supervisors, Jay Sarbry, Ernesto Lopez, Jaime Diaz, Juan Pina, Carlos Alfonso, David Feiss. Recording director, Gordon Hunt. Music by Hoyt Curtin. Musical direction by Paul DeKorte. Voices: George O'Hanlon, Penny Singleton, Mel Blanc, Daws Butler, Janet Waldo, John Stephenson, Don Messick and Jean VanderPyl (original characters); Frank Welker (Orbity); and Bob Arbogast, Rene Auberjonois, Gay Autterson, Jered Barclay, Dick Beals, Michael Bell, Greg Berger, Susan Blu, Carol Boen, Foster Brooks, Ruth Buzzi, Victoria Carroll, Didi Conn, Henry Corden, Dave Coulier, Peter Cullen, Brian Cummings, Julie Dees, Jerry Dexter, Selma Diamond, Paul Eiding, Dick Erdman, June Foray, Pat Fraley, Joan Gardner, Joan Gerber, Barry Gordon, Phil Hartman, John Ingle, Ralph James, Lauri Johnson, Stanley Jones, Zale Kessler, Lucy Lee, Peter Leeds, Allan Lurie, Jim MacGeorge, Kenneth Mars, Chuck McCann, Edie McClurg, Terry McGovern, Sonny Melendrez, Allan Melvin, Howard Morris, Frank Nelson, Cliff Norton, Tony Pope, Phil Proctor, Bob Ridgley, Roger Rose, Tim Rooney, Neilson Ross, Beverly Sanders, Marilyn Schreffler, Avery Schreiber, Andre Stojka, Fred Travalena, B. J. Ward, Frederica Weber, Lennie Weinrib, Paul Winchell, William Windom, Bill Woodson. (*See also* ASTRO AND THE SPACE MUTTS.)

The *Jetsons*, Hanna-Barbera's third prime time network cartoon series, was like *The Flintstones* (q.v.) predicated on time displacement. Reversing the stone age milieu in which the Flintstone family was planted, however, *The Jetsons* was set in the future — about a hundred years past its 1962 debut. Like most speculative fiction of the time, it was assumed that the world of the future would be dominated by aviation and outer space technology, and that lives would be governed by the flick of

a computer switch. Well, they got the computer part right, anyway.

The characters were introduced each week with what was probably the most easily memorizable cartoon theme song of all time. (Copyright 1962, Hanna-Barbera Music [BMI].) George Jetson was a computer operator at Spacely Sprockets, a business run by volcanic "Mr. Dithers" type Cosmo Spacely (whose name, like all the other character names on *The Jetsons*, had its base in jet-propulsion jargon). George's boy Elroy was a typical six-year-old schoolboy, a nice kid who divided his time equally between his homework videotapes and his anti-gravity playthings. Daughter Judy was 15, a traditionally curvaceous Hanna-Barbera teenager whose idea of a good time was to go space surfing or to attend a Martian rock concert.

Finally there was Jane Jetson, described in the ABC promo for *The Jetsons* as "a typical housewife . . . spends more than her husband earns." This wasn't the only sexist slur on *The Jetsons*, and it was this aspect that has tended to date the series for many modern viewers: Despite its 21st century trappings, the show relied all too heavily on such 1950s and 1960s bromides as lousy women drivers, battleaxe mothers-in-law, irrational jealousies and overextended department store charge accounts. Even jokes and plot situations that had no connection with the role expectations of men and women in 1962 had a tired look to them. *Variety* complained that the opening episode "Rosey the Robot" was predicated on "the oldest comedy chestnut known to man": bringing the boss home to dinner.

Oddly, *The Jetsons* plays better now than it did in 1962, when its suicide time slot opposite NBC's Disney series and CBS' *Dennis the Menace* condemned it to cancellation after only one season. Joe Barbera recently discovered through an independently conducted survey that the series clocked more laughs than the survey group had ever experienced with any other comedy program. Some of the laughs surely grew from the shock of recognizing that much of the 21st century gadgetry seen in *The Jetsons* has become commonplace in the last 30 years: wall-sized televisions, microwaved dinners, dehydrated food pills, exercise treadmills, and even prototypical versions of two-way TV telephones and robot servants (*The Jetsons'* infrequently seen Rosey the Robot was meant to be a takeoff on the popular live-action series *Hazel*, but the imitation has outlasted the original). There is also the nostalgia factor in seeing such 60s icons as Soupy Sales and Lawrence Welk retranslated in futuristic terms, just as *The Flintstones'* spoofs of Elvis Presley, the Beatles and *The Beverly Hillbillies* provide an instant cultural framework for its baby-boomer fans. And some jokes simply never lose their value, notably George Jetson's lament that he simply can't support his family on a measly annual income of $100,000; this gets a laugh today not so much from the concept that inflation will continue to gallop forever as from the suggestion that there will be any single-income families left in 2062.

Visually, *The Jetsons* represented no great advance in the art of animation, but it stands as one of Hanna-Barbera's most stylish projects. Hanna-Barbera's decisions to have the characters whisked from place to place via conveyor belt and to have all doors slide open may have been reached to save on animation time, but such choices added immeasurably to the streamlined 21st century texture of the series. Apart from this ongoing stylistic decision, one single episode, "A Date with Jet Screamer," included a brief musical number ("Eep-Opp-Ork-Ah-Ah") rendered in a brilliantly surrealistic, stream of consciousness fashion that couldn't help having had an effect on future MTV rock-video directors. Vignettes such as this make *Variety's* criticism that *The Jetsons* exhibited a "lack of style" incomprehensible.

A more traditional element of the series, the Jetson's family dog Astro, would turn out to have a profound effect on Hanna-Barbera's future. Astro was a gigantic Great Dane, surprisingly articulate (he began every word with an "R"; "Hello George" came out "Rello Rorge"), overly and sloppily affectionate, and very quick to cower when confronted with terror. The big mutt became quite popular with younger viewers, a fact not lost on Hanna-Barbera, who later reshaped the Astro character — with the creative input of CBS executive Fred Silverman and writers Joe Ruby and Ken Spears — into one of the studio's most durable properties, Scooby-Doo (q.v.).

Don Messick, future voice of Scooby-Doo, provided the growls and grunts of Astro. Messick was one of a highly talented team of voice artists who contributed mightily to *The Jetsons*. George O'Hanlon, longtime star of the "Behind the Eight Ball" series of one-reel theatrical shorts (O'Hanlon played hapless everyman Joe McDoakes), was ideally cast as George Jetson; the actor would later point with pride to the fact that his own children watched the series regularly in network reruns for 12 years. Jane was voiced by Penny Singleton, best known for her title role in the "Blondie" B-picture series, who in 1962 was emerging from a retirement forced on her by showbiz executives who didn't like her union activities on behalf of the American Guild of Variety Artists (Miss Singleton had lobbied successfully for more pay and better working conditions for chorus girls, which hardly endeared her to the mob-connected owners of several nightclubs). Forty-five-year-old Daws Butler successfully conjured up a preteen pitch for his role as Elroy Jetson (Lucille Bliss, the voice of *Crusader Rabbit* [q.v.], had been slated for this role, but cancelled due to illness), while Janet Waldo, who'd been portraying schoolgirls on radio and in films since the 1930s, once more convincingly adopted teenaged tones as Elroy's sister Judy. And as Mr. Spacely, Mel Blanc was untoppable: no one ever said "YOU'RE FIRED!" with as much blustery, earth-tremor conviction.

A footnote: early press releases concerning *The Jetsons* announced that Morey Amsterdam and Pat Carroll had been set for the voices of George and Jane. While such casting would have been fascinating, it is likely that this was mere publicity puff, since both of the above-mentioned comic actors were then employed as supporting actors on series telecast by ABC rival CBS (Amsterdam on *The Dick Van Dyke Show*, Carroll on *The Danny Thomas Show*), which were sponsored by General Foods and thus might have resulted in conflict with the advertisers on *The Jetsons*.

After its prime time exposure, the 24-episode *The Jetsons* began a more lucrative Saturday morning rerun career, which lasted 14 years on three different networks. Nothing new came from the *Jetsons* manifest (save for a spinoff of sorts, *Astro and the Space Mutts*, appearing in 1981 as a component of Hanna-Barbera's

Mr. Spacely uses 21st century technology to set employee relations back 100 years; George Jetson is the recipient of the Spacely spleen.

Space Stars [q.v.]) until 1985, when the enervated syndication market convinced the studio to make 41 new *Jetsons* half hours. In the manner of the original series, the new *Jetsons* juxtaposed cultural references of the 1980s into a futuristic setting, this time carefully avoiding the casual sexism of the 1960s version: When George Jetson tried to crack a woman driver joke on the later series, Jane put him down with

"That sort of humor went out three hundred years ago." The basic characters remained intact, and it was even possible to engage the same actors from the 1962 series to recreate their roles; the one new cast member was a pet alien named Orbity, voiced by Frank Welker. The rapidity of production required that the layouts for the new *Jetsons* be done quickly and inexpensively in Taiwan. This provided a golden opportunity for a young Hanna-Barbera employee named John Kricfalusi (see *Ren and Stimpy*), who supervised layout of the first 15 episodes, then was given his first-ever directing assignment on the episode titled "Hi-Tech Wreck."

The original *Jetsons* installments from 1962 were incorporated into the newer package to allow for a 65-episode manifest, suitable for stripping Monday through Friday. To make the old programs compatible with the new, Hanna-Barbera went to the expense of removing the intrusive, network-imposed laugh track on the initial *Jetsons* episodes, something that fans had been demanding without success for nearly a quarter of a century.

This redressed syndicated *Jetsons* property proved so successful that an additional ten episodes were filmed in 1987, and no fewer than three spinoff feature-length versions were produced. The first was a two hour TV movie, *The Jetsons Meet the Flintstones* (1987), which after a meandering and predictable first half managed to score potent satirical points concerning media hype and questionable big-business practices before fadeout time. *Rockin' with Judy Jetson* (1988) was the next TV special, an extension of the aforementioned 1962 *Jetsons* episode "A Date with Jet Screamer" dressed up for the MTV generation. The two TV movies were enjoyable, and critical response was warm if guarded.

Unfortunately, the 1990 theatrical feature *Jetsons: The Movie*, managed to dissipate much of the goodwill generated by the TV films. Animation was several steps up from the usual Hanna-Barbera standard, with some excellent extraterrestrial background art and eyepopping computer generated "3-D" effects courtesy of deGraf/Wahrman and Kroyer Films. But the story, an attenuated slam against corporate espionage and injurious business practices, weighed the proceedings down like a two-ton cartoon anvil. Fans of the series were unhappy when actress Janet Waldo was unceremoniously dumped as the voice of Judy Jetson in favor of a "hot" teenage singing star named Tiffany, who'd risen to celebrity through a series of shopping-mall concerts and appearances on the syndicated TV talent contest *Star Search*. This callously commercial casting turned out to be a harmful move when production delays forced *Jetsons: The Movie* to

premiere nearly three years after its inception, by which time Tiffany's fame had peaked and she'd been forgotten by all but her most fervent fans.

In fact, by the time the movie finally hit the screens, three of its voice artists — George O'Hanlon, Mel Blanc and Daws Butler — had died, compelling Hanna-Barbera to dedicate the picture to their memory. If asked, these three actors would probably have chosen a more lasting legacy; *Jetsons: The Movie* was a financial disappointment despite a strong opening week, posting a profit only after making the video-rental rounds — where it set a record for the shortest time elapsed between theatrical premiere and home video release.

JIM AND JUDY IN TELELAND. Syndicated: 1953 (produced 1949–50). Film Flash Productions/Television Screen Productions. Voices: Merrill Johls (Jim); Honey McKenzie (Judy). (Reissued in 1959 as BOB AND BETTY IN ADVENTURELAND.)

I may be the only man living who actually watched *Jim and Judy in Teleland* at the time it was originally syndicated. This series of 52 five-minute, black and white cliffhanging cartoons was run on a Cincinnati children's series, *The Bean's Clubhouse*, along with such other favorites as Laurel and Hardy, *Crusader Rabbit* (q.v.), and a bizarre live action simian detective spoof titled *The Chimps*.

What I remember best about *Jim and Judy in Teleland* was not its clever mixture of limited animation and hand manipulated cardboard cutouts, nor its espionage-laden storylines. No, my most vivid memory was the method in which the young protagonists Jim and Judy entered Teleland. This was accomplished by literally climbing into their TV set, through the screen.

Expectedly, adult "experts" complained that this last activity would encourage imitation at home. Well, I for one *never* tried to climb into my TV screen. I also never hanged myself by my cape playing "Superman" in a tree, nor did I carve a "Z" on anyone's chest while emulating Zorro, nor did I poke someone's eyes out in imitation of The Three Stooges. Where did those adult experts *find* such children? Not in *my* house.

JIM HENSON'S FRAGGLE ROCK *see* FRAGGLE ROCK

JIM HENSON'S MUPPET BABIES *see* MUPPET BABIES

JOHNNY CYPHER IN THE DI-MENSION ZERO. Syndicated: 1967. Joe Oriolo Films/Seven Arts. Voices: Paul Hecht (Johnny Cypher); Corinne Orr (Zina); Gene Allen (additional voices).

Johnny Cypher in the Dimension Zero was an exercise in TV Cartoon Literalism, in which all the characters looked like hand-tinted photographs of real people. Produced by Joe Oriolo Studios, *Johnny Cypher* was a series of 130 six-minute episodes, most of them cliffhangers, telling the story of a handsome Earth scientist who used his space-travel and time-travel powers and paraphernalia to defeat villains from all corners of the universe. Zina was Johnny's beautiful companion, and the principal heavy was named Rhom. "Dimension Zero" was the name given Cypher's ability to cross time and space barriers; the series' last episode brought events to an effective halt through its title "No More Dimension Zero." Tune in next week for a blank screen, friends.

JOKEBOOK. NBC: 4/23/1982–5/7/1982. Hanna-Barbera. Produced by Harry Love. Supervised by Marty Murphy. Voices: Henry Corden, Bob Hastings, Joan Gerber, Joyce Jameson, Don Messick, Sidney Miller, Robert Allan Ogle, Ronnie Schell, Marilyn Schreffler, Hal Smith, John Stephenson, Janet Waldo, Lennie Weinrib, Frank Welker.

Unheralded at the time of its release and ignored by diligent Hanna-Barbera chronicler Ted Sennett in his book on the studio, *Jokebook* was a desperate counterprogramming effort from beleaguered NBC to telecast something other than static opposite ABC's *Benson* and CBS' *Dukes of Hazzard* in the spring of 1982. Hanna-Barbera was responsible only for the wraparounds of this half hour prime-timer, which featured such forgettable recurring characters as The Nerd, Treeman, Eve and Adam, and a barbershop quartet called the Mount Rushmores (four singing presidential heads).

The body of each episode was a potpourri of theatrical short subjects produced worldwide, many of them award winners. What publicity there was for *Jokebook* did its best to hide the fact that the televised shorts were retreaded theatricals and not TV originals. The *TV Guide* listings would only say that the plotlines featured Noah vs. the Ark animals, an ungrateful damsel in distress who spurned her rescuer, a lawnmower run amok, and a scientist turning his nagging wife into a "shrinking violet"—without listing the titles of these various vignettes.

Per its title, *Jokebook* concentrated solely on cartoons that were distinguished by their punchlines. A prime example of this was the Oscar-winning *The Crunch Bird* (1971), already long established on the art house circuit, which spun a shaggy-dog story leading inexorably to a payoff—"Crunchbird my ass!"—which most male viewers had heard at summer camp 20 years earlier.

Supervised by magazine cartoonist Marty Murphy, who'd previously done character design work on such Hanna-Barbera series as *Wait Till Your Father Gets Home* (q.v.) and *Valley of the Dinosaurs* (q.v.), *Jokebook* prepared seven half hours for telecast. Four of these were actually scheduled. Only three were actually shown. For the rest of the 1981-82 season, NBC filled *Jokebook*'s Friday evening time slot with made-for-TV movies and busted pilots, while *Benson* and *Dukes of Hazzard* continued to sweep the ratings.

JONNY QUEST. ABC: 9/18/1964–9/9/1965 (switched nights 12/31/1964); 9/13/1970–9/2/1972 (reruns); CBS: 9/6/1967–9/5/1970; NBC: 9/7/1979–11/3/1979; 4/12/1980–9/6/1981. (*See also* GODZILLA.) Syndicated: 1986 (new episodes: *See also* FUNTASTIC WORLD OF HANNA BARBERA). Hanna-Barbera. Original 1964 version: Produced and directed by William Hanna, Joseph Barbera. Story director, Paul Sommer. Story supervisor, Arthur Pierson. Animation director, Charles A. Nichols. Animation supervisor, Irv Spence. Music by Hoyt Curtin. Voices: Tim Matthieson (Jonny Quest); Mike Road (Race Bannon); John Stephenson, Don Messick (Dr. Benton Quest); Don Messick (Bandit); Danny Bravo (Hadji); Vic Perrin (Dr. Zin, others); Cathy Lewis (Jezebel Jade); and Everett Sloane, Henry Corden, Sam Edwards, Keye Luke, and Doug Young.

—JONNY QUEST (1986 VERSION).

Executive producers, William Hanna and Joseph Barbera. Executive in charge of production, Jayne Barbera. Produced by Berny Wolf. Story editor, Mark Young. Creative design, Iwao Takamoto. Supervising director, Ray Patterson. Directed by Oscar Dufau, Don Lusk, Ray Patterson, Rudy Zamora. Animation directors: Rick Leon, Don Patterson, Jay Sarbry. Title design by Bill Perez. Music director, Hoyt Curtin. Animation facilities: Wang and Cuckoo's Nest. Voices: Scott Menville (Jonny); Don Messick (Quest, Bandit); Sonny Granville Van Dusen (Race); Rob Paulsen (Hadji); and Rene Auberjonois, Michael Bell, Candy Brown, Howard Caine, Roger C. Carmel, Peter Cullen, Jennifer Darling, Barry Dennen, Dick Erdman, Bernard Ehrhard, Dick Gautier, Ernest Harada, Dorian Harewood, Darryl Hickman, Georgi Irene, Aron Kincaid, Ruth Kobart, Keye Luke, Allan Lurie, Steve McGowan, Soon-Teck Oh, Rob Paulsen, Vic Perrin, Andre Stojka, George Takei, Jeff Tambor, Les Tremayne, B. J. Ward, Frank Welker, Stan Wojno, and Keone Young.

Jonny Quest, Hanna-Barbera's fourth prime time network series, was certainly the most atypical and ambitious of the lot. Unlike *The Flintstones* (q.v.) and *Top Cat* (q.v.), *Jonny Quest* wasn't a variation of earlier TV sitcoms; unlike *The Jetsons* (q.v.), it wasn't a spin on earlier Hanna-Barbera projects. *Jonny Quest* was a full-blooded return to the "boy's own adventure" school of pulp fiction, comic strip and movie and radio serials—the sort of fare that fiftysomething cartoon makers like Bill Hanna and Joe Barbera had grown up with.

The "adventure team" concept popularized on such novels as the *Doc Savage* series and such radio series as *Jack Armstrong* was redressed for *Jonny Quest*. In this instance, the team was headed by Dr. Benton Quest, a bearded, cultured scientist frequently enlisted by the government to investigate paranormal incidents throughout the world. Dr. Quest was a widower, and thus compelled to take his 11-year-old son Jonny along on many of his impromptu jet flights. Jonny's tutor-bodyguard was Roger "Race" Bannon, a Doc Savage lookalike whose brawn was relied upon when Dr. Quest's brain failed to extricate his team from their many life-threatening perils. Jonny's travelling com-

panions were a mystical Indian boy named Hadji—a rare instance of a non-caucasian treated as an equal on an early 1960s TV series—and his bulldog Bandit, so named because of the masklike markings around his eyes.

The characters on *Jonny Quest* were designed and developed by comic artist Doug Wildey, who was given a separate "signature" card on the series' closing credits. He certainly deserved the honor; after toiling for years on such comic books and newspaper action strips as *Hopalong Cassidy*, *Buffalo Bill*, and *The Outlaw Kid*, Wildey had accumulated a mental encyclopedia of sharp draftsmanship technique and thrill-inducing story construction. Wildey had also learned from his lengthy tenure on *The Saint* comic strip (based on the works of Leslie Charteris) how to adapt visually and expand upon other writers' creations. Milton Caniff's *Terry and the Pirates* villainess, "The Dragon Lady," was the model for the recurring *Jonny Quest* character of Jezebel Jade, while the insidious Dr. Zin, the Quest party's most frequent foe, was a cross between Sax Rohmer's Fu Manchu and Ian Fleming's Dr. No.

The stories on *Jonny Quest*, dealing with demented scientists, hostile natives (hardly acceptable in these more racially sensitive times), mutated lizard monsters, ex–Nazis, death rays, and the like, might have lent themselves to satire and "camp" had the series been produced after the live action *Batman* of 1966. To their credit, Hanna and Barbera played the proceedings straight and full out. The monsters were hideous and thus hideously disposed of; the villains were horrible, and thus were doomed to die horrible deaths (Even "good" characters were in jeopardy; in the opening episode, "The Mystery of the Lizard Men," the first thing we see is a harmless merchant steamer being blasted off the face of the earth!). While plotlines were frequently fantastic and scientifically impossible, Hanna-Barbera maintained a surface reality with its character design and story development. Even the traditional comic relief of Bandit the dog did not, as might have been expected, manifest itself in having the family pet assume human qualities. Despite a wide range of facial expressions, Bandit was drawn like a real quadrupedal dog, never behaving physically in any manner that a real dog would not behave.

Jonny Quest, enjoying the advantages of a friend who dabbles in mysticism; with Bandit (the dog), Hadji (with flute), and Race Bannon.

To digress a moment on the subject of Bandit: Doug Wildey had wanted to carry the "exotic" underpinnings of *Jonny Quest* into Jonny's pet, which he'd envisioned as a monkey or a cockatoo. But Hanna-Barbera vetoed this idea, noting that a pet dog would be more easily marketable as a toy. This might explain why virtually *every* subsequent Hanna-Barbera cartoon series featuring human characters included an arbitrary funny dog.

While a surprising number of daily newspaper critics recommended the series highly, *Jonny Quest*'s "all stops out" approach to its blood-and-thunder plotlines was inevitably attacked by those who felt that TV was already excessively violent, especially TV aimed at younger viewers. We must note that the principal tongue-cluckers were adults; most children, to quote *Variety*, were busy "ogling the TV set."

Had the nay-sayers paused to look at *Jonny Quest* objectively, they would have noted that the series was better animated and more elaborately mounted than any previous Hanna-Barbera effort. To be sure, character movement was still compartmentalized and limited, but it was brilliantly timed and preplanned; a simple detail such as a character's finger adjusting the lens of his binoculars made all the difference between quality limited animation and cheap "cartoons by the yard." And the background work was superb, particularly the renderings of the jungles, mountain passes, fjords and seascapes that figured so prominently in the half hour adventures. So riveting was this draftsmanship that viewers frequently wrote to Hanna-Barbera asking for reproductions of *Jonny Quest*'s background art.

Character voices matched the larger than life approach to *Jonny Quest*. As Jonny, Tim Matheson (his name then spelled Matthieson) was just beginning a career that would extend into adventure series and movies of the 1970s and 1980s. Mike Road, a minor leading man and past regular on ABC's *The Roaring 20s*, found in his characterization of Race Bannon a Hanna-Barbera niche as a specialist in hearty heroic types. John Stephenson was Dr. Benton Quest in the first few episodes, but prior commitments forced him to step down; his replacement was Hanna-Barbera stalwart Don Messick, taking full advantage of an opportunity to do a "straight" voice after years of Ranger Smith, Pixie Mouse and Reddy the Cat. Rounding out the cast, Danny Bravo brought the right blend of pragmatism and mystery to the role of Hadji.

By its very ambitious nature, and by virtue of the fact that a globetrotting group of heroes would never settle long enough in one place for background art to be used repeatedly in future episodes, *Jonny Quest* became almost prohibitively expensive. Fortunately, it did fairly well in Friday evening competition with CBS' *Rawhide* and NBC's *International Showtime*. Joe Barbera had previously gone on record promising that if a kid left his seat while viewing *Jonny Quest*, "I'll eat the chair!" For the first three months of the series' existence, there was no need for Mr. Barbera to alter his eating habits.

The problem was not *Jonny Quest* but *The Flintstones*, which during the 1964-65 season was being seen on Thursdays, where it was losing a lot of ground to CBS' *The Munsters* in its timeslot. Since *The Flintstones* had a greater offnet-rerun potential the longer it remained on the networks, Hanna-Barbera decided to move the series to the more preferable Friday evening berth occupied by *Jonny Quest*. This meant that *Quest* would be juggled to Thursdays—where, like *The Flintstones*

before it, it fell victim to *The Munsters*. The *Flintstones* was rescued for an additional season, while *Jonny Quest* lost its following and was cancelled by September of 1965. Still, there is nothing on record to indicate that Joe Barbera ever ingested a chair.

In keeping with the tradition set by *Top Cat* and *The Jetsons*, *Jonny Quest* spent the next seven years in Saturday morning rebroadcasts on all three major networks. In 1979, the 26 *Quests* were pulled from local syndication to pump up ratings on NBC's *Godzilla* (q.v.), compelling the 60-minute series to retitle itself *Godzilla and the Super 90*. And in 1986, a new cycle of 13 *Jonny Quest* episodes, heavily influenced by Spielberg's "Indiana Jones" theatrical films, were produced as a component of the weekend syndie *Funtastic World of Hanna-Barbera*.

The series' original cast was intact, looking none the worse for their 21 years' absence; in fact, Dr. Quest looked even more hale and hearty with a fuller beard. One new member of the Quest team was introduced in the episode "Monolith Man": Hardrok, a petrified warrior exhumed from the ruins of an ancient subterranean city and brought back to life with sonic rays. Hardrok possessed uncanny strength, evenly matched by his vast intellect and vocabulary. Of the principal voice actors, only Don Messick was back from the 1965 series in the dual roles of Dr. Quest and Bandit (though Vic Perrin made occasional return visits as the indomitable Dr. Zin). Scott Menville played Jonny Quest a year or two younger than Tim Matheson had, while Rob Paulsen did a joltingly accurate imitation of Danny Bravo in the part of Hadji.

Though expensively produced, the new *Quests* made few animation advances over the original program. This in itself wouldn't have been a problem had the original's thrill quotient been maintained, but the "sock" of the new series was muted by the overall downpedalling of violence in mid–1980s cartoons. (To compensate for the lack of physical action, Hadji was given vaster magical and mystical powers than in the original series, allowing the characters to escape their perils in a more peaceful manner.) In terms of raw excitement, the new *Jonny Quests* couldn't hold a candle to the original episodes, which also ran on *Funtastic World*.

In 1993, a two-hour TV movie, *Jonny*

and the Golden Quest, made its bow over the Family Channel cable service. This well-animated adventure succeeded in bringing the 30-year-old property into the 1990s (Paul Germain, writer for Nickelodeon's *The Rugrats* [q.v.], was not alone in observing that, much as he admired *Jonny Quest,* it hadn't weathered the years all that well); it also solved the long-standing mystery as to what happened to Jonny Quest's mother. Following the Family Channel's lead, TNT scheduled the original *Jonny Quest* as part of a daily hour long strip consisting principally of other Hanna-Barbera adventure efforts. As a postscript to this, a poll of cable viewers revealed that the character cartoon fans considered to be the "best mother figure" was not, as expected, Wilma Flintstone or Marge Simpson — but *Jonny Quest's* surrogate "mother" Race Bannon.

And finally, a note on titles. Despite the alphabetical entries in several previous television encyclopedias, this series was *never* called *The Adventures of Jonny Quest.* It was simply *Jonny Quest* on the screen, *Jonny Quest* on paper, and *Jonny Quest* in the TV listings. Before its debut, however, there was a slightly different title, perhaps invoking what was hoped would be fond memories of James Bond: *Jonny Quest — File 037.*

JOSIE AND THE PUSSYCATS.
CBS: 9/12/1970–9/2/1972; 9/6/1975–9/4/1976 (reruns).
—JOSIE AND THE PUSSYCATS IN OUTER SPACE. CBS: 9/9/1972–8/31/1974. Radio Comics/Hanna-Barbera. Produced by Alex Lovy. Creative producer, Iwao Takamoto. Animation director, Charles A. Nichols. Created by John and Richard Goldwater. Music by Hoyt Curtin. Songs written and arranged by Danny Janssen, Bob Ingerman and Art Hogell (Cala Productions). Voices (both series): Janet Waldo (Josie); Jackie Joseph (Melody); Barbara Pariot (Valerie); Jerry Dexter (Alan); Casey Kasem (Alexander Cabot III); Sherry Alberoni (Alexandra Cabot); Don Messick (Sebastian); Cathy Douglas, Patricia Holloway, Cherie Moore [Cheryl Ladd] (Vocalists for Pussycats). Additional voice, JOSIE AND THE PUSSYCATS IN OUTER SPACE: Don Messick (Bleep).

If Hanna-Barbera's *Josie and the Pussycats* resembled an all-girl version of *The Archies* (q.v.) at times, it's probably because both series shared the same pedigree. Archie Publications executives John and Richard Goldwater, together with artist/writer Dick DeCarlo, developed "Josie" (named after DeCarlo's wife) for the company's comic book line in 1963 — its target audience being little girls who liked to cut out paper dress designs and use "all–American teenager" Josie to model them. It was at the suggestion of CBS executive Fred Silverman that Hanna-Barbera (taking over from *The Archies'* home studio Filmation, then overloaded with product) reshape Josie into the lead singer of a rock group — hoping no doubt for a reprise of the success that greeted the Archies' hit single "Sugar Sugar." No such hit was forthcoming, though a 16-song record album tied in with the series sold reasonably well. Additionally, the female vocalists hired to provide the musical portions of each weekly half hour did produce at least one saleable commodity. Among the singers was Cheryl Jean Stopelmoor, who called herself "Cherie Moore" on *Josie and the Pussycats* in 1970, and who several years later achieved prominence using her married name, Cheryl Ladd.

Josie and the Pussycats was, as mentioned, all about a rock group, booked by its aggressive young manager Alexander Cabot III into an adventure-packed world tour. Cabot's somewhat timorous approach to life was countered by his smart-mouthed sister Alexandra, a dead ringer for *The Archies'* Veronica Lodge. The Pussycats, so named because of their brief feline-type costumes (tails and all), included redheaded leader Josie, ditsy blonde (was there any other kind in 1970?) Melody, and calm and practical Valerie. Much was made at the time over the fact that Valerie was black, the first instance of a recurring minority heroine in a cartoon series. Many found this laudatory, but the National Association for Better Broadcasting was apparently color blind. The NABB's sourball opinion of *Josie* was that the "characters are ugly. The production is crude. Unsuitable for children."

One overgrown child would certainly have contested this: Fred Silverman was very fond of the series, supervising its progress in minutest detail. One of the legends growing from the Silverman years at CBS concerned the time that Freddy was listening to a promotion tape for *Josie and the Pussycats* consisting of dialogue bites culled from the completed episodes. Suddenly he stopped the proceedings and exclaimed, "Josie wouldn't say that!" At Silverman's command, the offending snippet of dialogue was not only removed from the promo but re-recorded for the episode itself.

Another *Josie and the Pussycats* legend demonstrated the double-edged sword of network power—power that at once insisted upon having a cartoon series and then insisted that the series avoid what cartoons did best. In one of the *Josie* installments, writer-director Norman Maurer (see *The New Three Stooges*) had come up with a standard slapstick gag wherein a cat was dumped in a dish of spaghetti. That this could be offensive to anyone other than the owner of an Italian restaurant boggles the mind. Yet CBS ordered the gag removed. The argument? It was too easy for little kids at home to imitate. Imagine the anarchy that would have been wrought upon the nation had there been millions of pasta-stained pussycats.

Despite restrictions, there *was* some comic action on *Josie and the Pussycats,* with most of the adventures ending in an all-out slapstick chase, with Josie and others pursuing, or being pursued, by the villains. Many of the Pussycats' top musical numbers were heard as background accompaniment for these chases, a comic-counterpoint technique borrowed from the live-action series *The Monkees*—which in turn, had borrowed the routine from the Beatles movies *A Hard Day's Night* and *Help.*

After 16 episodes and two network seasons, *Josie and the Pussycats* was revamped to accommodate a sci-fi slant. On the inaugural episode of the 1972-73 season, the Pussycats, their manager, their manager's sister, their beefcake male friend Alan and their pet cat Sebastian were inadvertently locked in a NASA space capsule and launched into the stratosphere. *Josie and the Pussycats in Outer Space* played this concept for all it was worth, which in this case was 16 additional half hours. New to this incarnation of *Josie* was an alien from the planet Zelcor named Bleep, who like Sebastian the cat was voiced by the ineluctable Don Messick.

JOT. Syndicated: 1965–1970. Southern Baptist Radio-Television Commission. Created, produced and written by Ruth Byers and Ted Perry.

JOT, the first (and thus far only) cartoon series produced by the Radio and Television Commission of the Southern Baptist Convention, starred an anthropomorphic white dot. Little JOT—the name was always capitalized—bounced his way through life, altering his usually cheerful facial expression at a moment's notice whenever coming across something problematic, and in general learning spiritual and moral lessons in a deliberately soft-pedaled fashion. In the words of Ruth Byers, onetime director of children's productions at the Dallas Theatre Center, who created JOT with fellow Theatre Center employee Ted Perry, the dauntless dot "reflects a child's personality, sensitive to his inner world of thought and feeling. His conscience acts as a spiritual thermometer, registering thought and actions and calling attention to those that conflict with his spiritual well-being."

To convey this visually, JOT frequently changed shape and color whenever confronted with crises of conscience. To accommodate his circumstances and surroundings (drawn in an adolescent stick-figure fashion), JOT could become everything from a tree to a rabbit, even something as intangible as the wind. In this respect, the character had much in common with Terrytoons' Tom Terrific (q.v.), whose shape and color metamorphoses were manifested in a less spiritual fashion to get himself out of jams.

First telecast as a component of the religiously inclined Dallas kid's show *Peppermint Place* (which itself would be syndicated sporadically during the 1980s and 1990s), the first 13 four-and-a-half-minute episodes of *JOT* drew over 175,000 fan letters, not only from children but also from congratulatory adult church groups. A second batch of *JOT* episodes incorporated messages about racial tolerance and keeping one's faith in the increasingly dangerous big cities. During its heyday, the series was honored with several religious broadcasting awards—two of them bestowed by Roman Catholic organizations—and could be seen in Australia, Japan, and a handful of Western European cities. *JOT* was still being distributed into the 1980s, with several independent and religious stations running the series in half-hour installments, telecasting four to five *JOT* cartoons strung together.

JOURNEY TO THE CENTRE OF THE EARTH. ABC: 9/9/1967–8/30/1969. Filmation. Produced by Lou Scheimer and Norm Prescott. Directed by Hal Sutherland. Story editor, Ken Sobol. Music by Gordon Zahler. Voices: Ted Knight (Prof. Lindenbrook/Count Saccnusson); Jane Webb (Cindy Lindenbrook); Pat Harrington Jr. (Alec McEwen/Lar/Torg).

Jules Verne's fanciful 1864 novel *Voyage au Centre de la Terre* was a spectacular but straightforward account of Scots geologist Oliver Lindenbrook, who with a small but intrepid party travelled to the Earth's core to solve the mystery of a cryptic note left behind by previous inner Earth explorer Arne Sakknussem. It was enough 130 years ago merely to undertake so dangerous an expedition; no human villains were really necessary to sustain the novel's excitement quotient.

When Hollywood scenarist Charles Brackett took hold of the Verne original and converted it to the 1959 20th Century–Fox feature *Journey to the Centre of the Earth*, he must have recalled the oft-repeated words of former Fox executive Sol M. Wurtzel, who usually rejected a screenplay by shouting "Where's the menace?" So Brackett invented a menace in the form of Arne Sakknussem's evil brother, Count Sakknussem, who with a neanderthal-type henchman accompanied Lindenbrook to the middle of the Earth in order to megalomaniacally establish his own subterranean empire. That a beautiful girl would also go along for the ride was standard operating procedure for the Hollywood of 1959; Brackett's heroine was Carla Goetaborg, widow of the head of a rival Earth's-center expedition. And there was a sort of comedy relief in the form of Gertrude the Duck, the pet of Lindenbrook's Icelandic guide Hans. Only Hans, Lindenbrook, and the Professor's prize pupil and fellow explorer Alec McEwen were actual holdovers from the original novel.

Thus it was the film and not the book which acted as principal inspiration for the animated, half hour weekly *Journey to the Centre of the Earth* which premiered on ABC in 1967. Count Sakknussem was back, converted into "Count Saccnusson" but still fortified with hulking henchman Torg (an unnamed character in the movie), as was Gertrude the Duck—who as all of us who saw the movie when it first came out will remember was unchivalrously eaten by the villain (This moment induced far more nightmares than did the rather laid-back lizards who were photographically enlarged to double as dinosaurs). No such fate awaited the cartoon Gertrude, more's the pity. Carla Goetaborg disappeared, replaced on the expedition by Lindenbrook's pretty niece Cindy (her character had likewise been overlooked by Jules Verne, who might well have included her had the name "Cindy" existed in 1864). And of course, there was Oliver Lindenbrook, faithful guide Lars (originally Hans), and student Alec McEwen, the latter redrawn to conform to the "mod" 1960s.

I didn't see the 17-episode *Journey to the Centre of the Earth* when it made its TV bow, so I'll take fantasy-film historian Bill Warren's word for it when he notes in his book *Keep Watching the Skies* that the series was "poorly animated and not worth watching." At least it gave a few weeks' work to journeyman actor Ted Knight, who did the voices of both the heroic Lindenbrook and the wicked Saccnusson; this was, need we say, some time before Knight settled down with his regular job as vainglorious newsman Ted Baxter on *The Mary Tyler Moore Show*.

KANGAROO *see* **SATURDAY SUPERCADE**

KARATE KAT *see* **COMIC STRIP**

THE KARATE KID. NBC: 9/9/1989–9/1/1990. Jerry Weintraub Productions/DIC/Columbia Pictures TV. Executive producers, Jerry Weintraub and Andy Heyward. Co-executive producer, Robby London. Produced and directed by Larry Houston. Story editors, Dorothy Middleton and Michael Maurer. Based on characters created by Robert Mark Kamer. Adapted for animation by Dan Distefano. Animation director, Katsumi Takasuga. Executive in charge of production, Winnie Chaffee; assisted by Dawn Jackson and Stacy Gallishaw. Associate producer, Ken Duer. Script coordinators, Lori Crawford, George G. Robinson,

William A. Ruiz. Character design supervisor, Russ Heath. Music by Haim Saban and Shuki Levy; music production supervisor, Andrew Dimitroff. Voice director, Ginny McSwain. Title "Karate Kid" used with the consent of DC Comics, Inc. Voices: Joe Dedio (Daniel); Robert Ito (Miyagi Yakuga); Janice Kawaye (Taki); and Pat Morita, Charles Adler, James Avery, Bever-Leigh Banfield, Michael Bell, Bettina, Darlene Carr, Francois Chau, Cam Clarke, Townsend Coleman, Danny Cooksey, Jim Cummings, Brian Cummings, Debbi Derryberry, Shawn Donahue, Fernando Escandon, Ronald Feinberg, Takayo Fisher, Linda Gary, Ellen Gerstell, Ed Gilbert, Salim Grant, Edan Gross, Ernest Harada, Billie A. Hayes, Dana Hill, Michael Horton, Jerry Houser, Buster Jones, Dana Lee, Katie Leigh, Kadar Lewis, Sherry Lynn, Mary McDonald-Lewis, Joey Miyashima, Claudette Nevins, Toy Newkirk, Dyana Ortelli, Rob Paulsen, Diane Pershing, Brock Peters, Hal Rayle, Peter Renaday, Bob Ridgely, David Roberts, Joshua A. Rodine, Neil Ross, Kath Soucie, John Stephenson, Cree Summer, Brian Tocchi, Tamblyn Tomita, Marcelo Tubert, Chick Vennera, B. J. Ward, Anthony Watson, R. J. Williams, Anderson Wong, Keone Young.

The *Karate Kid*, a film in which highschool nebbish Daniel (Ralph Macchio) conquered the local bully constituency through karate skills honed under the tutelage of school janitor Miyagi Yakuga (Pat Morita), was the "feel good" movie of 1985. That two sequels followed virtually goes without saying (given the rubberstamp mentality of Hollywood in that era), and in 1989 a weekly animated *Karate Kid* half hour premiered, courtesy of DIC Enterprises.

Any resemblance between the movie and cartoon *Karate Kid*s ended with the principal characters and the martial-arts ambience. In keeping with the *Raiders of the Lost Ark* school popular amongst animation studios, DIC's *Karate Kid* was about the quest for a glowing shrine, carved from a blazing meteor and said to have mystical, healing qualities. The Shrine had vanished from its resting place on the island of Okinawa, so it was up to teenaged Daniel — a.k.a. "The Karate Kid" — his adult mentor Miyagi, and young Okinawan girl Taki to track the sacred artifact down, even if it meant visiting

the most exotic corners of the world. These locales were consummately illustrated, with expert character-design supervision by veteran comic book artist Russ Heath of *Sgt. Rock and the Easy Company* fame.

Taking a fresh approach to the timeworn *Karate Kid* concept was a good idea. The timing, alas, couldn't have been worse. The two theatrical *Kid* followups had scuttled the reputation of the original with cardboard characterizations, idiotically contrived plotlines and an overall wearing out of welcome. By 1989 nobody cared anything about the Kid and his elderly trainer, and it didn't help matters that NBC failed to advertise properly the significant changes made in the *Karate Kid* property for its cartoon incarnation. The 13-episode series ended up one of the very few failures in the DIC studios manifest, and was regularly kicked and chopped out of the ratings by the competing *Pee-wee's Playhouse* on CBS and *Slimer! And the Real Ghostbusters* (q.v.) on ABC.

KELLOGG'S PRESENTS THE BANANA SPLITS ADVENTURE HOUR *see* **THE BANANA SPLITS ADVENTURE HOUR**

KID 'N' PLAY. NBC: 9/8/1990–9/7/1991. Chris Cross Inc./Gordy de Passe Productions/Saban/Motown/Marvel Productions. Executive producers, Maynell Thomas and Joe Taritero. Produced by Larry F. Houston. Supervising director, Karen Peterson. Animation directors, Max Becraft, Brad Case, Joan Case, Consuela Cataldi, Bob Arkwright, Rudy Cataldi, Barbara Doumanian, Graham Morris. Eric Schmidt, Tom Tataranowicz. Developers and story editors, John Semper and Cynthia Friedlob. Director of production, Beth Gunn. Animation supervisor, Gerald Moeller. Music by Shuki Levy, Kussa Mahchi; music produced by Andrew Dimitroff. Rap Team: Romeo Rich, Stan "The Guitar" Man, Nye Tucker, Yutaka. Voice director, Ginny McSwain. Live action executive producers, Winston Richard and Ellen Levy. Live action director, Bill Parker. Executive in charge of production, Jim Graziano. Cast (Live action): Christopher Reid, Christopher Martin. Voices: Jack Angel, Tommy Davidson, Cree Summer Francks, Dorian Harewood, Alaina Reed Hall, J. D. Hall,

Martin Lawrence, Dawnn Lewis, Danny Mann, Brian Mitchell, Rain Pryor, Umberto Ortiz, Chris Hooks.

Kid 'n' Play was a two-man rap music group — Christopher Reid was "Kid," the one with the electrified hairdo, and Christopher Martin was "Play," the one with the buzz-cut — who hit big on a mass audience level with their 1989 feature film, *House Party*, which cost only $2.5 million but grossed over ten times that amount. The lead time between musical popularity and TV animation was getting shorter and shorter by 1990; thus it was that some 18 months after attaining fame, Kid 'n' Play got their own Saturday morning cartoon show.

The 13-episode series, set in what network publicity described as "an ethnically diverse New York neighborhood," emphasized the funnier — and cleaner — aspects of Kid 'n' Play's act. The group itself made wraparound live appearances (ingratiatingly mocking themselves and their image) on each program, in the manner of the like-vintage cartoon weekly *The New Kids on the Block* (q.v.). Kid 'n' Play's animated counterparts were somewhat younger than in real life, a "retro" device designed to appeal to preteen viewers. Featured in the youthful cartoon cast were the boys' goofy manager Herbie; three female backup dancers named Lela, Marika and Downtown Patty; Kid's tomboyish little sister Terry; and bad boys Acorn (short and sarcastic) and Pitbull (big and dumb), whose jealousy of Kid 'n' Play led to practical jokery and mild sabotage.

Kid 'n' Play themselves did not provide the cartoon voices, despite having proven themselves adequate actors in *House Party*. Still, the series' voice-cast boasted some respectable names: Rain Pryor, daughter of comedian Richard Pryor; Cree Summer Francks, onetime costar of the Bill Cosby–created situation comedy *A Different World* and previously the voice of Penny on *Inspector Gadget*; and comedian Martin Lawrence, formerly a *House Party* supporting player and later the controversial, occasionally censorable star of the Fox network sitcom *Martin*.

Kid 'n' Play emulated the earlier "urban" cartoon series *Fat Albert and the Cosby Kids* (q.v.) by stressing prosocial lessons within the context of the plots: respect for others' rights and beliefs, consideration for the elderly, belief in oneself, and avoid-

ance of crime activity (even Acorn and Terry stopped short of breaking the law, labelling such behavior "dumb"). One episode depicted the healing of a rift in the relationship between the kids and an elderly Jewish merchant — a plotline obviously inspired by contemporary real-life clashes between minority groups which occupied the headlines in the early 1990s. (It would be nice, but woefully inaccurate, to report that these differences were dissipated in the same spirit of goodwill as the *Kid 'n' Play* episode. Here was one instance where Real Life would have been better off had it been a cartoon.)

Unfortunately, the animated *Kid 'n' Play*, scheduled opposite CBS' invulnerable *Teenage Mutant Ninja Turtles* (q.v.) and ABC's powerhouse *Beetlejuice* (q.v.), was not a success, lacking even the staying power of the rappers' concurrently produced Sprite soft drink commercial. Nor could all the series' good intentions compensate for its shabby character design and abysmal animation. But the two "Kid 'n' Play" Christophers were able to weather this disappointment simply by counting their money and launching into a second starring film, innovatively titled *House Party 2*.

Kid Power at full steam; Connie (*right*) acts as valve.

KID POWER. ABC: 9/16/1972–9/1/1974. Rankin-Bass/Videocraft. Produced and directed by Arthur Rankin Jr. and Jules Bass. Associate producer, Basil Cox. Animation supervisors, Toru Hara and Tsuguyi Kubo. Music by Perry Botkin Jr.; theme song by Jules Bass and Perry Botkin

Jr. Songs performed by the Curbstones. Developed in consultation with the Bank St. College of Education. Based on "Wee Pals" by Morrie Turner. Voices: Charles Kennedy Jr. (Wellington); Jay Silverheels Jr. (Oliver); John Gardiner (Nipper); Allen Melvin (Jerry); Carey Wong (Connie); Guy Shapiro (Ralph); Michele Johnson (Sybil); Jeff Thomas (Diz); Greg Thomas (Albert); and April Winchell, and Donald Fullilove.

Created in 1965 by black comic strip artist Morrie Turner, Wee Pals can best be described as a multiracial Peanuts—and in fact was encouraged and endorsed as such by Peanuts mentor Charles Schultz. Turner's African American child characters included carefree Wellington, helpful Confederate-capped Nipper and budding businessperson Sybil; among the Caucasians were chubby Oliver, hoydenish blonde-haired Connie, and introspective Jewish boy Jerry. Together, these kids comprised an informal neighborhood fraternity known as the Rainbow Power Club.

Kid Power, the weekly animated half hour based on Wee Pals, retained the Rainbow Club and its members—though none were drawn to look much like the comic strip originals. Signed up for the duration of the series were such Pals regulars as Asian American George, sports-happy Randy, hipster Diz, studious Rocky and wiseguy Ralph (writing these entries is like writing a soap opera; we have to stretch to find a one-word encapsulation of each character). The obligatory funny cartoon animals created for the series were Polly the Parrot (they could've come up with a better one than that!) and General Lee the dog (that's better).

Like Turner's strip, the series stressed the positive results of ethnic balance and tolerance, with concern for the environment thrown in—and also like the strip, this was often accomplished with a heavy hand. The whole point of the series was to show a racially mixed group of kids who refused to be self-conscious about skin color. And yet, Kid Power's theme song rammed the repeated refrain "Red, Yellow, Black and White" down the audience's throats so ruthlessly that viewers couldn't do anything but notice the cosmetic differences among the Rainbow Club members.

Stylistically, Kid Power faltered in its overreliance on "psychedelic" musical numbers which looked like chintzy Yellow Submarine imitations, and in its use of one of the most obnoxious laughtracks in all of Saturday morning television. Such intrusive ingredients are what date this series most for modern-day viewers, though TV historians might get a kick out of the "Second Generation" voice-talent pool. The voice of Kid Power's Oliver was provided by Jay Silverheels Jr., son of the actor best remembered for his portrayal of Tonto on the Lone Ranger TV series (curiously, Oliver was not a Native American). And veteran ventriloquist Paul Winchell's very young daughter April made her TV-cartoon debut on Kid Power; two decades later, April Winchell was still on call for such roles as Peg on Goof Troop (q.v.) and Dylandra Piquel on Bonkers (q.v.).

Its faults aside, Kid Power upheld Morrie Turner's edict that his strip was essentially about kids having fun, and on this level the viewers were seldom disappointed. The 17-episode series, which coincidentally premiered the same year as its spiritual brother Fat Albert and the Cosby Kids (q.v.)—and which made its debut a week after its announced September 9 launch due to the 1972 Olympics—had a successful season's run opposite CBS's Flintstones Comedy Hour (see The Flintstones) and NBC's live-action Runaround. The second season of Kid Power consisted entirely of first-season reruns.

THE KID SUPER POWER HOUR WITH SHAZAM. NBC: 9/12/1981–9/11/1982. DC/Filmation. Produced and directed by Arthur Nadel. Directed by Bill Davis. Music by Yvette Blais, Jeff Michael. Announcer: Casey Kasem. Live-action producer, Arthur Nadel. Story editor/writer, Coslough Johnson. Components: 1. HERO HIGH. Voices: Christopher Hensel (Captain California); Becky Perle (Gorgeous Gal); Mayo McCaslin (Dirty Trixie); Jere Fields (Misty Magic); John Berwick (Rex Ruthless); John Greenleaf (Weatherman); John Venocour (Punk Rock); Alan Oppenheimer (Mr. Sampson); Erika Scheimer (Miss Grimm). 2. SHAZAM! Voices: Dawn Jeffery (Mary Marvel); Burr Middleton (Billy Batson-Captain Marvel); Barry Gordon (Freddie Freeman-Captain Marvel Jr.); Alan Oppenheimer (Tawny/Uncle Dudley/Dr. Sivana); Lou Scheimer (Sterling Morris); Norm Prescott (Narrator).

The Kid Super Power Hour with Shazam was a 60-minute cartoon weekly which included live action wraparounds featuring a seven-person rock group, whose animated likenesses appeared on the series' cartoon component *Hero High*. The gimmick here was to combine rock music with superhero activity, albeit the nonviolent brand preferred by network programmers of the early 1980s. Each of the two weekly *Hero High* vignettes outlined the humorous trials and tribulations in a specialty high school populated by aspiring superheroes like Captain California, Gorgeous Gal, Misty Magic and Weatherman—and a few incipient menaces, whose parents rather tactlessly gave such names as Rex Ruthless, Dirty Trixie and Punk Rock. If this sounds just a little like a spin on Filmation's *The Archies*, it's because "Hero High" was originally pitched as "Super Archies," but the characters had to be renamed and redesigned when Filmation's rights to the "Archie" property lapsed. The basic concept of a cartoon high school full of uniquely "gifted" teenagers turned out to have durability, for it was later adapted for 1985's *Galaxy High School* (q.v.) and 1990's *Rick Moranis in Gravedale High* (q.v.)—and, after a fashion, 1992's *X-Men* (q.v.), which as a concept actually predated all the above-mentioned properties.

The half-hour *Shazam* portion of the program featured Captain Marvel, who'd been created by artist C. C. Beck and writer Bill Parker as Fawcett Publications' *entrée* into the comic book field in 1939. The lead character was Billy Batson, an orphan boy who regularly invoked the combined powers of Solomon, Hercules, Atlas, Zeus, Achilles and Mercury with the anagrammatic cry of "Shazam!"—thereby converting himself into superpowered Captain Marvel. A Republic movie serial solidified the character's fame, and soon the "Big Red Cheese" was a major merchandising figure for Fawcett. Things came to a screeching halt when the competing National Periodicals comic concern refused to swallow Fawcett's insistence that Captain Marvel was patterned after movie star Fred MacMurray. National felt instead that Marvel was a direct steal from their own Superman, and the result was a long and bitter lawsuit, culminating in the end of Captain Marvel and the entire Fawcett comics line in a 1954 sellout to National.

Ironically, it was National who revived the character in the late 1960s for a comic book called *Shazam!*—so named because *another* Captain Marvel had been created in the meantime by Marvel Comics. It was under the title *Shazam!* that the "original" Captain made his 1974 live-action TV debut. This series was produced by the otherwise cartoon-oriented Filmation (Arthur H. Nadel supervised both this series and the later *Super Power Hour*) as part of an attempt by the networks to break the animated monopoly on Saturday mornings with worthwhile "real life" fare. Michael Gray played Billy Batson, with radio golden-ager Les Tremayne as his guardian Mentor (who also went by the name of Shazam, but in secret). Whenever Billy pulled a "Shazam!," Michael Gray disappeared and John Davey took over as Captain Marvel—until 1976, when Jackson Bostwick took over for John Davey. (A note for *Marvel* buffs: one episode set at the San Diego Zoo featured onetime child actor Frank Coghlan Jr., who was in 1974 on the zoo's public relations staff, and who in 1940 had originated the role of Billy Batson in the *Captain Marvel* serial.) Stressing moral and ethical values for teenaged viewers, *Shazam!* lasted two seasons, during which time it was combined with another live-action carryover from the comic books and became *The Shazam/Isis Hour.*

And then came *The Kid Super Power Hour with Shazam*, which used nothing from the live-action series but the dual character of Billy Batson and Captain Marvel. *Shazam!*, operating within the same nonviolent parameters as *Hero High*, revived several of the old comic book's supporting cast. Present were Billy Batson's twin sister Mary, who by invoking several Greek *goddesses* was still able to come up with the initials comprising "Shazam"—which was her cue to change into Mary Marvel. There was Freddie Freeman, an orphaned, crippled newsboy, who through machinations too complex to dwell upon here was adopted by Captain Marvel, was able to transform himself into a superhero by shouting the name of his foster father, and who adopted the alias "Captain Marvel Jr." And bringing up the rear in every sense was Uncle Dudley Batson, a rolypoly con man (given the requisite "W. C. Fields" voice by veteran Broadway actor Alan Oppenheimer) who was able to snooker everyone into believing that he, too, had super powers.

Other frequently seen characters included Tawky Tawny, a loquacious, business-suited tiger (!) who aided the Captain in his peacekeeping missions; Dr. Sivana, a master criminal whose extended family was almost as large as the Batsons'; Mr. Mind, a malevolent worm; and various other holdovers from the *Captain Marvel* glory days of the 1940s, among them Aunt Minerva, Mr. Atom, and King Kull. As anyone who's followed *Captain Marvel* over the last half-century can see, the cartoon series followed the comic book original as closely as possible under the strictures of 1981 kidvid, making it all the more amazing that several otherwise well-informed TV historians have insisted that Billy Batson turned himself into a character named "Shazam," that Freddie Freeman was in fact Captain Marvel Sr., and that Mary Marvel was really *Freddie's* sister.

All one need do is check out one of the many *Shazam!* videotapes from the local Blockbuster to verify the facts about *Kid Super Power Hour with Shazam!* Or failing that, try having a lifelong friend who knows the *Captain Marvel* saga better than he knows his own family tree (To cover all bets, I did both of the above).

KIDD VIDEO. NBC: 9/15/1984–4/4/1987; CBS: 9/19/1987–12/26/1987 (reruns). DIC/Saban. Executive producers, Andy Heyward, Haim Saban and Jean Chalopin. Animation produced by Rudy Zamora. Supervising director, Bernard Deyries. Live-action directed by Bud Schaetzle. Written by Jeff Book, Kevin Clyne, Carole Markin, Don McGlynn, Bud Schaetzle, Marty Wiley, Jim Carlson, Terrence McDonnel. Art directors, Kathe Klopp and Priscilla Beroud. Music by Haim Saban and Shuki Levy. Vocal direction by Michael Bell, Marsha Goodman and Ginny McSwain. Voices: Bryan Scott (Kidd Video, a.k.a. "KV"); Gabrielle Bennett (Carla); Robbie Rist (Whiz); Steve Alterman (Ash); Cathy Cavadini (Glitter); Pete Renaday (Master Blaster); Marshall Efron (Fat Cat); Robert Towers (Cool Kitty); Susan Silo (She-Lion).

Combining what was in 1984 perceived to be the younger viewers' two favorite pastimes — video games and rock music — DIC and Saban teamed to produce *Kidd Video*. In this one, a live-action rock group

led by Kidd Video (or "K.V.") was transported into the Flip Side, a fourth-dimensional cartoon world, by the evil Master Blaster. It was not the villain's intention to hurt or kill the group (TV was still not quite out of its most recent nonviolent phase) but to steal their popular musical sound; to do this, Master Blaster enlisted the aid of his own band, the Copy Cats (who were real cats — one of them, in fact, was a lion). The next two seasons of 27 half hours concerned K.V.'s quest to escape the Flip Side, restore himself to real rather than animated form, then return to Our World with his rockin' pals Ash, Whiz, Carla and Glitter.

Each episode featured at least one top-40 tune, "illustrated" with generic animated montage sequences. This technique, coupled with *Kidd Video's* jumps from live action to animation, would be redeployed by DIC for its 1985 networker *Hulk Hogan's Rock 'n' Wrestling* (q.v.). *Kidd Video* itself would be resurrected in 1989 in rerun form (with new musical numbers), and syndicated back-to-back with a similar network cartoon castoff, *Wolf Rock TV* (q.v.), under the overall title *Wolf Rock Power Hour.*

Point of interest: The director of *Kidd Video's* "live" sequences was Bud Schaetzle, whose subsequent assignments in the world of cinematized musical performance would include 1991's *This Is Garth Brooks.*

KIDEO TV. Syndicated: 1986. DIC Enterprises. Executive producers, Andy Heyward, Jean Chalopin, Tetsuo Katayama. Components: 1. THE GET-ALONG GANG. (See separate entry.) 2. THE POPPLES. DIC/Those Characters from Cleveland. Creative supervisor, Jean Chalopin. Associate producers, Sangbum Kim and Kenneth Y. Duer. Direction supervision by Masakazu Higuchi. Directed by James A. Simon, Katsumi Takasuga, Osamu Inoue. Character design and adaptation for animation, James A. Simon, Laureen Berger. Executive creative consultant, Cassandra Schafhausen. Story editors, Jack Mendelsohn and Bob Logan. Written by Jack Hanrahan, Eleanor Burian-Mohr, George Edwards, Bob Logan, Jody Miles Conner, Jina Bacarr, Sharman Divono, Sheree Guitar, Jack Olesker, Daniel Pitlik, Roger Scott, Michael D. Warren, Linda Woolverton.

Music by Haim Saban and Shuki Levy. Voices: Valrie Bromfield (Bonnie/Billy/ Mike); Donna Christie (Potato Chip); Jeannie Elias (Penny); Danny Mann (Punkster/Putter); Sharon Noble (Pancake); Louise Vallance (Party/Punkity/ Prize/Puffball); Maurice LaMarche (Puzzle); and Len Carlson, Diane Fabian, Dan Hennessey, Hadley Kaye, Jazmin Lausanne, Barbara Redpath, Pauline Rennie, Linda Sorenson, Noam Zylberman. **3. ULYSSES 31** (1986). Osmond International/DIC. Produced by Jean Chalopin and Yutaka Fujioka. **4. RAINBOW BRITE** (1987). Hallmark Cards/ DIC. Specials in 1984 and 1985. Directed by Rick Rudish. Creative director, Bernard Deyries. Executive in charge of production, Kevin O'Donnell. Script supervisor, Lori Crawford. Associate producer, Gaetano Vaccaro. Voice directors, Marsha Goodman and Howard R. Cohen. Animation supervisors, Shigeru Akagawa and Hiroshi Toita. Animation director, Satoshi Hirayama. Music by Shuki Levy and Haim Saban. Voices: Bettina (Rainbow Brite); Andre Stojka (Starlight); Robbie Lee (Twink/Indigo/Violet/Lala/Sprites); Peter Cullen (Murky/Monstromurk/Narrator); Pat Fraley (Lurky/Buddy/Evil Force); Scott Menville (Brian); Mona Marshall (Red/Patty/Canary); Rhonda Allman (Moonglow/Tickled Pink); and Jonathan Harris, David Mendenhall, and Marissa Mendenhall.

Kideo TV was a 90-minute syndicated cartoon block from DIC, comprised of something old, something new, and for a brief time, something borrowed.

The old material consisted of reruns from the half hour network series *The Get Along Gang* (q.v.). New to the manifest was the 30-minute *The Popples*, based on a series of dolls and toys created by American Greeting Cards' "Those Characters from Cleveland" division. Actually, it was "new" only if one could call this latest wrinkle on *Care Bears* (q.v.) and *Smurfs* (q.v.) new. The Popples were lovable little doll-like beings which, when their arms, legs and heads were contracted, appeared to be little balls of fabric. They earned their collective name from the "popping" sound made when squeezed and restored to full body size, and each one had an alliterative first name beginning with "P": Prize, Puzzle, Putter, Party, Pancake and so on. The Popples were all seemingly endowed with Felix the Cat's Bag of Tricks; to make their way through a large and frightening human world, the characters were able to pull such useful devices as roller skates, eating utensils and even facial makeup out of nowhere. Acting as the Popples' liaison to human society were preteens Bonnie and Billy. A second line of related toy figures introduced on this series were the Sport Popples, beings which "popped" full-grown from basketballs, baseballs, soccer balls, etc., with names like Pitcher, Dunker, Big Kick and T.D.

Almost too cutesy-wutesy for words, *The Popples* contained one neat "interactive" gimmick, albeit one borrowed from the old *Winky Dink and You* (q.v.). Whenever the Popples needed extra help, they'd ask the "kids in the audience" to reach towards the TV screen and set things right, whereupon an animated child's hand would indeed reach "into" the action and help out (resulting, no doubt, in a lot of sore knuckles in the living rooms of America).

The "borrowed" component of *Kideo TV* was *Ulysses 31*, a Japanese import which transposed the famed Homeric traveller into the 31st century. (This series had been ready for American release as early as 1981, but couldn't find a buyer at that time.) *Ulysses 31* was dropped after 13 weeks in favor of a home-grown series more compatible to the merchandising aspects of *The Get-Along Gang* and *The Popples*. This was *Rainbow Brite*, a character originally created by Hallmark in 1983 as a humanized distaff variation of American Greeting Cards' *Care Bears*. Little Rainbow Brite lived in the magic world of Rainbowland where she defended herself against the malevolent Murky Dismal, who hailed from the Land of Darkness, and Murky's beastly henchman Lurky (more dopey than demonic), by utilizing her special rainbow-generating belt.

While this light vs. dark concept had been done heaps better by Van Beuren Studios' *The Sunshine Makers* back in 1934 (which coincidentally was also bankrolled by a non-cartoon firm, Borden's milk), *Rainbow Brite* had played well as a series of greeting cards and as star of three TV specials: *Rainbow Brite: The Peril of the Pits* (1984), *Rainbow Brite: The Mighty Monstermurk Menace* (1984), and *Rainbow Brite: The Beginning of Rainbowland*

292   Kimba, the White Lion

(1985). Thus it was a logical step to weekly exposure—with all the attendant toy-store activity of Rainbow Brite, her flying horse Starlight, her little chum Twink the Sprite (the Sprites were a race of antennaed furballs who worked the "color mine" that yielded Rainbowland's valuable Color Crystals), and her equally cuddly playmates, the Color Kids.

KIMBA, THE WHITE LION. Syndicated: 1966. Mushi Productions/NBC Films. Created by Osamu Tezuka. Theme song by Bernie Baum, Bill Grant, Florence Kaye. Voice: Billie Lou Watt (Kimba). —LEO THE LION. Mushi Productions/ Sonic International. Available 1966; not released until CBN premiere 1984.

Kimba, the White Lion was an Americanization of *Jungle Tatei* ("Jungle Emperor"), an animated series based on a Japanese comic strip by Osamu Tezuka (see *Astroboy*). Tezuka's storyline, which began unravelling in October of 1950, was set in the African jungle. Its protagonist was Leo the white lion, son of "Jungle Emperor" Pancha. After his father was killed and his mother Raga captured by hunters, Leo was born in captivity in the London Zoo. En route to another zoo, Leo escaped and was adopted by a human boy named Kenichi, who raised the cub. Upon his return to Africa, Leo found himself balancing his predator instincts with lessons of beneficence and kindliness learned from his human master. The result was an animal civilization modelled after human society (of the "Utopian" variety), which dispensed justice among the creatures and formed an allied front against future human despoilers of the jungle. A mystical note was introduced with the Moonlight Stone, a strange and powerful energy source coveted by animals and humans alike.

Jungle Tatei ended its run in 1954, but remained popular enough in reprint form to inspire a 1965 cartoon series of the same title, produced by Osamu Tezuka's own Mushi Studios. The series numbered among its distinctions a 1967 International Children's Film Festival Award and the

fact that it was the first Japanese cartoon series to be colorcast in its home country. No sooner had the series premiered than NBC Films, hoping for a financial windfall comparable to its earlier acquisition of Tezuka's *Astro Boy*, licensed *Jungle Tatei* for American consumption. As with *Astro Boy*, the U.S. scenarists took it upon themselves to Americanize all the character names, coming up with such Yankee sobriquets as Dan'l Baboon, Pauley Cracker the Parrot, Roger Ranger and King Speckle Rex; Leo himself was now known as Kimba the White Lion, which was also this series' American title.

Such "improvements" didn't hurt the original Japanese series too much, mainly because it was hardly the original anymore itself. In translating *Jungle Tatei* to television, Osamu Tezuka had thrown out the original strip's backstory in favor of a fanciful soufflé about an ancient Egyptian "wisdom formula" passed on to an African tribe called the Kickapeels. The vessel of this passage was a white lion to whom Pharaoh "Tut Tut" had fed the formula. Handed down from generation to generation for nearly 4000 years, the animal kingdom founded upon high human intelligence was finally bestowed upon young Kimba by his dying father, Caesar (formerly Pancha). The story took off from there for a total of 52 half hour episodes.

Immediately after its initial Japanese run, *Jungle Tatei* was followed by a liketitled sequel, which charted the progress of the adult Leo/Kimba, his mate, and his two sons. This 26-week offering didn't get to the United States until purchased by the CBN cable service in 1984. Christian Broadcasting Network restored the main character's original name, and the sequel was run daily under the title *Leo the Lion.**

KING ARTHUR AND THE KNIGHTS OF JUSTICE. Syndicated: 1992 (as part of AMAZIN' ADVENTURES). Golden Films/Le Centre Nationale de la Cinematographie/Bohbot. Executive producers, Avi Arad, Allan Bohbot, Jean Chalopin, Diane Eskenazi. Produced by Allan Bohbot, Diane Eske-

In 1994, Disney studios released the theatrical cartoon feature The Lion King, *which though promoted as an "original story" was perceived by many Japanimation buffs to be more than a little beholden to* Kimba the White Lion. *Disney issued a statement that none of their animation staff had ever heard of* Kimba. *Uh huh. And Orson Welles never heard of William Randolph Hearst, either.*

nazi, Xavier Picard and Mark Taylor. Directed by Stephen Martiniere and Charlie Sansonetti. English story adaptation by Frank Olesker. Animation produced by KK C&D Asia. Music produced by Saban International. Voices: Kathleen Barr, Michael Beattie, Jim Byrnes, Gary Chalk, Michael Donovan, Lee Jeffrey, Willow Johnson, Andrew Kabadas, Scott McNeil, Venus Terzo, Mark Wilbreth.

Golden Films/Bohbot's *King Arthur and the Knights of Justice*, a 1992 half hour component of the weekend Bohbot compendium *Amazin' Adventures* (q.v.), was distinguished by a time-travel tangent. In this one, Merlin the Magician attempted to rescue Camelot from the scurrilous Lord Viperin and his Warlords. Since King Arthur and his knights had been banished by Arthur's wicked half-sister Morgana, Merlin had to "create" a new King and Round Table aggregation by transporting the New York Knights, a virtuous college football team of the 1990s whose quarterback was a certain Arthur King, back to the Middle Ages.

"Teen appeal" was the aim here, even unto redrafting Queen Guinevere as a campus-cutie "babe." The animation and artwork were passable, but virtually indistinguishable from the multitude of other sword and sorcery cartoon weeklies of its era. And, before you ask: The name "Mark Twain" appeared nowhere on the *King Arthur and the Knights of Justice* screen credits, despite the fact that the series' whole time displacement concept was pilfered from *A Connecticut Yankee in King Arthur's Court*.

THE KING FEATURES TRILOGY. Syndicated: 1963. King Features. Executive producer: Al Brodax. Incidental music by Win Sharples. Components: 1. BEETLE BAILEY. Paramount Cartoon Studios/King Features. Directed by Seymour Kneitel and Shamus Culhane. Theme music by Jay Livingston and Ray Evans. Voices: Howard Morris (Beetle Bailey/General Halftrack); Allan Melvin (Sgt. Snorkel). 2. SNUFFY SMITH. Paramount Cartoon Studios/King Features. Directed by Seymour Kneitel and Shamus Culhane. Voices: Paul Frees (Barney Google/Snuffy Smith); Penny Philips (Loweezy). 3. KRAZY KAT. Gene Deitch–Paramount/King Features. Directed by Gene Deitch. Voices: Penny Philips

(Krazy Kat); Paul Frees (Ignatz Mouse/ Offissa Pup).

The newly filmed *Popeye* (q.v.) TV cartoons had done well enough in 1960 for King Features to comb through other comic-strip properties for potential animation. The newspaper syndicate settled upon Mort Walker's peacetime-army comedy *Beetle Bailey*, launched in 1950; Fred Laswell's hillbilly saga *Barney Google and Snuffy Smith*, titled *Take Barney Google, for Instance* when created by Billy DeBeck in 1918, and later streamlined to *Barney Google*, with *Snuffy Smith* added to the billing in the mid–1940s; and George Herriman's surrealistic bouquet to the intelligentsia, *Krazy Kat*, which originally ran from 1913 until Herriman's death in 1944. The three above-named properties were the six-minute components for the syndicated *King Features Trilogy*.

Beetle Bailey was set in Camp Swampy, a post ignored by everyone including the Pentagon, where private Beetle Bailey carried on a war of nerves with his bombastic sergeant Orville Snorkel. A moonshine-brewing mountain man named Snuffy and his "honey pot" wife Loweezy were the stars of *Snuffy Smith*—and despite previous reports, the name *Barney Google* didn't appear in the credits, though the character of Barney Google, an incorrigible gambler who'd started as the star of the strip but who'd been shunted to the background during World War 2, made occasional guest appearances. And *Krazy Kat* was laid against the ever-changing desert backdrop of Kokonimo Kounty, where the androgynous Krazy loved brick-heaving, sociopathic mouse Ignatz—and was loved in turn by poetic patrolman Offisa Pupp.

As in the case of *Popeye*, the 150 *King Features* TV cartoons (50 per component) were ground out so swiftly that executive producer Al Brodax was forced to rely upon a couple of different animation studios. *Beetle Bailey* and *Snuffy Smith* were handled by director Seymour Kneitel at Paramount/Famous Studios, while *Krazy Kat* was the responsibility of Czechoslovakia-based Gene Deitch. The haste certainly showed. Both *Beetle* and *Snuffy* suffered from flip-picture animation, wearisome plotlines which robbed the original properties of their uniqueness, and some singularly irritating characters—most notably *Beetle's* General Halftrack, whose whistling speech impediment was enough to drive anyone up a wall. *Krazy Kat* was far better animated, and happily retained the calculatedly slapdash design of George Herriman's brilliant comic panels (a style all but ignored in the in-name-only *Krazy Kat* theatrical cartoons produced by Columbia/Screen Gems in the 1930s). But like *Beetle* and *Snuffy*, *Krazy* was laid low by banal plot contrivances, with the additional handicap of striving for "wacky" humor without the benefit of truly funny material.

The *King Features Trilogy* was completed by 1962, but didn't make it to TV until 1963. In the interim, Paramount Pictures leased 11 of the cartoons to fill out its commitment of theatrical releases for the 1962-63 season, utilizing the umbrella title *Comic Kings* (with one newly animated adventure of an old Paramount standby, *Little Lulu*, included in the package to make an even dozen). Financially, this wasn't a bad idea — there was virtually no competition at the time — but artistically it was a major goof. What might have been passable animation for television looked as amateurish as a kindergarten art class when blown up on a big, wide theatre screen. When the cartoons were finally distributed to TV, they were sent out with several helpful tips from the King Features promotion staff. It was suggested to local stations that the cartoons be showcased, rather than tossed in as "more of the same" on the nation's *Cartoon Carnivals* and *Kid's Klubs*. To this end, King Features dreamed up what was called a "hangout" format, wherein the local *Trilogy* hosts would dress up like soda jerks and their sets would be decked out like ice cream parlors. Most stations, cutting back on studio personnel in the face of mounting costs, ignored the hangout concept, preferring to do just what King Features had wanted to avoid— throwing the cartoons in as filler for odd nooks and crannies in their morning and afternoon "kiddie ghettos."

The color-TV boom of the late 1960s saved *The King Features Trilogy* from total obscurity. Local outlets, starving for first-run color product, eagerly pounced upon the package of cartoons that they'd previously (and sagaciously) disdained in favor of Three Stooges and Little Rascals comedies. But here as before, *The King Features Trilogy* failed to deliver a large audience— or even to *find* an audience. Adults who'd grown up with the original comic strips were invariably let down by the cartoons, while kids unfamiliar with *Beetle Bailey*, *Snuffy Smith* and *Krazy Kat* (the last-named hadn't been in the funny pages for over 20 years!) found other ways to fill their viewing time.

KING KONG. ABC: 9/10/1966–8/31/1969. Rankin-Bass. Produced by Arthur Rankin Jr. and Jules Bass. Music by Maury Laws.

Forget the Fay Wray–mauling, building-climbing *King Kong* of the classic 1933 fantasy film. The weekly, half hour cartoon *King Kong* was a pussycat among apes— the benign 60-foot-tall companion of precocious Bobby Bond. Bobby was the offspring of scientist Professor Bond, who'd come to the Javanese island of Mondo (what happened to Skull Island?) to do his research with his son and daughter Susan; Mondo also happened to be the domain of the title character, but you might have tumbled to that fact by now. Ever attempting to kidnap Kong for his own nefarious purposes was Dr. Who— no more a relation to the legendary British science fiction TV star than was Professor Bond a cousin to James. The *King Kong* series *did*, however, have its share of 1960s-style espionage in the person of Tom of T.H.U.M.B. (Tiny Humans Underground Military Bureau), a miniaturized secret agent who with his oriental sidekick Swinging Jack starred in his own separate six-minute cartoons.

King Kong was heralded in 1966 as the first network cartoon series made in Japan expressly for American TV— though it was certainly not the first such import job for Rankin-Bass, who'd been farming its animation out to Japan ever since the days of *The New Adventures of Pinocchio* (see *Pinocchio*) in 1960. Why any nation would have taken credit for the clumsy cartoonwork of *King Kong* or its sappy character design (the title character looked like a bloated version of Chim Chim the monkey from *Speed Racer* [q.v.]) is open to wonder. Audiences were warned what they were in for when *King Kong* was introduced the Friday before its official premiere in ABC prime time, but they watched anyway. Kids were probably attracted by what the National Association for Better Broadcasting found to be the series' worst element, a child character who was habitually "disrespectful" of his elders. *King Kong*'s now-middle-aged fans still have fond memories of the series, though when pressed for details, they won't remember anything about the 24-episode show beyond its strident theme song ("King KONG, You know the name of/King KONG, You know the fame of/KING KONG...").

KING LEONARDO AND HIS SHORT SUBJECTS. NBC: 10/15/1960–9/28/1963. Leonardo Productions/Total TV/Producers Associates of Television. Produced by Treadwell Covington, Peter Piech. Directed by Bob Schleh and Lu Guarnel. Animation director, Sam Kai. Written by Buck Biggers and Chet Stover. Animation by Gamma Productions, SA de CV. For Gamma: Harvey Siegel, chief of production. Jaime Torres V, administrator. Voices: Jackson Beck (Leonardo/Biggy Rat); Allan Swift (Odie Cologine/Itchy Brother/Tooter Turtle); Kenny Delmar (The Hunter); Ben Stone (The Fox); Frank Milano (Mr. Wizard); and George Irving, Sandy Becker, and Delo States.

King Leonardo and His Short Subjects was the first project for Total Television, formed in 1959 by writers Buck Biggers and Chet Stover, art director/designer Joe Harrington, sound recordist Treadwell Covington, and live-action children's show producer Peter Piech, the head man of Producers Associates of Television (P.A.T.). Total TV and its sister company Leonardo Television utilized the services of the same Mexico-based Gamma Studios where Jay Ward Productions (also releasing through P.A.T.) produced *Rocky and His Friends* (q.v.), so it's not surprising that the Leonardo and Ward product physically resembled one another. That, however, was where all relationship ended. *Rocky and His Friends* was a classic; *King Leonardo*, though occasionally funny, merely filled up the room.

Created at the behest of NBC and General Mills to fill a Saturday-morning gap vacated by Hanna-Barbera's *Ruff and Reddy* (q.v.), *King Leonardo* followed the Hanna-Barbera format of one main character sharing half hour space with two component cartoons. Leonardo, a talking lion, was the benevolent if befuddled ruler of Bongo Congo, an African monarchy subsisting on its sole import, bongo drums.

Leonardo's aide-de-camp was "true blue" Odie Cologine, an erudite skunk who sounded like Ronald Colman. The King's dominance was threatened by Edward G. Robinson-like gangster Biggy Rat, who kept company with Leonardo's beatnik sibling, Itchy Brother. In their efforts to topple Leonardo from his throne, Biggy and Itchy had two powerful allies: Professor Messer, a demented scientist who changed his accent with each cartoon, and Mr. Mad, a mystical villain who wanted to add the King and Odie to his "people collection" (Mad was truly mad if he thought a lion and a skunk were people, but this point was never dwelt upon). Each King Leonardo adventure was a four-part cliffhanger, two episodes per show, with the story resolved during the second week.

King Leonardo's and Biggy Rat's voices were supplied by Jackson Beck, erstwhile Bluto/Brutus of the old *Popeye* cartoons and a fixture of innumerable radio programs and commercials (he was still at it in 1993 with a string of Little Caesar's "Pizza-Pizza" ads). Though Beck would insist in the late 1980s that he'd never seen *King Leonardo* during production, this writer remembers the actor making a promotional appearance, with several *Leonardo* clips in hand, on a syndicated 1961 talk show hosted by former baseball star Roy Campanella.

The additional components of *King Leonardo and His Short Subjects* starred "The Hunter" and "Tooter Turtle." The Hunter was an intrepid dog detective, as famous for his motto "Have nose—will hunt" as he was for blowing an offkey trumpet whenever announcing his presence. Aligned with Officer Flim Flannigan and occasionally his nephew Horace, The Hunter regularly tracked the exploits of The Fox, a "wily clever criminal" whose crimes included snatching the Brooklyn Bridge and the Statue of Liberty. Total TV executive Treadwell Covington created the Hunter especially for actor Kenny Delmar, who revived the "Senator Claghorn" Southern bombast with which he'd risen to fame in the 1940s on NBC radio's *Fred Allen Show*. It was the first of many Leonardo Productions gigs for Delmar, who also provided the voices for Commander McBragg and Colonel Kit Coyote on the later *Tennessee Tuxedo* (q.v.) and *The Underdog Show* (q.v.).

Tooter Turtle was a Walter Mittyesque

amphibian who always wanted to be something he wasn't. To achieve this, Tooter would enlist the aid of Wizard the Lizard, a teutonic magician who'd reluctantly grant the turtle's wish and then narrate Tooter's adventures. These invariably ended with a chastened Tooter, overwhelmed by being out of his league in his later escapade, crying "Help! Mister Wizard!" — whereupon Wizard would break his spell, chanting "Trizzle trazzle truzzle trome. Time for this one to come home."

As with all General Mills–sponsored cartoon series of the 1960–1963 era, *King Leonardo* contained an additional component that hasn't been seen in years: the adventures of Twinkles the Elephant, produced by Leonardo TV and narrated by George S. Irving. The "Twinkles" cartoons were meant as tie-ins to a General Mills breakfast cereal which included as a sales incentive a complete, two-page "Twinkles" comic book story glued to the back of each box. For the benefit of those of you who were eating Gerber's baby food at the time, we'll note that the Twinkles adventures always ended with the elephant using his magic trunk to get his jungle pals out of their various scrapes.

All the *King Leonardo* components had a hip, UPA "look" to them, which was complemented by the flawless voicework of the aforementioned Jackson Beck, Kenny Delmar and George Irving, with the formidable backup work of such talent as New York kid's show host Sandy Becker and impressionist Allan Swift. But the series lagged badly in terms of plot values and joke content. *King Leonardo*'s exploits could never quite blend laughs and thrills with the deftness of its *Rocky and His Friends* role model; "The Hunter," though attractively designed, told the same story over and over again; and "Tooter Turtle," which with its barbs at popular media culture had the most satiric potential, sounded as though it was written by a 10-year-old fan of *Mad* magazine.

King Leonardo and His Short Subjects managed to hang on three network seasons and to do good business in 15-minute syndicated form under the title *The King and Odie Show*, but it wasn't half as laugh-provoking as Total TV obviously thought it was. Still, the company sentimentally retained the subsidiary name Leonardo Productions for its subsequent projects, including the company's most successful series, *Underdog*.

KISSYFUR. NBC: 9/13/1986–9/5/1987; 9/10/1988–8/25/1990. DIC Enterprises/ NBC Productions. (1987 episodes coproduced by Saban.) Executive producers, Andy Heyward and Jean Chalopin. Concept and characters created by Phil Mendez (creative consultant). Directed by Bernard Deyries, David Feiss and Marek Buchwald. Assistant director, Kenny Thompkins. Executives in charge of production, Kevin O'Donnell and Richard Raynis. Associate producers, Carol Corwin and Brian A. Miller. Animation production coordinator, Mitsuya Fujimoto. Story editors and adaptors for television, Len Janson, Chuck Menville (1986). Creative producers and story editors, John Semper and Cynthia Friedlob (1987). Animation produced by Tetsuo Katayama, Koichi Ishiguro, Yasumi Ishida, Masanori Kobayashi. Supervising animation director, Masaaki Osumi. Overseas direction, Mike Longden. Voice director, Stu Rosen. Music furnished by Shuki Levy and Haim Saban. Saban production staff (1987): Jerald E. Bergh, Eric S. Rollman. Saban music supervision, Andrew Dimitroff, Stuart Goetz. Saban's animation produced by Wang Film Production Co., Ltd. Voices: R. J. Williams, Max Meier (Kissyfur); Edmund Gilbert (Gus); Russi Taylor (Beehonie/Toot/Miss Emmy Lou/Cackle Sister/Bessie); Neilson Ross (Duane); Stu Rosen (Floyd/Stuckey); Devon Feldman (Toot); Terry McGovern (Jolene); Lennie Weinrib (Lenny/Charles); Frank Welker (Uncle Shelby/Howie/Claudette); Susan Silo (Ralph); and Marilyn Lightstone, Brian Cummings, Jeannie Elias, Ron Feinberg, Linda Gary, Barbara Goodson, Michael Horton, Mona Marshall, John Stephenson, and Jill Wayne.

Borrowing liberally from the "Bongo the Bear" episode in Disney's 1947 feature cartoon *Fun and Fancy Free, Kissyfur* was the weekly, half hour story of an eight-year-old bear cub who escaped from a circus in the company of his performing papa Gus (described accurately by Jeff Rovin as a Hoyt Axton type). Father and son try to set up a new life in the swampland kingdom of Paddlecab where they met any number of new friends and foes, from rabbits to hedgehogs to gators. To earn his keep, Gus became Paddlecab's ferryboat skipper. All of this backstory material was set up in a series of NBC one-shot specials in the 1985-1986 season before *Kissyfur* assumed its proper Saturday morning slot in the fall of 1986.

As indicated by his ooey-gooey name, Kissyfur was intended to be the launching pad of a merchandising blitz, and while the character never really took off in the non-TV marketplace, DIC Enterprises managed to keep *Kissyfur* in production for two years—though not *consecutive* years. It was cancelled by NBC in 1987, then brought back with new episodes one year later. Four programs from the 1986-87 season were reruns of the 1985 specials; the second production cycle, which commenced in 1987 and was telecast in 1988, was produced with the assistance of Saban International. Livening up the proceedings on all 26 *Kissyfur* installments were a handful of rousing musical numbers, always a high point of such DIC extravaganzas as *Hulk Hogan's Rock 'n' Wrestling* (q.v.) and *Kidd Video* (q.v.).

KLONDIKE KAT *see* **UNDERDOG**

KRAZY KAT *see* **THE KING FEATURES TRILOGY**

THE KWICKY KOALA SHOW. CBS: 9/12/1981–9/11/1982. Hanna-Barbera. Executive producers, William Hanna and Joseph Barbera. Produced by Art Scott. Directed by George Gordon, Rudy Zamora, Carl Urbano. Music by Hoyt Curtin. Music direction by Paul DeKorte. Character concept by Tex Avery. Components: 1. **KWICKY KOALA.** Voices: Robert Allan Ogle (Kwicky Koala); John Stephenson (Wilfred Wolf). 2. **DIRTY DAWG.** Voices: Frank Welker (Dirty Dawg); Marshall Efron (Ratso); Matthew Faison (Officer Bullhorn). 3. **CRAZY CLAWS.** Voices: Jim MacGeorge (Crazy Claws); Robert Allan Ogle (Rawhide Clyde); Peter Cullen (Bristletooth); Michael Bell (Ranger Rangerfield). 4. **THE BUNGLE BROTHERS.** Voices: Michael Bell (George); Allan Melvin (Joey).

Kwicky Koala was a Hanna-Barbera portmanteau distinguished by the creative guiding force behind the project. Director Tex Avery, a colleague of Hanna and Barbera's from the MGM days, should need no introduction to anyone who has laughed until crying at such theatrical-release classics as *Who Killed Who?*, *Batty Baseball*, *King Sized Canary* or *Bad Luck Blackie*. Avery's hyperbolic style, festooned with insane visual puns, ballistic facial and physical reactions (eyes expanding from their sockets, jaws dropping four feet to the floor, bodies stiffening suggestively in mid-air at the sight of feminine pulchritude) and uproariously violent, "everything *including* the kitchen sink" gag punchlines, has set the standard for such latter-day bouquets to the cartoons of old as the 1988 feature film *Who Framed Roger Rabbit?* and TV series like *Tiny Toon Adventures* (q.v.) and *Eek! The Cat* (q.v.). After the collapse of the Hollywood studio system in the mid–1950s, Tex Avery had gone into private business, utilizing his own small studio to turn out such bits of brilliance as the homicidal Raid bugspray commercials of the late 1950s and early 1960s. The director was in retirement when his old compadres Bill Hanna and Joe Barbera lured him back as a consultant and developer in 1979, giving him a grand welcome into their Cayuhenga Boulevard headquarters and promising him a free hand to do what he did best—within the economic dictates of commercial TV, of course.

The first thing Tex Avery came up with was a nod to Chuck Jones' "Road Runner" cartoons for Warner Bros. Avery's "Quicky Koala" was the story of a deceptively mild-mannered Koala bear, with a voice similar to that of Avery's Droopy Dog, who had no trouble literally popping in and out of the traps set by his chief predator, a hungry wolf named Wilfred. The director hoped to revert to the no-brakes policy of the MGM days, which wasn't entirely possible during American TV's nonviolence kick of the late 1970s and with Hanna-Barbera's verbally oriented, limited movement studio policy. To achieve his goals, Avery planned to film "Quicky Koala" in Canada, where costs were lower, and to syndicate the series to local markets, thereby circumventing network restrictions and interference.

This, alas, was not to be. When *Kwicky Koala* premiered in 1981, a year after Tex Avery's death, it was produced by Hanna-Barbera's own minimalist-animation staff, and it was broadcast on the CBS network, under strict nonviolence edicts—the like of which once moved Joe Barbera to moan, "If Charlie Chaplin, Buster Keaton and

Harold Lloyd had to work with NBC, CBS or ABC, they'd throw up their hands in disgust and walk away." To add insult to injury, the powers-that-were even spelled Tex Avery's original title differently.

To their credit, the seven-minute adventures of Kwicky Koala which appeared as the chief component of the half-hour series bearing his name contained a lot more energy and visual invention than was usual for the Hanna-Barbera product of the period; once in a while, the series induced genuine bellylaughs. But there were too many cut corners, too much extraneous dialogue, and way too much softening of the original concept: for example, Wilfred Wolf generally wanted to catch Kwicky not to devour him, but to keep him as a pet! None of these dilutions were really Hanna-Barbera's fault; they had to work with the staff trained for a different type of comedy, and also operate within the guidelines of the network heads. Still, one got the impression while watching Kwicky Koala that the material would have been infinitely better had Tex Avery lived to be the supreme guiding hand and had the harmless sadism of Avery's earlier work been acceptable in the kidvid climate of the era.

Kwicky Koala included two component cartoons. Crazy Claws starred a resourceful wildcat who sounded like Groucho Marx and who confronted every threat to his wellbeing with flippant wisecracks and propeller-like claws. The cat's nemeses were bearded mountaineer Rawhide Clyde and Bristletooth the hound, a Dastardly and Muttley combination (see *Dastardly and Muttley and Their Flying Machines*) whose efforts to trap Crazy Claws were about as successful as Wilfred Wolf's attempts to corner Kwicky Koala. Clyde and Bristletooth were in turn pursued by Ranger Rangerfield, a prissy young man constitutionally incapable of withstanding any physical exertion.

The "round robin chase" motif of *Crazy Claws* served Hanna-Barbera well, resulting in a concept much closer to the old Tex Avery style than the "main feature" *Kwicky Koala*. The best gags were liberally borrowed from earlier Warner Bros. and MGM Cartoons, and even from Hanna-Barbera itself—Bristle Hound could be bribed with a piece of beef jerky, which gave him the same sensual pleasure that Snuffles achieved from his "doggie bis-

cuits" on *Quick Draw McGraw* (q.v.)—but somehow there was a freshness and virtuosity to the tried-and-true material on *Crazy Claws* that put many other Hanna-Barbera lookalike efforts to shame.

Kwicky Koala's second component, *Dirty Dawg*, tried to be what the studio considered "street smart." Dirty Dawg, a Baron Munchausen-like talltale spinner who sounded like Howard Cosell, and his rodent pal Ratso (named, it is claimed, after Dustin Hoffman's fleabitten hustler in *Midnight Cowboy*, a film not terribly familiar to Hanna-Barbera's preteen audience) were disenfranchised street people. Their humorous struggles to attain a square meal despite the interference of helmeted officer Bullhorn—a goofy caricature of the cops who'd busted hippie heads during the 1968 Chicago Democratic Convention—aimed for an underlying cynical bite not often found in Saturday morning cartoons. The results were less cynical than typical, travelling the usual "outsmart the establishment" path that Hanna-Barbera had already worn smooth on *Top Cat* (q.v.) and *Yogi Bear* (q.v.). The laughs were there, but the intended "realistic" subtext wasn't.

The final *Kwicky Koala* component starred the Bungle Brothers, perhaps the dullest element of the series. This pair of showbiz-aspiring beagles (George and Joey Bungle) mercifully appeared only as one-minute buffers between the acts.

In all, *Kwicky Koala* was a mixed bag. Tex Avery had obviously inspired Hanna-Barbera to go beyond its own parameters towards a more radical, anarchic approach to humor, but the series invariably butted up against the brick wall of time constraints, budget limitations, and above all, the missives and modifications issued by a network rendered timorous by the "Clean Up TV" brigades.

LADY LOVELYLOCKS AND THE PIXIETAILS. Syndicated: 1987. Mattel/ Those Characters from Cleveland/DIC/ LBS. Produced by Andy Heyward and Tetsuo Katayama. Associate producer, Brian A. Miller. Directed by Bernard Deyries. Animation director, Kazuo Terada. Story editor, Jack Olesker. Written by Howard R. Cohen, Jody Miles Conner, Phil Harnage, Susan Leslie, Jack Olesker, Jeff Rose. Creative supervision by Robby London. Script coordinator, Lori Crawford. Executive creative consultant, Cassandra Schafhausen. Music by Haim Saban and Shuki Levy. Voices: Louise Vallance (Duchess Ravenwaves/Lady Curleycrown); Jeannie Elias (Maiden Fairhair/ Snags/Pixiebeauty); Tony St. Vincent (Lady Lovelylocks/Pixiesparkle); Danny Mann (Comb Gnome/Strongheart/Prince); Brian George (Shining Glory/Hairball/ Tanglet/Pixieshine).

Developed by American Greeting Cards' "Those Characters from Cleveland" division, the same folks who gave us *Care Bears* (q.v.), *Lady Lovelylocks and the Pixietails* was ostensibly designed to teach little girls the values of friendship, fidelity, and faith in oneself. What the half hour series actually did was suggest for 20 weeks that the perfect society was founded on the attractiveness of one's hairdo. Lady Lovelylocks, the kind and beneficent blonde ruler of the Land of Lovelylocks—where even the trees had coiffures—was locked in a power struggle with her wicked rival, brunette Duchess Ravenwaves. Lady Lovelylocks' trustworthy aides were the Pixietails, winged bunnies who in *Smurfs* (q.v.) fashion had character names amalgamating "Pixie" with personality: Pixiebeauty, Pixiesparkle, Pixieshine. The Duchess' main minion was an amorphous mound of split ends named Hairball. You still with us? Lady Lovelylocks' ladies-in-waiting were redhead Lady Curleycrown and brunette Maiden Fairhair. The heroines were lighthaired, the villainess had coal-black follicles. That's our lesson for today, girls.

There were a couple of male characters, just so we wouldn't consider the Land of Lovelylocks purely a matriarchy. The aged Shining Glory was a wizard with blank white eyes; he narrated the stories, or at least it sure sounded like him. A handsome prince also appeared, albeit one transformed by the evil Ravenwaves into a large dog.

The *Lady Lovelylocks* merchandising line (including expensive "personalized" videotapes) mercifully failed, and this animated Bad Hair Day was shorn after its first season.

LARIAT SAM see THE ADVENTURES OF LARIAT SAM

LASSIE'S RESCUE RANGERS.
ABC: 9/8/1973–8/31/1974; 9/8/1974–8/31/

1975. Wrather Productions/Filmation/ Rankin-Bass. Produced by Norm Prescott and Lou Scheimer. Associate producer, Robert F. Chenault. Directed by Hal Sutherland. Written by Jim Ryan, Bill Danch, Chuck Menville and Len Janson. Music by Yvette Blais and Jeff Michael. Voices: Ted Knight (Ben Turner/Narrator); Jane Webb (Laura Turner); Lane Scheimer, Keith Sutherland (Jackie Turner); Erika Scheimer (Susan Turner); Hal Harvey (Gene Fox/Ben Turner Jr.); Lassie [real name—Hey Hey] ("Herself").

Lassie, the noble female collie, had been created in 1938 by American author/ aviator Eric Knight. In her first incarnation, published by the *Saturday Evening Post* and later novelized as *Lassie Come Home*, the dog made a grueling 200-mile journey to be reunited with her master. Knight had written the story to please his young daughter and had no faith in its lasting value, so when approached by MGM for the rights, he let them go for a measly $8000. Five films resulted, all released after Knight's death in a 1943 air crash, and all of them were box office bonanzas for MGM. Rudd Weatherwax, trainer of Pal, the male dog who played Lassie (all subsequent Lassies were also male, because females tended to lose their coats when in heat), kept at it when the property was converted into a TV series in 1954. This one lasted 20 years both on network and in syndication, wearing down the talents of seven different Lassies and innumerable "stunt dogs."

It was in 1973, the live-action *Lassie's* penultimate year of existence, that series producer Jack Wrather contracted with Filmation and Rankin-Bass to create an animated, Saturday morning series centering around the Dog That Wouldn't Quit. Borrowing elements of the TV series' most recent years, in which Lassie was the responsibility of several forest rangers (the program was tied in promotionally with the U.S. Forest Service), and utilizing artwork and new characters previously seen on the 1972 *ABC Saturday Superstar Movie* (q.v.) entry "Lassie and the Spirit of Thunder Mountain," the production team came up with the weekly half-hour *Lassie's Rescue Rangers*. The human cast consisted of the Turner family. Ben Turner was patriarch of the clan and head of the Forest Force, an organization dedicated to conservation and avoidance of fires in the outdoors (the principal subject matter of the series' 30-second public service announcements). Ben's children, also of the Forest Force, were Ben Jr., Jackie, and Susan.

This "family affair" concept carried over to the offscreen world as well; three of the child actors working on the series were the offspring of Filmation executive Lou Scheimer and of *Rescue Rangers* director Hal Sutherland. Ted Knight, taking a breather from his chores on *The Mary Tyler Moore Show*, returned to the work that had sustained him in the pre-*Mary* days to give voice to Ben Turner. Lassie's bark was dubbed in by "Lassie" — actually Hey Hey, the most recent dog from the Weatherwax kennels to play the role. Rounding out the cast were fellow Ranger Jean Fox (voice by Hal Harvey) and two mascots, Robbie the Raccoon and Musty the Skunk (voices by no one).

Unfortunately, this was the first project in the 35-year saga of *Lassie* that didn't strike gold. Shaky animation and sagging storylines were only part of the problem on the 15-episode series. Rudd Weatherwax, who more than anyone qualified as America's foremost *Lassie* expert, took one look at *Rescue Rangers* and sniffed, "That's not Lassie. That's trash." A similar if elaborated statement was issued by the National Association for Better Broadcasting: "The manufacturers of this rubbish have incorporated violence, crime and stupidity into what is probably the worst show for children of the season."

Perhaps that assessment was a shade too strong — but it would have been worth it to throw this broadside at *Lassie's Rescue Rangers* just to wipe off the vacuous grin that the artists painted on the cartoon collie's face.

LAUREL AND HARDY. Syndicated: 1966. Larry Harmon Productions/Hanna-Barbera/Wolper. Music by Hoyt Curtin, based on themes by Larry Harmon and Marvin Hatley. Voices: Larry Harmon (Stan Laurel); Jim MacGeorge (Oliver Hardy); Paul Frees; Don Messick.

So much has been written about the comedy team of Stan Laurel and Oliver Hardy that to lavish any further praise would be preaching to the converted, and to analyze their films in minute detail would be retreading an already well-burrowed path. We'll assume you're familiar enough with the film antics of the skinny, simpleminded Laurel and the pudgy, pompous Hardy that we can move ahead to discuss the 130 five-minute cartoons based on their screen characters.

This cookie was a long time in the oven. As early as 1960, press releases were being issued by cartoon producer/entrepreneur Larry Harmon (see *Bozo the Clown*) that a new series of animated shorts based on the films of Laurel and Hardy were in preparation, and that Stan Laurel — the surviving member of the team and the one who worked hardest behind the scenes as gagman, editor and director-in-spirit — would function as Harmon's technical advisor. It was difficult for friends of Laurel to believe that the retired comedian would want to have anything to do with a project over which he wouldn't have total control, but there was an added incentive: A generous portion of profits accrued by these cartoons would be set aside for Laurel's wife and Oliver Hardy's widow as a sort of annuity.

When initial announcements about the project were made, Larry Harmon cast himself as the voice of Stan Laurel (reportedly at Stan's insistence), while Henry Calvin, the rotund Sgt. Garcia of the old Disney *Zorro* series, was to have been the voice of Oliver Hardy. Calvin in fact did supply a Hardy imitation for a 45 rpm children's record, a brief sketch based on "This Is Your Life" prepared in 1965, the year of Laurel's death (and of course Calvin portrayed Hardy onscreen in a memorable 1963 *Dick Van Dyke Show*). But when time came to record the sound tracks for the Laurel and Hardy cartoons, it was accomplished mimic Jim Mac-George who assumed the role of "Ollie."

This was in the sixth year of preparation for the L&H cartoons. During that time, Harmon had merrily merchandised the likenesses of the duo in coloring books, toys, dolls and games — but there'd been not one single cartoon made. Some fans of the team found this a blessing in light of the mediocrity of Harmon's *Bozo the Clown* cartoons, yet still they were anxious to see how Laurel and Hardy would adapt to animation. When the cartoons were finally produced, it was a complicated joint effort involving Harmon, Hanna-Barbera studios, and documentary producer David L. Wolper. In the fall of 1966 — one year after Stan Laurel's death — the new, full color *Laurel and Hardy* debuted in syndication.

It would be nice to say the cartoons were well worth the wait. Some devotees of the team, notably historian William K. Everson, bent over backward to find some value in the project. Everson was correct when he noted that the cartoons commendably captured some of the spirit of the original films, notably the basic premise of two likable bumblers who were forever flummoxed by a cold and cruel world, yet somehow remained undefeated. But all in all, the *Laurel and Hardy* cartoons, while not as slipshod and demeaning as the like-vintage *Abbott and Costello* (q.v.) cartoons, were a mile and a furlong away from being really good.

Part of the problem was style. In their best films, Laurel and Hardy could do 20 minutes on one single gag situation before getting to the punch line; they were the best "milkers" in the business. This was a luxury that the five-minute *Laurel and Hardy* cartoons could not afford. But the biggest stumbling block was Larry Harmon's and Hanna-Barbera's adherence to formula, cliché, and the easy laugh. Too often, characterization was forsaken in favor of an uncharacteristic one-line quip; and *far* too often, the cartoons consisted of Hardy getting stuck on some out-of-control mobile device—a lawn mower, an automobile, an airplane—while Laurel anxiously tried to rescue his pal. The animated Stan and Ollie were thus interchangeable with Harmon's Bozo and any one of Hanna-Barbera's legion of funny animals. A once highly individualized comic concept was reduced to assembly-line dimensions by throwing in gags and routines that any fourth rate comic personality could have done.

We could dwell upon the utter worthlessness of the *Laurel and Hardy* episodes wherein the characters emulated the *Batman* craze of 1966 and transformed into synthetic superheroes "Roosterman" and "Featherbrain." But enough space has already been squandered on a series of cartoons that served its purpose of entertaining small children and then was deservedly forgotten. Perhaps it's best to follow the advice of film critic and dyed-in-the-wool Laurel and Hardy buff Leonard Maltin: "To criticize these cartoons is pointless. Any imitation, even a good one, simply cannot be Laurel and Hardy . . .

No one can duplicate Laurel and Hardy's greatness because they were unique."

LAVERNE AND SHIRLEY IN THE ARMY. ABC: 10/10/1981–9/18/ 1982.
—LAVERNE AND SHIRLEY WITH THE FONZ (part of THE MORK AND MINDY/LAVERNE AND SHIRLEY/ FONZ HOUR). ABC: 9/25/1982–9/3/1983. Hanna-Barbera. Produced by Art Scott. Directed by George Gordon, Carl Urbano, Rudy Zamora, Bob Goe, Terry Harrison. Story editor, Duane Poole. Music by Hoyt Curtin; musical direction by Paul De-Korte. Executives in charge of production, Jayne Barbera and Margaret Loesch. Voices: Penny Marshall (Laverne); Lynn Marie Stewart (Shirley); Ken Mars (Sgt. Turnbuckle); Ron Palillo (Squealy); Henry Winkler (Fonzie [1982–83]); Frank Welker (Mr. Cool [1982–1983]). And Brad Crandall, Peter Cullen, Keene Curtis, Rick Dees, Dick Erdman, Joan Gerber, Bob Holt, Buster Jones, Zale Kessler, Henry R. Polic II, Lou Richards, Bob Ridgely, John Stephenson, Russi Taylor. (See also *Fonz and the Happy Days Gang* and *Mork and Mindy*.)

While manning the controls at ABC, Fred Silverman had encouraged developing a spinoff of the network's most precious commodity, *Happy Days*, with instructions to develop roughneck characters who'd be able to replace Fonzie (see *Fonz and the Happy Days Gang*) in the hearts of the viewers should actor Henry Winkler ever vacate that popular character. What *Happy Days* producer Gary Marshall came up with was a pair of wisecracking brewery employees, Laverne DeFazio and Shirley Feeney, who appeared as a couple of blind dates on a *Happy Days* episode before launching their own eponymous ABC series, *Laverne and Shirley*, in 1976. Those whose TV tastes were honed in the 1970s don't have to be told that *Laverne and Shirley* nearly surpassed *Happy Days* in viewer approval; from 1976 to 1983, ABC "owned" Tuesday evenings by kicking off that weeknight with *Happy Days* at 8 P.M. EST, and *Laverne and Shirley* at 8:30.

Like *Happy Days*, *Laverne and Shirley* was reshaped as a Hanna-Barbera Saturday morning cartoon—and like *Happy Days*, the *Laverne and Shirley* concept was reshaped to allow the lead characters to indulge in adventures they couldn't undergo in live action. The 13-episode *Laverne and Shirley in the Army* borrowed the premise of the 1981 Goldie Hawn feature film *Private Benjamin*, that of thrusting its heroine (or heroines) into the peacetime U.S. Army (the same premise was retreaded for H-B's *Popeye* [q.v.] spinoff *Private Olive Oyl*, also a 1981 issue). This allowed for a lot more "outdoor" slapstick than was permitted on the stagebound *Laverne and Shirley* original, which gave Hanna-Barbera free reign to broaden the series' already broad humor. Laverne and Shirley were given the traditional tough topkick, Sgt. Turnbuckle, who was later replaced by a noncom pig (!), Sgt. Squealy. Squealy appeared in *Laverne and Shirley in the Army*'s second season, which was bolstered with the "cast insurance" move of including the character of Fonzie from *Happy Days* (who ostensibly had joined the Army camp's motor pool), as well as Fonzie's cartoon-dog chum Mr. Cool, the latter a holdover from *Fonz and the Happy Days Gang*. With eight new episodes, the series was rechristened *Laverne and Shirley with the Fonz*.

To solidify the family ties with the two original live action series, Penny Marshall recreated her primetime role as the voice of Laverne, while Henry Winkler reassumed the mantle of the Fonz. Cindy Williams, the original Shirley, was having contract problems with the *Happy Days* production staff (she would walk off *Laverne and Shirley* in 1982), the result being that the cartoon Shirley was given speech by actress Lynne Marie Stewart. Another refugee from a popular ABC nighttimer, *Welcome Back Kotter*'s Ron ("Horshack") Palillo, launched what would be a lucrative cartoon voiceover career in the role of Sgt. Squealy.

As a means to (hopefully) dominate Saturday mornings in 1982, ABC rolled all its Garry Marshall Productions spinoffs into one big animated lump, scheduling the half-hour *Laverne and Shirley and the Fonz* back to back with Ruby-Spears' 30-minute cartoon *Mork and Mindy* (q.v.) and coming up with *The Mork & Mindy/Laverne & Shirley/Fonz Hour*. That said it all.

LAZER TAG ACADEMY. NBC: 9/13/1986–8/22/1987. Alchemy II/Worlds of Wonder Inc./Ruby-Spears. Executive producers, Joe Ruby and Ken Spears. Voices:

Brooker Bradshaw (Draxon Drear); Pat Fraley (Charlie/Skugg); Noelle Harding (Jamie Jaren); Billy Jacoby (Tom Jaren); Christina McGregor (Beth Jaren); Tress MacNeille (Genna Jaren); Sid McCoy (Olanga); Frank Welker (Andrew Jaren/Skugg); R.J. Williams (Nicky Jaren); and Susan Blu.

The Worlds of Wonder video arcade game *Lazer Tag* was the foundation of *Lazer Tag Academy*, an animated science fiction weekly. The series headlined Jamie Jaren, a 13-year-old girl from the year 3010, who in *Terminator* fashion journeyed back to the 20th century to confront evil time-traveller Silas Mayhem.

Mayhem—real name Draxon Dreer—was a prison escapee from the year 2010 who'd awakened 100 years later from suspended animation (as opposed to the limited animation seen on *Lazer Tag Academy*), stole a time machine, and headed backward to 1987. It was his intention to stop Jamie Jaren's ancestor Beth from developing a time travel machine, so that he'd be free from prosecution and thus be able to reshape the future to suit his own purposes. Jamie Jaren was then dispatched by the government-endorsed Lazer Tag Academy to stop Drexel Dreer/Silas Mayhem. (Why do cartoon villains with dangerously descriptive names always choose even more conspicuous phony monickers when travelling in disguise?)

Inasmuch as the cartoon-videogame format was (temporarily) faltering in 1987, *Lazer Tag Academy* was on and off in less time than it took to explain the plot.

THE LEGEND OF PRINCE VALIANT. The Family Channel: 9/3/1991–. Hearst/IDDH Groupe Bruno Rene Huchez/Polyphonfilmund Fernschgesellschaft mbH/Sei Young Studios/King Features/The Family Channel. Executive producers: William E. Miller, Jeffrey Schorr. Produced and developed for television by David J. Corbett. Associate producer, Mary Chojnowski Corbett. Line producer, Gwen Sandiff Wetzler. Directed by Michael Lyman, Marla Dall, Ron Myrick and Mike Kaweski. Based on the comic strip by Hal K. Foster. Story editor, Diane Dixon. Music by EXCHANGE (Steve Sexton, Gerald O'Brien). Lyrics by Marc Jordan. Theme performed by Jordan and Amy Sky. Voices: Robby Benson

(Prince Valiant); Michael Horton (Arn); Efrem Zimbalist Jr. (King Arthur); Samantha Eggar (Guinevere); Alan Oppenheimer (Merlin); Tim Curry (Sir Gawain); Noelle North (Rowanne); and Dorian Harewood, James Avery, John Corey, Jameson Parker, Tony Jay, Julian Holloway and Jack Lynch.

When he created *Prince Valiant* for the King Features Sunday comic supplement in 1937, artist Hal K. Foster's goal was to elevate the comic strip into Fine Art — as if it hadn't been up until then. Using a "continuing legend" format, a painstakingly accurate illustrative style, and a literary text written as captions to the art panels rather than as dialogue balloons, Foster wove a brilliant variation on the legend of King Arthur's Camelot, as seen through the exploits of the fearless and ever-chivalrous Prince Valiant. Though criticized by some comic strip historians for its ponderous prose and slow-moving story development, *Prince Valiant* has survived to the present day (it is now the responsibility of artist John Cullen Murphy), spawning a series of seven novels adapted from Foster's continuity, as well as a rousingly made 1954 Cinemascope feature film, in which a dutch-bobbed Robert Wagner acquitted himself excellently in the title role.

Perhaps it was the ambitiousness of the original strip that inspired the Family Channel cable service to pour as much effort and energy as it did in its 26-episode, animated *The Legend of Prince Valiant*. The project was a group effort involving Family Channel, Hearst Entertainment (King Features was a Hearst subsidiary), France's IDDH Groupe Bruno Rene Huchez, Germany's Polyphonfilmund Fernschgesellschaft mbH, and South Korea's Sei Young Animation Company, Ltd. Coordinating these various factions was producer David Corbett of Los Angeles. The *Legend of Prince Valiant* had been slated for a January 1992 debut, but Family Channel was so pleased with the results on the earliest episodes that Corbett was asked to move up the premiere to September 1991, allowing for a larger manifest of episodes. Family then chose to premiere the series in Tuesday night prime time, rather than confine it to weekend mornings (where it would eventually be rebroadcast, twice a week).

Despite attacks from cartoon purists like *Entertainment Weekly* columnist Ken Lynch, who complained that the series was "poorly animated" and had "all the drama of a high school pageant," Family Channel's pride in *Legend of Prince Valiant* was not all that misdirected. The series admirably emulated Hal K. Foster's superlative background art, even improving upon it with lush color schemes and shadings. The TV *Valiant* also retained the ongoing-legend concept of the original strip, telling its story in serialized fashion.

The series faltered a bit in its efforts at timeliness and in trying to cater exclusively to teens and preteens. Viewers could tolerate the "New Age" Camelot depicted in *Legend of Prince Valiant*, which King Arthur described as a place where misfits of all races and creeds could "start over." But it was a mistake to include a female character, Lady Rowanne, as one of the knights-in-training; what might have been politically correct in 1992 was way off the beam in the eighth century (and detrimental to the memory of Hal Foster, who always prided himself on the historical accuracy of his comic strip). And while it was instructive to show the young Prince Valiant learning his life's lessons through bouts of stubbornness, stupidity and barbarism, the results weakened the character considerably. Dwelling exclusively on Valiant's formative years may have pleased the youngest viewers, but robbed the older audience (already bemused when Prince Valiant's comic-strip son Arn was converted to his same-age best friend on TV) of seeing the full-flower Prince taking the positive lessons he'd learned from Arthur and the Round Table and carrying them over in benignly ruling his own subjects.

For a while, it looked as though *Legend of Prince Valiant* was going to have trouble finding any audience, old or young. But all problems had been smoothed out by the end of 1992, at which time the series had improved, entrenched itself, reclaimed its adult fans, and even won a few awards. Family Channel confidently commissioned 39 additional episodes in 1993, allowing for an ultimate Monday through Friday *Legend of Prince Valiant* strip.

THE LEGEND OF ZELDA *see* **SUPER MARIO BROS.**

LEO THE LION *see* **KIMBA, THE WHITE LION**

LINUS THE LIONHEARTED.
CBS: 9/26/1964–9/3/1966; ABC: 9/25/1966–8/31/1969. Ed Graham Productions/ Format Films/General Foods. Produced by Ed Graham and Herb Klynn. Voices: Sheldon Leonard (Linus); Carl Reiner (Sacha Grouse/Dinny Kangaroo/Rory Raccoon); Ed Graham (Billie Bird/So-Hi); Ruth Buzzi (Granny Goodwitch); and Jonathan Winters, Jerry Stiller and Anne Meara, among many others.

Linus the Lionhearted was one of the earliest, most blatant and most entertaining examples of the "thirty minute animated commercial." All the characters on the series were originally commissioned by General Foods to promote the company's line of breakfast cereals. Handling the package was the advertising agency of Benton and Bowles, and executing the results were B & B representative Gene Shinto and his partner Ed Graham—the latter a legend in Madison Avenue circles for scripting the classic Piel Beer animated commercials of the 1950s starring radio comedians Bob and Ray. Some of the cartoon "spokespersons" Shinto and Graham came up with in the years just prior to 1964 included Linus the Lionhearted, a friendly lion who promoted Post Krispy Kritters ("The one and only cer-e-al/that comes in the shape of an-i-mals," as the jingle went); Sugar Bear, representative for Post Sugar Crisps; So-Hi, a gently caricatured Chinese boy (the sort strictly avoided on TV these days) whose cereal of choice was Rice Krinkles; and Rory Raccoon, speaking on behalf of Post Toasties. A fifth character, a friendly postman (*Post* man, get it?) who huckstered Post Alphabits, had gone through an unsuccessful period as a fast-talking wise guy (voice by insult comic Jack E. Leonard) before the character was softened into the slightly effeminate Southern mailbearer Lovable Truly.

The weekly half hour *Linus the Lionhearted* was hosted by the title character, who appeared in his own component cartoon in the company of his loyal subjects Sacha Grouse, Billie Bird and Dinny Kangaroo. Linus' voice was supplied by Sheldon Leonard, an actor turned producer whose many prime time TV projects (*The Danny Thomas Show, The Andy Griffith Show, Gomer Pyle USMC*) enjoyed the sponsorial patronage of General Foods. Leonard's patented Damon Runyon gangster patois fit so well with the lines written

for him on the Krispy Kritters commercials of 1963 and 1964 that there was no question of his continuing the role when Linus graduated to his own series. Joining Leonard in the recording booth as Sacha Grouse and Dinny Kangaroo was Carl Reiner, whose own *Dick Van Dyke Show* was another appendage of the Sheldon Leonard TV sitcom empire. "They are friends and work for salary," said Ed Graham in 1966 of Reiner's and Leonard's participation in *Linus the Lionhearted*. "I just called them up and they said yes . . . I know that Leonard gets a big kick out of the fact that his grandchildren recognize his voice in *Linus*."

Of the remaining *Linus* components, the Sugar Bear and Lovable Truly cartoons were arguably the most amusing. Sugar Bear, who spoke in a cool, Bing Crosby manner, spent much of his cartoon time the same way he spent the time in his Sugar Crisp commercials—trying to wrest a free breakfast out of kindly sorceress Granny Goodwitch. Granny's voice represented the first regular series work by later *Laugh-In* star Ruth Buzzi. (Previously published reports giving Sterling Holloway voice credit for Sugar Bear are misleading; while Holloway originated the character in the earliest commercials, he was replaced early on by the Crosby imitation.)

Lovable Truly the postman was a likeable character, calling everyone—regardless of sex—"Dear," but the true star of his cartoons was the mellifluous Richard Harry Nearly, who described himself as "silent movie star and part-time dogcatcher." Nearly's strenuous efforts to capture Lovable Truly's little doggie friends paid off in Road Runner/Coyote style situations, and also in big laughs.

So-Hi's cartoons were conceived in the form of fables, with the little oriental sage relating a story with a message. At the end of each cartoon, he'd query his audience as to whether they'd gotten the point: "Moral of story, honorable children friends?" The So-Hi component was unremarkable save for some inspired voicework in one episode by Jonathan Winters, who played an accident prone giant. Whenever the giant stubbed his toe, he'd hop around in agony while Winters adlibbed such epithets as "Jumpin' Buddha!" and "Holy Pagoda!"

The final component of *Linus the Lionhearted*, featuring Rory Raccoon, was the weakest of the bunch, principally because the premise of a raccoon guarding a corn-field never seemed to lead anywhere beyond very standard "invading crow" gags.

Though never using "in" jokes or double-meaning references over the heads of the children, *Linus the Lionhearted* nonetheless had an edge of hipness to it, entertaining as many adults as kids. The clever limited animation was also of lasting value, reflecting the $87,000 per week budget (nearly triple the usual Saturday morning cartoon cost) lavished upon the series by General Foods. The 26 *Linus* episodes might well have been network-run forever had not the FCC horned in and decided that the series represented more advertising than entertainment. After being yanked off the networks in 1969, *Linus the Lionhearted* ran in syndication—but only after all the characters excepting Sugar Bear had been retired by General Foods.

LIPPY THE LION. Syndicated: 1962. Hanna-Barbera. Produced by William Hanna and Joseph Barbera. Voices: Daws Butler (Lippy the Lion); Mel Blanc (Hardy Har Har).

Lippy the Lion was a Munchausen-type blowhard whose tall tales ended disastrously when he was forced to put up or shut up. Lippy's companion, Hardy Har Har the nonlaughing hyena, could be counted upon to brood over the consequences of Lippy's lip, usually by shaking his head and moaning tremulously "Oh, dear. Oh, my." Daws Butler based his characterization of Lippy on cavern-mouth comedian Joe E. Brown. Lippy was a new Hanna-Barbera creation, while Hardy Har Har had already been established as a supporting character on several episodes of H-B's *Snooper and Blabber* (see *Quick Draw McGraw*). Hardy's voice was supplied by Mel Blanc, invoking happy memories of his whining, doomsaying postman ("Keep smiling!") from radio's *Burns and Allen Show*.

The 52 five-minute *Lippy the Lion* cartoons, together with *Wally Gator* and *Touche Turtle* (see notes on both), were sent out in syndication as part of a package titled *The Hanna-Barbera New Cartoon Series*. Unlike previous Kelloggs-sponsored Hanna-Barbera syndies, this package was sold sans advertising to local stations, who were expected to drum up

their own commercials. This gave the locals flexibility to run the new cartoons any way they chose—as separate entities, as 30-minute bundles, or as filler during baseball rain delays. The *New Hanna-Barbera Cartoon Series* also represented the studio's first syndicated property to be released in color; earlier programs like *Huckleberry Hound* and *Quick Draw McGraw* had been shot in color, but were printed in black and white. These series would have to wait until the commercial viability of tinted television to be proven in the mid- to late–1960s before color prints would be struck and distributed.

LIQUID TELEVISION. MTV: 6/2/1991–. (Colossal) Pictures/BBC/MTV. Created by Big Pictures and Noyes and Raybourn Entertainment. Executive producer, Abby Terkuhle. Creative producer, Japhet Asher. Produced by Prudence Fenton. Supervising producer for MTV, John Payson. Edited by Douglas Vines. Associate producer, Amy Cappen. Music by Mark Mothersbaugh. Musical interludes created by Oliver Harrison. Main titles and bumpers by Xaos, Inc.

When MTV signed on the air in August 1981, it was with the intention of offering the closest one could get to perpetual motion. To keep the action flowing from one rock video to the next, MTV commissioned animated logos and bumpers to be inserted between numbers—an ever-mobile visual style called "Interstitial Programming," which has since been adapted by virtually every TV station in the U.S. for local identification, news programs and commercials. When MTV began branching out into regular half-hour programming, the interstitial technique was maintained and expanded, thanks in great part to the network's creative director Judy McGrath. In 1991, McGrath wanted to inaugurate an animated TV series following the same nonstop philosophy as the rest of MTV. The avowed objective of this project was the same as the network itself: In order to keep people from switching the show off, the show would keep switching gears within itself. As McGrath put it, "Watch this and you won't have to change the channel." Hence the freeflowing title of the new series, *Liquid Television*, packaged in collaboration with Britain's BBC under the aegis of executive producer Abby Terkuhle.

A student of progressive, abstract European cartoonwork, Terkuhle craved "animation with an attitude"—the same sort of radical material he'd previously contributed to NBC's *Saturday Night Live*. To that end, Terkuhle handed the *Liquid Television* producer's reins to Prudence Fenton, who'd produced award-winning animated MTV I.D.'s in the first few years of the network's existence (Fenton had also had a hand in the inventive cartoon sequences on CBS' live-action *Pee-wee's Playhouse*). Fenton in turn knew just the right animation house to oversee production on *Liquid Television*: (Colossal) Films, so named and parenthesized because its creators, Gary Guitterez and Drew Takahashi, had found it amusing back in 1976 to have so many grandiose cartoon aspirations while working on a near-zero budget in a cluttered San Francisco basement.

But (Colossal) began living up to its name—minus parentheses—with its first major project, an advertisement for Levi's jeans in which hand-tinted live action stills were animated over a painted background—a process called Photomotion. This technique was later refined to a jumbled combination of live and cartoon action called "Blendo," described by Drew Takahashi as "a hyper jumping around from one completely different reality to another." Indeed, it was virtually impossible to ascertain where animation ended and "live" began, and this was the bewitching technique that (Colossal) would utilize throughout its advertising career (as in its series of frighteningly lifelike Pillsbury Doughboy ads), its contributions to opening-credit sequences of such films as *Peggy Sue Got Married* and *Top Gun* and its ultimate alliance with MTV, where director Mike Smith turned out terrific work on the network's interstitials. Disney Channel fans were also treated to the (Colossal) expertise with that cable service's famous "Mickey's Hands" bumpers.

There was going to be a *lot* of animation of this nature on each 30-minute *Liquid Television* installment, and (Colossal) was compelled to rely on the largesse of several independent cartoonmaking firms. This was clearly a labor of love—there certainly wasn't any money involved. A budget of only $150,000 per half hour was allotted by MTV for the first six episodes, meaning that Prudence Fenton, who'd been used to producing animation at $1000 per second,

would have to cajole her people to produce the mostest with the leastest.

Maybe MTV didn't contribute all that much financially, but it gave *Liquid Television* a superb kickoff for its June 6, 1991, premiere, preceding the event with a marathon of the best recent animated music videos (A frequent MTV featured artist, Mark Mothersbaugh of Devo, wrote *Liquid Television*'s interlude music, and later turned out the theme tunes for Nickelodeon's more mainstream *Rugrats* [q.v.]). Though barely mentioned in the "establishment" media, *Liquid Television*'s reputation was built up on the word of mouth of wide-eyed animation fans. Here at long last was a group of TV cartoons that refused to take the easy-outs of continuing characters, linear plotlines, standard Hanna-Barbera limited movement or adherence to traditional subject-matter taboos. Here was a program that was truly—per its name—liquid.

For the purposes of this book, we'll unfortunately have to shortchange the series' live-action vignettes. We recommend that you see for yourselves such flesh and blood projects as *Tim Boxell's Winter Steele*, a sociopathic biker-punk narrative enacted by huge puppets and costumed actors, directed by Cindra Wilson and scripted by San Francisco performance artists; the self-explanatory *Dog Boy*; *Art School Girls of Doom*, directed by *Liquid Television* coproducer Eli Noyes; and *Dangerous Puppets*, wherein directors Tim Boxell and Stuart Cudlitz guided us through a world of homicidal hand-puppets running amok on a cutesy kiddie show. Some of these segments were juiced up with animation (notably *Art School Girls*, which featured moving paper-cutout graphics and a chroma-key process called Ultimatte which removed those pesky blue lines around the superimposed figures of actors), but all were essentially "live" and thus outside the parameters of this book. If you *can't* catch these marvelous and challenging skits during their occasional rerun rounds, we invite you to read the chapters on (Colossal) in D.C. Denison's excellent book *As Seen on TV* (New York, 1992).

Liquid Television's cartoon sequences at first favored a "grab-bag" approach, with a variety of subjects and a tendency to emphasize gimmickry over characterization. *Soap Opera*, wherein "soap on a rope" was stop-motioned within the context of a daytime drama parody, was written by Ann Bernstein, directed by Don Smith, and animated by Michael Belzer, fresh from a stint with Art Clokey's *Gumby* (q.v.). *Miss Lidia's Make-Over to the Stars* was a "morphing" project, somewhat akin to the old *Changeable Charlie* hand toy. As Lidia Pryzluska's soothing "cosmetician" voice was heard on the soundtrack, celebrity caricatures would transform into the likenesses of other celebrities, with sometimes grotesque, sometimes androgynous results (it's lucky that people like Tom Cruise and Mel Gibson had a good sense of humor, considering the visual going-over they got on this one). The director was Gordon Clark, as far removed from his earlier work on Hanna-Barbera's *The Smurfs* (q.v.) as it was possible to get without leaving the planet.

Bill Plympton's *Plymptoons* were also sometimes spotlighted in the earliest *Liquid Televisions*. A critics' darling of the avant-garde animation movement, Plympton specialized in Daliesque landscapes, stream of consciousness (consciousness seemingly governed by controlled substances), mutilation, and an absolutely manic fascination in tight, distorted, yucky closeups of eyes, ears, mouths, tongues and especially noses. Plympton's best work has been developed outside the realm of TV for theatrical release (most of the clips seen on MTV were from his feature film *The Tune*), but his anarchistic style was certainly copacetic with the direction *Liquid Television* pursued its first season.

And then the public spoke. Judging by audience reaction, viewers loved *Liquid Television*, but were just a wee bit put off by cartoons that didn't concentrate on individual characters and some semblance of plot. Without losing any of its freeform integrity, the series began subtly shifting gears with its second season, giving more and more air time to "scenario" 'toons with ongoing characters.

One of the best of these was *Invisible Hands*, a Richard Sala–produced "comic strip" with multilayered, cutout animation, paced and plotted along the lines of a European detective/spy melodrama. Richard Sala, an admirer of the "great design sense" of the earliest Hanna-Barbera TV cartoons (like many fans of that studio, Sala's ardor cooled during the assembly-

line *Scooby-Doo* [q.v.] era), toiled to recreate those glory days with deliberately "clumsy," compartmentalized animation. Equally fascinating within the realm of cutout cartoonery was Mark Beyer and Dennis Morella's *Adventures of Thomas and Nardo*, which combined cardboard silhouettes and computer animation to tell the story of a talking, man-eating house and the self-abusive character relationships of its residents. (One of the voices was supplied by *Liquid Television* producer Prudence Fenton herself.)

The *Specialists*, a dual takeoff on Japanimation and *Mission: Impossible*, followed the spectacularly violent exploits of an invincibly inept crimefighting trio: Kitka, Mastermind and Samson. This beautifully colored recurring feature was cooked up by an impressive and international list of top animators, writers, and cartoon studios (including Pantomime Pictures, Riverton Studios, Devonshire Studios, Studio Z Productions) obviously working in concert for the sheer euphoria of it all. The talent included Fred (*Roger Ramjet*) Crippen, Chris (*Rocky and His Friends*) Jenkyns, DIC stalwart Thierry Laurin and Hanna-Barbera background design wizard Walt Peregoy, among many others.

Despite the series' taste for cluttered visuals, *Liquid Television* also fared well with some relatively simple vignettes. *Stick Figure Theatre*, produced by Ray Kissin and directed by (Colossal) regular Robin Steele, was one of the simplest—a single joke, but a good one. Utilizing child-like, crayoned stick figures on a lined, composition-paper background, *Theatre* offered comic enactments of scenes lifted bodily from the actual soundtracks of old motion pictures. It was hilarious and rather endearing to hear the tortured voices of Bette Davis and Leslie Howard from *Of Human Bondage* (1934) or Jimmy Stewart's last-reel exuberance from *It's a Wonderful Life* (1946) emanating from the mouths of goggle-eyed kindergarten drawings. Equally entertaining were the cartoons based on the tracks of *Night of the Living Dead* (1968) and the coming-attractions trailer for Hitchcock's *Psycho* (1960), wherein unspeakable horrors were reduced to the level of a day-care center "story hour." So popular was *Stick Figure Theatre* that Robin Steele was encouraged to develop the concept into a regular series independent of *Liquid Television*, with a continuing cast of characters and newly recorded (and as it turned out, less amusing) soundtracks.

Likewise slated for a weekly-series spin-off was Peter Chung's brilliant *Aeon Flux* — only here the appeal was in the concept's complexity and its strict *avoidance* of straight storytelling. Though produced in Los Angeles and Korea, the ambience and texture of *Aeon Flux* evoked the furthest fringes of radical Japanimation. The eponymous "heroine" was a ravishing, nearly nude guerilla fighter (what few clothes she wore were along the Frederick's of Hollywood "dominatrix" line) who decimated various murderous foes in a futuristic, extraterrestrial setting — only to be brutally killed off herself in each episode!

Viewers and critics alike luxuriated in what appeared to be *Aeon Flux*'s purpose — to devote all its screen time to never-ending movement without any plot or point whatsoever, forcing viewers to stare transfixed at a cartoon where no one has a clue of what's going on. Actually there *was* a throughline — Aeon Flux was on a search-and-destroy mission for a man carrying a deadly virus — and creator Peter Chung would take great umbrage with anyone who couldn't figure this out. Chung also was willing to explain why the series was offered *sans* dialogue and onscreen titles: "A lot of my motivation is to experiment with visual narrative, seeing how you can orchestrate images without text and try to invoke meaning." (Evidently the *Aeon Flux* school of wordlessness had enormous influence on Fox's mainstream *Batman: The Animated Series* [q.v.]; each episode opened with an action montage in which the name "Batman" was not shown or mentioned at all.) Alas, Peter Chung was persuaded to compromise this technique upon preparing *Aeon Flux* as a potential weekly series, with the intention of supplying the hitherto silent heroine with a low, guttural voice and several lines of dialogue.

At its weakest, *Liquid Television* was merely an elaboration on the Establishment animation it wished to satirize. At its best — with the above-mentioned projects and such added attractions as Robin Steele's *Wish You Were Here* and Bill Patterlite's *Psychograms* (both employing postcard art), John R. Dilworth's comic slant at child abuse (!) titled *Smart Talk with Raisin*, and briefies like *12 Dangers of*

Skydiving and *Speed Bump the Roadkill Possum* — the series was a living, breathing embodiment of the phrase "Cutting Edge." So much of *Liquid Television* was geared toward a higher intellectual plane than was found in most American TV animation, that it's ironic to close this essay by referring to the series' most successful spinoff to date: Mike Judge's doggedly *non*intellectual *Beavis and Butt-Head* (q.v.). Even so, *Beavis and Butt-Head* began like many other *Liquid Television* projects, poking fun at pop culture — and like many other *Liquid Television* projects, ended up becoming pop culture itself.

LITTL' BITS. Nickelodeon 8/3/1991–. Tatsunoko Productions Co. Ltd./Saban. Supervising producer, Winston Richard. Animation produced by Ippei Kuri. Writer (Japanese version): Shigera Yanagaua. Directed by Marayuki Hayaski. English version: Supervising writer, Robert V. Barron. Executive in charge of production, Jerald E. Bergh. Music by Haim Saban and Suki Levy. Musical supervision by Alex Dimitroff. Voices (English version): Arthur Grosser, Dean Hagopian, A. J. Henderson, Arthur Holden, Rick Jones, Liz MacRae, Walter Massey, Anik Matern, Terrence Scammel, Jane Woods.

The *Littl' Bits* pursued the "cutesy" formula already explored by *The Smurfs, Care Bears, Trollkins, Rainbow Brite* and oh so many other cartoons referred to in this book. Filmed and first released in Japan, the half hour series was set in a wintry, quasi–European setting known as Foothill Forest. Here dwelt the elflike Littl' Bits, who adhered to factory-tested formula by having descriptive character names deriving from their group appellation: Snoozabit, Lilabit, Williebit, Snagglebit, and on into the night. The inch-tall Bits governed their own community, maintained their own schools, produced their own goods (they had a healthy weaving industry), and learned their own lessons on how to cope with a world scaled for bigger folks.

The United States might have been spared this sublimely derivative series had not Saban decided to import *The Littl' Bits* and had not the Nickelodeon cable service deemed the series worthy of weekend morning play.

THE LITTLE CLOWNS OF HAPPYTOWN. ABC: 9/26/1987–7/16/1988.

Family Channel: 1989–1990. Murikami-Wolf-Swenson/Marvel/ABC Entertainment. Voices: Charlie Adler, Susan Blu, Danny Cooksey, Pat Fraley, Ellen Gerstel, Howard Morris, Ron Palillo, Josh Rodine, Frank Welker.

Geared for very small children, *The Little Clowns of Happytown* was a weekly half hour about a community called Itty Bitty City, populated exclusively by pintsized circus clowns with names like Geek and Blooper. Although the theme song wasn't "Don't Worry, Be Happy," it should have been, since the point of *Little Clowns* was to demonstrate the efficacy of having a positive outlook on life and to laugh as often as possible. To that end the producers engaged *Atlantic Weekly* editor Norman Cousins, who'd survived a bout with cancer by adopting a "laugh a day" policy, to act as *Little Clowns of Happytown*'s technical advisor.

But there was nothing to chortle or guffaw over when the ratings came in; *Little Clowns* was one of many "soft" cartoon series of the 1987-88 season overwhelmed by a glutted market. Its good intentions aside, *Little Clowns of Happytown* couldn't even raise a mild snicker against the competition of established people-pleasers *The Smurfs* (q.v.) on NBC and *Muppet Babies* (q.v.) on CBS.

LITTLE DRACULA. Fox: 9/3/1991–9/7/1991. Hahn Productions/Island Animation.

"Unlike his father, the young son of the Transylvanian count prefers to sink his fangs into rock and roll, and surfing." That's what *TV Guide* had to say about this half hour, five-episode miniseries based on the popular English children's book character *Little Dracula*, which got a week's worth of play on the Fox Children's Network afternoon lineup (with one Saturday showing) before flapping into obscurity. Like the previous season's *Rick Moranis in Gravedale High* (q.v.), *Little Dracula* seemed to demonstrate that semicomic junior monsters might look great on the drawing board, but would have to be a little more than adequate to succeed as TV cartoons. Besides, we already *had* a funny British cartoon vampire: *Count Duckula* (q.v.).

THE LITTLE KOALA *see* **THE ADVENTURES OF THE LITTLE KOALA**

THE LITTLE MERMAID. (The following entry covers both series based on this character.)
–1. SABAN'S ADVENTURES OF THE LITTLE MERMAID FANTASY. Syndicated: 1991. Bobot/Hexatol/Saban. Concept by Jean Chalopin. Produced by Eric S. Rollman, Koichi Sekizami, Satoshi Yashimoto, Keiko Tabana. Coproduced by Telescreen Japan, Ltd. Script editors: Robert V. Barron, Tony Oliver, Tim Reid. Animation director: Stephen Martiniere. Music by Haim Saban and Shuki Levy. Voices: Sonja Ball (Marina the Mermaid/Hedwig); Thor Bishopric (Prince Justin); Ian Finley (Dudhlee); Arthur Holden (Ridley); Gordon Masten (Chauncy); Anik Matern (Winnie); Aaron Tager (Anselm); Jane Woods (Narrator).
–2. DISNEY'S THE LITTLE MERMAID. CBS: 9/13/1992–. Walt Disney Productions (Japan). Supervised by Shigera Yamamoto. Produced and directed by Jamie Mitchell. Co-producers/story editors: Todd Anasti, Patsy Cameron. Directed by Mircea Marita. Music by Dan Follart. Theme song by Allan Menken; song "To the Edge of the Sea" by Silvesher and Silvesher, performed by Robby Melkin and Steve Gelfand. Voices: Jodi Benson (Ariel); Samuel E. Wright (Sebastian); Kenneth Mars (Triton); Edan Gross (Flounder); Mary Kay Bergman (Spot); and Tim Curry, Cheryl Bernstein, Jim Cummings, Pat Fraley, Michael Gough, and Hal Smith.

Hans Christian Andersen's 19th century fairy tale *The Little Mermaid* is no stranger to film adaptation, with several versions, mostly TV one-shots, made over the last 30 years. Only a handful of these adaptations adhered to the original bittersweet tale of a mermaid who gave up her voice in the course of true love; most chose the path of CBS' 1974 "Reader's Digest" animated *Little Mermaid* special, which allowed the heroine to experience romance and return to the sea intact. The best known of the cartoon *Little Mermaid*s was the 1989 Disney feature, an upbeat, musicalized version wherein the title character, now named Ariel, was an impulsive 16-year-old who swam ashore in defiance of her father to meet a handsome prince—and to very nearly forfeit her life and her father's to a fearsome sea witch named Ursula. The film, a welcome throwback to the old tried and true Disney animated formula of combining genuine horror with lighthearted humor, became the studio's most successful animated feature to date—and continued to uphold Disney tradition by yielding an Oscar-winning song, "Under the Sea."

The Disney adaptation was copyrighted, but the Hans Christian Andersen original was in public domain—meaning that, in the months before *Little Mermaid* went to the video stores, any number of fast-buck cassette dealers began issuing "official" cartoon versions of the old story, hoping to cash in on the Disney success before the public caught on. Saban International went so far as to slap together a 13-week *Little Mermaid* TV series—and when Disney griped, Saban invoked the "public domain" argument and pointed out that their version had nothing to do with Disney's (this didn't stop Saban from designing an opening credits sequence and theme song that bore a more than casual relationship to the Disney film). On the basis of title alone, *Saban's Adventures of the Little Mermaid Fantasy* achieved 85 percent coverage of the American TV syndicated market when the series was released in late 1991. (A random musing: Where did Saban come up with that title? How can a Fantasy have an Adventure?)

The studio was quite right in noting that the Saban *Little Mermaid* had nothing to do with the Disney film. It also had nothing to do with Hans Christian Andersen either. Instead, audiences were treated to a dizzy mélange combining parts of the King Arthur legend with generous samplings of every "sword and sorcery" opus seen on TV in the last ten years. The mermaid, here named Marina, spent more time on land with two legs than in sea with one fin. This earthbound mobility was accomplished by her downing a "potion of change," the better for her to visit handsome Prince Justin, a young nobleman learning life's values from his tutor, an ancient wizard named Anselm (who sounded just like Claude Rains—one of the few inventive touches in this otherwise pedestrian effort). The rest of the story ran along the lines of Saban's other "nursery story" series, full of cute humanized animals (Ridley the sea otter was the least offensive) and casually induced magic spells, with a mystical menace in the form of the sorceress Hedwig. It was hard to determine which was less interesting: the

stories or the animation. Whatever the case, *Saban's Adventures of the Little Mermaid Fantasy* had already been axed due to audience indifference by the time Disney decided to move in and show the folks how to *really* make a *Little Mermaid* series.

Disney's the Little Mermaid employed the characters, as well as the model sheets and the movement charts, that were utilized in the 1989 film. The series was a prequel to the movie; Ariel the mermaid was now 14, two years away from meeting her human prince. The stories were still motivated by her chafing at the restrictions and edicts imposed by her stern but loving father, King Triton, who saw to it that Ariel had a pair of chaperones in the person of Sebastian the crab and the overcautious Flounder.

Some of the half hour episodes showed how the disobedient Ariel swam where others feared to tread water, usually getting herself in a mess of trouble; these stories were balanced by plotlines in which the rigid Triton would be shown the value of tolerance and understanding by the freewheeling example set by his daughter. The series contained a great deal of original music, so it was a blessing that Disney engaged the same singing voices that had been heard in the feature film: Broadway musical comedy star Jodi Benson as Ariel and calypso specialist Samuel E. Wright as Sebastian (this latter character was spun off in his own starring series, which appeared as a component of Disney's 1993 networker *Marsupilami* [q.v.]).

The tightened TV budget, and the haste of completing 13 episodes in only eight months (the feature length *Mermaid*, which ran 83 minutes, took four years to complete), were reflected by the thicker border lines around the characters and the lessened fluidity of movement. There was also a nod to Saturday-morning traditionalism by introducing a couple of "kid" characters, a baby whale named Spot and a merboy named Urchin. The movie's malevolent Ursula was gone, replaced by such refugees from the Hanna-Barbera School of Pig-Bladder Humor as the "Lobster Mobster." Still, *Disney's the Little Mermaid* played like a first-string road show version of the film, with director James Mitchell compensating for animation deficiences with some ingenious background art touches—notably the characters' habit of decorating their domiciles with inventively recycled seaweed and shells. *Disney's the Little Mermaid* was a shining example of how farming out one's animation to Japan need not result in a second-rate effort—especially when all 38 Japanese artists were also on the Disney studios payroll, rather than the usual freelance "jobbers" who had little interest in sustaining studio integrity.

THE LITTLE PRINCE see THE ADVENTURES OF THE LITTLE PRINCE

THE LITTLE RASCALS:
—THE PAC MAN/LITTLE RASCALS/ RICHIE RICH SHOW. ABC: 9/5/1982– 9/3/1983.
—THE LITTLE RASCALS/RICHIE RICH SHOW. ABC: 9/10/1983–9/1/1984. King World Television/Hanna-Barbera. Executive producers, William Hanna and Joseph Barbera. Produced by Art Scott, Don Jurwich and Oscar Dufau. Directed by Ray Patterson, George Gordon, Bill Hutten, Bob Hathcock, Carl Urbano, Rudy Zamora, Bob Goe and Terry Harrison. Written by Mark Evanier, Bryce Malek, Jack Mendelsohn, Dick Robbins, Jan Green, Rick Fogel, Jim Simon, Tom Yakutis. Music by Hoyt Curtin. Voices (LITTLE RASCALS segments): Scott Menville (Spanky); Julie McWhirter Dees (Alfalfa/Porky/Woim); Patty Maloney (Darla); Shavar Ross (Buckwheat); B. J. Ward (Butch/Waldo); Peter Cullen (Officer Ed/Pete the Pup). *See* RICHIE RICH and PAC MAN for voice credits on those components.

The *Little Rascals* was the blanket title given to TV prints of the *Our Gang* short subjects produced by Hal Roach from 1929 through 1938 (the title was necessary to avoid confusion with the later *Our Gang* comedies filmed by MGM, which contractually were the only shorts permitted to retain that name). First released to television in 1954, these one- and two-reel shorts, featuring an ever changing group of mischievous children, remained in syndication for the next four decades—surviving accusations of bad taste and racism inherent in the depictions of the series' black children, and the subsequent butchering of the films to remove "offensive" material in the early 1970s.

Throughout the 1950s and 1960s, attempts were made by several producers— Hal Roach included—to revive *The Little Rascals* for TV with a new cast. Even Norman Lear got into the act with a late 1970s pilot film, which succeeded only in bringing Gary (*Diff'rent Strokes*) Coleman to the attention of Hollywood's dealmakers. All these latter-day *Rascals* attempts were doomed to failure, chiefly because none of the more recent crop of slick "professional kids" could match the roughhewn natural qualities of the original cast members.

Only the cartoon industry succeeded in getting a new *Little Rascals* on the tube— and then only by returning to the source with animated caricatures based on the original films. First there was NBC's *The Little Rascals Christmas Special* (1979), coproduced by King World Productions (the syndicators of the old Hal Roach shorts) and Murikami-Wolf-Swenson (later responsible for *Teenage Mutant Ninja Turtles* [q.v.]). Romeo Muller's script wisely returned to the milieu of the 1930s rather than attempting to update the Rascals. The gags were in the carefree, innocent spirit of the old films, and the drawings were reasonable facsimiles of the real kids (An added note of authenticity: two of the voices were provided by two original *Our Gang*-ers, Darla Hood and Mathew "Stymie" Beard—both of whom, sadly, were dead within a year of the special's telecast). The special was good enough to encourage a series spinoff, which occurred in 1983. Alas, in the intervening years, the property changed hands from young and eager Murikami-Wolf-Swenson to old and jaded Hanna-Barbera studios, then in one of its least inspired production periods.

Hanna-Barbera's weekly *Little Rascals* revival concentrated on the personalities of the children who appeared regularly in the series from 1935 through 1938, who'd proven to be the most popular characters with latter-day audiences. The cast included rotund lead Rascal George "Spanky" McFarland, cowlicked offkey crooner Carl "Alfalfa" Switzer, inseparable younger pals Billy "Buckwheat" Thomas (black) and Eugene Gordon "Porky" Lee (white), little heartbreaker Darla Hood, intellectual Darwood "Waldo" Kaye, and local bullies Tommy "Butch" Bond and Sidney "Woim" Kibrick. With scripts carefully monitored to avoid any of the so-called offensive elements of the Roach comedies (we weren't even permitted the He-Man Woman Haters Club), *The Little Rascals* premiered as a component of the 30-minute *Pac-Man/ Little Rascals/Richie Rich Show*, a new wrinkle on the *Richie Rich* (q.v.) saga which had been launched on TV in 1980, with the added fillip of the videogame star *Pac-Man* (q.v.). This was whittled down to *The Little Rascals/ Richie Rich Show* in 1983.

As expected, Hanna-Barbera lost most of the spontaneity and whimsy that had characterized the old two-reelers. The new series was also weighed down by some of the ugliest character art ever seen on Saturday-morning TV—surprising, in that attractively amusing caricature work was a Hanna-Barbera trademark. Somehow the studio managed to hang on to the property for two years, grinding out 34 11-minute installments (two per show) that made even the weakest Roach and MGM *Our Gangs* look like Oscar prospects. The new *Little Rascals* may have been inoffensive, but they also succeeded in being unfunny, uninvolving and totally unmemorable.

Well, unmemorable to all but those in the legal world, perhaps. In 1989, surviving Rascal "Porky" Lee sued Hanna-Barbera for nearly two million dollars, complaining that the company had exploited his screen character without his permission. According to *Little Rascals* historians Leonard Maltin and Richard Bann, Hanna-Barbera made a "sizable" settlement. There's no evidence that Porky responded to the judge's decision by shouting "O-tay!"

LITTLE ROSEY. ABC: 9/8/1990–8/13/ 1991. Nelvana. Story editor: Pam Sauder. Voice: Kathleen Laskey (Little Rosey).

Roseanne, ABC's megahit sitcom created by and starring comedienne Roseanne Arnold, was so grounded in the reality of the blue-collar "working poor" atmosphere that it's astounding anyone would consider transferring it to the patently unreal world of TV animation. The sharp thinking behind this move was of course the same logic that brought about cartoon spinoffs of *Dukes of Hazzard*, *Happy Days*, *Laverne and Shirley*, *Mork and Mindy*, *Star Trek*, and so many others: If they loved it once, they'll love it twice— and besides, if we get sore at a cartoon character, we can tear it up rather than renegotiate its contract.

Following the trend started by *Muppet Babies* (q.v.), *Little Rosey* took the principal character of *Roseanne* and shaved about twenty years off her age (according to one early report, she was originally supposed to have been a baby!). Little Rosey was now a preteen, cavorting with her sister Tess, her brother Tater, and her best pal Buddy. The cartoon series had little of the bite of the prime time TV series (in its third season when *Little Rosey* premiered in 1990), but there were glimmers of the original's edge with such lines as "Never put off until tomorrow what you can get your sister to do today." While the Rosey character looked uncomfortable joining the ranks of Typical Cartoon Kids, voice actress Kathleen Laskey offered an acceptable approximation of what the adolescent Roseanne might have sounded like.

Reports that Roseanne Arnold herself would assume the role for the series' second season proved groundless when it turned out there would be no second season (the replacement was ABC's reliable *Slimer! And the Real Ghostbusters*). That *Little Rosey* lacked the durability of its prime time model was only part of the reason for the cancellation. Roseanne had helped develop the cartoon show in hopes of making it as worthwhile as her "live" series, but found herself facing the formidable opposition of a cartoon firm (Nelvana) which had little sympathy for her "domestic goddess" comic persona (though curiously, Nelvana did just fine translating the skewed vision of *Beetlejuice* [q.v.] to television, which was certainly harder to animate than Roseanne's style) and with a network that "knew" what kids would want to see and didn't want to rock the boat with radical new ideas. Rather than threaten to sing or to stick obscene notes on the windshields of the ABC children's programming executives, Roseanne chose a more creative revenge. In the company of her husband Tom Arnold, she financed, produced, and supplied the starring voice for a half hour cartoon special, in which her travails with the Saturday morning sages were fictionalized. The special was better produced than *Little Rosey*, and might have been more interesting had it not been merely the latest example of the Arnolds' habitual public ego-tripping.

LITTLE SHOP. Fox: 9/7/1991–9/5/ 1992. Marvel/Saban. Produced by Tom

Tataranowicz. Developer/story editor, Mark Edward Evans. Executive producer: Haim Saban, Joe Taritero. Co-executive producers: Winston Richard, Ellen Levy. Creative consultant, Roger Corman. Music by Haim Saban and Shuki Levy. Executive in charge of music, Ron Kenan. Production facilities: Saban International NV, BIL, Gorfy Corp. Voices: Harvey Atkins, David Huban, Tamar Lee, Roland "Buddy" Lewis, Marlo Vola. Singing voices: Terry McGee (Junior Rap); Jana Lexxa (Seymour); Jennie Kwan (Audrey); Mark Ryan Martin (Paine); Michael Rawls (Mushnick).

Filmed in two days on a budget of $100,000, director Roger Corman's 1961 black comedy *The Little Shop of Horrors* went by virtually unnoticed on its first release. Gradually developing a reputation from repeated TV exposure, the film was being hailed as a cult classic by the early 1980s. Most of the credit went to the prolific Corman, but the real strength of *Little Shop* was Charles B. Griffith's screenplay, which deftly blended horror, satire, non sequitur, whimsy, and large doses of Yiddish-flavored dialect comedy. Any writer who can combine the potentially repellant story of a human-eating plant with lines like "How's the rain on the rhubarb?" and indelible vignettes like the sadomasochistic dentist office scene with a young Jack Nicholson, and *still* come up with a coherent, funny film, deserves some sort of gilt-plated plaque.

In 1982, a musical version of *Little Shop of Horrors*, written to a 1950s rock-and-roll beat by future Disney composers Howard Ashman and Allan Menken, opened off–Broadway. The libretto shamelessly bloated all the small, eccentric touches of Griffith's screenplay (without giving him any "original story" credit until the writer had to threaten to press charges), but this was the sort of aesthetic overkill craved by audiences of the 1980s. The play was a success, as was director Frank Oz' film version of 1986. It was this musicalized *Little Shop of Horrors*, rather than the 1961 original non-musical, that inspired the 1991 Fox network cartoon series, titled simply *Little Shop* due to its pruning of the original's horrific elements.

The basic characters of skid-row florist Mushnick, his nebbish assistant Seymour, Seymour's girl friend Audrey, and the talking carnivorous plant Audrey Junior were carried over to the cartoon series — but not without radical changes. Seymour and Audrey were now teenagers, Mushnick was now Audrey's father, and Audrey Junior was less interested in nibbling human flesh than in rendering a "rap" song or two each week. The sadistic dentist Dr. Farb of the original film, who'd already been re-vamped as a leather freak in the musical version, likewise regressed to childhood: he was now the school bully Paine, and his connection to dentistry was manifested in the outsized retainer worn on his buck teeth (Paine's dog was named Underbite!). The stories had no "horror" at all, but instead were banal little morality plays about status-seeking, dating, winning contests, and all the other nonesuch with which teens are presumed to fill their waking thoughts.

While the original premise of *Little Shop* was watered down, the program — commissioned because Fox Children's Network head Margaret Loesch felt the network needed a Saturday-morning musical — still had a lot of merit. The animation and background art was rendered in a cubist, 1950s-modern style evocative of the UPA cartoons of that period; movement was fluid, and the humor was largely of the visual-pun variety. The new songs weren't any great shakes, but weren't any worse than the lively but forgettable Ashman-Menken ballads upon which they were based. *Little Shop* lacked the engaging tastelessness, raucous humor and boundless spirit of both the Corman film and the stage musical, but at least it was consistently slick and stylish. But not slick or stylish enough, unfortunately, to survive opposite the cannonball competition of CBS' *Teenage Mutant Ninja Turtles* (q.v.).

LITTLE WIZARDS. ABC: 9/26/1987–9/3/1988. Janson and Melville/Marvel. Voices: Charlie Adler, Joey Camen, Peter Cullen, Katie Leigh, Danny Mann, Scott Menville, Amber Souza, Frank Welker.

An all-human variation of *Disney's Adventures of the Gummi Bears* (q.v.), *Little Wizards* was about a trio of teeny-tiny prestidigitators — Boo, Winkle and Gump — who helped average-sized Prince Dexter in his efforts to win back his kingdom from his usurping uncle, King Renwick. Magic was used more as a force of good than of evil on *Little Wizards*, perhaps to allay the accusations of wholesale witchcraft and sorcery on Saturday morning TV from fundamentalist media critics. This series lasted only one year; maybe with all the other pint-sized characters scampering underfoot on Saturday morning TV in 1988, the viewers were "littled" out.

THE LITTLES. ABC: 9/10/1983–9/6/ 1986. Tetsuo Katayama Productions/DIC/ ABC Entertainment. Executive producers: Jean Chalopin, Andy Heyward. Directed by Bernard Deyries. Based on the book by John Peterson. Developed by Woody Kling. Music by Haim Saban and Shuki Levy. Voices: Jimmy E. Keegan (Henry); Bettina Bush (Lucy); Donovan Freberg (Tom); Alvy Moore (Grandpa); Laurel Page (Mrs. Bigg); Robert David Hall (Mr. Bigg/ Dinky); B.J. Ward (Ashley); Patrick Fraley (Slick); and David Wagner.

John Peterson's Scholastic book series "The Littles" was the basis for this three-season ABC cartoon half hour weekly, described at the time by ABC children's programming head Squire Rushnell as "the first animated program designed to evoke emotions with which all children can identify." Like holding one's breath? No, like "loyalty, friendship and caring."

The title characters of *The Littles* were part of a microscopic community of pixieish humans with pointed ears and tails, who lived somewhere behind the walls of people's homes. Through the auspices of Henry Bigg, a normal-sized human boy, the Littles (foremost among them Lucy and Tom Little) were able to enter our world—actually all parts of the world, since Henry's father, George Bigg, was a globetrotting scientist. It was up to Henry to shield the Littles from the prying eyes of other humans, lest they be regarded as freaks and locked away in mason jars, while the Littles themselves had to avoid their own ruling fathers, because to cross over into the big world was against their laws.

Comparisons between *The Littles* and *The Smurfs* (q.v.) were inevitable. Perhaps in anticipation, an article was prepared for the September 17, 1983, issue of *TV Guide* ("Out of Sardine Cans and Into Battle"), wherein writer Ralph Schoenstein allegedly interviewed Lucy and Tom Little's second cousin Luther. On the subject of *The Smurfs*, Luther Little rose to his full height (about six inches) and proclaimed:

"If you think we're like *those* squeaky blobs, you must have trouble telling the Four Freshmen from the Seven Dwarfs. The Smurfs look like leftovers from a bakeoff. But the Littles are *real.*"

THE LONE RANGER. CBS: 9/10/ 1966–9/6/1969. Lone Ranger Television/ Format Films. Executive producer, Arthur Jacobs. Produced by Herb Klynn. Directed by Art Babbitt and Bill Tytla, among others. Animators: Virgil Ross, Hank Smith, A. Green. Background design by Walt Peregoy. Voices: Michael Rye (The Lone Ranger); Shep Menken (Tonto); Jackson Beck, Marvin Miller, William Conrad, Hans Conried, and others.

–**THE TARZAN/LONE RANGER ADVENTURE HOUR.** CBS: 9/13/1980– 9/5/1981.

–**THE TARZAN/LONE RANGER/ ZORRO ADVENTURE HOUR.** CBS: 9/12/1981–9/11/1982. Filmation. (*See* TARZAN for voice and production credits.)

The *Lone Ranger* was created for radio in 1933 by George W. Trendle and Fran Striker for Trendle's Detroit radio station WXYZ, whence the series was networkcast until 1954. While the Masked Rider of the plains merely appeared on his great white horse Silver without explanation in his earliest years, a "backstory" had to be developed for the purposes of a 1939 Republic movie serial based on the Lone Ranger character; this history was later refined on WXYZ in 1941 as part of a serialized story arc titled "The Legion of the Black Arrow." Here is where the world discovered that the Lone Ranger was actually Texas Ranger John Reid—left for dead in an ambush, nursed to health by "Kemo Sabe" Indian companion Tonto, and determined to fight for law and order as a free agent, hiding his true identity behind a mask. A rehash of the "legend" would serve as the three-part pilot for the *Lone Ranger* TV series in 1949, which ran until 1956 and starred Clayton Moore in the title role (briefly replaced during a contract dispute by John Hart) and Jay Silverheels as Tonto.

Executive Fred Silverman of CBS took the Lone Ranger out of mothballs in 1966 to counterattack ABC's Saturday morning ratings-rustler *The Beatles* (q.v.). Herb Klynn, late of *The Alvin Show* (q.v.), put his staff to work on the new 26 half-hour *Lone Ranger* installments, featuring three brief adventures per episode. Character animation was rudimentary, but the background art by Walt Peregoy—utilizing black marking-pencil borders and torn colored paper—was eyecatching and highly innovational. One could call the story material "innovational" too, but only in comparison to standard *Lone Ranger* scriptwork. The series' emphasis on robots, space aliens, death rays, weather machines and costumed villains like The Black Widow, The Fly, The Fire God and Dr. Destructo, had more in common with the 1966 *Batman* TV series than the Lone Ranger's customary "Thrilling Days of Yesteryear."

Youngsters thrived on this revised *Ranger*, but adults who'd grown up idolizing the character were less enthusiastic. One dim viewer was Charles Sopkin, author of *Seven Glorious Days, Seven Fun Filled Nights* (New York, 1968), an amusing if patronizing journey through a week's worth of television viewing. Obliged to watch seven TVs simultaneously in order to best observe the passing video parade in the New York market, Sopkin admitted to "snoring" through most of the current cartoon shows, but was motivated by curiosity to endure *The Lone Ranger*—the only animated series analyzed in his book. After detrimentally comparing the radio version (evidently a cherished memory) to the sample cartoon episode "The Rainmaker," in which the Masked Man and Tonto did battle with the despicable Dr. Vulcan, Sopkin declared "I am filled with a sense of nausea and grief."

Few other viewers were made physically ill by the cartoon *Lone Ranger*, but fewer still can remember any details of the series when grilled nowadays. Still, *Lone Ranger* had its redeeming qualities, not only the aforementioned Walt Peregoy background work but also its stirring full orchestra rendition of the characters' venerable theme music, Rossini's "William Tell Overture." In fact, when the old live action *Lone Ranger* series was repackaged for syndication in the 1980s, its TV ads used the cartoon version's "Tell" arrangement as background music.

When Filmation had its crack at *The Lone Ranger* as part of its 1980 "legendary superhero" package *The Tarzan/Lone Ranger Adventure Hour* (see *Tarzan*), later expanded to include the animated *Zorro*,

it was with the understanding that the series could feature none of the "wanton" violence of its 1966 predecessor. This was less a reaction to the earlier cartoon version than to a mid–1970s government probe concerning violent programming. One of the principal "violators" turned out to be the live-action *Lone Ranger*—and never mind that the hero's strict avoidance of killing and unnecessary fisticuffs was carefully established on WXYZ in the mid–1930s, as a "response" to even earlier parental complaints about media violence.

In the interests of self-defense, Filmation issued statements congratulating itself on how all gratuitous mayhem was weeded out of *The Lone Ranger*, almost as if the studio had been the first to do this. Also emphasized was the prosocial "history lesson" element of the new *Ranger*, who rubbed shoulders in his cartoon adventures with historical giants like Ulysses S. Grant and Wild Bill Hickok (and a few "fictionals" from the same period like Tom Sawyer). At the end of each half-hour adventure, the Masked Man would narrate 30-second history bites as a learning tool. Again, Filmation apparently felt it was pioneering in this respect, even though the radio Lone Ranger had been commiserating with the likes of Grant and Lincoln as far back as 1941, and had also featured an occasional "famous outlaw" episode throughout the rest of that decade.

One alteration to the Filmation *Lone Ranger* that *was* new to television was its giving the Ranger's friend Tonto a broader vocabulary than his "Get'um up scout" radio counterpart. This was the 1980s: TV Indians were now Native Americans, and they were as articulate as the next fellow. At times, Filmation's Tonto spoke better English than the Masked Man!

Animation on the 1980 *Lone Ranger* was typically better in its opening title logo than in the remainder of each episode, though the rotoscoping of live-action film in order to make the character movement more "realistic" was competently handled. The Filmation series returned to the "Days of Yesteryear" by reviving both the original "William Tell" orchestrations and the introductory narration ("From out of the past come the thundering hoof-beats . . ."). Also making a welcome return from radio's Golden Age was the voice of the Lone Ranger: William Conrad, of *Cannon* fame, whose own radio brush with the West was as Matt Dillon in the brilliant pre–TV *Gunsmoke* series. Conrad, who also did the opening narration, was billed as "J. Darnoc" in the closing credits. Ostensibly, Conrad did this to avoid hurting his reputation by "lowering" himself to TV cartoon work (Conrad of course had previously narrated Jay Ward's *Rocky and His Friends*), but the actor's voice was so well known to viewers at the time that one can't help feeling that "J. Darnoc" was merely a joke at the expense of the actor's millions of fans. One can envision Bill Conrad sitting at home and chuckling at the thought of viewers perusing the credits and then exclaiming "Who's this clown Darnoc stealing Conrad's style?"

The new *Lone Ranger* disappeared along with its *Tarzan* and *Zorro* cofeatures in 1982. The old, "real" *Lone Ranger* continues to thrive in reruns both on TV and on radio nostalgia programs, still galloping into the sunset with Tonto before the townsfolk have a chance to thank him.

LUNCH BOX. Disney Channel: 7/3/ 1989–. Various Production Companies.

Lunch Box was a daily portmanteau series packaged by cable's Disney Channel, highlighting several foreign-produced live-action and cartoon shorts. Some in the latter category were old favorites to American audiences, notably *Curious George* (q.v.) and *Paddington Bear* (q.v.).

Most of the other cartoon segments were relatively new to domestic audiences, though they'd been produced some time before *Lunch Box*'s premiere. *Rupert*, a 1988 issue from the BBC and Alfred Bestall Productions, was based on the longrunning British comic strip about a cute bear cub (see separate entry on this character). *Rupert* shared time on *Lunch Box* with *Will Quack Quack*, an adolescent duck created by Spud Houston, whose cartoon adventures were assembled in 1983 by Cardiff's Siriol Studios (see also *The Further Adventures of Superted* for more on Siriol). Another frequently seen component was Eric Hill's *The Adventures of Spot*, a storybook-design saga of a playful pup narrated by Paul Nicholas, originally produced for the BBC by Kingrollo Films. *Spot* was possibly *Lunch Box*'s best-known ingredient. The character, created by Hill in 1980 for a series of fold-out children's

books, was one of the most lucrative British literary properties of its time, selling some 22 million copies worldwide and spawning a package of high-grossing video tapes — plus scads and scads of toys, games, and miscellaneous merchandise.

MACRON 1. Syndicated: 1985. Saban/ Tamerlaine Publishing/Orbis. Executive producers: Haim Saban, Shuki Levy. Writing supervision and direction: Robert V. Barron. Creative supervisor, Dennys McCoy. Associate producer, Jonathan Braun. Production coordinators, Alex Dimitroff and Jeff P. Rubinstein. Written by Robert Barron, Greg Snow, Winston Richard, Richard Miller, Jason Klassi, Mike Reynolds, John Rust, Max Pynchon, Pam Hickey, Joe Hailey, Bob Cowley, Benjamin Lesko. Edited by Jonathan Braun, Mick Kollins, Sheila O'Callaghan. Editing facilities: Video Transitions. Music by Haim Saban, Shuki Levy; Top 40 music by original artists. Theme song "Reflex" performed by Duran Duran. Voices: Angela Rigamonti, Bill Laver, Christopher Eric, Octavia Beaumont, Tamara Shawn, Rich Ellis, Susan Ling, Oliver Miller.

Macron 1, a daily half hour sci-fi syndie, was cobbled together from two separate Japanese cartoon series, though American distributor Saban/Orbis did its best to hide this fact, removing all Japanese names from its production credits. The original series involved were *Go Shogun* (from Ashi Productions) and *Srungle* (production information unavailable); the two programs were linked thematically by a futuristic outer space setting and a "rebellion against oppression" throughline. Despite the Westernization efforts of its English-language adaptors, *Macron 1*'s country of origin was evident in its production and character design, and in its similarity to the like-vintage *Robotech* (q.v.) — which in the manner of *Macron* had been patched together by its American distributor from *three* separate Japanese series, one of them titled (what a coincidence!) *Macross*.

Set in the year A.D. 2545 (not in the 41st century that the series' publicity described), *Macron 1* was the story of a misguided teleportation experiment which hurled Earthling test pilot David Jance into a parallel universe — and in exchange, the evil Dark Star, leader of a terrorist cyborg-dominated army known as GRIP, wound up in our universe. From this point onward, David Jance and his *Star Wars*-like crew of rebellious teenagers and mutants—including a "Chewbacca" type first mate named Nok—flew on behalf of the parallel world's heroic Beta Command, led by Dr. Chagall. Beta Command's personnel (which received a lot more screen time than nominal hero Jance) included Nathan Bridger, the brilliant preteen son of late computer expert Dr. Bridger, whose scientific expertise placed him in a command post for which he was intellectually ready but psychologically ill-prepared. Also among the Beta group were several characters who, like the crew of Jance's "Flying Macstar," were echoes of *Star Wars*—right down to a cute "R2D2" robot named An-D and an erudite "C3PO" computer brain named Hugo.

"Macron 1" itself was a huge, flying space robot, formed whenever the Beta Command combined its energy and weaponry with the Flying Macstar. This Macron metamorphosis took place whenever the villains threatened to outpopulate the heroes—not all that distant a danger, since the GRIP contingent included the aforementioned Dark Star, the covetous Prince Maharn (who in the tradition of *Robotech* villain Lord Kyron sounded like British actor James Mason), the "avast, swabs!" space pirate Dr. Blade, a Nazilike mad scientist, and numerous skullheaded robot slaves.

Like *Robotech* at its best, *Macron 1* exuded a cocky wiseguy attitude, with its younger characters forever disregarding and mocking their superiors. Also like *Robotech*, *Macron* excelled in nailbiting outer-space battles, accomplished as much through rapid editing and bizarre camera angles as through clever limited animation. A major selling point to American markets was Saban/Orbis' inclusion of contemporary Top 40 tunes in *Macron 1's* soundtrack. These were illustrated in MTV fashion with flashy montage sequences, generically constructed to conform with any song that happened to be hot at the moment (the "neutral" quality of the montages came in handy when the distributors were forced by copyright restrictions to remove some of the songs when *Macron 1* was released to home video). The "rock" motif was often carried over into the straight action sequences; some of the most effective space battles

contained no sound effects at all, merely musical accompaniment.

Macron 1 scored where a lot of other Japanese imports struck out, combining the more sober and straightfaced characteristics of "Japanimation" with the cheerful Yankee Doodle cheekiness of Hollywood's best action-adventure films. But like its spiritual twin *Robotech*, *Macron 1* suffered by being scheduled in inappropriate early-morning and early-afternoon fringe timeslots—and by its nearly exclusive distribution to big city markets, leaving most potential southern and midwestern fans out in the cold.

THE MAD SCIENTIST TOON CLUB. Syndicated: 1993. Saban. Animation produced by Tatsunoko. Executive producer/creator, Eric S. Rollman. Supervising producer, Jeff Androsky. Produced and directed by Mark S. Pinsker. Produced by Armando Villalpando, Rhonda Barzon, David A. Chickering. Head writer, Rick Sandoval. Written by Lou DeCosta, Jonathan Shneidman. Story editor, Tod Himmel. Additional material, Michael Sorich. Science advisor: Alex Koperberg. Creative consultant, Karen Lee Copeland. Music by Shuki Levy and Kussa Mahchi. Music coordinated by David Hillenbrand. Executive in charge of production, Carol Sherman. Live-action sequences taped at Yeah! Studios. Animation produced by Bob Barron. Live action cast: Michael Sorich (Dr. Pi). Voices: Mikey Godzilla, Dave Molen, Wendy Swan, Steve Norton.

Saban's *The Mad Scientist Toon Club* was an imitation of such established "edutainment" efforts as *Beakman's World* and *Bill Nye the Science Guy*—programs calculated to satisfy the instructional requirements of the newly conscientious FCC of the 1990s. Like its above-mentioned predecessors, *Toon Club* starred an eccentric egghead—"Doctor Pi," played in live-action sequences by Michael Sorich—who conducted experiments, built workshop projects, explained and clarified scientific fact and theories, quizzed the home audience with historical factoids, and told relentlessly lousy jokes just to show he was a "regular guy" and not some aloof, ivory-tower pedant.

Each hour-long *Mad Scientist Toon Club* (also offered as two separate half hours) featured multiple appearances of two separate cartoon-short series from Japan's Tastunoko studios. The *Wacky World of Tic and Tac* spotlighted the pantomime adventures of a bird and a hippo, while *Eggzavier the Eggasaurus* was a do-gooder dinosaur who sounded like Ed Wynn. The cartoon components had nothing to do with the rest of *Mad Scientist Toon Club*, nor were they linked together thematically. They resembled one another only in their disjointed, inscrutable plotlines and appalling lack of humor.

MADELINE. Family Channel: 9/18/ 1993–. Family Channel/DIC Enterprises. Based upon characters created by Ludwig Bemelmans. Executive producers, Andy Heyward, Robby London, Saul Cooper and Pancho Kohner. Produced and directed by Stan Phillips. Story editor, Judy Rothman. Executive in charge of production for Family Channel: Bob Chmiel. Production executive: Thomas Halleen. Executive in charge of production for DIC: Brian A. Miller. Production supervisors, Stacy Gallishaw and RaNae Bonella. Associate producer, Lisa A. Salamone. Script coordinator, Lori Crawford. Art director, Sean Platter. Background design, Bob Dranko and Sean Platter. Color background: Joe Dempsey, Teri Shikasho. Music direction by Joanne Miller and Monica Wakefield. Music vocal direction by Louise Vallance. Music by Andy Street; lyrics by Judy Rothman (one or two original songs per show). Music editor, John Mortarotti. Animation facilities, Plus One Animation Co. Ltd. Overseas supervising director, Lee Choon Man. Voices: Tracey-Lee Smyth (Madeline); Louise Vallance (Miss Clavel/ Genevieve); Christopher Plummer (Narrator); and Vanessa King, Kelly Sheridan, Kristin Fairlie, A. J. Bond, Gary Chalk, French Tickner, Long John Baldry, Dale Wilson, Ian James Corlett, Corrine Koslo, Wezley Morris, Don McManus, Alec Willows, Kathleen Barr, Lufee Palmer, Brent Chapman, Jay Brazeau, Sam Manusco, Jim Byrnes, Danny Mann, Jane Mortifee, and Phil Hayes.

Created in 1939 by Austrian author/artist Ludwig Bemelmans, *Madeline* was the pintsized protagonist of several popular children's books. The smallest and bravest of the 12 young girls in Miss Clavel's strictly regimented Paris boarding school, Madeline (named for Bemelmans' wife) was featured in lighthearted, moralistic adventures written in verse. These were illustrated from an "overhead" point of view in a forced-perpective manner which was both easy to grasp for the kids and artistically complex for Madeline's many adult intellectual fans. The character was the subject of a 1952 UPA cartoon directed by Bobe Cannon, which drew critical praise for its meticulous recreation of the Bemelmans style (strikingly similar to the impressionistic background art in Chuck Jones' Pepe Le Pew cartoons being produced during the same period over at Warner Bros.).

Madeline's TV cartoon career began with a 1988 HBO special produced by DIC Enterprises. Two years later there followed a group of intermittently scheduled half-hour cable specials produced by Cinar Studios, and in 1993 a weekly *Madeline* cable series premiered, this one a joint project of DIC and the Family Channel. *Madeline* did so fine a job emulating the Ludwig Bemelmans books that, at first glance, one would think the series was produced by Nelvana/Ellipse, what with that studio's track record in animating children's-book material (see *Babar, Rupert* and *Tintin*). As it stood, *Madeline* was one of the most smoothly animated programs to come out of DIC since *Inspector Gadget* (q.v.).

By its very weekly nature, the series had to abandon the original Bemelmans stories early on in favor of situation-comedy and life-lesson stories from DIC's own staff writers. Still, the Continental literary style of the *Madeline* books (minus the rhymed couplets) was admirably maintained, even though homogenized for American audiences by a preponderance of breezy but forgettable songs, and by the characters' musical-comedy tendency to speak in exaggerated French accents, just to remind us that we were in Paris.

As in the case of the 1952 UPA version, critics fell over themselves praising DIC's *Madeline*, wearing out words like "delightful," "enchanting" and "engaging"—which is better than chanting the usual mantra of "violent" and "brainless." The warm narration by Christopher Plummer and the rich Gallic backdrops (unrealistic for the most part, but accurate when necessary—notably in one episode where Madeline's classroom made a trip to the Louvre) added immensely to *Madeline*'s charm. In a more equitable world, we might have even been able to report that the average preteen cartoon fan would choose the charming but low-watt *Madeline* over the more enticing network competition of ABC's *Sonic the Hedgehog* (q.v.) and Fox's live-action blockbuster *Mighty Morphin' Power Rangers*.

THE MAGICAL PRINCESS GIGI. Syndicated: 1985. Ashi Productions/Harmony Gold. Executive producer, Frank Agrama. Produced by Ahmed Agrama. Directed by Hiroshi Watanabe. Written by Greg Snegoff. Story by Carl Macek and Takeshi Shudo. Voices: Reva West, Lisa Paullette, Sal Russo, Abe Hurt, Betty Gustavson, Ryan O'Flannigan, Anita Pia, Sam Jones.

The five-part *Magical Princess Gigi* wasn't really a series but a reedited Japanese theatrical feature, *Magic Princess Miki Momo*. This story of a 12-year-old outer space princess from the planet of "Fairyland," who came to Earth in search of friends and kindred spirits, was directed by Hiroshi Watanabe, and released in some countries as *The Magical World of Gigi*.

MAGILLA GORILLA. Syndicated: 1964. ABC: 1/1/1966–9/2/1967. Hanna-Barbera/Ideal Toys/Screen Gems. Components: 1. **MAGILLA GORILLA.** Voices: Allan Melvin (Magilla Gorilla); Howard Morris (Mr. Peebles); Jean VanderPyl (Ogee). 2. **PUNKIN PUSS AND MUSH MOUSE.** Voices: Allan Melvin (Punkin Puss); Howard Morris (Mush Mouse). 3. **RICOCHET RABBIT.** Voices: Don Messick (Ricochet Rabbit); Mel Blanc (Deputy Droopalong). 4. **BREEZLY AND SNEEZLY.** (*See* PETER POTAMUS for details.)

Magilla Gorilla was the first of two syndicated liaisons between Hanna-Barbera and Ideal Toys (see also *Peter Potamus*). It was released with great fanfare, including an entertaining promotional half hour TV short in which announcer George Fenneman guided the viewers on a tour of the Hanna-Barbera studios, and managed to open in 151 markets during the week of January 14–21, 1964.

Like most other H-B syndies of the period, *Magilla Gorilla* was made up of three six-minute components. There has been some confusion over the years as to just which cartoon "stars" were seen on

Magilla. The following rundown is based upon contemporary *TV Guide* listings and the evidence of this writer's own 13-year-old eyes.

Headlining the series was Magilla Gorilla, a goodnatured gargantua who lived in Peebles' Pet Store. In a reversal of the Yogi Bear–Ranger Smith situation (see *Yogi Bear*), Peebles' mission was not to keep Magilla from escaping, but to get somebody to take the expensively hungry gorilla off his hands. The only person who *really* wanted Magilla was a little girl named Ogee (it was her favorite expletive—"Oh, gee!") who unfortunately couldn't meet Peebles' already marked-down asking price. *Magilla Gorilla's* second component, a joint takeoff of *Tom and Jerry* (q.v.) and the then-popular *Beverly Hillbillies*, starred Mush Mouse and Punkin Puss, a pair of feudin' mountain critters.

It was *Magilla Gorilla's* third component that has prompted inaccuracies in most current writeups on the series. When the show premiered, that third attraction was *Ricochet Rabbit*, from the *Quick Draw McGraw* (q.v.) school of TV-western parody. Sheriff Ricochet earned his name from his habit of bouncing from rock to rock in pursuit of miscreants (with a cry of "Bing—bing—biiiing!!!"). Assisting the rodent peacekeeper was Deputy Droopalong Coyote, a lampoon of *Gunsmoke's* deputy Chester Good, complete with Southern drawl and bad coffee.

Ricochet Rabbit appeared on *Magilla* until January of 1965, at which time Hanna-Barbera decided to pull a "crossover" to solidify the connection between this series and its other Ideal-sponsored syndie, *Peter Potamus*. The strategy was to make certain that *Magilla's* (q.v.) large audience would then spill over into *Potamus*, which wasn't doing quite so well in the ratings. Thus it was that *Ricochet Rabbit* moved to *Peter Potamus*, which in turn gave up one of its three components, *Breezly and Sneezly*, to *Magilla Gorilla*. In January of 1966, both *Magilla* and *Potamus* ended up on the ABC network weekend lineup (with new cartoons added to the existing syndicated manifest), swapping components so often that the relationship was nearly incestuous.

If one were to believe the aforementioned George Fenneman–hosted promo reel, *Magilla Gorilla* was the crowning achievement of the Hanna-Barbera mill, the ultimate goal for which all their previous projects were mere prologue. Many adult reviewers swallowed the bait: Ben Gross of the New York *Daily News* rhapsodized that "The producers of *The Flintstones* have another winner — it'll please the grownups and delight the youngsters." To some Hanna-Barbera fans, however, *Magilla Gorilla* seemed like warmed-over stew, with the best gags and central situations of their earlier series trotted out unimaginatively (save for the occasional clever visual pun) to fill up the half hour. Even the background music was recycled, evoking not so much laughter for *Magilla* as fonder memories of *Quick Draw McGraw* and *The Flintstones*. As for giving Magilla Gorilla a "Smarter than the average bear" type catch phrase, the best the writers could come up with was Magilla's put-upon complaint "I *resemble* that remark, sir."

Yet Hanna-Barbera's reputation, production polish and promotional expertise saved the day: *Magilla Gorilla* ended up the highest rated off-network kid's show in most of its markets, outperforming the far superior *Mickey Mouse Club* reruns. Perhaps this popularity was in great part the result of Ideal Toys' aggressive merchandising of tie-in *Magilla Gorilla* playthings — an aggressiveness brought on by the fact that the *Magilla* characters were specifically designed to be redefined in terms of dolls and toys, as a followup to the previous season's successful huckstering of Ideal's Pebbles Flintstone merchandise.

MANTA AND MORAY *see* **TARZAN**

MAPLE TOWN. Syndicated: 1987. Toei Animation/Tonka Toys/Saban-Maltese/Orbis. Executive producers, Haim Saban, Edd Griles and Ray Volpe. Supervising producer, Winston Richard. Executive in charge of production, Beth Broday. Vice president of production, J. Edward Bergh. Supervising director, Robert V. Barron. Associate director, Mike Reynolds. Written by Robert V. Barron, Mike Reynolds, Steve Kramer, Ben Lesko, Byrd Ehlman, Tom Weiner, Ardwright Chamberlain, Tony Oliver, Barbara Oliver. Live action produced and directed by Mary Jo Blue. Music by Haim Saban and Shuki Levy. Voices: Jeff Iwai, Wayne Kerr, Bebe Linet, Heidi Lenard,

Lou Pitt, John Zahler, Alice Smith. Live-action cast: Janice Adams (Mrs. Maple).

Maple Town was one of the few daily cartoon series of the 1980s to be syndicated with a live-action host. Janice Adams played Mrs. Maple, who'd greet the preschool home audience, delineate the lesson to be learned that day, then step aside and let the animation (just outside her kitchen window) take over.

Based on a line of cuddly Tonka toys, *Maple Town* spotlighted its titular, vaguely mittel European community (judging by costumes and props, the stories were set in the late 1920s), and the soft-and-squishy residents therein: Mrs. Raccoon, Bobby Bear, Patty Rabbit, Danny Dog, Mayor Lion, Funny Fox, Kevin Cat, Penny Pig, Susie Squirrel, the Beaver family — Bernard, Bitty and Bucky — and an unnamed bulldog sheriff. The almost oppressively cute atmosphere was occasionally (and thankfully) shattered by Maple Town's only criminal, Wilde Wolf, whose face was plastered on wanted posters all over town for the benefit of those animals who'd never seen a wolf before. In keeping with the overall gentility of the half hour series, Wilde Wolf's activities were more anarchistic than carnivorous: he'd rather break a window or tear down a house than chew on the Beaver family any day.

Produced within Saban's traditional boundaries of eye-pleasing graphic design and palsied animation technique, *Maple Town* ran for three whole weeks as a syndicated daily before the first rerun cycle settled in (there were only 15 episodes). After this, the half-hour program moved to cable TV, where it stayed put until the early 1990s.

MARINE BOY. Syndicated: 1966. Japan Telecartoons/K. Fujita Associates/Seven Arts. Produced by Minoru Adachi. Directed and written by Haruo Osanai. Background design by Akira Tomita. Art director, Yuichi Fukuhara. Music by Kenjiro Hirose and Setsuo Tsukahara. Theme music by Kenjiro Hirose. English version executive producer: Stanley Jaffee. English theme lyrics by Norman Gimble. Music by Norman Gould. Dubbing by Zavala/Riss. Dialogue adaptation by Peter Fernandez. Voices: Corinne Orr (Marine Boy/Neptina/Cli Cli); Jack Curtis (Dr. Mariner/various villains); Jack Grimes (Piper/Splasher/Dr. Fumble/Commander/

more various villains); Peter Fernandez (Bulton).

Earlier published reports that *Marine Boy* was among the first cartoon series to prepare scripts in the United States and then farm out the animation to Japan, were based on the American advertising campaign for *Marine Boy*, which stated as much. The ad copy was misleading. *Marine Boy* was not an American program produced in Asia; rather, it was a dual-country effort, released almost simultaneously in the United States and Japan in two separately dubbed versions.

The Asian version, produced between 1965 and 1968 by Minoru Adachi for Japan Telecartoons and distributed in its homeland by K. Fujita Associates, was titled *Kaitai Shonen Marine*. The title character (possibly patterned after National Periodicals' comic book character *Aquaman* [q.v.]) was the redheaded preteen son of underwater scientist Dr. Mariner, who under the aegis of the 21st century Ocean Patrol fought crime and oppression beneath the ocean waves. To sustain his air supply, the hero carried a supply of "Oxygum"— oxygen-packed tablets which when chewed would allow the chewer to breathe underwater (this element was left unexplained in many episodes, leading casual viewers to surmise that the human characters had all grown invisible gills). Kaitai Shonen Marine traversed the briny in his P-1 minisub in the company of crew members Bulton and Piper—who like all the other common seamen on this series incongruously wore French-style berets— as well as a hyperintelligent dolphin named Whity. He also had a vital underwater ally in the person of Neptina, a young mermaid who might well have been the first female TV cartoon character to appear "topless" (though she evidently had no breasts at all). To better battle his enemies, Kaitai Shonen Marine carried a lot of *Batman*-style hardware, notably his sonic boomerang, weapon-equipped boots, and electronic listening devices.

In its abundance of larger than life characters and florid dialogue exchanges, *Kaitai Shonen Marine* was as "sheer camp" as its American ad copy promised (after the premiere of *Batman* in 1966, the term "camp," once a vague reference to a film or TV series being corny or ridiculous without intending to be, was used as an umbrella term to describe any form of

deliberately exaggerated entertainment). It wasn't hard, then, for the American translating firm of Zavala/Riss to come up with dialogue that matched the dizzy exuberance of the Japanese scenarists. Nor was it hard to match the lip movements of the original cartoons, since the Japanese dialogue had adopted the same measured, deliberate pace as the animation, bypassing the usual translating problem of having the English-speaking actors talk at a super-accelerated pace to match the Japanese cadence.

Seven Arts Television domestically distributed the result, as had been planned by American producer Stanley Jaffee from the inception of *Kaitai Shonen Marine*; the U.S. title was *Marine Boy*. Unlike Japanese distributor K. Fujita, Seven Arts did not offer the series in a single package. To test the profitability of the syndicated market, only 26 episodes were offered at first, with a promise of 26 more should *Marine Boy* click. As it turned out, 75 half-hour color episodes made it into syndication, which many markets telecast on a Monday-through-Friday basis. *Marine Boy* enjoyed the formidable sponsorship of a major midwestern hamburger restaurant chain, and might have been the most successful Japanese import of the 1960s had not *Speed Racer* (q.v.)—also packaged in Japan by K. Fujita, though using different animation personnel—broken that record.

Little was changed beyond the spoken language when the series made its Pacific crossing; the only significant alteration was in the character names of the hero and of Whity the Dolphin, who became "Splasher" in the English version. Audiences in the U.S. were more than satisfied with *Marine Boy*. The series' limited animation technique and production design often exceeded American TV standards, with extra points scored by the elaborate undersea background art by Akira Tomita. The one main problem with domestic distribution of *Marine Boy* was the dilemma usually facing Japanese cartoons in the States; the violence, even the comic violence, was more intense than what was usually permissible in the late 1960s. Seven Arts was in fact compelled to remove three episodes from the original 78-program manifest due to excessive mayhem. What was left was still allegedly potent enough for the National Association for Better Broadcasting to kvetch that

Marine Boy was "one of the very worst animated shows. Child characters in extreme peril. Expresses a relish for torture and destruction of evil characters." In this instance, NABB chose to see only what it wanted to see. Rather than luxuriating in the demise of the villains, Marine Boy invariably tried to rescue his enemies from the perils that their own perfidy had gotten them into. When the baddies would ungratefully attempt to kill Marine Boy all the same, any fate that befell them was richly deserved. As was so often the case, the NABB had trouble differentiating wanton violence from standard dramatic story structure.

MARMADUKE see HEATHCLIFF

MARSUPILAMI. CBS: 9/18/1993–. Walt Disney Television Animation/Buena Vista. Produced by Ed Wexler, Bill Kopp, Jeff DeGrandis, Bob Hathcock. Director, MARSUPILAMI: Ed Wexler. Director, SEBASTIAN: Bob Hathcock. Story editors: Bill Matheny, Kevin Crosby Hoops. Voice directors: Ginny McSwain, Jaimie Thomason. Animation directors, Vincent Bassals, Marsh Lamore, James T. Walker. Direction supervisor: Karen Peterson. "Marsupilami" theme by John Beasley, John Vester, Ed Fournier. Additional themes by Ed Fournier, Alan Menken. Music by Stephen James Taylor and Mark Watters. Animation facilities: Akom Film Production Co., Ltd. Voices: Charlie Adler, Rene Auberjonois, Jim Cummings, Steve Mackall, April Winchell, Samuel E. Wright.

Le Marsupilami was a popular Belgian comic strip character created in the 1950s by Andre Franquin for *Spirou* magazine — the same publication that also unleashed Peyo's *The Smurfs* (q.v.) on the world. Redubbed simply "Marsupilami," Franquin's character was introduced to American TV audiences as one of two main components on Disney's *Raw Toonage* (q.v.) cartoon anthology in 1992. When this series was axed by CBS the following year, both *Marsupilami* and its companion feature *Bonkers* (q.v.) were split off into their own half hour programs. But while *Bonkers* went to daily syndication in a half-hour format, *Marsupilami* remained on CBS' Saturday morning schedule, still confined to short, 11-minute segments — again sharing its weekly, 30-minute slot with another Disney property.

The title character was a hyperkinetic, jungle-dwelling cheetah, who happened to have the world's longest tail (25 feet, give or take an inch). This appendage was utilized as a weapon, a climbing tool, a lasso, and any number of "Felix the Cat" type variations. Marsupilami could talk, which he did often and at the top of his voice. His musclebound pal Maurice the gorilla was nonverbal, but sure came in handy when fending off the various human hunters who tried to trap Marsupilami and cart him off to a zoo.

Sandwiched between the two weekly *Marsupilami* cartoons were the adventures of Sebastian the Crab, the Calypso-singing crustacean who costarred in the Disney film (and subsequent TV series) *The Little Mermaid* (q.v.). In the tradition of *Tale Spin* (q.v.) wherein animal characters from Disney's *The Jungle Book* were recast in essentially human roles, Sebastian was given the TV vocation of concierge at a lavish hotel, run by a Wagnerian human female closely resembling *Little Mermaid* villainess Ursula. Samuel E. Wright, the singer-actor who'd scored a hit with *Mermaid*'s Oscar-winning song "Under the Sea," was back to voice the TV Sebastian, as was fellow *Mermaid* alumnus Rene Auberjonois as the untrustworthy Chef Louie.

Both *Marsupilami* components bore less of the Disney influence than that of Warners' *Tiny Toon Adventures* (q.v.): innumerable sight gags and pop-cultural jokes at the expense of strong story values. But *Marsupilami* moved too quickly, and offered too many gut-level laughs, for audiences to complain that the plotlines were faulty. As of this writing, plans were finalized to further speed up the series' pace with a new component, developed by *Eek! The Cat* (q.v.) veteran Bill Kopp. I haven't seen Kopp's *Schnookums and Meat* (at least it wasn't on the *Marsupilami*s that I monitored just before this book's December 31, 1993, cutoff date), but studio and cartoon-industry enthusiasm concerning the property was high. "A dog and cat show where anything goes," was the assessment of *Marsupilami* producer Jeff DeGrandis, while Richard Pursel of *Wild Cartoon Kingdom* magazine described *Schnookums and Meat* as "a cross between old *Tom and Jerry* cartoons and *Mad* magazine's *Spy vs. Spy*." "Disney was great!" added Bill Kopp. "They left us alone to do what we needed to be funny."

Production stills and synopses indicate that *Schookums and Meat* might well stand as Disney's "answer" to *Ren and Stimpy* (q.v.), a suspicion strengthened by the presence on the production staff of *Ren and Stimpy*'s Lynne Naylor and Eddie Fitzgerald (cartoon collector and historian Mark Kausler handled character layout, another move in the right direction). But I wouldn't go as far as *Wild Cartoon Kingdom* did in describing the surrounding *Marsupilami* cartoons as a "Disney borefest." Fragmentary, yes. Incoherent, true. But *Marsupilami* was *never* boring.

THE MARVEL ACTION UNIVERSE. Syndicated: 1988. Marvel/ Orion/New World. Executive producers, Margaret Loesch Stimpson and Lee Gunther. Produced by Rick Hoberg, Larry Houston, Will Meugniot. Supervising producer, Stan Lee. Supervising director, Ray Lee. Animation directors: Neal Warner, Rudy Cataldi, Tom Ray, Eileen Dunn, Charlie Downs, Margaret Nichols, Stan Phillips. Story editors, Larry Parr, Will Meugniot, Larry Houston, Rick Hoberg. Storyboard direction: Hoberg, Houston, Meugniot. Voice director, Stu Rosen. Music by Rob Walsh. Executive in charge of production, Jim Graziano. Program administrator, Jean MacCurdy. Voices: Charlie Adler, Michael Bell, Robert Bockstael, Earl Boen, Barbara Budd, Wally Burr, Len Carlson, Andi Chapman, Cam Clarke, Joe Colligen, Peter Cullen, Shawn Donahue, Pat Fraley, Ronald Gans, Dan Gilvezan, Rex Hagon, Dan Hennessey, Ron James, Gordon Masten, Greg Morton, Noelle North, Allan Oppenheimer, Pat Pinney, Susan Roman, Neil Ross, Susan Silo, Kath Soucie, John Stephenson, Alexander Stoddart, Alan Stewart-Coates, Chris Ward, Frank Welker. (*See also* SPIDER-MAN for additional credits.)

The *Marvel Action Universe* was a syndicated, 90-minute weekend potpourri a la *Funtastic World of Hanna-Barbera* (q.v.), containing three separate half hour series which could be telecast all in one lump or separately on a weekday basis—the latter option chosen by most markets.

Component number one was a Spider-Man, a firmly established Marvel character who'd had already done service as two network series in 1967 and 1979 (see individual entry on this character) and as an abortive live action prime-timer. Spider-Man's 22-episode contribution to *Marvel Action Universe* consisted entirely of reruns from Marvel's 1979 network version.

The second component was derived from a "live" original: *RoboCop*, produced in association with Orion Pictures, was based on the very popular 1985 film about a 21st century Detroit policeman named Alex Murphy, who after his murder was converted by a shadowy computer products firm into an indestructible lawkeeping cyborg. The very presence of *RoboCop* pointed out the hypocrisy of the "R" rating bestowed upon the movie, for it was obvious that the youngsters in the audience were intimately familiar with a character whom they supposedly were prohibited from seeing (as this was television, the cartoon *RoboCop* was of course an "Officer Friendly" compared to the nihilistic cinema version).

The one wholly new component—albeit one based on a pretested formula—was *Dino Riders*, the exploits of 20th century adventurers thrust into prehistoric times. The heroic Dino Riders found plenty of trouble on their hands in the scaly person of Krulos, chief of the Vipers, who attempted to attach "brain boxes" to developmentally challenged T-Rexs in order to effect world domination. Most of the *Dino Riders* stories followed this fanciful pattern, with robot dinos designed by the series' toymaking sponsors thrown in, but there wasn't enough plot material nor strong enough characterizations to survive past 11 episodes, which was the most any of the *Marvel Action Universe* components lasted.

When first advertised, promises were made that *Action Universe* would include *five* half hour components, suitable for a weekday strip. Production schedule setbacks (animation was quite full, and somewhat cluttered at that) and the 1988 Hollywood writer's strike put the kibosh on those plans, but an intriguing—if overproduced—glimpse of what might have been was offered with a one-shot episode titled "Pryde of the X-Men"—the precursor to what would become Marvel's biggest TV hit of the 1990s, *X-Men* (q.v.).

THE MARVEL SUPERHEROES. Syndicated: 1966. Grantray-Lawrence/

Paramount/ARP/Krantz Films. Executive producer, Steve Krantz. Animation producer, Bob Lawrence. The *Marvel Superheroes* was a 1966 milestone in the world of cartoon kidvid. The series was one of the very few non-comedy projects offered on a syndicated, rather than network basis (*Gigantor* [q.v.] and most other adventure series were merely Japanese imports, while *Superheroes* was made by and for American TV), and one of the first mass-media acknowledgments that the comic book industry had developed a fan following above and beyond the comparatively innocuous Dell and Harvey lines previously committed to TV animation.

Five separate components made up the *Superheroes* package, each with a distinctive theme song and production staff, each based on the most popular of Marvel Comics characters (except for Spider-Man and the Fantastic Four, whose character rights had been committed to their own network starring series). *Sub-Mariner* was the oldest property of the batch, having been introduced by Marvel's predecessor Timely Comics in 1939. Created by Bill Everett, the Sub-Mariner was underwater-based Prince Namur of Atlantis, a sworn enemy of surface-level mankind. In his original adventures, Namur had no qualms about committing wholesale murder on land dwellers. He was in fact an antihero, who just happened to be on the side of Good because most of his enemies were nasty foreigners of indeterminate nationality who prattled on about world domination and the possibility of international war. The first incarnation of *Sub-Mariner* lasted until 1949. Marvel Comics and artist Gene Colan (working under the alias "Adam Austin") brought the character back to the comic pages in 1962 as a guest star in the "Fantastic Four" series, thence to his own starring comic book in 1965; no longer homicidal, Sub-Mariner still wrestled with contradictory alliances and attitudes when dealing with ordinary mortals.

Captain America, who before drinking a secret potion was spindly American G.I. Steve Rogers, had been created by Jack Kirby and Joe Simon for Timely Comics in 1941; after battling the Axis throughout the World War 2 decade, the Captain was dropped by Timely in 1949, save for a short desultory revival in 1954. Marvel reintroduced Captain America in 1963, ex-

plaining away the youthful physique of a middle aged man by claiming that the Captain had been placed in suspended animation 15 years earlier. The Captain's kid companion Bucky was de-emphasized in the *Captain America* cartoons, which concentrated more on the star's using his mighty magic shield against his principal wartime foe, the Red Skull.

The remaining *Marvel Superheroes* were of more recent vintage, mostly the brainchildren of Marvel chieftain Stan Lee. *The Incredible Hulk* was introduced by Lee and artist Jack Kirby in May of 1962. The eponymous star's alter ego was Doctor Bruce Banner, who became the green, shirtless, rocklike Hulk after being bombarded by gamma rays. Trouble was, Banner had no control over his other self, and was likely to turn into the Hulk at the most inopportune moments, usually wreaking destruction on anybody and anything that happened to be around. That the Hulk generally was more frightened than wicked, and that his victims usually were criminals who had it coming, were lost on the local constabulary which regarded the creature as a menace—which rested not at all well with the benighted Bruce Banner. This was the only *Superheroes* cartoon which made an effort to copy Stan Lee's irreverent and self-mocking style of captioning Marvel's comic book panels: *The Hulk's* theme song cheerily and with deliberate inaccuracy characterized the title character as "lovable" and "ever-lovin'."

The *Mighty Thor* was inspired by Norse legend (with a little of *Conan the Barbarian* added to the broth) and fleshed out in August of 1962 by Stan Lee, Lee's brother Larry Lieber and (again!) Jack Kirby. Another mild mannered doctor, this one named Donald Blake, turned into the mythological Thor when armed with a mystical walking stick—which metamorphosed into an all powerful "uru" hammer. Like his comic book counterpart, the cartoon Thor divided his time between earth and the celestial land of Asgard, where he commiserated with ruling god Odin and engaged in eternal conflict with the "god of mischief" Loki.

Iron Man was the alias for millionaire businessman Tony Stark, who in the comic book backstory had suffered a severe chest injury from a land mine in Vietnam, then was elevated to superstrength by an invincible iron flying suit originally built by

Communists as a weapon against the Americans. Stan Lee created *Iron Man* in 1963 (with the assistance of artist Don Heck) in the tradition of Lee's usual Achilles' heel–plagued heroes; Tony Stark was forced to be Iron Man because the armored suit had a device which kept his damaged heart beating. As with *Captain America*, Iron Man had a perpetual war-related nemesis, a modern Fu Manchu named the Mandarin.

Transferring the best of Marvel to the little screen was a project in development since 1965. The blockbusting popularity of *Batman* in 1966 prompted executive producer Steve Krantz to put the wheels in motion on *Marvel Superheroes* and to get 195 six-minute cartoons, budgeted at around $6000 each, committed to celluloid a.s.a.p.—September 1966 to be precise. This of course could not have been accomplished utilizing the old full-animation Hollywood methods, nor could the carefully preplanned corner-cutting Hanna-Barbera technique be properly utilized, since the time just wasn't there.

Bob Lawrence of Grantray-Lawrence Animation, a firm created in 1954 in association with longtime studio animators Grant Simmons and Ray Patterson to produce advertising cartoons, came up with the swiftest production method then available: Xerography. This was a copying process developed by Ub Iwerks which enabled the Disney Studio artists to transfer pencil sketches directly to animation cels for the 1961 cartoon feature *101 Dalmatians*. Working in concert with Marvel's Stan Lee, Bob Lawrence saw to it that several of the best Marvel Comics artists came up with fully articulated, action-posed drawings; these would then be Xerographed for the benefit of the cartoon inkers, painters, and animators.

The Marvel artwork far outshone most of the hit-and-miss character design then being seen on TV, which was more than could be said for the animation—though "animation" was perhaps too grandiose a term for a technique which frequently utilized camera pans and hand-jiggled cutouts to convey "movement." Grantray-Lawrence developed storyboards which allowed the cartoonmakers to work with extreme poses, which when intercut would give the *impression* of movement—very much the style then in vogue in Japan (see *Astro Boy*). For the most part the "ac-

tion" was confined to the characters' lip movements, and then it was merely a matter of opening lips on vowels and closing them on consonants.

Perhaps anticipating attacks from animation purists, Bob Lawrence insisted that the severely limited animation was actually *beneficial* for the "integrity and reality" of the characters—that by not fully animating the Superheroes, the producers were maintaining the charm and appeal the characters had had as immobile comic book personalities. Moreover, Lawrence suggested that by concentrating on suggested character movement, he was true to the Marvel "policy" of allowing the readers to give free reign to imagination. "The characters don't actually move," noted Lawrence in reference to the comic books, "and yet their actions seem to flow, catching the reader up in a current of activity." Theoretically, then, *The Marvel Super Heroes* encouraged the audience to create its *own* pictures of movement, thereby adding to the "fun." Bob Lawrence couldn't paint a rainbow, but he could sure spin a great description.

Fortunately, most of the artisans who worked on *Marvel Super Heroes* were able to transcend its tacky animation. Character designers Doug Wildey (see *Jonny Quest*) and Sparky Moore did a neat job streamlining Gene Colan's hard-to-imitate artwork of *Sub-Mariner* for the purposes of Xerography (though the animation itself was the weakest in the *Super Heroes* package). And the *Mighty Thor* cartoons had the inestimable advantage of being produced by the Shamus Culhane unit at Paramount Pictures. With an enthusiastic staff of Hollywood veterans and hungry "new blood" animators, Culhane was able to work around the strictures of Xerography to come up with some of the handsomest cartoons in all of 1966 television. The *Mighty Thor* still didn't move much, but he stood still so magnificently that no one really minded.

As it turned out, Bob Lawrence's cloaking himself in the banner of integrity was not as hollow a gesture as it seemed. Shorn of truly compelling animation, *Marvel Super Heroes* was obliged to rely heavily on its scripts—which, happily, were based on original stories by the superlative writing staff who'd placed Marvel Comics several cuts above the usual juvenile swill turned out by less adventuresome publishing firms. (Some plotlines were in fact based on comic book scenarios that had been written for the Marvel line but not yet published.) So as not to overly tax the staff, each *Superheroes* story was in the form of a cliffhanging serial—meaning that only one script was required for every three cartoon installments.

Riding into syndication on the capetails of *Batman*, *The Marvel Superheroes* managed choice timeslots in all the big cities and several medium-sized ones. Certain markets, like New York and Chicago, ran the full-color package in the next-to-prime slots between 6 and 7 P.M.—garnering excellent ratings thanks to younger viewers who were overwhelmed by the energy and willingness to please of the Marvel project (and who weren't bothered by the oversimplification of the original comic book plotlines, necessitated by the three-episode limit per adventure). As a tie-in, the series' distributors encouraged sales of the comic books by promoting their "Merry Marvel Marching Society," an informal fan club made up primarily of 12- to 15-year-old Stan Lee wannabes. This sort of promotional savvy on the part of Marvel was all the more profitable for the TV outlets who'd bought the series, since audience enthusiasm and involvement resulted in strong sponsor support.

Though generally out of favor with hardcore Marvel fans—so much so that Stan Lee, after initial public statements of how pleased he was with Grantray-Lawrence, was moved to eat his words and apologize for the cartoons—*The Marvel Superheroes* was a crucial factor in fomenting the "Animated Adventure" movement on TV in the years 1966 through 1968. This of course would ultimately boomerang in the form of negative reaction from the "Clean Up TV" activists, who might never have given Marvel's marvelously neurotic, nihilist comic characters a second glance had not younger viewers forced the issue by inviting the Hulk, Iron Man, Sub-Mariner, Captain America and Thor into the living room. (For more on *The Incredible Hulk*, see *Spider-Man*.)

M.A.S.K. Syndicated: 1985. Canada-France Co. Productions/DIC/ICC/Kenner-Parker/LBS. Executive producers, Jean Chalopin, Andy Heyward, Tetsuo Katayama. Produced by Jean Chalopin and Dennis Heroux. Creative supervisors, Jean Chalopin and Lori Crawford. Supervising chief directors, Bruno Bianchi and Bernard Deyries; assistant director, Michael Maliani. Supervising directors, Mineo Goto and Kazuo Terada. Story editors, Terrence McDonnell and Gary Warne. Music by Haim Saban and Shuki Levy. Voices: Doug Stone (Matt Tracker/ Nash Gorey/ Dusty Hayes/ Bruno Shepard/ Boris Bushkin/Max Mayhem); Mark Halloran (Buddy Hawkes/Ace Riker/Sly Rax); Brendon McKane (Alex Sector/Floyd Malloy/Miles Mayhem/Jacques LaFleur/Nevada Rushmore); Graeme McKenna (Brad/ Calhoun Burns/T-Bob); Sharon Noble (Gloria Baker/Vanessa Warfield); Brennan Thicke (Scott); Brian George (Lester Sludge/Jimmy Rashad).

M.A.S.K. was a five-a-week cartoon series chock-full of anagrammatic super-organizations, technohappy superheroes and supervillains, and futuristic transport vehicles and weaponry, all designed for the express purpose of having youngsters badger their parents for the accompanying line of Kenner toys. The letters of the title stood for Mobil Armored Strike Kommand, a secret (and evidently none too literate) crimefighting group headquartered in Central City and commandeered by Matt Tracker. M.A.S.K. was so nicknamed because of the group's propensity for donning specially designed masks, enabling them to carry out their activities with the added advantage of extraordinary powers; for example, Max Tracker wore a "spectrum" mask which gave him highly enhanced visual skills.

In emulation of *Mission: Impossible*, each *M.A.S.K.* episode opened with Max Tracker using a talking computer to help him choose the appropriate operatives for the job at hand—and, also like *Mission: Impossible*, those picked generally turned out to be the same people in each case. The M.A.S.K. team also had custom-designed vehicles to match their personalities (there's that merchandising creeping in again). Regulars included Buddy Hawkes, a master of disguise; Southerner Dusty Hayes, who drove a vehicle called "Gator"; driver/kung fu expert Gloria Baker; Brad Turner, hawkish driver of the "Condor" vehicle; Alex Sector, bearded computer whiz; Bruce Sato, technical genius, driver of "Rhino"; and weapons specialist Monk McLean, driver of "Firecracker." The team's special masks were kept secreted in an old mansion, and when the M.A.S.K.ers were assembled therein, their masks were installed mechanically (untouched by human hands; for what purpose, we don't know). Also around for the purpose of getting into mischief and being kidnapped was Max Tracker's son Scott, and Scott's pet robot T-Bob.

M.A.S.K.'s opposite number was a group calling itself V.E.N.O.M., populated by such public enemies as the overweight Max Mayhem and the dominatrix-like Vanessa Warfield. The acronym V.E.N.O.M. stood for Vicious Evil Network Of Mayhem. Wonder if they had a good dental plan? The plotlines had the air of déjà vu (especially to fans of *G.I. Joe*), but *M.A.S.K.* had a few points in its favor, notably the surprising low-key subtlety in the voice acting and some expertly rendered action sequences. The series' "prosocial" concession was a series of noncondescending safety tips that appeared at the end of each episode. Additionally, the 70-episode *M.A.S.K.* received some favorable press coverage in 1985 as the first syndicated cartoon series to be close-captioned for the hearing impaired. Now those so afflicted could finally see and fully appreciate such vital dialogue as "Look out!" "Ugghh!" and "Aiyeee!" It was odd that this particular program was selected for captioning, since the masks on *M.A.S.K.* were voice controlled, a gimmick that would have been lost on those who couldn't hear it.

One supposes that the Kenner Toy commercials were also close-captioned—for after all, the basic *raison d'être* of *M.A.S.K.*, once you stripped away its mask of entertainment value and instruction, was the sale and promotion of action figures.

MATTY'S FUNDAY FUNNIES *see* **BEANY AND CECIL**

MAX, THE 2000 YEAR OLD MOUSE. Syndicated: 1969. Krantz Animation/Quality Entertainment/ARP. Produced by Steve Krantz. Directed by Shamus Culhane.

Max, the 2000 Year Old Mouse was an engaging series of animated educational fillers, telecast as part of the weekday kidvid lineup so that local stations wouldn't be accused of total mindlessness. Produced for Steve Krantz by veteran Shamus Culhane (whose other, more elaborate collaborations with Krantz included *The*

Marvel Superheroes [q.v.] and *Spider-Man* [q.v.]), the four-minute spots featured a cheeky little mouse who didn't quite look the age designated him. In appropriate costume, Max would explain what world history topic would be discussed in the cartoon, then disappear while a narrator elucidated over the series of rare drawings, paintings, woodcuts and tintypes that followed. The purpose was to bring historical events into focus and perspective for children born long after the fact. Midway through the cartoon, Max would pop up in one of the vintage backgrounds, spout a pun or wisecrack, then defer to the narrator again.

It has been previously noted by both Jeff Lenburg and myself that the theme music for *Max the 2000 Year Old Mouse* was the same used for the later PBS movie-review series *Sneak Previews*. We should perhaps note further that the retreading of this theme demonstrated not only the tight budget of the original Siskel/Ebert *Sneak Previews* but of *Max* as well, since that particular composition was a stock public-domain piece that was in use on local TV stations long before *Max the 2000 Year Old Mouse* made its first appearance in 1969.

MAXIE'S WORLD. Syndicated: 1989. DIC/Claster. Executive producer, Andy Heyward. Produced by Cassandra Schafhausen. Supervising associate producer, John O'Sullivan Francis Jr. Directed by Marek Buchwald. Story editor, Judy Rothman. Script supervisors, Lori Crawford, Bill Ruiz, George Robinson. Written by Judy Rothman, Phil Harnage, Jack Olesker, David Ehrman, Sean Roche, Mike O'Mahoney, Kevin O'Donnell, Martha Moran, Pat Allee, Ben Hurst, Anthony Adams, Christina Adams, Betty G. Birney, Eleanor Burian-Mohr, Jack Hanrahan, Richard Glatzer, Doug Molitor, Celia Bonaduce, Lisa Maliani, Margaret Belgrade, Robin Lyons and Andrew Ollifer. Voice director, Paul Quinn. Music by Haim Saban and Shuki Levy. Lyrics by Joellyn Cooperman. Music supervision, Andrew Dimitroff. Vice president of creative affairs, Robby London. Executive in charge of production, Winnie Chaffee; assisted by Dawn Jackson, Stacey Miller. Voices: Loretta Jafelice (Maxie); Simon Reynolds (Rob); Tara Charendoff (Carly); Susan Roman (Ashley); Suzanne Coy (Simone); Nadine Rabinovitch (Jeri); Yannick Bisson

(Ferdie); Geoff Kahnert (Mushroom); John Stocker (Garcia); and Jeff Swanson, Gary Krawford, Diane Fabian. (See also *Beverly Hills Teens* and *It's Punky Brewster*.) *Maxie's World* was described by *TV Guide* as "a joint effort of Punky Brewster and *Beverly Hills Teens* [q.v.]." This did not mean that the established characters of the two above-mentioned series interacted with the newly minted characters on *Maxie's World*—merely that repeats of Ruby-Spears' *It's Punky Brewster* (q.v.) and DIC's *Beverly Hills Teens* rotated with first-run *Maxie's* episodes (also from DIC) to fill out the latter's 32-episode manifest, enabling the Hasbro-sponsored package to be syndicated on a Monday through Friday basis.

The half-hour *Maxie's World* featured a tall, tan teenaged girl named Maxie: "She's pretty . . . she's cool . . . she's exciting" exulted the ad copy. So were the rest of her beach-party friends at Surfside High School, all of whom had Malibu-bred names like Ashley, Rob and Simone (though they were more ethnically mixed than those names would suggest). As if her social life wasn't enough, Maxie was also a straight-A student and the host of her own weekly TV show! It was clear that any plot complications on *Maxie's World* would not grow from character imperfections on the part of Maxie, who was described expansively by the DIC promo staff as "the all-American teen" who was "probably the nicest, friendliest most unstuck-up person you'll ever meet."

One had the sneaking suspicion that "Maxie" was really supposed to be "Barbie." She well might *have* been the animated personification of Mattel Toys' popular dress-up doll, but Mattel had decided in 1988 not to license Barbie to DIC Enterprises for a daily cartoon series, fearing that the costume fashions depicted on such a program would become outdated and unsaleable after the first rerun cycle. Soon afterward, DIC aligned itself with Mattel rival Hasbro, and came up with an "almost" Barbie: *Maxie's World*.

MAYA THE BEE. Nickelodeon: 1/1/1990–12/31/1992. Produced 1982 and 1989. Apollo Film of Vienna/Zuge Elzo/Saban. Executive producer, Jerald E. Bergh. Associate producer, Eric S. Rollman. Music by Haim Saban and Shuki Levy. Musical direction by Alex Dimitroff. Based on "The

Adventures of Maya the Bee" and "Himmelsvolk" by Waldemar Bonsals. Voices: Pauline Little (Maya); Richard Dumont (Willie the Bee); R. J. Henderson (Flip the Grasshopper); Anna McCormick (Crimelda); Jane Woods (Cassandra).

Produced in Austria, *Maya the Bee* was based on characters created by children's novelist Waldemar Bonsals. The title character was a sprightly little female bee who did her best to carry on as normal a life as possible while foraging for sustenance and dodging natural predators. Maya's best friends included Willie, another adolescent bee, and Flip, a musical grasshopper.

Each half-hour *Maya the Bee* managed to tell a cogent story despite the frenetic pace imposed by the English-speaking voice actors' attempts to match the rapidity of the original Austrian lip movements. The series was full of wry little touches which "humanized" the animals and insects without taking them too far out of their true place in nature; for example, a band of soldier ants were shown to be as rowdy and disruptive as any overseas servicemen. The most disarming aspect of *Maya the Bee* was its depiction of Maya's "enemies"—the wasps, birds and other beings bent upon devouring her. These characters were not drawn as blackhearted villains simply because they were adhering to nature's food chain. They were quite reasonable creatures who enjoyed life and loved their families as much as Maya; it just happened that they were hungry, and bees had been on the menu for millions of years.

MEATBALLS AND SPAGHETTI. CBS: 9/18/1982–9/10/1983. Intermedia Entertainment/DePatie-Freleng/Marvel. Executive producers: David DePatie, Fred Silverman. Supervising producer, Jerry Eisenberg. Produced by Bob Richardson. Directed by Gerry Chiniquy, John Gibbs, Tom Ray. Music and lyrics by Steven DePatie. Written by Alex Lovy, Lew Marshall, Michael Jones, Jack Mendelsohn. Voices: Jack Angel, Wally Burr, Philip Clarke, Peter Cullen, Ronald Gans, Barry Gordon, David Hall, Sally Julian, Morgan Lofting, Ron Masak, Bill Ratner, Ronnie Schell, Marilyn Schreffler, Hal Smith, Frank Welker, Paul Winchell.

Meatballs and Spaghetti was an almost hallucinogenic animated attempt to duplicate the 1970s appeal of Sonny and

Cher. Meatball (one "s"), the fat husband, and Spaghetti, the thin wife, comprised a "mod" rock group, who found time for an original weekly song amidst some rather tepid comedy sequences. Costars on this short-lived half hour weekly were Clyde, Meatball's assistant, and Woofer, Spaghetti's dog. Was this *really* the best CBS could offer as competition for ABC's *Scooby and Scrappy-Doo?*

MEL-O-TOONS. Syndicated: 1960. New World Productions/United Artists Television.

Mel-O-Toons was a series of six-minute color fillers which used limited animation to illustrate preexisting children's records—those little yellow "45 rpm" discs with red labels that were tossed in free with the first record player you ever owned (remember?). Some cartoons featured famous legends, fairy tales and literary works, while others offered classical music as background to sugary animal stories, narrated by such top announcers as *The Jack Benny Program's* Don Wilson. The original intention of *Mel-O-Toons* was to highlight the works of Thornton Burgess (*Peter Cottontail, Paddy the Beaver,* etc.) with both live-action and cartoon segments. The series' expansion to 104 episodes necessitated going beyond Burgess for adaptable material.

METRIC MARVELS. NBC: Fall 1978–Fall 1979. Newall-Yohe.

Meter Man, Wonder Gram, Liter Leader and Super Celcius dispensed propaganda on behalf of the metric system (which people once upon a time believed would be unilaterally adopted in the United States) on *Metric Marvels*, a package of 150-second inserts scattered throughout NBC's 1978-79 Saturday morning schedule. The project was produced by Newall-Yohe, the same folks responsible for the similar instructional fillers *H.E.L.P.* (q.v.) for NBC and *Schoolhouse Rock* (q.v.) for ABC.

THE MICRO VENTURE *see* **BANANA SPLITS ADVENTURE HOUR**

MICRO WOMAN AND SUPER STRETCH *see* **TARZAN**

THE MIDNIGHT PATROL. Syndicated: 1990 (part of FUNTASTIC

WORLD OF HANNA-BARBERA). Hanna-Barbera/The Sleepy Kid Co., Ltd. Executive producers, William Hanna, Joseph Barbera, Paul Sabella. Executive producers for Sleepy Kids PLC and series creators: Martin Powell, Vivien Schrager-Powell. Executive in charge of production, Jayne Barbera. Supervising producer, Jeff Segal. Produced by Davis Doi. Executive producer on behalf of the BBC, Theresa Plummer-Andrews. Creative consultant, Mike Young. Supervising director, Ray Patterson. Directed by Don Lusk and Paul Sommer. Animation directors, Joanne Romersa, Sam Nicholson, Robert Alvarez, Joan Drake, Bill Hutten, Glen Kennedy, Ed Love, Tony Love, Irv Spence, Alan Wilzbach. Recording director, Gordon Hunt. Music by Michael Tavera. Background supervision, Al Gmuer, Pol Barona. Voices: Charlie Adler, Christina Avila, Michael Bell, Hamilton Camp, Brian Cummings, Jim Cummings, Judyanne Elder, Patrick Fraley, Dick Gautier, Joan Gerber, Dorian Harewood, Elizabeth Harnois, Whitby Hartford, Janice Kamaye, Emily Kuroda, George Lemore, David Lander, Marilyn Lightstone, Allan Lurie, Kenneth Mars, Scott Menville, Brian Mitchell, Howie Morris, Ron Palillo, Rob Paulsen, Henry Polic II, Clive Revill, Ronnie Schell, Tom Scott, Hal Smith, B. J. Ward, Frank Welker, Anderson Wong.

The 1990 edition of the *Funtastic World of Hanna-Barbera* (q.v.) weekend extravaganza scuttled *Paddington Bear* (q.v.) and *Superted* (q.v.) in favor of two new series. One of these was *Midnight Patrol,* a benign variation of the *Nightmare on Elm Street* concept of youngsters meeting one another in their dreams.

On this one, four suburban pre-teens would go to sleep each evening in their separate bedrooms, but not before promising to link up together in their collective "Dream Zone." The multiracial leading characters were African American Carter, an aspiring artist; bossy Rosie and her little brother Nick, the resident W.A.S.P.S.; and Asian American girl Kaiko, the most levelheaded of the bunch. Once in the Dream Zone, the kids united as the superpowered "Midnight Patrol," assigned to keep the peace in other children's dreams. Also part of the action was Carter's dog Potsworth, who upon attaining speech and intellect in the Dream Zone became an insufferable "Mr. Belvedere" know-all snob.

Potsworth and the kids would take their orders from the head of the Snooze Patrol (who answered to the Grand Dozer, a somnambulistic monarch dressed in Dr. Dentons). Their principal task was to protect the Dream Zone from the Nightmare Prince, who despite his forbidding name was a laughable loser with a domineering mother. The other major character was the Giant in charge of issuing props and fantasy surroundings for dream scenarios.

Midnight Patrol's concept originated in Britain as a tie-in to a line of children's sleepwear and bedroom playthings, all embossed with the image of Potsworth, who evidently was supposed to be the star (the series was retitled *Potsworth and Company* on videocassette). But neither the merchandising nor the series clicked. What might have been a surefire animation premise—the unfettered world of the subconscious imagination—was laid low by flat execution and misfire creative choices. Why, for example, did the "dream" world and the "real" world look exactly the same? Why was the "lovable" leading character Potsworth such an obnoxious upper class twit? Why would a program about sleeping kids be played out at such a drowsy pace?

THE MIGHTY HERCULES. Syndicated: 1963. Oriolo Studios/Adventure Cartoons for Television/Trans-Lux. Produced and directed by Joe Oriolo. Executive producer, Roger Carlin. Production coordinators, Arthur P. Brooks and "Big" Sid Ginsberg. Director of animation, Reuben Grossman. Animated by John Gentilella. Character design by George Peed. Story by George Kashman, Jack E. Miller. Background by Jim Vita. Edited by A. Rosenblum. Theme music sung by Johnny Nash. Music by Win Sharples. Voices: Jerry Bascombe (Hercules); Helene Nickerson (Helena); Jimmy Tapp (Newton/Tweet/Daedelus/Evil Wizard).

Hoping to capitalize on the popularity of the Italian *Hercules*, *Samson* and *Maciste* feature films making the neighborhood-movie rounds in the early 1960s, Joe Oriolo Studios assembled *The Mighty Hercules* as a full-color syndie package. A few liberties were taken with the Greek legend: Hercules now summoned strength by exposing his pinkie ring to lightning, he wasn't required to clean any stables, and he no longer worked solo. Now he was accompanied by the beauteous Helena of Calydon, the less beauteous Tweet the satyr, and Newton, that wimpy little centaur who drove viewers nuts by saying all of his lines twice ("Look at that over there, Herk . . . at that over there!"). The main villain, who skulked around covered by a blue hood, was Daedelus.

The Oriolo staff did wonders with the Learian Valley background art on *The Mighty Hercules*, and the character design—more "Captain Marvel" than Classic Greek—was clean-cut and precise. But the animation, though considerably better than Oriolo's previous *Felix the Cat* (q.v.) was less than Olympian. Nor were the storylines particularly Homeric, since they existed only as slender pegs on which to hang the wearisome hero-villain confrontations. In order to set up perils from which Our Hero could escape, the plotlines were often quite inconsistent with the "legend": If Hercules indeed had the strength of "ten ordinary men," as it was claimed in the opening titles, why did he usually wind up being stunned, trapped and threatened with imminent doom?

The 130 five-minute *Mighty Hercules* cartoons were heralded by a gushing, grandiose theme song, trilled by the golden-throated Johnny Nash: "Hercules, hero of song and story/Hercules, winner of ancient glory. . . ." The rest of the lyrics discussed such Herculean attributes as the softness of his eyes and the iron in his thighs, but I'll cut off here or else I'll be paying royalties. (See *Tarzan* and *Young Sentinels* for further cartoon variations on Hercules.)

THE MIGHTY HEROES. CBS: 10/29/1966–9/2/1967. Terrytoons/CBS Films. Created by Ralph Bakshi. Directed by Ralph Bakshi and Bob Taylor. Voices: Herschel Bernardi, Lionel Wilson.

In 1966, Ralph Bakshi, the young supervising director of Terrytoons, thought he'd have some fun with the burgeoning superhero craze inspired by the live-action *Batman*. At the same time, he'd show the contempt in which he held CBS, the network that had recently turned down several of Bakshi's non-superhero concepts. With *The Mighty Heroes*, Bakshi came up with a jovial justice league endowed with powers and personalities that were so ridiculous they made even the excesses of *Batman* look stodgily conservative.

The Mighty Heroes included Diaper Man, who'd have been more accurately named Diaper Baby, since that's all he was; a TV weathercaster who transformed into Tornado Man, not as fat as comic book artist Sheldon Mayer's "The Red Tornado" but just as clumsy; Cuckooman, who lived in a clock tower and looked like Charlie Chaplin dressed as a chicken in *The Gold Rush*; Ropeman, a onetime sailor who'd metamorphosed into a human lasso; and an ex–moving man called Strongman, the one character who actually looked dimly like a "real" superhero, albeit one with more brawn than brain. The Heroes' principal antagonist was the Junker, a run-down rapscallion who resembled an unholy amalgam of Snidely Whiplash and Quasimodo and whose cape was in dire need of patching. Other villains were wrought from the same mold: The Shrinker, The Stretcher, The Enlarger, and so forth.

Twenty five-minute episodes of *The Mighty Heroes* were bundled into half hour dollops for the CBS Saturday morning lineup during the 1966-1967 season. There they languished opposite the NBC competition: a near-lookalike "funny hero rally" from DePatie-Freleng called *The Super Six* (q.v.). Ralph Bakshi's earliest fans had a later opportunity to see this low-budget but highly uproarious project when 20th Century–Fox released ten of the *Mighty Heroes* episodes to theatres in 1969-1970. To anyone interested in sampling this engaging series, we suggest you keep an eye on the syndicated *Mighty Mouse* (q.v.) manifest currently offered by Viacom, of which *The Mighty Heroes* is sometimes a component.

MIGHTY MAX. Syndicated: 1993 (part of AMAZIN' ADVENTURES). Bluebird/ Canal + DA/Film Roman/Bohbot. Executive producer, Phil Roman. Co-executive producer, Rob Hudnut. Supervising producer/writer, Mark Zaslove. Produced by Gary Hartle. Executive in charge of production, Bill Schultz. Directed by Kyle James. Mighty Max character from Bluebird (U.K.). Developed for television by Rob Hudnut and Mark Zaslove, with inspiration from Breslow Morrison Terzan and Origin. Music by Cory Lerios and John D'Andrea. Executive in charge of production for Bohbot, Allen J. Bohbot. Animation facilities: Dong Yang Animation. Overseas supervisors, James Miko and Jeff Snow. Voices: Rob Paulsen (Max); Tony Jay (Virgil); Richard Moll (Norman); Tim Curry (Skullmaster); Tress MacNeille (Max's Mom); and Frank Welker, Corey Burton, Katie Leigh, Kath Soucie, Russi Taylor, among others.

Mighty Max was a weekly half hour expansion of a popular "pocket toy," small enough to stick in one's pocket until folded out for playing purposes. The player of the skull-shaped "Mighty Max" toy was obliged to guide its protagonist Max through a mazelike gauntlet to avoid being captured or terminated by the evil Skullmaster.

The TV Max was a typical preteen latch-key kid, left home alone by his working Mom to seek out his own amusements. To halt the Prosocial Police before they opened their mouths, the series' producers saw to it that Max had as much fondness for homework as for rock music and skateboarding—which was *not* how the character was depicted in the pre-release publicity, wherein Max was described as "intent on charming his way out of homework and household chores." In episode one, Max found himself the recipient of a mysterious package, containing an Egyptian statue embossed with a message written in hieroglyphics (which our studious hero was able to translate without stumbling over a single word) and a nondescript baseball cap.

The message lured Max to the local mini-mall, where he was introduced to Virgil, a talking bird who pompously called himself a "fowl" but whom Max (and the audience) took to be a small chicken. Virgil had waited 5000 years for The Chosen One: a hero with all the powers of good, the only person worthy of donning the "last cosmic cap to victory." This cap would enable the Chosen One to distribute virtue and wisdom throughout the world by means of a series of fourth-dimensional, invisible "portals." The anointed recipient of the cosmic cap turned out to be Mighty Max; "Mighty" was a "title of courtesy" which Virgil insisted upon and which Max despised. Once donning the cosmic cap, Max was endowed with awesome powers of magic and strength, and was also able to travel throughout time and space from portal to portal. Norman, a taciturn giant, was Max's official protector.

Max was prone to laugh off little Virgil until after barely escaping a fiery assault from the demonic, volcano-breath Skullmaster, master of Skull Mountain and Skull Dungeon (locales found in the foldout labyrinths of the original *Mighty Max* pocket game). Skullmaster had wiped out the portal-transit system through his own greed 10,000 years earlier, and was now determined to retrieve the cap and harness the Fourth Dimension for his own nefarious purposes. The Chosen Max had no choice but to join Virgil and Norman on dogooding missions spread out over a multitude of locales and timeframes. Eventually Max was joined on his quests by his mother, an attractive thirtysomething who went along for the ride so she could get in some shopping, and by his close friends Felix and Bea.

One of the best of the bountiful 1993 syndicated cartoon crop, *Mighty Max* was distinguished by sturdy story values, excellent computer animation effects and wholly credible background art. The "sword and sorcery" slant was offset by a sharp sense of humor and comic timing— especially on the part of Max, one of the most likeable of TV's animated adolescents—but the series never became so "jokey" or pop-culture conscious that it would become *outré* after the pocket game's popularity had dwindled. Most of the kidding was on the square, with Max letting off wisecracking steam after escaping innumerable near-fatal encounters with Skullmaster and his minions, the Lava Beasts. Conversely, the villains never kidded, and thus represented more genuine menace than was possible on, say, *Teenage Mutant Ninja Turtles* (q.v.), where the bad guys had evidently retained their own gagwriting staff.

The FCC-dictated "educational" aspect of *Mighty Max* was tied in with the hero's inveterate globetrotting. Each episode ended with a brief geography lesson, with Max using a map to point out where the story had taken place, and offering a quick rundown on that country's cultural heritage. These straightforward closing moments contained nary a trace of condescension or coyness; it was hard to believe that the same production company responsible for *Mighty Max* was also working concurrently on *Cro* (q.v.), which used its educational slant as an excuse to talk down to its audience.

THE MIGHTY MIGHTOR *see* **MOBY DICK**

MIGHTY MOUSE: 1. **MIGHTY MOUSE PLAYHOUSE** (All theatrical cartoons). CBS: 12/10/1955–10/2/1966. Terrytoons. 2. **NEW ADVENTURES OF MIGHTY MOUSE AND HECKLE AND JECKLE.** CBS: 9/8/1979–9/12/1982. Filmation. Executive producers, Lou Scheimer and Norm Prescott. Produced by Don Christensen. Directed by John Armstrong, Lou Zukor, Marsh Lamore, Gwen Wetzler, Kay Wright, Lou Kachivas, Marja Dahl, Ernie Schmidt. Written by Buzz Dixon, Sam Simon, Ted Pedersen, Bill Danch, Jim Ryan, Coslough Johnson. Music by George Mahana. Voices: Alan Oppenheimer (Mighty Mouse/Oil Can Harry); Diane Pershing (Pearl Pureheart); Frank Welker (Heckle/Jeckle/Quackula); Norm Prescott (Theodore H. Bear). 3. **MIGHTY MOUSE: THE NEW ADVENTURES.** CBS: 9/19/1987–9/2/1989. Ralph Bakshi Animation Productions. Directed and written by Ralph Bakshi, John Kricfalusi, Bob Jacques, Kent Butterworth, Mike Kazaleh, John Sparey. Artists included Tom Minton and Eddie Fitzgerald. Voices: Dana Hill, Beau Weaver, Patrick Pinney, Maggie Roswell.

The history of *Mighty Mouse* has been fully covered in other animation encyclopedias, so we'll just stick to basics here. In 1942, Terrytoons writer I. Klein became fascinated with Max Fleischer's *Superman* cartoons, and immediately set about concocting a comic parody of the Man of Steel. The first concept was Super Fly, rejected at the time but later fleshed out in the 1965 TV cartoon *Fearless Fly* (see *Milton the Monster*), and after a fashion, by the Hanna-Barbera 1965 TVer *Atom Ant* (q.v.). Paul Terry liked Klein's idea but felt a mouse was more appealing (he *always* felt a mouse was more appealing; take a look at Terry's rodent-ridden *Aesop's Fables* silent cartoons). The resultant cartoon, *The Mouse of Tomorrow*, had a mild-mannered mouse turn into a caped crimefighter after downing all the bodybuilding consumables in a supermarket—Super Soup, Super Cheese, etc. As "Super Mouse" the character appeared in several other Terrytoons before a licensing conflict with another Super Mouse (appearing in *Coo Coo Comics*) required a rechristening.

"Mighty Mouse," as the character was renamed, grew from a one-shot gag to Terrytoon's most popular star—even though, as Leonard Maltin has pointed out, the storylines were incredibly repetitious and the *deus ex machina* nature of the hero (he appeared at the tail end of most of his cartoons to rescue his mousy friends) meant that "Mighty Mouse . . . holds the distinction of spending less time on-screen than any other major cartoon star in history." Perhaps sensing the one-note quality of the character, the Terrytoons staff produced several diversions from the last-minute-rescue formula, mostly operatic melodramas (with dialogue sung rather than spoken) featuring Mighty Mouse saving his sweetie Pearl Pureheart from blackhearted machinations of top-hatted feline Oil Can Harry.

When Terry sold his entire *Mighty Mouse* manifest to CBS in 1955, the network, recalling the tremulous tenor used by the Mouse when singing his way through his "mellerdrammers," commissioned a theme song to open each half-hour weekly *Mighty Mouse Playhouse*. Over a montage of battle sequences, the kiddies were treated to an *a cappella* male chorus letting loose with the famous "Mister Trouble never hangs around/When he hears this might-y sound," whereupon Mighty Mouse (Tom Morrison) picked up the melody with "HEEERE I come to save the DAAAAYY"—which meant that Mighty Mouse was on the way. This opening, together with a few bumpers and a handful of Colgate Dental Cream commercials starring Mighty Mouse, comprised all that was new about *Mighty Mouse Playhouse*. Except for "Mighty Mouse Shows Where Your Pennies Go," an oft-rerun 1961 half hour cartoon on behalf of the UNICEF world relief fund, CBS was content to run 150 theatrical *Mighty Mouse* cartoons, together with a package of Terrytoons featuring other characters, for the next 12 years, with no new made-for-TV episodes included. And why should the network freshen up the package? *Mighty Mouse Playhouse* maintained an average 11.6 rating with a 45.8 percent audience share throughout its CBS run. No need to tamper with that kind of success.

But in 1967, the old Terrytoons were edged off the network and into syndication thanks to the up to date competition of superhero TV cartoons churned out by Hanna-Barbera and Filmation. It was the latter studio which, in tandem with CBS Films successor Viacom, brought *Mighty Mouse* back to life in 1979 with a package of brand-new cartoons, bundled together with the revival of another enduring Terrytoons property, the talking-magpie team of Heckle and Jeckle (who in the tradition of Mighty Mouse had had 104 of their theatrical releases played on CBS to excellent ratings from 1956 through 1961).

The 60-minute *New Adventures of Mighty Mouse and Heckle and Jeckle* followed TV-cartoon tradition of having the verbal humor carry the ball in lieu of brilliant animation, though the artwork was sprightly and in fact was a lot more energetic than some of the original Terrytoons. "Non violence" was the expected byword here: Mighty Mouse used his wits rather than his muscles to defeat Oil Can Harry, who in turn was motivated by greed and selfishness rather than lust in his tiltings with Pearl Pureheart. Likewise, Heckle and Jeckle were stronger on quips than on their patented mischief and practical jokes. And there was a new character wending its way through the program: Quackula, a vampire duck who slept in an egg-shaped coffin, and who, despite the producers' assurances that the character was "sure to be loved," was infinitely less lovable than Britain's *Count Duckula* (q.v.).

Mighty Mouse appeared in two weekly, cliffhanging seven-minute episodes set in Outer Space (it was the *Star Wars* era), plus one self-contained adventure; Heckle and Jeckle starred twice a week; and Quackula flapped about merely as a one-per-week filler (he disappeared, due to an obscure legal conflict with a similar comic book character, when the *New Adventures* was pared to a half hour for its second season). Additionally, Mighty Mouse was on hand to dispense the 30-second "environmental bulletins" and safety tips dictated by CBS, supervised by a team of academicians, and interwoven into the program between adventures.

Missing were all those operatic oratorios sung by Mighty Mouse in his theatrical-release heyday. "No more opera," insisted Filmation executive Norm Prescott in 1979. "I don't think that a singing superhero mouse would fly with contemporary audiences." Not even a flying superhero like Mighty Mouse.

Disregarding an overkill assessment of the series as "Mindless and monotonous" with "relentless violence-based humor" from a panel of children's TV experts assembled by *TV Guide*, the 16-week *New Adventures of Mighty Mouse and Heckle and Jeckle* was fun but antiseptic, just as Mighty Mouse himself had always been. Even if Filmation had *wanted* to be "relentlessly" violent, it was gagged and bound by the nonaggressive strictures imposed by CBS.

It would take former Terrytoons employee Ralph Bakshi (who'd directed some of *Mighty Mouse*'s valedictory episodes back in the early 1960s) to put some bite in this doggedly innocuous character. As part of an effort to expand its Saturday morning viewership past the 8 to 11 age range, CBS commissioned Bakshi to develop a new series for the 1986-1987 season: *Mighty Mouse: The New Adventures*. The three short cartoons per weekly half hour were the funniest and hippest *Mighty Mouse*s ever concocted. The Mouse of Tomorrow was hilariously introspective and self-doubting at times, making some of the episodes sound more like therapy sessions. His angst was doubled by his new "alter ego" identity as Mike Mouse, assembly line worker at Pearl Pureheart's factory. Being employed by his formerly helpless sweetheart was one of the many touches which dragged Mighty Mouse into the 1980s; another was his new pal Scrappy, an aggressively "ethnic" wise-guy character. With the help of an immensely talented director-writer staff including such old-timers as John (*Crusader Rabbit*) Sparey and relative newcomers like John Kricfalusi (see *Ren and Stimpy*), Ralph Bakshi managed to combine the mean streets quality of his and R- and X-rated cartoon feature films with the more restrictive sensibilities of children's television. (Kricfalusi and fellow *Mighty Mouse: The New Adventures* artisans Tom Minton and Eddie Fitzgerald had worked on the Filmation *Mouse* as part of a studio training program in the late 1970s. All three cartoonists would later comment that their unbridled wackiness on the Bakshi version was a form of "revenge" against the constrictions they'd suffered at Filmation, though in fact that studio's *Mighty Mouse* was funnier and more radically

animated than most of the studio's output.)

Most delectable were the parodies seen on *Mighty Mouse: The New Adventures*. The origin of Mighty Mouse was rewritten herein as a devastating lampoon of the Siegel-Shuster backstory for *Superman* (q.v.). *Alvin and the Chipmunks* (q.v.) was given a drubbing with "The Tree Weasels," three scrawny singing vermin who performed only because they lived in mortal fear of their ridiculously overaffectionate human owner. Best of all were the takeoffs on Terrytoons' own legacy. In "Ice Goose Cometh," Gandy Goose, Terrytoons star of the 1930s and 1940s, was thawed out after 40 years of suspended animation, only to fall victim to culture shock. After failing to redeem his World War II food ration stamps at a restaurant, Gandy ended up in the psychiatric ward, salvaged only after Mighty Mouse reunited the goose with his old cartoon costar Sourpuss the cat—who had become a skid row derelict! At the end, Mighty Mouse assumed his "reassimilation" job was over—until the thawing out of yet another Terrytoons hasbeen, Deputy Dawg (q.v.).

Then there was the now-notorious September 12, 1987, episode "The Littlest Tramp"—the one where a temporarily weakened Mighty Mouse renewed his strength by sniffing a white flower that had been doctored with health-inducing vegetables. What Religious Right media gadfly Rev. Donald Wildmon was doing watching *Mighty Mouse* that morning was anybody's guess, but the results were volcanic. Wildmon declared that the Mouse's reliance on a white flower was a thinly disguised paean to cocaine, exploiting Bakshi's past history as an icon of 1960s counterculture to bolster his argument. Charges and countercharges flew like warheads between Wildmon and CBS, but the victory was the reverend's: when "The Littlest Tramp" was rebroadcast, the "offensive" flower-sniffing bit was cut. (That same year, *Mighty Mouse* was honored with an award from another watchdog group, Action for Children's Television. Go figure.)

Some observers assume that it was Wildmon's censorial pressure that resulted in the ultimate cancellation of *Mighty Mouse* after only two seasons. Not so. The real reason was superbly summed up by TV critic Ron Powers, who noted that, although *Mighty Mouse: The New Adventures* was a hit with adult viewers (as intended), it failed to deliver the vital children's audience, which tuned to the ABC competition, *Animal Crack-Ups*. "The baby boomers were watching," noted Powers, "but the 2-to-11s weren't." Since it was that demographic group to whom sponsors were pitching their Saturday morning wares, *Mighty Mouse: The New Adventures* was cancelled. A syndicated-rerun revival is long overdue.

MIGHTY MR. TITAN. Syndicated: 1965. Mister Titan Productions/Trans-Lux. Producer: Richard H. Ullman.

Mighty Mr. Titan was apparently a package of three-and-a-half-minute color cartoons about a super-robot. Its existence is corroborated by the pages of *Broadcasting* magazine, which in the 1950s and 1960s kept a weekly tally of the number of sales made of various syndicated programs to local TV outlets. There we find a *Mighty Mister Titan* series, distributed by Trans-Lux (which also handled the animated *Felix the Cat* [q.v.] and *The Mighty Hercules* [q.v.]) and ostensibly produced by Richard H. Ullman of *Colonel Bleep* (q.v.) fame, which started toting up sales in April of 1965. After that, the rest is silence. Whether *Mighty Mr. Titan* was actually the American title of a long-forgotten Japanese offering, and whether the series actually attained release under *another* title from another distributor have been lost to posterity. The search for the full story goes on.

MIGHTY ORBOTS. ABC: 9/8/1984–8/31/1985. TMS Entertainment/MGM UA/Intermedia. Producer for MGM UA: Fred Silverman. Produced by George Singer, Tat Ikeuchi, Nobuo Inada. Supervising producer, Sachiko Tsuneda. Directed by Osamu Desaki and Yutaka Fujioka. Music by Yuji Ohno. Created by Barry Glasser. Story editor, Michael Reaves. Story consultant, Hideo Takayashi. Voice director, Howard Morris. Theme by Tom Chase and Steve Rucker. Associate producers, Marilyn Kouvalchuk, Mitsuo Yoshimura, Rikio Yoshida. Co-producer, Youichi Ikeda. Voices: Sherry Alberoni (Bo); Julie Bennett (Boo); Jennifer Darling (Dia); Barry Gordon (Robert Simmons); Jim MacGeorge (Bort); Robert Ridgely (Returns); Don Messick (Rondu/Crunch); Bill Martin (Umbra/Tor); Noelle North (Ohno); Gary Owens (Narrator).

One approaches *The Mighty Orbots* with a feeling of déjà vu, since so many of the program's ingredients have been seen so often elsewhere. Set in the 23rd century, the series' plot was motivated by its villain: Umbra, cyborg ruler of the Shadow Star, a multi-eyed computer sun. It was Umbra's mission to destroy the Earth, a goal blocked by the Galactic Patrol, headed by one Rondu. Geeky Galactic Patrol scientist Rob Simmons, who worshipped Rondu's daughter Dia from afar, demonstrated his devotion to both boss and boss' offspring by developing a team of five friendly robots, called "orbots" because of their space-flight propensity ("orbit" plus "robot").

The Orbot troop included both male and female cyborgs. Of the males, Tor looked and behaved like the earlier Japanese robot Gigantor (q.v.); Bort could metamorphose into any size and shape, occasionally suffering from an identity crisis as a result; and Crunch evidently earned his name from his habit of eating everything in sight (except humans). The females included Bo and Boo, twins distinguished by different colors; Bo could control the elements, while Boo was a metallic speed demon. And finally there was Ohno (the latter evidently named after Yuji Ohno, *Mighty Orbots*' musical director), an obnoxious little-girl cyborg who labored under the assumption that she was in charge of the Orbot squad. In moments of real peril, the five Orbots pooled their talents and united into a huge super-robot, and it's a wonder with all this heavy metal that Umbra survived 13 episodes—or that the audience did, for that matter.

With such similar cartoon properties as *Transformers, Voltron, Challenge of the Gobots* and *Macron 1* floating about (see individual entries on these series), it's surprising that *Mighty Orbots* retained any identity of its own. But while producer Fred Silverman indulged his usual mid-1980s tendency of imitating presold formulae, he gave *Mighty Orbots* a Tiffany setting which deflected its familiarity. The color scheme was eyecatchingly creative, with a particularly pleasing use of green hues. Animation was unusually elaborate for a 1984 Saturday morning series; there was an almost stereoscopic depth of field separating characters and hardware, while the background art swirled and rippled perpetually, like the Universe itself (or at least in the manner of a radar weather map). Some of the animation budget was amortized by heavy reliance on stock footage from earlier episodes (disguised as "flashbacks"), but this didn't really detract from the series' overall professional polish.

As for the producers' approach to the material, the series emulated *Mighty Orbot* member Bort: confused and a tad schizophrenic. No one seemed sure whether to take a straight, tongue-in-cheek, or outright camp point of view. One of the Orbots would go into what amounted to a comedy routine, then there'd be a dead serious plot development involving the villains, and then this would be undercut by narrator Gary Owens' mockingly pompous delivery of lines like "What a fiendish plan! Wait 'til our heroes hear about it!"

Mighty Orbots was derivative, but at least endeavored to carve its own individual niche, ragged though that niche was at times. Unfortunately, the series rammed up against the league-leading *Smurfs* (q.v.) on NBC and the new *Muppet Babies* (q.v.) on CBS — meaning that practically the only people watching were the immediate members of the Fred Silverman family.

THE MIGHTY THOR see MARVEL SUPERHEROES

MIGHTYMAN AND YUKK see PLASTICMAN

THE MILTON THE MONSTER SHOW. ABC: 10/9/1965–9/2/1967. Hal Seeger Productions. Produced by Hal Seeger. Directed by Shamus Culhane, Myron Waldman, James Tyler, Tom Golden, Arnie Levy (among others). Written by Jack Mercer and Kim Platt. Music by Win Sharples. Components: 1. **MILTON THE MONSTER.** Voices: Bob McFadden (Milton); Dayton Allen (Professor Weirdo); Larry Best (Count Kook). 2. **FEARLESS FLY.** Voices: Dayton Allen (Fearless Fly); Bev Arnold (Florrie Fly). 3. **PENNY PENGUIN.** Voices: Bev Arnold (Penny Penguin); Dayton Allen and Hettie Galen (Penny's parents, Chester and Beulah). 4. **STUFFY DURMA.** Voices: Dayton Allen (Stuffy Durma/Bradley

Brinkley). 5. **MUGGY DOO.** Voices: Larry Best (Muggy Doo). 6. **FLUKEY LUKE.** Voices: Dayton Allen (Flukey Luke); Larry Best (Two Feathers).

At first glance, 1965's *Milton the Monster*, a genteel parody of the *Shock Theatre* brand of old-time horror film, would seem to be a swipe from *The Munsters* and *The Addams Family*, two then-current sitcoms of a similar nature. Actually, *Milton* was in production long before either *Munsters* or *Addams* made their prime time debuts in 1964, and had originally been slated for a fall 1964 premiere. It was merely a series of production delays that caused *Milton the Monster* to make its appearance a year after the two above-mentioned live action series were established; originally, the cartoon program was less follower than leader.

The half dozen six-minute components seen on *Milton the Monster* represent the only consistently funny TV material ever bankrolled by producer Hal Seeger. Perhaps it was because *Milton* couldn't be adversely compared to an earlier prototype, as was Seeger's *Out of the Inkwell* (q.v.). Perhaps it was because the series didn't look like a cheap ripoff of someone else's bright idea, as did Seeger's *Batfink* (q.v.). Or perhaps it was because the talent lineup of *Milton's* production staff was comprised of the last courageous gasp of the old Paramount/Cartoon Studios regime, from directors Shamus Culhane (who dreamed up the name "Milton the Monster" in the first place) and Myron Waldman, to screenwriter Jack Mercer (see *Popeye* for more on Mercer).

The star component, *Milton the Monster*, was set on Horror Hill in Transylvania City (sic). Professor Weirdo (the short one) and Count Kook (the tall one with the pencil mustache), having populated their creepy castle with such mutants as Heebee and Jeebee (one was a hirsute cyclops, the other a skeleton, but I'm hard pressed to tell which was which), decided to concoct a fearsome, Frankensteinish man-monster. Unfortunately, far too much "Tincture of Tenderness" was spilled into the soup, and the result was the oversized Milton, who spoke in a Southern drawl reminiscent of character comedian Grady Sutton, and whose tender heart was matched only by his clumsiness and his voracious appetite. Milton tried to be helpful — he came in real handy roasting marshmallows with the little smokestack puffing out of his head—but mostly he was an expensive nuisance, and Prof. Weirdo and Count Kook stayed up nights wondering how to gently oust the big clod from the castle.

The *Milton the Monster* component was featured each week along with *Fearless Fly*, a Superman/Mighty Mouse mélange about a meek little cowboy-hatted fly named Herman who turned into the "fearless" galoot of the title whenever donning his atomic-powered glasses (a Hanna-Barbera super-insect creation of like vintage, *Atom Ant* [q.v.], took a similar metamorphic route). Herman/Fearless' girl friend was Flora Fly, his rival was Horsey Fly, and the villains (who had all the best lines and bits of business) were headed by the insidious but penurious Dr. Goo Fee and his hapless henchman Gung Ho. To keep things in the family, Professor Weirdo of the *Milton the Monster* episodes made a few "crossovers" into *Fearless Fly* territory—his sudden conversion into villainy explained by the narrator as a temporary "mad scientist" spell.

Four separate cartoon series took turns as *Milton the Monster's* third component. *Penny Penguin*, a self-styled "brat" of a little girl bird, was a chip off the old Paramount *Little Audrey* cartoons—the obnoxious kid whose efforts at helping her parents (Chester and Beulah Penguin) invariably resulted in catastrophe. Surprisingly, this basically toothless entry offered some of *The Milton the Monster Show*'s most pungent dialogue. When Penny's frog escaped in one episode by jumping into the blouse of a lady tourist, the woman giggled at the sensation, turned to her male companion, and said "Oh, you mad, impetuous boy!" Where was ABC's Standards and Practices *that* Saturday morning?

Penny Penguin wasn't always this clever, but it was a lot more worthwhile than its alternate components. *Flukey Luke* was a tiresome cowboy parody (undercover cowpoke vs. the notorious Spider Webb) redeemed only by the incongruous Irish brogue given Flukey Luke's faithful Indian companion Two Feathers; and *Muggy Doo* was a threadbare "softhearted con man" saga featuring a foxy cat. So dull were these characters that most of their adventures have been weeded out of the present *Milton the Monster* syndicated package.

The best we've saved till last: *Stuffy Durma*, the adventures of a pint sized hobo who inherited ten million dollars and was installed much against his will in a huge mansion. Despite the strenuous efforts of private secretary Bradley Brinkley to turn Stuffy Durma into a gentleman, a pillar of the community and a business tycoon, Mr. Durma preferred to surround himself in the trappings of indigence. Stuffy invited his hobo pals Stu Mulligan and Ashcan Annie to live with him; he kept his bindlestiff duds hidden in his sumptuous wardrobe; he required the butler to wake him up in the morning by tapping his feet with a billy club; and his transportation of choice was riding the "rails" (i.e. the running board) of his Rolls-Royce. *Stuffy Durma* was easily the most entertaining ingredient of *Milton the Monster*, as well as the most inventively designed; the "shallowness" of Stuffy's wealthy confreres and snooty servants was represented by drawing the characters like paper cutouts, revealing a pancake-flat face whenever turning their profiled heads from side to side.

The Milton the Monster Show was no *Rocky and His Friends* (q.v.), but it was a lot more fun than its present obscurity would suggest. Apparently ABC thought so as well, since the 28-week series was kept rerunning away in the network's Saturday morning lineup for two seasons.

THE MINI MONSTERS *see* **COMIC STRIP**

MISSION: MAGIC. ABC: 9/8/1973–8/31/1974. Filmation. Directed by Don Christensen, Hal Sutherland, Jack Townsley, Rudy Larriva, Bill Reed. Written by Mark Richards, Ben Starr, Jim Ryan, Bill Danch. Voices: Rick Springfield (Himself); Erika Scheimer (Miss Tickle); Lola Fisher (Carl/Kim); Lane Scheimer (Vickie/Franklin); Howard Morris (Harvey/Socks/Mr. Samuels/Tolamy/Tut-Tut).

Mission: Magic was spun off from "Teacher's Pet," an episode of Filmation's *The Brady Kids*, though it also owed something to the live-action series *Bewitched* and *Nanny and the Professor*. The protagonist of this weekly half hour was Miss Tickle, a schoolteacher whose magical powers enabled her prize pupils Harvey, Franklin, Carol, Vinnie, Kim, and Socks—not to mention her pet cat Tut

Tut—to pass through an enchanted chalk circle on her blackboard into a timeless fantasy world, much to the dismay of the "Mr. Weatherbee" type principal Mr. Samuels. Of interest was the network-imposed inclusion of popular Australian singer Rick Springfield, who provided voice to an adventuresome cartoon character named after him—nearly a decade before Springfield's "official" TV acting debut as a regular on the ABC soaper *General Hospital*. Like Miss Tickle, Rick Springfield had a pet animal, this one an owl named Tolamy (evidently Miss Tickle's curriculum contained small Latin and less Greek, otherwise she'd have taught Springfield how to spell the Greek name "Ptolemy").

Springfield also sang on the program. We mention this because of a comment made by the National Association for Better Broadcasting, which raked *Mission: Magic* over the coals for its "eerie settings and music." And while you're digesting the notion that Rick Springfield's crooning could in any way be eerie, we'll continue with the NABB condemnation: "Robbery, gangs and other sordid ingredients in cheap mediocre animation."

MISTER BOGUS. Syndicated: 1991. Y C Alligator Films/Zodiac/Calico Entertainment. Produced and directed by Tom and Claudia Zeitlin-Burton. Character created by Ghislain Honore and Michael Durieux. Series created by executive producer Peter Keefe. Music by Dale Schacker. Production facilities: Davinci Animation of Korea/Heiler-Lee Productions. Voices: Cam Clarke (Bogus); and Tress MacNeille, Pat Fraley, Jeanne Elias, Neil Ross, Jim Cummings, and Russi Taylor.

Mister Bogus was a "truly unruly" but goodnatured gremlin who resided in the walls of a typical American household. Instead of deliberately wreaking mischief on the human residents as gremlins are supposed to, Mister Bogus tried his misguided best to help the family, adopting numerous disguises along the way. It would have been frightfully original for his good deeds *not* to backfire—but then, there wouldn't have been any laughs that way.

The weekly half hour *Mister Bogus* was produced by Zodiac/Calico in the wake of the huge success of the 1990 Z-C release *Widget, the World Watcher* (q.v.). Unlike *Widget, Bogus* came with no ecological

message attached; its avowed mission was the audience's unbridled amusement. It succeeded in this and in being attractively animated and designed, with well produced stop-motion clay model "wraparounds" tying the *Mister Bogus* package into a pretty, profitable parcel. The series was the number one weekly syndicated program for two- to 11-year-old viewers in its first season. Two years later, Zodiac went from weekly to daily with *Mister Bogus*, with plans to expand the character into a group of theatrical animated shorts, designed as companion pieces for other studios' cartoon features.

MISTER MAGOO: 1. MISTER MAGOO. Syndicated: 1960. UPA. Produced by Henry G. Saperstein and Steve Bosustow. Directed by Abe Levitow. Voices: Jim Backus (Mister Magoo/Mother Magoo); Julie Bennett (Millie); Paul Frees (Tycoon Magoo, others); Richard Crenna (Hamlet); Jerry Hausner (Waldo/Prezley); Daws Butler (Prezley); and Mel Blanc, Henny Backus, June Foray, Joan Gardner, and Barney Phillips. **2. THE FAMOUS ADVENTURES OF MISTER MAGOO.** NBC: 9/19/1964–8/21/1965. UPA. Produced by Henry G. Saperstein. Directed by Abe Levitow, Robert McKimson, Gerald Baldwin, Steve Clark, Alex Lovy. Music by Carl Brandt. Voices: Jim Backus, Marvin Miller, Paul Frees, Shep Menken, Julie Bennett, Howard Morris, Joan Gardner, Everett Sloane. **3. WHAT'S NEW, MISTER MAGOO?** CBS: 9/10/1977–9/9/1979. DePatie-Freleng. Produced by David DePatie and Friz Freleng. Directed by Sid Marcus, Robert McKimson, Spencer Peel. Music by Doug Gordon, Eric Rogers, Dean Elliot. Voices: Jim Backus (Mister Magoo); Frank Welker (Waldo); Robert Ogle (McBarker). **4. MISTER MAGOO.** (all rebroadcasts from earlier UPA series) USA Network: 9/18/1989–1990.

Nearsighted Mr. Magoo is today widely regarded as one of the most lovable cartoon creations of all time. And that's the whole problem. He certainly didn't *start* that way. Once upon a time, he was funny.

Many stories have been told of the development of Magoo (no one currently subscribes to the 1950s party line that the character was dreamed up by self-aggrandizing UPA head Steve Bosustow). Animator John Hubley claimed he based the Myopic One on his own uncle Harry

Woodruff, a bombastic know-it-all who refused throughout his life to be confused by facts. Another theory is that Magoo was based on onetime Warner Bros. animation head Eddie Selzer, a "kicked upstairs" executive who was famous for his utter lack of knowledge of what went into cartoon production and for his angered response to a chucklesome story conference: "And just what the hell has all this laughter got to do with the making of cartoons?" And there are those who suggest that Magoo would never have come into full flower without the contributions of voice actor Jim Backus, whose cackling "boor in the club car" character (based, Backus claimed, on his own businessman father) had been heard on several radio series before Mr. Magoo's official debut in the 1949 UPA short *Ragtime Bear*.

It's probably unimportant how Magoo got there—the important thing is he *was* there. Though *Ragtime Bear* ostensibly starred a dumb-teenager type named Waldo, the show was stolen by Waldo's "Uncle" Magoo. In his earliest appearances, Magoo was frankly an old fart. The humor of his mistaking a bear for his nephew Waldo grew not so much from Magoo's nearsightedness as from the character's stubborn insistence upon seeing only what he *wanted* to see. Even if someone had told Magoo that his nephew was a bear, it wouldn't have mattered; Magoo's mind was a steel trap that had snapped shut years ago. To top it off, he was an unregenerate Eastern-seaboard snob, resistant to any sort of "radical" threat to his insulated lifestyle. It wasn't enough for him to mistake a dingy alley for his old college dance hall; Magoo had to pinpoint his snooty persona precisely by shouting, "By George, they've redecorated the ballroom without consulting the members!"

Audiences responded enthusiastically to this new cartoon antihero (just as audiences would respond to the similarly narrowminded Archie Bunker in the 1970s) and soon Mr. Magoo became UPA's most valuable property. The studio staffers went so far as to write up a biography for "the little jerk": He was a McKinley Republican, a 1902 graduate of ultraconservative Rutgers University, etc. The fact that Magoo was a direct attack on the sort of blind xenophobia that had brought about the Communist "witch hunt" of the early 1950s was lost on laughing moviegoers; they loved the ridicule heaped upon Magoo, and they wanted more. Nor were only the "have-nots" amused at the expense of the "haves." So democratic was the effect of *Mr. Magoo* on an audience that, during the 1960s and 1970s, a major Hollywood audience-testing firm would run a *Magoo* cartoon just before a new sitcom pilot episode was shown to a preview audience. The cartoon was meant as a "leveller"—a means of getting everyone laughing at once, to see how an equally entertained group of diverse public types would respond to the pilot.

The longer Mr. Magoo remained a series character, the less truculent and the more lovable he became. John Hubley resisted this metamorphosis, but fellow UPA director Pete Burness and others who worked on the Magoo series insisted upon softening the character in order to maintain his appeal with younger cartoon fans. Burness would later confess to Howard Rieder (whose Master's thesis on *Mr. Magoo* was developed into an article for *Cinema Journal*) that, in retrospect, he felt the character would have been stronger had the nastiness been retained. Audiences, however, tended not to mind a mellower Magoo, nor did the movie industry itself, which bestowed two Oscars on the character (*When Magoo Flew* [1954] and *Magoo's Puddle Jumper* [1956]). By the time UPA decided to enter the syndicated TV cartoon market opened up in 1958 by Hanna-Barbera's *Huckleberry Hound, Mr. Magoo* was the studio's hottest property and the most logical transferee to the small screen.

Under the aegis of UPA head Henry G. Saperstein—employing virtually none of the UPA personnel who'd worked on the Magoo vehicles in the 1950s—130 five-minute, full color *Mister Magoo* cartoons were produced for television between 1960 and 1962. Saperstein, who ran a merchandising firm called Television Personalities, was experienced in marketing cartoon characters for toy and game manufacturers, and applied these well-honed skills in getting the new *Magoo* series booked in all the top TV markets by the middle of 1960. The plan was for Kellogg's cereals to sponsor the property (to be shown in half-hour segments, four short cartoons per program) in much the same manner that Kellogg's was then underwriting Hanna-

Barbera's *Huckleberry Hound* and *Quick Draw McGraw*. But the cereal firm had a clause in its contract allowing it complete control in program content, meaning that Kellogg's would be allowed to veto any storylines or individual gags that failed to satisfy the company's advertising arm. Where UPA had had no qualms in making Mr. Magoo more likable for theatrical consumption, it refused any further compromises with the character on sponsorial grounds (see *Woody Woodpecker* for examples of the cereal company's interference). Kellogg's and UPA parted company, whereupon the studio marketed *Mr. Magoo* on a city-by-city basis on its own, drumming up local sponsorship — and being ever so careful not to have *Magoo* scheduled opposite another 1960 syndie, *Hot off the Wire*, which also starred Jim "Magoo" Backus! As for Kellogg's, the newly created gap in their 1960-1961 programming manifest was filled on demand by Hanna-Barbera's *Yogi Bear* (q.v.).

The decision by UPA to use stylized limited animation in its theatrical product was an artistic one; in TV, it was a matter of survival. *Mr. Magoo* was ground out so quickly that it's amazing anything of quality emerged. Most of the cartoons are enjoyable, but hampered by sloppy artwork, threadbare background design, and clumsy editing and sound recording. And Magoo himself (given the name "Quincy" for the first time in the TV cartoons) was a mere shadow of the fascinating character who debuted in *Ragtime Bear*. The subtext that his myopia was as much psychological as physical was all but lost: TV's Mr. Magoo was blind as a bat, and that was the series' only joke. The gags involving his inability to see anything for what it really was were so strained and exaggerated that at times Magoo appeared more senile than optically challenged. And, as movie encyclopedian Leslie Halliwell has noted, "[Magoo] quickly became a bore." Even Jim Backus, who in 1961 allowed that Magoo was a "fine old gentleman," confessed that after 12 years he was tired of him. (Two decades later, Backus' assessment was blunter: by that time, Magoo was a "pain in the posterior.")

To alleviate the sameness of his plots and the increasing dullness of his character, Magoo was given a varied supporting cast which at least energized the weaker efforts. New to the property were Mother Magoo, as bohemian and extroverted as her son was hidebound and conservative; Tycoon Magoo, the hero's millionaire uncle, who continually dispatched his butler Worcestershire to keep nephew Quincy from unwittingly wrecking one of Tycoon's property holdings; Magoo's household pets, a feuding dog-and-hamster duo named Caesar and Hamlet (the latter was given voice by the distinguished American character actor Richard Crenna, at the time costarring on the ABC sitcom *The Real McCoys*); and Charlie, Magoo's Chinese houseboy, whose thick Oriental dialect was offensive enough to be dubbed over when the *Mr. Magoo* cartoons were rerun on the USA cable network in the late 1980s — though nothing could be done to erase Charlie's demeaning buck teeth and pigtailed hair.

Waldo, Magoo's nephew and *Ragtime Bear* costar, was revived for the TV series, this time in the company of Prezley, a W.C. Fields-like con artist. Waldo and Prezley frequently appeared in their own separate adventures, which were always introduced by Magoo carrying on a phone conversation with his nephew — with Uncle Quincy's lips obscured by the receiver so that the introductory animation could be used repeatedly in future cartoons, with only the dialogue changed. This sort of amortization would be developed into a science by UPA for the studio's later *Dick Tracy* (q.v.) cartoon series.

While the large supporting cast kept the writers from getting into a rut with the increasingly tiresome Magoo, the series' overall dependence on formula and repetition was a fault that couldn't be completely overridden. And yet, the TV *Mr. Magoo* was a success, running in prime time in many markets and playing to strong ratings for years. Part of the reason was the fact that the series was in color, one of the few tinted syndies available at a time when local colorcasting was just beginning to take off. And there also was the perception that *Mr. Magoo* was geared more for adults than children, with plenty of "satire" in the scriptwork. This was during a period when most media satire was still on a *Mad* magazine level (that publication, in fact, was plugged with an "Alfred E. Neuman" caricature at the end of one *Magoo* cartoon); jokes about Madison Avenue executives, movie/TV moguls and beatniks were regarded as cutting-edge humor to everybody except genuine satirists like Mort Sahl and Lenny Bruce. *Mr. Magoo* tackled the abovementioned safe targets, got its quick shock-of-recognition laughs, and was hailed as being "above the heads" of most kiddies—and therefore a better than average cartoon outing.

To its credit, there was a refreshing *noir* humor streak to *Mr. Magoo*. In many of the cartoons, it was implied that Magoo's near-sightedness was responsible for the deaths—or at least the serious injuries—of innumerable sidelines characters; in *Racket Buster Magoo*, our hero led a vicious criminal gang on a fairly graphic spree of murdering rival gangs, all the while laboring under the assumption that the crooks were merely Boy Scouts working towards their merit badges! This comic morbidity was not enough, however, to redeem the more pedestrian aspects of the series, and though *Mr. Magoo* was profitable, the UPA people felt no real sense of accomplishment.

Things improved greatly on December 18, 1962, with an NBC one-hour special, *Mr. Magoo's Christmas Carol*, which featured a stellar voiceover cast (Jack Cassidy, Morey Amsterdam, Royal Dano, Les Tremayne, Paul Frees, Joan Gardner, Jane Kean and several other celebrated performers) and five sprightly original songs by Jule Styne and Bob Merrill—the best of which, "It's Great to Be Back on Broadway," is unfortunately missing from all syndicated and videocassette versions of *Christmas Carol*. By portraying Magoo as a famous Broadway actor who was returning to the stage in the role of Dickens' Ebenezer Scrooge, UPA at long last was able to reconcile the character's new lovableness with his old irascibility. Scrooge was the perfect "role" for Magoo, and the script did both him and Dickens full honor; the story was faithful enough to avoid complaints of distortion and misrepresentation, but still allowed Magoo a full range of characteristic nearsighted and "stubborn" jokes.

The play-within-a-play format of *Mr. Magoo's Christmas Carol* was recycled on the character's next project: a whole 26-week season of half hour literary adaptations (some of them presented as two- and three-part programs), *The Famous Adventures of Mr. Magoo*, which premiered over NBC in the fall of 1964. The animation was not UPA's best, while its character design was derived in great part from its 1959 theatrical feature film, *1001 Arabian Nights*, though it can be argued that re-using the character art over and over was an attempt to create a "repertory theatre" ambience to *Famous Adventures*. Still, it was intriguing and often rewarding to see Mr. Magoo tackle such roles as Sherlock Holmes' chronicler Dr. Watson, Cyrano de Bergerac, Don Quixote (an inspired casting choice!), William Tell, Robin Hood's companion Friar Tuck, and *all seven* of Snow White's dwarfs.

Less successful Magoo portrayals were those of Ishmael in *Moby Dick* and as the title character in *Gunga Din*, though both of these episodes had merit. The climactic death of Ahab in *Moby Dick* was handsomely rendered in the style of 1840s woodcuts, while *Gunga Din* combined the best elements of the Kipling poem and the 1939 Hollywood version while managing to graft on a new and wholly logical "motivation" for the titular Indian water carrier's loyalty to the British Empire.

One of the *Famous Adventures* drew its inspiration from another UPA property. *Magoo Meets Dick Tracy* contrived to have Tracy request that Mr. Magoo pose as his lookalike, master criminal "Squinty Eyes," in order to break up a crooked cartel consisting of the villains most often seen in UPA's *Tracy* cartoons: Flattop, B-B Eyes, Pruneface, Itchy, Mumbles, et al. The only other such example of cross-pollinating UPA characters was one of the 1960–1962 *Mr. Magoo* shorts, "Magoo Meets McBoing Boing."

The *Famous Adventures of Mr. Magoo* was UPA's most ambitious TV project since 1956's *Gerald McBoing Boing*, and while it still watered down the Magoo character, and stumbled as often as it succeeded in paring the "classics" down to TV standards, the series was one of the few oases of quality in the otherwise mediocre 1964-65 season. A footnote before moving on: As mentioned, UPA had in 1961 avoided scheduling the syndicated *Mr. Magoo* opposite the Jim Backus sitcom *Hot off the Wire*. But in early 1965, NBC decided to move *The Famous Adventures of Mr. Magoo* to a more preferable Saturday evening timeslot—smack dab opposite CBS' *Gilligan's Island*, which as even the most casual couch potato can tell you costarred Jim Backus as millionaire Thurston Howell III.

After 1965, *Mr. Magoo* left active production, with UPA content to resyndicate the five-minute cartoons and to bundle the *Famous Adventures* half hours into such ersatz "feature films" as *Mr. Magoo in the King's Service* and *Magoo at Sea*. On February 15, 1970, there was a one-shot revival, *Uncle Sam Magoo*, a patriotic cartoon special telecast over NBC. And then nothing until 1978, when DePatie-Freleng picked up the rights to the character from now-dormant UPA for a half-hour Saturday morning weekly, *What's New Mr. Magoo?* Twenty-six short Mr. Magoo cartoons were networkcast over a 13-week period, with Jim Backus returning to the role (despite his soured attitude on the old coot) and with a typical "kidvid" character added, a nearsighted dog named Mc-Barker who looked and acted just like his master. Despite the high hopes of Magoo's loyal fans and the usual high-grade De-Patie-Freleng production values, the answer to *What's New, Mr. Magoo?* was "not much, really."

Disregarding occasional TV commercial appearances in the manner of Magoo's G.E. lightbulb ads of the 1950s and early 1960s, this was the end of the Mr. Magoo saga. There were plans drawn up in the mid–1980s for a live-action "Magoo" feature film, but these were abandoned when Jim Backus died of Parkinson's disease in 1989.*

MISTER T. ABC: 9/17/1983–9/6/1986. Ruby-Spears. Produced by Joe Ruby and Ken Spears. Directed by Gary Shimokawa. Animation director, Rudy Larriva. Music by Dean Elliot. Voices: Mr. T (Himself); Amy Linker (Robin); Siu Ming Carson (Kim); Teddy S. Field III (Spike); Phillip LaMarr (Woody); Shawn Lieber (Jeff); Takayo Fisher (Miss Bisby).

Mr. T, who came into this world as Laurence Turand, was a godzillalike ex-bouncer who skyrocketed to fame as Sylvester Stallone's vicious ring opponent in *Rocky III*. "T"'s howitzer-shell temperament, coupled with his Mohawk haircut (actually a Mandinkan cut, as carefully noted by *Total Television* author Alex

McNeil) and his jewelry-bedecked chest and arms, made him a character difficult to forget, a fact that transcended his impressive lack of acting ability. Mr. T's popularity was cemented by his costarring role on the TV action series *The A-Team* (NBC, 1983–1987), where he played a character named "B. A.", which euphemistically stood for Bad Attitude. Mr. T struck a chord with the nine- to 12-year-olds, a demographic group whose affection for "T" was reciprocated by the star, who demonstrated a sensitive social consciousness by turning out a series of anti-drug public service ads.

It was Mr. T's preteen fan following which prompted NBC to commission a weekly half hour cartoon series from Ruby-Spears. *Mr. T* (what title did you expect? *Mr. Ed?*) cast the volatile muscleman as a gymnasium owner whose young multiracial neighborhood pals Robin, Kim, Spike, Woody, and Jeff were constantly involved in life-threatening adventures. As *Mr. T* was telecast in the "caring" early 1980s, there was a valuable moral at the end of each of the 30 episodes, usually delivered by Mr. T himself in his live-action program closings.

The whole affair resembled the earlier *I Am the Greatest—The Adventures of Muhammad Ali* (q.v.), right down to casting Mr. T to do the voice for his animated counterpart—an unusual move on the part of the cartoon makers, as witness the notes in this book on *Hulk Hogan's Rock 'n' Wrestling*, *New Kids on the Block* and *Prostars*. Perhaps because "T" read his lines with slightly more conviction than did Muhammad Ali, *Mr. T* clicked with viewers, and held on in first-run for three seasons.

Yow! Almost forgot. Mr. T's cartoon alter ego was given the obligatory pet dog, a "bull" named Dozer who sported the same Mandinkan hair-trim as his master.

MOBY DICK AND THE MIGHTY MIGHTOR. CBS: 9/9/1967–9/6/1969. Hanna-Barbera. Produced and directed by William Hanna and Joseph Barbera. Associate producer, Art Scott. Production supervisor, Howard Hanson. Animation director, Charles Nichols. Layout artists

*In 1994, talk of a full-length Magoo feature was reactivated thanks to a series of Nutra-Sweet commercials (which seamlessly grafted animation to live action) featuring a newly designed Magoo, with voicework by Greg Burson.

included Jerry Eisenberg, Iwao Takamoto. Animators included Irv Spence, Jerry Hathcock, Dick Lundy, Ed Barge, Kenneth Muse. Character design by Alex Toth. Musical director, Ted Nichols. Components: 1. MOBY DICK. Voices: Bobby Resnick (Tom); Barry Balkin (Tub); Don Messick (Scooby). 2. MIGHTY MIGHTOR. Voices: Paul Stewart (Mightor); Bobby Diamond (Tor); Patsy Garrett (Sheera); John Stephenson (Pondo/Ork/Tog/Rollo); Norma McMillan (Li'l Rock).

How thoughtless of Herman Melville not to include two cute kids and a funny seal when writing his allegorical novel *Moby Dick* in 1851. Not to worry! Hanna-Barbera corrected Melville's oversight when animating the Great White Whale for television in 1967. In addition to updating the story and adding the characters of Tom and Tubb, two preteen deep sea divers who'd been marooned by an underwater earthquake, and a seal named (prophetically for Hanna-Barbera) Scooby, the studio performed what amounted to drawing board evisceration by making the formerly vengeful and destructive giant Moby Dick into an economy-sized protective fighter for right. At least the cartoons were pleasing to look at, with more movement than usual for Hanna-Barbera, and with the enhancement of a "rippling" water effect over the action.*

Moby Dick turned out to have less screen time than its companion feature, *Mighty Mightor*, which was featured in two short cartoons per half hour program compared to Moby's single weekly entry. Caveman superhero Mighty Mightor was actually a young boy named Tor, who drew his strength from his magic club, a gift from an elderly shaman whose life Tor had saved. Something of a prehistoric *Superman*, Mightor's alter ego was seemingly a weakling. As such, he was an object of scorn for his "Lois Lane" leading lady Sheera, who like all other "primitives" on this series spoke perfect English and paid regular visits to a cosmetics consultant. The pulsating-pectoral design of the masked Mightor and his dinosaur/dragon companion Tog evinced the fine hand of artist Alex Toth, whose other super-

powered Hanna-Barbera character designs included *Birdman and the Galaxy Trio* (q.v.), *The Herculoids* (q.v.) and *Space Ghost and Dino Boy* (q.v.).

MONCHICHIS. ABC: 9/10/1983–9/1/1984. Mattel/Hanna-Barbera. Produced by George Singer and Kay Wright. Directed by Ray Patterson, Oscar Dufau, Carl Urbano, George Gordon, John Walker, Rudy Zamora. Music by Hoyt Curtin. Voices: Bobby Morse (Moncho); Laurel Page (Kyla); Ellen Gerstell (Tootoo); Frank Welker (Patchitt); Hank Saroyan (Thumkii); Sidney Miller (Horrg); Frank Nelson (Wizzar); Bob Arbogast (Snogs); Peter Cullen (Shreeker / Snitchitt / Gonker); Laurie Faso (Yabbot/Fassit/Scumgor); and Jack Angel, Carol Bacall, Dick Beals, Julie Bennett, Susan Blu, Bill Callaway, Victoria Carroll, Nancy Cartwright, Jeff Doucette, Walker Edmiston, Jennifer Ann Fujardo, Peggy Frees, Joan Gerber, Gary Goran, David Hollander, Hatti Lynn Hurtes, Erv Immerman, Buster Jones, Stanley Jones, Ham Larsen, Laurie Main, Patty Maloney, Julie McWhirter, Bill Martin, Gregg Marx, Scott Menville, Robert Ridgely, Shavar Ross, Rick Segal, B. J. Ward, Evie Williams, William Woodson, and Ted Ziegler.

Even Hanna-Barbera freely admitted that its *Monchichis* was yet another effort to duplicate the success of its earlier *The Smurfs* (q.v.) both in ratings and in ancillary toy sales via Mattel's "Happiness Dolls" and games. The Monchichis were tiny, tree-dwelling monkeylike humanoids, protected in their forest habitat by the kindly wizard Wizzar (voice by Frank Nelson, the "eeeyeessss" man from the old Jack Benny radio and TV series), and threatened by the truculent Grumplins of Grumplor, led by "His Loathsomeness" Horrg.

Hanna-Barbera historian Ted Sennett found the most "endearing" of the Monchichis to be Thumkii, who when excited had trouble finishing his sentences. Such indecisiveness didn't seem to plague the voice of Thumkii, Hank Saroyan, who in 1984 moved to Marvel Productions to become executive in charge of *The Muppet Babies* (q.v.) and later the producer/

According to former Hanna-Barbera scripter Michael Maltese, one writer for Moby Dick *became so incensed at the creative restrictions placed on him by CBS's Standards and Practices people that he quit cartoon work cold to open his own motion-picture memorabilia store in Van Nuys, California. And that, kiddies, is how Eddie Brandt's Saturday Matinee came into being.*

developer of Marvel's ultra-stylish *Rude Dog and the Dweebs* (q.v.).

MONSTER TAILS *see* **WAKE, RATTLE AND ROLL**

MOONDREAMERS *see* **MY LITTLE PONY**

MORK AND MINDY/LAVERNE AND SHIRLEY/FONZ HOUR. ABC: 9/25/1982–9/3/1983. Hanna-Barbera/Ruby-Spears/Paramount Television. MORK AND MINDY sequences produced by Joe Ruby and Ken Spears. Directed by John Kimball and Rudy Larriva. Music by Hoyt Curtin. Voices: Robin Williams (Mork); Pam Dawber (Mindy); Conrad Janis (Fred McConnell); Frank Welker (Doyng); Stanley Jones (Carruthers); Shavar Ross (Eugene); Ralph James (Orson); Mark Taylor (Hamilton); and Dennis Alwood, Jack Angel, Dave Coulier, Julie McWhirter Dees, Alan Dinehart, Walker Edmiston, Stan Freberg, Bob Holt, Katherine Leigh, Allan Melvin, Sidney Miller, Neilson Ross, Michael Rye, Steve Schatzberg, Marilyn Schreffler, Steve Spears, Larry Storch, Alan Young. (*See Laverne and Shirley in the Army* for additional voice credits.)

The Gary Marshall Successful Sitcom Foundry, which brought *Happy Days* and *Laverne and Shirley* into the world, also provided us with *Mork and Mindy*. Yet another *Happy Days* spinoff (reportedly prompted by a request from Gary Marshall's son that his dad develop a spaceman sitcom), *Mork and Mindy*, was about a manic extraterrestrial, Mork from Ork, who crashed to earth in a gigantic egg and was taken in (platonically) by a young Colorado woman named Mindy McConnell (Pam Dawber). Mork was a character made to order for improvisational monologist Robin Williams, who was elevated to superstardom by this series. *Mork and Mindy* had a rocky four-season ABC run (1978–1982) which was plagued by ill-advised cast and format changes, but by and large it performed well, and like the other Gary Marshall series enriched our pop-culture vocabulary with such catchphrases as Mork's "Shazbot!" and "Nanu-Nanu!"

Also like *Happy Days* and *Laverne and Shirley*, *Mork and Mindy* was ultimately converted into half hour cartoon form,

with its original cast intact as voiceover artists. This being a Hanna-Barbera project (coproduced with former H-B employees Joe Ruby and Ken Spears), it's hardly necessary to enumerate the alterations: Mork and Mindy were retrograded to teenagers, and Mork was given an Orkan doggie, a six-legged furball named Doyng.

The animated *Mork and Mindy* was foisted upon the public in the company of the remaining Gary Marshall cartoon derivations (see notes on *Laverne and Shirley* and *Fonz and the Happy Days Gang*), and the result was the 90-minute Saturday-morning extravaganza *The Mork and Mindy/Laverne and Shirley/Fonz Hour.*

MOST IMPORTANT PERSON. CBS: 4/3/1972–5/18/1973. Sutherland Learning Associates/H.E.W./Viacom. Produced by John Sutherland.

First seen as a component of CBS's *Captain Kangaroo, Most Important Person* was a package of 66 three-and-a-half-minute instructional inserts, illustrating how children could best deal with life's perplexities and to learn more about themselves. Three animated animals — Fumble, a philosophical ostrich; Hairy, a bell-ringing furball; and Bird, an excitable type whose name wrapped up *his* character — were aligned with a brace of human cartoon kids, Mike and Nicola. These characters were then intercut with live-action films of dancing and singing children to delineate such topics as Attitude, Communication, Self-Concept and Physical Powers. Songs featured on *Most Important Person* included such Hit Parade favorites as "Oops, I Made a Mistake!" and "Put Your Hands on Your Hair and Shake Them in the Air."

Not quite up to the level of PBS' *Sesame Street* and *Electric Company, Most Important Person* nonetheless warrants special recognition as the first network property financed by the Federal Government — specifically, the Department of Health, Education and Welfare.

MOTHER GOOSE AND GRIMM (a.k.a. GRIMMY). CBS: 9/14/1991–3/13/ 1993. Lee Mendelsohn Productions/Film Roman/Grimmy, Inc.–Tribune Media/ MGM UA. Executive producers: Lee Mendelsohn, Phil Roman and Mike Peters. Produced by Bob Curtis. Executive in

Most Important Person's cast: Hairy, Fumble, and Bird.

charge of production, Bill Schultz. Supervising director, Vincent Davis. Directed by Jeff Hall, Ron Myrick, Vincent Davis. Animation director, Glenn Kirkpatrick. Main title created by Mike Peters; directed by Phil Roman. Music by Ron Grant. Production facilities: Wang Film Production Co., Ltd./Cuckoo's Nest Studios. Voices: Mitzi McCall, Charlie Brill, Greg Burton, Gregg Berger.

Pulitzer Prize–winning political cartoonist Mike Peters decided in the mid–1980s to follow the lead of fellow editorial artist Jeff MacNelly, who had increased his newspaper saturation and his bank account with a daily comic strip, *Shoe*. Peters' own contribution to daily syndication was *Mother Goose and Grimm*, which maintained the artist's grotesque, wide-mouthed, bugle-nosed style and allowed him to turn out an endless flow of delectably "sick" humor and hideous puns. It also allowed Peters to pay regular homage to his idol, Warner Bros. cartoon director Chuck Jones.

Peter's Mother Goose was as ever the mistress of an enchanted animal domain, only now drawn more in the fashion of those "dirty old grannies" which graced the pages of *Playboy* magazine. Grimm, or "Grimmy," was a cynical and chronically hyper yellow dog, given to reacting with alarm at the least provocation, pausing to philosophize over the value of performing as a normal dog would, and trashing and devouring anything, or anyone, in his path. Grimmy's costars were a bedraggled, belligerent pussycat appropriately named Attila, and a bully bulldog named Thorp. Mike Peters' off-kilter menagerie was just what the 1980s was looking for, and by the 1990s, *Mother Goose and Grimm* was being distributed to 600 papers.

Reasoning that what had worked brilliantly for the comic strip creation *Garfield* (q.v.) would perform just ·as well for *Mother Goose and Grimm*, Tribune Media contracted with *Garfield*'s animator Film Roman for a weekly, half hour *Mother Goose and Grimm* series, to be telecast in CBS' ever-strengthening Saturday morning lineup. Film Roman transferred the original so flawlessly to celluloid that it seemed as though Mike Peters was inking, painting and animating the whole property all by himself. Grimm's weightier, sarcastic side was downplayed in favor of more traditional kidvid mayhem, usually involving the dog's foolhardy fascination with household appliances — a trait in common with creator Mike Peters, who claimed to have based Grimm on himself: "Good strips are correlations." Disregarding earlier, watch-out-for-the-pressure-groups network policies, the slapstick of *Mother Goose and Grimm* was played out full force, with less subtle "hip" humor than Film Roman's *Garfield* but with no less fun. The wackiness of the project extended to the series' closing credits, which listed as "dog trainer" Mike Peters' wife, Marian "Choke Chain" Peters.

In 1992, the series' name was changed to *Grimmy*, a decision made to attract young viewers who, according to CBS research, had originally shunned *Mother Goose and Grimm* on the belief that it was a puerile "nursery rhyme" weekly. It's possible the name change did more harm than good,

since *Grimmy* was abruptly cancelled in mid–March 1993.

MOTORMOUSE AND AUTOCAT *see* **THE CATTANOOGA CATS**

MUGGY DOO *see* **MILTON THE MONSTER**

MULTIPLICATION   ROCK   *see* **SCHOOLHOUSE ROCK**

MUMBLY *see* **TOM AND JERRY**

MUPPET BABIES. CBS: 9/15/1984–9/7/1992. Fox Network: 1991–. (reruns) —JIM HENSON'S MUPPETS, BABIES AND MONSTERS. CBS: 9/14/1985–5/1986. Jim Henson Productions/Marvel. Executive producers: Jim Henson, Margaret Loesch, Lee Gunther. Executive in charge of series: Hank Saroyan. Produced by Bob Richardson and John Ahern. Associate producers, Adam Bleibereau, Bob Shellhorn. Creative consultant, Michael K. Frith. Developed for televison by Jeffrey Scott. Supervising director, Bob Shellhorn. Directed by Norman McCabe, Gerry Chiniquy, Hank Saroyan, John Gibbs,· among others. Art director, Takashi. Music by Alan O'Day, Janis Liebhart. Production facilities, Toei Studios. Voices: Frank Welker (Kermit/Beaker); Howie Mandel, Dave Coulier (Animal); Howie Mandel, Frank Welker (Skeeter); Dave Coulier (Bunsen); Greg Berg (Fozzie/Scooter); Katie Leigh (Rowlf); Laurie O'Brien (Piggy); Russi Taylor (Gonzo); Barbara Billingsley (Nannie); and Peter Cullen.

The Muppets—part Marionette, part Puppet—had been created by Jim Henson in the 1950s as an "entertainment for all ages" attraction; indeed, what with the Muppets' regular 1960s appearances on such programs as *The Today Show*, *The Tonight Show*, *The Jack Paar Program*, *The Perry Como Kraft Music Hall* and *The Jimmy Dean Show*, Henson's troupe was generally regarded as an adult-satire aggregation. Once the characters began as regulars on PBS' *Sesame Street* in 1969, however, the Muppets became locked in to the consciousness of the industry as a children's entertainment—and as such, Henson in 1975 had difficulty marketing his weekly variety program *The Muppet Show* for a prime time slot (the series was

"Indiana Kermit" on *Muppet Babies*.

in fact rejected by ABC, only to be picked up for nonnetwork syndication, where it became the most popular variety show in the entire world!). With the weekly animated *Muppet Babies* of 1984, Henson managed to combine the most attractive elements of both the "adult" muppet characters seen on the nighttime show and the "kid's" muppets utilized on *Sesame Street*. The result, Jim Henson's first project without puppets, was — again — a property that pleased everyone in every age group.

The characters on *Muppet Babies* were all taken from the weekly nighttime variety show, and its spinoff theatrical feature films: Kermit the Frog, Miss Piggy, Gonzo, Rowlf, Fozzie Bear, Animal, Scooter, Bunsen and Beaker (a new character, Scooter's twin sister Skeeter, was created for *Babies* in order to give the series a second strong female character). Per the series' title, all the characters were regressed to nursery school age, and in fact they all lived in the same nursery. This "backtracking" device would later become too precious for its own good in such

Saturday morning efforts as *The New Archies* and *The Flintstone Kids*, but it worked beautifully on *Muppet Babies*. The characters retained the personalities that had won them fame in the first place, and by being cast as children, they were logically allowed unbridled rein of their imaginations so they could exploit those personalities in a limitless series of fantastic dream adventures. The characters would be inspired by a random comment or current fad or fancy to embark on exciting "faux" adventures without ever really leaving the nursery. It was a surefire concept, later successfully exploited by Fox's *Bobby's World* (q.v.) and Nickelodeon's *Doug* (q.v.) and *Rugrats* (q.v.), and one that met with universal approval from kidvid critics, who'd been saying all along that more programs were needed that encouraged using one's imagination.

Thanks to strong merchandising tie-ins, the Muppet Babies indulged in escapades inspired by the popular theatrical *Star Wars* and *Indiana Jones* features, even to the point of using licensed clips from those films. Otherwise, the Babies' imaginary adventures cast them in adult roles wherein they discovered that they had a lot to learn about behavior and relationships before tackling the grownup world (often depicted with background art comprised of "real" still photographs). These lessons could have been doled out in unsubtle, finger-waggling fashion (as indeed they were on other less accomplished cartoon programs), but Jim Henson, here as elsewhere, never talked down to his audience. And like Bill Cosby's *Fat Albert* (q.v.), the characters on *Muppet Babies* had a grand old time in the process of learning their lessons, not in spite of them.

While Jim Henson supervised the program, neither he nor longtime partner Frank Oz supplied his distinctive Muppet voice. Nevertheless, the superb voicework of such celebrated comic impressionists as Frank Welker, Dave Coulier and Howie Mandel did nothing but enhance the characters' appeal. One voice was particularly reassuring: Barbara Billingsley, the legendary June Cleaver of *Leave It to Beaver* fame, as the Babies' affectionate but no-nonsense Nanny (who like the other adult characters was seen only from the waist down — it wasn't *their* show, after all).

Muppet Babies opened in 1984 in a half

Muppet Babies: a yellow-brick fantasy with Fozzie, Miss Piggy, Kermit and Gonzo.

hour slot, with one adventure per program. In 1985, the program was expanded to an hour and retitled *Jim Henson's Muppets, Babies and Monsters.* New to the property were the "Little Muppet Monsters," three live-action cloth characters who endeavored to stage their own imaginary TV shows using props and costumes left over from previous *Muppet Show* episodes. Only three costly "Little Muppet Monster" half-hour adventures were produced; the title of the series reverted to simply *Muppet Babies* (and to its all-cartoon status) in 1986.

The following season, the series consumed a full 90 minutes—not by popular demand, but as a swift replacement for CBS' *Garbage Pail Kids*, which had met with so much prerelease adult resistance that the network buckled and flat-out cancelled the new program before it even began. *Muppet Babies* was back to a more manageable full hour for the 1988-89 season; the series left the network four years later, but that was hardly the end of the story. In 1989, the 65-episode *Muppet Babies* rerun package was established as an A-1 weekday syndicated attraction. Thereafter, it was telecast Monday through Friday as part of the Fox Children's Network syndicated lineup, and most recently over several different cable services.

There was something about the Jim Henson operation that attracted Emmy award nominations like a magnet. *Muppet Babies* was so honored in 1984, 1985, 1986, 1987, and 1988 (one for each year of full production), and managed to toddle away with statuettes in all but one of those years.

One of the true TV-cartoon giants, *Muppet Babies* had the humblest of inspirations: a TV executive noted a throwaway depiction of Kermit and Piggy as babies on a poster for the live-action movie *The Muppets Take Manhattan,* and brought the notion of diapered Muppets to the attention of Marvel Studios producer Margaret Loesch. Previous plans to animate the Muppets had always stalled because no one had found a good "hook" to make such a series substantially different from what Henson and company had already paraded before the TV public—and also because, up until the computer-driven early 1980s, Jim Henson had been unimpressed by the quality of TV animation.

Margaret Loesch would remain prideful of *Muppet Babies,* even long after production had closed down. Quoted in *Animation* magazine's Fall 1993 issue, Loesch, then in charge of the Fox Children's Network, recalled: "We put a lot of money and time into [*Muppet Babies*]. But I believed it would make TV more imaginative. Maybe I made kids laugh and stirred their imagination.... Maybe I did make a difference."

M*U*S*H *see* **UNCLE CROC'S BLOCK**

MY FAVORITE MARTIANS. CBS: 9/8/1973–8/30/1975. Filmation/Jack Chertok Television. Directed by Hal Sutherland, Don Townsley, Rudy Larriva, Lou Zukor, Hal Reed, Ed Solomon. Written by Ben Starr, Bill Danch, Marc Richards. Music by George Mahana. Voices: Jonathan Harris (Uncle Martin); Howard Morris (Tim O'Hara/Brennan/Brad/Tiny/Crumbs/Chump/Okey); Lane Scheimer (Andromeda); Jane Webb (Katey/ Lorelei Brown/Jan/Coral/Miss Casserole).

My Favorite Martian, CBS's Sunday evening replacement for *Dennis the Menace*, was a half hour fantasy sitcom which ran successfully from 1963 through 1966. Ray Walston played a misplaced Martian who was rescued and sheltered by earthbound reporter Tim O'Hara (Bill Bixby), who called the alien "Uncle Martin" to shelter him from prying government scientists. Hardly a bug-eyed monster, Uncle Martin was a kindly, erudite, highly intellectual humanoid, who could travel through time, build advanced futuristic contraptions (except for a machine that would repair his spaceship and allow him to go back to Mars), solve knotty mathematical problems in a wink, and even whip up a tasty soufflé when so inclined. Supporting characters on *My Favorite Martian* included Tim O'Hara's scatterbrained landlady Lorelei Brown (Pamela Britton), who carried a torch for Uncle Martin, and Lorelei's erstwhile boy friend, chronically suspicious detective Bill Brennan (Alan Hewitt).

My Favorite Martian was already in its seventh rerun cycle when a cartoon version appeared. The title was now pluralized to *My Favorite Martians* due to the additional extraterrestrial characters of Andromeda ("Andy"), who was the Martian's *real* nephew, and space dog Oakie Doakie. Uncle Martin was still his antennaed middle-aged self, but Tim O'Hara had been converted into a much younger man and given a miniskirted, teenybopper niece named Katy. Detective Brennan was also honored with an extraneous relative,

a snoopy son named Brad, who brought in tow his pet chimpanzee Chump. Only Lorelei Brown survived without a newly animated extended family.

New characters notwithstanding, the cartoon version followed almost exactly the same formula as the live action sitcom, albeit not with the original actors. One intriguing casting choice on the animated *Martians* was to replace Ray Walston as Uncle Martin's voice (Walston probably wouldn't have done it anyway, since he's publicly noted that *My Favorite Martian* put his career into a slump). Walston's substitute was Jonathan Harris, who at the time *My Favorite Martian* had originally been networkcast was appearing in *another* CBS sci-fi weekly, *Lost in Space*, as the villainous Dr. Smith.

Was animating the old property worth it? The National Association for Better Broadcasting didn't think so: "They threw out the baby and saved the dirty bath water. Everything bright and clever from the live-action *My Favorite Martian* is gone from this shoddy animated transition. Inane, silly and witless to the point of vulgarity."

Final score: *My Favorite Martian*, 107 half hour episodes. *My Favorite Martians*, 16.

MY LITTLE PONY AND FRIENDS. Syndicated: 1986. Sunbow/Wildstar/Starwild/Hasbro-Claster/Marvel. Executive producers: Joe Bacal, Margaret Loesch, Tom Griffin. Executive in charge of production, Lee Gunther. Creative director, Joe Bacal. Produced by Marja Miletic Dahl, Jeff Hall, Mike Joens. Supervisor of production, Ray Lee. Director of production, Jim Graziano. Directed by Bob Bemiller, Charlie Downs, Bob Kirk, Margaret Nichols, Bob Matz, Rudy Cataldi, Karen Peterson, Joe Morrison, Spencer Peel, Neal Warner, Lillian Evans, Stan Phillips, Norman McCabe, Gerry Chiniquy, Warren Batchelder, Bob Treat, Brad Case, Joan Case, John Freeman, Tom Ray, Bill Knoll, Milton Gray. Musical score by Robert J. Walsh. Title music by Ford Kinder and Anne Bryant; lyrics by Barry Harman. Additional songs by Tommy Goodman, Ray Eaton, Rich Meitlin and Barry Harman. Story editors: John Semper, Cynthia Friedlob, Martin Pasko, Rebecca Parr, Michael Reaves, J. Brynne Stephens. Voice director, Ginny McSwain.

Educational advisers: Robert L. Selman, Ph.D. Harvard; Anne P. Selman, M.A., educational consultant. Voices: Ginny Mc-Swain (Megan); and Susan Blu, Charlie Adler, Nancy Cartwright, Peter Cullen, Linda Gary, Scott Grimes, Keri Houlihan, Katie Leigh, Sherry Lynn, Ken Mars, Sarah Partridge, Frank Welker, Russi Taylor, Michael Bell, Bettina Bush, Jeannie Elias, Ian Freid, Susan Garbo, Ellen Gerstell, Melanie Gaffin, Skip Hinnant, Christina Lange, Jody Lambert, Kellie Martin, Anne Marie McEvoy, David Mendenhall, Scott Menville, Brecken Meyer, Laura Mooney, Andrew Potter, B. J. Ward, Jill Wayne, Frank Welker, Bunny Andrews, Bill Callaway, Adam Carl, Philip Clarke, Danny Cooksey, Jennifer Darling, Marshall Efron, Pat Fraley, Elizabeth Frazer, Liz Georges, Robert Ito, Renae Jacobs, Robin Kaufman, Danny Mann, Tress MacNeille, Terry McGovern, Michael Mish, Clive Revill, Stu Rosen, Neil Ross, Ken Sanson, Rick Segal, Judy Strangis, Len Weinrib, Charlie Wolfe, Ted Ziegler.

—MY LITTLE PONY TALES. Disney Channel: 2/28/1993–. Graz Entertainment/Wildstar/Starwild/Sunbow Productions. Creative producers: Jay Bacal, Tom Griffin, C. J. Kettler. Creative director: Jay Bacal. Executive in charge of production: Carole Weizman. Produced and story edited by Roger Slifer. Supervising animation directors, Karen Peterson and Graham Morris. Animation directors: Munir Bhatti, Rick Bowman, Rudy Cataldi, Barbara Doormashkin, J. K. Kim, Marlene May, Erik Peterson, Brian Ray, Mitch Rochon. Creative consultant/story editor: George Arthur Bloom. Music and lyrics by Tommy Goodman and Barry Harman. For Graz Entertainment: Executive in charge of production, Jim Graziano; producer, Terry Lennon. Production facilities: Akom Production Company. Akom directors: Seung Jin Oh, Kyung-Chook Sah, Nak-Jong Kim, Young-Soo Lee, Heung-Sun Oh. Voices: Brigitta Dau, Laura Harris, Willow Johnson, Lalainia Lindbherg, Shane Meier, Maggie O'Hara, Kate Robbins, Tony Sampson, Kelly Sheridan, Brad Swaile, Venus Terzo, Chiara Zanni.

Together with *G.I. Joe* (q.v.) and *He-Man* (q.v.), *My Little Pony* was Hasbro Toys' principal source of income in the mid–1980s. The *Pony* marketing strategy was founded on gender-role notions that purportedly were outdated by 1984: If boys would respond to a line of action-figure soldiers, girls would enthuse over an equally overpopulated line of toy horses. Perhaps it wasn't in the best interest of sexual equality to assume that girls would bypass warrior dolls to purchase toys that looked like pretty ponies, but that assumption proved accurate. This writer knows of several otherwise rational high school and college-age young ladies of 1994 (some within the family) who have My Little Ponies by the gross tucked away in their attics.

The characters weren't simply horses, of course, but humanized representations of various traits like vanity, pride, courage, and so forth (see *Care Bears*). All were gifted with magic powers, all were bedecked with flowing hair styles of various pastel colors, and all were evidently regular customers of Ponyland's Institute of Eyelash Elongation. Ponyland was of course the idyllic mythical land (with background art apparently based on the Beethoven Pastorale sequence in Disney's *Fantasia*) whence the tiny pony dolls owned by a human girl named Megan would retreat and come to life.

As expected, the heaven-on-earth of Ponyland was threatened by sinister forces, though none quite as sinister as the purple mass of goo called "The Smooze" which dominated the 1986 theatrical release *My Little Pony: The Movie*. For the most part, the villains on the *My Little Pony* daily syndicated TV series weren't terribly life-threatening, and some were even capable of learning lessons and reforming—indicative of the backstage overtime put in by the series' educational consultants, Harvard's Robert and Anne Selman. That the Selmans were capable of adapting their skills to any brand of children's entertainment is evidenced by the fact that they also performed the same advisory function on Hasbro/Sunbow's *G.I. Joe*, the militaristic theme song of which was written by the same folks who'd penned the lilting *My Little Pony* theme. *Lots* of versatility to go around here.

The first *My Little Pony* seven-minute episodes were shown in syndication on a daily cliffhanger basis (a 1985 "pilot" TV special, *My Little Pony: Escape from Catrina*, was sliced up in five installments to conform with the rest of the package).

The lead characters shared time with several other Hasbro products-cum-cartoons: *The Glo Friends, The Moondreamers* and *Potato Head Kids*. Like the *My Little Pony* episodes, all three of these components punctuated their seven-minute adventures with original songs, many of them actually hummable.

The Glo Friends were shimmering little insectlike entities with names like Glo-worm, Lovebug, Doodlebug and Glo-spider (and a few benign "mutants" like Globunny) who formed a united front against the evil Molligans, rodent rascals who coveted the protagonists' valuable Glo-Drops. The Moondreamers were cute pixielike extraterrestrials (Twinkle, Bucky, Whimzee, et al.) who were influenced in the nicest way by the lunar cycle. Occasional grown-up jokes (the Molligans' favorite clothes store was "Neiman Marsupial") did not alienate either *Glo-Friends* or *Moondreamers* from its four- to nine-year-old female target audience.

Potato Head Kids, a junior grade version of one of Hasbro's oldest and most durable toy products, Mr. and Mrs. Potato Head, was unlike the other *Pony* components geared more for boys than girls. Slapstick predominated in place of the genteel *Glo-Friends* and *Moondreamers* whimsy, causing this group of short cartoons to resemble a vegetable-counter *Little Rascals*. Main characters Spike, Big Chip, Pumpling, Smarty, and the inevitable Spud all wore characteristic headgear, in the manner of the 1980s singing group The Village People, whom the Potato Head Kids sounded like (a little) when warbling such hits as "Potato Pizazz" and "Go Go Potatoes." Mr. and Mrs. Potato Head themselves made token appearances in each story, holding down different jobs from cartoon to cartoon. In one installment, the elder Potato Heads were attorneys, confirming something we've suspected about the legal profession for years.

When *My Little Pony and Friends* moved to the Disney Channel pay-cable service in 1993, the *Friends* part was dropped (along with *Glo-Friends, Moondreamers*, and *Potato Head Kids*) and the title became *My Little Pony Tales*. Reruns were mixed in with newly filmed adventures wherein Ponyland had been tracted into a suburban community, complete with grade school, soda shop and mall.

Nonmagical ponies with names like Bon Bon, Scratch and Melody now wore preteen fashion togs, acted more human than ever, and commiserated with male ponies who looked like equestrian variants on the latest soap-opera and rock music heartthrobs. Even the theme music was rewritten to incorporate the lyric "Oh, wow!" Oh, mercy.

MY PET MONSTER. ABC: 9/12/1987–9/3/1988. Those Characters From Cleveland/Telefilm Canada/Nelvana Limited. Produced by Patrick Loubert, Clive A. Smith, Michael Hirsh. Supervising producer, Lenora Hume. Line producer, Peter Hudecki. Associate producers: Jack Chojnacki, Peter Sauder. Directed by Laura Shepherd. Animation directors: Steve Whitehouse, Mike Gerard. Story editor, Peter Sauder. Theme song by Marvin Dolgay and Kevan Staples. Score by John Welsman. Animation facilities: HanHo Heung Up Co. Voices: Sunny Bensen Thrasher (Max); Stuart Stone (Chuckie); Jeff McGibbon (Monster); Alyson Court (Jill); Dan Hennessey (Beastur); Colin Fox (Hinkle); Tracey Moore (Princess); Tara Charendoff (Ame); and Marv Long, Noam Zylberman, Simon Reynolds, Graham Haley, John Stocker, Maxine Miller, and Robert Cait.

My Pet Monster was like *Care Bears* (q.v.) a joint effort of Nelvana and American Greeting Cards, and was also based on a popular stuffed-doll plaything. Unlike *Care Bears, My Pet Monster* didn't have the overall feel of an extended commercial, and can thus be discussed on its own merits as a TV series now that the original toy has lost its currency.

The "Monster" was a squat, blue-skinned, spotted-nose biped who looked like a distant cousin of *The Muppet Babies'* (q.v.) Gonzo and who spoke in a guttural *Scooby-Doo* (q.v.) fashion. He was actually a doll come to life, owned by a boy named Max. Whenever Max slipped a pair of enchanted handcuffs on My Pet Monster, the character would revert to his non-live "toy" status (shades of the popular comic strip *Calvin and Hobbs*, with a bit of reverse *Wonder Woman* tossed in). Out of fear of losing his pet to a zoo or science lab, Max shared the secret of Monster's metamorphosis only with his Amerasian best friend Chuckie and with his sister Jill, who insisted upon calling the series' star

"Monzey." One other character, a nervous poodle named Princess, was witness to Monster's transformations, but was too hyper to say (or bark) anything. Complicating the weekly series was a bully named Leo, an amusingly self-aware reprobate who reprimanded other kids' shortcomings by saying things like "They expect *me* to cheat!" Leo craved the plaything version of Monster as a tear-up toy for his mean-spirted dog Spud (who borrowed a page from the Hanna-Barbera repertoire with his wheezing snicker).

Very well animated, *My Pet Monster* was unfortunately not as funny as its premise or production design seemed to promise, and its plotlines were too thinnish to sustain its full Saturday morning half hour timeslot. The series started strongly, but ultimately bowed to that ratings league leader, *Pee-wee's Playhouse.*

MYSTERIOUS   CITIES   OF GOLD. Nickelodeon: 6/30/1986–6/29/1990. MK Company Productions.

Telecast in the United States on the Nickelodeon cable service, the half hour *Mysterious Cities of Gold* was the only cartoon series released in an English-language version to deal exclusively with the legends of pre–Columbian Indian civilizations. Esteban, leader of the Children of the Sun, guided his young friends into the Central American "Mysterious Cities" of the title. The 39-episode series was telecast on a daily basis; it was introduced into the Nickelodeon lineup at 3:00 P.M. EST between *Belle and Sebastian* (q.v.) and *Danger Mouse* (q.v.) with little or no publicity fanfare, and is intriguingly obscure today despite its nationwide saturation and its relatively recent vintage.

NBC COMICS *see* TELE-COMICS

NELVANAMATION. Syndicated: 1977–1980. Nelvana/CBC/Viacom. Executive producers: Jeffrey Kirsch, Robert Foster, Ted Kernaghan, Nigel Martin. Produced by Patrick Loubert and Michael Hirsh. Head of animation, Frank Nissen. Directors included Ken Stephenson, Giano Franco Celestri, Greg Duffell. Music by John Sebastian, Sylvia Tyson, Rick Danko. 1. A COSMIC CHRISTMAS (1977). Voices: Joey Davidson (Peter); Martin Lavut (Dad/ Plutox/Santa Joe);

Intergalactic Thanksgiving of *Nelvanamation.*

Richard Davidson (Lexicon); Duncan Regehr (Amalthor); Patricia Moffat (Mom); Jane Mallett (Grandma); Marvin Goldhar (Police Chief Snerk); Greg Rogers (Marvin); Chris Wiggins (The Mayor); Nick Nichols, Marion Waldman (Townies). **2. THE DEVIL AND DANIEL MOUSE** (1978). Voices: Jim Henshaw (Daniel—speaking); John Sebastian (Daniel—singing/Rock Emcee); Annabelle Kershaw (Jan—speaking); Laurel Runn (Jan—singing); Chris Wiggins (B. L. Zebubb); Martin Lavut (Weez Weasel/ Pawnbroker); Diane Lawrence (Interviewer). **3. ROMIE-O AND JULIE-8** (1979). Voices: Greg Swanson (Romie-O); Donann Cavin (Julie-8); Max Ferguson (Mr. Thunderbottom); Marie Aloma (Ms. Passbinder); Nick Nichols (Gizmo); Bill Osler (Spare Partski, the junkman); and John Sebastian, Rory Block, and Richard Manuel (Singers). **4. INTERGALACTIC THANKSGIVING** (1979) (aka PLEASE DON'T EAT THE PLANET). Voices: Sid Caesar (King Goochie); Catherine O'Hara (Ma Spademinder); Chris Wiggins (Pa Spademinder); Jean Walker (Victoria Spademinder); Martin Lavut (Magic Mirror); Derek McGrath (Notfunyenuf); Al Waxman (The Bug); Toby Waxman (Bug Kid). **5. EASTER FEVER** (1980) (aka THE JACK RABBIT STORY). Voices: Garrett Morris (Jack); Maurice LaMarche

(Don Rattles/Steed Martin); Chris Wiggins (Santa Claus/Baker); Jeri Craden (Madama Malegg); Jim Henshaw (Aardvark); Catherine O'Hara (Scarlett O'Hare); Melleny Brown (Scrawny Chicken); Larry Mollin (Ratso Rat); Don Ferguson (Announcer). Music by John Sebastian. **6. TAKE ME UP TO THE BALLGAME** (1980). Voices: Phil Silvers (Irwin); Bobby Dermer (Beaver); Derek McGrath (Eagle); Don Ferguson (Commissioner); Paul Soles (Anoouncer); Anna Bourque (Edna); Maurice LaMarche (Jake); Melleny Brown (Mole); Rick Danko [of The Band] (Vocalist).

Nelvanamation was a blanket title given to six half-hour animated specials released between 1977 and 1980 in both Canada and the U.S. by Toronto's Nelvana Studios. It succeeded as the first major syndicated saturation for the young cartoon firm, though Nelvana would have to wait until 1983's *Care Bears* to score a real hit.

First on the manifest was *A Cosmic Christmas*, in which three extraterrestrial wise men visited a modern day earth to analyze the effect of the Christmas story. Like all future *Nelvanamation* specials, the program was telecast in America during "Access Time," the period between 7:30 and 8 P.M. (EST) that the FCC had wrested from the three networks in 1971 in order to encourage creative and innovative local programming. By 1977, Access Time had become a clearinghouse for game shows and silly contests like *The Gong Show*; thus, any programs remotely invoking those elusive abstractions "Culture" and "Quality," notably such syndicated weeklies as *In Search Of* and *Between the Wars*, were hailed by critics far beyond their real worth. *Cosmic Christmas* was likewise lauded for offering a half hour's worth of fresh, offbeat entertainment; in this instance, the praise was earned. The animation wasn't quite the "equal" to Disney that the animators had, according to Nelvana's publicity handouts, "set their sights on," but *Cosmic Christmas* exhibited a lot more care, production polish and heart than, say, *The Match Game*. As a result, the special received wide exposure and generous press coverage in 1977, encouraging Nelvana to continue producing seasonal specials aimed at both Canadian and U.S. viewers.

The *Devil and Daniel Mouse*, timed for the Halloween season, followed in 1978.

This surprisingly mature variation of "Faust" featured a duo of folksinging mice named Dan and Jan, rent asunder when Jan (the girl) signed her soul away to lizardlike B. L. ZeBubb in exchange for fame and fortune as a rock star. One of the cuter touches in *Devil and Daniel Mouse* was to recast Satan (ZeBubb) as a stereotypical Hollywood agent, with loud clothes, garish jewelry and all.

Romie-O and Julie-8 of *Nelvanamation*.

Romie-O and Julie-8, telecast in most U.S. markets during the Easter season of 1979, combined Shakespeare's starcrossed lovers with a sci-fi viewpoint: Both hero and heroine were robots, escapees from a junkyard planet overseen by the evil Spare Partski. The good-natured humor and above-average graphics of *Romie-O and Julie-8* allowed the scripters to pull off one of the oldest ones in the business when they offered as the special's punchline, "Oil's well that ends well."

For the first three Nelvana specials, a team of accomplished but comparatively unknown Canadian voice artists were used for the soundtracks (unknown below the border, that is; performers like Al Waxman, Chris Wiggins and Duncan Regehr were familiar names in the Great White North). The biggest names attached to the project were singers John Sebastian and Sylvia Tyson, the latter the wife of top Canadian country and western star Ian Tyson. The remaining three *Nelvanamation* installments, with larger budgets, chose to kowtow to American TV's demand for "star" names to buoy up sales. *Please Don't*

Eat the Planet (1979), released in the U.S. as *Intergalactic Thanksgiving*, top billed Sid Caesar as King Goochi, ruler of the planet Laffalot (and son of King Whoopie-cushion). This borscht-belt edge to the humor was carried over into its basic plotline, that of an outer-space wagon train, commandeering by two immigrant families—one hardworking, one selfish—looking for a planet to settle. In a variation of the "Ant and Grasshopper" story, the industrious settlers ended up rescuing the less noble family from a sloth-encouraging foodmaking machine, which ran amok and threatened to devour the whole of planet Laffalot.

The *Jack Rabbit Story*, which premiered in the U.S. under the title *Easter Fever* in March of 1980, featured as its comedy "star" former *Saturday Night Live* regular Garrett Morris, who recycled a variation of his "baseball has been good to me" catchphrase for the occasion, substituting "Easter" for "Baseball." Morris was the voice of Jack Rabbit, whose retirement from the Easter Bunny job prompted a zany celebrity roast (which managed to include takeoffs on Julia Child, *West Side Story*, and the whole Warner Bros. cartoon oeuvre), with veteran voiceman Maurice LaMarche offering dead-on imitations of Steve Martin and Don Rickles. Three cartoon directors worked to bring Larry Mollin's script for *The Jack Rabbit Story* to full satiric blossom. The musical portion of the program was in the capable hands of John Sebastian, who'd previously provided stellar vocal accompaniment to *Devil and Daniel Mouse* and *Romie-O and Julie-8*.

Rick Danko, former member of The Band, was musical contributor on the last *Nelvanamation* effort, *Take Me Up to the Ballgame* (1980), which like *Please Don't Eat the Planet* "starred" a comedy great, this time from TV's Golden Age: Phil Silvers, as an outer-space sports promoter who tried to set up an interplanetary all-star game. Though *Take Me Up to the Ballgame* started promisingly with solid visual gags (the "reporters" at an outer space baseball press conference were anthropomorphic tape recorders and movie cameras), this half hour spiralled downhill quickly. It was the weakest of the *Nelvanamation* series; even Rick Danko's tunes fell short of the project's usual standards.

Seen as a group—usually the only way one can see them nowadays, since the programs are generally offered in tandem for home video release—the *Nelvanamation* specials impress on a production-gloss level, but tend to fall prey to repetition, notably an overreliance on science fiction themes and protracted musical interludes. But the programs were meant to be seen individually at intervals of several months; as originally presented, the *Nelvanamation* specials appeared to contain a lot more variety than was actually the case. This last piddling criticism is not, however, enough to diminish the merits of the series. At a time when animated TV specials were chiefly confined to paste-up collections of old theatrical cartoons (cartoons that were good individually, but not designed for the "cluster" approach), *Nelvanamation* was a warm, welcome gust of creative originality from Nelvana's Toronto warehouse headquarters.

THE NEW ADVENTURES OF BATMAN see **BATMAN**

THE NEW ADVENTURES OF CAPTAIN PLANET see **CAPTAIN PLANET**

THE NEW ADVENTURES OF FLASH GORDON. CBS: 9/22/1979–9/20/1980. Filmation. Executive producers: Lou Scheimer, Norm Prescott. Produced by Don Christensen. Directed by Hal Sutherland, Marsh Lamore, Lou Kachivas, Kay Wright, Don Townsley, Gwen Wetzler, Lou Zukor, Ed Friedman. Music by Yvette Blais and George Mahana. Theme song by Marc Ellis and George Mahana. Voices: Robert Ridgely (Flash Gordon/ Prince Barin); Diane Pershing (Dale Arden); Alan Oppenheimer (Ming the Merciless/Dr. Zarkov); Melendy Britt (Aura/Fria); Allan Melvin, Ted Cassidy (Thun/Vultan); Lou Scheimer (Gremlin). Voices in pilot episode: Vic Perrin (Vultan); David Opatashu (Zarkov); Ted Cassidy (Thun).

Created in 1934, five years after *Buck Rogers, Flash Gordon* may have been the second major outer-space comic strip, but the excellent draftsmanship of artist/ writer Alex Raymond quickly moved it to first place in the genre. Its rapid climb to popularity was reflected when Universal Pictures, in association with the King Features syndicate, plunked down a record $350,000 for a 15-episode *Flash Gordon* serial in 1936, only two years after the strip's inception. While the action and acting in this serial seems alternately wooden and cardboard when seen today, it was handsomely mounted and made quite an impression in 1936; it was billed above its accompanying feature film on several movie house marquees, and even managed to get a laudatory review from *Time* magazine. Two sequels followed, both like their predecessor starring blonde former Olympic swimming star Buster Crabbe, who made such a mark for himself in the role that when a *Flash Gordon* TV series was filmed in 1952, star Steve Holland was cast as Flash primarily because he looked like Crabbe. The resemblance was the only real throwback to the elaborate Universal serials; the TV *Flash Gordon* was filmed very cheaply in Germany, utilizing warehouses full of papier-mâché for its sets and props.

The comic strip remained popular into the 1970s, though no further efforts were made to transfer that success to the movie or TV screen until George Lucas' *Star Wars* turned the industry on its ear in 1977. One of the stories circulating at the time was that Lucas had wanted to make a state-of-the-art version of *Flash Gordon*, but King Features wouldn't relinquish the rights, so he simply renamed all the characters and outlying planets; certainly the end product looked a lot like the *Gordon* serials, with their futuristic hardware, florid acting and fancy optical wipe-dissolves, albeit on a more expensive scale ($9,500,000).

Star Wars made the movie industry space-conscious in a way it hadn't been since the 1950s, and the result was a myriad of extraterrestrial adventures, including a new *Flash Gordon*, produced by the redoubtable Dino De Laurentiis (he's the man who teamed King Kong with Jessica Lange, if you need a reminder). At the same time De Laurentiis was at work, Filmation, in concert with King Features, set about producing an animated *Flash Gordon* feature, written by onetime *Star Trek* telewriter Samuel A. Peeples and slated for 1979 release. When it became apparent that this film wouldn't hold up theatrically, the cartoon was pitched to independent television stations as "the first full-length adult animated space fantasy for TV."

Acting out of self-protective instinct, De Laurentiis purchased theatrical exhibition rights to the Filmation effort, then shunted it away on back shelf so as not to provide competition for his own live-action *Gordon* (There's an alternate version to this account, wherein De Laurentiis was so impressed by Filmation's cartoon that he poured money into its budget and intended to release the property theatrically himself rather than suppress it; it's a sweet story, but it doesn't jibe with the typical modus operandi of Dino De Laurentiis). Filmation still had permission for TV exposure, so its feature film was chopped into 16 cliff hanging half hour episodes, with new footage wedged in for padding and several new voice actors hired to maintain continuity. This was what premiered on a weekly basis over CBS in the fall of 1979.

The *New Adventures of Flash Gordon* looked a lot like the old ones, with all the usual suspects: Flash, his lady love Dale Arden, cerebral Dr. Zarkov, the kindly Prince Barin and Queen Fria, lionlike Thun, the self-described Ming the Merciless and his equally merciless daughter Aura, all zapping around and zapping one another throughout the Universe.

In its favor, the series avoided the sappy attempts at using 1979 slang and cultural references that Dino De Laurentiis had employed to make his *Flash Gordon* accessible to younger audiences. But though its background and character design was every bit as sumptuous as the Alex Raymond original, the animation on *The New Adventures of Flash Gordon* was wildly uneven, alternating some excellently roto-scoped sequences (notably the perspective shots of model space vehicles in flight) with the usual stiff, strobelike movement that Filmation had been inflicting on Saturday morning for 15 years.

In fairness, the series does have its partisans, who forgive the animation technique on the basis of its character-design fidelity to the comic strip original. But I can't find anyone who truly enjoyed the incessant quips, one-liners and clumsy puns in the *New Adventures of Flash Gordon*'s dialogue sequences, which reduced such well-defined characters as Flash, Dale Arden and Ming the Merciless to the level of comedy club "amateur night" contestants.

After a year of bad ratings, the standard prerogative of all flagging Saturday morning shows was exercised on *Flash Gordon* with the addition of a funny pet, Gremlin the baby dragon, who could blow smoke in the shape of hearts and "smile" buttons. Gremlin lived up to his name by gumming up the proceedings even more than the series' earlier shortcomings. After *New Adventures of Flash Gordon* was cancelled, its better episodes were pared down and reassembled into a feature film, exhibited theatrically in Europe and finally telecast *in toto* over NBC as *Flash Gordon: The Greatest Adventure of All* on August 21, 1982. (For more on Flash Gordon, see *Defenders of the Earth*.)

THE NEW ADVENTURES OF GILLIGAN. CBS: 9/7/1974–9/4/1977. Filmation. Produced by Lou Scheimer and Norm Prescott. Executive consultant, Sherwood Schwartz. Creative director, Don Christensen. Directed by Don Townsley, Lou Zukor, Rudy Larriva and Bill Reed. Written by Marc Richards, Bob Ogle, Jim Ryan, Bill Danch, Chuck Menville, Len Janson. Music by Yvette Blais and Jeff Michael. Consultant: Dr. Nathan Cohen, UCLA. Voices: Bob Denver (Gilligan); Alan Hale (Skipper); Jim Backus (Thurston Howell III); Natalie Schafer (Lovey Howell); Russell Johnson (The Professor); Jane Webb (Ginger); Jane Edwards (Mary Ann); Lou Scheimer (Snubby).
—**GILLIGAN'S PLANET.** CBS: 9/1982–9/10/83. Production credits the same as above, with following change: Writers, Marc Richards, Paul Dini, Tom Ruegger, Robby London. Voice credits same as above, with following change: Voices of Ginger and Mary Ann: Dawn Wells.

Whatever *Gilligan's Island* had, it's a shame that its creator-producer Sherwood Schwartz didn't bottle it and sell it to other sitcom makers. Almost universally savaged by critics when it first appeared in 1964, this slapstick saga of a divergent group marooned on an uncharted tropical island lasted three seasons on CBS, and then became a perpetual cash machine in rerun syndication. Fan clubs, TV-movie revivals, master's theses, autobiographies written by its stars, and even an off–Broadway musical (*way* off, namely North Carolina) have been inspired in the last quarter century by the seven castaways of Gilligan's isle. Along the way, a couple of cartoon weeklies have appeared, conceived because Sherwood Schwartz had been unable in the early 1970s to convince shortsighted network executives that a live *Gilligan's Island* "reunion" would be commercially viable, and thus he was compelled to keep the property alive in another form.

Supervised by Schwartz, *The New Adventures of Gilligan* detailed the further exploits of the hapless passengers and crew of the S. S. *Minnow*. Gilligan, the Skipper, the wealthy Thurston Howells, the Professor, movie star Ginger Grant and secretary Mary Ann continued their efforts to make a home for themselves on their speck in the Pacific. The 24-episode cartoon series had a bit more support from the intelligentsia than its live action predecessor due to the presence of Dr. Nathan Cohen, UCLA educational consultant, who saw to it that the Filmation-produced series stressed the values of teamwork and tolerance.

Otherwise, it was the same old silliness, even unto hiring many of the series' regulars to do the voices. Bob Denver was Gilligan, Alan Hale Jr. the Skipper, Jim Backus (certainly no stranger to cartoondom, as witness *Mr. Magoo* [q.v.]) as Thurston Howell III, Natalie Schafer as Lovey Howell, and Russell Johnson as the Professor.

Conspicuous by their absences were Tina Louise and Dawn Wells, respectively, the original Ginger and Mary Ann. Dawn Wells was busy with a theatre tour in the Midwest; otherwise, she would have been more than happy to recreate the part that brought her more fan mail than anyone else on *Gilligan's Island*. Conversely, Tina Louise had always been contemptuous of her participation in the series and wanted nothing to do with the cartoon version. Therefore, the closing credits of *The New Adventures of Gilligan* listed Jane Webb as Ginger and Jane Edwards as Mary Ann.

In truth, both roles were played by the same actress, who used her maiden name (Webb) for one character and her married name (Edwards) for the other, maintaining the illusion of *seven* stranded castaways. This Webb/Edwards business has fooled many TV historians, who dutifully cite "both" actresses in *New Adventures'* credits. Evidently these writers weren't the only ones to fall for the deception. In his book on *Gilligan's Island*, actor Russell Johnson, who recreated his role as The Professor in the cartoon series, listed Jane

Webb and Jane Edwards as though "they" were different people.

The caricatures on *New Adventures of Gilligan* adhered faithfully to the live cast members, with the notable exception of Tina Louise's Ginger. Reports vary as to why the cartoon Ginger looked so different. According to the book *Animation by Filmation*, Tina Louise's disdain for the series was so profound that she refused permission to be caricatured by the Filmation artists. On the other hand, *Gilligan* executive producer Sherwood Schwartz claimed that Louise's likeness was not used because her animosity towards the property suggested that she *might* sue, thus the animated Ginger was redrawn on Schwartz' own volition. Whatever the case, *New Adventures of Gilligan*'s Ginger Grant was a platinum blonde Kim Novak lookalike as opposed to Titian-haired Tina Louise.

Enough on this subject! We haven't mentioned the one new character on *New Adventures of Gilligan*, that stalwart of Saturday morning animation, the Funny Animal: Gilligan's pet monkey Stubby.

Four years after the cancellation of *New Adventures of Gilligan* (which premiered as number one in its timeslot), a sequel of sorts appeared, this one dragging in a bit of the post–*Star Wars* interest in space travel. *Gilligan's Planet* had us believe that the Professor, who heretofore had been spectacularly unsuccessful in building a boat to get his friends off the island, was able to assemble a rocket ship from the flotsam and jetsam existent on that island. The space vessel then carried our heroes and heroines to the farthest reaches of the Final Frontier. Again, the voices were provided by a goodly portion of the original cast. This time Dawn Wells was back, as both Mary Ann *and* Ginger (she'd proven her ability to play both roles quite well in the 1967 *Gilligan's Island* episode "The Second Ginger Grant"). And this time, Dawn Wells was listed as "Dawn Wells" in both cases, proving that nobody really reads those closing credits after all.

Only 12 *Gilligan's Planet* episodes were filmed, but don't think for a moment that the concept was dead. Even as we speak in the summer of 1993, plans are being concocted for a *Gilligan's Island* theatrical feature film. It's up to you whether that's good news or bad.

THE NEW ADVENTURES OF HUCK FINN. NBC: 9/15/1968–9/7/1969. Hanna-Barbera. Produced by William Hanna and Joe Barbera. Directed by Charles Nichols. Music by Hoyt Curtin. Background art by Walt Peregoy. Cast (live-action): Michael Shea (Huck Finn); Kevin Schultz (Tom Sawyer); Lu Ann Haslam (Becky Thatcher); Ted Cassidy (Injun Joe); Dorothy Tennant (Mrs. Thatcher—first episode); Anne Bellamy (Aunt Polly—first episode). Voices: Ted Cassidy, Dennis Day, Hal Smith, Ted DeCorsia, Peggy Webber, Jack Kruschen, Paul Stewart, Mike Road, Vic Perrin, Charles Lane, Julie Bennett, Paul Frees, Marvin Miller, Joe Sirola, Keye Luke, Janet Waldo, John Myhers, Henry Corden, Don Messick, Daws Butler, Bernard Fox, Danny Bravo, Dayton Lummis, Jay Novello, Abraham Sofaer, Than Wynen, Bill Beckley.

The *New Adventures of Huck Finn* was at once Hanna-Barbera's most ambitious and most controversial project up to 1968. It wasn't that the studio delved into the serious issues of the day or had Huckleberry Finn spouting profanities (though it certainly would have been in character!). It was simply that *Huck Finn* had the gall to base itself on what is probably the greatest single American novel of the 19th century and come up with something that looked more like a warmed-over *The Time Tunnel*.

The 20-episode, weekly half hour series started conventionally enough, with Mark Twain's immortal characters Huck Finn, his pal Tom Sawyer and Tom's heartthrob Becky Thatcher being chased by a vengeful Injun Joe, who, determined to get even with Tom for testifying against him in court in a murder trial, had completely forgotten that he'd died in a cave at the end of *The Adventures of Tom Sawyer*. The protagonists and the antagonist ran into some sort of time warp vortex, with Injun Joe bellowing "I'll find you—wherever you go."

Up to this point, the program was live action (a first for Hanna-Barbera); once entering the realm of fantasy, Huck, Tom and Becky remained their "real" selves, but were now in a cartoon neverland populated by animated characters. The backgrounds and supporting characters changed from episode to episode. One week, the kids would be helping an Irish leprechaun guard his pot of gold; another week, Becky Thatcher would be holding a murderous caliph at bay by telling him stories à la Scheherazade; yet another week, the heroes and heroine would be surrounded by talking farm animals; yet still another week, it would be sword and sorcery time in a medieval kingdom. And at one point, the Twain characters even entered Cervantes territory for a tilt with Don Quixote! Through it all, an animated Injun Joe (retaining the voice of his "live" counterpart, actor Ted Cassidy) would skulk through the scene in various guises, all villainous, all vengeful.

Though Bill Hanna and Joe Barbera were familiar with the process of combining live actors and animation from their MGM days (as witness the Gene Kelly/ Jerry the Mouse dance in 1944's Anchors Aweigh), the process didn't come cheaply and easily, and it required the studio's hiring of new personnel to manage the trick, though some of this new breed had already been signed on for Hanna-Barbera's live/cartoon hybrid TV special, Jack and the Beanstalk (1966). While Huck Finn's trick photography was quite well done by TV standards, it wasn't hard to spot the blue matte lines around the real actors. Nor was there any attempt to truly "blend" the live footage with cartoon; as a result, the actors frequently looked as though they were walking past a stage backdrop rather than really being part of the action. This, however, was a deliberate stylistic decision, to enhance the fantasy feeling of the program. Onetime Hanna-Barbera background artist Walt Peregoy explained to Animato magazine: "The mistake would try to be to integrate the animated background, and make the illustration an attempt at photographic realism. Then you'd have trouble. Because then you're trying to fool, and this doesn't work."

The artificiality of the series was not what bothered viewers, or else they wouldn't have been tuning over to New Adventures of Huck Finn's Sunday evening competition, the even more unbelievable Irwin Allen opus Land of the Giants on ABC. What really grated was the fact that any resemblance to Mark Twain's original work was purely accidental—and this at a time when kidvid was under attack for deflecting children from reading books (was there ever a time when it wasn't under attack for this?). Critics complained

that some viewers might be tempted to pull the Cliff's Notes trick of using New Adventures as a substitute for reading the real Huckleberry Finn. Even worse to these critics was the distorted viewpoint taken when the Twain characters were hurled into situations completely foreign and unsuitable for them (though in fairness, it was Twain himself who invented this sort of "displacement" in his own A Connecticut Yankee in King Arthur's Court). In this manner, the literary characters were reduced to the level of any two-bit superhero or funny animal on Saturday morning TV.

Critic Cleveland Amory of TV Guide spotted an even more dangerous (to him) aspect of the series. By arbitrarily tossing in characters and situations from other great literary works and legends, the producers diminished those works and legends as much as they did Mark Twain. "In the La Mancha show," carped Amory, "it was really shocking to find that there was, in the concept of the character of Don Quixote, not one single whit of pathos, understanding or even point." Amory also found fault with the manner in which characters and situations were distorted into 1960s-TV style entertainment value. He cited the torturing of Sancho Panza by the villain (Injun Joe again, here called "Don Jose D'Indio") as horrendous, made doubly so by the bad guy's obsession with Don Quixote's wealth. Amory complained that by cheapening two timeless literary classics with mindless violence and lust for gold, this particular Huck Finn scenario was one of many examples of how "the whole thing does exactly the opposite of what it should do—i.e., bring to the child of today, if not the values and the virtues of yesterday, at least the simple sanities."

But Cleveland Amory's brutal words were unnecessary, since, when he wrote them in February of 1969, New Adventures of Huck Finn was already on its way out. Those that were attracted to the better than average Hanna-Barbera animation quickly tuned out when they learned that the upped quality did not include any real stylistic variety from week to week. The series also wilted from the competition of the aforementioned Land of the Giants and CBS' longrunning Lassie. The final ratings blow came with NBC's constant preemptions of New Adventures of Huckleberry Finn for sports events and specials—

one of these, the notorious 1968 TV movie version of *Heidi*, earning a great deal of castigation of its own for butting into the deciding final moments of a crucial Jets-Raiders football game. After its cancellation, *The New Adventures of Huck Finn* became just one more cog in the syndication wheel of the *Banana Splits and Friends* weekday package.

THE NEW ADVENTURES OF MIGHTY MOUSE AND HECKLE AND JECKLE see **MIGHTY MOUSE**

THE NEW ADVENTURES OF TIN-TIN see **TINTIN**

THE NEW ADVENTURES OF PI-NOCCHIO see **PINOCCHIO**

THE NEW ADVENTURES OF SU-PERMAN see **SUPERMAN**

THE NEW ADVENTURES OF WINNIE THE POOH. The Disney Channel: 1988. ABC: 9/10/1988–9/2/1989; 9/7/1990–9/4/1993.
—**DISNEY'S GUMMI BEARS/WIN-NIE THE POOH HOUR.** ABC: 9/8/1989–9/1/1990. Walt Disney Television Animation/Buena Vista. Produced and directed by Karl Geurs and Ken Kessel. Produced by Ed Ghertner and Russ Mooney. Story editors, Mark Zaslove and Carl Crocker. Animation directors: David Block and Terrence Harrison. Songs written by Steve Nelson and Tom Sharp; performed by Steve Nelson. Voices: Jim Cummings (Winnie the Pooh/Tigger); Michael Gough (Gopher); Tim Hoskins (Christopher Robin); Hal Smith (Owl); Paul Winchell (Tigger); Patty Parris (Kanga); Nicholas Melody (Roo); and John Fiedler, and Ken Sansom.

British novelist A. A. Milne's *Winnie the Pooh* tales of the 1920s grew out of bedtime stories he'd told his son, the model for *Pooh's* Christopher Robin. As such, these adventures of a little boy, his talking teddy bear and the various animal citizens of Pooh Corner who were based on children's toys were never designed to act as adult social satire, as many critics expected of Milne. The *Pooh* stories were kid's stuff, pure and simple, and though the preciousness of the character names — Eeyore, Piglet, Kanga and Roo — and the childlike spelling patterns ("hunny" for

"honey" and so forth) drove critics like Dorothy Parker up the proverbial wall, children were fascinated and enchanted. But movie and TV rights were elusive, thanks to Milne's proprietary hold on the property. It wasn't until 1960 that *Winnie the Pooh* would be given a live dramatization on NBC's *Shirley Temple Theatre*, and seven more years would pass before the Disney Studios' cartoon version of *Winnie the Pooh*.

Although rendered in the harsh, sketchy character lines of Disney's new Xerography process, the 25-minute *Winnie* short managed to convey all of the soft whimsy of the original stories. Outside of the inclusion of a new, nihilistic character named Gopher, who went about blowing up things as a calculated symbol of Vietnam-era violence, no real attempt was made to bring the characters or storylines up to date (though Christopher Robin was designed more along 1966 lines than 1920). With the irreplaceable Sterling Holloway as the voice of Winnie and the faultless direction of Disney veteran Wolfgang Reitherman, *Winnie the Pooh and the Honey Tree* was nominated for an Oscar; two years later, a sequel, *Winnie the Pooh and the Blustery Day* managed to win the Academy statuette. A third Oscar-nominated short, *Winnie the Pooh and Tigger Too*, rounded out the very brief *Pooh* series of 1966–1973; only the 1983 theatrical release *Winnie the Pooh and a Day for Eeyore* would be produced before the Milne characters would be prepped for television.

Premiering on ABC in 1988 after a brief run on the pay-cable Disney Channel, *The New Adventures of Winnie the Pooh* rapidly became a delightful eye of calm in a hurricane of hectic Saturday morning slapstick. Though by now the Disney company was farming out its animation overseas, there was only the slightest lessening of quality. The venerable property resisted the temptation to streamline and modernize (except for the occasional glancing reference to cowboys, detectives and other TV standbys); the lessons illustrated on the program of cooperation, tolerance, and the broadening of one's imagination were timeless, and offered in a far more subtle manner than the "beware the friendly stranger" prosocial snippets on other programs. And as the voice of Pooh, Jim Cummings managed the considerable task of recalling the wispy intonations of Sterling Holloway while still bringing his own off-kilter slant to the character.

An eager ABC commissioned 25 half-hour episodes of *New Adventures of Winnie the Pooh*, for the first season, rather than the standard 13 to 17. Disney not only gave the results the best production polish available, devoting a year's time to the process, but threw in original songs every few weeks in the bargain. The network was so pleased with the ratings that in 1989, it decided to create a Saturday morning "Disney block" comparable to the syndicated lineup of *DuckTales* and *Chip 'n' Dale's Rescue Rangers* (see separate notes on these programs). The result was *Disney's Gummi Bears–Winnie the Pooh Hour* (see *Disney's Adventures of the Gummi Bears*), which remained in tandem until 1990, when *Gummi Bears* moved to daily syndication.

The *New Adventures of Winnie the Pooh*, a two-time Emmy-winner in the "Outstanding Animated Program" category, was back on ABC as a solo act (new episodes intermixed with reruns) in the fall of 1990, remaining on the network's Saturday morning manifest until 1993. Innumerable children's-expert panels continued throughout the run to highly commend and recommend *New Adventures of Winnie the Pooh* to the three- to 10-year-old crowd, even growing tolerant enough to be amused rather than bemused by the "hunny/honey" spelling controversy.

THE NEW ARCHIES and THE NEW ARCHIE/SABRINA HOUR *see* **ARCHIE**

THE NEW CASPER CARTOON SHOW *see* **CASPER THE FRIENDLY GHOST**

THE NEW FANTASTIC FOUR *see* **THE FANTASTIC FOUR**

THE NEW FRED AND BARNEY SHOW *see* **THE FLINTSTONES**

NEW KIDS ON THE BLOCK. ABC: 9/8/1990–8/31/1991. Disney Channel: 1992. DIC/Big Step/Dick Scott Enterprises. Executive producers: Dick Scott, Andy Heyward, Maurice Starr. Co-executive producer, Robby London. Produced and directed by Mario Pilusco.

Associate producer, Jack Spillum. Music score by Murray McFadden, Timothy Mulholland. Musical supervisor, Joanne Miller. Executive in charge of production, Winnie Chaffee. Production supervisor, Brian Miller. Story editor, Kayte Kisch. Developer for TV/ Story editor: Sheryl Scarborough. Production facilities: Wang Film Production Company, Ltd. Live action producers, Kevin O'Donnell and Eric Schultz. Directed by Mario Pilusco. Cast (live action): Donnie Wahlberg, Jordan Knight, Jonathan Knight, Joe McIntyre, Danny Wood (The New Kids on the Block). Voices: David Coburn, Loren Lester, Scott Menville, Matt E. Mixer (The New Kids on the Block); and Dave Penny, J.P. Hall, Dorian Harewood, Janna Levenstein, Patricia Anne Albrecht, Susan Blu, Thom Gray, Hamilton Camp, Jennifer Darling, Patrick Fraley, Linda Gary, Gaille Heideman, Michael Horse, Clyde Kusutsu, Sherry Lynn, Ken Mars, Pat Musick, Samantha Paris, Rob Paulsen, Adam Phillipson, Maggie Roswell, Theresa Saldana, Leslie Speights, Cree Summer, Susan Ware, Joshua Luis Weiner, Michael Winslow.

The New Kids on the Block was a group of five young Bostonian musicians, white boys who could sing black Rhythm 'n' Blues. The Kids were the "flavor of the year" for all of 1990, selling nine million albums and making a TV series of some sort inevitable. The producers of the weekly animated *New Kids on the Block* labelled the program "the first MTV cartoon," in reference to the series' adoption of MTV's fast-cut rock video style, and the fact that each *New Kids* episode featured at least one new song in addition to live-action concert filmclips. Actually, the honor of "first MTV cartoon" should probably have gone to the syndicated *JEM* (q.v.), but *New Kids* was on the ABC network, and network TV still outranked syndication in the minds of many producers. So it was that *New Kids on the Block* was heralded without challenge as the innovator in this hybrid brand of cartoon-music entertainment.

The premise of the series was that each week the New Kids would be en route to a concert, but somehow always be side-tracked until the last possible moment. Caricatures of the five members—Danny Wood, Donnie Wahlberg, Joe McIntyre, and Jon and Jordan Knight—appeared in the cartoons. So did a drawn representation of their manager Dick Scott, who was probably the guiding force behind the TV depiction of Scott as a kindly, generous soul, good-natured despite assaults to his peaceability from the New Kids' screaming teenaged fans. These characters' voices were supplied by professional actors rather than the real Kids and Scott, though as a balm to their following, the singers were seen in live-action footage at the beginning and end of each episode, being interviewed on the topic explored by the week's episode. Most of these topics were designed to teach a valuable lesson about the importance of avoiding a swelled head, or of looking out for one's friends, or on how to get along with others without falling into peer-pressure pits. The series was careful to demonstrate that the life of a teen celebrity wasn't all roses. The kids were required to take schooling from a touring tutor nicknamed "Einstein," and had to be protected from their more rabid devotees by a tubby bodyguard, Biscuit (or "B-Man").

It wasn't all messages and morals, however. Though no better animated than most other DIC projects, *The New Kids on the Block* had its amusing moments: Particularly enjoyable were frequent cutaways to a "fan central" computer facility run by pretty teenage girls which monitored the movements of the Kids, and the occasional nonsequitur *Monkees*-style visual gag. And there was also a funny dog named Nikko, for those of you out there who couldn't get enough of funny cartoon dogs (aren't you satisfied *yet?*).

The *New Kids on the Block* lasted one season, which turned out to be longer than the success of its inspiration in the public eye. By the middle of 1991, the fan following had dwindled, and stories about the supposedly wholesome New Kids' trashing hotel rooms, undergoing violent domestic squabbles, and staging public exhibits of boorishness, were hard to keep out of the tabloids. The kiss of death came in 1992, when the New Kids made the talkshow route to deny trumped up charges that they'd lip-synched their concerts à la Milli Vanilli, and then proceeded to show off the "new," "adult" sound they would adopt in future concerts. Legend has it that when a showbiz phenomenon starts shouting back

at critics on nationwide TV and begins tinkering with its formula for past success, its phenomenon days are numbered. (Conversely, Mark Wahlberg, brother of "New Kid" Donnie, was skyrocketing to stardom by taking off his belt and changing his name to Marky Mark.) By the fall of 1992, *The New Kids on the Block* were the old fogies down the street, and their series was being seen only in unsponsored weekly doses on the Disney Channel.*

THE NEW PINK PANTHER SHOW *see* **PINK PANTHER**

THE NEW SCOOBY-DOO COMEDY MOVIES and **THE NEW SCOOBY-DOO MYSTERIES** *see* **SCOOBY-DOO**

THE NEW SHMOO. NBC: 9/22/1979–12/1/1979.
—**FRED AND BARNEY MEET THE SHMOO.** NBC: 12/8/1979–11/15/1980. Hanna-Barbera. Executive producers, William Hanna and Joseph Barbera. Produced by Art Scott. Directed by Charles Nichols. Music by Hoyt Curtin; musical direction by Paul DeKorte. Voices: Frank Welker (Shmoo); Delores Cantu-Primo (Nita); Chuck McCann (Billy Joe); Bill Idelson (Mickey).

The Shmoo was a character created in 1948 by Al Capp for his comic strip *Li'l Abner*. As originally conceived, the boneless, bowling pin–shaped Shmoo was the most bountiful creature on Earth: It tasted like chicken when fried and steak when broiled; it laid eggs already packaged in cartons and gave Grade-A milk already bottled; it entertained one and all with "Shmoozical Comedies"; and it defied extinction by multiplying its stock even as human beings slaughtered thousands of Shmoos for food. This, according to *Li'l Abner*'s liberal-slant continuity, posed such a threat for the capitalist system that it was vital to national security to wipe the Shmoo off the face of the Earth. While the Shmoo periodically reappeared in *Li'l Abner* throughout the 1950s and 1960s, it was conspicuous by its absence once Al Capp became a Born-Again Conservative.

The symbolic nature of the Shmoo was completely ignored when Hanna-Barbera produced *The New Shmoo* cartoon series in 1979. It was a funny looking character.

The Kids disbanded in 1994, after a brief spurt of activity under a "new" name—N.K.O.T.B.

Funny looking characters belong on Saturday morning. Case closed. (Note the almost microscopic tinyness of Al Capp's onscreen *New Shmoo* "created by" credit). Hanna-Barbera's Shmoo was a cute 'n' lovable crimefighter, a function later filled by Shmoolike spectre Casper the Friendly Ghost (q.v.) on *Casper and the Angels*. The star of *New Shmoo* helped the standard teenaged-reporter characters—Nita, Billy Joe and Mickey, stringers for "Mighty Mysteries" comics—investigate paranormal disturbances. The once unique Shmoo was now merely a weak-tea imitation of Terrytoons' *Tom Terrific* (q.v.), changing his shape and size depending on the dictates of the storylines.

Within months after its debut, *New Shmoo* was absorbed by a more successful H-B property, its title altered to *Fred and Barney Meet the Shmoo* (see *The Flintstones*). This in turn led to the Shmoo-populated Bedrock police force on *The Flintstones Comedy Hour*. To quote Li'l Abner, this denigration of a legendary comic strip property was "confoozin but not amoozin."

THE NEW THREE STOOGES. Syndicated: 1965. Cambria/Normandy/Heritage III. Executive producers: Norman Maurer (live action); Dick Brown (animation). Associate producer, Dave Detiege. Director (live action): Edward Bernds. Directors (animation): Eddie Rehberg, Sam Cornell, Dave Detiege. Written by Edward Bernds (live-action); Jack Miller, Sam Cornell, Art Diamond, Warren Tufts, Cecil Beard, Barbara Chaim, Jack Kinney, Nick George, Pat Kearin, Homer Brightman, Lee Orgel, Dave Detiege. Photography: Jerry Smith and Ed Gillette. Edited by William J. Faris. Music by Paul Horn. CAST (live action): The Three Stooges (Moe Howard, Larry Fine, Joe DeRita); and Emil Sitka, Peggy Brown/ Margaret Kerry, Emil Sitka, Harold Brauer, Jeffrey Maurer/Jeffrey Scott, Cary, Tina and Eileen Brown. Voices: Three Stooges (Themselves); and Hal Smith, Peggy Brown, and Ned Lefebvre.

Like its spiritual (though not identical) twin cartoon project *Laurel and Hardy* (q.v.), *The New Three Stooges* was several years in the making. There needs no ghost come from the grave to tell any comedy fan that the Three Stooges, a veteran knockabout comedy act formed in 1925,

enjoyed a renaissance in popularity when their 190 Columbia two-reel theatrical comedies were released to television in 1958. Suddenly the Stooges, who had been on the verge of retirement, were "hot" again, resulting in innumerable TV and personal appearances and a string of low-budget but enjoyable feature films.

Thanks to the efforts of senior stooge Moe Howard's son-in-law Norman Maurer, a major comic book artist/writer, it looked in 1960 as though the Three Stooges would also invade the animation medium. The plan was to film the Stooges—beatle-mopped Moe Howard, frizzy-haired Larry Fine and barrel-bellied Curly Joe DeRita (the newest member of the trio, taking the "patsy" role previously played by Curly Howard, Shemp Howard and Joe Besser)—in brief live sketches that would be used as wraparounds for five-minute cartoon sequences. According to authors Jeff and Greg Lenburg and Moe's daughter Joan Howard, the censorial leeway given TV cartoons at the time would permit the filming of all the destruction and mayhem that had made the Stooges famous, while the live portions would offer a more subdued form of comedy as a placebo to critics who deplored the team's violence.

The *Three Stooges Scrapbook* was the title for the 25-minute pilot film prepared by Norman Maurer's Normandy Productions. The pilot included a live vignette titled "Home Cooking" wherein the Stooges avoided their landlady, then foiled a Martian plot to steal an eccentric professor's flying machine, and still found time to host their own TV kiddie program. This last segment segued into the cartoon, which proposed that the Stooges and their pet parrot Feathers helped Columbus discover America.

Written by longtime Three Stooges collaborator Ellwood Ullman and directed by *Mickey Mouse Club* stalwart Sidney Miller, the live portion of the program was energetic and quite funny at times, bolstered by the antics of perennial Stooges supporting actor Emil Sitka as the befuddled professor. This was more than could be said for the cartoon segment, which although produced by the well-respected TV Spots, the company that in concert with Creston Studios had assembled the most recent batch of *Crusader Rabbit* (q.v.) episodes, looked more amateurish than any amateur cartoon could be. No one bought *Three Stooges Scrapbook* for television, so the property was given limited release as a theatrical short, and then was incorporated into the footage of a 1962 feature length comedy, *The Three Stooges in Orbit*. (The next time you see that film, you'll be able to spot immediately the *Three Stooges Scrapbook* sequences. They were filmed in color, then reprocessed in black and white along with the newly shot footage of *Three Stooges in Orbit*; consequently, the Stooges' facial makeup seems much deeper and thicker in the *Scrapbook* scenes than in the rest of the film.)

Now we move to 1965, the year that Norman Maurer struck a deal with Cambria Films, the company responsible for *Clutch Cargo*, *Captain Fathom* and *Space Angel* (q.v.). Cambria had an "in" with local TV outlets thanks to the success of their aforementioned cartoon series, so it was easier to sell a *Three Stooges* animated project this time around. Once more, the format of live action wraparounds and five-minute cartoon shorts was adhered to. Warner Bros. veteran Dave Detiege supervised the animated sequences, while oldtime Three Stooges colleague Edward Bernds wrote and directed the live sequences, most of which were filmed in and around the beach resort of Balboa, California. Again, the live sequences outclassed the animation, though the cartoons were far better produced than that wretched little exercise seen in *Three Stooges Scrapbook*. Filmed in full color on a budget of $1,500,000, *The New Three Stooges* was syndicated to 45 markets by Heritage Productions in the fall of 1965.

If you missed this series back then, you're in good company. The project was a disappointment for a couple of reasons. For one, only 40 live wraparounds were filmed, and then rotated as lead-ins for the 156 cartoons. Stooge member Curly Joe DeRita would note in later years that the casual viewer would tune in, see a live sequence that they'd seen a few days earlier, then assume it was a rerun and tune out, even though the cartoon may have been brand new. The second, and most deciding factor in the failure of *The New Three Stooges*, was that the Stooge craze had already peaked and was dying out. To paraphrase Joe DeRita again, by 1967 the Three Stooges couldn't even get booked into a bowling alley. Nobody came out

ahead with *The New Three Stooges*, least of all the team itself, which sued Heritage productions for allegedly not providing accurate earning statements on the series — and lost.

In the 1970s, many of the adult baby boomers whose 1950s enthusiasm had given the Three Stooges their "second career" had formed a cult around the team; where previously the Stooges had been written off as second-raters, they were now hailed to the skies as comic geniuses. Renewed interest in the team prompted fresh merchandising of anything remotely connected with the Stooges. That's when a number of videotape entrepreneurs discovered that several of the *New Three Stooges* segments had lapsed into public domain, and could be sold without paying a licensing fee. Throughout the late 1980s these worn, faded *New Three Stooges* prints flooded both video rental shelves and local TV outlets too parsimonious to pay for the more expensive cartoons from mainstream distributors. It could be said that *The New Three Stooges* has finally posted a profit — small comfort for the now-deceased members of the team or for Norman Maurer, who himself passed away in 1986. (See also *The Three Robonic Stooges*.)

In 1992, Maurer's son (and Moe Howard's grandson) Jeffrey Scott, having acquired the rights to the Stooges characters, repackaged *The New Three Stooges* utilizing bright new color prints, and released the property as a daily half hour strip through the distribution channels of DIC Enterprises. Why DIC? Because that company's CEO, Andy Heyward, was a lifelong fan of The Three Stooges. And *admitted* it.

THE NOOZLES. Nickelodeon: 11/8/ 1988–4/2/1993. Fuji Eight Co. Ltd./Saban. Executive producer, Haim Saban. Supervising producer, Winston Richard. Executive in charge of production, Jerald E. Bergh. Supervising director, Tom Wyner. Additional direction by Byrd Ehlmann, Tony Oliver, Dave Mallow. Written by Tom Wyner, R. Dwight, Benjamin Lesko, Wendy Mandel, Dave Mallow, Eric Early, Michael Santiago. Music by Haim Saban and Shuki Levy. Musical supervision by Andrew Dimitroff. No voice credits given.

Put simply, *The Noozles* were *The Care Bears* (q.v.) gone marsupial. Twelve-year-old Sandy discovered that by rubbing noses with her stuffed Koala bear Blinky, the creature became a live, magical being. Blinky was a refuge from Koalawallaland, a Heinleinesque alternate world where the citizens' movements were strictly governed by immigration-official kangaroos and police platypuses—and where no humans were allowed. Sandy was occasionally permitted entry into this "paradise" by donning a false koala nose, though as noted by cartoon historian Jeff Rovin (and most child observers), it's astounding that she'd want to visit such an oppressive society.

In addition to having the powers of speech and flight, Blinky also had a younger sibling, Pinky, whose rebellious nature caused no end of trouble in both Koalawallaland and the Real World. Woe would have been unto Blinky and Pinky should they have lost their magic compact-like device that enabled them to see through solid objects, or else they would have been easy prey for two scraggly villains, Spike and Frankie, who wanted to capture the Koalas and sell them to the highest bidder.

The 26 *Noozles* episodes were part of Nickelodeon's long lineup of "cute" cartoon imports (see also *The Adventures of the Little Koala*, *The Littl' Bits*, *Maya the Bee* and *The World of David the Gnome*) and were generally run on weekday afternoons.

THE NUTTY SQUIRRELS. Syndicated: 1960. Transfilm-Wilde.

Following the success of Ross Bagdasarian's "Chipmunk" albums in the late 1950s (see *Alvin and the Chipmunks*), there were quite a few fast-buck operators who pressed their own discs featuring speeded-up, Chipmunk-like voices singing popular songs. "The Nutty Squirrels" weren't exactly this sort of ripoff, but a different slant on the Bagdasarian premise.

The "Squirrels" were actually two well established musicians: jazzman Don Elliot and TV composer Alexander "Sascha" Burland (it was Burland who wrote the original theme for the CBS quiz show *What's My Line?*). Amused by the Chipmunks, Elliot and Burland decided that it would be intriguing to use the same recording technique for a hipper form of "scat" singing. What resulted was a brisk little ditty that went something like this:

"Uh-uh-uh-uh-UH-oh, UH oh, UH oh, doo-bee-yah!"

Playing far better than it reads, the song, officially titled "Uh-Oh!: Part Two," was picked up by a new label, Hanover-Signature records, owned in part by comedian and jazz aficionado Steve Allen. The single scored a novelty success, making it to number 14 in the Hit Parade for the week of December 28, 1959, almost exactly one year after Bagdasarian's "Chipmunk Song" made the same list.

Around the same time, plans were being drawn up in the Chipmunk camp for a cartoon series, plans which were snagged by budget problems and indecisions pertaining to character design. Transfilm-Wilde, a company specializing in animated commercials, decided to strike while the iron was hot and beat the Chipmunks to the drawing boards. The company secured TV rights to the Nutty Squirrels characters and songs, and by the fall of 1960, 100 five-minute *Nutty Squirrels* cartoons were sent out in syndication.

As evidenced by Transfilm-Wilde's ad campaign, the *Squirrels* efforts boasted an attractive, streamlined, UPA-like production design, with characters delineated in a minimalist style reminiscent of Jules Feiffer. The cartoons were immediately picked up by several big-city markets, notably Chicago, where they ran six days a week on WGN-TV. But *The Nutty Squirrels* failed to make any inroads in hinterland markets, where TV station managers were generally resistant to any form of "radical" entertainment, meaning jazz music. Those that did buy the package generally threw the *Squirrels* in arbitrarily with the rest of the "funny animal" characters in their Terrytoons and Walter Lantz packages. One station in South Bend, Indiana, used the *Nutty Squirrels* as "hosts" for their old, worn out *Farmer Alfalfa* theatrical cartoons, with the Squirrels themselves appearing as afterthoughts.

It's hard to determine whether or not the Squirrels deserved this cavalier treatment, since their cartoons are currently unavailable for reappraisal. At any rate, the vogue for *The Nutty Squirrels* was very brief. After a few other high-pitched singles with titles like "Salt Peanuts," "Ding Dong" and "Zowie," the "group" faded from view. Hanover-Signature records folded early in the 1960s, leaving Don

Elliot and Sascha Burland labelless. By 1964, the team broke up, returning to solo freelance work—just two more casualties of the record industry's "one hit wonder" syndrome.

THE ODDBALL COUPLE. ABC: 9/6/1975–9/3/1977. DePatie-Freleng. Executive producers, David DePatie and Friz Freleng. Directed by Lewis Marshall. Written by Robert Ogle, Joel Kane, Dave Detiege, Earl Kress, John W. Dunn. Music by Doug Goodwin. Voices: Paul Winchell (Fleabag); Frank Nelson (Spiffy); Joan Gerber (Goldie); and Frank Welker, Joe Besser, Don Messick, Sarah Kennedy, Bob Holt, and Ginny Tyler.

The *Oddball Couple* referred to two anthropomorphic animals. Fleabag, the dog, was a slob. Spiffy, the cat, was a neatnik. Neil Simon was on the phone with his attorney. Well, not really, but *The Oddball Couple* was indeed a Tom-and-Jerry lampoon of Simon's *The Odd Couple*, a very popular 1965 stage play about two mismatched roommates which became a very popular 1968 movie, which in turn became a very popular six-season ABC TV series that had been cancelled the very year that *Oddball Couple* entered the ABC Saturday morning sweepstakes. The *Oddball Couple* was not very popular.

Details: Fleabag (read "Oscar Madison") and Spiffy (read "Felix Ungar") were freelance reporters (on TV's *Odd Couple*, Oscar was a sportswriter, Felix a commercial photographer). Goldie (I guess this was supposed to be the character played on *Odd Couple* by Penny Marshall) was their secretary. For 16 half-hour episodes (two plotlines per program), Fleabag and Spiffy got mixed up in wacky adventures, much to the delight of the canned laughtrack.

Of marginal interest was the fact that some thought beyond ripoff actually went into the making of *Oddball Couple*. Originally the tidy Spiffy was to be named Sprucey, but this name was vetoed by the network on the grounds that kids wouldn't understand what "spruce" meant. The actual reason, speculated on by Walter Brasch in his book *Cartoon Monickers*, may have been the closeness of Sprucey to Bruce—a name that was in 1975 being avoided by TV because of its alleged homosexual connotations. So far as ABC was concerned, the kids of the seventies weren't ready for a gay pussycat.

The *Oddball Couple* was on a par with such other primetime ripoffs as *The Barkleys* (q.v.) and the *M*U*S*H* installments of *Uncle Croc's Block* (q.v.). And just what does that mean? To paraphrase Neil Simon:

READER: In other words, *The Oddball Couple* was bad.

ME: Not "in other words." Those are the *perfect words!*

OFF TO SEE THE WIZARD *see* **THE WIZARD OF OZ**

THE ORIGINAL GHOSTBUSTERS *see* **GHOSTBUSTERS**

THE OSMONDS. ABC: 9/9/1972–9/1/1974. Rankin-Bass. Directed by Arthur Rankin Jr., Tony Guy and Tony Zass. Animation facilities by Halas and Batchelor. Background musical orchestrations by Maury Laws. Voices: Allen, Jay, Jimmy, Donny, Merrill and Wayne Osmond (Themselves); Paul Frees (Fugi, the dog).

The *Osmonds* was a half-hour weekly cartoon series using the voices and likenesses of the singing Osmond boys from Utah: Allen, Jay, Jimmy, Donny, Merrill, and Wayne (this was a boys-only club, so Marie Osmond was absent). The premise was that the Osmonds were appointed by the United States Music Community (you remember them!) to tour the world as goodwill ambassadors. This they did, in the company of their talking dog Fugi, for 17 weeks (104 weeks, if you count the several rerun cycles). It wasn't the first regular TV series for the Osmonds (they appeared as supporting characters on the unlamented 1963 western *Travels of Jamie McPheeters*) and it sure wouldn't be the last.

Some activist groups of the 1970s accused ABC of commissioning *The Osmonds* in order to have a "whiteface" alternative for the network's popular Saturday morning *Jackson 5ive* (q.v.) cartoon series. Whether this was true or not, *The Osmonds* and *Jackson 5ive*, by virtue of sharing the same production company (Rankin-Bass) and some of the same comedy situations, did bear some resemblance. Certainly one bunch of adolescent singing kids sounded about the same as another bunch of adolescent singing kids to those who weren't fans of either group.

OUT OF THE INKWELL. Syndicated: 1962. Hal Seeger/Videohouse. Directed by Myron Waldman. Voices: Larry Storch.

Koko the Clown was just about the oldest animated property ever transferred to TV. The black-clad clown originally appeared as a nameless entity in a series of tests conducted by Max, David and Joe Fleischer in 1915. The Fleischers were attempting to recreate actual movement in cartoons, and developed a technique called Rotoscoping, which entailed tracing a live-action film frame by frame, then animating the traced pencil drawings. As the on-camera subject of these experiments, Dave Fleischer, who was able to dance and turn cartwheels, dressed in a white-buttoned harlequin suit.

From these tests grew a 1916 cartoon short, *Out of the Inkwell*, released by Paramount as part of the studio's "Bray Pictograph" animated series. No attempt was made to hide the fact that this and subsequent Rotoscoped cartoons were actually retraced live films, and this "open secret" resulted in a brief fan following for Dave Fleischer. Eventually the Clown was given his own starring series, and in due time a name, Koko (or Ko-Ko, as it was later spelled in avoidance of possible copyright infringement with Gilbert and Sullivan's *The Mikado*); he was also given a genuinely funny animal pet, a rubbery dog named Fitz. Released by several statesrights companies, the *Out of the Inkwell* series, so named because of Ko-Ko's initial emergence from the inkwell of live-action artist Max Fleischer in each cartoon, became internationally popular. In later years, such Ko-Ko vehicles as *Bedtime* (1923), *A Trip to Mars* (1925) and *Ko-Ko's Earth Control* (1927) would be hailed as masterpieces of hallucinogenic surrealism; audiences of the 1920s were more inclined to take them at face value and laugh till their sides ached.

The *Out of the Inkwell* "Ko-Ko the Clown" vehicles ended abruptly with the coming of sound in 1929; the character appeared as a supporting actor in the Fleischer *Betty Boop* cartoons of the early 1930s, then faded away. Television made Ko-Ko a star all over again in the 1950s when his silent escapades, with new musical scores attached, were released to the many "Uncle" and "Captain" kiddie shows throughout the USA. With the emergence of made-for-TV cartoons in the late 1950s, the old black and white Ko-Ko shorts were considered passé. Even so, Ko-Ko himself was deemed strong enough for a full-color revival.

Hal Seeger, a onetime Fleischer employee who'd struck out on his own as a TV animation producer, packaged a series of new *Out of the Inkwell* cartoons for off-network syndication in 1961. Another ex–Fleischer man, Myron Waldman, was engaged to direct, and even Max Fleischer himself was coaxed out of retirement to star in the pilot episode. Myron Waldman would in later years recall affectionately that the octogenarian Fleischer, eager to make one last good impression on the multitudes, wore an elaborate new toupee for his farewell *Out of the Inkwell* appearance.

Unfortunately, that was the only affectionate reminiscence Waldman would ever have about the project. Not given the time or the studio talent to let his imagination run unbridled, Waldman chafed at the restrictions imposed by mass-produced TV cartoonery. And then there was the tiresome adherence to Formula: As bad as it was to rob Ko-Ko of the fluid, humanlike movement that was once his trademark, it was even worse to saddle the Clown with a cast of all-too-typical cartoon pals, including a girlfriend named Kokette (who looked more like Honey Halfwitch, star of a 1960s package of second-rate Paramount Cartoon Studio theatrical shorts) and a villain named Mean Moe. As for Koko-Nut the dog, one expected the kids at home to rise as one and bellow "BRING BACK FITZ!"

After a misleadingly strong opener in which Ko-Ko not only coexisted with liveaction backgrounds but also led the audience in a "follow the bouncing ball" singalong (reviving yet another Fleischer creation), *Out of the Inkwell* went downhill very quickly. Myron Waldman did the best with the tools at hand, and Larry Storch was sometimes funny supplying all the voices, but the project was a major letdown, merely another mediocre entry in a TV world of mediocrities. And just try to find anyone who can remember seeing one of the new *Out of the Inkwell*s back in 1962. *I* couldn't.

THE PAC-MAN SHOW. ABC: 9/25/1982–9/3/1983.

−PAC-MAN/LITTLE RASCALS/ RICHIE RICH SHOW. ABC: 9/25/1982– 9/3/1983. Hanna-Barbera. Executive producers, William Hanna and Joseph Barbera. Creative producer, Iwao Takamoto. Produced by Kay Wright. Concept developed for television by Jeffrey Scott. Animation supervisors, Jay Sarbry and Joanna Romersa. Supervising director, Ray Patterson. Directed by George Gordon, Bill Hutten, Bob Hathcock, Carl Urbano, Rudy Zamora. Animation directors, Bob Goe and Terry Harrison. Story direction, Stephen Hickner, Mitchell Schauer, Thomas Tataranowicz, Wendall Washer, Roy Wilson. Recording directors, Gordon Hunt and Ginny McSwain. Music by Hoyt Curtin and Paul DeKorte. Background supervisor, Al Gmuer. Video game developed by Namco Ltd.; manufactured by Bally/Midway Mfg. Voices: Marty Ingels (Pac-Man); Barbara Minkus (Ms. Pepper Pac-Man); Russi Taylor (Baby Pac); Frank Welker (Chomp Chomp); Peter Cullen (Sour Puss); Alan Lurie (Mezmaron); Neilson Ross (Clyde Monster); Chuck McCann (Blinky and Pinky Monsters); Barry Gordon (Inky Monster); and Jodi Carlisle, Paul Kirby, Susan Silo, and Lennie Weinrib.

−THE PAC-MAN/RUBIK THE AMAZING CUBE HOUR. ABC: 9/10/ 1983–9/1/1984. Hanna-Barbera/Ruby-Spears. Hanna-Barbera production credits same as PAC-MAN. Ruby-Spears production credits: Executive producers, Joe Ruby and Ken Spears. Produced by Mark Jones and Steve Weiner. Directed by Rudy Larriva, John Kimball and Norman McCabe. Music by Dean Elliot. Voices of PAC-MAN installments: Same as above, with following additions: Lorenzo Music (Super-Pac); Daryl Hickman (Pac Junior). Voices of RUBIK installments: Ron Palillo (Rubik); Michael Saucedo (Carlos Rodriguez); Michael Bell (Renaldo/Ruby Rodriguez); Jennifer Fajardo (Lisa Rodriguez); Angela Moya (Marla Rodriguez).

−RUBIK THE AMAZING CUBE. ABC: 4/27/1985–8/31/1985. Ruby-Spears. Production and voice credits: see above.

Pac-Man was the first major videogame character aimed primarily at kids. Although the character's essential purpose in life was to eat his opponents and to avoid being eaten himself, the anthropomorphic white ball was essentially nonthreatening and childlike. Conversely, there was nothing terribly childlike about the joystick-operated character's origins. Pac-Man had been developed by an employee of Masaya Nakamura, owner of the Japan-based arcade firm Namco, who in turn sold the rights to Nintendo. The hapless Namco underling who'd invented this multi-million-dollar property was paid a miserly $3500 − and became so disgusted that he quit the video business altogether.

None of this corporate intrigue was allowed to intrude on the inevitable *Pac-Man* Saturday morning cartoon series, which starred the yellow, rounded, bouncing title character, along with wife Ms. Pepper Pac-Man (not "Mrs. Pac" − this was the 1980s), pacifier-sucking child Baby Pac, and their orb-shaped pets Chomp Chomp (the dog) and Sour Puss (the cat). Stuck with a videogame with a wafer-thin scenario (Pac-Man chomped his enemies, and that's about all there was to it), Hanna-Barbera was compelled to create a setting and format out of whole cloth. The Pac-Man family now lived in the crayon colored, forced perspective world of Pac-Land, where everything − trees, buildings, autos − was as ball-shaped as the protagonists. This world was energized by Power Pellets (providing "Pac Power"), which grew in the Power Forest, where Pac-Man was gainfully employed as Chief of Security.

With a treasure trove like the Power Forest at hand, it was only natural that there'd be dirty work afoot. The head villain was Mezmaron (a holdover from the videogame), a baldheaded comic-opera version of *Star Wars'* Darth Vader whose mission in life was to rob Pac-Land of its vital pellets. To this end, Mezmaron enlisted the aid of four tiny Ghost Monsters (three male, one female) who flitted about in multicolored shrouds. The battle of Pac-Man vs. Ghost Monsters would have to address the issue of the original arcade game's "cannibalism" somewhere along the line; after all, the basic appeal of Pac-Man was his indiscriminate ingestion of his foes. This was handled with such nonviolent dexterity that Hanna-Barbera could have written a textbook for Action for Children's Television on the subject. Pac-Man only chomped the Ghost Monsters when defending his loved ones or the Power Forest (as opposed to the videogame, where the lead character was on the offensive), and once chomped, the Ghost Monsters merely disappeared temporarily, re-emerging unscathed after picking up new shrouds from Mezmaron's wardrobe closet!

The *Pac-Man Show* could be a lot of fun if you were in the right mood, even though it leaned towards Hanna-Barbera's tendency to forsake story values in favor of a neverending chase. The starring voice of "Pakky" was supplied by Marty Ingels, a prominent comic actor of the 1960s and 1970s who'd left performing due to emotional problems and had become a powerful actors' agent. The story goes that Ingels was lining up talent for Hanna-Barbera, and in demonstrating how Pac-Man should talk, it was discovered that he was perfect for the role. This sort of story drives professional voice-people crazy. It's not *that* easy to land a leading role, even for veterans, though it's true that Marty Ingels turned out to be the ideal choice. (In his autobiography, Ingels intimated that this was his first cartoon work, though he'd done voices for a brace of earlier Hanna-Barbera properties: *Motormouse and Autocat* [see *The Cattanooga Cats*] and *Grape Ape* [see *Tom And Jerry*].) As it happened, Ingels' return to the performing end of the business resulted in *two* series stints: During its first season, the half-hour *Pac Man* was telecast back to back with the hourlong *The Pac-Man/Little Rascals/Richie Rich Show*, in which Pakky shared time with two other Hanna-Barbera animated properties (see individual entries on *The Little Rascals* and *Richie Rich*).

In 1983, *Pac-Man* and *The Little Rascals/Richie Rich Show* split off in two separate time slots. *Pac-Man* was teamed for an hour's airtime with another "craze" of the early 1980s, *Rubik the Amazing Cube* (q.v.). Created by Erno Rubik, the original cube was a maddening rebuslike plastic puzzle block; you had to align the movable colored squares on the block to "win," or have you forgotten? Through the auspices of Ruby-Spears, the nowanthropomorphic cube was given a voice (*Welcome Back Kotter*'s Ron "Horshack" Palillo) and a personality. He also became something of a Superblock, with wideranging talents including his ability to fly, alter his shape, and cast magic rays. The plotline captured the appeal of the original Rubik by contriving that the cartoon cube had to correctly line up the squares on his abdomen in order to perform his many feats (and woe be unto him

if his squares were ever lined up incorrectly).

The *Rubik* sequences themselves were unmemorable except for their prosocial content. Ruby-Spears chose to tap a previously underused ethnic group by making all of Rubik's friends Hispanic. The character's human companions were the Rodriguez children — Carlos, Lisa and Renaldo — and all were intensely involved in improving the standards of living in their neighborhood. In this respect, *Rubik the Amazing Cube* had a lot going for it; additionally, it was the only network cartoon series outside of Filmation's *Zorro* (see *Tarzan*) to acknowledge the existence of Saturday morning TV's strong Hispanic fan following.

As *The Pac-Man/Rubik the Amazing Cube Hour*, the series survived until 1984, at which time *Pac-Man* bounced into the sunset and *Rubik* remained on the air for a half-season of reruns.

PADDINGTON BEAR. PBS: 4/13/1981–5/18/1981. Disney Channel: 1989 (see notes on LUNCH BOX). G Films/Film Fair Productions. Produced by Graham Clutterback. Directed by Barry Leith. Voices: Michael Hordern. Host (American telecasts): Joel Grey.

—PADDINGTON BEAR. Hanna-Barbera: 1989 (As part of FUNTASTIC WORLD OF HANNA-BARBERA). Voices: Charlie Adler (Paddington Bear); John Standing (Mr. Brown); B. J. Ward (Mrs. Brown); Cody Everett (Jonathan Brown); Katie Johnson (Judy Brown); Georgia Brown (Mrs. Bird); R. J. Williams (David Russell); Hamilton Camp (Mr. Gruber); Tim Curry (Mr. Curry).

For whatever reason, London's Paddington Station, a humble railway depot, has given identity to two deathless fictional characters. The first was Lord Paddington, Stan Laurel's superintelligent alter ego in the 1940 Laurel and Hardy comedy *A Chump at Oxford*. The second was Paddington Bear, an urban "Winnie the Pooh" created by British children's author Michael Bond. A stuffed bear from Peru, the raincoated Paddington earned his name when discovered sitting on a suitcase in the selfsame railway station by a middle-class couple, Mr. and Mrs. Brown. The Browns adopted Paddington and took him for an extensive sightseeing tour of London, during which the ingenuous bruin caused all sorts of unintentional mischief, à la *Curious George* (q.v.). A favorite in Britain, the stop-motion animation of *Paddington Bear* was introduced to American audiences via a six-part series over PBS in 1981. Briton Michael Hordern narrated Paddington's adventures, while American entertainer Joel Grey was used as the celebrity host for the PBS telecasts.

Even as the original *Paddington Bear* was going the rerun route as part of the Disney Channel's daily *Lunch Box* (q.v.) in 1989, Hanna-Barbera put its own spin on the character with a series of 13 *Paddington* half hours, newly animated for the weekly syndicated omnibus *The Funtastic World of Hanna-Barbera* (q.v.). The studio did its utmost to retain the dry British wit and flavor of the first *Paddington Bear*, even though the benignly troublesome character was folded and spindled into fitting traditional Hanna-Barbera situation comedy formula. Author Michael Bond's original supporting characters of the Brown family, Gruber the antique shop owner and Mrs. Bird the housekeeper were kept on, in addition to a new, Americanized character, an overseas cousin named David Russell. Tim Curry, the British actor best known for his "Dr. Frank N. Furter" characterization in the cult classic *The Rocky Horror Picture Show*, began a long association with animated cartoons by providing the voice of Paddington's nemesis, a next door neighbor named — and this must have been the most blood-curdling cognomen Hanna-Barbera could come up with — Mr. Curry.

PANDAMONIUM. CBS: 9/18/1982–9/10/1983. Intermedia Entertainment/Marvel. Executive producer: Fred Silverman, David DePatie. Created by Fred Silverman and Jerry Eisenberg. Supervising producer, Jerry Eisenberg. Executive in charge of production, Lee Gunther. Produced by Tony Benedict. Animation directed by Art Vitello, Brad Case, Nelson Shin, Milt Gray, Norman McCabe, Kent Butterworth. Story editor, Jeffrey Scott. Written by Dennis Marks, Don Sheppard, Barry Caldwell, Alex Lovy, Gary Goldstein, Harry Forsyth. Voice director, Alan Dinehart. Music by Johnny Douglas. Animation facilities, Pam Sang East Co., Ltd. Voices: Jesse White (Chesty); Cliff Norton (Timothy); Walker Edmiston (Algernon); Katie Leigh (Peggy); Neilson Ross (Peter);

William Woodson (Mondraggor); Julie McWhirter Dees (Amanda Panda); and Rick Dees, Alan Dinehart, Janet Waldo, and David Banks.

Pandamonium combined the "Mythical Quest" concept with the contemporary — for 1982 — fascination with Asian panda bears (China had recently donated two pandas to the Washington Zoo, where their mating progress was closely monitored by the press). The weekly series' backstory took less time to set up than it does to explain: The evil Mondraggor, a faceless demon in a hooded cape, snuck aboard a faraway planet to steal the Pyramid of Power, which would enable Mondraggor to rule the universe. But the Pyramid apparently had a mind of its own. It resisted Mondraggor's grasp, hurled itself into space, and exploded into sundry particles, which were then scattered throughout the Earth. Witnessing the explosion by telescope was teenaged American scientist-in-training Peter Darrow. Peter and his sister Peggy, chartering a private plane with their parents' credit cards (was this the "educational" portion of the program?), sought out a Pyramid chunk located in Tibet, where there was a surprising absence of Communist guards. The Pyramid fragment was in the possession of three stoogelike talking Pandas: bullying Chesty, slowwitted Algernon and timorous Timmy.

When Pandas and Darrows met, Mondraggor appeared in a vision, explaining that the discovery of each Pyramid piece would lead to another piece. The race was both on Earth and in outer space between good guys and bad guy to reassemble the precious Pyramid. Mondraggor seemingly had the advantage with his ability to control the elements and to hypnotize people into doing his will. But the Pandas weren't exactly slouches; whenever threatened by Mondraggor, they'd merge into one all powerful "Poppapanda," which could counteract any mischief perpetrated by Mondraggor.

Thirteen weeks. That's all they got out of this one, despite its convoluted set-up. *Pandamonium* co-creator Fred Silverman may have been aiming for another copacetic combination of laughter and thrills in the tradition of *Scooby-Doo* (q.v.), but the magic was lacking this time around. No *Pandamonium* action figures or toys caught on, and neither the animation (surprisingly shoddy for the Marvel staff), the scripting nor the laughtrack-plagued comedy content was compelling enough to persuade kids to tune away from the competing *Incredible Hulk and Amazing Spiderman* (NBC) or *Scooby and Scrappy/ The Puppy's New Adventures* (ABC).

PARTRIDGE FAMILY: 2200 A.D. CBS: 9/9/1974–3/1/1975. Hanna-Barbera. Executive producers, William Hanna and Joseph Barbera. Creative producer, Iwao Takamoto. Directed by Charles Nichols. Music score by Hoyt Curtin. Voices: Joan Gerber (Connie Partridge); Chuck Mc-Clendon (Keith Partridge); Susan Dey (Laurie Partridge); Danny Bonaduce (Danny Partridge); Brian Forster (Christopher Partridge); Suzanne Crough (Tracy Partridge); Dave Madden (Reuben Kinkaid); Julie McWhirter (Marion); Frank Welker (Veenie); and Sherry Alberoni, Allan Melvin, Alan Oppenheimer, Mike Road, Hal Smith, John Stephenson, Lennie Weinrib.

The *Partridge Family*, a half hour series best described as a singing *Brady Bunch*, ran as a live-actioner on ABC from 1970 through 1974. The principal characters, a family singing troupe who travelled from engagement to engagement in a "psychedelic" multicolored bus, were based on a similar real life sibling aggregation, the Cowsills. Shirley Jones starred as Shirley Partridge, with her stepson David Cassidy as her TV son Keith. Cassidy of course was launched into Teen Idol Paradise with the series, though the only group member able to parlay her teenaged *Partridge* experience into an enduring television career was Susan Dey (Laurie Partridge), who in the 1980s and 1990s matured into a dependable leading lady in such series as *L.A. Law* and *Love and War*. The rest of the Partridges included Danny Bonaduce as Danny (whose later career as a radio disc jockey was occasionally interrupted by drug problems and public rowdiness), Jeremy Gelbwaks and later Brian Forster as Chris, and Suzanne Crough as Tracy. There was no Daddy Partridge, although the group's manager, Reuben Kincaid, (Dave Madden) functioned as surrogate father.

Though the last of the 96 *Partridge Family* episodes slipped off ABC and into syndication in 1974, the Family wasn't through with us yet. Hanna-Barbera cor-raled the series concept and most of its voice talent (minus Shirley Jones—whose character was renamed Connie Partridge even though she still looked a lot like Shirley—and David Cassidy) into a cartoon series. Per its title, *Partridge Family: 2200 A.D.* was set in the future, which in Saturday morning-ese translated to "outer space"; accordingly, the multicolored Partridge bus was traded in for a multicolored Partridge spaceship. Hanna-Barbera threw in its obligatory funny aliens: Venusian Veenie and Martian Marion. And there were songs aplenty, at least enough for a tune a week for 16 weeks.

Concurrent with their regular *2200 A.D.* appearances, several of the Partridge kids showed up as guest stars on another Hanna-Barbera cartoon outing, *Goober and the Ghost Chasers* (q.v.). Both *Goober* and *Partridge Family 2200 A.D.* were later incorporated into Hanna-Barbera's 1977 strip syndication package, *Fred Flintstone and Friends*.

THE PAW PAWS. Syndicated: 1985 (part of FUNTASTIC WORLD OF HANNA-BARBERA). Hanna-Barbera. Executives in charge of production, Jayne Barbera and Jean MacCurdy. Executive producers, William Hanna and Joseph Barbera. Produced by Berny Wolf. Creative supervisor, Joe Taritero. Creative directors, Iwao Takamoto and Judith Clarke. Supervising director, Ray Patterson. Directors: Art Davis, Oscar Dufau, Don Lusk, Carl Urbano, Rudy Zamora, Alan Zaslove. Animation directors: Don Alvarez, Bob Goe, Rick Leon, Don Patterson, Irv Spence, Tim Walker. Story editors, Don Nelson and Arthur Alsberg. Music by Hoyt Curtin and Paul DeKorte. Voices: Susan Blu (Princess Paw Paw); Thom Pinto (Brave Paw); Don Messick (Pupooch); Bob Ridgely (Mighty Paw); Sandy Stoddart (Laughing Paw); John Ingle (Wise Paw); Howard Morris (Trembly Paw); Stanley Ralph Ross (Dark Paw); Frank Welker (Bumble Paw); Ruth Buzzi (Aunt Pruney); and Scatman Crothers, Leo DeLyon, Jerry Dexter, Lauri Faso, Pat Fraley, Billie Hayes, Tom Kratochvil, Mitzi McCall, Rob Paulsen, Neilson Ross, and Marilyn Schreffler.

New in character if not in concept, *The Paw Paws* was the latest entry in the "cute little characters which hopefully will clean up as cute little toys" tradition, ex-

Dances with Doggies: the cast of *The Paw Paws*.

emplified by H-B's earlier *Smurfs, Shirt Tales, Trollkins, Monchichis, Biskitts* and *The Snorks* (see individual entries on these non-individualistic projects). The protagonists were tiny Native American bears, led by Princess Paw Paw, who were forced to make their way through an enchanted forest while in mild terror of their dreaded (but buffoonish) enemies, the equally tiny Meanos. The proverbial fine-toothed comb would not have been able to find

many genuine cultural trappings of Native Americans on *The Paw-Paws*. Beyond the occasional ancient tribal custom and ceremonial dance, the characters were more closely aligned to European Gypsies (the Meanos' Aunt Pruney practiced fortune-telling and magic spells) and 20th century computer fanatics (Dark Paw's teepee was cluttered with high-tech hardware).

Quotes from earlier sources abounded on *The Paw Paws*. There were flying horses, just like in *My Little Pony* (q.v.), Princess Paw Paw wore a "magic moonstone" around her neck, and the heroes were rainbow colored while the villains were hued in dull greys, in the manner of *The Care Bears* (q.v.). The characters, and their villages, were sylvan-sized, a la *The Smurfs*. And the principal villain Dark Paw wore an idiotic horned headpiece, apparently patterned after the escutcheon of the Loyal Order of Water Buffaloes in *The Flintstones* (q.v.). Some of the borrowings extended beyond the cartoon world: The Paw Paws' "Totem Man," a protective huge wooden statue, was straight out of the old Hebraic legend of "The Golem."

The Paw Paws was syndicated as part of the weekend block *The Funtastic World of Hanna-Barbera* (q.v.).

PEBBLES AND BAMM BAMM *see* THE FLINTSTONES

PENNY PENGUIN *see* MILTON THE MONSTER

THE PERILS OF PENELOPE PITSTOP. CBS: 9/13/1969–9/5/1970.
Hanna-Barbera. Produced and directed by William Hanna and Joseph Barbera. Associate producer, Alex Lovy. Animation director, Charles Nichols. Production designed by Iwao Takamoto. Written by Mike Maltese, Ken Spears and Joe Ruby. Story direction by Alex Lovy, Earl Klein, Bill Perez and Howard Swift. Music by Hoyt Curtin. Musical direction by Ted Nichols. Background art by Walt Peregoy. Voices: Janet Waldo (Penelope Pitstop); Paul Lynde (Sylvester Sneekly, alias the Hooded Claw); Mel Blanc (The Bully Brothers/Yak Yak/Chug-a-Boom); Paul Winchell (Clyde/Softy); Don Messick (Zippy/Pockets/Dum Dum/Snoozy); Gary Owens (Narrator).

The *Perils of Penelope Pitstop* was a spinoff from Hanna-Barbera's *Wacky Races* (q.v.), one of that studio's many "never-ending race" extravaganzas featuring peculiar characters driving colorful automobiles. Penelope Pitstop, a curvaceous redhead outfitted in a pink and red 1920s-style motoring outfit (helmet, goggles, gloves, hipboots) was navigator of the Compact Pussycat, which acted as an extension of its owner by bearing the same colors as Penelope's costume and even wearing long lashes on its headlights.

To this setup, Hanna-Barbera, in concert with staff writers Joe Ruby, Ken Spears and Michael Maltese, added plot twists stolen directly from the 1914 Pearl White serial *The Perils of Pauline* (which in one episode had plucky Pearl entering an auto race). Penelope was an heiress whose fortune would fall into the hands of her attorney should she suffer an early demise. The attorney, Sylvester Sneekly, was of course busy trying to engineer Penelope's death, utilizing a disguise and alternate identity, The Hooded Claw. Since both the Hooded Claw and Sneekly were voiced by distinctive character comic Paul Lynde, and since Sneekly's characteristic pince-nez was perched on his nose *outside* his Hooded Claw mask, no one was really fooled except the incredibly naive and trusting Penelope Pitstop, who never quite understood why disaster plagued her at each turn of the road, but who always serenely trusted in providence and her own resourcefulness to extricate her from her many perils.

Both heroine and villain had supporting characters aiding and abetting them. Penelope's protectors, who swung into action every time the poor girl was endangered, were the members of the Ant Hill Mob, seven dwarfish, softhearted gangster types who dogged the heroine's trail in their all-purpose limousine, the Chug-a-Boom. Bogart soundalike Clyde was top gun of the Mob, which included the sobbing Softy, the giggling Yak Yak, resourceful Pockets, fleetfooted Zippy, dumb dumb Dum Dum, and Snoozy, the asleep-at-the-wheel driver. Sneekly's stooges were the Bully Brothers, who looked alike, spoke in unison, and were every bit as inept as their vainglorious employer.

Stylistically, *The Perils of Penelope Pitstop* worked overtime maintaining the "feel" of silent movie serials (or at least what many people assume to be that feel), underlining the action with a rinky-dink piano score and having each episode begin as if it was the latest installment of a cliffhanger ("You remember in our *last* adventure . . ." intoned the narrator to an audience who didn't remember anything). The animation was vastly superior to most other late–1960s Hanna-Barbera offerings, and was abetted by excellent representational background art by Walt Peregoy, rendered in the style of road-company theatrical backdrops. While sight gags abounded, the bulk of the comedy was supplied by the writers, who forsook the usual Hanna-Barbera extraneous slapstick in favor of a deadpan "so serious it's silly" approach.

The scriptwork of *Perils of Penelope Pitstop* eventually became repetitious (the Ant Hill Mob stood upon each other's heads far too often to get a laugh every time), but maintained a fairly high standard throughout the series' 17 episodes. And here are two tips of the hat to the matchless voice cast: the aforementioned Paul Lynde (who strangely received no on-screen billing), Janet Waldo as the unflappable Penelope Pitstop, Mel Blanc as both Bully Brothers and the asthmatic Chug-a-Boom, Mel Blanc (again), Paul Winchell and Don Messick as various members of the Ant Hill Mob, and Gary Owens (hand cupped to ear, no doubt) as the declamatory, interactive narrator.

PETER PAN AND THE PIRATES (a.k.a. FOX'S PETER PAN AND THE PIRATES). Fox: 9/8/1990–9/11/1992. Southern Star Productions/TMS Entertainment/Fox Children's Network. Executive producer, Buzz Potamkin. Creative producer: Takashi. Coordinating producer, Lee Dannacher. Executive in charge of production, Robert D. Eastman. Story editors: Larry Carroll, David Carren, Chris Hubbell, Sam Graham, Matthew Malach, Michael Reaves. Musical direction by Steve Tyrrell. Music composed by Sam Wynans, Reg Powell, Paul Buckmaster, Bill Reichenbach. Theme music by Bill Reichenbach. Production facilities: Hinton Animation. Voices: Tim Curry, Chris Allport, Jack Angel, Michael Bacall, Adam Carl, Debi Deryberry, Linda Gary, Edmund Gilbert, Whitby Hartford, Tony Jay, Christina Lange, Aaron Lohr, Jack Lynch, Jason Marsden, Scott Menville, David Shaughnessy, Cree Summer, Josh Weiner, Eugene Williams, Michael Wise.

Peter Pan and the Pirates was based on characters first created in 1901 by British author James M. Barrie. The fanciful tale of a boy who refused to grow up and who became master of a domain chock full of lost children, pirates and Native Americans was formalized into a play in 1911, and it is this production that has inspired the *Peter Pan* film, TV and cartoon versions which have involved such talent over the

decades as Maude Adams, Betty Bronson, Jean Arthur, Mary Martin, Leonard Bernstein and Walt Disney. In 1989 and 1990, the movie industry was abuzz with anticipation of a new, updated version of the tale, *Hook*, starring Robin Williams as a grown-up Peter Pan, Dustin Hoffman as the boy's perennial foe Captain Hook, and Julia Roberts as the flying sprite Tinkerbell. The whole package was under the direction of Steven Spielberg, so how could it miss? This was evidently the thinking of the Fox Network, which commissioned a cartoon series, initially titled *The Never Told Tales of Peter Pan*, as the vanguard program of its new daily Fox Children's Network.

Most newly developed network children's divisions have at least a full year to make preparations. But three-year-old Fox was champing at the bit to be considered a serious contender in a four-network market; thus, only six months were allotted to patch together the new Children's Network. Even a streamlined cartoon operation like *Peter Pan*'s Southern Star Productions (which despite its name and Australian facilities was headquartered in Los Angeles) needed more time to cook up a daily animated series, but time was what both Fox and Southern Star had far too little of. With such other weekday projects as *Disney Afternoon* (q.v.), Warners' *Tiny Toon Adventures* (q.v.) and *Teenage Mutant Ninja Turtles* (q.v.) breathing down its neck, Fox not only had to have *Peter Pan* ready yesterday, but had to make the package attractive to independent TV stations whose afternoon schedules were already tight. So Fox offered a "make good" deal with the locals: Should *Peter Pan* not sweep the ratings, the network would forfeit one of the advertising minutes it was offering in syndication (which then stood at four commercial minutes for Fox, two for the local station per half hour episode), and make a financial settlement for any loss of local revenue.

To avoid comparison with such versions as the 1953 Disney cartoon feature and the like-vintage Mary Martin musical comedy adaptation, the production sheets of *Never Told Tales* looked nothing like any previous *Pan*. The characters and costumes seemed more suited to "Robin Hood" or "Last of the Mohicans" than to James M. Barrie. This was especially true in the case of Tinker Bell, who resembled a cross between Maid Marian and one of the tribeswomen in *Dances with Wolves.* To sidestep any resemblance to the copyrighted Disney version, all the characters were likewise redesigned, resulting in a polyglot of ethnic types, bizarre costumes and Dresden doll facial features. The only character retaining his already-established identity was Captain Hook, who was so broadly drawn in the grand tradition that audiences couldn't help gravitating to the villain as the most fascinating personality in the series. The virtuoso voicework of British actor Tim Curry, who won a well-deserved Emmy for his efforts, did nothing to diminish Hook's charisma and rapport with the viewers. This thing should have been called *Here's Hook.*

Perhaps the series could have succeeded on this level had it not been plagued with production indecision from the outset. Margaret Loesch had wanted *The Never Told Tales of Peter Pan* to be geared to smaller children, like her earlier CBS project *Muppet Babies* (q.v.). But the Fox affiliates, hoping for a *He-Man* or *G.I. Joe* to counterattack Disney's funny animals, insisted that the series exhibit (in the words of *Channels* magazine) a "masculine, adventurous edge." The first step in this direction was to replace the female voice artist who'd been playing Peter Pan (British stage tradition has dictated that Peter, who is supposed to be around 10 years old, should be played by a girl), redubbing the character so he'd pass as a macho male teen. The next move was to change the title to the more swashbuckling *Peter Pan and the Pirates.* The third, most debilitating "improvement" was to jettison most of the already filmed animation in order to toughen up the visuals and the storylines.

By August of 1990, a mere month before the series' premiere, potential *Peter Pan* advertisers had no completed film by which to judge the merits of the series and had to settle for production stills and animation cels. Southern Star Productions understandably couldn't deliver its quota of 65 episodes on time; in fact, barely two weeks' worth of patchily animated daily programs (some still in "rough cut" form with visible splices) were completed by the September air date. With virtually nothing in its manifest, and a blah advertising campaign which failed to entice youngsters into giving up Disney or Warner Bros., *Peter Pan and the Pirates* was marked for disaster before it even had a chance.

To counteract this gloomy advance word, Fox decided to heavily promote the opening episode with a one-shot Saturday morning showing, which would appear on more stations than had signed for the daily version. Fox bumped the debut episode for its *Piggsburg Pigs* (q.v.) weekender to give *Peter Pan* a head start, so that audiences would get a chance to sample the series before bowing to hearsay and avoiding its daily version.

But *Peter Pan and the Pirates* started small and stayed there. Although ratings improved somewhat by December, even those viewers fond of the show began dropping off when the inevitable premature reruns set in. By January, Fox, who'd been obliged to honor its "make good" promise of giving up a minute's commercial time at a loss, was making statements along the lines of "We expect to beat the other networks, but we do intend to boost our overall ratings." This "you can't win 'em all" strategy sounded more desperate than promissory to the already disenchanted Fox affiliates (disenchanted *and* ungrateful, since the affiliates themselves had ordered the changes that had slowed down *Pan*'s production).

Peter Pan and the Pirates' move back to Fox's lucrative Saturday morning schedule on January 26, 1991, replacing the network's weak-link *Zazoo U* (q.v.), did little to bolster its appeal; the series was pulled from the Saturday lineup in September, this time permanently. Hopes ran high that the 1991 release of Spielberg's *Hook* would have a salutary effect on Fox's daily *Peter Pan.* Instead, the overproduced, overlong theatrical feature turned out to be every bit as disappointing as the cartoon series. Fortunately for Fox, its more popular cartoon outings like *The Simpsons* (q.v.) and *Bobby's World* (q.v.) washed away the bitter taste of *Peter Pan,* as did the network's alliance with Warner Bros.' cartoon division in 1991 (onetime rival *Tiny Toon Adventures* was now a Fox attraction). But *Peter Pan and the Pirates* was a painful two-year lesson, one now spoken of only in cautionary whispers in the halls of the Fox Children's Network.

THE PETER POTAMUS SHOW.
Syndicated: 1964. ABC: 1/2/1966–1/24/ 1967. Hanna-Barbera. Produced and directed by Bill Hanna and Joseph Barbera. Music by Hoyt Curtin. Components: **1. PETER POTAMUS.** Voices: Daws Butler (Peter Potamus); Don Messick (So-So). **2. BREEZLY AND SNEEZLY** (1964). Voices: Howard Morris (Breezly); Mel Blanc (Sneezly); John Stephenson (Col. Fusby). **3. YIPPEE YAPPEE AND YA-HOOEY.** Voices: Doug Young (Yippee); Hal Smith (Yappee/King); Daws Butler (Yahooey). **4. RICOCHET RABBIT** (1965). (See MAGILLA GORILLA.)

Peter Potamus was the second of two syndicated 1964 liaisons between Hanna-Barbera and Ideal Toys, and like the first, *Magilla Gorilla* (q.v.), opened strongly in 151 markets. The Hanna-Barbera formula was once more followed to the letter: Each weekly half-hour program began with a bouncy theme song, then settled into three separate component cartoons, and closed with some bravura "goodbye" music—with the added voiceover invitation to tune in to *Magilla Gorilla* over most of these same stations.

The components were headlined by the title character, an anthropomorphic hippo bedecked in explorer's outfit and pith helmet. Befitting his cavernous oral extremity, Peter Potamus' voice characterization (courtesy Daws Butler) resembled another legendary movie bigmouth, Joe E. Brown; on occasion, Peter gave out with a "Hippo Howl" that sounded just like Brown's legendary "Eeeeyoowwww!" Peter Potamus travelled through the past, present and future in his flying balloon, accompanied by his friend and aide-de-camp, So-So the monkey.

The second component starred Breezly and Sneezly, a tall polar bear (who sounded like Bullwinkle Moose) and a short, bronchial seal who made life miserable for Arctic authority figure Col. Fusby; *Yogi Bear* on ice. *Peter Potamus'* third seven-minute attraction starred a trio of zanies known as the Three Goofy Guards: Yippee, Yappee and Yahooey. These humanized dogs were in the service of a pint-sized king, and the whole affair looked a lot like the 1939 film version of *The Three Musketeers* starring the Ritz Brothers, with echoes of another comedy team in the characterization of Yahooey, who sounded like Jerry Lewis.

To bolster viewership of both *Peter Potamus* and *Magilla Gorilla*, the two series staged a crossover in 1965: Breezly and Sneezly moved over to *Magilla Gorilla*, while the *Magilla* component "Ricochet Rabbit" was traded to *Peter Potamus*. All the various components traded off when both *Potamus* and *Magilla* left syndication in 1966 in favor of a brief ABC network run, with a handful of new episodes. Peter Potamus and So-So would be retreaded in 1973 as guest stars on Hanna-Barbera's *Yogi's Gang* (q.v.).

Incidentally, some sources list the official title of *Peter Potamus* as *Peter Potamus and His Magic Flying Balloon*. Perhaps it was so announced in the trade papers, but the extended title never appeared onscreen. This may not be a terribly fascinating sidenote, but neither was *Peter Potamus* terribly fascinating. Though produced and performed with the usual Hanna-Barbera slickness and verve, the series wasn't innovative or entertaining enough to enter the H-B pantheon with such greats as *Huckleberry Hound*, *Yogi Bear*, *Quick Draw McGraw* or *The Flintstones* (see individual entries on these series).

PIGGSBURG PIGS. Fox: 9/13/1990– 4/13/1991; 5/25/1991–6/29/1991; 8/10/1931– 8/31/1991. Ruby-Spears. Executive producers, Joe Ruby and Ken Spears. Produced by Sy Fischer.

Originally titled *Pig Out*, the Fox Network's *Piggsburg Pigs* was a 13-week half hour series vaguely reminiscent of the like-vintage *Barnyard Commandos* (q.v.) and the "U.S. Acres" component of *Garfield and Friends*. The series was set in Piggsburg, an all-swine metropolis located just behind a large barnyard, and featured such anthropomorphic porkers as the Bacon Brothers: Bo, Portley and Pighead. Piggsburg's principal villain was the gloriously named Rembrandt Proupork. (Did one of the series' writers actually wade through T. S. Eliot's "The Love Song of J. Alfred Prufrock" while attending English Literature 101?)

And that about covers it for *Piggsburg Pigs*. Inquiries to both the Fox Network and Ruby-Spears Productions have yielded no further program information beyond the previous paragraph. Though Ken Spears was able to tell this writer that the series' voicework was recorded in

376 The Pink Panther Show

Canada, all other production data on *Piggsburg Pigs* has passed into the hands of Turner Broadcasting, which purchased most of the Ruby-Spears backlog for Turner's new Cartoon Network cable service in 1992.

Alas, the Turner vaults are about as penetrable as those at Fort Knox, so we close by listing the basic scheduling facts concerning *Piggsburg Pigs*. Its Saturday morning debut was delayed by one week, pre-empted by a special presentation of Fox's *Peter Pan and the Pirates* (q.v.). Once *Piggsburg* did premiere, it wasn't terribly successful (it barely had a chance opposite CBS' *Teenage Mutant Ninja Turtles* [q.v.]) and was replaced in the spring of 1991 by DIC's *Swamp Thing* miniseries. This in turn was replaced (twice!) by reruns of *Piggsburg Pigs*, which finally died a quiet death ("Not with a bang, but a whimper," to further invoke T. S. Eliot) in September of 1991.

THE PINK PANTHER SHOW. NBC: 9/6/1969–9/5/1970. — **THE PINK PANTHER MEETS THE ANT AND THE AARDVARK.** NBC: 9/12/1970–9/11/1971. — **THE NEW PINK PANTHER SHOW.** NBC: 9/11/1971–9/4/1976. — **THE PINK PANTHER LAUGH AND 1/2 HOUR AND 1/2.** NBC: 9/11/1976–9/3/1977. — **THINK PINK PANTHER!** NBC: 2/4/1978–9/2/1978. DePatie-Freleng. Produced by David H. DePatie and Friz Freleng. Directed by Friz Freleng, Hawley Pratt, Gerry Chiniquy, Brad Case, Art Davis, Dave Detiege, Cullen Houghtaling, Art Leonardi, Sid Marcus, Robert McKimson, Bob Richardson. Most scripts written by John Dunn. Voices: John Byner, Dave Barry, Paul Frees, Rich Little, Marvin Miller, Arte Johnson, Arnold Stang, Tom Holland, Don Diamond. Live hosts (1969 season only): Lennie Schultz, The Ritts Puppets. — **THE ALL-NEW PINK PANTHER SHOW.** ABC: 9/9/1978–9/1/1979. DePatie-Freleng. Production credits basically same as above listing. Voices: Larry D. Mann (Crazylegs Crane); Frank Welker (Crane Jr./Dragonfly). — **PINK PANTHER AND SONS.** NBC: 9/15/1984–9/7/1985; ABC: 3/1/1986–9/6/1986. DePatie-Freleng/Hanna-Barbera. Voices: Billy Bowles (Pinky); B. J. Ward

(Panky/Punkin); Sherry Lynn (Chatta); Marshall Efron (Howl); Jeannie Elias (Anney/Liona); Frank Welker (Finko/Rocko); Gregg Berger (Bowlhead); Sonny Melendrez (Buckethead); Shane McCabe (Murfel). — **PINK PANTHER.** Syndicated: 1993. MGM Animation/Claster. Executive producers, Walter Mirisch, Marvin Mirisch, Paul Sabella and Mark Young. Produced and directed by Charles Grosvenor and Byron Vaughns. Creative consultants, David DePatie and Friz Freleng. Supervising story editors, Kelly Ward and Mark Young. Story editor, Sindy McKay. Staff writer, Thomas D. Hart. [46 writers! including the likes of Tony Benedict, Nick Meglin and Fred Crippen] Main title produced and directed by Paul Sabella. Theme song by Henry Mancini; arranged by Eddie Arkin. Additional music by Mark Watters, Albert Olson, James Stemple. Animation facilities, Wang Film Production Co., Ltd.; overseas animation supervisor, Shivan Ramsaran. Additional facilities: Phoenix Animation Ltd., Network of Animation Ltd., Bardel Animation Ltd., Funbag Animation Studios, Milimetros, Jaime Diaz Productions S.A., A-Film. Voices: Matt Frewer (Pink Panther); and Sheryl Bernstein, John Byner, Dan Castellaneta, Brian George, Jess Harnell, Joe Piscopo, Charles Nelson Reilly, Wallace Shawn, Kath Soucie, Jo Anne Worley, Ruth Buzzi, Hamilton Camp, Cathy Cavadini, Rickey D'Shon Collins, Troy Davidson, Phillip Glasser, Paige Gosney, Gerritt Graham, Maurice LaMarche, Steve Macell, Danny Mann, Kenneth Mars, Bradley Pierce, Hal J. Rayle, Gwen Sheperd, Susan Silo, Jean Smart, Elmarie Wendel, Tom Wilson.

The Pink Panther began not so much as a supporting character as a tertiary one in Blake Edwards' 1964 comedy-adventure film titled (was there any doubt?) *The Pink Panther*. The titular Panther was actually a rare jewel sought after by suave thieves David Niven and Robert Wagner, but for most viewers, the Pink Panther was personified by the smug, lanky animal character seen in the film's animated opening credits. By squeezing through and rubbing against the letters forming the names of the stars — the "E" in "Capucine" gave the overly familiar feline a resounding slap — the Panther made an unforgettable impression. He so overshadowed the early

A *Pink Panther* still autographed by Friz Freleng (courtesy of Wayne and Rita Hawk).

reels of the film that David Niven seriously considered taking legal action because his name and character were upstaged by a cartoon. (As it turned out, Niven's thunder would be stolen by costar Peter Sellers, making the first of several brilliant appearances as master bumbler Inspector Clouseau. It must have been particularly galling for Niven to play third fiddle to both Sellers *and* The Pink Panther.)

For the newly formed cartoon firm of DePatie-Freleng, the *Pink Panther* credit sequence was just another job, not nearly as lucrative as their advertising assignments. Little did Warner Bros. veterans David DePatie and Friz Freleng suspect that the Panther would not only hit big, but completely redefine the success and working methods of their studio. In answer to audience demands for more of that Pink Panther, United Artists engaged DePatie-Freleng to produce a six-minute starring vehicle, *The Pink Phink*. The cartoon opened with UA's *Kiss Me Stupid*, scoring so large an audience response that *Pink Phink* would soon be shipped out to virtually all of United Artists' big-city releases (this writer saw the cartoon in early 1965 as an intermission feature separating *Goldfinger* and *That Man From Rio* in Louisville, Kentucky). David DePatie would later note with swelling pride, "Our animated Pink Panther received billing on theatre marquees along with the feature. Many people said they went to the feature just to see the cartoon." An

Academy Award was icing on the cake, and further incentive for DePatie-Freleng to enter the theatrical cartoon-short business full time.

Subsequent *Pink Panther* cartoons were very funny but became increasingly strained as the series ground on; by 1968, writer John Dunn found story possibilities for the character running dry thanks to "Pinky's" comparatively tiny comic repertoire and the fact that he was nonverbal, a tough combination when one is expected to turn out a cartoon a month. Still, the Panther had a rapport with fans, and it was his insouciant personality (together with Henry Mancini's silky-smooth "Pink Panther" theme music) that secured bookings for such second-string efforts as *G.I. Pink* (1968) and *Pink Pest Control* (1969).

Those bookings began to decrease in 1969 and 1970, with a flock of "M," "R" and "X" rated films sapping the family market for whom the *Panther* cartoons were designed. United Artists was considering dropping the series when, in 1969, a backlog of DePatie-Freleng cartoons were licensed to NBC and run on Saturday mornings. Hosted by live-action comics Lenny Schultz and the Ritts Puppets, *The Pink Panther Show* featured the cream of the Panther crop, together with several Clouseau-inspired cartoons featuring a dimwitted police official known as The Inspector (who also appeared in newly animated buffers between cartoons). In later years, other DePatie-Freleng theatrical series made their way to weekend mornings under the *Pink Panther* banner, including the Spielberg-inspired "Misterjaw," "The Ant and the Aardvark," and "Texas Toads" (originally "The Tijuana Toads"). Thankfully, the least of the De-Patie-Freleng stable, the miserable "Dogfather" cartoons of 1974 and 1975, were not given TV play.

Even the idiotic addition of a sitcom laughtrack could not dampen the inherent quality of the 1960s cartoons, and *The Pink Panther Show* (and its variously retitled successors, listed above) scored a ratings success, the upshot of which was that the theatrical *Panther* series was given a shot in the arm and allowed to flourish until 1981, outlasting virtually all other non–TV animated shorts. Part of what kept the wheels of this series in motion was the sweetheart deal made by DePatie-Freleng with NBC, which guaranteed that the network would automatically purchase every one of the annual 17 *Panther* theatrical releases for television.

Meanwhile, DePatie-Freleng added to its TV manifest by producing *Pink Panther* episodes directly for the small screen, starting with ABC's *The All-New Pink Panther Show* in 1978. For this outing, three new characters were created: the Bullwinkle-like Crazylegs Crane, his smarter son Crane Jr., and Dragonfly. The writing remained sharp, and the animation, though not up to theatrical standards, was still above-average, a fact David DePatie attributed to the overall success of the *Pink Panther* cartoons. "That's the financial spine of our business," claimed DePatie in 1978. "We couldn't have the quality we do without it."

After a five year absence, during which the DePatie-Freleng studio was sold and renamed Marvel Productions, Hanna-Barbera brought the Pink Panther back to Saturday mornings by squeezing him into H-B's beloved "extended family" format. In *The Pink Panther and Sons*, "Pinky" Senior was still mute—earlier attempts to give him a "Cary Grant" or "Rex Harrison" voice were failures—but his offspring, who ranged from infant to preteen, made up for him in the loquacity department. Sons Pinky, Panky and Punkin were the "Huey, Dewey and Louie" of this effort, starring in two short episodes in each of the series' 13 half hours. In style and substance, *Pink Panther and Sons* more closely resembled

the cutesy *Biskitts* (q.v.) or *Pound Puppies* (q.v.) than the sophisticated *Panther* cartoons of bygone days. It was as if Cary Grant had suddenly become the star of *Full House.*

The *Pink Panther and Sons* was cancelled by NBC without regret in 1985, although it frankly wasn't any better or worse than its competition, CBS' *Get Along Gang* and ABC's *Superfriends.* After a brief rerun cycle in March of 1986, Pinky was put in mothballs, while his theatrical career had been squelched earlier by the 1980 shutdown of DePatie-Freleng and the 1981 death of Peter Sellers, who'd been starring in the *Pink Panther* sequels for which animated title sequences were "de rigueur." Except for a few specials from Marvel Productions, the character remained more or less dormant until a proposed 1989 *Pink Panther* special was assembled by Film Roman, wherein the hero left the screen and entered the real world a la Woody Allen's *Purple Rose of Cairo.* Though CBS liked the idea, it hated other aspects of the special, particularly a wise-guy reporter character in the "live" sequences, so this newest rebirth of the Pink Panther was aborted.

Repeats of the theatrical *Pink Panther* shorts over the TNT and TBS cable services in the early 1990s prompted renewed interest in the character, as did a Blake Edwards revival of the "Inspector Clouseau" series featuring computer-enhanced title art by MGM's new animation division. It was MGM/United Artists, together with the Claster Corporation, who put the wheels in motion for a 52-episode, daily syndicated *Pink Panther* series in the fall of 1993.

Unmindful of the aforementioned misfire attempts to give the character a voice, this latest Pink Panther would talk loudly and often thanks to actor Matt Frewer—best known for his interpretation of another computer-generated character, Max Headroom. The results illustrated the wisdom of an earlier executive decision elucidated by Friz Freleng: "[S]ince he was originally created for a main title and didn't speak, there wasn't any reason for him to ever speak." The excessive, expendable dialogue given the 1993 TV *Panther* added nothing to the character other than making him something of a *Garfield* (q.v.) clone.

Otherwise, the MGM/UA/Claster version was excellent, utilizing the talent and facilities of several animation houses to come up with a daily product that matched and sometimes surpassed the quality of the DePatie-Freleng originals. The humor was best when purely visual, with a rich variety of gags and marvelous "modernistic" character, color, and background design. Best of all, the 1993 *Pink Panther* managed to make such negligible DePatie-Freleng supporting characters as the Ant and the Aardvark and, yes, even The Dogfather (voice by Joe Piscopo) truly funny for a change. Not quite in the league of *Tiny Toon Adventures* (q.v.) or *DuckTales* (q.v.), the new *Pink Panther* was still one of the better character-revival cartoon series of the 1990s.

PINOCCHIO:
— THE NEW ADVENTURES OF PINOCCHIO. Syndicated: 1961. Rankin-Bass/Videocrafts International. Produced by Arthur Rankin Jr. and Jules Bass. Animation facilities: Toei Studios.
— SABAN'S ADVENTURES OF PINOCCHIO. HBO: 7/1/1992–. Tatsunoko Productions/Saban/Orbis. Supervising producer, Winston Richard. Produced by Eric S. Rollman. Executive in charge of production: Jerald E. Bergh. Script supervisor, Robert V. Barron. Music by Shuki Levy; supervised by Andrew Dimitroff; orchestrated by Steve Morrison. Animation created and produced by Tatsuo Yoshida. Stories written by Jingo Toriumi. Animation director, Ippei Kuri. Production facilities: Varitel Video, Starfax. No voice credits.

Pinocchio, the little wooden puppet who had to undergo numerous grueling and allegorical life experiences before he'd be permitted to transform into a human being, first appeared in 1881 in a series of children's magazine stories by Italian author Collodi (real name: Carlo Lorenzini). If you've always felt that the novelized version of the story has seemed to stop and start and go in circles, with Pinocchio remembering nothing that he'd learned in the last chapter, please remember that the story was originally serialized, and that Collodi was paid by the word. Stories with built-in anticlimaxes are perfect for adaptation into two- and three-act stage dramas, so *Pinocchio* became an early perennial on the children's theatre and puppet show circuit. A 60-minute cartoon, faithful to the source, was made of

the property in 1940 by Italy's Cartoni Animati Italiani studios, but it was Disney's animated 1939 *Pinocchio* that has solidified the elements — with an essentially lighthearted touch, despite its moments of genuine terror — that all future adaptations would use. This is particularly true in the case of Disney's Jiminy Cricket, appointed by the Blue Fairy to be Pinocchio's official conscience: In the original story, Pinocchio's conscience was an intangible narrative device, and when a cricket *did* appear to chastise the little woodenhead for a misdeed, the insolent insect was immediately crushed to death.

Other than a few live-action versions (one starring Mickey Rooney), television's first Pinocchio was also the first major project of Rankin-Bass Studios, a Canadian cartoon firm previously devoted to advertising and industrial films. The 130 five-minute *New Adventures of Pinocchio* episodes harked back to the Collodi original by being arranged in five-per-week cliffhanger form; local stations were advised by Rankin-Bass that the episodes could also be arranged into 26 half-hour weekly programs, in the manner of another cartoon serial of the era, Cambria Productions' *Clutch Cargo* (q.v.).

Inasmuch as Pinocchio was the story of a puppet, and in the interest of not courting lawsuits by following the Disney version too closely, *New Adventures* producers Arthur Rankin Jr. and Jules Bass opted for stop-motion puppet animation rather than ink and paint cartoonwork. Not quite ready for mass production, Rankin-Bass doled out most of its animation work to Japan, with storyboards prepared in Canada. The fine art of "overseas supervision" wasn't as well honed in 1960 as it would be in the 1990s, so the resulting work on *The New Adventures of Pinocchio* betrays a breakdown in communication between the idea men and the executors. The character design was appealing, and the movement as good as possible under the rushed circumstances, but the timing was invariably off. Jokes and plot points were often lost because the animation was too busy and cluttered, and characters would frequently float around and pointlessly bob their heads rather than exhibit "real" movement.

As mentioned, *New Adventures of Pinocchio* took great pains not to emulate Disney. The story was updated into the

1960s, Pinocchio traded his 19th century European togs for all–American T-shirt and shorts, and Cricket (not Jiminy Cricket) had a high, raspy voice and abrasive manner that was calculated to avoid imitating the brilliant voicework of Disney's Cliff Edwards (though, curiously, Rankin-Bass' Cricket wore a straw hat and carried a small guitar, not unlike Cliff Edwards when he appeared onstage as "Ukelele Ike"). Papa Gepetto, the woodcarver "father" of Pinocchio, narrated the stories in a calm, deliberate voice completely at odds with Disney's excitable, absentminded Gepetto.

As for the chief villains, the Fox and the Cat, Rankin-Bass retained the Collodi/Disney notion that they were devoted to exploiting Pinocchio for their own gains. In Collodi's book, the Fox and Cat hung Pinocchio from a tree so he'd regurgitate the gold coins he held in his mouth. In the Disney film, the characters (renamed J. Worthington Foulfellow and Gideon) sold Pinocchio first to an evil puppetmaster named Stromboli, then to a wicked horse trader who intended to transform the puppet into a donkey. Rankin-Bass' despicable duo were named Fibber Q. Fox and Cool S. Cat: the latter character was a hip-talking beatnik. No sooner had the cartoon series begun before Fibber and Cool signed Pinocchio away to an avaricious movie producer who intended to produce a picture where the leading character was really killed in the end.

The rest of The New Adventures of Pinocchio was likewise locked into 1960s cultural consciousness. At various junctures, Pinocchio met the Loch Ness Monster, a faux Communist spy named Rasputin Pasgoodnak (who sounded like "The Mad Russian" from the old Eddie Cantor radio series), and a Mexican lampoon of TV private eye Peter Gunn named Pedro Pistol. New Adventures sold well in 1961 and got laughs from its contemporary audience, but the series was virtually worthless ten years later when all the topical jokes had lost their lustre. Towards the end of the run, an attempt was made to spin off a new character, Willy Nilly, into his own series, but Willy Nilly died right along with The New Adventures of Pinocchio in 1962. However, Rankin-Bass stayed loyal to the concept of stop-motion animation, resulting in several enduring holiday TV specials, notably The Little Drummer

Boy, Rudolph the Red-Nosed Reindeer and Santa Claus Is Coming to Town (plus an animated cartoon one-shot revival of Pinocchio, 1980's Pinocchio's Christmas).

Nearly three decades passed before Pinocchio was regalvanized as a regular TV series. In 1990, Japan's Tatsunoko Productions, together with Canada's Saban International, cooked up The Adventures of Pinocchio, which superficially retained the spirit of the Collodi original. Pinocchio was returned to a period setting, he was drawn more like a marionette than a human, and he was so easily led into mischief by those wiser and wickeder than himself that he came across like the village idiot. The vision conjured up by Tatsunoko/Saban was crueler and grittier than Disney's, and more in keeping with Collodi's. Virtually everybody thought ill of Pinocchio and either tried to profit from his freakishness or to dispose of him. Typical was an episode in which several tough village kids conned Pinocchio into diving for a buried treasure because he had no need for oxygen. The kids, a truly scuzzy bunch, made no secret of their plans to leave Pinocchio in the briny deep once he retrieved the treasure. The story climaxed with the parents of the bullies accusing Pinocchio of leading their little darlings astray—this even after it was established that the puppet had rescued the miscreants. A bleak outlook indeed, leavened only by the unquenchable good spirits of Pinocchio, who never seemed to stop giggling.

As in both Collodi's original and Rankin-Bass' New Adventures of Pinocchio, the Saban half hours were serialized, though each week's story would resolve itself before the cliffhanger was introduced. Gepetto and the Cricket made token appearances, together with a likable mouse named Charley, perhaps as a means of counterbalancing the mean spirits of the rest of the supporting cast. The series was packaged by Orbis Productions for American syndication, but was first run in the United States as part of the weekend lineup of the HBO pay-cable service, where it remained for over a year and a half.

PIRATES OF DARK WATER. Syndicated: 2/25/1991–3/1/1991 (as five-part miniseries titled DARK WATER); 1992 (see FUNTASTIC WORLD OF HANNA-

BARBERA). ABC: 9/7/1991–9/5/1992. Fils-Cartoons, Inc./Tama Production Co./ Hanna-Barbera. Executive producer and creator, David Kirschner. Executive producers, Paul Sabella, Mark Young. Produced by Joey Dorman. Directed by Don Lusk. Written by Kristina Luckey and Laren Bright. Music by Tom Chase and Steve Rucker. Voices: Jodi Benson, Regis Cordic, Peter Cullen, Tim Curry, Hector Elizondo, Dick Gautier, Allan Lurie, George Newbern, Dan O'Herlihy, Brock Peters, Les Tremayne, Jessica Walter, Frank Welker.

Developed by Hanna-Barbera CEO David Kirschner just before his exit from the studio, *Pirates of Dark Water* (simply *Dark Water* when syndicated as a five-part "special event" several months before its official ABC premiere) was a noble attempt to bring a fantasy fiction style comparable to the best of J.R.R. Tolkien and Frank Herbert, coupled with the invention and complexity indigenous to Japanese animation, to Saturday morning American television.

Designed as a "quest" series, with each episode beginning where the last left off, *Pirates* was the saga of Mer, a faraway planet engulfed by a mighty ocean. The Kingdom of Octopon found itself endangered by the sinister forces of Dark Water, an intelligent and dictatorial liquid entity bent upon domination of the planet. According to the ancient seer Terradon, should Octopon be deluged, it would result in a domino effect spelling the end of Mer. Only the lost 14 treasures of Gor could save the planet from its soggy fate. Ren, prince of Octopon, was entrusted with the quest for the treasures, and to that end the teenaged regent set sail on the mighty vessel Maelstrom in the company of talking "monkey bird" Nidler.

Were the quest an easy one, it would have been wrapped up after the first chapter. But Ren's goal was complicated by the Constrictus, a wormlike sea creature (a dash of Frank Herbert's *Dune* here), and by wicked Dark Water pirate chieftain Blot and Blot's right hand man Commander Mantus. Nor was Ren totally at ease with his friends. Perhaps the female resistance leader Abagon could be trusted, but Maelstrom crew members Ios and Muli were out-and-out mercenaries, and the beauteous Tula from rival planet Andoris took the devil's own time letting us know which side she was really on.

Hanna-Barbera had the writing talent to pull this off but needed pumping up on the animation end, so most of the artwork was farmed out to the Philippines' Fils Cartoons. One look at *Pirates of Dark Water* and it was obvious that we were light years away from *Huckleberry Hound* or *Scooby-Doo*. The character movements and facial expressions were more realistic than those seen on some of ABC's nighttime live-action shows, while the story was told in an intricate and multilayered fashion (with an understated but deftly handled pro-ecology message, advising us to be kind to Mother Nature lest it result in mutations like Dark Water), demanding full attention and involvement from its audience. This was the definitive slap in the face to former FCC chieftain Mark Fowler's description of TV as a toaster with pictures.

In fact, it was the very excellence of *Pirates of Dark Water* that might have contributed to its downfall. The plot convolutions and MTV-like action sequences were cherished by its teen and adult fans, but smaller children tuning into a random episode had no idea what was going on, nor were they further enlightened after a few minutes' viewing. A little channel-surfing, and these kids were back on safer turf with CBS' *Teenage Mutant Ninja Turtles* (q.v.).

Like Ralph Bakshi's *Mighty Mouse: The New Adventures* (q.v.), *Pirates of Dark Water* worked so hard to please its older fans that it left out in the cold the 3-to-11 demographic group which the advertisers dearly coveted. Add to this the fact that the series was way too expensive to justify a non–prime time slot, and you have a good idea why the quest for the 14 treasures was over with in 13 weeks. After September of 1992, fans of *Pirates of Dark Water* would have to be satisfied with off-network reruns of the series, bundled into the weekend grab-bag *Funtastic World of Hanna-Barbera*.

PITFALL HARRY *see* **SATURDAY SUPERCADE**

PIXIE AND DIXIE *see* **HUCKLEBERRY HOUND**

THE PLASTICMAN COMEDY-ADVENTURE SHOW. ABC: 9/8/1979–9/27/1980; CBS: 11/12/1983–2/4/1984.

—THE PLASTICMAN/BABY PLAS SUPER COMEDY. ABC: 10/4/1980–9/5/1981. DC Comics/Ruby-Spears.

Executive producers, Joe Ruby and Ken Spears. Produced by Jerry Eisenberg. Directed by Charles Nichols Jr., Rudy Larriva, John Kimball, Manny Perez. Story editors, Mark Jones, Elaine Lesser, Cliff Ruby. Animation supervision, Ed Solomon. Voice director, Alan Dinehart. Consumer consultants, Wickie Chambers and Spring Asher. Music by Dean Elliot. Components: 1. PLASTICMAN. Voices: Michael Bell (Plasticman/Baby Plas); Melendy Britt (Penny/Chief); Joe Baker (Hoola Hoola). 2. MIGHTYMAN AND YUKK. Voices: Peter Cullen (Mightyman/Brandon Brucesty); Frank Welker (Yukk). 3. RICKETY ROCKET. Voices: Al Fann (Rickety); Bobby Ellerbee (Cosgrove); Dee Timberlake (Venus); Johnny Brown (Splashdown); John Anthony Bailey (Sunstroke). 4. FANGFACE AND FANGPUSS. Voices: Jerry Dexter (Fangface/Fangpuss); Susan Blu (Kim); Bart Braverman (Puggsy); Frank Welker (Biff). (See also FANGFACE.) Additional voices: John Stephenson, Marlene Aragon, Daws Butler, Ruth Buzzi, Henry Corden, Danny Dark, Takayo Doran, Walker Edmiston, Sam Edwards, Ron Feinberg, Shep Menkin, Chuck McCann, Julie McWhirter, Don Messick, Howard Morris, Gene Moss, Alan Oppenheimer, Stanley Ralph Ross, Michael Rye, Hal Smith, Joanie Gerber, Jerry Hausner, Johnny Haymer, Ralph Jones, Stanley Jones, Casey Kasem, Antonia Kotsaros, Keye Luke, Laurie Main, Allan Melvin, Harold J. Stone, Fred Travalena, Ginny Tyler, Herb Vigran, Janet Waldo, Len Weinrib, Nancy Wible, William Woodson, Alan Young.

Plasticman was introduced by Quality Comics artist Jack Cole in 1941's *Police Comics #1*. Originally a criminal named Eel O'Brien, the character assumed the ability to elasticize his body after falling into a tub of acid during the robbery of a chemical works. Cured of his criminal tendencies by a mysterious shaman at a religious retreat, O'Brien channeled his stretch-and-squash talents for the side of Right—specifically, the National Bureau of Investigation.

In its comic book heyday in the 1940s (and on into his DC Comics revival in the mid–1960s) the Plasticman character had a broad slapstick quality, satirizing the "super power" genre while at the same time honoring it. At the time Ruby-Spears adapted "Plas" for animation in 1979, the superhero vogue was resurfacing, but violence had been all but tabooed out of existence. What was needed, felt Ruby-Spears, was an all out comedy superhero: not a fabricated lampoon like *Roger Ramjet* (q.v.) or a campish corruption like the live-action *Batman* animated series, but a born caped comedian with a proven track record. Since the program wasn't allowed to display any real adventure or danger, the laughs (beyond those on the series' prerecorded laughtrack) were all that really mattered. Thus, Plasticman's elasticity was emphasized through such chucklesome metamorphoses as having Plas turn into cushions, waterhoses, periscopes, gangplanks, life preservers and toilet plungers. Here was one of the few full-out "cartoony" characters in a TV-animation world consisting mostly of "illustrated radio."

The *Plasticman Comedy-Adventure Show* headlined the title character and his two assistants: Penny, a Southern belle who openly lusted for Our Hero, and "jinxed" contact man Hoola-Hoola, a Hawaiian Lou Costello soundalike who replaced the comic book Plasticman's grotesquely hilarious sidekick Woozy Winks. This good guy team was dispatched to thwart an endless parade of mutant miscreants (The Weed, the Clam, Mr. Meteor, et al.) by The Chief, a beautiful, soft-spoken, sarcastic young woman. Twenty *Plasticman* adventures of various lengths were produced, then telecast two per week.

The rest of the *Comedy-Adventure Show* was populated by Ruby-Spears "originals," all of them takeoffs on established cartoon genres. *Mighty Man and Yukk* had a title both false and true: Mighty Man was really no larger than a thumbnail, but Yukk was per his name the ugliest dog in the world, so much so that he was compelled to wear a miniature doghouse over his head lest those who gaze on his Medusalike features literally fall to pieces. *Fangface and Fangpuss* were lycanthropic carryovers from an earlier Ruby-Spears series, *Fangface*, discussed in more detail in its own entry.

And *Rickety Rocket* was an ethnic *Space Kiddettes* (q.v.), with four black teenagers—Cosmo, Splashdown, Sunstroke and Venus—forming an interstellar detective agency, headquartered in a talking spaceship. In between all these short subjects were consumer safety tips from Plasticman (though it would have been more appropriate to offer nutritional tips, since Plas and his pals were almost always found eating long, cholesterol packed lunches during their adventures).

But you can't win for losing. Despite Ruby-Spears' heroic efforts to prune all "threatening" violent action from the series, a panel of children's experts quoted in *TV Guide* in 1980 chastised *Plasticman* as "discombobulated activity presented as adventure. Too frightening for many children." If so, it was the first time that Plasticman was ever frightening to anyone—even back when he was Eel O'Brien.

The *Plasticman Comedy-Adventure Show* was considered by ABC to be its hot-ticket new attraction, to be sandwiched between the established *Superfriends* (q.v.) and *Scooby-Doo* (q.v.) to complete a (hopefully) unbeatable adventure-comedy "block." The series opened opposite CBS' powerhouse *Bugs Bunny/Road Runner Show* in a one-hour slot, expanded to two hours two weeks later, then settled into 90 minutes in December of 1979. Only the *Plasticman* segments really clicked with the audience, however, so in 1980 the series was pared down to 30 minutes and retitled *The Plasticman–Baby Plas Super Comedy*. Here we had virtually the only nuclear superfamily on Saturday morning television: Plasticman had married Penny and fathered Baby Plas, who was a bendable chip off the old rubber tree and who starred in his own short adventure each week. Although the other components of *The Plasticman Comedy-Adventure Show* had bitten the dust, the consumer tips returned. Thirteen new half hours were filmed.

Following a network rerun cycle on CBS during the 1983-84 season, *Plasticman* entered daily strip syndication through Worldvision Enterprises in 1984. The episodes were the same old ones, linked together as they'd been on the network with live-action vignettes featuring a comic actor in a Plasticman costume.

The voice of the cartoon "Plas" was pro-vided throughout the series' run by the prolific Michael Bell, familiar to viewers of the 1970s as the off-camera "Butter . . . Parkay . . . Butter. . ." voice on the Parkay margarine commercials. When questioned in 1994, Neither Michael Bell nor Ruby-Spears' Ken Spears could remember who played the *live* Plasticman in the bumper sequences. Mr. Bell added that he hadn't given the on-camera Plasticman a second thought "as long as he didn't receive my residuals."

On a further monetary note, Ruby-Spears realized its biggest profits on the character when it went to reruns: *Plasticman* flourished for several seasons off-network, aced out only when Disney began encroaching upon afternoon reruns with its first-run *DuckTales* (q.v.) in 1987.

THE PLUCKY DUCK SHOW. Fox: 9/19/1992–11/7/1992. Spielberg/Warner Bros. TV. (*See* TINY TOON ADVENTURES for cast and credit details.)

This Fox Saturday morning entry consisted solely of selected repeats from Warner Bros.' *Tiny Toon Adventures* (q.v.), all spotlighting Daffy Duck's manic lookalike Plucky Duck. The title reverted in November to just plain *Tiny Toon Adventures*, with just plain more reruns.

POLE POSITION. CBS: 9/15/1984–8/30/1986. Namco, Ltd./DIC/LBS. Executive producers, Jean Chalopin and Andy Heyward. Produced by Chalopin, Heyward, Mitsuru Kaneko and Koichi Ishiguto. Executive in charge of production, Thierry P. Laurin. Developed by Michael Reaves and Jean Chalopin. Supervising director, Bernard Deyries. Written by Marc Scott Zicree, Chuck Lorre, Ted Petersen, Rowby Goren and Michael Reaves. Voice director, Ginny McSwain. Car and truck design by Eric Heshjong. Character design by Jesse Santos. Camera direction by Mushi Studios. Computer graphics by Japan Computer and MK Company. Music by Haim Saban and Shuki Levy. Voices: David Coburn (Dan Darret); Lisa Lindgren (Tess); Kaleena Kiff (Daisy); Marilyn Schreffler (Kuma); Darryl Hickman (Roadie); Jack Angel (Dr. Zachary); Mel Franklyn (Wheels); Helen Minniear (Teacher); and Neilson Ross, Paul Kirby, Phillip Clark, Jered Barclay, Brian Cummings, Irv Immerman, Steve Schatzberg,

Barry Gordon, Derek McGrath, Tony Pope, Hal Smith, and Bob Towers.

Pole Position was based on the popular video game created by Namco, Inc. The backstory of the 13 weekly half hours concerned a family of stunt motorists, the Darrets (No longer were the networks concerned over variations of the word "Dare," as NBC had been for the 1974 stunt-driver epic *Devlin* [q.v.]). Mom and Dad Darret were killed in a suspicious accident, leaving young adult offspring Dan and Tess and kid sister Daisy in charge of the Pole Position Stunt Show. The star automotive attractions were a brace of computerized cars, "Wheels" and "Roadie," which could travel by land, air and sea. And, just as in the live action series *Knight Rider*, the vehicles were endowed with computer-generated human voices and characteristics: Wheels was a reckless, laid-back "southerner" (the "action" sidekick) while Roadie was erudite and cautious (the "brains"). The Pole Position team divided its time between the racing circuit and crimefighting team, this at the behest of their Uncle Zach, head of the "Secret Force" for which the Darrets' late parents were special operatives.

Pole Position was weighed down with curiously unappealing characters; the worst was the "funny pet," a mutated cat/monkey named Kuma, which looked like a cat and did backflips like a monkey. (You don't want to know where she came from.) It was one of those programs where no one said anything funny but everybody was laughing at the fade-out. The series came to life only when emulating the original video game *Pole Position* with chase sequences shot from the driver's point of view. Otherwise, most viewers switched off *Pole Position* after its first commercial in favor of NBC's *Alvin and the Chipmunks* (q.v.). Why the series lasted two seasons (mainly reruns) is one of those unsolved TV mysteries which usually involve ironclad contracts and licensing commitments.

POLICE ACADEMY: THE SERIES. Syndicated: 1988. Ruby-Spears/ Warner Bros. Television. Executive producers: Joe Ruby, Ken Spears, Paul Mazlansky. Produced by Larry Huber. Supervising director, Charles A. Nichols. Directed by Cosmo Anzilotti, Bill Hutten, Tony Love. Senior story editor,

Michael Maurer. Story editors: Dorothy Middleton, Jack Mendelsohn. Music by John DeBray. Theme song performed by The Fat Boys. Animation facilities: Fils-Cartoons, Wang Film Production Company, Ltd. Voices: Ron Rubin (John Mahoney); Charles Gray (Hightower); Denise Pidgeon (Hooks/Callahan); Greg Morton (Jones); Dan Hennessey (Zed/ Tackaberry); Howard Morris (Sweetchuck/Professor); Greg Swanson (Proctor); Gary Crawford (Cmdr. Lassard); Dorian Joe Clark (House); and Catherine Gallant, Liz Hanna, Noam Zylberman and Len Carlson.

It's doubtful that the core audience for the R-rated 1985 comedy *Police Academy* wasted its time with cartoons on Saturday morning. In addition, we are shocked—*shocked*—at the notion that the film would be familiar to children's TV's target demographic; at least, three- to 11-year-olds weren't *supposed* to be watching a film in which the highlight featured a prostitute secretly servicing an unwitting police chief while he's giving a speech to his troops (I choose not to pursue this any further.) Regardless of who paid for the tickets, there were five *Police Academy* sequels, most as raunchy if not more so than the original. The level of humor and wit, substandard to begin with, descended with each sequel, even as profits soared. A cartoon series was as logical an extension as any.

The daily, half hour *Police Academy: The Series* was most emphatically not R-rated. It was barely a hard "G." Strictly for pre-teens and insatiable cartoon lovers was this saga of a group of misfits hired as Police Academy cadets through a misguided "equal opportunity" program. Commander Lassard oversaw the activities of such winning losers as amiable hunk Mahoney (played by Steve Guttenberg in most of the films), "human sound effects machine" Jones (originally played by golden-throated comic Michael Winslow), S.W.A.T. wanna-be Hightower, screaming zany Zed, phony macho Capt. Harris, and many others. The only truly efficient members of this squad were its female members: street smart Callahan and the deceptively meek Hooks.

Just as in most other TV adaptations of movie hits, the blueprint for these characters was etched indelibly long before Ruby-Spears got hold of *Police Academy*;

character development and nuance weren't part of the job description. What Ruby-Spears *did* contribute was a contingency of cartoony *Batman*-like villains, replacing the colorless baddies of the live-action films. Numbskull, Mr. Sleaze, and Lockjaw were the principal heavies of *Police Academy: The Series*, their names succinctly encapsulating their personalities. But where's the daily prosocial vignette, you ask? Ah, you're beginning to understand late–1980s kidvid. Each *Police Academy: The Series* included a 30-second safety tip. Actually, these were better done than usual, and even managed to raise a chuckle or two. And what about violence? Mayhem? Not on this voyage. *Police Academy* was played strictly for laughs. Often as not it got them.

Police Academy: The Series was nothing to be particularly proud of, but it wasn't anything to be ashamed of, either. At the very least it was better than most of the *Police Academy* movies, despite its palsied limited animation.

POPEYE THE SAILOR. (made-for-TV episodes only): Syndicated: 1960. King Features Television. Animation production companies: Larry Harmon Productions, Paramount Cartoon Studios, Jack Kinney Studios, Gene Deitch Studios, Rembrandt Films, TV Spots and Halas and Batchelor. Executive producer, Al Brodax. Producers: Larry Harmon, William L. Snyder, Gerald Ray. Directed by Jack Kinney, Paul Fennell, Seymour Kneitel and Gene Deitch. Written by Jack Mercer, Carl Meyer, Henry Lee, Ed Nofzinger, Al Bertino, Dick Kinney, Ralph Wright, Joe Grant, Milt Schaffer. Music (Paramount episodes): Win Sharples. Voices: Jack Mercer (Popeye/Wimpy); Mae Questel (Olive Oyl/Sea Hag/Swee'Pea); Jackson Beck (Brutus/others).
— **THE ALL-NEW POPEYE HOUR.** CBS: 9/9/1978–9/5/1981. King Features/Hanna-Barbera. Executive producers, William Hanna and Joseph Barbera. Animation director, Charles Cuddington. Produced by Alex Lovy. Directed by Ray Patterson, Carl Urbano. Creative producer, Iwao Takamoto. Story editor, Larz Bourne. Writers: Willie Gilbert, Jack Hanrahan, Jack Mercer, Bob Ogle, Chris Jenkyns, Doug Booth, Tom Dagenais, Don Heckman, Andy Heyward, Mark Jones, Glen Leopold, Kimmer Ringwald, Cliff

Roberts, Dalton Sandifer, David Villaire, Wally Wohl. Components: 1. **THE ADVENTURES OF POPEYE.** 2. **POPEYE'S TREASURE HUNT.** 3. **POPEYE'S SPORTS PARADE.** Voices: Jack Mercer (Popeye); Marilyn Schreffler (Olive Oyl/ Sea Hag); Allan Melvin (Bluto); Daws Butler (Wimpy). 4. **DINKY DOG.** Voices: Frank Welker (Dinky Dog); Frank Nelson (Uncle Dudley); Jackie Joseph (Sandy); Julie Bennett (Monica). Additional voices: Roger Behr, Ted Cassidy, Dick Erdman, Joan Gerber, Ross Martin, Don Messick, Frank Nelson, Pat Parris, William Schallert, Hal Smith, John Stephenson, and Jean VanderPyl.
— **THE POPEYE AND OLIVE SHOW.** CBS: 9/12/1981–11/27/1982. Production credits same as THE ALL-NEW POPEYE HOUR. Components: 1. **THE POPEYE SHOW.** 2. **PREHISTORIC POPEYE.** 3. **PRIVATE OLIVE OYL.** Voice credits same as ADVENTURES OF POPEYE segment on ALL-NEW ADVENTURES OF POPEYE, with the following additions: Jo Anne Worley (Sgt. Blast); Marilyn Schreffler (Alice the Goon); Hal Smith (Colonel Crumb).
— **POPEYE AND SON.** CBS: 9/19/1987– 9/10/1988. Hanna-Barbera/King Features. Voices: Maurice LaMarche (Popeye); Marilyn Schreffler (Olive Oyl/Lizzie/Puggy); Allan Melvin (Bluto/Wimpy); Josh Rodine (Popeye Jr.); David Markus (Tank); Penina Segall (Woody); Kaleena Kiff (Dee Dee); Don Messick (Eugene the Jeep).

Popeye, the taciturn one-eyed, muscle-heavy, spinach eating sailor man, was introduced as a secondary character in the Elzie Segar comic strip *Thimble Theatre* on January 14, 1929. The character served his purpose of guiding the strip's stars Ham Gravy, Ham's girlfriend Olive Oyl and Olive's brother Cole Oyl through a treacherous sea voyage, and then was supposed to leave the scene. You and I both know he didn't, so we can jump ahead to 1933, when Max Fleischer, house cartoon producer for Paramount Pictures, licensed the now-starring Popeye the Sailor for a series of animated shorts. Just as in the comic strip, Popeye debuted as an ostensible supporting character in a "Betty Boop" cartoon, but carried both the picture and the title, *Popeye the Sailor*. Olive Oyl was on hand, as well as a new character, a gargantuan bearded villain named Bluto. Twenty-three years and 234 cartoons later, Paramount sold the whole *Popeye* package, which by now was the mainstay of its cartoon output, to United Artists' TV subsidiary, Associated Artists Productions. If the words "Gold Mine" had not existed in 1956 and 1957, they would certainly have been coined for A.A.P.; *Popeye* turned out to be the biggest syndicated kids' attraction of its era, a position it would maintain until the release of Columbia's live-action Three Stooges shorts in the fall of 1958. Dancing in the streets should have been called for all around, but that's not the way King Features saw it. King Features was the newspaper syndicate who'd licensed *Popeye* to Paramount in 1933, but wasn't in on the TV bonanza at all. This status quo could not be allowed to remain status.

In 1960, when next we heard from King Features, official statements were being issued that the theatrical *Popeye*s had been run to death on TV, and that kids were beginning to tire of them. Yeh, right. Let's try this one: King Features wanted to downgrade the old *Popeye*s in order to build up its new *Popeye*s, which the syndicate would own outright and thus reap all the profits. Even as that "kids are tired of them" statement was being published in *TV Guide* in mid–1960, King Features was hard at work grinding out 210 new six-minute color *Popeye* cartoons, to be syndicated that October (not in October of 1961, as has been previously published). King Features chieftain Al Brodax very nearly struck a network deal with either NBC or CBS, but the networks weren't able to match the $65,000 already anted up by local stations as of January 1, 1960, on the strength of two *Popeye* pilot cartoons, "Hits and Missiles" and "Barbecue for Two." It would seem that, far from being tired of Popeye, the fans (and the local stations) couldn't get enough of him.

Since the new *Popeye*s would have to be mass-produced to get a decent manifest together by October, it was necessary to downplay visual humor in favor of verbal. Happily, all three of the voice actors who'd been with the theatrical series for the past several decades were still active. Jack Mercer was engaged to recreate Popeye, a role he'd been playing since 1935, as well as function in his original Fleischer studios capacity as a scriptwriter. Mae Questel, who'd been Olive Oyl for about as long as Mercer had been Popeye, took time from

her advertising schedule (she'd been busy in the last years of the 1950s as the voice of the Hasbro kid, Nabisco Wheat Honey's Buffalo Bee and the talking Fizzies soft-drink tablet, among many others) and her Broadway and movie work to provide the voice of Olive and the other female characters. And Jackson Beck, who'd been the blustering Bluto since the World War 2 years, likewise added to his crowded advertising, narration, radio and cartoon voiceover manifest as the new *Popeye*'s "new" nemesis Brutus.

Actually, Brutus wasn't new at all, merely Bluto rechristened. There's been a lot of discussion in recent years as to why King Features renamed the character, who'd been Bluto from the first 1933 cartoon onward. In an excellent 1993 *Animato* magazine article, Jim Korkis toted up the various Bluto/Brutus theories, starting off with the long-held (by the animation industry) theory that the Disney company advised King Features that "Bluto" sounded too much like "Pluto," the canine pet of Mickey Mouse. Korkis took recent character infringement lawsuits into consideration and noted that "even in 1960 the Disney studio did not hesitate to intimidate any imagined interlopers to the Disney heritage." This is true enough, but ten years before the Korkis article, Walter M. Brasch, author of *Cartoon Monickers*, doubted the Disney intervention simply by pointing out that the Bluto-Pluto "resemblance" had never bothered Disney throughout the 1930s, 1940s or 1950s, so why was it a problem in 1960?

Brasch elaborates on a second theory that is also proffered by Korkis: that the character names of "Popeye" and "Olive" were owned by King Features, but "Bluto" was owned by Paramount. *Animato* editor G. Michael Dobbs underlined this in a footnote to the Korkis article by pointing out that Bluto was developed by *Popeye* strip artist Elzie Segar at the request of Fleischer and Paramount to give Popeye a "consistent" villain. (The witchlike Sea Hag most often served this function in the comic strip, but the Hag would have been useless in the perennial "Popeye and Bluto fight over Olive Oyl" plotline that wove through the theatrical shorts.) This exclusivity-rights notion would seem to be the one that has the most credence with the closest observers. Bud Sagendorf, who for many years drew the *Popeye* daily strip,

Television's notion of Popeye, Olive Oyl, and Wimpy.

noted this theory in his "official" volume on the sailor's 50th anniversary in 1979; Bluto/Brutus' voice Jackson Beck told *Popeye* historian Fred Grandinetti that it was his understanding that Paramount owned the name Bluto; and *Popeye* executive producer Al Brodax, quoted in *Cartoon Monickers*, confirmed the words of Sagendorf and Beck.

But why "Brutus"? Al Brodax insisted that the name was drawn directly from Julius Caesar's assassin. Maybe that's what Brodax was told, but the truth is closer to a 1960 statement made by an anonymous *TV Guide* staff writer who noted that "In the first newspaper comics Brutus was the villain." Jim Korkis commented that *TV Guide* was not "entirely correct," but didn't elaborate, so I will here: In the earliest appearances of the Sea Hag, she was given a hulking son named Brutus, who didn't look like Bluto but who was decidedly on the unpleasant side.

And now that you've digested all that, here's another spanner in the works. In the *Popeye* pilot cartoon "Barbecue for Two," Brutus isn't given a name at all, merely the derogatory "Junior." This nickname wasn't plucked out of thin air. At the time that "Barbecue" was filmed (1959–1960), the Dell *Popeye* comic books, drawn by Bud Sagendorf, billed Bluto as "Sonny Boy"—the Sea Hag's son! This billing didn't last long, but it did bring things full circle, so to speak.

Let's get off this subject by noting that very little else on a surface level was altered in the new *Popeye* cartoons. The formerly scrawny Popeye was drawn with the huskier physique that he'd enjoyed since the war years, and was dressed in his white sailor ducks and cap from the same period, except in "Barbecue for Two," where he wore his comic strip wardrobe, a black and blue captain's uniform with red neckpiece and visored headgear. Olive Oyl was likewise sketched in pretty much the same manner that she'd appeared in the most recent theatrical cartoons, with fuller hairdo, longer lashes and an all-around more attractive appearance than the "schoolmarm" demeanor she'd borne in the earliest cartoons and was still bearing in the comic strip. She was, however, dressed in her old traditional floorlength dress, long sleeved blouse and clodhopper boots, forever relinquishing the "chic" clothing she'd been wearing at Paramount in the 1950s.

The most distinctive stamp made by King Features on the new *Popeye* was its resurrection of several comic-strip characters hitherto unseen in the cartoons: the aforementioned Sea Hag, her behemoth assistant Tor and her faithful vulture; Roughhouse the cook; eccentric inventor Professor O. G. WottaSnozzle; King Blozo of Spinachovia; the good-luck charm Wiffle Bird; and Geezil, the skuzzy nihilist who hated Popeye's hamburger-mooching pal J. Wellington Wimpy "to pieces"—though he never went so far as trying to murder Wimpy as he had in the strip!

Back in the fold were several other Elzie Segar–created characters who *had* appeared in the cartoons, though not as frequently as they would in the TV-made jobs: Wimpy, little Swee'Pea (Popeye's "adoptid infink"), Popeye's centenarian father Poopdeck Pappy, Eugene the magical Jeep, and Alice the Goon (whose "relatives" had appeared in the 1938 cartoon *Goon Island*, but who made her individual debut on TV).

The logistics of producing the 210 *Popeye* cartoons within a two-year period were beyond the resources of any single studio, so King Features shipped its storyboards, composed in their New York and Los Angeles offices, to five different outfits located throughout the world. The first people engaged by the syndicate were those who'd worked on the pilot films: Jack Kinney Studios, producers of "Barbecue for Two," and Paramount Cartoon Studios, which up until 1957 had been responsible for the theatrical *Popeye*s and which had used many of its old staffers to put together "Hits and Missiles." Kinney would make the greatest number of new *Popeye* shorts, 101 cartoons, while Paramount wasn't far behind with 63.

William L. Snyder, a cartoon producer whose Italian-based Rembrandt Films had been releasing through Paramount (including the Oscar-winning short *Munro*, a Jules Feiffer tale about a four-year-old military draftee), was engaged for 28 shorts, filmed variously at Britain's Halas and Batchelor studios and at the Prague headquarters of American expatriate Gene Deitch. Larry Harmon Productions, then busy with *Bozo the Clown* (q.v.), was responsible for 18 *Popeye*s, and Gerald Ray's TV Spots, an all-purpose animation factory comprised of several freelance operations (its best showing in the 1950s was *Crusader Rabbit* [q.v.]), put together 10 vehicles for America's favorite sailor man. The results belied the Nietzschean theory that out of chaos grows order: *Popeye* was the most schizophrenic cartoon series on television, one character in search of a style.

The Gerald Ray–produced *Popeye* shorts weren't very well made, but came closest to the spirit of the earliest theatrical *Popeye*s. They moved along at a fast clip, contained any number of culture-conscious jokes (one of Wimpy's favorite hamburger variations was the Ingrid Burger), had a scant regard for the lives and limbs of the characters (Bluto was smashed flat by a train in "Take It Easel," Sea Hag was blown to bits in "The Last Resort" and Popeye was beaten senseless by Olive's little niece Diesel in "Popeye's Junior Headache"), and contained dialogue delivered in nearly the same rapid-fire, deadpan style of the Fleischer 'toons. Credit for the scriptwork went to Henry Lee, who obviously cherished Popeye and his pals.

The Larry Harmon cartoons, directed by Paul Fennell with future Filmation mainstays Hal Sutherland and Lou Scheimer among the staffers, were on a par with Harmon's *Bozo* work, which in no way is a recommendation. The characters were drawn in an unattractive blocklike fashion, and the dialogue was burdened with those tiresome rhymes that inflicted Bozo's patter ("Gimme a gun, son," "I yam surrounded by ack-ack flack," ad nauseam). The cartoons were assembled with almost contemptuous laziness: When Brutus appeared as a college professor in "College of Hard Knocks," the animators decided it wasn't worth the bother giving him a wardrobe change, so he appeared before his student body wearing a mortar board and his traditional untucked sport shirt (he is similarly poorly attired as a "romantical" buccaneer in "The Irate Pirate"). Two Harmon cartoons with exactly the same background art, "Foola Foola Bird" and "Uranium on the Cranium," were released, and frequently telecast, back to back. A lot of kiddie viewers got awfully cynical *awfully* fast.

William L. Snyder/Rembrandt Films' *Popeye*s were produced at the very beginning and very end of the series' production schedule. On the whole, these were the best animated *Popeye*s of the bunch, but suffered the same faults as the Snyder/Gene Deitch *Tom and Jerry* shorts then being released by MGM. Characters moved too quickly with little sense of comic timing, and the scripts, though frequently witty, were on the insubstantial side. Probably the most endearing quality of the Rembrandt *Popeye*s was their quirkiness, from the hollow-sounding background music to such little oddball touches as the "new" voice of Brutus (Jack Mercer instead of Jackson Beck) in "Sea No Evil," the pint-sized, giggling villain in "Potent Lotion," Popeye and Olive's shared nightmare in "Intellectual Interlude," the outer space juvenile delinquents in "From Way Out," and Olive's massive poundage gain in "Weight for Me."

The Paramount Cartoon Studios offerings were by no means as well animated as the Snyder/Rembrandts, but at least were on the same level with what Paramount had been turning out for movie theatres in the last years of the 1950s. The pacing was poky but deliberate, and the cartoons had beginnings, middles and ends, their sturdy plotlines overcoming their overall lack of belly laughs. Paramount had the advantage of numerous animation sequences stockpiled from earlier cartoons, which were used frequently and creatively in their TV Popeyes, notably the closing "I'm Popeye the Sailor Man" musical renditions and an artfully rendered "explosion" effect. A welcome aspect to the Paramount-produced Popeyes was its reliance on storylines that had previously been seen in Segar's King Features comic strip continuity of the 1930s: The best of these were "Poppa Popeye," "Wimpy the Moocher," "Me Quest for Poopdeck Pappy" and especially "Myskery Melody" (not "Mystery Melody" as has sometimes been claimed), the last-named an effective seven minute paring down of a newspaper continuity that originally ran from December 1936 to April 1937.

Unfortunately, Paramount's dependency on the tried-and-true often worked against the cartoons. This was especially true in the studio's reliance on musical background themes composed years earlier by house musician Win Sharples. (Sharples now owned these themes in partnership with Hal Seeger, and spent the 1960s farming them out to several cartoon series, notably King Leonardo and His Short Subjects [q.v.], Tennessee Tuxedo [q.v.] and Milton the Monster [q.v.].) While the full, lavish orchestrations outclassed the stock themes heard in the Larry Harmon Popeyes and the shapeless agitatos of the Snyder/Rembrandts, they also tended to remind the viewer of the cartoons for which they'd originally been composed, thereby pulling the viewer out of the current cartoons rather than encouraging involvement in the storylines. It is, for example, very difficult to concentrate on Olive Oyl's shopping spree in the King Features Popeye "Popeye Goes Sale-ing" while the evocative musical score lifted from the 1951 Paramount Popeye "Swimmer Takes All" conjures up indelible memories of the English Channel swimming race in the earlier film.

And this brings us to the 100-plus Popeyes from the Jack Kinney Studios. On the credit side, the scripts for these were among the series' best, full of fresh storylines, clever one-liners and ingenious visual puns, trademarks of Kinney's work at Disney, which included the Goofy and Pluto cartoons. In fact, the 1961 Popeye cartoon "Uncivil War" is an engaging reworking of Kinney's award-winning Goofy vehicle, Motor Mania (1950). "After the Ball Went Over" comes to a climax after Popeye is outclassed by Brutus at a ping pong match, whereupon the sailor complains that the scriptwriters have let him down by forgetting his spinach! "Coffee House" is an amusing if familiar jibe at the Beat Generation, with Olive Oyl and Brutus adopting the traditional beatnik garb of horn-rimmed glasses and grungy clothes, then beginning all their sentences with "like." "Sea Hagracy" opened with Sea Hag being cleaned out by the I.R.S. for failing to pay her "Ill-Gotten Gains" tax. "Spinachoria" is told in the form of a Japanese "Noh" play, complete with Samurai warriors and Spinach Suki-Yaki. "Westward Ho-Ho" has wagon train scout Popeye running afoul of an Indian tribe called the Milwaukee Braves—whereupon we see a smoke signal in the shape of a beer bottle. "Through the Looking Glass" adroitly casts Swee'Pea in the role of Lewis Carroll's Alice and the rest of the Popeye stock company as the far-out denizens of Wonderland. And surely some sort of award was due the title of a whale-hunting epic: "Forever Ambergris."

On the debit side, Kinney's (admittedly necessary) overreliance on stock footage was maddening. Shots of Brutus laughing insanely, Popeye winking at the audience, Popeye reading Swee'Pea a bedtime story, Wimpy gesturing for a hamburger, and Prof. O. G. WottaSnozzle's "time-traveller machine" were trotted out so often that one wanted to reach through the screen, grab someone by the lapels and yell "STOP THAT!" Toward the end of the series, enough recyclable footage had been shot to enable production of that bane of all cartoon lovers, the "cheater": *Popeye's Testimonial Dinner*, which like Paramount's theatrical *Popeye's 20th Anniversary* (1953) was almost completely cobbled together from scenes of earlier cartoons (A *remake* of a cheater! The mind boggles). Even the sound tracks were repetitious, with one loop of Olive Oyl screaming "Help! Popeye! Save me!" dragged out at the flimsiest excuse.

The most appalling aspect of the Kinney *Popeyes* was the series' sloppiness. Even allowing for the fact that Kinney was denied the luxuries of time, budget and large staff, many of his *Popeye* cartoons were so clumsily made as to be unwatchable. Bluto would speak with Olive's voice, Popeye's pipe and hat would appear and disappear without warning, closeups failed to match medium shots (even the background art changed from shot to shot), characters would smile when upset and frown when happy, the narration and dialogue would comment upon sight gags that the animation staff had neglected to animate, and so on.

Alas, the very abundance of the Kinney *Popeyes* reflected badly on the rest of the series. Viewers tended to forget the good moments and recall only the bad, which is why the 210 King Features *Popeyes* have such a poor reputation among cartoon buffs today. Still, the package had the advantage of full-color photography (a leg up on the theatrical *Popeyes*, many of which were black and white—until Ted Turner got his mitts on them, the cad), and thus became extremely valuable in the late 1960s, when local TV stations were snatching up anything in any hue to fill the demands of the newly color conscious home viewers.

Except for the comic strip, the ongoing merchandising and a 1972 *ABC Saturday Superstar Movie* titled "Popeye and the Man Who Hated Laughter," the spinach-happy sailor kept a low media profile until 1978, when Hanna-Barbera was contracted by CBS for a *Popeye* Christmas special. The special was never produced, though a *Saturday Night Fever* takeoff, "Popeye Catches Disco Fever," did hit the airwaves. In the fall of 1978, *The All-New Popeye Hour* debuted on the CBS Saturday morning lineup. Jack Mercer was back as both the voice of Popeye (a role he

wouldn't relinquish until his death in 1984) and as a script and storyboard writer. Marilyn Schreffler, a Hanna-Barbera "regular" of the 1980s specializing in eccentrics and loopy teenagers, replaced Mae Questel as Olive Oyl, while veteran TV and movie character actor Allan Melvin (then also a regular on CBS' *Archie Bunker's Place*) was Bluto (the name reverted to the original with even less explanation than the switchover to Brutus in 1960). And Daws Butler's W.C. Fields-like reading of Wimpy wasn't entirely unprecedented, since a Fields imitation was being tried out for the character as early as Fleischer's "Plumbing Is a Pipe" (1938).

At its best, Hanna-Barbera's *Popeye* made the King Features efforts look like sidewalk chalkmarks. The animation was fuller and livelier than was expected of the studio, and the comedy content hit the audience full-wave. There *had* to be an upsurge in comedy because CBS' Standards and Practices had vetoed the violence and fisticuffs that had cemented Popeye's reputation back in the 1930s. Now Bluto was more concerned with outwitting Popeye than beating him up, and more preoccupied with winning races and coming out ahead financially than in seducing Olive Oyl. Likewise, Popeye never resorted to punching out Bluto; instead he used his spinach-sparked strength to outperform his opponent rather than outfight him. And at fade-out time, a chastened Bluto would usually admit that his reliance on cheating and cornercutting was wrong and Popeye's straight-arrow approach was right. The boys did everything but kiss and make up. Had the scripts not been funny, *The All-New Popeye Hour* would have drowned in its own syrup.

Each *All-New Popeye Hour* was subdivided into several components: "The Adventures of Popeye," "Popeye's Treasure Hunt" (the latest wrinkle on Hanna-Barbera's "never-ending contest" concept) and "Dinky Dog," the saga of a huge Marmaduke-like mutt who had never appeared in any earlier *Popeye* package and who after 1981 would vanish as completely as if he'd never existed. "Popeye's Sports Parade" was added to the series in 1979, with Wimpy refereeing while Popeye and Bluto competed at various athletic events. The prosocial portion of the program was manifested in the form of "Popeye's Safety Tips," featuring Popeye's lookalike nephews Peepeye, Pupeye and Pipeye; these 30-second bites were fun if you enjoyed Popeye saying such phrases as "electrukal applianskes." As part of this health- and safety-conscious attitude, it was made clear in the dialogue that Popeye no longer smoked his pipe. He merely used it as a toot-toot musical "instrumink."

In 1980, *The All-New Popeye Hour* shrank to 30 minutes and re-emerged as *The Popeye and Olive Comedy Show.* Added to the "Popeye" segments were two new components: "Prehistoric Popeye" enveloped the sailor man in Hanna-Barbera's beloved "anachronistic stone age" concept that had served them so well in *The Flintstones* (q.v.), while "Private Olive Oyl" teamed Olive with Alice the Goon as Army recruits, a nod to the 1980 Goldie Hawn comedy *Private Benjamin,* which also served as inspiration for H-B's *Laverne and Shirley in the Army* (q.v.). Though cancelled in 1983, this Hanna-Barbera *Popeye* package has been kept alive in reruns on cable's CBN and its successor, The Family Channel. The perpetuation of the Hanna-Barberas has enabled King Features Television and *its* successor, Hearst Entertainment, to pawn off its 1960s package of *Popeye* TV cartoons as "the original TV productions"—or sometimes, when the distributor is feeling particularly shameless, as "The Original *Popeyes.*"

In 1986, Hanna-Barbera was back at work with *Popeye and Son.* Popeye and Olive had married, settled down in a seaside cottage, and sired nine-year-old Popeye Jr., who didn't look like either one of them and who hated spinach (You just can't trust those sperm banks). Bluto had also married, perhaps on the rebound, to a bovine lady named Lizzie. Their son, Tank, was definitely genetically linked to the Bluto family: lazy, pugnacious, opportunistic, and a really sore loser.

Some storylines predictably centered on Popeye Jr. and his preteen pals, and we should at least be thankful that Hanna-Barbera didn't go its usual *Flintstone Kids* (q.v.) route and make Popeye, Olive and Bluto children themselves. As for the adults, the Popeye home was now a tobacco free zone, so the famous pipe remained unlit. Olive Oyl was no longer the imperiled heroine but an aerobics nut and civic leader. Bluto had the integrity to remain Bluto.

Replacing the late Jack Mercer as Popeye's voice was Canadian actor Maurice LaMarche, who held the job for a mere 13 half hours. Like the sailor's previous Hanna-Barbera incarnation, *Popeye and Son* also made the cable-rerun rounds after its network cancellation, but you'll notisk it ain't on much these days. Arf, Arf, Arf!

THE POPPLES *see* **KIDEO TV**

POP-UPS. NBC: 1/23/1971–8/28/1971. Educational Solutions Productions. Produced by Paul Klein.

Pop-Ups was a series of 12 one-minute educational bites designed to encourage reading. These were inserted sporadically in the NBC Saturday morning lineup throughout most of 1971.

POSSE IMPOSSIBLE *see* **THE C.B. BEARS**

POTATO HEAD KIDS *see* **MY LITTLE PONY**

POUND PUPPIES. ABC: 9/13/1986–9/19/1987. **—ALL-NEW POUND PUPPIES.** ABC: 9/26/1987–9/3/1988. Tonka Toys/Hanna-Barbera. Executive producers, William Hanna and Joseph Barbera. Executive in charge of production, Jayne Barbera. Produced by Kay Wright; associate producers, Berny Wolf and Lynn Hoag. Creative design, Iwao Takamoto. Supervising director, Ray Patterson. Directed by Art Davis, Don Lusk, Carl Urbano, Rudy Zamora. Animation directors, Jay Sarbry, Frank Andrina, Oliver Callahan, Joan Drake, Bob Goe, Rick Leon, Don Patterson, Joanna Romersa, Paul Sommer, Tim Walker. Story editors, Tom Ruegger and Charles M. Howell IV. Story directors, Dale Barnhart, Ric Estrada, Michael Kim, Art Leonardi, Jim Shull, Valeria Ventura, Jack White. Recording director, Gordon Hunt. Music by Hoyt Curtin. Animation facilities: Wang Film Production Co., Ltd., Cuckoo's Nest Studios. Production supervisor, Bob Marples. Voices: Dan Gilvezan (Cooler); Ruth Buzzi (Nose Marie); Bobby Morse (Howler); Nancy Cartwright (Brighteyes); B. J. Ward (Whopper); Ame Foster (Holly); Pat Carroll (Katrina Stoneheart); Frank Welker (Nabbit/Cat Gut); Adrienne Alexander (Brattina); June

Lockhart (Millie Trueblood); Chad Allen, Steve Bulen, Danny Cooksey, Peter Cullen, Brian Cummings, Barry Dennen, Bob DoQui, Casey Ellison, Dick Erdman, Pat Fraley, Joan Gardner, Linda Gary, Marilyn Lightstone, Chuck McCann, Haunani Minn, Clive Revill, Roger Rose, Ronnie Schell, John Stephenson, Patric Zimmerman.

—POUND PUPPIES SPECIAL. Voices included Ron Palillo, Henry Gibson, Sorrell Booke, Jonathan Winters, Garrett Morris, Ed Begley Jr., Jo Anne Worley, June Foray.

The Pound Puppies started as a line of stuffed dolls from Tonka Toys, then progressed to a Hanna-Barbera ABC network special aired in October of 1985. This one-shot was a genteel spoof of *The Great Escape*, with Pound Puppies leader Cooler, an "improv comic" type with an Eddie Murphy laugh, guiding his chums through an intricate escape route to free themselves from the Wagga-Wagga dog pound. Dabney Nabbitt was the hapless dogcatcher called upon to collar Cooler and cohorts Bright-Eyes, Scrounger, Howler, Tubbs and the rest. The 60-minute *Pound Puppies* special became one of the biggest renters on the videocassette scene, and additionally made a tiny niche in merchandising history as the first mainstream release processed exclusively in the VHS format, with no Beta counterpart.

When *Pound Puppies* graduated to a weekly half-hour series in the fall of 1986, only cool Cooler, his nervous cohort Howler (whose trademark was a gadget-laden hat), and the impressionable Bright-eyes were back at the pound. The property's premise and backstory were completely reshaped. The Pound Puppies now maintained a computer operated underground network in order to match deserving doggies with loving families. The so-called pound on the series was actually more of a sanctuary for homeless hounds, established on the front lawn of kindly millionaire Millicent Trueblood, who had the "Puppy Power" enabling her to talk to dogs. When Millicent died at age 101 (she didn't look a day over 95), her grandniece Katrina Stoneheart, a villain patterned after *101 Dalmatians'* Cruella DeVille, hoped to tear down the Trueblood mansion in order to erect condominiums for cat lovers only, and to oust the Puppies from the pound. Katrina was foiled by a proviso in Millie's will which left the mansion to Katrina but the pound and the soil beneath it to Katrina's young ward Holly, who also was gifted with Puppy Power. The remainder of the series boiled down to this: Pound Puppies and Holly versus Katrina, her nyaah nyaah-ing spoiled daughter Brattina (one must have some minor degree of sympathy for Hanna-Barbera characters whose personalities are dictated by the names chosen by their parents) and her pampered pussy Cat-Gut.

New arrivals to the *Pound Puppies* kennel were the infant pup Whopper, so named because of his "Jon Lovitz" lying technique, and vanity-ridden Southern belledog Nose Marie. Thirteen *Pound Puppies* episodes were filmed with this cast in 1986, amended by 20 more under the title *All-New Pound Puppies* in 1987; three of these all-new adventures ran the full half hour, while the remaining 20 were telecast two per week in 11-minute dollops. Each episode on both series ended with an easy to take "Pet Care Corner," offering advice to animal-loving kids.

While on surface merely a sales tool for the Pound Puppy toys, the series was elevated by some truly sharp scripting, usually the handiwork of future *Tiny Toons* (q.v.) and *Batman* (q.v.) writer-producer Tom Ruegger. *Pound Puppies* emulated the stream-of-consciousness patter of lead character Cooler, with instant movie and TV parodies that came and went so quickly that even the more jaded viewers, caught unawares, couldn't help dropping their resistance and chuckling knowingly. Cooler's costars were also given choice pop-cultural lines: When Nose Marie was rescued by alleycats, her first impulse was to coo "I've always depended upon the kindness of strangers." Precious moments like these, enhanced by the voice performances of Robert Morse (Howler), Ruth Buzzi (Nose Marie), Pat Carroll (Katrina), Nancy Cartwright (Whopper) and Dan Gilvezan (Cooler), not only transcended *Pound Puppies'* "commercial" angle, but also compensated for the Hanna-Barbera staff's tendency to overemphasize punch lines and throwaway gags and to toss in too many double-takes and gratuitous slapstick. (Tom Ruegger wouldn't completely escape this studio trait until after he'd left H-B for Warner Bros.)

Together with *Foofur* and *Pac-Man*, *Pound Puppies* was one of the best Hanna-Barbera cartoon adaptations of pre-established playthings.

POW WOW *see* **THE ADVENTURES OF POW WOW**

PRECIOUS PUPP *see* **ATOM ANT**

PRINCE PLANET. Syndicated: 1966. TCJ [Eiken Studios]/American-International. Produced by Mitsuteru Tokoyama. Created by Dentsu Advertising Ltd. and K. Fujita Associates. English-language version: Executive producers, James H. Nicholson and Samuel Z. Arkoff. Dialogue by Reuben Guberman. Music by Ronald Stein. Title song by Guy Hemrie and Jerry Styner. Vocals by the Carol Lombard Singers. Voice credits unavailable.

Prince Planet was standard-issue Japanimation: A 21st century setting, plenty of outer space hardware, characters with rounded eyes that appeared to be buttoned to the heads, and (in the U.S. version) a peppy theme song chanted by an all-kid chorus. Prince Planet (a.k.a. Prince of Planets), a preteen who hailed from the pacifistic planet Radion, was a member in good standing of the Universal Peace Corps. The Galactic Council of Planets chose Prince Planet as their delegate to Earth; the Council wanted to invite Earth to join up, but couldn't do so until the third planet from the sun was purged of warmongers and criminals. The Prince was selected as ambassador because of his advanced intelligence and his heightened sense of right and wrong.

After his spaceship crashed in the American southwest, Prince Planet was befriended by Diana Worthy, daughter of a wealthy but kindly oil tycoon. It was Diana who suggested the "ordinary everyday name" of Bobby as an alias for the Prince, who wanted to pass as an Earth boy when not on duty in order to avoid being pinned down as an "alien." Relocating in New Metropolis, Prince Planet carried on his fight against evil and cruelty, armed by a special pendant round his neck. Marked with a personalized "P," the pendant was powered by atomic energy from planet Radion which endowed the Prince with supernatural powers, extra body strength and the ability to fly. Maintaining his peacekeeping stance, Prince Planet

avoided fisticuffs, preferring to use strategy and speed to conquer his foes. From time to time, the Prince was spelled by two fellow Universal Peace Corps members, Haja Baba and Dynamo. The chief villains were weighted down with giveaway names like Warlock.

As with most Japanese imports, *Prince Planet* was clearly patterned after *Astro Boy* (q.v.), but with more elaborate background art and with better dubbing and script adapting from the English-version production team. Syndicated by American-International Pictures (whose head men James H. Nicholson and Samuel Z. Arkoff generously bestowed upon themselves an "executive producer" credit), *Prince Planet* performed best in big cities with large Asian populations. Elsewhere, the half-hour, 52-week *Planet* was handicapped by its retrogressive black and white photography, which has kept this exuberantly entertainment property off the videocassette shelves of the 1990s, and has confined its present existence to the dusty closets of private Japanimation collectors.

PROBLEM CHILD. USA: 9/1993–. D'Ocon Film Productions/Universal Cartoon Studios. Executive producers, Robert Simonds, Scott Alexander, Larry Karaczewski. Developed by Scott Alexander and Larry Karaczewski. Supervising producer/director, Antoni D'Ocon. Produced by Arthur Leonardi. Director of production, Gonzalo Castrillo. Associate producer, Kathi Castillo. Story editors, John Loy and John Ludin. Written by Wayne Kaatz, Ken Koonce, Mary Jo Ludin, John Ludin, Tom Mantke, Michael Merton. Music by Will Anderson. Voices: Gilbert Gottfried (Peabody); Nancy Cartwright (Junior Healy); and E. G. Daily, Ben Diskin, Jonathan Harris, John Kassir, Mark Taylor, Charlie Adler, John Astin, Gregg Berger, S. Scott Bullock, Rodger Bumpass, Corey Burton, Victoria Carroll, Dan Castellaneta, Marsha Clark, Jim Cummings, Debi Deryberry, Denny Dillon, Pat Fraley, Linda Gary, Dana Hill, Maurice LaMarche, Edie McClurg, Iona Morris, Hal Rayle, Bob Ridgely, Laraine Newman, Pamela Segall, Cree Summer, B. J. Ward, April Winchell.

The weekly, half-hour *Problem Child*, based on two truly reprehensible theatrical movies about a "bad seed" adopted child with a near-homicidal streak, premiered on TV with virtually no fanfare at all. Instead, the series snuck in like a thief on the USA cable service in tandem with *The Itsy Bitsy Spider* (q.v.) as part of the USA Cable Network's Sunday morning *Cartoon Express*. There was good reason not to trumpet this debut. If ever the clean-up-TV activists had a legitimate target, *Problem Child* was the bull's-eye, and even the most fervent civil libertarian would be hard put to blame them.

The Problem Child of the title was Junior Healy, a Bart Simpson without the charm. His co-conspirator was junior high classmate Cyndi, who collected bugs (she had a cockroach named Homer; do we detect jealousy directed at *The Simpsons* [q.v.]?). Junior also perpetrated his misdeeds with a pet monster (who knows *what* it was supposed to be?) named Yoji. Junior's policeman father didn't have any time for him, while the boy's wealthy grandfather flat-out despised him. And if these negative adult role models weren't enough, *Problem Child* also featured vengeful, prevaricating school vice principal Peabody (now we've stooped to attacking *Rocky and His Friends* [q.v.]), who was drawn—badly—to look like the actor who provided his voice, kvetching comic Gilbert Gottfried. Have we missed offending anyone yet? Well, here's another *Problem Child* stereotype: a developmentally disabled student named Murph, who'd been in the fourth grade so long that he had a driver's license.

Problem Child came off like a sick mockery of the majority of better produced, "prosocial" cartoons of the 1990s. The series had zero redeeming value, animation work on the level of a 1979 video arcade game, and utterly despicable leading characters. In fact, *Problem Child* may hold the record for most repellant characters within a single half hour. Attempts were made to "justify" Junior Healy's miserable behavior by pointing out that the adults were no better: One show featured a vengeful clown, while another had vice principal Peabody threaten corporal punishment in a school assembly, concluding his remarks with "Your word against mine!" The series also tried to emulate the pop-culture references and slapstick turns of comedy cartoon series like *Simpsons* and *Tiny Toon Adventures* (q.v.), but couldn't even get this right.

Why am I so steamed? Because *Problem Child* was produced by the new Universal Cartoon Studios, whose CEO Jeff Segal had in late 1993 publicly promised an unending stream of top-rank series based on the best material that the Universal story people could come up with (take a look at the tantalizing lineup of potential series ideas in our notes on Segal's pet project *Exo-Squad*). Funny that Segal never mentioned *Problem Child* in his press bites. Even *Beavis and Butt-Head* (q.v.) had more style and grace than this 13-week ribbon of wasted celluloid.

PROSTARS. NBC: 9/14/1991–7/25/1992. DIC Enterprises. Produced by Andy Heyward and Robby London. Concept by Michael Barnett. Opening title animation by Canvas Inc. Music by Eric Alaman. Additional music by Reed Robbins, Mark Simon. Music supervision by Joanne Miller. Animation facilities: Sei Young Productions. CAST (live action): Bo Jackson, Wayne Gretzky, Michael Jordan. VOICES: Townsend Coleman (Wayne Gretzky); Dave Fennoy (Bo Jackson); Dorian Harewood (Michael Jordan); Susan Silo (Mama); Diana Barrows (Denise); and Charlie Adler, Mary Albert, Jack Angel, Bill Callaway, Brian Cummings, Jim Cummings, Debi Deryberry, Pat Fraley, Mike Fratello, Ellen Gerstell, Dan Gilvezan, Edan Gross, Whitby Hartford, Dana Hill, Jerry Houser, Robert Ito, Richard Karron, Art Kimbro, David L. Lander, Katie Leigh, Sherry Lynn, Tress MacNeille, Candi Milo, Robert Morse, Rob Paulsen, Hal Rayle, Neil Ross, Ron Rubin, Justin Shenkerow, and R. J. Williams.

Originally conceived in 1990 for the ESPN cable service under the title *All-Stars*, DIC's *ProStars* premiered on NBC in 1991 after ESPN opted to remain an exclusively "live" sports events outlet. The new series did, however, retain the commercial ties with Nike shoes and General Mills that it would have enjoyed as *All-Stars* on cable.

In the tradition of *I Am the Greatest* (q.v.) and *Harlem Globetrotters* (q.v.), the weekly half hour *ProStars* was constructed around the likenesses and popularity of current sports icons, in this instance the National Hockey League's all-time leading scorer Wayne Gretzky, National Basketball Association top scorer Michael Jordan and baseball-football double threat Bo

Jackson. None of these men was a stranger to merchandising, so being turned into a cartoon was hardly a demeaning experience. The real athletes appeared in live-action at the beginning of each episode to set up the week's premise, a la DIC's *New Kids on the Block* (q.v.); and then, just like *New Kids*, the actual sports stars cleared a path for their animated likenesses, whose voices were provided by professional actors.

ProStars honored DIC's promise that Jackson, Jordan and Gretzky would be touted as "positive role models" by following the usual 1991 pro-ecology party line. The athletes would be assembled each week by their mentor Mama, a Dr. Ruth Westheimer soundalike who'd dispatch our heroes to various parts of the endangered globe, there to battle ecological threats with an arsenal of state-of-the-art gadgetry. Mama's loyal lieutenant Denise frequently accompanied the boys on their journeys, for the express purpose (it seemed) of getting kidnapped by the villain-pollutant of the week. The bad guys and bad gals fell into the *Captain Planet* (q.v.) mold of frothing unsubtlety, leading the more impressionable younger viewers to conclude that anyone who ever even considered cutting down a tree or damming a river was an automatic agent of Satan.

ProStars went into cable reruns — not on ESPN, but the Family Channel instead — after NBC decided to forego cartoons for news on Saturday morning.

PUNKIN PUSS AND MUSHMOUSE *see* MAGILLA GORILLA

PUNKY BREWSTER *see* IT'S PUNKY BREWSTER and MAXIE'S WORLD

A PUP NAMED SCOOBY-DOO *see* SCOOBY-DOO

THE PUPPY'S FURTHER ADVENTURES. ABC: 9/10/1983–11/10/1984.
—THE PUPPY'S GREAT ADVENTURES. ABC: 9/8/1984–11/10/1984; CBS: 9/13/1986–11/8/1986. Ruby/Spears. Executive producers, Joe Ruby and Ken Spears. Voices: Billy Jacoby (Petey the Pup); Nancy McKeon (Dolly); Michael Bell (Duke/Dash); Peter Cullen (Lucky); Tony O'Dell (Tommy); Josh Rodine (Glyder); Janet Waldo (Mother); John

Stephenson (Father). (*See also* SCOOBY-DOO.)

The "Puppy," whose name was Petey, was introduced in a children's book by Catherine Woolley, which was transferred to an *ABC Weekend Special* in May 1978 by Ruby-Spears, "The Puppy Who Wanted a Boy." Audiences responded to this 60-minute weeper about Petey's attachment to a lonely orphan boy, paving the way for three more *Weekend Specials*, shown between 1979 and 1981: "The Puppy's Great Adventure," "The Puppy's Amazing Rescue" and "The Puppy Saves the Circus." The encouraging rebroadcast ratings led to Ruby-Spears and ABC assembling a weekly series based on the character in 1982 — one that never seemed to fulfill the promise of the specials.

The *Scooby and Scrappy Doo/Puppy Hour* was an altogether copacetic arrangement between Hanna-Barbera and Ruby-Spears, since it was the popularity of Scooby-Doo (q.v.) that had enabled the dog's onetime writer-developers Joe Ruby and Ken Spears to declare independence from Hanna-Barbera and set up their own animation shop. The "Puppy's New Adventures" component of this series downplayed the human supporting cast, spotlighting Petey, his female friend Dolly, and his canine compadres Duke, Dash and Lucky, as they searched for Petey's lost family. Thirteen half-hour "New Adventures" were produced, with 10 more to come in the fall of 1983 under the title *The Puppy's Further Adventures*— run as a lead-in to Hanna-Barbera's *The All-New Scooby and Scrappy Doo Show*, forming one of those "comedy blocks" so beloved by Saturday morning schedule mavens.

In January 1984, *The Puppy's Further Adventures* was rerun as a separate half hour, then returned in a handful of existing episodes in the fall of 1984 as *The Puppy's Great Adventures*. Here, as throughout his series career, Petey the pup turned out to be less appealing on a weekly level than in his *Weekend Special* appearances; he ultimately lost the battle of the ratings in November 1984 in the competition of Hanna-Barbera's *Snorks* (q.v.) on NBC and that same studio's *Shirt Tales* (q.v.) on CBS. One year later, *The Puppy's Great Adventures* was picked up by CBS and rebroadcast for three months, hammocked as "soft" buffer between the more frenetic

Pee-wee's Playhouse and *Hulk Hogan's Rock 'n' Wrestling* (q.v.), and offered opposite ABC's *Ewoks* (q.v.) and NBC's *Foofur* (q.v.). CBS eventually forsook Petey in favor of the ever popular *Richie Rich* (q.v.). It's to the credit of strong sponsorial and prior-commitment contracts that a diverting but essentially forgettable property like the *Puppy* tales survived as long as it did without building any sort of acceptable audience.

Q*BERT *see* **SATURDAY SUPER-CADE**

Q. T. HUSH. Syndicated: 1960. Animation Associates/M & A Alexander/NTA. Q. T. Hush was a diminutive private eye whose cohorts were his own shadow, a towering, cigar-smoking independent entity named Quincy, and his deerstalker-wearing dog Shamus. Hush solved comically complex mysteries with both the aid and opposition of police Chief Muldoon. The all-color *Q. T. Hush* cartoon series was designed to run as either a daily cliffhanger or a weekly half hour: 10 plotlines, divided into 100 five-minute installments which could be strung together into 20 half-hour adventures. However, few local stations ran this enjoyable but slight property on its own. Most followed the lead of Chicago's WGN-TV, which spotted *Q.T. Hush* cartoons as an added attraction on its daily *Dick Tracy* (q.v.) program.

QUICK DRAW McGRAW. Syndicated: 1959. CBS: 9/28/1963–9/3/1966. Hanna-Barbera/Screen Gems. Produced and directed by William Hanna and Joseph Barbera. Associate producer, Alex Lovy. Animation director, Charles A. Nichols. Written by Warren Foster and Michael Maltese (among others). Music by Hoyt Curtin. Components: 1. QUICK DRAW McGRAW. Voices: Daws Butler (Quick Draw/Baba Looie/Snuffles); Julie Bennett (Sagebrush Sal); and Don Messick. 2. SNOOPER AND BLABBER. Voices: Daws Butler (Snooper/Blabber); and Don Messick. 3. AUGIE DOGGIE AND DOGGIE DADDY. Voices: Doug Young (Doggie Daddie); Daws Butler (Augie Doggie); and Don Messick.

The success of *Huckleberry Hound* (q.v.) spurred Hanna-Barbera and sponsor Kellogg's Cereals to develop a second weekly syndicated series in 1959. Taking into consideration the sizeable adult audience for *Huckleberry*, Hanna-Barbera decided to cater to a hipper crowd by giving its new series, *Quick Draw McGraw*, a keener satirical edge. The three six-minute cartoons incorporated into each half hour *Quick Draw* episode were deliberate takeoffs on the three most prevalent prime time TV genres of the period.

The host of the series was Quick Draw McGraw, a humanized horse who functioned as a frontier marshal — a lampoon of the flinteyed western heroes then glutting the TV marketplace. Quick Draw took the regimented behavior of these characters a step further into the ridiculous. His rigid obeisance to the Code of the West frequently allowed the less virtuously inclined bad guys to get the upper hand; in one episode, Quick Draw even took a chapter of the Maritime code of honor by "going down with the ship" when his prairie schooner began sinking into a sand dune. Like *Gunsmoke*'s Matt Dillon, Quick Draw had a deputy sidekick, a diminutive Mexican burro named Baba Looey. Former Warner Bros. scenarists Michael Maltese and Warren Foster borrowed from their Daffy Duck–Porky Pig movie genre parodies of the 50s by having Baba Looey behave more sensibly, and thereby reap better results, than his headstrong, doltish "boss."

The second component of *Quick Draw McGraw* featured the adventures of Super Snooper and Blabbermouse, a dog and cat detective team. This was Hanna-Barbera's "answer" to the overabundance of such private eye TV shows as *Peter Gunn*, *77 Sunset Strip* and *Michael Shayne*. As before, Snooper and Blabber fell into the standard Hanna-Barbera tall-guy leader and short-guy assistant mold. Augie Doggie and Doggie Daddy, a canine father-and-son contingent, comprised the third installment of each *Quick Draw* program. Their exploits constituted a spoof of the family sitcom genre that kept the private eye and Western shows company on late 1950s television.

Because there was a definite weekly throughline on this program, running gags abounded. These gags scored as much on audience anticipation as they did on execution. For example, whenever Quick Draw donned the disguise of the Zorrolike El Kabong — so named because his dispen-

Quick Draw McGraw rounds up some unusual suspects—including fellow Hanna-Barbera-ites Yogi Bear and Boo Boo!

sation of justice consisted of smashing a guitar on the miscreant's head with a shout of "Kabong!"—audiences were immediately tipped off that the rescued heroine would stop adoring and start shrieking the minute our horsey hero removed his hardly impenetrable face mask. And whenever Quick Draw enlisted the aid of a bloodhound named Snuffles, audiences started giggling even before Snuffles went through his ritual of begging for a "Doggie Bis-kitt," the consumption of which would send the delirious dog into an orgasmic fit of delight.

Since the animation was unremarkable, the series relied on verbal humor for its biggest laughs. While the writing of *Quick Draw* leaned towards the usual Hanna-Barbera overkill (when Quick Draw spots a reward poster for a bandit which lists any number of silly crimes and concludes with "we give Green Stamps," the joke is bludgeoned to death by having Quick Draw spend a full 30 seconds reading the poster out loud), there were times that the non-fan could fully understand why so much of the cartoon producers' audience was adult. A prime example: When a pampered dowager had her necklace stolen,

she instructed her husband to "find someone to scream for me."

With so much going for it in the script department, *Quick Draw McGraw* turned out to be voice actor Daws Butler's finest hour. Butler provided virtually all the principal voices on the series (the one exception was Doggie Daddy, who was given a clever approximation of Jimmy Durante's familiar rasp by Doug Young), and he rose to the occasion with some of his best work. Quick Draw McGraw's voice was close enough to Red Skelton's Clem Kadiddlehopper character that it's a wonder the litigation-happy Skelton didn't immediately ring up his attorney; Baba Looey was an affectionate parody of Desi Arnaz' rapid-fire Hispanic cadence (the character was in fact named after the Arnaz song hit "Baba Lu"); Super Snooper was a neat imitation of Archie the Manager, the Brooklynese character created by Ed Gardner for the *Duffy's Tavern* radio series; and the lisping Blabbermouse was reminiscent of nightclub comedian Buddy Hackett.

It was during *Quick Draw McGraw* that Butler developed another character who'd turn out to have enduring value; a Shakespearian lion (with Bert Lahr overtones) variously named Snagglepuss and Snaggletooth, who first appeared as a supporting character in such cartoons as Snooper and Blabber's *The Lion Is Busy* and who'd ultimately headline his own short subject series on the 1961 Hanna-Barbera syndie *Yogi Bear* (q.v.). A far more minor *Quick Draw* character, western damsel-in-distress Sagebrush Sal (who'd plead "Help, Help" in an utterly detatched manner while powdering her nose or applying lipstick), was the embryonic role model for the star of Hanna-Barbera's 1969 *The Perils of Penelope Pitstop* (q.v.).

Quick Draw McGraw remained in first run syndication until September of 1963, when the 45-episode package was sold, with Kellogg's sponsorship intact, to CBS for the network's Saturday morning lineup, where it flourished for three seasons (in some markets, the program continued playing off its syndication deals, even while CBS was running the series on weekends).

THE RACCOONS. Disney Channel: 1985-1992. Gillis-Wiseman/Atkinson Films-ARTS/CBC. Creator/producer-director/head writer: Kevin Gillis. Executive producer, Sheldon S. Wiseman. Co-director, Sebastian Gunstra. Story editors, Mary Crawford and Alan Templeton. Written by Kevin Gillis, Sheldon S. Wiseman, Alan Templeton, Jim Betts, Darson Hall, Sebastian Gunstra, Gerald Tripp. Songs by John Stroll, Steven Lunt, Kevin Gillis. Sung by Lisa Lougheed. Voices: Michael Magee (Cyril/Snag); Len Carlson (Bert, Prof. Smedley-Smythe, Pig #2, Pig #3); Bob Dermer (Ralph/Lady Baden-Baden); Susan Roman (Melissa); Nick Nichols (Pig #1); Sharon Lewis (Broo); Geoffrey Winter (Narrator).

The *Raccoons* were Ralph, Bert and Melissa, who lived in the Evergreen forest (in a "Raccoondominium") and ran the local newspaper, the *Evergreen Standard*. Bert, the leader, possessed a vivid imagination, which led to trouble when he fancied himself a detective or sportsman. The Raccoons jointly owned a dog, named Broo. Their principal opponent and social rival in the forest was Cyril Sneer, a wealthy wolf (who looked more like an anteater) whose principal fault was an overcompetitive streak. Cyril wasn't really a villain, just incurably greedy; perhaps some of his nicer qualities were inherited by his sensitive son Cedric. The Sneers also owned a dog, a vicious little snip named Snag. Their servants, three little unnamed pigs, were ever at the ready to do Cyril's bidding, but weren't above a little skullduggery on their own volition.

Created by Kevin Gillis, *The Raccoons* debuted on the Canadian CBC TV network in the late 1970s. Five years after a brace of 1980 American-run specials, "Christmas Raccoons" and "The Raccoons on Ice," *The Raccoons* became the first "new" cartoon project to run regularly on the Disney Channel cable service, where it remained until 1992.

RAGGEDY ANN AND ANDY *see* **THE ADVENTURES OF RAGGEDY ANN AND ANDY**

RAINBOW BRITE *see* **KIDEO TV**

RAMBO. Syndicated: 1986. Ruby-Spears/Carolco International NV. Worldvision. Executive producers, Joe Ruby and Ken Spears. Produced by Cosmo Anzilotti, Walt Kubiak. Directed by Charles A. Nichols and John Kimball. Production supervisor, Tom Morton. Story editors, Mike Chain and Jack Bornoff. Story direction by Kevin Altieri, Rich Chidlaw, Rick Hoberg, Dick Sebast. Series based on characters created by David Morrell. Creative consultants, Gil Kane, Jack Kirby and Doug Wildey. Voice director, Michael Hack. Music by Jerry Goldsmith. Additional music by Shuki Levy and Haim Saban. Voices: Neil Ross (Rambo); Michael Ansara (Warhawk); Allan Oppenheimer (Col. Trautman); Lennie Weinrib (Gripper); Peter Cullen (Sgt. Havoc); Mona Marshall (Kat); Frank Welker (Mad Dog); Robert Ito (Black Dragon); James Avery (Turbo); Edmund Gilbert (Nomad); and Michael Bell, Russi Taylor, and Dale Ishimoto.

Rambo was the Vietnam veteran gone ballistic played by Sylvester Stallone in the 1985 action film *First Blood*. Though he was subdued after a great deal of bloodletting (justified by a rambo-ling monologue toward the end of the film, explaining his frustration over how the Vietnam returnees were treated by an ungrateful America), the character was too lucrative to disappear—and he didn't, courtesy of two sequels. In these, Rambo was the unquestioned hero, rescuing fellow veterans from their Communist captors at the behest of the U.S. government.

Well, here we are again with an R-rated movie property whose principal appeal was with those young males who ostensibly weren't old enough for anything stronger than PG-13. And here we are with a larger than life personality who seemed best suited to the animated cartoon. What to do? Simply launder Rambo cleaner than he'd been in his theatrical sequels and put him in charge of a unit fighting tyranny of all sorts. Produced by Ruby-Spears, *Rambo* premiered in April of 1986 as a two-hour cartoon special, then settled into a Monday-through-Friday syndicated strip (30 minutes per episode) in the fall of that year.

Borrowing a page—actually several paragraphs—from the *G.I. Joe* (q.v.) concept, John J. Rambo was now in charge of The Force of Freedom, comprised of several musclebound members of various peacekeeping and combative talents: Kat (female master—or mistress—of disguise) Turbo (African American mechanical genius), Nomad, Sgt. Havoc and Mad Dog. The Force of Freedom answered to Colonel Trautman, the cartoon counterpart of the military character played by Richard Crenna in the *Rambo* films. Since *Rambo* was now *G.I. Joe* in everything but name, it was necessary for the series to have an equivalent to *Joe*'s villainous COBRA organization. *Rambo*'s principal foe was SAVAGE, commandeered by General Warhawk—who, in what must have been someone's private joke, looked and sounded a lot like General Douglas MacArthur!

Ruby-Spears' Rambo didn't resemble Sylvester Stallone much, either visually or vocally, and except for his tendency to strip to the waist (the cartoon series' opening titles offered several tantalizing closeups of the Rambo pecs) and his deployment of bows, arrows, and jagged knives, the animated Rambo acted not at all like his screen counterpart. This was a man who was moved to violence only after exhausting all other, more peaceful alternatives. He was frequently seen in the company of young, hero-worshipping children, whom he was called upon to rescue from the less politely inclined SAVAGE (The presence of youngsters was meant to appeal to the five- to 12-year-old crowd that *Rambo* was aimed at, a viewer-

ship that wouldn't have related to the M.I.A.s usually rescued in the "Rambo" movies). And he seemed to have a Princeton professor's knowledge of *everything* about the terrain, climate and wildlife of whatever country he happened to be visiting during his round-the-world adventures.

This knowledgeability satisfied *Rambo*'s "prosocial" obligations: without interrupting the action or plotline, Rambo was able to provide quickie geographical/ecological educational bites, all scrupulously accurate, and all beautifully complemented by the series' first-rate background art. Also laudatory was the painstaking character design, overseen by the same three-man "creative consultant" staff of comic book veterans (Gil Kane, Jack Kirby, Doug Wildey) that Ruby-Spears had previously employed on *Centurions* (q.v.). As for the animation—oh, well.

Despite its expurgations and educational aspirations, *Rambo* was just the sort of cartoon fare looked down upon by TV watchdog groups. Characters seemed to exist only to be transformed into toys and action figures; our government put the well-being of the world in the hands of vigilantes; the villains were ugly and loud; gunfire was rampant; little kids and old people were in constant jeopardy (at one point, SAVAGE even kidnapped a Santa Claus lookalike and strapped him to a buzzsaw!); and the plots were resolved by orgies of destruction—though no one was ever killed. Widely condemned at the time of its release, *Rambo* wasn't nearly as bad as its critics would have us believe. It simply wasn't distinguishable enough from the already-established *G.I. Joe* to have justified renewal beyond its initial 65-episode run.

RAW TOONAGE (a.k.a. DISNEY'S RAW TOONAGE). CBS: 9/12/1992–9/4/1993. Walt Disney TV Animation/Buena Vista. Supervising producer, Larry Latham. Produced by Larry Latham (*Bonkers*), Ed Wexler (*Marsupilami*). Story editors, Kevin Crosby Hoops, Tom Minton, Stephen James Taylor. Directed by Carole Beers, William Houchins, Marsh Lamore, James T. Walker. Written by Laraine Arkow, Terrie Collins, Robert Schechter, Gary Sperling. Theme song by Patrick DeRemer. Music by Ed Fournier, Mark Watters, Stephen James Taylor.

Animation facilities: Wang Film Production Company, Ltd. Voices: Jeff Bennett, Roger Bumpass, Jim Cummings, Steve Mackall, Terry McGovern, Marcia Wallace, Frank Welker.

The title (and publicized concept) of Disney's *Raw Toonage* suggested a half hour of unbridled cartoon experimentation, with brand new characters and situations each week. But Disney wasn't quite freewheeling enough for that, so the half hour series settled for two regular components. *He's Bonkers* was the story of a well-meaning bobcat, an unemployed cartoon star who tried his best to fit in with the "real" world as a delivery boy. *Marsupilami*, based on a long-established Belgian comic book character, was a cheetah with the talent, like Felix the Cat, of changing the shape of his tail (the world's longest—25 feet!) to suit the circumstances.

Bridging these weekly episodes was a rotating guest host, always an established Disney "star" drawn from the studio's other TV properties. On the first program, Ludwig Von Drake, a Teutonic professor type created in 1961 for *Walt Disney's Wonderful World of Color*, expostulated on cartoon technique for the edification of youngsters. The surprising thing was that Von Drake was funny, perhaps for the first time in his life. That first episode also introduced some hilarious spot-gag vignettes lampooning prime time television, notably "Doggie Schnauzer M.D." and "Totally Tasteless Video." Unfortunately, these little nuggets were discontinued early on so that the animators could concentrate their best work on Bonkers and Marsupilami.

In 1993, Disney dropped all of its existing Saturday morning network programs. This did not spell total doom for *Raw Toonage*, however, since both *Bonkers* and *Marsupilami* became half-hour series on their own. (See separate entries.)

THE REAL GHOSTBUSTERS. ABC: 9/13/1986–9/3/1988. Syndicated: 1987.

—SLIMER! AND THE REAL GHOSTBUSTERS. ABC: 9/10/1988–9/7/1992. DIC Enterprises/Columbia TV. Executive producers: Michael Gross, Joe Medjuck, Jean Chalopin. Producers: Jean Chalopin, Andy Heyward, Tetsuo Katayama, Len Janson, Chuck Menville. Coordinating producer, Robby London. Executive in charge of production, Brian Miller. Production supervisor, Stacy Gallishaw. Executive consultants, Ivan Reitman and Bernie Brillstein. Characters created by Dan Aykroyd and Harold Ramis. Produced and directed by Stan Phillips. Theme music composed by Ray Parker Jr.; performed by John Smith. Additional music by Haim Saban, Shuki Levy, John Goetz, Jim Mortarotti. Animation facilities: Sae Rom Plus One Productions (animation director, Pack Jun Nam). Voices: Arsenio Hall (Peter Venkman/Winston Zedmore—1986); Dave Coulier (Peter Venkman—1987 on); Edward L. Jones (Winston Zedmore—1987 on); Maurice LaMarche (Egon Spengler); Laura Summer, Kath Soucie (Janine Melnitz); Frank Welker (Slimer/Ray Stantz); Charlie Adler (Slimer/Rafael); Jeff Altman (Professor Dweeb); Fay De Witt (Mrs. Van Heuge); Cree Summer Francks (Chilly Cooper); Danny Mann (Linguini/Budd); Jeff Marder (Rudy); Alan Oppenheimer (Morris Grout); April Hong (Catherine); Katie Leigh (Jason); Danny McMurphy (Donald); and Lorenzo Music, Buster Jones, Luis Accinelli, Jess Dixon, J. P. Dixon, Brian George, and Robert Ito.

As we observed in our notes on *Ghostbusters* (q.v.), the year 1986 saw two different programs from two different production companies sharing that same basic title. But whereas Filmation's *Ghostbusters* was based on a 1975 live-action series, DIC's *Ghostbusters* drew its inspiration from the immensely popular 1984 theatrical comedy film which sparked the whole *Ghostbusters* TV imbroglio in the first place. In the interests of clarity and legality, DIC's series was titled *The Real Ghostbusters*, a distinction that seemed to subliminally murmur "accept no substitutes."

So far as it went, this series *was* the "real" thing in that the characters were lifted from the movie, which to many young viewers was the only *Ghostbusters* they'd ever known. It will be recalled that the film featured a team of paranormal investigators who operated a booming spook-eradication operation in Manhattan, only to find their talents strained to the utmost by an onslaught of horrifically demonic spirits. You may also remember that the Ghostbusters were frequently "slimed" for their efforts—covered with sticky goo by various sportive spirits and sometimes by their own Ghost-busting weaponry. All of this was incorporated in *The Real Ghostbusters*, including the character names and likenesses—though the animators were somewhat kinder to Dan Aykroyd, Bill Murray, Harold Ramis and company than Mother Nature had been, turning them into flawlessly handsome young hunks. Unlike the Filmation series, which concentrated on ghosts drawn from established legends and fairytales, *The Real Ghostbusters* did battle with brand-new ectoplasmic monstrosities.

In both movie and series, the Ghostbusters were Peter Venkman, Egon Spengler, Ray Stantz and Winston Zedmore, with ditzy little Janine Melnitz acting as secretary. None of the film's stars supplied the TV voices (the animated Zedmore's voice was provided by a fellow who left cartoon work for a slightly more fulfilling career elsewhere: Arsenio Hall), though *Ghostbusters* supporting actor Ray Parker Jr. was well represented by the theme music ("Who ya gonna call? GHOST-BUSTERS!") which he'd written for the movie and which was used on the series. Another important member of the Ghostbusters team was Slimer!, one of those green, bloblike spectres who'd been so destructive in the film. The TV Slimer! was a gentle, helpful little entity, though no less sloppy than his cinema counterpart. He was popular enough to warrant a title change on the series, which entered its third ABC network season as *Slimer! And the Real Ghostbusters* (the series had been on ABC as a weekly since 1986, and in daily syndication, with new episodes, since 1987).

At that time, the series also expanded to a full hour and added several preteen characters, presumably for preteen audience identification. *Slimer! And the Real Ghostbusters* survived the network wars until 1992, by which time the series had slipped comfortably into full-time cable TV exposure.

THE RELUCTANT DRAGON AND MR. TOAD.

ABC: 9/12/1970–9/3/1972. Rankin-Bass. Written by Romeo Muller and William J. Keenan; based on stories by Kenneth Grahame. Voices: Paul Soles, Donna Miller, Claude Rae, Carl Banas.

Several characters created in the early 20th century by British author Kenneth Grahame were spotlighted on the 17-episode, half hour *The Reluctant Dragon and Mr. Toad.* Tobias, the dragon of Willowmarsh Village, was a gentle soul, kept from harm by bumbling knight Sir Malcolm. If there was any antagonist at all, it was a cute little girl who brought Tobias daisies, which invariably brought on a sneezing fit (fire and all) from the allergic dragon. Mr. Toad was the funloving master of Toad Hall, whose extravagances and enthusiasms were ever at odds with his duties as a member of the Landed Gentry. These characters from *Wind in the Willows* were better handled by Disney in the 1940s, but *The Reluctant Dragon and Mr. Toad* was a harmless way for young couch potatoes to pass the time back in 1970. That is, if they weren't already glued to *Bugs Bunny/Road Runner* on CBS and *Heckle and Jeckle* on NBC.

THE REN AND STIMPY SHOW.

Nickelodeon: 8/11/1991–. (Also telecast on MTV.) Spumco Co. (1991); Games Animation (1992). Executive producer for Nickelodeon, Vanessa Coffey. Created, cowritten and coproduced by John Kricfalusi. Coproducer, Christine Danzo. Producer for Games Animation (1992): Bob Camp. Story editors, Bob Camp and Will McRobb. Written by Bob Camp, Vincent Waller, Will McRobb, Bill Wray, Jim Gomez, Chris Reccardi, Peter Avanzino, Mike Kim, Ron Hauge, Elinor Blake, Richard Purcel, Jim Smith. Animation facilities: Carbunkle Cartoons, Bon Art Company, Lakewood Productions. Executive in charge of production (Nickelodeon): Mary Harrington. Producer (Nickelodeon): Jim Ballantine. Voices: John Kricfalusi, Bob Camp (Ren); Billy West (Stimpy/Ren); Gary Owens (Powdered Toast Man); Michael Pataki (George Liquor); and Cheryl Chase, Edan Gross, Charles Haid, Sharon Mack, Harris Peet, Darrin J. Sargent, and various guest stars. Singers: Randy Crenshaw, Edan Gross, Lesa O'Donovan, Churlie Brissette.

Ren Hoek was an anemic-looking chihuahua whose voice suggested an unholy liaison between Peter Lorre and Raul Julia. Stimpson J. "Stimpy" Cat was a pot-shaped pussy with an obscenely large nose, the better for diligent picking. Ren and Stimpy lived in what appeared to be someone's basement, though Stimpy spent most of his time in his "Gritty Kitty" litter box. Ren devoured ice cream bars and romance novels, screamed a lot ("What EEEEZ it?," "You EEEdiot") and considered the day wasted if he couldn't break wind in the bathtub. Stimpy was an amiable, submissive punching bag for his dominant yet loving pal (whips and leather have yet to make an appearance on the series, but give the boys time); the crackbrained cat's pride and joy was his collection of "nose goblins." Together (they were utterly dysfunctional when *not* together), Ren and Stimpy underwent adventures that took them everywhere from a homicidal army camp to the literal gates of Hell. In one episode, Ren lost all his teeth, leaving only a mouthful of exposed nerves, while another episode was titled "Stimpy's First Fart" until Nickelodeon's Standards and Practices spoke up. This was not, repeat *not*, The Care Bears.

Ren and Stimpy was the creation of John Kricfalusi (pronounced Kriss-fal-loosee), a 35-year-old Ottawa native who spent his formative years sending bad drawings to Disney and other cartoon firms. After getting booted out of college in 1979, Kricfalusi secured a job as an animator, then spent the next 13 years of his life working on what he would later designate "some of the world's crappiest cartoons," including a personally frustrating stint on the short-lived 1988 revival of *Beany and Cecil* (q.v.). Kricfalusi was offered a more positive growth experience by Ralph Bakshi on 1987's ambitious *Mighty Mouse: The New Adventures* (q.v.). Still, Kricfalusi yearned for a project over which he'd have full control and unlimited range of imagination and experimentation — a "creator driven" project rather than the typical Saturday morning series wherein artwork was dictated by pre-existing cartoon characters, popular video games or overmerchandized action figures.

Entering into partnership with Bob Camp, another young writer/animator who after an unpleasantly restrictive experience at Warner Bros.' *Tiny Toon Adventures* (q.v.) yearned for a renaissance in creator-driven animation, Kricfalusi set up Spumco Productions (the animator claimed to have seen the word "spum" on a can of sardines, further claiming that it was Danish for "quality") and cooked up *Ren and Stimpy*. He was roundly refused by all the major commercial networks, but was accepted by the higher-ups at cable TV's Nickelodeon, after several bouts of wild, aggressive behavior at preliminary meetings — behavior which Kricfalusi admitted was patterned after his idol, hyperbolic actor Kirk Douglas.

Launching a weekly series about a sociopathic dog and an arrested-development cat who spent most of their screen time wallowing in their own body functions was quite a gamble for Nickelodeon, especially when the budget for *Ren and Stimpy* escalated to $400,000 per half-hour episode (compared to the Saturday-morning-network average of $250,000). Only six programs were completed for the first *Ren and Stimpy* season, each consisting of two 11-minute adventures and an occasional "commercial" for the stars' favorite product, "Log" (that's right — these were advertisements, done up in the flashy manner of the old "Slinky" commercials, for plain, everyday wooden logs). The series was broadcast on Nickelodeon's Sunday morning kiddie block, where it might have languished had it not caught the eye of that most trend-happy of target audiences, the College Crowd. Soon hundreds of thousands of 18- to 24-year-old collegians found themselves glued to the tube every Sunday morning, chanting along with Ren and Stimpy's cheer-up ditty "Happy Happy, Joy Joy," joining in when Ren admonished his pal (in John Kricfalusi's voice) to "Back Off, man!," and relishing each exploit of Stimpy's favorite TV cartoon star, an anthropomorphic, antisocial fish named Muddy Mudskipper.

Many theories were offered as to why the college contingent took to *Ren and Stimpy*. Perhaps it was the "gay" subtext indigenous to the stars' relationship (Kricfalusi frequently cited the influence of those old Bugs Bunny cartoons where Bugs would flirt with, kiss, or even marry Elmer Fudd); perhaps it was simply because the under-25 crowd thought that jokes about nose hair were funny. At any rate, the series became a 5.8-point ratings bonanza for Nickelodeon, an equally popular attraction when its episodes were rebroadcast on Nick's sister cable network MTV, and a merchandising boon for Spumco Productions; tie-in toys ranged from Ren and Stimpy dolls to a synthetic "Stimpy hairball." And a 1993 novelty song, "You Eediot!!," cracked the Top 200 list of popular recordings. All the while, John Kricfalusi received 5 percent of all merchandising profits, but had no say over how his characters would be used.

In the meantime, the scroungy dog-and-cat team had spawned a fervent fan club and was gracing the covers of many an establishment magazine. In the fall of 1992, Nickelodeon decided to cash in big-time by slotting *Ren and Stimpy* into its Saturday evening lineup. By September of 1993, at which time Kricfalusi's creation ranked seventh in the overall cable ratings, there emerged the ultimate form of TV-cartoon flattery: A *Ren and Stimpy* lookalike property from Hanna-Barbera, *Two Stupid Dogs* (q.v.).

But for John Kricfalusi, the mountains had crumbled long before 1993. There had always been friction between Spumco and Nickelodeon, partially over story content. Nickelodeon animation vice president Vanessa Coffey, while delighted over *Ren and Stimpy*'s good showing in the ratings, was still concerned that the series not push the envelope and become too gross and far-out for the kids (even though Coffey had publicly declared that the series was aimed at young adults!). Kricfalusi countered by pointing out that his program contained no *real* violence like knife fights or bloodletting, merely comic exaggeration. Nickelodeon wasn't completely convinced that such scenes as Ren's cousin Sven ripping out Ren's tongue and then eating it were models of humorous decorum, and ordered such scenes snipped before telecast.

There were many more instances in which *Ren and Stimpy* episodes would be bowdlerized by Nickelodeon for public consumption. The most notoriously pruned episode was "Powdered Toast Man," wherein a lampoonish superhero rescued the Pope from certain death and helped the President extricate himself from a zipper. These jolly happenings were witnessed with alarm by an angry viewer, who took her complaints straight to the FCC. When the episode was shown for a second time, the Pope was not identified by name, and the closing credits were rewritten to credit singer Frank Zappa as the voice of "that funny little guy with the pointed hat."

The biggest bone of contention between Kricfalusi and Nickelodeon was that Spumco seemed incapable of working within a budget or a deadline. Kricfalusi promised 13 new programs for the fall of 1992, but then had trouble producing any more than three very costly half hours, compelling Nickelodeon to trot out the "classic six" reruns that had been in constant play for well over a year. *Ren and Stimpy* head writer Bob Camp rationalized this by pointing out that each of the stylistically complex episodes took at least 12 months to make, "and we make them all at the same time. So it's impossible. . . . We're doing the best we can, and it's the absolute truth. And if we miss some airdates, that's just tough . . . because we're doing the best show on TV." John Kricfalusi claimed that it was Nickelodeon's fault that the series had habitually gone over budget and that new programs weren't being made, citing an instance in which an episode titled "Man's Best Friend," featuring a xenophobic, gun-obsessed character named George Liquor, was first approved by Nickelodeon, then vetoed at the very last moment.

The animator's argument might have carried more weight had Kricfalusi not already earned a reputation as the Slowest Drawer on the West Coast. Even before *Ren and Stimpy* had built up its audience, iconoclastic columnist Thelma Scumm noted in the Winter 1992 edition of *Animato* magazine that Kricfalusi "lacks something when it comes to comic timing and storytelling (and meeting deadlines)!" Scumm further noted that the cartoonist had a bad habit of surrounding himself with "yes men who think he's a genius," a statement apparently borne out by the increasingly self-indulgent Us Against the World attitude at Spumco.

By late September of 1992, Nickelodeon was fed up with Bob Camp's "artistic temperament" defense and John Kricfalusi's complaints of interference. Acting upon the fact that it owned the *Ren and Stimpy* property, the cable service fired Kricfalusi, then imposed budget slashes that resulted in the layoff of 35 Spumco employees. Writer Bob Camp and comedian Billy West, the voice of Stimpy, were among the few retained; Camp was in fact put in charge of the series, making him *persona non grata* with those Spumco staffers still loyal to Kricfalusi. Suits, countersuits and mutual recriminations were inevitable. Nickelodeon insisted that Kricfalusi had been warned of the consequences of failing to keep his end of the bargain; the network also relented a bit, offering to make the animator a "consultant" and to allow him to remain as the voice of Ren. Kricfalusi turned down these face-saving scraps from Nickelodeon and began issuing public statements that he was being persecuted and pilloried. "That's the reason Nickelodeon wanted new characters, so they could own them," was Kricfalusi's bitter response.

Sympathy and support from other animation firms was by and large directed at Kricfalusi, with Matt (*The Simpsons*) Groening speaking for many when he noted that the firing of *Ren and Stimpy*'s mentor was "like taking Dr. Frankenstein away from his monster." *Ren and Stimpy* fans also rallied behind Kricfalusi, and the tone of their letters to Nickelodeon began to take an ominous, threatening quality — not quite homicidal, but disquieting all the same. (One began, "Hello you scum sucking pigs," while other, less creative correspondents merely repeated Kricfalusi's own assessment of Nickelodeon as "the network of boogers and farts.")

Since portions of each new episode for the 1992-93 *Ren and Stimpy* season had been completed at the time of John Kricfalusi's dismissal, it was up to Nickelodeon to match the repellant but undeniably hilarious quality of these snippets with the Korean-animated work of the new, network-owned Games Animation division (which also produced what some considered a *Ren and Stimpy* stepchild, Joe Murray's *Rocko's Modern Life* [q.v.]). Series producer Bob Camp insisted that it was business as usual on *Ren and Stimpy*: "While most other companies are slinging fast food, we're making gourmet shows. As a creative artist, I couldn't hope for a better situation."

The Games Animation version of *Ren and Stimpy* utilized several topnotch scripts prepared during the Kricfalusi days, notably the screamingly funny "Stimpy's Cartoon Show," which featured a senile cartoon director whose nose and ears kept slipping off his face, and an "avant garde" cartoon like none other on the face of the Earth. Even though Bob Camp and crew still "pushed the envelope" with raucous comedy content, few censorship hassles resulted from these new cartoons, lending credence to the theory that Nickelodeon's fundamental

complaint with Kricfalusi had been his slowness rather than his sense of humor.

From what this writer has seen as of the winter of 1993, the new *Ren and Stimpy* was capable of being just as tastelessly uproarious as the original. This is not to take anything away from founding father John Kricfalusi — without whom, after all, there would have been no Ren and Stimpy. This is merely an observation that Kricfalusi's characters may very well be strong enough to stand on their own spindly legs without their Dr. Frankenstein.

RETURN TO THE PLANET OF THE APES. NBC: 9/6/1975–9/4/1976. DePatie-Freleng/20th Century–Fox. Directed by Doug Wilder. Written by Larry Spiegel, E. Jack Kaplan, John Buryett, Bruce Shelley, John Strong. Music by Dean Elliot, Eric Rogers. Voices: Tom Williams, Richard Blackburn (Bill); Claudette Nevins (Judy/ Nova); Austin Stoker (Jeff); Edwin Mills (Cornelius); Philipa Harris (Dr. Zera); Henry Corden (General Urko).

The 1968 *Planet of the Apes* theatrical film, based on the novel by Pierre Boule, told of a supposedly faraway planet wherein apes ruled and humans were subjugated and domesticated like animals. Ultimately, displaced Earth astronaut Charlton Heston discovered that this alien world was actually a post-apocalyptic earth. ("You blew it up! Damn you! Damn you to hell!") Somehow the 20th Century–Fox scenarists were able to milk this property for four sequels, through the simple expedient of having two of the talking-ape characters board a space ship and travel through a *backward* time warp, bringing them to a contemporary Earth, then starting the cycle all over again. The real attraction of the *Apes* films was the wholly convincing makeup worn by the actors playing the intellectual simians. The cosmetic process was a costly, time-consuming one, as everyone discovered when a live-action TV series, *Planet of the Apes*, surfaced briefly in 1974. Perhaps the producers should have gone directly to square one and turned the property into a cartoon series from the get-go; after all, cartoon characters don't have to sit in a makeup chair for four hours every morning.

DePatie-Freleng's *Return to the Planet*

of the Apes wasted no time reducing the concept to the "young audience identification" level common to Saturday morning. Replacing the thirty- and forty-something astronauts of the *Apes* movie was a trio of twentyish space travellers (what a hurry-up training program *that* must have been). Bill Hudson, Judy Franklin and Jeff Carter and their NASA craft, the "Venture," were sucked into a time vortex and deposited in the year 3810 A.D., some 1000 years after the time-frame of the first *Planet of the Apes* film. The apes were in the driver's seat, and the humanoids were segregated into a community called New City. Bill was brought to ape scientists Cornelius and Zera (the roles originally played by Roddy McDowall and Kim Hunter) for experimentation, but was saved from vivisection when he revealed his power of speech. The scientists then learned, just as they had in the film, that their government had kept the notion of intelligent humans a secret, for fear of sparking another atomic cataclysm. Bill was set free, and the series took off from there for 13 weeks' worth of episodes with titles like "Lagoon of Peril" and "Screaming Wings."

RICHIE RICH:
—RICHIE   RICH/SCOOBY-DOO HOUR. ABC: 11/8/1980–9/18/1982.
—THE PAC-MAN/LITTLE RASCALS/ RICHIE RICH SHOW. ABC: 9/5/1982–9/3/1983.
—THE LITTLE RASCALS/RICHIE RICH SHOW. ABC: 9/10/1983–9/1/1984.
—RICHIE RICH. CBS: 11/7/1986–12/17/1986.
—FUNTASTIC WORLD OF HANNA-BARBERA. Syndicated: 1988. Hanna-Barbera. Credits (RICHIE RICH segments only): Produced by Art Scott, Don Jurwich, Oscar Dufau. Directed by Ray Patterson, George Gordon, Bill Hutten, Bob Hathcock, Carl Urbano, Rudy Zamora, Bob Goe, Terry Harrison. Story editor, Norman Maurer. Written by Mark Evanier, Bryce Malek, Jack Mendelsohn, Dick Robbins, Jan Green, Rick Fogel, Jim Simon, Tom Yakutis. Music by Hoyt Curtin. Voices (RICHIE RICH segments only): Sparky Marcus (Richie Rich); Joan Gerber (Mrs. Rich/ Irona); Dick Beals (Reggie Van Goh); Bill Callaway (Prof. Keenbean); Nancy Cartwright (Gloria); Stanley Jones (Cadbury/ Mr. Rich); Frank Welker (Dollar); and Al Fann, Christian

Hoff, Joyce Jameson, and Marilyn Schreffer. (For further production information, see separate entries on *The Little Rascals*, *Pac-Man* and *Scooby-Doo*.)

"Do not—repeat, do not—subject your children to this cassette," warned media critic Harold Schechter regarding *Richie Rich* in 1986. Too late. The America of the 1980s was already in the clutches of the God of Conspicuous Consumption, and Richie Rich had been His prophet for a quarter of a century.

Richie Rich first appeared as a supporting character in Harvey Comics' *Little Dot* #6 in 1956, and one year later graduated to his own starring comic book. This fresh-faced blonde urchin in a Fauntleroy suit was billed as "the poor little rich boy," but he didn't look to be suffering as he enjoyed all the creature comforts of wealth: elaborate playthings, a rumpus room the size of Connecticut, the unquestioning servitude of Cadbury the butler, and a dog named Dollar, due to his "S" shaped markings. Even at an early age, I was aware that Harvey was doing everything in its power to depict Richie Rich as a nice boy, one who handled his wealth with kindheartedness and noblesse oblige rather than the smug snootiness of Rollo the Rich Kid in Ernie Bushmiller's *Nancy* or the overeducated arrogance of Waldo in the *Our Gang* comedies. The fact that Richie Rich was sweet and lovable did not alter the fact that I hated his guts. Apparently I was alone, since Richie became one of Harvey's hottest properties (he even graduated to "superhero" status in the *Batman*-dominated 1960s)—and this without an animated cartoon tie-in enjoyed by such other Harvey stalwarts as Casper the Friendly Ghost (q.v.), Little Audrey, Herman and Katnip and Baby Huey.

But an animated *Richie Rich* could not be held back much longer, especially not in the money-mad 1980s. Since Harvey's "house" cartoon company of Paramount had long since broken up, Hanna-Barbera was handed the job of transferring Richie Rich to the small screen. This H-B did, with Richie's supporting cast—Mother and Father, butler Cadbury, Dollar the dog, and best friends Gloria and Reggie—intact. Hanna-Barbera also endowed the series with a brush of the studio's own *The Jetsons* (q.v.) by including a robot maid named Irona and a whole staff of mechanical servants, some of whom malfunctioned

No filthy lucre in this house: *Richie Rich* (with faithful Cadbury).

from time to time, resulting in havoc, chaos and loud beeping sound èffects. At least they didn't steal the silverware and ask for Tuesdays off.

Richie Rich's sole purpose in life was to buy, buy, buy toys and spend, spend, spend his weekly $100,000 allowance. Could the kids at home resist such a role model? After all, he spoke their language—"Gimme!" And that's why *Richie Rich*, with only 13 full half hours to his name (broken down into 12-, seven- and four-minute segments), managed to survive on ABC for four seasons, CBS for one season, and in syndication for three more.

Perhaps sensing that the little capitalist creep couldn't sustain audience interest all by himself, Hanna-Barbera almost invariably coupled *Richie Rich* with other properties. The series went out as *The Richie Rich/Scooby-Doo Hour* in 1980, as *The Pac-Man/Little Rascals/Richie Rich Show* in 1982, *The Little Rascals/Richie Rich Show* in 1983, and finally as one of

several components of *The Funtastic World of Hanna-Barbera* in 1988.

Nausea alert! Richie Rich will be back, sooner than you'd want, in a big-budget motion picture. Starring Macaulay Culkin. But take heart. Maybe a comet will hit the planet first. (See also *The Little Rascals, Pac-Man* and *Scooby-Doo*.)

RICK MORANIS IN GRAVEDALE HIGH. NBC: 9/8/1990–9/7/1991. Turner Program Services. Voices: Rick Moranis (Mr. Schneider).

Following in the footsteps of Martin Short's *The Completely Mental Misadventures of Ed Grimley* (q.v.), Short's old *Second City Television* cohort Rick Moranis supplied the voice for his cartoon caricature on *Rick Moranis in Gravedale High*. Moranis portrayed a bowtied, bespectacled teacher named Mr. Schneider, who worked in a high school for monster teenagers. We'll avoid the obvious comment here. Suffice to say that these were *truly* monsters, in the fashion of the junior-grade horrors previously seen on *Drak Pack* (q.v.) and the *Mini-Monsters* segments of the syndicated *Comic Strip* (q.v.).

The decaying student body included Frankentyke, J. P. Blanche (an invisible kid), Vinnie Stoker (a teen vampire, apparently related to *Dracula* author Bram Stoker), Gill Waterman (scion of the "Gill Man" family of *Creature of the Black Lagoon* fame), and others with more nondescript cognomens like Sid, Cleofatra and Duzer. The headmistress of Gravedale High was Ms. Crone. This went on for half an hour a week (hammocked between two other NBC cartoon shows, *Captain N* [q.v.] and *Kid 'n Play* [q.v.]), and it's surprising that Mr. Schneider didn't apply for a transfer to a peaceful, quiet South Bronx high school, where one would merely risk a gunshot wound rather than a stake through the heart.

And that's all I can tell you. I am aware of some cute bits on *Gravedale High*, such as Vinnie Stoker wearing a bat insignia rather than a letter on his jacket, but I didn't get to watch the show; it was preempted in Milwaukee by reruns of another gang of young monsters, *The Little Rascals*. Evidently no one outside of Milwaukee watched *Gravedale High* either, because it was killed after a single season (reportedly by an mob of angry villagers) and replaced by *Prostars* (q.v.).

RICKETY ROCKET *see* **PLASTICMAN**

RICOCHET RABBIT *see* **MAGILLA GORILLA**

RING RAIDERS. Syndicated: 1989. DIC Enterprises/Those Characters from Cleveland/Bohbot. Executive producers, Andy Heyward and Robby London. Producer, director and art director: Turk Savage. Animation director, Dae Jung Kim. Adapted for animation and story edited by Phil Harnage. Executive in charge of production, Winnie Chaffee, assisted by Dawn Jackson and Stacy Gallishaw. Associate producer, Ken Duer. Creative consultant, Kevin S. Murray. Script coordinator, Lori Crawford; assistant, William A. Ruiz. Production coordinator, Vic Kephart. Voice director, Marsha Goodman. Music by Haim Saban and Shuki Levy. Music production super-

visor, Andrew Dimitroff. Voices: Dan Gilvezan (Victor Vector); Efrain Figueroa (Joe Thundercloud); Stuart Goetz (Hubbub); Ike Eisenmann (Cub Jones); Gregory Martin (Kirchov); Jack Angel (Mako); Chris Anthony (Jenny Gail); Roscoe Lee Browne (Max Miles); Roger Bumpass (Scorch); Townsend Coleman (Yasu Yakamura); Chuck McCann (Baron Von Clawdeitz); Susan Silo (Siren).

Ring Raiders was one of the very few two-hour DIC cartoon specials which only made it as far as a five-part daily without graduating to a series of its own. The story was an intriguing one, with a mystical team of aviators drawn from the ranks of the earliest lighter-than-air experimenters, World War 1 flying aces, World War 2 dive bombers, Vietnam, the present, and even the future, all aligned as the "Ring Raiders" under the command of Victor Vector. Vector, headquartered on the flying wing "Aircarrier Justice," led the raiders against the forces of the Skull Squadron and Skull Commander Scorch.

The miniseries (partially inspired by the success of the theatrical film *Top Gun*) promoted a "one world" allegiance among the disparate pilots, who were not only from different countries but from different ethnic groups (and different sexes) as well. This Global Village of the Sky was good for five episodes, but *Ring Raiders*, codeveloped by *Care Bears* (q.v.) creators Those Characters from Cleveland, never got beyond its syndicated "premiere" week in September of 1989.

ROBOCOP *see* **MARVEL ACTION UNIVERSE**

ROBOTECH. Syndicated: 1985. Tatsunoko/Harmony Gold/ZIV International. Executive producer, Ahmed Agrama. Produced by Carl Macek. Supervising director, Robert Barron. Written by Gregory Snegoff, Robert Barron, Greg Finley, Steve Kramer, Mike Reynolds, Jim Wager, Steve Flood. Music editor, John Mortarotti. Music by Ulnio Manolia Arlon Oser, Alberta Ruben Estevez. For Tatsunoko: Producer, Kenji Yushida. Director, Ippei Kuri. Voices: Greg Snow (Rick Hunter); and Reba West, Jonathan Alexander, Drew Thomas, Deanna Morris, Thomas Wyner, Brittany Harlow, Donn Warner, Axel Roberts, Tony Oliver, A. Gregory, Noelle McGraph, Sandra Snow, Guy Garrett, Jimmy Flinders, Anthony Wayne, Eddie Frierson, Leonard Pike, Aline Leslie, Shirley Roberts, Wendee Swan, Larry Abraham, Sam Fontana, Penny Sweet, Mary Cobb, Celena Banas, and Chelsea Victoria.

Perhaps *Robotech* never played any of the TV stations in your city, but that didn't stop the Japanese cartoon series from achieving cult status. In fact, for many years its very unavailability helped fire the "legend."

The property was developed by American animation-cel collector and dealer Carl Macek, who wanted to promote a cartoon series that would cut through the malaise of sameness on afternoon kidvid in the U.S. More than anything, Macek wanted to take one of the recent wave of Japanese serialized cartoons and compose a faithful translation for American audiences — more faithful than the recent watered-down *Battle of the Planets* (q.v.).

The Hollywood-based distribution firm Harmony Gold, anxious to capture the teenage audience that had made the *Star Wars* film trilogy a hit, learned of Macek's dream from other cartoon art collectors. Harmony Gold contracted Carl Macek for the purpose of preparing the Japanimation science fiction weekly *Macross* for English-language consumption. To that end, Macek aligned with Ahmed Agrama, who ran a translation and dubbing studio called Intersound Incorporated. Agrama had produced remarkably good results in translating the Japanese cartoon series *Captain Harlock* (q.v.), which though not quite ready for the public had caught the attention of Macek. The result was a feature-film adaptation of *Macross*, which encouraged Harmony Gold to give the green light for distributing the half hour episodes of the same property stateside.

The problem was that *Macross* ran only 36 episodes, falling short of the 65-episode minimum required for a daily strip. Carl Macek decided to incorporate two other series, *Southern Cross* and *Genesis Climber Mospeada*, to fill out the manifest with an additional 49 half hours. This was not the artistic stretch it might have been, since all three series were produced by Tatsunoko Studios and shared similarities in character, background design and story material. Macek conjured up a throughline about an ancient scientific method of generating and utilizing robotic personnel

and weaponry for extraterrestrial combat. Revell Toys, which owned the merchandising rights to *Macross*, came up with the name for this futuristic technology: "Robotech." Carl Macek re-christened the three separate series as Book One, Book Two and Book Three of the *Robotech* saga, bridging the stories together by developing interlocking family and fraternal ties among the principal characters.

Book One of *Robotech* retained the "Macross" designation. Set in 1999, the story told of the crash-landing on Earth of the Super Dimensional Fortress Macross, the vanguard vehicle of the Robotech Masters, whose awful warmaking capabilities were dearly coveted by a rival outerspace outfit, the Zentraedi. The thrust of the plot was the race of Earth's scientists to uncover the secrets of Robotech before suffering an apocalyptic Zentraedi invasion. Played out upon this tapestry were the personal affairs of Robotech Expeditionary Force officers Rick and Roy Hunter and Lisa Hayes, and of several civilians, notably a popular singer named Lynn Minmei. It was within this framework that the program took on soap-opera dimensions, with teary-eyed closeups of starcrossed lovers alternating with long shots of brutal outer space combat. As things came to a head and the Earth was on the brink of destruction, the subplots became more trenchant. The climactic moment wherein the participants of a romantic triangle bickered among themselves even as bombs decimated their cities is the litmus-paper test of *Robotech*. Fans of the series find this moment a profound example of the human spirit remaining unquenched even in the face of Doom. Detractors find the climax just plain dumb — to them, it looks like the old *Carol Burnett Show* "soap" parody "As the Stomach Turns."

After "The Macross Saga" ran its course, the "Southern Cross" portion of the series, set 20 years after "Macross," picked up the narrative. This portion — a tremendous improvement over "Macross" — was popularly known as "Dana's Story" after principal character Dana Sterling, a headstrong officer of the Armies of the Southern Cross, the organization entrusted by the Robotech Expeditionary Force to ward off any future invasions. The tenuous connection between the two narratives was explained by having Dana identified as the daughter of Max and Miriya Sterling, two of the young principals of "Macross."

Once "The Southern Cross" ended, "Genesis Climber Mospeada," variously retitled "The New Generation" and "Invid Invasion," took over the plot threads. Rick Hunter, from the "Macross" episodes, made a reappearance (via unseen voice-over) rallying the Robotech Expeditionary Force to ward off yet another invasion of Earth. This one had an even bleaker squint at the future than "Macross," with nearly the entire Expeditionary Force wiped out save for Scott Bernard, who carried on the fight with a ragtag group of Earthling youngsters and misfits. (An extension of the story, *Robotech II*, never achieved a TV syndie berth, but has become a hot property on the videocassette market.)

With innumerable characters and honeycomb-like storylines, this self-described "Multi Generational Space Soap Opera" offers no middle ground. You either love it or hate it. *Robotech* fans tend to be those who feel that "Japanimation," with its shattering of TV taboos with nudity, overt sexuality, and death scenes, is inherently better than American TV simply because it is so different. One could certainly revel in the somewhat perverse aura of *Robotech*, whose creators delighted in confounding all the plot and character predictability that American viewers have been lulled into. It was not uncommon for major, sympathetic characters to be killed off without warning — and just imagine the reaction of the kids of America were something like that to happen to Bugs Bunny. The fact that the villainous Zentraedi of the "Macross Saga" drew their strength from a South American rain forest could not have sat at all well with the ecological crowd who have had it all too much their own way on weekday animated TV. And never had there previously been the literal equivalent on American afternoon television of the "New Generation" character Lancer, a young man who, when not warding off enemy aliens, enjoyed a career as a *female* entertainer named Yellow Dancer!

In toto, however, *Robotech* wasn't nearly as perfect as its adherents insist. Though the adaptive transitions between the three separate series were done quite smoothly, and despite battle sequences which were excitingly staged and edited with razor-

sharp precision, the animation (particularly in the early "Macross" chapters) could be quite shabby at times — notably the artists' depiction of the aircraft vapor trails, which looked more like strands of warped spaghetti. As for the "adult" storylines, these were compromised by several downright childish dialogue sequences; at times, the characters sounded like the cast of *Speed Racer* (q.v.) reciting Damon Runyon after breathing helium. Let me add here that without prior prejudice, I sat through virtually all the *Robotech* episodes available on videotape. I was impressed by the imagination, energy and nuance of the whole project, especially the intricacies of plot and character development. Even so, it was an uphill task to get past the sappy banter and (sometimes) sloppy animation which plagued even the best episodes.

Still, a protective cult has built up around *Robotech*, part of it predicated by the assumption that its American distributor, Harmony Gold, "threw away" the project by stashing it in early morning and late afternoon hours rather than showcasing the series in the prime time slots it deserved. In fact, Harmony Gold did the best promotional job possible, given the tightness of the syndicated market of 1985. Remember that the new Fox network was still two years in the future, and many cities had no need for a fourth TV station on which to run the more esoteric syndie offerings. Even big cities were generally limited to one independent UHF outlet, since the big boom in new stations had died down earlier in the 1980s and some of those stations had already gone dark or been converted to music video or home shopping conduits. The lack of nighttime access for *Robotech* was due to the simple fact that the preteen market for cartoon series just wasn't watching at 8 P.M. — and if they were, it was a sitcom or an adventure program that would win out. (The *Simpsons* hadn't happened yet either.) Considering the glut of off-net reruns, old theatrical cartoons, and *He-Man* and *G.I. Joe*-type series on the market, it's miraculous that *Robotech* got on at all.

The cultists further argue that American TV was frightened of anything as innovative as *Robotech*, and that's why only a chosen few ever got to witness the series. *Of course* TV station managers shied away from the unorthodox in the morning and afternoon slots. That's because the unorthodox *never made money* in those slots— or hardly ever, anyway. When the great cartoon boom of the late 1980s came to be, it was accomplished with familiar, established properties from the Disney studios, *not* from a complex space serial involving galloping hormones or a powerful entity like Robotech which (to many viewers) was never clearly defined as being good or evil. *Robotech* had plenty of value, to be sure, but so did the cold-cash arguments against running the series in a choice timeslot.

Unique and challenging though it was, *Robotech* never soared as a syndicated daily. Its success in the United States has rested solely in the form of videocassette rentals and sales, allowing the series' hardcore fans to luxuriate in each twist and turn of plot with a steady finger on the pause button, and in ancillary sales of *Robotech* comic books and script novelizations.

Additionally, some of those aforementioned *Robotech* fans have recently gotten into the driver's seats of the major animation studios. The most conspicuous *Robotech* devotee in the past few seasons has been Jeff Segal, mentor of the weekly 1993 Universal Cartoon Studios syndie *Exo-Squad* (see individual entry for more details).

ROBOTIX *see* **SUPER SUNDAY**

ROCKET ROBIN HOOD. Syndicated: 1967. Trillium/Steve Krantz. Executive producers, Steve Krantz and Shamus Culhane. Voices: Carl Banas, Ed McNamara, Chris Wiggins, Bernard Cowan, Len Birman, Paul Kligman, Gillie Fenwick, John Scott.

Robin Hood, the 12th century nobleman turned bandit whose exploits have been told in song, legend and popular entertainment ever since "The Visions of Piers Plowman" in 1377, first made it to TV cartoons with none of his familiar surroundings extant. The milieu of Britain in the 1100s was exchanged for Outer Space in 3000 A.D. Sherwood Forest was now Sherwood Asteroid, a "solar powered" orb. And while Friar Tuck, Little John, Maid Marian, Allan A. Dale, Jiles and company were in attendance, the Sheriff of Nottingham now travelled under the name of Sheriff of N.O.T.T. Sir Robin of Locksley, propelled to this Brave New World by a

time machine, adapted to his surroundings by becoming "technology friendly" and calling himself Rocket Robin Hood.

It wasn't as contrived and corny as it sounds, not under the expert guidance of animation producer/director Shamus Culhane, who for *Rocket Robin Hood* was reunited with Steve Krantz, his executive producer during the *Marvel Super Heroes* (q.v.) days. And despite all the space-travel trappings, Rocket Robin Hood still dressed in the Lincoln green costume of old, while the theme music by Win Sharples evoked the tempo and rhythm of an ancient ballad.

The 156 five-minute episodes of *Rocket Robin Hood* were distributed by Canada's Trillium Ltd.—not in 1969 as has often been claimed—but as early as 1967. (See also *Funtastic World of Hanna-Barbera* for more on animating Robin Hood.)

ROCKO'S MODERN LIFE. Nickelodeon: 9/18/1993–. Games Animation. Creation, production, direction and character design by Joe Murray. Directed by Stephen Hillenberg, Doug Lawrence, Tim Berland, Jeff Marsh. Executive producers for NICK, Vanessa Coffey and Mary Harrington. Supervising producer for NICK, Linda Simensky. Associate producer, Melinda Wunsch. Story editor, Mitchell Kriegman. Writers: Joe Murray, Jeff "Swampy" Marsh, Nick Jennings, George Maestri, Stephen Hillenberg, Doug Lawrence, Vince Calandra (head writer), Ron Hauge, Martin Olsen. Line producer: Brad Gunther. Supervising art director, Roger Chiasson. Main title music, Sarah Frost-Goetz. Music editor, William B. Griggs. Music score by Pat Irvin. Main title animation by Joe Murray, Timothy Berglund, Shawn Murday. Background art by Nick Jennings. Overseas supervising director, Greg Hill. Animation facilities: Sunwoo Animation. Voices: Carlos Alazraqui (Rocko); Tom Kenny (Heffer); Charlie Adler (The Bigheads); and Doug Lawrence, Charlotte Booker.

Rocko's Modern Life was the first Nickelodeon-created production of Games Animation, the company formed by the cable service to take over production of John Kricfalusi's *Ren and Stimpy* (q.v.). The two Games series were in fact rather similar in terms of concept, character design and comic content. Rocko was a friendly, Hawaiian shirt–clad Australian wallaby trying to make a go at a new life in a typical American small town. Rocko's housemate/pets were Heffer, a gluttonous cow, and Spunky, a hyper dog. The character design was round and squat, with elongated noses and cantaloupe eyes. Much of the humor was of the gross-out variety involving intestinal closeups, flatulence and regurgitation, while the slapstick leaned toward the apocalyptic (one episode offered a neighborhood-eating vacuum cleaner). Given these ingredients, a casual viewer might switch on *Rocko's Modern Life* and think that he'd stumbled onto *Ren and Stimpy: The Lost Episodes.*

Not so, insisted *Rocko* creator Joe Murray, who stated emphatically that his series was in development before *Ren and Stimpy* had seen the light of the TV tube. The first reaction to this might be "Sure. It was just a cute coincidence that there were two cartoon creators who found the same body functions funny and developed the same visual style independently." But it turns out Murray spoke the truth. Long before either *Rocko* or *R and S*, a seminal "Rocko" (with the same bad taste in shirts) had starred in a comic strip called *Zak & Travis.* Joe Murray loosely adapted this strip's character design for his own proposed theatrical cartoon, *My Dog Zero,* about a man and his lobotomized pet. This was the concept which Nickelodeon bought in 1991, and it went through several revisions on the drawing board before its TV debut, hence its appearance on the scene after *Ren and Stimpy* rather than before. It is of course safe to assume that *Rocko's Modern Life* might not have appeared at all without *Ren and Stimpy* leading the way, but the fact is that the two series were thought up separately rather than one imitating the other.

If one *does* regard *Rocko* as an *R and S* derivation, one must be advised that despite the similarities, the two series charted different philosophical paths. *Ren and Stimpy* was determined to push the boundaries of good taste at the expense of story values; *Rocko* had strong, well-constructed scripts, in which even the supposedly nonsequitur gags fit into a deliberate plotline pattern. Where Ren and Stimpy worked day and night at their weirdness, Rocko was "alien" only because his new American environment was alien

to him. *R and S*'s John Kricfalusi believed that only animators were qualified to write animation scripts; *Rocko's* Joe Murray encouraged adlibbing at his recording sessions, and to that end hired stand-up comedians to do the voicework. Above all, *Ren and Stimpy* had a mile-wide mean streak; *Rocko's Modern Life,* no matter how cruel the gags or biting the satire, was about a nice wallaby maintaining his niceness despite the meanness of the world around him.

Joe Murray had picked a wallaby as his hero because he thought the animal was "cute," and this was part of the reason Nickelodeon was attracted to Murray's work; in his earlier independently made cartoons, he was able to function in the gonzo "Generation X" animation style in vogue in the early 1990s, without sacrificing the lovability of his characters. With this in mind, we can safely attribute some of the rawer moments in *Rocko's Modern Life* to director Doug Lawrence, best known for such intensely adult theatrical cartoons as *Looks Can Kill,* which starred a killer stripteaser with weaponry on her privates.

Whoever was responsible for *Rocko's Modern Life's* sorcerer's blend of appealing characterizations and hilariously grotesque sight gags, more power to them. The series hasn't been on long enough as of this writing to qualify as a classic, but the handful of available episodes prove that it's possible to speak to both the radicals and the conservatives in cartoon fandom without bringing down the wrath of either (they also prove that this sort of cartoonwork *can* be brought in on budget and schedule, which was not the case with the pre–Games Animation *Ren and Stimpy,* brilliant though it was). In keeping with Joe Murray's basic straight-line approach, many of the best *Rockos* were built around one-joke premises: going to the store, getting fired, etc. Others poked fun at the very sort of people who'd watch *Rocko* (perhaps an example of Joe Murray introspection), notably a running gag involving Rocko's employment at a comic-book store, populated by the sort of "wrap 'em in plastic and never read 'em" freaks one finds in such an establishment. Yet even these "throwaway" jokes were there for a plot-development reason, never mere gags for gags' sake.

My own favorite *Rocko's Modern Life —*

so far—is the 11-minute "Dirty Dog" (each half hour episode was divided into two short cartoons). Taking the basic premise of Rocko giving Spunky a much-needed bath, the episode managed to tell *two* stories within that single framework, simply by sporadically zooming in on closeups of the various parasites whose presence on Spunky's body precipitated the cleaning. As Spunky ran frightened around the bathroom, the camera cut to a group of bugs enacting a "bringing the boss home for dinner" routine staged like a 1950s sitcom, complete with laughtrack. Never losing focus, "Dirty Dog" kept us fascinated in Spunky's plight, all the while using the dog's insects to toss off pop-culture references involving such classic TV comedies as *The Honeymooners*, *The Patty Duke Show*, *The Mary Tyler Moore Show* and *Gilligan's Island*. And *just* when the simultaneous plotlines were both winding down, the camera zeroed in on the *tinier* parasites living on the bodies of Spunky's ringworms and tapeworms—who were stuck in the middle of an *I Love Lucy* episode!

If this last verbal overload has proven anything, it is that *Rocko's Modern Life* played better than it reads. Audiences in 1993 seemed to agree: Within a week of its September debut, *Rocko's Modern Life* had garnered a viewership of 2.3 million, cracking cable TV's "Top Ten" programs, only three notches below *Ren and Stimpy*.

ROCKY AND HIS FRIENDS. ABC: 9/29/1959–9/3/1961.
—**THE BULLWINKLE SHOW**. NBC: 9/24/1961–9/5/1964; ABC: 9/20/1964–9/2/1973; NBC: 9/12/1981–7/24/1982. Jay Ward Productions/Producers Associates of Television. Produced by Jay Ward and Bill Scott. Directed by Bill Hurtz, Pete Burness, Ted Parmalee, Lew Keller, Gerald Baldwin, Sal Fallaice and George Singer. Written by Chris Hayward, Lloyd Turner, Chris Jenkyns, George Atkins, Al Burns. Music by Fred Steiner, Frank Comstock, Dennis Farnon and George Steiner. Edited by Skip Craig. Producer for P.A.T., Peter Piech. Animation produced by Gamma Productions; animation producer, Bud Gourmley. Twinkles segments produced by Leonardo Television. Voices: Bill Scott (Bullwinkle/Mr. Peabody/Dudley Do-Right); June Foray (Rocky/Natasha Fatale/Nell Fenwick); Paul Frees (Boris

Badenov/Captain Peter Peachfuzz/Inspector Fenwick); William Conrad (Narrator); Edward Everett Horton (Narrator, "Fractured Fairy Tales"); Walter Tetley (Sherman); Hans Conried (Snidely Whiplash); Daws Butler (Aesop Jr.); Charlie Ruggles (Aesop).

In his espionage thriller *A Clear and Present Danger*, best selling novelist Tom Clancy described a fantastic new weapon: a silent explosive that could devastate whole communities without making a sound. So persuasive was Clancy's description of the device that he seemed to be privy to some actual government secret. When asked about this plot device, the author's explanation was surprising, but only to the wine-and-cheese literati who insisted that they only watched PBS. Tom Clancy revealed that he drew the inspiration for his silent bomb from "Hush-A-Boom"—a gimmick used on a 1962 episode of the cartoon series *The Bullwinkle Show*.

There can be no better proof of the influence on the TV generation exercised by Jay Ward Productions' *Bullwinkle Show*—and its lookalike predecessor, *Rocky and His Friends*. The foremost technothriller writer of the 1990s had watched *Rocky* in his youth, had never forgotten it, and had deliberately plucked from his memory one of the series' many devices that had stimulated his intellect in his formative years.

Tom Clancy spoke for many of us when tipping his hat to those Jay Ward Productions of yore. *Rocky and His Friends* is the first cartoon series that many of us can remember our parents laughing at. Beyond its traditional kidvid attractions of talking animals, punny dialogue and cliffhanging adventures, the series seemed to be working on a higher level. Many youngsters asked Mom and Dad what was so funny, and once the intellectual jokes and cultural references were explained, we suddenly seemed to be part of an "in" group that functioned on a different plane than the rest of the ultraconformist, ultranormal 1950s and early 1960s. We never deserted *Rocky*, and when we grew to adulthood and our collected life experiences allowed us to understand fully *all* the overflowing irreverent wit of the program, we revelled in the jokes and satire that had even flown over the heads of our elders 20 to 30 years earlier.

A SALUTE TO
ROCKY &
BULLWINKLE

With a cheery "Bleh-heh-heh," Boris Badenov (*right*) prepares some "hokey smoke" for Rocky and Bullwinkle, as Natasha checks her nail polish.

Rocky and His Friends burst onto the scene in 1959 after a decade's incubation. Fellow Californians Jay Ward and Alex Anderson had decided to go into the cartoon business in 1948, forming Television Arts Productions for that purpose. Out of several proposed concepts, Television Arts was only able to sell *Crusader Rabbit* (q.v.), a program so brilliant in itself that the qualification "only" is insulting. One of Television Arts' vetoed notions was a spoof of early local-TV broadcasting: *The Frostbite Falls Review* featured a cast of anthropomorphic animals who ran a spit-and-vinegar television station on the Minnesota-Canada border. Among the supporting characters were Rocket J. Squirrel, a flying rodent, and Bullwinkle — named after Clarence Bulwinkle, a California used-car dealer — described in the proposal as a "French Canadian Moose." The *Frostbite Falls Review* was registered for motion-picture copyright in 1950, then was all but forgotten in the rush to get *Crusader Rabbit* on the air. After several years of legal squabbles with *Crusader*'s distributor Jerry Fairbanks, during which the series made (in Ward's words) "oodles of money" for everyone but its creators, Ward and Anderson decided to get out of animation. Jay Ward sold real estate for several years, but never totally gave up his cartoon-industry connections (nor did he give up real estate, which he was still peddling even at the peak of *Bullwinkle*'s success in 1962!). In 1957, a new package of *Crusader Rabbit* cartoons, now owned by producer Shul Bonsall, made a great deal of headway in syndication, inspiring Jay Ward to give TV animation a second chance. This decison was partly prompted by a freak accident in which a car crashed into Ward's real estate office and broke both his legs — an event that might have been rejected as being too fanciful for a cartoon scenario.

Ward revived *Frostbite Falls Review* in concert with his new partner, onetime *Beany and Cecil* (q.v.) writer-actor Bill Scott, reshaping Rocky and Bullwinkle as the principal characters and patterning their personalities after Crusader Rabbit (short and scrappy) and Crusader's pal Rags the Tiger (tall and dopey). Ward and Scott were kindred spirits: Both enjoyed weaving labyrinthine adventure stories for their characters, and both delighted in injecting as much subtle social satire and lowbrow slapstick into their scenarios as traffic would allow.

Rocky and Bullwinkle would appear in only two four-minute cliffhanging episodes per each *Rocky and His Friends*, requiring additional components to pad out the rest of the half hour. Since several of Jay Ward Productions' writers and directors — Bill Scott, Bill Hurtz, Pete Burness, Ted Parmalee and Lew Keller — had recently broken away from UPA Studios, it was logical that "Fractured Fairy Tales," "Peabody's Improbable History" and the poetry-recital "Bullwinkle's Corner" would draw inspiration from UPA's "Fairy Tales," "Meet the Inventor" and "The

Twirlinger Twins" (see *Gerald McBoing Boing*). Additional creative input came from magazine illustrator Ted Key, who'd created "Hazel" for *The Saturday Evening Post*. It was Key who conceived the character of Mr. Peabody, a bespectacled, Clifton Webb-like genius who happened to be a dog. Peabody and his adopted boy Sherman would each week utilize their time-travelling "Waybac" machine to smooth the course of history.

The first four weeks' worth of *Rocky and His Friends* was completed by 1958, including the vocal track, which utilized some of the best comedy-voiceover talent then in harness. June Foray, fresh from several projects with satirist Stan Freberg, was engaged to play all the female characters on *Rocky and His Friends*, as well as the male role of Rocky. Bill Scott himself was Bullwinkle and Mr. Peabody, while Paul Frees, then more closely associated with radio and movie narration than cartoon work, provided innumerable voices, including the series' villain, Eastern-bloc spy Boris Badenov. Walter Tetley, a middle aged midget whose adolescent voice had been featured on such radio series as *The Great Gildersleeve* and *The Phil Harris–Alice Faye Show*, was engaged to play Mr. Peabody's "pet boy" Sherman. And yet another radio regular, Bill Conrad, took time out from his duties as star of radio's *Gunsmoke* and as staff producer at Warner Bros. studios to supply the ratatat narration of the "Rocky and Bullwinkle" segments. The biggest star hired for that 1958 session was Edward Everett Horton, who narrated "Fractured Fairy Tales."

The previously moribund TV cartoon market had cracked open in 1959 thanks to Hanna-Barbera's *Huckleberry Hound* (q.v.). While ABC was looking for product to fill the 5:30 P.M. daily timeslot vacated by the recently cancelled *Mickey Mouse Club*, General Mills Cereals was anxious to sponsor a new cartoon program that would do for them what *Huckleberry* had done for Kellogg's. All the pieces fell into place in October of 1959, when *Rocky and His Friends* joined live action reruns of *My Friend Flicka* and *Rin-Tin-Tin* in ABC's late afternoon lineup, right after the highly rated *American Bandstand* in most cities.

At first glance, *Rocky and His Friends* seemed a second-rate imitation of *Crusader Rabbit*, earmarked by the weaker aspects of UPA's "softer" cartoon projects.

The one-liners mostly fell flat and the characters didn't yet look and act like themselves. Everyone spoke in measured, muted tones instead of the series' later exaggerated rapidity; Bullwinkle's stupidity sounded tacked on rather than ingrained in his personality; and Boris Badenov was deadly serious, overweight, had bags under his eyes, and was nearly as tall as his aide Natasha Fatale. The first "Fractured Fairy Tales" was a disappointingly straightforward retelling of "Jack and the Beanstalk," with only the slightest comic content. Only the "Peabody's Improbable History" was up to snuff, with an introductory episode which set up the characters and explained that the Waybac machine had been built as a birthday present for Sherman; but even "Peabody" faltered, the victim of poor draftsmanship and sloppy sound recording.

Far worse was ABC's decision to "boost" the comic content of *Rocky and His Friends* with a canned sitcom laughtrack; the network even dubbed in applause at the end of the program! This insulting technical augmentation chortled its way throughout the next four weeks until it was mercifully dropped.

Yet if one stayed with all 40 episodes of the first adventure, "Jet Fuel Formula," one witnessed a metamorphosis. Within a picaresque plotline covering 20 weeks' time, *Rocky and His Friends* grew from a tentatively funny kid's program to the most sophisticated and hilarious cartoon series of its time. A topical satire of the U.S./U.S.S.R. space race, "Jet Fuel Formula," was the story of Bullwinkle's chocolate cake mix, which when garnished with the fruit of the rare Mooseberry bush was turned into a powerful rocket fuel. Yet like all future *Rocky* and *Bullwinkle* storylines, the plot was merely a peg upon which to hang Scott's and Ward's endearingly bizarre flights of fancy and devotion to "private" jokes.

Foremost of the producers' trademarks was their choice of character names. The two moonmen who didn't want Rocky and Bullwinkle to develop a formula that would incite an invasion of their home sphere were named Gidney and Cloyd. "Jay and I decided that the two names we would least like to have were Floyd and Sidney," recalled Bill Scott. "For the moonmen, we just changed the first letters." Captain Peter Peachfuzz, the

world's worst sailor, was named for Peter Piech, executive of Jay Ward's distributing company, Producer's Associates of Television (P.A.T.); Captain Peachfuzz' boat, the S. S. Andalusia, was named for the Andalusia Arms, an inexpensive hotel which served as Ward's headquarters. And the series' villain was named Boris Badenov, a twist on the protagonist in Mussorgsky's opera "Boris Godunov" — a joke lost on the average eight-year-old but immediately scooped up by the intellectuals who'd be the earliest and most fervent *Rocky* fans.

Boris' favorite curse word, "Raskolnikov!," was a vintage example of another series trademark, its highbrow-baiting humor; Raskolnikov was the name of the idealistic murderer-protagonist in Dostoyevski's novel *Crime and Punishment*. This and other similar nuggets made the audience feel privy to an extended inside joke, poking fun at the foibles and pretensions of the Eisenhower era. Rocky and Bullwinkle were unable to decipher a *Variety* headline reading "Moon Men Socko in Lost Wages" until running the "coded" message through a Univac machine. Boris and Natasha were trapped in the quicksilver of Iron Curtain bureaucracy, constantly having to cancel their last instructions to "Keel Moose and Squirrel" when the Moose and Squirrel became inexplicably valuable to their homeland of Pottsylvania. In Pottsylvania itself, the atmosphere was so paranoid that everyone was a spy, one needed a password to get into a tourist hotel, and the telephone book contained nothing but unlisted numbers. And in the next-to-last "Jet Fuel Formula" episode, we were introduced to a McCarthylike senator who wanted to pass a bill making it impossible for such aliens as "Canadians, Mexicans and Californians" to become U.S. citizens — and who was then yanked into space when his coat was caught in the door of a departing missile, but couldn't be removed from his shoulders because it "wouldn't be dignified."

Framing all this was the series' campy hyperbole, the one *Rocky* trademark which most clearly betrayed Ward and Scott's adoration of the pulp novels, weekly movie and radio serials, and blood-and-thunder Hollywood adventure films that they — and the older members of their audience — had grown up with. Bill Conrad narrated the program with a florid intensity that made Walter Winchell seem comatose. Each episode carried a main title and subtitle, in the manner of the old Horatio Alger novels ("Don't miss our next episode, 'Cheerful Little Pierful' or 'Bomb Voyage'"). The bad guys were deliciously broad stereotypes of traditional cinema heavies, especially Boris' boss Fearless Leader, who bore the monocle, dueling scar and Teutonic dialect of a movie Nazi. And the heroes were so doggedly true blue and patriotic that they very nearly got killed at every turn. When the narrator wondered at one point if a nasty turn of events had deterred Rocky and Bullwinkle, the pair turned to the camera, smiled inanely and replied, "Of *course* not. We're the *heroes!*" (This would later be refined to the point that Bullwinkle would refuse to come to the rescue of Rocky unless it was, as he described it, "just in the—ta da!—nick of time!")

And here we have the most affectionately remembered of Rocky and Bullwinkle trademarks: the traditional "Fourth Wall" meant nothing to these cartoon characters. Rocky, Bullwinkle, Boris et al. would converse regularly with the narrator, sometimes arguing with him, shushing him or threatening him with violence lest he impede the action or give away the plot. They would give "narrator man" dirty looks when his flowery prose got too precious, they'd ask him to repeat a particularly pungent piece of exposition, and at least once in later years would overpower him and slap a piece of adhesive tape over his mouth. This "it's only a cartoon, folks" ambience was what set *Rocky and His Friends* several levels higher than the standard play-it-safe, "realistic" TV storytelling of its era. And since the eyes of the narrator were traditionally meant to be the eyes of the audience, not only were we in on the jokes, but we were also participants in the storyline.

In the second serialized *Rocky and His Friends* adventure, the 12-episode "Box Top Bandits," Jay Ward and Bill Scott began displaying the "bite the hand that feeds you" insouiance that would ever after distinguish their TV work. This story of a nation's economy brought to its knees by a flood of counterfeit cereal box tops was a calculated dig at *Rocky* sponsor General Mills, which built most of its public relations image on box-top premiums and prizes. But what did Ward and

Scott have to lose? *Rocky and His Friends* wasn't exactly sweeping the ratings—ABC only had primary affiliates in half the country, and some of those outlets weren't even carrying *Rocky*—and it looked as though the first season would be the last. Certainly ABC itself had no stake in the program, generating little publicity on *Rocky*. But suddenly the viewership began growing; word of mouth spread the news that a "hip" new show was on the air, one with a comic content that left most of what passed for comedy in 1959 standing at the gate. *Rocky and His Friends* was renewed—and now both ABC and General Mills were more vigilant over story content.

Not that this intimidated Ward and Scott. With their second season opener, the 36-episode "Upsadasium," the producers focused their gunsights on military stupidity, Cold War competitiveness, the automobile industry and the government's tendency to promote rather than dismiss its more inept functionaries. This adventure was followed by "Metal Munching Mice," which dared to suggest that television had spawned a generation of zombies who'd be rendered helpless should their TV antennas be snatched away from them; the storyline also offered broad swipes at Disney's Mickey Mouse and Elvis' Colonel Parker.

Jay Ward Productions had put together enough programs by the middle of the 1960-61 season to allow for three full years of *Rocky and His Friends*. To do this, Ward was obliged to use the services of Mexico's Gamma cartoon studio, owned in part by Producer's Associates of Television. The communications breakdown between the Mexican studio and the Hollywood staff was obvious in some of the messiest TV animation ever (remember Boris Badenov's amazing disappearing moustache?). Meanwhile, the ABC network, which was never completely happy with Ward's unorthodox cartoon series which revelled in playing way over the target audience's heads, seemingly did its best to sabotage *Rocky* and hasten its cancellation. The program was run twice a week during its second season, dispensing with two years' worth of material in one year's time. And as if to express publicly its contempt for Ward and company, ABC ran the episodes out of sequence. "Metal Munching Mice" included a subplot involving Pottsylvania's head honcho Mister Big, which plainly didn't make any sense without its buildup in the earlier adventure "Upsadasium," which ABC ran *after* "Mice."

It's likely that ABC would have thrown in the towel if General Mills hadn't discovered the value of the Rocky and Bullwinkle characters as a merchandising tie-in—and back in 1960, the sponsor had the last word on renewal or cancellation. The downside of this was that Jay Ward Productions was obliged to mollify General Mills by including in each *Rocky and His Friends* half hour a 90-second commercial "adventure" starring Twinkles the elephant (see notes on *King Leonardo*), a cereal-box character whose exploits dragged the weekly proceedings down to the cutesy-poo level that Ward had been so successful in avoiding.

Except for "Twinkles," the changes made in the second-season *Rockys* were beneficial. "Fractured Fairy Tales" was replaced by "Aesop and Son," a looney package of updated fables narrated by an uncredited Charley Ruggles as Aesop and an equally unbilled Daws Butler as "Son." (Butler was busy with Hanna-Barbera's Kellogg-sponsored projects, and would have been in a conflict of interest bind had he been listed in the cast of a General Mills program; I honestly don't know why Ruggles wasn't billed.) And "Bullwinkle's Corner" was supplanted with "Mister Know-it-All," wherein Bullwinkle would come to weekly grief passing himself off as an expert problem-solver.

As the series matured, the writing got sharper and more pungent. Informed that he was the heir to the British mansion "Abominable Manor," Bullwinkle replied "That's nothing. I've been living in an abominable manner all my life." In another episode, Bullwinkle was discovered pedaling his bicycle up George Washington Hill, a promontory named not for the father of our country but for the onetime president of the American Tobacco Company.

The pointed hilarity extended to the other component cartoons on *Rocky and His Friends*. The "Aesop and Son" story "The Mice in Council" had one mouse suggest that his rodent pals escape a cat by moving to Disneyland, only to be admonished that "Cousin Mickey's got that place all sewn up!" (Disney was a pet Ward target. The "Fractured Fairy Tale" version

of "Sleeping Beauty" starred a handsome prince who looked just like Uncle Walt and who converted Beauty's castle into "Sleeping Beautyland.") And in "Peabody's Improbable History," conquistador Francisco Pizarro, accused by the Incan Indians of being an invading soldier, hastily retorted "No! I'm only an advisor from the U.N."

Despite ABC's indifference and so-so ratings, *Rocky and His Friends* became a national favorite, so much so that in 1961 NBC offered to pick up the program and showcase it in prime time, in emulation of ABC's success with *The Flintstones*. Furthermore, the series would be telecast in color, a bid to topple the dominance of CBS's black and white *Lassie* in the 7:00 P.M. Sunday night slot. In contrast to ABC, NBC planned to use its biggest promotional guns to hype the newly retitled *The Bullwinkle Show*, inspiring Jay Ward to hark back to his own real-estate experience and indulge in hilariously strident promo campaigns of his own (of which, more later).

The *Bullwinkle Show* retained most of the *Rocky and His Friends* components, adding a couple of new attractions. The first was "Dudley Do-Right," a rigidly heroic Canadian mountie who'd been in the developmental stages way back in the 1950 *Frostbite Falls Review* proposal. Dudley and his 37-year-old girl friend Nell Fenwick lampooned the Nelson Eddy–Jeanette MacDonald team in the 1936 "Mountie" musical film *Rose Marie*, while Nell's father, Inspector Fenwick, was a droll takeoff on British actor Eric Blore. The heavy of the piece was Snidely Whiplash, a tophatted "me proud beauty" type who had so many fingers in so many underhanded deeds that he had to keep an appointment book: Foreclose on widows and orphans at 11 P.M., tie woman to railroad tracks at 12:30, rob the Montreal bank at 2. Snidely's richly sneering voice was supplied by Hans Conried, the first of several Jay Ward assignments for this versatile comic dialectician. Last but not least of the "Dudley Do-Right" dramatis personae was Dudley's faithful horse Horse, who wore a Mountie uniform just like his master's and who was the true object of Nell Fenwick's romantic affections.

In many ways, "Dudley Do-Right" contained an even purer strain of satire than the "Rocky and Bullwinkle" installments because it zeroed in on a single basic premise. No one in the "Dudley" stories ever really accomplished anything because of their dogged adherence to the roles they'd been assigned in life. Dudley couldn't become an undercover agent because he was incapable of telling a lie; he couldn't accept any new development because he didn't understand anything that hadn't already happened to him; he couldn't even break the law when required to do so in one of the plotlines because he could only literally live up to his name and "do right." Nor was he able to be Nell Fenwick's true hero because of his obeisance to the letter of the law. When Nell, bound to a buzzsaw by Snidely in one episode, sent a letter to Dudley begging for help, the muttonheaded Mountie wouldn't accept delivery until he ran up to the sawmill, insisted that Nell affix a stamp to the letter, and then ran back to the Mountie camp to open the envelope. Even after rescuing Nell, Constable Do-Right was forced to clap her in prison for using a grocery store coupon instead of a stamp.

Similarly, Snidely Whiplash acted like a villain because he didn't know any better. In one bizarrely Freudian episode, Snidely went around binding women to railroad tracks in hopes of being captured, because his knot-tying had become an obsession—"This terrible *thing* with me." Whiplash's scheme to save himself was foiled by Nell Fenwick who, when ordered by her father to go away and read a book, picked up a law book, became Canada's top defense attorney, and won a "not guilty" vote from Snidely's jury.

This was one of the few instances in which Nell, the only character in the "Dudley Do-Right" episodes who seemed willing to try to better her lot in life, came out on top. More typical was the episode wherein, to prove her worth to her father, Nell arrested Snidely and marched him into the RCMP camp, whereupon Inspector Fenwick, his machismo threatened by his daughter's pluckiness, steadfastly insisted that he couldn't see Snidely and that Nell was hallucinating! You wouldn't find this sort of psychological complexity on *The Flintstones*. Nor would you get as many laughs. (Not everyone was laughing, of course. The Canadian goverment didn't find Dudley Do-Right an adequate representative of the RCMP. Canadian au-

diences, a little more responsive to the puncturing of uniformed authority figures, didn't seem to mind a bit.)

Also new to *The Bullwinkle Show* was a replacement for "Mister Know-it-All," "The Rocky and Bullwinkle Fan Club." Like "Dudley," it was a revival of the 1950 *Frostbite Falls Review* premise, with all the characters dropping their on-camera hostilities and behaving like actors on lunch break. Each "fan club" meeting consisted of trying to improve membership—which never got any larger than Rocky, Bullwinkle, Boris, Natasha and Captain Peachfuzz—or undertaking a group event like a potato sack race. (Peachfuzz forgot to remove the potatoes, while Bullwinkle got his sack stuck on his antlers.) Additionally, the first 13 weeks of *The Bullwinkle Show* featured a live-action Bullwinkle puppet operated and voiced by Bill Scott, who'd intro and outro each episode. Hard to believe such a harmless piece of cloth could stir up controversy, but that's just what happened.

On the first *Bullwinkle*, the puppet poked fun at the pretensions of NBC's *Walt Disney's Wonderful World of Color*, which subliminally suggested that anyone who didn't own a color set was, to quote *TV Guide*, "Socially retarded." The puppet suggested that the viewer create his or her "own color": "It's really very easy. First think of your income tax. Next Mr. Khrushchev's latest speech. Then think about what Mr. Disney said about your black-and-white set . . . Makes you see red, doesn't it?"

There was the jibe at Red Skelton, lawsuit-inciter supreme, who claimed that Bullwinkle was a ripoff of Skelton's own Clem Kadiddlehopper character: The puppet skewered that by showing the difference between Bullwinkle's and Clem's voices—by twice reciting a sentence *exactly* the same way.

But the limit came when the puppet suggested that kids help improve *The Bullwinkle Show*'s ratings by removing the TV control knobs: "In that way, we'll be sure to be with you next week." This was followed by a jocular solicitation that kids donate their parents' money for a 50-foot-tall Moose statue to be erected in front of Jay Ward Studios. Sure enough, NBC was besieged with angry missives about missing TV knobs and vanished money. The network demanded that Ward recant his statements. Thus, the Bullwinkle doll told the kids *not* to send in money, but to contribute their pennies to a skyscraper to be built in downtown Los Angeles — "50 feet tall, in the shape of a moose." And he advised the small fry to return the knobs to daddy's TV. It was simpler, he advised, to simply glue the controls into place.

And after that, it was simpler for NBC to drop the Bullwinkle puppet altogether; it was not to be seen again until a guest appearance on Jay Ward's 1963 syndicated comedy series *Fractured Flickers*, where oblivious host Hans Conried introduced the Moose as "Maureen O'Hara."

Ward didn't really need the puppet to keep *Bullwinkle* in the public eye. For the three years that the series remained on NBC, the producer conducted one gonzo publicity stunt after another, each one wackier than the last. There was Ward's "How to Kill Yourself" campaign, where contestants were promised big money if they'd suicidally assault Fidel Castro or Mao Tse-tung while shouting out plugs for *Bullwinkle* (try to imagine *that* one getting by in these copycat-crime days!). There were those two *Bullwinkle* premieres, where actors dressed in Salvation Army costumes picketed NBC studios with "Repent" and "Reform" signs, and box lunches were served, ostensibly serving roast peacock (NBC's color-TV trademark). There were special "gift lists" sent to disc jockeys, newspaper columnists, politicians and TV executives, offering a Jay Ward Pyramid Club (buy one Ward TV series, send chain letter to ad agency at the top of your list, and when your name reached the top, you'd get 2458 series for the price of one), and the "Sing Along with Bullwinkle" book, a nonpartisan satirical tome skewering Jackie Kennedy and Barry Goldwater alike. Some people receiving Ward's mailings didn't get the joke, writing back stiff, proper letters declining the producer's "gifts."

Others found it hilarious to be offered such bonuses as a "nonviolent" TV series package including *Peter Watergunn*, *Championship Hopscotch* and *Hamlet* with a happy ending; one thoroughly satisfied "customer" of the Ward line was FCC chairman Newton Minow, the principal advocate of TV nonviolence, who nevertheless delighted at being satirized by the *Bullwinkle* folks.

But NBC wasn't thrilled at jokes at their expense, notably Ward's publicly staged "singalongs" which featured ballads about the network's recent ratings decline. Every possible opportunity was taken by NBC to lash back at *Bullwinkle*, usually in the form of oppressive censorship. In one episode which found Rocky and Bullwinkle stewing in an African cooking pot, NBC forced Ward and Scott to tone down the cannibalism jokes ("Cannibalism? To eat a moose and squirrel?" was Ward's reaction), and to redraw the natives so as not to offend any minority group. The producers complied, redesigning the cannibals to look exactly like Jay Ward and Bill Scott. Ward took revenge by commenting on NBC's censorial excesses within his *Bullwinkle* scripts: In an episode wherein Rocky was about to be burned at the stake by an Indian, the plucky squirrel pulled out a "standards and practices" chart to check if stake-burning had been cleared and approved.

Bullwinkle did respectable business opposite *Lassie* (though still running second), and the sponsor was happy, so NBC couldn't drop the series altogether despite its clashes with Ward and Scott. So the network merely moved the program to a less advantageous Sunday-afternoon timeslot for its second season. The producers continued "business as usual," stirring up as much trouble as possible. One of the more notorious second-season stunts was built around "Moosylvania," a fictional mosquito-ridden island located between Canada and the U.S., which neither country wanted to claim. The *Bullwinkle Show* constructed two serialized escapades around Moosylvania (including the series' final episodes), but didn't stop there. Ward, sensing another headline-grabbing ploy, mounted an expensive publicity campaign to install Moosylvania as the 51st state, going so far as to transport a motorcade to the gates of the White House in October of 1962.

The producer was convinced that President Kennedy would find this *faux* campaign hilarious, but was nonplussed when the agitated White House guards told him to get out and stay out. It was only afterward that Ward discovered he'd chosen to invade the White House on the same day that the Cuban Missile Crisis broke loose!

The *Bullwinkle* series itself was showing signs of tiring out in its 1962-63 season, with long stretches of self-indulgent dialogue and misfire comedy setups. But before its NBC cancellation, the series was good for one last snatch of sheer brilliance, an adventure entitled "Wotsamatta U." Despite NBC's reliance on revenue from televised college football games, "Wotsamatta U" was a devastatingly funny attack on athletic scholarships and subsidies for "slow students" who happened to be gridiron champs. As a bonus, Ward persisted in censor-baiting. When Rocky asked college freshman Bullwinkle what he planned to do on his first date with a girl, there was a pregnant pause, then Bullwinkle looked at the camera and muttered "Boy, this really *is* a children's show, isn't it?"

And thus with a parting blast of irreverence, *The Bullwinkle Show* joined its ancestor *Rocky and His Friends* in Rerun Heaven. *Rocky* had been in local syndication since 1961 (first in a 15-minute version), while *Bullwinkle* remained on ABC's Saturday morning schedule from 1964 until 1973, with a return network engagement on NBC in 1982. In addition, the *Dudley Do-Right* episodes were deflected into their own network rerun package in 1969, bundled together with stray *Rocky* and *Bullwinkle* components and a few stragglers from Leonardo Productions' *King Leonardo* (q.v.). If the strength of cult worship is in the inaccessibility of the object of the cult, then perhaps *Rocky* and *Bullwinkle* don't qualify in this category. The two series have literally never stopped playing: Most recently, the Nickelodeon cable service picked up both series for its nightly 7:30 P.M. (EST) slot, where Ward's creations handily outperformed *Jeopardy*, *Wheel of Fortune*, *Entertainment Tonight* and *Current Affair* in several markets.

Rocky and *Bullwinkle* remain the crowning achievements of Jay Ward Productions.

The studio's subsequent cartoon series never quite attained the same plateau: 1964's *Hoppity Hooper* (q.v.) lacked the old satiric bite, while 1967's *George of the Jungle* (q.v.), which some aficionados consider to be Ward's funniest series, was denied the luxury of the serialized storylines which contributed so much to the charm of *Rocky* and *Bullwinkle*. By 1968, Jay Ward was out of the series business entirely, confining his activities

to cereal commercials. Burned by ceaseless network interference in the 1960s, the once-outgoing producer became a recluse, never granting interviews and emerging in public only to oversee his own licensed-merchandise stores which sold Rocky and Bullwinkle memorabilia (the "huckster" to the last!). On the subject of returning to the network rat race, Ward's only comment was related in absentia in 1977 by Ward Productions layout man Lou Kesler: "CBS doesn't like us. ABC hates us. NBC despises us."

Such animosity evidently exists only in the hallowed halls of the Big Three networks. It's hard nowadays to find anyone who doesn't adore *Rocky and His Friends* and *The Bullwinkle Show*, and equally hard to find a baby-boomer who can't recite reams of the series' dialogue verbatim. As further indication that we can't get enough *R* and *B*, witness the impressive sales records of Disney Video's *Rocky and Bullwinkle* cassettes, a sellout property since 1991. (Why don't viewers merely record the programs off the air and save $14? It's simple.)

The Disney people improved and enhanced the pictorial quality of the old *Rocky* negatives for video release, going so far as to redraw and re-animate several deteriorated sequences. If that isn't love, what is?

When we last left Our Heroes, they were back in the cartoon business in a series of eyecatching Taco Bell commercials directed by Bob Kurtz (with voice actress June Foray recreating Rocky and Natasha as though the 30 years were but an instant of Yesterday). They were also back in the headlines. After Jay Ward's death in 1989, his onetime *Crusader Rabbit* partner Alex Anderson reemerged from the shadows to claim that he'd been given a verbal agreement by Ward, securing Anderson a profit percentage of all Ward projects including *Rocky* and *Bullwinkle*.

This cash flow had been cut off abruptly upon Ward's demise, and Anderson took the case to court, where a confidential financial settlement was reached. Will this stop Rocky and Bullwinkle from entertaining generations yet to come? And what fiendish plan does Boris have in mind? Be sure to see our next thrill-packed episode, "Magistrate Moose" . . . or . . . "Oh, Say Can You Sue?"

ROD ROCKET. Syndicated: 1963. Jiro Entertainment/Victor Corporation. Produced by Lou Scheimer, Mark Lipsky. The all but forgotten *Rod Rocket* was a 130-episode syndicated package of serialized space adventures. In addition to the titular Rod Rocket, the series' regulars included Professor Argus, Rod's assistant Joey, and Joey's sister Casey. *Rod Rocket's* sole claim to fame is that it was the first independent production by the splinter group of animators who'd broken away from Larry Harmon Productions (see *Bozo the Clown*) and would eventually solidify into Filmation Studios.

ROGER RAMJET. Syndicated: 1965. Snyder-Koren Productions/Pantomime Pictures/CBS Films. Executive producer, Kenneth C. T. Snyder. Supervising director, Paul Shively. Coordinating producer, Fred Calvert. Associate producer, Dick Crippen. Produced and directed by Fred Crippen. Written by Gene Moss and Jim Thurman. Animation by Bill Hutten, Alan Zaslove, Fred Crippen, Don Schloat, George Nicholas. Backgrounds by Jack Hatter. Sound effects by Phil Kaye. Music by Ivan Dittmars. Voices: Gary Owens (Roger Ramjet); Dick Beals (Yank/Dan); Gene Moss (Doodle/Noodles Romanoff); Joan Gerber (Dee/Lotta Love); Bob Arbogast (Gen. G. I. Brassbottom/Ma Ramjet); Paul Shively (Lance Crossfire/Red Dog); Dave Ketchum (Announcer); and Ken Snyder, and Jim Thurman.

Only recently rediscovered on videotape, *Roger Ramjet* was a devastatingly funny superhero satire in the *Rocky and His Friends* (q.v.) vein. Roger Ramjet, a scientist-aviator invariably introduced as "Daredevil, Flying Fool and All-Around Good Guy" was the leader of the American Eagle Squadron, an all-kid escadrille headquartered in the town of Lompoc. Ramjet's squadron included Yank, Doodle, Dan and Dee. The last-named character was the only girl in the team, except when Roger's hyperthyroid Ma Ramjet or frustrated girlfriend Lotta Love paid a visit. A frequently deployed gimmick on the program, though not as frequently as has been claimed, was Roger Ramjet's cache of "proton pills," which gave him the strength of 20 atom bombs for 20 seconds. Reportedly, it was Roger's reliance on narcotic stimulants that kept *Roger Ramjet* off the market in the 1970s

and 1980s, though it may also have been a lack of interest from TV station executives who preferred the more lucrative returns from *Flintstones* and *Gilligan's Island* reruns.

That any TV market should have been denied *Roger Ramjet* either at the time of its 1965 release or in later years is criminal. The series was an unrelenting laugh factory, throwing puns, nonsequiturs and adult-oriented humor at the audience with such rapidity that at times it outstripped the gag quotient of the Jay Ward product (see *Rocky and His Friends, Hoppity Hooper* and *George of the Jungle*). The writers delighted in peppering the plotlines with Yiddishisms, showbiz "inside" chatter and old-movie references: Roger's chief rival was a Burt Lancaster clone named Lance Crossfire, while virtually every villain's henchman not only sounded like Lon Chaney Jr. in *Of Mice and Men* but came equipped with his own rabbit to pet. The scripts were also topheavy with throwaway asides like an army general's "I wish I'd become a musician like Mom wanted. Go try to save the world!" or a thwarted space invader's "This is very discouraging!"; and with deep-cutting lampoons of patriotic zealotry (practically every time Roger Ramjet was mentioned, an eagle, a flag, or a rotating circle of stars would crash on the screen, simultaneously celebrating and ridiculing Roger's blinkered Americanism).

Like the radio serials of the *Captain Midnight* vein which this series emulated, hyperbole was the order of the day on *Roger Ramjet*. The five-minute cartoons anticipated the 1966 live-action *Batman* by filling the screen with written sound effects like "Crash!" "Whack!" "Ouch!" "Think!" and "Goodbye Charlie!," and by including an exotic gallery of hoodlums, the most prevalent being gangster Noodles Romanoff. The mood was sustained brilliantly by the golden-toned voicework of Gary Owens as Roger Ramjet, and the throbbing musical score by organist Ivan Dittmars, the latter an unsung genius who'd built his reputation in radio as a "one man orchestra."

Unfortunately, for the most part *Roger Ramjet* was unceremoniously thrown in as a mere cog in various "Cartoon Carnival" potpourris by insensitve station managers who didn't realize they had a jewel on their hands. Perhaps if the series had performed better, producer Ken Snyder wouldn't have forsaken the satirical insanity of *Roger Ramjet* in favor of the by-the-numbers banality of *Hot Wheels* (q.v.) and *Sky Hawks* (q.v.).

ROMAN HOLIDAYS. NBC: 9/9/1972–9/1/1973. Hanna-Barbera. Executive producers, William Hanna and Joseph Barbera. Produced by Iwao Takamoto. Directed by Charles Nichols. Voices: Dave Willock (Gus Holiday); Shirley Mitchell (Laurie Holiday); Pamelyn Ferdin (Precocia Holiday); Stanley Livingston (Happius Holiday); Dom DeLuise (Mr. Evictus); Hal Smith (Mr. Tycoonus); Hal Peary (Herman); Janet Waldo (Henrietta); Judy Strangis (Groovius); Daws Butler (Brutus).

Roman Holidays proved the wisdom exercised by Hanna-Barbera when it decided to set *The Flintstones* (q.v.) in an indeterminate prehistoric era rather than a specific historical time and place. Like *Flintstones*, the 13 half-hour *Holidays* juxtaposed 1970s attitudes, foibles and creature comforts with the trappings of an earlier period, in this instance the Golden Age of the Roman Empire. It didn't work. Young viewers weaned on movies like *Ben-Hur* and *Spartacus* knew too much of actual Roman civilization to swallow the anachronisms of *Roman Holidays* without exclaiming, "But it didn't happen that way"—something these same kids would never have dreamed of doing when confronted by the pure fantasy of human beings coexisting with dinosaurs on *The Flintstones*.

For the record, the Roman Holidays of the title were Gus Holiday, an engineer with the Forum Construction Company (in real Roman life, he'd have been a slave); Laurie Holiday, his wife; and children Precocia and Happius. They lived in the Venus de Milo Arms. Their landlord was Mr. Evictus. They had a pet lion named Brutus. The Holiday kids' friends included a flower child named Groovius. You want more? In one episode the Holidays had the Emperor as a dinner guest, and everything went wrong. No, they weren't thrown to the lions, not even Brutus, but the viewers turned thumbs-down on *Roman Holidays* after a single season.

RUBIK THE AMAZING CUBE. ABC: 9/10/1983–9/1/1984; 5/4/1985–8/31/1985. Ruby-Spears.

After a season as the second half of *The Pac-Man/Rubik the Amazing Cube Hour*, the *Rubik* portion was telecast as a separate series, consisting entirely of reruns from its *Pac-Man* days. For further details—including production and voice credits—see *Pac-Man.*

RUDE DOG AND THE DWEEBS. CBS: 9/16/1989–9/1/1990. Sun Sportswear/Marvel Productions. Developed for TV and produced by Hank Saroyan. Executive in charge of production, Jim Graziano. Executive producers, Margaret Loesch Stimpson and Joe Taritero. Supervising producer, Bob Richardson. Story editor, Hank Saroyan. Music composed and conducted by Robert Irving and Hank Saroyan. Animation facilities: Akom Production Co. Voices: Rob Paulsen (Rude Dog); Dave Coulier (Barney); Jim Cummings (Satch); Ellen Gerstell (Kibble/Gloria); Hank Saroyan (Tweek); Mendi Segal (Reggie); Frank Welker (Caboose/Rot/Seymour).

Rude Dog and the Dweebs, created to promote a line of sportswear escutcheoned with a doggie trademark, was at least superficially more impressive than most 1989 network cartoon offerings. In illustrating the adventures of a cool Beverly Hills pooch who drove a vintage pink Cadillac and commandeered a gang of eccentric bowwows, Marvel Productions settled upon a cubist, neon-like production design, with "hot" pastel colors and radically stylized forced perpective background art.

Rude Dog, leader of the Dweebs, complemented his street-smart veneer by talking in a Brooklynese manner reminiscent of Archie the Manager on the old radio series *Duffy's Tavern*, a characterization previously used by Super Snooper on Hanna-Barbera's *Quick Draw McGraw* (q.v.). The Dweebs, who hung out in a spacious garage, included Britisher Winston, tiny Tweek, ladykiller Reggie (a Jack Nicholson soundalike), musically inclined Caboose, southerner Barney and dumb-dumb Satch. This mangy crew of male canines was frequently joined by Gloria, Rude Dog's girlfriend, and by hoydenish female Kibble.

Once the storylines on *Rude Dog and the Dweebs* got under way (two short scenarios per each week's half hour), the series' slick production design and hip ambience succumbed to several disheart-eningly traditional Saturday-morning car-toon situations. Most of these familiar convolutions were motivated by the vil-lains: Seymour the cat, Herman the dog-catcher and Herman's assistant Rot.

RUFF AND REDDY. NBC: 9/14/1957–9/24/1960; 9/29/1962–9/26/1964. Hanna-Barbera/Screen Gems. Produced and directed by William Hanna and Jo-seph Barbera. Voices: Don Messick (Ruff/Narrator/Others); Daws Butler (Reddy/Others).

Less than five months after getting their walking papers from MGM, William Hanna and Joseph Barbera had set up their own studio, in hopes of cracking the TV market. They wound up getting in as an afterthought. The NBC network had bought a package of color theatrical car-toons from Columbia Pictures, in hopes of realizing a merchandising bonanza com-mensurate with CBS' ownership of the old Terrytoons package. Unfortunately, the Columbias lacked a strong *Mighty Mouse* or *Heckle and Jeckle* starring character; the studio's main stars, the Fox and Crow, were amusing but uncharismatic, and hadn't made enough six-minute cartoons around which to build a weekly series. Other Columbias were one-shots of vary-ing quality, or failed attempts at continu-ing series, notably the disappointing *Li'l Abner* cartoons. What was needed was a newer, stronger cartoon property to "bookend" the older shorts.

At the same time as the NBC-Columbia deal, Hanna-Barbera had developed a serialized storyline starring a resourceful cat named Ruff and an amiable but slow-witted dog named Reddy. The project had been turned down by several distributors; only Screen Gems, Columbia's TV sub-sidiary, evinced any interest. John Mitch-ell, head of sales for Screen Gems, proposed to NBC that Hanna-Barbera's *Ruff and Reddy* be used as a wraparound for the old Columbia cartoons. Though NBC concurred, it was hesitant to entrust an entire Saturday morning half hour to cartoons alone; the network coupled the Hanna-Barbera and Columbia packages with an existing New York City children's show produced by Roger (*Howdy Doody*) Muir, which came equipped with human host Jimmy Blainé and puppet characters Rhubarb the parrot and Jose the Toucan.

Allotted a mere $2800 budget per five-minute cartoon (a far cry from its old MGM budgets of $45,000 to $65,000!). Hanna-Barbera established a policy of low-cost limited animation that would be honored by the studio for the next two decades. Movement was held to the barest minimum, with certain animated vignettes catalogued for re-use in future episodes; both Ruff and Reddy wore neck adorn-ments (the cat a bowtie, the dog a collar), to enable the animators to move the heads of the characters without having to animate the rest of the body. With little in the way of visual dynamics, Hanna-Bar-bera was forced to rely on dialogue and vocal characterization, resulting in long term engagements for two of the best voicemen in the business, Daws Butler and Don Messick.

More so than in later H-B projects, *Ruff and Reddy* was geared almost exclusively toward younger viewers. This meant that subtle and satirical humor was pretty much avoided, replaced by simplistic jokes and nurserylike rhyming dialogue—"That's tough, Ruff"; "Steady, Reddy," and so on—and chapter titles like "Smitten by a Kitten" and "Asleep While a Creep Steals Sheep." There was a strictly juvenile ap-proach to the character names as well: Professor Gizmo, Killer and Diller, the Goon of Glocca Mora, Scary Harry Safari, ad infinitum. Still, *Ruff and Reddy* man-aged to stay in step with current events with the very first adventure, a space travel jaunt to the metal-coated planet MuniMula ("Aluminum" spelled back-wards). Less than a month after *Ruff and Reddy's* debut, the launching of the Rus-sian Sputnik gave any TV program with an outer space theme a booster shot of au-dience appeal.

That audience wasn't around for the first few weeks of *Ruff and Reddy*, even though NBC had organized an elaborate ad cam-paign trumpeting Hanna-Barbera's recent alliance with MGM's *Tom and Jerry*, and despite the fact that the network had scheduled the new cartoon program in the half hour just following its highly rated *Howdy Doody*. Most youngsters didn't catch up with *Ruff and Reddy* until its competition, CBS' live action *Susan's Show*, was moved to a different timeslot one October morning, forcing the kids to seek gratification somewhere else on the dial. After that it was smooth sailing for

Ruff and Reddy, which was successful enough to put Hanna-Barbera in a stronger bargaining position when promoting its next project, *Huckleberry Hound* (q.v.).

Ruff and Reddy was cancelled in 1960 (on the same September day that we lost *Howdy Doody*), replaced by *King Leonardo and His Short Subjects* (q.v.). The property returned to NBC in 1962 with no worn-out Columbia theatrical cartoons cluttering up its path, but still with a live host, Captain Bob Cottle, and a new coterie of puppets. The series entered syndication in 1964, but didn't fare as well as it had on the network. Hanna-Barbera had progressed so far in terms of technique and comedy knowhow since 1957 that the groundbreaking *Ruff and Reddy* looked crude, awkward and uninvolving when compared to *Yogi Bear* (q.v.), *The Flintstones* (q.v.) and especially *Jonny Quest* (q.v.).

RUGRATS. Nickelodeon: 8/11/1991–. Klasky-Csupo Inc. Created by Arlene Klasky and Gabor Csupo. Supervising producers, Sherry Gunther and Mary Harrington. Creative producer/writers: Paul Germain, Charles Swenson. Produced by David Blum, Bee Beckman and Geraldine Clark. Directed by Norton Virgien, Howard Baker, Jim Duffy, Steve Socki, Jeff McGrath. Story editors: Craig Bartlett, Joe Ansolabehere, Steve Viksten, Peter Gaffney, Jonathan Greenberg, Rachel Lipman. Creative consultant, Chuck Swenson. Music by Mark Mothersbaugh, Dennis M. Hannigan. Executive producer for Nickelodeon, Vanessa Coffey. Voices: E. G. Daily (Tommy Pickles); Jack Riley (Stu Pickles); Melanie Chartoff (Didi Pickles); Kath Soucie (Phil/Lil/Betty); Cheryl Chase (Angelica); Michael Bell (Charles Sr./ Drew Pickles); Christine Cavanaugh (Chuckie); David Doyle (Grandpa); Cree Summer (Susie); Ron Glass (Randy); Lisa Dinkins (Lily).

Rugrats was one of a triumvirate of first-run Nickelodeon cartoons (see also *Doug* and *Ren and Stimpy*) all premiering over the Nickelodeon cable service on August 11, 1991. The series was created by Arlene Klasky and Gabor Csupo (pronounced CHEW-po), and developed by Paul Germain, whose inspiration grew from a profound disillusionment. Germain's favorite cartoon series of his youth was Hanna-

Barbera's *Jonny Quest* (q.v.), but upon reviewing the series some 20 years later, he was disappointed that it hadn't (to him) stood the test of time. What Germain wanted was an animated program that would appeal to children, then later down the line appeal to those same children after they'd grown up. And what better "leveller" than a series *about* children, told from a child's point of view and filtered through a child's unfettered imagination? It was a concept that kids could relate to and adults could regard with fond nostalgia.

Nothing is without precedent, and *Rugrats* had plenty of forerunners: UPA's *Christopher Crumpet* and Chuck Jones' similar series of "Ralph Phillips" cartoons on screen; animation writer Jack Mendelsohn's *Jackie's Diary* comic strip; and Sheldon Mayer's brilliant DC comic book *Sugar and Spike* (1955–1971), which many observers have cited as *Rugrat's* principal role model. More recently, *Muppet Babies* (q.v.) and *Bobby's World* (q.v.) had taken a successful kid's-eye squint at the world. But while both of these series had the built-in advantage of established characters ("Bobby" was the popular nightclub creation of comedian Howie Mandel), Paul Germain and the Klasky-Csupo cartoon firm constructed *Rugrats* from the ground up with brand new characters, based on the children of Germain and of animators Gabor Csupo and his "significant other" Arlene Klasky.

Rugrats' stars were one-year-old Tommy Pickles, his single-toothed pal Chuckie, his domineering older cousin (about 18 months older) Angelica, and infant twins Phil and Lil. Except for Angelica, none of the kids could talk — to adults, that is. Amongst themselves, however, Tommy, Chuckie and the twins commiserated at great length about life in general, mostly based on their own floor-level "eyewitness" testimony. So far as the Rugrats were concerned, eating from Spike the dog's supper dish could turn you into a dog; the toilet area was as forbidding a locale as the Korean DMZ; and when Dad said he spent his day at the office "pushing paper," that's *exactly* what the kids did when imagining themselves in the adult world.

While the bend-over-backward verbal puns of Jack Mendelsohn's *Jackie's Diary* and the slick visuals of Chuck Jones' Ralph Phillips cartoons tended to lean toward

Tommy Pickles: Public Rugrat No. 1.

preciousness, *Rugrats*, at least in its first season, refused to play "cute" with its kids. The viewers genuinely felt as though they were assimilating information by way of a brightly innocent one-year-old's mentality, rather than witnessing some clever adult writer's patronizing slant on babyhood. Klasky-Csupo's visual schematics helped to de-sentimentalize the proceedings, with squashed, lightly grotesque character design (especially Phil and Lil, who had heads like deflated volleyballs), though the Rugrats' essential lovability was never sacrificed. As a bonus, the adult voice actors on *Rugrats*—E.G. Daily, Christine Cavanaugh, Cheryl Chase, and the ubiquitous Kath Soucie—really sounded like preschoolers piecing together vocabulary for the first time, articulating the writers' "advanced" dialogue with the measured ingenuousness of uncomplicated children without lapsing into "goo-goo" caricatures. The gently naturalistic dialogue was complemented by the muted, synthesized background music, composed by Mark Mothersbaugh of the rock group Devo (who also contributed in a more characteristic manner to the soundtrack of MTV's rule-breaking *Liquid Television* [q.v.]).

Reflecting the general tone of 1990s animation, there were plenty of popular-culture jibes on *Rugrats*, though in its earliest episodes the more "knowing" humor was manifested in the adult characters. Tommy's dad was Stu Pickles, an underachieving toymaker who secretly yearned to have a commission with the profitable "Dummi Bears" (see *Care Bears* for examples of similar merchandising lampoons), while mom Didi was a lightly satirized social climber. Stu's brother Drew and sister-in-law Betty, Angelica's

parents, were grating, trend-chasing yuppies, advocates of "progressive" child care that benefited no one, especially their holy terror of a daughter. And Stu and Drew's dad, Grandpa Pickles, was every doting, spoiling grandparent on earth rolled into one. Other adults ran the gamut from Stu's harmless best friend Charles (Chuckie's dad) to smarmy TV directors, pompous ice-capade performers, combatative Jewish great-grandparents, martinet day care teachers, bullying toy company executives, and a pair of elderly recluses straight out of *Whatever Happened to Baby Jane?* and *Sunset Boulevard*.

While on surface quite straightforward and uncluttered, each *Rugrats* script went through a toilsome gestation period before filming. Six drafts per script were prepared, then refined for nearly three months before the animators began filming, with rough spots ironed out and the purity of concept retained. The final draft was then touched up by the producers, with little jokes added here and there for "punch," usually by inserting the aforementioned pop-culture gracenotes.

The producers were careful to avoid selfconscious cultural references when dealing with the kids themselves during the first season, reserving such humor for the grownup characters. By season two, however, the post-scripting punch-ups were becoming a bit mechanical and the Rugrats were behaving more like pocket edition adults, enacting such lampoonish scenarios as their takeoff on the 1952 western *High Noon* involving a playground bully who used sticky candy as a weapon. And though they still could only communicate with each other, the second-season *Rugrats* had suddenly developed the capacity to utilize household appliances and workbench tools, essential to the new plotlines but at odds with the original "infant" premise.

When the third season rolled around, there were even more alterations. Some, like the introduction of several African American characters—little girl Susie, her dad Randy (a writer for animated cartoons, specifically the "Dummi Bears") and mom Lily—helped broaden the series' appeal. But other new twists, like having Angelica plot to get attention by feigning a broken leg, or dumping hot sauce on the dinner so that her Dad's boss (the inevitable dinner guest) won't transfer her family, were better suited to standard-issue sitcoms like *I Love Lucy* than to a program about children trying to make sense of a world they never made.

Though the series suffered from ever-increasing cliché injections, *Rugrats* remained stylistically sublime. Visually, the series was a cartoon buff's dream, with ever-moving, multiple perpective backgrounds and intricate point of view travelling shots (almost always from floor level, just like the kids). Adding to the enjoyment was the carefully monitored color scheme, the scribbly, R. O. Blechman-like inklines around the characters, and the overall seemingly effortless flow of movement.

Rugrats' animation was completed in Korea, a potentially tricky proposition in that overseas production has often diluted or circumvented altogether the visual concepts of American producers. This was avoided in the case of *Rugrats* by sending out a computerized "animatic" board to the Korean studios, locking in Klasky-Csupo's movement guidelines for the benefit and edification of the overseas artists. The computer also "visualised" the ink and paint work, making certain that the cartoons wouldn't come back from Korea with inappropriate color or background design.

The extra effort was worth it: *Rugrats* won Nickelodeon its first Emmy award, and won Klasky-Csupo a lucrative contract with comedienne Lily Tomlin, who'd always resisted offers to animate her adolescent "Edith Ann" character until sampling some of K-C's superb *Rugrats* child's-eye animation. The series remained consistently in cable TV's top ten, becoming Nickelodeon's highest-rated cartoon series by early 1994. And though *Rugrats*, as mentioned, fell prey to arch cleverness as it moved along, the series still managed to toss off a gem or two in its fourth season. A recent treasured moment: Stu and Drew Pickles, flashing back to their own childhood, recalled that their favorite cartoon series had been *Blocky and Oxwinkle*. Not content with this exaggerated but affectionate bouquet to Jay Ward's *Rocky and His Friends* (q.v.), Klasky-Csupo even hired June Foray, the original "Rocky," to provide the voice of "Blocky" and of Natasha-like Russian spy "Svetlana"!

Our only reservation here was that the joke, uproarious though it was, ran far afield of the original *Rugrats* concept of concentrating on a playpen perspective of civilization. It's difficult to determine at this point whether Paul Germain's desire to create a series that would appeal to kids and later to those selfsame grownup kids will be realized. Catch us in about 20 years.

RUPERT. Disney Channel: July 1989–. (*See* LUNCH BOX.) Alfred Bestall Productions.

—RUPERT. Family Channel: September 6, 1993–. Ellipse/Nelvana/TVS/YTV. Executive producers: Michael Hirsh, Patrick Loubert, Philippe Gildar, Pierre Bertrand-Jaume, Clive A. Smith. Supervising producers: Stephen Hodgins, Philippe Grimond. Produced by Patricia R. Burns. Directed by Dale Schott. Story editor, Peter Sauder. Animation directors: Gary Hurt, Matios Marcos. Based on the characters in the *Daily Express*. Music score by Milan Kymlicka. Music produced by Cantus Productions Limited. Animation facilities: Hanho Heung Co. Ltd., Le Studio Ellipse. A Canada-France coproduction in association with TVS Television/YTV Canada, with participation of TeleFilm Canada, the Ontario Film Investment Program and le Centre National de la Cinematographie. Voices: Ben Sandford (Rupert); Torquil Campbell (Bill Badger); Oscar Hsu (Pong Ping); Hadley Kay (Pudgy Pig); Guy Bannerman (Mr. Bear); Lally Cadeau (Mrs. Bear); Keith White (Algy Pig); Colin Fox (The Professor); Stephanie Morgenstern (Tiger Lady); Wayne Robson (Sage of Um); and Colin O'Meara, Rick James, Tracy Moore, Richard Beasley, Graeme Campbell, Damon D'Olivera, Keith Knight, Julie Lemiere, Ross Manson, Sheila McCarthy, Allan Stewart-Coates, Tommy Van Kridge, Lisa Yamanaka, Philip Williams, Peter Waldman, William Colgate, Paul Haddad, Janie Brennan, Graham Haley, James O'Hegan, Jan Rubes, Valerie Bogle, John Winston Carroll, Don Dickinson, Steve Lederman, Kelly McGregor, Michael Stack, George Marmer, Stuart Stone, Chris Wiggins, Dennis Akigama, Ha Chew, Robert Bockstael, Elizabeth Dufresne, and Frank Proctor.

Mary Tourtel, the wife of the night editor of London *Daily Express*, was told in 1920 that the paper needed a children's comic strip. "The Little Lost Bear," written and illustrated by Tourtel, first appeared on November 8, 1920. When the serialized storyline ended, Tourtel moved on to other ideas, but the public had taken to the bear, whose name was Rupert. By popular demand, new Rupert continuities followed, with an attendant widely flung fan club called the Rupert League. The basic artistic style of *Rupert* allowed Mary Tourtel to spend several months on any one plotline, and to have a clear illustration field minus dialogue balloons. Each daily adventure comprised no more than two panels, numbered and titled like book chapters, while the narrative and dialogue were printed in text or verse beneath the picture (a British "comic cuts" tradition later utilized in such American strips as *Tarzan* and *Prince Valiant*). Most of the stories commented on past British traditions and current fads, but the artwork and dialogue were so stylized that even the "modern" stories of the 1930s and 1940s and the "contemporary" nature of the villains (smugglers, spies, etc.) don't date for comic fans of the 1990s. Mary Tourtel stayed with *Rupert* until her eyesight failed in 1935, at which time the strip was taken over by "Punch" cartoonist Alfred Bestall, who remained at his post for three decades until succeeded by Alex Cubie and Frederick Chaplain. Like *Nancy* in the U.S., *Rupert's* disarming innocence and simplicity sustained its popularity, with some offbeat ancillary results: The strip became a fad with the hippies of the 1960s, and even wound up in a *subrosa* pornographic version.

Rupert's TV career, concentrated on the British Broadcasting Corporation, began with a series of stop-motion puppet films in the 1970s, leading to a series of animated cartoon vignettes in 1988, both under the imprimatur of Alfred Bestall Productions. These harked back to the orginal strip's setting of the town of Nutwood, and the familiar supporting cast comprised of Rupert's upper-middle-class Mummy and Daddy and his best friends Bill Badger, Algy Pug and Edward Trunk the Elephant. They also retained little Rupert's trademarked garb of checked trousers, flowing scarf and turtleneck sweater. Missing was the strip's serial format; the 1980s cartoons were mere limited-animation skits, each one self contained. This made them ideal fare for

the Disney Channel's portmanteau daily series *Lunch Box*, which ran the *Rupert* cartoons in the U.S. beginning in 1989.

But *Rupert* had too lofty an international reputation to remain an "extra added attraction" for long. Canada's Nelvana Ltd. and Ellipse Productions, having done all right by themselves with half-hour cartoon versions of the popular European children's-adventure properties *Babar* (q.v.) and *Tintin* (q.v.), went the same route with a weekly *Rupert* in 1992, which premiered over YTV, a Canadian youth-oriented cable service. The series debuted below the Canadian border in 1993, telecast daily on U.S. cable's Family Channel in tandem with reruns of Nelvana's *Babar*.

The half hour format allowed Rupert more scope for his adventures than the two-panel-per-day strip, taking the bold little bear all over the world—Europe, Africa, Asia, the American West—usually in the company of his parents, his aforementioned pals, his older chum The Professor, or with one or other of his farflung relatives. The cartoon *Rupert* shared with its comic-strip source a sense of whimsical timelessness; though set in an indeterminate 1930s-like period, there is nothing than can pinpoint the year of production or the time-frames of the plots.

On the other hand, *Rupert's* artistic style and story material departed somewhat from the homely simplicity of Mary Tourtel and her successors. The series' lush background art, thin-lined character design and bottomless reserve of perilous situations made *Rupert* less an extension of its strip version and more an animal variation of Nelvana's *Tintin*. Indeed, both comic-based series shared many of the same animation staffers and voiceover talents. But since the original *Tintin* comic book was rather obviously influenced in part by the original *Rupert* comic strip, the fact that both TV series resembled one another can be considered a mutual *homage*.

SABAN'S ADVENTURES OF THE LITTLE MERMAID FANTASY *see* **THE LITTLE MERMAID**

SABAN'S AROUND THE WORLD IN EIGHTY DREAMS. Syndicated: 1992. Saban/Antenna 2/MBC/Brulsconi/ Telecino. Production executive producers: Winston Richard, Jacqueline

Tordj:nan, Vincent Chalvon-Demeruy. Produced by Eric S. Rollman. Directed by Bruno Bianchi. Story editor: Tony Oliver. Written by Jean Cheville and Alain Garcia. Animation director: Dae-Jung Kim. Music by Shuki Levy. Voices: Mark Camacho (Carlos); Rick Jones (Oscar/Grandma Tadpole); Pauline Little (Koki); Sonja Ball (A.J.); Patricia Rodriguez (Marianna).

The most delightful first-season component of Bohbot's weekend *Amazin' Adventures* (q.v.) package could trace its lineage to James Thurber's *The Secret Life of Walter Mitty*. Despite its title, *Saban's Around the World in Eighty Dreams* owed nothing to Jules Verne, but instead outlined the adventures of Carlos, a rolypoly bearded beachcomber who lived on a Caribbean island with his preteen friends A.J., Koki and Marianne, as well as several animal compadres, including a devil's-advocate parrot named Oscar.

Each week for 26 weeks, Carlos was compelled to prove the veracity of one of his tall tales by the magical Granny Tadpole (best described as a beneficent frog), who would whisk our hero and his youthful charges back to the point in time wherein Carlos' exploits were supposed to have occurred. The disarming comic whimsy of the series was best encapsulated by Granny Tadpole's credo: "Keep an open mind and believe that anything's possible—that's half the fun of being a kid."

SABAN'S GULLIVER'S TRAVELS.
Syndicated: 1992. Saban/Antenna 2/MBC/Silvio Brulsconi Communications/Telecino. Production executive producers: Winston Richard, Jacqueline Tordjman, Vincent Chalvon-Demeruy. Produced by Eric S. Rollman. Directed by Bruno Bianchi. Story editor: Tony Oliver. Written by Jean Cheville and Alain Garcia. Animation director: Dae-Jung Kim. Music by Shuki Levy. Voices: Terence Scammel (Gulliver); Danny Brochu (Rafael); Jessalyn Gilsig (Folia); Sonja Ball (Fosla); A. J. Henderson (Flim).

Saban's Gulliver's Travels, its title designed to identify the production company and to differentiate the project from earlier cartoon renditions of Jonathan Swift's 17th century masterpiece (see *The Adventures of Gulliver*), did its best within its simplistic children's television limits to emulate its satiric source material. Like previous animated *Gulliver* cartoons, the seafaring hero (here given a new ally, a cabin boy named Rafael) didn't get much farther than Lilliput; and as with many previous Saban productions, the animation work was somewhat threadbare.

The Saban *Gulliver* was one of the first-season components of the two-hour Bohbot weekender *Amazin' Adventures*.

SABER RIDER AND THE STAR SHERIFFS.
Syndicated: 1987. Calico/World Events. For Calico: Executive producer, Peter Keefe. Produced and directed by Franklin Cofod. Executive story editor, Marc Handler. Music by Dale Schacker. For Studio Pierrot Co., Ltd.: Produced by Yousi Nunokala, Yoshitaki Suzuki. Animation directors, Akira Shigino, Yorifusa Yamaguchi, Shigonori Kageyama. Voices: Townsend Coleman, Peter Cullen, Pat Fraley, Pat Musick, Rob Paulsen, Jack Angel, Michael Bell, Brian Cummings, Diane Pershing, Hal Smith, Alison Argo, Art Burghardt, Tress MacNeille, Neil Ross, B. J. Ward, Len Weinrib.

When *Saber Riders and the Star Sheriff* first ran in Europe and Asia in 1984, it was titled *Bismarck the Star Musketeers*. The English translation played up the "cowboy" trappings of the series' 51 half-hour episodes, which were released in the U.S. for daily syndication during the brief outer-space western cartoon spate of 1986–1987 (see also *Adventures of the Galaxy Rangers* and *Bravestarr*).

The plotline of *Saber Riders* was set in the extraterrestrial New Frontier, an untamed land where the law was in the hands of the Star Sheriffs, headquartered at space station "Cavalry Command." April, daughter of the head of the Star Sheriff unit, was in charge of a disparate group of dogooders: Saber Rider, a young man of mystery with an English accent; Colt, a bounty hunter and master of disguise; and Fireball, a hothead race driver (a nod to *Speed Racer*, perhaps). The villains were the renegade Outriders, led by such hombres as Vanquo, Nemesis and Razzle. Forming a united front against the Outriders, the Star Sheriff team piloted the "Ramrod," a sheriff-shaped space vehicle. (You read that right. The vehicle was in the shape of a sheriff. Keep going.)

The good guys were outfitted with electronic badge units, which were supposed to provide an interactive connection with the home viewers—that is, those kids who'd bought the necessary tie-in electronic Star Sheriff merchandise. The unluckier youngsters were left to scratch their heads and wonder why the program had so many gratuitous closeups of those badges. Outside of this distinctly American aspect, *Saber Riders and the Star Sheriff* betrayed its overseas origins by being more trigger-happy and fascistic than the general run of weekday cartoons.

Though it didn't survive past its first Monday through Friday season, *Saber Rider and the Star Sheriffs* was a valuable freshman lesson in cartoon syndication for Calico Entertainment, who'd later forsake distribution of readymade cartoons in order to develop its own projects: *Denver the Last Dinosaur, Widget, the World Watcher, Mr. Bogus, Bucky O'Hare and the Toad Wars* and *Twinkle the Dream Being* (see individual entries on these programs).

SABRINA AND THE GROOVIE GHOULIES. CBS: 9/12/1970–9/4/1971. —SABRINA THE TEENAGE WITCH. CBS: 9/1/1971–9/1/1973. —SABRINA, SUPERWITCH. NBC: 11/26/1977–1/28/1978. Filmation. Produced by Norm Prescott and Lou Scheimer. Creative director, Don Christensen. Directed by Don Townsley, Bill Reed, Lou Zukor and Rudy Larriva. Voices: Jane Webb (Sabrina/Aunt Hilda/Aunt Zelda); and Howard Morris, Larry Storch, and Larry D. Mann. (For additional information, see separate listings for ARCHIE and GROOVIE GOOLIES.)

Sabrina, the pretty teenaged witch introduced to Saturday morning audiences on *The Archie Show* (q.v.), has frequently and inaccurately been downpeddled as Filmation's rip-off of the live action sitcom *Bewitched*. Actually, Sabrina made her comic book debut in 1962, two years before *Bewitched*'s Samantha, so if she was inspired by anything it was by such earlier beautiful witches as Gillyan Holroyd in the John Van Druten play *Bell, Book and Candle* and the Veronica Lake character in the 1942 film *I Married a Witch*.

A Teen Witch 3rd Class in the *Archie* comics and a 15-year-old "apprentice witch" on TV, Sabrina generally utilized her prestidigitory skills to finish her homework and housework ahead of schedule. Her supporting cast included

her equally magical Aunts Hilda and Zelda, her warlock Uncle Ambrose, Salem the cat, and head witch Miss Della.

Of more lasting value was another group of *Sabrina* supporting characters, who shared billing in the title of her first, hourlong series: *The Groovie Goolies*, an unearthly rock band, which eventually was spun off into their own series (see separate entry), just as *Sabrina* had spun off from the Archies. This left *Sabrina the Teenage Witch* to star in her own half-hour series by her lonesome. The *Groovie Goolies* went into off-net syndication in 1978, the same year that NBC, desperate for ratings, reran 13 *Sabrina* episodes under the title *Sabrina, Superwitch*. Oddly, this last series, which collapsed under the weight of the failing attractiveness of the whole *Archie* concept, bore a most prophetic title. In 1984, Archie Comics took their Sabrina series and transformed the otherwise unprepossessing teenaged sorceress into a superheroine like Wonder Woman.

SAMSON AND GOLIATH. NBC: 9/9/1967–3/1968. —YOUNG SAMSON. NBC: 4/1968–8/31/1968. Hanna-Barbera. 26 episodes. Produced and directed by William Hanna and Joseph Barbera. Associate producer, Art Scott. Story by Tony Benedict, Walter Black, Dalton Sandifer, Ed Brandt. Music by Ted Nichols. Voices: Tim Mathieson (Young Samson); and Don Messick, John Stephenson, and Daws Butler.

Samson, a modern-day teenaged boy, and his dog Goliath were nonmercenary troubleshooters travelling from one dangerous assignment to another on a streamlined motorbike. Samson and Goliath were able to turn themselves into a superhero and lion respectively when Samson clasped his wrist bracelets together in *Wonder Woman* fashion, and then cried "I need Samson power!" This not only improved his posture and beefed up his biceps, but caused his voice to reverberate as though recorded in an echo chamber. As for Goliath, his dog-to-lion metamorphosis included the gift of flight, the power to use his eyes like lasers, and a grey left front paw (a cute artistic touch, even though it signified nothing). The only time Samson lost his bravado was when he wasn't able to connect his wrists and summon up his superstrength, a quandary similar to the number of times that Billy

Batson would be bound and gagged, and thus unable to cry "Shazzam" and transform into Captain Marvel (see *Kid Super Power Hour with Shazzam!*).

It's hard to find anyone who wholeheartedly adored *Samson and Goliath*. The standard adult complaint was that the series advocated the superiority of brawn over brain. Hanna-Barbera fans expecting top-drawer excitement in the *Jonny Quest* (q.v.) mode were let down by *Samson's* lack of strong story values. The monsters, even the well-designed ones (an "Aurora Borealis" creature was a neat takeoff on the animated "Id" in the 1956 science fiction flick *Forbidden Planet*), simply appeared out of nowhere and started busting things up, minus motivation or explanation of their existence. Samson confronted the monster a minute or so into the action, then spent the rest of the running time pummelling the miscreant when not being pummelled himself. His "character" was as dimensionless as the animation.

Kids liked *Samson and Goliath* at first, but soon tired of this derivative super-guy crowded into an overstocked Saturday morning TV barrel. In April of 1968, the weekly, half-hour series' title was altered to *Young Samson* so as to avoid confusion with the religious cartoon project *Davey and Goliath* (q.v.) — though few if any viewers ever got these two radically different programs mixed up. In syndication, the series was *Samson and Goliath* again, its 26 12-minute episodes (originally shown two per program) arbitrarily mixed in by the syndicator with reruns of Jay Ward's *Bullwinkle* (see *Rocky and His Friends*) and Leonardo Productions' *Tennessee Tuxedo* (q.v.).

SATURDAY SUPERCADE. CBS: 9/17/1983–8/24/1985. Ruby-Spears. Produced by Larry Huber. Directed by Charles Nichols and John Kimball. Theme music by Haim Saban and Shuki Levy. Musical director, Dean Elliot. Components: **1. DONKEY KONG.** Voices: Soupy Sales (Donkey Kong); Peter Cullen (Mario); Judy Strangis (Pauline). **2. DONKEY KONG JR.** Voices: Frank Welker (Donkey Kong Jr.); Bart Braverman (Bones). **3. FROGGER** (1984). Voices: Bob Sarlatte (Frogger); B. J. Ward (Fanny Frog); Marvin Kaplan (Shellshock "Shelly" Turtle); Ted Field Sr. (Tex); Alan Dinehart (Mac). **4. PITFALL HARRY**

(1984). Voices: Bob Ridgely (Pitfall Harry); Noelle North (Rhonda); Ken Mars (Quick Claws). **5. Q*BERT.** Voices: Billy Bowles (Q*Bert); Robbie Lee (Q*Tee/Q*Val); Julie McWhirter Dees (Q*Bertha/Q*Mom/Viper); Frank Welker (Q*Mungus/Q*ball/Q*Dad/Coilee Snake/Ugg/Wrongway/Sam Slick). **6. SPACE ACE** (1985). Voices: Jim Piper (Space Ace); Nancy Cartwright (Kimberly); Sparky Marcus (Dexter); Peter Renaday (Space Marshall Vaughn); Arthur Burghardt (Cmdr. Borf). **7. KANGAROO** (1985). Voices: Mea Martineau (Katy); David Mendenhall (Joey); Arthur Burghardt (Mr. Friendly); Marvin Kaplan (Sidney); Frank Welker, Pat Fraley (Monkey Biz Gang).

The videogame industry may have been suffering a dip in revenue in 1983 and 1984, but you'd never know it from the evidence on TV. Not only were there two live-action game shows built around the video arcade concept, Ted Turner's *Starcade* and Edwards-Billett's *Video Game*, but the most popular of ABC's 1983 Saturday morning animation efforts was *Pac-Man* (q.v.). For two successive seasons CBS tried to ape ABC's hold over weekend viewers with its own arcade extravaganza, *Saturday Supercade* — emphasis on the "Super," since the weekly program embraced five separate components within its hourly length.

The centerpiece of *Supercade* was *Donkey Kong*, whose history as a videogame was far more compelling than anything Ruby-Spears came up with on the animation table. This scenario of a giant ape's battle of wills and wits against a diminutive carpenter was created by Nintendo in 1981. The premise of the original game was that a dimwitted giant simian, named "Donkey" after Japanese slang for "stupid" and "Kong" after a certain 50-foot gorilla of movie fame, rebelled against the cruelties of his tiny human master Mario by kidnapping Mario's girlfriend, Princess Paulina. The videogame caught on like wildfire, prompting a lawsuit from MCA, which claimed it owned the rights to *King Kong*. Rather than back down, Nintendo's attorney tilted the mighty MCA windmill by proving that, while MCA may have bought the "Kong" property for a 1976 remake of the original 1933 film, the company had never registered the character name "King Kong" for copyright! *Donkey Kong* was not only the foundation of the Nintendo empire, but its legal contretemps proved that the Japanese-based video company was willing to take on any and all competition to protect its birthright. (Nintendo is now just as powerful as MCA, and has found itself the victim of potential usurpers.) Would that the cartoon *Donkey Kong* have conveyed some of the euphoria of Nintendo's courtroom victory. Instead, the animated version was made up of the very ordinary duck-and-run adventures of a circus escapee, with the scenario of the original game rewritten so that Princess Paulina was now Mario's niece Pauline and wasn't so much a victim of Donkey Kong as his stalker. Donkey Kong's voice was supplied by veteran kiddie-show host Soupy Sales, who once had gone on record complaining that "to my mind, cartoons are not television because the figures can't really be humorous like live show characters." Well, actors do get into bad habits like paying bills and eating. Worth noting is that the nominal "heavy" of *Donkey Kong*, Mario the carpenter, would evolve into Mario the plumber and become the central figure of another Nintendo arcade triumph (and subsequent cartoon series), *Super Mario Bros.* (q.v.). Incidentally, Mario got his name from Mario Sagali, a landlord who in 1981 had threatened to foreclose on Nintendo's principal warehouse.

The second *Saturday Supercade* component was another Nintendo creation, *Donkey Kong Jr.*; the younger Mr. Kong spent his screen time searching for his dad, in the company of his pal Bones. Component number three, *Frogger*, was predicated on a game created by Konami, a licensee of Nintendo who later was intimately involved in the marketing of another videogame-cum-cartoon series, *Double Dragon* (q.v.) as well as the cartoon series-cum-videogame *Teenage Mutant Ninja Turtles* (q.v.). Perhaps prophetically, one of the characters on the animated *Frogger* was Shelly Turtle, who with the titular amphibian hero and mutual chum Fanny Frog fought crime while publishing the muckraking "Swamp Gazette."

Pitfall was, like its videogame precursor, built around Pitfall Harry, dauntless explorer/treasureseeker. Harry, his niece Rhoda, and cowardly lion companion Quick Claws battled their way through the underbrush in search of gold. Alternating every other week with *Pitfall* on *Saturday Supercade* was an arcade protagonist marketed by the old pinball-game firm of D. Gottlieb: Q*Bert was the most "cartoonish" character in the bunch, a *Pac Man*-like anthropomorphic sphere (with a hose for a snout) who led a frantic teenage lifestyle in the town of Q*Berg. Q*Bert's girlfriend was Q*Tee, while his enemies were Coilee Snake and Coilee's confederates Viper, Ugh, and Wrong Way.

For its second season, *Saturday Supercade* dropped *Frogger* and *Pitfall* for a couple of newer videogame properties. *Space Ace*, illustrated in a more realistic manner than its companion components, was a *Star Wars*–influenced outing about a young space traveller and his lady friend Kimberly vs. the antagonistic Commander Borf. *Kangaroo* featured Joey, Katy, and Sidney, young Marsupial residents of a zoo terrorized by the Monkey Biz Gang. While this upgraded *Saturday Supercade* easily zapped its ABC competition (*Turbo Teen* [q.v.] and *Dragon's Lair* [q.v.]), it was regularly laid low by NBC's heavy hitter, *The Smurfs* (q.v.), which had been eating away *Supercade*'s ratings since season one and was utterly devouring them by season two. By the spring of 1985, *Saturday Supercade* was shifted to early Saturday afternoon, fighting for the 11- to 13-year-old demographic group against ABC's live-action *American Bandstand*, ultimately folding when the videogame-fostered cartoon craze (temporarily) wore itself out in September.

SCHOOLHOUSE ROCK. ABC: January 1973–September 1985; October 1993–. Newell/Yohe–Scholastic Rock, Inc. Executive producer, Tom Yohe. Produced by Radford Stone and George Newall. Based on an idea by David B. McCall. Music and lyrics by Bob Dorough, George Newall and Lynn Ahrens. Singers included Bob Dorough, Grady Tate, Lynn Ahrens, Jack Sheldon, Mary Sue Berry, Joshie Armstead and Maeretha Stewart. Animation: Kim & Gifford Associates, Phil Kimmelman and Associates. Components (premiere dates listed only): **MULTIPLICATION ROCK.** ABC: 1/6/1973. **GRAMMAR ROCK.** ABC: 9/8/1973. New episodes: 10/1993. **AMERICAN ROCK.** ABC: 9/7/1974. **BICENTENNIAL ROCK.** ABC: 1976. **SCIENCE ROCK.** ABC: 1978–79. **BODY ROCK.** ABC: 1979.

SCOOTER COMPUTER AND MR. CHIPS. ABC: Early 1980s.

In 1970, David McCall of the McCaffrey and McCall advertising agency discovered a fact of life that many parents had already tumbled to: McCall's 10-year-old son had less trouble memorizing rock music than he had learning numbers. This, coupled with the *Sesame Street* invasion of PBS in 1969, led McCall to conclude that combining music and multiplication would not only serve other children well, but would satisfy the FCC's demands that Saturday morning television occasionally dispense with frivolity and make with the book-learning.

McCall took the idea to future Disney CEO Michael Eisner, then in charge of ABC children's television, and Eisner's principal advisor, legendary animation director Chuck Jones. The result, developed in conjunction with the Bank Street College of Education, was ABC's "Multiplication Rock" (a.k.a. "Multiplication Is"), vanguard of a series of animated informational "bites" of 90 to 180 seconds' duration that would ultimately be labelled *Schoolhouse Rock*.

Shown six times weekly during and between the Saturday morning offerings of ABC's 1972-73 season, the 13 "Multiplication Rocks" bore such self-explanatory titles as "Zero, My Hero," "Two Elementary, My Dear," "Naughty Number Nine" and so on up to "Little Twelvetoes." Illustrated with animated figures of multiracial kids at work and play, the vignettes were scored by a number of top musicians, including frequent *Tonight Show* drummer Grady Tate, veteran "hillbilly jazz" composer Bob Dorough, and future Tony Award nominee Lynn Ahrens. Animation facilities were provided by cartoon-ad veterans Kim and Gifford Associates and Phil Kimmelman's studio. The project's motto was lifted from the *Sesame Street* book of instructions: Children learn best through repetition. Squire Rushnell, vice president of ABC children's programming, avoided the "repetition" tag by characterizing the series as "learning through entertainment."

Little difficulty was had by ABC in lining up General Foods, Kenner Toys and Nabisco to sponsor the FCC-friendly "Multiplication Rock," which despite a price tag of $12,000 per episode actually posted a profit for the network (it's always

nice when something good for you pays off). Galvanized, the series' producers formed Scholastic Rock, Inc., first as a subsidiary of McCaffrey-McCall and later as a separate production firm, for the purpose of sprinkling several more *Schoolhouse Rock* info-pellets throughout the morning. In the fall of 1973, "Grammar Rock" appeared, whisking its eager home audience through such adventures as "Lolly Lolly Lolly Adjectives Here" and "Verb: That's What's Happening," and making whistle stops at "Conjuction Junction" where, we were told, we could "unpack our adjectives."

In anticipation of the 1976 Bicentennial, 1974's *Schoolhouse Rock* package included the patriotic "American Rock," followed two years later by—no surprise here—"Bicentennial Rock." Most of the snippets in these two cycles, bearing such titles as "No More Kings," "I'm Just a Bill" and "Sufferin' Till Suffrage," were later given the catch-all label of "History Rock."

Nineteen hundred seventy-eight was the inaugural year of "Science Rock," enlightening while entertaining through such animated playlets as "Them Not So Dry Bones" and "Interplanet Janet." One "Science Rock" installment, "The Body Machine," inspired a whole new 1979 package, the three-episode "Body Rock." Dental care, meal preparations and protein supply were among the subjects covered therein. The last first-run *Schoolhouse Rock* segment reflected the emergence of the technosmart 1980s: "Scooter Computer and Mr. Chips" was prompted by the (mistaken) assumption that children would be intimidated by computers. Just before the debut of "Scooter Computer," *Schoolhouse Rock* producer Radford Stone, evidently using cognitive skills he'd picked up from his own series, figured that he and ABC had aired "2100 episodes [showings], each watched by about 3.24 million kids. And that works out to nearly seven billion child impressions."

Not all viewers were impressed by these impressions. Psychologist Bruno Bettelheim echoed the words of those who'd earlier been critical of the jump-cut *Sesame Street*, wondering if children really absorbed anything dispensed with such flash and rapidity. Other pundits felt that cartoons "distorted" the truth of the information, suggesting that puppets (more true to life than cartoons?) would have been better teachers. And more than a few observers replied with "Too little too late!" in response to ABC's attempt at adding substance to the standard Saturday-morning fare. On the subject of *Schoolhouse Rock* and other network "drop-in" vignettes like ABC's *H.E.L.P.!* (q.v.) and NBC's *Metric Marvels* (q.v.), *TV Guide* quoted Aimee Dorr of the Annenberg School of Communications in 1980: "I applaud the fact that each cartoon includes drop-ins on news, health, sports and so on, but these count for so little in the overall scope of the offerings. They do not redeem what is basically schlock."

May be. But the National Association for Better Broadcasting liked *Schoolhouse Rock*, while Action for Children's Television gave the series its coveted Achievement award. And the *Schoolhouse Rock* production staff were obliged to clear shelf space for their Emmy Awards in 1975, 1977, 1978, and 1979. The loudest appreciative accolades, of course, came from the viewers themselves. "More kids saw *Schoolhouse Rock* than ever watched *Sesame Street*," noted co-producer George Newall to *Wild Cartoon Kingdom* magazine in 1994. "And the big irony is that it was all done by a bunch of ad guys in their spare time."

The 41-episode *Schoolhouse Rock* manifest made the rounds until 1985 on ABC, in thick clusters or in thinnish, isolated spots depending upon whether or not the network felt the need to appease the TV watchdogs. The series was phased out during the regime of FCC head Mark Fowler, who tended to look the other way when networks overstocked the airwaves with presold properties based on popular movies and toys, at the expense of educational content. For the next few years, *Schoolhouse Rock* fans had to be satisfied with a Golden Book Video release of selected episodes, bogged down with gratuitous and irritating introductory sequences featuring Cloris Leachman and a bunch of strident singing professional kids.

After the FCC took a tougher regulatory stance with the Children's Television Act of 1990, ABC trotted out its "FCC Friendly" *Schoolhouse Rock* reruns. The official story for the series' return in the fall of 1992 was that the young parents who'd grown up on such fun/instructional lyrics as "Conjunction Junction, What's Your Function?" organized a letter-writing campaign to ABC demanding the reinstatement of *Schoolhouse Rock*. The network announced plans, in tandem with the animation firm of J. J. Sedelmaier (of *Beavis and Butt-Head* fame!), for a fresh new bundle of *Schoolhouse Rock* vignettes. Premiering in October 1993, the newest ones included "Busy P" (all about prepositions) and "A Tale of Mr. Morton" (lessons in prepositions, subject and predicate), the latter designed by Tom Yohe Jr., son of the original *Rock*'s executive producer.

And also in 1993, *Schoolhouse Rock* was honored with a stage revival. You heard right. The Chicago-based Theater Bam troupe, taking a cue from the then-popular staged readings of old *Brady Bunch* scripts (see notes on *The Brady Kids*), packed the house each evening with *Schoolhouse Rock Live*, offering in-person recreations of such classics as "Verb: That's What's Happening," "I'm Just a Bill" and—by popular demand—"Zero, My Hero."

SCOOBY-DOO. (The following is a list of all network programs featuring the character of Scooby-Doo.)

–SCOOBY-DOO, WHERE ARE YOU? CBS: 9/13/1969–9/2/1972; 9/8/1978–11/4/1978; ABC: 9/1974–8/1976; 10/6/1984–10/13/1984. Hanna-Barbera. Produced by William Hanna and Joseph Barbera. Associate producers, Alex Lovy, Lewis Marshall. Directed by Charles Nichols. Creative producer, Iwao Takamoto. Character design by Alex Toth. Story editor: Ray Parker. Original background stylings by Walt Peregoy. Writers included Joe Ruby, Ken Spears, Larz Bourne, David Ketchum, Norman Maurer, Dave Lutz and Willie Gilbert. Music by Hoyt Curtin. Musical direction by Ted Nichols and Paul DeKorte. Voices: Don Messick (Scooby-Doo); Frank Welker (Freddy); Heather North (Daphne); Casey Kasem (Shaggy); Nicole Jaffe, Pat Stevens (Velma); and John Stephenson, Henry Corden, Ann Jillian, Joan Gerber, Ted Knight, Olan Soule, Vincent Van Patten, Cindy Putnam, Pat Harrington Jr., Frances Halop, Jim MacGeorge, Mike Road, Bob Holt, Allan Melvin, Janet Waldo, Mickey Dolenz, Linda Hutson, Virginia Gregg, Alan Oppenheimer, Lennie Weinrib, and Steffania Christopherson.

–THE NEW SCOOBY-DOO COMEDY MOVIES. CBS: 9/9/1972–8/31/1974. Hanna-Barbera. Same production credits.

Same voice credits as above for Scooby-Doo, Freddy, Daphne and Velma. Additional voices: Jonathan Winters, Don Knotts, Phyllis Diller, Sonny and Cher, Davy Jones, Jerry Reed, Tim Conway, Don Adams, Cass Elliot, Dick Van Dyke, Olan Soule, Jim MacGeorge, Larry Harmon, Paul Winchell, Joe Baker, Scatman Crothers, Stu Gilliam, Richard Elkins, Eddie Anderson, Johnny Williams, Julie McWhirter, Joe Besser, Mel Blanc, Janet Waldo, Jackie Joseph, Barbara Pariot, John Astin, Carolyn Jones, Jackie Coogan, Ted Cassidy, Jodie Foster, Pat Harrington Jr., and Len Weinrib.

−THE SCOOBY-DOO/DYNOMUTT HOUR. ABC: 9/11/1976–9/3/1977. Hanna-Barbera. Executive producers, William Hanna and Joseph Barbera. Associate producer, Alex Lovy. Directed by Charles Nichols. "Dynomutt" created by Joe Ruby and Ken Spears. Creative producer, Iwao Takamoto. Storyboard direction, David Hannan, Tom Knowles, Michael O'Connor, Paul Sommer, Wendell Washer, Kay Wright. Story editor, Norman Maurer. Story by Earl Doud, Jeff Maurer, Lee Orgel, Haskell Barkin, Donald Glut, Orville Hampton, Michael Maurer, Dalton Sandifer, Deirdre Starlight. Character design, Alex Toth and Steve Nakagawa. Musical direction, Hoyt Curtin. Music supervision, Paul DeKorte. Unit director, Bill Kell. Production manager, Jayne Barbera. Same basic voice credits for "Scooby-Doo" with Nicole Jaffe as Velma. Additional voice: Daws Butler (Scooby-Dum). Additional component: DYNOMUTT, DOG WONDER. Voices: Frank Welker (Dynomutt); Gary Owens (The Blue Falcon). Additional voices, both components: Joan Gerber, Julie McWhirter, Pat Harrington, Daws Butler, John Stephenson, Alan Oppenheimer, Vic Perrin, Janet Waldo, Jim MacGeorge, Mike Road, Regis Cordic, Bob Holt, Ralph James, Henry Corden, Ron Feinberg, Larry McCormick, Pat Stevens, Len Weinrib, Allan Melvin.

−SCOOBY'S ALL-STAR LAFF-A-LYMPICS. ABC: 9/10/1977–9/2/1978.

−SCOOBY'S ALL-STARS. ABC: 9/9/1978–9/8/1979. Hanna-Barbera. Executive producers, William Hanna and Joseph Barbera. Associate producers, Art Scott, Alex Lovy and Don Jurwich. Creative producer, Iwao Takamoto. Directed by Charles Nichols. Story editor, Andy Hey-ward. Story by Neal Barbera and Tom Dagenais. Story direction by Bill Ackerman, Howard Swift and Alvaro Arce. Music by Hoyt Curtin; musical supervision by Paul DeKorte. Voices: Daws Butler (Snagglepuss/Yogi Bear/Huckleberry Hound/Hokey Wolf/Snooper and Blabber/Wally Gator/Quick Draw McGraw/Augie Doggie/Jinks/Scooby-Dum/Dirty Dalton); John Stephenson (Doggie Daddie/Dread Baron/The Great Fondoo); Don Messick (Scooby-Doo/Boo Boo/Pixie/Dastardly Dalton/Mumbly/Mr. Creepley/Announcer); Bob Holt (Grape Ape/Orfol Octopus/Dinky Dalton); Frank Welker (Mildew Wolf/Yakky Doodle/Dynomutt/Tinker/Sooey Pig/Magic Rabbit); Julie Bennett (Cindy Bear); Casey Kasem (Shaggy); Scatman Crothers (Hong Kong Phooey); Julie McWhirter (Jeannie); Joe Besser (Babu); Gary Owens (Blue Falcon); Mel Blanc (Captain Caveman/Speed Buggy); Marilyn Schreffler (Brenda Chance/Daisy Mayhem); Vernee Watson (Dee Dee Sykes); Laurel Page (Taffy Dare/Mrs. Creepley); and Alan Reed. (See SCOOBY-DOO/DYNOMUTT HOUR for additional voices. Cross reference the following series for further information on supporting characters on *Scooby's All-Star Laff-a-Lympics*: *Cattanooga Cats, Captain Caveman, Dastardly and Muttley, Hong Kong Phooey, Huckleberry Hound, Jeannie, Quick Draw McGraw, Speed Buggy, Tom and Jerry, Yogi Bear*.)

−SCOOBY AND SCRAPPY-DOO. ABC: 9/22/1979–11/1/1980. Associate producers, Alex Lovy and Don Jurwich. Directed by George Gordon, Ray Patterson, Charles A. Nichols, Carl Urbano and Oscar Dufau. Music by Hoyt Curtin. Voices: Same as original SCOOBY-DOO for Scooby, Shaggy, Fred and Daphne; Pat Stevens and Maria Frumkin as Velma. Additional voice: Len Weinrib (Scrappy-Doo).

−SCOOBY'S LAFF-A-LYMPICS. ABC: 6/12/1980–11/1/1980; 3/1986–9/1986 (check). (Reruns from SCOOBY'S ALL-STAR LAFF-A-LYMPICS and SCOOBY'S ALL-STARS.)

−THE RICHIE RICH/SCOOBY-DOO HOUR. ABC: 11/8/1980–9/19/1982. Produced by Art Scott and Don Jurwich. Directed by Ray Patterson. Music by Hoyt Curtin. (See RICHIE RICH for credits of that segment.)

−SCOOBY-DOO CLASSICS. ABC: 1981–1982; 1983–1984. (Reruns.)

—SCOOBY AND SCRAPPY-DOO/ PUPPY HOUR. ABC: 9/25/1982–1/1/ 1983. Hanna-Barbera/Ruby-Spears. *See* PUPPY'S FURTHER ADVENTURES for credits on that segment. For "Scooby and Scrappy-Doo" segments: Executives in charge of production: Jayne Barbera, Jean MacCurdy. Supervising executive, Margaret Loesch. Executive producers, Joseph Barbera and William Hanna. Produced by Art Scott. Creative producer, Iwao Takamoto. Story editor, Tom Ruegger. Directed by Oscar Dufau, George Gordon, Carl Urbano, John Walker and Rudy Zamora. Animation directors: Bob Goe, Bill Hutten, Tony Love, Don Lusk, Ann Tucker. Story directors: Jan Green, Alex Lovy, Lew Marshall and George Singer. Music by Hoyt Curtin. Musical direction by Paul DeKorte. Voices: Same for Scooby, Fred, Daphne, Shaggy. Pat Stevens as Velma, Don Messick as Scrappy. Additional voices: Adrienne Alexander, Jack Angel, Ed Begley Jr., Randy Bennett, Art Burghardt, Howard Caine, Phil Clarke, Henry Corden, Candace Craig, Brian Cummings, Jerry Dexter, Jeff Doucette, Cheri Eichen, Bernard Erhard, Ernest Harada, Joyce Jameson, Byron Kane, Phyllis Katz, Zale Kessler, Larry Mann, Bill Martin, Mickey McGowan, Joe Medalis, Michael Mish, John Paragon, Vic Perrin, Henry Polic II, Tony Pope, Neil Ross, Michael Rye, Marilyn Schreffler, Marla Scott, Michael Sheehan, Hal Smith, Tony Snyles, John Stephenson, Andre Stojka, Jean VanderPyl, Janet Waldo, Vernee Walton, Peggy Webber, Jimmy Weldon, Noni White, Alan Young, Mariah Zajac.

—THE   SCOOBY-DOO/PUPPY HOUR. ABC: 1/8/1983–9/3/1983. (Consists of reruns from various early programs.)

—THE ALL-NEW SCOOBY AND SCRAPPY-DOO SHOW.

—THE BEST OF SCOOBY-DOO. (Reruns.) ABC: 9/10/1983–9/1/1984.

—THE NEW SCOOBY-DOO MYSTERIES. ABC: 9/9/1984–9/31/1985. Hanna-Barbera. Same production credits as "Scooby and Scrappy-Doo/Puppy Hour." Same voices for Scooby, Shaggy and Daphne; Don Messick as Scrappy-Doo. Most additional voices the same as above listing. Additional voices included Rene Auberjonois, Joan Darling and Dena Dietrich, among many others.

—SCARY SCOOBY FUNNIES. ABC: 10/20/1984–8/31/1985. (Reruns.)

—THE THIRTEEN GHOSTS OF SCOOBY-DOO. ABC: 9/7/1985–9/6/1986. Hanna-Barbera. Executives in charge of production: Jayne Barbera, Jean MacCurdy. Story editor, Tom Ruegger. Creative design by Iwao Takamoto. Supervising director, Ray Patterson. Directed by Art Davis, Oscar Dufau, Tony Love, Don Lusk, Rudy Zamora, Alan Zaslove. Supervising animation director, Chris Cuddington. Animation directors: Robert Goe, Bill Hutten, Rick Leon, Jay Barby, Irv Spence, Tim Walker. Music by Hoyt Curtin. Musical direction by Paul DeKorte. Voices: Don Messick (Scooby-Doo/ Scrappy-Doo); Casey Kasem (Shaggy); Heather North (Daphne); Susan Blu (Flim Flam); Vincent Price (Vincent Van Ghoul); Arte Johnson (Weerd); Howard Morris (Bogel); and Bob Arbogast, Gay Autterson, Hamilton Camp, Vicki Carroll, Peter Cullen, Marshall Efron, Patricia Elliot, Dick Erdman, Bernard Ehrhard, Linda Gary, Joan Gerber, Phil Hartman, Alice Hirson, Bob Holt, Marilyn Lightstone, Kenneth Mars, Edie McClurg, Sid Miller, Alan Oppenheimer, Bob Ridgely, Michael Rye, John Stephenson, Russi Taylor, Les Tremayne, B. J. Ward, and Frank Welker.

—SCOOBY'S MYSTERY FUNHOUSE. ABC: 9/7/1985–2/22/1986. (Reruns.)

—A PUP NAMED SCOOBY-DOO. ABC: 9/10/1988–9/1/1990; 8/10/1991–8/31/ 1991; 9/12/1992–9/4/1993. Hanna-Barbera. Executive producers, William Hanna and Joseph Barbera. Executive in charge of production, Jayne Barbera. Produced by Craig Zukowski and Scott Jeralds. Supervising director, Ray Patterson. Directed by Don Lusk and Carl Urbano. Story producer, Bill Matheny. Creative design, Iwao Takamoto. Music by John DeBray. Production facilities: Wang Film Production Co., Ltd. and Fils-Cartoons. Voices: Don Messick (Scooby-Doo); Casey Kasem (Shaggy); Christina Lange (Velma); Kellie Martin (Velma); Carl Stevens (Freddy); Scott Menville (Red Herring); and Rene Auberjonois, Victoria Carroll, Bernard Ehrhard, Barry Gordon, Pat Harrington, Marilyn Lightstone, Lynne Moody, Pat Musick, Rob Paulsen, Robert Picardo, and B. J. Ward.

The man behind Hanna-Barbera's *Scooby-Doo* was not Hanna or Barbera,

From a 1988 TV special: Scooby, cradled in the arms of Shaggy, takes a night course in "Chicken 101."

but CBS children's programming executive Fred Silverman. Concerned in 1969 that the cartoon-superhero syndrome would soon die out, Silverman took stock of the popularity of 1968's *The Archies* (q.v.). This was the harbinger of the future: cartoon shows abounding with comic teenagers. Fred Silverman wanted a strong central series upon which to build his Saturday morning schedule, one that would draw on the comic strength of *The Archies* while still retaining the elements that had clicked on CBS' action-adventure cartoons.

From here on, the legends conflict. Either Silverman was a fan of the old radio thriller *I Love a Mystery*, which punctuated bloodcurdling storylines with wicked humor; or, he was a lifelong fan of Abbott and Costello's "haunted house" comedies, which likewise counterpointed terror with laughs. Either way, he wanted a cartoon weekly that would blend comedy with scares—*and* he wanted a program which would bear resemblance to another Fred Silverman personal favorite, the live action teenage sitcom *Dobie Gillis*. Thus the new show would have to follow the *Gillis* character pattern of goodlooking guy (Dobie Gillis type), a plain but smart girl (Dobie's erstwhile girlfriend Zelda Gilroy), a pretty but vacuous girl (Dobie's "dream" Thalia Menninger) and a scraggly comedy relief (Maynard G. Krebs).

The characters ultimately drawn up by Hanna-Barbera were handsome Freddy, pretty but airheaded Daphne, comparatively plain but intelligent Velma (her eyeglasses were, as always, a tipoff of mental acuity), and a bearded goofball named Shaggy. This foursome would (chastely) travel up and down the highway in a psychedelically painted van called "The Mystery Machine," solving crimes wherever they went, in the manner of the troubleshooting detective trio on *I Love a Mystery*. The tentative title was either *Who's Scared?* or *Mysteries Five*—"Five" because there was a fifth crimesolver, a typical Hanna-Barbera funny dog, meant to supply the occasional reaction shot or punchline, but not really a starring role. The CBS network didn't like the fright angle of the proposed new series, citing recent complaints about too much violence and intensity on Saturday mornings. Why not, CBS suggested, punch up the comedy

by concentrating on the teenagers' pet dog? Hanna-Barbera was agreeable, having had extensive experience with comedy canines. But what to name this newest member of the kennel? After all, they'd already used up such monikers as Snuffles, Bandit, and Astro. Credit for naming the animal went (again!) to Fred Silverman, who would later claim that his fondness of the Frank Sinatra song "Strangers in the Night" had compelled the refrain "Scooby Doobie Doo" to imbed itself in his subconscious.

Silverman may also have been harking back to his first major programming success while working for Manhattan's WPIX-TV in 1963. To engender audience interest, the producer had introduced a call-in contest, the catch phrase of which was "Oobie doobie! Oobie doobie!" Viewers were encouraged to call WPIX, substitute the phrase "Oobie Doobie" for "Hello," and then take a whack at solving a big-prize puzzle. The resultant tripling of WPIX's ratings cemented Silverman's reputation in the Big Apple. Thus it wasn't surprising that the alternate phrases "Ooby Doobie" and "Scoobie Doobie" represented the end of the rainbow for Fred Silverman. The next logical step was to name Silverman's cartoon dog Scooby-Doo.

As for Scooby himself, his character also harked back to a favorite Silverman conceit. One of the producer's pet notions at CBS was to develop mystery shows with seemingly harmless, guileless or nonathletic detectives who had more on the ball than they seemed to. *Barnaby Jones*, with an elderly, folksy private eye, and *Cannon*, with an overweight but aggressively self-reliant detective, came from this brand of thinking. Essentially, Fred Silverman was enamored of the "audience identification" concept of a nonglamorous gumshoe. What could be less glamorous than Scooby-Doo, an oversized, slobbering Great Dane who turned into jello at the sight of his own shadow?

Hanna-Barbera has always given Silverman full credit for the *Scooby-Doo* concept—though it was sometimes suggested that the notion of spotlighting Scooby developed on the air, with Joe Barbera noting that "Scooby-Doo was a sidekick who suddenly became a star," when in fact the dog was the top banana from the first episode onward. Once determining that the program would revolve around the canine, Hanna-Barbera knew just who would best develop the concept: the studio's two best comedy men, Joe Ruby and Ken Spears, who'd worked up the ranks from sequence editors to full writers. The basic *Scooby-Doo* format was virtually carved in marble. All ghosts and goblins on the program would turn out to be flesh-and-blood crooks, who'd ritualistically sputter that they would have gotten away with their crimes "if it hadn't been for you meddling kids!" So well-worn was this denouement that, when the 1991 film comedy *Wayne's World* offered a similar "*Scooby-Doo* ending" as one of its *three* fadeout wrapups, the scene got one of the movie's biggest laughs.

Another rule of *Scooby-Doo* was that it was usually Velma, the all-brain bespectacled one, who pieced the mystery together. Over the years, however, the mysteries became more complex, and sometimes Velma needed the help of her companions — but it was rare indeed when Scooby-Doo himself would solve the mystery. His function was to stumble over clues, scream in terror and gnash his teeth when confronting the series' synthetic ghosts, and growl his dialogue in the "Roobie Roo," "R-"dominated dialect which actor Don Messick had tried out on Astro the dog in 1962's *The Jetsons*.

Unwaveringly formula-bound though it was, *Scooby-Doo, Where Are You?* was a major success of the 1969-70 season, beating out its NBC competition, Hanna-Barbera's own *Banana Splits* (q.v.). This wasn't a fluke. In its first seasons, the series was quite funny (though not as funny as suggested by its buffoonish laughtrack), emphasizing sight gags over verbal humor. Before he'd been refined into the compleat coward, the early Scooby was more clever and resourceful in routing and confounding the villains. One aspect of Scooby's character in 1969 was his talent for producing comedy props, costumes and weaponry out of thin air, in the nonchalantly surreal manner of such oldtimers as Bugs Bunny, Daffy Duck, and Tom and Jerry. As amusing as these early character traits were, they tended to draw focus away from the mystery angle, so the later Scooby-Doo was more simplified — and more scared.

Fred Silverman, who loved to watch his "babies" nurture and grow, eagerly ordered new episodes of *Scooby-Doo* each season, avoiding the "instant rerun" syndrome that plagued many other cartoon series. And when it seemed in 1972 that the *Scooby-Doo* format was getting stale, Silverman took his prize pooch and plunked him in an all-new "guest star" format. *The New Scooby-Doo Comedy Movies* ran a full hour each week, one of the first 60-minute cartoon series to feature a single star, without cutaway components. For the next 13 episodes, Scooby and company would get tied up in mysteries involving actual celebrities' (including Don Knotts, Jonathan Winters, Phyllis Diller, and even Sonny and Cher!) supplying their own voices and comporting themselves with surprising fidelity to their public images. Also making guest appearances were ersatz versions of the Three Stooges and Laurel and Hardy (the latter drawn more life-size than in the earlier H-B *Laurel and Hardy* cartoons [q.v.]) and such fictional icons as Batman and Robin.

When Fred Silverman moved to ABC, he took *Scooby* with him. The 1976 *Scooby-Doo/Dynomutt Hour* gave viewers a funny-dog double dose with the introduction of an additional component, "Dynomutt, Dog Wonder," featuring a canine crime fighter who looked a lot like Scooby and sounded (and behaved) a lot like earlier Hanna-Barbera star Magilla Gorilla (q.v.). Dynomutt was the assistant of traditional cape-and-mask superhero The Blue Falcon, otherwise known as millionaire Bradley Crown. Dog and master dwelt in Falcon's Lair on the outskirts of Big City, battling various megalomaniac villains and their ingenious doomsday devices. Judging by his brusque attitude, the Blue Falcon might have been happier dispensing with Dynomutt's services entirely, save for the fact that the dog was endowed with life-saving "robonic" weaponry and body parts.

The animators emphasized Dynomutt's comedy contrast to the Blue Falcon by using a device already employed on *Scooby-Doo* and *Josie and the Pussycats* (q.v.), and later refined on H-B's *Jabberjaw* (q.v.) and *Snorks* (q.v.). The Blue Falcon and most other human characters were drawn and played "straight," while Dynomutt was illustrated in broad, cartoony strokes (the dichotomy was carried even farther by the series' laughtrack, which reacted *only* to Dynomutt). Overseeing most of the scripts was Norman Maurer, who later parlayed many of the robonic aspects of Dynomutt, namely his transistorized paws and spring-activated appendages, into the *Robonic Stooges* sequences on *Skatebirds* (q.v.). *Dynomutt* was more limited in story scope than *Scooby-Doo*, but did well on his own as the rerun series *Dynomutt, Dog Wonder*, though never as well as *Scooby*.

During the *Dynomutt* era, Hanna-Barbera and Silverman began introducing new characters in the *Scooby* sphere, funny relatives who could play off the big dog: Scooby-Dum, a country cousin type, and the female Scooby-Dee. This extended family failed to click, but otherwise *The Scooby-Doo/Dynomutt Hour* performed so well that it soon blanketed 90 minutes, with the word "Hour" replaced by "Show" in the title.

Scooby's All-Star Laff-a-Lympics was the 1977 edition of Hanna-Barbera's never-ending-race concept (see *Wacky Races*), adapting the studio's *Yogi's Gang* (q.v.) premise by rallying new and old H-B characters—45 in all—as contestants in a series of Olympic road competitions, held all over the world in all manner of vehicles. Going for the gold were the Yogi Yahooeys, captained by Huckleberry Hound and comprised of Hanna-Barbera characters created before 1968; the Scooby Doobies, headed by you-know-who, made up of H-B luminaries of the late 1960s and early 1970s; and the Really Rottens, wherein team captain Muttley (see *Dastardly and Muttley and Their Flying Machines*) led a raffish pack of such never-before-seen heavies as Sooey Pig, Orfol Octopus and Daisy Mayhem (even Hanna-Barbera's villainesses were sexy!).

Overwhelmingly entertaining if sometimes deficient in story values, *Laff-a-Lympics* was the first Saturday-morning cartoon series to spread over two full hours; its component cartoons included both first-run and rerun *Dynomutt* episodes as well as rebroadcasts from the original *Scooby-Doo, Where Are You?* and *Captain Caveman and the Teen Angels* (q.v.). At one point in 1978, CBS, whose competing series were being eaten alive by the ABC extravaganza, came up with the "throw in the towel" notion of programming old *Scooby-Doo* reruns (there were lots to go around at that point!) even while *Laff-a-Lympics* laffed its way to the bank.

Incidentally, *Scooby's All-Star Laff-a-Lympics* helped launch a career, not to mention a future Hanna-Barbera rival. In 1977, young Andy Heyward was employed as a Hanna-Barbera archivist, cataloging the studio's past program files. At the same time, *Laff-a-Lympics* executive producer Joe Barbera was faced with the daunting task of making certain all the various Hanna-Barbera "celebrities" on the series would retain their individual character traits and characteristic sight-gags. What was needed was an assistant who was not only intimately familiar with the many *Laff-a-Lympics* stars but with their unique comic repertoires as well. Knowing that Andy Heyward had become a walking encyclopedia of Hanna-Barbera personalities and gag material, Barbera tapped Heyward as his apprentice writer for *Laff-a-Lympics*, and by 1978 the young would-be scriptwriter would graduate to full story editor. After five years with Hanna-Barbera, Andy Heyward took what he'd learned at Joe Barbera's side and went to work on the promotional team of a small distribution house called DIC Audiovisuel. Under Heyward's executive guidance, DIC would develop into one of cartoondom's most prolific and powerful animation producers, churning out such popular series as *Inspector Gadget, Heathcliff, The Real Ghostbusters, Super Mario Bros.* and *Captain Planet and the Planeteers* (see individual entries on these programs).

Now back to the *Scooby-Doo* saga. After Scooby-Dum and Scooby-Dee proved inadequate, 1978's *Scooby and Scrappy-Doo* finally hit upon a "relative" who worked. Scooby's nephew Scrappy-Doo was an articulate little daredevil dog who idolized his uncle, and was blind to the elder "Doo's" basic cowardice. He worked beautifully as Abbott to Scooby's Costello, encouraging the producers to go the "relative" route again by featuring Scooby's gray-furred mom and dad (notably on 1988's *A Pup Named Scooby-Doo*). In 1982, a variation of Scooby-Dum, cowboy Yabba Doo, briefly surfaced.

Scooby was at this point ABC's insurance policy, always ready to plug up a Saturday-morning scheduling gap; throughout the 1980s the indestructible bowser appeared in tandem with such other cartoon properties as Richie Rich and The Puppy (see individual entries on these characters). These appearances were mostly reruns, but in the early 1980s the property enjoyed an influx of fresh comic ideas from H-B's new breed, including Tom Ruegger and Jean Mac-Curdy, both later with Warner Bros. animation, and Margaret Loesch, the future maven of the Fox Children's Network. The *New Scooby-Doo Mysteries* (1984) was a good example of this new-blood injection: the old formula, pepped up with fresh, witty gags and appealing supporting characters.

After another season of reruns, the new Scooby-Doo "team" came up with a foolproof concept: *Thirteen Ghosts of Scooby-Doo*, where at last the old characters were *genuinely* involved with the Supernatural, thanks to Vincent Van Ghoul (voice by Vincent Price). My favorite *Thirteen Ghosts* outing featured a miniaturized Scooby chasing a spectral villain through the funny pages, with each ersatz comic strip separately delineated with its own characters and catch-phrase dialogue (one of the strips was signed by Tom Ruegger, an in-joke later indigenous to Ruegger's work on *Tiny Toon Adventures* [q.v.] but a comparative rarity at Hanna-Barbera). A higher comic and creative plane was at work here, though network and Hanna-Barbera guidelines wouldn't let the *Thirteen Ghosts* creators blossom full force.

There was no Scooby at all in 1986, either first-run or rerun; a feature-length special, *Scooby-Doo Meets the Boo Brothers*, filled the slack in 1987 as part of the syndicated "Hanna-Barbera's Superstar Ten." Then came the Emmy-winning *A Pup Named Scooby-Doo* in the fall of 1988. Burdened with Hanna-Barbera's timeworm "retro" notion of exploring the childhood years of its established characters (see also *The Flintstone Kids* and *Yo Yogi*), *Pup* still managed to revitalize the old concept with wacky Tex Avery–style humor, parodies of rock videos, and spoofs of *Murder She Wrote* and other live-action sleuthers. Best of all, the series lampooned the Scooby-Doo format itself, deliberately overplaying such standbys as Velma's detective skills and the "you meddling kids" denouements. One amusing new angle was the continuing character Red Herring, who was always accused of the crime at hand but was never guilty. After nearly a full season of this, Red Herring

presented an award to the rest of the cast for guessing wrongly 13 weeks in a row.

But *A Pup Named Scooby-Doo* often as not read better than it was played, laid low by too-measured pacing and sledge-hammer "throwaway" jokes. The series represented the classic Hanna-Barbera dilemma of the late 1980s and early 1990s: vastly improved animation and technique and a hipper approach to jokes, compromised by too much extraneous talk and too many pointless gags (wait till we get to *Two Stupid Dogs* [q.v.] and *Droopy, Master Detective* [q.v.]).

A Pup Named Scooby-Doo was the last incarnation of the property to date; Scooby and friends still pop up in rerun on cable TV, while the *Pup* reruns briefly resurfaced to buoy weaknesses in the ABC Saturday morning lineups of 1991, 1992 and 1993. And don't forget the occasional one- and two-hour specials, the best of which remains 1979's *Scooby Goes Hollywood*, a blue ribbon satire of busted television pilot films.

Back in 1980, a panel of kiddie-TV experts assembled by *TV Guide* found Scooby-Doo "harmless but worthless." Whatever one's own feelings of its worth, *Scooby*'s lasting value to Hanna-Barbera, including two decades of profit-posting, has been immeasurable.

SCREWBALL   SQUIRREL   *see* **DROOPY, MASTER DETECTIVE**

SEABERT. HBO: 4/5/1987–6/30/1988. Sepp Inter/BZZ. Produced in 1985 in association with Antennae 2/FMI/Brussels Television. Produced by Freddy Monnickendam and Joop Visch. Original idea by Marc Tortarello. Original stories based on documents of C.E.P.P.A.F., adapted by Jacques Morel and Eric Turlot. Scripts adapted by Michael Jupp, John Armstrong, John Hays, Dirk Braat. Directed by John Armstrong and Al Lowenheim. Theme and incidental music by Jay Ferne. Animation by Mill Valley Animation Company. Voices: Diane Ellington, Melissa Freeman, Ron Knight, Bruce Robertson, Morgan Upton.

Seabert was a pro-ecology half hour which ran on cable's HBO a few years before the "save the environment" TV-cartoon trend really took hold. The first few episodes were set in Greenland, where Tommy, a young American boy of apparently limitless intellectual and financial resources, was visiting an Eskimo village. With the help of Eskimo girl Aura, Tommy rescued a baby seal named Seabert from club-wielding poachers, who were working on behalf of an underhanded fur coat manufacturer named Graphite. Tommy's new pet Seabert soon found his likeness being adopted for the logo of a Greenpeace-style ecological society. A base was set up in the Eskimo village, from which Tommy, Aura and Seabert would sally forth to rescue other endangered species. The organization was quite sophisticated, considering that its founder was a preteen kid: Not only could Tommy and his followers afford around the world trips, but they were also able to purchase radio-equipped snowmobiles which could travel across water. Aura was later rather chauvinistically left back in Greenland when Tommy and Seabert undertook further ecological rescue missions in Africa, Europe, Asia and Mexico.

Sepp International, the Belgian-based company responsible for *Seabert*, had evidently learned few tricks about comedy from its earlier coproduction tenure on Hanna-Barbera's *The Smurfs* (q.v.). Seabert, Tommy and the other characters tended to run in place before scooting off, a la Huckleberry Hound and Yogi Bear, and the series contained several long, gratuitous pantomime sequences wherein Seabert would indulge in some snowbound slapstick. Unfortunately, Sepp also learned the rudiments of Hanna-Barbera "overkill." The villains on *Seabert* were invariably depicted as ugly, scowling, or terminally stupid, while the good guys were seemingly only one step below the Archangels. As for the pro-ecology slant, *Seabert* displayed the typical faults of this genre. Tommy and his friends spoke in fluent tract, as though reading from mimeographed circulars. Meanwhile, Seabert would be magnanimously treated as though he were a human being, allowed to accompany his protectors on airplanes, in the jungle, and through city streets, with scant regard to the damage he might suffer by being taken out of his natural Arctic habitat. The hapless seal was even permitted to eat airline food—and this on a TV series that condemned cruelty to animals!

Nor were human characters free from such persecution. Captured by police, the evil fur mogul Graphite was severely punished by being forced to watch environmental propaganda films. The audience was treated in an equally merciless manner, with the narrator spewing out such phrases as "immoral," "unforgiveable" and "terrible wrongdoings" when describing such pursuits as hunting and trapping. One can assume that *Seabert* was not exactly a smash hit in Northern Wisconsin.

The animation on *Seabert* was rather attractive, but the visuals were constantly undercut by the poor English-language dubbing, which was as stilted and overemphatic as any *Hercules* movie. The background music didn't help matters any either. Attempts at invoking the lilting melodies heard on Sepp's earlier *Smurfs* sounded more like the shapeless "intermission" tunes once heard in drive-in movies.

Somehow, the 26 *Seabert* episodes were deemed worthy of a highly promoted showcase on HBO pay-cable in 1987. This had to have been a reaction to the series' noble eco-friendly intentions; the overall quality of *Seabert* certainly didn't warrant the same sort of preferential treatment given to such other pay-cable cartoon offerings as *Babar* (q.v.), *Tintin* (q.v.) and *Shelley Duvall's Bedtime Stories* (q.v.).

SEALAB 2020. NBC: 9/9/1972–9/1/1973. Hanna-Barbera. Executive producers, William Hanna and Joseph Barbera. Produced by Iwao Takamoto. Directed by Charles Nichols. Music by Hoyt Curtin. Voices: Ross Martin (Dr. Paul Williams); John Stephenson (Capt. Mike Murphy); Josh Albee (Bobby Murphy); Pamelyn Ferdin (Sally Murphy); Bill Callaway (Sparks); Jerry Dexter (Hal); Ann Jillian (Gail); Ron Pinckard (Ed); Olga James (Mrs. Thomas); Gary Shapiro (Jamie).

Sealab 2020 was a product from Hanna-Barbera's "realistic" phase in the early 1970s. The weekly half hour series was set in the 21st century. Dr. Paul Williams, a Chinook Indian—an early example of political correctness before the FCC forced the issue—was an oceanographer researching the depths from the vantage point of his high-tech underwater community called Sealab. This city beneath the waves was something of a waterlogged, immobile Starship Enterprise, fully computerized and with a 250-person crew. To further cement the similarities between this series and *Star Trek*, Dr. Williams' principal aides were three good-looking young astronaut types, here called oceanauts: Hal, Ed and Gail. As in Hanna-Barbera's earlier animated *Moby Dick*, several other characters, namely the Murphy family, were pulled into *Sealab 2020*'s plotlines by being rescued from a sinking ship. And just so we'd remember that the series was produced by Hanna-Barbera and not Gene Roddenberry, the cast included a comedy relief dolphin named Tuffy.

THE SECRET LIVES OF WALDO KITTY. NBC: 9/6/1975–9/4/1976. Filmation. Produced by Lou Scheimer and Norm Prescott. Directed by Don Christensen, Rudy Larriva. Based on an idea by Lorna Smith. Written by Jim Ryan and Bill Danch. Music by Yvette Blais and Jeff Michael. Voices: Howard Morris (Waldo Kitty/Wetzel/Lone Kitty/Catman/Catzan/Robin Cat/Captain Herc); Jane Webb (Felicia/Pronto/Sparrow/Lt. O-Hoo-Ha); Allan Melvin (Tyrone/Mr. Crock/Brennan Hench Dog/Dr. Moans).

Inspired by James Thurber's classic wish-fulfillment short story "The Secret Life of Walter Mitty," *The Secret Lives of Waldo Kitty* was introduced each week with live action footage of a male cat (Waldo), a female cat (Felicia) and a bullying bulldog (Tyrone). Waldo couldn't best the ferocious Tyrone in "real" life, so he would fantasize about being a fearless, invulnerable hero—and at this point the half hour program would switch over to animation. In his daydreams, Waldo would · metamorphose into such legendary felines as Catzan, The Lone Kitty, Catman, Robin Cat and "Captain Herc" of "Cat Trek." No animals were injured during the making of this 13-episode series. We wish we could say the same about James Thurber's reputation.

Not that the Thurber estate merely stood by looking askance when *Secret Lives of Waldo Kitty* premiered. In fact, the estate's attorneys sued Filmation for copyright infringement, forcing the company to retitle the series *The New Adventures of Waldo Kitty* (did I miss the *old* adventures?) when it went into syndication.

SECRET SQUIRREL *see* ATOM ANT and TWO STUPID DOGS

SECTAURS. Syndicated: 1985. Ruby-Spears. Voices: Dan Gilvezan (Dargon/Dragonflyer); Peter Renaday (Pinsor/Battle Beetle); Peter Cullen (Mantor/Skito/Toxid); Laurie Faso (Zak/Bitaur); Arthur Burghardt (Spidrax/Spiderflyer); Frank Welker (Skulk/Trancula/Raplor); Neil Ross (Waspax/Wingid).

Sectaurs was a syndicated miniseries, comprised of five half-hour segments. Symbion, an idyllic planet, fell victim to a misbegotten lab experiment. The resultant insectlike mutants, organized by leader Spridax into the Terror Troops, threatened to destroy the universe. The chastened lab scientists then created a humanoid race, the Sectaurs, to battle Spridax. So much for better living through chemistry.

SHAKE, RATTLE AND ROLL *see* C.B. BEARS

SHAKESPEARE: THE ANIMATED TALES. HBO: 11/5/1992–. Soyuzmultifilms Studios/HIT Communications (U.K.). Series director and producer, Dave Edwards. Production companies: Soyuzmultifilm, Christmas Films with S4C Channel 4 Wales in association with BBC Wales, HIT Entertainment PLC, HBO, Fujisankei, Dave Edwards Studios. Host: Robin Williams (winner 1993 Cable ACE award).

Shakespeare: The Animated Tales was the brainchild of Shakespearean scholar Leon Garfield. Broadcast in six-episode cycles over the HBO pay-cable service, these adaptations were each honed to 30 minutes, with surprisingly little damage done to the story threads (Shakespeare's multiplotted comedies were, traditionally, the trickiest to pare down) or the poetry. As a defense against potential howls from Shakespeare purists, Leon Garfield pointed out that truncating the Bard was hardly a new process, having been practiced from the 17th century onward, and that he was doing far less damage to the texts than those entrepreneur/censors of previous centuries who'd committed such artistic atrocities as tacking happy endings on *Romeo and Juliet* and *King Lear*. Garfield further deflected criticism by refusing to make the plays more "saleable" to 1990s audiences by updating or including modern slang, though series host Robin Williams, himself a Shakespeare aficionado, offered a comic (albeit respectful) slant to the classic material in his introductory comments. Voices for *Shakespeare: The Animated Tales* were supplied by members of the Royal Shakespeare Company, while the animation was in the hands of government-funded studio artists in Russia and Armenia, as well as the independent Cardiff, Wales, studios of producer Dave Edwards. Each drama endeavored to exhibit a different artistic style. The first program, "A Midsummer Night's Dream," was rendered in the manner of a Japanese watercolor. "Midsummer," "Romeo and Juliet" and "MacBeth" were produced with cel animation, while "Twelfth Night" and "Tempest" were brought to life with stop-motion puppets. "Hamlet" was the most visually striking (though the most sluggish in terms of animation) of the first season *Animated Tales*, with background art and several tableaux painted on translucent glass.

As of this writing, only six *Shakespeare: The Animated Tales* have been produced, at an astounding (for TV) budget of about $800,000 per episode. Should audience response warrant a second season, HBO and Leon Garfield have already drawn up plans for half hour versions of "Othello," "The Winter's Tale," "Richard III," "Julius Caesar," "As You Like It," and "Taming of the Shrew." Perhaps if they choose to risk an "R" rating, the producers might give us an animated "Titus Andronicus" someday.

SHAZAM *see* **KID SUPER POWER HOUR WITH SHAZAM**

SHAZZAN! CBS: 9/9/1967–9/6/1969. Hanna-Barbera. Produced and directed by William Hanna and Joseph Barbera. Associate producer, Lewis A. Marshall. Animation director, Charles Nichols. Story supervisor, Tom Dagenais. Story by Sloan Nibley, Walker Black and William Lutz. Production supervisor, Howard Hanson. Character design by Alex Toth. Musical director, Ted Nichols. Voices: Barney Phillips (Shazzan); Janet Waldo (Nancy); Jerry Dexter (Chuck); Don Messick (Kaboobie).

No relation to the *Captain Marvel*–inspired *Kid Super Power Hour with Shazam!* (q.v.), Hanna-Barbera's weekly half hour *Shazzan!* was a late–1960s slant on Scheherazade. Maine-born teenaged

twins Chuck and Nancy came across a mysterious divided ring while combing the coastline, which transported them to the days and locale of the Arabian Nights. When the two portions of the ring were connected, and the twins read its engraved message "Shazzan!," up popped Shazzan himself, a gentle giant genie who never stopped smiling or bellowing out his trademarked "Ho *Ho!*"

Shazzan could perform any feat of magic *except* returning Chuck and Nancy to Maine. To accomplish this, they would have to return the ring to its rightful owner. Armed with a "cloak of invisibility" (making life easier for the animators) and a magic rope, the young blonde siblings set on their mission astride the flying camel Kaboobie, who looked like an ad-design merger of Camel Cigarettes and Mobilgas. Eighteen half hours of *Shazzan!* were produced, each containing two 11-minute adventures.

According to Hanna-Barbera historian Ted Sennett, Fred Silverman, the man who commissioned *Shazzan!* for CBS, was ultimately sorry that he did. Silverman would observe that no one was aware of the "concept problem" until too late: "The genie had no weaknesses. Once you summoned him, the story was over. It was a very difficult show to do, and very expensive."

You'd never know it. *Shazzan!* was one of the tackiest and dreariest series ever to come out of Hanna-Barbera, weakened by flat character design (a real letdown from the usually reliable Alex Toth, though the fault could probably be traced to the animation table), dull background art, and "action" sequences with all the pace of a turtle wearing snowshoes. The studio would do a far more accomplished and eye-pleasing job with *Shazzan's* basic premise one year later, via the "Arabian Knights" component on *The Banana Splits Adventure Hour* (q.v.).

SHELLEY DUVALL'S BEDTIME STORIES. Showtime: 4/21/1992–. Think Entertainment/MCA Family Entertainment/Universal Cartoon Studios. Executive producer: Shelley Duvall. Co-producer, Carol Davies. Animation produced and directed by Arthur Leonardi. Computer-animated main titles by Metrolight Studios: produced by Jim Wheeler; animator, Mark Lasof. Live-action sequences produced and directed by Courtney P. Conte. Directed by Jeff Stein. Written by Shelley Duvall and Carol Davies. Executive in charge of production, Paul B. Strickland. Music by Jeff Silverman. Animation facilities: Rainbow Animation Group (Korea), Metracel Animation Studios (Hollywood; executive producer for Metracel, Mark A. Steeves). Pop-up set design, Arthur B. Leonardi.

By the time *Shelley Duvall's Bedtime Stories* made its April 1992 debut, actress Shelley Duvall, graduate of director Robert Altman's movie stock company, was a ten-year veteran of cable-TV children's programs. Starting with the live-action *Faerie Tale Theatre* in 1982 and continuing with *Shelley Duvall's Tall Tales and Legends*, *Nightmare Classics* and *Mother Goose Rock 'N' Rhyme*, Duvall's production company, Think Entertainment, exhibited enviable expertise at adapting famous children's stories capable of entertaining both kids and adults equally, without talking down to the older viewers or playing over the heads of the youngsters. Thanks to her professional clout, Shelley was able to inveigle several Hollywood celebrity chums to work for scale (union minimum) salary in her various projects. Casts of *Faerie Tale Theatre* et al. included the likes of Robin Williams, Paul "Pee-wee Herman" Reubens, Carl Reiner, James Coburn, Jennifer Beals, Jean Stapleton, Tatum O'Neal, Billy Crystal, Jim Belushi, Jeff Goldblum, Valerie Perrine, and Paul Simon (Simon was a former boyfriend of Duvall's; the lady must have been persuasive as all get out). The actress was also able to secure top-level talent behind the scenes. One *Faerie Tale* was directed by no less than Francis Ford Coppola.

Shelley Duvall's Bedtime Stories was the actress' first cartoon project, designed to introduce to the animation boards some of the lesser-known children's books—"The classics of the future" as she described them, though many of the stories had been in circulation for years (for example, "Millions of Cats" by Wanda Ga'g, which had been previously animated for *Captain Kangaroo* way back in 1962). Duvall appeared in the live-action introductions of each half-hour *Bedtime Stories* installment, lounging around an elaborate bedroom set that resembled a pop-up illustration from one of her favorite books. The set, which folded out at the beginning

of the show and back in again at the closing, was designed by old animation hand Arthur Leonardi, who also directed many of the Canadian-produced cartoon segments. Shelley Duvall had wanted to duplicate the "feel" of reading a book, and certainly succeeded so far as her surroundings were concerned. Less successful were Duvall's wraparound comments, which leaned toward syrupy patronization. This quality did not spill over into the excellent cartoon segments themselves, which in addition to being superbly produced also treated the kids at home as though they had a glimmer of intelligence and could enjoy the stories without suffering a golly-gee approach to the storytelling.

In the tradition of other Shelley Duvall projects, *Bedtime Stories* boasted a star-studded lineup of narrators. Each episode featured two to three individual stories, linked by theme or by author. The premier episode highlighted two tales by Audrey Wood: "Elbert's Bad Word," read by Ringo Starr, and "Weird Parents," read by Bette Midler. Episode number two had an "Alligator" throughline: Jean Stapleton read "Elizabeth and Larry," about a girl and her gator, while Dudley Moore read "Bill and Pete," which starred William Everett Crocodile and a bird named Pete who rescued the croc from capture.

The following *Bedtime Stories* installment contained an "anthropomorphic steam vehicle" theme (try saying that three times), with Rick Moranis reciting "Little Toot and the Loch Ness Monster" and Bonnie Raitt handling "Choo Choo." For its Halloween 1992 offering, Duvall's series showcased three "confronting one's fears" stories by Mercer Mayer, each with a different narrator: Michael J. Fox ("There's a Nightmare in My Closet"), Christian Slater ("There's an Alligator Under My Bed") and, best of the three, Sissy Spacek ("There's Something in My Attic"). Dinosaurs consumed the next *Bedtime Stories*, with Martin Short reading Carol and Donald Carrick's "Patrick's Dinosaurs" and "What Happened to Patrick's Dinosaurs." The series' first season closed out with a brace of "cat lover" yarns: John Candy narrated "Blumpoe the Grumpo Meets Arnold the Cat," while James Earl Jones was on hand for the venerable "Millions of Cats."

Even as the Showtime cable service began its reruns of *Shelley Duvall's Bed-*

time Stories, the first few episodes found their way into video stores—where some managers, associating Duvall with her earlier career with Robert Altman, instinctively shunted the cassettes to the "adult drama" section! The second *Bedtime Stories* cycle started up in the fall of 1992 with "Amos: the Story of an Old Dog and His Couch"; the third cycle showed up one year later. (As in season one, Showtime telecast the programs on a weekly basis in first run, then broke them up into monthly or bimonthly specials in rerun.) Contributors to subsequent seasons were Steve Martin, Candice Bergen, Charles Grodin and Billy Crystal, respectively reading "Tugford Wanted to Be Bad," "Little Penguin's Tale," "Rotten Island" (a natural for the lip-sneering Grodin!) and "My New Neighbors." Other celebrity storyspinners included Rhea Perlman ("Bootsie Barker Bites"), Mary Steenburgen ("Katy No-Pocket") and Shelley Duvall herself ("Ruby the Copycat," "The Little Rabbit Who Wanted Red Wings").

Showing no signs of halting production, Shelley Duvall was still springing out of her pop-up set as 1993 drew to a close; her introductions had by this time been shorn of the wide-eyed condescension which inflicted the earliest programs. *Shelley Duvall's Bedtime Stories* may turn out to have as long and healthy a run as the actress' inaugural independent project, *Faerie Tale Theatre*, meaning a strong afterlife on videocassette and in syndicated repeats. And Shelley's next project? Back to live action, with Jean Stapleton starring as Betty McDonald's magical babysitter Mrs. Piggle-Wiggle (what a cartoon *that* would have made!).

SHE-RA, PRINCESS OF POWER.
Syndicated: 1985. Filmation/Mattel/Group W. Executive producer, Lou Scheimer. Executive vice president, creative affairs, Arthur H. Nadel. Vice president in charge of production, Joe Mazzuca. Directed by Lou Kachivas, Ed Friedman, Marsh Lamore, Mark Glamack, Tom Sito, Tom Tataranowicz and Richard Trueblood. Character design supervisors, Herb Hazelton, Diane Keeler. Written by Larry Ditillio, Don Heckman, Francis Moss, Harvey Brenner, Michael Utvich, Michael Chase Walker and J. Michael Stracynski. Educational consultant, Donald F. Roberts. Voices: Melendy Britt (Princess Adora,

aka She-Ra/Madama Raxx/Frosta); George DiCenzo (Hordak); and Linda Gary (Castaspella/Glimmer/Shadow Weaver/Catra); John Erwin (Broom/He-Man); Alan Oppenheimer (Skeletor); Erik Gundin (Kowl/ Mantella/Leech); Erica Scheimer (Imp); Lou Scheimer (Lighthope/Sprint/Swiftwind/Horde Soldiers/Loo-Kee).

She-Ra, Princess of Power was a carefully timed and planned spinoff of Filmation/ Mattel's *He-Man and the Masters of the Universe* (q.v.). She-Ra was really Princess Adora, twin sister of He-Man, who lived in Etheria, a parallel world to her brother's Eternia. Adora defended the magic-source Crystal Castle against such villains as the Shadow Weaver and Hordak of the Horde World, who'd conquered Etheria. (Occasionally *He-Man's* Skeletor made crossover appearances.) Working in conjunction with the Friends of the Great Rebellion, Adora emulated her brother by holding her Sword of Protection high, shouting "For the honor of Greyskull!," and transforming into the superpowered She-Ra. Like He-Man, She-Ra possessed a magically gifted animal; hers was a horse named Swiftwind. Like He-Man's, She-Ra's adventures were carefully monitored for proper prosocial content by educational consultant Donald F. Roberts. And like He-Man, the "She-Ra" toys-and-games line was promoted by Richard Weiner Inc. on behalf of Mattel.

In fact, *She-Ra* wasn't so much a spinoff as an outright imitation of *He-Man*. The opening credit sequences on both episodes were virtually the same, shot for shot. She-Ra's incantation "For the Honor of Greyskull" was a variation on He-Man's "By the power of Grayskull," while her motto "I am She-Ra!" was a limp takeoff on her brother's "I have the Power!" Like He-Man, She-Ra shared her true identity with only three others: Lighthope, Madama Raxx and the winged Kowl were She-Ra's equivalents to her brother's Man at Arms, Sorceress and Orka. Even the villains had shared traits, albeit in reverse: Skeletor had a bony body and wore armor, Hordak had a metallic face and wore bones.

Perhaps perceiving that viewers would have trouble taking She-Ra seriously—she came off more like a drum majorette than a superwoman—her series had a lighter touch than *He-Man's*. Etheria boasted a zany, Daliesque landscape more suitable to the 1937 Warner Bros. cartoon *Porky in*

Wackyland than to traditional Sword and Sorcery. Whereas only one of He-Man's allies (Orka) could be considered comedy relief, two of She-Ra's friends, the eccentric Madama Raxx and a tiny spritelike character named Loo-Kee, were played for laughs. And the villainy was de-fanged by having Hordak and Skeletor squabble like envious siblings, hating one another more than they hated He-Man and She-Ra. Both baddies were forever trying to foist the troublesome superheroes into each other's worlds, just to "get even."

Unlike the situation prevalent in the sponsor-dominated world of 1950s television, Mattel didn't have a lot to say about *She-Ra*'s story content. The toy firm's principal responsibility was to think up potential action figures and playthings for inclusion within the storylines. One of She-Ra's principal means of transportation, Enchanta the Swan, was a prime example of a character which developed not on the animation board but in Mattel's "research and development" department, which then became a toy *only* after testing positively on the series.

A Filmation vice-president deflected accusations that *She-Ra: Princess of Power* was merely a distaff *He-Man* by insisting "We always wanted to do a series with resourceful women in the lead, women who did not need men to save them." In this, *She-Ra: Princess of Power* succeeded (more than can be said for the She-Ra toy line itself, which ended up a financial dud). But in format and technique, the 65-episode series couldn't help looking like *He-Man* in drag—and to make things dicier, *She-Ra* wasn't even as well animated as its predecessor.

Only in the "prosocial" closing 30 seconds of each episode did *She-Ra* offer anything that *He-Man* didn't. In these, She-Ra's faithful friend Loo-Kee dispensed the episode's moral, but only after challenging the home viewers to locate him lurking in the background during the action of the episode itself (not as hard as it sounded, since Loo-Kee was usually given a glaringly gratuitous closeup in the body of the story). This "find the hidden figure" technique would later be honed to perfection by artist Martin Handford in his children's books (and subsequent cartoon series) *Where's Waldo?* (q.v.).

THE SHIRT TALES. NBC: 9/18/1982–9/8/1984; CBS: 9/15/1984–5/23/1985.

Hanna-Barbera. Executive producers, William Hanna and Joseph Barbera. Produced by Kay Wright. Supervising director, Ray Patterson. Directed by George Gordon, Bob Hathcock, Carl Urbano, Rudy Zamora; assistant directors, Bob Goe, Terry Harrison, Bill Hutten. Story direction, Jan Green, Lew Saw, James Fletcher, Stephan Hickner, Roy Wilson, Jim Simon, Tom Yakutis. Story editor, Bob Ogle. Creative supervisor, Tony Pastor. Creative producer, Iwao Takamoto. Animation supervisors, Jay Sarbry and Bill Patterson; assistant, Joanna Romersa. Background supervision by Al Gmuer. Music by Hoyt Curtin; musical direction by Paul DeKorte. Executives in charge of production, Jayne Barbera and Margaret Loesch. Voices: Ronnie Schell (Rick Raccoon); Pat Parris (Pammy Panda); Robert Allan Ogle (Digger Mole); Fred Travalena (Bogey Orangutan); Steve Schatzberg (Tyg Tiger); Nancy Cartwright (Kip Kangaroo); Herb Vigran (Mr. Dinkle); and Richard Balin, Joe Besser, Brian Cummings, Walker Edmiston, Laurie Faso, Stanley Jones, Sherry Lynn, Tress MacNeille, Ken Mars, Joseph Medalis, Henry Polic II, Tony Pope, Bob Ridgely, Michael Rye, Marilyn Schreffler, R. J. Sagall, Michael Sheehan, John Stephenson, Andre Stojka, Frank Welker, William Woodson, and Ted Ziegler.

The *Shirt Tales*, based on animal characters created for a line of Hallmark greeting cards, was NBC's 1982 "counter" to its Saturday-morning competition *Sylvester & Tweety/Daffy & Speedy* on CBS and *The Pac-Man/Little Rascals/Richie Rich Show* (see separate entries on the last three titles) on ABC. The cutie-pie Shirt Tales were so named because selected bits of dialogue ("Okay," "Shhh," etc.) sprang from cryptic messages which popped up unexpectedly on their T-shirts. These ever-changing messages also reflected the personalities and emotions of the five "Tales": Rick Raccoon, Pammy Panda, Digger Mole, Tyg Tiger and Bogey Orangutan, the last so named because he spoke in a Bogart cadence and called everyone "shweetheart." A sixth character, the infantile Kip Kangaroo, was introduced during the series' second season.

The characters lived in an oak tree planted on the grounds of a public park, whence they were dispatched *Care Bear* (q.v.) style to spread goodwill and solve

Scooby-Doo (q.v.) type mysteries. Their main mode of transportation was the all-purpose Shirt Tales' Super-Sonic Transporter (The "STSST"), which spewed a solid, laserlike beam that sometimes functioned as a lasso or ladder. They were able to send holographic messages to one another by way of wristwatch communicators (do we detect *two* merchandising tie-ins in the last two sentences?), and their rallying cry whenever danger threatened was "It's shirt tale time"—whereupon the words SHIRT TALES would appear (sometimes misspelled, though never censorably so) on their chests. The one recurring human character on *The Shirt Tales* was park superintendent Dinkle, who was sometimes an ally, sometimes an opponent, but always the basically decent protector and shelterer of the Tales.

This half-hour opus (two short cartoons per episode) was simplistic enough to be a throwback to Hanna-Barbera's earliest days: extremely limited movement, inchwormlike pacing, sparse background art, and characters with frozen baby-doll facial expressions. Only Mr. Dinkle, the most typically "Hanna-Barbera" character, ever appeared to spring to life from the animation board, but even he was no cure for insomnia. As for story values *Shirt Tales* was the sort of program where a character could wander onto a missile base and accidentally launch himself into orbit without anybody around to stop him. Why bother animating additional characters who might confuse the plotlines with logic?

The *Shirt Tales* was easily the least of all Hanna-Barbera merchandise-into-cartoon series. Comparatively speaking, *Pound Puppies*, *The Biskitts*, and *Foofur* were Emmy Award material.

SILVERHAWKS. Syndicated: 1986. Rankin-Bass/Telepictures. Executive producers, Arthur Rankin Jr. and Jules Bass. Supervising producer, Lee Dannacher. Animation by Pacific Animation Corporation. In charge of production, Masaki Iisuka. Script supervisor, Peter Lawrence. Script editor, Lee Schneider. Project developed by Leisure Concepts Inc. Music by Bernard Hoffer. Character design, Michael Germakian. Secondary character design, Bob Camp. Scientific consultant, epilogue test segments: Dr. William A. Gutsch Jr., American Museum–Hayden Planetarium. Psychiatric consultant, Robert Kuisis, Ph.D. Voices: Robert McFadden, Earl Hammond, Larry Kenny, Maggie Jakobson, Peter Newman, Doug Preis, Adolph Caesar.

Rankin-Bass' *SilverHawks* was a daily half hour created in the image of the same studio's *ThunderCats* (q.v.). Like the earlier series (which ran back-to-back with *SilverHawks* in many local markets), this latest Rankin-Bass syndie existed primarily for the purpose of marketing toys, action figures, board games, T-shirts, and even a line of sports footwear. In the tradition of the half human/half lion Thunder-Cats, the SilverHawks were half human, half metal heroes, endowed with the wings of hawks.

Though not evident in the title, *Silver-Hawks* was something of an outer-space *Untouchables*, with an up-to-date rock music background score thrown in to touch as many audience-demographic bases as possible. Setting the plot in motion, the evil extraterrestrial gangster Mon Star had escaped prison in the land of Limbo. Commander StarGazer, Limbo's bionic chief lawman (and one of the ugliest "heroes" in all cartoondom, a rather refreshing contrast to the *He-Man* "Adonis" school), sought to thwart the Mon Star Mob with the aid of five ordinary humans, all recently transformed into peacekeeping SilverHawks. Jonathan Quick, renamed Quicksilver after his "machinization," was StarGazer's second in command; Emily and Will Hart, converted into the Steel Twins, were the group's resident scientists; Bluegrass was a combination country singer/ pilot/ robot; and Copper Kidd, the requisite young mascot, was a computerized human who spoke in synthesized tones. The SilverHawks' headquarters was Hawk Haven (a satellite sphere decorated with the group's trademark hawk escutcheon) whence they set forth in their space vehicle Tallyhawk to confront Mon Star, whose villainy was compounded whenever he invoked deadly powers from the Moonstar of Limbo.

Produced with the same low-level animation and overemphatic voice performances that distinguished *ThunderCats*, *SilverHawks* nonetheless improved upon the earlier program with stronger individual characterizations and better handled action sequences. There was also an amusing "Gangster B-Movie" undercurrent, notably in the Runyonesque character of Seymore, a space-alien cabbie. SilverHawks' tie-in with its merchandising was even more blatant than that on ThunderCats, going so far as exploiting that plotlines to demonstrate to the kids at home how the action figures worked: Commander StarGazer in fact had removable arms and legs, just like his toy counterpart! The fact that it was an unabashed extended commercial added to the shabby charm of SilverHawks, in much the same way that the ebullient host of a late-night "infotainment" program can be endearing if you're in the right frame of mind.

Each half hour SilverHawks concluded with a 90-second prosocial vignette, expansively called an "Epilogue." This consisted of an astronomy quiz, wherein the home viewers were invited to answer multiple choice questions about outer space, with points given for correct responses. It was an enjoyable twist on the usual syndicated cartoon episode-closing information "bite," though the questions asked on SilverHawks were so simplistic that the results were more ego-boosting than instructional.

THE SIMPSONS. Fox: 1/14/1990-. Klasky-Csupo (1990–91); Film Roman (1992–)/Gracie Films/20th Television. Executive producers: James L. Brooks, Matt Groening, Sam Simon, Phil Roman, David Mirkin. Created by Matt Groening. Creative consultants: James L. Brooks, David M. Stern. Creative producer, Sam Simon. Co-executive producer, Jace Richdale. Animation producers, Gabor Csupo, Sherry Gunther, Phil Roman. Producers: Richard Rayries, Michael P. Schoenbrun, John Vitti, John Swartzwelder, Conan O'Brien, J. Michael Mendel, Joseph A. Boucher, Richard Sakai, George Meyer, Frank Mula, David Sacks, Michael Scully, Bill Schultz, Mike Wolf, David Silverman. Coproducers, Margot Pipkin, Bill Oakley, Josh Weinstein. Directed by David Silverman, Jim Reardon, Rich Moore, Wes Archer, Susie Dieter, Carlos Baeza, Jeff Jynch, Bob Anderson, Mark Kirkland. Executive consultant: Brad Bird. Story editors: Jeff Martin, Brent Forrester, Bill Canterbury, David Cohen. Among the many writers: Conan O'Brien, John Collier, Rob Kushell, John Swartzwelder. Music by Danny Elfman. Musical direction by Alf Clausen. Animation facilities: Akom Studios, Korea. Voices: Dan Castellaneta (Homer Simpson/Krusty the Clown); Julie Kavner (Marge Simpson); Nancy Cartwright (Bart Simpson); Yeardley Smith (Lisa Simpson); Harry Shearer (Mr. Burns, Principal Skinner/Ned Flanders/Smithers/Otto/many others); Hank Azzaria (Abu/Moe/Chief Wiggum/Dr. Riviera); Marcia Wallace (Mrs. Karbappel); Elizabeth Taylor (Maggie Simpson—only once, so far); And Phil Hartman, Russi Taylor, Frank Welker, Maggie Roswell, June Foray, Jo Anne Harris, Pamela Hayden, Tress MacNeille, Chris Collins. Guest voices (as of now): Johnny Carson, Danny De Vito, Bob Hope, Linda Ronstadt, Albert Brooks, Larry King, Michael Jackson, Tony Bennett, Magic Johnson, Beverly D'Angelo, Joe Frazier, Harvey Fierstein, Jon Lovitz, Penny Marshall, Jackie Mason, Engelbert Humperdinck, Ringo Starr, David Crosby, The Ramones, Kelsey Grammer, Pamela Reed, Bette Midler, The Red Hot Chili Peppers, Aerosmith, Luke Perry, Michelle Pfeiffer, Robert Goulet, Tracy Ullman, Hugh Hefner, Tom Jones, Dr. Joyce Brothers, Jon Frazier, Sting, Adam West, James Taylor, Buzz Aldrin, Brooke Shields, Joe Mantegna, James Brown, Neil Patrick Harris, Kathleen Turner, Ernest Borgnine, Darryl Strawberry, Dustin Hoffman, Wade Boggs, Leonard Nimoy, Sara Gilbert, Cloris Leachman, James Woods, Conan O'Brien. (Dan Castellaneta was a 1993 Emmy winner in the "Best Voiceover" category. The series itself was a 1989-90 winner in the "Outstanding Animated Program: Nighttime" category—an admittedly sparse field.)

The Simpsons matured from a mere "filler" act to a full-fledged network megahit, and in so doing became one of the most popular and influential TV cartoon series of the 1990s.

The acorn for The Simpsons was a series of short animated buffers produced from 1987 through 1989, separating the live-action sketches on the Fox Network's Tracey Ullman Show. These "cartoonlettes," designed by artist Matt Groening in the manner of his surrealistic "Life in Hell" newspaper panels, were at first unfunny and intrusive. Things improved when Groening's buffers began concentrating on a grotesque bucktoothed family consisting of a short-tempered father, a beehive-haired mother, and three hyper children—foremost among them a repulsive brat of a son, whose haircut suggested that he'd stuck his head in the lawn mower. Gradually the cartoon sketches grew to be a benefit rather than a detriment to Tracey Ullman's variety weekly.

Sensing series potential, Fox urged Groening and *Ullman Show* producer James L. Brooks to expand the animated shorts into a half-hour weekly. Groening started the ball rolling by naming his cartoon family the Simpsons: The parents were dubbed Homer and Marge, and their daughters were christened Lisa and Maggie, names drawn from Groening's own parents and siblings. The central monsterson was named Bart, a character who insiders suggest represents the nihilistic aspects of Matt Groening's own personality. Voices for Homer and Marge were supplied by Dan Castellaneta and Julie Kavner, two supporting actors from Tracey Ullman's stock company. Fellow *Ullman Show* alumna Nancy Cartwright, an adult actress who specialized in children's voices, put the words in the mouth of 10-year-old Bart Simpson—including the soon-to-be-notorious catchphrases "Don't have a cow, man!," "Eat my shorts!," "Ay caramba!" and "I'm Bart Simpson: Who the hell are you?" Yeardley Smith, an actress who by 1991 would be doing double duty for Fox with a supporting part on the network's sitcom *Herman's Head*, portrayed eight-year-old Lisa. Maggie, the baby of the family, spoke not at all at first (nor could she have said much with that omnipresent pacifier jammed into her mouth), but in 1992 she mewled her first word, a punch line to a running gag, courtesy of an up and coming British actress by the name of Elizabeth Taylor.

James L. Brooks, with plenty of TV (*The Mary Tyler Moore Show*) and movie experience (*Terms of Endearment*) to his credit, gathered together Matt Groening's disparate elements and shaped them into coherence. There are those in Hollywood who have suggested that credit for all future *Simpsons* success was mainly due to Brooks' organizational and storytelling skills—skills that hadn't been that much evident in Groening's previous printed work, which consisted of scattershot immediate reaction gags. To build up Brooks' contribution at the expense of Groening is unfair (certainly Brooks would have had

nothing to work with without the artist's original conception), but it is true that *The Simpsons* was more consistently funny once the property stopped being a spotgag attraction and evolved into a "book" show.

Klasky-Csupo, a young cartoon firm later famous for *Rugrats* (q.v.), outbid several other companies—including Film Roman, reportedly Fox's first choice—to animate *The Simpsons* as a weekly half hour. The Simpson family's first full-fledged starring vehicle was a Christmas special, "Simpsons Roasting on an Open Fire," aired over Fox on December 17, 1989, priming enthusiastic audiences for the premiere of *The Simpsons* series proper on January 14, 1990. The special deliberately distorted an inherently sentimental story, wasting no time on pathos and introspection. The project's hallmark was speed, from the rapid fire editing to the laugh-per-second script and the waterbug movements of the principals.

Unfortunately, this momentum was not maintained for the premier *Simpsons* story, "Bart the Genius." All the episode had going for it were the apelike character designs and occasional "shock" gag. Otherwise, the lugubriously paced plotline, wherein Bart cheated his way into a school for gifted children, could have been done on any old live sitcom. Matt Groening has noted recently that *Simpsons* succeeded where other primetime cartoons of the 1990s failed (see *Capitol Critters*, *Family Dog* and *Fish Police*) because of the high quality of its writing. If so, this quality was manifested only after the writers stopped treating the Simpson family like the flesh and blood cast of *Roseanne* and started thinking of them as genuine *cartoon* characters.

The off-and-on quality of the first *Simpsons* season reflected not only problems on the writing staff but on the animation end as well. According to industry scuttlebutt, the animators started loading on heaps of "sick" humor and pointless throwaway gags because they felt the scripts weren't funny enough. Fox was so appalled by the results that the network ordered nearly 95 percent of the first season to be jettisoned and re-animated. Even after this, the network had qualms about the "censorable" material in *The Simpsons*—particularly Bart's vocabulary, which if anything reflected the way most 10-year-olds *really*

Bart Simpson in action; one of his sponsors was *not* Colgate.

talk—and attempted to whittle down the same cutting-edge humor that had sold them on the project in the first place.

But by the time the first season ended and the second began, all the winning elements began to jell. It became common knowledge that the Simpsons' home town of Springfield was a rundown community totally indebted to a faulty nuclear power plant run by Mr. Burns, a gnomish character who made Scrooge seem like Jimmy Stewart, where Homer "worked" as snoozing safety inspector. Wife Marge was a stay-at-home, except whenever venturing out into the community where she proved that, beyond her gravelly voice and Halloweenish appearance, she was fundamentally wiser and more decent than anyone else. Bart spent the majority of his time skateboarding past terrified pedestrians

and staying after school writing "I will not" punishments on the blackboard ("I will not belch the national anthem," "I will not yell 'she's dead' during roll call"—and, after an industry snub of *The Simpsons* went public, "I will never win an Emmy"). Lisa, a N.O.W. activist in the making, was the family's resident intellectual, whose chief form of expression was her saxophone. And baby Maggie's chief function in life was crawling around and requiring changes of wardrobe.

Subtle alterations over the first year made *The Simpsons* less of an outrageous freak attraction and more a welcome weekly visitor. The character design was softened from Matt Groening's "Quasimodo" approach, making the people simpler to draw as well as easier to watch. Homer Simpson, in the earliest episodes an "Archie Bunker" blowhard disciplinarian, developed into the quintessential couch potato, shaken from his ennui only when someone hid his pork rinds or lost the remote control. And Bart began to drop his catch-phrases the moment they became popular, as if perversely renouncing the commercialism of the lucrative Bart Simpson merchandising industry (T-shirts, dolls, balloons). In the self-mocking tradition established on *The Simpsons*, Bart converted his celebrity into a joke. While watching the Underdog balloon drift by during the televised Macy's Thanksgiving Parade, Bart complained about parade displays based on cartoon characters whose fame had long since deserted them—whereupon a Bart Simpson balloon bobbed down Fifth Avenue.

The *Simpsons* had scarcely signed on before the "clean-up-TV" predators began bearing down. On a surface level, there was a lot to complain about. Moralists weaned on "cute" cartoons were aghast that Homer and Marge were clearly enjoying an aggressive sex life. Educators were outraged that Bart declared himself "an underachiever—and proud of it." The Religious Right was incensed by the character of the Simpsons' next-door neighbor Ned Flanders, whose born-again Christianity went hand in hand with his overbearing personality and Peeping Tomism. The nuclear power industry was outraged that Homer spent most of his time napping on his job and that boss Mr. Burns was a scuzzbag who wasn't above coveting Homer's wife or kidnapping pop singer Tom Jones to provide free entertainment for an office party. Ethnic pride groups were insulted by the Simpsons' local convenience-store owner, a testy, barely coherent Third Worlder named Abu. And children's-television watchdogs were horrified by the character of Krusty the Clown, a TV host who snarled at his kiddie audience while shamelessly promoting his line of personality merchandise, and by the Simpson kids' favorite TV-cartoon characters, a homicidal cat and mouse team named Itchy and Scratchy.

Even viewers with no axes to grind had their Disney-nurtured sensibilities shattered by the series' mordant sense of humor. If someone fell off a building on *this* show, there was seldom any reassuring shot of the victim picking himself up unharmed. An expensive hospital stay was the kindest thing that happened to any accident prone character on *The Simpsons*.

After the initial shock to the senses had passed, viewers who stuck out the first year had to admit that there was more to *The Simpsons* than outrageousness. The misanthropy evident in the character concepts masked a potent understanding of human nature: In fact, the cast of *The Simpsons* were in their own way more "human" than the cast on most live action sitcoms. Mr. Burns, for example, was truly a creep, but he was motivated by a cynical mistrust of all humanity, and usually hurt himself more than anyone else. Marge Simpson was savvy to this when she was commissioned to paint a portrait of Burns to be displayed in the local art museum. Her depiction of Burns as a pathetic, shrivelled husk of a man elicited sympathy from a populace who previously had wholeheartedly hated Burns—who, in turn, enjoyed being pitied rather than feared.

In the same vein, most of the rest of the *Simpsons* characters were deeper than their stereotyped veneer. Abu the convenience-store man may have been all funny accent and misguided emotions, but he was a well-meaning and conscientious fellow, likable even when arresting Marge for shoplifting. And though Bible-thumping Ned Flanders was every agnostic's worst nightmare, he turned out to be the best friend Homer could ever have after rescuing the senior Simpson from a burning home.

As for the Simpsons themselves, we learned that Bart's underachiever status was due to a learning disability, that Homer's snack-stuffed body was capable of kicking him into middle age with a heart attack, and that Lisa's frequently irritating high-mindedness came in handy when saving Springfield from several corporate and ecological disasters. It was the sort of "reality check" that one would never have found on *The Flintstones*; just imagine Fred Flintstone in the E.R. ward with a coronary brought on by one too many bronto-burgers.

But in humanizing *The Simpsons*, the creators made certain we remembered that this was Fantasy Land, and that everyone would have forgotten any lesson he'd learned one week and be back to his old wayfaring ways the next. The scripters were emboldened at one point to have Bart Simpson inform his sister that they'd be back next week with another "wacky adventure" as though nothing had happened the previous week, then smile knowingly at the camera when a flashforward to the next episode proved him right. (The one surefire laugh-getter on *The Simpsons* was to satirize the conventions of TV situation comedy, usually with some pungent variation on the "everybody laughs at the end" cliché.)

The *Simpsons* got better and better as it rolled on. The comic focus shifted from Bart to the now more fascinating character of Homer Simpson, and thence past Homer and onto the ever-increasing Springfield supporting cast. When animation facilities moved from Klasky-Csupo to Film Roman in the third season (a result of labor problems at K-C), the animation became fuller and more consistent, while the character art, still ugly by prevailing standards, was less harshly delineated. By season three, with comedian Conan O'Brien and other top talents in the writing/producing pool, *Simpsons* was one of the best sitcoms of any kind, live or cartoon, as well as Fox's top-rated series. There was a density of visual and verbal wit unrivalled by almost any other animated program, even on those occasions when amortization required budgetary corner-cutting.

The beauty of *The Simpsons* was its ability to tickle and tease the cultural consciousness of its viewers, invoking pop-culture jokes which hit home for all age ranges, from baby boomer to grade-

Never steal Homer Simpson's pork rinds—especially the one with the hair cooked in it.

schooler. How many other cartoon shows have, within the space of a single calendar year, lambasted such targets as *Citizen Kane, A Streetcar Named Desire, One Flew Over the Cuckoo's Nest, Soylent Green,* the 1960 Kennedy-Nixon debates, hanky panky in the Kennedy family, Vice President Quayle's "family values" palaver, the L.A. riots, Andrew Lloyd Webber, Mason Williams' *Classical Gas,* Leonard Nimoy, the Fox Network's propensity toward raunchiness (let's bite our own hand here!), the bouncy but pointless 1930s cartoons of Ub Iwerks, the dismal avant garde East European animation of the 1960s, the deadline-meeting dilemmas of the cartoon series *Ren and Stimpy* (q.v.), the "repeated" background art on *The Flintstones* (q.v.), Johnny Carson's final *Tonight Show,* the "secret" of the film *The Crying Game,*

and that ubiquitous Spanish-language cable TV sitcom *Chesperito,* featuring the guy dressed in a bumblebee suit? (Puff-puff-puff.) *And,* how many other cartoon shows have done all this within the logical progressions of the storyline?

That's not as easy as it looks. Too many cartoons produced in *The Simpsons'* wake—*Cro* (q.v.) and *Problem Child* (q.v.) come to mind immediately—throw in "pop" jokes for the sake of a cheap laugh, and hang the storyline. Not so *The Simpsons.* After its first-season problems with mislaid non sequiturs, the scripters made sure that no so-called "throwaway" joke would show up unless it fit into the plot. The apotheosis of this technique was the 1992 episode in which the nuclear plant workers went on strike, despite all of Mr. Burns' underhanded scab tactics. Before we were aware it was happening, Burns began commenting on the workers' resilience in rhymed couplets. Suddenly the whole scene evolved into a parody of Dr. Seuss' *How the Grinch Stole Christmas*—and the central situation allowed this takeoff to grow naturally from the action, rather than being forced on it.

In the very same episode, we were treated to three parodies in rapid succession. The plotline had been sparked by Burns' veto of a dental plan—and of course, Lisa needed tooth work. In the inevitable dentist office scene, Lisa's dentist sounded like mass murderer Hannibal Lecter in *Silence of the Lambs*. Prior to oral surgery Lisa was knocked out by nitrous oxide, leading to a psychedelic dream right out of *Yellow Submarine*—complete with the Beatles. When Lisa woke up and wanted to see her braces, the staging was a direct steal (camera angles and all) from the Joker's "facial revelation" scene in *Batman: The Movie*. And it all *belonged*; no matter how "out of left field" the cultural reference, it was integral to the plotline.

The series invoked popular culture in a more direct manner by hiring celebrity voices, most of whom (such as the aforementioned Liz Taylor and Tom Jones) jumped at the opportunity of contributing to their favorite cartoon show. Part of the attraction is that voicework was (to those who didn't make a living at it) like stealing money. Boxer Joe Frazier, playing "himself," reacted to his *Simpsons* stint by noting "They called and said 'We got a paying job for you where you don't have to get hit.'" Even those who *did* subsist on their vocal chords had fun. Talk show host Larry King, who played the voice of God on the episode about Homer's heart attack, recalled "It's like doing radio. You get to work in jeans and T-shirt."

Unlike King, most celebrities portrayed themselves, partly out of amusement over how the animators caricatured them. "Actually, they made me look fairly good," observed Bob Hope. "Well, anyway, they made me look younger." Other actors took on *Simpsons* to let their hair down in non-characteristic roles: Oscar-nominated actress Michelle Pfeiffer played a nuclear plant co-worker of Homer's who could belch after downing a beer with the best of them.

Given that there was barely any money involved, the rich and famous guest voices on *Simpsons* did their bits as a sort of status symbol, in the manner of the "special guest villains" on the 1960s TV series *Batman*. To quote eminent psychologist Dr. Joyce Brothers: "There are three ne plus ultras in our culture: Being in the *New York Times* crossword puzzle, being on the cover of *Time*, and being a voice on *The Simpsons*."

As of this writing, the series is successfully pursuing its fourth season and landmark 100th episode. The writing had slackened a bit by 1993, leaning towards recycling what had worked in past episodes and pursuing too many gags beyond their worth. Nonetheless, for the most part *Simpsons'* comedy quotient was as sharp as ever, with definitely no letdown in commenting on mankind's ever expanding cultural-reference catalogue: Before the season was half over, we were treated to full-episode lampoons of *Cape Fear*, The Beatles' *Let It Be*, *Thelma and Louise* and *The Pink Panther*—not to mention passing gibes at *It's a Mad Mad Mad Mad World*, self-awareness groups, and (once again, but further developed this time around) Bart Simpson's "notoriety" brought on by his many catch-phrases.

Could anybody complain about *Simpsons* at this point? Tracey Ullman did. Insisting that *The Simpsons* was developed on her series and that it was she, not James L. Brooks, who had faith in the property's chances at a series, she sued the cartoon producers and the Fox network for several million dollars and a piece of the merchandising. And Julie Kavner, the voice of Marge Simpson, expressed disappointment that *The Simpsons'* new writers (replacing the old team, which had moved on to the 1994 prime-time cartoon series *The Critic*) had moved away from concentrating exclusively on the starring family. I could say "Don't have a cow, Julie." But I'm a grownup.

The *Simpsons* was much more than a Thursday night tradition by the end of 1993. In proving that TV animation could successfully challenge the boundaries of censorship and "good taste," and still manage to create enduring individual characters and to entertain the widest demographic age group ever to watch a nighttime cartoon since *The Flintstones*, *The Simpsons* opened the doors for the many risk-taking animated television series of the 1990s: *Ren and Stimpy* (q.v.), *Bat-*

man: The Animated Series (q.v.), *Liquid Television* (q.v.), and—for better or worse, as the cliché goes—*Beavis and Butt-Head* (q.v.).

SINBAD JR. Syndicated: 1965. Hanna-Barbera/American-International Television. Voices: Tim Matthieson (Sinbad Junior); Mel Blanc (Salty).

Despite previously published reports, the 100 five-minute *Sinbad Jr.* cartoons were not components of CBS' *The Alvin Show* (q.v.), though some markets ran *Sinbad* in conjunction with syndicated *Alvin* reruns. In the tradition of Hollywood's laundering process, Sinbad Jr. was not the pirate of legend, but an honest seaman who drew super strength from his magic belt. The lead character was a bit of a stick, so it was up to voice actor Mel Blanc to provide the best dialogue as Salty the parrot. Produced by Hanna-Barbera, *Sinbad Jr.* was a rare TV syndication release from American-International Pictures, better known for its Roger Corman–directed Edgar Allan Poe films and *Beach Party* flicks.

Another *Sinbad Jr.* from a different producer had been slated for 1960 release by the Trans-Artists company (see *Bucky and Pepito* and *Courageous Cat*), but apparently never got past the pilot-film stage.

THE SKATEBIRDS. CBS: 9/10/1977–1/21/1978; 9/1979–8/1980; 9/1980–1/25/1981.
—**THE THREE ROBONIC STOOGES.** CBS: 1/28/1978–9/6/1981. Hanna-Barbera. Executive producers, Joseph Barbera and William Hanna. Producer, "Mystery Island": Terry Morse Jr. Animation director, Charles A. Nichols. Live-action directors, Sidney Miller and Hollingsworth Morse. "Robonic Stooges" sequences written by Norman Maurer. Music by Hoyt Curtin. COMPONENTS (Animated): 1. **THE ROBONIC STOOGES / THREE ROBONIC STOOGES.** Voices: Paul Winchell (Moe); Frank Welker (Curly); Joe Baker (Larry); Ross Martin (Triple-Zero). 2. **WOOFER AND WIMPER, DOG DETECTIVES.** Voices: *See* CLUE CLUB. 3. **WONDER WHEELS.** Voices: Micky Dolenz (Willie Sheeler); Susan Davis (Dooley Lawrence). COMPONENTS (Live Action): 1. **THE SKATEBIRDS.** Voices: Don Messick (Scooter); Bob Holt (Satchel); Lennie Weinrib (Knock Knock); Scatman Cro-

thers (Scat Cat). 2. **MYSTERY ISLAND.** Cast: Stephen Parr (Chuck Kelly); Lynn Marie Johnston (Sue Corwin); Larry Volk (Sandy Corwin); Michael Kermoyan (Dr. Strange); Frank Welker (Voice of P.A.U.P.S.).

Skatebirds was a 1977 hour-long bid to revive the *Banana Splits* (q.v.) format of costumed actors' hosting cartoons, with one live-action adventure component thrown into the package. The newer series, linked with the skateboarding craze of the era, was hosted by several people in animal costume. The characters portrayed were Scooter Penguin, Satchel Pelican, Scat Cat and Knock Knock the Woodpecker (an animator's inside joke—the first *Woody Woodpecker* cartoon, filmed in 1941, was titled *Knock Knock*). To avoid the trap *Banana Splits* had fallen into, that of filming too many live sequences in front of the same backgrounds and thus leading viewers to conclude that they were watching nothing but reruns, the Skatebirds were filmed in a wide variety of theme-park locations.

The series' live-action component was "Mystery Island," a virtual replay of *Banana Splits*' "Danger Island," with the protagonists crash-landing on a Pacific isle rather than being shipwrecked by pirates. The young leads were scientists Chuck Kelly and Sue and Sandy Corwin, while the appropriately named Dr. Strange was the villain. An all-purpose robot, P.A.U.P.S. (sometimes spelled P.O.P.S.), was being airfreighted by the heroes in episode one. Strange required the robot for his world conquest agenda, so he forced Chuck, Sue and Sandy to crash land. Much too conventional in approach, "Mystery Island" perhaps could have used the improvisational guidance of "Danger Island" director Richard Donner.

Now to the cartoon components: *Wonder Wheels* was in the tradition of H-B's *Speed Buggy* (q.v.) (itself a reshuffling of the most workable elements of the Disney film *The Love Bug*): A speed-daffy motorcycle with a human personality helped teenaged journalist Willie solve crimes. *Woofer and Wimper, Dog Detectives*, were selected reruns from Hanna-Barbera's networker *Clue Club* (q.v.). And then there were *The Robonic Stooges*.

This last-named component is a fair indication of what might have happened if the live-action Three Stooges' perennial director Jules White, and not Glen Larson, had produced the 1970s adventure series *The Six Million Dollar Man*. Larry, Moe and Curly, more appealingly designed than they'd been in the 1965 cartoon syndie *The New Three Stooges* (q.v.), augmented their traditional poking, slapping and nose-tweaking with newly installed robonic, stretchable arms, legs and eyes. The Robonic Stooges were secret agents who answered to Triple-Zero (voiced by *Wild Wild West* costar Ross Martin), applying their roughhouse tactics on behalf of national security. Story material ranged from modernistic to legendary, with the Tempestuous Trio mixed up with everyone from Goldfingerlike master spies to the Giant of the Beanstalk. The whole affair was overseen by Norman Maurer, who was senior stooge Moe Howard's son-in-law and a highly respected cartoonist in his own right. "Robonic Stooges" represented a springback from an earlier, rejected Maurer cartoon proposal, "Super Stooges."

Conspicuously missing were the original Stooges' voices: Moe Howard and Larry Fine had both been gathered to the Big Pie Fight in the Sky in 1975, while Curly Joe DeRita was retired save for a few appearances at fan conventions (no matter, since the "Curly" on "Robonic Stooges" was based on the *real* one, the immortal Curly Howard). Voice artists Frank Welker, Paul Winchell and Joe Baker upheld the grand "Nyuk nyuk," "Spread Out!" and "I'm sorry, Moe, it was an accident!" tradition as Curly, Moe and Larry.

According to Stooge historians Jeff and Greg Lenburg, the initial ratings of *The Skatebirds* indicated a ho-hum audience reaction to most of the components, with the spectacular exception of "The Robonic Stooges." As a result, the 32 five-minute "Robonic" installments were spun off into their own half hour weekly in 1978, *The Three Robonic Stooges* (with *Woofer and Wimper* along for the ride). This revamped version was networkcast until the last week of 1979.

Reaction was swift and brutal from adults, who'd never liked the Stooges anyway (until it became fashionable to do so in the nostalgically inclined 1990s). "Terrible! A waste of any child's time!" was the predictable condemnation from a panel of professorial know-alls assembled by *TV Guide* in 1980. But *The Three*

Robonic Stooges persevered, enjoying a hearty rerun afterlife in international distribution, while the rest of the original *Skatebirds* plodded along in Sunday-morning network reruns before languishing in Cartoon Limbo.

SKY COMMANDERS. Syndicated: 1987. Kenner Toys/Hanna-Barbera. Executive producers, William Hanna and Joseph Barbera. Voices: Bob Ridgely (Mike Summit); William Windom (Cutter Kling); Darryl Hickman (R. J. Scott); Lauren Tewes (Red McCullough); Bernard Erhard (General Plague); Richard Boyle (Books Baxter); Dorian Harewood (Jim Stryker); Tristan Rogers (Spider Reilly); Dick Gautier (Mordax); Paul Eiding (Raider Rath); Charlie Adler (Kreeg); B. J. Ward (Dr. Erica Slade).

In 1987, the two-hour weekend omnibus *Funtastic World of Hanna-Barbera* (q.v.) consisted of *Yogi's Treasure Hunt* (see *Yogi Bear*), reruns of *Jonny Quest* (q.v.) and *The Snorks* (q.v.), and a new commodity, *Sky Commanders*, which can best be redubbed *Stars Wars Yet Once More*. Back we went to outer space, this time in the company of Sky Commander leader Mike Summit and his band of renegades, who manned their 21st century space vehicles to thwart another omnipotent villain, General Plague of the High Frontier.

Kenner Toys coproduced *Sky Commanders*, and we'll assume the reader is intelligent enough to comprehend the merchandising significance of this fact. In this instance, the toys came first.

SKY HAWKS. ABC: 9/6/1969–9/4/1971. Ken Snyder Productions/Pantomime Pictures. Executive producer, Ken Snyder. Produced by Paul Shively, Jean Lindsay, Charles Phalen, Dick Reed, Fred Crippen and Ed Smarden. Directed by George Singer, Fred Crippen, Joe Bruno, Irv Spector. Written by Tony Asher, Larry Thor, Peter Dixon. Music by Jack Fascinato. Theme song performed by Mike Curb and the Curbstones. Voices: Michael Rye (Mike Wilson); Iris Rainer (Carolyn Wilson); Casey Kasem (Steve Wilson/Joe Conway); Dick Curtis (Pappy/Red); Melinda Casey (Cynthia); Joan Gerber (Maggie); Bob Arbogast (Devlin).

Like Ken Snyder's other "straight" cartoon series of 1969, *Hot Wheels* (q.v.), *Sky Hawks* was tied in with a line of Mattel

Toys (though in keeping with then-current network policy, those toys were not advertised during *Sky Hawks* itself). The series drew its title from an air transport/rescue/secret-mission service run by the multigenerational Wilson family. Mike "Cap" Wilson, head of Sky Hawks Inc., had been a World War 2 air force colonel, while Pappy Wilson was a World War I ace. Somehow the youngsters of the group, Steve and Carolyn Wilson and Pappy's foster kids Red and Cynthia Hughes, managed to avoid Korea and Vietnam. Maggie McNally was Cap Wilson's girlfriend, no slouch in the cockpit herself. In keeping with *Hot Wheels* tradition, the Wilson clan espoused safe aviation practices in their weekly adventures (two per half hour), which was more than could be said for Sky Hawks Inc.'s principal rival Buck Devlin.

There was little attempt to insert humor into the 17-episode *Sky Hawks*, since it was designed as ABC's sober-sided "answer" to CBS's slapsticky *Dastardly and Muttley and Their Flying Machines*. It was also supposed to be ABC's counterprogramming ammunition against its network timeslot opponents *The Archies* (q.v.) and *Banana Splits* (q.v.), both of which stressed comedy. Since the fate of *Sky Hawks* was dictated by Mattel and not by the ratings, the series graduated to a second (all-rerun) season in 1970, still offering a stylistic alternative to the more comedic servings on the other networks: the *Archies* again on CBS, *Here Comes the Grump* (q.v.) on NBC.

SLIMER! AND THE REAL GHOST-BUSTERS *see* **THE REAL GHOST-BUSTERS**

THE SMOKEY BEAR SHOW. ABC: 9/9/1969–9/5/1970; 9/13/1970–9/12/1971 (reruns). Rankin-Bass/Videocraft. Production facilities: Toei Productions. Music by Maury Laws. Voices: Jackson Weaver (Smokey); and Billie Richards, Paul Soles, and Carl Banas.

Smokey Bear, the ranger-hatted mascot bruin of the Department of Agriculture's Forest Service, had his roots in wartime propaganda. During World War II, a Japanese submarine managed to shell a wooded area in Southern California, sparking threats of a forest fire. The Forest Service immediately drew up plans for a fire-prevention campaign, along the lines of local Civil Defense units, as a means of convincing the "home front" that it was aiding the war effort by avoiding woodland conflagrations. When the campaign swung into action in 1944, it was decided that an animal mascot was needed to publicize the effort. The original mascot was Walt Disney's Bambi (there had, after all, been a spectacular forest fire in the Disney cartoon feature based on Felix Salter's deer protagonist), but the character's licensing costs proved prohibitive. Jim Felton, of the Cone and Belding ad agency, developed Smokey Bear, a character based on an actual bear cub who'd been rescued from a fire and raised by forest rangers. Artist Albert Staehle designed the humanized "Smokey," who soon found his likeness popping up on trees, bulletin boards and magazine ads everywhere, together with his motto "Remember. Only *you* can prevent forest fires."

Throughout the 1950s and 1960s, Smokey's animated cartoon appearances were confined to a series of fondly remembered TV public service announcements, which costarred a safety-savvy little boy and were narrated by Marvin Miller. These were animated by Disney staffers, who also managed to sneak Smokey into an unbilled cameo in the Disney "Humphrey the Bear" cartoon *In the Bag* (1956). In addition, Smokey appeared in a strange series of Dell comic books from 1955 through 1961, costarring with Smokey Bear Jr. and several comic-relief talking animals. This series was one of the most morbid in all Dell history, concentrating on truly nasty forest despoilers and plunderers, all portrayed by anthropomorphized animals. In one adventure, the forest is threatened by two Communist spies, both bears, one of whom meets a horrible death; in another, a pair of cynical weasel photojournalists decide to feed a baby bird to a wildcat in order to stage a "tragic" photo that will bring big bucks from their magazine.

Many of these grim comic book scenarios were adapted for television's *The Smokey Bear Show*, a weekly half hour which debuted on ABC in 1969. Thankfully, Rankin-Bass studios toned down some of the darker aspects of the plots, pumped up the comedy content, and improved upon the repellant animal caricatures in the comic book. But the unpleasant aftertaste remained, and *The Smokey Bear Show*, despite its jovial theme song, built-in safety tips, and 8:30 A.M. Saturday time slot, was not altogether suitable for the small children for which it was intended. The series lasted 17 episodes, which were regularly torched in the ratings by two oldtimers: CBS' *Bugs Bunny/Road Runner* (see *The Bugs Bunny Show*) and NBC's *Heckle and Jeckle* (see *Mighty Mouse*).

THE SMURFS. NBC: 9/12/1981–8/25/1990. Syndicated (reruns retitled THE SMURFS' ADVENTURES): 1986. Hanna-Barbera/Sepp International S.A. Executive producers, William Hanna, Joseph Barbera. Executives in charge of production, Jayne Barbera, Jean MacCurdy. Producer/story editor, Gerald Baldwin. Created by Peyo (Pierre Culliford). Written by Gerald Baldwin, Peyo, Yvan Delporte, Len Janson, Chuck Menville, among others. Animation supervisor, Jay Sarbry. Music editors, Cecil Broughton, Daniele McLean, Terry Moore, Joe Sandusky. Voices: Don Messick (Papa Smurf/Azrael/Dreamy/Sleepy/others); Lucille Bliss (Smurfette); Danny Goldman (Brainy); Frank Welker (Hefty/Poet/Peewit/Clockwork/Puppy); June Foray (Jokey/Mother Nature); Michael Bell (Lazy/Handy/Grouchy/Johan); Hamilton Camp (Greedy/Harmony); Paul Winchell (Gargamel/Nosey/Baby/others); Brenda Vaccaro (Scruple); Jonathan Winters (Grandpa); Bill Callaway (Clumsy/Painter); Alan Oppenheimer (Vanity/Hominbus); Bob Holt (King); Linda Gary (Dame Barbara); Marshall Efron (Sloppy); Alan Young (Scaredy/Farmer); Julie Dees (Baby/Sasette); Susan Blu (Nanny); Pat Musick (Snappy); Charlie Adler (Nat); Noelle North (Slouchy); Paul Kirby, Kris Stevens (Narrators); and Arte Johnson, Avery Schreiber, Janet Waldo, Jack Angel, Ed Begley Jr., Walker Edmiston, Leo De-Lyon, Peter Cullen, William Christopher, Russi Taylor, Phil Proctor, B. J. Ward, John Stephenson, Phil Hartman, Michael Rye, Bob Ridgely, Rene Auberjonois, Tress MacNeille, Alexandra Stoddart, Bob Arbogast, Sidney Miller, Dick Erdman, Ronnie Schell, Marvin Kaplan, Les Tremayne, Susan Tolsky, Paul Riding, Clare Peck, Bernard Ehrhard, Henry Polic II, Allan Melvin, Jennifer Darling, Vic Perrin, Peggy Walton Walker, Fred Travalena,

Bob Holt, Selette Cole, Roger C. Carmel, Norma McMillan, Peter Brooks, Henry Corden, Sorrell Booke, Ray Walston, Michael Lembeck, Edie McClurg, Lynnanne Zager, Susan Silo, Henry Gibson, Ruth Buzzi, Pat Fraley, Joey Camden, Bernard Behrens, Patti Parris, Mimi Seton, Richard Dysart, Lewis Arquette, Neil Ross, Keene Curtis, Patti Deutsch, Dick Gautier, Joe Ruskin, Amanda McBroom, Barry Gordon, Cindy McGee, Bever-Leigh Banfield, Peggy Webber, Francine Wilkin, Gregg Berger, Zale Kessler, Victoria Carroll, Andre Stojka, Diane Pershing, Marilyn Schreffler, Dee Stratton, Marlene Aragon, Joy Grdnic, Kath Soucie, Mary Jo Catlett, Allen Lurie, Joe Medalis, Tandy Cronyn, Ruta Lee, Patty Maloney, Justin Gocke, William Schallert, Jess Doucette, Aron Kincaid, Jerry Houser, John Ingle, and Will Ryan.

Using the pen name "Peyo," Belgian magazine artist and onetime animation studio employee Pierre Culliford created the medieval comic-book character *Johan* in 1947. Peyo went on to work for the Brussels-based comic weekly *Spirou*, where he revamped Johan as *Johan et Pirlouit*, saddling his hero with a funny sidekick. Ten years into this project, Peyo introduced a batallion of background supporting characters: the tiny, blue, elflike "Schtroumpfs," their collective name a slang word for "Watchamaycallit," based upon an inside joke shared by Peyo and fellow *Spirou* artist Andre Franquin (see *Marsupilami*). The "three apples tall" Schtroumpfs gradually developed their own following, and in 1960 graduated to their own separate *Spirou* feature. Though drawn in 1950s modernist fashion, the mushroom-dwelling Schtroumpfs were very much geared to ancient European "little people" legends, while the storylines were full of typical Euro-threats like would-be charismatic dictators, pirates and foreign invaders.

Peyo was fond of explaining that he picked blue as the Schtroumpfs' skin hue because it was "a child's color"; he'd already vetoed yellow, which made him think of illness, and red, which to Peyo represented war and death. The artist's instincts were evidently on target, as witness the international popularity of the Schtroumpfs. Like Mickey Mouse before them, the characters were christened with different names in different countries:

A Smurf, ushering in nine years of NBC solvency.

Strunfs in Brazil, Lah-Shin-Lings in China, and Smurfies, or Smurfs, in English-speaking countries. Even with this first burst of success, Peyo was inclined to dismiss his creations: "Three years from now, no one will think of them anymore."

Nine *Schtroumpfs* theatrical animated cartoons (bearing such titles as *Le Voleur de Schtroumpf*, *Les Schtroumpfs Noir* and *Schtroumpf et le Dragon*) were produced in Belgium between 1960 and 1966 by Eddy Ryssack and Maurice Rosy, with Peyo exerting creative control. A cartoon feature, *V'la les Schtroumpfs*, was produced by Studios Belvision in the late 1970s, with Johan and Pirlouit (renamed Peewit) retaining star status, and the Schtroumpfs in support. None of these cartoons were distributed to the United States upon their initial release; the American reputation of the Schtroumpfs as it was, rested upon the "Smurf" toys licensed in the U.S. throughout the 1970s.

Enter NBC network head man Fred Silverman, who became interested when he saw his daughter playing with Smurf dolls in 1979. The executive's fabled "Golden Gut" was exercising its instinctual prerogative: Silverman sensed something BIG in the Smurfs, and he was desperately in need of something REALLY BIG for Saturday mornings in 1981—something to keep the NBC vice presidents from

obliterating the network's failing cartoon schedule in favor of expanding its early-morning *Today Show* to weekends. Silverman told his favorite cartoon firm Hanna-Barbera that they'd have a firm Saturday-morning commitment once they'd secured TV rights for the Smurfs.

With Peyo still wielding the mighty sword/pen of creative supervision, the artist collaborated with Hanna-Barbera and Belgium's Sepp International in working up a weekly, half-hour *Smurfs* series, bowing to merchandising dictates by introducing a female "Smurfette" to the previously boys-only fraternity, the better to appeal to little girl toy consumers. The cartoon studio then launched its most elaborate project in years, swiftly Hanna-Barberizing the Smurfs by commissioning a jolly introductory song ("La, La, La, La-la-la-lahhhh") and personalizing the otherwise lookalike leading characters. Under the patronization of "Papa Smurf" (the "Grand Schtroumpf" in the Peyo original), the various Smurfs all had distinct personalities, their character traits (in *Snow White* tradition) encapsulated by their names: Dreamy, Vanity, Grouchy, Brainy, Hefty, Poet, Greedy, Nosey, on and on and on.

But we were still on Hanna-Barbera turf, and the company had learned from long past experience that it was less expensive to hire different voice artists to differentiate the characters than it was to create a new, time-consuming character design for each Smurf. Gordon Clark, who worked as a Hanna-Barbera animator before moving on to more aesthetically satisfying projects with the Industrial Light & Magic special-effects firm (and later to the avant-garde excesses of MTV's *Liquid Television* [q.v.]), would recall fondly in the early 1990s that *The Smurfs* was a breeze of an assignment: "All the characters look alike. They just wear different hats." As a break from the drawing-board monotony, the artists seemed to revel in bringing to life the decidedly non–Smurflike villain of the piece, wicked wizard Gargamel. Still, even Gargamel seemed to function within a Hanna-Barbera mindset: when creating the "Smurfette" for the original intention of luring the taste-tempting Smurfs into his stewpot, Gargamel could do no better than to come up with a Smurf in a skirt.

That the characters may have been

cookie-cutter bothered the audience not one scintilla: *The Smurfs* was an instant hit, garnering the highest ratings of any NBC Saturday morning show in 11 years. Scrapping its weekend-news plans, NBC built its whole Saturday kiddie-TV schedule around *The Smurfs.* In 1982, the series was expanded to 90 minutes; Peyo's original stars Johan and Pee Wee (formerly Peewit, formerly Pirlouit) were added in component cartoons, but never gained the U.S. popularity of the Smurfs. Keeping the lines of demarcation drawn, the series' "big" humans existed only in relation to the cruel real world, and could visit Smurf Village only when guided in by the Smurfs themselves (just as the normal-sized home viewers were being lured to Saturday mornings).

In 1983, *Smurfs* was back to 60 minutes. Keeping the program fresh and avoiding as many reruns as possible, the producers introduced a handful of new characters, principally Baby Smurf (who like his "ageless" village elders would remain a baby at least four centuries), perhaps as a marketing reaction to 1983's top-selling Cabbage Patch Kids. Also making her *Smurfs* debut was one of TV cartoondom's first handicapped characters, hearing impaired wood elf Laconia—a full decade before Disney Animation Studios congratulated itself for introducing a "pioneering" deaf character on *The Little Mermaid* (q.v.). On to 1984: NBC's number one Saturday show inspired the belated release of the Belgian feature cartoon *V'la les Schtroumpfs,* retitled *Smurfs and the Magic Flute,* distributed by Atlantic Releasing Company and voiced mostly by Canadian talent.

As a means of getting more "kid" characters in the show, several grownup Smurfs fell into Father Time's "Backward Clock" in 1985 and became Smurflings. Along the way, another female character was introduced, a balm to feminists who'd taken to newsprint bemoaning the overall paucity of distaff characters on *Smurfs* (Excuse me, ma'am, but there must be more significant fish to fry than children's programs).

Reruns of the first five seasons entered daily, off-network syndication in 1986 as *The Smurfs' Adventures,* where thanks to the lack of network license fees the series made more money than ever before. Also in 1986, Gargamel, having carried on his villainy virtually solo in past seasons (save for his pet "hen-cat" Azriel), was given a clumsy assistant, wizard-school dropout Scruple. And *also* in 1986, Jonathan Winters, as Grandpa Smurf, joined the network series' enormous voice cast. Sidenote: In discussing 1992's star-studded *Batman: The Animated Series* (q.v.), Warner Bros. voice-casting director Andrea Romano noted, "Over the years I've had contact with a lot of different celebrities who have said to me that they wanted to do animation, but they didn't want to do *Smurfs.*" If this is the case, then such stellar *Smurfs* talent as Jonathan Winters, Ed Begley Jr., Rene Auberjonois, Tandy Cronyn, Sorrell Booke and Ray Walston — to name but a few—just wouldn't have measured up to *Batman*'s Snob Brigade. (P.S.: Ed Begley Jr. did both *Smurfs* and *Batman.* Does that make him a part-time snob?)

Taking into consideration the series' success in daily syndie reruns, Hanna-Barbera continued producing new *Smurfs* episodes (some 12-minute, some 30-minute) into the program's eighth and ninth seasons. As late as 1988, the series was introducing fresh new characters like Nancy Smurf and the wizard Nemesis. And for their last first-run season in 1989, the Smurfs left their cloistered community to make round-the-world journeys and backward-forward time trips.

Defining any popular cartoon series' appeal is not easy, since the very elements that many people love in a program are the selfsame things that others wholeheartedly despise. Certainly this was true in the case of *Smurfs.* For every viewer that doted on the series' assembly-line character design, syrupy storybook ambience, overdoses of the color blue, and that omnipresent "Smurfspeak" ("Have a smurfy day," "I'm going to smurf down to the store," and so forth), there was another viewer to whom the very name "Smurf" was just cause for a hasty retreat back under the covers on Saturday morning.

On the whole, the television industry looked beyond criticism, bestowing one award after another on *The Smurfs.* The series won Emmies in 1982 and 1983 as "Outstanding Children's Entertainment Series." Also toting up honors were the many prime-time *Smurfs* specials. *The Smurfs Springtime Special* (1982) won the Bronze Award for Best Children's Special at the International Film Festival; so did 1984's *The Smurfic Games.*

The best evidence of *The Smurfs'* impact on the TV world were the many imitation *Smurfs* clotting the airwaves throughout the 1980s: *The Littles, Litt'l Bits, Monchichis, Pac-Man, Shirt Tales, The Snorks, The Wuzzles* (see individual entries on these series). As late as 1993, a year in which *The Smurfs* was confined to cable-TV reruns, a Smurflike village full of pointy-eared humanoids was the focal point of Calico/Zodiac's *Twinkle, The Dream Being* (q.v.).

In 1990, *The Smurfs* was cancelled by NBC, a victim of attrition and the upsurge in cartoons based on videogames. Two years later, a *Smurf*-less NBC, having ridden high on the smurftails of the series for nearly a decade, fell back on its original 1981 plan and cancelled all its Saturday cartoon programs in favor of an expanded *Today Show.* In piquant coincidence, the NBC cartoon lineup was not the only 1992 casualty. Pierre "Peyo" Culliford died that same year, on Christmas Eve.

SNAGGLEPUSS *see* **YOGI BEAR**

SNEEZLY AND BREEZLY *see* **PETER POTAMUS**

SNIP SNAP. Syndicated: 1961. Halas and Batchelor/Interstate Films.

Released in the U.S. simultaneously with the same British studio's *Foo Foo* (q.v.), Halas-Batchelor's *Snip Snap* was a stop-motion animation property about a paper dog and a pair of scissors. In each of the 18 episodes, the scissors, named "Snip," would cut "Snap" out of a sheet of newspaper, then join the ersatz pooch in his tabletop adventures (26 episodes of this project were originally released in Britain under the title *Snip the Magic Scissors,* co-starring *three* dogs: Snap, Snarl and Sniff). The plotlines, to put it mildly, were incomprehensible, and since they were played out in pantomime, there was no voice to explain to us what the hey was going on. The episodes always ended with Snap winking at the audience, satisfied no doubt at having thoroughly confounded us for the past six minutes.

SNOOPER AND BLABBER *see* **QUICK DRAW McGRAW**

THE SNORKS. NBC: 9/15/1984–9/3/1988. Syndicated: 1989 (*see* FUNTASTIC WORLD OF HANNA-BARBERA). Hanna-Barbera/Sepp SA. Executive producers: Joseph Barbera, William Hanna and Freddy Monnickendam. Executives in charge of production: Jayne Barbera, Jean MacCurdy. Creative producer, Iwao Takamoto. Produced by Gerald Baldwin; associate producer, Larry Latham. Created by Freddy Monnickendam. Supervising director, Ray Patterson. Directed by Carl Urbano; assistant directors, Bob Goe, Don Lusk and Bob Patterson. Story editor, John Bradford. Art director, Bob Singer. Animation supervisor, Sean Newton. Music by Hoyt Curtin. Music director, Paul DeKorte. International promotion, Joop Visch. Voices: Michael Bell (Allstar/Elder 4); Frank Welker (Tooter/Occy); Brian Cummings (Dimmy); Frank Nelson (Gov. Wetworth); Barry Gordon (Junior Wetworth); B. J. Ward (Casey); Joan Gardner (Mrs. Wetworth); Nancy Cartwright (Daffney); Edie McClurg (Mrs. Seaworthy); Clive Revill (Galeo); Peter Cullen (Elders 1, 2, 3); Gail Matthius (Baby Smallstar); Fredricka "Freddie" Weber (Willie); Bob Holt (Mr. Seaworthy); Mitzi McCall (Auntie Marina); Joan Gerber (Mrs. Kelp); Bob Ridgely (Mr. Kelp).

Question: what cartoon series was based on a Belgian comic book, in which the leading characters used their names as adjectives in every other sentence? The answer: *The Smurfs,* with the principals bandying about phrases about "smurfy" this and "smurfy" that. Yes, that's what first comes to mind for most of us—and that's what Hanna-Barbera and Sepp International were banking on with their 1984 *Smurfs* derivation, *The Snorks.*

Created by Freddy Monnickendam (see also *Foofur*), the weekly half hour *Snorks* was founded on the notion that in 1643, a merchant ship was sunk by pirates, but an airpocket in one of the cabins rescued the captain. While submerged, the captain witnessed the spectacle of a microscopic underwater civilization, populated by strange, tiny creatures who seemed human save for their fishlike facial features and the snorkels emanating from their heads. Once rescued, the captain spread his tale of "Snorks" no bigger than his thumb to a skeptical world—while in a parallel situation, the Snorks' Uncle Galeo perpetrated the legend of gigantic, oddly shaped alien surface dwellers (living in "Dry Space") who might pose a threat to his species' wellbeing.

After this was established in the "teaser," viewers were swept to the 20th century, a time in which the Snorks had developed their culture on a level comparable to mankind's in the 1980s. The Snorks enjoyed split-level homes, a progressive school system, movies, fast-food restaurants serving "kelp-burgers," amusement parks, and so on. The *Snorks* centered on high schooler Allstar, his girlfriend Casey, and his best pals Dimmy (male), Daffney (female), and Tooter, who spoke only in flutelike sound effects. Their particular nemesis was Junior Wetworth, snotty son of Snorkland's pompous mayor. This being an underwater Hanna-Barbera item, Allstar possessed a funny pet, an octopus named Occy (*you'd* name him Rover?). And as mentioned in the first paragraph, the word "snork" was affixed to practically everything: "Have a snorky day," a state called South Snorkolina, and movies with titles like "Snorkbusters."

The plotlines on *Snorks* were waterlogged by standard sitcom trappings (some stories rehashed Hanna-Barbera's earlier *The Flintstones*), inevitably leading to a moral lesson at plot's end that could have just as effectively been adapted to any old environment, wet or dry. Still, the series was well drafted and animated in the tradition of *Smurfs*, often surpassing that earlier program. The underwater "smear" so prevalent on Hanna-Barbera's earlier *Moby Dick* (q.v.) was handled quite well to convey the deep-sea ambience of *Snorks*, not so much during the episodes themselves as in the rippling optical wipe-dissolves from one scene to another. The best stylistic choice was one of dramatic contrast: The Snorks were drawn in a traditional cartoony manner, while the "Dry Space" humans and non-Snork sea life were illustrated in a realistic fashion.

After three seasons of cruising through NBC's shipping channels, *The Snorks* entered daily syndication with a combination of repeats and new episodes, some running 12 minutes, others the full 30. In 1990, all existing *Snorks* were netted together as a component of *The Funtastic World of Hanna-Barbera* (q.v.).

SNUFFY SMITH *see* KING FEATURES TRILOGY

SONIC THE HEDGEHOG:

—ADVENTURES OF SONIC THE HEDGEHOG. Syndicated: 1993. Sega of America Inc./DIC Enterprises/Bohbot. Executive producers, Andy Heyward and Robby London. Executive in charge of production, Brian A. Miller. Executive in charge for Bohbot, Allen J. Bohbot. Produced and directed by Kent Butterworth. Production supervisor, Stacy Gallishaw. Story editors, Reed and Bruce Shelley. Developed for TV by Reed and Bruce Shelley, Phil Harnage and Kent Butterworth. Written by Reed and Bruce Shelley and Jeffrey Scott. "Sonic Says" segments written by Kevin Donahue and Phil Harnage. Main title theme by Clark Gassman. Music score by Reed Robbins, Mark Simon. Musical supervision, Joanne Miller. Animation facilities: Rainbow Animation, Hong Ying Animation, Sae Rom Production Co., Ltd., Tokyo Movie Shinsha Co. Ltd. Voices: Jaleel White (Sonic); and Long John Baldry, Gary Chalk, Ian James Corlett, Phil Hayes, Christopher Welch, Kathleen Barr, Michael Benyaer, Jay Brazeau, Jim Byrnes, Babz Chula, Jennifer Copping, Mike Donovan, Terry Klassen, Wally March, Scott McNeil, Shane Meier, Jane Mortifee, Paula Newstone, John Stocker, Jayleen Stonehouse, Venus Terzo, French Tickner, Lee Tocker, Louise Vallance, Dave Ward, Cathy Weseluck, Alec Williams, Dale Wilson, Kyle Fairlie, and John Tench.

— SONIC THE HEDGEHOG. Weekly ABC: 9/18/1993–. DIC Animation City/ Sega of America. Executive producers, Andy Heyward and Robby London. Produced and directed by Dick Sebast. Executive in charge of production, Brian A. Miller. Production supervisors, Stacy Gallishaw and RaNae Bonella. Voice director, Virginia K. McSwain. Associate producer, Antran Manoogian. Script coordinator, Lori Crawford. Music by Michael Tavera. Main title theme performed by Noisy Neighbors. Music supervision, Joanne Miller. Animation facilities: Sae Rom and Millimetros Dibujos Animatos. Overseas supervisor, Doug Williams. Character names licensed from Sega of America, Inc. Voices: Jaleel White (Sonic), Kath Soucie (Sally); and Charlie Adler, Mark Ballou, Christine Cavanaugh, Jim Cummings, Rob Paulsen, Bradley Pierce, David Doyce, Gailee Heideman, Dana Hill, Danny Mann, Jason Marsden, Charlie

Schlatter, Frank Welker, and William Windom.

Sonic, the roundheaded, wicked-eyed blue hedgehog of videogame fame, was created by Sega in 1991 to compete against Nintendo's league-leading Super Mario Bros (q.v.). Cuter, faster and better designed than the Marios, Sonic soon dominated the marketplace, thanks in great part to Sega's sophisticated 16-bit computer system, which far outperformed most existing Nintendo machines. Not only was Sonic the fastest videogame star around, but he let you know it: He'd scowl and tap his foot with mounting impatience when a game player wasn't quick enough on the control button.

That the inevitable Sonic the Hedgehog cartoon series was produced by DIC Enterprises, the very studio responsible for the earlier Super Mario Bros. series, is not all that remarkable. It was a bit unusual that Sonic premiered on ABC as a Saturday morning weekly simultaneously with the property's September 1993 debut in daily strip syndication. Andy Heyward, DIC president, was quick to note that the dual Sonic intro was "the first time since Ghostbusters [see listing for The Real Ghostbusters] that a character will debut in syndication and on a network at the same time. [Teenage Mutant] Ninja Turtles did it, but only after the syndicated show was a success did the network buy it."

Strangely, Heyward didn't trumpet the single most astonishing aspect of the two Sonic the Hedgehogs: Beyond sharing the same lead character and the same lead voice actor—Jaleel White, the nerdish "Urkel" on the nighttime sitcom Family Matters—the network Sonic was an entirely different program than the syndicated Sonic.

Premiering some five days before the networker, the 65-episode syndicated Adventures of Sonic the Hedgehog was geared to the under-12 bunch, with slapstick and nonthreatening situations predominant. Sonic, portrayed as an adolescent, was costarred with his videogame companion Tails, a two-tailed Fox. Darting around a storybook landscape as prettified as a Smurfs (q.v.) setting, Sonic both learned and dispensed softpedalled lessons about caring, sharing, honesty and personal integrity. Besides Tails, two other trademarks of the original Sonic game popped up on the syndie: the giant rings

which appeared onscreen as score-toting tokens, and the villain, good-scientist-gone-sour Dr. Robotnik, a comic figure who looked like a constipated walrus. Each Adventures of Sonic the Hedgehog ended with a 30-second "Sonic Says" prosocial bite.

Contrasting with this lighthearted Sonic was the shadow-dominated network weekly, titled simply Sonic the Hedgehog. Suddenly we were thrust through the stratos to Sonic's home planet Morbius, a forbidding netherworld straight out of Star Wars, the Alien films, and TV's Batman: The Animated Series (q.v.). With beetle-browed sobriety and even less patience than his videogame counterpart ("I'm waiting!" was his exasperated catchphrase), Sonic, now apparently a teenager, battled the omnipotent Dr. Robotnik—here a monstrous, moundlike beast resembling Return of the Jedi's Jabba the Hutt. The lovable Tails was nowhere to be found, replaced by a more mature dramatis personae. Princess Sally, an all-but-naked female hedgehog, was a "holographic computer" expert who spent most of the series searching for her father in the company of her nervous major domo Antoine. Sonic, who piloted the outsized space vehicle which propelled Princess Sally on her quest, had a reckless buddy named Katt.

Befitting its dark and brooding style, ABC's Sonic was slower moving than the buoyant syndicated version; in this it succeeded better than the syndie in emphasizing Sonic's hyperspeed, simply by having everything around him stand still. And while its overall morbidity would seem to open the door to graphic violence, the network Sonic admirably featured a hero who preferred ingenuity over fisticuffs in extracting himself from danger. Whenever faced with a seemingly inescapable predicament, Sonic would merely state that "the Hedgehog knows"—and, fortunately, he did. Only in emulating the verbal humor of the syndicated Sonic did the ABC version falter: While puns and one-liners were vital to the sillier syndie situations, they seemed woefully out of place on Planet Morbius.

No official statement was issued as to why the two Sonic the Hedgehogs were so radically different, but it's safe to assume that DIC was simply hedging its bets, testing both lighter and grittier approaches to see which would be more likely to succeed in the quicksilver TV-cartoon market of the early 1990s.

SPACE ACE *see* **SATURDAY SUPER-CADE**

SPACE ANGEL. Syndicated: 1962 (copyright date: 1964). Cambria Studios/ T.V. Comics. Produced and directed by Dick Brown and Clark Haas. Created by Dik Darley and Dick Brown. Character design and execution by Alex Toth, Jim Mabry, Hy Mankin, Saul Trapani. Director of photography, Ed Gillette. Art director, Clark Haas. Special effects, Scotty Thomas. Music by Paul Horn. Writers included Warren Tufts and Dave Detiege. Voices: Ned Lefebvre, Jim Chandler (Scott McCloud); Margaret Kerry; Hal Smith.

Children have a tendency to lump bad experiences together with the good. As a youth, I had avoided *Space Angel* because I wasn't fond of *Clutch Cargo* (q.v.); both programs were products of Cambria Studios, and both utilized the SyncroVox technique of superimposing actual "live" lip movements on the faces of the cartoon characters. *Clutch Cargo* struck me as crude and tiresome, and so I wasn't willing to give *Space Angel* a chance—not until nearly 30 years later, when I caught up to the series on videocassettes. Far from a waste of time, *Space Angel* was one of the finest, most accomplished animated series of the 1960s, and it's of little importance that there was barely any real animation.

An outer-space epic set in the Near Future, *Space Angel* starred eyepatch-wearing pilot Scott McCloud, who commandeered the rocketship Starduster. McCloud was known to his superiors on Earth only as Space Angel, troubleshooter and dogooder par excellence, dispatched from Earth to purge the Cosmos of megalomaniac villains and invading alien hordes. Space Angel's true identity was shared by the crew of the Evening Star, McCloud's space station: Taurus, a brash, bearded Scottish pilot/mechanic, and the beauteous science expert/navigator Crystal Mace, daughter of renowned egghead Professor Mace, who'd invented most of the high-tech hardware utilized on the Evening Star.

The series was created by Dik Darley, who was also responsible for *Space Patrol*, a popular live action TV sci-fi weekly of the 1950s. Dick Brown, the guiding force of Cambria Studios, had done some of his earliest work as co-director of *Space Patrol* with Darley; ten years later, the two innovators reunited for *Space Angel*, an updated version of the space-peacekeeper concept. Darley and Brown decided that a more realistic artistic approach than the representational, caricatured style of *Clutch Cargo* was needed for *Space Angel*, which was targetted to an older audience who, weaned on the recent NASA space shots, demanded a higher degree of accuracy. The Cambria team engaged comic book artist Alexander Toth, already established in the "serious" comics field through his work on DC's superhero line and Dell's illustrated adaptations of popular recent movies.

Toth's graphic design for *Space Angel* was infinitely superior to the customary kiddie TV fare in 1961: Fully articulated human forms, pitch-black shadows alternating with subtle shadings, and an overall sense of composition wherein the busily detailed backgrounds never detracted from what the artist wanted the reader to focus upon. (This technique was decidedly superior to the "chicken salad" artwork on some of the Japanese action cartoons of the 1980s, where one has to stare intently before figuring out where one's attention is supposed to be.)

Alex Toth's friend and colleague Warren Tufts (they'd worked together on the daily adventure strip *Casey Ruggles*) was engaged to work on the *Space Angel* scripts, as was Disney alumnus Dave Detiege, who'd later collaborate with Dick Brown on Cambria/Heritage's *New Three Stooges* (q.v.) cartoons. Toth had wanted Tufts to help out with the artwork, but the latter had too many prior commitments. Seeking out artists who'd be sympatico with the space-aviation trappings of *Space Angel*, Toth called upon Ray Vinella, an illustrator for Lockheed Missiles' promotional and educational material, and Jim Mabry, who'd performed bascially the same artistic function for the U.S. Air Force. Hy Mankin and Sal Trapani, two freelancers with extensive experience with science-fiction comics, were also signed on. This luminous talent lineup explains why *Space Angel* was one of the best looking series of *any* kind on the air in 1962. (Incredibly, the cartoons carried *no* on-screen credits. I can't believe these guys didn't have ego enough to blow their own horns!)

As mentioned in the notes on *Clutch Cargo*, the Cambria people preferred to call their product "motorized movement" rather than animation. *Space Angel* was motorized movement at its zenith. Sliding doors, dial indicators and rocket launches were hand-operated or manipulated with strings and pulleys. Blastoffs, gunfire and fog were enhanced with actual smoke. The illusion of ceaseless space-station activity was handled by a multitude of blinking lights and machine-rotated equipment. Space flights were depicted by keeping the vessels in one fixed place, then moving the background or panning the camera. For landings on mountainous terrains, Cambria's patented four-layer multiplane camera (created by Ed Gillette) was used, resulting in the pleasingly plausible "3-D" effect of the Starduster casting a shadow upon the background, while hills and peaks zoomed past the camera in proper foreground perspective. Shots like these were remarkably similar to the battle sequences in *Star Wars*, which wouldn't be filmed for another decade and a half (and at a considerably inflated budget!).

Some effects were accomplished by simply adjusting the camera's focus. These ranged from the standard fuzzy backgrounds (suggesting great distance), to such sophisticated effects as the manner in which Space Angel's "Leader" was seen issuing orders on a two-way TV screen. The screen would always be just slightly out of focus and too bright, establishing a plane of action independent from the rest of Space Angel's control room.

While this may sound ponderous and overly mechanical, it didn't play that way. Whenever a *Space Angel* special effect threatened to remain onscreen too long to remain convincing, the action would cut instantly to something else. The timing of the editing was razor-sharp, while the action panels themselves were drawn with so rich a variety of angles and perspective that the still pictures seemed to "move" without movement (this was the same approach taken, after a fashion, on 1966's *Marvel Superheroes*).

Space Angel looked clumsy only when it employed actual cel animation, such as an explosion or a change of pose within the same frame. The series was most convincing when it didn't try to be a "cartoon."

The Syncrovox technique still gave the lip movements a disembodied quality, as on *Clutch Cargo*, but now the skin color of the voice actors was artificially enhanced to match the complexions of the cartoon characters, avoiding *Clutch*'s "edged" look. At any rate, Syncrovox was de-emphasized on *Space Angel*, so that process never stayed on screen long enough to appear ludicrous. As often as possible, the characters' lip movements were adroitly obscured by microphones, helmets, props, etc. As with the motorized movement technique, it was the editing and camera angling that gave the impression of smooth conversation between the *Space Angel* characters.

So much space has been given to *Space Angel* technique that we've almost forgotten to mention the excellence of its content. Though the series occasionally relied upon established space-jockey clichés — the alien creatures were almost invariably villains (notably the recurring antagonist Queen Zora), and Crystal Kane, despite her intellectual credentials, existed primarily to scream and get kidnapped — *Space Angel* contained some of the best thought-out fantasy writing seen on early 1960s television. The dialogue was spare and mature, never talking down to its audience (this was occasionally a drawback when the series was shunted to the early-morning preschooler TV ghetto). The technological terminology was worked into the dialogue casually, as if the characters had been dealing with space travel all their lives. And the "futuristic" trappings were remarkably prescient (except, of course, for the colonization of planets). Practically every electronic device and creature comfort seen on *Space Angel* represented a logical rather than farfetched improvement upon existing 1962 paraphernalia. In fact, much of the hardware — two way TVs, satellite dishes, home computers — have indeed graduated to reality in the three decades since *Space Angel*'s production.

Space Angel began production in 1961 and stayed there until 1963. In all, 260 four-minute cliffhanger episodes were produced, which (as in the case of *Clutch Cargo*) could be organized into 52 weekly half hours. Viewers who, like myself, dismissed the series during its first run as "childish" on the basis of the inferior *Clutch Cargo*, are strongly advised to rent one of the *Space Angel* cassettes readily available in most video stores. So superior was *Space Angel* to virtually all science-fiction cartoon efforts of its era (and of future eras), that one can't help feeling a sense of loss that Cambria's staff had disbanded before getting a crack at 1974's faithful but artistically disappointing *Star Trek* cartoons.

SPACE GHOST AND DINO BOY.
CBS: 9/10/1966–9/7/1968.
– SPACE GHOST/FRANKENSTEIN JR. SHOW NBC: 11/27/1976–9/3/1977. Hanna-Barbera. Produced and directed by Joseph Barbera and William Hanna. Production supervisor, Howard Hanson. Animation director, Charles A. Nichols. Story directors: Lew Marshall, Paul Sommer, Bill Perez. Layout artists included Alex Toth. Animators included Jerry Hathcock, Bill Hutten. Musical director, Ted Nichols. Components: 1. SPACE GHOST. Voices: Gary Owens (Space Ghost); Tim Matthieson (Jayce); Ginny Tyler (Jan); Don Messick (Blip). 2. DINO BOY. Voices: Johnny Carson (Dino Boy); Mike Road (Ugh); Don Messick (Bronto). (*See* FRANKENSTEIN JR. AND THE IMPOSSIBLES for additional voice credits. *See also* SPACE STARS.)

Space Ghost was a vital segment of CBS executive Fred Silverman's counter-programming strategy: A "Superhero Morning" versus ABC's Saturday morning comedy cartoons, specifically *The Beatles* (q.v.). The CBS series was also significant as the first of Hanna-Barbera's "straight" superhero efforts. Prior to 1966, most of the studio's programs (with the spectacular exception of *Jonny Quest* [q.v.]) were comedies. Among H-B's writers, only Joe Ruby and Ken Spears were truly comfortable in the science fiction–adventure mode, so it was the Ruby-Spears team that was put in virtual charge of *Space Ghost*. Since the series was a special pet of Fred Silverman's, he also contributed mightily in its pre-production days, helping Hanna-Barbera select the proper costume colors and participating in the selection of the "Space Ghost" name itself.

Space Ghost, who though not really "deceased" was inspired in part by the previous "dead" DC comic book character *The Spectre*, was a husky, muscular extraterrestrial, outfitted in a white costume, yellow cape and black hood. He also sported a red Inviso-Belt which allowed him to disappear when necessary. (This was the color scheme chosen by Hanna-Barbera and Silverman out of some 20 possibilities. It seems so "right" when seen today that it's amazing it wasn't the first selection.) While cloaked in invisibility, Space Ghost enjoyed Inviso-Power, imbuing him with extraordinary strength, weaponlike fists and the ability to fly. Speeding through the universe in his space vehicle "The Phantom Cruiser," Space Ghost was assisted in his villain-thwarting missions by masked twin teenagers Jan and Jayce and by an alien monkey named Blip (which was the only word in his vocabulary). Questions as to why Space Ghost needed such tiresome characters as Jan, Jayce and Blip hanging around were quickly answered in practically every episode: Space Ghost had to rescue the twins and the monkey from outer-space monstrosities (The Black Widow, The Sorceror, the Creature King and company), or else there would have been a half hour of nothing more than starscapes, modernistic hardware and talking heads.

The full title of this half-hour weekly series was *Space Ghost and Dino Boy*, the main character appearing in two short weekly adventures bracketing Dino Boy's single weekly appearance. Utilizing the music, background art and several plot devices from *Jonny Quest*, the "Dino Boy" component featuring a young 20th century boy named Tod, who parachuted into a remote, retrogressive jungle full of dinosaurs, cavemen and prehistoric meanies like the Mighty Snow Creature, the Tree Men and the Rocky Pigmies. A remarkably imperturbable lad, Tod, a.k.a. Dino Boy, immediately adapted to his surroundings and to his new comrades, a caveman named Ugh and a "pup" dinosaur named Bronty.

Scoring on its character design by Hanna-Barbera mainstay Alex Toth (see *Space Angel*) and its nonstop action content, *Space Ghost* entertained even those who would have preferred sturdier story values and more substantial characters. The series, slated opposite ABC's *Beatles* (q.v.) and NBC's *Space Kiddettes* (another Hanna-Barbera space opera, albeit in a lighter vein), was an instantaneous hit, inspiring innumerable imitations and, by the end of 1967, virtually eradicating comedy cartoons on the Saturday morning scene. In the words of Lone Ranger (q.v.) producer Alan Ducovny, Space Ghost "set the industry on its ear."

The industry never forgot the rabbit's-foot factor of Space Ghost. In 1976, NBC purchased reruns of Space Ghost to replace the faltering Krofft live action weekly Land of the Lost (see Valley of the Dinosaurs for more on this program), combining the property with rebroadcasts of another 1966 CBS success, Frankenstein Junior and the Impossibles (q.v.), the result being The Space Ghost/Frankenstein Jr. Show. And as part of a 1981 effort to forestall NBC's plans to eliminate its Saturday morning cartoon lineup in favor of an expanded Today Show, Fred Silverman, now in charge of NBC programming, revived Space Ghost in 1981, with new episodes, and golden-larynxed Gary Owens back as the voice of Space Ghost, as a component of H-B's Space Stars. This time, however, comedy was king, at the expense of action-adventure: Space Stars died, while The Smurfs (q.v.) rescued NBC cartoonery for the next decade.

But Space Ghost survived this setback, flourishing both in rerun form and on videocassette. The character's most recent re-emergence was in April 1994, as the animated Letterman-like host of Space Ghost Coast-to-Coast, a live-action cable talk show on Ted Turner's Cartoon Network. This tantalizing project had been slated for a fall 1993 debut, but was shelved when Space Ghost's intended co-host, onetime Fantasy Island star Herve Villechaize, committed suicide just before the series' premiere.

SPACE KIDDETTES. NBC: 9/10/1966–9/2/1967. Hanna-Barbera. Produced and directed by William Hanna and Joseph Barbera. Co-producer, Alex Lovy. Animation directed by Charles Nichols. Story by Tony Benedict. Music by Hoyt Curtin. Voices: Chris Allen (Scooter); Lucille [billed as Lou] Bliss (Snoopy); Don Messick (Countdown/Pupstar); Janet Waldo (Jenny); Daws Butler (Captain Skyhook).

Hanna-Barbera's Space Kiddettes was patterned after Hal Roach's Our Gang comedies (see notes on The Little Rascals), or so the studio claimed in its publicity copy. Superficially, that's what it was: four space-age little rascals who congregated in an orbiting clubhouse, planet-hopped with jet powered backpacks, and piloted the void in a small jerry-built rocket cruiser with their dog Pupstar tethered behind the vehicle. The milieu was a child's-eye redo of The Jetsons, with some of the same background art.

But the four tiny Space Kiddettes — Countdown, Snoopy, Scooter, and Jenny — were eminently forgettable. All of them took a back seat to Space Kiddettes' genuine leading player: Captain Skyhook, the best Hanna-Barbera "heavy" since Mr. Jinks (see Huckleberry Hound). Skyhook, a bearded space buccaneer who sounded like actor Robert Newton (the "arr matey" Long John Silver in Disney's Treasure Island), coveted a treasure map that was in the possession of the goody-goody Kiddettes. He wasn't homicidal, he simply wanted to come out on top, and in this spirit advised his "Mr. Smee-" like aide de camp Static to invent something "humane but diabolical" to thwart the space urchins and steal the map. Already drawn in such broad, brash strokes that he couldn't help dominating the proceedings, Captain Skyhook further stamped Space Kiddettes as his own by narrating the introductions and the opening titles. He even sneeringly invited the kids at home to enjoy the "'orrible fate" awaiting the Kiddettes after the cliffhanging middle commercial break.

There was no real danger, of course, since Space Kiddettes was strictly geared to the four- to eight-year-old crowd. All of Skyhook's schemes were predestined to fail, and there would always be a point in the plot when the Captain found himself in the position of having to rescue the Kiddettes from a nastier predator — or having to be rescued by them. Space Kiddettes was produced in the twilight days of "comic violence" on Saturday morning TV, just before the Clean TV zealots would purge the weekend hours of the harmless sadism that was a Hanna-Barbera trademark. Thus we still were permitted to witness Skyhook being bammed and blasted by such classic cartoon props as anvils, dynamite sticks, spring-activated boxing gloves, sledgehammers, and even an occasional intergalactic pie in the puss.

Of interest are Space Kiddettes' unintentional links with the cartoon work of Jay Ward. Beyond the adoption of the "cliffhanger" and "funny villain" byplay usually associated with Ward's *Rocky and His Friends* (q.v.), the Hanna-Barbera series featured voice work by Chris Allen, who played Ward's *Hoppity Hooper* (q.v.) and Lucille Bliss, who as *Crusader Rabbit* (q.v.) was Jay Ward's very first "star."

Always on the move and very well designed, *Space Kiddettes* nonetheless would have been better as a series of seven-minute shorts rather than a weekly half hour; the 30-minute spread got pretty thin before the closing credits. Also, the program was hampered by the usual Hanna-Barbera formula-bound plotlines, which when seen in a group appear to be the same story told over and over again. But the show was designed for very small children, who seemed to dote on repetition, and worked just fine within those limits. Unfortunately the older kids commandeered the ratings: *Space Kiddettes* lasted but twenty episodes, beaten out by ABC's *The Beatles* (q.v.), and (a logjam here?) Hanna-Barbera's own *Space Ghost* (q.v.) on CBS.

SPACE SENTINELS *see* **YOUNG SENTINELS**

SPACE STARS. NBC: 9/12/1981–9/11/1982. Hanna-Barbera. Executive producers, William Hanna and Joseph Barbera. Directed by Oscar Dufau, Charles Nichols. Animation directed by Carl Urbano, Rudy Zamora, George Gordon. Announcer: Casey Kasem. Music by Hoyt Curtin. New components: **1. TEEN FORCE.** Voices: Darryl Hickman (Kid Comet); David Hubbard (Moleculad); B. J. Ward (Elektra); Mike Winslow (Plutem); Alan Lurie (Uglor). **2. ASTRO AND THE SPACE MUTTS.** Voices: Don Messick (Astro); Frank Welker (Cosmo); Len Weinrib (Dipper); Mike Bell (Space Ace). **3. HERCULOIDS.** Voices: Mike Road (Zandor/Tundro/Zok/Igoo); Virginia Gregg (Tara); Sparky Marcus (Dorno); Don Messick (Gloop and Gleep); Keene Curtis (Narrator). **4. SPACE GHOST.** Voices: Gary Owens (Space Ghost); Alexandra Stewart (Jan); Steve Spears (Jace); Frank Welker (Blip); Keene Curtis (Narrator). (Cross references: *Space Ghost and Dino Boy* and *Herculoids*; see also *The Jetsons*.)

The weekly, 60-minute *Space Stars* was a lazy effort by Hanna-Barbera to cash in on the success of its own *Superfriends*

(q.v.) and *Scooby-Doo* (q.v.). (Ironically, the program ran opposite *Scooby* on Saturday morning.) The series was comprised of two components drawn from the studio's archives, with two new features thrown in—"new" being a relative term.

"Teen Force" was not only a retread of the "Junior Justice League" featured on *Superfriends*, itself a derivation of the "Teen Titans" seen on Filmation's *Superman/Aquaman Hour of Adventure* (see *Superman*), but also a variation on *Fantastic Four* (q.v.), the "Super Seven" segment of *Tarzan and the Super Seven* (see *Tarzan*), and even the Robin Hood legend! Kid Comet, Moleculad and Elektra travelled the universe leaving scores of good deeds and abused villains in their wake. Of marginal interest was the presence in the cast of Mike Winslow, the "human sound effects" comedian of *Police Academy* (q.v.) fame.

"Astro and the Space Mutts" was the *Scooby-Doo* ripoff this time around, with a little of *Casper and the Angels* (see *Casper the Friendly Ghost*) in the stew. Astro, the large and clumsy dog first introduced on H-B's *The Jetsons* (q.v.), was now a smaller but still clumsy canine, teamed with a couple of doggie pals, cottonwitted Cosmo and pugnacious Dipper, on behalf of the crimefighting Space Ace, a mustachioed Burt Reynolds clone (complete with weary wisecracks).

The remaining components were newly produced episodes of old favorites *The Herculoids* (q.v.) and *Space Ghost* (q.v.)—both properties, especially *Herculoids*, losing considerable quality in the resuscitation process. Most of the various *Space Stars* cast members were rallied for the series' closing "Space Stars Finale," a weekly battle against cosmic enemies.

Space Stars was a cluttered bulletin board of past good ideas, offering some of the sloppiest Hanna-Barbera animation in recent memory (one could even detect thumb indentations on the cels!). The series was a particularly inadequate lead-in to NBC's Saturday morning lineup for Marvel's far superior *Spider-Man and His Amazing Friends* (see *Spider-Man*). Happily, *Space Stars* was one of the last of Hanna-Barbera's halfhearted "potboiler" series before the studio's creative renaissance in the mid–1980s.

SPACECATS. NBC: 9/14/1991–7/25/1992. Paul Fusco Productions/Marvel.

Executive producers: Paul Fusco and Bernie Brillstein. Created by Paul Fusco. Produced by Leslie Ann Podkin. Creative consultant, Judy Rothman. Story editor, Rowby Goren. Animation producer, Richard Trueblood. Animation associate director, Karen Peterson. Music theme by Leslie Ann Podkin, Alf Clausen. Music by Shuki Levy. Production facilities: Akom Productions. Voices: Charles Nelson Reilly (DORC); and Paul Fusco, Townsend Coleman, Pat Fraley, Rob Paulsen, Bob Ridgely, Jack Angel, Gregg Berger, Sheryl Bernstein, Susan Blu, Hamilton Camp, Cam Clarke, Jennifer Darling, Walker Edmiston, Jeannie Elias, John Erwin, Lea Floden, Brad Garrett, Barry Gordon, Pat Musick, Jan Rabson, Hal Rayle, Maggie Roswell, Susan Silo, Kath Soucie, John Stephenson, Lennie Weinrib.

SpaceCats was an uneasy combination of animation and hand-and-string puppetry from the same production team responsible for the live action sitcom *Alf* and its cartoon spinoff *Alf Tales* (q.v.). Executive producers Paul Fusco and Bernie Brillstein had already had experience with puppets on *Alf* and with animation on *Alf Tales,* but *SpaceCats* didn't exhibit the skill of Henson/Marvel's *Dog City* (q.v.) in successfully merging the two entertainment forms, even though Brillstein had once been *Muppet* maven Jim Henson's manager.

Each weekly half-hour *SpaceCats* was introduced with live footage (interspersed with cartoon backgrounds and computerized hardware) set on Triglyceride 7, a planet populated by cats. The top banana of this kitty community was a human being, the Disembodied Omnipotent Ruler of Cats, or D.O.R.C. (a richly deserved appellation). The D.O.R.C. had dispatched a crack space-travel team—Captain Catgut and his aides Tom, Scratch and Sniff—to Earth, in a vaguely defined attempt to save the planet from predators, with the less altruistic secondary motive of seeking out "catfood without that fishy aftertaste." The earthbound adventures were animated, and much funnier than critics suggested. ("Turn it off" was the hipshot comment from *Entertainment Weekly.*)

The series' principal saving grace was its voice cast, featuring Charles Nelson Reilly as the supremely bitchy D.O.R.C. and Paul Fusco, formerly the voice of "Alf," in an expository role. Still, it was clear even to the youngest viewer that *SpaceCats* was creeping on little cat feet down a path already smoothed by *Teenage Mutant Ninja Turtles* (q.v.), and the former suffered mightily in comparison.

Undaunted by the thinnish 13-week lifespan of *SpaceCats,* Hanna-Barbera undertook a similar felinized *Turtles* with 1993's *Swat Kats* (q.v.), which was an improvement if only in terms of draftsmanship.

SPARTAKUS AND THE SUN BENEATH SEA. Nickelodeon: 10/11/1986–7/28/1991. RMC Audio Visual/Monte Carlo Productions.

Spartakus and the Sun Beneath Sea had nothing to do with the ancient Roman slave revolt. This was an "Atlantis" style half hour cartoon series, produced in Europe and released in America on the Nickelodeon Cable Service. *Spartakus'* story springboard was the Terra, an underground sun, which provided energy for the center-of-the-earth-dwelling Arcadians. When the Terra faltered, the Arcadians (dressed in Greco-Roman fashion, keeping with Hollywood's standard treatment of the Atlantis story) had to use special forbidden powers to summon the beautiful Arkanna to go to the Earth's surface—also forbidden—for help. The 52-episode *Spartakus* was similar to the texture and atmosphere of *Mysterious Cities of Gold,* another foreign-produced animated series run by Nickelodeon in the mid–1980s.

SPEED BUGGY. CBS: 9/8/1973–8/31/1974; ABC: 9/6/1975–9/4/1976; CBS: 2/4/1978–9/2/1978; CBS: 9/18/1982–1/29/1983. Hanna-Barbera. Produced by Iwao Takamoto. Directed by Charles Nichols. Music by Hoyt Curtin. Musical direction by Paul DeKorte. Written by Jack Mendelsohn, Larz Bourne, Len Janson, Joel Kane, Jack Kaplan, Woody Kling, Norman Maurer, Chuck Menville, Larry Rhine. Voices: Mel Blanc (Speed Buggy); Arlene Golonka (Debbie); Phil Luther Jr. (Tinker); Mike Bell (Mark); and Chris Allen, Hal Smith, Michelle Road, Sid Miller, Ron Feinberg, Virginia Gregg, John Stephenson, and Ira Paran.

Speed Buggy (not *Speedy Buggy,* as sometimes reported) was a weekly, half hour Hanna-Barbera emulation of both the *Speed Racer* (q.v.) cartoon series and the Disney feature film *The Love Bug*. Debbie, Tinker and Mark were the *Scooby Doo*–inspired teenagers on this outing. They travelled the world seeking out adventure and mystery in their custom built, remote control–operated Speed Buggy, an anthropomorphic vehicle which chugged and wheezed in the manner of Jack Benny's old Maxwell. As it happened, both Speed Buggy and the Maxwell were voiced by Mel Blanc, the difference being that Speed Buggy could also talk in addition to sputtering. *And* he could fly, a handy talent considering the scrapes his teen owners got themselves into.

Most sources quote the original *TV Guide* listings in describing Speed Buggy as having a "St. Bernard-like personality." One might suppose *Speed Buggy* would have needed a St. Bernard to rescue it from its stiff first-season network competition of *Brady Kids* (q.v.) and the live-action *Sigmund and the Sea Monsters*, but the Hanna-Barbera series managed to speed along for 16 first-run episodes, which ran on two different networks over an off-and-on period of ten years! While the original *Speed Buggy* half hours aren't easy to come by, the character can be seen in the occasional guest-star spot on reruns of *Scooby's All Star Laff-a-Lympics* (see *Scooby-Doo*).

SPEED RACER. Syndicated: 1967. MTV: 1993. Tatsunoko and Yokino/K. Fujita/Trans-Lux, then Alan Enterprises. Produced, directed and created by Tatsuo Yoshida. Music by Nobuyoshi Koshibe. Animation and art direction by Ippei Kuri and Hiroshi Sasagawa. English adaptation written and directed by Peter Fernandez. Japanese production supervision by K. Fujita. Anerican production supervision by Zavala-Riss. Voices: Jack Grimes (Speed Racer); Corinne Orr (Trixie/Spridal/Mrs. Racer); Jack Curtis (Racer X/Pops Racer); and Peter Fernandez.

—THE NEW ADVENTURES OF SPEED RACER. Syndicated: 1993. Fred Wolf Films/Speed Racer Entertainment/ MWS Inc./Group W. Executive producer, Fred Wolf. Produced by Walt Kubiak and Michael Algar. Supervising director, Bill Wolf. Story editor, David Wise. Sequence directors: Kent Butterworth, Bill Hutten, Tony Love, Neal Warner. Music score by Dennis C. Brown and Larry Brown. Theme music by Dennis C. Brown and

Maxine Sellers. Overseas animation supervisors, Mik Casey and Shivan Ramsaran. No voice credits.

Once seen in childhood, *Speed Racer* is never forgotten, which can be a bogy or a blessing depending on one's attitude. Devotees of the daily, half hour series can't get enough of Speed Racer and his adventures both on and off the race track. Non-fans find the program ridiculous in the extreme, its "funny" artwork jarringly at odds with its "straight" plotlines. Either way, the series has remained in healthy distribution since its 1967 American release—representing for many viewers the quintessential Japanese animated import.

The archeology of *Speed Racer* has been meticulously traced by Japanimation buff Fred Patten (see "Speed Racer: Still in the Lead," *Animation* magazine, Winter 1993, pp. 16–17). In the original 1960s Japanese comic book created by Tatsuo Yoshida, Speed Racer's high-tech car was the star, as indicated by the title *Mach Go Go Go*; "Go" is the Japanese word for "Five," which explains the number 5 emblazoned on the side of the auto. Speed's original name was Go Mifune, after legendary Japanese film star Toshiro Mifune, and *that* explains the letter "M" on Speed's helmet and jacket. Go Mifune competed in worldwide racing events on behalf of his father Daisuke's Mifune Motors, much in the manner of his spiritual predecessor, France's Michel Vaillant (see *Heroes on Hot Wheels*). Working on behalf of Daisuke's organization was his wife Aya, Go's kid brother/mascot Kuo, and an extended family of close friends and coworkers: Go's girlfriend Michi Shimua, mechanic Sabu, and a comedy relief monkey (complete with cute cap) named Senpei. Casting an ominous shadow over the action was a mystery figure, the Masked Racer, who popped up sporadically to save Go Mifune from the various dishonest racers, master criminals and foreign spies that plagued the hero. Unbeknownst to Go, the Masked Racer was actually his older brother Kenichi, who for a complexity of top-secret reasons (including an implied death sentence from his own government!) was compelled to divorce himself from the rest of the Mifune family.

Profits from the *Mach Go Go Go* comic book enabled Tatsuo Yoshida to set up his own animation firm in 1965: Tatsunoko, the first Japanese cartoon company de-

Speed Racer (*right*), the Special Formula Mach 5, and the mysterious Racer X—all given an artistic overhaul for the series' 1993 "comeback."

voted exclusively to TV work. Just as fellow artist Osamu Tezuka used his bread-and-butter star *Astro Boy* (q.v.) as the inaugural attraction of Tezuka's Mushi Studios, so too did Yoshida adapt his moneyspinning *Mach Go Go Go* as *his* first cartoon series. The serialized program, distributed by K. Fujita Associates, ran in prime time on Japanese television, then was picked up by American distributor Trans-Lux for stateside distribution in 1967, in hopes of matching the U.S. success of another Fujita animated release, *Marine Boy* (q.v.).

As was usually the case with made-in-Japan cartoonery, Trans-Lux retained only the physical series, altering all the character names for domestic consumption. Go Mifune, as mentioned, was transformed into Speed Racer; his girl Michi became Trixie; mechanic Sabu was changed (logically) into Sparks; little brother Kuo was changed (who knows why?) into Spridal; and Senpei the monkey was now Chim Chim. The mysterious Masked Racer was altered to the mysterious Racer X, while parents Daisuke and Aya Mifune were left with merely Pops and Mom Racer (evidently Trans-Lux lost its "name the baby" dictionary).

Once the names were changed, Trans-

Lux began to recondition *Speed Racer's* interior. The Japanese version piled steaming heaps of tense violence atop its standard intrigues of gangsters and secret agents. The really rough stuff would have to be weeded out for the American version, a job entrusted to writer/actor Peter Fernandez, a former radio juvenile performer and a "regular" in the world of redubbed Japanese cartoons. Two decades after this assignment, Fernandez was still proud of the fact that in *his* variation of *Speed Racer*, no one was ever killed. This may explain those arbitrarily inserted shots of prone and supine bad guys with comic-book planets and stars circling around their heads, indicating that although they were down, they were not permanently out.

The one aspect of *Speed Racer* blessedly left intact was Speed's car, known in the U.S. version as the Special Formula Mach Five. If you can't quite remember the function of each button on the Mach Five's steering wheel, the pilot episode "The Great Plan" (readily available on home video) lays it all out. Button "A" activated the auto's jets; "B" handled the special grip tires for tough roads; "C" operated the rotating saws that could cut a swath through wooded terrain (hmmm—not very pro-ecological, there); "D" activated the deflecting mechanism, principally the bulletproof and crashproof windshield; "E" provided long-range headlight illumination; "F" was for underwater driving, operating the oxygen and periscope (Boy! was this the *neatest*!); and "G" released a little birdlike robot, ideal for sending and receiving messages. The most remarkable feature of the Special Formula Mach Five was that it boasted the only push-button transmission in the history of the automobile industry that never jammed.

As I said at the outset, virtually everyone who's seen it has vivid memories of the 52-episode *Speed Racer*, notably of its insistent theme song ("Here he comes/Here comes Speed Racer/He's a de-mon on wheels..."), but I've yet to come across anyone unequivocally in love with its production values. Even its truest fans are hard put to justify fully *Speed Racer*'s dizzying kaleidoscope of clumsy animation, inordinately wide-eyed character design, ragged bursts of violence, comic characters uneasily rubbing shoulders with deadly serious opponents, and that eardrum-piercing voice given the allegedly amusing kid brother Spridal. And there's hardly a baby boomer alive who didn't want to ram Spridal's head upside his body whenever he and monkey pal Chim Chim stowed away in Speed's car, thereby adding to the hero's already overloaded peril quotient. The one firm element in *Speed Racer*'s everlasting favor is that it truly lived up to its American title; the damned thing never stopped moving, making it an ideal recent entry in the schedule of the MTV cable network, a service specializing in rapid-fire, "short attention span" musical material.

In the early 1990s, plans were formed to update *Speed Racer*. A live-action feature film, directed by Richard (*Lethal Weapon*) Donner, was promised, but the most immediate result of these plans was the 13-week, syndicated *New Adventures of Speed Racer*, from Fred Wolf productions (Wolf's previous big-money cartoon entry had been *Teenage Mutant Ninja Turtles* [q.v.]). The characters and the Special Formula Mach Five were given a new, streamlined design courtesy of artist George Goodchild, and a fresh sci-fi angle was introduced with Speed's ability to travel through time. Unfortunately, either

out of necessity or misguided *homage*, the animation quality was on the level of the original series. This might have been forgivable, and *New Adventures of Speed Racer* might have had a better chance at survival past its first season, had not the series committed the ultimate sacrilege: It changed the theme music! You won't catch *me* getting up at 6 in the morning to watch a *Speed Racer* that denies me the pleasure of chanting along with "Go, Speed Racer/ Go, Speed Racer/ Go, Speed Racer GOOOOOO!"

SPIDER-MAN. ABC: 9/9/1967–8/30/1969; 3/22/1970–9/6/1970. Grantray Lawrence Animation/Krantz Films. Executive producers, Robert L. Lawrence and Ralph Bakshi. Produced by Ray Patterson. Directed by Grant Simmons, Sid Marcus and Clyde Geronimi. Assistant director, Cos Anzilotti. Story editor, June Patterson. Story supervisor, Ralph Bakshi. Written by Bill Danch, Al Bertino, Phil Babet, Dick Cassarino, Dick Robbins. Production supervisor, Robert "Tiger" West. Story and art consultants, Smilin' Stan Lee and Jazzy Johnny Romita. Theme song by Bob Harris, Paul Francis Webster. Music by Ray Ellis. Voices: Bernard Cowan and Paul Soles (Peter Parker, aka Spiderman); Peg Dixon (Betty Brandt); Paul Kligman (Jameson).

—**SPIDER-MAN AND HIS AMAZING FRIENDS.** NBC: 9/12/1981–9/11/1982; 9/15/1984–9/6/1986.
—**THE INCREDIBLE HULK AND THE AMAZING SPIDER-MAN.** NBC: 9/18/1982–9/10/1983.
—**AMAZING SPIDER-MAN AND THE INCREDIBLE HULK.** NBC: 9/17/1983–9/8/1984. Marvel Productions. Executive producers, David DePatie and Lee Gunther. Produced by Dennis Marks and Art Vitello. INCREDIBLE HULK produced by Don Jurwich. Directed by Gerry Chiniquy, Steve Clark, John Gibbs, Sid Marcus, Nelson Shin, Art Vitello, Bob Richardson, Tom Ray, Dan Thompson, Sam Weiss, Arnie Wong, Kent Butterworth, Milt Gray. Supervising director, Don Jurwich. Written by Creighton Barnes, Doug Booth, Francis H. Deighen, Donald P. Glut, Jack Hanrahan, Christy Mark, Larry Parr, Jeffrey Scott. Storyboard directors included Will Meugniot, Michael Swanigan and Doug Wildey. Music composed and conducted by John Douglas. Created for

TV by Stan Lee. Voices: Anne Lockhart, George DiCenzo, Alan Dinehart, Jerry Dexter, Michael Evans, Walker Edmiston, Alan Young, Dennis Marks, William Woodson, John Haymer, Keye Luke, Allan Melvin, Sally Julian, Casey Kasem. Additional voices, INCREDIBLE HULK AND AMAZING SPIDER-MAN: Stan Lee (narrator); Jack Angel, Mike Bell, Lee Brilley, Bill Boyett, Corey Burton, Susan Blu, Wally Burr, Bill Callaway, Hamilton Camp, Victoria Carroll, Phil Clarke, Hans Conried, Regis Cordic, Henry Corden, Brad Crandall, Roberto Cruz, Peter Cullen, Brian Cummings, Jeff David, Jack DeLeon, Jerry Dexter, Michael Evans, Al Fann, Ron Feinberg, Elliot Field, June Foray, Pat Fraley, Brian Fuld, Kathy Garver, Linda Gary, Dan Gilvezan, Bob Holt, Michael Horton, Ralph James, Lynn Johnson, Stanley Jones, Lee Lampson, Morgan Lofting, Mona Marshall, John Mayer, Shephard Menken, Don Messick, Vic Perrin, Tony Pope, Richard Ramos, Bob Ridgely, Neilson Ross, Gene Ross, Stanley Ralph Ross, Michael Rye, Marilyn Schreffler, John Stephenson, Ted Schwartz, Gary Seeger, Michael Sheehan, Andre Stojka, Janet Waldo, B. J. Ward, Frank Welker, Paul Winchell, William Woodson.

—MARVEL ACTION UNIVERSE. Syndicated: 1988. (See separate listing for this program.)

Spider-Man, first and foremost of Marvel Comics' angst-driven superheroes, was created for *Amazing Fantasy #15* in 1962 by Stan Lee and Steve Ditko. Peter Parker, a goodlooking but shy and withdrawn teenager, was bitten by a spider during a school lab experiment. The result was Peter's attaining the strength and agility of a spider, manifested in the ability to climb walls, leap great heights, and support himself on webs spun from a special spider fluid. Parker also found himself with a heightened "Spidersense," warning him of impending danger at every turn.

In keeping with Marvel's policy of adding depth to otherwise two-dimensional characters, Lee and Ditko saddled Peter Parker/Spider-Man with heavy personal and emotional "excess baggage." Being Spider-Man didn't advance Peter financially, since no bank would cash a check made out to Spider-Man without proper identification. Despite his every effort to thwart crime, Spider-Man was wrongly regarded as a criminal himself, thanks to a vitriolic, and unmotivated, campaign conducted by powerful *Daily Bugle* editor J. Jonah Jameson (for whom Parker worked as an underpaid freelance photographer). And with his Spider-powers came a tragic price tag: While Peter Parker was grandstanding on a TV show for publicity, his uncle was murdered by crooks because Spider-Man wasn't around to prevent it.

Few of the personal hang-ups plaguing Peter Parker were explored in the 1967 cartoon series *Spider-Man*, though other superficial elements of the comic book— Spidey's red, web-motif costume, Jameson's dislike of the "Wall Crawler," and Peter Parker's on-and-off romance with reporter Betty Brandt (a character killed off in the comics, but for some reason continually resurrected on TV)—were retained. The weekly, half hour series was an outgrowth of Marvel/Krantz Films' syndicated *Marvel Superheroes* (q.v.) of 1966, and in fact Spider-Man had been slated to make his debut on *Superheroes* before the ABC network's proprietary commitment on the character. One of the several animation houses working on behalf of Grantray-Lawrence productions for *Superheroes*, Shamus Culhane's Paramount Cartoon Studios, was originally approached to bring *Spider-Man* to life, but the Paramount higher-ups didn't want to expend time and money on the "dying" cartoon market. Culhane quit Paramount shortly thereafter, so Grantray-Lawrence contracted his successor, Ralph Bakshi, who assembled several Paramount animators to work independently on *Spider-Man*. (Bakshi, whose name would carry considerably more weight in the cartoon field of the early 1970s, received no billing in any of the *Spider-Man* episodes I've seen, perhaps due to Paramount's reluctance in being associated with the project.)

A vast improvement over the still-life *Marvel Superheroes*, *Spider-Man* managed both to invoke the original Marvel artwork and develop a method whereby the limited animation technique would benefit rather than injure the project. There wasn't much in the way of intricate movement (except for some fine work on such intangibles as water and wind), but what movement there was was bold and deliberate, sustaining audience interest until the next burst of action. Buoying the "dead" spots were the first-rate character

Spider-Man takes on a "comic book *noir*" look for his 1994 series.

design, exuberant voice-acting performances, and well-knitted scenarios.

Best of all, *Spider-Man* retained the inner lining of humor which distinguished
the Marvel comics line; not campy or self-
conscious jokery detracting from the
seriousness of the stories, but comedy
growing naturally from character and
situation — most often in the form of
wisecracks at the expense of a particularly
pompous villain like The Sorceror. Some
of the better examples of this subliminal
lightheartedness were the methods by

which Peter Parker used J. Jonah Jameson's animosity to his advantage, convincing the editor to do exactly what
Spider-Man wanted by insisting that it
wasn't what Spider-Man wanted.

Otherwise, it was "down to business" on
Spider-Man, with little gratuitous kidding
around except for the nicknames in the
closing credits (Smilin' Stan Lee and Jazzy
John Romita) and the tongue-in-cheek
theme song, "Friendly Neighborhood
Spider-Man," cowritten by Paul Francis
Webster, who in earlier collaboration with

Sammy Fain had penned "Secret Love," the Oscar-winning song hit of 1953! The 52 *Spider-Man* installments paid their way for two first-run seasons and one repeat season on ABC (holding its own during its maiden season opposite Hanna-Barbera's *Shazzan!* on CBS and *Flintstones* reruns on NBC), then played for what seemed like forever in syndication.

Twixt and tween the first and second network cartoon *Spider-Man*, the character appeared under his nickname "Spidey" in several prosocial vignettes on PBS' *Sesame Street*, and was also the protagonist of a live-action CBS miniseries (later restructured into a brace of ersatz "movies") starring Nicholas Hammond. By the time the character returned to Saturday mornings in 1981, DC/Hanna-Barbera's rival *Superfriends* (q.v.) had taken hold, hence the evocative title *Spider-Man and His Amazing Friends*. Those "amazing" compadres were Peter Parker's college chums Firestar, also known as Angelica Jones, and Iceman, a.k.a. Bobby Drake (a character lifted from Marvel Comics' *X-Men*). The "new" *Spider-Man* was produced by Marvel's recently created animated cartoon division, which in honor of its founding father was using Spidey in the corporate logo.

Back in the fold were (of course) Spider-Man/Peter Parker, Betty Brandt and J. Jonah Jameson. The artwork was even more faithful to the Marvel comics pages than the 1967 version had been, with a multitude of forced-perspective shots, off-kilter camera angles, and deep, foreboding shadows. A welcome addition to the proceedings (carried over from the comics) was Peter Parker's basic discomfiture at being a Spider-Man Without Honor—especially since an on-call superhero was permitted very little social life. Though it wasn't so stated, Peter's relationship with Betty, continually disrupted by crime-fighting, was one long coitus interruptus. To make matters worse, the citizenry had adopted a "What have you done for me lately?" attitude. After saving the world in one episode, Spidey was given a ticket for dumping a criminal in the river without a license! What else could Spider-Man do but shrug and smile wearily at the audience?

In 1982, The Incredible Hulk, a Marvel character created the same year as Spider-Man (1962), was added to the series.

Previously animated in 1966 as part of *Marvel Superheroes* (see listing on this series for the Hulk's backstory), the Hulk had in the intervening years gained prominence on a live-action TV series (1978–1982) starring Lou Ferrigno in the title role and Bill Bixby as the Hulk's alter-ego Dr. David Banner. In deference to his prime time celebrity status, the Hulk was given top billing on the new *Incredible Hulk and the Amazing Spider-Man*—new only in the case of the Hulk's cartoon episodes, since Spider-Man's adventures were all repeats. The following year, Spidey regained star status when the one-hour show was *re*-retitled *The Amazing Spider-Man and the Incredible Hulk*. One suspects that Spider-Man's agent had threatened to sue.

The *Incredible Hulk* adventures not only blew away the stiff poses of the 1966 *Hulk* cartoons, but in terms of animation finesse and rich color design threatened to overshadow the *Spider-Man* sequences. The Banner-to-Hulk transformations (trotted out repeatedly as stock footage) were first rate, counterpointing smooth "abnormal growth" closeups with heartstopping lightning bolts. This Hulk was truer to the comic books than the Bill Bixby vehicle had been: His alter ego was once more Dr. *Bruce* Banner (the surname "David" had been substituted on the Bixby series so as not to invite comparison to *Batman's* Bruce Wayne); the Doctor worked as researcher on a military base (Bixby's Banner was a fugitive from the law); his girlfriend was his comic-book *amour* Betty Ross; and the one person who shared the secret of Banner's hidden identity was laid-back hippie type Rick Jones, another carryover from the comics. Unlike earlier TV *Hulks*, this version of the leaping green giant wasn't altogether sociopathic. He busted up the joint, true, but only when severely provoked, and he had the sense to seek out allies like Rick Jones whenever his "Hulk-outs" threatened to get too dicey. The most enjoyable feature of *Incredible Hulk* was the breathless narration of Stan Lee himself—not hokey enough to be a lampoon, but just a degree or so overcooked to indicate that this show was meant to be entertainment, not rocket science.

The Hulk disappeared from the series in 1983, and the series shrank back to half an hour, again titled *Spider-Man and His*

Amazing Friends. Since the series was exclusively comprised of reruns at this point, none of the episodes touched upon the comic-book *Spider-Man*'s reinvention, wherein the character flew off to fight wrongdoing on an "Alternate Earth." Nor was this new, improved Spidey an element of the 24 *Spider-Man* episodes featured on the syndicated 1988 weekend omnibus *Marvel Action Universe*, since, once again, all those episodes were repeats of the 1981 network run.

In 1993, Marvel announced that a state-of-the-art *Spider-Man*, emulating the recent Warner Bros. cartoon hit *Batman: The Animated Series* (see *Batman*) was on the horizon. The plan was to release a *Spider-Man* miniseries in 1994, which if successful would matriculate into a weekly, and then a daily by 1995. Whatever the cartoon studio came up with, it would have to be an improvement on the daily *Spider-Man* newspaper strip, which by 1993 had settled into soulless rehashes of earlier plotlines and round-robin continuities which slowed the once energetic Marvel pace to a crawl—and *not* a "wall crawl." (See also *Spider-Woman*.)

SPIDER-WOMAN. ABC: 9/22/1979–3/1/1980. DePatie-Freleng/Marvel Productions. Executive producers, David DePatie and Friz Freleng. Created for television by Stan Lee. Produced by Lee Gunther. Directed by Bob Richardson, Gerry Chiniquy, Sid Marcus, Dave Detiege. Written by Jeff Scott. Voice directors, Peter Cullen and Bruce Houghtaling. Storyboard direction by Mario Piluso. Graphic design, George Goode. Title design, Arthur Leonardi. Music by Eric Rogers. Voices: Joan Van Ark (Spider-Woman, aka Jessica Drew); Bruce Miller (Jeff Hunt); Bryan Scott (Billy Drew); Lou Krugman (Police Chief); Larry Carroll (Detective Miller); Dick Tufield (Announcer); and John Mayer, Vic Perrin, Ilene Latter, Tony Young, Karen Machon, and John Milford.

As part of an ongoing effort to appeal to the female reading public generally frozen out of the "superhero" market, Marvel head man Stan Lee created Spider-Woman, a distaff variation of Marvel's league-leading *Spider-Man* (q.v.). The weekly, half hour animated version of *Spider-Woman* left a few complications out of the "backstory" that Lee had concocted for the comic-book introduction of the character in February 1977's *Marvel Spotlight #32*—notably the fact that Spider-Woman wasn't really a human being!—but in general followed the basic scenario.

As a child, Jessica Drew was bitten by a venomous spider in her scientist father's lab. Desperate for an antidote, Dr. Drew treated his daughter with untested secret serum "No 34." The results were pretty much the same as those attending Spider-Man's alter ego Peter Parker: Jessica developed the ability to crawl walls, spin webs, and summon up several times her normal strength. Unlike the neurotic Parker, however, Jessica adjusted more gracefully to her unusual talents. She became the powerful publisher of *Justice* magazine, a far cry from Peter's journeyman existence as a freelance photographer. Jessica may have had a better self-image because her "spider" talents far exceeded those of Peter Parker's: She could fly (when not relying upon her Justice Jet Copter), she was able to use "venom" rays in the manner of laser blasts, and her telepathic powers, or "spider sense," was developed to the point that she could see events transpiring in all corners of the world, and could even communicate with real spiders when the need arose.

In short, the animated *Spider-Woman* wasn't as compelling as *Spider-Man* because she lacked those neuroses and vulnerabilities that afflicted "Spidey" and other more memorable Marvel creations. In order to give her *some* reason to be wary of the villains, the series introduced two eminently kidnappable male characters: chauvinistic *Justice* magazine photographer Jeff, and Jessica's boy-genius nephew Billy. On occasion, she was also called upon to bail out Spider-Man himself when the going got tough. While all this sounds like a calculated nod to Feminism, *Spider-Woman* tended to counteract the positive role-model established by Jessica Drew by having her pretend to need Jeff's macho assistance. At one point, she even pretended to be frightened of a spider!

Spider-Woman's TV life wasn't as long as that of her male counterpart, perhaps because she came off like a board of directors' notion of what would attract female viewers. Additionally, she was derivative all down the line: Her red costume was seemingly cut from the same pattern as

Batgirl's (see *Batman*), while her "spin-around" method of transforming into Spider-Woman was right out of *Wonder Woman* (see *Superfriends*). Modern TV viewers will probably find *Spider-Woman* worth viewing only for its voice casting. Joan Van Ark, later costar of *Knots Landing*, was both Jessica Drew and Spider-Woman—and in fine (if sexually inappropriate) cartoon tradition, Van Ark's voice lowered when making the switchover to superheroine.

THE SPIRAL ZONE. Syndicated: 1987. Atlantic-Kushner-Locke/The Maltese Companies/Orbis Communications. Executive producers, Donald Kushner and Peter Locke. Associate producers, Edd Grilles and Ray Volpe. Produced by Diana Dru Botsford; assisted by Brenda K. Kyle. Supervising directors, Pierre Decelles and Georges Grammat; assisted by Elayne Shina, Joe Cisi, Chiou Wen Shian. Executive story editors, Jim Carlson, Terrence McDonnell. Story editor, Mark Edens. Music by David Kitay, Richard Kosinski, Sam Wynans, Ashley Hall, Steve Tyrrell. Lyrics by Stephanie Tyrrell. Theme performed by Steve Tyrrell, Max Gronenthal, Ashley Hall. Executive producer for Tonka, Mark Ludke. Animation facilities: Visual 80 Productions, Akom Productions. Voices: Dan Gilvezan (Dirk Courage); Hal Rayle (Max); Denny Delk (General McFarland/Reaper); Frank Welker (Dr. Lawrence/Razorback); Michael Bell (Hiro); Mona Marshall (Katarina/Mommy); Neil Ross (Overlord/Tank/Bandit).

Spiral Zone was set in The Future. The Overlord, a renegade scientist, had created the "Spiral Zone," a curlicue-shaped green cosmic cloud which laid waste to huge cities and turned everyone exposed to it into zombielike slaves. With most of the Earth held captive beneath the Zone, Overlord and his "Black Widow" minions had it all their own way until Cmdr. Dirk Courage and his five Zone Riders were dispatched to free the world. Operating on behalf of General McFarland from a "free" zone called the MCC (which appeared to be what was left of San Francisco), Courage and his multicultural subordinates—Max, Katarina, Razorback, Tank and Hiro—fought the Black Widows with every piece of weaponry, flying machinery and raw courage at their com-

mand. The 65 half hour *Spiral Zone* adventures hurled the Zone Riders all over the world, where they encountered any number of allies, traitors and oppressed common citizens.

Telecast daily in syndication, *Spiral Zone* was touted as "High Gloss adventure for the High Tech Generation." (It could also have been heralded as *Star Wars: 1986* by virtue of the warp-speed air battles and the "Darth Vader" look and demeanor of the Overlord.) Coproduced by Tonka Toys, the series was obviously designed to push merchandise, which makes it all the more puzzling that *Spiral Zone* was hardly suitable for anyone under the age of ten. The series was unrelentingly grim and excessively violent, with both good guys and bad guys dropping like flies in the heat of the many laser-weapon battles. As for the vehicles and weaponry, their deployment in *Spiral Zone* was so impossibly elaborate and spectacular that the kids at home couldn't even begin to duplicate the toys' on-screen activity (in comparison, the toys "advertised" on *Transformers* [q.v.] did change from robot to vehicle and back again, just as seen on TV).

And if the main characters were meant to be converted into action figures, *Spiral Zone* really missed the boat by making Dirk Courage and company emotionless ciphers. The audience couldn't "pull" for anyone since the heroes refused to open themselves up for empathy. Not that they were given anything to work with; the "plots" on *Spiral Zone* consisted of a 30-second setup, three minutes of explosions and combat, a few breathing spaces to advance the plot, then several more bloodthirsty battle scenes leading to an indecisive climax. This was the sort of program that would normally have had the "clean up TV" people up in arms. Perhaps they just didn't bother with *Spiral Zone* because it wasn't successful, and therefore not as high-profile a target as the comparatively benign *Teenage Mutant Ninja Turtles* (q.v.) or *He-Man* (q.v.).

In all fairness, *Spiral Zone*'s animation and artwork were excellent; the problem lay in what was done with them. One could probably stay awake through a single *Spiral Zone* half hour, but the deadening sameness of the violent sequences, the empty leading characters, and the non-think plotlines would make getting through the *next* episode rough sledding indeed.

SPIRIT OF FREEDOM. Syndicated: 1975. Shamus Culhane Productions. The *Spirit of Freedom* was a series of three-minute animated fillers conceived for America's Bicentennial in the spirit of Shamus Culhane's earlier *Max the 2000 Year Old Mouse* (q.v.) and *The Wonderful Stories of Professor Kitzel*. This time, a spectral Yankee Doodle type introduced vignettes of American history, with background art lifted from magazine illustrations, paintings and engravings from the 18th and 19th centuries.

SPORT BILLY. Syndicated: 1982. NBC: 7/31/1982–9/11/1982. Filmation. Executive producers, Norm Prescott and Lou Scheimer. Directed by Ed Friedman, Marsh Lamore, Lou Kachivas, Kay Wright, Lou Zukor. Written by Paul Aratow, Jack Hanrahan, Paul Dini, Marsha Humphreys, Dan DiStefano, Coslough Johnson, Barry Gaines, Tom Ruegger. Voices: Lane Scheimer (Sport Billy); Joyce Bulifant (Vanda/Lilly); Frank Welker (Sporticus XI/Willie).

Sport Billy was a half hour weekly about a young, clean-living, otherworldly athlete. Sport Billy was dispatched to Earth by Sporticus XI, ruler of Olympus, to protect fair play throughout the Universe and to shield athletes from the evil Queen Vanda, who committed every underhanded foulplay trick short of bribing basketball players to shave points. The hero was accompanied by his girlfriend Sport Lilly, and by a dog named Willie (not "Sport Willie," more's the suprise). Sport Billy also toted an "Omni-Sack," which like Felix the Cat's bag of tricks contained an endless supply of vital props and supplies.

The hero was originally designed as a mascot character for a West German sports organization, and in fact *Sport Billy* was designed to premiere in that country, where the character was already a popular figure. However, the series was written and performed in English, with Sport Billy's voice supplied by Lane Scheimer, son of a Filmation executive—an incongruously nepotistic note to a series conceived in the spirit of "fairness." Produced in 1979 and 1980, the 16-episode *Sport Billy* was first syndicated in the United States in mid–1982, then popped up in July

of that year as an eight-week Saturday afternoon offering on NBC. Very few NBC affiliates outside the network's owned-and-operated stations ran *Sport Billy*, due to previous commitments to *actual* sports events.

SPUNKY AND TADPOLE. Syndicated: 1958. Beverly Hills Productions/TV Cinema Sales/Guild Films. Owner of show, Barnet Films. Voices: Joan Gardner, Don Messick, Ed Janis.

Spunky and Tadpole starred, respectively, a little oval-headed boy and his big talking teddy bear. Their series of 150 five-minute cliffhanging adventures (10 episodes per storyline) were produced in the minimalist *Crusader Rabbit* (q.v.) manner, meaning that the "animated" characters moved every five seconds or so, and then only when absolutely necessary.

Ultra-chintzy both in concept and execution (the artwork resembled an extended junk food commercial), *Spunky and Tadpole* was given a big-bucks promotional sendoff in 1958 by its first syndicator, Guild Films. A major TV distributor of the period thanks to such valuable properties as *The Liberace Show* and the Warner Bros. *Looney Tunes* theatrical cartoons, Guild secured bookings for *Spunky and Tadpole* in several top markets, promising a series that would appeal equally to grownups and children. Competition from stronger syndies like *Huckleberry Hound* (q.v.) and the *Three Stooges* shorts caused *Spunky and Tadpole* to fall by the wayside, and when Guild disappeared in a merger at the end of the 1950s, the cartoons were shunted around to several minor distributors. Offered at bargain rates to less affluent stations in smaller markets, *Spunky and Tadpole* continued to play unobtrusively into the mid–1960s.

The series' one balm to cartoon fans of the 1990s was its pre–Hanna/Barbera display of virtuosity from voice actor Don Messick, who not only played Tadpole but most of the secondary villains and authority figures.

SQUIDDLY DIDDLY *see* **ATOM ANT**

STARBLAZERS. Syndicated: 1979. Office Academy and Sunwagon Productions/Claster (American distributor) and Westchester Corporation. Produced by

Yoshinobu Nishizaki. Directed and created by Reiji Matsumoto. The history of *Starblazers*, up to 1981, was admirably chronicled by George Woolery in his own book on TV cartoons, and it is Woolery's notes which we've used as guideline for this expanded entry on the series. *Starblazers* began in Japan in 1974 as a serialized weekly under the title *Space Battleship Yamato* ("Uchu Senkan Yamato"), the titular vehicle named for a legendary World War 2 Japanese sea vessel. Reiji Matsumoto, later the guiding force of *Captain Harlock* (q.v.), created the half hour series and the comic book upon which it was based; both were set in the year 2199.

The plot: the Earth was being radiation-bombed by the planet Gamilon, led by the despotic Desslok. The faraway planet Iscandar, headed by good Queen Starsha, offered help to our beleaguered globe in the form of the formidable defense cruiser Yamato. Earth's Star Force, led by Admiral Jyuzo Okita and his aide Sosumu Kodai, set out for Iscandar in their state-of-the-art spaceship Argo. The Star Force included Daisuke Shima, chief of operations; ship's doctor Sado; and Kodai's lady friend, radar operator Yuki Moro. The crew also included a comic-relief robot, IQ-9, and a cyborg mechanic, Sandor (these characters, incidentally, were created long before the *Star Wars* films, so Matsumoto cannot be accused of rip-off, unlike many of his contemporary cartoonmakers. There is however a lot of "Flash Gordon" inherent in this series, just as there was in *Star Wars*).

The first 26 episodes of *Space Battleship Yamato*, subtitled "Quest for Iscandar," chronicled the battle to save earth. This *Yamato* package performed admirably on Japanese TV, and even better after *Star Wars* sparked a renewal of enthusiasm for space operas. At that time (1977), *Space Battleship Yamato* was revived with a new group of 26 half hours, "The Comet Empire," wherein the evil Desslok aligned with Prince Zodar, ruler of Empire City, a cometlike metropolis which drew its strength by devouring other planets for fuel. This time it was the Earth Defense Fleet which sent out the Argo rescue team, prompted by a cry for help from the planet Telazart (one of whose residents, the beauteous Trelaina, became Daisuke Shima's sweetheart).

It was the above-mentioned 52 episodes which Claster Studios, envisioning marketing tie-ins on behalf of its Hasbro Toys division, bundled together in 1979 and syndicated to selected big cities in the U.S. as a Monday-through-Friday strip. The title *Starblazers* was not the first choice: Claster dallied briefly with *Star Force*, which was vetoed as sounding a shade *too* much like *Star Wars*.

Claster toned down the more violent passages of *Space Battleship Yamato* and redid the character names. Admiral Okita was now Captain Avatar, Sosumu Kodai was Derek Wildstar (prophetic in that Wildstar would later be the name of Claster's music division), Daisuke Shima was Mark Venture, Dr. Sado was Dr. Sane, and Yuki Moro was Nova. The robot IQ-9 was redubbed Tin-Wit, a reflection of the robot's tendency to wisecrack and toss off abysmal jokes.

Wisely, Claster avoided some of the less judicious cuts that producer Sandy Frank made in adapting another popular Japanese cartoon series, *Gatchaman*, into the Americanized *Battle of the Planets* (q.v.). *Starblazers* retained the plot and character complexities that were trademarks of *Space Battleship Yamato*, and as such was welcomed enthusiastically by the Japanimation fans who'd been disappointed by *Planets*.

Unfortunately, the decision to limit syndication to only the most important markets resulted in a lukewarm ratings showing for *Starblazers*. The series didn't really pick up steam until it went out in the 1980s to medium-sized cities with substantial Asian populations. At that time, Claster included 25 more episodes to the *Starblazers* manifest, comprised of the final *Space Battleship Yamato* story arc of 1980, "Bolar Wars." Originally telecast in Japan as *Yamato: The New Voyage*, "Bolar Wars" was named after the Bolar Federation, whose war with the Gamilons over the conquest of the Milky Way threatened to annihilate the Earth and all other "peaceful" planets.

STARCOM: THE US SPACE FORCE. Syndicated: 1987. Family Channel: 9/19/1993–. DIC Enterprises/Coca-Cola Television. Executive producer, Andy Heyward. Produced by Richard Raynis. Directed by Marek Buchwald. Animation director, Kazumi Fukushima.

Creative supervisor, Robby London. Script coordinator, Lori Crawford. Story editors, Byrnne Stephens and Lydia Marano. Associate producer, Kenneth Y. Duer. Produced for KK DIC by Tetsuo Katayama. Music by Haim Saban and Shuki Levy. Starcom licensed through Coleco. Developed in cooperation with the Young Astronauts Council. Voices: Rob Cowan (Dash); Robert Cait (Crowbar/Torvak); Phil Aikin (Slim); Neil Munro (Dark); Susan Roman (Kelsey); Marvin Goldhar (Vondar); Elva May Hoover (Malvanna); Don Francks (Col. Brinkley); Dan Hennessey (Klag); Louis DiBianco (Romak); and Marla Lukovsky, John Stocker, Greg Swanson, Jank Aszman, Hardee Lineham, Linda Sorenson, Doug Stratton, and Christopher Ward.

Starcom was developed by DIC in conjunction with the Young Astronauts Council, an international organization created by journalist Jack Anderson to encourage classroom study of outer-space travel and technology. Its academic credentials aside, the weekly, half-hour *Starcom* was fundamentally another *Star Wars* wannabe, right down to its "Darth Vader" counterpart, emperor Dark of the Shadow Force. The syndicated series also emulated such Japanimation efforts as *Robotech* (q.v.), notably in its crazy-quilt plotlines and its intimate interrelations among its characters. Virtually all the members of the peacekeeping Starcom fleet were related to one another: Dash, the hero, had a mother and sister who were space scientists, his sidekick Slim had a niece who flew with Dash, and so on.

Crowded with well-illustrated robot drones, space-cruiser hardware, laser weaponry and exotic planets, *Starcom* was often a feast for the eyes, with notably excellent background graphics and lovingly detailed skyscapes. But the characters and storylines leaned toward the ploddish, wearying the young viewers for whom the tie-in line of *Starcom* action figures, toys, and video games was designed. The series ended after a 13-week run, though an early–1990s renewal of interest in outer space heroics warranted a *Starcom* rerun cycle in 1993 on cable's Family Channel.

STAR TREK. NBC: 9/8/1973–8/30/1975. Filmation/Norway/Paramount. Executive producer, Gene Roddenberry. Produced by Norm Prescott and Lou Scheimer. Assistant producer and story editor, D. C. Fontana. Directed by Hal Sutherland. Art director, Don Christensen. Written by D. C. Fontana, Marc Daniels, Margaret Armen, David Gerrold, James Schmerer, Walter Koenig, Larry Brody, Len Janson, Chuck Menville, Stephen Kandel, Joyce Perry, Samuel A. Peeples, Howard Weinstein, Russell Bates, David Wise, John Culver (aka Fred Bronson), Paul Schneider, Larry Niven, David P. Harmon, Dario Finelli. Music by Yvette Blais and Jeff Michael. Voices: William Shatner (Capt. James T. Kirk); Leonard Nimoy (Mr. Spock); DeForest Kelley (Dr. Leonard "Bones" McCoy); James Doohan (Chief Engineer Montgomery "Scotty" Scott); Majel Barrett (Nurse Christine Chapel); George Takei (Lt. Sulu); Nichelle Nichols (Uhura); Roger C. Carmel, and Ted Knight.

Star Trek—the original series, that is—was not so much watched as devoured by its fans. Though cancelled by NBC after three seasons in 1969 for inadequate ratings, the futuristic space-travel series had built up so loyal a following that the program quickly became the number one attraction on the rerun circuit, one of the very few hour long series outside of *Perry Mason* to succeed in a syndie market geared to the half hour form. Almost from the outset, the faithful kept alive rumors that somehow, somewhere, *Star Trek* would be revived, with the original cast and its original high quality intact. The legend began gathering real momentum in the early 1970s, when the first of the many *Star Trek* conventions was launched and the "Trekkers" began hobnobbing with numerous *Trek* cast members, most of whom would have welcomed steady work again.

The first *Star Trek* redo was not the feature length film promised by producer Gene Roddenberry (that wouldn't come until 1978), but a weekly, half hour cartoon series, produced jointly by Roddenberry and Filmation. At the 1972 *Trek* convention, Filmation executives Norm Prescott and Lou Scheimer appeared to make a solemn oath to fans that their series would be faithful to the original, enlisting as many original cast and writing people as possible and maintaining the lofty standards set by Roddenberry back in 1964. The cartoon producers even asked the NBC network that their *Star Trek* be scheduled at a later hour on Saturday mornings so that the scripts could be targetted to older children and young adults rather than the under-10 viewers who dominated the earlier Saturday timeslots. This would result in a 50 percent drop in potential audience, although the slack would be made up by the true blue Roddenberry disciples who (then as now) couldn't get enough *Star Trek* and could be depended upon as weekly tune-ins.

Though surely unnecessary, a few notes about the *Star Trek* premise are offered here as a frame of reference. The series was set in the 23rd century, on board the Federation of Planets' starship Enterprise. Boldly going where no man had gone before in pursuit of the Enterprise's three-year mission to seek out intelligent and (potentially) friendly extraterrestrial life forms, were William Shatner as Captain James T. Kirk; Leonard Nimoy as Vulcan/Human science officer Spock; DeForest Kelley as Dr. Leonard (Bones) McCoy; James Doohan as Montgomery (Scotty) Scott, chief engineer; Nichelle Nichols as communications officer Lt. Uhura; Majel Barrett (Roddenberry's real-life wife) as chief nurse Christine Chapel; George Takei as Asian helmsman Mr. Sulu; and from the second season on, Walter Koenig as Russian-born navigator Ensign Pavel Chekhov. True to their word, the Filmation people were able to round up all the above-mentioned principals for voicework on the cartoon *Star Trek*, with the exception of Walter Koenig, who nonetheless wrote one of the animated version's scripts.

It was certainly the prerogative of the home viewers to envision the happy cast reunions during the *Star Trek* recording sessions. But according to Filmation executive Norm Prescott, quoted in Gary Grossman's *Saturday Morning TV*, the *Star Trek* principal actors seldom saw one another. Prescott and Lou Scheimer were committed to a 1973 opening date, and didn't have time to assemble all the stars in one place—nor were they able to, since many of the actors, notably Shatner and Nimoy, had moved on to other projects. So the producers were forced to track down and record dialogue whenever and wherever their cast was handy. This meant instant looping sessions in airline terminals, clubhouse locker rooms, *Trek* conventions, and men's rooms (one hopes that

discretion ruled when the ladies were tape-recorded). For the record, Filmation historians Michael Swanigan and Darrell McNeil have refuted the notes in the previous sentences, commenting that most *Star Trek* recording sessions occurred with the cast working as an ensemble. Personally, I like Norm Prescott's version better. Imagine Leonard Nimoy elucidating logic in a toilet stall.

The resulting 22 *Star Trek* cartoon half hours did their best within their $75,000-per-episode budget to satisfy the series' cultists, even though there were carpers who weren't happy with the less than fluid movements of the animated Enterprise and the loss of Alexander Courage's compelling theme music. Foremost of the series' plusses was its superior writing staff, which included such veteran *Star Trek* scriveners as D. C. Fontana (the original *Trek*'s story editor, who worked in this capacity and as associate producer for the cartoon version at Gene Roddenberry's insistence), David Gerrold, Samuel A. Peeples and Stephen Kandel. Though none of the individual animated *Treks* has truly entered the canon along with the classic 78 "live" episodes, their scripts did get novelized for the paperback trade by *Star Trek Log* author Alan Dean Foster—who, according to legend, never bothered to watch the cartoon series!

Like the live version, the animated *Star Trek* was written with the assumption that the viewers could grasp concepts more complex and mature than the usual Saturday-morning status quo of flashy flying saucers, garish gadgetry and costumes, bug-eyed monsters, and indiscriminate laser blasts. Educators and TV watchdog groups were pleased by the series' script values and avoidance of excess violence. The TV industry as a whole also liked *Star Trek*: Its first episode, "Yesteryear," won a 1975 Emmy Award in the Outstanding Entertainment Children's Series category.

In one respect, the animated *Star Trek* had a major advantage over the original in its wider range of nonhuman characters, including several reptilian, canine and feline types in both the hero and villain contingencies; this variety wasn't always possible on the live series, which had to fight NBC's resistance against alien characters on the principle that the audience couldn't "identify" with a Venusian or Martian. The cartoon series also was more generous in the amount of dialogue given its supporting actors. Lt. Uhura in particular was allowed to toss off bizarre non sequitur quips whenever escaping the villainous Klingons (perhaps a result of actress Nichelle Nichols' ongoing complaints during the filming of the series that she was being shortchanged in terms of dialogue).

Whether or not the cartoon *Star Trek* was really a *great* show is as moot a point as is whether or not the original series was the best TV program ever produced in the history of humankind. Many discriminating Trekkers will give the animated series an appreciative nod, then move on to other things. The cartoon *Trek* was mentioned only in passing in the earliest *Star Trek* published histories, and virtually not at all in more recent volumes, wherein most space is taken up with the original series' *live* followups, *Star Trek: The Next Generation* and *Star Trek: Deep Space Nine.* But to those bleary-eyed viewers for whom *Star Trek* is the Alpha and Omega, the cartoon series could do no wrong. For such diehard devotees, the memory of the original clouded their perception of the cartoon, and it was virtually impossible to assess critically the Filmation version without the rosey nostalgic glow of the live *Star Trek* affecting their opinions.

Less sentimental were the editors of the iconoclastic 1993 magazine *Wild Cartoon Kingdom,* who in Issue One had several "burning questions" regarding the cartoon *Star Trek*: "Why doesn't Kirk's weight fluctuate like the real show? Why is it that the only thing that moves is the characters' mouths? Why do all the aliens look like fish?"

STEVEN SPIELBERG PRESENTS ANIMANIACS *see* **THE ANIMANIACS**

STEVEN SPIELBERG PRESENTS TINY TOON ADVENTURES *see* **TINY TOON ADVENTURES**

THE STONE PROTECTORS. Syndicated: 1993. Ace Novelty Co. Inc./ Fantasy, Ltd./Liu Concept Design and Associates/Graz Entertainment/Sachs TV Enterprises. Executive producer, Stephanie Graziano. Produced by Michael Hack. Story editor, Peter Lawrence. Director of

production, Doreen Rich. Supervising animation director, Richard Bowman. Animation directors, Bob Nesler and Sue Peter. Background design by Dennis Venizelos, Kim Ellis. Voice director, Susan Blu. Music composed by Steve Zuckerman; performed by "The Stone Protectors." Overseas animation studio, Liberty Bell Productions (division of Hyun Young Enterprises). Overseas supervisor, Barry Anderson. Voices: Don Brown, Ted Cole, Scott McNeil, Cathy Weseluck, Rob Morton, Jim Byrnes, Ian Corlett, John Tench, Terry Klassen, Louise Vallance, Cam Lane.

The daily, half hour *The Stone Protectors* was so cynical a grab-bag of past cartoon series ideas that it seems superfluous to cross-reference the properties ripped off herein. Perhaps perusing the pages of this book, one can determine just how many *Stone Protectors* elements were lifted from earlier animated series.

The five major characters were grungy teenaged boys who comprised a street rock band, "short on talent and long on nerve." The boys' physical and personal properties were jumbled up by the arrival of five extraterrestrial, multicolored gemstones, which streaked through the earth's atmosphere and crashed directly into the band during a performance. Kazango! The five rock wannabes were instantly transformed into musclebound, troll-like creatures, renamed "Stone Protectors" once the boy/trolls left the earth by way of an outer-space vortex.

The stones being protected, the five multicolored gems were actually fragments of the all-powerful Great Crystal of the planet Mythrandir. It had been shattered and sent to earth as a last ditch effort by Mythrandir's Empress Opal to keep it out of The Wrong Hands—which in this case belonged to the evil usurping warlords Zok and Zinc (who looked like "mean" trolls, in contrast to the "nice" Stone Protectors). I think you can pick up the storyline from here. The Teenaged Mutant Ninja, er Stone Protectors, found themselves aligned with Princess Opal in the fight against Zok and Zinc. And once in a while (though not a long enough while) the five S.P.'s sang a rock song.

You've gone this far with me—now comes the Stone Protectors roll call, complete with a tally of their individual "special powers." Yellow-haired Cornelius (the band's leader/vocalist) was the intellectual samurai specialist. Blue-haired Clifford (on drums) was a rock climber. Blond Scotsman Angus (on keyboard) was the "soldier" of the bunch. Redheaded Maxwell (lead guitar) was the swiftfooted "accelerator." And another red-top, Chester (bass and sax) was the wrestler.

Stone Protectors' TV premiere was preceded by plenty of merchandising from Ace Novelty Co., including a comic book—which, unique among such tie-ins, actually had worse artwork than the cartoon series itself (no small accomplishment). Evidently the property was patched together so quickly that the "research and development" people hadn't completely coordinated all the various *Stone Protectors* merchandising aspects; for example, Empress Opal, a brunette on TV, was a blonde in the comic book. It's one thing to follow the same concept–packaging procedures established by *Teenage Mutant Ninja Turtles* (q.v.). It's another thing to do it right.

Since this book covers only the TV cartoons which appeared up to December 31, 1993, *Stone Protectors* almost didn't make it. However, the series managed to sneak onto the airwaves the very last week of 1993.

STORYBOOK CLASSICS. Showtime: 1989–1991. Rabbit Ears Video. Produced by Mark Sottnick.

Storybook Classics began appearing in 1987 as a series of videocassettes, produced by Rabbit Ears Video. Like the company's *American Heroes and Legends* (q.v.) and *We All Have Tales* (q.v.), these half hours were not animated *per se*, but instead concentrated on the verbal. Well-known movie, stage and TV personalities were engaged to narrate classic children's stories; these were then illustrated with lovingly detailed still pictures, which through the utilization of quick dissolves, flat cuts, camera pans and hand-operated cardboard cutouts were given the illusion of movement. Eighteen *Storybook Classics* would be produced between 1988 and 1990, all of them telecast over the Showtime cable service on an irregular basis, sometimes concurrently with their home-video release.

Nine *Classics* were seen in 1989, the first year of the Showtime telecasts, including *Brer Rabbit and the Tar Baby* (narrated by

Danny Glover), *The Fisherman and His Wife* (Jodie Foster), Rudyard Kipling's *The Elephant's Child* (Jack Nicholson, who also read the subsequent Kipling "Just So Stories" adaptation of *How the Leopard Got His Spots*) and *The Steadfast Tin Soldier* (Jeremy Irons). Other *Storybook Classics* spotlighted such luminaries as Kelly McGillis, Holly Hunter, Meg Ryan and John Gielgud, reciting illustrated tales running the gamut from *Thumbelina*, to *Three Billy Goats Gruff*, to *The Emperor's New Clothes*. Most of the stars stuck to the script, with the conspicuous, and hilarious, exceptions of inveterate adlibbers Jonathan Winters (*Paul Bunyan*) and Robin Williams (*Pecos Bill*).

Storybook Classics' 1991 Christmas-week offering was something of a "full circle" for Rabbit Ears. As mentioned in the notes on *American Heroes and Legends*, the company's inaugural production, 1985's *Velveteen Rabbit*, was narrated by Meryl Streep. The actress was recalled three years later for a delectable rendition of Beatrix Potter's *Tailor of Gloucester* (illustrated by David Jorgenson, with music by Ireland's The Chieftains), which was duly broadcast over Showtime in 1989. *Tailor of Gloucester* received an encore performance in Showtime's stellar Christmas '91 attraction, one of the last *Storybook Classics* telecast.

The production represented not only an ending but a beginning, as an unofficial kickoff for a two-year Centennial celebration of Beatrix Potter's *Peter Rabbit* stories. The same week that Rabbit Ear's *Tailor of Gloucester* was cablecast, a live action version of the story was seen on PBS. Within the next two seasons, the story did yeoman service as ballet and theatrical presentations. Finally in 1993, *Tailor of Gloucester* was recreated for *another* series of animated videocassettes-turned-cable specials: *The World of Peter Rabbit and Friends* (q.v.).

THE STREET FROGS *see* **COMIC STRIP**

STUFFY DURMA *see* **MILTON THE MONSTER**

STUNT DAWGS. Syndicated: 9/28/1992–. Rainforest Entertainment/Claster. Executive producers, Jeff Franklin, Steve Waterman. Produced by Kevin O'Donnell. Executive consultant, Steve Bel. Story editors: Cliff MacGillvray, Jeffrey McNickel Rose. Directed by John Grusd, Blair Peters. Supervising director, Michael Maliani. Music composed by Allaman. Production supervisor, Stacy Gallishaw. Executive in charge of production, Brian Miller. Copyrighted by Franklin/Waterman 2, Licensees of Seabrook Productions, Inc. Produced in association with Reteitalia and Telecino. Production facilities: Milimatos, SaeRom, Big Star, Point Animation, Woo Nam. Voices: Neil Crone (Needham/Whizkid); John Stocker (Fungus); Greg Morton (Splatter/Crash/Velda); Greg Swanson (Lucky/Skiddd); Ron Rubin (Airball/Slyme); Harvey Atkin (Badyear/Half-a-Mind); Lenore Zann (Sizzle); Barbara Budd (Nina Newscaster).

Stunt Dawgs was a half hour cartoon daily inspired by the 1980 film Hooper, which starred Burt Reynolds as a dauntless movie stuntman and was directed by former stuntman Hal Needham. On the 40-episode Stunt Dawgs, a handsomer-than-the-original "Needham" was head of a group of stuntpersons (not "dawgs," but humans), who doubled as crimefighters while motoring from one location shoot to another in their hi-tech truck. Needham's Dawgs included African American Crash, preppie Splatter, gorgeous female member Sizzle, and Lucky, who, true to inverse-nickname logic, was the unluckiest of the bunch.

The villains, with fingers in dirty pies ranging from jewel robbery to ecological plundering, were members of a renegade band of Tinseltown athletes called The Stunt Scabs. They were headed by reckless movie producer/director Richard P. Fungus, who in the Stunt Dawgs pre-release publicity was originally named Peter Bogus, harking back to an abrasive character played by Robert Klein in Hooper, allegedly a caricature of Peter Bogdanovich. Beyond the strong possibility of legal action from the real-life "inspiration," Peter Bogus would have to be rechristened because there was already a Mr. Bogus (q.v.) cartoon series in 1992. No changes were required with the names of Richard Fungus' main assistants: French-accented Airball, "Scabs" bearing such monickers as Badyear and Half-a-Mind, and a corrupt lawyer named Slyme, who was poised to press the Stunt Dawgs to honor their potentially fatal contractual commitments to Fungus Studios.

Syndicated to 85 stations within the confines of the 7–8:30 A.M. and 3:30–5:30 P.M. timeslots, Stunt Dawgs passed the time, but funnier satirical jibes at Hollywood, and classier artwork, could be found any day on Tiny Toon Adventures (q.v.).

SUB-MARINER see THE MARVEL SUPER HEROES

SUPER DAVE. Fox: 9/12/1992–8/28/1993. Blye-Einstein Productions/DIC/Reteitalia Ltd. Executive producers: Andy Heyward, Bob Einstein, Allan Blye, Robby London. Produced by Mike Maliani. Adapted for animation by Reed and Bruce Shelley, Mike Maliani, Bob Einstein, Allan Blye. Directed by Joe Barruso. Story editors, Reed and Bruce Shelley. Music by Tom Worral, Murray McFadden, Mike Watt, Clark Gassman, Reed Robbins, and Mark Simon. Animation facilities: Hung Long Animation Co., Ltd., SaeRom Plus One Co., Ltd. Voices: Bob Einstein (Super Dave); Art Irizawa (Fuji); and Charlie Adler, Jack Angel, Jesse Corti, Brian George, Don Lake, Susan Silo, Kath Soucie, Louise Vallance, B. J. Ward, and Frank Welker.

Variations of comedian Bob Einstein's "Super Dave" character had first popped up on the late–1960s Smothers Brothers Comedy Hour, the writing staff of which included Einstein and his longtime partner Allan Blye. Basically a parody of those blunt, humorless "experts" who showed up at high school assemblies to explain the rights and wrongs of health, hygiene and home safety, Super Dave was honed to perfection on the R-rated Showtime cable comedy sketch series Bizarre (1980–85), resulting in the spinoff Super Dave Showtime offering in 1987. The character's appeal was his living-cartoon quality: Super Dave, a fearless products tester and the premier proponent of "safety first," was invariably (and spectacularly) run over, blown up and shredded in the tradition of cartoondom's Wile E. Coyote.

The next move must have seemed like a natural to Einstein, Allan Blye, DIC and the Fox Network. Since Super Dave was one step removed from a cartoon, why not make him literally a cartoon in his own weekly half hour? The resultant Super Dave did just that—and promptly lost all the charm it had had as a live-actioner. While it was absurdly funny to see a flesh

Stunt Dawgs: for a change, funny humans.

SKIDDD   SIZZLE   SPLAT

More Stunt Dawgs.

and blood human being treated in the fanciful manner of an animated figure, there was nothing absurd at all to see a cartoon character treated in this fashion — and the less absurd, the less amusing.

Grasping at past-success straws to pump up *Super Dave*, the producers aimed at a *Roger Ramjet* (q.v.) approach. Like *Ramjet*, *Super Dave* exploited a "Red, White and Blue" motif (Dave and was a freelance secret agent for the Good Ol' USA) and a dependence on ripe vocal hyperbole. The series also aped the "funny mutant" approach of *Attack of the Killer Tomatoes*, *Teenage Mutant Ninja Turtles* and *Toxic Crusader* (see individual entries on these series), with a pinch of *Superman* (q.v.) tossed in. Super Dave's rival daredevil was the evil Slash Hazard, whom Dave had accidentally pushed into a car compressing machine (a lampoon of the lab accident which spawned *Superman* villain Lex Luthor), and who was then transformed into a vengeful half-man, half-automobile. It was theoretically a great notion, but the execution was only so-so.

Even the funnier *Super Dave* moments (most of them at the expense of Dave's superiors, President Bush and Vice President Quayle) were unintentionally compromised by the hint of racism. Dave's sidekick Fuji was conceived as a positive Asian character, but soon lapsed into retrogressive stereotype by mispronouncing his "L's" and "R's" and exhibiting an obsessive affection for computers and gadgetry. The fact that a genuine Asian actor provided Fuji's voice did not completely compensate for this unfortunate "Goofy Jap" characterization.

Each *Super Dave* closed with a sidesplitting clip from Dave's live action Showtime series, reminding us only too well just what the animated *Super Dave* wasn't.

The cartoon *Dave* was cancelled by Fox in 1993, not because of its flaws but because it occupied the choice timeslot following the vastly superior *X-Men*. Fox planned to bracket *X-Men* with another comic strip derivation, *Phantom 2040*, but at the last minute decided to go "FCC Friendly" with a more prosocial series, a cartoon version of PBS' live-action *Where in the World Is Carmen Sandiego?* Even this series failed to materialize (it was rescheduled for early 1994) because Margaret Loesch was unhappy with the

pilot. Which raises the nagging question: Loesch was *happy* with *Super Dave?*

SUPER FRIENDS. ABC: 9/8/1973–8/30/1975; 2/21/1976–9/3/1977.
—**ALL-NEW SUPER FRIENDS HOUR.** ABC: 9/10/1977–9/2/1978.
—**CHALLENGE OF THE SUPERFRIENDS.** ABC: 9/8/1978–9/15/1979.
—**THE WORLD'S GREATEST SUPERFRIENDS.** ABC: 9/22/1979–9/27/1980.
—**SUPERFRIENDS HOUR.** ABC: 10/4/1980–9/3/1983. DC Publications/Hanna-Barbera. Executive producers, William Hanna and Joseph Barbera. Produced by Iwao Takamoto (1973–75) and Don Jurwich (1977–80). Directed by Charles Nichols, Carl Urbano, Ray Patterson, Oscar Dufau and George Gordon. Written by Jeffrey Scott, Rich Hoberg, Will Meugniot, Don Sheppard, Emilie Kong, and Larry Latham. Music by Hoyt Curtin. Supervised by Alex Toth. Voices: Danny Dark (Superman); Olan Soule (Batman); Casey Kasem (Robin); Shannon Farnon (Wonder Woman); Norman Alden, Bill Callaway (Aquaman/Green Lantern/Plastic Man); Frank Welker (Marvin/Wonder Dog); Sherry Alberoni (Wendy); John Stephenson (Col. Wilcox). Additional voices after 1977: Mike Bell (Zan/Gleeck); Liberty Williams (Jayne); Casey Kasem (Computer); Buster Jones (Black Vulcan); Michael Rye (Apache Chief/Green Lantern); Frank Welker (Marvel the wonder dog); Sherry Alberoni (Wendy). LEGION OF DOOM: Stan Jones (Luthor); Ted Cassidy (Brainiac/Black Manta); Frank Welker (Toyman); Ruth Forman (Giganta); Marlene Aragon (Cheeta); Mike Bell (Riddler); Dick Ryal (Captain Cold); Vic Perrin (Sinestro); Don Messick (Scarecrow); Bill Callaway (Bizarro); Jimmy Weldon (Solomon Grundy); Stanley Ross (Grodd the Gorilla). Narrators: Ted Knight (1973–77); Bob Lloyd (1977–78); William Woodson (1977–78, 1980); Stanley Ross (1978–79).
—**SUPER FRIENDS: THE LEGENDARY SUPER POWERS SHOW.** ABC: 9/8/1984–8/31/1985. Hanna-Barbera. Executives in charge of production: Jayne Barbera, Jean MacCurdy. Directed by Charles Nichols, Ray Patterson, Carl Urbano, Oscar Dufau, George Gordon. Creative producer, Iwao Takamoto. Written by Alan Burnett (among others).

Voices: Danny Dark (Superman); B. J. Ward (Wonder Woman); Adam West (Batman); Casey Kasem (Robin); Mark Taylor (Firestorm); Ernie Hudson (Cyborg); Frank Welker (Darkseid/Kabilak); Rene Auberjonois (Desaad).
—SUPER POWERS TEAM: GALACTIC GUARDIANS. ABC: 9/7/1985–9/30/1986. Hanna-Barbera. Credits basically the same as SUPER FRIENDS: THE LEGENDARY SUPER POWERS SHOW. (Cross reference *Batman, Plastic Man* and *Superman*.)

Super Friends was a (very) delayed offshoot of *The Justice Society of America*, a comic book concept created by Sheldon Mayer and Gardner Fox for National Periodicals' All-American Comics division in 1940. The original strategy behind all this was to sustain reader interest in National's second-echelon superheroes (Superman and Batman didn't need this sort of boost) by lumping them together in a team. The first "Justice Society" lineup, appearing in *All-Star #3*, were the Flash, the Green Lantern, Hawkman, Hourman, Sandman, Dr. Fate, Spectre and Atom, each appearing in separate adventures tentatively tied together by the "team" concept. As popularity of National's individual stars fluctuated, so too did the Justice Society membership. Guest stars, a handful lasting longer than a few issues, included Wonder Woman, The Black Canary, Johnny Thunder, the Red Tornado, and as a circulation-boosting ploy, the first teaming of Superman and Batman.

The Justice Society was disbanded after 57 issues, but when superheroes became "hot" again in 1960, Gardner Fox revivified the concept, this time in collusion with editor Julius Schwartz and artist Mike Sekowsky. The result was *The Justice League of America*, again designed to sustain interest in National/DC's characters in between their own starring comics, which premiered in *Brave and Bold #28*. This time around, the floating membership roster included Wonder Woman, Hawkman, The Green Arrow, The Black Canary, J'onn J'onnz, and other less familiar National/DC properties.

When the *Justice League* matriculated to TV animation as part of *The Superman/Aquaman Hour of Adventure* (see *Superman*), the team lineup included Superman, The Green Lantern, the Atom, and Hawkman. Only three *Justice League* car-

toon shorts were produced (though the aforementioned heroes were spotlighted elsewhere on *Superman/Aquaman*), but the concept refused to die. A 1973 revival of interest in TV superheroes all but decreed a return of *Justice League of America*. But *not* with that title! Considering that America was reeling from its disastrous Vietnam experience, the ABC network and Hanna-Barbera wanted to avoid a title that smacked of overzealous patriotism. *Super Friends* was decided upon; the title was—well, it was super-friendlier. Also, ABC wished to sidestep the usual clean-up-TV admonitions of "mindlessness" and "gratuitous violence." *Super Friends* would be a caped and cowled learning seminar, wherein the Heroes would stress and practice teamwork, trust and cooperation. Thus, Dr. Haim Ginott, a "pop" child psychologist familiar on the talk-show trail thanks to his bestselling book *Between Parent and Child*, was engaged to act as *Super Friends'* psychological advisor.

The first *Super Friends* cast list included old reliables Superman and Aquaman and Green Lantern, together with Batman (see this character's separate entry) and Robin. Appearing for the first time in TV animation was Wonder Woman (a.k.a. Diana Prince), the golden-lasso-wielding heroine originally created in 1942 by psychologist William Moulton Marston (a.k.a. Charles Moulton—does *everyone* in the comic book industry travel under two names?). Wonder Woman had been created to give young girls a positive comic book role model, and in this spirit many latter-day feminists have rallied around this character, despite the property's uncomfortable S&M subtext, which encompassed bondage, domination, male-bashing and even subliminal lesbianism. Thankfully for ABC's and Hanna-Barbera's purposes, the comic book Wonder Woman had been "cleaned up" long before *Super Friends*. Echoing William Moulton Marston's intent, W.W.'s inclusion on the cartoon series' lineup was as a balm to critics who'd complained about the paucity of self-reliant female characters on Saturday morning TV.

A second new-to-TV DC favorite made sporadic *Super Friends* appearances: *Plastic Man*, who'd be seen to better effect on his own Ruby-Spears series (which see) in 1979. *Super Friends* rounded out its membership with a trio of freshly minted characters, in the tradition of *Justice League*'s Teen Titans: Wendy and Marvin, Junior Super Friends, and their *Scooby Doo*-ish pet Wonder Dog.

The weekly half hour *Super Friends* represented Hanna-Barbera's only comic book derivation of the 1970s; the series was itself adapted by D.C. into a *Super Friends* comic book in November 1976, which read like a kiddie-matinee *Justice League of America*. The healthy success of *Super Friends* was due in no small part to the creative input of comic book artist Alex Toth (see *Space Angel*), who oversaw Hanna-Barbera's Australian production facilities. After the first production cycle shut down, reruns of *Super Friends* resurfaced in 1976 in response to the primetime popularity of *Wonder Woman* (the live action version with Lynda Carter) and *Six Million Dollar Man*; then, the property was freshened with new episodes in 1977 under the title *The All-New Super Friends Hour*. New cast members were added to the Super Friends roster, albeit at the expense of the wimpish Junior Justice League: Zan (male) and Janya (female), the Wonder Twins, who had the dubiously beneficial talent of turning themselves into icelike statues. The various stars appeared in their own separate adventures, rallying for the "League of Justice" component. The weekly *All-New Super Friends Hour* was capped by FCC-dictated health and safety tips.

Challenge of the Super Friends followed in 1978, with the ever-expanding Good Guy team (which now included Black Vulcan, Apache Chief, Samurai and Hawkman) pitted against the Legion of Doom, populated by such dear old DC scoundrels as Lex Luthor, Brainiac, Bizarro, Toyman and The Riddler. As in previous *Super Friends* incarnations, violence was sidestepped if not avoided altogether, and the positive aspects of teamwork played up.

Not that this satisfied the National Association of Better Broadcasting, which pegged the series as a wolf in sheep's clothing, advocating vigilantism over police authority: "[*The Super Friends*] always save us. We don't need anybody else. Everything is settled by the violent use of super power. That's the message." Nor were a group of children's experts gathered together by *TV Guide* in 1980 satisfied by the series, which by then was

travelling under the title *The World's Greatest Superfriends*: "Old cartoons hiding behind a new title. A tremendous amount of destructive behavior." The hostile reaction against *Super Friends* is hard to fathom (unless we accept the opinion of many animation producers that the "experts" never bothered to watch any cartoon past the opening titles), since the producers' guidelines against violence were as rigid as the opinions of the NABB or the *TV Guide* panel. Animators were even advised that they couldn't show anyone shaking a fist at anyone else on *Super Friends*—and if a fly was swatted, it couldn't be killed!

After three seasons of reruns, a new batch of *Super Friends* adventures was put together and networkcast in 1984 as *Super Friends: The Legendary Super Powers Hour*, easily the best designed and animated series in this saga to date. Backstage contributors this time around were producer Jean MacCurdy and writer Alan Burnett, who several years later collaborated on Warners' *Batman: The Animated Series* (q.v.). For Burnett, the *Super Friends* gig was a mixed blessing; he loved the close contact with his favorite comic book characters, but despaired when Hanna-Barbera ordered the staff to change characters and storylines to conform with the *Super Friends* toy and action figure spinoffs.

The pared-down *Legendary Super Power Show* cast included returnees Batman, Robin, Superman and Wonder Woman. Newcomers to the project were, like their predecessors, comic-book veterans. The bionic Cyborg, the first African American member of the Superfriends, had earlier been introduced in print as one of the "Teen Titans" (see *Superman* for more on this aggregation). And Firestorm, a "nuclear" character who had no fewer than *two* alter egos (he was the combination of a scientist's brain power and a teenager's strength and enthusiasm), had also debuted in the DC comics line of the 1980s. Gone were most of the old-line villains (though veteran *Superman* foe Mr. Mxyzptlk made a welcome appearance), replaced by extraterrestrials Darkseid and Desaad, superpowered "Darth Vader" types created and designed by longtime Marvel mainstay Jack Kirby.

The outer space trappings prevalent on

this go-round were underlined when the series returned in 1985 under a new title, *Super Powers Team: The Galactic Guardians*. Despite its shiny new veneer, this last *Super Friends* variation adhered faithfully to DC tradition with a "Bizarro Super Powers Team" episode, featuring slapsticky doppelganger versions of the stars. After one *Galactic Guardians* season, which ran a distant second to NBC's omnipotent *Smurfs* (q.v.), *Super Friends* retreated to rerun syndication. As for the principals, Superman's licensing passed on to Ruby-Spears for an animated 1988 revival; Batman was optioned by Warner Bros. for his spectacular cartoon return in 1992; and Wonder Woman, Cyborg and Firestorm were once more exclusively the property of the comic pages.

THE SUPER GLOBETROTTERS *see* **THE HARLEM GLOBETROTTERS**

SUPER MARIO BROTHERS SUPER SHOW. Syndicated: 1989. Nintendo/DIC/Viacom. Produced and conceived by Andy Heyward. Coordinating producer, Robby London. Animation director, SUPER MARIO segments: Dan Riba. Director, ZELDA segments: John Grusd. Music supervision: Joanne Miller, Andy Heyward, Saban Productions. Animation facilities: Reteitalia, Sei Young. Story editors, Reed and Bruce Shelley. Live action sequences directed by Kevin O'Donnell. CLUB MARIO created by Kevin O'Donnell, Eric Schultz. Music composed by Eric Alaman. Components: 1. SUPER MARIO BROS. Voices: Captain Lou Albano (Mario); Danny Wells (Luigi); Harvey Atkin (King Koopa/ Mushroom Mayor/ Tryclyde/ Sniffet); John Stocker (Toad/ Mouser/ Troopa/ Beezo/Flurry); Jeannie Elias (Princess Toadstool/Shyguy). 2. LEGEND OF ZELDA. Voices: Cyndy Preston (Zelda); Jonathan Potts (Link); Len Carlson (Ganon); Colin Fox (Harkinian); Elizabeth Hanna (Triforce of Wisdom); Allan Stewart Coates (Triforce of Power); Len Carlson (Moblin). Additional voices: Robert Bockstael, Dorian Joe Clark, Rob Cowan, Denise Pigeon, Paulina Gillis, Greg Morton, Greg Swanson, Dianne Fabian, Marilyn Lightstone, Marla Lukovsky. CLUB MARIO live-action sequences: Captain Lou Albano (Mario); Danny Wells (Luigi); Chris Coombs (Tommy Treehugger);

Michael Anthony Rawlins (Evil Eric); Kurt Weldon (Dr. Know It All); Victoria Delany (Tammy Treehugger); James Rose (The Big Kid); James Abbott (The Band); Shanta Kahn (Princess Centauri).

—CAPTAIN N AND THE ADVENTURES OF SUPER MARIO BROS. 3. NBC: 9/8/1990–9/7/1991.

—CAPTAIN N AND THE NEW SUPER MARIO WORLD. NBC: 9/14/ 1991–7/25/1992. (See above credits— minus live action sequences—and entry for CAPTAIN N: THE GAME MASTER. Tony Rosato replaced Captain Lou Albano in the role of Mario.)

Nintendo's *Super Mario Bros.* video game was a spinoff from the company's earlier "Donkey Kong" (see *Saturday Supercade*). The antagonist of that game was an abusive little carpenter named Mario, who made life for his pet gorilla Donkey Kong a Living Heck. Observers at the time noted that the mustachioed, red overall–clad Mario looked more like a plumber than a carpenter; thus it was as a plumber that Mario graduated to his own series of arcade and home-video games. For the purpose of having at least one more saleable character commodity, Mario was given a tall, green-overalled brother named Luigi. With a scenario that began with the Brothers being flushed down a Brooklyn sewer, then emerging into the alternate-world Mushroom Kingdom, *Super Mario Bros.* was unveiled in 1983. Coming at a time when the videogame business was in a slump, the topselling *Super Mario* was credited as the concept which singlehandedly rescued a megamillion-dollar industry.

Continuous improvements were made in the basic circuitry over the next six years. Whereas the first *Super Mario Bros.* used weapons to fight villains in the Mushroom Kingdom, *Super Mario Bros. 2* added humor to the proceedings by trading in guns and clubs for ripe, throwable vegetables. In 1989 we were introduced to *Super Mario Bros. 3*, with bells, whistles, and the Brothers' newfound ability to fly added to the recipe. This was the most successful variation yet, selling seven million units in the U.S. and four million in Nintendo's home base of Japan.

Now the *Mario* phenomenon was too big to be ignored by non-videogame fans. Inevitably, the cognoscenti grabbed the character by the scruff of the neck and tried to shake some "relevancy" into it. The San Francisco *Examiner* explained that Mario was an "existential hero," trapped in a world he never made. That's the sort of thing written by newspaper reporters seeking to justify their hanging around the local arcade.

Of more practical value than dissecting *Super Mario*'s appeal was transferring it to the cartoon drawing board. The daily, half hour *Super Mario Bros. Super Show*, syndicated by DIC, borrowed liberally from all existing versions of the original game. Mario and Luigi, stranded in the Mushroom Kingdom, were obliged to rescue the luscious Princess Toadstool and her aide Toad from the reptilian scoundrel King Koopa. The series strove to emphasize humor over violence, failing to be truly impressive in either department. *Super Mario Bros. Super Show* garnered ratings thanks to the built-in reputation of the videogames, but added little to the concept that wasn't already there. Even the constantly shifting backgrounds which complicated the *Super Mario* episodes, though attractively designed, weren't any more effective than those seen on the arcade screen. Unlike Hanna-Barbera's enjoyable earlier *Pac-Man, Super Mario Bros.* was merely an adjunct to its parent game rather than an expansion.

A secondary *Super Mario Bros.* component, also based on a Nintendo game, was actually more fun to watch than the *Mario* segments. *The Legend of Zelda* featured a 15-year-old princess who lived in the world of Cri. Ganon, evil wizard of the Kingdom of Hyrule, was engaged in a mazelike race with Zelda for the great "Source of Wisdom" that would enable him to rule all he surveyed. Zelda was aided by Link, a young adventurer the same age as the princess, while Ganon was armed with the magical assistance of an evil talking mirror. Basic *He-Man* and *She-Ra* stuff, to be sure, but handled with finesse. *Legend of Zelda* popped up on a weekly, serialized basis in the body of the daily *Super Mario Bros.*

Both *Mario* and *Zelda* took a back seat to the most entertaining aspect of *Super Mario Bros. Super Show*: the live-action wraparounds, set at teen-trendy Club Mario and featuring such members as "Tommy and Tammy Treehugger" and "Evil Eric." The Club Mario scenes were delightful sendups of "typical" local live action kiddie shows, replete with resident scientist Dr. Know It All and a one-man "Band." Captain Lou Albano, a popular professional wrestler, showed up from time to time at the Club, bringing to life his voiceover role as the cartoon Mario (Albano's gargantuan likeness—minus his voice—had previously been used by DIC on *Hulk Hogan's Rock 'n' Wrestling* [q.v.]). "Club Mario's" finest moment was its interview segment with DIC president Andy Heyward, who was aggressively grilled to determine just what it was he did for a living.

All *Super Mario Bros. Super Show* material, minus the live wraparounds, was incorporated with new material into the network Nintendo derivation *Captain N and the Super Mario Bros.* in 1990 (see *Captain N: The Game Master*). This in turn was retooled with still newer episodes, including adventures of still another Nintendo character based on the "Gameboy" pocket computer, as *Captain N and the New Super Mario World* in 1991. This state of affairs remained intact until NBC dropped practically all its cartoons in August of 1992, the better to expand its Monday-through-Friday *Today Show* to weekends. The animated *Super Mario Bros.* and its companion pieces were consigned to cable-TV rerun play, but show business wasn't quite finished with the property. In the summer of 1993, a live-action film version of *Super Mario* made the rounds, with Bob Hoskins (replacing both Dustin Hoffman and Danny DeVito) as Mario and Dennis Hopper beautifully typecast as the lizardlike King Koopa. But this time around, even the goodwill engendered by the still-flourishing videogame couldn't save *Super Mario Bros.* from gurgling down the pipes to box-office disaster.

SUPER POWERS TEAM: GALACTIC GUARDIANS *see* **SUPER FRIENDS**

SUPER PRESIDENT AND SPY SHADOW. NBC: 9/16/1967–9/14/1968. DePatie-Freleng. Executive producers, David H. DePatie and Friz Freleng. Voices: Paul Frees (President James Norcross); Daws Butler (Richard Vance); and Ted Knight, June Foray, Paul Frees, Shep Menken, Don Menken, Don Messick, Lorrie Scott, Mark Scor.

You may not believe it unless you've actually seen it (which I have, damn my eyes), but there really was a weekly half hour series back in 1967 called *Super President and Spy Shadow*. The second-billed component character was a more serious variation of *Q. T. Hush* (q.v.) about private eye Richard Vance and his independently functioning shadow. Never mind that— you *really* want to get to the "Super President" part, don't you?

James Norcross, chief executive of the United States, was transformed into a Superhero by fallout from a cosmic storm (consider yourself warned about that acid rain). In between conducting press conferences and lighting the White House Christmas tree, Super President flew through the sky without the help of Air Force One, spending most of his time rescuing his vice president from various grisly fates. Perhaps Humphrey, Agnew and Quayle were fans of the show, but they wouldn't admit it. Well, maybe Quayle would.

Beyond the fact that a series about an invulnerable president was ill-advised (at best) a scant four years after the Kennedy assassination, *Super President and Spy Shadow* was jaw-dropping in its awfulness. The NABB laid it on a bit thick, but said it best: "An all-time low in bad taste, with the President of the United States in a Superman role. NBC was responsible for this direct ideological approach to totalitarianism. We fear that there may be other broadcasters who are irresponsible enough to keep it in circulation."

Not if its creators, DePatie-Freleng, could help it. To quote David DePatie: "I think it was really the worst thing we've ever made. It was a real turkey. We tried to put our comedy people on it, but it really looked terrible."

Rival producers Hanna-Barbera might possibly have cast the series in a more favorable light. After all, *Super President* made its Saturday morning network competition, Hanna-Barbera's *Fantastic Four* (q.v.) and *The Herculoids* (q.v.), look brilliant by comparison.

SUPER SIX. NBC: 9/10/1966–9/6/1969. DePatie-Freleng/Mirisch-Rich. Produced by David H. DePatie and Friz Freleng. Directed by Art Davis, Dave Detiege, Art Leonardi, Hawley Pratt. Voices: Daws Butler (Magnet Man); Paul Stewart (Ele-

vator Man); Arte Johnson (Super Scuba); Lyn Johnson (Granite Man); Charles Smith (Super Bwoing); Paul Frees (Captain Zammo); Daws Butler, Paul Frees (The Brothers Matzoriley); and Pat Carroll, June Foray, Joan Gerber, and Diana Maddox.

Super Six, DePatie-Freleng's first TV cartoon series, was a weekly half hour starring a bunch of futuristic oddball characters working for Super Services Inc., a "hero for hire" operation. The "Super Services" segments featured Elevator Man, Super Scuba, Magnet Man, Granite Man, and Captain Zammo. (Earlier reports on *Super Six* have included an additional character, Super Stretch, who was evidently dropped or renamed before the series premiere.) Super Bwoing, an inept singing-cowboy type reminiscent of Hanna-Barbera's "El Kabong" (see *Quick Draw McGraw*), and the ethnically jumbled Brothers Matzoriley, were the stars of the series' two companion components.

If you had to have funny superheroes with offbeat and endearingly pointless special powers, you were well served in 1966, with *Super Six* on NBC and Ralph Bakshi's similar *The Mighty Heroes* (q.v.) on CBS—which as luck would have it briefly ran opposite each other on Saturday mornings. The 21-episode *Super Six* was pleasant enough entertainment put together by seasoned cartoon pros, but it was unsteady Saturday morning competition for CBS' ratings champ *Mighty Mouse Playhouse* (see *Mighty Mouse*)—so much so, in fact, that many NBC affiliates preempted *Super Six* in favor of local programs. Nevertheless, the network had to schedule *something* other than a test pattern from 9 to 9:30 A.M. (EST), so it stuck with *Super Six* through two subsequent rerun seasons, where the series continued to finish third opposite such CBS and ABC rivals as *The New Casper Cartoon Show* (see *Casper the Friendly Ghost*), *Frankenstein Jr. and the Impossibles* (q.v.), and *The Bugs Bunny/Road Runner Show* (see *Bugs Bunny*).

SUPER SUNDAY. Syndicated: 1985. Marvel/Sunbow/Claster. Executive in charge of production, Lee Gunther. Creative director, Jay Bacal. Executive producers, Joe Bacall, Margaret Loesch, Tom Griffin. Title songs by Kinder and Bryant. Producers: Don Jurwich, Alex

Lovy. Director of production, Jim Graziano. Story editor, Alan Swayze. For Sunbow: Associate producers, Doug Booth and Roger Slifer. Directors: Gerry Chiniquy, Norman McCabe, Tom Ray, Bob Matz, Brad Case, Joan Case, Warren Batchelder, Karen Peterson, Al Kouzel, M. Flores Nichols, Bob Kirk, Bob Shellhorn, Bob Treat, Bill Exter. Voices: Charlie Adler, Michael Bell, Arthur Burghardt, Susan Blu, Cory Burton, Bill Callaway, Victoria Carroll, Nancy Cartwright, Fred Collins, Brad Crandall, Peter Cullen, Pat Fraley, Linda Gary, Dick Gautier, Ed Gilbert, Chris Latta, Jason Naylor, Neil Ross, Stanley Ralph Ross, Richard Sanders, Susan Silo, John Stephenson, Frank Welker. (See also *JEM* and *Inhumanoids*.)

Super Sunday was Marvel Productions' first foray into weekend block programming, in the manner of *The Funtastic World of Hanna-Barbera*. The syndicated package consisted of three separate half-hour weeklies, all related to toys and action figures from the Hasbro/Milton Bradley plants.

The first component, *Robotix*, was *Super Sunday*'s slant on the already established *Transformers* (q.v.), with elements of such live-action movie/TV properties as *Star Wars, Invasion of the Body Snatchers, Alien* and the long-forgotten Harlan Ellison TVer *Starlost* woven into the proceedings. *Robotix* was set on the planet Skalorr, where the reptilian-humanoid populace was divided into enemy camps: the "good" Protectons and the "bad" Terrakons. The Terrakons had developed the deadly superweapon Terrastar, which could only be activated when conjoined with the Protectons' central intelligence computer Compucor. Just when both factions had reached a truce, Skalorr's sun turned into a supernova, threatening mass destruction. A plan was drawn up to "bottle" the citizenry in stasis tubes, but radiation threatened this notion, so Compucor transformed the "life essences" of the Skalorrians into huge guardian robots, or Robotix (pronounced "ro-*bah*-tix," to avoid confusion with the Japanese cartoon series *Robotech* [q.v.]). Even as robots, the denizens of Skalorr were split into heroes and villains, with such characters as Argus, Bront, Koncor and Nara on the "right" side, and Tyrannix, Narok, Jarark, Stegar and Goon among the opposition.

Three million years later—to make a long story short—a space vehicle from earth, piloted by Commander Exeter, was forced to crash land on Skalorr, where the Protectons and Terrakons were carrying on their ages-old struggle through the auspices of the Robotix. To survive on Skalorr, the earthlings were forced to "interface" with the robots, and even here the battle lines were drawn: Exeter's group aligned with the Protectons, while covetous, Klingon-like crewman Kanark led his stooges into the Terrakon camp. Since *Robotix* was told in serialized fashion, all this backstory was spread out over several weeks. The remaining episodes were taken up with such complications as Compucor's fluctuating loyalties and the heroes' and villains' life-essences bouncing back and forth between the good and bad machines. Potentially enthralling, the 15-episode *Robotix* was undercut by an overload of computer terminology (which sounded like Korean hi-fi instructions to computer "illiterates"), the sameness of character design, the lumbering pace, and way too many closeups of machines talking to one another.

Simpler, shorter, and more attractively designed was *Super Sunday*'s second component. *Bigfoot and the Muscle Machine* starred "monster truck" driver Yank Justice and his super-trucker friends. While described in the theme song as "Big, Bad, Dirty and Mean," Yank Justice couldn't have been more generous in protecting an innocent young man and woman from the perfidy of evil industrialist Mr. Big. The object of the nine-episode cliffhanger plotline was a lost treasure, with clues to its whereabouts revealed on a secret map. It was hoped that the home viewers would play along with the *Big Foot* protagonists and antagonists, using their own tie-in toystore hardware.

While both *Robotix* and *Bigfoot and the Muscle Machine* were serialized, the third *Super Sunday* component was not: *JEM*, a tale of a beautiful young rock star who doubled on magic and mysticism, proved so popular that it branched off into its own separate weekly series (which see). *JEM*'s replacement was another chapter-play, *Inhumanoids* (q.v.), which likewise was spun off as a self-contained entry when the rest of the *Super Sunday* package was cancelled in the fall of 1986.

Though most of the *Super Sunday* components failed to click either as series or merchandising tools, the success of *Jem* encouraged Marvel to go the "block program" route again with the 1988 portmanteau weekender *Marvel Action Universe* (q.v.).

SUPERBOOK. Syndicated: 1982. CBN/ Tatsunoko Productions. Produced by Warren Marcus and Jason Vinley. English version by Echo Productions. Theme music: Live Oak Sounds. Written by Ray Owens. Voices: Billie Lou Watt, Sonia Owens, Helene Van Koert, Ray Owens, Bill Mack.
  —FLYING HOUSE. Syndicated: 1982. CBN/Tatsunoko Productions. Production supervised by Warren Marcus, Ned Vankervich. Production associate, Greg Cummings. English version by Echo Productions. Written by Ray Owens. Theme music: Live Oak Sounds. Voices: Billie Lou Watt, Sonia Owens, Hal Studer, Helene Van Koert, Peter Fernandez, Ray Owens, George Gunneau.
  Syndicated in 1982 by the Christian Broadcasting Network and cablecast at the same time over the CBN service (now known as Family Channel), *Superbook* and *Flying House* were the first nationally distributed religious cartoon series since 1960's *Davey and Goliath*. The two interrelated CBN series originally aired on Japanese television, where the 26-episode *Superbook* had been titled *Animated Parent and Child Theatre* (the literal English translation of a somewhat less prosaic Japanese cognomen) and the 52-episode *Flying House* was called *Tondera House* (or *Great Adventures of Amazing House*). Both programs involved three precocious children—two boys and a girl—and an "R2D2" style talking robot, who wore a cross on his chest so we wouldn't lose track of the theological throughline. In both series, the kids and the robot were transported to biblical times. *Superbook* transported them through the Old Testament by way of a huge, fourth-dimensional Bible, while in *Flying House*, the titular residence, actually a scientist's combination laboratory/ spaceship, whisked the protagonists back to the events of the New Testament.
  The twin series were animated by Tatsunoko studios, the same Japanese outfit responsible for *Robotech* (q.v.) and *Speed Racer* (q.v.), and as a result *Superbook* and *Flying House* shared a strong family resemblance to those more sectarian projects. The children were wide-eyed, chipmunk-toothed "cartoony" characters, while the biblical personalities were drawn realistically, though still with eyes far rounder than those found among residents of Jerusalem. The programs themselves evoked the bizarre, unsettling atmosphere common to many Japanimation projects, with quirky tidbits of inappropriate humor, sudden jolts of violence, stop-and-go animation, grotesque facial expressions, and offpaced editing.
  And as for the dialogue, during the *Flying House* scene in which Jesus is nailed to the cross (yes, that was in there, too), the Son of Man murmurs, somewhat ahead of schedule, "Father, forgive them. They know not what they do." Whereupon one of the Roman officers (who looks like a *Speed Racer* villain) stops hammering, glares at Jesus and snarls, "Are you implying that we don't know our job?"
  Superbook and *Flying House* seldom cracked the major TV commercial outlets, but can still be seen on local UHF religious channels and on such Christian cable services as the Trinity Broadcasting Network. A third biblical series produced by Tatsunoko, featuring the same leading characters as in *Superbook* and *Flying House*, was seen in Japan, but has not to my knowledge been shown in the U.S.

SUPERBOY *see* **SUPERMAN**

SUPERMAN:
  —THE NEW ADVENTURES OF SUPERMAN. CBS: 9/10/1966–9/2/1967; 9/13/ 1969–9/5/1970.
  —THE SUPERMAN / AQUAMAN HOUR OF ADVENTURE. CBS: 9/9/ 1967–9/7/1968. Ducovny Productions/ Filmation/National Periodicals Productions. Executive producer, Allen Ducovny. Produced by Lou Scheimer, Norman Prescott. Directed by Hal Sutherland, Norman McCabe, Lou Zukor. Story editor, Mort Weisinger. Art director, Don Christensen. Music by John Marion. COMPONENTS: 1. SUPERMAN and SUPERBOY. Voices: Bud Collyer (Clark Kent and Superman); Joan Alexander (Lois); Ted Knight (Perry White/Superboy Narrator); Bob Hastings (Superboy); Janet Waldo (Lana Lane); Jackson Beck (Super-

man Narrator); and Jack Grimes, Julie Bennett, Janet Waldo, and Cliff Owens. **2. AQUAMAN.** Voices: Marvin Miller (Aquaman); Ted Knight (Imp/Tusky/Narrator); Jerry Dexter (Aqualad); Diana Maddox (Mera). **3.** Voices for additional components: Cliff Owens (The Flash); Tommy Cook (Kid Flash); Julie Bennett (Wonder Girl); Gilbert Mack (Hawkman); Pat Harrington Jr. (The Atom/Speedy); Gerald Mohr (Green Lantern); Paul Frees (Kyro/ Guardian of the Universe).

—THE BATMAN/SUPERMAN HOUR. CBS: 9/14/1968–9/6/1969. Same basic production credits as NEW ADVENTURES OF SUPERMAN, minus SUPERBOY credits. *See also* BATMAN.

—SUPER FRIENDS (and sequels). 1973–1986. (See individual listings under this title.)

—SUPERMAN. CBS: 9/17/1988–9/12/ 1989. Ruby-Spears/DC Comics. Voices: Beau Weaver (Superman and Clark Kent); Ginny McSwain (Lois Lane); Mark Taylor (Jimmy Olsen); Stanley Ralph Ross (Perry White); Michael Bell (Lex Luthor); Lynn Marie Stewart (Jessica Morganberry); Tress MacNeille (Ma Kent); Alan Oppenheimer (Pa Kent).

Must we? Doesn't everyone know the *Superman* backstory by now? Well, once more into the breach:

Back in 1938, two lean and hungry artist/writers named Jerry Siegel and Joe Shuster pulled together story elements from such material as the *Doc Savage* pulps and Phillip Wylie's novel *The Gladiator*, added a dash of *Flash Gordon* and *Buck Rogers* and several doses of their own vivid imaginations, and came up with a comic strip character named Superman. The sole survivor of the doomed planet Krypton, Superman was only a baby when he was stuffed into a spaceship by his Kryptonian father Jor-El and sent hurtling to earth, where he was discovered and adopted by rural couple Jonathan and Martha Kent, and given the name Clark. As he grew into manhood, Clark Kent discovered that he had powers "far beyond those of mortal men," principally superstrength, virtual invulnerability (except when exposed to Kryptonite from his home planet, which rendered him helpless), and the ability to fly. As an adult, Clark was hired as a reporter for the *Daily Planet*, which though billed as a "great metropolitan newspaper" apparently had

only three full-time employees: blowhard editor Perry White, dauntless investigative reporter Lois Lane, and callow cub reporter Jimmy Olsen. Once in a while, Clark Kent or one of his coworkers would be overwhelmed by the criminal element or by natural and supernatural disasters: That's when Clark would run off to the broom closet, remove his glasses, declare "This looks like a job for Superman"—and, once exchanging his baggy street clothes for blue-and-red tights and cape, Superman he would become. Nobody ever caught on that Clark Kent and Superman were one and the same; the best comment on this matter was made by Jay Leno, who questioned Lois Lane's investigative abilities when she couldn't even see through Clark's bargain-rate Lenscrafters.

Almost from inception, *Superman* has leaped off the comics pages into other media. A radio program commenced in 1941, starring future gameshow host Clayton "Bud" Collyer as the Man of Steel. Collyer also provided the voice for most of the 17 *Superman* theatrical cartoons, magnificently assembled between 1941 and 1943 by the Fleischer studios for Paramount release. The fondest memory most fans have of Collyer's interpretation was his ability to go instantly from the reedy, wimpy Clark Kent voice used for "This looks like a job . . . ," to the resonant, deeply masculine intonation for the end of that phrase, ". . . for *Superman!*" Bud Collyer's daughter Cynthia would recall years later that her father was able to make this sudden tone-switch by swallowing a gulp of air, and then literally burping out the "for *Superman*" coda.

Collyer didn't play Superman when Columbia Pictures fashioned two serials out of the property in 1948 and 1949; these starred Kirk Alyn, who many have noted was better as Clark Kent than as Superman. The actor most closely associated with the role was George Reeves, superb as both Clark *and* Superman in the 104-episode *Superman* TV series, produced between 1951 and 1958, which is *still* turning a profit on the Nickelodeon cable network. Later TV and movie *Supermen*, and a few adolescent "Superboys," have included Christopher Reeve, John Haymes Newton, Gerard Christopher, and Dean Cain.

The 1966 TV-cartoon version of *Superman* was a pet project of CBS executive

Fred Silverman's, who wanted to use the warhorse property to go up against comedy cartoons like ABC's *The Beatles* (q.v.) and make Saturday morning TV genuinely competitive, rather than a neglected afterthought in network schedule conferences. Silverman's strategy worked, and *The New Adventures of Superman* ended up scoring the highest ratings shares in the history of Saturday morning network cartoonery, though it would be a *Superman* derivation, Hanna-Barbera's *Space Ghost* (q.v.) which would put CBS firmly on top.

The *New Adventures of Superman* represented Filmation Studios' first foray into network television — and in fact, the company's first-ever half hour cartoon series. With *Superman*, Filmation established its future *modus operandi* in dealing with animated adaptations from other media. For one, the artwork faithfully recreated the DC Comics staff's renditions of Superman and his friends (the character actually looked more like "himself" than he had in the Fleischer's). For another, Filmation engaged several of DC's *Superman* writers, notably George Kashdan, Leo Dorfman and Bob Haney, to script the series. As a result, the *Superman* cartoons had more fidelity to their source than any other movie or TV incarnation, and as a bonus revived such long-standing *Superman* supporting villains as Brainiac, Mr. Mxyzptlk, and The Toyman. Filmation's establishment of strong bridges between original comic-book or "live" properties and their TV cartoon incarnations would be maintained in such future efforts as *The Archies, Batman, Star Trek* and *The New Adventures of Gilligan* (see individual entries on these series).

To some purists, however, simply *looking* like Superman wasn't enough. Unfortunately, Filmation's habit of failing to bring its characters to life fully also established itself on *New Adventures of Superman*. Outside of the occasional smooth loop-the-loop flying sequences, the cartoon Superman/Clark Kent moved like the Steadfast Tin Soldier. The artwork was as inconsistent as the animation, with characters' heads changing size in relation to their bodies from one scene to the next, and the extent of Superman's muscularity likewise fluctuating wildly from shot to shot. And though Filmation's deployment of classic *Superman* opponents was certainly welcome, these potentially fasci-

nating characters seldom held any interest beyond their costumes.

But to less demanding younger fans, *Superman* was just what was needed to satiate a late–1960s appetite for costumed superheroes, an appetite whetted by excessive exposure to ABC's live-action *Batman* series. The aforementioned excellent ratings that greeted *New Adventures of Superman* not only broadened to Saturday mornings the comic-book-to-cartoon market, but also firmly solidified Filmation as one of TV's foremost animation factories.

Two internal elements distinguished the weekly half-hour *New Adventures of Superman*. One was the inclusion of *Superboy* adventures, sandwiched between two six-minute *Superman* cartoons appearing on each program. The Superboy concept, that of depicting the childhood years of Clark Kent in a contemporary setting (thus suggesting that the young Superman and the older one lived at exactly the same time!), had been developed in the postwar era for the DC Comics line, but only an abortive 1960 *Superboy* TV pilot film had ever made it to any other entertainment form. Filmation's *Superboy* cartoons were the first weekly depiction of this character for television, though Clark Kent was so mature-looking in the *Superboy* episodes that he might as well have been called SuperYoungMan. (Voice-actor Bob Hastings did not, as did Bud Collyer, drop his voice when changing from Clark to Superboy. Evidently puberty hadn't yet set in.) These brief episodes also brought two other comic-book characters to "life" for the first time: Clark's erstwhile high school sweetheart Lana Lang, and his dog Krypto, the latter another superpowered survivor of Krypton. It was nice to have the old gang back, especially in the expertly written *Superboy* scripts of George Kashdan, but the animation and draftsmanship were just as haphazard as on the *Superman* cartoons.

The second distinguishing element of *New Adventures of Superman* was its utilization of voice talent from the 1940s radio series. Jackson Beck was commissioned to narrate and play various good and bad guy roles, just as he had on radio; Joan Alexander was back as Lois Lane; and Bud Collyer, then a very popular high-paid TV personality, willingly took a more modest salary for the privilege of recreating Clark Kent/Superman, right down to the old vocal gear-shift during transformation scenes. Apparently Collyer got the most enjoyment and personal fulfillment out of this gig. Joan Alexander saw herself as merely a working actress, who couldn't remember any details of her earlier Lois Lane work when interviewed in the late 1960s, while Jackson Beck reportedly kept his distance from Collyer due to political differences stemming from the "Blacklist" era of the 1950s.

In 1967, Superman's cartoon vehicle was retitled *The Superman/Aquaman Hour of Adventure*, introducing another DC property to the small screen. Aquaman was created for November 1941's *More Fun* #73 by comic-book craftsmen Paul Morris and Mort Weisinger (Weisinger, longtime editor of the *Superman* comics, functioned as *New Adventures of Superman*'s liaison between Filmation and DC). Conceived as National Periodicals' "answer" to Timely Comics' underwater hero *Sub-Mariner* (see *Marvel Super Heroes*), Aquaman was the son of an Earth scientist who'd learned to live in the soggy kingdom of Atlantis and had married one of its residents. Establishing the "surface" identity of Arthur Curry, Aquaman straddled — or paddled — two worlds, one beneath the ocean as "King of the Seven Seas." The character treaded water in support of other National/ DC stars until attaining his own headlining comic book in 1962; perhaps making up for lost time, Aquaman met and married fellow Atlantan Mera, and, a respectable four issues later, Aquababy, later known as Aqualad, was born. This backstory was ignored on TV: Aquaman simply "was," *sans* explanation or dual identity.

The *Aquaman* component of *The Superman/Aquaman Hour of Adventure* featured Aqualad as a companion rather than a son; Mera barely appeared at all. Also costarring were the hero's trusty seahorse Storm, Aqualad's mount Imp and comic-relief pet walrus Tusky. (Contrary to previously published accounts, only Tusky was specifically created for TV; Storm and Imp had both appeared in the comic books, albeit without regular character names.) Unlike *Superman*, *Aquaman* was campy in nature, *Batman* style: Stentorian narration (by Ted Knight, a la Ted Baxter); Aqualad's oft-repeated "Holy Halibut"; frequent references to an Aquacave and the "Aquaduo"; and special guest villains like

the Black Manta, the Fisherman, and Mephisto. The cartoons also borrowed from *Tarzan* by having Aquaman occasionally call all other sea-life to swim to the rescue. *Aquaman*'s animation was an improvement on *Superman*'s, though it could have used a superimposed "ripple" effect to convince us that the limber-limbed characters were underwater.

After a year in tandem with Superman, Aquaman was spun off into his own all-rerun CBS weekly in 1968. Upon parting company with Superman, Aquaman took with him a number of other *Superman/ Aquaman Hour of Adventure* component cartoons, starring various and sundry DC "guest" celebrities, listed herewith. The Green Lantern, invented in 1940 by National Comics laborers Martin Nodell and Bill Finger, was Alan Scott when in mufti, his superskills generated by a power ring. Hawkman, also from 1940 courtesy of artist/writers Gardner Fox and Dennis Neville, was actually Carter Hall, winged reincarnation of Egyptian Prince Khufu (his anti-gravity belt would be "appropriated" by Hanna-Barbera's *Space Ghost*); Hawkman had a girlfriend, named — amazingly enough — Hawkgirl. Two other DC stars, the superfast Flash and the fissioned-powered Atom (both introduced in that incredibly busy year of 1940, then renovated with new "origin" stories by DC in 1956 and 1961, respectively) made cameo appearances as members of the "Justice League of America" (see *Superfriends*) on both *The Superman/Aquaman Hour* and the *Aquaman* spinoff half hour.

"The Teen Titans" were likewise introduced on the hour version of the series, then continued in rerun form to costar with Aquaman. When originally created for the comic books in 1964, the Teen Titans were Aqualad, Robin, Wonder Girl and Kid Flash (son of the Flash); later on, the Green Lantern's youthful sidekick Speedy joined the club. All but one of the comic-page Titans appeared on the cartoon series: Filmation didn't have the character rights to Batman's young companion Robin when *Superman/Aquaman* was produced, so the series went along without him.

Meanwhile, Superman was appearing in first-run cartoons as part of 1968's *Batman/ Superman Hour*. Character design was stronger and more consistent this time around, and story values were improved by adopting a two-part cliffhanger format (*Superboy* was dropped, giving both caped cavorters more airtime). The series returned to a half hour format in 1969, again as *New Adventures of Superman* (not "new" but reruns), a title which remained in effect until its 1970 cancellation. Eventually, Aquaman, Hawkman and the Green Lantern would rejoin Superman and other DC headliners as fixtures of Hanna-Barbera's *Superfriends* and its various incarnations (see separate listings) from 1973 through 1986.

Superman soared back solo in 1988 with a Ruby-Spears *Superman* half hour weekly, created as a tie-in to the Man of Steel's 50th anniversary. At that time, comic book fanciers were revelling in the "darker" Superman that had recently surfaced in several graphic comics from the DC factory. But this complex, somewhat sinister character was not welcome on TV in the pre–*Batman: The Animated Series* era, so our hero was restored to the bright, optimistic ambience of the 1960s.

Thankfully, the animation of the 1988 version was on a far higher level than in the Filmation days—in fact, Superman hadn't moved this well since the Fleischer efforts back in the early 1940s. Unfortunately, the storylines were stuck in a retread mode: It appeared that virtually every Ruby-Spears *Superman* would set up a supposedly altruistic Metropolis benefactor whom Superman would ulimately expose as a villainous fraud. Nonetheless, there were cherished moments along the way. Wonder Woman (see *Super Friends*) guested on one episode, teaming with Superman to thwart a particularly nasty foe; and in a pleasant recurring feature, "The Superman Family Album," the audience was treated to gentle blackout gags showing Superboy's growing awareness of his own strength and his place in the world.

Ruby-Spears' *Superman* lasted only 13 episodes, done in not by Kryptonite but by a deadlier double-dose of Disney: *Gummi Bears* on NBC, *Winnie the Pooh* on ABC. Perhaps it's just as well that this relatively cheerful variation on the "Up, up, and away" theme wasn't around in 1993, when the cartoon producers would have been pressed to come to grips with the comic-book *Superman*'s highly publicized "death"—and subsequent circulation-boosting "rebirth."

SUPERTED *see* **FUNTASTIC WORLD OF HANNA-BARBERA**

SWAMP THING. Fox: 4/20/1991–5/18/1991; 7/6/1991–8/3/1991. Batfilm Productions Inc./DIC. Executive producers, Benjamin Melniker, Michael E. Uslan. Co-executive producers, Andy Heyward, Michael Maliani, Robby London. Associate producers, Ken Duer, Kenneth T. Ito, Kevin Schmidt (Batfilms). SWAMP THING created by Len Wein and Berni Wrightson; based upon characters appearing in magazines published by DC Comics, Inc. Directed by Chuck Patton. Story editors, Reed and Bruce Shelley. Executive in charge of production, Winnie Chaffee. Production supervisor, Brian A. Miller. Script coordinators, Lori Crawford, William A. Ruiz. Voice directors, Paul Quinn, Marsha Goodman. Music by Michael Tavera; musical supervisors, Joanne Miller, Judy Sampson-Brown, Melissa Gentry. Voices: Len Carlson (Swamp Thing); Harvey Atkin (Tomahawk); Phil Aikin (Bayou Jack); Don Francks (Arcane); Errol Slue (Dr. Deemo); Gordon Masten (Skin Man); Joe Matheson (Weed Killer); Paulina Gillis (Abby); Richard Yearwood (J.T.); Jonathan Potts (Delbert); Stuart Stone; Eva Almos.

Swamp Thing was created in 1972 as a one-shot DC comic book by Len Wein and Berni Wrightson. This delightfully slimy horror tale of a man turned into an amorphous vegetative beast owed a little of its inspiration to the classic 1940s comic character "The Heap," but was fresh and intriguing enough for 1970s readers to demand more. When *Swamp Thing* was revived as a regularly published DC star in 1974, the story concerned researcher Alec Holland who, transformed by a foolish lab accident into the Swamp Thing, slogged through the Louisiana bogs doing good deeds that went unrewarded because of his hideous appearance. Numerous sideline characters were introduced over the next two decades, notably the evil scientist Arcane, as was a plot-motivating "hook": the Biorestorer, which might provide the only means for the foliage-laden Swamp Thing's return to full humanhood.

Given the basic material, Hollywood could have gone "straight" or "camp" when adapting *Swamp Thing* to movies. Hollywood did both. The first *Swamp Thing* (1982) handled the premise with respect, and the Beauty-and-Beast romance between the mossy Dr. Holland and his lady love with reverence and a touch of sweetness; meanwhile, Louis Jourdan bit large bites out of the scenery as the wicked Arcane. *Return of Swamp Thing* (1989) opted for full-out lampoon, exemplified by Heather Locklear's overboard performance as Dr. Arcane's stepdaughter. This unsuccessful sequel also served to introduce two obnoxious small boys who befriended the beast, and with whom the kids in the audience were supposed to identify. Variations of these youngsters were carried over into USA Network's live-action weekly *Swamp Thing* series, and also into the Fox Network's cartoon version—which is what this entry is supposed to be about.

Produced by DIC Enterprises, the animated *Swamp Thing* tinkered a bit with the original and came up with the following backstory: In the early 1980s, Dr. Alec Holland invented a plant-growing formula that was supposed to stem world hunger. But Anton Arcane wanted the formula for his own nefarious purposes, and to this end sent his mutant "Unmen" (Crocodile Man, Scorpion Man, Mosquito Mike, Lizard Liz, Zombie, Black Magic, and Toxic) to blow up Holland's lab and steal the precious discovery. The explosion doused Holland with the formula, and after running screaming into the Louisiana swamplands, the good doctor discovered that he'd transmogrified into walking "plant life"— while still retaining his scientific intellect. This was Swamp Thing, a green, seven-foot Man of Muck who'd henceforth devote his time to battling Arcane and his Unmen.

Considered only a legend by the locals and thus left alone to his own devices, Swamp Thing operated a hi-tech "Tree-Lab" to continue his experimentation. He maintained his connections with the outside world through several human friends: Abby, the evil Dr. Arcane's nice, ecologically correct stepdaughter; Tracker, a Native American game warden; Cajun Jack, a Vietnam veteran who'd become a swamp hermit after the war; and those two aforementioned "audience-identification" kids, Delbert and J.T., described respectively by DIC as a "Cajun 'Spanky' from *Our Gang*" and "a ten-year-old version of Eddie Murphy."

When pitching *Swamp Thing* to Fox, story editors Reed and Bruce Shelley outlined eight potential plotlines, involving such out-of-swamp experiences as space aliens, witches and lost Indian tribes. Only five costly half hours were filmed, however; these were given a trial run as a miniseries in April of 1991 as a replacement for the failed Fox endeavor *Piggsburg Pigs*. *Swamp Thing* eschewed parody for larger-than-life adventure, endeavoring admirably to honor the spirit (and the vine-encrusted visuals) of the original DC Comics, but no one was watching. No matter how hard the DIC staff tried (and this was one of the company's better efforts), it would take more than a talking shrubbery to pry viewers away from CBS' *Teenage Mutant Ninja Turtles*. Though given two tries in April and July of 1991, *Swamp Thing* was replaced both times by reruns of *Piggsburg Pigs*, the very thing it had been assigned to supplant.

Still, DIC didn't completely give up on the Leafy One. A caricature of *Swamp Thing* still occasionally appears in the studio's trade-magazine advertising, keeping company with such certified DIC moneyspinners as *Inspector Gadget* (q.v.) and *Dennis the Menace* (q.v.). And in 1993, the existing *Swamp Thing* episodes were released to home video.

SWAT KATS: THE RADICAL SQUADRON. Syndicated: 1993. TBS Superstation: 9/12/1993–. Hanna-Barbera/ Turner Program Services. Created by Yvon Tremblay and Christian Tremblay (also given credit for "visual stylization"). Executive producer, Buzz Potamkin. Produced by Davis Doi. Directed by Robert Alvarez. Developed for television by Glenn Leopold and Davis Doi. Story editor, Glenn Leopold. Theme music and score by Matt Muhoberac and John Zucker. Sound editing by EFX Systems and Tom Gedemer. Re-recording mixers: Terry O'Bright and Bill Freesh. Supervising editor, Pat Foley. Animation directors, Joanna Romersa, Ken Southworth, Allan Wilzbach, Rick Bowman, Joan Drake, Frank Andrina. Design coordinator, Lance Falk. Design head, Tony Sgroi. Produced in association with Mook Co., Ltd.; overseas animation supervisor, Kunio Shimiamura. Voices: Charlie Adler, Frank Birney, Earl Boen, Keene Curtis, Jim Cummings, Linda Gary, Edmund Gilbert, Barry Gordon, Tress MacNeille, Gary Owens, Frank Welker.

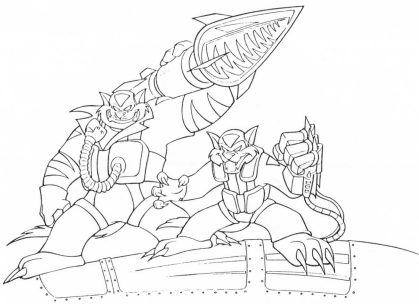

"Funny-animal" superheroes *du jour:* 1993's *Swat Kats.*

Swat Kats, a 1993 addition to *Funtastic World of Hanna-Barbera* (q.v.), was set in Megakatt City. One would think that a metropolis entirely populated by humanized cats would be phenomenon enough, yet Megakatt City was festooned with phenomena of the psychic, ecological and extraterrestrial variety: black holes, sorcerers, humongous blobs, even dinosaurs. Megakatt's mayor Meggs and female deputy mayor Kalley Briggs were compelled to rely on the protection of Cmdr. Farrell and his Enforcers, a group of gung-ho *G.I. Joe* lampoons so wrapped up in their own egos that they hindered more than helped. Far more beneficial were two humble garage mechanics, Chance Furlong and Jack Clawson. When things looked bleakest, Chance and Jack donned disguise to become, respectively, "T-Bone" and "Razor," the vigilante Swat Kats. In their land-air-sea Turbokatt vehicle, the Swat Kats were more than a match for the various cat-astrophes inflicting Megakatt City.

A little bit of this, a little bit of that. I credit my 10-year-old son and his friends for spotting the "liftings" from other cartoon half hours which popped up on *Swat Kats.* The title logo and "dark deco" veneer of Megakatt City were straight out of *Batman: The Animated Series.* (This at least was acknowledged by Hanna-Barbera, whose CEO Fred Seibert allowed that *Swat Kats* was "not unlike *Batman.*") The notion of a modern burg in which animals, reptiles and the like assumed all the human roles could have been seen anywhere in 1992-1993, notably on *Dog City* (q.v.) and *Adventures of T-Rex* (q.v.), and long before that in the comics, vis-à-vis Scrooge McDuck's Duckburg and Krazy Kat's Kokonimo Kounty. The "vigilante vs. supernatural" angle was already being thoroughly explored by the 1992 hit *X-Men* (q.v.) (*Swat Kats* included a closing-credits invitation to its viewers to inaugurate an *X-Men* style fan club), and the same angle had been picked over in the 1980s, after a fashion, by both cartoon versions of *Ghostbusters* (q.v.). And, of course, the whole notion of nonhuman superheroes can be tracked directly back to the Mother of Them All, *Teenage Mutant Ninja Turtles* (q.v.). *Swat Kats* was in fact the *second* such animated series to substitute cats for turtles, as witness *SpaceCats* (q.v.).

Hanna-Barbera even borrowed from itself in at least one respect: All the female characters on *Swat Kats* had trim legs that the *Sports Illustrated* supermodels would have sold their souls for.

Disregarding the series' multiple TV-cartoon ancestors, the publicity for the weekly *Swat Kats* suggested that its creators had worked in a virtually TV-less vacuum. The series was conceived by Yvon and Christian Tremblay, two brothers from Montreal who'd forsaken that city's university because it didn't have an art department to their liking. Studying all the painting and draftsmanship reference books they could get their hands on (from Renaissance to Rodin to Disney), the Tremblays squirreled themselves away in their parents' basement and taught themselves to be artists. When struck by the notion to create a cartoon property, the brothers based the Swat Kats, so they said, on their own personalities; the character of "Razor" was an alleged takeoff on Yvon Tremblay. And instead of memorizing the entire Saturday-morning cartoon schedule, the Tremblays learned the art of storytelling by reading magazines and classical literature.

When setting out to find jobs for themselves, the Tremblays utilized their research knowhow by drawing up a list of animation producers from various industry publications and sent out resumes. Hanna-Barbera's Fred Seibert, on the lookout for fresh talent, took the brothers under his wing. When offered *Swat Kats*, Seibert accepted the notion, with a laissez-faire "You create it, you take care of it." The Hanna-Barbera production team dressed up the results with some of the studio's most evocatively moody artwork and most intricate animation (no off-camera collisions represented by merely shaking the camera on *this* show), and to achieve that end lured independent animation producer Buzz (*Berenstain Bears*) Potamkin back into the cartoon-studio system.

In addition, Seibert promised the public a "Brian May" type musical score, adding that "The soundtrack is really going to be different for a cartoon." This time, there might actually *have* been a justification for the word "different" when speaking of *Swat Kats*. Indeed, the property's full-stereo sound quality was only a tiny step below movie-theatre level, virtually strongarming audiences into paying attention. It might have even seemed innovative had not *Biker Mice from Mars* (q.v.), *Cadillacs and Dinosaurs* (q.v.) and *Mighty Max* (q.v.) premiered the same year

as *Swat Kats*—each from a different producer, and each with its own superlative audio system, collectively yanking TV sound out of the "tin can" era.

Excellent draftsmanship and sound quality notwithstanding, the first reaction one had to *Swat Kats* was "But we've been here before." Hanna-Barbera produced an above-average derivation of earlier cartoon series, no denying that: but it was still a derivation. It would have been nice if Fred Seibert's hiring practices had equated fresh talent with fresh ideas.

SWISS FAMILY ROBINSON. Family Channel: 9/9/1989–8/30/1992. Nippon Animation/PMT. Executive producer, Koichi Metohashi. Produced by Takaji Matsudo. Directed by Yoshio Kurada. Music: Koichi Sakata. Screenplay by Shozo Matsuda. English version: Supervising producers, Peter Maris, Mark H. Tuttle. English version directed by Richard Epsar. Theme song by Ron Kruger. Voices: Jeremy Platt (Ernest); Reba West (Becca); R. Dwight (Fritz); Grace Michaels (Jack); Wendee Swann (Anna); and Montenni Moon, Ellyn Epcar, Sox Walcox, Jonathan Alexander, and Jacqueline Elizabeth.

Johann David Wyss' novel *Swiss Family Robinson* (1895) was the tale of a shipwrecked family struggling to survive and maintain civilized decorum on a tropical island. The story was Hollywoodized in 1940, Disney-fied in 1960, and transformed into no fewer than two mid–1970s live action weeklies, one of them produced by "Master of Disaster" Irwin Allen. Like the novel, all these movie-TV adaptations concentrated on the Robinsons' trials and tribulations after their shipwreck.

The weekly, half hour animated *Swiss Family Robinson* was produced for Japanese TV in 1989 and released in the U.S. that same year as part of the Family Channel's weekend "Funtown" lineup (which included the live-action *Gerbert* and *Something Else*). The first few episodes were "prequels" to the novel, taking place in the months before the family was marooned. In the cartoon version, the Robinsons were in the process of emigrating from Switzerland to America before the weather started getting rough and their tiny ship was tossed. Herein we saw the

Robinson children learning vital life lessons about trust, misunderstanding, looking beyond face value, etc., that would ultimately serve them well when subsisting on coconuts and wild berries in their new tropical homestead. Though Japanese both in production staff and animation style, *Swiss Family Robinson* was careful not to rob the characters of their mid–European charm and social graces—something often forgotten by movie and TV adaptations of the property, which tended to Anglicize or (even worse) Americanize the Robinsons.

THE SYLVANIAN FAMILIES. Syndicated: 1987. DIC/C.C.T. Executive producer, Andy Heyward. Supervising producer, Robby London. Associate producers, Gaetano Vaccaro and Yolanda Gorick. Production supervisor, Winnie Chaffee. Executives in charge of production, Thierry Laurin and Mark M. Galvin. Directed by Christian Choquet. Animation director, Kazuo Terada. Supervising director, James A. Simon. Story editor, Phil Harnage. Script coordinator, Lori Crawford. Adapted for animation by Phil Harnage. Voice direction by Victor Villegas. For K.K. DIC: Producer, Tetsuo Katayama. Production managers, Shigeru Akagawa and Hiroshi Toita. Production coordinators, Yasuhiro Takei and Hironobu Ohtsuki. Music by Haim Saban and Shuki Levy. Individual characters copyright 1986 Epoch Co. Ltd.; usage herein by agreement with Epoch and Coleco Industries Inc. Voices: Frank Proctor (Woodkeeper), Len Carlson (Packbat/ Papa Herb Wildwood), John Stocker (Gatorpossum/Grandpa Smoky Wildwood), Jeri Craden (Mama Honeysuckle Evergreen), Thick Wilson (Papa Ernest Evergreen), Ellen-Ray Hennessey (Grandma Primrose Evergreen), Michael Fantini (Preston Evergreen), Noam Zylberman (Rusty Wildwood), Catherine Gallant (Holly Wildwood), Brian Belfry (Papa Slick Slydale), Diane Fabian (Mama Velveter Slydale/Grandma Flora Wildwood/ Mama Ginger Wildwood), Jeremiah McCann (Buster Slydale), Lisa Coristine (Scarlette Slydale), and Chuck Shamata.

Based (prepare for a shock!) on a children's toy line, the weekly *Sylvanian Families* was set in a *Smurf*ish glade. The Sylvanians were not talking light bulbs, as might be assumed, but instead tiny forest animals and anthropomorphized fauna. They were able to make the wishes of human children come true, usually by proving to the kids (in "Wizard of Oz" fashion) that they'd had their heart's desire all along but just didn't realize it. Thus, a little boy who wished for physical strength would discover the value of *mental* strength through his strategic methods of rescuing the Sylvanians from a bursting dam. Other plotlines would transport children to the Sylvanian Forest to clear up childish misconceptions and half-truths. In one episode, a girl who felt that her divorced dad didn't love her anymore learned through her adventure in the Forest that love doesn't end just because people are apart.

Seldom preaching or talking above the heads of its under-10 target audience, *Sylvanian Families* was a satisfactory effort to bolster the self esteem of children plagued by physical disabilities, poverty, loneliness, jealousy, misguided values, peer pressure and other societal woes. Thirteen *Sylvanian Families* half hours (two adventures per episode) came skipping down the syndication pike in 1987. The "wish come true" premise would have another crack at the kiddie market four years later with DIC's *Wishkid Starring Macaulay Culkin* (q.v.), then again in 1993 with Calico/Zodiac's *Twinkle, the Dream Being* (q.v.).

TALE SPIN. Syndicated: 1990. Disney/ Buena Vista. Supervising producer and story editor, Jymn Magnon. Produced and directed by Robert Taylor, Larry Latham, Jamie Mitchell and Tim Walker. Co-producer/story editor, Mark Zaslove. Story editors, Ken Koonce, David Wiemers, Duane Capizzi, Karl Geurs and Bruce Talkington. Written by Mark and Michael Evans. Original music by Christopher L. Stone. "Tale Spin" theme by Silvesher and Silvesher. Animation facilities: Walt Disney Animation France, Walt Disney Animated UK, Limited. Voices: Sally Struthers (Rebecca Cunningham); Edmund Gilbert (Baloo); Jim Cummings (King Louie/Don Karnage); Tony Jay (Shere Khan); Patrick Fraley (Wild Cat); Janna Michaels (Molly); R. J. Williams (Kit Cloudkicker); Chuck McCann (Dumptruck); Charlie Adler (Maddog); Lorenzo Music (Dunder); Michael Gough (Spigot); and Dan Gilvezan. *Tale Spin*, a 1990 Monday-through-

Friday addition to the syndicated "Disney Afternoon" (see also *DuckTales, Chip 'n' Dale's Rescue Rangers, The Goof Troop, Bonkers* and *Disney's Gummi Bears*), was based upon characters appearing in the 1967 Disney cartoon feature *The Jungle Book*. That's where all resemblance to the source material ended: In the half-hour TV series, the principal *Jungle Book* characters of Baloo the Bear, Shere Khan the Tiger and King Louie the Gorilla were swept away from their jungle habitat and plunked down in a contemporary action-adventure setting. In fact, *Tale Spin* had less to do with Rudyard Kipling than it did with the old Richard Arlen–Chester Morris "soldiers of fortune" B-pictures of the 1940s.

Easygoing charter pilot Baloo, who operated the Higher for Hire transport service out of the port city of Cape Suzette, had lost his business through a series of financial missteps and professional booboos. The lovely Rebecca (who like Baloo was a humanized bear) took over Baloo's business and tried to run it "by the book," something your slovenly, what-the-hell hero was by nature incapable of doing. Most of the adventures transpired high above the clouds aboard Baloo's ragtag amphibian plane, the Sea Duck. Joining the adult characters in their comic exploits were Baloo's bear-cub partner Kit Cloudkicker, and Rebecca's daughter Molly. Baloo's favorite hangout was the canteen run by the excitable Louie, who with his tendency to be sucked in by Baloo's wilder moneymaking schemes was reminiscent not so much of *Jungle Book*'s King Louie as he is of Louie Dumbrowski, the gullible sweetshop proprietor in the *Bowery Boys* films. The Good Guys' principal nemesis was larcenous fat cat businessman Shere Khan, who owned everything in Cape Suzette—except, of course, "Higher for Hire."

Like many daily "strip" cartoons of the late 80s–early 90s, *Tale Spin* was introduced via a two hour pilot film, which was later chopped up into a five part cliffhanger and incorporated in the series' 65-episode manifest. *Tale Spin* maintained the standard set by its companion Disney programs *DuckTales* and *Rescue Rangers* through its first rate animation and graphics, and its Spielberg-like tongue-in-cheek approach to the various perils and calamities dreamed up by the scriptwriters. And like the other Disney dailies of its period, *Tale Spin* emphasized several strong, positive female role models for its younger viewers.

TALES FROM THE CRYPTKEEPER. ABC: 9/18/1993–. EC/Tales from the Crypt Holdings Inc./Nelvana. Executive producers: Richard Donner, David Giler, Walter Hill, Joel Silver, Robert Zemeckis. Co-executive producer, Toper Taylor. Produced by Michael Hirsh, Patrick Loubert. Originated by William H. Gaines in E.C. Comics. Supervising producer, Stephen Hodgins. Producers: Alex Collett, Patricia R. Burns, Pamela Slavin. Directed by Laura Shepherd. Story editor, Peter Sauder. Additional dialogue, Terry Black. Cryptmaster based on design by Kevin Yagher. Theme performed by Heart Times Coffee Cups Equals Lightning. Background music by Amin Bhatia; music produced by David Greene. Production facilities: Wang Film Prod. Co., Ltd., Funbag Productions, Bardel Productions, Medallion-PFA Film and Video, International Image, Studio 306. Overseas director, John DeKlein. Voices: John Kassir (Cryptkeeper). Cast varied from episode to episode.

Tales from the Crypt was the title of an HBO horror anthology, based very liberally on the E.C. Comics tales of the early 1950s that brought down the wrath of dogooders and led to the "cleaning up" of the comic book industry. Superbly illustrated by such E.C. talent as Johnny Craig, Jack Davis and the legendary Graham "Ghastly" Ingels, the original "Tales" usually involved repulsive people's receiving revolting comeuppance for their crimes: the compulsive neatnik hacked to death by his wife, who then tidily preserved her husband's remains in carefully labelled jars; the sadistic lobster eater abducted by extraterrestrials, who split the "hero" down the middle and served him up in butter sauce; and most notoriously, the homicidal ballplayer whose victim was avenged by his teammates, resulting in the killer's body parts being chopped into baseball equipment. This "hoist on your own petard" throughline of the E.C. horror comics was once defined by publisher William Gaines as "You sharpen the pencils, then the pencils sharpen your head."

Home Box Office's all-star *Tales from the Crypt*, which debuted in 1989, maintained

Baloo (*right*), with the rest of "Higher for Hire," Kit Cloudkicker: from *Tale Spin*.

the spirit of the old comic books, with extra doses of sex and profanity tossed in. Presiding over these grimly funny half hours was the skeletal Cryptkeeper, an animatronic puppet who loved to make horrendously punning wisecracks concerning the grisly but well-deserved fate of the week's protagonist. (The Cryptkeeper's voice was provided by comedian John Kassir, who'd once been a winner on *Star*

Search. So *that's* where those guys end up.) The program was strictly for adults, but that didn't stop the kids from breaking into mom and dad's cable box to wallow in the Cryptkeeper's lousy jokes and bonechilling morality plays.

The ABC network and Nelvana Studios saw cartoon possibilities in *Crypt*, though there'd have to be a lot of laundering before the property would be acceptable for

Death takes a holiday: the Cryptkeeper, from the "*Tales of....*"

Saturday mornings. Then there was the problem of making deals with the five producer-directors who, between them, had bought up all the entertainment and exploitation rights for the old E.C. *Crypt* stories. This is why ABC's weekly, half hour *Tales from the Cryptkeeper* bore in its credits the names of filmmakers Richard Donner, Walter Hill, Robert Zemeckis, Joel Silver and David Giler.

While *Cryptkeeper* was nowhere near as graphic as the live action HBO version, ABC and Nelvana proudly touted the cartoon series as having more meat than the usual Saturday morning offering. Toper Taylor, senior vice president of Nelvana, noted that the typical "last minute rescue" would not be an ingredient of the series. "In this particular show," said Taylor, "if a child slimes the monster, the monster keeps coming." Jennie Trias, president of children's programs for ABC, likened the thrill factor on the show to "a roller coaster." And the program's psychological advisor, Dr. Brian Newmark of Massachusetts General Hospital, cautioned that while *Tales from the Cryptkeeper* had been mellowed, adults were advised to watch the program for themselves before permitting their kids to take a peek.

There was no real need for concern. Even at its most horrific, *Tales from the Cryptkeeper* had all the bite of a jack-o-lantern. The mordant nature of the live action series was discarded in order to offer a weekly "wonder-filled morality lesson." Example: two kids who enjoyed torment-

ing ants at a picnic were suddenly miniaturized, then forced to see the ant's point of view on survival. What promised to be a stomach-churning affair segued into a classroom lecture on the feeding and organizational habits of ants, including one of the kids' page-by-page recitation from a book on insects. The boys learned their lesson at the end; no blood was shed, no head sharpened.

Despite assurances that some characters on *Cryptkeeper* would pay for their misdeeds with their lives, most episodes ended with everyone sitting around and agreeing to straighten out their attitudes. Even when there was a shock ending in the grand tradition, such as the story of a brutal fisherman who wound up being hooked by a family of fish and then canned like a sardine, the effect was blunted with lame verbal humor.

It is certainly understandable that ABC and Nelvana would want to deflect the wrath of the "clean up TV" activists. And it isn't that one would really *enjoy* seeing rotting corpses and splattered guts all over the Saturday morning landscape. But some viewers, promised a ripsnorting *Tales from the Cryptkeeper* in the fabled E.C. tradition, were inevitably let down by a harmlessly prosocial half hour that wouldn't scare an eight-month-old baby.

The best part of the cartoon series was the Cryptkeeper himself, who retained his gruesome integrity and perverse sense of humor. Surrounded by screeching zombies and werewolves, the Cryptkeeper gleefully introduced his "car-tombs" with disgusting one-liners and puns, emphasizing allusions to death and burial. But the self-censoring network couldn't even leave this genial grotesquerie alone. One sequence, in which the Cryptkeeper used his arm as bait to catch a piranha and then pulled back a bony stump, was bowdlerized by changing the bait to a juicy pork chop. The message of *Tales from the Cryptkeeper* diminished from "You sharpen the pencils, the pencils sharpen your head" to "You blunt the concept, you mollify the pressure groups."

Though it didn't quite live up to its publicity (which was later rewritten to admit that its scare quotient was minimal), *Tales from the Cryptkeeper* was consummately and professionally turned out, with a budget of $400,000 per episode, some $150,000 more than the Saturday network norm. It never frightened, but it always entertained. And given the puerile R-rated excesses that often inflicted HBO's *Tales from the Crypt*, it's perhaps just as well that the cartoon series charted its own course. Poor taste and excessive obscenities were *never* charges that could be levelled on the amusingly antiseptic *Tales from the Cryptkeeper*.

TALES OF LITTLE WOMEN. HBO: 7/3/1988–12/1990. Toei Animation/ Harmony Gold. Produced by Ahmed Agrama. Directed by Byrd Ehlmann. Written by Norman Siderow.

Based on the 19th century novel by Louisa May Alcott, *Tales of Little Women* was a genteel animated serialization of the lives of the March sisters. The half-hour weekly series concentrated on the familiar Alcott characters Meg, Amy, Jo and Beth March, young Massachusetts girls left temporarily fatherless during the American Civil War. *Tales* was filmed in English by Japan's Toei Animation, which betrayed its prior fondness for graphic science fiction and fantasy (see *Tranzor Z*) only in the grim montage sequences devoted to wartime battle and the cruelties of slavery.

According to Japanimation expert Fred Patten, *Tales of Little Women* was one of several cartoon adaptations of Western literature produced for both the Japanese and North American markets. According to the *TV Guide* listings of 1988–90, it was also one of the few such programs actually to get American play.

TALES OF THE WIZARD OF OZ *see* **THE WIZARD OF OZ**

TARO, GIANT OF THE JUNGLE. Syndicated: 1969. Global Productions.

A Japanese weekly half hour, *Taro, Giant of the Jungle* was about a young Tarzan type who gained super powers from exposure to a radioactive tree. The series should not be confused with Toei's *Taro, the Dragon Boy*, based on an ancient Japanese legend about a young boy whose mother was transformed into a dragon!

TARZAN:
—**TARZAN, LORD OF THE JUNGLE.** CBS: 9/11/1976–9/3/1977; 2/11/1984–9/8/ 1984. Filmation. Executive producers, Lou Scheimer and Norm Prescott. Produced by Don Christensen. Directed by

Ed Friedman, Gwen Wetzler, Kay Wright, Marsh Lamore, Lou Zukor. Music by Yvette Blais, Jeff Michael. Voices: Robert Ridgely (Tarzan); Lou Scheimer (N'Kima); and Linda Gary, Joan Gerber, Ted Cassidy, Barry Gordon, Allan Oppenheimer, and Jane Webb.
—**THE BATMAN/TARZAN ADVENTURE HOUR.** CBS: 9/10/1977–9/2/1978. Filmation. Same production and voice credits, with additional voices: Adam West (Batman); Burt Ward (Robin); Lennie Weinrib (Bat-Mite).
—**TARZAN AND THE SUPER SEVEN.** CBS: 9/9/1978–8/30/1980. Filmation. Same production and voice credits. Additional components: 1. **ISIS AND THE FREEDOM FORCE.** Voices: Diane Pershing (Isis); Bob Denison (Hercules); Michael Bell (Merlin/Sinbad/Super Samurai). 2. **MICROWOMAN AND SUPER STRETCH.** Voices: Kim Hamilton (Microwoman); Ty Henderson (Super Stretch). 3. **WEB WOMAN.** Voices: Linda Gary (Kelly Webster); Lou Scheimer (Spinner). 4. **MANTA AND MORAY.** Voices: Joe Stern (Manta); Joan Van Ark (Moray). 5. **JASON OF STAR COMMAND** (Live-action sequences). Created, produced and directed by Arthur H. Nadel. Story editor: Samuel Peeples. Cast: Craig Littler (Jason); James Doohan, John Russell (The Commander); Charlie Dell (Prof. E. J. Parsafoot); Tamara Dobson (Samantha); Susan O'Hanlon (Nicole Davidoff); Sid Haig (Dragos); Larry Storch (Voice of Twiki); and Peepo the Robot.
—**TARZAN/LONE RANGER ADVENTURE HOUR.** CBS: 9/13/1980–9/5/1981.
—**TARZAN/LONE RANGER/ZORRO ADVENTURE HOUR.** CBS: 9/12/1981– 9/11/1982. Filmation. Produced by Lou Scheimer and Norm Prescott. Produced by Don Christensen. Story editor, Arthur C. Brown. Written by Arthur Browne Jr., Marty Warner, Robby London. Music by Yvette Blais and George Michael. 1. **TARZAN.** Voices: Robert Ridgely (Tarzan). 2. **LONE RANGER.** Voices: J. Darnoc [William Conrad] (The Lone Ranger/ Opening Announcer); Ivan Naranjo (Tonto). 3. **ZORRO.** Voices: Henry Darrow (Don Diego, aka Zorro); Christine Avila (Maria); Don Diamond (Sgt. Gonzales); Eric Mason (Capt. Ramon); Julio Medina (Amigo/Miguel); East Carlo (Frey Gaspar); Socorro Valdez (Lucia); Carlos Rivas (Don Alejandro/Governor General).

Tarzan, human king of the apes who in reality was landed-gentry Lord Greystoke, first appeared in the pages of *All-Story Magazine* in 1912. Author Edgar Rice Burroughs may not have known much about the African jungle (his references to tigers in that region have been carefully weeded out of the reprints), but he was a persuasive story constructionist who thoroughly understood his audience. The subsequent Burroughs canon included 24 *Tarzan* novels, movie after movie about the "ape man" in both the silent and sound eras, and various radio and TV series, on into the 1980s.

Filmation's weekly animated *Tarzan, Lord of the Jungle*, like Ron Ely's *Tarzan* TV series of the 1960s, restored the protagonist to the erudite, educated character of the Burroughs books (the "Me Tarzan— You Jane" patois didn't develop until Johnny Weissmuller was introduced as the movie Tarzan in 1932), and also got rid of Tarzan's lovely "mate" Jane. The pumped-up muscular character design was deliberately based on the comic-pages work of Burne Hogarth, who had drawn the *Tarzan* daily strip from 1937 through 1947, succeeding Hal K. Foster of *Prince Valiant* fame (see *The Legend of Prince Valiant*). To allow for reasonable smoothness of movement (at least in the opening-credits sequence), Filmation traced its artwork over live-action footage of a male athlete; this extra care was complemented by above-average background art. In keeping with the dramatic value of his physique, the cartoon Tarzan was cast in the cartoon-superhero mode, fighting on the side of Virtue with the obligatory animal mascot, Nikima the spider monkey. *Tarzan, Lord of the Jungle* was consistently fun to look at, but less enjoyable when it came to its penny-dreadful dialogue and plotlines.

As it turned out, Tarzan was better served by the lampoonish *George of the Jungle* (q.v.) than he was by Filmation. At least George was definitely the star of his own series, whereas Tarzan was deemed not to be strong enough to handle his program himself. The problem lay in the licensing of related *Tarzan* toys and action figures. Cy Schneider, a seasoned veteran of the plaything-marketing business, has pointed out that Tarzan "isn't a great licensed character. How much can you do with a leopard-skin loincloth and a rubber knife?" As a result, more marketable superheroes, both old and new, were enlisted to help out *Tarzan* as "guest" components.

After a "solo" season, Tarzan returned with six new half hour episodes (plus reruns) as part of *The Batman/Tarzan Adventure Hour* (see *Batman*). In 1978, the series was reconditioned as *Tarzan and the Super Seven*, a 90-minute block designed as CBS' ammunition against ABC's Saturday-morning comedy cartoon lineup. A handful of new *Tarzan*s were added to the character's ever-growing rerun manifest. (So much stock footage had been built up by this point that, according to the book *Animation by Filmation*, one 1978 *Tarzan* contained no new animation whatsoever!) The "Super Seven" consisted of Batman (also in new episodes) and a whole slew of characters created by Filmation itself, thus free of licensing fees: "The Freedom Force," "Superstretch and Microwoman," "Web Woman" and "Manta and Moray."

These "originals" were not all that original in concept. "The Freedom Force" featured Hercules (a holdover from Filmation's earlier *Young Sentinels* [q.v.]), god of strength, who mixed his legends by riding the winged horse Pegasus; Isis, goddess of the elements, last seen in live-action form on Filmation's *Shazam/Isis Hour* and *Isis*, both series starring Joanna Cameron; Super Samurai, "giant of justice," whose milder alter ego was young kid Toshi (echoes of such cartoon properties as *Captain Marvel*, *Mighty Mightor* and *Samson and Goliath*, as well as a bid for the affections of Bruce Lee fans); Merlin, long-established "master of magic"; and Sinbad, legendary Master of the Seven Seas. (Sinbad's "actual" career as a bloodthirsty buccaneer was not alluded to.) This team concept was a blatant attempt by Filmation to capture the *Superfriends* (q.v.) crowd with wholly studio-owned characters, and with an eye on future toystore sales.

The rest of the "Super Seven" also ached to be embraced with the same affection (and marketing) that greeted proven animated properties. "Superstretch and Microwoman," starring tiny female crimefighter Christy Cross and her elasticized husband Chris Cross, borrowed elements from *Plasticman* (q.v.), *Inch High Private Eye* (q.v.), *The Fantastic Four* (q.v.) and the "Tom of THUMB" segments from the cartoon *King Kong* (q.v.). The single nuance of

"Microwoman and Superstretch" was that both characters were African American.

"Web Woman" was something of a distaff *Spider-Man* (q.v.), which itself would undergo a spiritual gender-change within a few seasons as *Spider-Woman* (q.v.). The Web Woman of the title was NASA scientist and weekend gardener Kelly Webster, who after rescuing a spider from a grisly death, was endowed with the combined strength of all insects and arachnids—which when magnified to human proportions would of course translate to superstrength. Kelly Webster/Web Woman was dispatched to all parts of the world on dogooding missions by her contact/mentor Scarab, an extraterrestrial; accompanying her on these journeys was alien being Spinner, named for his ability to roll himself into a ball (I was unaware that there was much call for this talent).

"Manta and Moray" was Filmation's version of *Aquaman* (see *Superman*) and *Sub-Mariner* (see *Marvel Super Heroes*). Manta was the last of a water-breathing civilization of humans; his female friend Moray was rescued from a shipwreck by a benign whale (see *Moby Dick and the Mighty Mitor* for another spin on this premise).

Filling out the hour-and-a-half *Tarzan and the Super Seven* was a 15-minute live-action property, *Jason of Star Command*, about a 22nd century space traveller (Toujours *Star Wars*). This segment was eventually spun off into its own half hour, which ran on CBS from September 15, 1979, through August 29, 1981, and was worth noting for two of its cast members: James Doohan, "Scotty" of *Star Trek* (an earlier live-to-cartoon Filmation project), and Susan O'Hanlon, daughter of *Jetsons* (q.v.) voice star George O'Hanlon. *Jason* was inspired by the success of another Filmation live-actioner, *Space Academy*, even unto sharing the same robot, "Peepo." Series like *Jason of Star Command*, *Space Academy* and the aforementioned *Shazam/Isis* were all part of a concerted effort by Filmation to branch off into non-cartoon projects, partly as a defense against those media meddlers who wanted to purge Saturday morning of all animation. Ultimately, the plan was defeated by the exigencies of finance: The average *Jason* cost $220,000 plus actors' residuals, while the standard Filmation cartoon half hour clocked in at $165,000.

The studio decided to hack through the animation wilds for just a bit longer.

But we were talking about *Tarzan*, weren't we? In 1980, all the "Super Seven" animated components were dropped, bundled into a separate rerun entity, *Batman and the Super Seven*. Tarzan wasn't alone for long, however. That same year, CBS unveiled *The Tarzan/Lone Ranger Adventure Hour*, cofeaturing the Masked Rider of the Plains and his Indian companion Tonto (see *The Lone Ranger*). Sixteen half hours each of *Tarzan* and *Lone Ranger* were produced, with an additional 16 11-minute "shorts" headlining each character. The new *Lone Ranger*, like the new *Tarzan*, was well illustrated, with expert rotoscoping of live-action film and attractive character design. Otherwise, the *Adventure Hour* shared the same shortcomings of most other Filmations: uneven animation, protracted "talking heads" closeup sequences, and miles and miles of recycled stock footage.

Tarzan/Lone Ranger did well enough for Filmation to resuscitate another pulp-novel hero of old, Johnson MacCulley's benevolent bandit Zorro. Introduced in the 1919 short story "The Curse of Capistrano," the masked, black-clad, sword-wielding Robin Hood of Spanish California was committed to celluloid by Douglas Fairbanks in 1920's *Mark of Zorro*, launching an off-again, on-again flow of Zorro features and serials for the next three decades. The character's longest-sustained media success was in Disney's *Zorro* TV series of the late 1950s, starring the magnificent Guy Williams in the "dual" role of Zorro and his foppish alter ego Don Diego.

Filmation's *Tarzan/Lone Ranger/Zorro Adventure Hour* constituted Zorro's first cartoon appearance. The series bore the credit-sequence warning that the "distinctive likeness" of Zorro was copyrighted by Filmation, but failed to note (as the audience did) that this likeness was eerily similar to Disney's Guy Williams. It's too bad that actor Basil Rathbone had never copyrighted his distinct likeness, otherwise Filmation would have been prevented from drawing its *Zorro* villain Captain Ramon as the spitting image of the Rathbone character in the 1940 Tyrone Power version of *Mark of Zorro*.

Nor were the characters the only "quotes" from earlier *Zorros*. Though network publicity insisted that the hero's swordplay would be downgraded in keeping with the nonviolent tenor of the times, Filmation's Zorro still opened with a montage of carved "Z's" (rotoscoped over live footage of a CBS executive who was a fencing enthusiast!), just like in the Disney days. Equally Disneyesque was the series' title logo, which emulated the lightning stroke design of the Guy Williams version.

Some changes *were* made for the cartoonization, however. In place of the comedy-mute manservant played in Disney's *Zorro* by pantomimist Gene Sheldon, Filmation's Zorro had a handsome-hunk family retainer named Miguel, who acted as Don Diego's "Tonto" during his midnight forays aginst tyranny and oppression. In contrast to Disney's lovable, harmless Sgt. Garcia, bound by law to battle Zorro but basically sympathetic to the bandit's cause, the cartoon Zorro was antagonized by Sgt. Gonzalez, just as dumb and as fat as Garcia but not at all lovable or even likable. And in keeping with the pacifistic tone set by *Tarzan* and *The Lone Ranger*, who never shirked from a fight but never instigated one either, Filmation's Zorro refused to kill or seriously injure anyone. His philosophy was that Sgt. Gonzalez's soldiers were just "doing their duty" when engaged in swordsmanship against him. To make sure the audience would understand the difference between defending oneself and fighting for the hell of it, a secondary bandit was introduced: sexy female pirate Lucia, whose plundering of Spanish gold was strictly for her own benefit.

As in the presence of radio's "Matt Dillon" William Conrad as the voice of Filmation's Lone Ranger, the voice-cast of *Zorro* included several crossovers to other similar series. Henry Darrow, the voice of Zorro, would later portray the freedom fighter in the 1983 Disney TV comedy series *Zorro and Son*; and Don Diamond, the cartoon series' Sgt. Gonzalez, had been prominently featured in the 1950s *Zorro* weekly as Corporal Reyes, fall guy to that program's Sgt. Garcia.

Incidentally, both Darrow and Diamond were Hispanic, as was the rest of the voice talent on *Zorro*; the series was the only cartoon series of the 1980s outside of Ruby-Spears' *Rubik the Amazing Cube* to employ an all–Latin cast. In a related note, each *Zorro* episode ended with a prosocial 30-second coda wherein the hero would teach the audience a Spanish word or phrase, or elucidate a piece of history about old California. Like the 30-second jungle-oriented info-bites on *Tarzan* and the old-west historical snippets heard on *Lone Ranger*, these prosocial vignettes were frequently the best written segments on the show.

Tarzan and its various 1980s cofeatures represented the first time that Filmation went outside its own studios for animation help, enlisting the talents of Japan's TMS (Tokyo Movie Shinsha) studios. Filmation historians Michael Swanigan and Darrell McNeil regard this move as the beginning of the end for the studio, which previously had prided itself on its "All-American" animation work. At the risk of sparking an argument, it must be noted that the work on *Tarzan* was actually superior to most earlier Filmations, managing to realize several of the storyboard artists' more intricate concepts (floor-level camera angles, well composed overhead shots, breathless action montages) without giving the impression that the artist's ambitions were stifled by corner-cutting animation. It wasn't flawless, what with Filmation's tendency to shortchange its expository sequences with mis-timed animation, and to wear down its best-animated sequences through extensive stock-footage repetition. Still, *Tarzan* and its companion *Lone Ranger* and *Zorro* projects indicated that the studio was on the verge of consisent class-A product before a series of corporate buyouts forced its permanent shutdown at the end of the 1980s.

Since this essay began with *Tarzan* alone, it also ends that way. In 1984, *Tarzan* reruns were brought back to CBS as a solo act, just as in the series' beginning.

TAZ-MANIA. Fox: 9/7/1991–. Warner Bros. Television. Executive producers, Jean MacCurdy, Tom Ruegger. Executive in charge of production, Tom Sarnoff. Producer and story editor, Art Vitello. Directed by Douglas McCarthy. Theme music by Richard Stone. Music by J. Eric Schmidt, Don Davis and Harvey Cohen. Production facilities: Akom Film Production Co. Ltd., Startoons (Chicago). Overseas animation supervisor, Dev Ramsarian. Voices: Jim Cummings (Taz); Debi Derryberry, Miriam Flynn, Maurice

LaMarche, Kellie Martin, Rob Paulsen, Dan Castellaneta, John Astin, others. Warner Bros. cartoon director Robert McKimson came up with the slobbering, gibberish-spouting Tasmanian Devil for the 1954 Bugs Bunny cartoon *Devil May Hare*. Inspiration typically came from desperation: McKimson and staff simply couldn't think of any animal that they hadn't yet transferred to celluloid, until someone pulled the name "Tasmanian Devil" from the deep recesses of his subconscious. The ultravicious character appeared in only five theatrical cartoons, always in support of Bugs Bunny, but somehow his destructive tendencies and antisocial demeanor struck a chord with disenfranchised younger viewers. It wasn't long before the Warners' animation studio was besieged with fan letters addressed to The Tasmanian Devil, or just simply "Taz."

After a brief period in the early 1990s when a younger version of the character, "Dizzy Devil," made occasional appearances in Warners' TV series *Tiny Toon Adventures* (q.v.), the diabolical marsupial was awarded his own Saturday morning Fox series, *Taz-Mania*. Renamed "Taz," perhaps in tribute to his first fan following, the character no longer tore things apart just for the hell of it, nor did he pounce upon and devour timid woodland creatures. Taz was simply a little wild and very unintelligible, but "civilized" enough to hold down a job as bellhop for the down-under Hotel Tazmania, owned by human Aussie Bushwacker Bob. Most of his weekly adventures involved his extended family, who except for their furry bodies and razor sharp teeth might well have been mistaken for a typical sitcom gathering from the 1960s. Taz's father Hugh was a laid-back Bing Crosby/Dean Martin type, who preferred reading his Sunday paper to ripping trees out by the roots. Mom Jean was an aproned homemaker, devoted to her hobbies. Sister Molly talked like a Valley Girl ("Fer sure," "dream on," and so forth), while baby brother Jake generally just gurgled.

As with the other Warners' TV cartoon outings of the 1990s, *Taz-Mania* worked best when lampooning other forms of popular entertainment. One of the best episodes, a dual parody of Jane Goodall's National Geographic specials and the 1988 film *Gorillas in the Mist*, featured a female anthropologist who "adopted" Taz' family.

Oblivious to the fact that everyone except Taz spoke perfect English and behaved with utter normality, the pompous researcher insisted upon bestowing condescending names like "Bright Eyes" upon members of the Devil family, read evolutionary significance in their every movement, and finally came to the conclusion that Taz was the smartest and most "human" of the bunch!

Most of the *Taz-Mania* episodes were 30-minute playlets, while some episodes were divided up into components featuring several other denizens of the Australian continent. The Platypus Brothers, Daniel and Timothy, were sort of a combination of Daffy Duck (the lisps and the duck-bills) and of another Warner Bros. property, the Goofy Gophers (spouting gratuitous and flowery terms of endearment for each other). Their adventures were insanely stream-of-consciousness at best, tiresomely overdone at worst, but at least they had the self-awareness of *knowing* when they were beating a joke or plot situation to death and were considerate enough to inform the audience. Didgeri Dingo was a monumentally selfish creature despite his plaintive catch-phrase "Sometimes I think I care too much!," and not above exploiting Taz for his own personal comfort. Bull and Axel Gator were a pair of inept (and sometimes introspective) trappers, doing their best to capture Taz for "the little zoo kids." The Bushrats, despite their Australian homeland, spoke in thick *Hogan's Heroes* style German accents. Other *Taz-Mania* supporting characters included Wendell T. Wolf, Willy Wombat (a flea!), Bushwacker Bob and his Mum, Kiwi, Constance and Thickly (a koala and a wallaby), Buddy Boar, Francis X. Bushlad of the Mud Men, and Dog the Turtle. And there were occasional cameo appearances by past Warner Bros. cartoon greats, from the famous to the obscure. (Marvin Martian returns!)

Unlike other Warners series like *Tiny Toon* and *Animaniacs*, which were appreciated and enjoyed by the public at large, *Taz-Mania* was not universally beloved. Cartoon purists applauded the full animation, intricate background design, and freewheeling comedy content. Others, such as the reviewer for *Entertainment Weekly*, found the program repetitious and the "Taz" character too limited to carry his own series. The final court of public opinion, the ratings, shouted down the detractors, allowing *Taz-Mania* to enjoy two full first-run seasons on Fox and (as of this writing) an additional season of network reruns.

TEDDY RUXPIN *see* **THE ADVENTURES OF TEDDY RUXPIN**

TEEN FORCE *see* **SPACE STARS**

TEEN WOLF. CBS: 9/13/1986–8/27/1988; 10/29/1988–9/2/1989. Southern Star Productions/Hanna-Barbera Australia/Kushner-Locke Company/Clubhouse Pictures/Atlantic Entertainment Group. Produced by Buzz Potamkin and Jonathan Dana. Produced and directed by Gordon Kent. Creative director, Chris Cuddington. Animation directors, Jon McClenahan, Darrell Van Citters. Story editor, Buzz Dixon. Executive in charge of production, Keith Amor. Music themes by David Kitay and Richard Kosinski, Wells Christie, John Lewis Parker, James Donnellan. Opening theme by John Lewis Parker, Barry Mann and Steve Tyrrell. Closing music by Ashley Hall and Stefanie Tyrrell; sung by Ashley Hall. Voices: Townsend Coleman (Scott Howard); Jeannie Elias (Boof); June Foray (Grandma/Mrs. Sesslick); Stacy Keach Sr. (Grandpa); James Hampton (Harold); Donny Most (Stiles); Craig Schaffer (Mick); Will Ryan (Chuck); and Sheryl Bernstein, Ellen Gerstell, Mona Marshall, and Frank Welker.

Teen Wolf was a 1985 Michael J. Fox film vehicle about high school "outsider" Scott Howard, who gained popularity only after his classmates discovered that he was a werewolf. Too raunchy for most adult tastes, the comedy was a big hit with teen and preteen moviegoers—which of course meant "Sequel Time." *Teen Wolf II* didn't immediately materialize, but a weekly, half hour cartoonization of *Teen Wolf* filled the demand in the fall of 1986.

Well animated by the same team responsible for *The Berenstain Bears* (q.v.), *Teen Wolf* expectedly threw out the sex and profanity that had "distinguished" the movie, and also jettisoned most of the rest of the film's premise. The cartoon series was set in Wolverton, where the tourist trade was totally dependent upon the town's history of werewolf sightings. Unlike the circumstances in the film, Scott Howard's lycanthropy was not common

knowledge. Scott didn't want to be the freakish object of gawking tourists, nor did he want to risk incarceration by scientists or zoologists, so his secret was shared only with his best friends Styles (male) and Boof (female). Nor did Scott become a werewolf merely when angered, as was the case in the movie; TV's *Teen Wolf* also "wolfed out" during the traditional full moon.

Further departing from the film, in which only Scott and his father Harold were wolf-guys, the cartoon *Teen Wolf*'s family was comprised *entirely* of lycanthropes. Grandma Howard had pointy ears and hailed from Transylvania, as did fuzz-faced Grandpa, a proud veteran of the wartime Canine Corps! Little sister Lupe wasn't quite as "far gone" as the rest of the family, though she did enjoy dressing up in a dog suit and chasing cats.

Borrowing from the "Gladys Kravitz" character on the live action sitcom *Bewitched*, the Howard family had a snoopy neighbor, cat-loving Mrs. Sesslick, who was wise to the Howards' werewolfery but was unable to convince anyone except her bumbling newspaper-reporter son Waldo. Scott Howard suffered additional antagonism from high school jock Mick, though this grew less from Scott's tendency to grow fangs in the moonlight than from his rivalry with Mick over campus vamp Pam (who never quite caught on why her pet dog showed such unnatural affection toward Scott).

James Hampton, as Scott's dad Harold, was the only actor from the *Teen Wolf* movie to provide voiceover talent on the cartoon series. As in the case of *Back to the Future* (q.v.), Michael J. Fox seemed to be making a career out of not appearing in the animated versions of his films.

Though limited in concept and scope (as the disastrous theatrical sequel *Teen Wolf II* would demonstrate), *Teen Wolf* kept its paws above water with clever dialogue, logical plotlines (under the circumstances), and well-rounded characterizations. In a very tough late-1980s Saturday morning ratings war, the series managed to hang on to its network berth for three full seasons.

TEENAGE MUTANT NINJA TURTLES. Syndicated: 1987. CBS: 9/8/1990–. Murikami-Wolf-Swenson (later Fred Wolf Prod.)/Group W. Supervising producer and supervising director, Fred Wolf. Executive producer, Mark Freedman. Produced by Walt Kubiak. Animation directors: Bill Wolf, Walt Kubiak, Tony Love, Bill Hutten, Kent Butterworth. Sequence directors: Bill Hutten, John Kafka, Walt Kubiak, Tony Love, Neal Warner, Ron Myrick, Richard Trueblood, Bob Shellhorn. Executive story editor, Bill Wolf. Story editors, David Wise and Jack Mendelsohn. Voice director, Susan Blu. Music by D. C. Brown and Chuck Lorre. Musical supervision, John Mortarotti. Created by Kevin Eastman and Peter Laird (c. 1985 Mirage Studios). Characters courtesy of Surge Licensing. Additional production facilities: IDDH. Additional direction, Rene Huchez. Voices: Townsend Coleman (Michaelangelo); Cam Clarke (Leonardo); Barry Gordon (Donatello); Rob Paulsen (Rafael); James Avery (Shredder); Pat Fraley (Krang); Renae Jacobs (April O'Neil); Peter Renaday (Splinter); Jennifer Darling (Irma); and Greg Berg, Jim Cummings, Joan Gerber, Dorian Harewood, Tress MacNeille, Nicholas Omana, Thom Pinto, Maggie Roswell, and Beau Weaver.

In 1983, 19-year-old Kevin Eastman and 28-year-old Peter Laird were just two more unsuccessful artists hoping to crack the big time. The well had run dry on new comic strip concepts, they'd been told. While kidding around for lack of any good ideas, Eastman doodled a turtle in Japanese ninja warrior costume, just to get a laugh from his partner. Then, as though a dam had broken, out flowed the inspiration: a satire of Samurai action films, with turtles rather than humans in the starring roles. Later on, Eastman and Laird would smooth out their story, claiming that they'd thought of turtles because the amphibians had become exotically "rare" due to their being removed from pet stores for fear of spreading disease. I like better that bit about scribbling a ninja turtle out of boredom.

As the concept began to grow, so did the backstory for the proposed Eastman-Laird comic book. The original version featured a rat (real, not figurative) named Splinter, the pet of the human Ninja Master Hamato Yoshi. Oroko Saki of the "Foot Clan," settling an old grudge, murdered Yoshi, but before making his escape was bitten by Splinter. Setting off after Oroko Saki, who'd come to America and set up villainous shop under the name of Shredder,

Splinter was shpritzed with radioactive waste called Mutagen, which rendered him into a part-human. The mutant later discovered four baby turtles, who'd also undergone the radioactive glop treatment and had taken on human traits. Splinter, by now a full-fledged Ninja expert, raised the turtles as surrogate sons, naming them after his four favorite artists: Leonardo, Michaelangelo, Raphael and Donatello. The turtle-boys matured into typical teenagers, complete with pimples, raging hormones and a fondness for pizza and beer. They also became as Ninja-savvy as Splinter, joining their mentor in the fight against the covetous, megalomaniac Shredder on American soil.

Though they looked alike, as turtles are wont to do, each Mutant Ninja developed his own distinct personality and martial arts specialty. Leonardo, the leader, was master of katana (flat sword); Michaelangelo, the prankster, specialized in karate and nunchaku (chain and club—the same weapon preferred by Splinter); Raphael, the jokester and rebel, used the sai (dagger); and Donatello, the technical whiz, was most efficient fighting with the bo (staff). (On the TV version, the Turtles were further personalized with different colored masks and initialed belts.)

Originally printed in black and white on cheap stock, *Teenage Mutant Ninja Turtles* was the sole asset of Eastman and Laird's Mirage Studios—so named because it accurately described their office space. Only 175 copies of Issue Number One were printed up and distributed at comic book conventions. Sales were all but nonexistent until a UPI reporter, amused by the concept, brought Mirage to the attention of the public at large. This resulted in 3000 copies and 3000 sales, netting Eastman and Laird a princely hundred dollars. But word of mouth was a force to be conjured with, and before the 1980s were half over, the independent version of *Teenage Mutant Ninja Turtles* boasted 150,000 readers. That's when the Archie Comics line stepped in, together with the action-figure merchandising firm of Playmate Toys. Archie and Playmate convinced Eastman and Laird that the appeal of *Turtles* could be broadened with a slicker, better distributed product, and this could be best expedited by prettying it up a bit. The first move was to remove any overt killing from the storylines; the

Teenage Mutant Ninja Turtles: Leonardo (thumbs up), Michaelangelo (holding pizza), Donatello (in sewer), and Raphael ("ta-da" gesture).

second was to change the Turtles' beverage of preference from beer to root beer.

When Murikami-Wolf-Swenson entered the picture in 1987 for the *Teenage Mutant Ninja Turtles* cartoon pilot, the "laundering" process continued. "I've always loved monster shows," noted Fred Wolf to *Animation* magazine in 1992, "but this was so bizarre." The un-bizarring process commenced when Wolf changed the Turtles' backstory. Yoshi was not murdered, but instead discredited by Oroko/Splinter as part of a power struggle over control of the Foot Clan; falsely accused of attempting to murder his superior, Yoshi was forced to flee Japan. Survival, not revenge, was the motivating factor, a more digestible concept for American kidvid.

And there was no pet rat named Splinter this time around; instead, Yoshi and Splinter were one and the same.

It's easier to watch the pilot episode than explain it, but here goes. Exiled to the sewers of New York, Yoshi made friends with four turtles who'd been abandoned by a teenaged boy. When Mutagen was spilled this time, there happened to be a rat in the vicinity. Yoshi merged with the rat and became Splinter, while the turtles, who'd been around humans since birth, simply adopted the combined attitudes of Yoshi and the teenager who'd once owned them.

The TV Teenage Mutant Ninja Turtles (hereafter called *T.M.N.T.* so I won't overload the word processor), and indeed the entire concept, was played more for laughs than the more graphic, funereal comic book. Fred Wolf's intent was to lighten up the darkness, to make the Turtles friendlier and more approachable for the kids in the audience, with de-emphasis on the horrific aspects of mutation. Murikami-Wolf-Swenson redrew the Turtles as rounder, nicer-looking characters. And even though the Turtles had never been truly human, Fred Wolf emphasized the 'humanness' of *T.M.N.T.*: "The turtles are vulnerable," said Wolf. "When they're cut, they bleed."

Still, the emphasis was on comedy instead of carnage, avoiding any "straight" violence. The scriptwriters always undercut the horror or threat of death of any given situation with wisecracks and sight gags. The *T.M.N.T.* carefully plucked the curse out of any danger with a *Rocky and His Friends*-like toppling of the Fourth Wall separating audience from story, and story from credibility. A formidable feat of strength or dazzling martial-arts display would be followed by the Turtles' turning to us and warning, "Remember, kids. Don't try this at home. We're professionals." While climbing a wall, the Turtles would bemoan the fact that they weren't wearing the suction boots "from Episode Six." And if a turn of events seemed even more ridiculous than the whole Mutant Ninja concept, one of the Turtles would shrug and sigh "Hey, waddya want from us? It's a cartoon."

Even the villainy was played for yocks. The wicked Darth Vader–like Foot Clan warrior Shredder was often shown grovelling like a fourth assistant vice president before his own superior, Krang from Dimension X—a pink, disembodied brain, toted around as a belt accessory by a mindless humanoid flunkey. Krang's world-conquering aspirations were tempered by the fact that he was the most luckless cartoon villain since Boris Badenov. His Technodrome, a huge space station vehicle designed as Krang's weapon and control center, wound up sinking beneath the earth's surface and festering there for the remainder of the series like a sliver in a pimple. Understandably, Krang had a miserable disposition, and took out most of his invective on Shredder. At times, the two groused so much to each other about their misfire schemes and dislike for one another that

they sounded like the ageing vaudeville team in Neil Simon's *The Sunshine Boys*.

The loudest of the villains' recriminations were reserved for Shredder's henchmen: Bebop and Rock Steady, street punks who'd been mutated with zoo animals. Despite their fearsome appearance, the two baddies were as senseless as their bosses, spending less time at their villainy than at griping over how being sent to do Shredder's dirty work robbed them of their principal vocation of loafing and eating. In one marvelous episode, Bebop and Rock Steady appeared to have found their proper niche in life when they were mistakenly promoted to network TV executives, scheduling a prime-time season by throwing darts at a bulletin board (our suspicions are confirmed).

The *T.M.N.T.'s* heroine was April O'Neil, a TV reporter for *Channel 6 Happy Hour News* who befriended the "heroes on a half shell" and acted as their liaison between their sewer headquarters and the outside world. April had appeared peripherally in the *T.M.N.T.* comic books, but her "conduit" function was created for the cartoon series. Fred Wolf turned April into the link between sewers and surface to remove the other-worldly "weirdness" of the original *T.M.N.T.* concept: "Once we established these characters in the real world, anything was possible."

Though frequently plunked into peril, April was one of the most resilient and self-reliant of all cartoon heroines of the 1980s. Indeed, Rock Steady and Bebop visibly cringed whenever ordered to kidnap the girl, knowing they'd be in for more than a few lumps ("Just like the last 19 times we kidnapped her this season"). The remaining human regular characters were as buffoonish as the villains, notably Vernon, a "Ted Baxter" anchorman who always tried to take credit for April's scoops, and Irma, a scatterbrained TV station employee who never seemed to have a grip on any plot point at any time—even when she herself was the focus of the storyline.

Other subordinate characters remained laughable, no matter how frightening they hoped they were. Casey Jones, self-styled vigilante who hated the Turtles unto death, was flexible enough to become the romantic lead in the first live-action *T.M.N.T.* movie. The Rat King was a self-styled dictator who commandeered armies of rats to wreak havoc on the human world; he had a pet rodent named Mickey, explaining to no one in particular "that's an inside joke." Gadgetman was a paunchy unemployed middle-ager who tried his ineptest to become a superhero himself before resigning himself to a job as the Turtles' erstwhile hardware inventor. And Baxter Stockman was a nerdish half-human/half-fly—who of course got to say "Help Meeee!" when stuck in a spider's web.

The Rat King's "Mickey," Baxter Stockman's glancing reference to the 1959 film *The Fly*, and a trio of extraterrestrials named Klatu, Barada and Nikto (remember *Day The Earth Stood Still?*), were among the many *T.M.N.T.* in-jokes involving popular culture, which ranged from movie parodies to the Turtles' rallying cry "Cowabunga"—a surfing phrase to the under 20 bunch, but a phrase that had a lot more meaning to us baby boomers who'd grown up watching *Howdy Doody*. In the manner of *Rocky and His Friends* (q.v.), many of the jokes were generic enough to get a laugh from all age groups, while some were deliberately over the heads of the youngest viewers. Some of the jokes were *so* "in" that even diligent trivia collectors needed a scorecard. Most people got the point when an insane collector of Turtle memorabilia explained that his obsession was to compensate for the fact that his mother threw away his pet turtle "Rosebud." But only the most monklike of TV worshippers would have understood why this villain's henchmen were named Clyde and Adler. Oh, you didn't know? Clyde Adler was the voice of "White Fang" and "Black Tooth" on the *Soupy Sales Shows* of the 1960s and 1970s.

The writing *had* to be *T.M.N.T.'s* strong suit; the scripters couldn't rely on the animation, which varied in quality depending on production facilities, and was never more than serviceable. At that, *T.M.N.T.* looked better than many of its contemporary programs when it first appeared as a miniseries in 1987 and 1988. The excellent response to the project's first run encouraged branching out to a weekly syndicated *Turtles* in 1988, and finally a daily in 1989, which almost instantly grabbed 73 percent of the audience.

Something which pleased so many children couldn't *possibly* be good for them, so despite all of Fred Wolf's efforts to "cleanse" the Turtles, their series was under adult-group attack from the outset.

Most vocal in their attacks were members of the Religious Right, who bombarded *T.M.N.T.* as anti–Christian because of the occult overtones of Kung Fu and Ninja practice. One writer, taking his cue from obscure clues found in the comic books rather than the series, complained that the form of Ninja practiced by the Turtles was Kung Pau, which allegedly exercised a form of "mind control" over its practitioners. The notion that kids responded to *T.M.N.T.* because they were attracted to the uniqueness of the concept, the comedy content, and the ancillary toys and action figures, was foreign to this born-again critic, who evidently believed that viewers' minds were being governed by ultra-violet rays emanating from the Turtles' animation cels. While the series wasn't above criticism, *T.M.N.T.* certainly never condoned godlessness or brain damage. In fact, the first *T.M.N.T.* theatrical film, released in the spring of 1990, came out *against* mind control by offering a Fagan-like villain who seduced street kids into crime with hypnotic video games.

That initial *Turtles* feature film, by the way, established for good and all the marketplace value of the concept. The film netted $115,000,000, which not only opened the door for two sequels, but actually saved the cartoon version of *T.M.N.T.* from extinction. Murikami-Wolf-Swenson's Dublin-based studios, beset by overhead problems, were on the verge of closing down in 1990. But when the CBS network took a glance at the success of the *Turtles* movie, it pumped its own money into the project on the promise of a fall CBS 60-minute Saturday morning slot. Thus *T.M.N.T.* became one of the very few cartoon series to open on a network with new episodes, even while first-run half hours were still running in daily syndication. There was no reason for CBS to rue its decision: *T.M.N.T.* turned out to be the number one Saturday networker, garnering the Big Eye its best ratings in kiddie-show history.

As enjoyable as the Turtles can be, the "super-creature" concept and its attendant self-mocking, pig-bladder comic style can lapse into archness, as proven by the many *T.M.N.T.* wannabes we've witnessed in the last few years. Clutching for the surplus *Turtles* market with variable results have been such lookalike one-shots as *Barnyard Commandos* (q.v.) and such soundalike series as *The Adventures of T-Rex* (q.v.), *Bucky O'Hare and the Toad Wars* (q.v.) (which admittedly predated *Turtles* as a comic book, but wound up an imitation when adapted to television), *Stone Protectors* (q.v.), and *Swat Kats* (q.v.). And there have been innumerable comic-book parodies, most of them about as funny as their titles: *Cold Blood Chameleon Commandos, Geriatric Gangrene Jujitsu Gerbils, Mildly Microwaved Pre-Pubescent Kung Pu Gophers, Nuclear Spawned Martial Arts Frogs,* and *Pre-Teen Dirty Gene Kung Fu Kangaroos.*

In the spirit of "everybody's doing it," even *T.M.N.T.* offered a takeoff on itself: the "Punk Frogs," mutants created by Shredder and named (perhaps out of desperation) after famous political usurpers Attila the Hun, Genghis Khan, Napoléon, and Rasputin. The hands-down best *T.M.N.T.* parody occurred on Warner Bros.' *Tiny Toon Adventures* as part of a half-hour satire on cartoon merchandising: "The Immature Radioactive Samurai Slugs," who bore names like Grandma Moses and Rockwell, and whose snail-shaped automobile left a slimy silver trail behind it.

By 1991, the *T.M.N.T.* property was worth one billion dollars in revenue and merchandising. It lagged a bit in 1992, with only a few measly hundred million in the coffers. That's when Marvel Productions moved in to promise the *Turtles* franchisers that they would come up with a series deliberately designed as a successor: *Biker Mice from Mars* (q.v.). But the Turtles hadn't turned over on their backs yet. In 1993, CBS commissioned eight new episodes, with 14 in production for future use. And though the series was dropped in syndication, the USA Network accrued blockbuster ratings when they began daily broadcasts of *Teenage Mutant Ninja Turtles* reruns, launched by a powerhouse 24-hour episode marathon.

Unlike other series that have gained popularity while justifiably irritating and offending millions of nonfans (remember the live-action *Three's Company?*), I for one can think of few reasons to begrudge *Teenage Mutant Ninja Turtles* its success. Perhaps my mind *has* been controlled, at that.

TELE-COMICS. Syndicated: 1949.
—NBC COMICS. NBC: 9/18/1950–3/30/1951. Vallee Video. Voices: Bob Bruce, Howard McNear, Pat McGeeham, Lurene Tuttle.

Tele-Comics was essentially what its title described: filmed comic-strip panels, with the camera panning from one panel to the next as the story progressed. Most reports insist that the project contained no movement whatsoever, but the snippets I've seen, coupled with my own childhood memories, indicate that occasionally there was an isolated piece of animation such as a rocket blast or the shifting of a character's eyes. However, the series was never meant to be regarded as an actual cartoon; it was designed as a cheap early-TV alternative to filming more expensive live-action adventure programs.

Whatever the extent of actual movement, *Tele-Comics*, released for limited syndication in 1949, has to be regarded along with *Crusader Rabbit* (q.v.) as one of the first cartoon series ever produced for television. And when the property was picked up by NBC in 1950 and retitled *NBC Comics*, this series of three-minute vignettes made broadcast history as the first made-for-TV network cartoon program.

Under the original *Tele-Comics* label, the series featured four serialized stories: "Brother Goose," "Joey and Jug," "Rick Rack Secret Agent" and "Su Lah." Not much is known about these continuities, but the properties seen during the *NBC Comics* run have been better chronicled. A few episodes have in fact made it into the hands of private collectors and have been prepared for home video distribution.

Among the *NBC Comics* features were "Johnny and Mr. Do-Right," no relation to Jay Ward's later "Dudley Do-Right" (see *Rocky and His Friends*) but instead the adventures of a boy and his dog. "Danny March," set in Metro City (a popular fictional locale, as witness the much-later *Inspector Gadget* [q.v.] and *Double Dragon* [q.v.]), was the tale of a juvenile delinquent who turned himself around; unable to become a cop because of his height, Danny March chose to become a private detective, and in this capacity functioned as the mayor's personal gumshoe. "Kid Champion" was a prizefight saga sired out of *Golden Boy* and *They Made Me a Criminal.* Hero Eddie Hale was a musician who (in a novel story twist) was urged by his dad to become a boxer. When Eddie mistakenly believed he'd killed a man, he changed his identity to Kid Champion, refusing to discuss his past with anyone. The *NBC Comics* component which got the most circulation (I can remember it being run in the Cincinnati market at least until 1959) was "Space Barton," all about a Chuck Yeager–like jet pilot who underwent special training to prepare himself for outer space maneuvers.

After its NBC run, the whole *NBC Comics* package was resyndicated under its original *Tele-Comics* title and continued to run as "filler" for live-action children's programs. Very occasionally, *Tele-Comics* was telecast as its own separate 15-minute component; in 1955, for example, a UHF station in Hartford, Connecticut, was showing the series nightly at 7 P.M., just before its target audience was sent out of the room so the grownups could watch TV. *Tele-Comics* faded from view as made-for-TV cartoons entered the (comparatively) more sophisticated Hanna-Barbera era, and was never revived in the 1960s due to its black and white photography.

TENNESSEE TUXEDO AND HIS TALES. CBS: 9/28/1963–9/3/1966. Leonardo Television/Total TV Productions. Executive producers, Peter Piech and Treadwell Covington. Directed by Pete Dakis, Sal Faillace, Lu Guarnier, Bob Schleh. Written by Chet Stover and Buck Biggers. Animation by Gamma Studios. Music (stock themes): Win Sharples. Voices: Don Adams (Tennessee Tuxedo); Larry Storch (Mr. Whoopee); Bradley Bolke (Chumley); Kenny Delmar (Yak/ Baldy/Commander McBragg); and Jackson Beck, Ben Stone, Allen Swift, Delo States, Norman Rose, Mort Marshall, and George Irving.

Tennessee Tuxedo and His Tales, a Leonardo Productions weekly starring a wise-lipped penguin, was touted by CBS as "educational," and in fact acquitted itself quite well in that department. Each episode had Tennessee Tuxedo—advertised as "sarcastic," though voice actor Don Adams (see *Inspector Gadget*) sounded only mildly cynical—and his walrus pal Chumley became involved in some activity at Stanley Livingston's Megopolis Zoo which involved knowledge beyond their ken. The penguin and the walrus would then have to escape the zoo and visit all-knowing Mr. Whoopee for advice,

who'd illustrate cogent educational points on his collapsible "3.D.B.B." (three-dimensional blackboard). Despite the comic surroundings, the information was provided straightforwardly, minus the usual Saturday-morning condescension.

Comedian Larry Storch (see *Out of the Inkwell*), Don Adams' lifelong pal, had reportedly substituted for Frank Morgan in the late 1940s whenever that bibulous comic actor was indisposed for a radio appearance. On *Tennessee Tuxedo*, Storch (brilliantly) imitated Morgan again as Mr. Whoopee. His appearances were high points in the short *Tennessee* adventures, which otherwise featured such unmemorable characters as Yak, Baldy (an Eagle) and Flunkey, Stanley Livingston's assistant.

The surrounding components on *Tennessee Tuxedo* were reruns culled from the earlier *King Leonardo and His Short Subjects*. New to the series was "The World of Commander McBragg," which remained a regular on the next Leonardo TV project, *Underdog* (q.v.), and in all of that studio's syndicated packages—and even Jay Ward Productions' *Hoppity Hooper* (q.v.). Why, we couldn't tell you. The central character, a longwinded Baron Münchhausen type named Commander McBragg, wasn't new when his ancestor appeared in the 1937 Warner Bros. cartoon *The Major Lied Till Dawn*. Each 90-second segment featured the Commander boring a clubroom companion with reminiscences of improbable adventures in McBragg's questionable past. The sequence was ritualistically unfunny, elevated only by the voicework of Kenny Delmar (see *King Leonardo*), and the nostalgic wit of the Total Television artists, who drew McBragg as a caricature of British character actor C. Aubrey Smith.

Outside of the drudgery-laden "Commander McBragg," *Tennessee Tuxedo* was one of the better Leonardo Television works, spritely and attractive despite its lookalike plotlines (and thank heaven, no incessantly repeated catch phrases such as those afflicting *Underdog*). The series was also worthwhile as a pioneer in the cartoon "educational entertainment" field, enlightening children without whacking them over the head with dry factoids.

THESE ARE THE DAYS. ABC: 9/7/ 1974–9/5/1976. Hanna-Barbera. Produced by William Hanna and Joseph Barbera. Creative producer, Iwao Takamoto. Directed by Charles Nichols. Story consultant, Myles Wilder. Story editor, Ed Jurist. Music by Hoyt Curtin. Voices: June Lockhart (Martha Day); Pamelyn Ferdin (Kay Day); Jack E. Haley [Jackie Earle Haley] (Danny Day); Henry Jones (Grandpa Jeff Day); Andrew Parks (Ben Day); Frank Cady (Homer); and Julie Bennett, Henry Corden, Micky Dolenz, Moosie Drier, Dennis Duggan, Sam Edwards, June Foray, Joan Gerber, Virginia Gregg, Allan Melvin, Don Messick, Vic Perrin, William Schallert, Betsy Slade, John Stephenson, Irene Tedrow, Michele Tobin, Lurene Tuttle, Janet Waldo, Jesse White, and Paul Winchell.

The Days of *These Are the Days* were a farm family, widow Martha Day and her three children, living in the sleepy rural village of Elmsville. The series was set in an indeterminate past, but must have been circa 1910, since Ben Day, the oldest son, owned a Model T Ford. Grandpa Jeff Day represented the conduit between the Day farm and the Elmsville populace by managing the Day General Store.

These Are the Days was obviously inspired by the popular CBS live-action series *The Waltons*, though the half-hour cartoon weekly was set about 20 years earlier than the action on Waltons' Mountain. *Days* represented some of Hanna-Barbera's best work of the mid–1970s, boasting excellent production design and non-exaggerated characters—one of the few times that Hanna-Barbera's simulated reality in the *Jonny Quest* (q.v.) tradition was successfully pulled off. Storylines were very gentle, emphasizing situation over comedy. And, behold, there were no funny dogs! *These Are the Days* did however contain a cute inside joke: the character name "Ben Day" was taken from a cartoonist's technical term for a method of comic-strip shading and shadowing.

Sixteen episodes of *These Are the Days* were first-run on Saturdays in 1974, then rerun on Sundays the following year.

THE THING see **FRED AND BARNEY MEET THE THING**

THIRTEEN GHOSTS OF SCOOBY-DOO see **SCOOBY-DOO**

THIS IS AMERICA, CHARLIE BROWN. CBS: 10/21/1988–11/11/1988; 2/10/1989; 3/10/1989; 4/19/1989; 5/23/1989; 5/30/1990–7/25/1990. Lee Mendelson–Bill Melendez Productions/Charles M. Schultz Creative Organization/United Features Syndicate. Written by Charles M. Schultz and Lee Mendelson. Directed by Sam Jaimes. Musical contributions by Wynton Marsalis, Dave Brubeck, John Philip Sousa, George M. Cohan, Irving Berlin, Vince Guaraldi. Voices: Erin Chase, Jason Rifle (Charlie Brown); Ami Foster, Eric Gayle (Lucy); Jeremy Miller, Brandon Stewart (Linus); Christina Lange, Brittany Thorton (Sally Brown); Jason Mendelson (Peppermint Patty); Curtis Anderson (Schroeder); Keri Houlihan, Marie Lynn Wise, Tani Taylor Powers (Marcie); Hakeem Abdul Samad, Grant Gelt (Franklin); and Bud Davis, Shepard Menken, Chuck Olsen, Hal Smith, Frank Welker, Gregg Berger, Alissa King, Julie Payne, Kristy Baker, Tiffany Billings, Sean Collins, Ami Jane Foster, Nichole Buda, Cam Clarke, Desiree Goyette, Lou Rawls, Christopher Collins, Sean Mendelson, Carvin Winans, Marvin Winans, Michael Winans, Ronald Winans, and Brandon Horne.

Promoted as the first cartoon miniseries, *This Is America, Charlie Brown* was a group of eight half hours featuring Charles Schultz's usual gang of goobers: Charlie Brown, Lucy, Linus, Snoopy, Schroeder, Sally and Peppermint Patty. Unlike the earlier weekly *Peanuts* series *The Charlie Brown and Snoopy Show*, *This Is America* owed little allegiance to the original comic strip beyond the characters and Schultz' scripts. For the first time, the Peanuts gang appeared in period costume, popping up at various crucial points of past American history. And for the first time in *Peanuts* history, adults appeared on-camera, rather than as cacophonous off-stage entities. Though the alterations did seem jarring to Schultz purists, the programs were assembled with a lot more allegiance to historical fact than, say, the condescending *U.S. of Archie* (see *The Archies*) or the 1993 fact-corrupter *Cro* (q.v.). As such, the series was tied in with CBS' "Read More About It" program, a cooperative venture between the network and the libraries of America.

The first program on October 21, 1988,

"The Mayflower Voyagers," featured Charlie Brown and friends at work and play aboard the Pilgrims' America-bound vessel, with Snoopy posting watch in the crow's nest. Without stooping to galloping anachronisms, the children stayed in character, even to Lucy's reacting to a stormtossed sea by grousing "I've got a few choice words for the Captain of this ship." The next week brought "The Birth of the Constitution," with cameo appearances by George Washington, John Hancock et al., and with Charlie Brown taking time off outside Philadelphia's convention hall to invent stickball.

Part three interrupted the "historical" flow with a modern day story, "The NASA Space Station," which cast our heroes and heroines as astronauts. The episode, which contained more comedy than the others, was rather unnecessarily explained away as a dream of Linus'. Back in the "past" groove was the next episode, "The Wright Brothers at Kitty Hawk." The gang's appearance at the First Flight was explained away by Linus' visit to his cousin Dolly, who happened to be a neighbor of the Brothers Wright. This episode was introduced with a brief but colorful look at lighter-than-air experiments prior to 1903, and was highlighted by the lighter-than-light jazz score of Wynton Marsalis.

It's likely the weekly format of This Is America, Charlie Brown would have continued had the Hollywood screenwriter's strike, which had retarded the opening of the 1988-89 TV season, remained unresolved. But by November things were patched up, and CBS' live action adventure series Beauty and the Beast overtook Charlie Brown's Friday 8 P.M. slot. Three months went by before This Is America picked up again in February of 1989, this time as a monthly rather than a weekly.

"The Building of the Transcontinental Railroad," which aired February 10, transported the kids back to the laying of the Golden Spike in 1869. "The Great Inventors" (telecast March 10) included Alexander Graham Bell, Thomas Edison, the motoring Duryea brothers, and, as a balm to Snoopy, the fellow who invented the pizza. "The Smithsonian and the Presidency," telecast April 19, had as its high points reenactments of the Gettysburg Address and FDR's "Nothing to fear but fear itself" inaugural speech. This Is America, Charlie Brown concluded on May 23, 1989,

with "The Music and Heroes of America," an homage to past musical greats Stephen Foster, John Philip Sousa, George M. Cohan and Irving Berlin. The episode concluded with an affectionate "in" joke when Charlie Brown noted that one of his favorite composers was Vince Guaraldi — the man who'd scored most of the Charlie Brown TV specials of the 1960s and 1970s.

In the summer of 1990, CBS reran This Is America, Charlie Brown, again as a weekly. The program was not then any more a ratings champion than it had been in 1988-89, nor was it intended to be. Compelled to offer educational programming from time to time, CBS offered This Is America as its contribution for the year. Happily, the reasoning behind This Is America was that there was no law against entertaining while teaching, and succeeding in both departments.

THE THREE MUSKETEERS see BANANA SPLITS ADVENTURE HOUR

THREE ROBONIC STOOGES see THE SKATEBIRDS

THUNDARR THE BARBARIAN. ABC: 10/4/1980–9/18/1982; CBS: 4/9/1983–9/8/1984. Ruby-Spears. Executive producers, Joe Ruby, Ken Spears. Produced by Jerry Eisenberg. Directed by Rudy Larriva, Charles Nichols, John Kimball and Bill Reed. Written by Buzz Dixon, Mark Evanier, Steve Gerber, Martin Pasko, Ted Pedersen, Christopher Vane, Jeffrey Scott, Ray Thomas. Special material by Chuck Couch. Supervising story director, John Dorman. Story direction: Cullen Blaine, Scott Jeralds, Bob Nesler, Mitch Schauer, Bob Taylor, Roy Wilson. Story editor, Steve Gerber. Character design by Jerry Eisenberg, Jack Kirby and Alex Toth. Music by Dean Elliot. Voices: Robert Ridgely (Thundarr); Nellie Bellflower (Princess Ariel); Henry Corden (Ookla); and Rachel Baker, Marilyn Schreffler, Julie McWhirter, Joan Van Ark, Keye Luke, Stacy Keach Sr., Alan Dinehart, Shep Menken, and Alan Oppenheimer.

Thundarr the Barbarian was set 2000 years after a comet destroyed all civilization on earth. Far beneath the ruined city of Man-Hat, the evil Great Gemini, a two-faced mutant with 20th century laser technology at his command, dispatched his ratlike henchmen to enslave the world.

Thundarr, an ex-slave from an earlier totalitarian regime, battled Gemini mostly out of self preservation (in the manner of *Thundarr's* spiritual ancestor, Conan the Barbarian [q.v.]), and only incidentally on behalf of the good guys. The musclebound Thundarr was abetted in his struggles by his Sun Sword, which bestowed upon him supernatural powers. Thundarr's principal ally was the gorgeous Princess Ariel, a part-time sorceress and fulltime wiseacre who continually chided Thundarr because of his limited intellect and who was given to sniping "What kept you so long?" when being rescued. Ookla the Mok was Thundarr's lionlike aide, who in contrast to Ariel merely grunted his dialogue. Others aligned against Gemini were the survivors of the "normal" human race, the Groundlings.

"Sword, Sorcery and Lasers Too" is the clearest way to define *Thundarr the Barbarian*. The series boasted some deft time-displacement material, such as Thundarr's misinterpreting a series of movie posters as depictions of actual past events. The setting of a long-dead Manhattan was likewise cleverly employed, though given the younger audience to whom *Thundarr* was ostensibly aimed, one could question the wisdom of showing a demonic, vengeful Statue of Liberty.

Joe Ruby and Ken Spears, producers of *Thundarr the Barbarian*, demonstrated that they'd kept their eyes and ears open while working for Hanna-Barbera, particularly in the adroit handling of props and the well-defined character design (including a Hanna-Barbera-like sexy female lead). But Ruby-Spears also repeated a major Hanna-Barbera shortcoming in *Thundarr*: No matter how well written the script, the climax was invariably a pointless, violent confrontation in which the characters never really learned anything about their world or their roles in that world.

Though a ratings success which spawned more than a few copycat programs, *Thundarr the Barbarian* was an unsatisfying blend of social satire and wanton destruction, its superior production values squandered on second-rate story resolutions. The whole "future barbarianism" concept would be better handled a decade later by Nelvana's *Cadillacs and Dinosaurs* (q.v.).

THUNDERBIRDS 2086. Showtime: 1983–1986. Syndicated: 1986. ITC Entertainment. Executive in charge of production, Robert Mandell. Executive producers, Banjiro Uemura and Shinji Nakagaua. Technical supervisor, David Gregg. Dialogue recording supervision by Peter Fernandez. Storymen: Owen Lock, Robert Mandell. Music composed by Kentaro Haneda. Theme music composed by Koji Makaino. Performed by the Columbia Symphony Orchestra. Produced in cooperation with ITC Entertainment (Japan) Ltd. Voices: Joan Audiberti, Paollo Audiberti, John Belluci, Laura Dean, Earl Hammond, Ira Lewis, Keith Mandell, Alexander Marshall, Lori Martin, Terry Vantell.

The original 1966 *Thunderbirds* series was a Gerry and Sylvia Anderson "Supermarionation" production. Introduced embryonically in the 1961 weekly series *Supercar*, Supermarionation was a marionette process combining the traditional strings with electronic impulses that allowed the plastic puppets to move their eyes, blink, raise their eyebrows and move their lips in a reasonably lifelike fashion. *Supercar* was rather crude-looking, with painfully obvious wires supporting the figures, frozen facial expressions on the marionettes, and laughable special effects, but the process improved enormously for the next Anderson production, the outer space adventure *Fireball XL-5* (1963). The remarkably realistic marionette movement was complemented by convincingly scaled-down futuristic sets and backgrounds — though it wouldn't be until the Andersons' 1965 *Stingray* that the .005-inch-thick strings would be completely undetectable.

Like most of the British-produced Supermarionation projects, *Thunderbirds* was released to the U.S. a year or so after its English debut, then shown exclusively in nonnetwork syndication (only *Fireball XL-5* attained a national network slot). The Andersons' most elaborate project to date, *Thunderbirds* was set in the 21st century, and detailed the exploits of International Rescue, an impossible missions force located on a farflung Pacific atoll. Jeff Tracy headed the Thunderbirds team, which embarked in high-tech vehicles loaded with supersophisticated equipment to rescue those unfortunates trapped in seemingly inextricable circumstances, and to prevent interplanetary criminals from pulling off their "foolproof" crimes. The adventures of Tracy and his staff (which included several members of Jeff's immediate family) were offered either as full one-hour episodes or as two half-hour cliffhangers; most U.S. markets opted for the 30-minute version, the better to strip the series Monday through Friday.

Thunderbirds 2086, the long-delayed animated version of this property, was copyrighted 1983 and telecast daily over Showtime pay-cable in the U.S. that same year. No mention was made of Gerry and Sylvia Anderson in the credit titles, and none of the original characters appeared on the animated version. In place of the all–W.A.S.P. Tracy family, the new *Thunderbirds* International Rescue Organization was a five-person team of unrelated, multicultural adventurers: Jesse (redhead), Dillon (dark-haired), Johnny (African American), Grant (middle-aged authority figure, silver-haired), and Callan (girl, blonde). The squareheaded, beady-eyed Anderson character design was skipped for standard "Japanimation" renditions: attractive, wild-haired characters with round or almond-shaped eyes.

Operating (per the series' title) in 2086, this *Thunderbirds* crew all had personalized shuttle vehicles and versatile backpacks. As in the Supermarionation *Thunderbirds*, five main vehicles were utilized for search and rescue: Thunderbird-1 was a shuttle, TB-2 a hypersonic transport, TB-5 a drilling vehicle, etc. While this holdover from the original was maintained, the cliffhanger structure was not; all stories on *Thunderbirds 2086* were self-contained half hours, packing in plenty of action and suspense while keeping a well-measured pace, neither strident at one extreme nor tiresome at the other. The technological advances presented on the series were quite logical given our present rate of spaceware progress, so that the futuristic ambience of *Thunderbirds 2086* looked more like intelligent speculation rather than farfetched "Sci Fi." Plots were cut from the *Star Trek* cloth, but were well enough constructed to avoid imitation. The strictly business storylines, which cut out all slack and flab, allowed for a bare minimum of spectacular effects, and resorted to violence only as a logical extension of the action, were ideally suited to the series' limited animation. Even the

overdependence on computer animation (as opposed to handcrafted artwork) fit the premise because of the extensive use of computer technology in the *Thunderbirds* plotlines themselves. An excellent deployment of shadows and perspective in the draftsmanship compensated for any gaps in movement.

In keeping with the Andersons' original *Thunderbirds*, the characters on the cartoon version behaved cooly and professionally, with none of the unnecessary histrionics or gratuitous kidding around which often weakened American-produced extraterrestrial cartoons. Teamwork was emphasized, as opposed to the maverick types on Japanimation efforts like *Robotech* and *Captain Harlock*. Under the direction of actor/writer Peter Fernandez, the voice acting on the English language version was realistic, far more so than that on such previous Fernandez projects as *Speed Racer* (q.v.), while the adapted dialogue neither condescended to nor played over the heads of younger viewers.

To sum up, *Thunderbirds 2086* was extremely well done, and a significant improvement on the already commendable Supermarionation version. But though its level of maturity fit right in with the HBO schedule, *Thunderbirds 2086* was less successful opposite such child-oriented competition as *He-Man* (q.v.) and *G.I. Joe* (q.v.) when syndicated commercially in 1986 and 1987.

THUNDERCATS. Syndicated: 1985. Rankin-Bass/Lorimar Telepictures. Executive producers, Arthur Rankin Jr. and Jules Bass. Supervising producer, Lee Dannacher. Characters created by Ted Wolf; project developed by Leisure Concepts, Inc. Head writer, Leonard Starr. Music by Bernard Hoffer. Animation facilities: Pacific Animation Corporation; in charge of production, Masaki Izuka. Psychological consultant, Robert Kuisis M.D. Voices: Robert McFadden (Snarf/S-S-Slithe); Earl Hammond (Mumm-Ra/Vultureman/Jaga); Larry Kenny (Lion-O/Jackalman); Lynne Lipton (Cheetara/Wilykit); Peter Newman (Wilykat/Monkian/Ben-Gali/Tygra); Earle Hyman (Panthro); Gerianne Raphael (Pumyra); and Doug Preis.

Rankin-Bass' *ThunderCats* was set on "Third Earth." The heroes were huge members of the Cat family, endowed with human bodies and characteristics: Lion-O (the leader), Tygra, Panthro, Cheetara, Jaga and Pumyra. The villain threatening Third Earth's equilibrium was Mumm-Ra, a mummy come to life.

Props essential to the action were the Thundertank, the Eye of Thundera pendant (which warned of danger), "The Driller" (half drill, half human), and Thundera the sword, which glowed magically when a ThunderCat would shout "Thunder . . . Thunder . . . THUNDER!" The crystal on the sword's hilt became an all-seeing third eye when Lion-O declared "Give me sight beyond sight!" All the above-mentioned paraphernalia was unabashedly trotted out on each daily *ThunderCats* episode as a merchandising ploy for the tie-in toys manufactured by the LJN company. (See also *Hello Kitty's Furry Tale Theatre* and *Bionic Six*.)

First peddled to the syndication marketplace by Telepictures in 1983, *ThunderCats* was offered to selected stations on a percentage-of-profits basis, predicated on the toy sales. While some TV outlets took the bait, others, fearful over their own "untainted" reputations in the area of "serving the public interest" (and incidentally wary over possible FCC intervention), balked. The more cautious stations went for Telepictures' alternate deal of profiting only off the 65 *ThunderCats* episodes themselves, so as not to be accused of fostering "thirty minute commercials." *He-Man and the Masters of the Universe* (q.v.) hadn't yet taken hold in early 1983 to show that animated advertising dressed up as entertainment would be considered acceptable by the newly lax FCC of Mark Fowler.

In fact, it wouldn't be until 1985, two years after *He-Man* had set the trend and one year after *Transformers* (q.v.) had helped stake out the territory, that Telepictures considered *ThunderCats* "safe" enough to debut nationwide. Keeping up the *He-Man* connection, *ThunderCats* was preceded by a one-hour special, which would later be chopped up into two half hours for compatibility in the series proper. By the time the next special, the two-hour *ThunderCats Ho!*, premiered in 1987, the parent *ThunderCats* was the top-rated cartoon in strip syndication.

If all these dry business statistics make *ThunderCats* sound more cut-and-dried

than inspired, the series itself will only strengthen that assessment. So clumsily animated that it made *He-Man* look like Disney's *Beauty and the Beast, ThunderCats* was obliged to keep the audience awake with overripe voiceover performances, suggesting that all the actors had just graduated from the Ted Baxter Famous School of Broadcasting. But what price quality, so long as the ThunderCats toys cleared the shelves? *ThunderCats* worked well enough as a marketing conduit that Rankin-Bass/Telepictures had a similarly packaged cartoon property signed, sealed and syndicated in less than a year: *The Silverhawks*.

TIGERSHARKS *see* **COMIC STRIP**

TINTIN. Syndicated in U.S.: 1963, 1971. Tele-Hatchette and Belvision Productions/NTA (1963); Tele-Features (1971). Adapted by Charles Shows. Directed by Ray Gossens. From Herge's Albums (Casterman Publisher). Voices, U.S. version: Larry Harmon (Tintin); and Paul Frees.

–THE NEW ADVENTURES OF TINTIN. HBO: 12/21/1991–. Ellipse/Nelvana. Executive producers, Patrick Loubert, Michael Hirsh, Clive A. Smith, Philippe Gildar, Pierre Bertrand-Jaume, Simon Hart. Supervising producers: Philippe Grimond (Ellipse), Stephen Hodgins (Nelvana). Produced by Robert Rea. Directed by Stephane Bernasconi. Unit director, Peter Hudrek. Story editor, Dennise Fordham. Consultant, Philippe Goddin. Based on the character created by Herge (Georges Remi); published by Methuen/Little, Brown and Co. Directors of Animation: Serge Eisraider, Laurent Cordon. Art director, Thierry Fournier. Music editors: Stephen Hudecki, Peter Branton, Asha Daniere. Music theme and score by Roy Parker, Jim Morgan and Tom Szczesniak. Production facilities: HanHo Heung Up Studios, Canada-France Productions. Produced in association with Le Fondation Herge. Production participation by Telefilm Canada. Produced in association with HBO/FR3/Madrid Participations/Family Channel (Canada)/Global Television Network. Voices: Colin O'Meara (Tintin); David Fox (Haddock); Wayne Robson (Calculus); John Stocker (Thompson); Dan Hennessey (Thomson); Susan Roman (Snowy); and Denis Akiyama, Graham

Haley, Keith Hampshire, Michael Lempart, Verna Chapman, Robert Coit, Paul Haddad, Ray Londry, Marvin Ishmael, Elizabeth Dufresne, Graeme Campbell, Keith Knight, Tom Kneebone, Frank Proctor, and Maureen Forrester.

Tintin, the fearless cowlicked teenaged reporter, was created for the pages of Belgium's Le Vingtième Siècle in 1929. Artist Georges Remi, who signed himself Herge (the phonetic pronunciation of the initials "R. G."), was well grounded in the "Boys Own Adventure" school of comic art, having done similar work for a French boy-scout newspaper in his teens (he was only 23 when Tintin came to be). Though Remi/Herge created a number of other youth-oriented properties, it was Tintin upon which he built his fame and fortune.

Drawn in a deceptively simplistic, "funny" style (reminiscent of such serious but "cartoony" American strips as Little Orphan Annie and Captain Easy), Tintin was easily the most popular of Europe's serialized strips, especially with preteens who identified like mad with the farflung adventures of the hero. In the grand tradition, Tintin used his reporter's credentials to function as everything from a private detective to an outer-space espionage agent, his good cheer and unflappability enabling him to wriggle out of the most horrendous dangers. He travelled everywhere with his white fox terrier Milou and was frequently allied with such remarkable characters as twin detectives Dupont and Dumond, post-deaf Professor Calculus, and cantankerous Captain Haddock. The clean-lined artwork and detailed plot intricacies set a standard for European comic strips and books, frequently called "The Brussels School" in honor of Herge's heritage. (There was an unfortunate tendency to draw the Tintin villains with semitic facial features in the 1930s and 1940s, but this was a common failing of European art in those xenophobic times.)

Tintin at its peak was translated into 30 languages: The English version changed several character names, notably those of Milou ("Snowy" in English) and Dupont and Dumond (Thomson and Thompson). The strip's popularity resulted in 22 illustrated novels, a stage play, two live-action features, and, inevitably, several cartoons. In assessing the character's popularity, some contemporary sociologists choose to ignore the wish-fulfillment in-

herent in a teenager who moves with impunity and reciprocal respect in an adult world and attribute Tintin's success to "hidden messages." One recent theory postulates that Tintin is an androgynous character (huh?), and thus appeals to closet gender-switch yearnings within Us All!

Discounting an aborted plan by Hollywood's Larry Harmon Productions to animate a Tintin series in 1959—no great loss, considering the mediocrity of such Harmon projects as Bozo the Clown (q.v.) and Laurel and Hardy (q.v.)—the first group of Tintin cartoons were produced in France and Belgium from 1961 through 1966 and offered in American syndication by NTA as early as 1963. Few U.S. markets bit at this time (if they wanted a "Foreign Job," they had Astroboy [q.v.]), though the character's worldwide popularity remained unabated. The series did a little better stateside when picked up by Tele-Features in 1971, a time when a whole new crop of independent UHF stations was panting for first-run color product (earlier published reports that the first Tintins were black and white are incorrect).

Packaged as a serialized half-hour daily, Tintin was faithful in character and background design to Herge's original artwork, but bore the shortcomings of most early 1960s animation: stilted movement, overemphasis on gratuitous slapstick, and uncomfortable lurches from fast-paced action to dull expository sequences. The American voice dubbing did little to improve the project. Though Larry Harmon Productions, as mentioned, had nothing to do with the animation, it was obvious that Harmon's company was responsible for the American voicework. An unbilled Larry Harmon was Tintin himself, utilizing an inappropriate Bozo-like adolescent pitch, while fellow Bozo alumnus Paul Frees rapidly depleted his repertoire by enacting all the other roles. Both Harmon and Frees were overcome by an acute attack of hyperbole on Tintin, diminishing a property that had previously thrilled both adults and children down to a Romper Room level.

The New Adventures of Tintin (1991) was infinitely superior. In fact, it was everything an adventure cartoon should be: literate, exciting, funny, intensely faithful to its comic-book source, and capable of entertaining children and adults without insulting the intelligence of either group. The series was produced on behalf of Le Fondation Herge by the Canadian-French concern Nelvana/Ellipse—appropriately, since the bulk of the Ellipse product (see individual entries on *Babar*, *Doug* and *Rupert*) was so obviously influenced by Herge's "Brussels School." Scripts for *Tintin* were prepared in both French and English, but neither version betrayed any clumsiness of translation (a standard fault of American-dubbed "Japanimation" series like *Gigantor* and *Robotech*).

The narrative of this half-hour *Tintin* was lifted virtually verbatim from the characters' earlier comic stories, with all characters and situations adhering to established formula. Tintin operated on bold but intelligent instincts, never showing a whit of fear even when faced with certain death. His friends were eccentric, sometimes irritating, but basically lovable. The villains were dead serious, stopping at nothing, including threatening mayhem to the hapless dog Snowy, but almost invariably tripped up by their own stupidity or vanity. And in keeping with Herge's always lofty standards, *Tintin*'s artwork, from character movement to background design, was flawless; every penny of the series' $350,000-per-episode budget (made possible by licensing fees from various international cable firms) showed on the small screen.

The *New Adventures of Tintin* was first telecast over Canada's Family Channel cable service, then shipped to the U.S. via pay-cable's HBO in 1991; HBO had staked some of the budget money, and thus had proprietary interest. Though its affiliation with a pay service limited its viewership, at least *Tintin* wasn't plagued with commercial interruptions (the ad-breaks were, however, built into the program for future syndication). Still, HBO managed a great deal of first-season audience saturation with their weekly *Tintin*, culminating in a publicity ploy in April of 1992 that was straight out of *Where's Waldo?* (q.v.). The cable company invited home viewers to send in postcards for the privilege of playing an interactive "Search for Snowy" contest, with viewers' pinpointing the geographical location wherein Tintin's dog was hidden by pressing the strategic buttons of their touch-tone telephones.

TINY TOON ADVENTURES. Syndicated: 1990. Fox: 9/19/1992–. (As THE PLUCKY DUCK SHOW until 11/24/92.) Amblin/Warner Bros. Executive producer, Steven Spielberg. Produced by Tom Ruegger. Associate producer, Alfred Gimeno. Executive in charge of production, Jean MacCurdy. Production executives: Kathleen Kennedy, Frank Marshall. Directed by Art Vitello, Rich Arons, Byron Vaughns, Ken Boyer, Alfred Gimeno, David West, Arthur Leonardi. Animation director, Dave Marshall. Story editors, Tom Minton, Jim Reardon. Theme music by Bruce Broughton. Music score by Steve Bramson. Title animation by Tokyo Movie Shinsha Co. Production facilities: Wang Film Production Co., Ltd. Voices: Charlie Adler, John Kassir (Buster Bunny); Tress MacNeille (Babs Bunny); Joe Alaskey (Plucky Duck); Danny Cooksey (Montana Max); Cree Summer (Elmyra); Maurice LaMarche (Taz, aka Dizzy Devil); Gail Matthius (Shirley); Don Messick (Hampton Pig); and Frank Welker, June Foray, Kath Soucie, Jeff Bergman, John Hilner, Sally Struthers, Jim Cummings, Rob Paulsen, Roger Rose, Brian Mitchell and Greg Burson (and many others).

Tiny Toon Adventures producer Jean MacCurdy has always attributed the Disney company's successful entree into daily cartoon syndication (see *DuckTales*) for creating the market that made her own series possible. *Tiny Toon* was designed as the harbinger for the TV future of the young Warner Bros. Animation firm. If the series succeeded, the sky was the limit for Warner Animation.

Well, with executive producer Steven Spielberg involved, *Tiny Toon* wouldn't be permitted to fail, and that's all there was to it. Spielberg pumped $350,000 per episode into the Warner budget—some $100,000 more than the Disney efforts. The producer then wangled a CBS network "sneak preview" for the new series on September 14, 1990, just before the *Tiny Toon* syndicated premiere. And in concert with Warners, Spielberg saw to it that one of the most appealing aspects of Disney's *DuckTales* and *Chip 'n' Dale's Rescue Rangers* (q.v.), the deployment of established, universally popular cartoon characters, would be emulated on *Tiny Toon Adventures*.

To straddle the tastes of both older Warner Bros. animation fans and pre-teen

Tiny Toon toonsters, on a roll. (Could that be "Rosebud" in a guest appearance?)

viewers, *Tiny Toon* risked the wrath of cartoon purists by adopting the "retro" concept seen on several like-vintage Hanna-Barbera series. To wit, the producers redesigned the "grownup" Warner cartoon stars as children. Actually, it wasn't as simple or as derivative as that. The *Tiny Toon* characters may have looked like old Warners favorites Bugs Bunny, Daffy Duck, Porky Pig, Wile E. Coyote et al. at an earlier age, but in point of fact, these seven- to 14-year-old characters were completely new inventions—and most of them, the program's publicity was careful to point out, weren't even related to the older characters whom they resembled.

The principal residents of *Tiny Toon*'s Acme Acres (explaining the significance of the name "Acme" to the Warners cartoon canon is surely unnecessary) were such adolescents as Buster Bunny and Babs Bunny (as in Bugs), Plucky Duck (as in Daffy) and Hamton Pig (as in Porky). Each character had his or her own fresh bag of tricks, but withal evinced the character traits of Acme Acres' "Founding Fathers."

Plucky Duck was green rather than black, but still evoked memories of Daffy in respect to greediness and jealousy. Hamton Pig was a little more lively but no less speech-impaired than P-p-p-porky. Fifi Le Pew the skunk invariably left rows of wilted flowers in her wake, in the tradition of her aromatic forebear Pepe. And Calamity Coyote was as luckless and foredoomed as Wile E., just as the lisping Furball Cat was as unsuccessful in "getting thuthtenance" as his equally hungry father figure Sylvester. The most compelling "inheritance" was manifested in Bugs' counterparts Buster and Babs Bunny. Each character exhibited separate aspects of Bugs' complex personality: Buster was the "man's home is his castle" type, benign unless threatened, while Babs was fond of heckling her foes and indulging in instant character transformations.

The two most memorable "human" characters in the theatrical WB cartoons, Yosemite Sam and Elmer Fudd, were not directly imitated by their younger *Tiny*

Toon counterparts, save for retaining an antagonistic stance against Acme Acres' funny animals. The short-fused, rabbit hatin' Yosemite Sam was retooled as Montana Max, the richest and most obnoxious youngster in all Acme Acres. Montana's one-upmanship efforts were as disastrous to him as were Yosemite's claim-jumping and train-robbing exploits in the classic Warner shorts of the 1940s and 1950s. Conversely, Elmyra, Elmer Fudd's younger incarnation, was on surface a sugary sweet little girl who wanted to "hug and love" all her cartoon contemporaries. Unfortunately, she did this with the same thoughtless aggression exhibited whenever Elmer Fudd hunted down Bugs and Daffy during "Wabbit Season/Duck Season." In fact, if left to her own devices, Elmyra would have loved everyone to death!

In pursuit of tighter story values, the characters of *Tiny Toon Adventures* had a common meeting ground: the hallowed campus of Acme Looniversity. Once the series stars stepped through Acme's concentric-circle doorway (a visual echo of the old "Looney Tunes and Merrie Melodies" opening credit design), they were instructed in the finer points of being cartoon characters by a tenured staff consisting of established WB luminaries like Bugs, Daffy, Porky, Elmer Fudd, Foghorn Leghorn, and even Tweety Pie's sweet old mistress Granny, who in a superb twist was redefined as a granite-voiced martinet. The Looniversity faculty guided our heroes through such varied undergraduate curricula as How to Get Hit by an Anvil, Standing in Mid-Air, and Surviving a Stick of TNT (for advanced students only).

Further unifying *Tiny Toon* thematically was the device of having the two to three short cartoons per episode contain some sort of common throughline: getting a job, dreaming, "the great outdoors," dinosaurs, and so forth. Steven Spielberg and crew were savvy enough to know that the Disney TV series which inspired *Tiny Toon* had scored as much on strong story values as on appealing characters.

While the animation style was state-of-the-art, *Tiny Toon* contained enough trademarks of past Warner theatrical cartoons to satisfy long-standing fans, but always with a new slant to keep events locked into the 1990s. *Tiny Toon* revelled in quickie celebrity parodies, with newer stars replacing such past Warners "regulars" as

Jerry Colonna, Jack Benny, Rochester and Joe Penner. Perhaps there were too many Shirley MacLaine jokes and not enough Roseanne Arnold jokes, but the *Tiny Toon* staff was on the right track with such gags as having Kevin Costner dance with wolves at a Hollywood party. And in the tradition of Warners' intramural "Jack Warner" and "Leon Schlesinger" gags in the earlier theatrical cartoons (*I Ought to Be in Pictures* and *The Scarlet Pumpernickle* come most readily to mind) *Tiny Toon* bit the hand that fed it with jibes at Steven Spielberg—and in "equal opportunity" fashion, there were snippy jokes about competing Disney bosses Michael Eisner and Jeff Katzenberg (both of whom were shown wearing Mouseketeer hats).

Also, the studio's well-worn "reaction" gags—woebegone facial reactions, bug-eyed double takes, hyperbolic sexual arousal—were back in harness, seasoned with quirky 1990s twists. When Calamity Coyote fell victim to yet another malfunctioning Acme product, he imitated his role model Wile E. Coyote by silently holding up a reaction sign reading "Why Me?" Whereupon *Tiny Toon*'s junior-version Road Runner, evidently having taken a post-graduate course in existentialism, held up another sign reading "Why Not?"

And what would a Warner Bros. cartoon be without a nod to popular culture? *Tiny Toon* had such nods in abundance, from biting takeoffs on the toy-marketing ploys on rival cartoon series like *Transformers* and *Teenage Mutant Ninja Turtles*, to a lunatic, full half hour black-and-white *Citizen Kane* parody, complete with an aged Bugs "Jed Leland" Bunny asking the offscreen reporter "Ya haven't got a good carrot on you, have ya?" Lest it seem at this juncture that *Tiny Toon* was a stranger to subtlety, be assured that throwaway gags were peppered throughout each half hour, including such fleeting vignettes as the Jewish menorah resting on the mantle in the home of Hamton Pig, and the daily "hidden punchline" in the *Tiny Toon* closing credits.

Deliberately designed to go toe to toe with Disney in the syndie marketplace, *Tiny Toon* scored a ratings coup when another Disney rival, the Fox network, plucked the series from syndication and installed it in the daily Fox lineup. The move was welcome but somewhat superfluous: *Tiny Toon Adventures* was a hit from the outset, and by the end of its first season was being shown worldwide in several languages. (A minor hitch here. The French viewers couldn't see any humor in the amorous Fifi Le Pew, at least not until the adaptors changed her into a Spanish rather than Gallic skunk.) Reviewers virtually fell over one another in their praise, all of them citing the series' Spielberg-dictated "full animation" (as opposed to standard Hanna-Barbera limited movement) as the series' strongest selling point.

Ironically, this aspect of *Tiny Toon* was the one that disturbed its production staff the most. To their way of thinking, the series had *too much* great animation. According to the animators, Spielberg's insistence on perpetual movement merely resulted in clutter, bereft of the artful posing, nuance of characterization, and pauses for comic effect that distinguished the earlier Warner classics of Chuck Jones and Friz Freleng.

"But what's *wrong* with perpetual movement?" you well may ask. Many cartoon fans tend to regard full animation as the end-all and be-all of "good" toonwork. But most animators will argue that quality isn't measured by the *amount* of animation but by what is done within the animation at hand, whether it be full or limited. "Literally, every drawing is moving," Warner storyboard artist Bruce Timm observed in an interview for *Not of This Earth* magazine. ". . . [I]t was just characters moving their arms and being in motion all the time. It's hard to look at. It's not acting or telling the story, it's just moving." The stark minimalism of Bruce Timm's later work as producer on Warners' *Batman: The Animated Series* was a reaction — almost a retort — to *Tiny Toon*.

Bob Camp, who bolted the Warners animation team for John Kricfalusi's *Ren and Stimpy* (q.v.) also felt hamstrung at *Tiny Toon*. Quoted in *Wild Cartoon Kingdom* magazine, Camp recalled "The writers had all the power and none of the talent. You couldn't change things, it was all written out. The writers were writing sight gags, which is something you need to work out physically by drawing — not by some guy at the typewriter who doesn't know how to draw." Camp was laying it on a bit thick here, since the *Tiny Toon* writers included bona fide artists like Paul Dini (also a later *Batman* contributor), but

his basic assessment holds up. *Tiny Toon*, even at its best, had a chicken-salad look to it that might have been avoided had the artists been in fuller control.

Still, *Tiny Toon* undeniably worked harder at pleasing the crowd than almost any other animated TV series — and in pursuing its "anything goes" policy, some of the material was bound to be wildly funny. When the staff was exhausted and inspiration flagged, however, the jokes were frankly dragged out beyond their value. An example of this was "Anvil Chorus," a plodding parody of the musical "Oklahoma." The episode's single gag — anvils dropping from the sky on the unlucky Plucky Duck — fluttered between Irritating and Boring on the audience interest scale.

The series made up for these brief moments of lethargy by piling joke upon joke based on audience familiarity with the older theatrical WB cartoons. Michigan J. Frog, the enigmatic singing amphibian of Chuck Jones' imperishable *One Froggy Evening* (1956) made an encore appearance on *Tiny Toon*, this time as a supposedly dead lab specimen. In answer to many "how does he get those wonderful toys?" inquiries, *Tiny Toon* permitted us to witness the delivery of Wile E. Coyote's Acme catalog, which was the size of a Greyhound bus and had to be lowered to the anxious customer by four helicopters. And in a gentle jab at the sort of cult worship which fostered the Warners cartoon legend in the first place, a minor WB cartoon character from the 1950s, Elmer the Elephant, was reborn on *Tiny Toon* as a Jerry Lewis–like French film idol!

Perhaps the most controversial harkback to the Warners of old was *Tiny Toon*'s 1990 *Field of Dreams* takeoff, "Fields of Honey," which revived (in appropriate black and white) the first Looney Tunes stars of the 1930s, Bosko and Honey. Continual references were made to the fact that no one had ever been certain what kind of character Bosko was ("A dog? A bug?"), a nebulous quality which would later extend into the "generic" stars of Warners' *Animaniacs* (q.v.). But the Political Correctness Patrol complained that the TV producers didn't "confront" the fact that Bosko was originally a caricatured black child — just as if *Tiny Toon* was a kiddie version of *Phil Donahue* or *Oprah Winfrey*. Can you say "lighten up"?

Production on *Tiny Toon Adventures* ended in 1992, after 100 episodes. Several of these were rerun on the Fox Network's 1992-93 Saturday morning schedule as *The Plucky Duck Show*, before reverting to the original title after a few months. Even after its production shutdown, *Tiny Toon* remained an eminently saleable commodity, winning Emmy Awards in 1992 and 1993 for "Outstanding Animated Children's Program." Meanwhile, the series had served its purpose of establishing the Warners animation unit, and the new "Termite Terrace" was firmly and (it is hoped) permanently entrenched in the old Lorimar Building in the San Fernando valley. The Warners staff—300 strong by 1992, including Jean MacCurdy, Paul Dini, Bruce Timm, Tom Ruegger and Eric Radomski—was permitted to digest the lessons learned from *Tiny Toon* and move onward and upward to *Batman* and *Animaniacs*.

TOM AND JERRY (made-for-TV cartoons only):
—THE TOM AND JERRY/GRAPE APE SHOW. ABC: 9/6/1975–9/4/1976.
—THE TOM AND JERRY/GRAPE APE/MUMBLY SHOW. ABC: 9/11/1976–11/27/1976.
—THE TOM AND JERRY/MUMBLY SHOW. ABC: 12/4/1976–9/3/1977.
—THE GREAT GRAPE APE. ABC: 9/10/1977–9/3/1978. Hanna-Barbera. Executive producers: William Hanna, Joseph Barbera. Produced by Iwao Takamoto. Directed by Charles Nichols. Music by Hoyt Curtin and Paul DeKorte. Voices: Marty Ingels (Beagle); Bob Holt (Grape Ape); Don Messick (Mumbly); John Stephenson (Schnooker); and Henry Corden, Joan Gerber, Bob Hastings, Virginia Gregg, Cathy Gori, Alan Oppenheimer, Allan Melvin, Hal Smith, Joe E. Ross, John Stephenson, Jean VanderPyl, Janet Waldo, Lurene Tuttle, Paul Winchell, Frank Welker, and Lennie Weinrib.
—THE TOM AND JERRY COMEDY SHOW. CBS: 9/6/1980–9/4/1982. Filmation. Produced by Lou Scheimer and Norm Prescott. Creative director, Don Christensen. Art director, Robert Kline. Voices: Frank Welker, Lou Scheimer (Droopy).
—TOM AND JERRY KIDS. Fox: Weekly: 9/8/1990–10/2/1993. Daily: 9/14/1992–. Hanna-Barbera/Turner Program Services. Produced by Joseph Barbera and Don Jurwich. Directed by Carl Urbano, Don Lusk, Paul Sommer. Story editors: Neal Barbera and Don Jurwich. Head writer: Sandy Fries. Music by Tom Worrall and Gary Lionelli. Production facilities: Wang Film Production Co., Ltd./Mr. Big Cartoons/Fils-Cartoons Inc. Voices: Brandon Adams, Charlie Adler, Joe Alaskey, Rene Auberjonois, Gregg Berger, Nicole Brown, Greg Burson, William Callaway, Hamilton Camp, Danny Cooksey, Peter Cullen, Jim Cummings, Tim Curry, Teresa Ganzel, Brad Garrett, Kathy Garver, Dick Gautier, Joan Gerber, Phil Hartman, Jerry Houser, Tony Jay, Arte Johnson, Vicki Juditz, Kip King, David Lander, Tress MacNeille, Chuck McCann, Edie McClurg, Don Messick, Brian Mitchell, Bibi Osterwald, Henry Polic II, Kimmy Robertson, Sally Struthers, Frank Welker, Lee Wilkoff, Jo Anne Worley, Patric Zimmerman.

For both of you who've never seen Tom and Jerry: Tom was an easily offended but resourceful grey house cat, while Jerry was a lovably arrogant little brown mouse. Throughout the 114 theatrical cartoons written and directed for MGM by William Hanna and Joseph Barbera from 1939 through 1957, the characters were generally nonspeaking (contrary to popular belief, they were occasionally given voices, usually as punctuation to a gag). Without dialogue, their personality traits were revealed through their zip-zap chases, their vast repertoire of facial reactions and double-takes, and their endless, often exquisitely violent games of one-upmanship.

We won't delve too deeply into the argument as to whether or not Tom and Jerry were too violent for their own good. They were, after all, cartoon characters, with the resilience of that species which allowed them to survive unscathed from every frying pan, billiard ball and dynamite stick tossed their way. Audiences of the 1940s demanded an outlet for the pent-up hostilities brought about by war shortages, the tyrannies of local draft boards and civil defense units, and the ever-present real-life nemeses like bosses, noisy neighbors and mooching relatives. Just like the live-action Three Stooges, Tom and Jerry committed deliberately exaggerated violence that the audience, through laughing uproariously, could "participate" in at a safe and sane distance.

Certainly the Academy of Motion Picture Arts and Sciences were judging the merit rather than the mayhem in the *Tom and Jerry* cartoons when the organization bestowed seven Oscars upon the series between 1943 and 1952.

Hanna and Barbera stayed with the series until MGM disbanded its animation unit and fired the team in 1957. The studio brought back Tom and Jerry in 1961 with a bizarre, unsatisfying cluster of cartoons produced in Czechoslovakia by Gene Deitch and Rembrandt Productions (see *Popeye* for more on this production unit). A later group of *Tom and Jerry*s, directed by Warner Bros. veteran Chuck Jones for MGM release, is widely regarded as a low point in both Jones' and the characters' careers (something Jones will readily concur); this mannered, meandering version of the property ran from 1963 through 1967.

Even as the Chuck Jones *Tom and Jerry*s were busy boring theatre audiences, the MGM/Hanna-Barbera *Tom and Jerry* backlog from the 1940s and 1950s were licensed to television. These cartoons, together with a selection of other MGM animated shorts, ran from September 1965 to September 1972 on CBS' Saturday morning lineup, accruing excellent ratings all the while. Though this period was one of many during which the Watchdog Brigades were blasting kidvid for its supposed overemphasis on violence, *The Tom and Jerry Show* was surprisingly spared the censor's scissors. The only notable expurgation was the redrawing and redubbing of the series' recurring housemaid character Mammy Two Shoes, changing her from an offensive black stereotype to an Irish stereotype (which *itself* would be considered offensive a decade or so later).

In the mid–1960s, the Hanna-Barbera studio was going full blast with its own platoons of cartoon characters, some of them falling into the "big animal vs. little animal" format Bill Hanna and Joe Barbera had honed to an art in *Tom and Jerry*, most notably Pixie and Dixie and Mr. Jinks (see *Huckleberry Hound*) and Mushmouse and Punkinpuss (see *Magilla Gorilla*). The producers' hearts had always been with Tom and Jerry, however, and in 1975 they jumped at the opportunity to revive the series for television. Out of respect for the characters who'd established their reputations, Hanna and Barbera refused to compromise those characters' most distinctive trait: unlike most other TV cartoon animals of the period, the "new" Tom and Jerry would not speak. Yes, it meant overtime on the animation boards to convey communication minus dialogue (production time cut down a trifle by "fragmenting" Jerry's movements, separating head from body with a bowtie) but the cat and mouse deserved to retain their mute integrity.

And that's about *all* they were allowed to retain. Hanna-Barbera pitched the notion of a made-for-TV *Tom and Jerry* by screening the best of their theatrical cartoons for a group of ABC network executives. As Leonard Maltin has reported, the ABC people "laughed heartily" at the old cartoons, then sighed that it was too bad they couldn't accept anything that violent for their Saturday morning schedule. The Watchdogs had finally attained Big Brother status, and even the slightest hint of animated aggressiveness was being whittled down to the point of emasculation.

So in order to survive the tenor of the times, TV's Tom and Jerry became close buddies rather than friendly enemies, wandering (on two feet rather than all fours) from one harmlessly slapstick situation to another. Any "threatening" gesture would be made by the cardboard villains against whom Tom and Jerry would align on behalf of Goodness and Truth. And while Tom and Jerry didn't talk, the supporting characters *did*, and with far too much to say.

The official name of the new weekly, 60-minute Hanna-Barbera series was *The Tom and Jerry/Grape Ape Show*, with the "older" stars appearing in short segments, sharing airtime with their new companion component star Grape Ape. This 30-foot-tall talking gorilla, whose name was derived from his purple skin color and favorite catch-phrase (he'd end his sentences with a superfluous "grape ape!," so we wouldn't confuse him with King Kong), was not as repetitious as he seemed at the time, but the basic joke of people intimidated by a giant but harmless simian got tired early on. Grape Ape's cohort was Beegle Beagle (or Beegily Beagley, as Ape called him), his buddy and interpreter. Their short cartoons exhibited the slapdash 1970s Hanna-Barbera style at its weakest, merely rehashing previously

Tom (*at right*) and Jerry: double duty as "Kids" and Crimestoppers.

proven formulae: parodied he-man heroics, a big dumb ape who doesn't know his own strength, and so on.

In 1976, reruns of *Tom and Jerry* and *Grape Ape* were joined with another uninspired creation, a trenchcoated private eye dog named Mumbly, who with assistant Schnooker took on various tiresome criminals with alliterative names, most of whom spouted dialogue like "I'll be back in a flash with the cash." Been there, done that. *The Tom and Jerry/Grape Ape/Mumbly Show* limped along until December of 1976, when Grape Ape was spun off into his own all-rerun half hour series (*The Great Grape Ape Show*), leaving behind the 30-minute *Tom and Jerry/ Mumbly Show.* The whole affair disappeared in 1978; Tom and Jerry retreated to the Old Toons Home, while Mumbly went on to a more rewarding career as a recurring villain on Hanna-Barbera's *Scooby's All-Star Laff-a-Lympics* (see *Scooby-Doo*), in which Grape Ape and Beegle also made guest appearances.

By 1980, cartoon producers had taught themselves to work around network Standards and Practices, enabling the makers of such series as *The All-New Popeye Hour* (see *Popeye*) and *The Heathcliff and Dingbat Show* (see *Heathcliff*) to create the illusion of nonstop slapstick without offending anyone's sensibilities (except those of old-time cartoon fans who couldn't shake

memories of the Golden Days). Into this atmosphere stepped Filmation, which in association with MGM put together *The Tom and Jerry Comedy Show.* Filmation restored the blessed "cat chases mouse" formula of old, ignoring the buddy-buddy concept forced by ABC upon Hanna-Barbera back in 1975. The difference in 1980 was that instead of laying waste to the neighborhood in trying to eradicate one another, Tom and Jerry were rechanneled into "safe" rivalry: athletic events, competition at the workplace, and the like.

Filmation also brought back from the Void several other MGM favorites of the 1940s and 1950s, who appeared in component cartoons: Droopy the Dog (see *Droopy, Master Detective*), his nemesis The Wolf, here named "Slick," and father-and-son canines Spike and Tyke. Tom and Jerry remained as silent as ever, while Frank Welker did the vocal honors on the remaining component characters (except during a 1980 industry strike, at which time all voices were provided by *Tom and Jerry Comedy Show* co-producer Lou Scheimer).

Filmation chroniclers Michael Swanigan and Darrell McNeil have reported that the series generated an esprit de corps in the Filmation headquarters, with many artists developing unscripted sight gags right on the storyboards as part of a genial rivalry with the writing staff. This overall sense of euphoria carried over into the cartoons themselves: Though hobbled by stock footage, limited animation and network censorship, *The Tom and Jerry Comedy Show* was, for Filmation at least, a remarkably fast-moving and funny program. It wasn't the "true" Tom and Jerry, and never would be, but it was an acceptable bush league facsimile.

As the many *Tom and Jerry* TV cartoons from both Hanna-Barbera and Filmation ran their network course, they were absorbed into Turner Television's MGM package along with the theatrical originals. The most recent regeneration of the T and J saga came from Turner and (again) Hanna-Barbera in 1990. Conceived in the spirit of the Disney TV character revivals from the same period (see *DuckTales* and *Chip 'n' Dale's Rescue Rangers*), with the "retro" stars-as-kids concept previously used by Hanna-Barbera's *A Pup Named Scooby-Doo* (see *Scooby-Doo*) and *Flintstone Kids* (see *The Flintstones*) thown in, *Tom and Jerry Kids* premiered as part of the first Fox Children's Network Saturday morning manifest. Tom and Jerry were younger, smaller and distressingly cuter, but the full animation movement and pell-mell pacing were back, as were several artistic earmarks of the vintage MGM days: highly polished kitchen floors, living rooms right out of *Better Homes and Gardens*, weaponlike household appliances, "zing-pow-boing" sound effects, and wall to wall *agitato* background music.

Tom and Jerry Kids won a whole legion of new fans by virtue of its production gloss and energy level. Indeed, the half hour series performed so well for Fox that it was instrumental in convincing NBC, whose once-popular *Super Mario Bros. 3* was plowed over in the ratings by *T & J Kids*, to drop out of the four-way weekend cartoon race altogether. (This success also encouraged Fox to expand *Kids* to weekdays in 1992 with 39 new episodes.) There were, however, classic cartoon purists who despaired at the series' reducing of Tom and Jerry to petulant children, a gimmick which robbed the characters of their old urbanity and limited the degree of comic violence. And few were enchanted by scripters' attempts to bring the characters into the 1990s, chiefly through misfire doses of pop-culture humor. At least there was the consolation that the new Tom and Jerry were permitted to hold their tongues; no matter how much the other characters spoke (look at the enormous voice-cast list at the beginning of this entry!), the stars refused to compromise their established personae by speaking.

Some of the better moments on *Tom and Jerry Kids* belonged to the wacko Tex Avery–style component features, starring a host of new characters: Wild Mouse, Slow Poke Antonio, the Mouse Scouts and the Gator Brothers. Back for a second TV round were *Tom and Jerry Comedy Show* veterans Spike, Tyke and the Wolf. Also returning to TV was Droopy, teamed with lookalike son Dripple in a variable series of seven-minute globetrotting adventures. Though on balance the Droop's cartoons weren't the true highpoints of *Tom and Jerry Kids*, his was the only character whose audience rapport warranted a spinoff series: 1993's *Droopy, Master Detective* (q.v.).

Tom and Jerry Kids was but one aspect of the many plans formulated to exploit these time-tested favorites in the 1980s and 1990s. Ted Turner made several announcements that he'd produce a *live-action* Tom and Jerry vehicle (With a real cat and mouse? And maybe colorized?), while at one point Hanna-Barbera intended to collaborate with Andrew Lloyd Webber for a musical cartoon (*Le Tom?*). Unfortunately, outside of *Tom and Jerry Kids*, the only plan to reach full fruition was a feature-length theatrical cartoon, *Tom and Jerry: The Movie*, produced by Film Roman and Turner Entertainment in 1993. It's no sweat at all to tick off the many miscalculations of this benighted project: Tom and Jerry were teamed as bosom buddies again, they helped a treacly little girl, they swilled in political correctness, and—blasphemy!—they talked and talked and talked. (Film Roman trumpeted this film as the first time Tom and Jerry ever spoke, neither an accurate statement nor anything that I'd be particularly proud of.)

Resigned to the fact that latter-day producers will insist upon exhuming *Tom and Jerry* whether asked to or not, we rate *Tom and Jerry Kids* as the best of the new breed, with the Filmation *Tom and Jerry Comedy Show* a distant second best.

TOM TERRIFIC. CBS: 6/10/1957–late 1960s. Terrytoons/CBS Films. Produced by Gene Deitch. Voices: Lionel Wilson.

When the CBS network acquired Terry-toons full-out in 1955, the studio began hastily assembling TV cartoons for its new master. The first and perhaps best project was *Tom Terrific*, networkcast exclusively as a component of CBS' daily, live action children's series *Captain Kangaroo*.

Developed by Terrytoons' resident "genius" Gene Deitch (so anointed because his stylistic theatrical cartoons had won the studio its first-ever recognition from film critics and prestigious animation festivals), *Tom Terrific* starred an energetic young boy who wore a magical funnel-shaped cap. This unusual headwear enabled Tom to transform himself into anything from "a plane on high" to "a Diesel train . . . roaring by" to "a bumblebee, or a tree," or so the opening theme song informed us. The self-styled "greatest hero ever," Tom Terrific fought all forms of evil, usually personified by human antagonist Crabby Appleton, "rotten to the core." Tom's ever-faithful companion was Mighty Manfred the Wonder Dog, who was more interested in settling down for a long nap than in saving the world.

Denied anything like a budget on *Tom Terrific* (there wasn't even enough money for background music, forcing the cartoons to rely on a banjo and harmonica combo), Gene Deitch used his diminished resources to his advantage. The characters on the daily, five-minute cliffhanging *Tom Terrific* were transparent line drawings laid against the sparsest of backgrounds — very simple but very, very stylish. The lack of elaborate animation trappings forced the Terrytoons staff to concentrate on clever dialogue (some of it supplied by future newspaper cartoonist Jules Feiffer), the solidity of the storylines, and the principal characters' personalities and byplay, to sustain audience involvement. All of this was something new to Terrytoons, which for years had relied on repetitious, childish sight gags rather than strength of characterization or scriptwork. But the staff rose to the occasion, and the result was one of the best TV cartoon projects of its era. As a bonus, Tom Terrific's calculatedly hyperbolic adventures could be enjoyed both by children (on their own merits) and adults (for the gentle satire of movie and radio serials the adults had grown up with).

And even though Gene Deitch's limited budget would not seem to allow for it, *Tom Terrific* was an ideal *visual* concept. The notion of a scribbled-down little boy who could in a twinkling metamorphose into a tornado or a telephone pole was a refreshing throwback to the days when cartoons moved just for the sake of moving. As Leonard Maltin has observed, Tom was welcome contrast to the "static TV cartoon stars who followed."

Since the CBS eye was virtually color-blind in the 1950s, most of the *Tom Terrific* cartoons were filmed in black and white. The package remained on *Captain Kangaroo* at least until 1965, far beyond the "official" termination date of September 1961 listed in most reference books, and were eased out only when the monochrome installments were deemed outmoded for the all-color late 1960s. By this time *Captain Kangaroo* had become an agreeable conduit for several other high-quality cartoon components, including *The Adventures of Lariat Sam* (q.v.) and *The Adventures of Pow Pow* (q.v.), and would continue to feature brief animation vignettes into the 1970s and 1980s, notably *Most Important Person* (q.v.) and *CBS Storybreak* (q.v.). None of these, however, have insinuated themselves into the subconscious of the baby boomer generation to the extent of *Tom Terrific*, which at its peak had a viewership of 3.5 million, and which still stands as a crowning TV achievement for the otherwise lackluster Terrytoons Studio.

THE TOMFOOLERY SHOW. NBC: 9/12/1970–9/4/1971. Rankin-Bass/Halas and Batchelor. Produced by Arthur Rankin Jr. and Jules Bass. Music by Maury Laws. Voices: The Maury Laws Singers, Peter Hawkins, Bernard Spear.

Tomfoolery was a weekly, half hour collection of cartoon shorts based on the "nonsense" verse of 19th century authors Edward (*The Owl and the Pussycat*) Lear and Lewis (*Alice in Wonderland*) Carroll, with side glances at the likes of Henry Wadsworth Longfellow and Ogden Nash. The series was a noble attempt at "quality" children's programming that just didn't jell. Combining the whimsical convoluted-logic poetry of Lear and Carroll with the disjointed, flash-gag style of *Rowan and Martin's Laugh-In* only resulted in one comic style cancelling out the other. Nor were there any compelling continuing characters for the home viewer to latch onto. Instead, we had the amusing but unapproachable Youngie Bungie Bow (whose head was bigger than his body), the Scroovy Snake, the Umbrageous Umbrella Maker, the Fastidious Fish, the Outrageous Ostrich, the Worrying Whizzing Wasp and the Enthusiastic Elephant.

Seventeen half-hour *Tomfoolery* episodes came and went, ignominiously shot down by the less aesthetically satisfying but frankly more bankable *Sabrina* (q.v.) on CBS and (the unkindest cut of all) ABC's live-action *Lancelot Link, Secret Chimp*.

TOOTER TURTLE see **KING LEONARDO**

TOP CAT. ABC: 9/27/1961–9/26/1962; 10/6/1962–3/30/1963; NBC: 4/3/1965–12/31/1968. Hanna-Barbera/Screen Gems. Produced and directed by Joseph Barbera and William Hanna. Associate producer, Alan Dinehart. Production supervisor, Howard Hanson. Backgrounds by Fernando Montealegre. Music by Hoyt Curtin. Theme song by Hanna and Barbera. Animation director, Charles A. Nichols. Animation by Kenneth Muse and Jerry Hathcock. Voices: Arnold Stang (Top Cat); Allen Jenkins (Officer Dibble); Maurice Gosfield (Benny the Ball); Marvin Kaplan (Choo Choo); Leo de Lyon (Spook/The Brain); John Stephenson (Fancy Fancy); and Daws Butler, Don Messick, Paul Frees, Jean VanderPyl, Bea Benaderet, and GeGe Pearson.

In 1961, the two most popular exnetwork sitcoms in nighttime rerun syndication were Jackie Gleason's *The Honeymooners* and *The Phil Silvers Show* (a.k.a. *You'll Never Get Rich*, and informally known as *Sgt. Bilko*). Hanna-Barbera had already done its take on *Honeymooners* with its first ABC primetime cartoon series *The Flintstones* (q.v.); the studio's second such program, *Top Cat*, would give the pen-and-ink treatment to *Phil Silvers*. The ABC network, which a year or so earlier might have had second doubts about a weekly 8:30 P.M. series starring a cast of anthropomorphic alley cats, was so pleased with the ratings on *The Flintstones* that Joe Barbera was able to sell the network *Top Cat* on the basis of one single drawing of the character!

Prerelease publicity indicated that the new half hour cartoon was to have been titled *Tomcat*, but this was probably rejected not only because it would have infringed on MGM's *Tom and Jerry* (q.v.) but because the original title's sexual subtext would have brought down the wrath of the censors — a headache no one needed in the year that FCC chairman Newton Minow had made his "vast wasteland" speech about television. The renamed Top Cat was a fastlipped con-artist feline, who resided with his ragtag band of followers in an alley in New York City's 13th Precinct. Forever promoting scams and get-rich-quick schemes, "T.C." (as his close friends knew him) relied on wits and witticisms to keep one step ahead of the series' human antagonist, police officer Dibble. Top Cat's loyal companions were the intellectual Choo-Choo, lovable patsy Benny the Ball, hipster Spook, ladies' cat Fancy-Fancy, and The Brain, whose "duuuhhh" demeanor rather negated his nickname.

Those familiar with *The Phil Silvers Show* will recognize the strong links between that series and *Top Cat*: the wheeler-dealer head man (Sgt. Bilko/Top Cat), the uniformed authority figure (Colonel Hall/Officer Dibble), the gang's resident schlemiel (Pvt. Doberman/Benny the Ball) and the variegated supporting chums (*Silvers*' Papperelli, Ritzik, Henshaw, Fender etc. and *Top Cat*'s above-named contingent). Hanna-Barbera not only encouraged such comparisons, but underlined them. Where *The Flintstones* merely used *Honeymooners* as a reference and then went off on its own tangent, *Top Cat* was a carbon copy *Phil Silvers*: the same types of con jobs, the same speech rhythms (both Bilko and T.C. were masters of sudden improvisation when a well-plotted plan went awry, and of fawning false flattery designed to throw their antagonists off the track), and the same denouements, where the hero would play his cards so smartly that he'd wind up outsmarting himself.

The resemblances were further emphasized in the voicework. Comic actor Arnold Stang, who played Top Cat, sounded so much like Phil Silvers' Bilko in the earlier episodes that one of the sponsors complained that they'd okayed the hiring of Stang for his *own* talents, not for his gift of mimicry. (The role of T.C. had first been offered to H-B stalwart Daws Butler, whose "Bilko" was even more on target than Stang's, but Butler had too many prior voiceover commitments.) Maurice Gosfield, the voice of Benny the Ball, had little control over the fact that he reminded viewers of *Phil Silvers'* Doberman—mainly because it was Gosfield who'd created the Doberman role on the earlier series.

Everyone involved had high hopes for *Top Cat*, and understandably so. The series was better animated and more attractively drawn than *The Flintstones*, with particularly felicitous background art designed by H-B regular Fernando Montealegre, whose work would later elevate such otherwise pedestrian cartoon series as *Inch High Private Eye* (q.v.) and *Wheelie and the Chopper Bunch* (q.v.). The dialogue was flippant and funny, succinctly capturing the street-hustler atmosphere. (When one episode threatened to end with a wearisome "everybody's laughing" fadeout, Top Cat stopped, reconsidered the one-liner he'd just dispensed, then frowned and muttered "Ahhhh . . . nothin'!") And the characters were sharply etched as genuinely distinctive personalities instead of suffering the "walk-alike talk-alike" syndrome afflicting many other Hanna-Barbera funny animals.

The voice cast was another booster shot to the overall quality of *Top Cat*. In addition to the aforementioned Arnold Stang and Maurice Gosfield, veteran movie toughguy Allen Jenkins was right in his element as the gravelly Officer Dibble, delivering a performance every bit as *con brio* as in the actor's glory days at Warner Bros. in the 1930s. Of the secondary characters, Hanna-Barbera regular John Stephenson did his usual smooth job as Fancy-Fancy, whom Stephenson described (and played) as "the Cary Grant of Brooklyn," while owleyed character actor Marvin Kaplan, best known to modern audiences for his recurring role on the 1970s sitcom *Alice*, provided the perfect combination of milquetoast trepidation and Manhattan street savvy as Choo-Choo.

Yet despite its many virtues, and even opposite such soft prime-time competition as CBS' detective series *Checkmate* and NBC's eternal ratings-loser *The Joey Bishop Show*, *Top Cat* was a major disappointment. Just what went wrong can be attributed to many factors. First off, the principal charm of the original *Phil Silvers Show* was its nose-thumbing at military rules and regulations, something a mid-1950s audience largely comprised of exservicemen could readily appreciate. Most World War 2 veterans in the *Silvers* audience lived their fantasies vicariously through Sgt. Bilko, who regularly outfoxed the hated Brass and lived like a king despite his olive-drab Army camp surroundings. What grownup in 1961, however, could "identify" with a gang of alley cats who tried to flummox a musical-comedy cop? The *Flintstones* appealed to adults because it mirrored adult situations; the whole "smart animals vs. human establishment" conceit on *Top Cat* was, so far as most adults of the period were concerned, mere kid's stuff.

Once perceived as a children's show, *Top Cat* was at a disadvantage because of its Wednesday night timeslot. One hour earlier on the same weeknight, CBS telecast its own cartoon prime-timer, *The Alvin Show* (q.v.). "You've already seen your cartoon tonight," one can hear the Moms and Dads of America saying on any Wednesday evening in early 1962. "Now turn off that foolishness and do your homework." (The same situation vexed ABC's like-vintage *Calvin and the Colonel* [q.v.], which had the misfortune of spending its first few weeks on Tuesday evenings, an hour after the same network's *Bugs Bunny Show* [q.v.].)

But the killer blow for *Top Cat* was manifested in its story values—or lack of them. The same production team that regularly served up satisfying, well-knit plotlines for *The Flintstones* couldn't seem to construct a completely coherent 30-minute scenario for *Top Cat*. Typical was an episode titled "The Maharajah of Pookajee." After spending several minutes showing a diligent Officer Dibble guarding a visiting potentate, two out-of-nowhere jewel thieves—dressed in *Guys and Dolls* black shirt and white tie, just so the audience won't miss the fact that they're crooks—encounter no resistance sneaking into the visitor's hotel suite and pulling a heist. The reason? Simply to bloat a workable 20-minute story into a full half hour. And surely some sort of "lost tangent" award was due *Top Cat's* very first episode, "The $1,000,000 Derby," in which, after painstakingly establishing the plot point that a worn-out horse would be galvanized into winning a race only by the sound of a factory whistle, Top Cat and his friends whipped the horse into a frenzy of speed with the totally unrelated sound of an ambulance bell! *Top Cat* survived only 30 episodes in prime time. It enjoyed a more successful rerun life on Saturday mornings, where all plotline flab was sliced away to make room for more commercials and where children were more likely to get to see the show. The series remained a profitable weekend attraction on two different networks until 1968, then continued to rake in the green in syndication. Top Cat himself would guest on various Hanna-Barbera specials and "all star" rallies of the 1980s: His best showing was on *Yogi's Treasure Hunt* (see *Yogi Bear*), where as "Treasure Captain" he set the weekly plot in motion. And in 1990, Top Cat and his lieutenant Choo-Choo were prominently featured as auto race contestants on the "Fender Bender 500" segment of Hanna-Barbera's *Wake, Rattle and Roll* (q.v.), complete with the undiminished vocal talents of sexagenarians Arnold Stang and Marvin Kaplan.

TOUCHE TURTLE. Syndicated: 1962. Hanna-Barbera. Produced by William Hanna and Joseph Barbera. Music by Hoyt Curtin. Voices: Bill Thompson (Touche Turtle); Alan Reed (Dum Dum); and Daws Butler, and Don Messick.

Touche Turtle was a variation on a theme explored by the "El Kabong" episodes on Hanna-Barbera's *Quick Draw McGraw*: the fearless swashbuckler of unprepossessing demeanor and unpretty face. The tiny Touche Turtle, decked out in a plumed hat and wearing a sheathed sword, roamed the countryside in search of villains to vanquish and maidens to rescue with the help of his larger companion, bipedal sheepdog Dum Dum. Touche's 52 five-minute adventures had been offered for syndication in 1960, but weren't picked up until two years later, and then as part of the *Hanna-Barbera New Cartoon Series* package which included *Lippy the Lion* (q.v.) and *Wally Gator* (q.v.). Once past the undeniably funny image of a wizened little amphibian swinging from the balcony shouting "Touche Away!," *Touche Turtle* was merely one of many "small and tall" animal combos which the Hanna-Barbera studio conveyer-belted out to the world in the 1960s.

Distinguishing *Touche Turtle* from the rest of the Hanna-Barbera factory look-alikes was the voicework by two seasoned "Golden Age of Radio" veterans. As Touche, Bill Thompson squeaked out his best "Wallace Wimple" voice (a character created for *Fibber McGee and Molly* and later modified as the MGM cartoon star *Droopy*), while Alan Reed took time away from *The Flintstones* (q.v.) to employ his patented "moron" cadence as Dum Dum.

TOXIC CRUSADERS. Syndicated: Fall 1991 (Test marketed in January 1991 as a five-part miniseries). Murikami-Wolf-Swenson/Sachs Family Entertainment/ Troma, Inc. Executive producer, Fred Wolf. Produced for Troma by Lloyd Kaufman, Michael Herz and Jeffrey W. Sass. Produced by Walt Kubiak. Directed by Bill Hutten and Tony Love. Animation directors: John Kavka, Ed Love, Bill Hutten. Story editor: Jack Mendelsohn. Based on the TOXIC AVENGER films created by Lloyd Kaufman and Michael Herz. Original songs by Dennis C. Brown and Chuck Lorre. Background music by Dennis C. Brown and Larry Brown. Voices: Gregg Berger, Susan Blu, Paul Eiding, Chuck McCann, Roger Bumpass, Rad Rayle, Susan Silo, Kath Soucie, Ed Gilbert, Patric Zimmerman and Michael J. Pollard.

Toxic Crusaders, a weekly half hour syndie, was based on the live action "Toxic Avenger" films produced by New Jersey-based Troma Films—but not, we hasten to add, *too* literally. Troma, created in 1974 by Lloyd Kaufman and Michael Herz, would at one time have been the last candidate for the cartoon field, inasmuch as their entire product consisted of R-rated "B" pictures, brimmed to overflowing with profanity, amply endowed females and sexual single entendres. Figuring that most low-grade R product of the early 1970s took itself too seriously (and violently), Troma decided to create an open market for itself by concentrating on raucous comedy, switching over to semi-horror and adventure only when the big studios muscled into the R-comedy field with such raunchy parades as *Animal House* and *Porky's*. Among the "classic" Troma epics of its first decade are such epics as *Squeeze Play*, *When Nature Calls (You've Gotta Go)*, *A Nymphoid Barbarian in Dinosaur Hell*, *Chopper Chicks in Zombietown* and *Class of Nuke 'Em High*. Fellini and Kurosawa would pale with envy.

Naturally, such an illustrious lineup

automatically assured Troma Films a cult status amongst film buffs. The British Film Institute staged a salute to Troma in 1990, the same year that the American Film Institute assembled a week-long "Aroma de Troma." And the Cinemax cable service served up "Troma Presents the Year of the Woman" in 1993, scheduling such incisive feminist manifestos as *Ferocious Female Freedom Fighters*. It's hard to tell if the cinema cognoscenti took all this seriously. It's clear that Troma didn't. The company wallowed in sleaze and cheapness, exhibiting no artistic pretensions nor expecting anyone to read hidden meaning into their films. Kaufman and Herz were having a ball churning out their slimy masterpieces, and they expected the audience to share the fun.

The most popular Troma output was its aforementioned "Toxic Avenger" flicks, a quartet of films made between 1985 and 1992 about a 90-pound nerd named Melvin Junko, who by his own admission was "hideously deformed" into a mutant by toxic waste. Junko took his revenge in the form of good deeds, usually at the expense of the greedy, polluting fatcat business executives of Tromaville. There were violence and gore to spare in the "Avenger" pictures (*Toxic Avenger I, Toxic Avenger II, Toxic Avenger III: The Last Temptation of Toxie*, and *Toxic Avenger IV: Mr. Toxic Goes to Washington*) but also a healthy share of intentional laughs. Predictably, the series was a big hit with preteens, who evidently planted false mustaches on themselves when entering the theatres or drugged their babysitters and then plunked their rented *Toxic Avenger* (q.v.) cassettes in their VCRs. They *couldn't* have seen these films any other way, for as we all know, it's illegal for kids under the age of 18 to attend R-rated movies unescorted.

Whatever the case, it was felt that a presold *Toxic Avenger* cartoon series would tap the mutant-cartoon market already opened by *Teenage Mutant Ninja Turtles* (q.v.); no surprise, then, that the *Turtles*' animators Murikami-Wolf-Swenson undertook the task of bringing Tromaville to the small screen. That the property was heavily expurgated for Saturday morning consumption was instantly evident in its title: An "Avenger" no more (getting even was still something of a forbidden issue on children's TV), the hero was now the Toxic Crusader.

"Toxi" now took on the task of punishing polluters with several fellow mutants, all of them reminding the audience (and each other) in every other spoken sentence that they were "hideously deformed": No Zone, Junkyard, and the two-headed Headbasher (Benderman and Fenderman), all human beings melded into auto parts, scrap iron, and other castaway garbage. The normal humans, who on a series like this wound up being abnormal, included Major Disaster, a military man who joined the pro-eco fight because of his unnaturally obsessive love of plants; Toxi's mom, better known to one and all as Toxi's Mom; and Toxi's bubblebrained girlfriend Yvonne.

The baddies were led by Zarzoza, a controlling force from the planet Smogula, and Zarzoza's lieutenants: Dr. Killemoff, Bonehead, Psycho, and Tromaville's graft-driven Mayor Grody. The Smogulans operated from nearby Islet City, which looked like a rundown New Jersey factory town.

By virtue of its premise and the Murikami-Wolf-Swenson staff input, *Toxic Crusaders* was not without its chuckles, but it pushed too hard, ending up more forced than funny. The series also fell into the same trap that tended to lessen the impact of other cartoon series based on schlock movies (see *Attack of the Killer Tomatoes* and *Little Shop*). By the very nature of 1990s economics, even the least expensive cartoon series is bound to look slicker and more costly than a B picture. Somehow it just didn't seem right for *Toxic Crusaders* to look as professional and accomplished as it did (and that wasn't so much to begin with). For full effect, the series should have had the wretched acting, the family-member extras, the fluffed lines, the tawdry motel-room "sets," the dangling overhead microphones, and the overall gloriously grungy veneer of the "best" Troma films.

Toxic Crusaders managed a considerable number of first-season sales, but that didn't guarantee a second season. The series was hideously deactivated after 13 episodes.

TRANSFORMERS. Syndicated: 1984. Marvel/Sunbow/Claster/Hasbro (Griffin Bacal Inc.). Executive producers: Lee Gunther, Margaret Loesch and Tom Griffin. Produced by Nelson Shin. Creative director, Joe Bacal. Directed by John Walker. Segment directors: John Gibbs, Norm McCabe, Jeff Hall and Brad Case. Story editors: Dick Robbins, Bryce Malek. Written by Douglas Booth, Don Glut, Alfred A. Pegal, Larry Struss, Earl Kress, Reed Robbins, Peter Salas. Additional dialogue by Ron Friedman. Title music by Ford Kinder and Ann Bryant. Music by Johnny Douglas. Voices: Michael Bell (Prowler/Scrapper/Swoop/Junkion); Peter Cullen (Optimus Prime/ Ironhide); Jack Angel (Astro Train); Gregg Berger (Grimlock); Susan Blu (Arcee); Arthur Burghardt (Devastator); Roger C. Carmel (Cyclonus); Scatman Crothers (Jazz); Brad Davis (Dirge); Walker Edmiston (Inferno); Paul Eiding (Perceptor); Ed Gilbert (Blitzwing); Dan Gilvezan (Bumblebee); Buster Jones (Blaster); Stan Jones (Scourge); Casey Kasem (Cliffjumper); Chris Latta (Star Scream/Cobra Commander); David Mendenhall (Daniel); Don Messick (Gears); John Moschitta (Blurr); Judd Nelson (Hot Road/Rodimus); Hal Rayle (Shrapnel); Clive Revill (Kickback); Neil Ross (Bone Crusher/Hook/Springer/Slag); Frank Welker (Soundwave/Megatron/Galatron/Rumble/Frenzy/Wheelie); and Corey Burton, John Stephenson, and Ken Sansom.

—TRANSFORMERS: GENERATION II. Syndicated: 1993. Sunbow/Claster. Same production credits as TRANS-FORMERS. Additional credits for "Cybernet Space Cube" enhancements: For Sunbow Productions: Associate creative director, Rob Travalino. Producer/art director, Sam Register. Creative producer, Steve Goldfine. Main Title and Bumpers: Lamb and Company. For Tapestry Productions: Production supervisor, Paul Fisher. 3-D Modeling: Steve Sullivan, Vincent Musarella. Effects supervisor, Jim Burgess. Cube Animation by Doro Motion. Animation director, Doros Evangelides. Animation by Carl Edwards.

The *Transformers* was tied in with a Hasbro line of "morphing" toys—robots which could turn into automotive vehicles, and vice versa (see also *Challenge of the GoBots* for a like-vintage example of this). The series' premise was laid out in the theme song, which assured us that the characters were "More Than Meets the Eye."

On the planet of Cybertron, Optimus Prime was the leader of Autobots, the

"good" branch of the Transformer family. Megatron, the main villain, was head of the Decepticons. A centuries-long battle on Cybertron has compelled both Autobots and Decepticons to move their battleground to planet Earth in the year 2005. The warring camps, of course, managed to find human allies for both causes, and of course the "good" guys were easier on the eye. Among the Autobots were Smoke Screen, Tracks, Hoist, Inferno, Red Alert and Grapple. (Many of these characters had distinctive ethnic and regional accents and personality traits, a cute variation of the "All American platoon" cliché in World War II movies.) Decepticons were stuck with downer names like Thrust and Dirge.

Animation on the daily *Transformers* was well above average for the mid–1980s, setting a precedent that Marvel has not always been able to maintain. The company *has*, however, continued to emulate *Transformers*' strong story values and character development, as witness the recent *X-Men*. And though the series was at base a half-hour commercial, merchandising of the various *Transformers* hardware was built into the storyline without sore-thumb prominence. The paraphernalia flowed naturally from the action rather than being crudely imposed upon it. This relative restraint was in contrast to the property's gonzo ad campaign, which looked as though it had been assembled by former flea-circus hucksters.

Transformers spawned a 1986 theatrical feature with an all-star voice cast, including Robert Stack, Leonard Nimoy, Eric Idle, Lionel Stander, and Orson Welles in one of his last gigs as the voice of "Unicron," an evil *planet*. The animation style that passed muster on TV seemed inadequate when blown up to the 35-foot dimensions of a movie screen. The film's ear-shattering rock music score was also a drawback. Leonard Maltin has dropped a "BOMB" on *Transformers: The Movie* in his film ratings book. I wouldn't go that far, but I also wouldn't have gone as far as to plunk down five dollars to see the film back in 1986 either.

The "new," weekly *Transformers: Generation II* of 1993 consisted merely of 13 old half hour episodes from the 1980s, redressed with computer-enhanced bumpers and scene transitions.

TRANZOR Z. Syndicated: 1985. Toei Animation/3B Productions/T. E. N. Executive producer, Bunker Jenkins. Directed by Chris Henderson. Written by Dick Strome, Sandy Childs and Bunker Jenkins. Music by Doug Lackey. Voices: Gregg Berger, Mona Marshall, Paul Ross, Willard Jenkins, Pat Pinney, Robert A. Gaston, James Hodson, Willard Lloyd Davis.

Ready for the backstory of *Tranzor Z*? Fasten your seat belts.

Dr. Demon was an evil sorceror who looked like Moses(!) and who told anyone who would listen that he planned to rule the world. For this purpose, Demon fortified himself with the "Fork of Fury," a magic staff, and the Doom Machines, evil giant robots. He also had at his disposal the submarine fortress Barracuda (which sucked battleships into a vortex) and the Air Fortress (which used a deadly cloud to destroy aircraft). Evidently this fiend could be stopped only by kindly Dr. Wells, an American scientist who'd found a way to harness volcano energy. Wells was also the inventor of Alloy Z, an impenetrable metal. But Dr. Demon's minions eventually burned down Wells' lab, destroying most of his equpiment. Found dying in his cellar by nephews Tommy (handsome hero) and Toad (tousle-haired kid), Wells revealed his creation of the volcano-powered, Alloy Z–crafted giant "super robot" Tranzor Z.

Though mortally wounded, Wells delivered a spirited five-minute expository speech. Tranzor Z, he explained, had detachable rocket fists, a boomerang breastplate, atomic hurricane breath which disintegrated the enemy, a flying scrambler which attached wings to the robot, and laser rays emanating from its fingertips and eyes. Wells stubbornly managed to stave off death until he'd had a chance to utter the obligatory "If this should ever fall in the wrong hands. . . ." The right hands, it turned out, belonged to Tommy, who became the flying Tranzor Z's pilot.

The remainder of *Tranzor Z* was Tommy vs. Dr. Demon. On Tranzor Z's side were female robot (with breasts!) Aphrodite A, operated by Tommy's girlfriend Jessica; and Mobilbot, a hot rod operated by funny tough-guy Bobo. The humans were capable of being injured or kidnapped, and their hardware was prone to damage and breakdown, but Tranzor Z himself was so invulnerable that he became a dullard very early on.

The series featured typically uneven Japanimation design and movement. The plotlines were unsettling combinations of starkly realistic action with downright silliness. Campy, ripe acting and character design were juxtaposed with grisly scenes of wholesale slaughter of innocent bystanders. But if one was able to sidestep its splotchy production values and confusing point of view, *Tranzor Z* could be a lot of fun, especially if one concentrated on the villainy. For example, Dr. Demon didn't waste time exercising the typical cartoon-villain prerogative of speaking in double meanings or euphemisms: "Destroy every city in America!" he'd command with admirable directness.

Tranzor Z's best moments were such oddball vignettes as having one of Demon's henchmen being haunted by the "ghosts" of all the Doom Machines destroyed by Tranzor Z. And although conceived in comic-opera terms, Demon's lieutenants were fascinating. Dr. DeCapito was a Nazi type who screamed all his lines and whose monocled, goateed head was disembodied, floating independently as DeCapito skulked about.

Unique in the annals of Japanese cartoons released to mainstream American television was Demon's other assistant: Devilene the "She-Man." Not only was Devilene half man and half woman—divided down the middle, carnival style—but "with the worst elements of both!," so the narrator told us. (Does this mean that Devilene left the toilet seat up *and* stockings hanging on the bathroom shower curtains?) The character spoke in two voices and was addressed by his/her hopelessly confused flunkeys as "Sir Ma'am." Even the transvestite nightclub singer on the Japanese *Robotech* (q.v.) wasn't this kinky.

Its childish dialogue at odds with its grim wanton violence, and with wacked-out characters the like of which may never pass this way again, the daily *Tranzor Z* never quite found a "base" audience. Perhaps it would have worked with a demographic group comprised of giant, conscience-stricken transvestite Nazi robots.

T-REX *see* **THE ADVENTURES OF T-REX**

THE TROLLKINS. CBS: 9/12/1981–
9/4/1982. Hanna-Barbera. Executive producers, William Hanna and Joseph
Barbera. Produced by Kay Wright. Supervising director, Ray Patterson. Directed
by Rudy Zamora, Carl Urbano, George
Gordon; assistant directors, Bob Goe,
Terry Harrison. Story supervisor, Ray
Parker. Supervising story editor, Hank
Saroyan. Story direction, Edward Fitz-
gerald, Gary Goldstein, Cullen Hough-
taling, Lewis Sow, Mitchell Schauer, Roy
Wilson, Kay Wright. Animation super-
visor, Jay Sarbry. Background supervisor,
Al Gmuer. Recording directors, Gordon
Hunt and Ginny McSwain. Creative su-
pervisor, Iwao Takamoto. Music direction
by Hoyt Curtin. Musical supervision by
Paul DeKorte. Executives in charge of
production, Jayne Barbera and Margaret
Loesch. Voices: Alan Oppenheimer
(Sheriff Pudge Trollson); Jennifer Darling
(Pixie Trollson/Deputroll Dolly); Steve
Spears (Blitz Plumkin); Frank Welker
(Flooky/Bogg/Top Troll); Michael Bell
(Grubb Trollmaine); Paul Winchell
(Mayor Lumpkin); Marshall Efron (Depu-
troll Flake); Hank Saroyan (Afid); Bill
Callaway (Slug); and Jarad Barclay, Mel
Blanc, Scatman Crothers, Peter Cullen,
Billie Hayes, Ken Mars, Don Messick,
Robert Allan Ogle, Bob Sarlatte, Marilyn
Schreffler, Rick Segal, Hal Smith, Steve
Spears, John Stephenson, Lennie Wein-
rib, and Alan Young.

Trollkins was *The Smurfs* (q.v.) cross-
bred with *Dukes of Hazzard* (q.v.). Appearing in two short adventures per weekly
half hour, the teeny-tiny Trollkins lived in
Trolltown, located in the trunk of a hollow
tree. Leading the community was Mayor
Lumpkin, an apoplectic hairball who
spoke in tongue-tied spoonerisms: "Bum-
suddy" for "somebody," "wandshield whip-
per" for "windshield wiper," "Treen Groll
Road" for "Green Troll Road," and so it
went. Lumpkin was a stupe, but no worse
than his seconds-in-command, Sheriff
Pudge Trollson and "Deputroll" Flake,
who were eager to slip their "nose-cuffs"
on any suspected felon but who usually
bore the brunt of their own clumsiness. A
variety of younger folks dotted the landscape, but only the Mayor's daughter Pixie
Trollson could be described as attractive;
the rest may not have looked like the
wizened, bearded trolls of European
legend, but were fairly grotesque all the

same. And of course there was a funny dog.
This one was Flooky, who communicated
in sound effects and sign language: When
spotting a UFO, he turned his head into a
space helmet and hummed the theme
from *Close Encounters of the Third Kind.*

Like "Smurfspeak" in *Smurfs,* the
Trolltown language was a quasi–English
vernacular in which the speaker's ethnic
origin was mentioned in every other word:
"Troll-diculous," "Trollerskating," and you
get the drift. Adding to *Trollkins'* rustic
flavor was the fact that everyone spoke in
thick Southern accents (even a resurrected mummy in one episode sounded
like something out of *Deliverance*). Unlike
Smurfs, the characters were multicolored
instead of standard-issue blue. In fact, the
color scheme and background design (by
the always reliable Al Gmuer) were the
most memorable aspects of *Trollkins.*
While the series scored on its peppy
country-western background music and
its comedy content (mostly pop-cultural
references and the convoluted monologues of Mayor Lumpkin), the characters
were unmemorable, with no *Smurf*like
magical or unique powers to grab the audience. Nor did the tie-in *Trollkin* action
figures and toy vehicles have the marketplace staying power of the similar *Smurfs*
merchandise.

We've mentioned *Smurfs* so often that
one would think *Trollkins* was merely a
Smurfs imitation, perhaps produced a year
or so after the more popular Hanna-
Barbera series had taken hold. But the fact
is that both *Trollkins* and *Smurfs* premiered on the same Saturday morning in
1981—in the same timeslot on competing
networks! Perhaps the two series influenced each other due to like minds
within the same studio. Whatever the
case, *Smurfs* lasted nine seasons, while
Trollkins barely got through one. It was
one of the few instances in which Hanna-
Barbera gained popularity for one of its
programs by stepping on itself.

TURBO TEEN. ABC: 9/8/1984–8/31/
1985. Ruby-Spears. Executive producers,
Joe Ruby and Ken Spears. Produced by
Larry Huber and Michael Hack. Directed
by John Kimball. Voice direction by
Howard Morris and Alan Dinehart. Music
by Udi Harpaz. Voices: Michael Mish
(Brett Mathews); T. K. Carter (Alex);
Pamela Hayden (Pattie); Frank Welker

(Flip/Rusty); Pat Fraley (Eddie); and Clive Revill.

The title of the weekly, half-hour *Turbo Teen* referred to series hero Brett Mathews, a journalism major and racing enthusiast. In the opener, a bolt of lightning forced Brett's car to crash through the wall of a government science lab, where a hush-hush fusion experiment was in progress. Result: Whenever his body temperature rose beyond normal, Brett Mathews transformed into a turbocharged racing car. Suspicions prevail that the 12 mystery-busting adventures of Turbo Teen and his "normal" friends Alex and Pattie were trying to promote a tie-in toy vehicle.

Viewers' choices opposite *Turbo Teen* included CBS' *Dungeons and Dragons* (q.v.) and NBC's *The Smurfs* (q.v.). Pick the winner and you get a stuffed blue doll (no coaching from the audience, please!).

TWINKLE, THE DREAM BEING. Syndicated: 1993. Sei Young/MBC Productions/Calico/Zodiac. Executive producer/creator, Peter Keefe. Supervising producers, Choi An Hee, Claudia Zeitlin-Burton, Paul Vitello. Senior executives in charge of production, No Seung Woo and Choi Kwang Am. Animation production design, Calico Enterprises. Directed by Claudia Zeitlin-Burton. Executives in charge for Calico, Lee Mann and Tom Burton. Music by Dale Schacker. Voices: Tress MacNeille (Twinkle); and Pat Fraley, Russi Taylor, and Cam Clarke.

Twinkle, the Dream Being was set on the Possible Planet (The Land of Possibility was the main borough) which had its own Wishing Star. Twinkle, denizen of that glimmering spectral orb, granted wishes to the Possible Planet citizenry. While most such fulfillments were beneficial, there was the implicit warning to the greedy: "Be careful what you wish for; you just might get it!"

Forever spouting expletives like "Blazing Stars" and "Sizzling Starbursts," Twinkle could strengthen his body by invoking the magic phrase "Starbright, Starlight, Starnight!" Twinkle's "star" motif included the stellar shape of his body, his mode of transportation (he'd ride in on a star) and the talking star on his antenna. At times, watching this program was the equivalent of being kicked in the head.

Twinkle had a girlfriend named Jedda, and counted among his friends the Oogies (Mother and Son), metamorphosing members of the "Urg" family, who could change into anything. For the benefit of both the home viewers and the FCC, Twinkle and the "good" characters constantly encouraged reading, ecology, health, and other parent-approved niceties.

The villain was Miss Diva Weed, a.k.a. "The Queen of Mean" (her method of locomotion was a buzzard) who wanted to keep Possible Planet stupid and subservient; thus, a prosocial, pro-intelligence type like Twinkle was someone to be thwarted. Fortunately, Diva's magical powers generally backfired, but the residents of Possible Planet were perfectly capable of exhibiting ignorance without Diva's encouragement, notably by wishing for things from Twinkle that served a selfish rather than altruistic purpose. And when Twink wasn't around, they'd squander their money on the overpriced, useless wares of Hot-Shot the travelling salesman.

Designed to replace Calico/Zodiac's *Mr. Bogus* (q.v.) weekly syndie (just as *Bogus* had replaced the same studio's earlier *Widget, the World Watcher* [q.v.]), *Twinkle, the Dream Being* played like a combo of *Muppet Babies* (q.v.) and *Smurfs* (q.v.), both in theme and visual design. Each half hour was comprised of loosely basted individual skits related by a basic "moral." As such, *Twinkle* didn't have the strong story values of its Calico/Zodiac predecessor *Widget*, nor could it boast the solid laugh content of the studio's *Mr. Bogus*. In addition, the principal characters were oddly unattractive, so much so that the best-looking person on the program was the villainess.

Nevertheless, as a result of a massive, year-long promotional buildup, including filming a full season's worth of 26 half hour programs before the first sale was even made to assure local stations that there'd be plenty of product handy, *Twinkle, the Dream Being* was widely syndicated in its inaugural season. The leading character had a strong "out of TV" tie-in as the mascot of International Expo 93, a Korea-based ecological and sociological celebration which functioned on behalf of the "Global Family." Sei Young studios, which animated *Twinkle* on behalf of Calico/Zodiac, hoped that the weekly series would act as a catalyst for the Korean animation industry, leading to more homegrown projects and less American-commissioned work.

TWO STUPID DOGS. Syndicated: 1993. TBS: 9/12/1993–. Hanna-Barbera/ Turner Program Services. Executive producer, Buzz Potamkin. Produced and directed by Donovan Cook and Larry Huber. Story editor/co-developer: Mark Saraceni. Principal writers: Mark Saraceni and Roberts Gallaway. Art direction by Craig McCracken and Paul Rudish. Supervising animation director, Joanna Romersa. Animation directors: Gennoy Tartanovsky, Joan Drake, Frank Andrina, Allen Wilzbach, Rick Bowman, Vince Waller, Robert Alvarez. Theme music by Chris Desmond and Tom Seufert. Music by Vaughn Johnson and Guy Moon. Overseas production supervision by Bob Marples. Animation facilities: Mr. Big Cartoons (Australia); Wang Film Production Co., Ltd. (Taiwan). COMPONENTS: 1. TWO STUPID DOGS. Voices: Brad Garrett (Big Dog); Mark Schiff (Little Dog); Brian Cummings (Hollywood). 2. SUPER SECRET SQUIRREL. Voices: Jess Harnell (Secret Squirrel); Jim Cummings (Morocco Mole); Tony Jay (Chief). Additional voices, both components: Charlie Adler, Yoshio Be, Jeff Bennett, Greg Burson, Ruth Buzzi, Carol Channing, Donna Cherry, Paul Eiding, Bernard Erhard, June Foray, John Frost, John Garry, Mark Hamill, Haven Hartman, Whitby Hartford, Casey Kasem, Jean Kasem, Jarrett Lennon, Pat Lentz, Tress MacNeille, Rose Marie, Roddy McDowall, Scott Menville, Candi Milo, Pat Musick, Gary Owens, Rob Paulsen, Kimmy Robertson, Roger Rose, Stu Rosen, Neil Ross, Susan Silo, Kath Soucie, Ben Stiller, Tawni Tamietti, B. J. Ward, Derek Webster.

Two Stupid Dogs, a 1993 entry in the weekend package *The Funtastic World of Hanna-Barbera* (q.v.), represented H-B's much-heralded break from its old style (which had been trumpeted 35 years earlier as a break from an even older style) and its entree into the new, progressive animated world of squat, angular artwork and toilet humor.

The series was created by 25-year-old California Institute of the Arts graduate Donovan Cook, a lifelong cartoon junkie; Cook's idol was H-B animator Ed Benedict, the principal architect behind the studio's flat, two-dimensional visual style

(anyone who admits to *admiring* that style gets five points on guts alone). But Cook didn't get the artistic "bug" until the 1983 creation of cable's Disney Channel, which seemed to herald the opening of innumerable doors for fresh, unbounded talent. After working as assistant production manager on the Mickey Mouse short subject *Prince and the Pauper* (1990), Donovan Cook was brought into the Hanna-Barbera fold by the studio's new CEO Fred Seibert, who at the time was on the prowl for a new-breed animation staff to counter the onslaught of Disney and Warner Bros. on the cartoon market.

The time was prime for Donovan Cook to pull out several ideas he'd mulled over with his industry pals — the best of which was about two terminally moronic dogs. This notion had already been pitched to several companies, most of whom enjoyed the premise, but wondered "what do you do with it?" Cook, never one to hide his ego under a bushel, would invariably reply, "Well, you put three of them together and you get a half hour." Steven Spielberg's Amblin Entertainment would have seemed in the early 1990s to be most responsive to funny-animal 'toons (as witness *Tiny Toon Adventures* [q.v.]), but according to Cook, Amblin "ran screaming" from *Two Stupid Dogs* due to the company's ceaseless headaches over their long-delayed, benighted *The Family Dog* (q.v.). Hanna-Barbera, however, said "go with it," and go with it Donovan Cook did.

Two Stupid Dogs, which premiered almost simultaneously on Turner's TBS superstation and in local syndication, featured a brace of cretinous canines, identified only as "Big Dog" and "Little Dog." It would have better been titled *One Stupid Dog*, since it was invariably the Little Dog, all bravado and no brains, who led his lugubrious bigger companion into disaster. Their impressionistically illustrated adventures were underscored by jazz music, and their comedy was of the nose-booger, funny-underwear, body-secretion variety (the logo for the series was in the shape of a fireplug).

Say, doesn't that sound just a teeny bit like Nickelodeon's ground-breaking *Ren and Stimpy* (q.v.)? And isn't it peculiar that *Two Stupid Dogs* didn't get the green light until after *Ren and Stimpy* had been entrenched for two seasons? Fred Seibert was prepared for this critical reaction with a rock-band analogy. Comparing *Two Stupid Dogs* to *Ren and Stimpy*, Seibert noted, was "like Pearl Jam worrying about being compared to Nirvana."

Whether or not *Dogs* was designed as H-B's answer to *R and S* might be hotly contested by Seibert, but the fact is that *Two Stupid Dogs* bore many of the earmarks that had been popularized by the Nickelodeon series. Characters never spoke when screaming hysterically would do; one character, a behemoth of a man named "Hollywood," would interrupt the proceedings at regular intervals by bellowing "But that's WROOOONNNNG," while those about him would batten down against the hurricane breeze from his mouth. (This character's name grew from narrator Gary Owens' frequent comment that "Hollywood" was against the creation of *Two Stupid Dogs*. Get it? Hollywood?) A generous amount of time was devoted to exploring the Two Stupid Dogs' nostrils and bloodshot eyes, with various other orifices making cameo appearances. And, just like *Ren and Stimpy*, storylines were frequently not so much skimpy as nonexistent: In the very first episode, the Little Dog spent five full minutes trying to figure out the mechanics of a supermarket's automatic door.

Perhaps to avoid a total breakaway from the Hanna-Barbera of old, Donovan Cook burrowed through the studio's past properties to come up with a component feature, to be sandwiched between the two *Two Stupid Dogs* seven-minute cartoons appearing on each weekly half hour. Cook decided to resuscitate 1965's Secret Squirrel (see *Atom Ant*). This may well have been a creative self-challenge, since Secret Squirrel was one of the least pliable of all H-B characters: Not only was he locked into the "James Bond" craze of the mid–1960s, but his original cartoons had been exercises in dreariness, failing to exploit fully the spoofable aspects of spydom and relying instead on repetitious spot gags. As it turned out, Donovan Cook's *Super Secret Squirrel* segments were a decided improvement on the original, with a riveting character design (Secret Squirrel now looked like a Picasso painting, while his immediate superior was a demonlike bull) and a fascinating spin on the character of Secret's assistant Morocco Mole. The 1965 version had given Morocco a "Peter Lorre" voice

(courtesy Paul Frees) and let it go at that; Donovan Scott's version played the imitation for all it was worth, allowing his Morocco (Jim Cummings) to revert occasionally to a gibbering, raving lunatic, in the best bugeyed tradition of the "real" Lorre.

While *Super Secret Squirrel*, along with the rest of *Two Stupid Dogs*, still played like a road-company *Ren and Stimpy*, it was clear that Donovan Scott had The Right Stuff for the TV-cartoon business. And perhaps someday, Scott will cast off the shackles of Hanna-Barbera and become his own producer, in the footsteps of *R and S*'s John Kricfalusi.

ULYSSES 31 *see* **KIDEO TV**

UNCLE CROC'S BLOCK. ABC: 9/6/ 1975–2/14/1976. Filmation. Produced and directed by Mack Bing (live-action). Animation producer, Don Christensen, Lou Scheimer, Norm Prescott. Music by Yvette Blais and Jeff Michael. Cast (live-action): Charles Nelson Reilly (Uncle Croc); Jonathan Harris (Basil Bitterbottom); Johnny Silver and Alfie Wise (Rabbit Ears); Bob Ridgely (The $6.95 Man); and Huntz Hall. Cartoon Components: 1. **FRAIDY CAT.** Voices: Alan Oppenheimer (Fraidy Cat/Tinkey/Dog/Moose/Hokey); Lennie Weinrib (Tonka/Wizard/ Capt. Kitt/Sir Walter Katt/Winston). 2. **M*U*S*H.** Voices: Robert Ridgely (Bullseye/Trooper Joe/Sonar/Hilda); Kenneth Mars (Sideburns/Coldlips/Col. Flake/ General Upheaval). 3. **WACKY AND PACKY.** Voices: Allan Melvin.

"Sophisticated satire for children" was the promise made by the press releases for *Uncle Croc's Block*. What we got was trenchant, flatfooted "comedy" unsuitable for anyone.

Uncle Croc was a live-action character, a meanspirited lampoon of the "typical" kiddie host. He wore a crocodile suit, exuded phony enthusiasm, and was bolstered by a threadbare supporting cast including the likes of "Rabbit Ears" and "The 6.95 Man" (one of the fleeting cast members was "Mr. Mean Jeans," which couldn't have rested well with image-conscious Captain Kangaroo). The principal gag here was that Uncle Croc (played with more spirit than the role deserved by Charles Nelson Reilly) made no secret on the air that he hated his job, hated his boss (*Lost in Space* veteran Jonathan Harris),

Two Stupid Dogs compound their foolishness by bolting down deadly theater popcorn.

and—are you ready?—*hated kids*. Maybe this was a new concept when Ernie Kovacs was doing it back in the 1950s; but then, given the famous "That oughta hold the little bastards" urban legend concerning radio's Uncle Don (which dated back at least to 1939), maybe Kovacs was also coughing up an old bromide.

Even allowing for the fact that New Jersey's like-vintage *Uncle Floyd Show* was gaining laughs and a national reputation by satirizing cheap local children's programming, *Uncle Croc's Block* was doomed from the start by targetting a form of entertainment all but dead and buried by 1975. Old fashioned kiddie hosts had by this time been pretty much squeezed out by *Sesame Street*, with recent governmental rulings that such hosts couldn't promote commercial products within the bodies of their programs finishing off whatever *Sesame Street* hadn't squashed. Funny though Charles Nelson Reilly could be at times, his series was ravaging a corpse; it was as if a 1975 nightclub comic were suddenly to begin joking about Eisenhower, Khrushchev and the Edsel (CBS' 1980s series *Pee-wee's Playhouse* was infinitely more successful in spoofing 1950s children's shows—simply by applying affection and nostalgia rather than cynicism and contempt).

The Filmation cartoon shorts hosted by Uncle Croc were rather better than the live stuff, but at base derivative and plodding. *Fraidy Cat*, the story of a timorous feline whose eight previous lives have teamed up in the Great Beyond to get their most recent incarnation to join them in death, was just a retread of Filmation's earlier *Secret Lives of Waldo Kitty* (q.v.) — even down to the lookalike character design of the leading cat's various alternate personalities. Some admittedly amusing moments occurred due to Fraidy Cat's avoidance of saying the numbers 1 through 8 lest he conjure up one of his past lives, and strict avoidance of saying "9," which of course would cause forfeiture of his own life.

Wacky and Packy, the second *Uncle Croc* component, likewise was good for a laugh or two. This was the tale of two neanderthals — caveman Wacky and pet mastodon Packy — who through a timewarp were thrust into the 20th century and subsequently forced to forage through the concrete jungles of the Modern World in search of food. *Wacky and Packy* was not bad at all; still, Hanna-Barbera had cornered the market (and most of the better writers) for cartoon cavemen vis-à-vis *The Flintstones* and *Captain Caveman* (see individual entries).

The one *Uncle Croc's Block* component to receive even worse press reviews than the live wraparounds was *M*U*S*H*, an execrable parody of the top-rated CBS sitcom *M*A*S*H*. The letters in the cartoon acronym stood for Mangy Unwanted Shabby Heroes, which could have been the motto for the rest of *Uncle Croc*. Instead of a mobile hospital administering to Korean War casualties, the M*U*S*H humanized-dog personnel were mounted policemen in a godforsaken snowbound outpost. One can assess the inherent humor of this property with a roll-call of the parodied character names: Bullseye, Trooper Joe, Major Sideburns, Sonar, Colonel Flake, and Cold Lips. This one would have fallen apart even under its original title, *MUSH Puppies*. You might get a snicker out of a *M*U*S*H* videocassette (they're on the rental shelves, caked with dust) but only if you happen to despise Alan Alda.

Oddly, when poor ratings (brought about by the stronger competition of Filmation's own live action *Shazam-Isis*

Hour on CBS) compelled ABC to pare down *Uncle Croc's Block* from an hour to 30 minutes, its weakest component, *M*U*S*H*, was the only one retained. Ratings continued to plummet; even 13-year-old reruns of *The Jetsons* (q.v.) were beating out *Uncle Croc*. By February 1976, halfway through its first season, ABC dropped the show entirely, replacing it with the reliable *American Bandstand*. According to Filmation chroniclers Swanigan and O'Neal, ABC was so disgusted by *Uncle Croc's Block* that it never bought anything from the studio again. We can think of all sorts of extenuating reasons for ABC's decision: Try watching Filmation's *Lassie's Rescue Rangers* or *My Favorite Martians* sometime.

UNCLE WALDO *see* **HOPPITY HOOPER**

UNDERCOVER ELEPHANT *see* **C.B. BEARS**

UNDERDOG. NBC: 10/3/1964–9/3/1966; 9/7/1968–9/1/1973; CBS: 9/7/1966–9/2/1967. Leonardo Television/Total TV Productions. Produced by Peter Piech and Treadwell Covington. Directed by Pete Dakis, Sal Faillace, Lu Guarnier, Bob Schleh. Written by Buck Biggers and Chet Stover. Animation by Gamma Studios. Voices: Wally Cox (Underdog); Norma McMillan (Sweet Polly Purebred); George Irving (Narrator/Ruffled Feathers); Sandy Becker (The Sergeant); Kenny Delmar (The Hunter/Col. Kit Coyote/Commander McBragg) and Mort Marshall, Delo States, Ben Stone, and Allen Swift.

Underdog was the most popular cartoon series produced by Total Television/Leonardo Productions (see *King Leonardo and His Short Subjects*), and at the same time its most repetitious and predictable. If there's a correlation there, then that must be why *most* Saturday morning cartoon shows of the 1960s and 1970s were repetitious and predictable.

The half-hour series was broken up into several components. The *Underdog* segments featured "humble and lovable" anthropomorphized dog Shoe Shine Boy, who, whenever there was a call for help, became ("in real life," narrator George Irving solemnly informed us) the superpowered Underdog. While togged in his "Underdog" cape and costume (a huge "U" on the shirt, so we'd recognize him), the character spoke in rhyme: "When danger threatens, I am not slow/ So it's hip, hip, hip, and awaaaay I go!"

Underdog's "Lois Lane" counterpart in his serialized seven-minute adventures was Sweet Polly Purebred, a doggie parody of the helpless damsel-in-distress so vital to oldtime melodramas. Sweet Polly was a TV reporter (how she got through broadcasting school without losing her simpering tone is a mystery), who, whenever danger threatened, helped matters not at all by reminding her viewers that Underdog was their only hope. She heralded her hero by singing "Oh, where, oh where has my Underdog gone?/ Oh, where, oh where can he be?"—no challenge to Underdog's status as his series' poet laureate.

Evidently, Sweet Polly couldn't go out for coffee and doughnuts without being kidnapped by one of the many *Underdog* villains, who'd imperil the city with weather machines, "forget" gas, phony phone booths that turned people into zombies, and dynamited gold trains. Minor baddies like the Marbleheads and the Molemen took second place to the series' two chief antagonists: Riff Raff, a gangsterish wolf whose neck was apparently welded to his shirt collar, and Simon Bar Sinister, a Lionel Barrymore soundalike who introduced all his evil doomsday devices by intoning "Simon Says!"

It's easy to remember all this from long-ago viewings because the writers on *Underdog* never told us anything less than three times. Most of the four-part adventures sounded as though the voice tracks were recorded on loops, then played over and over to make sure those who came in late wouldn't miss a trick. Riff Raff would chuckle "Crash! the gold will be mine!" and the wicked witch in another episode would cackle "Ah hah! Ee hee! Sweet Polly will sleep for one hunnnndred years!" so often that it took on the droning dimensions of the brainwashing technique in *The Manchurian Candidate*. One expected Simon Bar Sinister to invite Underdog to pass the time with a little game of solitaire.

Similarly, the storylines had a knack of looking alike: One oft-repeated ploy was forcing Underdog to be in two places at once so that he couldn't thwart the villainy

at hand. Unfortunately, the scripts frequently substituted repetition for genuine humor. Small wonder that journalists commenting upon the frequent *Underdog* movie-theatre revivals of the early 1990s would confess sheepishly that the show wasn't quite as hilarious as they remembered it. But little children—as those journalists once were—are less picky when it comes to funny-looking characters and hilariously hyperbolic voice work: Wally Cox, bespectacled comic actor of *Mr. Peepers* fame, and Norma McMillan (see also *Davey and Goliath*) were tops as Underdog and Sweet Polly, though rumors persist that Cox was occasionally replaced by mimic Allan Swift. Thanks to audience turnover, *Underdog* is as popular today as he was in 1965 when he first appeared as a balloon in the Macy's Thanksgiving parade.

The series' first-season companion components were older Total/Leonardo properties. Lifted from *King Leonardo* was "The Hunter," the relentless dog detective voiced by Kenny "Senator Claghorn" Delmar. The Hunter's *Underdog* adventures went beyond his standard battle of wits with the "wily clever" criminal The Fox, concentrating on the gumshoe's tiltings with his precocious nephew Horace, and at one point offering an unexpected and delightful "opéra bouffe," a musical version of "Little Boy Blue." Also borrowed from an earlier show was "Commander McBragg" (see *Tennessee Tuxedo*), as droningly unfunny as ever.

In 1966, *Underdog* moved from NBC to CBS (as a replacement for Leonardo/Total's own *Tennessee Tuxedo*), losing "The Hunter" in the process. In its place was another humanized-animal romp, "Go Go Gophers," described succinctly by one cartoon fan as a comedy about genocide. The two surviving members of the Gopher Indian tribe were Ruffled Feathers, who spoke in gibberish, and Running Board, a Tonto type who interpreted his tribesman's ravings. The Go Go Gophers were the bane of the existence of Col. Kit Coyote, a Teddy Roosevelt type (voice by Kenny Delmar again), who wanted to rid the west of the pesky Indians in as permanent a manner as possible. Col. Coyote's plans were always doomed to failure (perhaps he was a distant cousin of the equally luckless Wile E.) because the Gophers were smarter, faster, and perpetually one step ahead of the Colonel. Not all "white" animals were as xenophobic as Coyote; his sergeant, an easygoing John Wayne type, tried to be the voice of reason, but gave up when he saw the Colonel was going to mess himself up anyway. He then invited the kids at home to tune in next week to see if the Gophers had left yet (They hadn't). Seen today, "Go Go Gophers" is as moderately offensive as most comedy westerns of the 1960s, but at least the "non–Indians" were always the butt of the humor.

The other new *Underdog* component of 1966, "Klondike Kat," was the worst of all the Total/Leonardo creations, bar none. Klondike Kat was a terminally stupid mountie, sent on a weekly mission by Major Minor (a Terry-Thomas takeoff) to capture cheese-stealing French Canadian mouse Savoir Faire. The six-minute cartoons seemed to be nothing but wall-to-wall annoying catchphrases: "Klondike Kat always gets his mouse"; "Savoir Faire eez every-whaire"; and, knocking the needle off the Nausea Meter, "OOOOOH! I'll make MINCEMEAT outa that mouse!" Both the "Klondike Kat" and "Go Go Gophers" reruns were bundled together into a separately telecast half hour in 1968, CBS' *Go Go Gophers*. That same year, a pared-down *Underdog*, consisting of four episodes per program starring the titular flying pooch, returned in rerun form to NBC, where it remained a top-rater until 1973.

In syndication, the various *Underdog* components were frequently packaged with those of Jay Ward Productions' *Rocky and His Friends* (q.v.) and *Hoppity Hooper* (q.v.). As mentioned in the notes on *Hoppity*, the fact that Ward and Leonardo/Total used the same Mexico-based Gamma Studios facilities gave the two companies' series a superficial resemblance to one another (at one point, in fact, the playful Gamma folks stuck Bullwinkle into a "Go Go Gophers" adventure). This in turn has led many viewers to believe that the Ward and Leonardo/Total series were made by the same producers.

For once and for all, and despite the emphatic statement of at least one newspaperman TV "expert" that Jay Ward created *Underdog*, Jay Ward Productions and Total Television/Leonardo Productions were *not* produced by the same writing and production talent pool. Just

look at the shows once. Do you really think the creator of "Dudley Do-Right" would have blasphemed that character with "Klondike Kat"?

THE UPA CARTOON SHOW *see* **MR. MAGOO** and **THE GERALD McBOING BOING SHOW**

U.S. OF ARCHIE *see* **THE ARCHIES**

VALLEY OF THE DINOSAURS. CBS: 9/7/1974–9/4/1976. Hanna-Barbera. Executive producers, William Hanna and Joseph Barbera. Creative producer, Iwao Takamoto. Directed by Charles Nichols. Executive story consultant, Myles Wilder. Story editor, Sam Roega. Written by Peter Dixon, Peter Germano, James Henderson, Ernie Kahn, Don Masselink, Dick Robbins, Henry Sharp, Jerry Thomas. Storyboard editors, Clark Haas, Cullen Houghtaling, Lew Marshall, Paul Sommer, Irv Spector, Howard Swift. Animation director, Peter Luschiwitz. Character design, Marty Murphy. Recording director, Wally Burr. Music by Hoyt Curtin. Voices: Mike Road (John Butler); Shannon Farnon (Kim Butler); Margene Fudenna (Katie Butler); Jackie Earle Haley (Greg Butler); Alan Oppenheimer (Gorak); Joan Gardner (Gera); Melanie Baker (Tana); Steacy Bertheau (Lock); and Andrew Parks.

Hanna-Barbera's *Valley of the Dinosaurs* was a "straight" half hour cartoon that came out the same year (1974) as the strangely similar live-actioner *Land of the Lost* (which has in recent years been revived with new episodes). Both the Butler family of *Valley of the Dinosaurs* and the Marshall family of *Land of the Lost* were contemporary vacationers (the Butlers were in South America, the Marshalls in Colorado) who, while traversing river rapids, were sucked by a vortex into a Stone Age setting.

Valley's Butlers—dad John, mom Katie, son Greg and daughter Kim—met a similarly structured cave family: father Gorak, mother Gera, son Lock and daughter Tana. The two family units even had complementary pets: the Butlers' dog Digger and the cave folks' pet stegosaurus Glomb. Though *Valley of the Dinosaurs* was advertised as semi-educational, Hanna-Barbera had no qualms of resurrecting its *Flintstones* (q.v.) conceit of humans' co-existing with dinosaurs. The company got away with this historical gaffe by never making clear whether the Butlers had actually gone back in time or whether they'd simply surfaced in a parallel fantasy world. One publicly avowed purpose of the weekly *Valley of the Dinosaurs* was to explore "a variety of scientific principles and their applications." This was the alleged similar purpose of Krofft's like-vintage *Land of the Lost*, which was created by a linguistics professor and sought to investigate the mysteries of how language and communications developed. Hanna-Barbera's own live-actioner *Korg: 70,000 B.C.*, which *also* premiered in 1974, checked out the accuracy of its depiction of Neanderthal life with natural history museum curators (this, again, was from the folks who brought us *Flintstones*). All this Saturday-morning fascination in the Dawn of Mankind occurred two decades before the much-heralded ABC/Children's Television Workshop cartoon series *Cro* (q.v.), an "educational entertainment" set in the Cro-Magnon era. In point of fact, all three 1974 series did a better, less pretentious job than the self-congratulatory *Cro*.

Valley of the Dinosaurs was particularly deft at demonstrating the proper application of such "new" discoveries as fire, cooking, clothing, utensils and weaponry, all within the natural progression of its well-knit storylines. *Valley* also showed—in a downpedalled, non-strident fashion—how both the Butlers and the cave people could learn from one another. The cave people had to shed their distrust of the "Outsiders" and to rely more on common sense than superstition and blind adherence to retrogressive customs. Conversely, John Butler had to overcome his condescending attitude and genuinely respect the cave people before trying to teach them the ways of civilization. In traditional fashion, it was the wives and the kids from each group—the ones with least clout in a patriarchal society—who got along best and learned to coexist the quickest. Thus, the program came out on the side of women and youth without stooping to proselytizing, and without demeaning the adult male population.

Of course, this *was* 1974 television and *Valley of the Dinosaurs* was a Hanna-Barbera project, so the series wasn't quite free from flaws. While the dinosaur animation was well above average, character animation and design were sketchy and the artwork on the level of a second-grade historical textbook. The writers dragged out the old "jungle movie" cliché of having the cave folks speaking in flowery, metaphoric sentences, minus such contractions as "I'm" and "You're." The Butler children, particularly daughter Kim, wisecracked far too often for their own good and at the most inappropriate moments. And has anyone ever found *genuinely* funny a Hanna-Barbera "funny pet" like the bothersome Digger?

Still, the 16-episode *Valley of the Dinosaurs* was a laudatory example of melding entertainment with education, a marked contrast to its 1993 grandchild, the wildly overrated *Cro*. Without bombarding the viewer with "message" dialogue or prosocial propaganda, *Valley of the Dinosaurs* did a topnotch job demonstrating how divergent cultural groups could live together by learning together.

VIDEO POWER. Syndicated: 1990. Saban/Acclaim/Bohbot. Created by Allen J. Bohbot. Produced by Winston Richard. Developed by Jack Diesker. Animation directed by Stephen Martiniere. Story editor, Jack Olesker. Written by Gregory E. Fishbach, Robert Holmes. Written by Winston Richard, Gregory E. Fishbach, Robert Holmes. Animation facilities: KK C&D Asia. Live action produced and directed by Kevin S. Murray; written by Frank Marrone, McPaul Smith and John TenEyck. Live action cast: Stivi Paskoski (Johnny Arcade). Voices: Mike Donovan, Terry Klassen, Richard Newman, Lee Jeffrey, Jason Michas, John Novak, Dale Wilson.

Video Power was a partly live-action, partly animated arcade of the air; in fact, the hero, a joystick-wielding videogame junkie, was named Johnny Arcade.

Portrayed in the live-action wraparounds by Stivi Paskoski, Johnny Arcade introduced the daily, half hour *Video Power*'s cartoon sequences, then showed up at the end of each episode to display filmclips and offer critiques of the newest video games on the market. Johnny also showed up in pen-and-ink form in the animated segment, which took up most of the program, wherein we were witness to the "team" adventures of several superpowered characters—all, of course, based on established arcade games.

From the Acclaim video company (coproducer of the series) came Kuros, a Sword 'n' Sorcery type, and Kwirk, a little Pac-Man-type humanized ball with glasses and crewcut (something of a precursor to Sega's *Sonic the Hedgehog* [q.v.]). From the Midway Magic Factory came Tyrone, a limber basketball player. Big Foot, an anthropomorphic "monster truck," was the property of Bigfoot 4×4 Ltd. And Max Force, a ninja, had been invented by Williams Electronics—the company also responsible for *Video Power*'s villains Mr. Big, Joe Rockhead and Spike Rush.

Video Power lasted two seasons—more than can be said for the cartoon portion of the show, which all in all was the series' least appealing aspect. For season two, the program went fully live-action as an audience participation series, still hosted by "Johnny Arcade," who was still portrayed by Stivi Paskoski.

VISIONARIES: KNIGHTS OF THE MAGICAL LIGHT. Syndicated: 1987. Marvel/Sunbow/Hasbro-Claster/TMS Productions. Executive producers: Joe Bacal, Yutaka Fujioka, Tom Griffin. Creative director, Jay Bacal. Creative consultant, Osamu Dezaki. Production executives: Eiji Katayama, Sander Schwartz. Produced by Jim Duffy, Tadahito Matsumoto. Supervising producers, Barry Glasser and Sachiko Tsuneda. Animation directors, Yoshinori Kanada and Osamu Nabeshima. Music composed and conducted by Thomas Chase and Steve Rucker. Title song by Ford Kinder and Anne Bryant. Animation facilities, Tokyo Movie Co. Ltd. Original concept licensed by Abrams/Gentile Entertainment Inc. Voices: Neil Ross (Leoric); Michael McConnohie (Ectar/Lexor); Bernard Erhard (Cyrotek); Jim Cummings (Witterquick/Bearer of Knowledge); Hal Rayle (Arzon/Wisdom Owl); Beau Weaver (Feryl); Susan Blu (Galadria); Chris Latta (Darkstorm/Cravex); Jonathan Harris (Mortredd); Peter Cullen (Cindarr); Roscoe Lee Browne (Reekon); Jennifer Darling (Virulina); Malachi Throne (Narrator); and Ellen Gerstel.

Visionaries had a curious pre-release "teaser" at the American International Toy Fair in New York in February 1987. A representative of Hasbro, dressed as an extraterrestrial, set up a booth to display similarly garbed toy action figures, each decorated with holographic designs. At the end of his pitch, the ersatz alien added, almost as an afterthought, "As you know, all of these toys will be backed up with a new half-hour show this fall called *The Air Raiders/Visionaries Show.*" The man from Hasbro was half right. The show premiered as *Visionaries: Knights of the Magical Light.*

The premise of this 13-week, half-hour syndicated series would have had us believe that the many suns around which the planet Prysmos orbited suddenly formed an alignment. Results were disastrous: The cosmic upheavals threw the technologically sophisticated Prysmos back to "Dark Ages" where magic ruled (this "old" world was a hemstitched combination of Medieval and Machine Age). Merklyn, master of magic incarnate, rallied the Knights of the Magical Light, or "Spectral Knights," or "Visionaries" (choose one, and no looking at your neighbor's paper), to fight the wicked Darkling Lords, for whoever controlled the magic controlled the world.

Despite the Darklings, the tone on *Visionaries* was light. The vanity-ridden villains bitched at each other, while the Spectrals were stymied with protocol, red tape and self-serving "citizens guilds" whenever going about the mundane business of saving their world. The "Bearer of Knowledge," an oracle who motivated the plots, was a pompous bore, causing both the good guys and the bad guys to doze off. Heroes and villains also expressed equal distate and impatience with the many rhymed oaths, deep curses and secret spells through which they had to wade to get to the end of a plotline. Even Merklyn was a bellyacher, grumbling that he was only able to afford the "cheap, abridged" version of the Book of Magic.

One felt while watching *Visionaries*, however, that Hasbro would have been satisfied had the series dispensed with its bursts of originality and simply stuck to pitching the toys and action figures. The major selling angle on each Visionaries costume was a holographic emblem, exhibiting a simulated 3-D picture, just like their toystore counterparts. The characters also carried holographic banners, likewise duly converted into playthings—which, I've been told by preteen experts in the plaything-consumption field, were quite fragile, and not nearly as sturdy as those seen on TV.

At least *Visionaries* made a valiant effort to look like a separately functioning cartoon entity rather than a mere advertising adjunct. Still, we'd have to wait for *Teenage Mutant Ninja Turtles* (q.v.) before both cartoon and toys could score long-lasting success with equanimity on their own individual merits.

VOLTRON: DEFENDER OF THE UNIVERSE. Syndicated: 1984. World Events. Executive producer, Peter Keefe. Produced by Steve Sterling. Written by Jameson Brewer, Howard Albrecht, Coslough Johnson, Stan Oliver, Jack Paritz, Michael Walker and Sol Weinstein. Music by Dale Schacker. Original animation by Toei Co. Ltd. Voices: Jack Angel, Michael Bell, Peter Cullen, Neil Ross, B. J. Ward, Lennie Weinrib.

The Japanese-produced *Voltron* was set on the Planet Arus in the 25th century. A giant, flying samurai robot was transformed by covetous space witch Merla into five individual units, each in the shape of a lion. Meanwhile, reptile alien Zarkon (who wore French Court dress, like the rest of the "nobles" on this series) endeavored to overtake Arus, with the help of Merla. The five-person Space Explorers team, led by young Lance, were compelled to journey to the Castle of Lions to reassemble Voltron as an "Ultimate Super Robot," to be used against Zarkon and the Dark Forces (such robot-reclamation jobs were frequent in the world of Japanimation). Along for the ride as a Space Explorer was Arus' young Princess Alura (read "Princess Leia," as in *Star Wars*), abetted by her loyal retainers Coran and Nanny.

First seen on Japanese television in the early 1980s under the title *Voltus 5*, *Voltron*'s animation was rendered in the time-honored Toei Studios technique of dissolving from one extreme pose to another. The project was test marketed in the U.S. as a 90-minute special in 1983, then syndicated by the World Events company as a half hour daily to 76 markets the following season. The series followed the *Transformers* and *He-Man* pattern of being built into the merchandising of such toy weaponry as the "Electrothermoblaster." The previously built-up *Star Wars* momentum enabled *Voltron* to have reasonable success, both in first run and as a weekend rerun attraction on cable's Family Channel into the 1990s.

VOYAGES OF DR. DOOLITTLE. Syndicated: 1984. A Knack Television Production/20th Century–Fox. Voices: John Stephenson (Dr. Doolittle); B. J. Ward (Tommy Stubbins); Jeannie Elias (Maggie Thompson); and G. Stanley Jones, William Callaway, Ralph James, Jerry Dexter and Linda Gary.

Voyages of Dr. Doolittle would have been bracketed in this book with the other cartoon series based on Hugh Lofting's "talk to the animals" physician (see *Further Adventures of Dr. Doolittle*), had my research been able to determine exactly when and where *Voyages* was syndicated. Short of that, I can only repeat what cartoon historian Jeff Lenburg has written about the 13-episode *Voyages of Dr. Doolittle* in his encyclopedia of cartoons. Reportedly, this half hour weekly series paired Dr. Doolittle with two young folks, Tommy Stubbins and Maggie Thompson, in a round-the-world journey wherein they touched bases with such curious creatures as the Pushmi-Pullyu (two heads, no tail) and "The Dragon of Barbary."

Voyages of Dr. Doolittle was not, so far as I can determine, syndicated in the Milwaukee or Chicago area, so I'll trust the reliable Mr. Lenburg that the information in the preceding paragraph is correct.

VYTOR THE STARFIRE CHAMPION. Syndicated: 1989. Calico/World Events. Voices: Michael Horton (Vytor); Liz Georges (Skyla/Lyria); Peter Cullen (Myzor); Peter Cullen (Eldor); Neil Ross (Targil); Allison Argo (Baboose); Patrick Fraley (Windchaser/Mutoids).

Vytor the Starfire Champion was the first collaborative production for the Calico and Zodiac cartoon concerns, though *Widget, the World Watcher* (q.v.) was the first such collaboration to become successful. The five-part miniseries *Vytor* spotlighted the teenaged title character and his girlfriend Skyla, both *Star Wars*-type space travellers. *Vytor* was thematically linked to Calico-Zodiac's later environmentally correct *Widget* in that Vytor had to reclaim the Starfire Orb, a pro-ecology energy source, from the hands of plunderers.

WACKY AND PACKY see **UNCLE CROC'S BLOCK**

WACKY RACES. CBS: 9/14/1968–9/5/1970. Hanna-Barbera/Heatter-Quigley. Executive producers, William Hanna and Joseph Barbera. Creative producer, Iwao Takamoto. Directed by Charles Nichols. Background styling by Walt Peregoy. Music by Hoyt Curtin. Voices: Daws Butler (Peter Perfect/Sergeant/Big Gruesome/ Red Max/Rufus Ruffcut/Rock and Gravel Slag); Paul Winchell (Dick Dastardly/Private Pinkley); Don Messick (Muttley/Sawtooth/Prof. Pat Pending/"Ring-a-Ding"/ Little Gruesome); John Stephenson (Luke and Blubber Bear/General); Janet Waldo (Penelope Pitstop); Mel Blanc (The Ant Hill Mob); David Willock (Narrator).

Wacky Races was the first of Hanna-Barbera's "never ending race" programs, the purpose of which was to keep things moving and the audience involved without being encumbered by such nuisances as strong plotlines and first-rate animation. The series was also part of Fred Silverman's plan to bring a full-bodied return of comedy to the Saturday morning cartoon field after several seasons of Superhero domination.

The point of the cross-country race (to earn the coveted title of "World's Wackiest Racer"), and the individual storylines of the 13 Wacky Races half hours, were essentially unimportant. What stuck in the memory banks of the home audience was the rich variety of unorthodox characters and goofy automotive vehicles.

Most of the contestants were eccentric but basically "clean" racers. Professor Pat Pending, an inventor, drove the Ring a Ding Convert-a-Car, an anthropomorphous contraption. The Ant Hill Mob, toughlooking but toothless midget mobster types, tooled about in their Bulletproof Bomb. Hillbillies Luke and Blubber Bear putputted about in their Arkansas Chugabug. Rufus Ruffcut and Sawtooth maintained their sawmill motif with their Buzz Wagon. A pair of militarists known only as the General and the Sergeant were chauffeured by Private Pinkley in the Army Surplus Special (Hanna-Barbera's comment on Vietnam? I don't think so). Cavemen Rocky and Gravel Slag took a cue from fellow Hanna-Barbera contractee Fred Flintstone by utilizing a Bouldermobile. Peter Perfect, a takeoff on

Tony Curtis' dazzlingly dauntless Great Leslie in Wacky Races' movie inspiration The Great Race (1965), piloted the modestly named Turbo Terrific. The Red Max, a Baron Von Richthofen ripoff, was landbound in his Crimson Haybailer. And the Gruesome Twosome, 1968's variation on The Addams Family (q.v.), rounded the curbs in the Creepy Coupe.

That all these characters and their vehicles were defined in bold, intensely individualized strokes would suggest that Fred Silverman was casting about for potential star material, to be spun off into one or more separate series — a trick Silverman was up to in prime time into the 1970s, as witness such All in the Family stepchildren as Maude and The Jeffersons and such Happy Days progeny as Laverne and Shirley and Joanie Loves Chachi. But the only Wacky Races participants who were able to stand on their own as series headliners were the ones we've saved till last: Pearl White–like heroine Penelope Pitstop, who drove her Compact Pussycat (with the Ant Hill Mob in support) into her own Perils of Penelope Pitstop (q.v.); and Dick Dastardly, the only blatantly dishonest Wacky Races contestant — he drove the weapon-laden Mean Machine, accompanied by a sniggering dog named Muttley — whose first of many Hanna-Barbera spinoffs was 1969's Dastardly and Muttley and Their Flying Machines (see also Yogi Bear and Wake, Rattle and Roll for more on the dastardly Dastardly).

While Fred Silverman kept one eye on the future by using Wacky Races as galloping pilot series, he also drew on what had worked for him in the past. Recalling his successful promotional efforts to attract viewership during his days in local Chicago and New York City television, Silverman saw to it that Wacky Races was tied in with a home-participation contest. The winners would receive genuine plastic action figures of the Wacky Races stars, suitable for losing behind the davenport.

WAIT TILL YOUR FATHER GETS HOME. Syndicated: 1972. Hanna-Barbera/Rhodes Communications. Executive producers, William Hanna and Joseph Barbera. Produced by R. S. Allen and Harvey Bullock. Associate producer, Zoran Janjic. Animation director, Peter Luschwitz. Production design, Iwao Takamoto. Character design, Marty Mur-

550   Wait Till Your Father Gets Home

phy. Story director, Don Christensen. Dialogue director, Alan Dinehart. Music by Richard Bowden. Voices: Tom Bosley (Harry Boyle); Joan Gerber (Irma Boyle); Lennie Weinrib (Chet Boyle); Tina Holland (Alice Boyle); Jackie [Earle] Haley, Willie Aames (Jamie Boyle); Jack Burns (Ralph); and Pat Harrington Jr., Gil Herman, Don Adams, Jonathan Winters, Monty Hall, Phyllis Diller, Joe E. Ross, Don Knotts, and Rich Little.

Wait Till Your Father Gets Home was Hanna-Barbera's contribution to the Prime Time Access Rule of 1971. This controversial FCC legislation dictated that the three networks, who once had commandeered a full three-and-one-half hours of each evening's TV schedule, were compelled to give back a half-hour's airtime to the locals per evening, usually from 7:30 to 8 P.M. EST. Local stations in the top 50 television markets weren't permitted to broadcast the off-network reruns that had proved so lucrative in the past in the new "access" slot, but were instead urged to telecast original, first-run programming. The FCC's strategy behind this was to encourage fresh ideas and concepts in the 7:30 P.M. slot, in an effort to mollify politicians and lobbyists who complained that TV was a copycat medium. Before the economic pressures of television proved the critics correct and the Prime Time Access offerings dwindled down to lookalike game shows (*Wheel of Fortune*), newsmagazines (*Entertainment Tonight*) and tabloids (*Hard Copy*), syndicators tried their best to meet the demands of diversification. The years 1971–1981 saw a handful of 7:30 P.M. smash hits like *The Muppet Show, Sha Na Na, In Search Of* and *Wild Wild World of Animals,* countered by countless misses like *Don Adams' Screen Test, Dusty's Trail,* and *Ozzie's Girls* — and a few modest successes, lasting beyond the usual single season, like *Wait Till Your Father Gets Home.*

This series was not only the first Hanna-Barbera prime time cartoon since 1970's unlamented *Where's Huddles?* (q.v.) but also the *only* weekly animated property spawned by the Prime Time Access Rule. (Disney's syndicated *The Mouse Factory,* also from 1972, was as much live-action as animation.) *Wait Till Your Father Gets Home* can be summed up as a suburban spin on the CBS live-actioner *All in the Family,* featuring the Boyle family rather

than the Bunkers. Harry Boyle, conservative manager of a restaurant supply firm, found himself perpetually at odds with his broadminded wife Irma and his shaggy-haired liberal children Alice and Chet. Harry's long-suffering dialogue was ideally recited by voice actor Tom Bosley, in what was practically a dress rehearsal for Bosley's longer sitcom-dad hitch on *Happy Days.*

Unlike *All in the Family,* where we were encouraged to regard Archie Bunker as an object of ridicule, Harry Boyle was drawn sympathetically; he couldn't *help* being sympathetic considering how revolting, and homely, his kids were. In fact, audiences viewing the pilot episode (run as an installment of the comedy anthology *Love, American Style* in early 1972) felt that Harry was so unfairly endowed with a dysfunctional family that a third child, youngest son Jaimie Boyle, was hastily written into the series. Harry had an ally in Jaimie, the only Boyle who adhered to the "Father Knows Best" theory.

Since Harry Boyle was essentially the hero of *Wait Till Your Father Gets Home,* he was never as abusive or ignorant as *All in the Family*'s Archie. That particular knee-jerk role was assumed by the Boyle family's jerk-jerk neighbor, a "Commies under the bed" type named Ralph who wore survivalist-style camouflage and a full magazine of bullets, and who constantly hid in the bushes for fear of enemy reprisal. Ralph's paranoia-peppered voice was flawlessly supplied by actor/writer/producer Jack Burns.

Superficially, *Wait Till Your Father Gets Home* looked nothing like a "typical" Hanna-Barbera series. The old-line sameness that had encroached upon their character design in the early 1970s was replaced by the James Thurber–like figure stylings conceived by magazine cartoonist Marty Murphy, while the background art eschewed the studio's usual "safe" representational technique for a bold, European-cartoon sparseness. And even though the series suffered its studio's usual overreliance on repetition, cliché and pointless slapstick, *Wait Till Your Father Gets Home* contained some of the best and most mature comedy writing Hanna-Barbera ever exhibited. Sample: when teenaged Alice Boyle is lured into a commune by a phony guru, dad Harry goes off to retrieve her. The guru turns to his

Harry Boyle expresses disdain for the 70s; in this he's not alone. From Hanna-Barbera's *Wait Till Your Father Gets Home.*

henchman and says, "I'll bet you ten dollars I know the first thing he's going to say to her." Cut to Harry and daughter. Harry softly remonstrates "I can't begin to tell you what this is doing to your mother." Cut back to the guru, who smirkingly collects his ten-spot.

At times, the tone of *Wait Till Your Father Gets Home* was so adult that the series appeared to be functioning as a steam valve for all of Hanna-Barbera's past "standards and practices" problems on the networks. Glancing at the episode which subliminally suggested that the Boyles' neighbors were drug-indulging, wife-swapping "senior swingers," or at the weekly opening-credits montage which intimated that Alice Boyle had been date-raped, the average viewer felt an acute disorientation: Could this be the same studio that brought us the *Flintstones* and *Scooby-Doo*?

The National Association for Better Broadcasting likewise seemed out of character in its assessment of *Wait Till Your Father Gets Home*, suggesting that perhaps its standards were more liberal than indicated in earlier cartoon-series critiques: "Whatever else can be said about this show, it is unquestionably the most intriguing half-hour weekly series on television, including anything they do for the children on Saturday mornings. The characters are clear-cut; the dialogue is sharp and satiric. It's for adults, but mature youngsters will enjoy it too."

Perhaps the establishment-oriented

NABB was responding to *Father's* basic status-quo ideological slant: No matter how "liberal" the dialogue and situations, the characters would emerge from their experiences by returning to the common-sense conservatism of Harry Boyle. Hanna and Barbera could talk like Norman Lear, but way deep down could not think like him.

The audience appeal of *Wait Till Your Father Gets Home* was broadened by a guest-star policy, featuring the voices and animated facsimiles of such evergreen celebrities as Phyllis Diller, Don Adams, Jonathan Winters and Rich Little. There were also occasional *à clef* lampoons of well known 1970s personalities—one of which led to a lawsuit from a prominent California used car dealer, who felt that he was being maligned by a caricatured crooked auto huckster.

Nationally sponsored by Chevrolet and picked up in syndication by the five NBC owned-and-operated stations and thereafter by virtually all major and secondary markets, *Wait Till Your Father Gets Home* lasted two seasons—48 episodes in all, the most successful Hanna-Barbera prime time series since *The Flintstones* (q.v.). However, many stations in smaller markets, already overloaded with Prime Time Access product in 1973, purchased *Father's* first season only.

WAKE, RATTLE AND ROLL. Syndicated: 1990. Disney Channel (retitled JUMP RATTLE AND ROLL): 1991. Four Point Entertainment/Hanna-Barbera. Executive producers: David Kirschner, Sholi Ghalayini, Ron Ziskin. Animation producers: David Kirschner, Paul Sabella. Producer, live-action: Bruce McKay. Producer, FENDER BENDER 500: Kay Wright. Producer, MONSTER TAILS: Cos Anzilotti. Director, live-action: Doug Ivens. Story editors, Bill Matheny, Don Dougherty. Puppeteers: Alan Coulter, Mark Eyer. Music by Bob Mithoff. Components: **1. Live-action sequences.** CAST: R. J. Williams (Sam); Ebonie Smith (K. C.); Terri Ivens (Debbie); Avery Schreiber (Grandpa Quirk); Tim Lawrence (DECKS); Rob Paulsen (Voice of DECKS). **2. FENDER BENDER 500.** Voices: Greg Burson (Yogi Bear); Arnold Stang (Top Cat); Marvin Kaplan (Choo Choo); Paul Winchell (Dick Dastardly); Don Messick (Muttley); Shadoe Stevens

(Announcer); and John Mariano, Allan Melvin, Neil Ross, John Stephenson, Janet Waldo, and Patric Zimmerman. 3. **MONSTER TAILS.** Voices: Charlie Adler, Tim Curry, Dick Gautier, Pat Musick, Frank Welker, Jonathan Winters.

Wake, Rattle and Roll, slated for early morning syndication by Hanna-Barbera, was a daily half hour collection of cartoons—some old, some new—with live action wraparounds. In the live (actually taped) segments, R. J. Williams portrayed computer-happy teen Sam Baxter, who hung out in his family's basement, watching cartoons courtesy of D.E.C.K.S., a "Yo, dude!" talking robot built mostly from old VCR remnants. Occasional visitors to Sam's private sanctum were his friend K. C., a young African American girl; Sam's Grandpa Quirk, a certified (and certifiable) eccentric; and Sam's older sister Debbie, a tyrannical tyro whose entrances were presaged by D.E.C.K.S.' "Debbie Detector," which allowed Sam time to run for cover.

Somewhere in the basement was a sort of time machine, which frequently spewed forth famous visitors from the past and a few odd ducks from the future. These appearances would segue into the educational portion of *Wake, Rattle and Roll*, which consisted of painless historical, geographical and scientific lessons elucidated and illustrated by D.E.C.K.S. "This is clearly the freshest idea that Hanna-Barbera had had in years," noted John Kiesewetter of the Cincinnati *Enquirer*, "proof positive that the company's president, David Kirschner, has big plans for the little Flintstones factory." It was also the sort of "edu-tainment" that would more or less evaporate after Kirschner and the Flintstones factory parted company a few years later.

Two principal cartoon components interrupted the live action on *Wake, Rattle and Roll*. "Fender Bender 500" was Hanna-Barbera's by-now standard "never ending race" with the equally standard allstar cast: Yogi Bear, Huckleberry Hound, Top Cat, Dastardly and Muttley, and most of the rest of the Hanna-Barbera menagerie (see individual entries for more on the characters mentioned in the previous sentence). Shadoe Stevens, erstwhile D. J./actor and offscreen announcer for the 1980s edition of *Hollywood Squares*, assumed the narrator role usually taken in these celebrity-race cartoons by Gary Owens. Nothing really new here, except the occasional good throwaway gag, such as a long shot of the hills of Scotland, which were landscaped in plaid.

The second animated component, "Monster Tails," was a zoological variation of the "sons and daughters and cousins of movie monsters" format previously seen in such efforts as *The Drak Pack* (q.v.) and the "Mini-Monsters" segment of *Comic Strip* (q.v.). This time we were introduced to the famous monsters' *pets*, all displaying their masters' mordant character traits. The names were fairly self-explanatory, but we'll belabor the obvious here: Catula was Dracula's pet feline; Frankenhound and Elsa were the Frankenstein Monster's dogs (the name Elsa, and the character's cotton-candy hairdo, were of course inspired by actress Elsa Lanchester, "leading lady" of the 1935 film *Bride of Frankenstein*); Dr. Heckell was another dog, who like his master occasionally lapsed into a snarling alter ego, "Mr. Snide"; and on it went, all under the watchful eye of Igor Jr., the nerdy son of Dr. Frankenstein's hunchbacked assistant.

When *Wake, Rattle and Roll* resurfaced in 1991 on the Disney Channel, it was moved to a later timeslot with its title logically altered to *Jump, Rattle and Roll*. Included in this package were reruns of several earlier Hanna-Barbera creations, including *The Flintstones* (q.v.) and "Undercover Elephant" (see *The C. B. Bears*).

WALLY GATOR. Syndicated: 1962. Hanna-Barbera. Voices: Daws Butler (Wally Gator); Don Messick (Mr. Twiddles).

One-third of the *Hanna-Barbera New Cartoons* package released to TV in 1962 (see also *Lippy the Lion* and *Touche Turtle*), *Wally Gator* was that project's variation on H-B's *Yogi Bear* (q.v.). Perhaps recognizing this, several local stations, more prominently Chicago's WGN, ran the trio of new cartoons under the blanket title *Wally Gator and Friends* or some such variation, hoping that the *Yogi* ratings lightning would strike again. Tribune Broadcasting, WGN's parent company, covered its bets by having its sister newspaper, the Chicago *Tribune*, shamelessly plug *Wally* at the slightest provocation — even in the "Letters to the Editor" column. Wally Gator was a bipedal alligator who sounded like comedian Ed Wynn (a special favorite of cartoonmakers, as witness Terrytoons' theatrical star Gandy Goose, and Captain Peter Peachfuzz on Jay Ward's *Rocky and His Friends*). The opening title sequence of Wally's cartoons showed him darting through the Everglades in a motorboat, while a chorus sang a paean to "the swingin' alligator in the swamp." Curious this was, because the Wally Gator we saw in his 52 five-minute starring cartoons was firmly ensconced in a city zoo, whence he constantly plotted his escape, with nary a swamp or boat in sight. In the tradition of role-model Yogi Bear, Wally wore a hat and necktie, and spent most of his waking hours trying to outwit his "Ranger Smith" counterpart, in this instance zookeeper Mr. Twiddles.

WE ALL HAVE TALES. Showtime: May 1991–. Rabbit Ears Video. Executive producers, Mark Sottnick and Mike Pogue. Produced by Ken Hoin. Directed by C. W. Rogers. Animation camera/editor: Mark Forker.

We All Have Tales was a group of half hours based on children's stories from all over the world, produced by Rabbit Ears Video for simultaneous TV and videocassette release. Like other projects in the Rabbit Ears manifest (see *American Heroes and Legends* and *Storybook Classics*), these *Tales* weren't technically animated, but instead utilized dissolves, camera pans and swift cuts from one still picture to another. The illustrations were lovingly rendered in the style appropriate to each story: For example, the Japanese tale "The Boy Who Drew Cats" was drawn in black ink on rice paper.

Also like other Rabbit Ears productions, *We All Have Tales* boasted celebrity narrators. William Hurt read the aforementioned "Boy Who Drew Cats"; Robin Williams recited "The Fool and the Flying Ship"; Catherine O'Hara lent a convincing brogue to the story of "Finn McCoul"; and, as a Christmas-season attraction, Michael Caine was heard relating the fable "King Midas and the Golden Touch."

Others on the *Tales* honor roll included Ben Kingsley, Max von Sydow, Whoopi Goldberg, and Michael Palin. The celebrity reciters were selected not only for their talents but for their kinship to the material. African American actress Whoopi Goldberg was matched up with

"Kai and the Kola Nuts," an African folktale (which she rattled off in an astonishing display of vocal calisthenics, enacting roles ranging from small boy to village elder), while Ben Kingsley, of East Indian descent, was called upon to read "The Tiger and the Brahmin."

We All Have Tales was telecast irregularly on the Showtime cable service over a two-year period—13 "tales" in all. (The series began introducing new episodes in early 1994.)

WHAT'S NEW, MR. MAGOO? *see* **MR. MAGOO**

WHEELIE AND THE CHOPPER BUNCH. NBC: 9/7/1974–8/30/1975. Hanna-Barbera. Executive producers, William Hanna and Joseph Barbera. Creative producer, Iwao Takamoto. Directed by Charles Nichols. Executive story consultant, Myles Wilder. Story editor, Ray Parker. Written by Larz Bourne, Len Janson, Chuck Menville, Robert Ogle, Dalton Sandifer. Character design by Jerry Eisenberg and David High. Music by Hoyt Curtin. Musical director, Paul DeKorte. Voices: Frank Welker (Wheelie/Chopper); Judy Strangis (Rota Ree); Don Messick (Scrambles); Paul Winchell (Revs); Lennie Weinrib (Hi-Riser); and Rolinda York.

Collectively, *Wheelie and the Chopper Bunch* and Hanna-Barbera's other anthropomorphic-automobile series (see *Wonder Wheels* and *Speed Buggy*) tend to make one's mind wander back to all those theatrical cartoons of the 1930s, 1940s and 1950s in which cars would act out human plots and exhibit human traits and emotions. Note that none of these earlier one-shot cartoons resulted in starring series for any of those funny autos. That's because the joke is good for about, oh, six minutes. *Wheelie and the Chopper Bunch*, however, lasted 13 episodes, one half hour per week.

Title-car Wheelie looked like a Volkswagen, perhaps as a nod to the Disney feature film *The Love Bug*. He didn't speak, expressing himself instead with a series of horn blasts and a versatile windshield which displayed his inner impulses and emotions: a beating heart, an "idea" light bulb, the illuminated word "CHARGE," and so forth.

Not content with borrowing from *The*

Love Bug, Wheelie also lifted a bit from the motorcycle gang "B" movies of the late 1960s in having the protagonist menaced by the villainous Choppers, a gang of rebel motorbikes; Chopper, the leader, wore a spiked German helmet on his handlebars. In contrast to Wheelie, the Choppers had reams of dialogue, notably the gang's silliest member Revs, for whom voice actor Paul Winchell provided his patented "woo-woo" imitation of character comedian Hugh Herbert. Wheelie's lookalike "girl" friend was Rota Ree (*not* Rota Lee, as has sometimes been claimed; that would have been baiting a defamation suit from real-life actress Ruta Lee). She spoke in the voice of actress Judy Strangis, who was also employed at the time of *Wheelie and the Chopper Bunch* as Mean Mary Jean, spokesperson in the live-action Dodge car commercials. Strangis may well have been the only performer of 1974 who pitched automobiles for one studio and then portrayed one in another.

You know where the rest of this is going. The "law" on *Wheelie* consisted of talking police cars; a fork lift performed manual labor; an old Model T was in danger of being carted off to a senior citizens' home. We repeat, it was about six minutes' worth of a premise. As boredom inevitably set in, viewers of *Wheelie and the Chopper Bunch* could treat themselves to Fernando Montealegre's superb background art, rendered in an American Primitive style with eyecatching, opaque color spheres representing hills and foliage. Ideally of course, one is not supposed to be watching the background, but that's about all *Wheelie and the Chopper Bunch* had to offer past its first episode.

WHERE'S HUDDLES? CBS: 7/1/ 1970–9/9/1970; 7/1971–9/5/1971. Produced by William Hanna, Joseph Barbera and Alex Lovy. Directed by Hanna, Barbera and Charles Nichols. Principal writers, Harvey Bullock and Ray Allen. Music by Hoyt Curtin. Voices: Cliff Norton (Ed Huddles); Mel Blanc (Bubba McCoy); Marie Wilson (Penny McCoy); Paul Lynde (Claude Pertwee); Alan Reed (Mad Dog Maloney); Jean VanderPyl (Marge Huddles); Herb Jeffries (Freight Train); Dick Enberg (Announcer).

Hanna-Barbera's weekly, half hour *Where's Huddles?* was a quickie summer replacement for CBS's prime-time *Glen Campbell Goodtime Hour.* The *Huddles* characters were mostly members of the Rhinos (not *really* rhinos, but human beings), a professional football team. Ed Huddles was the star player, Bubba McCoy his "Barney Rubble" best chum, and Mad Dog Maloney his coach. Stories revolved around Ed's and Bubba's home life, and their efforts to raise money in order to augment their low salaries as football players (this was evidently intended as the "fantasy" element of the series).

Several of the *Flintstones* (q.v.) personnel were back on microphone: Mel Blanc as Bubba, Alan Reed as Mad Dog, and Jean VanderPyl as Marge Huddles. Comic actor Paul Lynde, rapidly becoming a Hanna-Barbera regular (see *The Perils of Penelope Pitstop* and *The Cattanooga Cats*), was heard as Ed Huddles' prissy neighbor Pertwee. Newcomers to the voiceover fold included Cliff Norton, versatile monologist of *Garroway at Large* and *Funny Manns* fame, as Ed. Marie Wilson, the archetypal "dumb blonde" of many a 1930s, 40s and 50s movie and TV show, played Penny McCoy; it was Wilson's last role before her death in 1972 (the series reunited the actress with Alan Reed, a costar from her days as radio's *My Friend Irma*). And Herb Jeffries, a popular singer, former vocalist for the Duke Ellington orchestra, and one of Hollywood's few black cowboy stars of the 1930s, portrayed Rhinos teammate Freight Train.

The visual design of *Where's Huddles?* was typical of Hanna-Barbera's 1970s work: rough-hewn and scribbly, as though the producers had decided to film the pencil tests rather than the cels. As for the plotlines, originality was hardly a consideration. Virtually every story had been used before on *The Flintstones* or some other H-B effort. The most outrageous remake was the *Where's Huddles?* episode "To Catch a Thief," a virtual scene-by-scene copy of the 1961 *Flintstones* installment "Wilma's Vanishing Money," which had *previously* been reworked in 1964 as an episode of *The Danny Thomas Show!*

The eminently forgettable 1970 summer appearance of *Where's Huddles?* was supposed to have been a trial run for a projected CBS nighttime slot starting in January of 1971. But except for a cycle of reruns in the summer of that year, *Where's Huddles* vanished after ten episodes. It would be the last Hanna-Barbera prime time network cartoon series until the 1980 revival of *The Flintstones.*

WHERE'S WALDO? CBS: 9/14/1991–9/7/1992. Waldo Film Company/DIC. Executive producers, Martin Handford, Andy Heyward, Peter Orton. Created by Martin Handford. TV Concept: Phil Harnage. Story editor, Bill Matheny. Music by Jeff Barry. Animation facilities: Sei Young Animation. Voices: Townsend Coleman, Jim Cummings, Julian Holloway, Dave Workman, Joe Alaskey, Jack Angel, Jeff Bennett, Gregg Berger, Susan Blu, Carol Channing, Cam Clarke, Brian Cummings, Jennifer Darling, Jeanne Elias, Pat Fraley, Maurice LaMarche, Mary McDonald Lewis, Michele Mariana, John Mariano, Chuck McCann, Pat Musick, Alan Oppenheimer, Rob Paulsen, Jan Rabson, Roger Rose, Susan Silo, Frank Welker.

Created in 1987 by British artist Martin Handford, "Where's Waldo" was a spectacularly popular hidden-picture puzzle book, selling some 15 million copies worldwide. Waldo, a gangly young man wearing glasses, striped turtleneck sweater, and tam-o'-shanter, would be plunked by Handford into a painstakingly rendered illustration aswarm with tiny people and cluttered with shrubbery, machinery, staircases and similar obstructive detail. The reader's mission was to locate the semi-camouflaged Waldo within a set period of time. Handford's best-selling "Waldo" children's books soon begat games, puzzles, a comic strip, and ultimately a weekly half-hour network cartoon series. (And just in case you're wondering how the character earned his name, Martin Handford explained to *TV Guide* that the British nickname for Waldo was Wally, which was "slang for simpleton.")

Your first thought might be that a property which relied upon intensive study of still pictures might not be all that adaptable to animation. We'll bypass snide commentary on previous cartoon series comprised almost exclusively of still pictures (see *Clutch Cargo* and *Speed Racer*) and note that *Where's Waldo* underwent the transition to Saturday morning TV with admirable smoothness. Each week, Waldo, his pet dog Woof, and sometimes his girlfriend Wilma would be off to a far corner of the world, en route to adventure

or a good-samaritan mission. The menace was personified by Waldo's doppelganger, a villainous lookalike named Odlaw. The storylines weren't any great shakes, but were pulled off swiftly and enjoyably, with the narrator utilizing the *Rocky and His Friends* (q.v.) and *Danger Mouse* (q.v.) device of trading quips and insults with the onscreen characters, who gave back as good as they got.

The basic gimmick of the "Where's Waldo?" books was manifested in two weekly "Waldo Minutes," during which the action would freeze for a full 60 seconds while the kids at home were invited to spot Waldo, or a significant clue to the denouement of the week's adventure, within a cluttered picture. This, we were told by CBS, was to encourage other lethargic children to interact with *Where's Waldo*, the better to sharpen their cognitive and deductive powers.

WIDGET, THE WORLD WATCHER. Syndicated: 1990. Calico/Zodiac. Original story and "Widget" character created by Peter Keefe. Supervising producer, Claudia Zeitlin-Burton. Produced and directed by Tom Burton. Produced in association with Kroyer Films, KBS Media Enterprises and Sei Young Animation Co., Ltd. Music by Dale Schacker. Voices: Russi Taylor (Widget); Jim Cummings (MegaBrain); Kath Soucie (Brian/Christine); Dana Hill (Kevin); and Tress MacNeille, Brian Cummings, Cam Clarke, Pat Fraley, Peter Cullen, Cree Summer, Townsend Coleman.

Widget, the World Watcher, like *Captain Planet and the Planeteers* (q.v.), was meant to represent the cartoon industry's battle against worldwide ecological disaster, vintage 1990. But where *Captain Planet* pounded home its statement with a sledgehammer, *Widget* tickled the funny bone—and only *after* amusing its audience did it make its statement.

The title of the series (originally announced in the trade papers as "Widget the *Whale*-watcher," possibly by a publicist with Greenpeace on the brain) was inspired by a derisive comment made by a British network executive. While in the process of turning down the half-hour animated series, the executive told the British-rooted Zodiac Productions (a partnership involving Peter Keefe, Brian Lacey and England's Central Television) that he

Widget, the World Watcher emulates Popeye (with pesticide-free spinach, of course).

wasn't interested in underwriting any character that would result in toy merchandising: "We're not in the business of making widgets, factory things, we're broadcasters in England."

Widget was no "factory thing," but a tiny flying alien being who with his domelike head and squirrel-sized body somewhat resembled *The Flintstones'* (q.v.) "Great Gazoo." Like Gazoo, Widget was an observer from outer space; his concerned planet had appointed him the "world-watcher," sent to earth to battle eco-villains, as well as such non-environmental evils as prejudice, greed and sloth. Widget travelled in the company of his cousin Half-Pint, also an airborne alien; the two were assisted by Mega-Brain, a floating, transparent robot comprised solely of a head and a pair of hands.

While on Earth, Widget enlisted the aid of humans Brian, Kristine and Kevin. After monitoring the safety of zoo animals, wildlife, the terrain and those oppressed, Widget hopscotched to other planets, where the "good" and "bad" characters were drawn in broad, representational strokes, a la *Captain Planet*, but never in such an annoyingly preachy style. If Widget could make his point with lighthearted-ness and laughter, he did so, and left the heavy messages to the pundits and prophets. Perhaps as a result, *Widget, the World Watcher* received an Environmental Media Award long before *Captain Planet* did. And it was Widget, not Captain Planet, who was appointed "official

spokes-alien" by Earth Day International. Additionally, *Widget* both looked and sounded better than the much-vaunted but ponderous *Planet*, doing the young firm of Zodiac proud in its second year of syndication existence. Final proof of *Widget's* superiority over *Planet* came from the marketplace: During the last months of 1990, *Widget, the World Watcher* attained a 3.1 overall rating, compared to *Captain Planet's* 2.2—and this at a time when Zodiac/Calico hadn't the clout of *Planet's* mentor Ted Turner in insisting upon the best local timeslots.

In fact, Zodiac/Calico was then building up goodwill by virtue of its *lack* of clout. In a period during which the Disney company was averse to selling its new *Tale Spin* (q.v.) unless the buying stations also purchased *DuckTales* (q.v.) and *Chip 'n' Dale's Rescue Rangers* (q.v.), local station managers were pleased to deal with a company like Zodiac which didn't insist upon "block booking." One manager spoke for many when he noted "I like [*Widget, the World Watcher*], but I really liked dealing with a distributor who didn't try to run my station for me."

Widget, the World Watcher became a daily strip in 1991. Its place on weekend schedules was taken by another Zodiac/Calico project, *Mr. Bogus* (q.v.).

WILD WEST C.O.W.-BOYS OF MOO MESA. ABC: 9/13/1992–. Gunther-Wahl Productions (1992); Ruby-Spears (1993)/RC Bee/Greengrass Productions/King World. Gunther-Wahl credits: Executive producers, Lee Gunther, Michael Wahl. Supervising producer, Mark Freedman. Produced by Mitch Schauer. Directed by Jeff Hall, Bill Knoll, Lynn Larson. Creative consultants/story editors, Cliff Ruby, Elana Lesser. Developed for television by Bob Carrau. Main title music performed and conducted by Billy Dean. Background music by Gordon Goodwin. Created by Ryan Brown. Ruby-Spears credits: Executive producers, Joe Ruby, Ken Spears. Supervising producer, Mark Freedman. Produced by Glen Hill. Directed by Rich Collado, Daniel De La Vega, Bobtown Productions. Story editors, Rick Fogel and Mark Seidenberg. Animation facilities: Wang Film Production Co., Ltd.; overseas supervisor, Mik Casey. Main title music composed and conducted by Billy Dean. Background music by Dan

Wild West C.O.W.-Boys: and you thought I was making this up.

Savant, Gordon Goodwin and Lisa Goodwin. Voices: Jeff Bennett, Troy Davidson, Pat Fraley, Bill Farmer, Michael Horse, Charity James, Kay Lenz, Danny Mann, Joe Piscopo, Neil Ross (1992-93 and 1993-94 episodes); Robby Benson, Tim Curry, Michael Gough, Michael Greer, Kath Soucie, Sally Struthers and Russi Taylor (1992-93 episodes); Charlie Adler, Jack Angel, Michael Bell, Corey Burton, Ruth Buzzi, Jodi Carlisle, Jim Cummings, David Doyle, Brad Garrett, Ellen Gerstell, Mark Hamill, Dorian Harewood, Kate Mulgrew, Rob Paulsen, Stu Rosen (1993-94 episodes).

One of a brace of 1992 cartoon westerns (see also *Fievel's American Tails*), *Wild West C.O.W.-Boys of Moo Mesa* may well be the only "frontier mutant" series in network cartoon history. We can live with that.

The premise of this weekly half hour was that a crashing comet in Moo Mesa resulted in cows, bulls and various other desert varmints (coyotes, pigs, scorpions, lizards) mutating into humanoids. The heroes were the C.O.W.-Boys, the initials standing for "Code Of the West." Mooing Marshal Moe Montana, aided by deputies Tenderfoot (the talkative one) and the Dakota Dude (the taciturn Eastwood type) as well as the maverick Cowlorado Kid,

protected the tiny bovine community of Cow Town. On the side of wrong were the Wild Wild Bullies and the Gila Hooligans, whose dirty deeds would have continued unlassoed had it been left to corrupt Mayor Bulloney and bumbling Sheriff Terribull. The ladies (heifers?) of the town included demure Miss Lilly, raucous Calamity Kate, and some surprisingly frank depictions of saloon gals, albeit horned and hooved ones.

It sure sounded funny and the background draftsmanship sure captured the old west as we all remember it from the movies, but *Wild West C.O.W.-Boys* was best described by *Entertainment Weekly* as "a bum steer." Viewers were made uncomfortable by the grotesquely musclebound cow characters, who looked as though they'd been pumped full of growth hormones in preparation for a trip to the slaughterhouse. The series' home animation studio, Gunther-Wahl, wasn't happy either, what with *C.O.W.-Boys'* beautifully rendered landscape paintings butting up against the messy plotlines, overripe dialogue and nonexistent character development. Gunther-Wahl vamoosed from the project after one season, citing "creative differences" with ABC.

Ruby-Spears took over for season two with promises of an "all new style," consisting mainly of *all old* slapstick setpieces and sillier storylines, with more attractive character design (a big step forward) and tackier background art (two steps backward). At the very least, Ruby-Spears' *Moo Mesa* animation did move faster than it had in the series' inaugural season, while the new scripts delivered a satisfying supply of laughs.

A note on the title. Officially, the program was *Wild West C.O.W.-Boys of Moo Mesa*, and remained as such on the opening credit logo and in most TV listings. So far as its advertising and publicity were concerned, however, the "Wild West" part went thataway, and the series was known as simply *C.O.W.-Boys of Moo Mesa*.

WILDFIRE. CBS: 9/13/1986–9/5/1987. Hanna-Barbera. Executive producers, William Hanna and Joseph Barbera. Music by Jimmy Webb. Voices: Georgi Irene (Princess Sara); John Vernon (Wildfire); David Ackroyd (John); Jessica Walter (Diabolyn); Rene Auberjonois (Alvinar); Bobby Jacoby (Dorin); Lilly Moon (Ellen); Susan Blu (Brutus); Billy Barty (Dweedle); Victoria Carroll (Mrs. Ashworth).

Straightforward and realistically illustrated, *Wildfire* was a 13-week half hour Hanna-Barbera networker geared to young horse-loving girls. Heroine Sara, a 12-year-old living on a Montana ranch, was whisked away to the other-dimensional land of Dar-Shan by the talking horse Wildfire. Here Sara found she was really a princess, sent to the mortal world during her infancy to protect her from villains. An amulet Sara wore around her neck both protected her from harm and gave her supernatural powers. Wicked sorceress Diabolyn wanted the amulet, and this was where the plotline took off. Assisting Sara in warding off Diabolyn and regaining the throne of Dar-Shan were Wildfire's equestrian companions Dorin, Brutus and Alvinar.

WILL THE REAL JERRY LEWIS PLEASE SIT DOWN? ABC: 9/12/1970–9/2/1972. Filmation. Produced by Lou Scheimer and Norm Prescott. Directed by Hal Sutherland. Written by Bill Danch, Bill Ryan, Len Janson, Chuck Menville, Jack Mendelson, and (allegedly) Jerry Lewis. Music by Yvette Blais and Jeff Michael. Voices: David L. Lander (Jerry Lewis); Jane Webb (Geraldine Lewis/

Rhonda); Howard Morris (Mr. Blunderbuss/Ralph Rotten Lewis/Won Ton Son/ Prof. Lewis/Hong Kong Lewis/Uncle Seadog).

Will the Real Jerry Lewis Please Sit Down? came at the tail end of Lewis' movie popularity—in fact, it was released at the same time as the comedian/director's last feature film for a decade, the dismal *Which Way to the Front?* Whether or not the weekly cartoon series would have succeeded had Jerry Lewis still been the hot property of his glory days in the 1950s and early 1960s is questionable. So cartoonlike were the Lewis films themselves (many were directed by ex-Warner Bros. animator Frank Tashlin) that any attempt to imitate that style with pen and ink would have been inadequate.

Various characters created by Jerry Lewis during his screen and TV career—the Nutty Professor, The Kid, Ralph Rotten, and several of the Lewis alter egos portrayed by the comedian in his 1965 film *The Family Jewels*—appeared on the 17-episode *Will the Real Jerry Lewis Please Sit Down?* Somehow these multiple personalities were connected with the cartoon Jerry's jerk-of-all-trades job at the Oddjob Employment Agency, run by Mr. Blunderpuss. Also poking around from time to time were Jerry's kid sister Jerraldine (*there's* a chilling thought), his girlfriend Rhonda, and his pet frog Spot.

Although Jerry Lewis himself developed the series in conjunction with Filmation, the comedian's voice on *Will the Real Jerry Lewis Please Sit Down?*, expertly wailing such Lewisisms as "Oh, ladyyyy!" and "Waaah, I dropped the . . . stuff . . . all over . . . the place!", was provided by future *Laverne and Shirley* costar David L. (Squiggy) Lander. The various "other" Lewises were, however, voiced by Howard Morris, who ironically had played Jerry's father in 1963's *The Nutty Professor.*

WINKY DINK AND YOU. CBS: 10/ 10/1953–4/27/1957. Syndicated: 1969. Ariel Productions/Barry-Enright/W. J. Seidler. Syndicated version produced by Fred Calvert. Voices: Mae Questel (Winky Dink); Dayton Allen (Woofer).

Winky Dink and You was one of those "Golden Days" kiddie shows with which people over 40 regularly bore their children by evoking its memory. The series originally ran weekly from 1953 to 1957 on CBS' Saturday morning schedule. Prolific game show producer/host Jack Barry (*Tic Tac Dough*, *The Joker's Wild*) emceed on camera; behind the scenes Barry produced the program with long-time partner Dan Enright and with Ed Friendly.

Outside of several short comic sketches involving Jack Barry and sidekick Dayton Allen, the central attraction of *Winky Dink* was its manifest of limited-animation cartoons featuring star-shaped Winky (who resembled a more recent animated hero, 1993's *Twinkle, the Dream Being* [q.v.]) and his dog Woofer. The animation and writing were elementary; it was the gimmick that grabbed 'em. In the course of each *Winky Dink* episode, the hero would find himself in an inescapable situation — a room with no door, a high wall with no ladder, a skydive with no parachute. It was up to the kids at home, cued by the magic word "WINKO!", to supply the missing "rescue" prop, simply by drawing the necessary convenience right on the TV screen.

Well, many of us *did* apply crayon to screen, much to the dismay of our parents. What we were *supposed* to do was draw upon a special, transparent cellophane screen covering, part of a 50-cent "Winky Dink" kit mail-ordered from Jack Barry and CBS. Once the drawing had served its purpose, the kids were encouraged to clean the screen with a "magic cloth," also supplied in the Winky Dink kit.

Though it wasn't so labelled at the time, *Winky Dink and You* was the very first "interactive" cartoon, encouraging the home audience to participate in the action. Beyond the obvious merchandising windfall, Jack Barry had high educational hopes for the concept, announcing that his "working screen" could also be applied to classroom use. Certainly this was feasible since *Winky Dink* had a large fan following, although it was regularly beaten in the ratings by its NBC competition. However, more than one youngster was ultimately disillusioned by the program when discovering (usually by visiting the home of an older relative who hadn't the inclination to purchase the Winky Dink kit) that Winky was able to scale those walls and pass through those invisible doors *without* having them drawn for him.

After 12 years' hibernation, *Winky Dink and You* was trotted out in a new syndicated cartoon package, part of the nostalgia craze of the late 1960s — and once more, the kids were prodded to purchase the necessary kits in order to interact with Winky. This time, however, the program failed to click. Jack Barry commented at the time that rumors of children suffering illness due to sitting too close to the TV screen had prevented the new *Winky Dink*'s success. The actual reason might have been that the 1969 cartoons were even more primitive and less amusing than the originals, despite the production knowhow of *Roger Ramjet* (q.v.) veteran Fred Calvert. No attempt was made at this time to turn out new cartoons spotlighting the original *Winky Dink and You*'s animated co-features: "Mike McBean," a young time traveller, and "Dusty Dan," a cowboy.

WINNIE THE POOH *see* **NEW ADVENTURES OF WINNIE THE POOH**

WINSOME WITCH *see* **ATOM ANT**

WISHKID STARRING MACAULAY CULKIN. NBC: 9/14/1991–9/7/1992. Family Channel: 1992–1993. Macaulay Culkin Productions/DIC. Executive producers, Andy Heyward and Robby London. Produced and directed by Chuck Patton. Story editor, Jeffrey Scott. Live action sequences produced and directed by Christopher Brough. Animation facilities: Hong Kong Animation, Point Animation, Cartooneurs. Music by Clark Gassman. Voices: Macaulay Culkin, Quinn Culkin, Paul de la Rosa, Paul Haddad, Marilyn Lightstone, Judy Marshak, Andrew Sabiston, Stuart Stone, James Rankin, Harvey Atkin, Tara Charendoff, Joe Matheson, Benji Plener, Catherine Gallant, Susan Roman, Greg Swanson.

Wishkid Starring Macaulay Culkin spotlighted the voice, the drawn likeness, and, at the beginning of each episode, the in-the-flesh presence of the titular preteen superstar of the *Home Alone* pictures.

Contrary to the series title, Macaulay Culkin didn't star as "himself" but as young Nick McClary, whose reporter father and real estate agent mother couldn't seem to find any time for him. Left to his own devices, Nick didn't boobytrap his house like his *Home Alone* counterpart; instead, he devoted his energies to his baseball glove. Stop what you're thinking right there! The glove was not self-gratifying but magical, one that granted Nick's every wish and whisked him off to Fantasy Land — "but only," we were told by the star, "once a week." Thirteen weeks, to be exact. Nick had a baby sister named Peggy, a best friend named Darryl, a dog named Slobber, and a bully nemesis named Frankie. You can fill in the rest of the blanks yourself. Blindfolded.

Wishkid Starring Macaulay Culkin was as pat and predictable as I hope I've made it sound. Strangely enough, when NBC dropped its cartoon programs on August 1, 1992, to make way for the two-hour *Saturday Today Show*, *Wishkid* was the only such series spared — which means it well may own the distinction of being the very last cartoon series ever telecast on NBC's weekend schedule. A whimper of a climax, indeed, for an animated legacy which began with *The NBC Comics* (q.v.) way back in 1950.

Wishkid could have been a worthier climax, and the viewers might have had more fun, in a twisted sort of way, had we been offered a closer-to-home Macaulay Culkin cartoon project. Perhaps one which featured the adventures of a young overpaid film star whose manager/father demanded enormous concessions, such as a pointless and unwarranted animated TV series with a substantial voice part reserved for the star's younger sister, so that his kid would deign to appear in big budget movie sequels.

WIZARD OF OZ:
—TALES OF THE WIZARD OF OZ. Syndicated: 1961. Rankin-Bass/Videocrafts. Produced by Arthur Rankin, Jr. and Jules Bass. Music by Maury Laws. Animation facilities: Toei Studios. Voices (probable): Alfie Scopp, Carl Banas, Larry Mann.
—OFF TO SEE THE WIZARD. ABC: 9/8/1967–9/20/1968. MGM Television. Animated wraparounds produced by Chuck Jones and Abe Levitow.
—WONDERFUL WIZARD OF OZ. HBO: 5/6/1990–6/30/1992. Videocassette title: *OZ.* Cinar Productions. Filmed 1987–1988. Produced by Micheline Charest,

Ronald A. Weinberg. Associate producer, Elizabeth Klinck. Directed by Tim Reid. Written by Don Arioli and Tim Reid; based on the works of L. Frank Baum. Animation director, Gerald Potterton. Animation supervisor, Christine LaRocque. Education and psychological consultant, Margie Golick, Ph.D. Music composed by Hagood Hardy, Tom Sczesniak, Ray Parker. "Searchin' for a Dream" performed by Parachute Club; music and lyrics by Hagood Hardy. Voices: Morgan Hallett (Dorothy); George Morris (Tinman); Neil Shee (Lion); Richard Dumont (Scarecrow); Margot Kidder (Narrator); and Stephen Bednarski, Harvey Berger, Maria Bircuer, Mark Denis, Kathleen Fee, Carol Ann Francis, Gayle Garfinkle, Susan Glover, Arthur Grosser, Dean Hagopian, A. J. Henderson, Adrian Knight, Terrence Labrosse, Linda Lonn, Liz MacRae, Bronwen Massey, Gordon Masten, Steve Michaels, Carla Napier, Linda O'Dwyer, Barbara Pogemiller, Rob Roy, Michael Rudder, Howard Ryshpan, Vlasta Vrana, Tim Webber, and Jane Woods.
—THE WIZARD OF OZ. ABC: 9/7/1990–9/6?/1991. Syndicated: 1992 (part of AMAZIN' ADVENTURES). Turner Entertainment/DIC. Executive producer: Andy Heyward. Supervising producer: Michael Maliani. Co-ordinating producer: Robby London. Adapted for animation by Cliff Ruby and Elana Lesser. Layout consultant: Stacy Gallishaw. Art director: Kurt William Connor. Animation produced by Pacific Rim Productions. Music supervision by Joanne Miller. Music by Tom Worral, based on original songs by E. Y. Harburg and Harold Arlen. Voices: Charlie Adler, Liz Georges, David Lodge, Tress MacNeille, Alan Oppenheimer, Hal Rayle, B. J. Ward, Frank Welker, Jack Angel, Hamilton Camp, Pat Fraley, Bibi Osterwald, Rob Paulsen, Ken Sansom, Susan Silo.

Rankin-Bass' 1961 *Tales of the Wizard of Oz* was the Canadian studio's first cartoon series to get nationwide syndication in the U.S. (*Pinocchio* [q.v.], released simultaneously, was stop-motion rather than cel animation), and also the first of four attempts to animate *Wizard of Oz* for television. The principal characters in the 150 five-minute Rankin-Bass cartoons were drawn from those created by L. Frank Baum for his first *Oz* book, written in 1900: These had lapsed into public domain, allowing Rankin-Bass to sidestep exorbitant licensing fees.

The cartoon version was careful not to imitate MGM's classic 1939 filmization of *The Wizard of Oz*, even though the basic characters — Wizard, Dorothy, Toto, Scarecrow, Tin Man, Cowardly Lion, Wicked Witch of the West and the Munchkins — were the same. First off, all the non-human *Oz* characters were given new first names: Rusty the Tin Man, Socrates the Straw Man, Dandy the Lion. For another, their personalities were far removed from those of the MGM's cast lineup. Rusty's heartlessness was conveyed by a nasty temper rather than actor Jack Haley's melancholia. Socrates was more a slow-witted Mortimer Snerd type than the loose-limbed, eccentric Scarecrow created by Ray Bolger. Dandy Lion was not at all like Bert Lahr (just as well, since Lahr was one of Hollywood's most notorious sue-ers, with a battery of lawyers poised to pounce at the slightest hint of nonauthorized imitation); Dandy sounded more like the tremulous Captain Huffenpuff on *Beany and Cecil* (q.v.). And the Munchkins were Singer Midgets no more; the Rankin-Bass Munchkins spoke in gibberish and resembled the amoebalike animated dirt spots seen in liquid detergent commercials.

As for the humans, Dorothy was a non-singing non–Judy Garland, while The Wizard sounded like W. C. Fields rather than Frank Morgan — ironic, since the role of the Wizard in the 1939 film had been written with Fields in mind, and in fact the film would have starred Fields had not W. C. been committed to a screenplay for Universal Studios. And The Wicked Witch was a wart-covered "child" of the 1960s, complete with a Cape Canaveral–style launching pad for her broom.

The best elements of *Tales of the Wizard of Oz* were the character design and forced-perspective backgrounds. You can take your pick of its worst elements: the poor timing and coordination of the animation, the sound effects which never seemed to match the action, or the feeble updating attempts. This last yielded the greatest number of misfire ideas: The Tin Man, Straw Man and Lion were drafted in the army; the Straw Man participated in a TV quiz show; the Wizard built a three-stage rocket to send Dorothy back to Kansas. Anachronisms can be funny (look at *The Flintstones*) but on *Tales of the Wizard of Oz* they leaned toward the precious and boring. Still, *Tales* was popular enough for a reasonably good NBC spin-off special, *Return to Oz* (1964), which retained Rankin-Bass' design but harked back to MGM by having the Lion sound like Bert Lahr and the Wizard like Frank Morgan again. *Return to Oz* also had the salutary effect of launching Rankin-Bass in the seasonal-special business, which resulted in such perennials as *The Little Drummer Boy* and *Rudolph the Red-Nosed Reindeer*.

Peripherally related to this and future *Wizard of Oz* cartoon series was an MGM prime time series of 1967, a weekly, hourlong ABC network potpourri titled *Off to See the Wizard*. Chuck Jones and Abe Levitow directed the animated buffers and wraparounds for this series, which spotlighted the familiar *Oz* denizens. Since MGM produced the program, the character designs and voices of Dorothy, the Wizard, Scarecrow, Lion and Tin Man were carbon copies of those seen in the 1939 movie, while the TV series' theme music was a lilting combination of E. Y. Harburg/Harold Arlen's "Off to See the Wizard" and "Over the Rainbow." But the *Oz* characters weren't really the stars; they were "hosts" for a 26-week package of live action properties. Except for featuring a few new specials like the all-star "Who's Afraid of Mother Goose" and a handful of busted TV pilots like "Mike and the Mermaid," *Off to See the Wizard* aped Walt Disney by telecasting serialized or heavily re-edited versions of such MGM theatrical films as *Flipper*, *Lili*, *Zebra in the Kitchen*, *The Glass Slipper*, and the 1960 version of *The Adventures of Huckleberry Finn*. *Wizard* even emulated the worst aspect of the Disney series, the narrative intrusions of the highly unamusing Ludwig Von Drake, by having the Wizard of Oz's Frank Morgan–like voice dubbed over Walter Pidgeon's narration of *Glass Slipper*. *Off to See the Wizard* perished opposite CBS' *Wild Wild West* and NBC's *Tarzan* in the Friday night ratings battle — small compensation for the heinous crime of exploiting L. Frank Baum's immortal characters for the sake of a graceless Disney rip-off.

The next regularly telecast animated *Oz* appeared two decades later. Cinar's *Wonderful Wizard of Oz* was first broadcast in Canada in 1987; it premiered in early 1990 in the U.S. over the HBO pay-cable service, first as a weekly, then as an early morning strip. Narrated by Margot Kidder, the Cinar *Wonderful Wizard* half hours were serialized, going beyond the original *Wizard of Oz* and branching out to the *Oz* sequels written by L. Frank Baum in the early 20th century. As with Rankin-Bass' *Oz*, Cinar confined itself only to those Baum works in the public domain: "The Wonderful Wizard of Oz," "The Marvelous Land of Oz," "Ozma of Oz" and "The Emerald City of Oz." This meant that such marvelous Baum characters as Ozma, the Gnome King, Jack Pumpkinhead and General Ginger were given their first animated-cartoon exposure. As a bonus, the episodes based on "Wonderful Wizard of Oz" itself included sequences and characters from the book excised from the MGM film: The grandmotherly Good Witch of the North, Tin Man's flashback to his days as a genuine human being, the attack of the Kalidahs (half-bear, half-tiger) in the forest, the Wicked Witch's enslavement of Dorothy as kitchen help, the Witches' magic golden cap, the Wizard's ersatz "brain," "heart" and "courage," assembled from household articles, and the kindly assistance of the Flying Monkeys in transporting Dorothy to Glinda.

Storylines occasionally went a bit afield from Baum, but unlike the Rankin-Bass version, Cinar's *Oz* embroidered within the author's framework rather than completely jettisoning the original. Character design owed nothing to any previous adaptation: Tin Man was chubby with metal curls in his hair, the Witch was a white-haired harridan with glowing red eyes, and the Wizard looked like perennial Laurel and Hardy supporting actor Jimmy Finlayson.

Overall, Cinar's *Wonderful Wizard of Oz* did an admirable job capturing the spirit of the original, alternating whimsy, pathos and light satire with moments of genuine horror (the "melting" of the Wicked Witch was enough to send adults scurrying under the bed!). The Cinar staff didn't quite manage fluidity of animation, but the series boasted individual setpieces of real accomplishment, such as the opening tornado sequence and the rafting trip of Dorothy and her friends on a turbulent river. If you'd like to check out this worth-while endeavor yourself sometime, all 26

Wonderful Wizard of Oz episodes are available on videocassette, under the simplified title *Oz*. The series' HBO run came to an end in mid–1992, when it was replaced by Saban's animated *Pinocchio* (q.v.).

Running almost simultaneouly with the Cinar version was DIC's *The Wizard of Oz*, which premiered in 1990 as part of ABC's Saturday morning schedule. The series was produced in conjunction with Turner Entertainment, the company which controlled the rights to MGM's 1939 film version of *Oz*. As such, permission was granted (as it had been for 1967's *Off to See the Wizard*) to pattern the animated characters, and the voices, after their classic movie counterparts: Garland (Dorothy), Bolger (Scarecrow), Haley (Tin Woodsman), Lahr (Cowardly Lion), Morgan (The Wizard) and Margaret Hamilton (The Wicked Witch of the West). Even the Munchkins were drawn in the manner of the *Oz* film's Singer Midgets, complete with accurate voice impersonations of our old friends the Mayor, the Coroner and the Lollipop Guild. Like Cinar's series, DIC/Turner's *Wizard of Oz* ran 26 episodes, covering a number of the adventures and characters appearing in L. Frank Baum's original *Oz* books, though many more liberties were taken than in the Cinar version. The whole project was inevitably derivative, but was refreshingly ambitious and attractively produced. It was too bad *Wizard of Oz* was expected to duke it out with CBS' *Muppet Babies* and NBC's *Captain N/Super Mario Bros. 3*.

Reruns of DIC's *Wizard of Oz* became a component of Bohbot's syndicated *Amazin' Adventures* (q.v.) in 1992.

WOLF ROCK TV. ABC: 9/8/1984–10/13/1984. DIC/Dick Clark Productions. Produced by Jean Chalopin, Dick Clark, Andy Heyward, Toshitsugu Mukaitsubo, Kiyoshi Ieno. Story editors, Len Janson, Chuck Menville. Creative supervision, Jean Chalopin and Lori Crawford. Executive in charge of production, Thierry P. Laurin; associate producer, James P. Finch. Written by Mike O'Mahoney, Chuck Lorre, J. Johnson, Len Udes, Warren Taylor and Dennis Marx. Supervision director, Bernard Deyries, assisted by Rita Rokisky. Animation directed by Kazumi Fukushima. Voice director, Ginny McSwain. Music videos courtesy of EMI

America, MCA Records, Polygram Records. Music by Shuki Levy and Haim Saban. Voices: Wolfman Jack (Himself); Siu Ming Carson (Sunny); Noelle North (Sarah); Robert Vega (Ricardo); Jason Bernard (Mr. Morris); Frank Welker (Bopper); and William Callaway, Danny Mann, Linda Gary, Tress MacNeille, Pat Fraley, Fred Travalena, and Barbara Goodson.

Wolf Rock TV was an animated vehicle for popular "outlaw" deejay Wolfman Jack (real name: Bob Smith). The bearded Wolfman had built his 1950s and 1960s reputation over super-powered Mexican "border radio" stations, playing songs ignored or banned on more conservative outlets and giving teens of the era a "clandestine" conduit to what was then an alternative form of rock and roll. When the outsiders in the musical world became the insiders in the 1970s, Wolfman Jack entered the establishment mainstream thanks to frequent TV appearances and a guest role in the 1973 film *American Graffiti*. By 1984, the once rebellious Wolfman was practically the Gray Eminence of Rock.

Wolfman Jack's weekly, half hour cartoon series *Wolf Rock TV* featured the star's voice and caricature, with ample screen time given to teen characters Sarah, Sunny and Ricardo, and their pet bird Bopper. The kids ran an MTV-type TV station on behalf of apoplectic station manager Mr. Morris and easygoing station owner Wolfman Jack. The plotlines involved the expected "Will they make it to the station in time for the sign-on?" complications. Actual music videos (the cleaner ones!) and interviews with recording artists appeared throughout this eight-episode endeavor, which was produced by another rock-n-roll elder statesman, Dick Clark.

In 1989, *Wolf Rock TV* reruns were syndicated in tandem with episodes of another former network music-video cartooner, *Kidd Video* (q.v.), under the blanket title *Wolf Rock Power Hour*.

THE WONDERFUL STORIES OF PROFESSOR KITZEL. Syndicated: 1972. M G Animation/Worldvision. Produced by Shamus Culhane.

The Wonderful Stories of Professor Kitzel were three-minute information bites produced by Shamus Culhane, combining cartoon wraparounds with still photographs and period illustrations of famous historical events.

A student of old-time radio might think that the titular Professor was named after the Hebraic Mr. Kitzel of *Jack Benny Program* fame, who in the 1940s popularized the nonsense catchphrase "pickle in the middle and the mustard on top." Actually both Jack Benny and Culhane drew the name Kitzel from the Yiddish slang word for "tickle." Unlike Benny, Shamus Culhane wasn't Jewish, but had grown up in prominently Jewish neighborhoods and had retained a lifelong affection for the colorful Yiddish jargon prevalent in those communities.

Culhane had intended *The Wonderful Stories of Professor Kitzel* series to be run as an in-classroom service, but a barter deal with Bristol-Myers enabled Worldvision to syndicate the series to local TV stations. The stylized limited animation of *Kitzel* closely resembled the like-vintage American Dental Association public service announcements—also produced by Shamus Culhane. (See also *Max the 2000 Year Old Mouse* and *The Spirit of Freedom*.)

WONDERFUL WIZARD OF OZ *see* **THE WIZARD OF OZ**

THE WOODY WOODPECKER SHOW. ABC: 10/31/1957–9/25/1958. Universal/MCA/Kellogg's. Thereafter syndicated.

By rights, Woody Woodpecker doesn't belong in a book about made-for-TV cartoons. The red-topped, blue-feathered Woodpecker is practically the only major animated star whose career was limited exclusively to theatrical releases (though plans for a new *Woody Woodpecker* from Universal Cartoon Studios may change this). He is included herein because of the valuable service rendered to incipient cartoonists by *The Woody Woodpecker Show*. This 1957 package of old cartoons was commissioned by ABC and Kellogg's as part of a daily afternoon kid's strip, supplanting the first half hour of the originally 60-minute *Mickey Mouse Club* (other programs in this Monday-through-Friday outing were live-action repeats of *Superman*, *Wild Bill Hickok*, *Sir Lancelot* and *The Buccaneers*). Walter Lantz, Woody's creator, could have simply licensed the cartoons to ABC/Kellogg's and let it go at that. Instead, he decided to emulate the "behind the scenes" installments of the nighttime *Disneyland* series. Thus Lantz shot new, live footage, to be inserted between the three theatrical shorts on each *Woody* half hour, wherein he revealed the secrets of cartoon animation.

In imitating Disney, however, Lantz turned out to be better than his role model. Sometimes, admittedly, Lantz tried to cloud a few facts in Disneylike mythos. The classic example of this was his "re-enactment" of the 1941 creation of Woody, who was allegedly inspired by a bothersome woodpecker who disturbed Lantz on his honeymoon, which in fact took place a year *after* Woody's screen debut in *Knock Knock*. Otherwise, the producer generally stuck to nuts-and-bolts facts. One week he'd show the folks at home how a storyboard was put together; the next, he'd give a crash course on painting cels; the week after that, there'd be a glance at the sound effects department; and the following week, he'd demonstrate how a cartoon's timing could be determined by something as simple as a ticking metronome.

Walter Lantz may not have been as charismatic as Disney, who (as mentioned) also occasionally explored the technical end of the business on his own series, but Lantz was more successful in demystifying and clarifying the process. Disney tended to trot out the equipment, tell the viewers how much time and money it took to put together a few minutes' animation, then jump straight to the finished product. Lantz felt that people were more interested in seeing *how* it was done, rather than hearing how much it cost or a tally of man-hours.

In short: As a host, Walt Disney was like your dad's boss, giving up a bit of his valuable time to guide you through his suite of plush offices, point out the progress charts on the wall, and end up before a glassed-in display of bonds and dividend samples. "Look how big and rich we are," was the message, "but keep your hands off!" Conversely, Walter Lantz was the friendly next-door neighbor who invited you into his workshop, showed off his bird feeders and ash trays, and then let you hammer and plane and whittle a bit yourself. "Any one can do this with a little hard work and persistence" was the message — and I'd venture a bet that more

aspiring cartoonists were prompted to continue in the profession through Walter Lantz's humble little information bites than Walt Disney's glorified stockholders' meetings.

We said at the beginning that the *Woody Woodpecker* cartoons (together with the other Lantz productions seen on this series) were not made for television; the only newly animated material included Woody's between-the-acts bumpers and his weekly introduction of "My boss, Walter Lantz." In truth, however, the 51 cartoons telecast during the original *Woody Woodpecker Show* were remade for television: that is, they were carefully scrutinized by the Kellogg's Cereal censors and trimmed for network consumption. "Kellogg's doesn't want to make any enemies," said Wally Ruggles, production manager for the Leo Burnett Company, the cereal firm's ad agency. It's hard to imagine a less offensive group of cartoons than the 50-year manifest of Walter Lantz Studios, yet in two separate articles, one published in a 1957 *Hollywood Reporter*, the other ("Censorship Invades the Animal Kingdom") in the January 4, 1958, edition of *TV Guide*, Lantz ruefully explained how 25 separate sequences were pared down or cut out altogether.

First to go were all scenes involving drinking: The besotted horse in *Musical Moments* and the inebriated mouse in *Mousie Come Home* were seen weaving to and fro, but the scenes showing them *getting* drunk were snipped, rendering their behavior pointless. The next expurgation involved sex. A wriggling harem girl in *Abu Ben Boogie* was removed from the action, prompting Lantz to pull the cartoon from the package completely; while in other cartoons, no animal could be shown kissing a "human" character. (It's a darn good thing that Kellogg's didn't sponsor the cross-kissing Bugs Bunny.) Other expulsions included a tobacco-spitting grasshopper; the climactic gag in *Knock Knock* which suggested that Woody Woodpecker was a genuine (instead of apparent) lunatic; and a cartoon titled *Three Blind Mice*, which was adjusted to the more "sensitive" *Three Lazy Mice*.

Lantz concurred that certain older cartoons produced before the Hollywood Production Code could use censorship, and also went along with the understandable decision to eliminate any cartoons

Woody Woodpecker: what did Kellogg's censors think of those bedroom eyes?

tours of the cartoon world would be included for the proposed made-for-TV *Woody Woodpecker* from the Universal Cartoon Network.*

THE WORLD OF DAVID THE GNOME. Nickelodeon: 1/4/1988–. Cinar Films/Miramax/BRB Internacional/Uneboer NVV. Executives in charge of production, Bob and Harvey Weinstein. Created for TV by executive producer Claudio Biern Boyd. Produced by Michelle Charest and Ronald A. Weinberg. Directed by Luis Ballestes. English version adapted and directed by Ernest Reid. Based on "The Gnomes" and "The Secret of the Gnomes" by Rien Poortvliet and Wil Huygen. Animation facilities: BRB Internacional SA, T.V.E. Music by Pierre Daniel Rheault, Bob Jewett, Jack Maeby. Title song by Savier Losada. Performed by Normand Giroux. Voices, English version: Tom Bosley (David the Gnome); Jane Woods (Lisa); Vlasta Vrana (Swifty the Fox); Barbara Pogemiller (Susan); Richard Dumont (King). TROLLS: A. J. Henderson (Holler); Adrian Knight (Pit); Rob Roy (Pat); Marc Denis (Pot). First episode narrated by Christopher Plummer.

with overt racial stereotypes (though *100 Pygmies and Andy Panda,* hardly a salutary glance at African life, was left unscathed); but the producer was aghast and astonished, as he'd been during the heyday of the Production Code, at the removal of relatively harmless gags. Even into the 1970s the normally amiable Lantz would bristle when it was suggested that his cartoons could be considered violent or offensive by modern standards.

At least *one* questionable bit slipped by the Kellogg's censors. On the very first *Woody Woodpecker Show,* the climactic cartoon segment featured a closeup of a lengthy, unpaid hotel bill. One of the room-service entries was a large dollar amount for "Cocaine." To quote Mr. Woodpecker, "Hah Hah Hah *Hah* Huh!"

The original *Woody Woodpecker Show* package remained in syndication until 1960. Three years later, a new color package emerged for the offnetwork market, this one untouched by censorial hands. In 1970 and 1976, several more Lantz cartoons were bundled up for Saturday morning network runs; and also in 1976, the series re-entered syndication, where it remains to this day. Unfortunately, none of these latter-day *Woody Woodpecker Shows* featured any live action animation tips narrated by Walter Lantz. Mr. Lantz' death in 1994 scotched any hopes that his guided

David the Gnome was a physician, married to lady gnome Lisa, living in one of those sylvan glades so common to European children's stories. The *World of David the Gnome* was in fact European, both in origin and production staff. The series' 26 half hours were based on two best-selling books by Dutch writers Rien Poortvliet and Wil Huygen, and were produced in studio locations ranging from France to Spain. Cinar Productions shipped out the series on the wave of *The Smurfs'* (q.v.) popularity, but the only resemblance between the two properties was the presence of little people with sometimes magic powers. Once in America, *David the Gnome* happily resisted any attempts at Americanization, outside of casting *Happy Days* costar Tom Bosley as the voice of David. The series retained its Old World ambience, while the artistic style (similar to other Cinar productions) resembled the watercolor illustrations so common to European children's literature.

In October of 1964, Walter Lantz hosted a Woody Woodpecker *Halloween special (labelled a "Spookenanny"), which was telecast by the 185 local stations then carrying the weekly syndicated* Woody *series.*

As a bonus, *The World of David the Gnome* satisfied sensitive children (and their sensitive parents) by playing away from violence and terror as often as possible. No matter how nasty the opponent, be it evil troll or slavering spider, David the Gnome was unflappable, always certain that right would prevail—and always prepared to dodge his way out of trouble rather than put up his diminutive dukes. Despite the potentially declamatory presence of narrator Christopher Plummer, there was seldom a shout heard on *The World of David the Gnome*. The series, run weekdays by cable's Nickelodeon, was perfectly suited to the three- to seven-year-old demographic class often overlooked by the superhero/wacky animal-dominated syndicated cartoon series.

THE WORLD OF PETER RABBIT AND FRIENDS. Family Channel: 3/28/1993–. TVC London Production for Frederick Warne and Co./BBC. Produced in association with Pony Canyon Inc. and Fuji Television Inc. Executive producer, Jonathan Peel. Produced by John Coates, Catrin Unwin, Ginger Gibbons and Nick Comley. Directed and written by Dianne Jackson. Animation directors, Jack Stokes, Geoff Dunbar, Mike Stuart and Dave Unwin. Art director, Rosalind Henderson. Music by Colin Towns. "Perfect Day" sung by Miriam Shockley. Animation facilities: Jumping Jack Animation Ltd., TVC, Grand Slam Partnership, Stuart Brooks Animation. Live action produced and directed by Dennis Abbey. Starring Niamh Cusack as Beatrix Potter. Voices include: Niamh Cusack, Derek Jacobi, Prunella Scales, Rory Carry, Andrew Clitherne, Alan Bowe, Mary Jane Bowe, Jenny Moore, Rosemary Leach, Patricia Routledge, Sue Pollard, Dinsdale Landen, Enn Reitel, Selma Cadell, June Whitfield, Richard Wilson, June Watson, Sara Woolcock, Moir Lesley.

The *World of Peter Rabbit and Friends* was prepared for the British Broadcasting Corporation in 1992 as part of the centennial celebration of Beatrix Potter's *Peter Rabbit* storybooks, a year-long festival that took shape elsewhere in the form of ballets, museum exhibitions and toy merchandising. The *Peter Rabbit* cartoon series, representing nine Beatrix Potter books, expertly whittled down to six half hours, was the single most expensive

British TV-animation series to date, employing the talents of four animation studios at a budget of 11 million dollars.

Potter had been approached for animation rights to her stories as early as 1935, but she didn't feel at the time that her watercolor illustrations would properly translate to the screen. The 1992 series proved it not only could be done, but could be done brilliantly. The animators employed watercolors for its backgrounds, then gave the same delicately shaded texture to the character-animation cels by overlaying them with separate cels, upon which the shadings were drawn with soft pencil. This "rendered animation" style (as the producers called it) was every bit the equal to the Potter originals. In the eyes of at least one critic, *Premiere* magazine's Davina Parnet, the cartoon renditions were superior to Potter's "always-too-little" printed pictures.

Hosted and narrated in exquisitely photographed live action sequences by actress Niamh Cusack (as Beatrix Potter herself, in proper 1890s costume), *The World of Peter Rabbit* sextet was launched with "The Tale of Peter Rabbit and Benjamin Bunny," the familiar story of Peter's forbidden foray into Mr. MacGregor's garden, and his last-minute escape from a rabbit pie. The second program, "Tale of Samuel Whiskers and the Roly-Poly Pudding," was the gently cautionary tale of a kitten named Tom nearly baked into a dessert by the Whiskers, a pair of landed-gentry rats. (Beatrix Potter had a ladylike obsession with cute little animals barely escaping ingestion.) "Tale of Tom Kitten and Jemima Puddleduck" was next, all about an adolescent cat (Tom again), a foolish goose, a duplicitous fox with eyes for the goose's tasty eggs, and a stalwart dog.

This was followed by "The Tailor of Gloucester," a variation on the "elves and the shoemaker" legend that had been previously adapted on several programs, including Rabbit Ears Video's animated *Storybook Classics* (q.v.). Number five was "Tale of Pigling Bland," with a naive rural pig at the mercy of smooth-talking predator Mr. Piperson. *World of Peter Rabbit and Friends* was rounded out with "Tale of Mrs. Tiggy-Winkle and Mr. Jeremy Fisher," wherein a little girl named Lucy spends a warm afternoon with the title characters, a talkative hedgehog housekeeper and "a most elegant and gentlemanly" frog.

All six episodes were fully and meticulously animated, the Beatrix Potter canon literally springing to life. Thankfully, any temptation to "improve" the originals by updating them, or by downplaying the fleeting but genuine moments of terror, was religiously avoided. The characters dressed precisely in period, with knickers on the "boys" and pinafores on the "girls," and even the most willful of the children used well-bred phrases like "If you please." (The younger voices were supplied by real British children rather than adult kid imitators, another nice touch.) The dangers facing the more foolhardy characters were played full out with no regard to viewers' potential nightmares, even though the villainous characters did take the trouble to cloak their intentions in proper Victorian euphemisms. And in maintaining faithfulness to the Beatrix Potter originals, the cartoons politely refused to sugarcoat the occasional ironic consequences suffered by Potter's animals. Jemima Puddleduck's eggs were rescued from the Fox, only to be sucked dry by the dogs who'd been sent to save them. The gentlemanly lead dog watched the sorry spectacle, then comforted Jemima with a resigned "It's just the nature of things."

In the United States, the Family Channel cable service ran *World of Peter Rabbit and Friends* as a series of six specials over a period of 13 months, beginning in March of 1993. Just prior to the series' American cable premiere, the *World of Peter Rabbit and Friends* package was released as a group of home videocassettes, extensively advertised on television with an "infotainment" half hour commercial hosted by Angela Lansbury—a carefully produced and tasteful venture in itself. (For other projects prepared for dual cable/cassette release, see *American Heroes and Legends*, *HBO Storybook Musicals*, *Storybook Classics* and *We All Have Tales*.)

THE WORLD'S GREATEST SUPERFRIENDS *see* **THE SUPERFRIENDS**

WOWSER. Family Channel: 9/4/1989–9/14/1990. Telecable Benelux/Saban. A production of Telecable Benelux BV, TV Tokyo Channel 12 Ltd., Les editions du Lombard S.A., and Luc Dupa. Telecable

Benelux credits: Executive producer of animation, Dennis Livson. Animation producer, Kazuo Tabata. Director of animation, Hiroshi Sasagawa. Original stories by Matsue Jimbo. Animation facilities, Telescreen Japan, Ltd., Teleimage, Ltd. Original ideas and character designs, [Luc] Dupa. Saban credits: Executive producer, Haim Saban. Supervising producer, Winston Richard. Associate producer, Eric S. Rollman. ADR director, Tom Wyner. ADR script coordinator, Kelly Griffin. Music by Haim Saban and Shuki Levy. No voice credits.

Coproduced in Europe and Japan in 1988, *Wowser* was readied for U.S. distribution by Saban International the following year, enjoying a 12-month daily run on the Family Channel cable service. More slapstick oriented than the usual Saban release, *Wowser* was all about the title character, a large white sheepdog (who looked more like a bear), and his master, eccentric Professor Dinghy. The bushy-headed Professor was the erstwhile inventor of such novel but unwieldy gadgets as a walking car, a bone-shaped dirigible, a mountain-climbing bicycle and a mouse-powered shoeshine machine. Wowser acted as "guinea dog" for the dingy Dinghy, letting his discomfiture be known in an endless stream of wisecracks and insults.

During the course of each half hour (two short adventures per episode), Wowser and Dinghy would cross the paths of such friends and neighbors as Linda Lovely, Linda's housekeeper-mother Beatrice, and steadfast Officer Whistle, so named because he "spoke" by tooting the police whistle around his neck. The monkeywrench of Wowser's existence was Ratso the cat, who delighted in playing sadistic practical jokes on all concerned, then heaping the blame on the hapless dog.

While the uncredited voice cast did its best to Americanize the series (both Wowser and Linda Lovely had pronounced New York accents), *Wowser* was transparently "overseas" in origin. The melon-eyed character design gave away its Japanese heritage, while the topography and trappings of the production design—cobblestone streets, twin-stacked chimneys, geese wandering unmolested through major thoroughfares—betrayed its European roots.

In one respect, the fact that the series was an import enhanced its comic value. The English-language actors were forced to speak very rapidly in order to match the foreign lip movements, and the result was an exhilarating verbal pace, brimming with overlapping punchlines and throw-away asides. This intensified pacing was maintained by *Wowser's* sight gags, with one hilariously violent vignette following another in a machine-gun manner reminiscent of the best Tex Avery and Bob Clampett theatrical cartoons of the 1940s. The hesitant animation style wasn't quite up to the swiftness of the visual humor, but this was circumvented with split-second film editing.

With an uninhibited comedy content ranging from simple hammers on the noggin to an elaborate satire of "Disneyland Mentality" (in that particular episode, a covetous land developer planned to convert Loch Ness into a theme park— "Cheap and commercial, for the benefit of cheap and commercial people like myself"), *Wowser* was well above average, especially for a Saban product. The series certainly deserved a more accessible showcase than the red-eye 8:00 A.M. slot bestowed upon it by Family Channel. But even at that early hour, *Wowser* might have succeeded—had it had a different title. "Wowser," you see, also happened to be a catch-phrase on the DIC cartoon series *Inspector Gadget* (q.v.). The upshot of this was that many viewers, glancing casually at the *TV Guide* listing for *Wowser*, probably mistook it for a package of retitled *Inspector Gadget* reruns and switched the channel.

THE WUZZLES. CBS: 9/14/1985–9/6/1986; ABC: 9/13/1986–9/5/1987. (Telecast on Disney Channel following network run.) Produced and directed by Fred Wolf. Associate producer, Tom Ruzicka. Animation supervisor, Vincent Davis. Written by David Wiemers and Ken Koonce. Theme song composed and performed by Stephen Geyer. Music composed and performed by Tom Chase, Steve Rucker. Animation facilities: Walt Disney Pictures TV Animation Group, TMS (Tokyo Movie Shinsha) Entertainment. Voices: Brian Cummings (Bumblelion/Flizard); Henry Gibson (Eleroo/Girafbra); Jo Anne Worley (Hoppopotamus); Bill Scott (Moosel/Brat); Alan Op-

penheimer (Rhinokey/Croc/Pack-Cat); Kathy Helppie (Butterbear); Tress MacNeille (Mrs. Pedigree); Stan Freberg (Narrator).

The stars of Disney's *The Wuzzles* lived on the Isle of Wuz, which makes sense. The premise of the series—which some religious fundamentalists condemned in print as being "demonic"—was that each little Wuzzle was a mutation of two different animals. The various species were implicit in the character names: Bumblelion, EleRoo, Hoppopotamus, Girafbra, Rhinokey, Butterbear. The villains were non-mutated "outsiders," usually sorcerors or plunderers.

What could have been oppressively cute was refreshingly irreverent thanks to the comic expertise of the writing staff. Whenever events on the *Wuzzles* threatened to descend into childish gooeyness, the audience was brought back to earth by the deliberately pompous narration of satirist Stan Freberg. One of Freberg's most endearing traits was to tell the kids at home all the excitement that they'd missed while the commercial was on. (Another welcome voice-talent was Bill Scott of *Bullwinkle* fame [see *Rocky and His Friends*], here appropriately cast as "Moosel.")

The half hour, 13-episode *The Wuzzles* turned out to be a crucial stepping stone for the animation firm of Murikami-Wolf-Swenson. Producer/director Fred Wolf's studio was subcontracted by Disney to work on *The Wuzzles*, which led to a longer stint for Wolf on Disney's *Duck-Tales* (q.v.). This in turn gave Fred Wolf the industry reputation for being able to "kid on the square" successfully with basic adventure material, which enabled the producer to push through Murikami-Wolf-Swenson's most profitable property to date: *Teenage Mutant Ninja Turtles* (q.v.).

X-MEN. Fox: 10/10/1992–. Marvel/Saban/Graz Entertainment. Created by Stan Lee. Executives in charge of production, Eric S. Rollman and Jim Graziano. Executive producers, Winston Richard, Joseph Calimari, Stan Lee. Co-executive producer, Richard Ungar. Supervising producer, Will Meugniot. Animation directors, Karen Peterson, Graham Morris. Music by Shuki Levy. Animation facilities: Akom Production Company. Voices: Phil Aiken, Lawrence Bayne, Rick Bennett, George

Wolverine from *X-Men*.

Buza, Lally Cadeau, Robert Coit, Randall Carpenter, John Colicos, Rod Coneybaer, Brett Halsey, David Hemblen, Dan Hennessey (also voice director), Judy Marshak, George Mercer, Jim Millington, Stephen Ouimette, Ross Petty, Chris Potter, Alyson Court, Jennifer Dale, Catherine Diener, Cal Dodd, Adrian Egan, Barry Flatman, David Fox, Don Francks, Cathy Gallant, Paul Haddad, Jeremy Hutchford, Iona Morris, Ron Rubin, Cedric Smith, Norm Spencer, Stuart Stone, Marc Strange, Kay Trembley, Lenore Zann, Graham Haley.

X-Men, a weekly half hour animated adventure, was a long time coming. It officially debuted as a semi-special on October 10, 1992, and began regular weekly telecasts on January 2, 1993, after five years of false starts—and 30 years after the birth of the Marvel comic book which inspired the series.

Created by Stan Lee and Jack Kirby in the summer of 1963, *X-Men Number One* centered upon five troubled Westchester County teenagers, students at Charlie Xavier's School for Gifted Youngsters. "Gifted" hardly covered the story. The youthful quintet were mutants, each endowed by technology from the far-off

Shi'ar Galaxy with astounding skills and powers that could make them either international heroes or a group menace to society. Charlie Xavier was really the wheelchair-bound, telepathic Professor X, who knew their secret and (hopefully) how to harness the teens' energy for good instead of evil. "The point is made in the books that power is as much a burden as a gift," noted Jim Lee, an *X-Men* writer of the 1980s.

Latter-day theorists have observed that most of Dr. X's charges had begun mutating around the age of 13, suggesting that this was a deliberate analogy to the confusing hormonal changes afflicting real kids during those awkward years when no young boy or girl feels completely "normal." While this might have been the intention of Kirby and Lee when creating *X-Men* in 1963, it's also likely that the writers were simply using teen heroes so that teens would buy the comic books. Commercialism has always been as potent a creative force as sociology.

The earliest *X-Men* incarnation often reflected the alienation of teenagers in an insensitive adult society (read: Kids vs. Vietnam), but surprisingly failed to strike a sympathetic chord with its target audience and was cancelled in 1970. Neal Adams was the artist who really gave *X-Men* the boost into cultism with a brooding "noir" style, but cultists didn't make up a large enough consumer group back then. The reputation of the property was improved somewhat through reprints and guest appearances by various X-People in other Marvel Comics, resulting in a resurgence of interest in 1975, the year that a new *X-Men* comic was inaugurated for Marvel by artist David Cockrum and writer Chris Claremont.

Perhaps this time around there were more young readers who felt like outsiders, and thus were in concert with these "cast off" Marvel heroes; whatever the reason, the Cockrum-Claremont revival of *X-Men* was soon outselling all its competition. Devotees of the series particularly cherished the "jump in and start swimming" narrative device fostered by Claremont, in which long-winded expository scenes were dispensed with on the assumption that the reader had been following the story up to the most recent chapter. Confusing to some, this device was delectable to most readers, many of whom felt for the first time in their lives like part of an "in crowd." (David Byrne succeeded Cockrum in 1977, retaining his predecessor's style without a ripple in the water.)

The original "X-Men" of 1963 — not *all* men, by the way — included Slim Summers, whose encounter with space aliens left him with "solar," energy-storing eyes, hence the nickname Cyclops; Hank McCoy, a onetime science student who retained his intellect and erudition even after being transformed into the hideous, gorilla-muscled "Beast"; Iceman, formerly Bobby Drake, a freeze-inducing character who later popped up on the animated *Spider-Man and His Amazing Friends* (see *Spider-Man*); Angel, who before sprouting wings was young millionaire Warren Kenneth Worthington III; and Jean Grey, a female telepathic, who took on the name Marvel Girl (no relation to Captain Marvel).

In the 1975 revival, Cyclops and Dr. Xavier returned; many of the other charter X-ers had drifted to their own magazines, while Marvel Girl/Jean Gray, suffering guilt over being transmorphed briefly into the villaious Dark Phoenix, had killed herself! (It was not the only suicide amongst the X-Men, nor was Mr. Death a stranger to the group; even Dr. Xavier was "killed off" after a time.) Newer additions to the team anticipated the multiculturalism prevalent in comic books and cartoon series of the 1980s and 1990s. There was the Canadian Wolverine, previously introduced in one of the *X-Men* guest-star stints in 1973; formerly a secret agent named Logan, Wolverine was inflicted with "Weapon X" under his skin, which gave him metal claws, an understandably violent temper and an unregenerate cigarette habit. Orono Munroe, a princess of African heritage, was redubbed Storm due to her frightening control over the Elements. And in the spirit of glasnost, there was Colossus, aka Peter Rasputin, the seven-foot-tall son of Russian farmers. (A list of additional X-Men can be found in Jeff Rovin's excellent book on cartoon superheroes.)

Normally, *X-Men*'s popularity would have resulted in instant early–1960s transmutation to television, but the networks, nervous about a property that suggested an unfriendly imbalance in the relationship between superheroes and the normal world (which might extend to rifts between real-life parents and children, as if such rifts didn't already exist), preferred to stick to "friendly," assimilated characters like Superman, Batman and Plasticman. A decade would pass before creation of an *X-Men* animation cartoon. By the late 1980s, the wheel had turned and a new "lost generation" had developed: children of baby-boomers who'd grown up listening to their parents' disillusionment with the world, and had inherited the feeling that they would always be on the outside looking in when it came to social acceptance and financial security. Sociologists labelled these post–1962 children "Generation X" (a phrase invented by Canadian novelist Douglas Coupland, to his everlasting regret) — so what better set of role models than a superhero team with the letter "X" already built in to its name?

The first move into TV was a pilot episode shown as part of the 1988 syndicated potpourri *Marvel Action Universe* (q.v.): "Pryde of the X-Men." Kitty Pryde, a 14-year-old mutant "phaser" (and at the time a popular *X-Men* comics character), was located by Professor X's "Cerebro" computer and invited to join the professor's select group. In this half-hour, the X-Men included the aforementioned Cyclops, Colossus, Wolverine and Storm, as well as recent additions Nightcrawler (a German youth with "line of sight teleportation") and Dazzler (Alison Blair, a young lady who could turn sound into light). These oddly unattractive characters all spoke with thick ethnic accents; the Canadian Wolverine, for example, sounded Irish. Heading the villains was Magneto, a onetime colleague of Dr. Xavier's. Magneto (whose bad-guy motives were unexplained here, though they'd later be outlined in full on the series) was in charge of "Brotherhood of Mutant Terrorists," an echo of the "villain cartel" motif popularized in the 1970s and 1980s on Hanna-Barbera's *Super Friends*.

With the benefit of hindsight, it's easy to see why this first *X-Men* pilot didn't catch on. Though beautifully designed and animated, the story was much too busy and confusing; so much was thrown at the viewer all at once that even the explanatory voiceover narration of Stan Lee himself couldn't make heads or tails of things for those unfamiliar with the *X-Men* comic book. Writer Chris Claremont's leap-into-plot technique worked better on paper, where the reader could re-read and digest matters, than it did on TV, where the images were gone before the viewer could figure out who was doing what and why it was being done. Marvel recalled the *X-Men* TV version for retooling, with the intention of allowing non-fans of the original to catch up (and catch on!) to events in the second pilot film.

The year 1991 would have been ideal for the premiere of an *X-Men* series: it was the year that the *X-Men* comic book itself was redesigned and slicked up in the looming-shadow fashion of the contemporary *Batman* (q.v.) "graphic novels." This new, improved *X-Men* was launched with a printing of 7.5 million copies, extensive merchandising, and a massive publicity blitz in mainstream magazines and newspapers (the project made everyone involved, including the artists and writers, enormously wealthy—a far cry from the old "left in the lurch" days of *Superman* [q.v.] creators Siegel and Shuster). So where was the new *X-Men* TV series, announced with fulsome fanfare as the newest addition to the Fox Network Saturday morning lineup? Production glitches and post-production tinkering so delayed this much-anticipated project that executives of local Fox affiliates wore out their telephone ears responding to months of anxious calls from *X-Men* devotees. But delays and production tinkering resulted in anxious phone calls to Fox Network affiliates from the property's fans. At long last the weekly half-hour *X-Men* was introduced with a 60-minute pilot, tantalizingly available prior to telecast as a best-selling home video.

Characters on the new cartoon series included several carryovers from "Pryde": Professor X, Cyclops, Storm (more modestly dressed than her bare-midriffed counterpart on "Pryde") and Wolverine. Back from the earliest *X-Men* comics were Jean Grey (never referred to as Marvel Girl) and the Beast. New to TV were Jubilee, really Chinese-American adoptee Jubilation Lee, who inadvertently caused things to explode (her story was related in the opening episode when she joined the X-ers in the manner of Kitty Pryde; handshakes and vocal introductions were as good a way as any to identify logically all the characters by name); Rogue, a country gal with the ability to absorb the strength of anybody near her; and Gambit, a Cajun-accented worthy who altered things around him with kinetic explosive charges.

Except for Jubilee, the *X-Men* were not identified as teens but as nebulously younger than the powers-that-be, in the manner of the popular Fox prime time series *Beverly Hills 90210*. The character design was less forbidding and threatening than in the like-vintage comic books, and the mortality rate was held in check (although one new character named Morph was introduced in the pilot specifically for the plot-motivating purpose of being killed, just like the many faceless "Lieutenant Smiths" on the old live-action *Star Trek*), but there were still enough trademarks and trappings of the comics to satisfy hard-core *X* fans. Retained was the "outside looking in" approach to the characters' relationship with the Establishment, and the social pressures that sparked rivalries among the heroes themselves. And Wolverine, ever defiant in the face of mounting political correctness, still lost his temper when he felt like it and still continued to chain-smoke. Not surprisingly, Wolverine was one of the series' most popular characters.

Some "experts" suggested that *X-Men* was a pulp variation of the alienated-teen novels of S. E. Hinton, though this was the sort of pseudo-intellectualism that often justified the sociological studying of comic books (few pedants and professors want to admit that they read comics, because they actually *enjoy* them). Less subliminal were the TV series' allusions to the Civil Rights Movement of the 1950s and 1960s. The ruling class on *X-Men* didn't really come out and say that they hated mutants and planned to use existing laws against them, but there was an undeniable "Jim Crow" and "de facto segregation" atmosphere to the restraints put on the mutant underclass. A "Mutant Control Agency," ostensibly designed to protect the X-ers and their kind from persecution, was actually a repressive organization which sent out huge Sentinel robots to round up and contain those who were "different."

The civil rights theme was carried into the depiction of head villain Magneto. Originally Dr. Magnus, a kindly colleague of Professor Xavier's who shared Xavier's desire to battle prejudice against the mutants, Magneto began developing extraordinary powers himself—the ability to magnetize—and with them a sense of megalomania. Where Xavier wanted to set up coexistence between humans and mutants, Magneto desired to conquer the human race and set up his own rule. This division of interests was uncomfortably similar to the fracturing of the civil rights leadership in the 1960s, with the movement sagging under the weight of Moderates vs. Extremists. The power struggle affected the X-Men themselves, who fought among each other over what constituted "right," and challenged Xavier's wish to eradicate Magneto after the X-ers had been warned *not* to seek revenge on society.

Plenty of hidden meanings herein, but the *X-Men* series adroitly avoided the confusion inherent in the pilot episode. The extra time spent on pre-production helped the writers to sort out messages, motives and plotlines for the denser viewers (like myself)—and no matter how convoluted the plot or contradictory the characters, it was always a relatively easy matter to determine "who, what and why" on *X-Men*. The visual style was just as cluttered as on the "Pryde" pilot—some critics have accused the producers of deliberate murki-

ness to hide the second-rate animation—but *X-Men* pulled off the not inconsiderable trick of retaining the complexity of the comic books while simplifying events for the benefit of the casual viewer. (Of course, once the series got rolling and the audience settled into the weekly tune-in habit, the plots could and did become as intricate and multilayered as the writers wished.)

The results couldn't have been more salutary: *X-Men* wound up its first season as the second-highest-rated Saturday morning cartoon, and the number one animated series on Fox. The program had barely finished its first episode before thousands of viewers were answering Stan Lee's closing-credits invitation to join the *X-Men* fan club (a solicitation blatantly copied by Hanna-Barbera's *SwatKats* [q.v.]). And inevitably, multitudes of *X-Men* imitators came marching over the TV horizon as 1993 drew to a close—a list of animated series that will probably someday fill a book in itself.

YAKKY DOODLE *see* **YOGI BEAR**

YIPPEE, YAPPEE AND YAHOOEY *see* **PETER POTAMUS**

YOGI BEAR. (The following is a list of all cartoon series starring or featuring Yogi Bear.)
—**HUCKLEBERRY HOUND.** Syndicated: 1958. (See separate listing for details.)
—**THE YOGI BEAR SHOW.** Syndicated: January 1961. Hanna-Barbera/ Screen Gems. Produced and directed by William Hanna and Joseph Barbera. Written by Alex Lovy, Michael Maltese, and Warren Foster, among others. Music by Hoyt Curtin. Components: 1. **YOGI BEAR.** Voices: Daws Butler (Yogi Bear); Don Messick (Boo Boo/Ranger Smith); Julie Bennett (Cindy Bear). 2. **SNAGGLE-PUSS.** Voices: Daws Butler (Snagglepuss/ Major Minor). 3. **YAKKY DOODLE.** Voices: Jimmy Weldon (Yakky Doodle); Pinto Colvig (Chopper); Daws Butler (Fibber Fox).
—**YOGI'S GANG.** ABC: 9/8/1973–8/30/ 1975. Hanna-Barbera. Executive producers, William Hanna and Joseph Barbera. Directed by Charles Nichols. Music by Hoyt Curtin. Technical advisor: psychologist Dr. Tom Robischon. Voices: Same as

THE YOGI BEAR SHOW for Yogi Bear, Boo Boo, Ranger Smith, Snagglepuss. Additional voice credits: Daws Butler (Huckleberry Hound/Quick Draw McGraw/Augie Doggie/Wally Gator/Peter Potamus); Don Messick (Touche Turtle/Squiddly Diddly/Atom Ant/So-So); Henry Corden (Paw Rugg); John Stephenson (Doggie Daddy); Mel Blanc (Secret Squirrel). (Cross-reference: *Atom Ant, Banana Splits, Huckleberry Hound, Peter Potamus, Quick Draw McGraw, Wally Gator, Touche Turtle.*)
—SCOOBY'S ALL-STAR LAFF-A-LYMPICS. ABC: 9/10/1977–9/2/1978.
—SCOOBY'S ALL-STARS. ABC: 9/9/1978–9/8/1979.
—SCOOBY'S LAFF-A-LYMPICS. ABC: 6/12/1980–11/1/1980. (See *Scooby-Doo* for details on the three abovementioned series.)
—YOGI'S SPACE RACE. NBC: 9/9/1978–3/3/1979. Hanna-Barbera. Produced by Iwao Takamoto. Directed by Charles Nichols. Music by Hoyt Curtin. Components: 1. YOGI'S SPACE RACE. 2. GALAXY GOOF-UPS. Voices: Daws Butler (Yogi Bear/Huckleberry Hound); Joe Besser (Scarebear); John Stephenson (Captain Snerdly); Mel Blanc (Quack-Up); Frank Welker (Jabberjaw—on YOGI'S SPACE RACE only). 3. THE BUFORD FILES. 4. THE GALLOPING GHOST. (See listing on BUFORD AND THE GALLOPING GHOST for information on the two above listed components). (Cross-reference *Huckleberry Hound* and *Jabberjaw.*)
—YOGI'S TREASURE HUNT. Syndicated: 1985 (as component of FUNTASTIC WORLD OF HANNA-BARBERA). Hanna-Barbera. Executives in charge of production: Jayne Barbera, Jean MacCurdy. Executive producers, William Hanna, Joseph Barbera. Produced by Bob Hathcock; associate producer, Jeff Hall. Creative supervisor, Joe Taritero. Supervising director, Ray Patterson. Directed by Oscar Dufau, Tony Love, Rudy Zamora, Bill Hutten and Alan Zaslove. Animation directors: Bob Alvarez, Bob Goe, Bill Hutten, Rick Leon, Tony Love, Tim Walker and Irv Spence. Story direction by Ron Campbell, Jeff Hall, Alex Lovy and Jean Marshall. Story editors, Tom Ruegger and John K. Ludin. Creative design by Iwao Takamoto. Music by Hoyt Curtin; musical direction by Paul

DeKorte. Animation supervision by Willard Kitchen and Mike Langden. Animation facilities: Wang Film Production Co., Ltd., Cuckoo's Nest Studios. Computer animation consultant, Dr. Don Greenberg. Voices: Daws Butler (Yogi Bear/Huckleberry Hound/Quick Draw McGraw/Snooper/Blabbermouse/Augie Doggie/Snagglepuss); Don Messick (Boo Boo/Ranger Smith/Muttley); Arnold Stang (Top Cat); John Stephenson (Doggie Daddy); Paul Winchell (Dastardly); and Dick Erdman, Dick Gautier, Arlene Golonka, Bob Holt, Stacy Keach Sr., Gail Matthius, Don Messick, Rob Paulsen, Joni Robbins, Ann Ryerson, Andre Stojka, Janet Waldo, and Jonathan Winters. (Cross-reference the following series: *Dastardly and Muttley in Their Flying Machines, Huckleberry Hound, Quick Draw McGraw, Top Cat.*)
—YOGI BEAR. Syndicated: 1988. Hanna-Barbera. Executive producers: William Hanna, Joseph Barbera. Voices: Greg Burson (Yogi Bear); Don Messick (Boo Boo/Ranger Smith).
—FENDER BENDER 500. Syndicated: 1990. (*See* WAKE, RATTLE AND ROLL for details.)
—YO, YOGI! ABC: 9/14/1991–7/25/1992 (afterward on Family Channel). Syndicated: 1992 (FUNTASTIC WORLD). Hanna-Barbera. Executive producers, William Hanna and Joseph Barbera. Associate producers, Paul Sabella and Mark Young. Supervising director, Ray Patterson. Directed by Don Lusk, Paul Sommer, Carl Urbano, Jay Sarbry, Joanna Romersa. Main title music by Joe Christie; lyrics by Duncan Pain. Musical score by Jonathan Wolff. Animation facilities: Wang Film Production Co., Ltd., Fils-Cartoons. Voices: Greg Burson (Yogi Bear); Don Messick (Boo Boo); and Charlie Adler, Lewis Arquette, Greg Berg, Charlie Brill, Bernard Erhard, Pat Fraley, Pat Harrington Jr., Matt Hurwitz, Arte Johnson, Nancy Linari, Gail Matthius, Mitzi McCall, Allan Melvin, Howard Morris, Roger Nolan, Rob Paulsen, Henry Polic II, Neil Ross, Ronnie Schell, Hal Smith, Kath Soucie, John Stephenson, Sally Struthers, B. J. Ward, Lennie Weinrib, Frank Welker, Patric Zimmerman.
When Bill Hanna and Joe Barbera first pitched *The Huckleberry Hound Show* (q.v.) to Kellogg's Cereals in 1958, no cartoon had yet been filmed. All the pro-

ducers had were embryonic notions of the component stars of the new series: Huckleberry Hound, Pixie and Dixie the mice, and, in Joe Barbera's words, "two itinerant bears." Details could be filled in later on the secondary characters; it was Huckleberry whom Hanna and Barbera were promoting.

Within a few weeks of the *Huckleberry* premiere, it was clear that the series' nominal star was, in the minds of many viewers, coming off second best to those "itinerant" bears, who between concept and execution had evolved into Yogi Bear and his little pal Boo Boo. Three years after that fateful meeting with the Kellogg's folks, Yogi Bear was the biggest star in the Hanna-Barbera stable—a classic example of the scene-stealing supporting player who winds up getting all the bows.

Yogi Bear, carefree denizen of fictional Jellystone Park, was drawn in typical Hanna-Barbera compartmentalized fashion, a necktie and collar separating his head from his body so that full animation of the bruin's entire pelt would be unnecessary. His voice, supplied by Daws Butler, was patterned after Art Carney's Ed Norton character on *The Honeymooners* (very obviously so in the earliest cartoons). And his name was patterned after...

Well, there's a bit of controversy here. Hanna-Barbera has always claimed that several names were tested out, including Yo-Yo Bear and even Huckleberry Bear, before "Yogi" popped up arbitrarily in a story session and just happened to fit. By an allegedly unforeseen coincidence, this freshly minted cognomen just happened to sound a lot like baseball star Yogi Berra. Mr. Berra was also sensitive to the comparison, and failed to see the humor of it. Unhappy with being linked to a buffoonish cartoon character (and one with a better vocabulary at that), Berra threatened to take his discomfiture to his attorney. Legend has it that Yogi the First was talked out of his suit by friends who pointed out that "Yogi" was, after all, not his given name. Had Hanna-Barbera christened their character Lawrence Peter Bear, the ballplayer might have had a case. (As a footnote, one of Yogi Bear's proposed names was revitalized years later, when reruns of H-B's *The Hair Bear Bunch* was retitled *Yo Yo Bears* for syndication. As the "real" Yogi might have put it, it was déjà vu all over again.)

Hanna-Barbera tested Yogi in several story formats before his basic style was nailed down. In cartoons like "The Stout Trout," the bear was a Goofy-like fumbler. In "Duck in Luck" and "Foxy Hound Dog," he was a good samaritan, sheltering a baby duck for the winter in the first cartoon, rescuing a fox from a "yowp-ing" dog and pompous British sportsman in the second. Some plotlines had good-natured Yogi exploited by thoughtless humans: destructive little-kid tourists, big game hunters, bank robbers, mad scientists, and that most heinous of all predators, movie directors. Audiences were amused by the whole panorama, but responded best to those *Yogi Bear* cartoons in which Yogi, sometimes solo but most often in the company of his little bow-tied, nasal-voiced pal Boo Boo, did his utmost to filch every "pic-a-nic basket" in Jellystone Park.

Yogi saw himself as "Smarter than the av-er-age bear," to quote one of Hanna-Barbera's most tolerable catchphrases. He was certainly far smarter than most any other species, notably his principal human opposition, park ranger John Smith (who contrary to previously published reports was named "Smith" as early as 1958 and was *not* an unnamed entity until the early 1960s, though his character design was inconsistent in the first few cartoons). While he may have had a ballplayer's name and a voice from the *Honeymooners*, Yogi Bear's essential characterization was reminiscent of Phil Silvers' "Sergeant Bilko" character: grovelling in the face of Authority, snickering behind Authority's back, gleefully scamming everyone in sight to further his own comfort, and never losing rapport with an audience who'd give anything to get away with what Yogi got away with.

What the earliest *Yogi Bear* cartoons lacked in production finesse they made up for in droll, deadpan humor, some of the best verbiage in all of Hanna-Barbera. Out of innumerable choice bits of dialogue (mostly written by longtime Warner Bros. wordsmiths Michael Maltese and Warren Foster), my favorite is a line in 1959's "Show Biz Bear": Having been hired by a fly-by-night filmmaker to play "The Bear from Outer Space," Yogi was handed a script and told laconically to "look over the bear's part."

At the end of *Huckleberry Hound*'s second season, Yogi Bear had clearly outgrown his "also appearing" status and was

Yogi Bear does his patented suck-up job on Ranger Smith.

ready for his own cartoon series. Originally, Hanna-Barbera had intended to
premiere *The Yogi Bear Show* in the fall of
1961, but a falling-out between Kellogg's
and United Productions of America had
terminated the cereal firm's syndicated
sponsorship of *Mister Magoo* (q.v.) in October 1960. Stuck for a new series, Kellogg's requested that Hanna-Barbera
speed up Yogi's spinoff program, the result
being that *The Yogi Bear Show* made its
bow several months earlier than planned,
in January 1961. Yogi's replacement on
Huckleberry Hound was still another con-
artist forest creature, Hokey Wolf.

As full-fledged star, Yogi Bear dropped
the reactive, pantomimic stance he'd
adopted in some of his earlier adventures,
relying almost exclusively on dialogue to
carry the humor. The writing was, fortunately, sharper than ever, and the
animation and background design of *The
Yogi Bear Show* constituted Hanna-
Barbera's most accomplished 1961 work
outside of *The Flintstones* (q.v.).

Following the proven *Huckleberry
Hound* format, the half-hour *Yogi Bear
Show* headlined Yogi in his own weekly
adventure, with the rest of the program in
the hands of two component characters —
who, like Yogi, had been test-marketed on
earlier Hanna-Barbera projects. Snagglepuss, the Shakespearian lion whose
getaways were invariably heralded with a
theatrical "Exit . . . stage left," had appeared under his own name and as Snaggletooth in several *Quick Draw McGraw*
(q.v.) episodes, playing a comic villain opposite both Quick Draw and the cat-and-
mouse detective team Snooper and Blabber. In his own cartoons, Snagglepuss was
a tame, poetic gentleman lion, usually the
quarry of C. Aubrey Smith–like hunter Major Minor. Unlike Yogi Bear, Snagglepuss
was best enjoyed in small doses in other
characters' cartoons; as a star, his artistic
pretensions, fatuous monologues and too-
precious catchphrases ("Heaventh to
Murgatroyd") rapidly wore down one's patience. Significantly, Snagglepuss would

Yogi's Treasure Hunt. **In foreground: Boo Boo, Yogi. Digging: Doggie Daddy. In background: Ranger Smith, Quick Draw McGraw, Snagglepuss, Huckleberry Hound.**

stage a successful comeback on such Hanna-Barbera "gang" projects as *Yogi's Treasure Hunt* and *Scooby's All-Star Laff-a-Lympics* (see *Scooby-Doo*) where he had to share airtime with a passel of other H-B luminaries, and thus wasn't allotted enough time to become boring.

The remaining *Yogi Bear* component,

Yakky Doodle the diminutive duckling, was introduced as an unnamed quackster in one of the very first *Yogis* of 1958, the aforementioned "Duck in Luck." Actually, his roots went back farther than that: a seminal Yakky had appeared in several Hanna-Barbera *Tom and Jerry* theatrical cartoons of the 1950s, usually as a baby duck who'd lost "My Mamma." Jimmy Weldon, the voice of this earlier infant fowl, was hired by Hanna-Barbera to stick tongue in cheek and recreate his quasi-Donald Duck act as Yakky Doodle. The "Yakky" cartoons costarred Chopper, a golden-hearted bulldog who sounded like Wallace Beery (thanks to veteran voicemaster Pinto Colvig, who for many years had played Goofy for Walt Disney). As if to underline the resemblance, some of the dog's dialogue parodied the Beery–Jackie Cooper exchanges in such 1930s films as *The Champ*, with Chopper tearfully telling Yakky Doodle "You 'n' me can't be pals no more." Chopper's function was to protect the taste-tempting Yakky from the oven of hungry Fibber Fox, who, sustaining the celebrity-takeoff tone established on these cartoons, sounded like a cross between Groucho Marx and Shelly Berman. The "Yakky Doodle" segments were funnier than "Snagglepuss," but both paled in comparison to Yogi Bear's adventures. Yogi was the star, appropriating the best material by *droit du seigneur*.

Like many Hollywood biggies before him, Yogi Bear found himself functioning as studio goodwill ambassador in the early 1960s. In addition to box-office duty in the Kellogg's commercials, Yogi was mascot to many a military installation and submarine base, not to mention the unofficial spokesman of several state and national parks. He also went in for public service work, at least according to a 1962 *TV Guide* article about voice actor Daws Butler. When a bear escaped from a Seattle zoo in 1959, a local radio station avoided public panic by inveigling Butler, as Yogi, to tape-record a disclaimer: "Duh, it's not me, folks — it's some kind of impostor."

In another *TV Guide* article, in 1963, readers learned that at least one personality in Yogi's orbit had achieved notoriety by osmosis. Real-life ranger H. P. "Denny" Smith of real-life Yellowstone Park was convinced that constant tourist queries about somebody named "Yogi" were some sort of practical joke; he'd never seen the show! Once apprised that some impressionable youngsters had been persuaded that he was the "Ranger Smith" of TV fame, Denny Smith basked in the glory, giving autographs and sometimes "growling" behind rocks as Yogi for the benefit of fans. But like Daws Butler in Seattle, the "real" Ranger Smith was concerned that

kids would confuse lovable Yogi with Yellowstone's less lovable genuine bruins, so he found himself giving impromptu lectures on park safety — always careful not to impugn Yogi's reputation.

Two seasons' worth of new *Yogi Bear* cartoons were filmed for Yogi's own series, plus a half hour "Birthday Party" special syndicated in 1963. This, in addition to constant reruns of earlier *Yogis* on the Saturday-morning CBS live action series *Magic Land of Allakazam* and a prime time syndie package of 1962, *The Best of Huck and Yogi*, would seem to have brought the character to oversaturation level. Nay, no, m' lord. Less than a year after production had shut down on his series, Yogi was starred in Hanna-Barbera's first-ever theatrical cartoon feature, *Hey There, It's Yogi Bear* (1964). Never straying so far from accepted "Yogi Bear" formula as to alienate his fans, *Hey There, It's Yogi Bear* was still able to pull a feature's worth of value out of the character and his TV friends without undue strain. The film was distinguished by several pleasant songs, a non-syrupy romance involving Yogi and Cindy Bear (whose character had been barely visible on TV), and several well-wrought comedy situations, capped by a neat closing gag borrowed from the 1930 Harold Lloyd film *Feet First*. *Snow White* it wasn't, of course, but with fuller animation than audiences had come to expect from Hanna-Barbera, *Hey There, It's Yogi Bear* proved a moneymaker (it became a kiddie matinee and church-basement perennial), and also demonstrated that Yogi was a solid enough personality to please the crowd for any length of screen time, from six minutes to 90.

For the next few years, Yogi's appearances were concentrated in reruns, comic books and tie-in merchandise. Then in 1973 came *Yogi's Gang*, heralded by the 1972 pilot episode "Yogi's Ark Lark" on *The ABC Saturday Superstar Movie* (q.v.). The series was the first of many "monster rallies" of past Hanna-Barbera stars brought together for a single program. Yogi captained a flying ark, in the company of Boo Boo, Snagglepuss, Wally Gator, Augie Doggy and Doggy Daddy, and various personalities culled from such H-B series as *Atom Ant* (q.v.) and *Banana Splits* (q.v.). The purpose of this air journey was prosocial and pro-ecological, long before those movements had overtaken Saturday morning TV in the late 1980s: Yogi and friends did battle with such environmental/sociological ravagers as "Mr. Pollution," "Mr. Bigot" and "Lotta Litter." The stories were as subtle as the character names, but *Yogi's Gang* was a lot more palatable than the smug self-righteousness of the later *Captain Planet and the Planeteers* (q.v.).

Yogi's Space Race came along four years later (Yogi had appeared in the interim as part of the ensemble on *Scooby's All-Star Laff-a-Lympics*, discussed in detail in the notes on *Scooby-Doo*). *Space Race*, a 90-minute effort to latch onto the *Star Wars* bandwagon, adopted the never-ending *Wacky Races* (q.v.) format, with formerly top-billed Huckleberry Hound reduced to a supporting role, and a new character replacing Boo Boo, Scarebear (voiced by ex–Three Stooges patsy Joe Besser). Seen as a component feature each week was "The Galaxy Goof-Ups," wherein Yogi, Huck, Scarebear, Quack-Up the duck and Jabberjaw the Shark (see *Jabberjaw*) fought extraterrestrial lawbreakers under the guidance of Captain Snerdley. "Galaxy Goof-Ups" was spun off into a separate series, as were two other *Space Race* components, *Buford and the Galloping Ghost* (q.v.).

Yogi's natural charisma was stretched to the breaking point on *Yogi's Gang* and *Yogi's Space Race*. Both projects were handicapped by ragged artwork, poorly planned animation and a Laughtrack From Hell. The bear regained pride of place with the comparatively elaborate *Yogi's First Christmas*, a two-hour 1980 TV movie produced for a syndicated potpourri called "Operation Prime Time." Sentiment was ladled on straight from the buckets, as it would be again for the half hour 1982 CBS special *Yogi Bear's All-Star Comedy Christmas Caper*, but Yogi and his friends Huck Hound, Augie and Daddy, and Snagglepuss were in top form. Additional *Yogi Bear* specials included a brace of 1987 syndie one-shots, *Yogi and the Magical Flight of the Spruce Goose* and *Yogi's Great Escape*, both for "Hanna-Barbera's Superstar 10" package; a final "Superstar 10" in 1988, *Yogi and the Invasion of The Space Bears*; and a belated "answer" to *First Christmas*, 1994's *Yogi, the Easter Bear*.

Yogi remained off-network for his next major project: *Yogi's Treasure Hunt* (1985) was a half hour component of the weekend extravaganza *Funtastic World of Hanna-Barbera*, blending the "quest" format popularized by the *Indiana Jones* films with the social consciousness of *Yogi's Gang*. Taking his orders directly from old Hanna-Barbera hand Top Cat (q.v.), Yogi and a full cadre of H-B stars were sent to seek out the lost or stolen cash and valuables of deserving people before those pesky submarine pirates Dastardly and Muttley (see *Dastardly and Muttley in Their Flying Machines*) could retrieve the riches for their own use. Expensive-looking but uninspired, *Yogi's Treasure Hunt* managed to plod on for two seasons, proof that Yogi could still pack the house after 25 years even in a lesser vehicle (though by now his delightfully larcenous side was all but buried).

In 1988, a new batch of *Yogi Bear* five-minute cartoons were filmed to pad out the rerun manifest. Daws Butler had died, so Greg Burson took over as Yogi, doing a commendable if slightly perfunctory job. The new *Yogi Bear*s were back-to-basics slapstick, heightened by a few enjoyable self-conscious gags, the sort of "in" humor that is only possible when an audience is familiar to the point of intimacy with the characters. For example, when Boo Boo packs to leave Yogi's cave, his suitcase contains nothing but his trademarked bowties.

Fender Bender 500 (1990) starred Yogi and other H-B regulars in yet another shot at the "never ending chase" conceit—with Dastardly and Muttley back again as antagonists. This daily, serialized project was one of two components of Hanna-Barbera's cartoon/live action "strip" *Wake, Rattle and Roll* (q.v.).

The most recent *Yogi Bear* series was also the weakest: 1991's *Yo Yogi*, a demeaning "retro" project along the lines of *Flintstone Kids* (see *Flintstones*) and *A Pup Named Scooby-Doo* (q.v.). In this weekly network half hour, teenaged versions of Yogi, Boo Boo, Huck Hound, Snagglepuss and Dastardly and Muttley (won't they *ever* go home?) cruised "Jellystone Mall" (what happened to all that 1970s pro-ecology?). Three guesses as to the level of humor on this one. *Yo Yogi's* sole distinction was its advertising tie-in with a breakfast cereal; each box contained a premium set of polarized plastic glasses, so that the viewers could watch a weekly 3-D highlight sequence of Yogi and his friends.

Produced by the Nuoptix company, this *Yo Yogi* gimmick didn't immediately lead to an onslaught of televised 3-D, indicating that perhaps neither cereal nor series was a worldbeater. (The next prominent utilization of 3-D animation would occur on 1993's *The Bots Master* [q.v.], another Nuoptix project.)

We can, thankfully, be permitted to treat *Yo Yogi* as a temporary aberration. The original *Yogi Bear* is still with us in syndication and on cable, enhanced by amusing wraparound montage sequences of past cartoon highlights, complemented with semi-satiric narration. Like *The Flintstones*, *Yogi Bear* has matured from a novelty to a national institution. Maybe he wasn't really smarter than the av-er-age bear, but he was a lot more appealing and enduring.

YOUNG ROBIN HOOD. Syndicated: 1991–92. (Part of FUNTASTIC WORLD OF HANNA-BARBERA.) Cinar/Hanna-Barbera. A Cinar/France Animation/Antennae 2 Production, in association with: Crayon Animation/France Animation/Fils-Cartoons/Global Television Network/Family Channel (Canada)/Centre National de la Cinematographie/Sofica Confirmage 3. Supervising producer, Cassandra Schafhausen. Produced by Ronald A. Weinberg and Christian Davin. Executive consultants: Paul Sabella, Jayne Barbera, Kay Wright. Creative consultant: Bruce D. Johnson, Mark Young. Story editors: Peter Landecker, Christophe Izard. Music by Leon Aronson. Voices: Sonja Ball (Will Scarlet); Thor Bishopric (Robin Hood); Kathleen Fee (Mathilda); Jessalyn Gilsig (Gertrude of Griswold); A. J. Henderson (Sheriff of Nottingham); Anik Matern (Maid Marian); Bronwen Mantel (Hagalah); Michael O'Reilly (Alan-A-Dale); Michael Rudder (Prince John); Terrence Scammell (Little John); Harry Standjofsky (Brother Tuck).

The only new 1991 addition to the *Funtastic World of Hanna-Barbera* (q.v.) weekend cartoon marathon was the Euro/American coproduction *Young Robin Hood*. Originally produced in Canada and France in 1989 under the auspices of Hanna-Barbera creative consultant Mark Young, and first telecast in the Western hemisphere by Canada's Family Channel cable service in 1990, *Young Robin Hood* was brought to the States in 1991 to cash in

on the popularity of Kevin Costner's recent theatrical film version of the Robin Hood legend. The animated series followed a Hanna-Barbera pattern established on *Flintstone Kids* (see *The Flintstones*) and *A Pup Named Scooby-Doo* (see *Scooby-Doo*), depicting a group of well-known fictional characters at an earlier point of their lives. This time around, Young Robin Hood and his Merrie Men were teens and preteens — even "Brother" Tuck. Robin was 14 years old, Maid Marian and Tuck were both 13, and Will Scarlet was so young (12, to be exact) that his voice was provided by an actress! In true "generation gap" fashion, Prince John was older than the good guys — all of 19 years old.

In keeping with this fountain-of-youth approach, *Young Robin Hood*'s pressbook was careful to note that the series was designed to explore the "origin" of Robin Hood's "mission." And in keeping with the usual Hanna-Barbera predilection for improving upon the studio's source material, a whole Sherwood Forest full of new characters was introduced. Mathilda was Marian's nurse, along for the ride as an (implicit) escort for her blossoming mistress. Hagalah, Robin Hood's "surrogate mother," was a kindly sorceress. Seventeen-year-old Gilbert of Griswold was the "jock" assistant to the Sheriff of Nottingham, as well as Robin's rival for Marian (nurse Mathilda sure had her work cut out for her). Gilbert's sister was Gertrude, whose sole function was to emit jealous thought-waves at the very sight of poor Marian. And to make up for the fact that the anonymous 14th-century authors of the Robin Hood legend had overlooked the inclusion of funny animals, Hanna-Barbera took up the slack by introducing three non-human *Young Robin Hood* cast members: Robin's falcon Arrow, Hagalah's white cat Miranda, and Gilbert's surly mastiff Bruno.

Even so, *Young Robin Hood* did no more damage to the legend than had Kevin Costner's "New Age" film version. At least the cartoon series didn't give us a Robin Hood with an Oklahoma accent, nor subject us to a gratuitous shot of Costner's stuntman's bare backside.

Animation magazine singled out *Young Robin Hood* as an example of the "subtle changes" the TV cartoon industry was then undergoing, noting that the series was "a

Young Robin Hood, with younger Maid Marian.

departure from [Hanna-Barbera's] familiar line of comedy critters and the ever popular *Flintstones* and *Jetsons* series." A departure it was, as well it should have been, since Hanna-Barbera had virtually nothing to do with *Young Robin Hood's* European animation work—nor even its voiceover work, which was produced in Canada. (See also *Rocket Robin Hood*.)

THE YOUNG SENTINELS (SPACE SENTINELS). NBC: 9/10/1977–9/2/1978. Filmation. Executive producers: Norm Prescott, Lou Scheimer. Produced by Don Christensen. Directed by Hal Sutherland. Written by J. Michael Reaves, Kathleen Barnes, Jerry Winnick, Don Glut, David Wise. Music by Yvette Blais and Jeff Michael. Voices: George DiCenzo (Hercules/Sentinel One); Dee Timberlake (Astrea); Evan Kim (Mercury); and Ross Hagen (M. O.).

The *Young Sentinels* (1977) combined the outer-space concept recently regalvanized by the first *Star Wars* film with elements of Greco/Roman legend. This weekly, half hour Filmation series was a last-gasp entry in the "superhero" genre, which had been dying out on Saturday mornings in the past couple of seasons;

Young Sentinels was in fact the *only* new superhero program to appear on the 1977-78 Saturday morning map.

The backstory: Sentinel One, a life force from another galaxy, landed on Ancient Earth, whence he chose three teenagers as potential saviors for the future. These three, given extraordinary powers by Sentinel One, were Hercules, a WASP-ish blonde of enormous strength; Mercury, a swift-of-foot Asian; and Astrea, a young black woman with the ability to metamorphose into any shape or life form. (Like many Filmation productions of the era, *The Young Sentinels* stressed multiculturalism, but this was one of the first instances that the studio actually hired minority actors to do the voices of the minority characters.) The three Young Sentinels were transported back to earth after being "superpowered" by Sentinel One; their space vessel landed in a volcano, wherein the trio awaited being called upon to protect the oppressed and to safeguard the environment (anticipating the much-later series *Captain Planet* [q.v.].) Maintaining the link to *Star Wars* was the robot M.O. (Maintenance Operator), Sentinel One's chief assistant.

In mid-season, *The Young Sentinels*,

which had been lagging far behind ABC's *Scooby's All-Star Laff-a-Lympics* (see *Scooby-Doo*), was moved to a different timeslot—and simultaneously retitled *Space Sentinels*. It has been suggested that the name change was prompted by NBC's seeking what it called a "stylistic linkup" with the live-action Filmation show *Space Academy*, then on CBS. It's more likely, however, that the network was worried that kids were tuning out because (a) the original *Young Sentinels* didn't tip off the series' outer space trappings, and (b) most younger viewers didn't know what a "Sentinel" was. Whatever the case, *Space Sentinels* couldn't stand up to the ratings challenge of CBS' *Isis* (also produced by Filmation) and ABC's *Krofft SuperShow*. All that ended up being retained from the moribund *Space Sentinels* was its artists' rendition of Hercules, who in 1978 co-starred in the "Freedom Force" component on Filmation's *Tarzan and the Super Seven* (q.v.).

ZAZOO U. Fox: 9/8/1990–1/19/1991; 2/2/1991–8/31/1991. Phil Mendez Productions/Hanna-Barbera.

Zazoo U, a self-styled "socially conscious" Fox weekly, took place in a university for anthropomorphic animals. The student body included the likes of Boink, Tess, Grizzle, and Bully. I can't say that I remember much of the brief glimpse I had of *Zazoo U's* debut episode (my six-year-old son insisted I change the channel, and chances are his instincts were correct). The Fox Network would probably like to forget *Zazoo U* as well, since it proved to be lame competition for *Muppet Babies* (q.v.) on CBS—not to mention the less formidable opposition of NBC's *Captain N* (q.v.) and ABC's *Wizard of Oz* (q.v.).

After four months, *Zazoo U's* timeslot was appropriated by Fox's *Peter Pan and the Pirates* (q.v.). One week later, *Zazoo* was back, this time so early in the morning that its few fans needed a couple of strong slugs of java to get through the whole half hour. This, added to the fact that many Fox affiliates weren't even carrying the show at this point, led to the unilateral shutdown of *Zazoo U's* curriculum by the time the next semester rolled around.

ZORAN, SPACE BOY. Syndicated: 1966. Global Productions.

The Japanese-produced *Zoran, Space Boy* featured the saucer-eyed title character and his pet squirrel, who came to earth in search of Zoran's sister. Ninety-six half hour episodes managed to elude most middle-sized American markets, while getting limited play in large cities with heavy Asiatic populations. The principal function of *Zoran, Space Boy* seems to be not as entertainment but to provide a final entry in virtually every piece on TV cartoons ever written—as it does here.

ZORRO *see* **TARZAN**

Closing Credits:
Cartoon Voices

The success of a fully animated theatrical cartoon can be attributed to the director, animators, background artists, storyboard staff, and musical arranger. The success of a barely animated TV cartoon frequently rests on the shoulders of those hardy souls who stand before a microphone and pay the bills by pretending to be mice, hounds, ducks and hedgehogs. Denied lavish animation budgets for the most part, TV cartoons have had to rely on dialogue. From *Crusader Rabbit* onward, the strength of the made-for-TV cartoon has been in its voice talent.

At first, this was a thankless vocation. Historically, cartoon producers have been averse to doling out on-screen credit to anyone, figuring (like Walt Disney) that a solo credit was the divine right of the producer. Animators and other technical people fought long and hard to get their names on screen, but voice actors were ignored in the battle. There have been many theories as to why these actors were cloaked in anonymity, but most performers hold to the belief that the studios refused to bestow credit so that no one performer would feel indispensable. "Don't hold us up for salary! We can get anyone to play Popeye (or Droopy, or Bugs) and the public will never know the difference." Mel Blanc changed all that in 1942. After several years of providing virtually all the voices of Warner Bros.' *Looney Tunes* and *Merrie Melodies*, Blanc was denied a well-deserved salary hike. "Well," Mel responded, "if you won't give me a raise, how about at least giving me a screen credit?" The studio balked, but then realized that this concession would cost nothing. Thereafter, every cartoon issued by Warner Bros. would carry the credit "Voice characterization by Mel Blanc."

For many years, however, Blanc was virtually alone in his recognition, as both theatrical and TV cartoons went on blissfully ignoring voice actors in their credits. On the 1949 edition of *Crusader Rabbit* only distributor Jerry Fairbanks received screen billing; ignored were the series' physical producer/animators Jay Ward and Alex Anderson, and Lucille Bliss as Crusader.

583

With the TV entree of Hanna-Barbera studios in 1957, actors began to attain on-screen recognition—actually *two* actors, Daws Butler and Don Messick, who did so much work for Hanna-Barbera in the late 1950s that the producers would have been both foolish and ungrateful not to give credit where due. *Rocky and His Friends* producer Jay Ward also recognized the value of his voice people, especially since one of them was his business partner Bill Scott; there was a longer actors' credit list on Ward's productions than on any previous TV cartoon. Still, not every voice actor was afforded billing. It was more cost efficient for the producers of such series as *Huckleberry Hound*, *The Alvin Show* and *Calvin and the Colonel* to film one single closing-credit segment per year, listing only the principal voice personalities who performed on a regular weekly basis and bypassing freelance "guest stars." In other instances, actors were unheralded because of conflicting contractual commitments. Daws Butler was easily recognizable in his various roles on *Rocky and His Friends* and *The Bullwinkle Show*, but both of these series were sponsored by General Mills—and to give Butler credit would compromise his commitment to Hanna-Barbera (where he *was* billed), whose syndicated series were sponsored by Kellogg's Cereals.

From the late 1960s onward, changes in Screen Actors' Guild rules required that billing be awarded to anyone with five lines or more per program. Accordingly, voice credits on cartoons began to be double-columned, alphabetized to avoid scraps over "top billing." Some studios, notably Hanna-Barbera, were so overloaded with cartoon assignments in the 1970s and 1980s that they could not keep relying solely on their core voice talent (Daws Butler, Don Messick, Paul Frees, June Foray, et al.), especially since union regulations permitted only four hours per recording session. Nor did the producers have the luxury of directing those sessions themselves, as they once had. Thus, more and more performers were added to the roster, and a new supervisory position, "voice director," was created to handle the traffic.

Hanna-Barbera's Gordon Hunt, hired in 1980, was the industry's first fulltime voice director. While he appreciated and recognized the "regulars" in the business, Hunt also wanted to inject some new blood into the voice pool, so he brought in several stage actors who had not had a lot of on-screen experience but who could be relied upon for versatile vocal calisthenics. The resulting overpopulated voice sessions were costly, not so much in terms of up-front money as in residual payments, those union-dictated fees paid to actors on an annual basis for the first seven reruns of a filmed or taped TV performance. To avoid this financial drain, some parsimonious cartoon producers of the 1980s and 1990s began relying on less expensive voicework recorded in Canada, where actors were paid only once for their efforts, *sans* residuals. Actors likewise began trekking north of the border, also for financial reasons. While Canadian recording sessions afforded no residuals, the payments per diem were frequently higher than in Hollywood.

Whether the actors are congregated in Canada or California these days, they are still at the mercy of indifferent, downright ignorant typesetters and computer processors when it comes to screen credit. No one (except, of course, the actor) seems to care if the name is spelled right, so long as the union obligation is fulfilled and the name shows up on screen. Lucille Bliss suffered the indignity of being rechristened "Lou Bliss" by Hanna-Barbera when the studio wanted to sustain the illusion that the little boy character whom she was portraying was in fact a male child, but this is a rare example of a deliberate misrepresentation. Perhaps it is understandable if not condonable that performers like Rene Auberjonois and Andre Stojka find infinite variations on their surnames. And perhaps Maurice LaMarche's well-deserved special billing on Nelvana's *Easter Fever* took some of the sting out of seeing his name spelled "LaMarsh." But how can one forgive such gaffes as "Len Mars" for Ken Mars or "Maggie Boswell" for Maggie Roswell?

Few performers have had the letters of their name rearranged and mangled with more frequency than Kath Soucie, an actress who has contributed a rich variety of characterizations on such programs as *Rugrats, Captain Planet and the Planeteers, Sonic the Hedgehog, Tiny Toon Adventures* and *Darkwing Duck*. Over the past decade Ms. Soucie has been billed as Kathy E. Soucie, Cathy Soucie, Cathy Souci, Kath E. Souci, and so on (I may have even spotted a "Katy Sousie," but I can't bet on it). Could this conceivably have been a *calculated* ploy of the actress to draw attention to herself, perhaps changing the spelling with each character as a publicity stunt? The answer is no, non, nyet, nada. When asked, Kath Soucie graciously but emphatically denied a "master plan" in these misspellings, attributing the many variations on her professional cognomen to "plain old carelessness."

Voice actors may take their billing seriously, but tend to loosen up a bit (or more than a bit) when it comes to the job itself. Descriptions of the atmosphere surrounding cartoon recording sessions range from sedate to certifiably insane. Barry Gordon welcomed "the relaxed setting" and the flexible hours of his work as Donatello on *Teenage Mutant Ninja Turtles*; in contrast, another actor likened a recording session directed by the extroverted Ginny McSwain to "working with the Mad Hatter." McSwain, herself a voice actress who had once been Gordon Hunt's assistant, was legendary in cartoon circles for directing the most manic recording gigs this side of a Guns N' Roses album. "I'm pretty rough on people, even some of the good ones get a workout from me. I'm not there to pamper or stroke them and I don't have time for anyone who can't keep up."

Not that Ginny McSwain brandishes a whip and chair. It is simply that her actors are verbally pummelled and cajoled into giving their very best. If an actor is capable of coming up with a louder, deeper, whinier, funnier or more threatening voice for his character, Ginny McSwain and other like-minded vocal directors will prod, poke and pounce until the actor exceeds his or her own expectations. And far from resenting the forced extra effort, most voice specialists thoroughly enjoy this sort of near-cathartic intensity. April Winchell (*Bonkers, Goof Troop*) sums up her work thusly: "For me, it's therapeutic because I'm screaming all day. I'm making my PMS work for me."

Though voice actors occasionally resent the qualifying word "voice," preferring to be regarded as actors pure and simple, they are with some justification adjudged a breed apart by the rest of the acting community. Movie and TV stars, used to relying on movement and physical attributes to contribute to their characterizations, often sign up for cartoon work expecting to breeze through the experience without sweat. These on-camera actors just as often walk out of recording sessions shaking their heads in amazement over the amount of effort, body language and raw, uninhibited energy expended by the regular voice artists. Voice director Kris Zimmerman notes, "Some people think cartoons are so easy to do, and then you put them in a room with [voice actors] Frank Welker and Charlie Adler and Rob Paulsen and Jim Cummings, and watch their faces. Big name celebrities with their mouths hanging open, going 'Oh, my God, how do they do that?'"

Sometimes voice people themselves can be amazed. June Foray, the longtime voice of Rocky, Natasha and many others on Jay Ward's *Rocky and His Friends*, was hired in the early 1990s to recreate those roles for a series of Taco Bell commercials. Just as she had done in the *Rocky* heyday of the 1960s, Foray switched from character to character without pausing for breath. "At one point," noted commercial director Bob Kurtz, "she made the change so quickly she actually stepped on her own line! Frank Welker was working with her and he said, 'How does she do that?'" The same Frank Welker whose list of voice credits is as long as June Foray's.

Welker, Foray and others of their ilk are obliged to be astonishingly versatile in order to eat. There was a time when the voiceover corps was a small one, but the influx of talent engendered by Gordon Hunt turned the profession into as competitive an endeavor as professional football. While Daws Butler was forced at one point in the early 1960s to turn down work from his own home studio of Hanna-Barbera (no ego trip, he was simply too busy), voice artists of the 1990s do not have that luxury. "You have to do something better than anyone else," noted casting director Andrea Romano. "I was always looking for new talent, but not talent that was just new—they had to be brilliant, they had to compete with people like Frank Welker, Tress MacNeille, Rob Paulsen and all these wonderful actors and actresses who do this all the time."

Bob McFadden, an "A-List" veteran of the cartoon voice business (the title role on *Milton the Monster* was one of his many gigs), underlined this competitive spirit when discussing his job as the "Ring around the collar!" parrot in a series of early–1980s detergent commercials. When called for the role, McFadden did the "standard" parrot character, then regaled the director with several varieties of parrots. "I was showing the director my versatility. You're always trying to get some extra edge on your competitors." Russi Taylor, the voice of Huey, Dewey and Louie in *DuckTales*, has secured a demand for her services in the international TV market of the 1990s through her fluency in four different languages. And it is said that when an equally prominent voice actress of the 1960s answered the call to play an animated big toe, she immediately won the part over many other aspirants by demurely asking the director, "The left toe or the right toe?"

Who are these people?

Many actors had a propensity for vocal versatility at a very early age. Several had been professional performers since childhood, among them Dick Beals (*Funny Company, Frankenstein Jr.*), Walter Tetley ("Sherman" on *Rocky and His Friends*), Susan Silo (many roles, including a *male* mad scientist on *Biker Mice from Mars*), Janet Waldo (*The Jetsons, Perils of Penelope Pitstop*), and Barry Gordon (*Teenage Mutant Ninja Turtles*). Some were even stars in adolescence. Barry Gordon won a Tony nomination at age 14 for the stage play *A Thousand Clowns*, while Janet Waldo played the teenaged lead on radio's *Meet Corliss Archer*.

Radio has always been a prime breeding ground for voice artists; when one relies almost exclusively on one's larynx to make a living in the first place, providing voices for anthropomorphic animals, vegetables and minerals should cause no great trepidations. The aforementioned Mel Blanc and June Foray, along with Don Messick (*Scooby-Doo* and virtually the entire Hanna-Barbera output) and Paul Frees (zillions of voices), all started in radio's "Golden Age" of the 1930s and 1940s, making their marks in an overcrowded profession with programs wherein they played all the roles. Blanc and Messick hosted daily free-form comedy programs in their home towns; Foray wrote and acted in a Los Angeles series called *Lady Make Believe* when she was barely out of high school; and Frees, billed as "America's most versatile actor," was heard in a syndicated one-man mystery anthology, *The Player*.

Others who built their reputations on radio include Julie Bennett, who played most of the female and adolescent roles in the early Hanna-Barbera cartoons and in the TV output of UPA (*Mr. Magoo, Dick Tracy*); the still very young Bennett was the only American outside of Orson Welles to be heard on the British Broadcasting Corporation's *Sherlock Holmes* radio series of the early 1950s. Lucille Bliss (*Crusader Rabbit*) was a fixture of such San Francisco–based programs as *Candy Matson* and *Pat Novak for Hire* in the late 1940s, and had almost won the plum role of Charlie McCarthy's "teenaged foil" on Edgar Bergen's popular radio program when Chase and Sanborn abruptly cancelled the show. And Hal Smith, a prolific voice man for such programs as *Clutch Cargo* and *Davey and Goliath* (and best known for his on-screen role as Otis Campbell on *The Andy Griffith Show*), spent most of the 1940s as a radio writer, singer and disc jockey.

Likewise graduating from "platters 'n' chatters," albeit more recently, was Townsend Coleman, whose radio-emcee reputation was so solid in 1985 that he hosted a nationally syndicated music video weekly, *The Dance Show*. This of course was before Coleman settled down to do such celebrated cartoon voices as "Michaelangelo" on *Teenage Mutant Ninja Turtles*. Even more recently, Billy West, "Stimpy" of *Ren and Stimpy* and "Doug" in the cartoon series of the same name, built up his fan following as a regular contributor to "shock jock" Howard Stern's radio talkfest.

Before that, however, Billy West appeared before live audiences as a comedian, a profession that has yielded many other voice artists. Howard Morris was a comic fixture of Sid Caesar's many TV variety offerings of the 1950s and of the entire CBS sitcom manifest of the 1960s (*The Andy Griffith*

Show, The Dick Van Dyke Show, The Danny Thomas Show); all the while, his voice could be heard in an exhausting variety of guises on such cartoon ventures as *The Flintstones, The Jetsons, Beetle Bailey* and *The Famous Adventures of Mr. Magoo*. Hamilton Camp, who had been at his craft since appearing in the Boris Karloff fright film *Bedlam* at the age of 12, achieved prominence as a comic actor in films and TV in the 1960s and 1970s (he was the funny apartment super on the Dick Benjamin–Paula Prentiss "cult" sitcom *He and She*, and was supposed to be a regular on the notorious one-episode flop *Turn On*), enjoying additional exposure as an "improv" comedy player on producer Paul Sills' syndicated *Story Theatre*. Camp's many cartoon assignments include *The Smurfs, DuckTales* and *The Incredible Hulk*; recently, the actor came full circle with another child role on *The Flintstone Kids*.

Probably the best known "reformed" comic in the cartoon industry is Frank Welker, whose standup act opened for such musical performers as Sergio Mendez, Brasil 66 and the Righteous Brothers in the 1960s. Later on, Welker was an ensemble sketch comic on *The Don Knotts Show* (1971) and *Laugh Trax* (1982). Cartoon devotees hold Frank Welker in highest esteem for his long and fruitful career as a "funny animal" specialist, wherein he has provided a wealth of amusing and endearing barks, growls, whimpers, purrs, and even one "Curly Howard" shark (*Jabberjaw*). Nowadays, Welker is deservedly honored with star billing for such roles as "Itsy Bitsy Spider" in the series of the same name.

Along with comedians, many "straight" actors with years of classical training behind them have made the transition to animation. Prominent among contemporary theatrical artists who have "gone cartoon" is Cornell University graduate Pat Fraley, who toured Australia in Shakespearean repertory before settling in Los Angeles for such cartoon assignments as the title roles in *Denver the Last Dinosaur* and *Bravestarr*. Tony Jay, who achieved American fame with his multiple roles in the Royal Shakespeare Company's marathon staging of *Nicholas Nickelby*, remained in demand throughout the 1980s and 1990s both on camera and in the sound booth, providing smooth erudition (both heroic and villainous) to such animated projects as *Tale Spin*, *Wild West C.O.W.-Boys of Moo Mesa*, and *Mighty Max*.

Tony Jay's specialty in his cartoon work has been a remarkably succinct imitation of movie leading man George Sanders. In this, Jay is copacetic with most other voice masters, who if asked could turn out celebrity imitations by the yard. Paul Frees certainly did so, and in fact was called upon to substitute for well known actors when they were indisposed for post-dubbing—even recording the dialogue of one TV series actor (Peter Deuel) who had committed suicide before his production schedule had wrapped! Phil Hartman, a regular on *Saturday Night Live* and contributor to such animated fare as *Dennis the Menace* and *The Simpsons*, currently counts 99 voices, many of them celebrity takeoffs, in his repertoire.

Yes, these very special actors *could* get by on imitation alone in their cartoon work—but do not ever tell *them* that. If there is one thing any self-respecting voice actor hates, it is being told that he is merely a shadow of someone else's vocal chords. Not only does it suggest a lack of creativity, but it also tends to limit the work possibilities. Discussing such legendary voice people as Daws Butler and Don Messick for an *Animato* magazine interview, Billy West noted, "To me these guys are the geniuses. . . . I think you had to twist their arm to do impressions. And I understand why today. Because impressionists can put you out of business in two seconds. Once the hard work is done creating something, that's the hard thing, and then there's loads of people who can do it once it's established."

Daws Butler realized this. He had started in show business as part of a 1940s nightclub act ("The Three Short Waves") doing parodies of well known radio actors, and his first major national exposure came with an imitation of *Dragnet* co-star Ben Alexander on Stan Freberg's classic comedy record "St. George and the Dragonette." But when told to come up with a voice for Hanna-Barbera's Yogi Bear that sounded like Art Carney's Ed Norton character from *The Honeymooners*, Butler knew that if he locked himself into an impression, any decent Carney imitator could take the job away from him. Thus, while Art Carney may have provided the springboard for Yogi Bear, the ultimate characterization was deepened and enriched until it was firmly Daws Butler's alone. The same applied to Butler's "almost" imitations of Bert Lahr for the cartoon character Snagglepuss, of Marlon Brando for Jinx the Cat, and of 1930s movie comedian Charles Butterworth for Cap'n Crunch. The celebrity inspirations were clear, but thanks to the genius of Daws Butler, the cartoon personalities emerged as pure, and beloved, originals.

The best of the voiceover brigade not only deal in originality, but can even shape the destinies of the characters they have been hired to play. Mel Blanc's amorous skunk Pepe Le Pew was basically a single-note personality, and his cartoons told the same story over and over again. Yet the viewer never tired of Pepe, simply because Blanc had the knowhow to find little nuances and fresh shadings in each cartoon. The actor's creative input helped to make a character intended to be a one-shot into one of Warner Bros.' most enduring properties. In more recent times, Jim Cummings, often called the "Mel Blanc of Disney," has seen several of his cartoon roles (Bonkers T. Bobcat, Darkwing Duck, Winnie the Pooh) take on the facial expressions and body English of Cummings himself. The notoriously difficult to please Ginny McSwain was once moved to remark "Do you know how much Jim Cummings has contributed to the writing and mannerisms of any character he's given?"

In a similar "It's what you bring to your work that counts" vein, Nancy Cartwright has taken the character of Bart Simpson, who started his tenure on Fox's *The Simpsons* as a flat-out obnoxious creep, and developed a multi-faceted characterization that manages to be loveable even when damnable. In so doing, Cartwright (with of course the considerable input of her writers) has gone a long way towards taking the "shocking" onus off the irreverent Bart for those early *Simpsons* critics who condemned the program as irredeemably offensive. And even as Nancy Cartwright's emotional range as an actress has rubbed off on Bart Simpson, a little of Bart has rubbed off on her.

When confronting her series' non-fans, Cartwright has been known to respond, in character, "It's a cartoon, man! It's for your entertainment! It's not the Bible!"

Despite Nancy Cartwright's feigned insouciance, the voice-acting fraternity includes some of show business' most caring individuals. Daws Butler once voluntarily defused a public panic over an escaped zoo bear in Seattle by going on radio and assuring the listeners that the escapee *wasn't* Yogi. June Foray, a longtime advocate of improving the standards of children's entertainment and TV animation, has over the years served with such organizations as the Motion Picture Academy's Board of Governors (she was chairperson of the Academy's Student Film Awards) and the Advisory Board of Turner Broadcasting's Cartoon Network. And practically any cartoon voiceperson can be counted on for "above and beyond" compassionate service to her or his fans. *Teenage Mutant Ninja Turtles* costars Rob Paulsen ("Raphael") and Cam Clarke ("Leonardo") have contributed to Famous Fone Friends, a telephone service that allows seriously ill children to converse with their favorite cartoon stars. "I'm blessed with a healthy son," notes Paulsen, "and if hearing from a 'Turtle' can help just one youngster feel better, I'll gladly offer my services."

So many people, so many stories, so little space. We do not mean to minimize the contributions of those voice actors whom we have not mentioned in this chapter. Alas, like a typical afternoon cartoon show, we have spent so much time with the "body" of the story that we are left with very little time to run the credits. Herewith we offer a rapid tip of the hat to such luminescent vocal stars as Hans Conried, Dal McKennon, Julie McWhirter, Doug Young, Michael Bell, Scott Menville, Susan Blu, Pauline Little, Bill Callaway, Katie Leigh, Dan Hennessey, Jean VanderPyl, John Stocker, Jeanne Elias, Greg Burson, Jim MacGeorge, Debi Deryberry, Allen Swift, George S. Irving, Walker Edmiston, Marilyn Schreffler, Edmund Gilbert, Chuck McCann, Terry McGovern, Michael Rye, Marilyn Lightstone, Neil Ross, Corey Burton, Sid Raymond, Corinne Orr . . .

The list goes on, and unfortunately we do not have the space to make it all-inclusive, so we will wrap it up with a viewer alert. If you have a quick eye and a quicker finger on the remote control button, you just might see as well as hear some of the best cartoon voice people, any hour of the day, thanks to the miracle of cable TV. Be on the lookout for Cree Summer, "Penny" on *Inspector Gadget*, as college coed Freddie Brooks on the Bill Cosby–produced sitcom *A Different World*; Joe Alaskey, "Plucky Duck" on *Tiny Toon Adventures*, as the hilariously feckless Beano Froelich on the weekly fantasy show *Out of This World*; John Stephenson, "Mr. Slate" on *The Flintstones*, as arrogant attorney Roger Crutcher on the vintage Jackie Cooper series *The People's Choice*; Dan Castellaneta, "Homer" on *The Simpsons*, as a comedy-ensemble regular on the variety series *The Tracey Ullman Show*; and "Space Ghost" and "Roger Ramjet" himself, Gary Owens, as the unctuous announcer of *Rowan and Martin's Laugh-In*.

Finally, a few personal glimpses:

After a hectic recording session featuring Frank Welker with a group of child actors on their first job, one of the kids went up to Welker and asked, "Do you have to go back to work after this?"

Jim Cummings, reading a bedtime story to his daughter Livia, was stopped in mid-characterization by the surfeited young lady, who sighed, "Dad, it's getting late. Just read the story. Don't do voices, okay?"

Lucille Bliss, commenting on competition in the voicework field: ". . . [E]xpect a lot of rejection. Treat the job like a streetcar. Let the car go by, there will be another car . . . Jump on the next one, and go for it."

Rob Paulsen on the subject of *Teenage Mutant Ninja Turtles*: "I'm proud to be a part of something that has essentially become part of the culture."

And Rob Paulsen again, overcoming his sudden attack of reverence, on the subject of his career: "I'm getting paid to do what used to get me thrown out of school—making wacky noises. What could be better?"

Selected Bibliography

BOOKS

Adamson, Joe. *Tex Avery: King of Cartoons.* New York: Popular Film Library, 1975.
_____. *The Walter Lantz Story.* New York: Putnam, 1985.
Allen, Robert C. *Channels of Discourse, Reassembled: Television and Contemporary Criticism.* Second edition. Chapel Hill, NC: University of North Carolina Press, 1987, 1992.
Beck, Jerry, and Will Friedwald. *Looney Tunes and Merrie Melodies.* New York: Henry Holt, 1988.
Becker, Stephen. *Comic Art in America.* New York: Simon and Schuster, 1959.
Bedell, Sally. *Up the Tube: Prime Time TV and the Silverman Years.* New York: Viking Press, 1981.
Bianculli, David. *Teleliteracy: Taking Television Seriously.* New York: Continuum, 1992.
Blanc, Mel. *That's Not All, Folks! My Life in the Golden Age of Cartoons.* New York: Warner Bros., 1988.
Brasch, Walter M. *Cartoon Monickers: An Insight into the Animation Industry.* Bowling Green, OH: Bowling Green University Popular Press, 1983.
Brion, Patrick. *Tom and Jerry: The Definitive Guide to Their Animated Adventures.* New York: Harmony/Crown, 1990. (Originally published in France as *Tom et Jerry.* Editions du Chêne, 1987.
Carbaga, Leslie. *The Fleischer Story.* New York: DaCapo Press, 1988.
Cawley, John, and Jim Korkis. *Encyclopedia of Cartoon Superstars: From A to (Almost) Z.* Las Vegas: Pioneer Press, 1990.
Coghlan, Frank "Junior." *They Still Call Me Junior: Autobiography of a Child Star, with a Filmography.* Jefferson, NC: McFarland, 1993.
Culhane, Shamus. *Talking Animals and Other People.* New York: St. Martin's Press, 1986.
Denison, D. C. *As Seen on TV.* Photos by Flint Born. New York: Fireside/Simon and Schuster, 1992.
Eisner, Joel, and David Krinsky. *Television Comedy Series: An Episode Guide to 153 Sitcoms in Syndication.* Jefferson, NC: McFarland, 1983.
Erickson, Hal. *Syndicated Television: The First Forty Years.* Jefferson, NC: McFarland, 1989.
Fireman, Judy. *TV Book: The Ultimate Television Book.* New York: Workman Publishing, 1977.
Fischer, Stuart. *Kid's TV: The First 25 Years.* New York: Facts on File, 1983.

Gerani, Gary, with Paul H. Schulman. *Fantastic Television: A Pictorial History of Sci-Fi, the Unusual and the Fantastic.* New York: Harmony Books, 1977.

Grossman, Gary H. *Saturday Morning TV.* New York: Dell, 1981.

Horn, Maurice, ed. *World Encyclopedia of Comics.* New York: Chelsea House, 1976.

Kaplan, Louis, and Scott Michaelsen, in harmony with Art Clokey. *Gumby: The Authorized Biography of the World's Favorite Clayboy.* New York: Harmony Books, 1986.

Kaye, Evelyn. *The Family Guide to Children's Television: What to Watch, What to Miss, What to Change and How to Do It.* Written under the guidance of ACT with the cooperation of the American Academy of Pediatrics. Illustrations by Edward Frascino. New York: Pantheon Books, 1974.

Lenburg, Jeff. *The Encyclopedia of Animated Cartoons.* Foreword by Gary Owens. New York: Facts on File, 1991.

_____.*The Great Cartoon Directors.* Jefferson, NC: McFarland, 1983.

_____, with Joan Howard Maurer and Greg Lenburg. *The Three Stooges Scrapbook.* Secaucus, NJ: Citadel, 1982.

Lupoff, Dick, and Don Thompson, eds. *All in Color for a Dime.* New York: Ace Books, 1970.

_____. *The Comic Book Book.* New Rochelle, CT: Arlington House, 1973.

McNeil, Alex. *Total Television.* Third edition. New York: Penguin, 1992.

Maltin, Leonard. *The Laurel and Hardy Book.* New York: Popular Press, 1973.

_____. *Of Mice and Magic.* Revised edition. New York: Plume Books, 1981, 1987.

_____, and Richard Bann. *The Little Rascals: The Lives and Times of Our Gang.* Revised edition. New York: Crown, 1977, 1992.

Mulholland, Jim. *The Abbott and Costello Book.* New York: Popular Library, 1975.

Perry, George, and Alan Aldridge. *The Penguin Book of Comics.* Revised edition. Middlesex, England: Penguin Press, 1971.

Phillips, Phil. *Saturday Morning Mind Control.* Nashville: Oliver Nelson Publishers, 1991.

Powers, Ron. *The Beast, the Eunuch and the Glass-Eyed Kid: Television in the '80s.* New York: Harcourt Brace Jovanovich, 1990.

Robie, Joan Hake. *Turtles Exposed: A Critical Analysis.* Lancaster, PA: Starburst Publications, 1991.

Rovin, Jeff. *Encyclopedia of Superheroes.* New York: Facts on File, 1985.

_____. *The Illustrated Encyclopedia of Cartoon Animals.* New York: Prentice Hall, 1991.

Schechter, Harold, Ph.D. *Kidvid: A Parent's Guide to Children's Videos.* New York: Pocket Books, 1986.

Schneider, Cy. *Children's Television: The Art, the Business and How It Works.* Intro. by Fred Silverman. Lincolnwood, IL: NTC Business Books, 1987.

Sennett, Ted. *The Art of Hanna-Barbera.* New York: Viking, 1989.

Sheff, David. *Game Over: How Nintendo Zapped an American Industry, Captured Your Dollars and Enslaved Your Children.* New York: Random House, 1993.

Sopkin, Charles. *Seven Glorious Days, Seven Fun Filled Nights.* New York: Simon and Schuster, 1968.

Stephenson, Ralph. *Animation in the Cinema.* London: A. Zwimmer Ltd., 1967.

Swanigan, Michael, and Darrell McNeil. *Animation by Filmation.* Edited by John Reed and Joshua Lou Friedman. Simi Valley, CA: Black Bear Press, 1993.

Terrace, Vincent. *Encyclopedia of Television: Series, Pilots and Specials (1937–1984).* Three volumes. New York: Zoetrope, 1986.

Turow, Joseph. *Entertainment, Education and the Hard Sell: Three Decades of Network Children's Television.* New York: Praeger, div. of CBS, 1981.

Walt Disney Productions. *Donald Duck*. Foreword by Carl Barks. New York: The Abbeville Press, 1978.
Warren, Bill. *Keep Watching the Skies! American Science Fiction Movies of the Fifties*. Two volumes. Jefferson, NC: McFarland, 1982, 1986.
Wilmut, Roger. *From Fringe to Flying Circus: Celebrating a Unique Generation of Comedy*. London: Methuen, 1983.
Woolery, George. *Children's Television: The First Thirty-Five Years*. Two volumes. Metuchen, NJ: Scarecrow Press, 1983.

PUBLISHED ARTICLES

Altman, Mark A. "The Dark Knight Conquers the Screen." *Not of This Earth*, October 1993.
Bauer, Patricia E. "Babe in Toyland." *Channels*, July/August 1987.
Cerone, Daniel. "How Nicktoons Were Drawn to Success." Los Angeles *Times* Service; printed in the Milwaukee *Journal*, November 7, 1993.
_____. "Not Your Typical Kiddie Host: Cryptkeeper of HBO's Adult Series Will Emcee ABC Cartoon." Los Angeles *Times* Service; printed in the Milwaukee *Journal*, August 2, 1993.
Cohen, Howard. "What's Hot? MTV's Lewd, Crude Toons, Beavis and Butt-Head." Knight and Ridder; printed in the Milwaukee *Sentinel*, August 19, 1993.
Donlin, Brian. "Fox, Pied Piper of Saturdays." *USA Today*, April 14, 1993.
_____. "On cable, more education joins the 'toons and goons." *USA Today*, September 10, 1992.
Duarte, Roger "Rad," and Jim Swallow. "The Robotech Generation." *Anime UK* magazine, April/May 1993.
Duston, Diane. "More Positive Cartoons on the Way?" Associated Press; printed in the Milwaukee *Journal*, December 21, 1993.
Engelhardt, Tom. "The Shortcake Strategy." In Gitlin, Todd, ed., *Watching Television*. New York: Pantheon Books, 1986.
"FCC Restricts Ads During Shows for Children, But Not Toy Tie-ins." NY Times Service; reprinted in the Milwaukee *Journal*, April 14, 1991.
Graham, Jefferson. "*Animaniacs:* Toons Whose Time Is Coming." *USA Today*, July 30, 1993.
Gross, Edward. "*Cadillacs and Dinosaurs* Roars to Saturday Morning." *Not of This Earth*, October 1993.
Jankiewicz, Pat. "*Exo-Squad:* They're Battling the Next Stage of Human Animation." *Comics Scene*, October 1993.
"Kidvid: A National Disgrace." *Newsweek*, October 17, 1983.
Mangan, Jennifer. "Rodents Run Amok: Senseless 'Biker Mice from Mars' Cartoon Lands in Chicago." Chicago *Tribune*, September 19, 1993.
_____. "'Small Talk' a Sound Investment for Voice Artists." Chicago *Tribune* "TV Week" magazine, July 18, 1993.
Metych, John III. "A Talk with Tim Eldred." *MangaNewswatch*, No. 3, 1993.
Natale, Richard. "Horror Takes a Holiday." Chicago *Tribune*, October 10, 1993.
Parnett, Davina. "Potter Training." *Premiere* magazine, February 1994.
Schmeltzer, John. "3 Mice from Mars a Cause for Hype, Hope." Chicago *Tribune*, September 19, 1993.
"Show-Length Ads: Why Johnny Wants a Gobot." *Christian Science Monitor*, May 20, 1985.
"Spielberg, 'Family Dog' Have Their Day." Los Angeles *Times*; reprinted in Milwaukee *Sentinel*, June 15, 1993.

Wax, Roberta. "Something to CRO About." *Emmy* magazine, October 1993.
"Why Children's TV Turns Off So Many Parents." *US News and World Report,* February 18, 1985.
Wilke, John, and Amy Duncan. "Are the Programs Your Kids Watch Simply Commercials?" *Business Week,* March 25, 1985.

PERIODICALS (PRINCIPAL SOURCES)

The following magazines have been sifted through so often for my research that to list articles singly would be superfluous.

Animation magazine. Thoren Publications, Agoura Hills CA.
Animato magazine. Springfield MA.
Broadcasting magazine (aka *Broadcasting and Cable*). Washington DC.
Electronic Media. Crain Communications, Chicago IL.
Entertainment Weekly. Entertainment Weekly/Time Inc., New York NY.
Filmfax. Evanston IL.
Toon magazine (to date, one edition: Spring 1993). Black Bear Press, Simi Valley CA.
TV Guide. News America Publications, Radnor PA.
Variety. New York NY.
The Whole Toon Catalog. Issaquah WA.
Wild Cartoon Kingdom. LPF Inc., Beverly Hills CA.

Index

Numbers in **boldface** refer to pages with photographs.

597

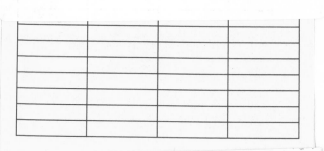